THE DANZIG TRILOGY

OTHER BOOKS BY
GÜNTER GRASS

THE TIN DRUM
CAT AND MOUSE
DOG YEARS

GÜNTER GRASS

THE DANZIG TRILOGY

Translated by Ralph Manheim

A HELEN AND KURT WOLFF BOOK
HARCOURT, INC.
San Diego   New York   London
PANTHEON BOOKS, INC.
New York

Requests for permission to make copies of any part of *The Tin Drum* should
be mailed to: Pantheon Books, a division of Random House, Inc., 201 East 50th Street,
New York, N.Y. 10022. Requests for permission to make copies of any part of *Cat and
Mouse* or *Dog Years* should be mailed to: Permissions Department, Harcourt, Inc.,
6277 Sea Harbor Drive, Orlando, Florida 32887-6777.

Library of Congress Cataloging-in-Publication Data
Grass, Günter, 1927–
The Danzig trilogy.
"A Helen and Kurt Wolff book."
Contents: The tin drum—Cat and mouse—Dog years.
I. Title.
PT2613.R338D2713   1987   833'.914   87-8725
ISBN 0-15-123816-2

Designed by Francesca M. Smith
Printed in the United States of America
First United States edition
K J I H G F E D C B

Contents

The Tin Drum   1

Cat and Mouse   467

Dog Years   557

THE TIN DRUM

For Anna Grass

Contents

BOOK ONE

The Wide Skirt   7
Under the Raft   15
Moth and Light Bulb   25
The Photograph Album   34
Smash a Little Windowpane   43
The Schedule   52
Rasputin and the Alphabet   61
The Stockturm. Long-Distance Song Effects   71
The Rostrum   80
Shopwindows   93
No Wonder   101
Good Friday Fare   110
Tapered at the Foot End   121
Herbert Truczinski's Back   129
Niobe   140
Faith, Hope, Love   150

BOOK TWO

Scrap Metal   161
The Polish Post Office   171
The Card House   182
He Lies in Saspe   191
Maria   200
Fizz Powder   209
Special Communiqués   219
How Oskar Took His Helplessness to Mrs. Greff   227
165 Lbs.   237

Bebra's Theater at the Front   247

Inspection of Concrete, or Barbaric, Mystical, Bored   256

The Imitation of Christ   270

The Dusters   281

The Christmas Play   290

The Ant Trail   299

Should I or Shouldn't I?   309

Disinfectant   319

Growth in a Freight Car   328

BOOK THREE

Firestones and Tombstones   339

Fortuna North   351

Madonna 49   361

The Hedgehog   372

In the Clothes Cupboard   381

Klepp   389

On the Fiber Rug   398

In the Onion Cellar   407

On the Atlantic Wall, or Concrete Eternal   420

The Ring Finger   432

The Last Streetcar, or Adoration of a Preserving Jar   441

Thirty   453

Glossary   463

Book
One

The Wide Skirt

Granted: I am an inmate of a mental hospital; my keeper is watching me, he never lets me out of his sight; there's a peephole in the door, and my keeper's eye is the shade of brown that can never see through a blue-eyed type like me.

So you see, my keeper can't be an enemy. I've come to be very fond of him; when he stops looking at me from behind the door and comes into the room, I tell him incidents from my life, so he can get to know me in spite of the peephole between us. He seems to treasure my stories, because every time I tell him some fairy tale, he shows his gratitude by bringing out his latest knot construction. I wouldn't swear that he's an artist. But I am certain that an exhibition of his creations would be well received by the press and attract a few purchasers. He picks up common pieces of string in the patients' rooms after visiting hours, disentangles them, and works them up into elaborate contorted spooks; then he dips them in plaster, lets them harden, and mounts them on knitting needles that he fastens to little wooden pedestals.

He often plays with the idea of coloring his works. I advise him against it, taking my white enamel bed as an example and bidding him try to imagine how this most perfect of all beds would look if painted in many colors. He raises his hands in horror, tries to give his rather expressionless face an expression of extreme disgust, and abandons his polychrome projects.

So you see, my white-enameled, metal hospital bed has become a norm and standard. To me it is still more: my bed is a goal attained at last, it is my consolation and might become my faith if the management allowed me to make a few changes: I should like, for instance, to have the bars built up higher, to prevent anyone from coming too close to me.

Once a week a visiting day breaks in on the stillness that I plait between the white metal bars. This is the time for the people who want to save me, whom it amuses to love me, who try to esteem and respect themselves, to get to know themselves, through me. How blind, how nervous and ill-bred they are! They scratch the white enamel of my bedstead with their fingernail scissors, they scribble obscene little men on it with their ballpoint pens and blue pencils. No sooner has my lawyer blasted the room with his hello than he slaps his nylon hat down over the lower left-hand bedpost—an act of violence that shatters my peace

7

of mind for the duration of his visit, and lawyers find a good deal to talk about.

After my visitors have deposited their gifts beneath the water color of the anemones, on the little white table covered with oilcloth, after they have submitted their current projects for my salvation, and convinced me, whom they are working indefatigably to save, of the high quality of their charity, they recover their relish in their own existence, and leave me. Then my keeper comes in to air the room and collect the strings from the gift packages. Often after airing he finds time to sit by my bed for a while, disentangling his strings, and spreading silence until I call the silence Bruno and Bruno silence.

Bruno Münsterberg—this time I mean my keeper, I've stopped playing with words—has bought me five hundred sheets of writing paper.

Should this supply prove insufficient, Bruno, who is unmarried and childless and hails from the Sauerland, will go to the little stationery store that also sells toys, and get me some more of the unlined space I need for the recording of my memories—I only hope they are accurate. I could never have asked such a service of my visitors, the lawyer for instance, or Klepp. The solicitous affection prescribed in my case would surely have deterred my friends from bringing me anything so dangerous as blank paper and making it available to this mind of mine which persits in excreting syllables.

"Oh, Bruno," I said, "would you buy me a ream of virgin paper?" And Bruno, looking up at the ceiling and pointing his index finger in the same direction by way of inviting a comparison, replied: " You mean white paper, Herr Oskar?"

I stuck to "virgin" and asked Bruno to say just that in the store. When he came back late in the afteroon with the package, he gave the impression of a Bruno shaken by thought. Several times he looked fixedly up at the ceiling from which he derived all his inspiration. And a little later he spoke: "That was the right word you told me. I asked for virgin paper and the salesgirl blushed like mad before getting it."

Fearing an interminable conversation about salesgirls in stationery stores, I regretted having spoken of virgin paper and said nothing, waiting for Bruno to leave the room. Only then did I open the package with the five hundred sheets of writing paper.

For a time I weighed the hard, flexible ream in my hands; then I counted out ten sheets and stowed the rest in my bedside table. I found my fountain pen in the drawer beside the photograph album: it's full, ink is no problem, how shall I begin?

You can begin a story in the middle and create confusion by striking out boldly, backward and forward. You can be modern, put aside all mention of time and distance and, when the whole thing is done, proclaim,

8

or let someone else proclaim, that you have finally, at the last moment, solved the space-time problem. Or you can declare at the very start that it's impossible to write a novel nowadays, but then, behind your own back so to speak, give birth to a whopper, a novel to end all novels. I have also been told that it makes a good impression, an impression of modesty so to speak, if you begin by saying that a novel can't have a hero any more because there are no more individualists, because individuality is a thing of the past, because man—each man and all men together— is alone in his loneliness and no one is entitled to individual loneliness, and all men lumped together make up a "lonely mass" without names and without heroes. All this may be true. But as far as I and Bruno my keeper are concerned, I beg leave to say that we are both heroes, very different heroes, he on his side of the peephole, and I on my side; and even when he opens the door, the two of us, with all our friendship and loneliness, are still far from being a nameless, heroless mass.

I shall begin far away from me; for no one ought to tell the story of his life who hasn't the patience to say a word or two about at least half of his grandparents before plunging into his own existence. And so to you personally, dear reader, who are no doubt leading a muddled kind of life outside this institution, to you my friends and weekly visitors who suspect nothing of my paper supply, I introduce Oskar's maternal grandmother.

Late one October afternoon my grandmother Anna Bronski was sitting in her skirts at the edge of a potato field. In the morning you might have seen how expert my grandmother was at making the limp potato plants into neat piles; at noon she had eaten a chunk of bread smeared with lard and syrup; then she had dug over the field a last time, and now she sat in her skirts between two nearly full baskets. The soles of her boots rose up at right angles to the ground, converging slightly at the toes, and in front of them smouldered a fire of potato plants, flaring up asthmatically from time to time, sending a queasy film of smoke out over the scarcely inclined crust of the earth. The year was 1899; she was sitting in the heart of Kashubia, not far from Bissau but still closer to the brickworks between Ramkau and Viereck, in front of her the Brenntau highway at a point between Dirschau and Karthaus, behind her the black forest of Goldkrug; there she sat, pushing potatoes about beneath the hot ashes with the charred tip of a hazel branch.

If I have made a special point of my grandmother's skirt, leaving no doubt, I hope, that she was sitting in her skirts; if indeed I have gone so far as to call the whole chapter "The Wide Skirt," it is because I know how much I owe to this article of apparel. My grandmother had on not just one skirt, but four, one over the other. It should not be supposed that she wore one skirt and three petticoats; no, she wore four skirts; one supported the next, and she wore the lot of them in accordance with a definite system, that is, the order of the skirts was changed from day to day. The one that was on top yesterday was today in second place; the second became the third. The one that was third yesterday was next to her skin today. The one that was closest to her yesterday clearly disclosed its pattern today, or rather its lack of pattern: all my grandmother Anna Bronski's skirts favored the same potato color. It must have been becoming to her.

Aside from the color, my grandmother's skirts were distinguished by a lavish expanse of material. They puffed and billowed when the wind came, crackled as it passed, and sagged when it was gone, and all four of them flew out ahead of her when she had the wind in her stern. When she sat down, she gathered her skirts about her.

In addition to the four skirts, billowing, sagging, hanging down in folds, or standing stiff and empty beside her bed, my grandmother possessed a fifth. It differed in no way from the other four potato-colored garments. And actually the fifth skirt was not always fifth. Like its brothers—for skirts are masculine by nature—it was subject to change, it was worn like the other four, and like them when its time had come, took its turn in the wash trough every fifth Friday, then Saturday on the line by the kitchen window, and when dry on the ironing board.

When, after one of these Saturdays spent in housecleaning, baking, washing and ironing, after milking and feeding the cow, my grandmother immersed herself from top to toe in the tub, when after leaving a little of herself in the soapsuds and letting the water in the tub sink back to its normal level, she sat down on the edge of the bed swathed in a great flowery towel, the four worn skirts and the freshly washed skirt lay spread out before her on the floor. She pondered, propping the lower lid of her right eye with her right index finger, and since she consulted no one, not even her brother Vincent, she quickly made up her mind. She stood up and with her bare toes pushed aside the skirt whose potato color had lost the most bloom. The freshly laundered one took its place.

On Sunday morning she went to church in Ramkau and inaugurated the new order of skirts in honor of Jesus, about whom she had very set ideas. Where did my grandmother wear the laundered skirt? She was not only a cleanly woman, but also a rather vain one; she wore the best piece where it could be seen in the sunlight when the weather was good.

But now it was a Monday afternoon and my grandmother was sitting by the potato fire. Today her Sunday skirt was one layer closer to her person, while the one that had basked in the warmth of her skin on Sunday swathed her hips in Monday gloom. Whistling with no particular tune in mind, she coaxed the first cooked potato out of the ashes with her hazel branch and pushed it away from the smouldering mound to cool in the breeze. Then she spitted the charred and crusty tuber on a pointed stick and held it close to her mouth; she had stopped whistling and instead pursed her cracked, wind-parched lips to blow the earth and ashes off the potato skin.

In blowing, my grandmother closed her eyes. When she thought she had blown enough, she opened first one eye, then the other, bit into the potato with her widely spaced but otherwise perfect front teeth, removed half the potato, cradled the other half, mealy, steaming, and still too hot to chew, in her open mouth, and, sniffing at the smoke and the October air, gazed wide-eyed across the field toward the nearby horizon, sectioned by telegaph poles and the upper third of the brickworks chimney.

Something was moving between the telegraph poles. My grandmother closed her mouth. Something was jumping about. Three men were darting between the poles, three men made for the chimney, then round in front, then one doubled back. Short and wide he seemed, he took a fresh start and made it across the brickyard, the other two, sort of long and thin, just behind him. They were out of the brickyard, back between the telegraph poles, but Short and Wide twisted and turned and seemed to be in more of a hurry than Long and Thin, who had to double back to the chimney, because he was already rolling over it when they, two hands' breadths away, were still taking a start, and suddenly they were gone as though they had given up, and the little one disappeared too, behind the horizon, in the middle of his jump from the chimney.

Out of sight they remained, it was intermission, they were changing their costumes, or making bricks and getting paid for it.

Taking advantage of the intermission, my grandmother tried to spit another potato, but missed it. Because the one who seemed to be short and wide, who hadn't changed his clothes after all, climbed up over the horizon as if it were a fence and he had left his pursuers behind it, in among the bricks or on the road to Brenntau. But he was still in a hurry, trying to go faster than the telegraph poles, he took long slow leaps across the field; the mud flew from his boots as he leapt over the soggy ground, but leap as he might, he seemed to be crawling. Sometimes he seemed to stick in the ground and then to stick in mid-air, short and wide, time enough to wipe his face before his foot came down again in the freshly plowed field, which bordered the five acres of potatoes and narrowed into a sunken lane.

He made it to the lane; short and wide, he had barely disappeared into the lane, when the two others, long and thin, who had probably been searching the brickyard in the meantime, climbed over the horizon and came plodding through the mud, so long and thin, but not really skinny, that my grandmother missed her potato again; because it's not every day that you see this kind of thing, three full-grown men, though they hadn't grown in exactly the same directions, hopping around telegraph poles, nearly breaking the chimney off the brickworks, and then at intervals, first short and wide, then long and thin, but all with the same difficulty, picking up more and more mud on the soles of their boots, leaping through the field that Vincent had plowed two days before, and disappearing down the sunken lane.

Then all three of them were gone and my grandmother ventured to spit another potato, which by this time was almost cold. She hastily blew the earth and ashes off the skin, popped the whole potato straight into her mouth. They must be from the brickworks, she thought if she thought anything, and she was still chewing with a circular motion when one of them jumped out of the lane, wild eyes over a black mustache, reached the fire in two jumps, stood before, behind, and beside the fire all at once, cursing, scared, not knowing which way to go, unable to turn back, for behind him Long and Thin were running down the lane. He hit his knees, the eyes in his head were like to pop out, and sweat poured from his forehead. Panting, his whole face atremble, he ventured to crawl closer, toward the soles of my grandmother's boots, peering up at her like a squat little animal. Heaving a great sigh, which made her stop chewing on her potato, my grandmother let her feet tilt over, stopped thinking about bricks and brickmakers, and lifted high her skirt, no, all four skirts, high enough so that Short and Wide, who was not from the brickworks, could crawl underneath. Gone was his black mustache; he didn't look like an animal any more, he was neither from Ramkau nor from Viereck, at any rate he had vanished with his fright, he had ceased to be wide or short but he took up room just the same, he forgot to pant or tremble and he had stopped hitting his knees; all was as still as on the first day of Creation or the last; a bit of wind hummed in the potato fire, the telegraph poles counted themselves in silence, the chimney of the brickworks stood at attention, and my grandmother smoothed down her uppermost skirt neatly and sensibly over the second one; she scarcely felt him under her fourth skirt, and her third skirt wasn't even aware that there was anything new and unusual next to her skin. Yes, unusual it was, but the top was nicely smoothed out and the second and third layers didn't know a thing; and so she scraped two or three potatoes out of the ashes, took four raw ones from the basket beneath her right elbow, pushed the raw spuds one after another into the hot ashes, covered them over with more ashes, and poked the fire till the smoke rose in clouds—what else could she have done?

My grandmother's skirts had barely settled down; the sticky smudge of the potato fire, which had lost its direction with all the poking and thrashing about, had barely had time to adjust itself to the wind and resume its low yellow course across the field to southwestward, when Long and Thin popped out of the lane, hot in pursuit of Short and Wide, who by now had set up housekeeping beneath my grandmother's skirts; they were indeed long and thin and they wore the uniform of the rural constabulary.

They nearly ran past my grandmother. One of them even jumped over the fire. But suddenly they remembered they had heels and used them to brake with, about-faced, stood booted and uniformed in the smudge, coughed, pulled their uniforms out of the smudge, taking some of it along with them, and, still coughing, turned to my grandmother, asked her if she had seen Koljaiczek, 'cause she must have seen him 'cause she was sitting here by the lane and that was the way he had come.

My grandmother hadn't seen any Koljaiczek because she didn't know any Koljaiczek. Was he from the brickworks, she asked, 'cause the only ones she knew were the ones from the brickworks. But according to the uniforms, this Koljaiczek had nothing to do with bricks, but was short and stocky. My grandmother remembered she had seen somebody like that running and pointed her stick with the steaming potato on the end toward Bissau, which, to judge by the potato, must have been between the sixth and seventh telegraph poles if you counted westward from the chimney. But whether this fellow that was running was a Koljaiczek, my grandmother couldn't say; she'd been having enough trouble with this fire, she explained, it was burning poorly, how could she worry her head about all the people that ran by or stood in the smoke, and anyway she never worried her head about people she didn't know, she only knew the people in Bissau, Ramkau, Viereck, and the brickworks—and that was plenty for her.

After saying all this, my grandmother heaved a gentle sigh, but it was enough of a sigh to make the uniforms ask what there was to sigh about. She nodded toward the fire, meaning to say that she had sighed because the fire was doing poorly and maybe a little on account of the people standing in the smoke; then she bit off half her potato with her widely spaced incisors, and gave her undivided attention to the business of chewing, while her eyeballs rolled heavenward.

My grandmother's absent gaze told the uniforms nothing; unable to make up their minds whether to look for Bissau behind the telegraph poles, they poked their bayonets into all the piles of potato tops that hadn't been set on fire. Responding to a sudden inspiration, they upset the two baskets under my grandmother's elbows almost simultaneously and were quite bewildered when nothing but potatoes came rolling out, and no Koljaiczek. Full of suspicion, they crept round the stack of potatoes, as though Koljaiczek had somehow got into it, thrust in their bayonets as though deliberately taking aim, and were disappointed to hear no cry. Their suspicions were aroused by every bush, however abject, by every mousehole, by a colony of molehills, and most of all by my grandmother, who sat there as if rooted to the spot, sighing, rolling her eyes so that the whites showed, listing the Kashubian names of all the saints—all of which seemed to have been brought on by the poor performance of the fire and the overturning of her potato baskets.

The uniforms stayed on for a good half-hour. They took up positions at varying distances from the fire, they took an azimuth on the chimney, contemplated an offensive against Bissau but postponed it, and held out their purple hands over the fire until my grandmother, though without interrupting her sighs, gave each of them a charred potato. But in the midst of chewing, the uniforms remembered their uniforms, dashed a little way out into the field along the furze bordering the lane, and scared up a hare which, however, turned out not to be Koljaiczek. Returning to the fire, they recovered the mealy, steaming spuds and then, wearied and rather mellowed by their battles, decided to pick up the raw potatoes and put them back into the baskets which they had overturned in line of duty.

Only when evening began to squeeze a fine slanting rain and an inky twilight from the October sky did they briefly and without enthusiasm attack a dark boulder at the other end of the field, but once this enemy had been disposed of they decided to let well enough alone. After flexing their legs for another moment or two and holding out their hands in blessing over the rather dampened fire, they coughed a last cough and dropped a last tear in the green and yellow smudge, and plodded off coughing and weeping in the direction of Bissau. If Koljaiczek wasn't here, he must be in Bissau. Rural constables never envisage more than two possibilities.

The smoke of the slowly dying fire enveloped my grandmother like a spacious fifth skirt, so that she too with her four skirts, her sighs, and her holy names, was under a skirt. Only when the uniforms had become staggering dots, vanishing in the dusk between the telegraph poles, did my grandmother arise, slowly and painfully as though she had struck root and now, drawing earth and fibers along with her, were tearing herself out of the ground.

Suddenly Koljaiczek found himself short, wide, and coverless in the rain, and he was cold. Quickly he buttoned his pants, which fear and a boundless need for shelter had bidden him open during his stay beneath the skirts. Hurriedly he manipulated the buttons, fearing to let his piston cool too quickly, for there was a threat of dire chills in the autumn air.

My grandmother found four more hot potatoes under the ashes. She gave Koljaiczek three of them and took one for herself; before biting into it she asked if he was from the brickworks, though she knew perfectly well that Koljaiczek came from somewhere else and had no connection with bricks. Without waiting for an answer, she lifted the lighter basket to his back, took the heavier one for herself, and still had a hand free for her rake and hoe. Then with her basket, her potatoes, her rake, and her hoe, she set off, like a sail billowing in the breeze, in the direction of Bissau Quarry.

That wasn't the same as Bissau itself. It lay more in the direction of Ramkau. Passing to the right of the brickworks, they headed for the black forest with Goldkrug in it and Brenntau behind it. But in a hollow, before you come to the forest, lay Bissau Quarry. Thither Joseph Koljaiczek, unable to tear himself away from her skirts, followed my grandmother.

Under the Raft

It is not so easy, lying here in this scrubbed hospital bed under a glass peephole with Bruno's eye in it, to give a picture of the smoke clouds that rose from Kashubian potato fires or of the slanting October rain. If I didn't have my drum, which, when handled adroitly and patiently, remembers all the incidentals that I need to get the essential down on paper, and if I didn't have the permission of the management to drum on it three or four hours a day, I'd be a poor bastard with nothing to say for my grandparents.

In any case, my drum tells me this: That afternoon in the year 1899, while in South Africa Oom Kruger was brushing his bushy anti-British eyebrows, my mother Agnes, between Dirschau and Karthaus, not far from the Bissau brickworks, amid smoke, terrors, sighs, and saints' names, under four skirts of identical color, under the slanting rain and the smoke-filled eyes of two rural constables asking uninspired questions, was begotten by the short but stocky Joseph Koljaiczek.

That very night my grandmother Anna Bronski changed her name; with the help of a priest who was generous with the sacraments, she had herself metamorphosed into Anna Koljaiczek and followed Joseph, if not into Egypt, at least to the provincial capital on the river Mottlau, where Joseph found work as a raftsman and temporary peace from the constabulary.

Just to heighten the suspense, I'm going to wait a while before telling you the name of the city at the mouth of the Mottlau, though there's ample reason for mentioning it right now because it is there that my mama first saw the light of day. At the end of July, 1900—they were just deciding to double the imperial naval building program—my mother was born under the sign of Leo. Self-confident, romantic, generous, and vain. The first house, known also as *domus vitae*, the sign of the

15

ascendant: Pisces, impressionable. The constellation of the sun in opposition to Neptune, seventh house or *Domus matrimonii uxoris*, would bring confusion. Venus in opposition to Saturn, which is termed the sour planet and as everyone knows induces ailments of the liver and spleen, which is dominant in Capricorn and meets its end in Leo, to which Neptune offers eels and receives the mole in return, which loves belladonna, onions, and beets, which coughs lava and sours the wine; it lived with Venus in the eighth house, the house of death; that augured accidental death, while the fact of being begotten in the potato field gave promise of hazardous happiness under the protection of Mercury in the house of relatives.

Here I must put in a protest from my mama, for she always denied having been begotten in the potato field. It was true—this much she admitted—that her father had done his best on that memorable occasion, but neither his position nor that of Anna Bronski had been such as to favor impregnation. "It must have happened later that night, maybe in Uncle Vincent's boxcart, or maybe still later in Troyl when the raftsmen took us in."

My mama liked to date the beginnings of her existence with words such as these, and then my grandmother, who must have known, would nod patiently and say: "Yes, child, it must have been in the cart or later in Troyl. It couldn't have been in the field, 'cause it was windy and raining all getout."

Vincent was my grandmother's brother. His wife had died young and then he had gone on a pilgrimage to Częstochowa where the Matka Boska Częstochowska had enjoined him to consider her as the future queen of Poland. Since then he had spent all his time poking around in strange books, and every sentence he read was a confirmation of the Virgin Mother's claim to the Polish throne. He had let his sister look after the house and the few acres of land. Jan, his son, then four years of age, a sickly child always on the verge of tears, tended the geese; he also collected little colored pictures and, at an ominously early age, stamps.

To this little farm dedicated to the heavenly Queen of Poland, my grandmother brought her potato baskets and Koljaiczek. Learning the lay of the land, Vincent hurried over to Ramkau and stirred up the priest, telling him to come quick with the sacraments and unite Anna and Joseph in holy wedlock. Scarcely had the reverend father, groggy with sleep, given his long yawned-out blessing and, rewarded with a good side of bacon, turned his consecrated back than Vincent harnessed the horse to the boxcart, bedded the newlyweds down in straw and empty potato sacks, propped up little Jan, shivering and wispily weeping beside him on the driver's seat, and gave the horse to understand that he was to put straight out into the night: the honeymooners were in a hurry.

The night was still dark though far advanced when the vehicle reached the timber port in the provincial capital. There Koljaiczek found friends and fellow raftsmen who sheltered the fugitive pair. Vincent turned about and headed back to Bissau; a cow, a goat, the sow with her porkers, eight geese, and the dog demanded to be fed, while little Jan had developed a slight fever and had to be put to bed.

Joseph Koljaiczek remained in hiding for three weeks. He trained his hair to take a part, shaved his mustache, provided himself with unblemished papers, and found work as a raftsman under the name of Joseph Wranka. But why did Koljaiczek have to apply for work with the papers of one Joseph Wranka, who had been knocked off a raft in a fight and, unbeknownst to the authorities, drowned in the river Bug just above Modlin? Because, having given up rafting for a time and gone to work in a sawmill at Schwetz, he had had a bit of trouble with the boss over a fence which he, Koljaiczek, had painted a provocative white and red. Whereupon the boss had broken one white and one red slat out of the fence and smashed the patriotic slats into tinder over Koljaiczek's Kashubian back. To Koljaiczek this had seemed ground enough for setting red fire to the brand-new, resplendently whitewashed sawmill the very next night, a starry night no doubt, in honor of a partitioned but for this very reason united Poland.

And so Koljaiczek became a firebug, and not just once, for throughout West Prussia in the days that followed, sawmills and woodlots provided fuel for a blazing bicolored national sentiment. As always where the future of Poland is at stake, the Virgin Mary was in on the proceedings, and there were witnesses—some of them may still be alive—who claimed to have seen the Mother of God, bedecked with the crown of Poland, enthroned on the collapsing roofs of several sawmills. The crowd that always turns up at big fires is said to have struck up the hymn to the Bogarodizica, Mother of God—Koljaiczek's fires, we have every reason to believe, were solemn affairs, and solemn oaths were sworn.

And so Koljaiczek was wanted as an incendiary, whereas the raftsman Joseph Wranka, a harmless fellow with an irreproachable past and no parents, a man of limited horizon whom no one was looking for and hardly anyone even knew, had divided his chewing tobacco into daily rations, until one day he was gathered in by the river Bug, leaving behind him three daily rations of tobacco and his papers in the pocket of his jacket. And since Wranka, once drowned, could no longer report for work and no one asked embarrassing questions about him, Koljaiczek, who had the same build and the same round skull, crept first into his jacket, then into his irreproachable official skin, gave up pipe-smoking, took to chewing tobacco, and even adopted Wranka's most personal and characteristic trait, his speech defect. In the years that followed he played the part of a hardworking, thrifty raftsman with a slight stutter, rafting whole forests down the Niemen, the Bobr, the Bug, and the Vistula. He even rose to be a corporal in the Crown Prince's Leib-Hussars under Mackensen, for Wranka hadn't yet done his military service, whereas Koljaiczek, who was four years older, had left a bad record behind him in the artillery at Thorn.

In the very midst of their felonious pursuits the most desperate thieves, murderers, and incendiaries are just waiting for an opportunity to take up a more respectable trade. Whether by effort or by luck, some of them get the chance: under the identity of Wranka, Koljaiczek was a good husband, so well cured of the fiery vice that the mere sight of a match gave him the shakes. A box of matches, lying smugly on the kitchen table, was never safe from this man who might have invented matches. He threw the temptation out of the window. It was very hard for my grandmother to serve a warm meal on time. Often the family sat in the dark because there was nothing to light the lamp with.

Yet Wranka was not a tyrant. On Sunday he took his Anna Wranka to church in the lower city and allowed her, his legally wedded wife, to wear four superimposed skirts, just as she had done in the potato field. In winter when the rivers were frozen over and the raftsmen were laid off, he sat quietly at home in Troyl, where only raftsmen, longshoremen, and wharf hands lived, and supervised the upbringing of his daughter Agnes, who seemed to take after her father, for when she was not under the bed she was in the clothes cupboard, and when there were visitors, she was under the table with her rag dolls.

The essential for little Agnes was to remain hidden; in hiding she found other pleasures but the same security as Joseph had found under Anna's skirts. Koljaiczek the incendiary had been sufficiently burnt to understand his daughter's need for shelter. When it became necessary to put up a rabbit hutch on the balcony-like appendage to their one-and-a-half-room flat, he built a special little house to her measure. Here sat my mother as a child, playing with dolls and getting bigger. Later, when she went to school, she is said to have thrown away the dolls and shown her first concern with fragile beauty in the form of glass beads and colored feathers.

Perhaps, since I am burning to announce the beginning of my own existence, I may be permitted to leave the family raft of the Wrankas drifting peacefully along, until 1913, when the *Columbus* was launched in Schichau; for it was then that the police, who never forget, caught up with Wranka.

The trouble began in August, 1913 when, as every summer, Koljaiczek was to help man the big raft that floated down from Kiev to the Vistula by way of the Pripet, the canal, the Bug, and the Modlin. Twelve raftsmen in all, they boarded the tugboat *Radaune*, operated by their sawmill, and steamed from Westlich Neufähr up the Dead Vistula to Einlage, then up the Vistula past Käsemark, Letzkau, Czattkau, Dirschau, and Pieckel, and tied up for the night at Thorn. There the new manager of the sawmill, who was to supervise the timber-buying in Kiev, came on board. By the time the *Radaune* cast off at four in the morning, word got around that he had come on. Koljaiczek saw him for the first time at breakfast in the galley. They sat across from one another, chewing and slopping up barley coffee. Koljaiczek knew him right off. Broad-shouldered and bald, the boss sent for vodka and had it poured into the men's empty coffee cups. In the midst of chewing, while the vodka was still being poured at the far end, he introduced himself: "Just so you know what's what, I'm the new boss, my name is Dückerhoff, I like order and I get it."

At his bidding, the crew called out their names one after another in their seating order, and drained their cups so their Adam's apples jumped. Koljaiczek drank first, then he said "Wranka," looking Dückerhoff straight in the eye. Dückerhoff nodded as he had nodded each time and repeated "Wranka" as he had repeated the names of the rest of the crew. Nevertheless it seemed to Koljaiczek that there was something special about Dückerhoff's way of saying the dead raftsman's name, not exactly pointed, but kind of thoughtful.

The *Radaune* pounded her way against the muddy current, deftly avoiding sandbanks with the help of changing pilots. To right and left, behind the dikes the country was always the same, hilly when it wasn't flat, but always reaped over. Hedges, sunken lanes, a hollow overgrown with broom, here and there an isolated farm, a landscape made for cavalry attacks, for a division of Uhlans wheeling in from the left across the sandbox, for hedge-leaping hussars, for the dreams of young cavalry officers, for the battles of the past and the battles to come, for heroic painting. Tartars flat against the necks of their horses, dragoons rearing, knights in armor falling, grand masters in blood-spattered mantles, not a scratch on their breastplates, all but one, who was struck down by the Duke of Mazowsze; and horses, better than a circus, bedecked with tassels, sinews delineated with precision. nostrils dilated, carmine red, sending up little clouds and the clouds are pierced by lowered lances hung with pennants, sabers part the sky and the sunset, and there in the background—for every painting has a background—pasted firmly against the horizon, a little village with peacefully smoking chimneys between the hind legs of the black stallion, little squat cottages with moss-covered walls and thatched roofs; and in the cottages the pretty little tanks, dreaming of the day to come when they too will sally forth into the picture behind the Vistula dikes, like light foals amid the heavy cavalry.

Off Wloclawek, Dückerhoff tapped Koljaiczek on the shoulder: "Tell me, Wranka, didn't you work in the mill at Schwetz a few years back?

The one that burned down?" Koljaiczek shook his head heavily, as though he had a stiff neck, and managed to make his eyes so sad and tired that Dückerhoff kept any further questions to himself.

When Koljaiczek at Modlin, where the Bug flows into the Vistula and the *Radaune* turned into the Bug, leaned over the rail as the raftsmen did in those days and spat three times, Dückerhoff was standing beside him with a cigar and asked for a light. That little word, like the word "match," had a strange effect on Koljaiczek. "Man, you don't have to blush because I want a light. You're not a girl, or are you?"

It wasn't until after they left Modlin behind them that Koljaiczek ost his blush, which was not a blush of shame, but the lingering glow of the sawmills he had set on fire.

Between Modlin and Kiev, up the Bug through the canal that joins the Bug and the Pripet, until the *Radaune,* following the Pripet, found its way to the Dniepr, nothing happened that can be classified as an exchange between Koljaiczek-Wranka and Dückerhoff. There was surely a bit of bad blood aboard the tug, among the raftsmen, between stokers and raftsmen, between helmsman, stokers, and captain, between captain and the constantly changing pilots; that's said to be the way with men, and maybe it really is. I can easily conceive of a certain amount of backbiting between the Kashubian logging crew and the helmsman, who was a native of Stettin, perhaps even the beginning of a mutiny: meeting in the galley, lots drawn, passwords given out, cutlasses sharpened. But enough of that. There were neither political disputes, nor knife battles between Germans and Poles, nor any mutiny springing from social grievances. Peacefully devouring her daily ration of coal, the *Radaune* went her way; once she ran aground on a sandbank—a little way past Plock, I think it was—but got off on her own power. A short but heated altercation between Captain Barbusch from Neufahrwasser and the Ukrainian pilot, that was all—and you wouldn't find much more in the log.

But if I had to keep a journal of Koljaiczek's thoughts or of Dückerhoff's inner life, there'd be plenty to relate: suspicion, suspicion confirmed, doubt, hesitation, suspicion laid at rest, more suspicion. They were both afraid. Dückerhoff more than Koljaiczek; for now they were in Russia. Dückerhoff could easily have fallen overboard like poor Wranka in his day, or later on in Kiev, in the timberyards that are so labyrinthine and enormous you can easily lose your guardian angel in their mazes, he could somehow have slipped under a suddenly toppling pile of logs. Or for that matter, he could have been rescued. Rescued by Koljaiczek, fished out of the Pripet or the Bug, or in the Kiev woodyard so deplorably short of guardian angels, pulled at the last moment from the path of an avalanche of logs. How touching it would be if I could tell you how Dückerhoff, half-drowned or half-crushed, still gasping, a glimmer of death still barely discernible in his eyes, had whispered in the ostensible Wranka's ear: "Thank you, Koljaiczek, thanks old man." And then after the indispensable pause: "That makes us quits. Let bygones be bygones."

And with gruff bonhomie, smiling shamefacedly into each other's manly eyes with a twinkle that might almost have been a tear, they would have clasped one another's diffident but horny hands.

We know the scene from the movies: the reconciliation between two enemy brothers, brilliantly performed, brilliantly photographed, from this day onward comrades forever, through thick and thin; Lord, what adventures they'll live through together!

But Koljaiczek found opportunity neither to drown Dückerhoff nor to snatch him from the jaws of death. Conscientiously, intent on the best interests of the firm, Dückerhoff bought his lumber in Kiev, supervised the building of the nine rafts, distributed a substantial advance in Russian currency to see the men through the return trip, and boarded the train, which carried him by way of Warsaw, Modlin, Deutsch-Eylau, Marienburg, and Dirschau back to his company, whose sawmill was situated in the timber port between the Klawitter dockyards and the Schichau dockyards. Before I bring the raftsmen down the rivers from Kiev, through the canal and at last, after weeks of grueling toil, into the Vistula, there is a question to be considered: was Dückerhoff sure that this Wranka was Koljaiczek the firebug? I should say that as long as the mill boss had Wranka, a good-natured sort, well liked by all despite his very medium brightness, as his traveling companion on the tug, he hoped, and preferred to believe, that the raftsman was not the desperado Koljaiczek. He did not relinquish this hope until he was comfortably settled in the train. And by the time the train had reached its destination, the Central Station in Danzig—there, now I've said it—Dückerhoff had made up his mind. He sent his bags home in a carriage and strode briskly to the nearby Police Headquarters on the Wiebenwall, leapt up the steps to the main entrance, and, after a short but cautious search, found the office he was looking for, where he submitted a brief factual report. He did not actually denounce Koljaiczek-Wranka; he merely entered a request that the police look into the case, which the police promised to do.

In the following weeks while the logs were floating slowly downstream with their burden of reed huts and raftsmen, a great deal of paper was covered with writing in a number of offices. There was the service record of Joseph Koljaiczek, buck private in the so-and-soeth West Prussian artillery regiment. A poor soldier, he had twice spent three days in the guardhouse for shouting anarchist slogans half in Polish and half in German while under the influence of liquor. No such black marks were to be discovered in the record of Corporal Wranka, who had served in the second regiment of Leib-Hussars at Langfuhr. He had done well; as battalion dispatch runner on maneuvers, he had made a favorable impression on the Crown Prince and had been rewarded with a Crown Prince thaler by the Prince, who always carried a pocketful of them. The thaler was not noted in Corporal Wranka's military records, but reported by my loudly lamenting grandmother Anna when she and her brother Vincent were questioned.

And that was not her only argument against the allegation of arson. She was able to produce papers proving that Joseph Wranka had joined the volunteer fire department in Danzig-Niederstadt as early as 1904, during the winter months when the raftsmen are idle, and that far from lighting fires he had helped to put them out. There was also a document to show that Fireman Wranka, while fighting the big fire at the Troyl railroad works in 1909, had saved two apprentice mechanics. Fire captain Hecht spoke in similar terms when called up as a witness. "Is a man who puts fires out likely to light them?" he cried. "Why, I can still see him up there on the ladder when the church in Heubude was burning. A phoenix rising from flame and ashes, quenching not only the fire, but also the conflagration of this world and the thirst of our Lord Jesus! Verily I say unto you: anyone who sullies the name of the man in the fire helmet, who has the right of way, whom the insurance companies love, who always has a bit of ashes in his pocket, perhaps because they dropped into it in the course of his duties or perhaps as a talisman—anyone, I say, who dares to accuse this glorious phoenix of arson deserves to have a millstone tied round his neck and . . ."

Captain Hecht, as you may have observed, was a parson, a warrior of the word. Every Sunday, he spoke from the pulpit of his parish church of St. Barbara at Langgarten, and as long as the Koljaiczek-Wranka investigation was in progress he dinned parables about the heavenly fireman and the diabolical incendiary into the ears of his congregation.

But since the detectives who were working on the case did not go to church at St. Barbara's and since, as far as they were concerned, the word "phoenix" sounded more like *lèse-majesté* than a disculpation of Wranka, Wranka's activity in the fire department was taken as a bad sign.

Evidence was gathered in a number of sawmills and in the town halls of both men's native places: Wranka had first seen the light of day in Tuchel, Koljaiczek in Thorn. When pieced together, the statements of older raftsmen and distant relatives revealed slight discrepancies. The pitcher, in short, kept going to the well; what could it do in the end but break? This was how things stood when the big raft entered German territory: after Thorn it was under discreet surveillance, and the men were shadowed when they went ashore.

It was only after Dirschau that my grandfather noticed his shadows.

He had been expecting them. It seems to have been a profound lethargy, verging on melancholia, that deterred him from trying to make a break for it at Letzkau or Käsemark; he might well have succeeded, for he knew the region inside out and he had good friends among the raftsmen. After Einlage, where the rafts drifted slowly, tamping and thumping, into the Dead Vistula, a fishing craft with much too much of a crew ran along close by, trying rather conspicuously not to make itself conspicuous. Shortly after Plehnendorf two harbor police launches shot out of the rushes and began to race back and forth across the river, churning up the increasingly brackish waters of the estuary. Beyond the bridge leading to Heubude, the police had formed a cordon. They were everywhere, as far as the eye could see, in among the fields of logs, on the wharves and piers, on the sawmill docks, on the company dock where the men's relatives were waiting. They were everywhere except across the river by Schichau; over there it was all full of flags, something else was going on, looked like a ship was being launched, excited crowds, the very gulls were frantic with excitement, a celebration was in progress—a celebration for my grandfather?

Only when my grandfather saw the timber basin full of blue uniforms, only when the launches began crisscrossing more and more ominously, sending waves over the rafts, only when he became fully cognizant of the expensive maneuvers that had been organized all for his benefit, did Koljaiczek's old incendiary heart awaken. Then he spewed out the gentle Wranka, sloughed off the skin of Wranka the volunteer fireman, loudly and fluently disowned Wranka the stutterer, and fled, fled over the rafts, fled over the wide, teetering expanse, fled barefoot over the unplaned floor, from log to log toward Schichau, where the flags were blowing gaily in the wind, on over the timber, toward the launching ceremony, where beautiful speeches were being made, where no one was shouting "Wranka," let alone "Koljaiczek," and the words rang out: I baptize you H.M.S. *Columbus*, America, forty thousand tons, thirty thousand horsepower, His Majesty's ship, first-class dining room, second-class dining room, gymnasium, library, America, His Majesty's ship, modern stabilizers, promenade deck. *Heil dir im Siegerkranz,* ensign of the home port. There stands Prince Heinrich at the helm, and my grandfather Koljaiczek barefoot, his feet barely touching the logs, running toward the brass band, a country that has such princes, from raft to raft, the people cheering him on, *Heil dir im Siegerkranz* and the dockyard sirens, the siren of every ship in the harbor, of every tug and pleasure craft, *Columbus*, America, liberty, and two launches mad with joy running along beside him, from raft to raft, His Majesty's rafts, and they block the way, too bad, he was making good time, he stands alone on his raft and sees America, and there are the launches. There's nothing to do but take to

23

the water, and my grandfather is seen swimming, heading for a raft that's drifting into the Mottlau. But he has to dive on account of the launches and he has to stay under on account of the launches, and the raft passes over him and it won't stop, one raft engenders another: raft of thy raft, for all eternity: raft.

The launches stopped their motors. Relentless eyes searched the surface of the water. But Koljaiczek was gone forever, gone from the band music, gone from the sirens, from the ship's bells on His Majesty's ship, from Prince Heinrich's baptismal address, and from His Majesty's frantic gulls, gone from *Heil dir im Siegerkranz* and from His Majesty's soft soap used to soap the ways for His Majesty's ship, gone from America and from the *Columbus,* from police pursuit and the endless expanse of logs.

My grandfather's body was never found. Though I have no doubt whatever that he met his death under the raft, my devotion to the truth, the whole truth, compels me to put down some of the variants in which he was miraculously rescued. According to one version he found a chink between two logs, just wide enough on the bottom to enable him to keep his nose above water, but so narrow on top that he remained invisible to the minions of the law who continued to search the rafts and even the reed huts until nightfall. Then, under cover of darkness—so the tale went on—he let himself drift until, half-dead with exhaustion, he reached the Schichau dockyard on the opposite bank; there he hid in the scrap-iron dump and later on, probably with the help of Greek sailors, was taken aboard one of those grimy tankers that are famous for harboring fugitives.

Another version is that Koljaiczek, a strong swimmer with remarkable lungs, had not only swum under the raft but traversed the whole remaining width of the Mottlau under water and reached the shipyard in Schichau, where, without attracting attention, he had mingled with the enthusiastic populace, joined in singing *Heil dir im Siegerkranz*, joined in applauding Prince Heinrich's baptismal oration, and after the launching, his clothes half-dried by now, had drifted away with the crowd. Next day—here the two versions converge—he had stowed away on the same Greek tanker of famed ill fame.

For the sake of completeness, I must also mention a third preposterous fable, according to which my grandfather floated out to sea like a piece of driftwood and was promptly fished out of the water by some fishermen from Bohnsack who, once outside the three-mile limit, handed him over to a Swedish deep-sea fisherman. After a miraculous recovery he reached Malmö, and so on.

All that is nonsense, fishermen's fish stories. Nor would I give a plugged nickel for the reports of the eyewitnesses—such eyewitnesses are to be met with in every seaport the world over—who claim to have seen my grandfather shortly after the First World War in Buffalo, U.S.A.

Called himself Joe Colchic, said he was importing lumber from Canada, big stockholder in a number of match factories, a founder of fire insurance companies. That was my grandfather, a lonely multimillionaire, sitting in a skyscraper behind an enormous desk, diamond rings on every finger, drilling his bodyguards, who wore firemen's uniforms, sang in Polish, and were known as the Phoenix Guard.

Moth and Light Bulb

A man left everything behind him, crossed the great water, and became rich. Well, that's enough about my grandfather regardless of whether we call him Goljaczek (Polish), Koljaiczek (Kashubian), or Joe Colchic (American).

It's not easy, with nothing better than a tin drum, the kind you can buy in the dimestore, to question a river clogged nearly to the horizon with log rafts. And yet I have managed by drumming to search the timber port, with all its driftwood lurching in the bights or caught in the rushes, and, with less difficulty, the launching ways of the Schichau shipyard and the Klawitter shipyard, and the drydocks, the scrap-metal dump, the rancid coconut stores of the margarine factory, and all the hiding places that were ever known to me in those parts. He is dead, he gives me no answer, shows no interest at all in imperial ship launchings, in the decline of a ship, which begins with its launching and sometimes goes on for as much as twenty or thirty years, in the present instance the decline of the H.M.S. *Columbus*, once termed the pride of the fleet and assigned, it goes without saying, to the North Atlantic run. Later on she was sunk or scuttled, then perhaps refloated, renamed, remodeled, or, for all I know, scrapped. Possibly the *Columbus*, imitating my grandfather, merely dived, and today, with her forty thousand tons, her dining rooms, her swimming pool, her gymnasium and massaging rooms, is knocking about a thousand fathoms down, in the Philippine Deep or the Emden Hollow; you'll find the whole story in Weyer's *Steamships* or in the shipping calendars—it seems to me that the *Columbus* was scuttled, because the captain couldn't bear to survive some sort of disgrace connected with the war.

I read Bruno part of my raft story and then, asking him to be objective, put my question to him.

"A beautiful death," Bruno declared with enthusiasm and began at once to transform my poor drowned grandfather into one of his knotted spooks. I could only content myself with his answer and abandon all harebrained schemes of going to the U.S.A. in the hope of cadging an inheritance.

My friends Klepp and Vittlar came to see me. Klepp brought me a jazz record with King Oliver on both sides; Vittlar, with a mincing little gesture, presented me with a chocolate heart on a pink ribbon. They clowned around, parodied scenes from my trial, and to please them I put a cheerful face on it, as I always did on visiting days, and managed to laugh even at the most dismal jokes. Before Klepp could launch into his inevitable lecture about the relationship between jazz and Marxism, I told my story, the story of a man who in 1913, not long before the shooting started, was submerged under an endless raft and never came up again, so that they had never even found his body.

In answer to my questions—I asked them in a very offhand manner, with an affectation of boredom—Klepp dejectedly shook his head over an adipose neck, unbuttoned his vest and buttoned it up again, made swimming movements, and acted as if he were under a raft. In the end he dismissed my question with a shake of his head, and said it was too early in the afternoon for him to form an opinion.

Vittlar sat stiffly, crossed his legs, taking good care not to disturb the crease in his pin-striped trousers, and putting on the expression of eccentric hauteur characteristic only of himself and perhaps of the angels in heaven, said: "I am on the raft. It's pleasant on the raft. Mosquitoes are biting me, that's bothersome. I am under the raft. It's pleasant under the raft. The mosquitoes aren't biting me any more, that is pleasant. I think I could live very nicely under the raft if not for my hankering to be on the top of the raft, being molested by mosquitoes."

Vittlar paused as usual for effect, looked me up and down, raised his already rather lofty eyebrows, as he always did when he wished to look like an owl, and spoke in piercing theatrical tones: "I assume that this man who was drowned, the man under the raft, was your great-uncle if not your grandfather. He went to his death because as a great-uncle, or in far greater measure as a grandfather, he felt he owed it to you, for nothing would be more burdensome to you than to have a living grandfather. That makes you the murderer not only of your great-uncle but also of your grandfather. However, like all true grandfathers, he wanted to punish you a little; he just wouldn't let you have the satisfaction of pointing with pride to a bloated, water-logged corpse and declaiming: Behold my dead grandfather. He was a hero. Rather than fall into the hands of his pursuers, he jumped in the river. Your grandfather cheated the world and his grandchild out of his corpse. Why? To make posterity and his grandchild worry their heads about him for many years to come."

Then, with a quick transition from one brand of pathos to another, he bent slightly forward and assumed the wily countenance of a purveyor of false consolation: "America! Take heart, Oskar. You have an aim, a mission in life. You'll be acquitted, released. Where should you go if not to America, the land where people find whatever they have lost, even missing grandfathers."

26

Sardonic and offensive as Vittlar's answer was, it gave me more certainty than my friend Klepp's ill-humored refusal to decide between life and death, or the reply of Bruno, my keeper, who thought my grandfather's death had been beautiful only because it had been immediately followed by the launching of the *Columbus*. God bless Vittlar's America, preserver of grandfathers, goal and ideal by which to rehabilitate myself when, weary of Europe, I decide to lay down my drum and pen: "Go on writing, Oskar. Do it for your grandfather, the rich but weary Koljaiczek, the lumber king of Buffalo, U.S.A., the lonely tycoon playing with matches in his skyscraper."

When Klepp and Vittlar had finally taken their leave, Bruno drove their disturbing aroma out of the room with a thorough airing. I went back to my drum, but I no longer drummed up the logs of death-concealing rafts; no, I beat out the rapid, erratic rhythm which commanded everybody's movements for quite some time after August, 1914. This makes it impossible for me to touch more than briefly on the life, up to the hour of my birth, of the little group of mourners my grandfather left behind him in Europe.

When Koljaiczek disappeared under the raft, my grandmother, her daughter Agnes, Vincent Bronski, and his seven-year-old son Jan were standing among the raftsmen's relatives on the sawmill dock, looking on in anguish. A little to one side stood Gregor Koljaiczek, Joseph's elder brother, who had been summoned to the city for questioning. Gregor had always had the same answer ready for the police: "I hardly know my brother. All I'm really sure of is that he was called Joseph. Last time I saw him, he couldn't have been more than ten or maybe twelve years old. He shined my shoes and went out for beer when mother and I wanted beer."

Though it turned out that my great-grandmother actually did drink beer, Gregor Koljaiczek's answer was no help to the police. But the elder Koljaiczek's existence was a big help to my grandmother Anna. Gregor, who had spent most of his life in Stettin, Berlin, and lastly in Schneidemühl, stayed on in Danzig, found work at the gunpowder factory, and after a year's time, when all the complications, such as her marriage with the false Wranka, had been cleared up and laid at rest, married my grandmother, who was determined to stick by the Koljaiczeks and would never have married Gregor, or not so soon at least, if he had not been a Koljaiczek.

His work in the gunpowder factory kept Gregor out of the peacetime and soon the wartime army. The three of them lived together in the same one-and-a-half-room apartment that had sheltered the incendiary for so many years. But it soon became evident that one Koljaiczek need not necessarily resemble another, for after the first year of marriage my grandmother was obliged to rent the basement shop in Troyl, which happened to be available, and to make what money she could selling miscellaneous items from pins to cabbages, because though Gregor made piles of money at the powder works, he drank it all up; what he brought home wasn't enough for the barest necessities. Unlike Joseph my grandfather, who merely took an occasional nip of brandy, Gregor was a real drinker, a quality he had probably inherited from my great-grandmother. He didn't drink because he was sad. And even when he seemed cheerful, a rare occurrence, for he was given to melancholia, he didn't drink because he was happy. He drank because he was a thorough man, who liked to get to the bottom of things, of bottles as well as everything else. As long as he lived, no one ever saw Gregor Koljaiczek leave so much as a drop in the bottom of his glass.

My mother, then a plump little girl of fifteen, made herself useful around the house and helped in the store; she pasted food stamps in the ledger, waited on customers on Saturdays, and wrote awkward but imaginative missives to those who bought on credit, admonishing them to pay up. It's a pity that I possess none of these letters. How splendid if at this point I could quote some of my mother's girlish cries of distress —remember, she was half an orphan, for Gregor Koljaiczek was far from giving full value as a stepfather. Quite the contrary, it was only with great difficulty that my grandmother and her daughter were able to conceal their cashbox, which consisted of a tin plate covered by another tin plate and contained more copper than silver, from the sad and thirsty gaze of the gunpowder-maker. Only when Gregor Koljaiczek died of influenza in 1917 did the profits of the shop increase a little. But not much; what was there to sell in 1917?

The little room which had remained empty since the powder-maker's death, because my mama was afraid of ghosts and refused to move into it, was occupied later on by Jan Bronski, my mother's cousin, then aged about twenty, who, having graduated from the high school in Karthaus and served a period of apprenticeship at the post office in the district capital, had left Bissau and his father Vincent to pursue his career at the main post office in Danzig. In addition to his suitcase, Jan brought with him a large stamp collection that he had been working on since he was a little boy. So you see, he had more than a professional interest in the post office; he had, indeed, a kind of private solicitude for that branch of the administration. He was a sickly young man who walked with a slight stoop, but he had a pretty oval face with perhaps a little too much sweetness about it, and a pair of blue eyes that made it possible for my mama, who was then seventeen, to fall in love with him. Three times Jan had been called to the colors, but each time had been deferred because of his deplorable physical condition, a circumstance which threw ample light on Jan Bronski's constitution in those days, when every male who could stand halfway erect was being shipped to Verdun to undergo a radical change of posture from the vertical to the eternal horizontal.

Their flirtation ought reasonably to have begun as they were looking at stamps together, as their two youthful heads leaned over the perforations and watermarks. Actually it began or, rather, erupted only when Jan was called up for service a fourth time. My mother, who had errands in town, accompanied him to district headquarters and waited for him outside the sentry box occupied by a militiaman. The two of them were both convinced that this time Jan would have to go, that they would surely send him off to cure his ailing chest in the air of France, famed for its iron and lead content. It is possible that my mother counted the buttons on the sentry's uniform several times with varying results. I can easily imagine that the buttons on all uniforms are so constituted that the last to be counted always means Verdun, the Hartmannsweilerkopf, or some little river, perhaps the Somme or the Marne.

When, barely an hour later, the four-times-summoned young man emerged from the portal of the district headquarters, stumbled down the steps, and, falling on the neck of Agnes, my mama, whispered the saying that was so popular in those days: "They can't have my front, they can't have my rear. They've turned me down for another year"—my mother for the first time held Jan Bronski in her arms, and I doubt whether there was ever more happiness in their embrace.

The details of this wartime love are not known to me. Jan sold part of his stamp collection to meet the exigencies of my mama, who had a lively appreciation of everything that was pretty, becoming to her, and expensive, and is said to have kept a diary which has unfortunately been lost. Evidently my grandmother tolerated the relations between the young people—which seem to have been more than cousinly—for Jan Bronski stayed on in the tiny flat in Troyl until shortly after the war. He moved out only when the existence of a Mr. Matzerath became undeniable and undenied. My mother must have met this Mr. Matzerath in the summer of 1918, when she was working as an auxilary nurse in the Silberhammer Hospital near Oliva. Alfred Matzerath, a native of the Rhineland, lay there wounded—the bullet had passed clear through his thigh—and soon with his merry Rhenish ways became the favorite of all the nurses, Sister Agnes not excluded. When he was able to get up, he hobbled about the corridor on the arm of one of the nurses and helped Sister Agnes in the kitchen, because her little nurse's bonnet went so well with her little round face and also because he, an impassioned cook, had a knack for metamorphosing feelings into soup.

When his wound had healed, Alfred Matzerath stayed in Danzig and immediately found work as representative of the Rhenish stationery firm where he had worked before the war. The war had spent itself. Peace treaties that would give ground for more wars were being boggled into shape: the region round the mouth of the Vistula—delimited roughly by a line running from Vogelsang on the Nehrung along the Nogat to Pieckel, down the Vistula to Czattkau, cutting across at right angles as far as Schönfliess, looping round the forest of Saskoschin to Lake Ottomin, leaving Mattern, Ramkaus and my grandmother's Bissau to one side, and returning to the Baltic at Klein-Katz—was proclaimed a free state under League of Nations control. In the city itself Polani was given a free port, the Westerplatte including the munitions depot, the railroad administration, and a post office of its own on the Heveliusplatz.

The postage stamps of the Free City were resplendent with red and gold Hanseatic heraldry, while the Poles sent out their mail marked with scenes from the lives of Casimir and Batory, all in macabre violet.

Jan Bronski opted for Poland and transferred to the Polish Post Office. The gesture seemed spontaneous and was generally interpreted as a reaction to my mother's infidelity. In 1920, when Marszalek Pilsudski defeated the Red Army at Warsaw, a miracle which Vincent Bronski and others like him attributed to the Virgin Mary and the military experts either to General Sikorski or to General Weygand—in that eminently Polish year, my mother became engaged to Matzerath, a citizen of the German Reich. I am inclined to believe that my grandmother Anna was hardly more pleased about it than Jan. Leaving the cellar shop in Troyl, which had meanwhile become rather prosperous, to her daughter, she moved to her brother Vincent's place at Bissau, which was Polish territory, took over the management of the farm with its beet and potato fields as in the pre-Koljaiczek era, left her increasingly grace-ridden brother to his dialogues with the Virgin Queen of Poland, and went back to sitting in four skirts beside autumnal potato-top fires, blinking at the horizon, which was still sectioned by telegraph poles.

Not until Jan Bronski had found and married his Hedwig, a Kashubian girl who lived in the city but still owned some fields in Ramkau, did relations between him and my mother improve. The story is that the two couples ran into each other at a dance at the Café Woyke, and that she introduced Jan and Matzerath. The two men, so different by nature despite the similarity of their feeling for Mama, took a shine to one another, although Matzerath in loud, unvarnished Rhenish qualified Jan's transfer to the Polish Post Office as sheer damn-foolishness. Jan danced with Mama, Matzerath danced with the big, rawboned Hedwig, whose inscrutable bovine gaze tended to make people think she was pregnant. After that they danced with, around, and into one another all evening, thinking always of the next dance, a little ahead of themselves in the polka, somewhat behind hand in the English waltz, but at last achieving self-confidence in the Charleston and in the slow foxtrot sensuality bordering on religion.

In 1923, when you could paper a bedroom with zeros for the price of a matchbox, Alfred Matzerath married my mama. Jan was one witness, the other was a grocer by the name of Mühlen. There isn't much I can tell you about Mühlen. He is worth mentioning only because, just as the Rentenmark was coming in, he sold Mama and Matzerath a languishing grocery store ruined by credit, in the suburb of Langfuhr. In a short time Mama, who in the basement shop in Troyl had learned how to deal with every variety of nonpaying customer and who in addition was favored with native business sense and ready repartee, managed to put the business back on its feet. Matzerath was soon obliged to give up his job—besides, the paper market was glutted—in order to help in the store.

The two of them complemented each other wonderfully. My mother's prowess behind the counter was equalled by Matzerath's ability to deal with salesmen and wholesalers. But what made their association really perfect was Matzerath's love of kitchen work, which even included cleaning up—all a great blessing for Mama, who was no great shakes as a cook.

The flat adjoining the store was cramped and badly constructed, but compared with the place in Troyl, which is known to me only from hearsay, it had a definite middle-class character. At least in the early years of her marriage, Mama must have felt quite comfortable.

There was a long, rather ramshackle hallway that usually had cartons of soap flakes piled up in it, and a spacious kitchen, though it too was more than half-full of merchandise: canned goods, sacks of flour, packages of rolled oats. The living room had two windows overlooking the street and a little patch of greenery decorated with sea shells in summer. The wallpaper had a good deal of wine-red in it and the couch was upholstered in an approximation of purple. An extensible table rounded at the corners, four black leather-covered chairs, a little round smoking table, which was always being moved about, stood black-legged on a blue carpet. An upright clock rose black and golden between the windows. Black against the purple couch squatted the piano, first rented then purchased in installments; and under the revolving stool lay the pelt of some yellowish-white long-haired animal. Across from the piano stood the sideboard, black with cut-glass sliding panels, enchased in black eggs-and-anchors. The lower doors enclosing the china and linen were heavily ornamented with black carvings of fruit; the legs were black claws; on the black carved top-piece there was an empty space between the crystal bowl of artificial fruit and the green loving cup won in a lottery; later on, thanks to my mama's business acumen, the gap was to be filled with a light-brown radio.

The bedroom ran to yellow and looked out on the court of the four-

31

story apartment house. Please believe me when I tell you that the canopy over the citadel of wedlock was sky-blue and that under its bluish light a framed, repentant, and flesh-colored Mary Magdalene lay in a grotto, sighing up at the upper right-hand edge of the picture and wringing so many fingers that you couldn't help counting them for fear there would be more than ten. Opposite the bed stood a white-enameled wardrobe with mirror doors, to the left of it a dressing table, to the right a marble-covered chest of drawers; the light fixture hung on brass arms from the ceiling, not covered with satin as in the living room, but shaded by pale-pink porcelain globes beneath which the bulbs protruded.

I have just drummed away a long morning, asking my drum all sorts of questions. I wished to know, for instance, whether the light bulbs in our bedroom were forty or sixty watts. The question is of the utmost importance to me, and this is not the first time I have asked it of myself and my drum. Sometimes it takes me hours to find my way back to those light bulbs. For I have to extricate myself from a forest of light bulbs, by good solid drumming without ornamental flourishes I have to make myself forget the thousands of lighting mechanisms it has been my lot to kindle or quench by turning a switch upon entering or leaving innumerable dwellings, before I can get back to the illumination of our bedroom in Labesweg.

Mama's confinement took place at home. When her labor pains set in, she was still in the store, putting sugar into blue pound and half-pound bags. It was too late to move her to the hospital; an elderly midwife who had just about given up practicing had to be summoned from nearby Hertastrasse. In the bedroom she helped me and Mama to get away from each other.

Well, then, it was in the form of two sixty-watt bulbs that I first saw the light of this world. That is why the words of the Bible, "Let there be light and there was light," still strike me as an excellent publicity slogan for Osram light bulbs. My birth ran off smoothly except for the usual rupture of the perineum. I had no difficulty in freeing myself from the upside-down position so favored by mothers, embryos, and midwives.

I may as well come right out with it: I was one of those clairaudient infants whose mental development is completed at birth and after that merely needs a certain amount of filling in. The moment I was born I took a very critical attitude toward the first utterances to slip from my parents beneath the light bulbs. My ears were keenly alert. It seems pretty well established that they were small, bent over, gummed up, and in any case cute, yet they caught the words that were my first impressions and as such have preserved their importance for me. And what my ear took in my tiny brain evaluated. After meditating at some length on what I had heard, I decided to do certain things and on no account to do certain others.

"It's a boy," said Mr. Matzerath, who presumed himself to be my father. "He will take over the store when he grows up. At last we know why we've been working our fingers to the bone."

Mama thought less about the store than about outfitting her son: "Oh, well, I knew it would be a boy even if I did say once in a while that it was going to be a girl."

Thus at an early age I made the acquaintance of feminine logic. The next words were: "When little Oskar is three, he will have a toy drum."

Carefully weighing and comparing these promises, maternal and paternal, I observed and listened to a moth that had flown into the room. Medium-sized and hairy, it darted between the two sixty-watt bulbs, casting shadows out of all proportion to its wing spread, which filled the room and everything in it with quivering motion. What impressed me most, however, was not the play of light and shade but the sound produced by the dialogue between moth and bulb: the moth chattered away as if in haste to unburden itself of its knowledge, as though it had no time for future colloquies with sources of light, as though this dialogue were its last confession; and as though, after the kind of absolution that light bulbs confer, there would be no further occasion for sin or folly.

Today Oskar says simply: The moth drummed. I have heard rabbits, foxes and dormice drumming. Frogs can drum up a storm. Woodpeckers are said to drum worms out of their hiding places. And men beat on basins, tin pans, bass drums, and kettledrums. We speak of drumfire, drumhead courts; we drum up, drum out, drum into. There are drummer boys and drum majors. There are composers who write concerti for strings and percussion. I might even mention Oskar's own efforts on the drum; but all this is nothing beside the orgy of drumming carrried on by that moth in the hour of my birth, with no other instrument than two ordinary sixty-watt bulbs. Perhaps there are Negroes in darkest Africa and others in America who have not yet forgotten Africa who, with their well-known gift of rhythm, might succeed in imitation of African moths—which are known to be larger and more beautiful than those of Eastern Europe— in drumming with such disciplined passion; I can only go by my Eastern European standards and praise that medium-sized powdery-brown moth of the hour of my birth; that moth was Oskar's master.

It was in the first days of September. The sun was in the sign of Virgo. A late-summer storm was approaching through the night, moving crates and furniture about in the distance. Mercury made me critical, Uranus ingenious, Venus made me believe in comfort and Mars in my ambition. Libra, rising up in the house of the ascendant, made me sensitive and given to exaggeration. Neptune moved into the tenth house, the house of middle life, establishing me in an attitude between faith in miracles and disillusionment. It was Saturn which, coming into opposition to Jupiter in the third house, cast doubt on my origins. But who sent the moth and allowed it, in the midst of a late-summer thunderstorm roaring like a high school principal, to make me fall in love with the drum my mother had promised me and develop my aptitude for it?

Outwardly wailing and impersonating a meat-colored baby, I made up my mind to reject my father's projects, in short everything connected with the grocery store, out of hand, but to give my mother's plan favorable consideration when the time came, to wit, on my third birthday.

Aside from all this speculation about my future, I quickly realized that Mama and this Mr. Matzerath were not equipped to understand or respect my decisions whether positive or negative. Lonely and misunderstood, Oskar lay beneath the light bulbs, and figuring that things would go on like this for some sixty or seventy years, until a final short circuit should cut off all sources of light, he lost his enthusiasm even before this life beneath the light bulbs had begun. It was only the prospect of the drum that prevented me then from expressing more forcefully my desire to return to the womb.

Besides, the midwife had already cut my umbilical cord. There was nothing more to be done.

The Photograph Album

I am guarding a treasure. Through all the bad years consisting only of calendar days, I have guarded it, hiding it when I wasn't looking at it; during the trip in the freight car I clutched it to my breast, and when I slept, Oskar slept on his treasure, his photograph album.

What should I do without this family cemetery which makes everything so perfectly clear and evident? It has a hundred and twenty pages. On each page, four or six or sometimes only two photographs are carefully mounted, sometimes symmetrically, sometimes less so, but always in an arrangement governed by the right angle. It is bound in leather and the older it grows the stronger it smells of leather. At times my album has been exposed to the wind and weather. The pictures came loose and seemed so helpless that I hastened to paste them back in their accustomed places.

What novel—or what else in the world—can have the epic scope of a photograph album? May our Father in Heaven, the untiring amateur who each Sunday snaps us from above, at an unfortunate angle that makes for hideous foreshortening, and pastes our pictures, properly exposed or not, in his album, guide me safely through this album of mine; may he deter me from dwelling too long on my favorites and discourage Oskar's penchant for the tortuous and labyrinthine; for I am only too eager to get on from the photographs to the originals.

So much for that. Shall we take a look? Uniforms of all sorts, the styles and the haircuts change, Mama gets fatter and Jan gets flabbier, some of these people I don't even know, but I can guess who they are. I wonder who took this one, the art was on the downgrade. Yes, gradually the art photo of 1900 degenerates into the utilitarian photo of our day. Take this monument of my grandfather Koljaiczek and this passport photo of my friend Klepp. One need only hold them side by side, the sepia print of my grandfather and this glossy passport photo that seems to cry out for a rubber stamp, to see what progress has brought us to in photography. And all the paraphernalia this quick photography takes. Actually I should find fault with myself even more than with Klepp, for I am the owner of the album and should have maintained certain standards. If there is a hell in wait for us, I know what one of the more fiendish torments will be: they will shut up the naked soul in a room with the framed photographs of his day: Quick, turn on the pathos: O man amid snapshots, passport photos. O man beneath the glare of flash bulbs, O man standing erect by the leaning tower of Pisa, O photomaton man who must expose his right ear if he is to be worthy of a passport! And—off with the pathos. Maybe this hell will be tolerable because the worst pictures of all are not taken but only dreamed or, if they are taken, never developed.

Klepp and I had these pictures taken and developed during our early days in Jülicher-Strasse, when we ate spaghetti together and made friends. In those days I harbored plans for travel. That is, I was so gloomy that I resolved to take a trip and, to that end, apply for a passport. But since I hadn't money enough to finance a real trip, including Rome, Naples, or at least Paris, I was glad of the lack of cash, for what could have been more dismal than to set out on a trip in a state of depression? But since we had enough money to go to the movies, Klepp and I in those days attended motion picture theaters where, in keeping with Klepp's taste, Wild West films were shown, and, in response to my needs, pictures where Maria Schell was the tearful nurse and Borsche, as the surgeon, played Beethoven sonatas by the open window after a difficult operation, and displayed a lofty sense of responsibility.

We were greatly dissatisfied that the performances should take only two hours. We should have been glad to see some of the programs twice. Often we arose at the end, determined to buy tickets for the next showing. But once we had left the hall and saw the line waiting outside the box office, our courage seeped away. Not only the thought of a second encounter with the ticket-seller but also the insolent stares with which total strangers mustered our physiognomies shamed us out of lengthening the line.

The upshot was that after nearly every show we went to a photo studio not far from the Graf-Adolf-Platz and had passport pictures taken. We were well known and our entrance was greeted with a smile; however, we were paying customers and treated politely as such. As soon as the booth was free, we were pushed into it by a young lady—all I remember about her is that she was nice. She deftly set our heads at the right angle, first mine, then Klepp's, and told us to fix our eyes on a certain point, and a moment later a flash of light and a bell synchronized with it announced that six succesive likenesses had been transferred to the plate.

Still stiff around the corners of the mouth, we were pressed into comfortable wicker chairs by the young lady, who nicely, but no more than nicely, and nicely dressed too, asked us to be patient for five minutes. We were glad to wait. For now we had something to wait for—our passport pictures—and we were curious to see how they would turn out. In exactly seven minutes the still nice but otherwise nondescript young lady handed us two little paper envelopes and we paid.

The triumph in Klepp's slightly protuberant eyes! As soon as we had our envelopes, we had ipso facto an excuse for repairing to the nearest beer saloon, for no one likes to look at his own passport pictures on the open, dusty street, standing amid all the noise and bustle and blocking the traffic. Just as we were faithful to the photo studio, we always went to the same saloon in Friedrichstrasse. We ordered beer, blood sausage, onions, and rye bread, and, even before our order came, spread out the slightly damp photographs over the little round table and, while partaking of our beer and blood sausage, which had arrived in the meantime, immersed ourselves in our own strained features.

We always brought along other photographs taken on the occasion of previous movie shows. This gave us a basis for comparison and where there is a basis for comparison, there is also ground for ordering a second, third, fourth glass of beer, to create merriment, or, as they say in the Rhineland, *ambiance*.

I am not tryng to say that a passport photo of himself can cure a gloomy man of a gloom for which there is no ground; for true gloom is by nature groundless; such gloom, ours at least, can be traced to no identifiable cause, and with its almost riotous gratuitousness this gloom of ours attained a pitch of intensity that would yield to nothing. If there was any way of making friends with our gloom, it was through the photos, because in these serial snapshots we found an image of ourselves which, though not exactly clear, was—and that was the essential—passive and neutralized. They gave us a kind of freedom in our dealings with ourselves; we could drink beer, torture our blood sausages, make merry, and play. We bent and folded the pictures, and cut them up with the little scissors we carried about with us for this precise purpose. We juxtaposed old and new pictures, made ourselves one-eyed or three-eyed, put noses on our ears, made our exposed right ears into organs of speech or silence, combined chins and foreheads. And it was not only each with his own

36

likeness that we made these montages; Klepp borrowed features from me and I from him: thus we succeeded in making new and, we hoped, happier creatures. Occasionally we gave a picture away.

We—I am speaking only of Klepp and myself, setting aside all synthetic photo-personalities—got into the habit of donating a photo to the waiter, whom we called Rudi, every time we saw him, and that happened at least once a week. Rudi, a type who ought to have had twelve children and at least eight wards, appreciated our distress; he had dozens of profiles of us and still more full-faced views, and even so his eyes were full of sympathy and he said thank you when after long deliberation and a careful process of selection we handed him his photo.

Oskar never gave any pictures to the waitress at the counter or to the redheaded young thing with the cigarette tray; it's not a good idea to give women pictures, for you never know what use they may make of them. Klepp, however, who with all his easygoing corpulence was a setup for the fair sex, who was communicative to the point of folly and required only a feminine presence to make him spill his innermost guts, must have given the cigarette girl a photo unbeknownst to me, for he became engaged to the snippety little thing and married her one day, because he wanted to have his picture back.

I have gotten ahead of myself and devoted too many words to the last pages of my album. The silly snapshots don't deserve it; however, if taken as a term of comparison, they may give you an idea how sublimely grandiose, how artistic if you will, the album still seems to me.

Short and stocky he stands there behind a richly carved coffee table. Unfortunately he had himself photographed not as a firebug, but as Wranka the volunteer fireman. But the tight-fitting fireman's uniform with the rescue medal and the fireman's helmet that gives the table the aspect of an altar almost take the place of the incendiary's mustache. How solemn is his gaze, how full of all the sorrow of those sorrowful years. That proud though tragic gaze seems to have been popular and prevalent in the days of the German Empire; we find it again in Gregor Koljaiczek, the drunken gunpowder-maker, who looks rather sober in his pictures. Taken in Częstochowa, the picture of Vincent Bronski holding a consecrated candle is more mystical in tone. A youthful portrait of the sickly Jan Bronski is a record of self-conscious melancholy, achieved by the methods of early photography.

The women of those days were less expert at finding the expression suited to their personality. In the photographs taken shortly before the First World War even my grandmother Anna, who, believe me, was somebody, hides behind a silly glued-on smile that carries not the slightest suggestion of her four great, asylum-giving skirts.

During the war years they continued to smile at the photographer as he danced about beneath his black cloth. From this period I have a picture, double postcard size on stiff cardboard, of twenty-three nurses, including my mother, clustering timidly round the reassuring solidity of an army doctor. The nurses seem somewhat more relaxed in a picture of a costume ball attended by convalescent warriors. Mama ventures a wink and a rosebud mouth which despite her angel's wings and the tinsel in her hair seem to say that even angels have a sex. Matzerath is seen kneeling at her feet in a costume that he would have been only too glad to wear every day: he has on a starched chef's hat and he is even brandishing a ladle. But when wearing his uniform adorned with the Iron Cross Second Class, he too, like Koljaiczek and Bronski, peers into the distance with a wittingly tragic look, and in all the pictures he is superior to the women.

After the war the faces changed. The men look rather demobilized; now it is the women who rise to the occasion, who have grounds for looking solemn, and who, even when smiling, make no attempt to conceal an undertone of studied sorrow. Melancholy was becoming to the women of the twenties. With their little black spit curls they managed, whether sitting, standing, or half-reclining, to suggest a harmonious blend of madonna and harlot.

The picture of my mama at the age of twenty-three—it must have been taken shortly before the inception of her pregnancy—shows a young woman with a round, tranquil face slightly tilted on a firm, substantial neck. But tilted or not, she is always looking you straight in the eye. Good solid flesh, but the effect of solidity is called into question by the melancholy smile of the day and by those eyes, more gray than blue, which seem to look upon the souls of her fellow men— and her own soul as well—as solid objects, something like teacups or cigarette holders. I should say that the look in my mama's eyes is something more than soulful.

Not more interesting, but easier to appraise and hence more revealing, are the group photos of that period. How beautiful, how nuptial the wedding dresses were in the days of the Treaty of Rapallo. In his wedding photo Matzerath is still wearing a stiff collar. A fine figure of a man, he looks distinctly elegant, almost intellectual. His right foot is thrust forward, and he rather resembles a movie actor of the day, Harry Liedtke perhaps. The dresses were short. My mama's wedding dress, white and accordion-pleated, reaches barely below the knee, showing her shapely legs and cunning little dancing feet in white buckled shoes. Other pictures show the whole bridal assemblage. Surrounded by people who dress and pose like city dwellers, my grandmother Anna and her grace-favored brother Vincent are always conspicuous for their provincial gravity and a confidence-inspiring air of unsureness. Jan Bronski, who like my mama stems from the same potato field as his father and his Aunt Anna, manages to hide his rural Kashubian origins behind the festive elegance of a Polish postal official. He is small and frail amid these robust occupiers of space, and yet the extraordinary look in his eyes, the almost feminine regularity of his features, make him the center of every picture, even when he is on the edge of it.

For some time now I have been looking at a group picture taken shortly after the marriage. I have been compelled to take up my drum and drumsticks and, gazing at the faded brownish rectangle, attempt to conjure up the dimly visible three-cornered constellation.

The picture must have been taken in the Bronski flat in Magdeburger-Strasse not far from the Polish Students' House, for in the background we perceive a sunlit balcony of a type seen only in the Polish quarter, half-concealed by the vinelike foliage of pole beans. Mama is seated, Matzerath and Jan Bronski are standing. But how she sits and how they stand! For a time I foolishly tried to plot the constellation of this triumvirate—for she gave the full value of a man—with the help of a ruler, a triangle, and a school compass that Bruno had to go out for. Starting with the angle between neck and shoulder, I drew a triangle; I spun out projections, deduced similarities, described arcs which met significantly outside the triangle, i.e., in the foliage, and provided a point, because I needed a point, a point of vantage, a point of departure, a point of contact, a point of view.

All I accomplished with my metaphysical geometry was to dig a number of small but annoying holes in the precious photo with the point of my compass. What, I cannot help wondering, is so remarkable about that print? What was it that made me seek and, if you will, actually find mathematical and, preposterously enough, cosmic references in it? Three persons: a woman sitting, two men standing. She with a dark marcel wave, Matzerath curly blond, Jan chestnut brown, combed back flat from the forehead. All three are smiling, Matzerath more than Jan Bronski; and both men a good deal more than Mama, for their smile shows their upper teeth while of her smile there is barely a trace in the corners of her mouth and not the least suggestion in her eyes. Matzerath has his left hand resting on Mama's right shoulder; Jan contents himself with leaning his right hand lightly on the back of the chair. She, her knees slightly to one side but otherwise directly facing the camera, has in her lap a portfolio which I took years ago for one of Jan's stamp albums, later reinterpreted as a fashion magazine, and more recently as a collection of movie stars out of cigarette packages. Her hands look as if she would begin to leaf through the album the moment the picture was taken. All three seem happy, as though congratulating one another on their immunity to surprises of the sort that can arise only if one member of the triumvirate should acquire a secret life—if he hasn't had one all along.

In their tripartite solidarity, they have little need of the fourth person, Jan's wife Hedwig Bronski née Lemke, who may at that time have been pregnant with the future Stephan; all they needed her for was to aim the camera at them, so perpetuating their triangular felicity, photographically at least.

I have detached other rectangles from the album and held them next to this one. Scenes showing either Mama with Matzerath or Mama with Jan Bronski. In none of these pictures is the immutable, the ultimate solution so clearly discernible as in the balcony picture. Jan and Mama by themselves: this one smacks of tragedy, money-grubbing, exaltation turning to surfeit, a surfeit of exaltation. Matzerath and Mama: here we find an atmosphere of conjugal weekends at home, a sizzling of cutlets, a bit of grumbling before dinner and a bit of yawning after dinner; jokes are told before going to bed, and the tax returns are discussed: here we have the cultural background of the marriage. And yet I prefer such photographed boredom to the distasteful snapshot of later years, showing Mama seated on Jan Bronski's lap in the Forest of Oliva near Freudenthal; because this last picture with its lewdness—Jan's hand has disappeared under Mama's skirt—communicates nothing but the mad passion of this unhappy pair, steeped in adultery from the very first day of Mama's marriage; Matzerath, I presume, was the disabused photographer. Here we see none of the serenity of the balcony picture, none of the delicate, circumspect little gestures which seem to have been possible only when both men were together, standing behind or beside Mama or lying at her feet as on the bathing beach at Heubude; see photo.

There is still another picture which shows the three protagonists of my early years forming a triangle. Though it lacks the concentration of the balcony scene, it emanates the same tense pace, which can probably be concluded only among three persons. We may get pretty sick of the triangle situations in plays; but come to think of it, what can two people do if left to themselves on the stage except dialogue each other to death or secretly long for a third? In my picture the three of them are together. They are playing skat. That is, they are holding their cards like well-organized fans, but instead of looking at their trumps and plotting their strategy, they are looking into the camera. Jan's hand lies flat, except for the raised forefinger, beside a pile of change; Matzerath is digging his nails into the tablecloth; Mama is indulging in a little joke which strikes me as rather good: she has drawn a card and is showing it to the camera lens but not to her fellow players. How easy it is with a single gesture, by merely showing the queen of hearts, to conjure up a symbol that is not too blatant; for who would not swear by the queen of hearts?

Skat—as everyone should know, skat can only be played three-handed—was not just a handy game for Mama and the two men; it was their refuge, their haven, to which they always retreated when life threatened to beguile them into playing, in one combination or another, such silly two-handed games as backgammon or sixty-six.

That's enough now for those three, who brought me into the world though they wanted for nothing. Before I come to myself, a word about Gretchen Scheffler, Mama's girl friend, and her baker consort Alexander Scheffler. He bald-headed, she laughing with her great equine teeth, a good half of which were gold. He short-legged, his feet when he is sitting down dangling several inches above the carpet, she always in dresses she herself had knitted, with patterns that could not be too intricate. From later years, photos of both Schefflers in deck chairs or standing beside lifeboats belonging to the "Strength through Joy" ship *Wilhelm Gustloff*, or on the promenade deck of the *Tannenberg* (East Prussian Steamship Lines). Year by year they took trips and brought souvenirs from Pillau, Norway, the Azores, or Italy safely home to their house in Kleinhammer-Weg, where he baked rolls and she embroidered cushion covers. When Alexander Scheffler was not talking, he never stopped moistening his upper lip with the tip of his tongue, a habit which Matzerath's friend, Greff the greengrocer who lived across the way, thought obscene and disgusting.

Although Greff was married, he was more scout leader than husband. A photo shows him broad, healthy, and unsmiling, in a uniform with shorts, wearing a scout hat and the braid of a leader. Beside him in the same rig stands a blond lad of maybe thirteen, with rather too large eyes. Greff's arm is thrown affectionately over his shoulder. I didn't know the boy, but I was later to become acquainted with Greff through his wife Lina and to learn to understand him.

I am losing myself amid snapshots of "Strength through Joy" tourists and records of tender boy-scout eroticism. Let me skip a few pages and come to myself, to my first photographic likeness.

I was a handsome child. The picture was taken on Pentecost, 1925. I was eight months old, two months younger than Stephan Bronski, who is shown on the next page in the same format, exuding an indescribable commonplaceness. My postcard has a wavy scalloped edge; the reverse side has lines for the address and was probably printed in a large edition for family consumption. Within the wide rectangle the photograph itself has the shape of an oversymmetrical egg. Naked and symbolizing the yolk, I am lying on my belly on a white fur, which must have been the gift of a benevolent polar bear to an Eastern European photographer specializing in baby pictures. For my first likeness, as for so many photos of the period, they selected the inimitable warm brownish tint which I should call " human" in contrast to the inhumanly glossy black-and-white photographs of our day. Some sort of hazy greenery, probably artificial, provides a dark background, relieved only by a few spots of light. Whereas my sleek healthy body lies flat and complacent on the fur, basking in polar well-being, my billiard-ball skull strains upward and peers with glistening eyes at the beholder of my nakedness.

A baby picture, you may say, like all other baby pictures. Consider the hands, if you please. You will have to admit that my earliest likeness differs conspicuously from all the innumerable records of cunning little existences you may have seen in photograph albums the world over. You see me with clenched fists. You don't see any little sausage fingers playing with tufts of fur in self-forgetful response to some obscure haptic urge. My little claws hover in earnest concentration on a level with my head, ready to descend, to strike. To strike what? The drum!

It is still absent, the photo shows no sign of that drum which, beneath the light bulbs of my Creation, had been promised me for my third birthday; yet how simple it would be for anyone experienced in photo-montage to insert a toy drum of the appropriate size. There would be no need to change my position in any way. Only the ridiculous stuffed animal, to which I am not paying the slightest attention, would have to be removed. It is a disturbing element in this otherwise harmonious composition commemorating the astute, clear-sighted age when the first milk teeth are trying to pierce through.

After a while, they stopped putting me on polar-bear skins. I was probably about a year and a half old when they pushed me, ensconced in a high-wheeled baby carriage, close to a board fence covered by a layer of snow which faithfully follows its contours and convinces me that the picture was taken in January, 1926. When I consider it at length, the crude construction of the fence, the smell of tar it gives off, connect me with the suburb of Hochstriess, whose extensive barracks had formerly housed the Mackensen Hussars and in my time the Free City police. But since I remember no one who lived out there, I can only conclude that the picture was taken one day when my parents were paying a visit to some people whom we never, or only seldom, saw in the ensuing period.

Despite the wintry season, Mama and Matzerath, who flank the baby carriage, are without overcoats. Mama has on a long-sleeved embroidered Russian blouse: one cannot help imagining that the Tsar's family is having its picture taken in deepest, wintriest Russia, that Rasputin is holding the camera, that I am the Tsarevich, and that behind the fence Mensheviks and Bolsheviks are tinkering with homemade bombs and plotting the downfall of my autocratic family. But the illusion is shattered by Matzerath's correct, Central European, and, as we shall see, prophetic shopkeeper's exterior. We were in the quiet suburb of Hochstriess, my parents had left the house of our host just for a moment—why bother to put coats on?—just time enough to let their host snap them with little Oskar, who obliged with his cunningest look, and a moment later they would be deliciously warming themselves over coffee, cake, and whipped cream.

There are still a dozen or more snapshots aged one, two, and two and a half, lying, sitting, crawling, and running. They aren't bad; but all in all, they merely lead up to the full-length portrait they had taken of me in honor of my third birthday.

Here I've got it. I've got my drum. It is hanging in front of my tummy, brand-new with its serrated red and white fields. With a solemnly resolute expression, I hold the sticks crossed over the top of it. I have on a striped pull-over and resplendent patent leather shoes. My hair is standing up like a brush ready for action and in each of my blue eyes is reflected the determination to wield a power that would have no need of vassals or henchmen. It was in this picture that I first arrived at a decision which I have had no reason to alter. It was then that I declared, resolved, and determined that I would never under any circumstances be a politician, much less a grocer, that I would stop right there, remain as I was—and so I did; for many years I not only stayed the same size but clung to the same attire.

Little people and big people, Little Claus and Great Claus, Tiny Tim and Carolus Magnus, David and Goliath, Jack the Giant Killer and, of course, the giant; I remained the three-year-old, the gnome, the Tom Thumb, the pigmy, the Lilliputian, the midget, whom no one could persuade to grow. I did so in order to be exempted from the big and little catechism and in order not, once grown to five-foot-eight adulthood, to be driven by this man who face to face with his shaving mirror called himself my father, into a business, the grocery business, which as Matzerath saw it, would, when Oskar turned twenty-one, become his grownup world. To avoid playing the cash register I clung to my drum and from my third birthday on refused to grow by so much a finger's breadth. I remained the precocious three-year-old, towered over by grownups but superior to all grownups, who refused to measure his shadow with theirs, who was complete both inside and outside, while they, to the very brink of the grave, were condemned to worry their heads about " development," who had only to confirm what they were compelled to gain by hard and often painful experiance, and who had no need to change his shoe and trouser size for year after year just to prove that something was growing.

However, and here Oskar must confess to development of a sort, something did grow—and not always to my best advantage—ultimately taking on Messianic proportions; but what grownup in my day had eyes and ears for Oskar, the eternal three-year-old drummer?

Smash a Little Windowpane

I have just described a photograph showing Oskar full length with a drum and drumsticks, and at the same time disclosed what decisions, having had three years in which to mature, were definitely taken by Oskar as he was being photographed at his birthday party, not far from a cake with three candles. But now the album lies silent beside me, and I must speak of certain events about which it has nothing to say. Even if they do not explain why I continued to be three years old, there is no doubt that they happened, and what is more, that I made them happen.

From the very beginning it was plain to me: grownups will not understand you. If you cease to offer them any discernable growth, they will say you are retarded; they will drag you and their money to dozens of doctors, looking for an explanation if not a cure for your deficiency. Consequently I myself, in order to keep the consultations within tolerable limits, felt obliged to provide a plausible ground for my failure to grow, even before the doctor should offer his explanation.

A sunny day in September, my third birthday. An atmosphere of late summer reverie; even Gretchen Scheffler's laughter was muffled. Mama at the piano intoning airs from the *Gypsy Baron*, Jan standing behind her, his hand grazing her shoulder, giving himself an air of following the music. Matzerath in the kitchen, already getting supper. Grandma Anna with Hedwig Bronski and Alexander Schleffler moving over to sit with Greff, because the greengrocer always knew stories, boy-scout stories full of loyalty and courage; and in the background, the upright clock which didn't miss a single quarter-hour of that finespun September day. And since, like the clock, they were all so busy, and since a line ran from the Gypsy Baron's Hungary by way of Greff's boy scouts (who were touring the Vosges Mountains), past Matzerath's kitchen, where Kashubian mushrooms with scrambled eggs and tripe were sputtering in the frying pan, down the hallway to the shop, I, vaguely improvising on my drum, followed it. Soon I was in the shop, standing behind the counter—piano, mushrooms, and Vosges already far behind me. There I notice that the trap door leading to the cellar was open; Matzerath, who had gone down to get a can of mixed fruit for dessert, must have forgotten to close it.

It was a moment before I realized what that trap door demanded of me. Not suicide, certainly not. That would have been too simple. The alternative, however, was difficult and painful; it demanded sacrifice, and even then, as has been the case ever since when a sacrifice has been required of me, such an idea brought the sweat to my forehead. Above all, no harm must come to my drum; I would have to carry it carefully down the sixteen worn-down steps and lodge it among the flour sacks, so motivating its unharmed condition. Then back up again as far as the eighth step, no, the seventh, no, actually the fifth would do just as well. But from that height it would be impossible to combine safety with plausible injury. Back up again, too high this time, to the tenth, then finally, from the ninth step, I flung myself down, carrying a shelf laden with bottles of raspberry syrup along with me, and landed head first on the cement floor of our cellar.

Even before the curtain passed over my consciousness, I registered the success of my experiment: the bottles of raspberry syrup which I had intentionally taken with me in my fall made clatter enough to bring Matzerath from the kitchen, Mama from the piano, and the rest of the birthday party from the Vosges, all running into the shop, to the open trap door, and down the stairs.

Before they arrived, I had time to enjoy a whiff of the raspberry syrup, to observe that my head was bleeding, and to wonder—by now they were already on the stairs—whether it was Oskar's blood or the raspberries that smelled so sweet and sleepy-making, but I was delighted that everything had gone off smoothly and that, thanks to my foresight, the drum had suffered no injury.

I think it was Greff who carried me upstairs. It was only in the living room that Oskar emerged from a cloud which consisted no doubt half of raspberry syrup and half of his juvenile blood. The doctor had not arrived yet; Mama was screaming and flailing out at Matzerath, who was trying to pacify her, striking him in the face, and not just with her palm but with her knuckles as well, calling him a murderer.

And so with a single fall, not exactly without gravity but its degree of gravity calculated by myself in advance, I not only supplied a reason —repeatedly confirmed by the doctors and in general satisfactory to the grownups who simply have to have their explanations for things—for my failure to grow, but in addition and without any real intention on my part, transformed our harmless, good-natured Matzerath into a guilty Matzerath. He had left the trap door open, my mother put all the blame on him, and for years to come he incurred Mama's merciless, though not too frequent reproaches.

My fall brought me four weeks in the hospital and after that, apart from the weekly visits to Dr. Hollatz later on, relative peace from the medical profession. On my very first day as a drummer I had succeeded in giving the world a sign; my case was explained even before the grownups so much as suspected the true nature of the condition I myself had induced. Forever after the story was: on his third birthday our little Oskar fell down the cellar stairs, no bones were broken, but he just wouldn't grow any more.

And I began to drum. Our apartment house had four stories. From the ground floor to the attic I drummed up and down stairs. From Labesweg to Max-Halbe-Platz, thence to Neuschottland, Marienstrasse, Kleinhammer Park, the Aktien Brewery, Aktien Pond, Fröbel Green, Pestalozzi School, the Neue Markt, and back again to Labesweg. The drum stood up well under the strain, the grownups around me not quite so well, they were always wanting to interrupt my drum, to cross it up, to crimp my drumsticks—but nature looked out for me.

45

The ability to drum the necessary distance between grownups and myself developed shortly after my fall, almost simultaneously with the emergence of a voice that enabled me to sing in so high-pitched and sustained a vibrato, to sing-scream so piercingly that no one dared to take away the drum that was destroying his eardrums; for when the drum was taken away from me, I screamed, and when I screamed, valuable articles burst into bits: I had the gift of shattering glass with my singing: my screams demolished vases, my singing made windowpanes crumple and drafts prevail; like a chaste and therefore merciless diamond, my voice cut through the doors of glass cabinets and, without losing its innocence, proceeded inside to wreak havoc on harmonious, graceful liqueur glasses, bestowed by loving hands and covered with a light film of dust.

It was not long before my talents became known the whole length of our street, from Brösener-Weg to the housing development by the airfield. Whenever I caught the attention of the neighborhood children, whose games—such as "Pickled herring, one, two, three" or "Where's the Witch, black as pitch?" or "I see something you don't see"—didn't interest me in the slightest, the whole-unwashed chorus of them would begin to squeal:

Smash a little windowpane,
Put sugar in the beer,
Mrs. Biddle plays the fiddle,
Dear, dear, dear.

It was a silly, meaningless jingle and troubled me very little; I took up the simple rhythm, which was not without charm, and drummed my way from start to finish, through the little pieces and through Mrs. Biddle. Thus drumming, I marched down the street and though I was not the Pied Piper, the children followed in my wake.

Even today, when Bruno is washing my windows, for instance, my drum, as often as not, will find a moment for the rhythm of that little jingle.

More irritating than the children's lyrical mockery, especially for my parents, was the costly fact that every windowpane broken in the entire neighborhood by rowdies big or little was blamed on me and my voice. At first Mama conscientiously paid for the breakage, most of which was the work of slingshots, then at last she saw what was what and, putting on her frosty businesslike look, demanded proof when damages were claimed. And indeed, I was unjustly accused. Nothing could have been more mistaken at the time than to suppose that I was possessed by a childlike passion for destruction, that I was consumed by an unreasoning hatred of glass and glassware. Only children who play are destructive out

46

of mischief. I never played, I worked on my drum, and as for my voice, its miraculous powers were mobilized, in the beginning at least, only in self-defense. It was only when my right to drum was threatened that I made weapons of my vocal cords. If with the same tones and techniques I had been able to cut up Gretchen Scheffler's beastly, intricately embroidered tablecloths or to remove the somber polish from the piano, I should gladly have left all glassware intact. But tablecloths and varnish were impervious to my voice. It was beyond my powers to efface the pattern of the wallpaper with my screams, or by rubbing together two long-drawn-out tones as our Stone Age ancestors rubbed flints, to produce the heat that would produce the spark needed to kindle decorative flames in the tinder-dry curtains, spiced with tobacco smoke, of our living room windows. I never sang the leg off a chair in which Matzerath or Alexander Scheffler was sitting. I should gladly have defended myself in less destructive, less miraculous ways, but no other weapon was available; only glass heeded my commands, and had to pay for it.

It was shortly after my third birthday that I staged my first successful performance of this nature. I had been in possession of the drum for about four weeks and, conscientious as I was, I had pretty well worn it out. The serrated red and white cylinder still held top and bottom together, but the hole in the playing surface could not be overlooked; since I scorned to use the other side, it became larger and larger, spread out in all directions, and developed fierce jagged edges. Bits of tin worn thin by my drumming broke off, fell inside the drum, and at every beat set up a disgruntled clatter of their own; white specks of enamel, unequal to the hard life the drum had been leading, took up residence on the living room rug and the red-brown flooring of the bedroom.

It was feared that I would cut myself on the sharp edges. Particularly Matzerath, who had become exceedingly safety-minded since my fall from the cellar stairs, pleaded with me to be careful. Since, when I drummed, my violently agitated wrists were always close to the jagged edge of the crater, I must own that Matzerath's fears were not groundless, though they may have been exaggerated. Of course they could have forestalled all danger by giving me a new drum; but this was not their plan; they simply wanted to deprive me of my good old drum, which had taken the fall with me, which had gone to the hospital with me and come home with me, which accompanied me upstairs and down, over cobblestones and sidewalks, through "Pickled herring, one two three" and past "I see something you don't see" and "Where's the Witch"—yes, they wanted to take it away from me and give me nothing in return. They tried to bribe me with some silly old chocolate. Mama held it out to me, pursing her lips. It was Matzerath who, with a show of severity, laid hands on my decrepit instrument. I clung to it with all my might. He pulled. My strength, which was barely enough for drumming, began to give out. Slowly, one red tongue of flame after another, the cylinder was slipping from my grasp. At this moment Oskar, who until then had passed as a quiet, almost too well-behaved child, succeeded in emitting that first annihilating scream: the polished round crystal which protected the honey-colored dial of our clock from dust and moribund flies burst and fell to the floor (for the carpet did not reach all the way to the base of the clock), where the destruction was completed. However, the inside of the precious mechanism incurred no harm; serenely the pendulum continued on its way, and so did the hands. Not even the chimes, which otherwise reacted almost hysterically to the slightest jolt, which would be thrown off kilter by the passage of a beer truck, were one bit dismayed by my scream; it was only the glass that broke, but it did a thorough job of it.

"The clock is broken!" cried Matzerath and let go of the drum. With a brief glance I convinced myself that nothing had happened to the clock proper, that only the glass was gone. But to Matzerath, as well as to Mama and Uncle Jan Bronski, who was paying his usual Sunday afternoon call, it seemed that the damage must be much more serious. They blanched, exchanged shifty, helpless glances, and reached for the nearest solid object, the tile stove, the piano, the sideboard. There they stood fast, afraid to budge. Jan Bronski's eyes were filled with supplication and I could see his parched lips move. I still believe that he was inwardly muttering a prayer, perhaps: "O Lamb of God, Who taketh away the sins of the world, *miserere nobis.*" Three of these, followed by a "Lord, I am not worthy that Thou shouldst enter under my roof; say but the word . . . "

Naturally the Lord didn't say a thing. Besides, the clock wasn't broken, but just the glass. However, there is something very strange and childish in the way grownups feel about their clocks—in that respect, I was never a child. I am willing to agree that the clock is probably the most remarkable thing that grownups ever produced. Grownups have it in them to be creative, and sometimes, with the help of ambition, hard work, and a bit of luck they actually are, but being grownups, they have no sooner created some epoch-making invention than they become a slave to it.

What, after all, is a clock? Without your grownup it is nothing. It is the grownup who winds it, who sets it back or ahead, who takes it to the watchmaker to be checked, cleaned, and when necessary repaired. Just as with the cuckoo that stops calling too soon, just as with upset saltcellars, spiders seen in the morning, black cats on the left, the oil portrait of Uncle that falls off the wall because the nail has come loose in the plaster, just as in a mirror, grownups see more in and behind a clock than any clock can justify.

At length, Mama, who with all her flightiness had a cool head on her shoulders and whose very frivolity led her to put optimistic interpretations on all ostensible signs or portents, found words to save the situation.

"Shards are good luck!" she cried, snapping her fingers, brought dustpan and brush, and swept up the good luck.

If Mama's words are taken at face value, I brought my parents, relatives, friends, and even a good many total strangers plenty of good luck by screaming or singing to pieces any glassware belonging to or being used by persons who tried to take my drum away, including windowpanes, crystal bowls full of artificial fruit, full beer glasses, empty beer bottles, or those little flacons of vernal fragrance that laymen call perfume bottles, in short, any product whatever of the glass blower's art.

To limit the damage, for I have always been a lover of fine glassware, I concentrated, when they tried to take my drum away at night instead of letting me take it to bed with me, on shattering one or more of the four bulbs in our living room lamp. On my fourth birthday, at the beginning of September, 1928, I threw the whole assembled company— my parents, the Bronskis, Grandma Koljaiczek, the Schefflers, and the Greffs, who had given me everything conceivable, tin soldiers, a sailboat, a fire engine, but no drum; who wanted me to play with tin soldiers and waste my time with this fool fire engine, who were planning to rob me of my battered but trusty old drum, to steal it away from me and leave me, in its place, this sailboat, useless in itself and incorrectly rigged to boot—as I was saying, I threw the whole lot of them, who had eyes for the sole purpose of overlooking me and my desires, into primeval darkness with a circular scream that demolished all four bulbs in our hanging lamp.

Ah, grownups! After the first cries of terror, after the first almost desperate demands for light, they grew accustomed to the darkness, and by the time my Grandma Koljaiczek, who aside from little Stephan Bronski was the only one who had nothing to gain by the darkness, had gone to the shop, with blubbering little Stephan hanging on her skirts, for candles and returned to the room bearing light, the rest of the company, by now in an advanced state of intoxication, had paired off strangely.

As was to be expected, Mama, with disheveled corsage, was sitting on Jan Bronski's lap. It was the opposite of appetizing to see Alexander Scheffler, the short-legged baker, almost submerged amid the billows of Mrs. Greff. Matzerath was licking Gretchen Scheffler's gold horse teeth. Only Hedwig Bronski sat alone with her hands in her lap, her cow's eyes pious in the candlelight, close but not too close to Greff the greengrocer, who, though he had had nothing to drink, was singing in a sad sweet voice, full of languor and melancholy. Turning toward Hedwig Bronski, he invited her to join him in a duet and together they sang a boy-scout song about a scoutmaster named Rübezahl whose spirit haunted the mountains of Bohemia.

I had forgotten. Under the table sat Oskar with the ruins of his

49

drum, coaxing a last vestige of rhythm from it. My feeble but regular drumbeats may well have been welcome to the ecstatically displaced persons who were sitting or lying about the room. For, like varnish, my drumming covered over the persistent sounds of smacking and sucking.

I stayed under the table when my grandmother came in like an angel of wrath with her candles, beheld Sodom and Gomorrah in the candlelight, flew into a rage that made her candles tremble, called them pigs the whole lot of them, and put an end both to the idyll and to Rübezahl's excursions in the mountains by sticking the candles on saucers, taking skat cards out of the sideboard, and throwing them down on the table, all the while comforting Stephan, who was still blubbering. Soon Matzerath put new bulbs in the old fixtures of our lamp, chairs were moved, beer bottles popped open; over my head, a game of skat began for a tenth of a pfennig a point. Mama proposed at the very start that the stakes be raised to a quarter of a pfennig, but this struck Uncle Jan as too risky and the game continued on this niggardly level except when the stakes were raised by a double count or an occasional grand with four.

I felt fine under the table, in the shelter of the tablecloth. Lightly drumming, I fell in with the sounds overhead, followed the developments of the game, and in exactly an hour announced skat: Jan Bronski had lost. He had good cards, but he lost all the same. It was no wonder; he wasn't paying attention. His mind was on very different things than his diamonds without two. Right at the start, while still talking with his aunt, trying to tell her that the little orgy in the dark was nothing to get excited about, he had slipped off one shoe, and thrust forward, past my head, a gray sock with a foot in it, searching for, and finding, my mama's knee. Thereupon Mama had moved closer to the table and Jan, who, in response to Matzerath's bid, had just passed, lifted the hem of her dress with his toe, so enabling his entire inhabited sock, which luckily he had put on fresh that same day, to wander about between her thighs. I have to hand it to my mother, who in spite of this woolen provocation beneath the table managed, up there on the crisp tablecloth, to execute the most daring games, including clubs without four, accompanied by a flow of the sprightliest talk, and won while Jan, growing more and more intrepid under the table, lost several games which even Oskar would have carried to a successful conclusion with somnambulistic certainty.

Later on poor tired little Stephan joined me under the table and, quite at a loss to know what his father's trouser leg was doing under my mama's skirt, soon fell asleep.

Clear to slightly cloudy. Light showers in the afternoon. The very next day Jan Bronski came over, took away the wretched sailboat he had given me, and exchanged it for a drum at Sigismund Markus' toystore. Slightly wilted from the rain, he came back late in the afternoon with a brand-new drum of the model with which I had grown so familiar, with the same red flames on a white field, and held it out to me, at the same time withdrawing my old wreck, which had retained only the barest vestiges of its paint. As Jan gripped the tired drum and I the new one, the eyes of Jan, Mama, and Matzerath were glued on Oskar; I almost had to smile, goodness, did they think I clung to tradition for its own sake, that I was burdened by principles?

Without emitting the cry expected by all, without so much as a note of glass-destroying song, I relinquished the relic and devoted myself with both hands to the new instrument. After two hours of attentive drumming, I had got the hang of it.

But not all the grownups around me proved as understanding as Jan Bronski. Shortly after my fifth birthday, in 1929—there had been considerable talk about the stock market crash in New York and I had begun to wonder whether my grandfather Koljaiczek, with his lumber business in far-off Buffalo, had also suffered losses—Mama, alarmed at my by now quite obvious failure to grow, took me by the hand and inaugurated our Wednesday visits to the office of Dr. Hollatz in Brünshofer-Weg. His examinations were interminable and exasperating, but I put up with them, because even at that tender age I was very much taken with the white dress of Sister Inge, Dr. Hollatz' assistant, which reminded me of Mama's much-photographed wartime activity as a nurse. Intense concentration on the new system of pleats in her uniform enabled me to ignore the stream of words, by turns sternly authoritative and unpleasantly uncle-ish, that poured from the doctor's lips.

His spectacles reflecting the furnishings of his office—lots of chrome, nickel, and smooth enamel; shelves and glass cabinets with neatly labeled bottles containing snakes, toads, salamanders, and the embryos of humans, pigs, and monkeys—Hollatz, after each examination, shook his head thoughtfully, leafed through my case history, questioned Mama about my fall, and quieted her when she began to vilify Matzerath, guilty now and forever of leaving the trap door open.

One Wednesday, after this had been going on for months, when Dr. Hollatz, probably in order to convince himself and perhaps Sister Inge as well that his treatment was bringing results, tried to take my drum away, I destroyed the greater part of his collection of snakes, toads, and embryos.

This was the first time Oskar had tried his voice on a whole set of filled and carefully sealed glasses. The success was unique and overwhelming for all present, even for Mama, who knew all about my private relation to glassware. With my very first trim, economical scream, I cut the cabinet in which Hollatz kept his loathsome curiosities wide open, and sent an almost square pane of glass toppling to the linoleum floor where, still preserving its square shape, it cracked into a thousand pieces. Then, lending my scream greater relief and throwing economy to the winds, I shattered one test tube after another.

The tubes popped like firecrackers. The greenish, partly coagulated alcohol squirted and splashed, carrying its prepared, pale, gloomy-eyed contents to the red linoleum floor, and filling the room with so palpable a stench that Mama grew sick to her stomach and Sister Inge had to open the windows.

Dr. Hollatz managed to turn the loss of his collection to his advantage. A few weeks after my act of violence, he published an article about me, Oskar M., the child with the glass-shattering voice, in a medical journal. The theory with which Dr. Hollatz succeeded in filling more than twenty pages is said to have attracted attention in medical circles both in Germany and abroad, and led to a whole series of articles by specialists, both in agreement and disagreement. He sent Mama several copies of his article and the pride she took in it gave me food for thought. She never wearied of reading passages from it to the Greffs, the Schefflers, her Jan, and, regularly after dinner, to Matzerath. Even her customers were subjected to readings and were filled with admiration for Mama, who had a strikingly imaginative way of mispronouncing the technical terms. As for me, the first appearrance of my name in periodical literature left me just about cold. My already keen skepticism led me to judge Dr. Hollatz' opusculum for what it essentially was: a long-winded, not unskillfully formulated display of irrelevancies by a physician who was angling for a professorship.

Today as he lies in his mental hospital, unable to damage even his toothbrush glass with his singing, with doctors of the same type as Hollatz coming in and out, giving him Rorschach tests, association tests, and tests of every other conceivable kind in the hope of finding a high-sounding name for the disorder that led to his confinement, Oskar likes to think back on the archaic period of his voice. In those early days he shattered glass only when necessary, but then with great thoroughness, whereas later on, in the heyday and decadence of his art, he exercised it even when not impelled by outward circumstances. Succumbing to the mannerism of a late period, he began to sing out of pure playfulness, becoming as it were a devotee of art for art's sake. He employed glass as a medium of self-expression, and grew older in the process.

The Schedule

Klepp often spends hours drawing up schedules. The fact that while doing so he regularly devours blood sausage and warmed-over lentils, confirms my thesis, which is simply that dreamers are gluttons. And the assiduity with which he fills in his hours and half-hours confirms another theory of mine, to wit, that only first-class lazybones are likely to turn out labor-saving inventions.

This year again Klepp has spent more than two weeks trying to schedule his activities. He came to see me yesterday. For a while he behaved mysteriously, then fished an elaborately folded sheet of paper out of his breast pocket and handed it to me. He was obviously very pleased with himself: another of his labor-saving schemes.

I looked through his handiwork, there was nothing very new about it: breakfast at ten; contemplation until lunchtime; after lunch a nap (one hour), then coffee, in bed if transportation was available; flute playing in bed (one hour); get up; play bagpipes while marching round the room (one hour); more bagpipes out in the courtyard (half an hour). Next came a two-hour period, spent every other day over beer and blood sausage and the alternate day at the movies; in either case, before the movies or over the beer, discreet propaganda for the illegal Communist party of Germany, not to exceed half an hour, mustn't overdo it. Three nights a week to be spent playing dance music at the Unicorn; on Saturday, beer and propaganda transferred to the evening, afternoon reserved for a bath and massage in Grünstrasse, followed by hygiene with girl (three-quarters of an hour) at the "U 9," then with the same girl and her girl friend coffee and cake at Schwab's, a shave and if necessary a haircut just before the barber's closing time; quick to the Photomaton; then beer, blood sausage, Party propaganda, and relaxation.

I admired Klepp's carefully custom-made schedule, asked him for a copy, and inquired what he did to fill in occasional gaps. "Sleep, or think of the Party," he replied after the briefest reflection.

Naturally this led me to Oskar's first experience with a schedule.

It began quite harmlessly with Auntie Kauer's kindergarten. Hedwig Bronski called for me every morning and took me, along with her Stephan, to Auntie Kauer's place in Posadowski-Weg, where we and six to ten other little urchins—a few were always sick—were compelled to play ad nauseam. Luckily my drum passed as a toy, I was never obliged to play with building blocks, and I was constrained to mount a rocking horse only when an equestrian drummer in a paper helmet was required. My drumming score was Auntie Kauer's black silk, extraordinarily button-some dress. Several times a day I unbuttoned her on my drum and once her dress was open buttoned it up again. She was all wrinkles and very skinny, I don't think it was her body I had in mind.

The afternoon walks down avenues bordered with chestnut trees to Jeschkentaler Forest, past the Gutenberg Monument, and up to the Erbs-berg were so pleasantly tedious and angelically silly that even today I should be very glad to go on one of those picture-book outings, guided by Auntie Kauer's papery hand.

First we were harnessed, all six, eight, or twelve of us. The shaft was a pale-blue strip of knitted wool. To each side were attached six woolen bridles with bells, room for twelve children in all. Auntie Kauer held the reins, and we trotted along ahead of her tinkling and twittering, I sluggishly drumming, through the autumnal suburban streets. Now and then Auntie Kauer struck up "Jesus, for thee we live, Jesus, for thee we die" or "Star of the Sea, I greet thee." We filled the clear October air with "O Mary, help me" and "Swe-e-e-t Mother of God," and the passers-by found it very touching. When we came to the main street, the traffic had to stop for us. Street cars, automobiles, horse-drawn vehicles stood motionless as we carried the Star of the Sea across the avenue. There was a crackling as of paper when Auntie Kauer waved her hand to thank the policeman who had directed our crossing.

"Our Lord Jesus will reward you," she promised with a rustle of her silk dress.

Actually I was sorry when Oskar, in the spring of his seventh year, had to leave Fräulein Kauer and her buttons along with and because of Stephan. Politics was at the bottom of it, and where there is politics, there is violence. We had just reached the Erbsberg. Auntie Kauer removed our woolen harness, the leaves glistened, and new life was stirring in the treetops. Auntie Kauer sat on a moss-covered road marker indicating the various spots that could be reached on foot in one, one and a half, and two hours. Like a young girl in whom the spring has awakened unidentified feelings, she began to sing tra-la-la with the spasmodic movements of the head that one would ordinarily expect of a guinea hen, knitting the while a new harness, which was to be flaming red. Unhappily, I never got to wear it, for just then cries were heard from the bushes, Fräulein Kauer fluttered to her feet and, drawing red yarn behind her, raced on stiltlike legs into the thicket. I followed her and the yarn, which was not as red as the sight that soon met my eyes: Stephan's nose was bleeding profusely and a boy named Lothar, with curly hair and fine blue veins on his temples, was kneeling on the sickly little fellow's chest, resolutely belaboring his nose.

"Polack!" he hissed between blows. "Polack!" When, five minutes later, Auntie Kauer had us back in our light-blue harness—I alone ran free, winding up the red yarn—she uttered a prayer that is normally recited between Consecration and Communion: "Bowed with shame, full of pain and remorse . . . "

We descended the Erbsberg and halted at the Gutenberg Monument. Pointing a long finger at Stephan, who was whimpering and holding a handkerchief to his nose, she remarked gently: "He can't help it if he's a little Pole." On Auntie Kauer's advice, Stephan was taken out of kindergarten. Though Oskar was not a Pole and was no great admirer of Stephan, he made it clear that if Stephan couldn't go, he wouldn't either.

Then Easter came and they resolved to give school a try. Dr. Hollatz decided behind his horn-rimmed glasses that it could do no harm, and this was also his spoken opinion: "It can do little Oskar no harm."

Jan Bronski, who was planning to send his Stephan to Polish public school after Easter, refused to be dissuaded. Over and over again he pointed out to my mama and Matzerath that he was a Polish civil servant, receiving good pay for good work at the Polish Post Office. He was a Pole after all and Hedwig would be one too as soon as the papers came through. Besides, a bright little fellow like Stephan would learn German at home. As for Oskar—Jan always sighed a little when he said "Oskar"—he was six years old just like Stephan; true, he still couldn't talk properly; in general, he was quite backward for his age, and as for his size, enough said, but they should try it just the same, schooling was compulsory after all—provided the school board raised no objection.

The school board expressed misgivings and demanded a doctor's certificate. Hollatz said I was a healthy child; my physical development, he had to admit, was that of a three-year-old and I didn't talk very well, but otherwise I was not mentally inferior to a normal child of five or six. He also said something about my thyroid.

I was subjected to all sorts of examinations and tests. But I had grown accustomed to that kind of thing and my attitude ranged from benevolent to indifferent, especially as no one tried to take my drum away. The destruction of Hollatz' collection of snakes, toads, and embryos was still remembered with awe.

It was only at home that I was compelled to unsheathe the diamond in my voice. This was on the morning of my first school day, when Matzerath, against his own better judgment, demanded that I leave my drum at home and moreover pass through the portals of the Pestalozzi School without it.

When at length he resorted to force, when he attempted to take what did not belong to him, to appropriate an instrument he did not know how to play and for which he lacked all feeling, I shattered an empty and allegedly genuine vase. When the genuine vase lay on the carpet in the form of genuine fragments, Matzerath, who was very fond of it, raised a hand to strike me. But at this point Mama jumped up and Jan, who had dropped in for a moment with Stephan and a large ornate cornucopia, intervened.

"Alfred, please, please!" he said in his quiet unctuous way, and Matzerath, subdued by Jan's blue and Mama's gray gaze, dropped his hand and thrust it into his trousers pocket.

The Pestalozzi School was a new brick-red, three-story, flat-roofed, boxlike edifice, decorated with sgraffiti and frescoes, which had been built by the Senate of our prolific suburb at the vociferous insistence of the

Social Democrats, who at the time were still exceedingly active. I rather liked the box, except for its smell and the Jugendstil athletes in the sgraffiti and frescoes.

In the expanse of gravel outside the gate stood a few trees so unnaturally diminutive that one was startled to find them beginning to turn green; they were supported by iron stakes that looked like croziers. From all directions poured mothers holding colored cornucopias and drawing screaming or model children after them. Never had Oskar seen so many mothers tending toward a single point. They seemed to be on their way to a market where their first- or second-born could be offered for sale.

In the entrance I already caught a whiff of that school smell which has been described often enough and which is more intimate than any perfume in the world. In the lobby four or five huge granite bowls, in a rather casual arrangement, were affixed to the tile floor. From deep down within them water spouted from several sources at once. Surrounded by boys, including some of my own age, they reminded me of my Uncle Vincent's sow at Bissau, who would occasionally lie down on one flank and tolerate the equally thirsty and violent assault of her piglets.

The boys bent over the bowls with their vertical geysers, allowing their hair to fall forward and the streams of water to gush into their open mouths. I am not sure whether they were playing or drinking. Sometimes two boys stood up almost simultaneously with bloated cheeks, and with a disgusting gurgle spat the mouthwarm water, mixed, you may be certain, with saliva and bread crumbs, into each other's faces. I, who on entering the lobby had unsuspectingly cast a glance through the open door of the adjoining gymnasium, caught sight of the leather horse, the climbing bars, the climbing rope, and the horrible horizontal bar, crying out as always for a giant swing. All this made me desperately thirsty and like the other boys I should gladly have taken a gulp of water. But it was hardly possible to ask Mama, who was holding me by the hand, to lift Oskar the Lilliputian up to one of the fountains. Even if I had stood on my drum, the fountain would have been beyond my reach. But when with a quick jump I managed to glance over the edge and noted that the drain was blocked with greasy remnants of bread and that the bottom of the bowl was full of a noxious sludge, the thirst I had accumulated in spirit, while my body was wandering in a desert of gymnastic apparatus, left me.

Mama led me up monumental stairs hewn for giants, through resounding corridors into a room over the door of which hung a sign bearing the inscription I-A. The room was full of boys my own age. Their mothers pressed against the wall opposite the window front, clutching in their arms the colored cornucopias covered with tissue paper that were traditional on the first day of school. The cornucopias towered above me. Mama was also carrying one of them.

As my mother led me in, the rabble laughed and the rabble's mothers as well. A pudgy little boy wanted to beat my drum. Not wishing to demolish any glass, I was obliged to give him a few good kicks in the shins, whereupon he fell down, hitting his well-combed head on a desk, for which offense Mama cuffed me on the back of my head. The little monster yelled. Not I, I only yelled when someone tried to take my drum away. Mama, to whom this public performance was very embarrassing, pushed me down behind the first desk in the section by the windows. Of course the desk was too high. But further back, where the rabble was still more freckled and uncouth, the desks were still higher.

I let well enough alone and sat calmly, because there was nothing to be uncalm about. Mama, who it seemed to me was still suffering from embarrassment, tried to disappear among the other mothers. Here in the presence of her peers she probably felt ashamed of my so-called backwardness. The peers all behaved as though their young dolts, who had grown much too quickly for my taste, were something to be proud of.

I couldn't look out the window at Fröbel's Meadow, for the level of the window sill was no more appropriate to my stature than was the size of the desk. Too bad. I would have been glad to gaze out at the meadow where, as I knew, scouts under the leadership of Greff the greengrocer were pitching tents, playing lansquenet, and, as befitted boy scouts, doing good deeds. Not that I was interested in their fulsome glorification of camp life. What appealed to me was the sight of Greff in his short pants. Such was his love of slender, wide-eyed, pale boys that he had donned the uniform of Baden-Powell, father of the boy scouts.

Cheated of the coveted view by the insidious architecture, I gazed up at the sky and was soon appeased. New clouds kept forming and drifting southwestward, as though that direction had some special attraction for clouds. I wedged my drum firmly between my knees and the desk, though it had never for so much as a beat thought of wandering off to southwestward. Oskar's head was protected in the rear by the back rest. Behind me my so-called schoolmates snarled, roared, laughed, wept, and raged. They threw spitballs at me, but I did not turn around; it seemed to me that the tranquil purposive clouds were better worth looking at than a horde of grimacing, hopelessly hysterical louts.

Class I-A calmed down at the entrance of a person who subsequently introduced herself as Miss Spollenhauer. I had no need to calm down for I was already calm, awaiting things to come in a state of almost complete self-immersion. To be perfectly truthful, Oskar gave barely a thought to what the future might hold in store, for he required no distraction. Let us say, then, that he was not waiting but just sitting at his desk, pleasantly aware that his drum was where it belonged and otherwise preoccupied with the clouds behind the paschally polished windowpanes.

Miss Spollenhauer had on an angularly cut suit that gave her a desiccated mannish look, an impression that was enhanced by the narrow stiff collar, of the kind, it seemed to me, that can be wiped clean, which closed round her Adam's apple, creating deep furrows in her neck. No sooner had she entered the classroom in her flat walking shoes than she felt the need to make herself popular and asked: "Well, my dear children, are we up to singing a little song?"

The response was a roar which she must have taken to mean yes, for she embarked at once, in a mincing high-pitched voice, on "This Is the Merry Month of May," though it was only the middle of April. Her premature announcement of the month of May was all it needed to make hell break loose. Without waiting for the signal to come in, without more than the vaguest notion of the words, or the slightest feeling for the simple rhythm of the song, the rabble behind me began to shake loose the plaster from the walls with their howling.

Despite her bilious complexion, despite her bobbed hair and the man's tie peering out from behind her collar, I felt sorry for la Spollenhauer. Tearing myself away from the clouds which obviously had no school that day, I leapt to my feet, pulled my drumsticks out from under my suspenders, and loudly, emphatically, drummed out the time of the song. But the populace had neither ear nor feeling for my efforts. Only Miss Spollenhauer gave me a nod of encouragement, smiled at the line of mothers glued to the wall, with a special twinkle for Mama. Interpreting this as a go-ahead signal, I continued my drumming, first quietly and simply, then displaying all my arts and burgeoning into rhythmic complexities. The rabble behind me had long ceased their barbaric howls. I was beginning to fancy that my drum was teaching, educating my fellow pupils, making them into my pupils, when la Spollenhauer approached my desk. For a time she watched my hands and drumsticks, I wouldn't even say that her manner was inept; she smiled self-forgetfully and tried to clap her hands to my beat. For a moment she became a not unpleasant old maid, who had forgotten her prescribed occupational caricature and become human, that is, childlike, curious, complex, and immoral.

However, when she failed to catch my rhythm, she fell back into her usual rectilinear, obtuse, and to make matters worse underpaid role, pulled herself together as teachers occasionally must, and said: "You must be little Oskar. We have heard so much about you. How beautifully you drum! Doesn't he, children? Isn't our Oskar a fine drummer?"

The children roared, the mothers huddled closer together, Miss Spollenhauer was herself again. "But now," she piped with a voice like a pencil sharpener, "we shall put the drum in the locker; it must be tired and want to sleep. Then when school is out, you will have it back again."

Even before she had finished reeling off this hypocritical nonsense, she bared her close-clipped teacher's fingernails and ten close-clipped fingers tried to seize my drum, which, so help me, was neither tired nor sleepy. I held fast, clutching the red and white casing in the sleeves of my sweater. At first I stared at her, but when she kept on looking like a stencil of a public school teacher, I preferred to look through her. In Miss Spollenhauer's interior I found enough interesting material for three scabrous chapters, but since my drum was in danger, I tore myself away from her inner life and, my gimlet eyes drilling between her shoulder blades, detected, mounted on well-preserved skin, a mole the size of a gulden with a clump of long hairs growing in it.

I can't say whether it was because she felt herself seen through or whether it was my voice with which I gave her a harmless warning scratch on the lens of her right eyeglass: in any case, she suspended the show of force that had already blanched her knuckles. It seems likely that she could not bear the scraping on the glass, probably it gave her gooseflesh. With a shudder she released my drum and, casting a look of reproach at my mama, who was preparing to sink into the earth, declared: "Why, you are a wicked little Oskar." Thereupon she left me my wide-awake drum, about-faced, and marched with flat heels to her desk, where she fished another pair of spectacles, probably her reading glasses, from her briefcase, briskly took off her nose those which my voice had scraped as one scrapes windowpanes with one's fingernails, with a grimace which seemed to imply that I had profaned her spectacles, put on the other pair, straightening herself up so you could hear the bones rattle, and, reaching once again into her briefcase, announced: "I will now read you your schedule!"

What issued from the briefcase this time was a little bundle of cards. Keeping one for herself, she passed the rest on to the mothers, including Mama, and at length communicated the schedule to the already restive class. "Monday: religion, writing, arithmetic, play; Tuesday: arithmetic, penmanship, singing, nature study; Wednesday: arithmetic, writing, drawing, drawing; Thursday: geography, arithmetic, writing, religion; Friday: arithmetic, writing, play, penmanship; Saturday: arithmetic, singing, play, play."

Proclaimed in a stern voice that neglected not one jot or tittle, this product of a solemn faculty meeting assumed the force of irrevocable fate. But then, remembering what she had learned at Normal School, Miss Spollenhauer became suddenly mild and mellow. "And now, my dear children," she cried in an outburst of progressive merriment, "let us all repeat that in unison: Now: Monday?"

The horde shouted "Monday."

"Religion?" And the baptized heathen roared "religion." Rather than strain my voice, I for my part beat out the syllables on my drum.

Behind me, spurred on by la Spollenhauer, the heathen bellowed:

59

"Writing!" Boom-boom went my drum. "A-rith-me-tic!" That was good for four beats.

Before me la Spollenhauer's litany, behind me the howling of the mob. Putting a good face on a sorry and ludicrous business, I beat out the syllables, with moderation I should say, and so it continued until la Spollenhauer, goaded by some inner demon, leapt up in palpable fury, but not over the Tartars behind me; no, it was I who sent the red blotches to her cheeks; Oskar's poor little drum was her stumbling block, her bone of contention; it was I she chose to rebuke.

"Oskar, you will now listen to me: Thursday, geography?" Ignoring the word Thursday, I drummed four beats for geography, four beats for arithmetic, and two for writing; to religion I devoted not four, but, in accordance with sound theological principles, three triune and only-saving drumbeats.

But la Spollenhauer had no ear for subtleties. To her all drumming was equally repugnant. Once again she bared her ten truncated fingernails and once again they tried to seize my drum.

But before she had so much as touched it, I unleashed my glass-demolishing scream, which removed the upper panes from the three oversized windows. The middle windows succumbed to a second cry. Unobstructed, the mild spring air poured into the classroom. With a third shriek I annihilated the lower windowpanes, but this I admit was quite superfluous, pure exuberance as it were, for la Spollenhauer had already drawn in her claws at the discomfiture of the upper and middle panes. Instead of assaulting the last remaining windowpanes out of pure and, from an artistic standpoint, questionable malice, Oskar would have done more wisely to keep an eye on la Spollenhauer as she beat a disorderly retreat.

Lord only knows where she found that cane. In any case it was suddenly at hand, vibrant in the classroom air now mingled with spring-time air. Through this atmospheric mixture she whished it, endowing it with resiliency, with hunger and thirst for bursting skin, for the whistling wind, for all the rustling curtains that a whishing cane can impersonate. And down it came on my desk so hard that a violet streak sprang from my inkwell. Then, when I wouldn't hold out my hand to be whipped, she struck my drum. She struck my darling. She, la Spollenhauer, struck my instrument. What ground had she to strike? And if she was bent on hitting something, why my drum? What about the yokels behind me? Did it have to be my drum? By what right did she, who knew nothing, nothing whatsoever, about the drummer's art, assault and batter my drum? What was that glint in her eye? That beast ready to strike? What zoo had it escaped from, what did it lust for, what prey was it after? The very same beast invaded Oskar; rising from unknown depths, it rose up through the soles of his shoes, through the soles of his feet, rose and rose, investing his vocal cords and driving him to emit a rutting cry that would have sufficed to unglass a whole Gothic cathedral resplendent with the refracted light of a hundred windows.

In other words, I composed a double cry which literally pulverized both lenses of la Spollenhauer's spectacles. Slightly bleeding at the eyebrows, squinting through the empty frames, she groped her way backward, and finally began to blubber repulsively, with a lack of self-control quite unbefitting an educator, while the rabble behind me fell into a terrified silence, some sitting there with chattering teeth, others vanishing beneath their desks. A few of them slid from desk to desk in the direction of the mothers. The mothers for their part, perceiving the extent of the damage, looked round for the culprit and were about to pounce on my mother. They would surely have torn her to pieces had I not gathered up my drum and rushed to her assistance.

Past the purblind Miss Spollenhauer, I made my way to my mama, who was menaced by the Furies, seized her by the hand, and drew her out of the drafty headquarters of Class I-A. Resounding corridors, stone stairs for giant children. Crusts of bread in gushing granite fountains. In the open gymnasium boys were trembling beneath the horizontal bar. Mama was still holding her little card. Outside the portals of the Pestalozzi School, I took it from her and transformed a schedule into a speechless wad of paper.

However, Oskar allowed the photographer, who was waiting for the new pupils and their mothers between the doorposts, to take a picture of him and of his cornucopia, which for all the tumult had not been lost. The sun came out, classrooms buzzed overhead. The photographer placed Oskar against a blackboard on which was written: My First School Day.

Rasputin and the Alphabet

I have just been telling my friend Klepp and Bruno my keeper, who listened with only half an ear, about Oskar's first experience with a school schedule. On the blackboard (I said) which provided the photographer with the traditional background for postcard-size pictures of six-year-old boys with knapsacks and cornucopias, these words were inscribed: My First School Day.

Of course the words could only be read by the mothers who, much more excited than their children, were standing behind the photographer. The boys, who were in front of the blackboard, would at best be able to decipher the inscription a year later, either at Easter time when the next first grade would turn up at school or on their own old photographs. Then and only then would they be privileged to read that these lovely pictures had been taken on the occasion of their first school day.

This testimonial to a new stage in life was recorded in Sütterlin

61

script that crept across the blackboard with malignant angularity. However, the loops were not right, too soft and rounded. The fact is that Sütterlin script is especially indicated for succinct, striking statements, slogans for instance. And there are also certain documents which, though I admit I have never seen them, I can only visualize in Sütterlin script. I have in mind vaccination certificates, sport scrolls, and handwritten death sentences. Even then, I knew what to make of the Sütterlin script though I couldn't read it: the double loop of the Sütterlin M, with which the inscription began, smelled of hemp in my nostrils, an insidious reminder of the hangman. Even so, I would have been glad to read it letter for letter and not just dimly guess at what is said. Let no one suppose that I drummed in revolutionary protest and shattered glass so highhandedly at my first meeting with Miss Spollenhauer because I had already mastered my ABC's. Oh, no, I was only too well aware that this intuition of mine about Sütterlin script was not enough, that I lacked the most elementary school learning. It was just unfortunate that Miss Spollenhauer's methods of inculcating knowledge did not appeal to Oskar.

Accordingly, when I left the Pestalozzi School, I was far from deciding that my first school day should be my last, that I had had my fill of pencils and books, not to mention teacher's dirty looks. Nothing of the sort. Even while the photographer was capturing my likeness for all eternity, I thought: There you are in front of a blackboard, under an inscription that is probably important and possibly portentous. You can judge the inscription by the character of the writing and call forth associations such as solitary confinement, protective custody, inspector, and hang-them-all-by-one-rope, but you can't read the words. And yet, with all your ignorance that cries out to the overcast heavens, you will never again set foot in this schedule-school. Where, oh where, Oskar, are you going to learn your big and little alphabet?

Actually a little alphabet would have been plenty for me, but I had figured out that there must be a big as well as a little one, among other things from the crushing and undeniable fact of the existence of big people, who called themselves grownups.

In the next few months, neither Matzerath nor Mama worried about my education. They had tried to send me to school, and as far as they were concerned, this one attempt, so humiliating for Mama, was quite sufficient. They behaved just like Uncle Jan Bronski, sighed as they looked down on me, and dug up old stories such as the incident on my third birthday: "The trap door! You left it open, didn't you? You were in the kitchen and before that you'd been down in the cellar, hadn't you? You brought up a can of mixed fruit for dessert, didn't you? You left the cellar door open, didn't you?"

Everything Mama held up to Matzerath was true, and yet, as we know, it was not. But he took the blame and sometimes even wept, for he was a sensitive soul at times. Then Mama and Jan Bronski had to comfort him, and they spoke of me, Oskar, as a cross they had to bear, a cruel and no doubt irrevocable fate, a trial that had been visited on them, it was impossible to see why.

Obviously no help was to be expected from such sorely tried cross-bearers and victims of fate. Nor could Aunt Hedwig, who often took me to Steffens-Park to play in the sand pile with her two-year-old Marga, have possibly served as my preceptor. She was good-natured enough, but as dull-witted as the day is long. I also had to abandon any ideas about Dr. Hollatz' Sister Inge, who was neither dull-witted nor good-natured, for she was no common door-opener but a real and indispensable doctor's assistant and consequently had no time for me.

Several times a day I tramped up and down the steps of the four-story apartment house—there were more than a hundred of them—drumming in quest of counsel at every landing. I sniffed to see what each of the nineteen tenants was having for dinner, but I did not knock at any of the doors, for I recognized my future preceptor neither in old man Heilandt nor in Laubschad the watchmaker, and definitely not in the corpulent Mrs. Kater nor, much as I liked her, in Mother Truczinski.

Under the eaves dwelt Meyn the trumpet player. Mr. Meyn kept four cats and was always drunk. He played dance music at "Zinglers Höhe" and on Christmas Eve he and five fellow sots plodded through the snow-clad streets battling the frost with carols. One day I saw him in his attic: clad in black trousers and a white evening shirt, he lay on his back, rolling an empty gin bottle about with his unshod feet and playing the trumpet just wonderfully. He did not remove his instrument from his lips, but merely squinted vaguely round at me for a moment. He acknowledged me as his drummer accompanist. His instrument was no more precious to him than mine to me. Our duet drove his four cats out on the roof and set up a slight vibration in the gutter tiles.

When the music was finished and we lowered our instruments, I drew an old copy of the *Neueste Nachrichten* from under my sweater, smoothed out the paper, sat down beside the trumpeter, held out my reading matter, and asked him to instruct me in the big and little alphabets.

But Mr. Meyn had fallen directly from his trumpeting into a deep sleep. His spirit recognized only three repositories: his bottle of gin, his trumpet, and his slumber. It is true that for quite some time after that —to be exact, until he joined the band of the Mounted SA and temporarily gave up gin—we would quite frequently play unrehearsed duets in the attic for the benefit of the roof tiles, the chimneys, the pigeons, and the cats; but I could never get anything out of him as a teacher.

I tried Greff the greengrocer. Without my drum, for Greff didn't appreciate it, I paid several visits to the basement shop across the way. The wherewithal for thorough and many-sided study seemed to be at hand. In every corner of the two-room flat, all over the shop, under and behind the counter, even in the relatively dry potato cellar, lay books, adventure stories, song books, *Der Cherubinische Wandersmann*, the works of Walter Flex, Wiechert's *Simple Life*, *Daphnis and Chloë*, monographs about artists, piles of sport magazines and illustrated volumes full of half-naked youths, most of whom, for some unfathomable reason, were chasing after a ball amid sand dunes, exhibiting oiled and glistening muscles.

Even then Greff was having a good deal of trouble in the shop. The inspectors from the Bureau of Weights and Measures had not been quite satisfied with his weights. There was talk of fraud. Greff had to pay a fine and buy new weights. He was bowed down with cares; his books and scout meetings and weekend excursions were his only cheer.

He was making out price tabs when I came in and hardly noticed me. Taking advantage of his occupation, I picked up three or four white squares of cardboard and a red pencil and, in the hope of attracting his attention, made a great show of zeal copying his handiwork in my own version of Sütterlin script.

But Oskar was clearly too little for him, not pale and wide-eyed enough. I dropped the red pencil, picked out a book full of the nudities that so appealed to Greff, and pretended to be very busy, inspecting photographs of boys bending and boys stretching and twisting them about so he could see them.

But when there were no customers in the shop asking for beets or cabbages, the greengrocer had eyes only for his price tabs. I tried to arouse his interest in my unlettered presence by clapping book covers or making the pages crackle as I turned them.

To put it very simply: Greff did not understand me. When scouts were in the shop—and in the afternoon there were always two or three of his lieutenants around him—Greff didn't notice Oskar at all. And when Greff was alone, he was quite capable of jumping up in nervous irritation and dealing out commands: "Oskar, will you leave that book alone. You can't make head or tail of it anyway. You're too dumb and you're too little. You'll ruin it. That book costs more than six gulden. If you want to play, there's plenty of potatoes and cabbages."

He took his nasty old book away and leafed expressionlessly through the pages, leaving me standing amid potatoes and several representatives of the cabbage family, white cabbage, red cabbage, savoy cabbage, Brussels sprouts, and kohlrabi, wretchedly lonely, for I had left my drum at home.

There was still Mrs. Greff, and after her husband's brush-off, I usually made my way to the matrimonial bedroom. Even then Mrs. Lina Greff would lie in bed for whole weeks, vaguely ailing; she smelled of decaying nightgown and though her hands were very active, one thing she never touched was a book that might have taught me anything.

It was not without a suspicion of envy that Oskar, in the weeks that followed, looked upon his contemporaries and their schoolbags from which dangled importantly the little sponges or cloths used for wiping off slates. Even so, he cannot remember having harbored such thoughts as: you've made your own bed, Oskar, you should have put a good face on the school routine; you shouldn't have made an everlasting enemy of la Spollenhauer. Those yokels are getting ahead of you. They have mastered the big or at least the little alphabet, whereas you don't even know how to hold the *Neueste Nachrichten* properly.

A suspicion of envy, I have said, and that is all it was. A little smell test is all that was needed to disgust me with school for all time. Have you ever taken a sniff of those inadequately washed, worm-eaten sponges appended to peeling, yellow-rimmed slates, those sponges which somehow manage to store up all the effluvia of writing and 'rithmetic, all the sweat of squeaking, halting, slipping slate pencils moistened with saliva? Now and then, when children on their way home from school laid down their bags to play football or Völkerball, I would bend down over those sponges steaming in the sun, and the thought came to me that if Satan existed, such would be the acrid stench of his armpits.

Certainly I had no yearning for the school of slates and sponges. But, on the other hand, it would be an exaggeration to say that Gretchen Scheffler, who soon took his education in hand, was the precise answer to Oskar's dreams.

Everything about the Scheffler dwelling behind the bakery in Kleinhammer-Weg set my teeth on edge. Those ornamental coverlets, those cushions embroidered with coats-of-arms, those Käthe Kruse dolls lurking in sofa corners, those plush animals wheresoever one turned, that china crying out for a bull, those ubiquitous travel souvenirs, those beginnings of knitting, crocheting, and embroidery, of plaiting, knotting, and lacework. The place was too sweet for words, so cunning and cozy, stiflingly tiny, overheated in winter and poisoned with flowers in summer. I can think of only one explanation: Gretchen Scheffler was childless; oh, if she had had some little creature to knit for, who can say whether she or Scheffler was to blame, oh, how happy she would have been with a little sugarplum baby, something she could love to pieces and swathe in crocheted blankets and cover with lace and ribbons and little kisses in cross-stitch.

This is where I went to learn my big and little alphabets. I made a heroic effort to spare the china and the souvenirs. I left my glass-destroying voice at home and bore it meekly when Gretchen expressed the opinion

65

that I had drummed enough for now and, baring her equine gold teeth in a smile, removed my drum from my knees and laid it among the teddy bears.

I made friends with two of the Käthe Kruse dolls, clutched the little dears to my bosom, and manipulated the lashes of their permanently startled eyes as though I were madly in love with them. My purpose in this display of affection for dolls, which seemed sincere just because it was so completely false, was to knit a snare round Gretchen's knitted, knit two purl two, heart.

My plan was not bad. It took only two visits before Gretchen opened her heart; that is, she unraveled it as one unravels a stocking, disclosing a long crinkly thread worn thin in places. She opened all her cupboards, chests, and boxes and spread out all her beaded rubbish, enough baby jackets, baby pants, and bibs to clothe a set of quintuplets, held them up against me, tried them on, and took them off again.

Then she showed me the marksman's medals won by Scheffler at the veterans' club and photographs to go with them, some of which were identical with ours. Then she went back to the baby clothes and at long last, while searching for heaven knows what cute little object, she unearthed some books. That was what Oskar had been building up to. He fully expected her to find books under the baby things; he had heard her talk about books with Mama; he knew how feverishly the two of them, while still engaged and after their early and almost simultaneous marriages, had exchanged books and borrowed books from the lending library by the Film-Palast, in the hope of imparting wider horizons and greater luster to their grocery store and bakery marriages.

Gretchen had little enough to offer me. Like Mama, who had given up reading in favor of Jan Bronski, she who no longer read, now that she spent all her time knitting, had evidently given away the sumptuous volumes of the book club, to which both had belonged for years, to people who still read because they did not knit and had no Jan Bronski.

Even bad books are books and therefore sacred. What I found there can only be described as miscellaneous; most of it came, no doubt, from the book chest of Gretchen's brother Theo, who had met a seaman's death on the Dogger-Bank. Seven or eight volumes of Köhler's *Naval Calendar*, full of ships that had long since sunk, the *Service Ranks of the Imperial Navy, Paul Beneke, the Naval Hero*—these could scarcely have been the nourishment for which Gretchen's heart had yearned. It seemed equally certain that Erich Keyser's *History of the City of Danzig* and *A Struggle for Rome*, which a man by the name of Felix Dahn seems to have fought with the help of Totila and Teja, Belisarius and Narses, had arrived at their present state of dilapidation beneath the hands of the seafaring brother. To Gretchen's own collection I attributed a book by Gustav Freytag about

Debit and Credit, something by Goethe about *Elective Affinities*, and a copiously illustrated thick volume entitled: *Rasputin and Women*.

After long hesitation—the selection was too small to permit me to make up my mind quickly—I picked out first Rasputin and then Goethe. I had no idea what I was taking, I was just following the well-known inner voice.

The conflicting harmony between these two was to shape or influence my whole life, at least what life I have tried to live apart from my drum. To this very day—and even now that Oskar in his eagerness for learning is gradually plowing his way through the whole hospital library—I snap my fingers at Schiller and company and fluctuate between Rasputin and Goethe, between the faith healer and the man of the Enlightenment, between the dark spirit who cast a spell on women and the luminous poet prince who was so fond of letting women cast a spell on him. If for a time I inclined more toward Rasputin and feared Goethe's intolerance, it was because of a faint suspicion that if you, Oskar, had lived and drummed at his time, Goethe would have thought you unnatural, would have condemned you as an incarnation of anti-nature, that while feeding his own precious nature—which essentially you have always admired and striven for even when it gave itself the most unnatural airs—on honey-buns, he would have taken notice of you, poor devil, only to hit you over the head with *Faust* or a big heavy volume of his *Theory of Colors*.

But back to Rasputin. With the help of Gretchen Scheffler he taught me the big and little alphabets, taught me to be attentive to women, and comforted me when Goethe hurt my feelings.

It was not so easy to learn how to read while playing the ignoramus. It proved even more difficult than impersonating a bed-wetter, as I did for many years. In wetting my bed, after all, I merely had to offer purely material proof each morning of a disorder that I did not really need in the first place. But to play the ignoramus meant to conceal my rapid progress, to carry on a constant struggle with my nascent intellectual pride. If grownups wished to regard me as a bed-wetter, that I could accept with an inner shrug of the shoulders, but that I should have to behave like a simpleton year in year out was a source of chagrin to Oskar and to his teacher as well.

The moment I had salvaged the books from the baby clothes, Gretchen cried out for joy; she had sensed her vocation as a teacher. I succeeded in disentangling the poor childless woman from her wool and in making her almost happy. Actually she would have preferred for me to choose *Debit and Credit* as my reader; but I insisted on Rasputin, demanded Rasputin when she produced a common primer for our second lesson, and finally resolved to speak when she kept coming up with fairy tales such as *Dwarf Longnose* and *Tom Thumb*. "Rasputin!" I would cry, or occasionally:

"Rashushin!" Sometimes Oskar would lay it on really thick with "Rashu, Rashu!" The idea was to make it perfectly clear what reading matter I desired but at the same time to leave her in ignorance of my awakening literary genius.

I learned quickly and regularly without much effort. A year later I had the impression of living in St. Petersburg, in the apartments of the Tsar of all the Russias, in the nursery of the ailing Tsarevich, amid conspirators and popes, an eyewitness to Rasputin's orgies. The tone of the thing appealed to me; here, I soon saw, was a dominant figure. How dominant was also made evident by the contemporary engravings scattered through the book, showing the bearded Rasputin with the coal-black eyes, surrounded by ladies wearing black stockings and nothing else. His death made a deep impression on me: they poisoned him with poisoned cake and poisoned wine; then, when he wanted more cake, they shot him with pistols, and when the lead in his chest made him feel like dancing, they bound him and lowered him into the Neva, through a hole in the ice. All this was done by officers of the male sex. The ladies of St. Petersburg would never have given their little father Rasputin poisoned cake, though they would have given him anything else he wanted. The women believed in him, whereas the officers had to get rid of him if they were ever again to believe in themselves.

Is it any wonder that I was not the only one to delight in the life and death of the athletic faith healer? Little by little Gretchen recovered her old pleasure in reading. Sometimes, as she read aloud, she would break down completely; she would tremble at the word "orgy" and utter it with a special sort of gasp; when she said "orgy" she was ready and willing for an orgy, though she certainly had very little idea of what an orgy might be.

Things took a salty turn when Mama came with me and attended my lesson in the flat over the bakery. Sometimes the reading degenerated into an orgy and became an end in itself; little Oskar's lesson was quite forgotten. Every third sentence produced a duet of giggles, which left the ladies with parched lips. Beneath Rasputin's spell the two of them moved closer and closer to one another; they would begin to fidget on the sofa cushions and press their thighs together. In the end, the giggling turned to moaning. Twelve pages of Rasputin produced results that they had hardly expected in mid-afternoon but were perfectly glad to accept. In any case Rasputin would not have minded; on the contrary, he may be counted on to distribute such blessings free of charge for all eternity.

At length, when both ladies had said "goodness, goodness" and sat back in embarrassment, Mama expressed some misgiving: "Are you sure little Oskar doesn't understand?" "Don't be silly," Gretchen reassured her, "you can't imagine how hard I work over him, but he just doesn't learn. My honest opinion is that he'll never be able to read."

As an indication of my incorrigible ignorance, she added: "Just imagine, Agnes, he tears the pages out of our Rasputin and crumples them up. They just disappear. Sometimes I feel like giving up. But when I see how happy he is with the book, I let him tear and destroy. I've already told Alex to get us a new Rasputin for Christmas."

As you have no doubt suspected, I succeeded very gradually, over a period of three or four years—Gretchen Scheffler went on teaching me that long and a bit longer—in carrying away over half the pages of Rasputin. I tore them out very carefully while putting on a wanton destructiveness act, crumpled them up, and hid them under my sweater. Then at home in my drummer's corner, I would smooth them out, pile them up, and read them in secret, undisturbed by any feminine presence. I did the same with Goethe, whom I would demand of Gretchen every fourth lesson with a cry of "Doethe." I didn't want to stake everything on Rasputin, for only too soon it became clear to me that in this world of ours every Rasputin has his Goethe, that every Rasputin draws a Goethe or if you prefer every Goethe a Rasputin in his wake, or even makes one if need be, in order to be able to condemn him later on.

With his unbound book Oskar would repair to the attic or hide behind the bicycle frames in old Mr. Heilandt's shed, where he would shuffle the loose leaves of *Rasputin* and *The Elective Affinities* like playing cards, so creating a new book. He would settle down to read this remarkable work and look on with intense though smiling wonderment as Ottilie strolled demurely through the gardens of Central Germany on Rasputin's arm while Goethe, seated beside a dissolutely aristocratic Olga, went sleighing through wintry St. Petersburg from orgy to orgy.

But let us get back to my schoolroom in Kleinhammer-Weg. Even if I seemed to be making no progress, Gretchen took the most maidenly pleasure in me. Thanks to me, though the invisible but hairy hand of the Russian faith healer also had something to do with it, she blossomed mightily and even imparted some of her newfound vitality to her potted trees and cactuses. If Scheffler in those years had only seen fit once in a while to take his fingers out of his dough, to relinquish his bakery rolls for a human roll! Gretchen would gladly have let him knead her and roll her, brush her with egg white and bake her. Who knows what might have come out of the oven. Perhaps, in the end, a baby. Too bad. It was a pleasure she had coming to her.

As it was, she sat there after an impassioned reading of Rasputin with fiery eyes and slightly tousled hair; her gold horse teeth moved but she had nothing to bite on, and she sighed mercy me, thinking of flour and dough, flour and dough. Since Mama, who had her Jan, had no way of helping Gretchen, this part of my education might have ended in grief if Gretchen had not been so buoyant of heart.

She would leap into the kitchen and come back with the coffee mill;

embracing it like a lover, she would sing with melancholy passion while grinding, "Dark Eyes" or "Red Sarafan," and Mama would join in. Taking the Dark Eyes into the kitchen with her, she would put water on to boil; then as the water was heating over the gas flame, she would run down to the bakery and, often over Scheffler's opposition, bring back cakes and pastries, set the table with flowered cups, cream pitchers, sugar bowls, and cake forks, and strew pansies in the interstices. She would pour the coffee, hum airs from *The Tsarevich,* pass around the sand tarts and chocolate dewdrops. A soldier stands on the Volga shore, coffee ring garnished with splintered almonds, Have you many angels with you up there?, topped off with meringues filled with whipped cream, so sweet, so sweet. As they chewed, the conversation would come back to Rasputin, but now things appeared to them in their proper perspective, and once glutted with cake, they were even able to deplore, in all sincerity, the abysmal corruption of court life under the tsars.

I ate much too much cake in those years. As the photographs show, I grew no taller, just fat and lumpy. After the cloying sweetness of those lessons in Kleinhammer-Weg I would often sneak into our shop and await my opportunity. As soon as Matzerath had his back turned, I would tie a string around a piece of dry bread, dip the bread in the pickled herring barrel, and remove it only when the bread was saturated with brine. You can't imagine what a blissful emetic that was for one who had eaten too much cake. In the hope of reducing, Oskar would often vomit up a whole Danzig gulden's worth of Scheffler's cake in our toilet. That was a lot of money in those days.

I paid for Gretchen's lessons in still another way. With her passion for sewing, knitting, or crocheting baby clothes, she used me as a dressmaker's dummy. I was compelled to try on little frocks and little bonnets, little pants and little coats with and without hoods, in all styles, colors, and materials.

I do not know whether it was Mama or Gretchen who transformed me, on the occasion of my eighth birthday, into a little tsarevich who fully deserved to be shot. Their Rasputin cult was then at its height. A photo taken that day shows me standing beside a birthday cake hedged about by eight dripless candles; I am wearing an embroidered Russian smock, a Cossack's cap perched at a jaunty angle, two crossed cartridge belts, baggy white breeches, and low boots.

Luckily my drum was allowed to be in the picture. Another bit of luck was that Gretchen Scheffler—possibly I had asked her to do so— tailored me a suit which, cut in the unassuming, electively affinitive style of the early nineteenth century, still conjures up the spirit of Goethe in my album, bearing witness to the two souls in my breast, and enables me, with but a single drum, to be in St. Petersburg and in Weimar at once, descending to the realm of the Mothers and celebrating orgies with ladies.

The Stockturm. Long-Distance Song Effects

Dr. Hornstetter, the lady doctor who drops in on me almost every day just long enough to smoke a cigarette, who is supposed to be taking care of me but who, thanks to my treatment, leaves the room after every visit a little less nervous than she was when she came, a retiring sort who is intimate only with her cigarettes, keeps insisting that I suffered from isolation in my childhood, that I didn't play enough with other children.

Well, as far as other children are concerned, she may be right. It is true that I was so busy with Gretchen Scheffler's lessons, so torn between Goethe and Rasputin, that even with the best of intentions I could have found no time for ring-around-a-rosy or post office. But whenever, as scholars sometimes do, I turned my back on books, declaring them to be the graveyards of the language, and sought contact with the simple folk, I encountered the little cannibals who lived in our building, and after brief association with them, felt very glad to get back to my reading in one piece.

Oskar had the possibility of leaving his parents' flat through the shop, then he came out on Labesweg, or else through the front door that led to the stairwell. From here he could either continue straight ahead to the street, or climb four flights of stairs to the attic where Meyn the musician was blowing his trumpet, or, lastly, go out into the court. The street was paved with cobblestones. The packed sand of the court was a place where rabbits multiplied and carpets were beaten. Aside from occasional duets with the intoxicated Mr. Meyn, the attic offered a view and that pleasant but deceptive feeling of freedom which is sought by all climbers of towers and which makes dreamers of those who live in attics.

While the court was fraught with peril for Oskar, the attic offered him security until Axel Mischke and his gang drove him out of it. The court was as wide as the building, but only seven paces deep; in the rear it was separated from other courts by a tarred board fence topped with barbed wire. The attic offered a good view of this maze which occupied the inside of the block bordered by Labesweg, by Hertastrasse and Luisenstrasse on either side, and Marienstrasse in the distance. In among the irregularly shaped courts that made up the sizable rectangle there was also a cough-drop factory and several run-down repair shops. Here and there in the yards one could discern some tree or shrub indicative of the time of year. The courts varied in size and shape, but all contained rabbits and carpet-beating installations. The rabbits were present and active every day; carpets, however, as the house regulations decreed, were beaten only

71

on Tuesdays and Fridays. On Tuesdays and Fridays it became evident how large the block really was. Oskar looked and listened from the attic as more than a hundred carpets, runners, and bedside rugs were rubbed with sauerkraut, brushed, beaten, and bullied into showing the patterns that had been woven into them. With a great display of bare arms a hundred housewives, their hair tied up in kerchiefs, emerged from the houses carrying mounds of carpets, threw the victims over the rack supplied for that very purpose, seized their plaited carpet beaters, and filled the air with thunder.

Oskar abhorred this hymn to cleanliness. He battled the noise with his drum and yet, even in the attic, far away from the source of the thunder, he had to admit defeat. A hundred carpet-beating females can storm the heavens and blunt the wings of young swallows; with half a dozen strokes they tumbled down the little temple that Oskar's drumming had erected in the April air.

On days when no carpets were being beaten, the children of our building did gymnastics on the wooden carpet rack. I was seldom in the court. The only part of it where I felt relatively secure was Mr. Heilandt's shed. The old man kept the other children out but admitted me to his collection of vises, pulleys, and broken-down sewing machines, incomplete bicycles, and cigar boxes full of bent or straightened nails. This was one of his principal occupations: when he was not pulling nails out of old crates, he was straightening those recovered the day before on an anvil. Apart from his salvaging of nails, he was the man who helped on moving day, who slaughtered rabbits for holidays, and who spat tobacco juice all over the court, stairs, and attic.

One day when the children, as children do, were cooking soup not far from his shed, Nuchi Eyke asked old man Heilandt to spit in it three times. The old man obliged, each time with a cavernous clearing of the throat, and then disappeared into his shanty, where he went on hammering the crimps out of nails. Axel Mischke added some pulverized brick to the soup. Oskar stood to one side, but looked on with curiosity. Axel Mischke and Harry Schlager had built a kind of tent out of blankets and old rags to prevent grownups from looking into their soup. When the brick gruel had come to a boil, Hänschen Kollin emptied his pockets and contributed two live frogs he had caught in Aktien Pond. Susi Kater, the only girl in the tent, puckered up her mouth with disappointment and bitterness when the frogs vanished ingloriously into the soup without the slightest attempt at a swan song or a last jump. Undeterred by Susi's presence, Nuchi Eyke unbuttoned his fly and peed into the one-dish meal. Axel, Harry, and Hänschen Kollin followed suit. Shorty tried to show the ten-year-olds what he could do, but nothing came. All eyes turned toward Susi, and Axel Mischke handed her a sky-blue enamel cook pot.

Oskar was already on the point of leaving. But he waited until Susi, who apparently had no panties on under her dress, had squatted down on the pot, clasping her knees, looking off expressionlessly into space, and finally crinkling her nose as the pot emitted a tinny tinkle, showing that Susi had done her bit for the soup.

At this point I ran away. I should not have run; I should have walked with quiet dignity. Their eyes were all fishing in the cook pot, but because I ran, they looked after me. I heard Susi Kater's voice: "What's he running for, he's going to snitch on us." It struck me in the back, and I could still feel it piercing me as I was catching my breath in the loft after hobbling up the four flights of steps.

I was seven and a half. Susi may have been nine. Shorty was just eight. Axel, Nuchi, Hänschen, and Harry were ten or eleven. There was still Maria Truczinski. She was a little older than I, but she never played in the court; she played with dolls in Mother Truczinski's kitchen or with her grown-up sister Guste who helped at the Lutheran kindergarten.

Is it any wonder if to this day I can't abide the sound of women urinating in chamberpots? Up in the attic Oskar appeased his ears with drumming. Just as he was beginning to feel that the bubbling soup was far behind him, the whole lot of them, all those who had contributed to the soup, turned up in their bare feet or sneakers. Nuchi was carrying the pot. They formed a ring around Oskar, Shorty arrived a moment later. They poked each other, hissing: "Go on, I dare you." Finally, Axel seized Oskar from behind and pinned his arms. Susi laughed, showing moist, regular teeth with her tongue between them, and said why not, why shouldn't they. She took the tin spoon from Nuchi, wiped it silvery on her behind, and plunged it into the steaming brew. Like a good housewife, she stirred slowly, testing the resistance of the mash, blew on the full spoon to cool it, and at length forced it into Oskar's mouth, yes, she forced it into my mouth. Never in all these years have I eaten anything like it, the taste will stay with me.

Only when my friends who had been so concerned over my diet had left me, because Nuchi had been sick in the soup, did I crawl into a corner of the drying loft where only a few sheets were hanging at the time, and throw up the few spoonfuls of reddish brew, in which I was surprised to find no vestiges of frogs. I climbed up on a chest placed beneath the open attic window. Crunching powdered brick, I looked out at distant courts and felt an urge for action. Looking toward the distant windows of the houses in Marienstrasse, I screamed and sang in that direction. I could see no results and yet I was so convinced of the possibilities of long-distance action by singing that from then on the court and all the many courts became too small for me. Thirsting for distance, space, panorama, I resolved to take advantage of every opportunity to leave our suburban Labesweg, whether alone or with Mama, to escape from the pursuits of the soup-makers in the court that had grown too small.

Every Thursday Mama went into the city to shop. Usually she took me with her. She always took me along when it became necessary to buy a new drum at Sigismund Markus' in Arsenal Passage off the Kohlenmarkt. In that period, roughly between the ages of seven and ten, I went through a drum in two weeks flat. From ten to fourteen I demolished an instrument in less than a week. Later, I became more unpredictable in my ways; I could turn a new drum into scrap in a single day, but then a period of mental balance might set in, and for as much as three or four months I would drum forcefully but with a moderation and control that left my instrument intact except for an occasional crack in the enamel.

But let us get back to the days when I escaped periodically from our court with its carpet beating and its soup chefs, thanks to my mama, who took me every two weeks to Sigismund Markus' store, where I was permitted to select a new drum. Sometimes Mama let me come even when my old drum was in relatively good condition. How I relished those afternoons in the multicolored old city; there was always something of the museum about it and there was always a pealing of bells from one church or another. Usually our excursions were pleasantly monotonous. There were always a few purchases to be made at Leiser's, Sternfeld's, or Machwitz'; then we went to Markus'. It had got to be a habit with Markus to pay Mama an assortment of the most flattering compliments. He was obviously in love with her, but as far as I know, he never went any further than to clutch my mother's hand, ardently described as worth its weight in gold, and to impress a silent kiss upon it—except for the time I shall speak of in a moment, when he fell on his knees.

Mama, who had inherited Grandma Koljaiczek's sturdy, imposing figure and her lovable vanity tempered with good nature, put up with Markus' attentions. To some extent, no doubt, she was influenced by the silk stockings—he bought them up in job lots but they were of excellent quality—which he sold her so cheap that they were practically gifts. Not to mention the drums he passed over the counter every two weeks, also at bargain prices.

Regularly at half-past four Mama would ask Sigismund if she might leave me, Oskar, in his care, for it was getting late and she still had a few important errands. Strangely smiling, Markus would bow and promise with an ornate turn of phrase to guard me, Oskar, like the apple of his eye, while she attended to her important affairs. The mockery in his tone was too faint to give offense, but sometimes it brought a blush to Mama's cheeks and led her to suspect that Markus knew what was what.

As for me, I knew all about the errands that Mama characterized as important and attended to so zealously. For a time she had let me accompany her to a cheap hotel in Tischlergasse, where she left me with the landlady and vanished up the stairs for exactly three-quarters of an hour. Without a word the landlady, who as a rule was sipping half-and-half, set a glass of some foul-tasting soda pop before me, and there I waited until Mama, in whom no particular change was discernible, returned. With a word of good-by to the landlady, who didn't bother to look up from her half-and-half, she would take me by the hand. It never occurred to her that the temperature of her hand might give me ideas. Hand in overheated hand, we went next to the Café Weitzke in Wollwebergasse. Mama would order mocha, Oskar lemon ice, and they would wait, but not for long, until Jan Bronski should happen by, and a second cup of mocha should be set down on the soothingly cool marble table top.

They spoke in my presence almost as though I were not there, and their conversation corroborated what I had long known: that Mama and Uncle Jan met nearly every Thursday to spend three-quarters of an hour in a hotel room in Tischlergasse, which Jan paid for. It must have been Jan who objected to these visits of mine to Tischlergasse and the Café Weitzke. Sometimes he was very modest, more so than Mama, who saw no reason why I should not witness the epilogue to their hour of love, of whose legitimacy she always, even afterward, seemed to be convinced.

At Jan's request, then, I spent almost every Thursday aftenoon, from half-past four to shortly before six o'clock, with Sigismund Markus. I was allowed to look through his assortment of drums, and even to use them—where else could Oskar have played several drums at once? Meanwhile, I would contemplate Markus' hangdog features. I didn't know where his thoughts came from, but I had a pretty fair idea where they went; they were in Tischlergasse, scratching on numbered room doors, or huddling like poor Lazarus under the marble-topped table at the Café Weitzke. Waiting for what? For crumbs?

Mama and Jan Bronski left no crumbs. Not a one. They ate everything themselves. They had the ravenous appetite that never dies down, that bites its own tail. They were so busy that at most they might have interpreted Markus' thoughts beneath the table as the importunate attentions of a draft.

On one of those afternoons—it must have been in September, for Mama left Markus' shop in her rust-colored autumn suit—I saw that Markus was lost in thought behind his counter. I don't know what got into me. Taking my newly acquired drum, I drifted out into Arsenal Passage. The sides of the cool dark tunnel were lined with sumptuous window displays: jewelry, books, fancy delicatessen. But desirable as these articles may have been, they were clearly beyond my reach. They did not hold me; I kept on going, through the passage and out to the Kohlen-markt. Emerging in the dusty light, I stood facing the Arsenal. The basalt gray façade was larded with cannon balls dating back to various sieges, which recorded the history of the city of Danzig for the benefit of all who should pass by. The cannon balls were of no interest to me, particularly as I knew that they had not stuck in the wall of their own accord, that there lived in the city of Danzig a mason employed and paid conjointly by the Public Building Office and the Office for the Conser-vation of Monuments, whose function it was to immure the ammunition of past centuries in the façades of various churches and town halls, and specifically in the front and rear walls of the Arsenal.

I decided to head for the Stadt-Theater, whose portico I could see on the right, separated from the Arsenal only by a short unlighted alley. Just as I had expected, the theater was closed—the box office for the evening performance opened only at seven. Envisaging a retreat, I drummed my way irresolutely to leftward. But then Oskar found himself between the Stockturm and the Langgasser Gate. I didn't dare to pass through the gate into Langgasse and turn left into Grosse Wollwebergasse, for Mama and Jan Bronski would be sitting there; and if they were not there yet, it seemed likely that they had just completed their errand in Tisch-lergasse and were on their way to take their refreshing mochas on the little marble table.

I have no idea how I managed to cross the Kohlenmarkt, to thread my way between the streetcars hastening to squeeze through the arch or popping out of it with a great clanging of bells and screeching round the curve as they headed for the Holzmarkt and the Central Station. Probably a grownup, perhaps a policeman, took me by the hand and guided me through the perils of the traffic.

I stood facing the Stockturm, steep brick wall pinned against the sky, and it was only by chance, in response to a faint stirring of boredom, that I wedged my drumsticks in between the masonry and the iron mounting of the door. I looked upward along the brickwork, but it was hard to follow the line of the façade, for pigeons kept flying out of niches and windows, to rest on the oriels and waterspouts for the brief time it takes a pigeon to rest before darting downward and forcing my gaze to follow.

Those pigeons really got on my nerves with their activity. There was no point in looking up if I couldn't follow the wall to its end in the sky, so I called back my gaze and, to dispel my irritation, began in earnest to use my drumsticks as levers. The door gave way. It had no need to open very far, already Oskar was inside the tower, climbing the spiral staircase, advancing his right foot and pulling the left one after it. He came to the first dungeons and still he climbed, on past the torture chamber with its carefully preserved and instructively labeled instruments.

At this point he began to advance his left foot and draw the right one after it. A little higher he glanced through a barred window, estimated the height, studied the thickness of the masonry, and shooed the pigeons away. At the next turn of the staircase he met the same pigeons. Now he shifted back to his right foot and after one more change reached the top. He felt a heaviness in his legs, but it seemed to him that he could have kept on climbing for ages. The staircase had given up first. In a flash Oskar understood the absurdity, the futility of building towers.

I do not know how high the Stockturm was (and still is; for it survived the war). Nor have I any desire to ask Bruno my keeper for a reference work on East German brick Gothic. My guess is that it must measure a good 150 feet from top to toe.

I was obliged—because of the staircase that lacked the courage of its convictions—to stop on the gallery that ran around the spire. I sat down, thrust my legs between the supports of the balustrade, and leaned forward. I clasped one of the supports in my right arm and looked past it, down toward the Kohlenmarkt, while with my left hand I made sure that my drum, which had participated in the whole climb, was all right.

I have no intention of boring you with a birds'-eye view of Danzig —venerable city of many towers, city of belfries and bells, allegedly still pervaded by the breath of the Middle Ages—in any case you can see the whole panorama in dozens of excellent prints. Nor shall I waste my time on pigeons, or doves as they are sometimes called, though some people seem to regard them as a fit subject for literature. To me pigeons mean just about nothing, even gulls are a little higher in the scale. Your "dove of peace" makes sense only as a paradox. I would sooner entrust a message of peace to a hawk or a vulture than to a dove, which is just about the most quarrelsome animal under God's heaven. To make a long story short: there were pigeons on the Stockturm. But after all, there are pigeons on every self-respecting tower.

At all events it was not pigeons that held my eyes but something different: the Stadt-Theater, which I had found closed on my way from the Arsenal. This box with a dome on it looked very much like a monstrously blown-up neoclassical coffee mill. All the Temple of the Muses lacked was a crank with which to grind up its contents, actors and public, sets and props, Goethe and Schiller, slowly but exceeding small. The building annoyed me, especially the column-flanked windows of the lobby, sparkling in the rays of a sagging afternoon sun which kept mixing more and more red in its palette.

Up there on the tower, a good hundred feet above the Kohlenmarkt with its streetcars and throngs of homeward-bound office workers, high above Markus' sweet-smelling shop and the Café Weitzke with its cool marble table tops, two cups of mocha, far above Mama and Jan Bronski, above all courtyards, all bent and straightened nails, all juvenile soup-makers—up there on the tower, I who had hitherto screamed only for good and sufficient reason, became a gratuitous screamer. Until the day when I took it into my head to climb the Stockturm I had projected my cutting notes upon glasses, light bulbs, beer bottles, but only when someone wanted to take away my drum; now on the tower I screamed though my drum was not even remotely threatened.

No one was trying to take Oskar's drum away, and still he screamed. No pigeon had sullied his drum with its droppings. Near me there was verdegris on copper plates, but no glass. And nevertheless Oskar screamed. The eyes of the pigeons had a reddish glitter, but no one was eying him out of a glass eye; yet he screamed. What did he scream at? What distant object? Did he wish to apply scientific method to the experiment he had attempted for the hell of it in the loft after his meal of brick soup? What glass had Oskar in mind? What glass—and it had to be glass—did Oskar wish to experiment with?

It was the Stadt-Theater, the dramatic coffee mill, whose window-panes gleaming in the evening sun attracted the modernistic tones, bordering on mannerism, that I had first tried out in our loft. After a few minutes of variously pitched screams which accomplished nothing, I succeeded in producing an almost soundless tone, and a moment later Oskar noted with joy and a blush of telltale pride that two of the middle panes in the end window of the lobby had been obliged to relinquish their share of the sunset, leaving two black rectangles that would soon require attention from the glazier.

Still, the effect had to be verified. Like a modern painter who, having at last found the style he has been seeking for years, perfects it and discloses his full maturity by turning out one after another dozens of examples of his new manner, all equally daring and magnificent, I too embarked on a productive period.

In barely a quarter of an hour I succeeded in unglassing all the lobby windows and some of the doors. A crowd, from where I was standing one would have said an excited crowd, gathered outside the theater. But the stupidest incident draws a crowd. The admirers of my art made no particular impression on me. At most they led Oskar to discipline his art, to strive for greater formal purity. I was just getting ready to lay bare the very heart of things with a still more daring experiment, to send a very special cry through the open lobby, through the keyhole of one of the loge doors into the still darkened theater, a cry that should strike the pride of all subscribers, the chandelier with all its polished, facetted, light-reflecting and refracting hardware, when my eye lit on a bit of rust-brown material in the crowd outside of the theater: Mama was on her way back from the Café Weitzke, she had had her mocha and left Jan Bronski.

Even so, it must be admitted that Oskar aimed a cry at the chandelier.

But apparently it had no effect, for the newspapers next day spoke only of the windows and doors that had burst asunder for unknown, mysterious reasons. For several weeks purveyors of scientific and semiscientific theories were to fill the back pages of the daily press with columns of fantastic nonsense. The *Neueste Nachrichten* spoke of cosmic rays. The unquestionably well-informed staff of the local observatory spoke of sunspots.

I for my part descended the spiral staircase as quickly as my short legs would carry me and, rather out of breath, joined the crowd outside the theater. Mama's rust-brown autumn suit was nowhere to be seen, no doubt she was in Markus' shop, telling about the destruction wrought by my voice. And Markus, who took my so-called backwardness and my diamond-like voice perfectly for granted, would be wagging the tip of his tongue and rubbing his yellowed white hands.

As I entered the shop the sight that met my eyes made me forget all about my success as a singer. Sigismund Markus was kneeling at Mama's feet, and all the plush animals, bears, monkeys, dogs, the dolls with eyes that opened and shut, the fire engines, rocking horses, and even the jumping jacks that guarded the shop, seemed on the point of kneeling with him. He held Mama's two hands in his, there were brownish fuzzy blotches on the backs of his hands, and he wept.

Mama also looked very solemn, as though she were giving the situation the attention it deserved. "No, Markus," she said, "please, Markus. Not here in the store."

But Markus went on interminably. He seemed to be overdoing it a little, but still I shall never forget the note of supplication in his voice. "Don't do it no more with Bronski, seeing he's in the Polish Post Office. He's with the Poles, that's no good. Don't bet on the Poles; if you gotta bet on somebody, bet on the Germans, they're coming up, maybe sooner maybe later. And suppose they're on top and Mrs. Matzerath is still betting on Bronski. All right if you want to bet on Matzerath, what you got him already. Or do me a favor, bet on Markus seeing he's just fresh baptized. We'll go to London, I got friends there and plenty stocks and bonds if you just decide to come, or all right if you won't come with Markus because you despise me, so despise me. But I beg you down on my knees, don't bet no more on Bronski that's meshugge enough to stick by the Polish Post Office when the Poles are pretty soon all washed up when the Germans come."

Just as Mama, confused by so many possibilities and impossibilities, was about to burst into tears, Markus saw me in the doorway and pointing five eloquent fingers in my direction: "Please, Mrs. Matzerath. We'll take him with us to London. Like a little prince he'll live."

Mama turned toward me and managed a bit of a smile. Maybe she was thinking of the paneless windows in the theater lobby or maybe it was the thought of London Town that cheered her. But to my surprise she shook her head and said lightly, as though declining a dance: "Thank you, Markus, but it's not possible. Really it's impossible—on account of Bronski."

Taking my uncle's name as a cue, Markus rose to his feet and bowed like a jackknife. "I beg your pardon," he said. "That's what I was thinking all along. On account of him you couldn't do it."

It was not yet closing time when we left the shop, but Markus locked up from outside and escorted us to the streetcar stop. Passers-by and a few policemen were still standing outside the theater. But I wasn't the least bit scared, I had almost forgotten my triumph. Markus bent down close to me and whispered, more to himself than to us: "That little Oskar! He knocks on the drum and hell is breaking loose by the theater."

The broken glass had Mama worried and he made gestures that were intended to set her mind at rest. Then the car came and he uttered a last plea as we were climbing into the trailer, in an undertone for fear of being overheard: "Well, if that's the case, do me a favor and stay by Matzerath what you got him already, don't bet no more on that Polisher."

When today Oskar, lying or sitting in his hospital bed but in either case drumming, revisits Arsenal Passage and the Stockturm with the scribbles on its dungeon walls and its well-soiled instruments of torture, when once again he looks down on those three windows outside the lobby of the Stadt-Theater and thereafter returns to Arsenal Passage and Sigismund Markus' store, searching for the particulars of a day in September, he cannot help looking for Poland at the same time. How does he look for it? With his drumsticks. Does he also look for Poland with his soul? He looks for it with every organ of his being, but the soul is not an organ.

I look for the land of the Poles that is lost to the Germans, for the moment at least. Nowadays the Germans have started searching for Poland with credits, Leicas, and compasses, with radar, divining rods, delegations, and moth-eaten provincial students' associations in costume. Some carry Chopin in their hearts, others thoughts of revenge. Condemning the first four partitions of Poland, they are busily planning a fifth; in the meantime flying to Warsaw via Air France in order to deposit, with appropriate remorse, a wreath on the spot that was once the ghetto. One of these days they will go searching for Poland with rockets. I, meanwhile, conjure up Poland on my drum. And this is what I drum: Poland's lost, but not forever, all's lost, but not forever, Poland's not lost forever.

The Rostrum

It was in singing away the lobby windows of our Stadt-Theater that I sought and found my first contact with the Thespian art. Despite Markus' attentions Mama must have observed my direct tie with the theater that afternoon, for when the Christmas holidays came, she bought four theater tickets, for herself, for Stephan and Marga Bronski, and for Oskar, and the last Sunday of Advent she took us to see the Christmas play. The fancy chandelier over the orchestra did its best to please, and I was glad I hadn't sung it to pieces.

Even in those days there were far too many children. In the balcony there were more children than mothers, while the balance was about even in the orchestra frequented by the more prosperous citizens, who were more cautious in their begetting and conceiving. Why can't children sit still? Marga Bronski, who was sitting between me and the relatively well-behaved Stephan, slid off her seat that promptly folded up, made a stab at climbing back again, but found it more interesting to do gymnastics on the balcony rail, got stuck in her folding seat, and started to scream, though no louder than the other little demons around us and only briefly, because Mama wisely poured candy into her open mouth. Sucking candy and tuckered out by her struggles with her seat, Marga fell asleep soon after the performance began, but had to be awakened after each act to clap, which she did with enthusiasm.

The play was *Tom Thumb,* which obviously had a special appeal for me and gripped me from the start. They did it very cleverly. They didn't show Tom Thumb at all, you only heard his voice and saw the grownups chasing around after him. He was invisible but very active. Here he is sitting in the horse's ear. Now his father is selling him to two tramps for good money, now he is taking a walk, very high and mighty, on the brim of one of the tramps' hats. Later he crawls into a mousehole and then into a snail shell. He joins a band of robbers, lies down with them, and along with a mouthful of hay makes his way into the cow's stomach. But the cow is slaughtered because she speaks with Tom Thumb's voice. The cow's stomach, however, with Tom inside it, is thrown out on the dump heap, and gobbled up by the wolf. Tom cleverly persuades the wolf to pillage his father's storeroom and starts to scream just as the wolf is getting to work. The end was like the fairy tale: The father kills the wicked wolf, the mother cuts open the wolf's stomach with her scissors, and out comes Tom Thumb, that is, you hear his voice crying: "Oh, father, I've been in a mousehole, a cow's stomach, and a wolf's stomach: now I'm going to stay home with you."

The end touched me, and when I looked up at Mama, I saw that she was hiding her nose in her handkerchief; like me, she had identified herself with the action on the stage. Mama's feelings were easily stirred, and for the next few weeks, especially for the remainder of the Christmas holidays, she kept hugging and kissing me and, laughing or wistful, calling me Tom Thumb. Or: My little Tom Thumb. Or: My poor, poor Tom Thumb.

It was not until the summer of '33 that I went to the theater again.

81

Because of a misunderstanding on my part, the venture turned out badly, but it was a profound experience that stayed with me. The thundering surge still rings in my ears. No, I am not exaggerating, all this took place at the Zoppot Opera-in-the-Woods, where summer after summer Wagner was poured forth upon nature beneath the night sky.

It was only Mama who actually cared anything about opera. Even operettas were too much for Matzerath. Jan took his lead from Mama and raved about arias, though despite his musical appearance he was completely tone deaf. However, he was friends with the Formella brothers, former schoolmates at Karthaus High School, who lived at Zoppot, had charge of the floodlights illuminating the lakeside path and the fountain outside the Casino, and also attended to the lighting effects at the Opera-in-the-Woods.

The way to Zoppot led through Oliva. A morning in the Castle Park. Goldfish and swans, Mama and Jan Bronski in the famous Whispering Grotto. Afterward more goldfish and swans, obviously working hand in glove with a photographer. While the picture was being taken, Matzerath let me ride on his shoulders. I rested my drum on the top of his head, that was always good for a laugh, even later after the picture had been pasted in the album. And then good-by goldfish, good-by swans, good-by Whispering Grotto. Not only in the Castle Park was it Sunday but also outside the gate and in the streetcar bound for Glettkau, and in the Glettkau Casino, where we had lunch, while the Baltic, as though it had nothing else to do, held out an invitation to bathe; everywhere it was Sunday. As we approached Zoppot along the beach promenade, Sunday came out to meet us and Matzerath had to pay admission for the lot of us.

We bathed at South Beach because it was supposedly less crowded than North Beach. The men undressed in the men's cabins, Mama took me to a ladies' cabin where she, who was already beginning to overflow her banks, poured her flesh into a straw-colored bathing suit. I was expected to go naked. To put off my encounter with the thousands of eyes on the beach, I shielded my private parts with my drum and later lay down on my belly in the sand. The waters of the Baltic were inviting but I had no desire to go in, preferring to play the ostrich and shelter my modesty in the sand. Both Matzerath and Jan Bronski looked so ridiculous verging on pathetic with their incipient potbellies that I was glad when, late in the afternoon, we returned to the bath houses and, having anointed our sunburns, slipped back into Sunday civilian dress.

Coffee and cake at the Seestern. Mama wanted a third helping of the five-story cake. Matzerath was against, Jan was for and against. Mama ordered her cake, gave Matzerath a bite, fed Jan a spoonful, and, having provided for the well-being of her men, crammed the rest of the buttery-sweet wedge into her stomach, spoonful by spoonful.

O sacred butter cream, O clear to slightly cloudy Sunday afternoon dusted with powdered sugar! Polish nobles sat behind blue sunglasses and intense soft drinks that they did not touch. The ladies played with their violet fingernails and the sea breeze wafted over to us the mothflake smell of the fur capes they rented for the season. Matzerath thought the fur capes were idiotic. Mama would have loved to rent one, if only for a single afternoon. Jan maintained that the boredom of the Polish nobility had risen to such heights that despite mounting debts they had stopped speaking French and out of sheer snobbery taken to conversing in the most ordinary Polish.

We couldn't sit forever at the Seestern, studying the blue sunglasses and violet fingernails of the Polish nobility. Replete with cake, my mama needed exercise. We repaired to the Casino Park, where I had to ride a donkey and pose for another picture. Goldfish and swans—what nature won't think of next—and more goldfish and swans, what else is fresh water good for?

Amid clipped yew trees which, however, did not whisper as they are supposed to, we met the Formella Brothers, illuminators of the casino grounds and of the Opera-in-the-Woods. First the younger Formella had to reel off all the jokes that came his way in the course of his illuminating professional activities. The elder Formella brother knew all the jokes by heart but brotherly love made him laugh contagiously at the right places, showing one more gold tooth than his younger brother, who had only three. We went to Springer's for a drop of gin, though Mama would have preferred the Kurfürst. Then, still dealing out jokes from an inexhaustible stock, the generous younger brother invited us all to dinner at the Papagei. At the Papagei we met Tuschel, who owned half of Zoppot, a share in the Opera-in-the-Woods, and five movie theaters. He was also the Formella brothers' boss and was glad to make our acquaintance, just as we were glad to make his. Tuschel kept twisting a ring on his finger, but it couldn't have been a wishing ring or a magic ring, for nothing happened at all, except that Tuschel in turn began telling jokes, the same Formella jokes we had heard before, though he made them more complicated because he had fewer gold teeth. Even so, the whole table laughed, because Tuschel was doing the telling. I alone remained solemn, trying to puncture his punch lines with the straightness of my face. Ah, how those salvos of laughter, like the bull's-eye panes in the partition of our dining corner, fostered well-being, even if they were not genuine. Tuschel was visibly grateful, told a few more, ordered Goldwasser, and suddenly, floating in laughter and Goldwasser, turned his ring around a different way. This time something happened. Tuschel invited us all to the Opera-in-the-Woods; unfortunately he couldn't attend, an appointment and that kind of thing, but would we kindly accept his seats, they were in a loge with upholstered seats, the little fellow could sleep if he was tired; and with a silver mechanical pencil he wrote a few words in Tuschel's hand on Tuschel's visiting card; it would open all doors, he said—and so it did.

What happened next can be related in a few words: A balmy summer evening, the Opera-in-the-Woods was sold out, full of foreigners. Even before it started, the mosquitoes were on hand. And only when the last mosquito, which always comes a little late, just to be chic, announced its arrival with a bloodthirsty buzzing, did the performance really get under way. It was *The Flying Dutchman*. A ship, looking more like a poacher than a pirate, drifted in from the woods that had given the Opera-in-the-Woods its name. Sailors began to sing at the trees. I fell asleep on Tuschel's upholstery, and when I woke up, the sailors were still singing, or maybe they were different sailors: Helmsman, keep watch . . . but Oskar fell asleep once more, happy even in dozing off that Mama, gliding with the waves and heaving in the true Wagnerian spirit, was taking so much interest in the *Dutchman*. She failed to notice that Matzerath and her Jan had covered their faces with their hands and were sawing logs of different thicknesses and that I too kept slipping through Wagner's fingers. Then suddenly Oskar awoke for good, because a woman was standing all alone in the forest, screaming for all she was worth. She had yellow hair and she was yelling because a spotlight, probably manipulated by the younger Formella, was blinding her. "No!" she cried. "Woe's me!" and: "Who hath made me suffer so?" But Formella, who was making her suffer, didn't divert the spotlight. The screams of the solitary woman— Mama referred to her afterward as a soloist—subsided to a muffled whimper, but only to rise again in a silvery bubbling fountain of high notes which blighted the leaves of the trees before their time but had no effect at all on Formella's spotlight. A brilliant voice, but its efforts were of no avail. It was time for Oskar to intervene, to locate that importunate source of light and, with a single long-distance cry, lower-pitched than the persistent buzzing of the mosquitoes, destroy it.

It was not my plan to create a short circuit, darkness, flying sparks, or a forest fire which, though quickly put out, provoked a panic. I had nothing to gain. Not only did I lose my mama and the two roughly awakened gentlemen in the confusion; even my drum got lost.

This third of my encounters with the theater gave my mama, who had begun, after that evening at the Opera-in-the-Woods, to domesticate Wagner in easy arrangements on our piano, the idea of taking me to the circus. It was put into effect in the spring of '34.

Oskar has no intention of chewing your ear off about trapeze artists darting through the air like streaks of silver, about ferocious tigers or the incredible dexterity of the seals. No one fell headlong from the dome. Nothing was bitten off any of the animal-tamers. The seals did just what they had been taught: they juggled with balls and were rewarded with live herring which they caught in mid-air. I am indebted to the circus for many happy hours and for my meeting, which was to prove so important in my life, with Bebra, the musical clown, who played "Jimmy the Tiger" on bottles and directed a group of Lilliputians.

We met in the menagerie. Mama and her two cavaliers were letting the monkeys make monkeys of them. Hedwig Bronski, who for once had come along, was showing her children the ponies. After a lion had yawned at me, I foolishly became involved with an owl. I tried to stare him down, but it was the owl that stared me down. Oskar crept away dismayed, with burning ears and a feeling of inner hurt, taking refuge between two blue and white trailers, because apart from a few tied-up dwarf goats, there were no animals here.

He was in suspenders and slippers, carrying a pail of water. Our eyes met as he was passing and there was instant recognition. He set down his pail, leaned his great head to one side, and came toward me. I guessed that he must be about four inches taller than I.

"Will you take a look at that!" There was a note of envy in his rasping voice. "Nowadays it's the three-year-olds that decide to stop growing." When I failed to answer, he tried again: "My name is Bebra, directly descended from Prince Eugene, whose father was Louis XIV and not some Savoyard as they claim." Still I said nothing, but he continued: "On my tenth birthday I made myself stop growing. Better late than never."

Since he had spoken so frankly, I too introduced myself, but without any nonsense about my family tree. I was just Oskar.

"Well, my dear Oskar, you must be fourteen or fifteen. Maybe as much as sixteen. What, only nine and a half? You don't mean it?"

It was my turn to guess his age. I purposely aimed too low.

"You're a flatterer, my young friend. Thirty-five, that was once upon a time. In August I shall be celebrating my fifty-third birthday. I could be your grandfather."

Oskar said a few nice things about his acrobatic clown act and complimented him on his gift for music. That aroused my ambition and I performed a little trick of my own. Three light bulbs were the first to be taken in. Bravo, bravissimo, Mr. Bebra cried, and wanted to hire Oskar on the spot.

Even today I am occasionally sorry that I declined. I talked myself out of it, saying: "You know, Mr. Bebra, I prefer to regard myself as a member of the audience. I cultivate my little art in secret, far from all applause. But it gives me pleasure to applaud your accomplishments." Mr. Bebra raised a wrinkled forefinger and admonished me: "My dear Oskar, believe an experienced colleague. Our kind has no place in the audience. We must perform, we must run the show. If we don't, it's the others that run us. And they don't do it with kid gloves."

His eyes became as old as the hills and he almost crawled into my

85

ear. "They are coming," he whispered. "They will take over the meadows where we pitch our tents. They will organize torch-light parades. They will build rostrums and fill them, and down from the rostrums they will preach our destruction. Take care, young man. Always take care to be sitting on the rostrum and never to be standing out in front of it."

Hearing my name called, Mr. Bebra took up his pail. "They are looking for you, my friend. We shall meet again. We are too little to lose each other. Bebra always says: Little people like us can always find a place even on the most crowded rostrum. And if not on it, then under it, but never out in front. So says Bebra, who is descended in a straight line from Prince Eugene."

Calling Oskar, Mama stepped out from behind a trailer just in time to see Mr. Bebra kiss me on the forehead. Then he picked up his pail of water and, swaying his shoulders, headed for his trailer.

Mama was furious. "Can you imagine," she said to Matzerath and the Bronskis. "He was with the midgets. And a gnome kissed him on the forehead. I hope it doesn't mean anything."

To me that kiss on the forehead was to mean a good deal. The political events of the ensuing years bore him out: the era of torchlight processions and parades past rostrums and reviewing stands had begun.

I took Mr. Bebra's advice, and Mama, for her part, followed a part of the advice Sigismund Markus had given her in Arsenal Passage and continued to repeat every Thursday. Though she did not go to London with Markus—I should not have had much objection to the move—she stayed with Matzerath and saw Bronski only in moderation, that is, in Tischlergasse at Jan's expense and over the family skat games, which became more and more costly for Jan, because he always lost. Matzerath, however, on whom Mama had bet, on whom, following Markus' advice, she let her stakes lie though she did not double them, joined the Party in '34. But though he espoused the forces of order at a relatively early date, he never attained any higher position than unit leader. Like all unusual happenings, his promotion was the occasion for a family skat game. It was then that Matzerath introduced a new note of severity mingled with alarm into the warnings he had long been meting out to Jan Bronski on the subject of his activity in the Polish Post Office.

Otherwise there was no great change. The picture of the gloomy Beethoven, a present from Greff, was removed from its nail over the piano, and Hitler's equally gloomy countenance was hung up on the same nail. Matzerath, who didn't care for serious music, wanted to banish the nearly deaf musician entirely. But Mama, who loved Beethoven's slow movements, who had learned to play two or three of them even more slowly than indicated and decanted them from time to time, insisted that if Beethoven were not over the sofa, he would have to be over the sideboard.

So began the most sinister of all confrontations: Hitler and the genius, face to face and eye to eye. Neither of them was very happy about it.

Little by little Matzerath pieced together the uniform. If I remember right, he began with the cap, which he liked to wear even in fine weather with the "storm strap" in place, scraping his chin. For a time he wore a white shirt and black tie with the cap, or else a leather jacket with black armband. Then he bought his first brown shirt and only a week later he wanted the shit-brown riding breeches and high boots. Mama was opposed to these acquisitions and several weeks passed before the uniform was complete.

Each week there were several occasions to wear the uniform but Matzerath contented himself with the Sunday demonstrations on the Maiwiese near the Sports Palace. But about these he was uncompromising even in the worst weather and refused to carry an umbrella when in uniform. "Duty is duty and schnaps is schnaps," he said. That became a stock phrase with him and we were to hear it very often. He went out every Sunday morning after preparing the roast for dinner. This put me in an embarrassing situation, for Jan Bronski quickly grasped the new Sunday political situation and, incorrigible civilian that he was, took to calling on my poor forsaken mama while Matzerath was drilling and parading.

What could I do but make myself scarce? I had no desire to disturb the two of them on the sofa, or to spy on them. As soon as my uniformed father was out of sight and before the civilian, whom I already looked upon as my presumptive father, should arrive, I consequently slipped out of the house and drummed my way toward the Maiwiese.

Did it have to be the Maiwiese? you may ask. Take my word for it that nothing was doing on the waterfront on Sundays, that I had no inclination to go walking in the woods, and that in those days the interior of the Church of the Sacred Heart still had no appeal for me. There were still Mr. Greff's scouts, to be sure, but even at the risk of being thought a fellow traveler I must admit that I preferred the doings on the Maiwiese to the repressed eroticism of the scout meetings.

There was always a speech either by Greiser or by Löbsack, the district chief of training. Greiser never made much of an impression on me. He was too moderate and was later replaced as Gauleiter by a Bavarian named Forster, who was more forceful. But for Löbsack's humpback, it would have been hard for the Bavarian to get ahead in our northern seaport. Recognizing Löbsack's worth, regarding his hump as a sign of keen intelligence, the Party made him district chief of training. He knew his business. All Forster knew how to do was to shout "Home to the Reich" in his foul Bavarian accent, but Löbsack had a head for particulars.

He spoke every variety of Danzig Plattdeutsch, told jokes about Boller-mann and Wullsutzki, and knew how to talk to the longshoremen in Schichau, the proletariat in Ohra, the middle class of Emmaus, Schidlitz, Bürgerwiesen, and Praust. It was a pleasure to hear the little man, whose brown uniform lent a special prominence to his hump, stand up to the feeble heckling of the Socialists and the sullen beer-drinker's aggressive-ness of the Communists.

Löbsack had wit. He derived all his wit from his hump, which he called by its name; the crowd always likes that. Before the Communists would be allowed to take over he would lose his hump. It was easy to see that he was not going to lose his hump, that his hump was there to stay. It followed that the hump was right and with it the Party—whence it can be inferred that a hump is an ideal basis for an idea.

When Greiser, Löbsack, or later Forster spoke, they spoke from the rostrum. This was one of the rostrums that little Mr. Bebra had com-mended. Consequently I long regarded Löbsack, who was humpbacked and gifted and spoke from a rostrum, as an emissary from Bebra, one who stood brown-clad on the rostrum fighting for Bebra's cause and mine.

What is a rostrum? Regardless of whom it is built for, a rostrum must be symmetrical. And that rostrum on our Maiwiese was indeed striking in its symmetry. From back to front: six swastika banners side by side: then a row of flags, pennants, standards; then a row of black-uniformed SS men who clutched their belt buckles during the singing and the speeches; then, seated, several rows of uniformed Party comrades; behind the speaker's stand more Party comrades, leaders of women's associations with motherly looks on their faces, representatives of the Senate in civilian garb, guests from the Reich, and the police chief or his representative.

The front of the rostrum was rejuvenated by the Hitler Youth or, more precisely, by the Regional Bands of the Hitler Young Folk and the Hitler Youth. At some of the demonstrations a mixed chorus, also sym-metrically arranged, would recite slogans or sing the praises of the east wind, which, according to the text, was better than any other wind at unfurling banners.

Bebra, who kissed me on the forehead, had also said: "Oskar, never be a member of the audience. Never be standing out in front. The place for our kind is on the rostrum."

Usually I was able to find a place among the leaders of the women's associations. Unfortunately the ladies never failed to caress me for pro-paganda purposes during the rally. I couldn't slip in between the drums and trumpets at the foot of the platform because of my own drum, which the trooper musicians rejected. An attempt to enter into relations with Löbsack, the district chief of training, ended in failure. I had been sorrily mistaken in the man. Neither was he, as I had hoped, an emissary from Bebra, nor, despite his promising hump, had he the slightest understanding of my true stature.

On one of those rostrum Sundays I went up to him as he stood near the pulpit, gave him the party salute, looked brightly up at him for a moment, and then whispered with a wink: "Bebra is our leader!" But no light dawned. No, he patted me just like the ladies of the National Socialist women's associations and finally had Oskar removed from the platform—after all he had a speech to make. I was taken in hand by two representatives of the League of German Girls, who questioned me about my papa and mama all through the speech.

Thus it will come as no surprise when I tell you that by the summer of '34 I began to be disillusioned with the party—the Roehm putsch had nothing to do with it. The longer I contemplated the rostrum from out in front, the more suspicious I became of its symmetry, which was not sufficiently relieved by Löbsack's hump. Of course Oskar's criticism was leveled first of all at the drummers and horn-blowers; and one sultry demonstration Sunday in '35, I tangled with the young drummers and trumpet-players at the foot of the reviewing stand.

Matzerath left home at nine o'clock. To get him out of the house on time, I had helped him shine his brown leather puttees. Even at that early hour it was intolerably hot, and even before he went out in the sun, there were dark and spreading spots of sweat under the arms of his Party shirt. At half past nine on the dot Jan Bronski arrived in an airy, light-colored summer suit, tender-grey, pierced oxfords, and a straw hat. Jan played with me for a while, but even as he played, he could not take his eyes off Mama, who had washed her hair the night before. I soon realized that my presence inhibited their conversation; there was a stiffness in her bearing and an air of embarrassment in Jan's movements. It was plain that he felt cramped in those summer trousers of his. And so I made off, following in the footsteps of Matzerath, though I did not take him as my model. Carefully I avoided streets that were full of uniformed folk on their way to the Maiwiese and for the first time approached the drill ground from the direction of the tennis courts which were beside the Sports Palace. Thanks to this indirect route, I obtained a rear view of the rostrum.

Have you ever seen a rostrum from behind? All men and women—if I may make a suggestion—should be familiarized with the rear view of a rostrum before being called upon to gather in front of one. Everyone who has ever taken a good look at a rostrum from behind will be immunized ipso facto against any magic practiced in any form whatsoever on rostrums. Pretty much the same applies to rear views of church altars; but that is another subject.

Oskar was already inclined to thoroughness; he did not content himself with viewing the naked ugliness of the scaffolding. Remembering the words of Bebra his mentor, he made his way to the rostrum. This rostrum was meant to be viewed only from the front, but he approached its uncouth rear. Clutching his drum, without which he never went out, he squeezed between uprights, bumped his head on a projecting beam, and gashed his knee on a protruding nail. He heard the boots of the party comrades overhead, and a moment later the little shoes of the women's associations. Finally he reached the place where the August heat was most stifling. At the foot of the stand he found a nook where, hidden behind a slat of plywood, he was able to enjoy the accoustical delights of the political rally at his ease, free from the optical irritation of banners and uniforms. And so I huddled under the speaker's stand. To the left and right of me and above me stood the younger drummers of the Young Folk and the older drummers of the Hitler Youth, squinting, as I knew, beneath the blinding sunlight. And then the crowd. I smelled them through the cracks in the planking. They stood there rubbing elbows and Sunday clothes. They had come on foot or by streetcar; some had brought their fiancées, to give them a treat; all these people wanted to be present while history was being made, even if it took up the whole morning.

No, said Oskar to himself. It wouldn't be right if they had come for nothing. He set an eye to a knothole in the planking and watched the hubbub approaching from the Hindenburg-Allee. *They* were coming! Commands rang out over his head, the band leader fiddled with his baton, the musicians set their polished and gleaming trumpets to their lips and adjusted their mouthpieces. And then the grim trumpeting of the young troopers began. "Poor SA Man Brand," said Oskar to himself in bitter pain, "and poor Hitler Youth Quex, you have died in vain."

As though to confirm Oskar's sorrowful obituary for the martyrs of the movement, a massive pounding on taut calfskin mingled with the trumpets. Down the lane leading through the crowd to the rostrum, I dimly saw uniforms approaching in the distance. "Now, my people," Oskar cried out. "Now, my people. Hearken unto me!"

The drum was already in place. Supplely and tenderly I manipulated the sticks, imprinting an artful and joyous waltz rhythm upon it. Conjuring up Vienna and the Danube, I beat more and more loudly until the first and second bass drums of the troopers were drawn to my waltz and the kettledrums of the older boys took up my prelude with varying skill. Here and there, of course, there was a diehard, hard also of hearing no doubt, who went on playing boom-boom, whereas what I had in mind was the three-four time so beloved of the simple folk. Oskar was on the point of giving up when the trumpets saw the light and the fifes, oh, Danube, oh, how blue they blew! Only the leaders of the trumpeters' and the drummers' corps refused to bow to the waltz king and kept shouting their exasperating commands. But I had deposed them, the music was mine. The simple folk were full of gratitude. Laughter rang out close to the rostrum, here and there I heard singing, oh, Danube, and across the whole field so blue, as far as the Hindenburg-Allee so blue and the Steffens-Park so blue, my rhythm went hopping, amplified by the wide-open microphone above me. And when, still energetically drumming, I looked out into the open through my knothole, I saw that the people were enjoying my waltz, they were hopping about merrily, they had it in their legs: already nine couples and yet another couple were dancing, brought together by the waltz king. Only Löbsack, who appeared on the meadow followed by a long brown train of party dignitaries, Forster, Greiser, Rauschning, and others, whose passage to the rostrum was blocked by the crowd, stood there fuming and surprisingly disgruntled by my three-quarter time. He was used to being escorted to the rostrum by rectilinear march music. These frivolous sounds shook his faith in the people. Through the knothole I observed his sufferings. A draft was blowing through the hole. Though threatened with an inflammation of the eye, I felt sorry for him and changed over to a Charleston: "Jimmy the Tiger." I took up the rhythm that Bebra the clown had drummed in the circus on empty seltzer siphons; but the young troopers out in front didn't dig the Charleston. They belonged to a different generation. What could they know of the Charleston and "Jimmy the Tiger"? What those drums were pounding —oh, Bebra, my dear friend—wasn't Jimmy the Tiger, it was pure chaos, and the trumpets blew Sodom and Gomorrah. It's all one to us, thought the fifes. The trumpet leader cursed in all directions. And nevertheless the troopers drummed, piped, and trumpeted for all they were worth, bringing joy to Jimmy's heart in the sweltering tigery August heat, and at last the national comrades who were crowding round the stand by the thousands caught on: it's Jimmy the Tiger, summoning the people to the Charleston.

All those who were not yet dancing hastened to snatch up the last available partners. But Löbsack had to dance with his hump, for near him there was not a single member of the fair sex to be had, and the NS ladies who might have come to his help were far away, fidgeting on the hard wooden benches of the rostrum. Nevertheless—as his hump advised him—he danced, trying to put a good face on the horrible Jimmy music and to save what could still be saved.

But the situation was beyond saving. The national comrades danced away from the Maiwiese and soon the grassy field, though badly trampled, was quite deserted. The national comrades had vanished with Jimmy the Tiger in the spacious grounds of the nearby Steffens-Park. There they found the jungle that Jimmy promised; there tigers moved on velvet paws, an ersatz jungle for the sons and daughters of the German nation, who only a short while before had been crowding round the rostrum. Gone were law and order. The more culture-minded element repaired to the Hindenburg-Allee, where trees had first been planted in the eighteenth century, where these same trees had been cut down in 1807 when the city was being besieged by Napoleon's troops, and a fresh set had been planted in 1810 in honor of Napoleon. On this historic ground, the dancers were still able to benefit by my music, because no one turned off the microphone above me. I could be heard as far as Oliva Gate. In the end the excellent lads at the foot of the rostrum succeeded, with the help of Jimmy's unleashed tiger, in clearing the Maiwiese of everything but daisies.

Even when I gave my instrument a well-deserved rest, the drummer boys kept right on. It was quite some time before my musical influence wore off.

Oskar was not able to leave his hiding place at once, SA men and SS men spent more than an hour kicking at the planks, poking into crannies, tearing holes in their brown and black uniforms. They seemed to be looking for something under the rostrum, perhaps a Socialist or a team of Communist saboteurs. I shall not describe my dodges and maneuvers. Suffice it to say that they did not find Oskar, because they were no match for him.

At least it was quiet in my wooden labyrinth, which was about the size of the whale's belly where Jonah sat staining his prophet's robes with blubber. But Oskar was no prophet, he was beginning to feel hungry. There was no Lord to say: "Arise, go unto Nineveh, that great city, and preach unto it." For me the Lord saw no need to make a gourd grow and send a worm to destroy it. I lamented neither for a biblical gourd nor for Nineveh, even if its name was Danzig. I tucked my very unbiblical drum under my sweater and concentrated on my own troubles. Carefully avoiding overhanging beams and protruding nails, I emerged by my own resources from the bowels of a rostrum intended for meetings and rallies of all sorts and which happened only by the merest accident to have the proportions of a prophet-swallowing whale.

Who would have noticed a wee mite of a three-year-old, whistling as he skirted the Maiwiese in the direction of the Sports Palace. Behind the tennis courts my boys from the rostrum were hopping about with their bass drums and kettledrums, their fifes and trumpets. Punitive drill, I observed, as they hopped about in response to their leader's whistle. I felt only moderately sorry for them. Aloof from his assembled staff, Löbsack was walking up and down, alone with his hump. About-facing on the heels of his boots, he had managed to eradicate all the grass and daisies at the extremities of his course.

Dinner was on the table when Oskar reached home. There was meat loaf with boiled potatoes, red cabbage, and for dessert chocolate pudding with vanilla sauce. Matzerath didn't say a word. Mama's thoughts were somewhere else. But that afternoon there was a family quarrel hinging on jealousy and the Polish Post Office. Toward evening came a refreshing storm, a cloudburst accompanied by a fine drum solo of hail. Oskar's weary instrument was able to rest and listen.

Shopwindows

For several years, until November, '38, to be exact, my drum and I spent a good bit of our time huddling under rostrums, observing successful or not so successful demonstrations, breaking up rallies, driving orators to distraction, transforming marches and hymns into waltzes and fox trots.

Today I am a private patient in a mental hospital, and all that has become historical, old stuff, dead as a doornail, though still much debated and discussed. It has become possible for me to see my drumming under rostrums in proper perspective, and it would never occur to me to set myself up as a resistance fighter because I disrupted six or seven rallies and threw three or four parades out of step with my drumming. That word "resistance" has become very fashionable. We hear of the "spirit of resistance," of "resistance circles." There is even talk of an "inward resistance," a "psychic emigration." Not to mention those courageous and uncompromising souls who call themselves Resistance Fighters, men of the Resistance, because they were fined during the war for not blacking out their bedroom windows properly.

Let us cast one more glance beneath Oskar's rostrums. Did Oskar drum for the people? Did he, following the advice of Bebra his mentor, take the action in hand and provoke the people out in front of the rostrum to dance? Did he confound and perplex Löbsack, the shrewd and able chief of training? Did he, on a one-dish Sunday in August, 1935 and on several occasions thereafter, break up brown rallies on a drum which though red and white was not Polish?

Yes, I did all that. But does that make me, as I lie in this mental hospital, a Resistance Fighter? I must answer in the negative, and I hope that you too, you who are not inmates of mental hospitals, will regard me as nothing more than an eccentric who, for private and what is more esthetic reasons, though to be sure the advice of Bebra my mentor had something to do with it, rejected the cut and color of the uniforms, the rhythm and tone of the music normally played on rostrums, and therefore drummed up a bit of protest on an instrument that was a mere toy.

In those days it was possible to reach the people on and in front of a rostrum with a wretched toy drum, and I must admit that I perfected

93

this little trick, as I had my long-distance, glass-shattering song, for its own sake. For it was not only demonstrations of a brown hue that I attacked with my drumming. Oskar huddled under the rostrum for Reds and Blacks, for Boy Scouts and Spinach Shirts, for Jehovah's Witnesses, the Kyffhäuser Bund, the Vegetarians, and the Young Polish Fresh Air Movement. Whatever they might have to sing, trumpet, or proclaim, my drum knew better.

Yes, my work was destructive. And what I did not defeat with my drum, I killed with my voice. In the daytime I assaulted the symmetry of rostrums; at night—this was in the winter of '36 to '37—I played the tempter. My earliest instruction in the tempting of my fellow men was provided by my grandmother Koljaiczek, who in that hard winter opened a stand at the weekly market in Langfuhr: there she sat in her four skirts, crying plaintively: "Fresh eggs, golden creamy butter, geese not too fat, not too thin." Every Tuesday was market day. She took the narrow-gauge railway from Viereck; shortly before Langfuhr she removed the felt slippers she wore in the train, donned a pair of shapeless galoshes, took up her two baskets, and made her way to the stall in Bahnhofstrasse. Over it hung a sign: Anna Koljaiczek, Bissau. How cheap eggs were in those days! You could get two and a half dozen of them for one gulden, and Kashubian butter cost less than margarine. My grandmother's place was between two fish vendors who called: "Fresh flounder and cod!" The cold made the butter hard as stone, kept the eggs fresh, turned fish scales into extra-thin razor blades, and provided work for a one-eyed man named Schwerdtfeger who heated bricks over a charcoal fire, wrapped them in newspaper, and rented them out to the market women.

Every hour on the dot Schwerdtfeger pushed a hot brick under my grandmother's four skirts with an iron rake. He pushed the steaming package under the scarcely lifted hems, discharged it, caught hold of the brick of the preceding hour, which was almost cold by now, and pulled it out.

How I envied those bricks wrapped in newspaper, those storehouses and bestowers of warmth! To this day I wish I could be a toasty warm brick, constantly exchanged for myself, lying beneath my grandmother's skirts. What, you will ask, can Oskar be after beneath his grandmother's skirts? Does he wish to imitate his grandfather Koljaiczek and take liberties with an old woman? Is he searching for oblivion, a home, the ultimate Nirvana?

Oskar replies: I was looking for Africa under the skirts, or perhaps Naples, which, as we all know, one must have seen before dying. This was the watershed, the union of all streams; here special winds blew, or else there was no wind at all; dry and warm, you could listen to the whishing of the rain; here ships made fast or weighed anchors; here our

94

Heavenly Father, who has always been a lover of warmth, sat beside Oskar; the Devil cleaned his spyglass, and the angels played blindman's buff; beneath my grandmother's skirts it was always summer, even when it was time to light the candles on the Chrismas tree or to hunt for Easter eggs; even on All Saints' Day. Nowhere could I have been more at peace with the calendar than beneath my grandmother's skirts.

But she seldom let me take shelter under her tent, and never at market. I sat beside her on a crate, receiving a kind of warmth from her arm, and looked on as the bricks came and went. Here it was that I learned my grandmother's trick of tempting people. Her equipment consisted of Vincent Bronski's old pocketbook with a string tied to it. She would toss the pocketbook out on the hard-packed snow of the sidewalk. Against the gray sand strewn over the slipperiness no one but my grandmother and I could see the string. Housewives came and went. Cheap as her wares were, they were not in the mood to buy; they wanted the merchandise for nothing, if possible with a little premium thrown in. In this state of mind, a lady would bend down to pick up Vincent's pocketbook, her fingers were already touching it. And then my grandmother would pull in the hook, drawing a well-dressed, slightly embarrassed fish over to her stall: "Well, my dear lady, would you like a little butter, golden creamy, or a few eggs, two and a half dozen for a gulden?"

This was how Anna Koljaiczek sold her produce. I for my part learned the magic of temptation, not the kind of temptation that lured the fourteen-year-olds on our block down to the cellar with Susi Kater to play doctor and patient. That tempted me not at all, I avoided it like the plague after the little monsters, Axel Mischke and Nuchi Eyke, in the role of serum donors, and Susi Kater playing the doctor, had used me as a patient, making me swallow medicines that were not so sandy as the brick soup but had an aftertaste of putrid fish. My temptation was almost disembodied and kept its distance from its victims.

Long after nightfall, an hour or two after the shops closed, I slipped away from Mama and Matzerath and went out into the winter night. Standing in a doorway sheltered from the wind, I would peer across the silent, almost deserted streets at the nearby shopwindows, displays of delicatessen, haberdashery, shoes, watches, jewelry, all articles both desirable and easy to carry. All the windows were not illuminated. Indeed, I preferred those that were half in darkness, beyond the beam of the street lamps, because light attracts everyone, even the most commonplace people, while only the elect choose to linger in the penumbra.

I was not interested in the kind of people who in strolling by cast a glance into brightly lit shopwindows, more concerned with the price tags than the merchandise; nor did I concern myself with those who looked at themselves in the plate-glass panes to see if their hats were on right. The kind for whom I lurked in wait on crisp dry nights, on nights when the air was full of great silent snowflakes, or beneath the waxing wintry moon, were the kind who stopped to look in a shopwindow as though in answer to a call; their eyes did not wander about aimlessly, but quickly came to rest on a single object.

I was the hunter, they were my game. My work required patience, coolness, and a sure eye. It was my voice which felled the victim, painlessly and without bloodshed. By temptation. What sort of temptation?

The temptation to steal. With my most inaudible cry I made a circular incision in the shopwindow on a level with the bottommost displays, close to the coveted article. And then, with a last vocal effort, I toppled the cut-out disk into the interior of the showcase. It fell with a quickly muffled tinkle, which however was not the tinkle of breaking glass. I did not hear it, Oskar was too far away; but the young woman in the threadbare brown coat with the rabbit collar heard the sound and saw the circular aperture, gave a start that sent a quiver through her rabbit fur, and prepared to set off through the snow, but stood still, perhaps because it was snowing and everything is permitted when it is snowing, provided it is snowing hard enough. Yet she looked round, suspicious of the snowflakes, looked round as though behind the snowflakes there were something else beside more snowflakes, and she was still looking round when her right hand slipped out of her muff, which was also made of bunny fur. Then she stopped looking round and reached through the circular hole, pushed aside the glass disk which had fallen on top of the desired object, and pulled out first one then the other black suede pump through the hole without scratching the heels, without cutting her hand on the sharp edge of the aperture. One to the left, one to the right, the shoes vanished into her coat pockets. For a moment, for the time it takes five snowflakes to fall, Oskar saw a pretty but insignificant profile; perhaps, the thought flashed through his mind, she was a model at Sternfeld's; and then she had vanished into the falling snow. She was once more briefly visible in the yellow glow of the next street lamp and then, emancipated model or newly wedded wife, she was gone for good.

My work done—and believe me it was hard work to lurk undrummingly in wait and to sing so neat a hole into the icy glass—I too made my way home, without spoils but with a hot flame and a cold chill in my heart.

My arts of seduction were not always crowned with such unequivocal success. One of my ambitions was to turn a couple into a couple of thieves. Either both were unwilling, or even as he stretched out his hand, she pulled it back; or it was she who had the courage while he went down on his knees and pleaded, with the result that she obeyed and despised him forever after. Once I seduced a young couple who in the falling snow

96

seemed particularly young. This time it was a perfumer's shop. He played the hero and seized a bottle of cologne. She whimpered and said she didn't want it. However, he wanted her to be fragrant and had his way up to the first street lamp. But there in the lamplight the young thing stood up on tiptoe and kissed him—her gestures were as blatantly demonstrative as if her purpose had been to annoy me—until he retraced his steps and put the bottle back in the window.

I had several similar experiences with elderly gentlemen, of whom I expected more than their brisk step in the wintry night promised. An old fellow would stand gazing devoutly into the window of a cigar store; his thoughts were in Havana, Brazil, or the Brissago Islands, and when my voice produced its custom-made incision and an aperture appeared directly opposite a box of "Black Wisdom," a jackknife folded up in his heart. He turned about, crossed the street waving his cane, and hurried past me and my doorway without noticing me, giving Oskar an opportunity to smile at his stricken countenance, yes, he looked as if the Devil had been giving him a good shaking. But there was a tinge of anxiety in my smile, for the poor old gentleman—and most of these veteran cigar-smokers were very very old—was visibly in a cold sweat and especially in changing weather I was afraid he might catch his death of cold.

Most of the stores in our suburb were insured against theft, and that winter the insurance companies had to pay out considerable indemnities. Though I never engineered any depredations on a large scale and purposely made my apertures so small that only one or two objects could be removed from the displays at a time, so many burglaries were reported that the police scarcely had a moment's rest and were nevertheless treated very harshly by the press. From November, '36 to March, '37, when Colonel Koc formed a National Front government in Warsaw, sixty-four attempted and twenty-eight successful burglaries of the same type were listed. Of course the majority of those salesmen, housemaids, old ladies, and pensioned high school principals had no vocation for theft and the police were usually able to recover the stolen articles next day; or else the amateur shoplifter, after the object of his desires had given him a sleepless night, could think of nothing better than to go to the police and say: "Mm, I beg your pardon. It will never happen again. Suddenly there was a hole in the glass and by the time I had halfway recovered from my fright and was three blocks away, I discovered to my consternation that I was illegally harboring a pair of wonderful calfskin gloves, very expensive I'm sure, in my coat pocket."

Since the police did not believe in miracles, all who were caught and all who went to the police of their own free will were given jail sentences ranging from four to eight weeks.

I myself was punished occasionally with house arrest, for of course Mama suspected, although she did not admit it to herself and—very wisely—refrained from communicating with the police, that my glass-cutting voice had something to do with the crime wave.

Now and then Matzerath would put on his stern, law-abiding face and try to question me. I refused to reply, taking refuge more and more astutely behind my drum and the undersized backwardness of the eternal three-year-old. After these hearings Mama would always cry out: "It's the fault of that midget that kissed him on the forehead. Oskar never used to be that way. The moment I saw it I knew something would go wrong."

I own that Mr. Bebra exerted a lasting influence on me. Even those terms of house arrest could not deter me from going AWOL for an hour or so whenever possible, time enough to sing the notorious circular aperture in a shopwindow and turn a hopeful young man, who happened to be drawn to a certain window display, into the possessor of a pure silk, burgundy necktie.

If you ask me: Was it evil that commanded Oskar to enhance the already considerable temptation offered by a well-polished plate-glass window by opening a passage through it?—I must reply: Yes, it was evil. If only because I stood in dark doorways. For as everyone should know, a doorway is the favorite dwelling place of evil. On the other hand, without wishing to minimize the wickedness of my acts, I am compelled, now that I have lost all opportunity or inclination to tempt anyone, to say to myself and to Bruno my keeper: Oskar, you not only contented the small and medium-sized desires of all those silent walkers in the snow, those men and women in love with some object of their dreams; no, you helped them to know themselves. Many a respectably well-dressed lady, many a fine old gentleman, many an elderly spinster whose religion had kept her young would never have come to know the thief in their hearts if your voice had not tempted them to steal, not to mention the changes it wrought in self-righteous citizens who until that hour had looked upon the pettiest and most incompetent of pickpockets as a dangerous criminal.

After I had lurked in wait for him several evenings in a row and he had thrice refused to steal but turned thief the fourth time though the police never found him out, Dr. Erwin Scholtis, the dreaded prosecuting attorney, is said to have become a mild, indulgent jurist, a hander-down of almost humane sentences, all because he sacrificed to me, the little demigod of thieves, and stole a genuine badger-hair shaving brush.

One night in January, '37 I stood for a long while shivering, across the way from a jeweler's shop which, despite its situation in this quiet suburban street bordered with maple trees, was regarded as one of the best in town. The showcase with its jewelry and watches attracted a number of possible victims whom I should have shot down without hesitation if they had been looking at the other displays, at silk stockings, velour hats, or liqueurs.

That is what jewelry does to you. You become slow and exacting, adapting your rhythm to endless circuits of beads. I no longer measured the time in minutes but in pearl years, figuring that the pearl outlasts the neck, that the wrist withers but not the bracelet, that rings but not fingers are found in ancient tombs; in short, one window-shopper struck me as too pretentious, another as too insignificant to bestow jewels on.

The showcase of Bansemer's jewelry store was not over-crowded. A few choice watches, Swiss quality articles, an assortment of wedding rings on sky-blue velvet, and in the center six or seven of the choicest pieces. There was a snake in three coils, fashioned in multicolored gold, its finely chiseled head adorned and made valuable by a topaz and two diamonds, with two sapphires for eyes. I am not ordinarily a lover of black velvet, but the black velvet on which Bansemer's snake lay was most appropriate, and so was the gray velvet which created a provocative quietness beneath certain strikingly harmonious articles of hammered silver. There was a ring with a gem so lovely that you knew it would wear out the hands of equally lovely ladies, growing more and more beautiful in the process until it attained the degree of immortality which is no doubt the exclusive right of jewels. There were necklaces such as no one can put on with impunity, necklaces that wear out their wearers; and finally, on a pale yellow velvet cushion shaped like a simplified neck base, a necklace of infinite lightness. Subtly, playfully woven, a web perpetually broken off. What spider can have secreted gold to catch six small rubies and one large one in this net? Where was the spider sitting, for what was it lurking in wait? Certainly not for more rubies; more likely for someone whose eye would be caught by the ensnared rubies which sat there like modeled blood—in other words: To whom should I, in conformity with my plan or the plan of the gold-secreting spider, give this necklace?

On the eighteenth of January, 1937, on crunching hard-trodden snow, in a night that smelled like more snow, the kind of night that is made to order for one who wishes to hold the snow responsible for anything that may happen, I saw Jan Bronski crossing the street not far from my observation post; I saw him pass the jeweler's shop without looking up and then hesitate or rather stop still as though in answer to a summons. He turned or was turned—and there stood Jan before the showcase amid the quiet maple trees topped with white.

The handsome, too handsome Jan Bronski, always rather sickly, submissive in his work and ambitious in love, a dull man enamored of beauty; Jan Bronski, who lived by my mother's flesh, who, as to this day I believe and doubt, begot me in Matzerath's name—there he stood in his fashionable overcoat that might have been cut by a Warsaw tailor, and became a statue of himself, a petrified symbol. Like Parsifal he stood in the snow, but whereas Parsifal's attention had been captured by drops of blood on the snow, Jan's gaze was riveted to the rubies in the golden necklace.

I could have called or drummed him away. My drum was right there with me. I could feel it under my coat. I had only to undo a button and it would have swung out into the frosty night. I had only to reach into my coat pockets and the sticks would have been ready for action. Hubert the huntsman withheld his arrow when that very special stag entered his field of vision. Saul became Paul. Attila turned back when Pope Leo raised his finger with the ring on it. But I released my arrow, I was not converted, I did not turn back, I, Oskar, remained a hunter intent on my game; I did not unbutton my coat, I did not let my drum swing out into the frosty night, I did not cross my drumsticks over the wintry white drumhead, I did not turn that January night into a drummer's night, but screamed silently, screamed as perhaps a star screams or a fish deep down in the sea. I screamed first into the frosty night that new snow might fall at last, and then into the glass, the dense glass, the precious glass, the cheap glass, the transparent glass, the partitioning glass, the glass between worlds, the virginal, mystical glass that separated Jan Bronski from the ruby necklace, cutting a hole just right for Jan's glove size, which was well known to me. I made the cutout fall inward like a trap door, like the gate of heaven or the gate of hell: and Jan did not flinch, his fine leather hand emerged from his coat pocket and moved heavenward; from heaven or hell it removed a necklace whose rubies would have satisfied all the angels in the world, including the fallen. Full of rubies and gold, his hand returned to his pocket, and still he stood by the gaping window although to keep standing there was dangerous, although there were no more bleeding rubies to tell him, or Parsifal, which way to look.

O Father, Son, and Holy Spirit. It was high time the spirit moved, or it would be all up with Jan, the father. Oskar the son unbuttoned his coat, reached quickly for his drumsticks, and made his drum cry out: Father, father, until Jan Bronski turned and slowly, much too slowly, crossed the street, and found me, Oskar, in the doorway.

How wonderful it was that just as Jan, still frozen in his trance but about to thaw, turned to look at me, snow began to fall. He held out a hand, but not the glove that had touched the rubies, to me and led me silent but undismayed home, where Mama was worrying about me, and Matzerath, not quite seriously but with his usual show of severity, was threatening to call the police. Jan offered no explanation; he did not stay long and was disinclined to play skat, though Matzerath put beer on the table and invited him. In leaving, he caressed Oskar and Oskar was at a loss to know whether it was discretion or friendship he was asking for.

A few days later Bronski gave my mother the necklace. Surely knowing where it came from, she wore it only when Matzerath was absent, either for herself alone or for Jan Bronski, and possibly for me.

Shortly after the war I exchanged it on the black market in Düsseldorf for twelve cartons of Lucky Strikes and a leather briefcase.

No Wonder

Today as I lie here in my mental hospital, I often regret the power I had in those days to project my voice through the wintry night to thaw frost flowers on glass, cut holes in shopwindows, and show thieves the way.

How happy I should be, for example, to unglass the peephole in my door so that Bruno my keeper might observe me more directly.

How I suffered from the loss of this power during the year before my commitment to the hospital! From time to time I would dispatch a cry into the wretched Düsseldorf suburb where I was living. When despite my eagerness for success nothing happened, I, who abhor violence, was quite capable of picking up a stone and flinging it at a kitchen window. I would have been so glad to put on a show, especially for the benefit of Vittlar the window dresser. It was past midnight when I saw him behind the plate-glass window of a men's fashions store or perhaps of a perfumer's shop. From the waist up he would be hidden by a curtain, but I recognized him by his green and red socks. And though he is or might be my disciple, I desired passionately to sing his window to pieces, because I did not know then and still do not know whether to call him John or Judas.

Vittlar is noble and his first name is Gottfried. When after my humiliating vain vocal effort I called his attention to myself by drumming lightly on the unharmed plate glass and he stepped outside for a few minutes to chat with me and make light of his decorative abilities, I was reduced to calling him Gottfried because my voice could not perform the miracle that would have entitled me to call him John or Judas.

The exploit of the jewelry store, which made Jan Bronski a thief and my mama the possessor of a ruby necklace, put a temporary end to my singing outside of shopwindows with desirable displays. Mama got religion. How so? No doubt it was her association with Jan Bronski, the stolen necklace, the delicious misery of an adulterous woman's life, that made her lust after sacraments. How easily the routine of sin establishes itself. Ah, those Thursdays: rendezvous in town, deposit little Oskar with Markus, strenuous exercise, usually satisfactory, in Tischlergasse, mocha and pastry at the Café Weitzke, pick up the boy along with a few of Markus' compliments and a package of sewing silk, sold at a price which made it more a present than a purchase, and back again to the Number

5 streetcar. Smiling and far away in her thoughts, my mama enjoyed the ride past Oliva Gate through Hindenburg-Allee, scarcely noticing the Maiwiese where Matzerath spent his Sunday mornings. She gritted her teeth on the curve round the Sports Palace—how ugly that boxlike structure could be immediately after a beautiful experience!—another curve and there behind dusty trees stood the Conradinum with its red-capped schoolboys—how lovely if little Oskar could have been there in a red cap with a golden C; he would be twelve and a half, in the first year of high school, just starting in on Latin, cutting the figure of a regular little Conradinian, a good student, though perhaps a bit cocky.

After the underpass, as the car moved on toward Reichskolonie and the Helene Lange School, Mrs. Matzerath's thoughts of the Conradinum and her son Oskar's lost opportunities seeped away. Another curve to leftward, past Christ Church with its bulbiform steeple. Then at Max-Halbe-Platz, we would get out, just in front of Kaiser's grocery store. After a glance into the competitor's window, my mama turned into Labesweg, her calvary: what with her nascent ill humor, this freak of a child, her troubled conscience, and her impatience to begin all over again, my mama, torn between not enough and too much, between aversion and good-natured affection for Matzerath, plodded wearily down Labesweg with me and my drum and her package of dirt-cheap silk thread, toward the store, toward the rolled oats, the kerosene by the herring barrel, the currants, raisins, almonds, and spices, toward Dr. Oetker's Baking Powder, toward Persil Washes White, Maggi and Knorr, Kaffee Hag, Kühne's Vinegar, and four-fruit jam, toward the two strips of flypaper, buzzing in different keys, which hung honeysweet over our counter and had to be changed every other day in the summer, whereas Mama, always with the same honeysweet soul, which summer and winter, all year long, attracted sins buzzing high and buzzing low, repaired each Saturday to the Church of the Sacred Heart, where she confessed to the Right Reverend Father Wiehnke.

Just as Mama took me with her to the city on Thursday to share as it were in her guilt, she led me on Saturday over cool and Catholic flagstones through the church door, having previously stuffed my drum under my sweater or overcoat, for without my drum I would not budge, and without my drum I should never have touched my forehead, chest, and shoulders, making the Catholic cross, nor should I ever have bent my knees as though to put on my shoes and, with holy water slowly drying on the bridge of my nose, sat still and behaved on the polished wooden bench.

I could still remember this church from my baptism: there had been trouble over the heathen name they were giving me, but my parents insisted on Oskar, and Jan, as godfather, took the same position. Then

Father Wiehnke blew into my face three times—that was supposed to drive Satan out of me. The sign of the cross was made, a hand was imposed, salt was sprinkled, and various other measures were taken against Satan. At the baptismal chapel the party stopped again. I kept still while the Credo and the Lord's Prayer were dished out to me. Afterward Father Wiehnke saw fit to say another "Satan depart," and touched my nose and ears, fancying that by so doing he was opening up the senses of this child, Oskar, who had known what was what from the very first. Then he wanted one last time to hear it loud and plain and asked: "Dost thou renounce Satan? And all his works? And all his pomp?"

Before I could shake my head—for I had no intention whatsoever of renouncing—Jan, acting as my proxy, said three times: "I do renounce."

Without my having said anything to spoil my relations with Satan, Father Wiehnke anointed me on the breast and between the shoulder blades. By the baptismal font another Credo, then at last I was dipped thrice in the water, my scalp was anointed with chrism, they clothed me in a white dress to make spots on, the candle for dark days was bestowed on Uncle Jan, and we were dismissed. Matzerath paid, Jan carried me outside the Church, where the taxi was waiting in fair to cloudy weather, and I asked the Satan within me: "Did you get through it all right?"

Satan jumped up and down and whispered: "Did you see those church windows? All glass, all glass!"

The Church of the Sacred Heart was built during the early years of the German Empire and its style could consequently be identified as Neo-Gothic. Since the brickwork had quickly darkened and the copper covering of the steeple had promptly taken on the traditional verdegris, the differences between medieval and modern brick Gothic were embarrassingly evident only to connoisseurs. Confession was heard in the same way in churches old and new. Just like the right Reverend Father Wiehkne, a hundred other Right Reverend Fathers sat down in their confessionals on Saturdays after business hours, pressing their hairy sacerdotal ears to the shiny black grating, and the members of the congregation did their best to slip their strings of sins, bead after bead of tawdry sinfulness, through the wire meshes into the priest's ear.

While Mama, by way of Father Wiehnke's auditory canal, was communicating her commissions and omissions, her thoughts, words, and works, to the supreme authorities of the only-saving Church, I, who had nothing to confess, slipped off the wooden bench, which was too smooth for my liking, and stood waiting on the stone floor.

I must admit that the floors of Catholic churches, the smell of a Catholic church, in fact everything about Catholicism still fascinates me in some inexplicable way, just as redheaded girls fascinate me though I should like to change the color of their hair, and that Catholicism never ceases to inspire me with blasphemies which make it perfectly clear that I was irrevocably though to no good purpose baptized a Catholic. Often I surprise myself in the course of the most commonplace acts, while brushing my teeth, for instance, or even while moving my bowels, muttering commentaries on the Mass: In Holy Mass Christ's blood sacrifice is renewed, his blood is shed again for the remission of your sins. The chalice of Christ's blood, the wine is transformed whenever Christ's blood is shed, the true blood of Christ is present, through the vision of his most sacred blood the soul is sprinkled with the blood of Christ, the precious blood, washed in the blood, in the consecration the blood flows, the bloodstained flesh, the voice of Christ's blood rings through all the heavens, the blood of Christ diffuses fragrance before the face of God.

You will admit that I have maintained a certain Catholic tone. There was a time when I couldn't wait for the streetcar without thinking of the Virgin Mary. I called her blessed, full of grace, virgin of virgins, mother of divine grace, Thou blessed among women, Thou who are worthy of all veneration, Thou who hast borne the . . ., mother most amiable, mother inviolate, virgin most renowned, let me savor the sweetness of the name of Jesus as Thou savoredst it in thy heart, for it is just and meet, right and for our salvation, Queen of Heaven, thrice-blessed . . .

Sometimes, and especially on those Saturdays when Mama and I went to the Church of the Sacred Heart, that little word "blessed" was so poisonously sweet in my heart that I thanked Satan for living through my baptism within me, for providing me with an antidote which enabled me to stride, blaspheming like a Catholic but still erect, over the flagstones of Sacred Heart.

Jesus, after whose heart the church was named, was manifested not only in the sacraments and in the bright-colored little pictures of the Calvary; there were also three colored sculptures showing him in different poses.

One was of painted plaster. He stood there, long-haired, on a golden pedestal in a Prussian-blue robe and sandals. He opened his robe over his chest and, in defiance of all physiology, disclosed in the middle of his thorax a tomato-red, glorified, and stylized bleeding heart, so enabling the church to be named after this organ.

The very first time I examined this open-hearted Jesus, I couldn't help noticing an embarrassing resemblance between the Saviour and my godfather, uncle, and presumptive father Jan Bronski. The same dreamy blue eyes full of naive self-confidence. That blossoming rosebud mouth, always on the point of tears. The manly suffering in the line of the eyebrows. The full sanguine cheeks demanding to be chastised. Both had that face which men feel rather inclined to punch in the nose but which wrings caresses from women. And then there were the tired effeminate hands, well manicured and averse to manual labor, with their stigmata displayed like the prize pieces of a court jeweler. I was deeply troubled by those Bronski eyes, those eyes that misunderstood me like a father, which had been painted into Jesus' face. For my own eyes had that same blue look which can arouse enthusiasm but not convince.

Oskar turned away from the bleeding heart in the nave, hastened from the first station of the Cross, where Jesus takes up the Cross, to the seventh station where he falls for the second time beneath its weight, and on to the high altar over which hung the second sculptured image of Jesus. Perhaps he was tired or perhaps he was just trying to concentrate—in any case, this Jesus had his eyes closed. What muscles the man had! At the sight of this decathlon-winner I forgot all about Sacred-Heart Bronski. There I stood, as often as Mama confessed to Father Wiehnke, gazing devoutly at the athlete over the high altar. You can believe me that I prayed. Athlete most amiable, I called him, athlete of athletes, world's champion hanger on the Cross by regulation nails. And never a twitch or a quiver. The perpetual light quivered, but he displayed perfect discipline and took the highest possible number of points. The stop watches ticked. His time was computed. In the sacristy the sexton's none-too-clean fingers were already polishing his gold medal. But Jesus didn't compete for the sake of honors. Faith came to me. I knelt down as best I could, made the sign of the Cross on my drum, and tried to associate words like "blessed" or "afflicted" with Jesse Owens and Rudolf Harbig and last year's Olympic Games in Berlin; but I was not always successful, for I had to admit that Jesus had not played fair with the two thieves. Forced to disqualify him, I turned my head to the left, where, taking new hope, I saw the third statue of the divine athlete in the interior of the church.

"Let me not pray until I have seen thrice," I stammered, then set my feet down on the flags and followed the checkerboard pattern to the left-side altar. At every step I had the feeling: he is looking after you, the saints are looking after you, Peter, whom they nailed to a cross with his head down, Andrew whom they nailed to a slanting cross—hence the St. Andrew's cross. There is also a Greek cross, not to mention the Latin, or Passion, cross. Double crosses, Teutonic crosses, and Calvary crosses are reproduced on textiles, in books and pictures. I have seen the patty cross, the anchor cross, and the cloverleaf cross overlapping in relief. The Moline cross is handsome, the Maltese cross is coveted, the hooked cross, or swastika, is forbidden, while de Gaulle's cross, the cross of Lorraine, is called the cross of St. Anthony in naval battles. This same cross of St. Anthony is worn on a chain, the thieves' cross is ugly, the Pope's cross is papal, and the Russian cross is also known as the cross of Lazarus. In addition there is the Red Cross. And the anti-alcoholic Blue Cross. Yellow cross is poison, cross spiders eat one another. At the crossroads you crossed me up, crisscross, cross-examination, cross purposes, crossword puzzles. And so I turned round, leaving the Cross behind me; turned my back on the crucified athlete, and approached the child Jesus who was propped up on the Virgin Mary's right thigh.

Oskar stood by the left side-altar of the left aisle of the nave. Mary had the expression that his mama must have worn when as a seventeen-year-old shopgirl in Troyl she had no money for the movies, but made up for it by gazing spellbound at posters of Asta Nielsen.

She took no interest in Jesus but was looking at the other boy on her right knee, whom, to avert misunderstandings, I shall identify at once as John the Baptist. Both boys were my size. Actually Jesus seemed perhaps an inch taller, though according to the texts he was even younger than the little Baptist. It had amused the sculptor to make the three-year-old Saviour pink and naked. John, because he would later go out into the desert, was wearing a shaggy, chocolate-colored pelt, which covered half his chest, his belly, and his watering can.

Oskar would have done better to stay by the high altar or to mind his business in the vicinity of the confessional than to venture into the company of these two boys with that precocious look in their eyes which bore a terrifying resemblance to his own. Naturally they had blue eyes and his chestnut-brown hair. The likeness would have been complete if only the barber-sculptor had given his two little Oskars a crew cut and chopped off those preposterous corkscrew curls.

I shall not dwell too long on the boy Baptist, who pointed his left forefinger at Jesus as though counting off to see who should play first: "Eeny meeny miny mo . . ." Ignoring such childish pastimes, I take a good look at Jesus and recognize my spit and image. He might have been my twin brother. He had my stature and exactly my watering can, in those days employed exclusively as a watering can. He looked out into the world with my cobalt-blue Bronski eyes and—this was what I resented most—he had my very own gestures.

My double raised both arms and clenched his fists in such a way that one wanted desperately to thrust something into them, my drumsticks for example. If the sculptor had done that and put a red and white plaster drum on his pink little thighs, it would have been I, Oskar's very own self, who sat there on the Virgin's knee, drumming the congregation together. There are things in this world which—sacred as they may be —cannot be left as they are.

Three carpeted steps led up to the Virgin clad in green and silver, to John's shaggy, chocolate-colored pelt, and to the boy Jesus whose coloring suggested boiled ham. In front of them there was an altar outfitted with anemic candles and flowers at all prices. All three of them—the green Virgin, the brown John, and the pink Jesus—had halos the size of dinner plates stuck to the backs of their heads—expensive plates adorned with gold leaf.

If not for the steps before the altar, I should never have climbed up. Steps, door handles, and shopwindows had a power of seduction for Oskar in those days, and though today he has no need of anything but his hospital bed, they still do not leave him indifferent. He let himself be seduced from one step to the next, though always on the same carpet. He came close enough to tap the group, at once disparagingly and respectfully with his knuckles. He was able to scratch it with his fingernails in the way that discloses the plaster under the paint. The folds in the Virgin's drapery could be followed along their devious course to the toes resting on the cloud bank. A succinct intimation of the Virgin's shin suggested that the sculptor had first created flesh and then submerged it in draperies. When Oskar felt the boy Jesus' watering can, which should have been circumcised but wasn't, when he stroked it and cautiously pressed it as though to move it, he felt a pleasant but strangely new and disturbing sensation in his own watering can, whereupon he left Jesus' alone in the hope that Jesus would let his alone.

Circumcised or uncircumcised, I let matters rest there, pulled out my drum from under my sweater, removed it from my neck, and, taking care not to nick Jesus' halo, hung the drum round his neck. In view of my size, this took a bit of doing. I had to climb up on the sculpture and stand on the cloud bank that served as a pedestal.

This did not happen in January, '36, on Oskar's first visit to church after baptism, but during Holy Week of the same year. All that winter his mama had been hard put to it to keep abreast of her dealings with Jan Bronski in the confessional. Consequently Oskar had plenty of Saturdays in which to mature his plan, to reject, justify, and revise it, to examine it from all sides, and finally, with the help of the stations of the Cross on the Monday of Holy Week, to discard all previous variants, formulate a new one, and carry it out with the utmost simplicity and directness.

Since Mama felt the need to confess before the Easter to-do should reach its climax, she took me by the hand on the afternoon of Passion Monday and led me down Labesweg to the Neue Markt and Elsenstrasse, down Marienstrasse past Wohlgemuth's butcher shop, turning left at Kleinhammer-park, through the underpass always dripping with some disgusting yellow ooze, to the Church of the Sacred Heart across from the railway embankment.

It was late when we arrived. There were only two old women and a frightened young man waiting outside the confessional. While Mama was examining her conscience—leafing through her missal with a moistened thumb as though searching a ledger for the figures she would need in preparing her tax returns—I slipped out of the pew and, managing to avoid the eyes of the open-hearted Jesus and the Athlete on the Cross—made my way to the left side-altar.

Although I had to move quickly, I did not omit the Introit. Three steps: *Introibo ad altare Dei.* To God who giveth joy to my youth. Dragging out the Kyrie, I removed the drum from my neck and climbed up on the cloud bank; no dawdling by the watering can, no, just before the Gloria, I hung the drum on Jesus, taking care not to injure the halo. Down from the cloud bank—remission of sins, pardon, and forgiveness—but first I thrust the drumsticks into Jesus' hands that were just the right size to receive them, and one, two, three steps, I lift my eyes unto the hills, a little more carpet, then at last the flags and a prayer stool for Oskar, who knelt down on the cushion and folded his drummer's hands before his face—*Gloria in Excelsis Deo* awaited the miracle: will he drum now, or can't he drum, or isn't he allowed to drum? Either he drums or he is not a real Jesus; if he doesn't drum now, Oskar is a realer Jesus than he is.

If it is miracles you are after, you must know how to wait. And so I waited. In the beginning at least I waited patiently, though perhaps not patiently enough, for the longer I repeated the words "All eyes attend thee, O Lord"—substituting ears for eyes as the occasion demanded—the more disappointed Oskar became as he knelt on his prayer stool. He gave the Lord all sorts of opportunities, closed his eyes on the supposition that Little Lord Jesus, afraid that his first movements might be awkward, would be more likely to begin if no one were looking, but finally, after the third Credo, after Father, Creator of Heaven and Earth of things visible and invisible, and the only begotten Son, begotten not made by Him, true Son of true Father, consubstantial with Him, through Him, who for us men and our salvation, descended from Heaven, became incarnate, was made man, was buried, rose again, sitteth at the hand of the Father, the dead, no end, I believe in, together with the Father, spoke by, believe in the one Holy, Catholic, and . . .

Well, my Catholicism survived only in my nostrils. My faith was just about washed up. But it wasn't the smell I was interested in. I wanted something else: I wanted to hear my drum, I wanted Jesus to play something for my benefit, I wanted a modest little miracle. I wasn't asking for thunder that would send Vicar Rasczeia running to the spot and Father Wiehnke painfully dragging his fat to witness the miracle; I wasn't asking for a major miracle that would demand reports to the Diocese at Oliva and impel the bishop to submit a testimonial to the Vatican. No, I was not ambitious. Oskar had no desire to be canonized. All he wanted was a little private miracle, something he could hear and see, something that would make it clear to him once and for all whether he should drum for or against; all he wanted was a sign to tell him which of the two blue-eyed identical twins was entitled and would be entitled in future to call himself Jesus.

I sat and waited. I also began to worry: Mama must be in the confessional; by now she must have the sixth commandment behind her. The old man who is always limping about churches limped past the main altar and then past the left side-altar, saluting the Virgin with the boys. Perhaps he saw the drum but without understanding. He shuffled on, growing older in the process.

Time passed, but Jesus did not beat the drum. I heard voices from the choir. If only no one starts playing the organ, I thought anxiously. If they start practicing for Easter, the organ will drown out the first feeble, hesitant drumbeats.

But no one touched the organ. Nor did Jesus drum. There was no miracle. I rose from my cushion with a cracking in my knee joints. Desolate and morose, I moved over the carpet, pulled myself up from step to step, but neglected all the gradual prayers I knew. I climbed up on the plaster cloud, upsetting some medium-priced flowers. All I wanted was to get my drum back from that preposterous naked kid.

I admit it and I always will: it was a mistake to try to teach him anything. I can't imagine what gave me the idea. Be that as it may, I took the sticks but left the drum. Softly at first, but then with the impatience of an impatient teacher, I showed little pseudo-Jesus how to do it. And finally, putting the drumsticks back into his hands, I gave him his chance to show what he had learned from Oskar.

Before I had time to wrench drum and drumsticks away from this most obstinate of all pupils without concern for his halo, Father Wiehnke was behind me—my drumming had made itself heard throughout the length and breadth of the church—Vicar Rasczeia was behind me, Mama was behind me, the old man was behind me. The Vicar pulled me down, Father Wiehnke cuffed me, Mama wept at me, Father Wiehnke whispered at me, the Vicar genuflected and bobbed up and took the drumsticks away from Jesus, genuflected again with the drumsticks and bobbed up again for the drum, took the drum away from Little Lord Jesus, cracked his halo, jostled his watering can, broke off a bit of cloud, tumbled down the steps, and genuflected once more. He didn't want to give me the drum and that made me angrier than I was before, compelling me to kick Father Wiehnke and shame my mama, who indeed had plenty to be ashamed about by the time I had finished kicking, biting, and scratching and torn myself free from Father Wiehnke, the Vicar, the old man, and Mama. Thereupon I ran out in front of the high altar with Satan hopping up and down in me, whispering as he had at my baptism: "Oskar, look around. Windows everywhere. All glass, all glass."

And past the Athlete on the Cross, who kept his peace and did not so much as twitch a muscle, I sang at the three high windows of the apse, red, yellow and green on a blue ground, representing the twelve apostles. But I aimed neither at Mark nor Matthew. I aimed at the dove above them, which stood on its head celebrating the Pentecost; I aimed at the Holy Ghost. My vocal chords vibrated, I battled the bird with my diamond. Was it my fault? Was it the dauntless Athlete who intervened: Was that the miracle, unknown to all? They saw me trembling and silently pouring out my powers against the apse, and all save Mama thought I was praying, though I was praying for nothing but broken glass. But Oskar failed, his time had not yet come. I sank down on the flagstones and wept bitterly because Jesus had failed, because Oskar had failed, because Wiehnke and Rasczeia misunderstood me, and were already spouting absurdities about repentance. Only Mama did not fail. She understood my tears, though she couldn't help feeling glad that there had been no broken glass.

Then Mama picked me up in her arms, recovered the drum and drumsticks from the Vicar, and promised Father Wiehnke to pay for the damage, whereupon he accorded her a belated absolution, for I had interrupted her confession: even Oskar got a little of the blessing, though I could have done without it.

While Mama was carrying me out of the Sacred Heart, I counted on my fingers: Today is Monday, tomorrow is Tuesday, then Wednesday, Holy Thursday, Good Friday, and then it will be all up with that character who can't even drum, who won't even give me the pleasure of a little broken glass, who resembles me but is false. He will go down into the grave while I shall keep on drumming and drumming, but never again experience any desire for a miracle.

Good Friday Fare

Paradoxical: That might be the word for my feelings between Passion Monday and Good Friday. On the one hand I was irritated over that plaster Boy Jesus who wouldn't drum; on the other, I was pleased that the drum was now all my own. Though on the one hand my voice failed in its assault on the church windows, on the other hand that intact multicolored glass preserved in Oskar the vestige of Catholic faith which was yet to inspire any number of desperate blasphemies.

And there was more to the paradox than that: On the one hand I managed to sing an attic window to pieces on my way home from the Church of the Sacred Heart just to see if it was still within my powers, but from that time on, on the other hand, the triumph of my voice over profane targets made me painfully aware of my failures in the sacred sector. Paradox, I have said. The cleavage was lasting; I have never been able to heal it, and it is still with me today, though today I am at home neither in the sacred nor the profane but dwell on the fringes, in a mental hospital.

Mama paid for the damage to the left side-altar. Business was good at Easter although the shop, on the insistence of Matzerath, who was a Protestant, had to be closed on Good Friday. Mama, who usually had her way, gave in on Good Fridays and closed up, demanding in return the right to close on Catholic grounds for Corpus Christi, to replace the gingerbread in the window by a gingerbread Virgin with electric lights and to march in the procession at Oliva.

We had a cardboard sign with "Closed for Good Friday" on one side and "Closed for Corpus Christi" on the other. On the Good Friday following that drumless and voiceless Monday of Holy Week, Matzerath hung out the sign saying "Closed for Good Friday," and immediately after breakfast we started for Brösen on the streetcar. To run our word into the ground, the scene in Labesweg was also paradoxical. The Protestants went to church, the Catholics washed windows and beat everything vaguely resembling a carpet so vigorously and resoundingly in the courtyards that one had the impression thousands of Saviours were being nailed to thousands of Crosses all at once.

Our Holy Family however—Mama, Matzerath, Jan Bronski, and Oskar—left the Passiontide carpet-beating behind us, settled ourselves in the Number 9 streetcar, and rode down Brösener-Weg, past the airfield, the old drill ground and the new drill ground, and waited on a siding near Saspe Cemetery for the car coming in the opposite direction, from Neufahrwasser-Brösen, to pass. Mama took the wait as an occasion for gloomy, though lightly uttered observations. The abandoned little graveyard with its slanting overgrown tombstones and stunted scrub pines was pretty, romantic, enchanting, she thought.

"I'd be glad to lie there if it was still operating," she said with enthusiasm. But Matzerath thought the soil was too sandy, found fault with the thistles and wild oats. Jan Bronski suggested that the noise from the airfield and the nearby streetcar switches might disturb the tranquility of an otherwise idyllic spot.

The car coming from Neufahrwasser-Brösen passed round us, the conductor rang twice, and we rode on, leaving Saspe and its cemetery behind us, toward Brösen, a beach resort which at that time, toward the end of April, looked mighty dismal: the refreshment stands boarded over, the casino shut tight, the seaside walk bereft of flags, long lines of empty bathhouses. On the weather table there were still chalk marks from the previous year: Air: 65; water: 60; wind: northeast; prospects: clear to cloudy.

At first we all decided to walk to Glettkau, but then, though nothing was said, we took the opposite direction to the breakwater. Broad and lazy, the Baltic lapped at the beach. As far as the harbor mouth, from the white lighthouse to the beacon light on the breakwater, not a soul to be seen. A recent rainfall had imprinted its regular pattern on the sand; it was fun to break it up with our footprints; Mama and I had taken off our shoes and stockings. Matzerath picked up smooth little disks of brick the size of gulden pieces and skipped them eagerly, ambitiously over the greenish water. Less skillful, Jan Bronski looked for amber between his attempts to skip stones, and actually found a few splinters and a nugget the size of a cherry pit, which he gave Mama, who kept looking back, as though in love with her footprints. The sun shone cautiously. The day was cool, still and clear; on the horizon you could make out a stripe that meant the Hela Peninsula and two or three vanishing smoke trails; from time to time the superstructure of a merchant ship would bob up over the horizon.

In dispersed order we reached the first granite boulders of the break-water. Mama and I put our shoes and stockings back on. Matzerath and Jan started off into the open sea, hopping from stone to stone, while she was still helping me to lace my shoes. Scraggly clumps of seaweed grew from the interstices at the base of the wall. Oskar would have liked to comb them. But Mama took me by the hand and we followed the men, who were gamboling like schoolboys. At every step my drum beat against my knee; even here, I wouldn't let them take it away from me. Mama had on a light-blue spring coat with raspberry-colored facings. She had difficulty in negotiating the granite boulders in her high-heeled shoes. As always on Sundays and holidays, I was wearing my sailor coat with the gold anchor buttons. The band on my sailor hat came from Gretchen Scheffler's grab bag; s.m.s. *Seydlitz*, it said, and it would have fluttered if there had been any breeze. Matzerath unbuttoned his brown overcoat. Jan, always the soul of fashion, sported an ulster with a resplendent velvet collar.

We hopped and hobbled as far as the beacon at the end of the breakwater. At the base of the little tower sat an elderly man in a long-shoreman's cap and a quilted jacket. Beside him there was a potato sack with something wriggling and writhing in it. The man—I figured he must be from Brösen or Neufahrwasser—was holding one end of a clothes-line. The other end, caked with seaweed, vanished in the brackish Mottlau water which, still unmixed with the clear open sea, splashed against the stones of the breakwater.

We were all curious to know why the man in the longshoreman's cap was fishing with a common clothesline and obviously without a float. Mama asked him in tones of good-natured mockery, calling him "Uncle." Uncle grinned, showing tobacco-stained stumps; offering no explanation, he spat out a long, viscous train of tobacco juice which landed in the sludge amid the granite boulders, coated with tar and oil, at the base of the sea wall. There his spittle bobbed up and down so long that a gull circled down and, deftly avoiding the boulders, caught it up and flew off, drawing other screaming gulls in its wake.

We were soon ready to go, for it was cold out there and the sun was no help, but just then the man in the longshoreman's cap began to pull in his line hand over hand. Mama still wanted to leave. But Matzerath couldn't be moved, and Jan, who as a rule acceded to Mama's every wish, gave her no support on this occasion. Oskar didn't care whether we stayed or went. But as long as we were staying, he watched. While the longshoreman, pulling evenly hand over hand and stripping off the seaweed at every stroke, gathered the line between his legs, I noted that the merchantman which only half an hour before had barely shown its superstructure above the horizon, had changed its course; lying low in the water, she was heading for the harbor. Must be a Swede carrying iron ore to draw that much water, Oskar reflected.

I turned away from the Swede when the longshoreman slowly stood up. "Well, s'pose we take a look." His words were addressed to Matzerath, who had no idea what it was all about but nodded knowingly. "S'pose we take a look," the longshoreman said over and over as he continued to haul in the line, now with increasing effort. He clambered down the stones toward the end of the line and stretched out both arms into the foaming pond between the granite blocks, clutched something—Mama turned away but not soon enough—he clutched something, changed his hold, tugged and heaved, shouted at them to make way, and flung something heavy and dripping, a great living lump of something down in our midst: it was a horse's head, a fresh and genuine horse's head, the head of a black horse with a black mane, which only yesterday or the day before had no doubt been neighing; for the head was not putrid, it didn't stink, or if it did, then only of Mottlau water; but everything on the breakwater stank of that.

The man in the longshoreman's cap—which had slipped down over the back of his neck—stood firmly planted over the lump of horsemeat, from which small light-green eels were darting furiously. The man had trouble in catching them, for eels move quickly and deftly, especially over smooth wet stones. Already the gulls were screaming overhead. They wheeled down, three or four of them would seize a small or medium-sized eel, and they refused to be driven away, for the breakwater was their domain. Nevertheless the longshoreman, thrashing and snatching among the gulls, managed to cram a couple of dozen small eels into the sack which Matzerath, who liked to be helpful, held ready for him. Matzerath was too busy to see Mama turn green and support first her hand, then her head, on Jan's shoulder and velvet collar.

But when the small and medium-sized eels were in the sack and the longshoreman, whose cap had fallen off in the course of his work, began to squeeze thicker, dark-colored eels out of the cadaver, Mama had to sit down. Jan tried to turn her head away but Mama would not allow it; she kept staring with great cow's eyes into the very middle of the longshoreman's activity.

"Take a look," he groaned intermittently. And "S'pose we!" With the help of his rubber boot he wrenched the horse's mouth open and forced a club between the jaws, so that the great yellow horse teeth seemed to be laughing. And when the longshoreman—only now did I see that he was bald as an egg—reached both hands into the horse's gullet and pulled out two at once, both of them as thick and long as a man's arm, my mother's jaws were also torn asunder: she disgorged her whole breakfast, pouring out lumpy egg white and threads of egg yolk mingled with lumps of bread soaked in *café au lait* over the stones of the breakwater. After that she retched but there was nothing more to come out, for that was all she had had for breakfast, because she was overweight and wanted to reduce at any price and tried all sorts of diets which, however, she seldom stuck to. She ate in secret. She was conscientious only about her Tuesday gymnastics at the Women's Association, but on this score she stood firm as a rock though Jan and even Matzerath laughed at her when, carrying her togs in a drawstring bag, she went out to join those comical old biddies, to swing Indian clubs in a shiny blue gym suit, and still failed to reduce.

Even now Mama couldn't have vomited up more than half a pound and retch as she might, that was all the weight she succeeded in taking off. Nothing came but greenish mucus, but the gulls came. They were already on their way when she began to vomit, they circled lower, they dropped down sleek and smooth; untroubled by any fear of growing fat, they fought over my Mama's breakfast, and were not to be driven away —and who was there to drive them away in view of the fact that Jan Bronski was afraid of gulls and shielded his beautiful blue eyes with his hands.

Nor would they pay attention to Oskar, not even when he enlisted his drum against them, not even when he tried to fight off their whiteness with a roll of his drumsticks on white lacquer. His drumming was no help; if anything it made the gulls whiter than ever. As for Matzerath, he was not in the least concerned over Mama. He laughed and aped the longshoreman; ho-ho, steady nerves, that was him. The longshoreman was almost finished. When in conclusion he extracted an enormous eel from the horse's ear, followed by a mess of white porridge from the horse's brain, Matzerath himself was green about the gills but went right on with his act. He bought two large and two medium-sized eels from the longshoreman for a song and tried to bargain even after he had paid up.

My heart was full of praise for Jan Bronski. He looked as if he were going to cry and nevertheless he helped my mama to her feet, threw one arm round her waist, and led her away, steering with his other arm, which he held out in front of her. It was pretty comical to see her hobbling from stone to stone in her high-heeled shoes. Her knees buckled under her at every step, but somehow she managed to reach the shore without spraining an ankle.

Oskar remained with Matzerath and the longshoreman. The longshoreman, who had put his cap on again, had begun to explain why the potato sack was full of rock salt. There was salt in the sack so the eels would wriggle themselves to death in the salt and the salt would draw the slime from their skin and innards. For when eels are in salt, they can't help wriggling and they wriggle until they are dead, leaving their slime in the salt. That's what you do if you want to smoke the eels afterward. It's forbidden by the police and the SPCA but that changes nothing. How else are you going to get the slime out of your eels? Afterward the dead eels are carefully rubbed off with dry peat moss and hung up in a smoking barrel over beechwood to smoke.

Matzerath thought it was only fair to let the eels wriggle in salt. They crawl into the horse's head, don't they? And into human corpses, too, said the longshoreman. They say the eels were mighty fat after the Battle of the Skagerrak. And a few days ago one of the doctors here in the hospital told me about a married woman who tried to take her pleasure with a live eel. But the eel bit into her and wouldn't let go; she had to be taken to the hospital and after that they say she couldn't have any more babies.

The longshoreman, however, tied up the sack with the salted eels and tossed it nimbly over his shoulder. He hung the coiled clothesline round his neck and, as the merchantman put into port, plodded off in the direction of Neufahrwasser. The ship was about eighteen hundred tons and wasn't a Swede but a Finn, carrying not iron ore but timber. The longshoreman with the sack seemed to have friends on board, for he waved across at the rusty hull and shouted something. On board the Finn they waved back and also shouted something. But it was a mystery to me why Matzerath waved too and shouted "Ship ahoy!" or some such nonsense. As a native of the Rhineland he knew nothing about ships and there was certainly not one single Finn among his acquaintances. But that was the way he was; he always had to wave when other people were waving, to shout, laugh, and clap when other people were shouting, laughing, and clapping. That explains why he joined the Party at a relatively early date, when it was quite unnecessary, brought no benefits, and just wasted his Sunday mornings.

Oskar walked along slowly behind Matzerath, the man from

Neufahrwasser, and the overloaded Finn. Now and then I turned around, for the longshoreman had abandoned the horse's head at the foot of the beacon. Of the head there was nothing to be seen, the gulls had covered it over. A glittering white hole in the bottle-green sea, a freshly washed cloud that might rise neatly into the air at any moment, veiling with its cries this horse's head that screamed instead of whinnying.

When I had had enough, I ran away from the gulls and Matzerath, beating my fist on my drum as I ran, passed the longshoreman, who was now smoking a short-stemmed pipe, and reached Mama and Jan Bronski at the shore end of the breakwater. Jan was still holding Mama as before, but now one hand had disappeared under her coat collar. Matzerath could not see this, however, nor could he see that Mama had one hand in Jan's trouser pocket, for he was still far behind us, wrapping the four eels, which the longshoreman had knocked unconscious with a stone, in a piece of newspaper he had found between the stones of the breakwater.

When Matzerath caught up with us, he swung his bundle of eels and boasted: "He wanted one fifty. But I gave him a gulden and that was that."

Mama was looking better and both her hands were visible again. "I hope you don't expect me to eat your eel," she said. "I'll never touch fish again as long as I live and certainly not an eel."

Matzerath laughed: "Don't carry on so, pussycat. You've always known how they catch eels and you've always eaten them just the same. Even fresh ones. We'll see how you feel about it when your humble servant does them up with all the trimmings and a little salad on the side."

Jan Bronski, who had withdrawn his hand from Mama's coat in plenty of time, said nothing. I drummed all the way to Brösen so they wouldn't start in again about eels. At the streetcar stop and in the car I went right on drumming to prevent the three grownups from talking. The eels kept relatively quiet. The car didn't stop in Saspe because the other car was already there. A little after the airfield Matzerath, despite my drumming, began to tell us how hungry he was. Mama did not react, she looked past us and through us until Jan offered her one of his Regattas. While he was giving her a light and she was adjusting the gold tip to her lips, she smiled at Matzerath, for she knew he didn't like her to smoke in public.

At Max-Halbe-Platz we got out, and in spite of everything Mama took Matzerath's arm and not Jan's as I had expected. While Matzerath was opening up the apartment, Mrs. Kater, who lived on the fourth floor next door to Meyn the trumpeter, passed us on the stairs. A rolled brownish carpet was slung over her shoulder, and she was supporting it with her upraised arms, enormous and meat-red. Her armpits displayed flaming bundles of blond hair, knotted and caked with sweat. The carpet hung down in front of her and behind her. She might just as well have been carrying a drunken man over her shoulder, but her husband was no longer alive. As this mass of fat moved past us in a shiny black house smock, her effluvia struck me: ammonia, pickles, carbide—she must have had the monthlies.

Shortly thereafter the rhythmic reports of carpet-beating rose from the yard. It drove me through the apartment, it pursued me, until at last I escaped into our bedroom clothes cupboard where the worst of the pre-paschal uproar was damped out by the winter overcoats.

But it wasn't just Mrs. Kater and her carpet-beating that sent my scurrying to the clothes cupboard. Before Mama, Jan, and Matzerath had even taken their coats off, they began to argue about the Good Friday dinner. But they didn't stick to eels. As usual when they needed something to argue about, they remembered me and my famous fall from the cellar stairs: "You're to blame, it's all your fault, now I am going to make that eel soup, don't be so squeamish, make anything you like but not eels, there's plenty of canned goods in the cellar, bring up some mushrooms but shut the trap door so it doesn't happen again or something like it. I've heard enough of that song and dance, we're having eels and that's that, with milk, mustard, parsley, and boiled potatoes, a bay leaf goes in and a clove, no, no, please Alfred, don't make eels if she doesn't want them, you keep out of this, I didn't buy eels to throw them away, they'll be nicely cleaned and washed, no, no, we'll see when they're on the table, we'll see who eats and who don't eat."

Matzerath slammed the living room door and vanished into the kitchen. We heard him officiating with a demonstrative clatter. He killed the eels with a crosswise incision in the backs of their necks and Mama, who had an over-lively imagination, had to sit down on the sofa, promptly followed by Jan Bronski. A moment later they were holding hands and whispering in Kashubian. I hadn't gone to the cupboard yet. While the three grownups were thus distributing themselves about the apartment, I was still in the living room. There was a baby chair beside the tile stove. There I sat, dangling my legs while Jan stared at me; I knew I was in their way, though they couldn't have done much, because Matzerath was right next door, threatening them invisibly but palpably with moribund eels that he brandished like a whip. And so they exchanged hands, pressed and tugged at twenty fingers, and cracked knuckles. For me that was the last straw. Wasn't Mrs. Kater's carpet-beating enough? Didn't it pierce the walls, growing no louder but moving closer and closer?

Oskar slipped off his chair, sat for a moment on the floor beside the stove lest his departure be too conspicuous, and then, wholly preoccupied with his drum, slid across the threshold into the bedroom.

I left the bedroom door half-open and noted to my satisfaction that no one called me back. I hesitated for a moment whether to take refuge under the bed or in the clothes cupboard. I preferred the cupboard because under the bed I would have soiled my fastidious navy-blue sailor suit. I was just able to reach the key to the cupboard. I turned it once, pulled open the mirror doors, and with my drumsticks pushed aside the hangers bearing the coats and other winter things. In order to reach and move the heavy coats, I had to stand on my drum. At last I had made a cranny in the middle of the cupboard; though it was not exactly spacious, there was room enough for Oskar, who climbed in and huddled on the floor. I even succeeded, with some difficulty, in drawing the mirror doors to and in jamming them closed with a shawl that I found on the cupboard floor, in such a way that a finger's-breadth opening let in a certain amount of air and enabled me to look out in case of emergency. I laid my drum on my knees but drummed nothing, not even ever so softly; I just sat there in utter passivity, letting myself be enveloped and penetrated by the vapors arising from winter overcoats.

How wonderful that this cupboard should be there with its heavy, scarcely breathing woolens which enabled me to gather together nearly all my thoughts, to tie them into a bundle and give them away to a dream princess who was rich enough to accept my gift with a dignified, scarcely perceptible pleasure.

As usual when I concentrated and took advantage of my psychic gift, I transported myself to the office of Dr. Hollatz in Brunshöfer-Weg and savored the one part of my regular Wednesday visits that I cared about. My thoughts were concerned far less with the doctor, whose examinations were becoming more and more finicky, than with Sister Inge, his assistant. She alone was permitted to undress me and dress me; she alone was allowed to measure and weigh me and administer the various tests; in short, it was Sister Inge who conscientiously though rather grumpily carried out all the experiments to which Dr. Hollatz subjected me. Each time Sister Inge, not without a certain irony, reported failure which Hollatz metamorphosed into "partial success." I seldom looked at Sister Inge's face. My eyes and my sometimes racing drummer's heart rested on the clean starched whiteness of her nurse's uniform, on the weightless construction that she wore as a cap, on a simple brooch adorned with a red cross. How pleasant it was to follow the folds, forever fresh, of her uniform! Had she a body under it? Her steadily aging face and rawboned though well-kept hands suggested that Sister Inge was a woman after all. To be sure, there was no such womanish smell as my mama gave off when Jan, or even Matzerath, uncovered her before my eyes. She smelled of soap and drowsy medicines. How often I was overcome by sleep as she auscultated my small, supposedly sick body: a light sleep born of the folds of white fabrics, a sleep shrouded in carbolic acid, a dreamless sleep except that sometimes in the distance her brooch expanded into heaven knows what: a sea of banners, the Alpine glow, a field of poppies, ready to revolt, against whom, Lord knows: against Indians, cherries, nosebleed, cocks' crests, red corpuscles, until a red occupying my entire field of vision provided the background for a passion which then as now was self-evident but not to be named, because the little word "red" says nothing, and nosebleed won't do it, and flag cloth fades, and if I nonetheless say "red," red spurns me, turns its coat to black. Black is the Witch, black scares me green, green grow the lilacs but lavender's blue, blue is true blue but I don't trust it, do you? Green is for hope, green is the coffin I graze in, green covers me, green blanches me white, white stains yellow and yellow strikes me blue, blue me no green, green flowers red, and red was Sister Inge's brooch: she wore a red cross, to be exact, she wore it on the collar of her nurse's uniform; but seldom, in the clothes cupboard or anywhere else, could I keep my mind on this most monochrome of all symbols.

Bursting in from the living room, a furious uproar crashed against the doors of my cupboard, waked me from my scarcely begun half-slumber dedicated to Sister Inge. Sobered and with my heart in my mouth I sat, holding my drum on my knees, among winter coats of varying length and cut, breathed in the aroma of Matzerath's party uniform, felt the presence of sword belt and shoulder straps, and was unable to find my way back to the white folds of the nurse's uniform: flannel and worsted hung down beside me, above me stood the hat fashions of the last four years, at my feet lay big shoes and little shoes, waxed puttees, heels with and without hobnails. A faint beam of light suggested the whole scene; Oskar was sorry he had left a crack open between the mirror doors.

What could those people in the living room have to offer me? Perhaps Matzerath had surprised the two of them on the couch, but that was very unlikely for Jan always preserved a vestige of caution and not just when he was playing skat. Probably, I figured, and so indeed it turned out, Matzerath, having slaughtered, cleaned, washed, cooked, seasoned, and tasted his eels, had put them down on the living room table in the form of eel soup with boiled potatoes, and when the others showed no sign of sitting down, had gone so far as to sing the praises of his dish, listing all the ingredients and intoning the recipe like a litany. Whereupon Mama began to scream. She screamed in Kashubian. This Matzerath could neither understand nor bear, but he was compelled to listen just the same and had a pretty good idea of what she was getting at. What, after all, could she be screaming about but eels, leading up, as everything led up once my mama started screaming, to my fall down the cellar stairs. Matzerath answered back. They knew their parts. Jan intervened. Without him there could have been no show. Act Two: bang, that was the piano lid being thrown back; without notes, by heart, the three of there all at once but not together howled out the "Huntsmen's Chorus" from *Freischütz*: "What thing on earth resembles . . . " And in the midst of the uproar, bang shut went the piano lid, bang went the overturned piano stool, and there was Mama coming into the bedroom. A quick glance in the mirror of my mirror doors, and she flung herself, I could see it all through the cleft, on the marriage bed beneath the blue canopy and wrung her hands with as many fingers as the repentant gold-framed Mary Magdalene in the color print at the head end of the matrimonial fortress.

For a long time all I could hear was Mama's whimpering, the soft creaking of the bed, and faint murmurs from the living room. Jan was pacifying Matzerath. Then Matzerath asked Jan to go and pacify Mama. The murmuring thinned down, Jan entered the bedroom. Act Three: he stood by the bed, looking back and forth between Mama and the repentant Mary Magdalene, sat down cautiously on the edge of the bed, stroked Mama's back and rear end—she was lying face down—spoke to her soothingly in Kashubian—and finally, when words were no help, inserted his hand beneath her skirt until she stopped whimpering and he was able to remove his eyes from the many-fingered Mary Magdalene. It was a scene worth seeing. His work done, Jan arose, dabbed his fingers with his handkerchief, and finally addressed Mama loudly, no longer speaking Kashubian and stressing every word for the benefit of Matzerath in the kitchen or living room: "Now come along, Agnes. Let's forget the whole business. Alfred dumped the eels in the toilet long ago. Now we'll play a nice game of skat, for a quarter of a pfennig if you like, and once we've all forgotten and made up, Alfred will make us mushrooms with scrambled eggs and fried potatoes."

To this Mama said nothing, stood up from the bed, smoothed out the yellow bedspread, tossed her hair into shape in front of my mirror doors, and left the bedroom behind Jan. I removed my eye from the slit and soon heard them shuffling cards. I think Jan was bidding against Matzerath, who passed at twenty-three. Whereupon Mama bid Jan up to thirty-six; at this point he backed down, and Mama played a grand which she just barely lost. Next Jan bid diamond single and won hands down, and Mama won the third game, a heart hand without two, though it was close.

Certain that this family skat game, briefly interrupted by scrambled eggs, mushrooms, and fried potatoes, would go on far into the night, I scarcely listened to the hands that followed, but tried to find my way back to Sister Inge and her white, sleepy-making uniforms. But I was not to find the happiness I sought in Dr. Hollatz' office. Not only did geen, blue, yellow, and black persist in breaking into the redness of the Red Cross pin, but the events of the morning kept crowding in as well: whenever the door leading to the consultation room and Sister Inge opened, it was not the pure and airy vision of the nurse's uniform that presented itself to my eyes, but the longshoreman at the foot of the beacon on the Neufahrwasser breakwater, pulling eels from the dripping, crawling horse's head, and what set itself up to be white, so that I tried to connect it with Sister Inge, was the gulls' wings which for barely a moment covered the horse's head and the eels in it, until the wound broke open again but did not bleed red, but was black like the black horse, and bottle-green the sea, while the Finnish timber ship contributed a bit of rust color to the picture and the gulls—don't talk to me of doves—descended like a cloud on the sacrifice, dipped in their wingtips and tossed the eel to Sister Inge, who caught it, celebrated it, and turned into a gull, not a dove, but in any case into the Holy Ghost, let it take the form of a gull, descending cloudlike upon the flesh to feast the Pentecost.

Giving up the struggle, I left the cupboard. Angrily pushing the doors open, I stepped out and found myself unchanged in front of the mirrors, but even so I was glad Mrs. Kater had stopped beating carpets. Good Friday was over for Oskar, but it was only after Easter that his Passion began.

Tapered at the Foot End

And Mama's as well. On Easter Sunday we went with the Bronskis to visit Grandma and Uncle Vincent in Bissau. It was after that that her sufferings began—sufferings that the smiling spring weather was powerless to attenuate.

It is not true that Matzerath forced Mama to start eating fish again. Quite of her own accord, possessed by some mysterious demon, she began, exactly two weeks after Easter, to devour fish in such quantities, without regard for her figure, that Matzerath said: "For the Lord's sake stop eating so much fish like somebody was making you."

She started in at breakfast on canned sardines, two hours later, unless there happened to be customers in the shop, she would dig into a case of Bohnsack sprats, for lunch she would demand fried flounder or codfish with mustard sauce, and in the afternoon there she was again with her can opener: eels in jelly, rollmops, baked herring, and if Matzerath refused to fry or boil more fish for supper, she would waste no breath in arguing, but would quietly leave the table and come back from the shop with a chunk of smoked eel. For the rest of us it was the end of our appetites, because she would scrape the last particle of fat from the inside and outside of the eel's skin with a knife, and in general she took to eating her fish with a knife. She would have to vomit at intervals throughout the day. Helplessly anxious, Matzerath would ask: "Maybe you're pregnant, or what's the matter with you?"

"Don't talk nonsense," said Mama if she said anything at all. One Sunday when green eels with new potatoes swimming in cream sauce were set on the table, Grandma Koljaiczek smacked the table with the flat of her hand and cried out: "What's the matter, Agnes? Tell us what's the matter? Why do you eat fish when it don't agree with you and you don't say why and you act like a lunatic?" Mama only shook her head, pushed the potatoes aside, pulled out an eel through the sauce, and set to with relentless determination. Jan Bronski said nothing. Once when I surprised the two of them on the couch, they were holding hands as usual and their clothing was normally disarranged, but I was struck by Jan's tear-stained eyes and by Mama's apathy, which, however, suddenly shifted into its opposite. She jumped up, clutched me, lifted me up and squeezed me, revealing an abyss of emptiness which apparently nothing could fill but enormous quantities of fried, boiled, preserved, and smoked fish.

A few days later I saw her in the kitchen as she not only fell upon the usual accursed sardines, but poured out the oil from several cans she had been saving up into a little saucepan, heated it over the gas, and drank it down. Standing in the doorway, I was so upset that I dropped my drum.

That same evening Mama was taken to the City Hospital. Matzerath wept and lamented as we were waiting for the ambulance: "Why don't you want the child? What does it matter whose it is: Or is it still on account of that damn fool horse's head? If only we'd never gone out there. Can't you forget it, Agnes? I didn't do it on purpose."

The ambulance came, Mama was carried out. Children and grownups gathered on the sidewalk; they drove her away and it soon turned out that Mama had forgotten neither the breakwater nor the horse's head, that she had carried the memory of that horse—regardless of whether his name was Hans or Fritz—along with her. Every organ in her body stored up the bitter memory of that Good Friday excursion and for fear that it be repeated, her organs saw to it that my mama, who was quite in agreement with them, should die.

Dr. Hollatz spoke of jaundice and fish poisoning. In the hospital they found Mama to be in her third month of pregnancy and gave her a private room. For four days she showed those of us who were allowed to visit her a face devastated by pain and nausea; sometimes she smiled at me through her nausea.

Although she tried hard to make her visitors happy, just as today I do my best to seem pleased when visitors come, she could not prevent a periodic retching from seizing hold of her slowly wasting body, though there was nothing more to come out of it except, at last, on the fourth day of that strenuous dying, the bit of breath which each of us must give up if he is to be honored with a death certificate.

We all sighed with relief when there was nothing more within her to provoke that retching which so marred her beauty. Once she had been washed and lay there in her shroud, she had her familiar, round, shrewdly naive face again. The head nurse closed Mama's eyes because Matzerath and Bronski were blind with tears.

I could not weep, because the others, the men and Grandma, Hedwig Bronski and the fourteen-year-old Stephan, were all weeping. Besides, my mama's death was no surprise to me. To Oskar, who went to the city with her on Thursdays and to the Church of the Sacred Heart on Saturdays, it seemed as though she had been searching for years for a way of breaking up the triangle that would leave Matzerath, whom perhaps she hated, with the guilt and enable Jan Bronski, her Jan, to continue his work at the Polish Post Office fortified by thoughts such as: she died for me, she didn't want to stand in my way, she sacrificed herself.

With all the cool calculation the two of them, Mama and Jan, were capable of when it was a question of finding an undisturbed bed for their love, they nevertheless revealed quite a talent for romance: it requires no great stretch of the imagination to identify them with Romeo and Juliet or with the prince and princess who allegedly were unable to get together because the water was too deep.

While Mama, who had received the last sacraments in plenty of time, lay submissive to the priest's prayers, cold and impervious to anything that could be said or done, I found it in me to watch the nurses, who were mostly of the Protestant faith. They folded their hands differently from the Catholics, more self-reliantly I should say, they said the Our Father with a wording that deviates from the original Catholic text, and they did not cross themselves like Grandma Koljaiczek, the Bronskis, and myself for that matter. My father Matzerath—I sometimes call him so even though his begetting of me was purely presumptive—prayed differently from the other Protestants; instead of clasping his hands over his chest, he let his fingers pass hysterically from one religion to another somewhere in the vicinity of his private parts, and was obviously ashamed to be seen praying. My grandmother knelt by the deathbed beside her brother Vincent; she prayed loudly and vehemently in Kashubian, while Vincent only moved his lips, presumably in Polish, though his eyes were wide with spiritual experience. I should have liked to drum. After all I had my mother to thank for all those red and white drums. As a counterweight to Matzerath's desires, she had promised me a drum while I lay in my cradle; and from time to time Mama's beauty, particularly when she was still slender and had no need for gymnastics, had served as the model and subject matter for my drumming. At length I was unable to control myself; once again, by my mother's deathbed, I re-created the ideal image of her gray-eyed beauty on my drum. The head nurse protested at once, and I was very much surprised when it was Matzerath who mollified her and took my part, whispering: "Let him be, sister. They were so fond of each other."

Mama could be very gay, she could also be very anxious. Mama could forget quickly, yet she had a good memory. Mama would throw me out with the bath water, and yet she would share my bath. When I sang windowpanes to pieces, Mama was on hand with putty. Sometimes she put her foot in it even when there were plenty of safe places to step. Sometimes Mama was lost to me, but her finder went with her. Even when Mama buttoned up, she was an open book to me. Mama feared drafts but was always stirring up a storm. She lived on an expense account and disliked to pay taxes. I was the reverse of her coin. When Mama played a heart hand, she always won. When Mama died, the red flames on my drum casing paled a little; but the white lacquer became whiter than ever and so dazzling that Oskar was sometimes obliged to close his eyes.

My mama was not buried at Saspe as she had occasionally said she would like to be, but in the peaceful little cemetery at Brenntau. There lay her stepfather Gregor Koljaiczek the powder-maker who had died of influenza in '17. The mourners were numerous, as was only natural in view of my mama's popularity as a purveyor of groceries; in addition to the regular customers, there were salesmen from some of the wholesale houses, and even a few competitors turned up, such as Weinreich Fancy Groceries, and Mrs. Probst from Hertastrasse. The cemetery chapel was too small to hold the crowd. It smelled of flowers and black clothing seasoned with mothballs. My mother's face, in the open coffin, was yellow and ravaged. During the interminable ceremony I couldn't help feeling that her head would bob up again any minute and that she would have to vomit some more, that there was something more inside her that wanted to come out: not only that fetus aged three months who like me didn't know which father he had to thank for his existence; no, I thought, it's not just he who wants to come out and, like Oskar, demand a drum, no, there's more fish, not sardines, and not flounder, no, it's a little chunk of eel, a few whitish-green threads of eel flesh, eel from the battle of the Skagerrak, eel from the Neufahrwasser breakwater, Good Friday eel, eel from that horse's head, possibly eel from her father Joseph Koljaiczek who ended under the raft, a prey to the eels, eel of thine eel, for eel thou art, to eel returnest . . .

But my mama didn't retch. She kept it down and it was evidently her intention to take it with her into the ground, that at last there might be peace.

When the men picked up the coffin lid with a view to shutting in my mama's nauseated yet resolute face, Anna Koljaiczek barred the way.

Trampling the flowers round the coffin, she threw herself upon her daughter and wept, tore at the expensive white shroud, and wailed in Kashubian.

There were many who said later that she had cursed my presumptive father Matzerath, calling him her daughter's murderer. She is also said to have spoken of my fall down the cellar stairs. She took over the story from Mama and never allowed Matzerath to forget his ostensible responsibility for my ostensible misfortune. These accusations never ceased although Matzerath, in defiance of all political considerations and almost against his will, treated her with a respect bordering on reverence and during the war years supplied her with sugar and synthetic honey, coffee and kerosene.

Greff the vegetable dealer and Jan Bronski, who was weeping in a high feminine register, led my grandmother away from the coffin. The men were able to fasten the lid and at last to put on the faces that pallbearers always put on when they lift up a coffin.

In Brenntau Cemetery with its two fields on either side of the avenue bordered by elm trees, with its little chapel that looked like a set for a Nativity play, with its well and its sprightly little birds, Matzerath led the procession and I followed. It was then for the first time that I took a liking to the shape of a coffin. Since then I have often had occasion to gaze upon dark-colored wood employed for ultimate ends. My mama's coffin was black. It tapered in the most wonderfully harmonious way, toward the foot end. Is there any other form in this world so admirably suited to the proportions of the human body?

If beds only had that narrowing at the foot end! If only all our habitual and occasional lying could taper off so unmistakably toward the foot end. For with all the airs we give ourselves, the ostentatious bulk of our head, shoulders, and torso tapers off toward the feet, and on this narrow base the whole edifice must rest.

Matzerath went directly behind the coffin. He carried his top hat in his hand and, despite his grief and the slow pace, made every effort to keep his knees stiff. I always felt sorry for him when I saw him from the rear; that protuberant occiput and those two throbbing arteries that grew out of his collar and mounted to his hairline.

Why was it Mother Truczinski rather than Gretchen Scheffler or Hedwig Bronski who took me by the hand? She lived on the second floor of our house and apparently had no first name, for everyone called her Mother Truczinski.

Before the coffin went Father Wiehnke with a sexton bearing incense. My eyes slipped from the back of Matzerath's neck to the furrowed necks of the pallbearers. I had to fight down a passionate desire: Oskar wanted to climb up on the coffin. He wanted to sit up there and drum. However, it was not his tin instrument but the coffin lid that he wished to assail with his drumsticks. He wanted to ride aloft, swaying in the rhythm of the pallbearers' weary gait. He wanted to drum for the mourners who were repeating their prayers after Father Wiehnke. And as they lowered the casket into the ground, he wished to stand firm on the lid. During the sermon, the bell-ringing, the dispensing of incense and holy water, he wished to beat out his Latin on the wood as they lowered him into the grave with the coffin. He wished to go down into the pit with Mama and the fetus. And there he wished to remain while the survivors tossed in their handfuls of earth, no, Oskar didn't wish to come up, he wished to sit on the tapering foot end of the coffin, drumming if possible, drumming under the earth, until the sticks rotted out of his hands, until his mama for his sake and he for her sake should rot away, giving their flesh to the earth and its inhabitants; with his very knuckles Oskar would have wished to drum for the fetus, if it had only been possible and allowed.

No one sat on the coffin. Unoccupied, it swayed beneath the elms and weeping willows of Brenntau Cemetery. In among the graves the sexton's spotted chickens, picking for worms, reaping what they had not sowed. Then through the birches. Hand in hand with Mother Truczinski. Ahead of me Matzerath, and directly behind me my grandmother on the arms of Greff and Jan; then Vincent Bronski on Hedwig's arm, then little Marga and Stephan hand in hand, then the Schefflers. Then Laubschad the watchmaker, old Mr. Heilandt, and Meyn the trumpeter, but without his instrument and relatively sober.

Only when it was all over and the condolences started, did I notice Sigismund Markus. Black-clad and embarrassed, he joined the crowd of those who wished to shake hands with me, my grandmother, and the Bronskis and mumble something. At first I failed to understand what Alexander Scheffler wanted of Markus. They hardly knew each other, perhaps they had never spoken to one another before. Then Meyn the musician joined forces with Scheffler. They stood beside a waist-high hedge made of that green stuff that discolors and tastes bitter when you rub it between your fingers. Mrs. Kater and her daughter Susi, who was grinning behind her handkerchief and had grown rather too quickly, were just tendering their sympathies to Matzerath, naturally—how could they help it?—patting my head in the process. The altercation behind the hedge grew louder but was still unintelligible. Meyn the trumpeter thrust his index finger at Markus' black façade and pushed; then he seized one of Sigismund's arms while Scheffler took the other. Both were very careful that Markus, who was walking backward, should not stumble over the borders of the tombs; thus they pushed him as far as the main avenue, where they showed him where the gate was. Markus seemed to thank them for the information and started for the exit; he put on his silk hat and never looked around at Meyn and the baker, though they looked after him.

Neither Matzerath nor Mother Truczinski saw me wander away from them and the condolences. Assuming the manner of a little boy who has to go, Oskar slipped back past the gravedigger and his assistant. Then, without regard for the ivy, he ran to the elms, catching up with Sigismund Markus before the exit.

"If it ain't little Oskar," said Markus with surprise. "Say, what are they doing to Markus? What did Markus ever do to them they should treat him so?"

I didn't know what Markus had done. I took him by his hand, it was clammy with sweat, and led him through the open wrought-iron gate, and there in the gateway the two of us, the keeper of my drums and I, the drummer, possibly his drummer, ran into Leo Schugger, who like us believed in paradise.

Markus knew Leo, everyone in town knew him. I had heard of him, I knew that one sunny day while he was still at the seminary, the world, the sacraments, the religions, heaven and earth, life and death had been so shaken up in his mind that forever after his vision of the world, though mad, had been radiant and perfect.

Leo Schugger's occupation was to turn up after funerals—and no one could pass away without his getting wind of it—wearing a shiny black suit several sizes too big for him and white gloves, and wait for the mourners. Markus and I were both aware that it was in his professional capacity that he was standing there at the gate of Brenntau Cemetery, waiting with slavering mouth, compassionate gloves, and watery blue eyes for the mourners to come out.

It was bright and sunny, mid-May. Plenty of birds in the hedges and trees. Cackling hens, symbolizing immortality with and through their eggs. Buzzing in the air. Fresh coat of green, no dust. Bearing a tired topper in his left gloved hand, Leo Schugger, moving with the lightness of a dancer, for grace had touched him, stepped up to Markus and myself, advancing five mildewed gloved fingers. Standing aslant as if to brace himself against the wind, though there was none, he tilted his head and blubbered, spinning threads of saliva. Hesitantly at first, then with resolution, Markus inserted his bare hand in the animated glove. "What a beautiful day!" Leo blubbered. "She has already arrived where everything is so cheap. Did you see the Lord? *Habemus ad Dominum.* He just passed by in a hurry. Amen."

We said amen. Markus agreed about the beautiful day and even said yes he had seen the Lord.

Behind us we heard the mourners buzzing closer. Markus let his hand fall from Leo's glove, found time to give him a tip, gave me a Markus kind of look, and rushed away toward the taxi that was waiting for him outside the Brenntau post office.

I was still looking after the cloud of dust that obscured the receding

Markus when Mother Truczinski took my hand. They came in groups and grouplets. Leo Schugger had sympathies for all; he called attention to the fine day, asked everyone if he had seen the Lord, and as usual received tips of varying magnitude. Matzerath and Jan Bronski paid the pallbearers, the gravedigger, the sexton, and Father Wiehnke, who with a sigh of embarrassment let Leo Schugger kiss his hand and then proceeded, with his kissed hand, to toss wisps of benediction after the slowly dispersing funeral company.

Meanwhile we—my grandmother, her brother Vincent, the Bronskis with their children, Greff without wife, and Gretchen Scheffler—took our seats in two common farm wagons. We were driven past Goldkrug through the woods across the nearby Polish border to the funeral supper at Bissau Quarry.

Vincent Bronski's farm lay in a hollow. There were poplars in front of it that were supposed to divert the lightning. The barn door was removed from its hinges, laid on saw horses, and covered with tablecloths. More people came from the vicinity. It was some time before the meal was ready. It was served in the barn doorway. Gretchen Scheffler held me on her lap. First there was something fatty, then something sweet, then more fat. There was potato schnaps, beer, a roast goose and a roast pig, cake with sausage, sweet and sour squash, fruit pudding with sour cream. Toward evening a slight breeze came blowing through the open barn, there was a scurrying of mice and of Bronski children, who, in league with the neighborhood urchins, took possession of the barnyard.

Oil lamps were brought out, and skat cards. The potato schnaps stayed where it was. There was also homemade egg liqueur that made for good cheer. Greff did not drink but he sang songs. The Kashubians sang too, and Matzerath had first deal. Jan was the second hand and the foreman from the brickworks the third. Only then did it strike me that my poor mama was missing. They played until well into the night, but none of the men succeeded in winning a heart hand. After Jan Bronski for no apparent reason had lost a heart hand without four, I heard him say to Matzerath in an undertone: "Agnes would surely have won that hand."

Then I slipped off Gretchen Scheffler's lap and found my grandmother and her brother Vincent outside. They were sitting on a wagon shaft. Vincent was muttering to the stars in Polish. My grandmother couldn't cry any more but she let me crawl under her skirts.

Who will take me under her skirts today? Who will shelter me from the daylight and the lamplight? Who will give me the smell of melted yellow, slightly rancid butter that my grandmother used to stock for me beneath her skirts and feed me to make me put on weight?

I fell asleep beneath her four skirts, close to my poor mama's beginnings and as still as she, though not so short of air as she in her box tapered at the foot end.

Herbert Truczinski's Back

Nothing, so they say, can take the place of a mother. Soon after her funeral I began to miss my poor mama. There were no more Thursday visits to Sigismund Markus' shop, no one led me to Sister Inge's white uniforms, and most of all the Saturdays made me painfully aware of Mama's death: Mama didn't go to confession any more.

And so there was no more old city for me, no more Dr. Hollatz' office, and no more Church of the Sacred Heart. I had lost interest in demonstrations. And how was I to lure passers-by to shopwindows when even the tempter's trade had lost its charm for Oskar? There was no more Mama to take me to the Christmas play at the Stadt-Theater or to the Krone or Busch circus. Conscientious but morose, I went about my studies, strode dismally through the rectilinear suburban streets to the Kleinhammer-Weg, visited Gretchen Scheffler, who told me about Strength through Joy trips to the land of the midnight sun, while I went right on comparing Goethe with Rasputin or, when I had enough of the cyclic and endless alternation of dark and radiant, took refuge in historical studies. My old standard works, A *Struggle for Rome*, Keyser's *History of the City of Danzig*, and Köhler's *Naval Calendar*, gave me an encyclopedic half-knowledge. To this day I am capable of giving you exact figures about the building, launching, armor, firepower, and crew strength of all the ships that took part in the battle of the Skagerrak, that sank or were damaged on that occasion.

I was almost fourteen, I loved solitude and took many walks. My drum went with me but I was sparing in my use of it, because with Mama's departure a punctual delivery of tin drums became problematic.

Was it in the autumn of '37 or the spring of '38? In any case, I was making my way up the Hindenburg-Allee toward the city, I was not far from the Café of the Four Seasons, the leaves were falling or the buds were bursting, in any event something was going on in nature, when whom should I meet but my friend and master Bebra, who was descended in a straight line from Prince Eugene and consequently from Louis XIV.

We had not seen each other for three or four years and nevertheless we recognized one another at twenty paces' distance. He was not alone, on his arm hung a dainty southern beauty, perhaps an inch shorter than Bebra and three fingers' breadths taller than I, whom he introduced as Roswitha Raguna, the most celebrated somnambulist in all Italy.

Bebra asked me to join them in a cup of coffee at the Four Seasons. We sat in the aquarium and the coffee-time biddies hissed: "Look at the midgets, Lisbeth, did you see them? They must be in Krone's circus. Let's try to go." Bebra smiled at me, showing a thousand barely visible little wrinkles.

The waiter who brought us the coffee was very tall. As Signora

Roswitha ordered a piece of pastry, he stood there beside her, like a tower in evening clothes.

Bebra examined me: "Our glass-killer doesn't seem happy. What's wrong, my friend? Is the glass unwilling or has the voice grown weak?"

Young and impulsive as I was, Oskar wanted to give a sample of his art that was still in its prime. I looked round in search of material and was already concentrating on the great glass façade of the aquarium with its ornamental fish and aquatic plants. But before I could begin to sing, Bebra said: "No, no, my friend. We believe you. Let us have no destruction, no floods, no expiring fishes."

Shamefacedly I apologized, particularly to Signora Roswitha, who had produced a miniature fan and was excitedly stirring up wind.

"My mama has died," I tried to explain. "She shouldn't have done that. I can't forgive her. People are always saying: a mother sees everything, a mother forgives everything. That's nonsense for Mother's Day. To her I was never anything but a gnome. She would have got rid of the gnome if she had been able to. But she couldn't get rid of me, because children, even gnomes, are marked in your papers and you can't just do away with them. Also because I was *her* gnome and because to do away with me would have been to destroy a part of herself. It's either I or the gnome, she said to herself, and finally she put an end to herself; she began to eat nothing but fish and not even fresh fish, she sent away her lovers and now that she's lying in Brenntau, they all say, the lovers say it and our customers say so too: The gnome drummed her into her grave. Because of Oskar she didn't want to live any more; he killed her."

I was exaggerating quite a bit, I wanted to impress Signora Roswitha. Most people blamed Matzerath and especially Jan Bronski for Mama's death. Bebra saw through me.

"You are exaggerating, my good friend. Out of sheer jealousy you are angry with your dead mama. You feel humiliated because it wasn't you but those wearisome lovers that sent her to her grave. You are vain and wicked—as a genius should be."

Then with a sigh and a sidelong glance at Signora Roswitha: "It is not easy for people our size to get through life. To remain human without external growth, what a task, what a vocation!"

Roswitha Raguna, the Neapolitan somnambulist with the smooth yet wrinkled skin, she whose age I estimated at eighteen summers but an instant later revered as an old lady of eighty or ninety, Signora Roswitha stroked Mr. Bebra's fashionable English tailor-made suit, projected her cherry-black Mediterranean eyes in my direction, and spoke with a dark voice, bearing promise of fruit, a voice that moved me and turned me to ice: "*Carissimo*, Oskarnello! How well I understand your grief. *Andiamo*, come with us: Milano, Parigi, Toledo, Guatemala!"

My head reeled. I grasped la Raguna's girlish age-old hand. The Mediterranean beat against my coast, olive trees whispered in my ear: "Roswitha will be your mama, Roswitha will understand. Roswitha, the great somnambulist, who sees through everyone, who knows everyone's innermost soul, only not her own, *mamma mia*, only not her own, *Dio!*"

Oddly enough, la Raguna had no sooner begun to see through me, to X-ray my soul with her somnambulist gaze, than she suddenly withdrew her hand. Had my hungry fourteen-year-old head filled her with horror? Had it dawned on her that to me Roswitha, whether maiden or hag, meant Roswitha? She whispered in Neapolitan, trembled, crossed herself over and over again as though there were no end to the horrors she found within me, and disappeared without a word behind her fan.

I demanded an explanation, I asked Mr. Bebra to say something. But even Bebra, despite his direct descent from Prince Eugene, had lost his countenance. He began to stammer and this is what I was finally able to make out: "Your genius, my young friend, the divine, but also no doubt the diabolical elements in your genius have rather confused my good Roswitha, and I too must own that you have in you a certain immoderation, a certain explosiveness, which to me is alien though not entirely incomprehensible. But regardless of your character," said Bebra, bracing himself, "come with us, join Bebra's troupe of magicians. With a little self-discipline you should be able to find a public even under the present political conditions."

I understand at once. Bebra, who had advised me to be always on the rostrum and never in front of it, had himself been reduced to a pedestrian role even though he was still in the circus. And indeed he was not at all disappointed when I politely and regretfully declined his offer. Signora Roswitha heaved an audible sigh of relief behind her fan and once again showed me her Mediterranean eyes.

We went on chatting for a while. I asked the waiter to bring us an empty water glass and sang a heart-shaped opening in it. Underneath the cutout my voice engraved an inscription ornate with loops and flourishes: "Oskar for Roswitha." I gave her the glass and she was pleased. Bebra paid, leaving a large tip, and then we arose.

They accompanied me as far as the Sports palace. I pointed a drumstick at the naked rostrum at the far end of the Maiwiese and—now I remember, it was in the spring of '38—told my master Bebra of my career as a drummer beneath rostrums.

Bebra had an embarrassed smile, la Raguna's face was severe. The Signora drifted a few steps away from us, and Bebra, in leave-taking, whispered in my ear: "I have failed, my friend. How can I be your teacher now? Politics, politics, how filthy it is!"

Then he kissed me on the forehead as he had done years before when

I met him among the circus trailers, Lady Roswitha held out her hand like porcelain, and I bent over it politely, almost too expertly for a fourteen-year-old.

"We shall meet again, my son," said Mr. Bebra. "Whatever the times may be, people like us don't lose each other."

"Forgive your fathers," the Signora admonished me. "Accustom yourself to your own existence that your heart may find peace and Satan be discomfited!"

It seemed to me as though the Signora had baptized me a second time, again in vain. Satan, depart—but Satan would not depart. I looked after them sadly and with an empty heart, waved at them as they entered a taxi and completely vanished inside it—for the Ford was made for grownups, it looked empty as though cruising for customers as it drove off with my friends.

I tried to persuade Matzerath to take me to the Krone circus, but Matzerath was not to be moved; he gave himself entirely to his grief for my poor mama, whom he had never possessed entirely. But who had? Not even Jan Bronski; if anyone, myself, for it was Oskar who suffered most from her absence, which upset, and threatened the very existence of, his daily life. Mama had let me down. There was nothing to be expected of my fathers. Bebra my master had found his master in Propaganda Minister Goebbels. Gretchen Scheffler was entirely taken up with her Winter Relief work. Let no one go hungry, let no one suffer cold. I had only my drum to turn to, I beat out my loneliness on its once white surface, now drummed thin. In the evening Matzerath and I sat facing one another. He leafed through his cookbooks, I lamented on my drum. Sometimes Matzerath wept and hid his head in the cookbooks. Jan Bronski's visits became more and more infrequent. In view of the political situation, both men thought they had better be careful, there was no way of knowing which way the wind would blow. The skat games with changing thirds became fewer and farther between; when there was a game, it was late at night under the hanging lamp in our living room, and all political discussion was avoided. My grandmother Anna seemed to have forgotten the way from Bissau to our place in Labesweg. She had it in for Matzerath and maybe for me too; once I had heard her say: "My Agnes died because she couldn't stand the drumming any more."

Despite any guilt I may have felt for my poor mama's death, I clung all the more desperately to my despised drum; for it did not die as a mother dies, you could buy a new one, or you could have it repaired by old man Heilandt or Laubschad the watchmaker, it understood me, it always gave the right answer, it stuck to me as I stuck to it.

In those days the apartment became too small for me, the streets too long or too short for my fourteen years; in the daytime there was no occasion to play the tempter outside of shopwindows and the temptation to tempt was not urgent enough to make me lurk in dark doorways at night. I was reduced to tramping up and down the four staircases of our apartment house in time to my drum; I counted a hundred and sixteen steps, stopped at every landing, breathed in the smells, which, because they too felt cramped in those two-room flats, seeped through the five doors on each landing.

At first I had occasional luck with Meyn the trumpeter. I found him lying dead-drunk among the bed sheets hung out in the attic to dry, and sometimes he would blow his trumpet with such musical feeling that it was a real joy for my drum. In May, '38 he gave up gin and told everyone he met: "I am starting a new life." He became a member of the band corps of the Mounted SA. Stone sober, in boots and breeches with a leather seat, he would take the steps five at a time. He still kept his four cats, one of whom was named Bismarck, because, as might have been expected, the gin gained the upper hand now and then and gave him a hankering for music.

I seldom knocked at the door of Laubschad the watchmaker, a silent man amid a hundred clocks. That seemed like wasting time on too grand a scale and I couldn't face it more than once a month.

Old man Heilandt still had his shop in the court. He still hammered crooked nails straight. There were still rabbits about and the offspring of rabbits as in the old days. But the children had changed. Now they wore uniforms and black ties and they no longer made soup out of brick flour. They were already twice my size and were barely known to me by name. That was the new generation; my generation had school behind them and were learning a trade: Nuchi Eyke was an apprentice barber, Axel Mischke was preparing to be a welder at the Schichau shipyards, Susi was learning to be a salesgirl at Sternfeld's department store and was already going steady. How everything can change in three, four years! The carpet rack was still there and the house regulations still permitted carpet-beating on Tuesdays and Fridays, but by now there was little pounding to be heard and the occasional explosions carried an overtone of embarrassment: since Hitler's coming to power the vacuum cleaner was taking over; the carpet racks were abandoned to the sparrows.

All that was left me was the stairwell and the attic. Under the roof tiles I devoted myself to my usual reading matter; on the staircase I would knock at the first door left on the second floor whenever I felt the need for human company, and Mother Truczinski always opened. Since she had held my hand at Brenntau Cemetery and led me to my poor mother's grave, she always opened when Oskar plied the door with his drumsticks.

"Don't drum so loud, Oskar. Herbert's still sleeping, he's had a rough night again, they had to bring him home in an ambulance." She pulled me into the flat, poured me imitation coffee with milk, and gave me a piece of brown rock candy on a string to dip into the coffee and lick. I drank, sucked the rock candy, and let my drum rest.

Mother Truczinski had a little round head, covered so transparently with thin, ash-grey hair that her pink scalp shone through. The sparse threads converged at the back of her head to form a bun which despite its small size—it was smaller than a billiard ball—could be seen from all sides however she twisted and turned. It was held together with knitting needles. Every morning Mother Truczinski rubbed her round cheeks, which when she laughed looked as if they had been pasted on, with the paper from chicory packages, which was red and discolored. Her expression was that of a mouse. Her four children were named Herbert, Guste, Fritz, and Maria.

Maria was my age. She had just finished grade school and was living with a family of civil servants in Schidlitz, learning to do housework. Fritz, who was working at the railway coach factory, was seldom seen. He had two or three girl friends who received him by turns in their beds and went dancing with him at the "Race Track" in Ohra. He kept rabbits in the court, "Vienna blues," but it was Mother Truczinski who had to take care of them, for Fritz had his hands full with his girl friends. Guste, a quiet soul of about thirty, was a waitress at the Hotel Eden by the Central Station. Still unwed, she lived on the top floor of the Eden with the rest of the staff. Apart from Monsieur Fritz' occasional overnight visits, that left only Herbert, the eldest, at home with his mother. Herbert worked as a waiter in the harbor suburb of Neufahrwasser. For a brief happy period after the death of my poor mama, Herbert Truczinski was my purpose in life; to this day I call him my friend.

Herbert worked for Starbusch. Starbusch was the owner of the Sweden Bar, which was situated across the street from the Protestant Seamen's Church; the customers, as the name might lead one to surmise, were mostly Scandinavians. But there were also Russians, Poles from the Free Port, longshoremen from Holm, and sailors from the German warships that happened to be in the harbor. It was not without its perils to be a waiter in this very international spot. Only the experience he had amassed at the Ohra "Race Track"—the third-class dance hall where Herbert had worked before going to Neufahrwasser—enabled him to dominate the linguistic volcano of the Sweden Bar with his suburban Plattdeutsch interspersed with crumbs of English and Polish. Even so, he would come home in an ambulance once or twice a month, involuntarily but free of charge.

Then Herbert would have to lie in bed for a few days, face down and breathing hard, for he weighed well over two hundred pounds. On these days Mother Truczinski complained steadily while taking care of him with equal perseverance. After changing his bandages, she would extract a knitting needle from her bun and tap it on the glass of a picture that hung across from Herbert's bed. It was a retouched photograph of a man with a mustache and a solemn steadfast look, who closely resembled some of the mustachioed individuals on the first pages of my own photograph album.

This gentleman, however, at whom Mother Truczinski pointed her knitting needle, was no member of my family, it was Herbert's, Guste's, Fritz', and Maria's father.

"One of these days you're going to end up like your father," she would chide the moaning, groaning Herbert. But she never stated clearly how and where this man in the black lacquer frame had gone looking for and met his end.

"What happened this time?" inquired the gray-haired mouse over her folded arms.

"Same as usual. Swedes and Norwegians." The bed groaned as Herbert shifted his position.

"Same as usual, he says. Don't make out like it was always them. Last time it was those fellows from the training ship, what's it called, well, speak up, that's it, the *Schlageter*, that's just what I've been saying, and you try to tell me it's the Swedes and Norskes."

Herbert's ear—I couldn't see his face—turned red to the brim: "God-damn Heinies, always shooting their yap and throwing their weight around."

"Leave them be. What business is it of yours? They always look respectable when I see them in town on their time off. You been lecturing them about Lenin again, or starting up on the Spanish Civil War?"

Herbert suspended his answers and Mother Truczinski shuffled off to her imitation coffee in the kitchen.

As soon as Herbert's back was healed, I was allowed to look at it. He would be sitting in the kitchen chair with his braces hanging down over his blue-clad thighs, and slowly, as though hindered by grave thoughts, he would strip off his woolen shirt. His back was round, always in motion. Muscles kept moving up and down. A rosy landscape strewn with freckles. The spinal column was embedded in fat. On either side of it a luxuriant growth of hair descended from below the shoulder blades to disappear beneath the woolen underdrawers that Herbert wore even in the summer. From his neck muscles down to the edge of the underdrawers Herbert's back was covered with thick scars which interrupted the vegetation, effaced the freckles. Multicolored, ranging from blue-black to greenish-white, they formed creases and itched when the weather changed. These scars I was permitted to touch.

What, I should like to know, have I, who lie here in bed, looking

135

out of the window, I who for months have been gazing at and through the outbuildings of this mental hospital and the Oberrath Forest behind them, what to this day have I been privileged to touch that felt as hard, as sensitive, and as disconcerting as the scars on Herbeh Truczinski's back? In the same class I should put the secret pads of a few women and young girls, my own pecker, the plaster watering can of the boy Jesus, and the ring finger which scarcely two years ago that dog found in a rye field and brought to me, which a year ago I was still allowed to keep, in a preserving jar to be sure where I couldn't get at it, yet so distinct and complete that to this day I can still feel and count each one of its joints with the help of my drumsticks. Whenever I wanted to recall Herbert Truczinski's back, I would sit drumming with that preserved finger in front of me, helping my memory with my drum. Whenever I wished—which was not very often—to reconstitute a woman's body, Oskar, not sufficiently convinced by a woman's scarlike parts, would invent Herbert Truczinski's scars. But I might just as well put it the other way around and say that my first contact with those welts on my friend's broad back gave promise even then of acquaintance with, and temporary possession of, those short-lived indurations characteristic of women ready for love. Similarly the symbols on Herbert's back gave early promise of the ring finger, and before Herbert's scars made promises, it was my drumsticks, from my third birthday on, which promised scars, reproductive organs and finally the ring finger. But I must go back still farther. I was still an embryo, before Oskar was even called Oskar, my umbilical cord, as I sat playing with it, promised me successively drumsticks, Herbert's scars, the occasionally erupting craters of young and not so young women, and finally the ring finger, and at the same time in a parallel development beginning with the boy Jesus, watering can, it promised me my own sex which I always and invariably carry about with me—capricious monument to my own inadequacy and limited possibilities.

Today I have gone back to my drumsticks. As for scars, tender parts, my own equipment which seldom raises its head in pride nowadays, I remember them only indirectly, by way of my drum. I shall have to be thirty before I succeed in celebrating my third birthday again. You've guessed it no doubt: Oskar's aim is to get back to the umbilical cord; that is the sole purpose behind this whole vast verbal effort and my only reason for dwelling on Herbert Truczinski's scars.

Before I go on describing and interpreting my friend's back, an introductory remark is in order: except for a bite in the left shin inflicted by a prostitute from Ohra, there were no scars on the front of his powerful body, magnificent target that it was. It was only from behind that they could get at him. His back alone bore the marks of Finnish and Polish knives, of the snickersnees of the longshoremen from the Speicherinsel, and the sailor's knives of the cadets from the training ships.

When Herbert had had his lunch—three times a week there were potato pancakes, which no one could make so thin, so greaseless, and yet so crisp as Mother Truczinski—when Herbert had pushed his plate aside, I handed him the *Neueste Nachrichten*. He let down his braces, peeled off his shirt, and as he read let me question his back. During these question periods Mother Truczinski usually remained with us at table: she unraveled the wool from old stockings, made approving or disapproving remarks, and never failed to put in a word or two about the—it is safe to assume—horrible death of the man who hung, photographed and retouched, behind glass on the wall across from Herbert's bed.

I began my questioning by touching one of the scars with my finger. Or sometimes I would touch it with one of my drumsticks. "Press it again, boy. I don't know which one. It seems to be asleep." And I would press it again, a little harder.

"Oh, that one! That was a Ukrainian. He was having a row with a character from Gdingen. First they were sitting at the same table like brothers. And then the character from Gdingen says: Russki. The Ukrainian wasn't going to take that lying down; if there was one thing he didn't want to be, it was a Russki. He'd been floating logs down the Vistula and various other rivers before that, and he had a pile of dough in his shoe. He'd already spent half his shoeful buying rounds of drinks when the character from Gdingen called him a Russki, and I had to separate the two of them, soft and gentle the way I always do. Well, Herbert has his hands full. At this point the Ukrainian calls me a Water Polack, and the Polack, who spends his time hauling up muck on a dredger, calls me something that sounds like Nazi. Well, my boy, you know Herbert Truczinski: a minute later the guy from the dredger, pasty-faced guy, looks like a stoker, is lying doubled-up by the coatroom. I'm just beginning to tell the Ukrainian what the difference is between a Water Polack and a citizen of Danzig when he gives it to me from behind—and that's the scar."

When Herbert said "and that's the scar," he always lent emphasis to his words by turning the pages of his paper and taking a gulp of coffee. Then I was allowed to press the next scar, sometimes once, sometimes twice.

"Oh, that one! It don't amount to much. That was two years ago when the torpedo boat flotilla from Pillau tied up here. Christ, the way they swaggered around, playing the sailor boy and driving the little chickadees nuts. How Schwiemel ever got into the Navy is a mystery to me. He was from Dresden, try to get that through your head, Oskar my boy, from Dresden. But you don't know, you don't even suspect what it means for a sailor to come from Dresden."

Herbert's thoughts were lingering much too long for my liking in the fair city on the Elbe. To lure them back to Neufahrwasser, I once again pressed the scar which in his opinion didn't amount to much.

"Well, as I was saying. He was a signalman second class on a torpedo boat. Talked big. He thought he'd start up with a quiet kind of Scotsman what his tub was in drydock. Starts talking about Chamberlain, umbrellas and such. I advised him, very quietly the way I do, to stow that kind of talk, especially cause the Scotsman didn't understand a word and was just painting pictures with schnaps on the table top. So I tell him to leave the guy alone, you're not home now, I tell him, you're a guest of the League of Nations. At this point, the torpedo fritz calls me a 'pocketbook German,' he says it in Saxon what's more. Quick I bop him one or two, and that calms him down. Half an hour later, I'm bending down to pick up a coin that had rolled under the table and I can't see 'cause it's dark under the table, so the Saxon pulls out his pickpick and sticks it into me."

Laughing, Herbert turned over the pages of the *Neueste Nachrichten*, added "And that's the scar," pushed the newspaper over to the gumbling Mother Truczinski, and prepared to get up. Quickly, before Herbert could leave for the can—he was pulling himself up by the table edge and I could see from the look on his face where he was headed for—I pressed a black and violet scar that was as wide as a skat card is long. You could still see where the stitches had been.

"Herbert's got to go, boy. I'll tell you afterwards." But I pressed again and began to fuss and play the three-year-old, that always helped.

"All right, just to keep you quiet. But I'll make it short." Herbert sat down again. "That was on Christmas, 1930. There was nothing doing in the port. The longshoremen were hanging around the streetcorners, betting who could spit farthest. After midnight Mass—we'd just finished mixing the punch—the Swedes and Finns came pouring out of the Seamen's Church across the street. I saw they were up to no good, I'm standing in the doorway, looking at those pious faces, wondering why they're playing that way with their anchor buttons. And already she breaks loose: long are the knives and short is the night. Oh, well, Finns and Swedes always did have it in for each other. But why Herbert Truczinski should get mixed up with those characters, God only knows. He must have a screw loose, because when something's going on, Herbert's sure to be in on it. Well, that's the moment I pick to go outside. Starbusch sees me and shouts: 'Herbert, watch out!' But I had my good deed to do. My idea was to save the pastor, poor little fellow, he'd just come down from Malmö fresh out of the seminary, and this was his first Christmas with Finns and Swedes in the same church. So my idea is to take him under my wing and see to it that he gets home with a whole skin. I just had my hand on his coat when I feel something cold in my back and

Happy New Year I say to myself though it was only Christmas Eve. When I come to, I'm lying on the bar, and my good red blood is running into the beer glasses free of charge, and Starbusch is there with his Red Cross medicine kit, trying to give me so-called first aid."

"What," said Mother Truczinski, furiously pulling her knitting needle out of her bun, "makes you interested in a pastor all of a sudden when you haven't set foot in a church since you was little?"

Herbert waved away her disapproval and, trailing his shirt and braces after him, repaired to the can. His gait was somber and somber was the voice in which he said: "And that's the scar." He walked as if he wished once and for all to get away from that church and the knife battles connected with it, as though the can were the place where a man is, becomes, or remains a freethinker.

A few weeks later I found Herbert speechless and in no mood to have his scars questioned. He seemed dispirited, but he hadn't the usual bandage on his back. Actually I found him lying back down on the living-room couch, rather than nursing his wounds in his bed, and yet he seemed seriously hurt. I heard him sigh, appealing to God, Marx, and Engels and cursing them in the same breath. Now and then he would shake his fist in the air, and then let it fall on his chest; a moment later his other fist would join in, and he would pound his chest like a Catholic crying *mea culpa, mea maxima culpa*.

Herbert had knocked a Latvian sea captain dead. The court acquitted him—he had struck, a frequent occurrence in his trade, in self-defense. But despite his acquittal the Latvian remained a dead Latvian and weighed on his mind like a ton of bricks, although he was said to have been a frail little man, afflicted with a stomach ailment to boot.

Herbert didn't go back to work. He had given notice. Starbusch, his boss, came to see him a number of times. He would sit by Herbert's couch or with Mother Truczinski at the kitchen table. From his briefcase he would produce a bottle of Stobbe's 100 proof gin for Herbert and for Mother Truczinski half a pound of unroasted real coffee from the Free Port. He was always either trying to persuade Herbert to come back to work or trying to persuade Mother Truczinski to persuade her son. But Herbert was adamant—he didn't want to be a waiter any more, and certainly not in Neufahrwasser across the street from the Seamen's Church. Actually he didn't want to be a waiter altogether, for to be a waiter means having knives stuck into you and to have knives stuck into you means knocking a Latvian sea captain dead one fine day, just because you're trying to keep him at a distance, trying to prevent a Latvian knife from adding a Latvian scar to all the Finnish, Swedish, Polish, Free-City, and German scars on Herbert Truczinski's lengthwise and crosswise belabored back.

"I'd sooner go to work for the customs than be a waiter any more in Neufahrwasser," said Herbert. But he didn't go to work for the customs.

Niobe

In '38 the customs duties were raised and the borders between Poland and the Free City were temporarily closed. My grandmother was unable to take the narrow-gauge railway to the market in Langfuhr and had to close her stand. She was left sitting on her eggs so to speak, though with little desire to hatch them. In the port the herring stank to high heaven, the goods piled up, and statesmen met and came to an agreement. Meanwhile my friend Herbert lay on the couch, unemployed and divided against himself, mulling over his troubles.

And yet the customs service offered wages and bread. It offered green uniforms and a border that was worth guarding. Herbert didn't go to the customs and he didn't want to be a waiter any more; he only wanted to lie on the couch and mull.

But a man must work. And not only Mother Truczinski was of that opinion. Although she resisted Starbusch's pleas that she persuade Herbert to go back to waiting on tables in Neufahrwasser, she definitely wanted to get Herbert off that couch. He himself was soon sick of the two-room flat, his mulling had become purely superficial, and he began one fine day to look through the Help Wanted ads in the *Neueste Nachrichten* and reluctantly, in the Nazi paper, the *Vorposten*.

I wanted to help him. Should a man like Herbert have to look for work other than his proper occupation in the harbor suburb? Should he be reduced to stevedoring, to odd jobs, to burying rotten herring? I couldn't see Herbert standing on the Mottlau bridges, spitting at the gulls and degenerating into a tobacco chewer. It occurred to me that Herbert and I might start up a partnership: two hours of concentrated work once a week and we would be made men. Aided by his still diamond-like voice, Oskar, his wits sharpened by long experience in this field, would open up shopwindows with worthwhile displays and stand guard at the same time, while Herbert would be quick with his fingers. We needed no blowtorch, no passkeys, no tool kit. We needed no brass knuckles or shootin' irons. The Black Maria and our partnership—two worlds that had no need to meet. And Mercury, god of thieves and commerce, would bless us because I, born in the sign of Virgo, possessed his seal, which I occasionally imprinted on hard objects.

There would be no point in passing over this episode. I shall record it briefly but my words should not be taken as a confession. During Herbert's period of unemployment the two of us committed two medium-sized burglaries of delicatessen stores and one big juicy one—a furrier's:

the spoils were three blue foxes, a sealskin, a Persian lamb muff, and a pretty, though not enormously valuable, pony coat.

What made us give up the burglar's trade was not so much the misplaced feelings of guilt which troubled us from time to time, as the increasing difficulty of disposing of the goods. To unload the stuff profitably Herbert had to go back to Neufahrwasser, for that was where all the better fences hung out. But since this locality inevitably reminded him of the Latvian sea captain with the stomach trouble, he tried to get rid of the goods everywhere else, along Schichaugasse, on the Bürgerwiesen, in short everywhere else but in Neufahrwasser, where the furs would have sold like butter. The unloading process was so slow that the delicatessen finally ended up in Mother Truczinski's kitchen and he even gave her, or tried to give her, the Persian lamb muff.

When Mother Truczinski saw the muff, there was no more joking. She had accepted the edibles in silence, sharing perhaps the folk belief that the theft of food is legitimate. But the muff meant luxury and luxury meant frivolity and frivolity meant prison. Such were Mother Truczinski's sound and simple thoughts; she made mouse eyes, pulled a knitting needle out of her bun, and said with a shake of the needle: "You'll end up like your father," simultaneously handing her Herbert the *Neueste Nachrichten* or the *Vorposten*, which meant, Now go and get yourself a job and I mean a regular job, or I won't cook for you any more.

Herbert lay for another week on his mulling couch, he was insufferable, available neither for an interrogation of his scars nor for a visit to promising shopwindows. I was very understanding, I let him savor his torment to the dregs and spent most of my time with Laubschad the watchmaker and his time-devouring clocks. I even gave Meyn the musician another try, but he had given up drinking and devoted his trumpet exclusively to the tunes favored by the Mounted SA, dressed neatly and went briskly about his business while, miserably underfed, his four cats, relics of a drunken but splendidly musical era, went slowly to the dogs. On the other hand, I often, coming home late at night, found Matzerath, who in Mama's lifetime had drunk only in company, sitting glassy-eyed behind a row of schnaps glasses. He would be leafing through the photograph album, trying, as I am now, to bring Mama to life in the little, none too successfully exposed rectangles; toward midnight he would weep himself into an elegiac mood, and begin to apostrophize Hitler or Beethoven, who still hung there looking each other gloomily in the eye. From the genius, who, it must be remembered, was deaf, he seemed to receive an answer, while the teetotaling Führer was silent, because Matzerath, a drunken little unit leader, was unworthy of Providence.

One Tuesday—so accurate is my memory thanks to my drum— Herbert finally made up his mind. He threw on his duds, that is, he had Mother Truczinski brush his blue bell-bottom trousers with cold coffee, squeezed into his sport shoes, poured himself into his jacket with the anchor buttons, sprinkled the white silk scarf from the Free Port with cologne which had also ripened on the duty-free dungheap of the Free Port, and soon stood there ready to go, stiff and square in his blue visor cap.

"Guess I'll have a look around for a job," said Herbert, giving a faintly audacious tilt to his cap. Mother Truczinski let her newspaper sink to the table.

Next day Herbert had a job and a uniform. It was not customs-green but dark gray; he had become a guard in the Maritime Museum.

Like everything that was worth preserving in this city so altogether deserving to be preserved, the treasures of the Maritime Museum occupied an old patrician mansion with a raised stone porch and a playfully but substantially omamented façade. The inside, full of carved dark oak and winding staircases, was devoted to records of the carefully catalogued history of our seaport town, which had always prided itself on its ability to grow or remain stinking rich in the midst of its powerful but for the most part poor neighbors. Ah, those privileges, purchased from the Teutonic Knights or from the kings of Poland and elaborately defined in elaborate documents! Those color engravings of the innumerable sieges incurred by the fortress at the mouth of the Vistula! There within the walls of the city stands Stanislaw Leszczynski, who has just fled from the Saxon anti-king. The oil painting shows exactly how scared he is. Primate Potocki and de Monti the French ambassador are also scared out of their wits, because the Russians under General Lascy are besieging the city. All these scenes are accurately labeled, and the names of the French ships are legible beneath the fleur-de-lys banner. A legend with an arrow informs us that on this ship King Stanislaw Leszczynski fled to Lorraine when the city was surrendered on the third of August. But most of the exhibits consisted of trophies acquired in wars that had been won, for the simple reason that lost wars seldom or never provide museums with trophies.

The pride of the collection was the figurehead from a large Florentine galleon which, though its home port was Bruges, belonged to the Florentine merchants Portinari and Tani. In April, 1473, the Danzig city-captains and pirates Paul Beneke and Martin Bardewiek succeeded, while cruising off the coast of Zeeland not far from Sluys, in capturing the galleon. The captain, the officers, and a considerable crew were put to the sword, while the ship with its cargo were taken to Danzig. A folding "Last Judgment" by Memling and a golden baptismal font—both commissioned by Tani for a church in Florence—found a home in the Marienkirche; today, as far as I know, the "Last Judgment" gladdens the Catholic eyes of Poland. It is not known what became of the figurehead after the war. But in my time it was in the Maritime Museum.

A luxuriant wooden woman, green and naked, arms upraised and hands indolently clasped in such a way as to reveal every single one of her fingers; sunken amber eyes gazing out over resolute, forward-looking breasts. This woman, this figurehead, was a bringer of disaster. She had been commissioned by Portinari the merchant from a sculptor with a reputation for carving figureheads; the model was a Flemish girl close to Portinari. Scarcely had the green figure taken its place beneath the bow-sprit of a galleon than the girl, as was then customary, was put on trial for witchcraft. Put to the question before going up in flames, she had implicated her patron, the Florentine merchant, as well as the sculptor who had taken her measurements so expertly. Portinari is said to have hanged himself for fear of the fire. As to the sculptor, they chopped off both his gifted hands to prevent him from ever again transforming witches into figureheads. While the trials were still going on in Bruges, creating quite a stir because Portinari was a rich man, the ship bearing the fig-urehead fell into the piratical hands of Paul Beneke. Signor Tani, the second merchant, fell beneath a pirate's poleax. Paul Beneke was the next victim; a few years later he incurred the disfavor of the patricians of his native city and was drowned in the courtyard of the Stockturm. Ships to whose bows the figurehead was affixed after Beneke's death had a habit of bursting into flames before they had even put out of the harbor, and the fire would spread to other vessels; everything burned but the figure-head, which was fireproof and, what with her alluring curves, always found admirers among shipowners. But no sooner had this woman taken her place on a vessel than mutiny broke out and the crew, who had always been a peaceful lot until then, decimated each other. The unsuccessful Danish expedition of the Danzig fleet under the highly gifted Eberhard Ferber in the year 1522 led to Ferber's downfall and bloody insurrection in the city. The history books, it is true, speak of religious disorders— in 1523 a Protestant pastor named Hegge led a mob in an iconoclastic assault on the city's seven parish churches—but we prefer to blame the figurehead for this catastrophe whose effects were felt for many years to come; it is known at all events that the green woman graced the prow of Ferber's ship.

When Stefan Batory vainly besieged the city fifty years later, Kaspar Jeschke, abbot of the Oliva Monastery, put the blame on the sinful woman in his penitential sermons. The king of the Poles, to whom the city had made a present of her, took her with him in his encampments, and she gave him bad advice. To what extent the wooden lady affected the Swedish campaigns against the city and how much she had to do with the long incarceration of Dr. Aegidius Strauch, the religious zealot who had con-spired with the Swedes and also demanded that the green woman, who had meanwhile found her way back into the city, be burned, we do not know. There is a rather obscure report to the effect that a poet by the

143

name of Opitz, a fugitive from Silesia, was granted asylum in the city for some years but died before his time, having found the ruinous wood carving in an attic and having attempted to write poems in her honor.

Only toward the end of the eighteenth century, at the time of the partitions of Poland, were effective measures taken against her. The Prussians, who had taken the city by force of arms, issued a Royal Prussian edict prohibiting "the wooden figure Niobe." For the first time she was mentioned by name in an official document and at the same time evacuated or rather incarcerated in that Stockturm in whose courtyard Paul Beneke had been drowned and from whose gallery I had first tried out my long-distance song effects. Intimidated perhaps by the presence of the choice products of human ingenuity of which I have spoken (for she was lodged in the torture chamber), she minded her business throughout the nineteenth century.

When in '25 I climbed to the top of the Stockturm and haunted the windows of the Stadt-Theater with my voice, Niobe, popularly known as "the Green Kitten," had long since and thank goodness been removed from the torture chamber of the tower. Who knows whether my attack on the neoclassical edifice would otherwise have succeeded?

It must have been an ignorant museum director, a foreigner to the city, who took Niobe from the torture chamber where her malice was held in check and, shortly after the founding of the Free City, settled her in the newly installed Maritime Museum. Shortly thereafter he died of blood poisoning, which this overzealous official had brought on himself while putting up a sign saying that the lady on exhibition above it was a figurehead answering to the name of Niobe. His successor, a cautious man familiar with the history of the city, wanted to have Niobe removed. His idea was to make the city of Lübeck a present of the dangerous wooden maiden, and it is only because the people of Lübeck declined the gift that the little city on the Trave, with the exception of its brick churches, came through the war and its air raids relatively unscathed.

And so Niobe, or "the Green Kitten," remained in the Maritime Museum and was responsible in the short space of fourteen years for the death of three directors—not the cautious one, he had got himself transferred—for the demise of an elderly priest at her feet, the violent ends of a student at the Engineering School, of two graduates of St. Peter's Secondary School who had just passed their final examinations, and the end of four conscientious museum attendants, three of whom were married. All, even the student of engineering, were found with transfigured countenances and in their breasts sharp objects of a kind to be found only in maritime museums: sailor's knives, boarding hooks, harpoons, finely chiseled spearheads from the Gold Coast, sailmakers' needles; only the last of the students had been obliged to resort first to his pocketknife and then to his school compass, because shortly before his death all the sharp objects in the museum had been attached to chains or placed behind glass.

Although in every case the police as well as the coroner spoke of tragic suicide, a rumor which was current in the city and echoed in the newspapers had it that "The Green Kitten does it with her own hands." Niobe was seriously suspected of having dispatched men and boys from life to death. There was no end of discussion. The newspapers devoted special columns to their readers' opinions on the "Niobe case." The city government spoke of untimely superstition and said it had no intention whatsoever of taking precipitate action before definite proof was provided that something sinister and supernatural had actually occurred.

Thus the green statue remained the prize piece of the Maritime Museum, for the District Museum in Oliva, the Municipal Museum in Fleischergasse, and the management of the Artushof refused to accept the man-crazy individual within their walls.

There was a shortage of museum attendants. And the attendants were not alone in refusing to have anything to do with the wooden maiden. Visitors to the museum also avoided the room with the amber-eyed lady. For quite some time utter silence prevailed behind the Renaissance windows which provided the sculpture with the necessary lateral lighting. Dust piled up. The cleaning women stopped coming. As to the photographers, formerly so irrepressible, one of them died soon after taking Niobe's picture; a natural death, to be sure, but the man's colleagues had put two and two together. They ceased to furnish the press of the Free City, Poland, Germany, and even France with likenesses of the murderous figurehead, and even went so far as to expunge Niobe from their files. From then on their photographic efforts were devoted exclusively to the arrivals and departures of presidents, prime ministers, and exiled kings, to poultry shows, National Party Congresses, automobile races, and spring floods.

Such was the state of affairs when Herbert Truczinski, who no longer wished to be a waiter and was dead set against going into the customs service, donned the mouse-grey uniform of a museum attendant and took his place on a leather chair beside the door of the room popularly referred to as "the Kitten's parlor."

On the very first day of his job I followed Herbert to the streetcar stop on Max-Halbe-Platz. I was worried about him.

"Go home, Oskar, my boy. I can't take you with me." But I stood there so steadfast with my drum and drumsticks that Herbert relented: "Oh, all right. Come as far as the High Gate. And then you'll ride back again and be a good boy." At the High Gate I refused to take the Number 5 car that would have brought me home. Again Herbert relented; I could come as far as Heilige-Geist-Gasse. On the museum steps he tried again to get rid of me. Then with a sigh he bought a child's admission ticket. It is true that I was already fourteen and should have paid full admission, but what people don't know won't hurt them.

We had a pleasant, quiet day. No visitors, no inspectors. Now and then I would drum a little while; now and then Herbert would sleep for an hour or so. Niobe gazed out into the world through amber eyes and strove double-breasted toward a goal that was not our goal. We paid no attention to her. "She's not my type," said Herbert disparagingly. "Look at those rolls of fat, look at that double chin she's got."

He tilted his head and began to muse: "And look at the ass on her, like a family-size clothes cupboard. Herbert's taste runs more to dainty little ladies, cute and delicate like."

I listened to Herbert's detailed description of his type and looked on as his great shovel-like hands kneaded and modeled the contours of a lithe and lovely person of the fair sex, who was to remain for many years, to this very day as a matter of fact and even beneath the disguise of a nurse's uniform, my ideal of womanhood.

By the third day of our life in the museum we ventured to move away from the chair beside the door. On pretext of cleaning—the room really was in pretty bad shape—we made our way, dusting, sweeping away spiderwebs from the oak paneling, toward the sunlit and shadow-casting green wooden body. It would not be accurate to say that Niobe left us entirely cold. Her lures were heavy but not unshapely and she wasn't backward about putting them forward. But we did not look upon her with eyes of covetousness. Rather, we looked her over in the manner of shrewd connoisseurs who take every detail into account. Herbert and I were two esthetes soberly drunk on beauty, abstract beauty. There we were, studying feminine proportions with our thumbnails. Niobe's thighs were a bit too short; aside from that we found that her lengthwise measurements—eight head lengths—lived up to the classical ideal; beam-wise, however, pelvis, shoulders, and chest demanded to be judged by Dutch rather than Greek standards.

Herbert tilted his thumb: "She'd be a damn sight too active in bed for me. Herbert's had plenty of wrestling matches in Ohra and Fahrwasser. He don't need no woman for that." Herbert's fingers had been burnt. "Oh, if she was a little handful, a frail little thing that you've got to be careful not to break her in two, Herbert would have no objection."

Actually, if it had come to brass tacks, we should have had no objection either to Niobe and her wrestler's frame. Herbert was perfectly well aware that the degree of passivity or activity he liked or disliked in naked or half-clad women is not limited to the slender type to the exclusion of the buxom or stout; there are slim young things who can't lie still for a minute and women built like barrels who show no more current than a sleepy inland waterway. We purposely simplified, reducing the whole problem to two terms and insulting Niobe on principle. We were unforgivably rude to her. Herbert picked me up so I could beat her breasts with my drumsticks, driving absurd clouds of sawdust from her sprayed and therefore uninhabited wormholes. While I drummed, we looked into her amber eyes. Not a quiver or twinge, no sign of a tear. Her eyes did not narrow into menacing, hate-spewing slits. The whole room with everything in it was reflected perfectly though in convex distortion in those two polished, more yellowish than reddish drops of amber. Amber is deceptive, everyone knows that. We too were aware of the treacherous ways of this ennobled, ornamental wood gum. Nevertheless, obstinately classifying all things womanly as active and passive in our mechanical masculine way, we interpreted Niobe's apparent indifference in a manner favorable to ourselves. We felt safe. With a malignant cackle, Herbert drove a nail into her kneecap: my knee hurt at every stroke, she didn't even flick an eyelash. Right under her eyes, we engaged in all sorts of silly horseplay. Herbert put on the overcoat of a British admiral, took up a spyglass, and donned the admiral's hat that went with it. With a little red jacket and a full-bottomed wig I transformed myself into the admiral's pageboy. We played Trafalgar, bombarded Copenhagen, dispersed Napoleon's fleet at Aboukir, rounded this cape and that cape, took historical poses, and then again contemporary poses. All this beneath the eyes of Niobe, the figurehead carved after the proportions of a Dutch witch. We were convinced that she looked on with indifference if she noticed us at all.

Today I know that everything watches, that nothing goes unseen, and that even wallpaper has a better memory than ours. It isn't God in His heaven that sees all. A kitchen chair, a coat-hanger, a half-filled ash tray, or the wooden replica of a woman named Niobe, can perfectly well serve as an unforgetting witness to every one of our acts.

We came to work in the Maritime Museum for two weeks or more. Herbert made me a present of a drum and twice brought Mother Truczinski home his weekly wages, which included a danger bonus. One Tuesday, for the museum was closed on Monday, the cashier refused to sell us a child's ticket; he refused to admit me altogether. Herbert asked why. Grumpily but not without benevolence, the cashier told us that a complaint had been made, that children could no longer be admitted; the little boy's father was against it; he didn't mind if I waited down by the ticket window, since he, as a businessman and widower, had no time to look after me, but he didn't want me in the Kitten's Parlor any more, because I was irresponsible.

Herbert was ready to give in, but I pushed him and prodded him. On the one hand he agreed that the cashier was right, on the other hand, he said I was his mascot, his guardian angel; my childlike innocence would protect him. In short, Herbert almost made friends with the cashier and succeeded in having me admitted "one last time," those were the cashier's words, to the Maritime Museum.

Once again my big friend took me by the hand and led me up the ornate, freshly oiled winding staircase to the second floor where Niobe lived. The morning was quiet and the afternoon still more so. Herbert sat with half-closed eyes on his leather chair with the yellow studs. I sat at his feet. My drum remained silent. We blinked up at the schooners, frigates, and corvettes, the five-masters, galleons, and sloops, the coastal sailing vessels and clippers, all of them hanging from the oak paneling, waiting for a favorable wind. We mustered the model fleet, with it we waited for a fresh breeze and dreaded the calm prevailing in the parlor. All this we did to avoid having to look at and dread Niobe. What would we not have given for the work sounds of a wood worm, proof that the inside of the green wood was being slowly but surely eaten away and hollowed out, that Niobe was perishable! But there wasn't a worm to be heard. The wooden body had been made immune to worms, immortal. Our only resource was the model fleet, the absurd hope for a favorable wind. We made a game out of our fear of Niobe, we did our very best to ignore it, to forget it, and we might even have succeeded if suddenly the afternoon sun had not struck her full in the left amber eye and set it aflame.

Yet this inflammation need not have surprised us. We were quite familiar with sunny afternoons on the second floor of the Maritime Museum, we knew what hour had struck or was about to strike when the light fell beneath the cornice and lit up the ships. The churches round about did their bit toward providing the dust-stirring movements of the sun's beam with a clock-time index, sending the sound of their historical bells to keep our historical objects company. Small wonder that the sun took on a historical character; it became an item in our museum and we began to suspect it of plotting with Niobe's amber eyes.

But that afternoon, disinclined as we were to games or provocative nonsense, Niobe's flaming eye struck us with redoubled force. Dejected and oppressed, we waited out the half-hour till closing time. The museum closed on the stroke of five.

Next day Herbert took up his post alone. I accompanied him to the museum, but I didn't feel like waiting by the ticket window; instead I found a place across the street. With my drum I sat on a granite sphere which had grown a tail that grownups used as a banister. Small need to say that the other side of the staircase was guarded by a similar sphere with a similar cast-iron tail. I drummed infrequentiy but then hideously loud, protesting against the passers-by, female for the most part, who seemed to take pleasure in stopping to talk with me, asking me my name, and running their sweaty hands through my hair, which though short was slightly wavy and already looked upon as attractive. The morning passed. At the end of Heilige-Geist-Gasse the red and black brick hen of green-steepled St. Mary's brooded beneath its great overgrown bell tower. Pigeons kept pushing one another out of nooks in the tower walls; alighting not far away from me, they would chatter together; what nonsense they talked; they hadn't the faintest idea how long the hen would go on brooding or what was going to hatch, or whether, after all these centuries, the brooding wasn't getting to be an end in itself.

At noon Herbert came out. From his lunchbox, which Mother Truczinski crammed so full that it couldn't be closed, he fished out a sandwich with a finger-thick slice of blood sausage and handed it to me. I didn't feel like eating. Herbert gave me a rather mechanical nod of encouragement. In the end I ate and Herbert, who did not, smoked a cigarette. Before returning to the museum, he went, with me tagging after him, to a bar in Brotbänken-Gasse for two or three drinks of gin. I watched his Adam's apple as he tipped up the glasses. I didn't like the way he was pouring it down. Long after he had mounted his winding staircase, long after I had returned to my granite sphere, Oskar could still see his friend Herbert's Adam's apple jumping up and down.

The afternoon crept across the pale polychrome façade of the museum. It sprang from cornice to cornice, rode nymphs and horns of plenty, devoured plump angels reaching for flowers, burst into the midst of a country carnival, played blindman's buff, mounted a swing festooned with roses, ennobled a group of burghers talking business in baggy breeches, lit upon a stag pursued by hounds, and finally reached the second-story window which allowed the sun, briefly and yet forever, to illuminate an amber eye.

Slowly I slid off my granite ball. My drum struck hard against the stone. Some bits of lacquer from the white casing and the red flames broke off and lay white and red on the stone steps.

Possibly I recited something, perhaps I mumbled a prayer, or a list: a little while later the ambulance drew up in front of the museum. Passersby gathered round the entrance. Oskar managed to slip in with the men from the emergency squad. I found my way up the stairs quicker than they, though by that time they must have begun to know their way around the museum.

It was all I could do to keep from laughing when I saw Herbert. He was hanging from Niobe's façade, he had tried to jump her. His head covered hers. His arms clung to her upraised, folded arms. He was bare to the waist. His shirt was found later, neatly folded on the leather chair beside the door. His back disclosed all its scars. I read the script, counted the letters. Not a one was missing. But not so much as the beginning of a new inscription was discernible.

The emergency squad who came rushing in not far behind me had difficulty in getting Herbert away from Niobe. In a frenzy of lust he had torn a double-edged ship's ax from its safety chain; one edge he had driven into Niobe and the other, in the course of his frantic assault, into himself. Up top, then, they were perfectly united, but down below, alas, he had found no ground for his anchor and his member still emerged, stiff and perplexed, from his open trousers.

When they spread the blanket with the inscription "Municipal Emergency Service" over Herbert, Oskar, as always when he incurred a loss, found his way back to his drum. He was still beating it with his fists when the museum guards led him out of "the Kitten's parlor," down the stairs, and ultimately stowed him in a police car that took him home.

Even now, in the mental hospital, when he recalls this attempted love affair between flesh and wood, he is constrained to work with his fists in order to explore once more Herbert's swollen, multicolored back, that hard and sensitive labyrinth of scars which was to foreshadow, to anticipate everything to come, which was harder and more sensitive than anything that followed. Like a blind man he read the raised script of that back.

It is only now, now that they have taken Herbert away from his unfeeling carving, that Bruno my keeper turns up with that awful pear-shaped head of his. Gently he removes my fists from the drum, hangs the drum over the left-hand bedpost at the foot end of my iron bed, and smoothes out my blanket.

"Why, Mr. Matzerath," he reproves me gently, "if you go on drumming so loud, somebody's bound to hear that somebody's drumming much too loud. Wouldn't you like to take a rest or drum a little softer?"

Yes, Bruno, I shall try to dictate a quieter chapter to my drum, even though the subject of my next chapter calls for an orchestra of ravenous wild men.

Faith, Hope, Love

There was once a musician; his name was Meyn and he played the trumpet too beautifully for words. He lived on the fifth floor of an apartment house, just under the roof, he kept four cats, one of which was called Bismarck, and from morning to night he drank out of a gin bottle. This he did until sobered by disaster.

Even today Oskar doesn't like to believe in omens. But I have to admit that in those days there were plenty of omens of disaster. It was approaching with longer and longer steps and larger and larger boots. It was then that my friend Herbert Truczinski died of a wound in the chest inflicted by a wooden woman. The woman did not die. She was sealed up in the cellar of the museum, allegedly to be restored, preserved in any case. But you can't lock up disaster in a cellar. It drains into the sewer pipes, spreads to the gas pipes, and gets into every household with the gas. And no one who sets his soup kettle on the bluish flames suspects that disaster is bringing his supper to a boil.

When Herbert was buried in Langfuhr Cemetery, I once again saw Leo Schugger, whose acquaintance I had made at Brenntau. Slavering and holding out his white mildewed gloves, he tendered his sympathies, those sympathies of his which made little distinction between joy and sorrow, to all the assembled company, to Mother Truczinski, to Guste, Fritz, and Maria Truczinski, to the corpulent Mrs. Kater, to old man Heilandt, who slaughtered Fritz' rabbits for Mother Truczinski on holidays, to my presumptive father Matzerath, who, generous as he could be at times, defrayed a good half of the funeral expenses, even to Jan Bronski, who hardly knew Herbert and had only come to see Matzerath and perhaps myself on neutral cemetery ground.

When Leo Schugger's gloves fluttered out toward Meyn the musician, who had come half in civilian dress, half in SA uniform, another omen of disaster befell.

Suddenly frightened, Leo's pale glove darted upward and flew off, drawing Leo with it over the tombs. He could be heard screaming and the tatters of words that hovered in the cemetery air had no connection with condolences.

No one moved away from Meyn the musician. And yet, recognized and singled out by Leo Schugger, he stood alone amid the funeral company. He fiddled embarrassedly with his trumpet, which he had brought along by design and had played beautifully over Herbert's grave. Beautifully, because Meyn had done what he hadn't done for a long time, he had gone back to his gin bottle, because he was the same age as Herbert and Herbert's death, which reduced me and my drum to silence, had moved him.

There was once a musician; his name was Meyn, and he played the trumpet too beautifully for words. He lived on the fifth floor of an apartment house, just under the roof; he kept four cats, one of which was called Bismarck, and from morning to night he drank out of a gin bottle until, late in '36 or early in '37 I think it was, he joined the Mounted SA. As a trumpeter in the band, he made far fewer mistakes but his playing was no longer too beautiful for words, because, when he slipped on those riding breeches with the leather seat, he gave up the gin bottle and from then on his playing was loud and sober, nothing more.

When SA Man Meyn lost his long-time friend Herbert Truczinski, along with whom during the twenties he had paid dues first to a com-munist youth group, then to the socialist Red Falcons; when it came time for his friend to be laid in the ground, Meyn reached for his trumpet and his gin bottle. For he wanted to play beautifully and not soberly; his days in the equestrian band hadn't destroyed his ear for music. Arrived at the cemetery, he took a last swig, and while playing he kept his civilian coat on over his uniform, although he had planned to play in Brown, minus the cap, of course.

There was once an SA man who, while playing the trumpet too beautifully for words after drinking plenty of gin, kept his overcoat on over his Mounted SA uniform. When Leo Schugger, a type met with in all cemeteries, came forward to offer condolences, everyone else came in for his share of sympathy. Only the SA man was not privileged to grasp Leo's white glove, because Leo, recognizing the SA man, gave a loud cry of fear and withheld both his glove and his sympathies. The SA man went home with a cold trumpet and no sympathy. In his flat under the roof of our apartment house he found his four cats.

There was once an SA man, his name was Meyn. As a relic of the days when he drank gin all day and played the trumpet too beautifully for words, Meyn still kept four cats, one of which was called Bismarck. One day when SA Man Meyn came home from the funeral of his old friend Herbert Truczinski, sad and sobered, because someone had withheld his sympathies, he found himself all alone in the flat with his four cats. The cats rubbed against his riding boots, and Meyn gave them a newspaper full of herring heads. That got them away from his boots. That day the flat stank worse than usual of the four cats who were all toms, one of which was called Bismarck and was black with white paws. But Meyn had no gin on hand and that made the stench of the cats more unacceptable. He might have bought some gin in our store if his flat hadn't been on the fifth floor, right under the roof. But as it was, he dreaded the stairs and still more he dreaded the neighbors in whose presence and hearing he had sworn on numerous occasions that never again would a drop of gin cross his musician's lips, that he had embarked on a new life of rigorous sobriety, that from now on his motto was order and purpose, away with the vapors of a botched and aimless youth.

There was once a man, his name was Meyn. One day when he found himself all alone in his flat under the roof with his four tomcats, one of which was called Bismarck, the smell was most particularly distasteful to him, because he had had an unpleasant experience earlier in the day and also because there was no gin on hand. When his thirst and displeasure and with them the cat smell had reached a certain point, Meyn, a musician by trade and a member of the Mounted SA band, reached for the poker that was leaning against the cold stove and flailed out at the cats until it seemed safe to assume that though the cat smell in the flat had lost none of its pungency, all of them, including the one named Bismarck, were dead and done for.

Once there was a watchmaker named Laubschad who lived on the second floor of our apartment house in a two-room flat, with windows overlooking the court. Laubschad the watchmaker was unmarried, a member of the National Socialist Welfare Organization and of the SPCA. He was a kindly man who liked to help all tired humans, sick animals, and broken clocks back on their feet. One afternoon as the watchmaker sat pensively at his window, thinking about the neighbor's funeral he had attended that morning, he saw Meyn the musician, who lived on the fifth floor of the same building, carry a half-filled potato sack, which was dripping and seemed wet at the bottom, out into the court and plunge it into one of the garbage cans. But since the garbage can was already three-quarters full, the musician had trouble getting the lid back on.

There were once four tomcats, one of which was called Bismarck. These tomcats belonged to a musician by the name of Meyn. Since the tomcats, which had not been fixed, emitted a fierce, uncompromising smell, the musician clouted them with a fire poker one day when for particular reasons he found the smell particularly distasteful, stuffed their remains in a potato sack, carried the sack down four flights of stairs, and was in a great hurry to stow the bundle in the garbage can in the court beside the carpet rack, because the burlap was not water- nor bloodproof and began to drip before he was even half down the stairs. But since the garbage can was a bit full, the musician had to compress the garbage and his sack in order to close the lid. No sooner had he left the court in the direction of the street—for he had no desire to go back to his flat which though catless still stank of cats—than the compressed garbage began to expand, raised the sack, and with it the lid of the garbage can.

Once there was a musician, he slew his four cats, buried them in a garbage can, left the house, and went out to visit friends.

There was once a watchmaker who sat pensively by his window, looking on as Meyn the musician stuffed a half-filled sack in the garbage can and quickly left the court. A few moments after Meyn's departure, he saw the lid of the garbage can beginning to rise and slowly go on rising.

There were once four tomcats; because they smelled particularly strong on a certain particular day, they were knocked dead, stuffed into a sack, and buried in a garbage can. But the cats, one of which was called Bismarck, were not quite dead; they were tough customers, as cats tend to be. They moved in the sack, set the lid of the garbage can in motion, and confronted Laubschad the watchmaker, who still sat pensively at the window, with the question: what can there be in the sack that Meyn the musician threw in the garbage can?

There was once a watchmaker who could not look on with indifference while something was moving in a garbage can. He left his flat on the second floor, went down into the court, lifted up the lid of the garbage can, opened the sack, took the four badly damaged but still living tomcats home with him, and cared for them. But they died the following night under his watchmaker's fingers. This left him no other course than to enter a complaint with the SPCA, of which he was a member, and to inform the local party headquarters of a case of cruelty to animals which could only impair the party's reputation.

There was once an SA man who did four cats in with a poker. But because the cats were not all-the-way dead, they gave him away and a watchmaker reported him. The case came up for trial and the SA man had to pay a fine. But the matter was also discussed in the SA and the SA man was expelled from the SA for conduct unbecoming a storm trooper. Even his conspicuous bravery on the night of November 8, which later became known as Crystal Night, when he helped set fire to the Langfuhr synagogue in Michaelisweg, even his meritorious activity the following morning when a number of stores, carefully designated in advance, were closed down for the good of the nation, could not halt his expulsion from the Mounted SA. For inhuman cruelty to animals he was stricken from the membership list. It was not until a year later that he gained admittance to the Home Guard, which was later incorporated in the Waffen SS.

There was once a grocer who closed his store one day in November, because something was doing in town; taking his son Oskar by the hand, he boarded a Number 5 streetcar and rode to the Langasser Gate, because there as in Zoppot and Langfuhr the synagogue was on fire. The synagogue had almost burned down and the firemen were looking on, taking care that the flames should not spread to other buildings. Outside the wrecked synagogue, men in uniform and others in civilian clothes piled up books, ritual objects, and strange kinds of cloth. The mound was set on fire and the grocer took advantage of the opportunity to warm his fingers and his feelings over the public blaze. But his son Oskar, seeing his father so occupied and inflamed, slipped away unobserved and hurried off in the direction of Arsenal Passage, because he was worried about his tin drums with their red and white lacquer.

There was once a toystore owner; his name was Sigismund Markus and among other things he sold tin drums lacquered red and white. Oskar, above-mentioned, was the principal taker of these drums, because he was a drummer by profession and was neither able nor willing to live without a drum. For this reason he hurried away from the burning synagogue in the direction of Arsenal Passage, for there dwelt the keeper of his drums; but he found him in a state which forever after made it impossible for him to sell tin drums in this world.

They, the same firemen whom I, Oskar, thought I had escaped, had

154

visited Markus before me; dipping a brush in paint, they had written "Jewish Sow" obliquely across his window in Sütterlin script; then, perhaps disgusted with their own handwriting, they had kicked in the window with the heels of their boots, so that the epithet they had fastened on Markus could only be guessed at. Scorning the door, they had entered the shop through the broken window and there, in their characteristic way, they were playing with the toys.

I found them still at play when I, also through the window, entered the shop. Some had taken their pants down and had deposited brown sausages, in which half-digested peas were still discernible, on sailing vessels, fiddling monkeys, and on my drums. They all looked like Meyn the musician, they wore Meyn's SA uniform, but Meyn was not there; just as the ones who were there were not somewhere else. One had drawn his dagger. He was cutting dolls open and he seemed disappointed each time that nothing but sawdust flowed from their limbs and bodies. My

I was worried about my drums. They didn't like my drums. My own drum couldn't stand up to their rage; there was nothing it could do but bow down and keep quiet. But Markus had escaped from their rage. When they went to see him in his office, they did not knock, they broke the door open, although it was not locked.

The toy merchant sat behind his desk. As usual he had on sleeve protectors over his dark-grey everyday jacket. Dandruff on his shoulders showed that his scalp was in bad shape. One of the SA men with puppets on his fingers poked him with Kasperl's wooden grandmother, but Markus was beyond being spoken to, beyond being hurt or humiliated. Before him on the desk stood an empty water glass; the sound of his crashing shopwindow had made him thirsty no doubt.

There was once a drummer, his name was Oskar. When they took away his toy merchant and ransacked the shop, he suspected that hard times were in the offing for gnomelike drummers like himself. And so, in leaving the store, he picked out of the ruins a whole drum and two that were not so badly injured, hung them round his neck, and so left Arsenal Passage for the Kohlenmarkt to look for his father, who was probably looking for him. Outside, it was a November morning. Beside the Stadt-Theater, near the streetcar stop, some pious ladies and strikingly ugly young girls were handing out religious tracts, collecting money in collection boxes, and holding up, between two poles, a banner with an inscription quoted from the thirteenth chapter of the First Epistle to the Corinthians. "Faith . . . hope . . . love," Oskar read and played with the three words as a juggler plays with bottles: faith healer, Old Faithful, faithless hope, hope chest, Cape of Good Hope, hopeless love, Love's Labour's Lost, six love. An entire credulous nation believed, there's faith for you, in Santa Claus. But Santa Claus was really the gasman. I believe—such is my faith—that it smells of walnuts and almonds. But it smelled of gas. Soon, so they said, 'twill be the first Sunday of Advent. And the first, second, third, and fourth Sundays of Advent were turned on like gas cocks, to produce a credible smell of walnuts and almonds, so that all those who liked to crack nuts could take comfort and believe:

He's coming, He's coming. Who is coming? The Christ child, the Saviour? Or is it the heavenly gasman with the gas meter under his arm, that always goes ticktock? And he said: I am the Saviour of this world, without me you can't cook. And he was not too demanding, he offered special rates, turned on the freshly polished gas cocks, and let the Holy Ghost pour forth, so the dove, or squab, might be cooked. And handed out walnuts and almonds which were promptly cracked, and they too poured forth spirit and gas. Thus it was not hard, amid the dense blue air, for credulous souls to look upon all those gasmen outside department stores as Santa Clauses and Christ children in all sizes and at all prices. They believed in the only-saving gas company which symbolizes destiny with its rising and falling gas meters and staged an Advent at bargain prices. Many, to be sure, believed in the Christmas this Advent seemed to announce, but the sole survivors of these strenuous holidays were those for whom no almonds or walnuts were left—although everyone had supposed there would be plenty for all.

But after faith in Santa Claus had turned out to be faith in the gasman, an attempt was made, in disregard of the order set forth in Corinthians, to do it with love: I love you, they said, oh, I love you. Do you, too, love yourself? Do you love me, say, do you really love me? I love myself too. And from sheer love they called each other radishes, they loved radishes, they bit into each other, out of sheer love one radish bit off another's radish. And they told one another stories about wonderful heavenly love, and earthly love too, between radishes, and just before biting, they whispered to one another, whispered with all the sharp freshness of hunger: Radish, say, do you love me? I love myself too.

But after they had bitten off each other's radishes out of love, and faith in the gasman had been proclaimed the state religion, there remained, after faith and anticipated love, only the third white elephant of the Epistle to the Corinthians: hope. And even while they still had radishes, walnuts, and almonds to nibble on, they began to hope that soon it would be over, so they might begin afresh or continue, hoping after or even during the finale that the end would soon be over. The end of what? They still did not know. They only hoped that it would soon be over, over tomorrow, but not today; for what were they to do if the end came so suddenly? And then when the end came, they quickly turned it into a hopeful beginning; for in our country the end is always the beginning and there is hope in every, even the most final, end. And so too is it written: As long as man hopes, he will go on turning out hopeful finales.

For my part, I don't know. I don't know, for example, who it is nowadays that hides under the beards of the Santa Clauses, nor what Santa Claus has in his sack; I don't know how gas cocks are throttled and shut off; for Advent, the time of longing for a Redeemer, is flowing again, or flowing still, I do not know. Another thing I don't know is whether I can believe that, as I hope, they are polishing the gas cocks lovingly, so as to make them crow, what morning, what evening, I don't know, nor know I whether the time of day matters; for love knows no time of day, and hope is without end, and faith knows no limits, only knowing and not knowing are subject to times and limits and usually end before their time with beards, knapsacks, almonds, so that once again I must say: I know not, oh, I know not, for example, what they fill sausage casings with, whose guts are fit to be filled, nor do I know with what, though the prices for every filling, fine or coarse, are legibly displayed, still, I know not what is included in the price, I know not in what dictionaries they find the names for fillings. I know not wherewith they fill the dictionaries or sausage casings, I know not whose meat, I know not whose language: words communicate, butchers won't tell, I cut off slices, you open books, I read what tastes good to me, but what tastes good to you? Slices of sausage and quotations from sausage casings and books—and never will we learn who had to be reduced to silence before sausage casings could be filled, before books could speak, stuffed full of print, I know not, but I surmise: It is the same butchers who fill dictionaries and sausage casings with language and sausage, there is no Paul, the man's name was Saul and a Saul he was, and it was Saul who told the people of Corinth something about some priceless sausages that he called faith, hope, and love, which he advertised as easily digestible and which to this very day, still Saul though forever changing in form, he palms off on mankind.

As for me, they took away my toy merchant, wishing with him to banish all toys from the world.

There was once a musician, his name was Meyn, and he played the trumpet too beautifully for words.

There was once a toy merchant, his name was Markus and he sold tin drums, lacquered red and white.

There was once a musician, his name was Meyn and he had four cats, one of which was called Bismarck.

There was once a drummer, his name was Oskar, and he needed the toy merchant.

There was once a musician, his name was Meyn, and he did his four cats in with a fire poker.

There was once a watchmaker, his name was Laubschad, and he was a member of the SPCA.

There was once a drummer, his name was Oskar, and they took away his toy merchant.

There was once a toy merchant, his name was Markus, and he took all the toys in the world away with him out of this world.

There was once a musician, his name was Meyn, and if he isn't dead he is still alive, once again playing the trumpet too beautifully for words.

Book
Two

Scrap Metal

Visiting Day: Maria has brought me a new drum. After passing it over the bars enclosing my bed, she wished to give me the sales slip from the store, but I waved it away and pressed the bell button at the head end of the bed until Bruno my keeper came in and did what he always does when Maria brings me a new drum. He undid the string, let the blue wrapping paper open of its own accord, solemnly lifted out the drum, and carefully folded the paper. Only then did he stride—and when I say stride, I mean stride—to the washbasin with the new drum, turn on the hot water, and, taking care not to scratch the red and white lacquer, remove the price tag.

When, after a brief, not too fatiguing visit, Maria prepared to go, she picked up the old drum, which I had pretty well wrecked during my saga of Herbert Truczinski's back, my stories about the figurehead, and my perhaps rather arbitrary interpretation of the first Epistle to the Corinthians. She was going to take it home to store in our cellar, side by side with all the other worn-out instruments that had served my professional or private purposes. "There's not much room left in the cellar," she said with a sigh. "I'd like to know where I'm going to put the winter potatoes." I smiled, pretending not to hear this plaint of the housekeeper in Maria, and gave her my instructions: the retired drum must be numbered in black ink and the brief notes I had made on a slip of paper about the drum's career must be transferred to the diary which has been hanging for years on the inside of the cellar door and knows all about my drums since 1949.

Maria nodded in resignation and kissed me good-by. She never did understand this passion of mine for order; in fact it strikes her as almost insane. Oskar can see how she feels, for he himself is at a loss to account for the pedantry he puts into collecting battered tin drums. The strangest part of it is that he never wants to lay eyes on that pile of scrap metal in the potato cellar again as long as he lives. For he knows from experience that children despise their father's collections and that his son Kurt will look with indifference at best on all those pitiful drums he will one day inherit.

What is it then that makes me, every three weeks, give Maria instructions which, if regularly followed, will one day take up all the room in our cellar and expel the potatoes?

The idea which lights up in my mind now and then, though more and more infrequently, that a museum might one day take an interest in my weary instruments, came to me only after several dozen of them had found their way to the cellar; hence it cannot have been at the root of my collector's passion. The more I think of it, the more I veer toward a very simple motive: fear, fear of a shortage, fear that tin drums might be prohibited, that existing stocks might be destroyed. One day Oskar might be obliged to unearth a few of the less damaged ones and have them repaired as a stopgap to carry him through a period of bleak and terrible drumlessness.

The doctors at the mental hospital offer a similar explanation, though they put it differently. Dr. (Miss) Hornstetter was even curious to know the exact date when my complex was born. I told her at once: November 9, 1938, for that was the day when I lost Sigismund Markus, who had kept me supplied with drums. After my mother's death, it had already become difficult to obtain a new drum when I needed one; there were no more Thursday visits to Arsenal Passage, Matzerath's interest in my drum supply was very halfhearted, and Jan Bronski came to see us more and more infrequently. Now that the toystore was smashed to bits, my situation became truly desperate. The sight of Markus sitting at his empty desk made it very clear to me: Markus won't give you any more drums, Markus won't be selling any more toys, Markus has broken off business relations with the makers of your beautiful red and white drums.

At the time, however, I was not yet prepared to believe that the relatively serene and playful days of my childhood had ended with Markus' death. From the ruins of the toystore I selected a whole drum and two that were dented only at the edges and, running home with my treasures, imagined that I was secure against hard times.

I was very careful with my drums, I drummed seldom and only in cases of absolute necessity; I denied myself whole afternoons of drumming and, very reluctantly, the drumming at breakfast time that had hitherto made my days bearable. Oskar had turned ascetic; he lost weight and was taken to see Dr. Hollatz and Sister Inge, his assistant, who was getting steadily bonier. They gave me sweet, sour, bitter, and tasteless medicine and put the blame on my glands, which in Dr. Hollatz' opinion had upset my constitution by alternating between hyperfunction and hypofuncton.

To escape from Dr. Hollatz' clutches, Oskar moderated his asceticism and put on weight. By the summer of '39, he was his old three-year-old self again, but in filling out his cheeks he had irrevocably demolished the last of Markus' drums. The object that hung on my belly was a pitiful wreck, rusty and full of gaping holes; the red and white lacquer was nearly gone and the sound was utterly lugubrious.

There was no point in appealing to Matzerath for help, though he was a helpful soul and even kindly in his way. Since my poor mother's death, he thought of nothing but his Party occupations; when in need of distraction, he would confer with other unit leaders. Or toward midnight, after ample consumption of spirits, he would carry on loud though confidential conversations with the black-framed likenesses of Hitler and Beethoven in our living room, the genius speaking to him of destiny and the Führer of providence. When he was sober he looked upon the collecting of Winter Aid as the destiny allotted him by providence.

I don't like to think about those collection Sundays. It was on one of them that I made a futile attempt to possess myself of a new drum. Matzerath, who had spent the morning collecting outside the Art Cinema in Hauptstrasse and Sternfeld's Department Store, came home at noon and warmed up some meatballs for our lunch. After the meal—I can still remember that it was very tasty—the weary collector lay down on the couch for a nap. No sooner did his breathing suggest sleep than I took the half-full collection box from the piano and disappeared into the store. Huddled under the counter, I turned my attention to this most preposterous of all tin cans. Not that I intended to filch so much as a penny. My absurd idea was to try the thing out as a drum. But however I beat, however I manipulated the sticks it gave but one answer: Winter Aid, please contribute. Let no one be cold or hungry. Winter Aid, please contribute.

After half an hour I gave up; I took five pfennigs from the cash drawer, contributed them to the Winter Aid, and returned the collection box thus enriched to the piano, so that Matzerath might find it and kill the rest of his Sunday shaking it for the cold and hungry.

This unsuccessful attempt cured me forever. Never again did I seriously attempt to use a tin can, an overturned bucket, or the bottom of a washbasin for a drum. If I nevertheless did so from time to time, I try my best to forget these inglorious episodes, and give them as little space as possible on this paper. A tin can is simply not a drum, a bucket is a bucket, and a washbasin is good for washing yourself or your socks. There was no more substitute then than there is now; a tin drum adorned with red flames on a white field speaks for itself and no one can speak for it.

Oskar was alone, betrayed and sold down the river. How was he to preserve his three-year-old countenance if he lacked what was most necessary to his well-being, his drum? All the deceptions I had been practicing for years: my occasional bed-wetting, my childlike babbling of evening prayers, my fear of Santa Claus, whose real name was Greff, my indefatigable asking of droll, typically three-year-old questions such as: Why have cars got wheels?—all this nonsense that grownups expected of me I now had to provide without my drum. I was soon tempted to give up. In my despair I began to look for the man who was not my father but had very probably begotten me. Not far from the Polish settlement on Ringstrasse, Oskar waited for Jan Bronski.

My poor mama's death had put an end to the relations, sometimes verging on friendship, between Matzerath and my uncle, who had meanwhile been promoted to the position of postal secretary. There was no sudden break, but despite the memories they shared they had gradually moved apart as the political crisis deepened. The disintegration of my mama's slender soul and ample body brought with it the disintegration of the friendship between these two men, both of whom had mirrored themselves in her soul and fed on her body. Deprived of this nourishment and convex mirror, they found no substitute but their meetings with men who were dedicated to opposing political ideas though they smoked the same tobacco. But neither a Polish Post Office nor meetings with unit leaders in shirtsleeves can take the place of a beautiful, tender-hearted woman. Despite the need for caution—Matzerath had to think of his customers and the Party and Jan had the postal administration to consider—my two presumptive fathers met several times between my poor mama's death and the end of Sigismund Markus.

Two or three times a month, toward midnight, we would hear Jan's knuckles tapping on our living room window. Matzerath would push the curtain aside and open the window a crack; both of them would be thoroughly embarrassed until one or the other found the saving word and suggested a game of midnight skat. They would summon Greff from his vegetable store or, if he was disinclined, which he often was on Jan's account, because as a former scout leader—he had meanwhile disbanded his troop—he had to be careful and besides he was a poor player and didn't care much about skat in the first place, they usually called in Alexander Scheffler, the baker, as third. Scheffler himself was none too enthusiastic about sitting at the same table with Jan, but a certain affection for my poor mama, which had transferred itself like a kind of legacy to Matzerath, and a firm conviction that retailers should stick together, induced the short-legged baker to hurry over from Kleinhammer-Weg in response to Matzerath's call, to take his place at our living room table, to shuffle the cards with his pale, worm-eaten, floury fingers and distribute them like rolls to the hungry multitude.

Since these forbidden games did not as a rule begin until midnight, to break off at three in the morning when Scheffler was needed in the bakery, it was only on rare occasions that I managed to rise from my bed unseen, unheard, and drumless, and slip into the shady corner beneath the table.

164

As you have been doubtless noticed by now, I had always, under tables, been given to the easiest kind of meditation: I made comparisons. How things had changed since my poor mama's death. No longer did Jan Bronski, cautious up top and yet losing game after game, but intrepid below, send out his shoeless sock on expeditions between my mother's thighs. Sex, not to say love, had vanished from the skat table. Six trouser legs in various fishbone patterns draped six masculine legs, some bare and more or less hairy at the ankles, others affecting long underwear. Down below, all six made every effort to avoid the slightest contact, however fortuitous, while up above their extensions—trunks, heads, arms—busied themselves with a game which should have been forbidden on political grounds, for every hand lost or won admitted of such baleful or triumphant reflections as: Poland has lost a grand hand, or, the Free City of Danzig has taken a diamond single for the German Reich.

It was not hard to foresee a day when these war games would come to an end, transformed, as is the way with war games, into hard realities.

Early in the summer of '39 it became clear that Matzerath, in the course of his weekly party conferences, had found skat partners less compromising than Polish postal officials and former scout leaders. Jan Bronski remembered—he was forced to remember—the camp to which fate had assigned him; he began to stick to his post-office friends, such as Kobyella, the crippled janitor who, since his service in Marszalek Pilsudski's legendary legion, had one leg an inch or more shorter than the other. Despite his limp, Kobyella was an excellent janitor, hence a skillful repair man who might, it seemed to me, be kind enough to make my sick drum well again. The path to Kobyella led through Jan Bronski. That was the only reason why I took to waiting for Jan near the Polish settlement toward six in the evening. Even in the most stifling August heat I waited, but Jan, who normally started punctually for home at closing time, did not appear. Without explicitly asking myself what does your presumptive father do after work? I often waited until seven or half-past. And still he did not come. I could have gone to Aunt Hedwig's. Possibly Jan was sick; maybe he had fever or he had broken a leg and had it in plaster. Oskar stayed right where he was and contented himself with staring from time to time at the windows and curtains of the postal secretary's flat. Oskar felt a strange reluctance about visiting his Aunt Hedwig, whose motherly cow's eyes made him sad. Besides, he was not especially fond of the Bronski children, his presumptive half brother and sister. They treated him like a doll. They wanted to play with him, to use him for a toy. What right had Stephan, who was just fifteen, scarcely older than himself, to treat him with the condescension of a father or schoolmaster? And ten-year-old Marga with those braids and that face that rose like a fat full moon, what gave her the right to look upon Oskar as a dummy to be dressed, combed, brushed, adjusted, and lectured at by the hour? To both of them I was nothing but a freak, a pathetic midget, while they were normal and full of promise. They were also my grandma Koljaiczek's favorites, but then I have to own that I made things pretty hard for her. I showed little interest in fairy tales and picture books. What I expected of my grandmother, what even today I dream of in the most pleasurable detail, was very clear and simple, and for that reason hard to obtain: the moment he saw her, Oskar wanted to emulate his grandfather Koljaiczek, to take refuge beneath her skirts and, if possible, never again draw a breath outside of their sheltering stillness.

What lengths I went to to gain admittance to that tent! I don't believe that she actually disliked to have Oskar sitting there. But she hesitated and usually refused me; I think she would gladly have granted refuge to anyone who halfway resembled Koljaiczek; it was only I who, having neither his build nor his ready hand with matches, was constrained to think up stratagems.

I can see Oskar playing with a rubber ball like a real three-year-old; by pure chance the ball rolls under her skirts and Oskar, in pursuit of the spherical pretext, slips in before his grandmother can see through his ruse and give back the ball.

When the grownups were present, my grandmother never tolerated me under her skirts for very long. The grownups would make fun of her, reminding her, often in rather crude terms, of her betrothal in the autumnal potato fields, until my grandmother, who was not pale by nature, would blush loud and long, which was not unbecoming to her with her hair which by then—she was past sixty—was almost white.

But when my grandmother Anna was alone—as she seldom was, and I saw her more and more rarely after my poor mama's death, and scarcely ever since she had been obliged to give up her stall at the weekly market in Langfuhr—she was more willing to let me take shelter beneath her potato-colored skirts and let me stay longer. I didn't even need the silly trick with the rubber ball. Sliding across the floor with my drum, doubling up one leg and bracing the other against the furniture, I made my way toward the grandmotherly mountain; arrived at the foot, I would raise the fourfold veils with my drumsticks and, once underneath, let them fall, all four at once. For a moment I remained perfectly still, breathing in with my whole soul the acrid smell of slightly rancid butter, which, unaffected by the changing of the seasons, pervaded this chosen habitat. Only then did Oskar begin to drum. Knowing what his grandmother liked to hear, I called forth sounds of October rain, similar to what she must have heard by the smouldering potato plants, when Koljaiczek, smelling like a hotly pursued firebug, came to her for shelter. I would make a fine slanting rain fall on the drum, until above me I could hear sighs and saints' names, and it is up to you to recognize the sighs and saints' names that were uttered in '99 when my grandmother sat in the rain and Koljaiczek sat dry in the tent.

As I waited for Jan Bronski outside the Polish settlement in August, '39, I often thought of my grandmother. Possibly she was visiting with Aunt Hedwig. But alluring as the thought may have been to sit beneath her skirts, breathing in the smell of rancid butter, I did not climb the two flights of stairs, I did not ring the bell under the name plate marked "Jan Bronski." What had Oskar to offer his grandmother? His drum was broken, it made no music, it had forgotten the sound of the rain, the fine rain that falls aslant on a fire of potato plants. And since these autumnal sound effects were his only way of appealing to his grandmother, he stayed out on Ringstrasse, gazing at the Number 5 cars as they approached or receded, clanging their bells in their course along the Heeresanger.

Was I still waiting for Jan? Had I not already given up? If I was still standing on the same spot, was it not simply that I had not yet thought up an acceptable way of leaving? Long waiting can be quite educational. But a long wait can also make one conjure up the awaited encounter in such detail as to destroy all possibility of a happy surprise. Nevertheless Jan surprised me. Resolved to take him unawares, to serenade him with the remains of my drum, I stood there tense, with my sticks at the ready. If only the groans and outcries of my drum could make my desperate situation clear to him, there would be no need of any longwinded explanations. Five more streetcars, I said to myself, three more, just this one; giving shape to my anxieties, I imagined that the Bronskis, at Jan's request, had been transferred to Modlin or Warsaw; I saw him as postmaster in Bromberg or Thorn. Then, in disregard of all my promises to myself, I waited for one more streetcar, and had already turned to start for home when Oskar was seized from behind. A grownup had put his hands over Oskar's eyes.

I felt soft hands that smelled of expensive soap, pleasantly dry, men's hands; I felt Jan Bronski.

When he let me loose and spun me round toward him with an overloud laugh, it was too late to demonstrate my disastrous situation on the drum. Consequently I inserted both drumsticks under the linen suspenders of my filthy knickers, filthy and frayed around the pockets because in those days there was no one to take care of me. That left my hands free to lift up my drum, to raise it high in accusation, as Father Wiehnke raised the host during Mass, I too might have said: this is my body and blood, but I said not a word; I just held up the battered metal. I desired no fundamental or miraculous transubstantiation; all I wanted for my drum was a repair job, nothing more.

Jan's laughter was plainly hysterical. He must have felt it to be out of place for he stopped it at once. He saw my drum, he couldn't very well help it, but soon turned away from it to seek my bright, three-year-old eyes, which at that time still had a look of candor. At first he saw nothing but two expressionless blue irises full of glints and reflections, everything in short that eyes are said to be full of, and then, forced to admit that the reflections in my eyes were no better or worse than those that can be seen in any first-class puddle, summoned up all his good will, concentrated his memory, and forced himself to find in my orbits my mama's gray, but similarly shaped eyes which for quite a few years had reflected sentiments ranging from benevolence to passion for his benefit. Perhaps he was disconcerted to find a shadow of himself, though this would not necessarily mean that Jan was my father or, more accurately, my begetter. For his eyes, Mama's, and my own were distinguished by the same naively shrewd, sparkling, inept beauty as those of nearly all the Bronskis, of Stephan, of Marga, though in lesser degree, but above all of my grandmother and her brother Vincent. Yet despite my blue eyes and black lashes, there was no overlooking a dash of incendiary Koljaiczek blood in me—how else account for my delight in shattering glass with song?—whereas it would have been hard to discern any Rhenish, Matzerath traits in me.

At that moment, when I lifted my drum and put my eyes to work, Jan himself, who preferred to sidestep such questions, would, if asked directly, have had to confess: it is his mother Agnes who is looking at me. Or perhaps I am looking at myself. His mother and I had far too much in common. But then again it might be my uncle Koljaiczek, who is in America or on the bottom of the sea. In any case it is not Matzerath who is looking at me, and that is just as well.

Jan took my drum, turned it about, tapped it. He, the impractical butterfingers, who couldn't even sharpen a pencil properly, assumed the air of a man who knows something about repairing tin drums. Visibly making a decision, which was rare with him, he took me by the hand, quite to my surprise because I had never expected things to move that quickly, and led me across Ringstrasse to the Heeresanger streetcar stop. When the car came, he pulled me after him into the trailer where smoking was permitted.

As Oskar suspected, we were going into the city, to the Hevelius-Platz, to the Polish Post Office, to see Janitor Kobyella, who possessed the tools and the skill that Oskar's drum was so sorely in need of.

That streetcar ride in the jingling, jangling Number 5 might have been a quiet pleasure jaunt if it had not taken place on the day before September 1, 1939. At Max-Halbe-Platz, the car filled up with weary but vociferous bathers from the beach at Brösen. What a pleasant summer evening would have awaited us, drinking soda pop through a straw at the Café Weitzke after depositing the drum, if the battleships *Schleswig* and *Schleswig-Holstein* had not been riding at anchor in the harbor mouth across from the Westerplatte, displaying their grim steel flanks, their double revolving turrets, and casemate guns. How lovely it would have been to ring at the porter's lodge of the Polish Post Office and leave an innocent child's drum for janitor Kobyella to repair, if only the post office had not, in the course of the last few months, been fitted out with armor plate and turned into a fortress garrisoned by the hitherto peace-loving post-office personnel, officials, clerks, and mail carriers, who had been devoting their weekends to military training at Gdingen and Oxhöft.

We were approaching Oliva Gate. Jan Bronski was sweating profusely, staring at the dusty green trees of Hindenburg-Allee and smoking more of his gold-tipped cigarettes than his economical nature would ordinarily have permitted. Oskar had never seen his presumptive father sweat so, except for two or three times when he had watched him on the sofa with his mama.

But my poor mama had long been dead. Why was Jan Bronski sweating? When I saw how he prepared to leave the car at every approaching stop but each time remembered my presence at the last moment, when I realized that if he resumed his seat it was because of me and my drum, I knew why he was sweating. It was because Jan, as an official, was expected to help defend the Polish Post Office. He had already made his getaway, but then he had run into me and my scrap metal on the corner of Ringstrasse and the Heeresanger, and resolved to follow the call of duty. Pulling me, who was neither an official nor fit to defend a post office, after him, he had boarded the car and here he sat smoking and sweating. Why didn't he get out? I certainly would not have stopped him. He was still in the prime of life, not yet forty-five, blue of eye and brown of hair. His trembling hands were well manicured, and if he hadn't been perspiring so pitifully, the smell that came to Oskar's nostrils as he sat beside his presumptive father would have been cologne and not cold sweat.

At the Holzmarkt we got out and walked down the Altstädtischer Graben. It was a still summer night. The bells pealed heavenward as they always did toward eight o'clock, sending up clouds of pigeons. "Be True and Upright to the Grave," sang the chimes. It was beautiful and made you want to cry. But all about us there was laughter. Women with sunburned children, terry-cloth beach robes, bright-colored balls and sailboats alit from the streetcars bearing their freshly bathed multitudes from the beaches of Glettkau and Heubude. Girls still drowsy from the sun nibbled raspberry ice. A fifteen-year-old dropped her ice cream cone and was about to pick it up, but then she hesitated and finally abandoned the rapidly melting delicacy to the paving stones and the shoe soles of future passers-by; soon she would be a grownup and stop eating ice cream in the street.

At Schneidermühlen-Gasse we turned left. The Hevelius-Platz, to which the little street led, was blocked off by SS Home Guards standing about in groups: youngsters and grown men with the armbands and rifles of the security police. It would have been easy to make a detour around the cordon and get to the post office from the Rähm. Jan Bronski went straight up to the SS men. His purpose was clear: he wanted to be stopped under the eyes of his superiors, who were certainly having the Hevelius-Platz watched from the post office, and sent back. He hoped to cut a relatively dignified figure as a thwarted hero and return home by the same Number 5 streetcar that had brought him.

The Home Guards let us through; it probably never occurred to them that this well-dressed gentleman leading a three-year-old child by the hand meant to go to the post office. They politely advised us to be careful and did not shout "Halt" until we were through the outside gate and approaching the main entrance. Jan turned irresolutely. The heavy door was opened a crack and we were pulled inside: there we were in the pleasantly cool half-light of the main hall.

The greeting Jan Bronski received from his colleagues was not exactly friendly. They distrusted him, they had probably given him up. Some, as they declared quite frankly, had even begun to suspect that he, Postal Secretary Bronski, was going to shirk his duties. Jan had difficulty in clearing himself. No one listened. He was pushed into a line of men who were busy hauling sandbags up from the cellar. These sandbags and other incongruous objects were piled up behind the plate-glass windows; filing cabinets and other items of heavy furniture were moved close to the main entrance with a view to barricading it in case of emergency.

Someone asked who I was but had no time to wait for Jan's answer. The men were nervous; they would shout at one another and then suddenly, grown overcautious, start whispering. My drum and its distress seemed forgotten. Kobyella the janitor, on whom I had counted, whom I expected to rehabilitate the mass of scrap metal hanging from my neck, was not to be seen; he was probably on the second or third floor of the building, feverishly at work like the clerks and postmen around me, piling up sandbags that were supposed to resist bullets. Oskar's presence was obviously embarrassing to Bronski. The moment a man, whom the others called Dr. Michon, came up to give Jan instructions I slipped away. After cautiously circumnavigating this Dr. Michon, who wore a Polish steel helmet and was obviously the postmaster, I looked about and finally found the stairs leading to the second floor. Toward the end of the second-floor corridor, I discovered a medium-sized, windowless room, where no one was hauling crates of ammunition or piling sandbags. In fact, the room was deserted.

A number of baskets on rollers had been pushed close together; they were full of letters bearing stamps of all colors. It was a low-ceilinged room with ocher-red wallpaper. I detected a slight smell of rubber. An unshaded light bulb hung from the ceiling. Oskar was too tired to look for the switch. Far in the distance the bells of St. Mary's, St. Catherine's, St. John's, St. Bridget's, St. Barbara's, Trinity, and Corpus Christi announced: It is nine o'clock. You must go to sleep now, Oskar. And so I lay down in one of the mail baskets, bedded down my drum that was as tired as I was by my side, and fell asleep.

The Polish Post Office

I slept in a laundry basket full of letters mailed in Lodz, Lublin, Lemberg, Thorn, Krakau, and Tschenstochau or addressed to people in Lodz, Lublin, Lwow, Toruń, Krakow, and Częstochowa. But I dreamed neither of the Matka Boska Częstochowska nor of the Black Madonna. In my dreams I nibbled neither on Marszalek Pilsudski's heart, preserved in Cracow, nor on the gingerbread that has made the city of Thorn so famous. I did not even dream of my still unrepaired drum. Lying dreamless in a laundry basket on rollers, Oskar heard none of the whispering, twittering, and chattering that allegedly fill the air when many letters lie in a heap. To me those letters didn't breathe a word, I wasn't expecting any mail, and no one could have had the slightest ground for regarding me as an addressee, let alone a sender. Lordly and self-sufficient, I slept with retracted antennae on a mountain of mail gravid with news, a mountain which might have been the world.

Consequently I was not awakened by the letter which a certain Lech Milewczyk in Warsaw had written his niece in Danzig-Schidlitz, a letter alarming enough to have awakened a millenarian turtle; what woke me up was either the nearby machine-gun fire or the distant roar of the salvos from the double turrets of the battleships in the Free Port.

All that is so easily written: machine guns, double turrets. Might it not just as well have been a shower, a hailstorm, the approach of a late summer storm similar to the storm that had accompanied my birth? I was too sleepy and speculation of this sort was not in my repertory. With the sounds still fresh in my ears, I guessed right and like all sleepyheads called a spade a spade: They are shooting, I said to myself.

Oskar climbed out of the laundry basket and stood there wobbling on his pins. His first thought was for the fate of his sensitive drum. With both hands he scooped out a hole in the letters that had sheltered his slumbers, but he was not brutal about it; though loosely piled, the letters were often dovetailed, but he did not tear, bend, or deface, no, cautiously I picked out the scrambled letters, giving individual attention to each single envelope with its "Poczta Polska" postmark—most of them were violet—and even to the postcards. I took care that none of the envelopes should come open, for even in the presence of events so momentous as to change the face of the world, the secrecy of the mails must remain sacred.

As the machine-gun fire increased, the crater in the laundry basket deepened. Finally I let well enough alone, laid my mortally wounded drum to rest in its freshly dug bed, and covered it well, with ten, perhaps twenty layers of envelopes fitted together in overlapping tiers, as masons fit bricks together to build a solid wall.

I had no sooner completed my precautionary measures, with which I hoped to protect my drum from bullets and shell fragments, when the first antitank shell burst against the post office façade, on the Hevelius-Platz side.

The Polish Post Office, a massive brick building, could be counted on to absorb a good many such hits. There seemed to be no danger that the Home Guard would quickly open up a breach wide enough to permit the frontal attack they had often rehearsed.

I left my safe, windowless storeroom enclosed by three offices and the corridor, to go looking for Jan Bronski. In searching for Jan, my presumptive father, there is no doubt that I was also looking, perhaps with still greater eagerness, for Kobyella, the crippled janitor. For, after all, had I not gone without supper the evening before, had I not taken the streetcar to the Hevelius-Platz and braved the soldiery to enter this post office building which under normal conditions left me cold, in order to have my drum repaired? If I should not find Kobyella on time, that is, before the all-out attack that was surely coming, it seemed scarcely possible that my ailing drum would ever get the expert treatment it needed.

And so Oskar thought of Kobyella and looked for Jan. His arms folded across his chest, he paced the long, tiled corridor and found nothing but solitude. Amid the steady not to say lavish gunfire of the Home Guard, he could make out single shots that must have been fired from inside the building, but the economy-minded defenders had no doubt stayed right in their offices, having merely exchanged their rubber stamps for other implements that could also do a stamp job of sorts. There was no one sitting, standing, or lying in the corridor in readiness for a possible counterattack. Oskar patrolled alone; drumless and defenseless he faced the history-making introitus of the early, far too early hour, which carried plenty of lead but, alas, no gold in its mouth.

The offices on the court side were equally empty. Very careless, I thought. The building should have been guarded there too, for there was only a wooden fence separating the Police Building on Schneidermühlen-Gasse from the post office court and the package ramp—for the attackers, indeed, the layout was almost too good to be true. I pattered through the offices, the registered letter room, the money order room, the payroll room, the telegraph office. And there they lay. Behind sandbags and sheets of armor plate, behind overturned office furniture, there they lay, firing very intermittently.

In most of the rooms the windows had already made contact with the Home Guard's machine-gun fire. I took a quick look at the damage, making comparisons with the windowpanes that had collapsed in quiet, deep-breathing times of peace, under the influence of my diamond voice. Well, I said to myself, if they ask me to do my bit for the defense of the Polish Post Office, if this wiry little Dr. Michon approaches me not as postmaster but as military commander of the post office building, if he tries to enlist me in the service of Poland, my voice will do its duty. For Poland and for Poland's untilled but perpetually fruitful economy, I would gladly have shattered the windows of all the houses on the other side of the Hevelius-Platz, the transparent house fronts on the Rähm, the windows of Schneidermühlen-Gasse, including Police Headquarters; carrying my long-distance technique to new heights and lengths, I should gladly have transformed every sparkling windowpane on the Altstädtischer Graben and Ritter-Gasse into a black, draft-fomenting hole. That would have created confusion among the Home Guard and the onlookers as well. It would have had the effect of several machine guns and, at the very outset of the war, given rise to talk of secret weapons. But it would not have saved the Polish Post Office.

Oskar's abilities were not put to the test. This Dr. Michon with the Polish steel helmet and the directorial countenance did not enlist me; instead, when, having run down the stairs to the main hall, I got tangled up in his legs, he gave me a painful box on the ear and immediately afterwards, cursing loudly in Polish, resumed his military duties. I could only swallow my chagrin. Obviously all these people, and most of all Dr. Michon, who bore the responsibility, were very excited and scared; I had to forgive them.

The clock in the main hall told me that it was 4:20. When it was 4:21, I inferred that the first hostilities had left the clockwork unharmed. The clock was running, and I was at a loss to know whether this equanimity on the part of time should be taken as a good or bad omen.

In any case, I remained for the present in the main hall, looking for Jan and Kobyella and keeping out of Dr. Michon's way. I found neither my uncle nor the janitor. I noted damage to the glass windows and also cracks and ugly holes in the plaster beside the main entrance, and I had the honor of being present when the first two wounded were carried in. One of them, an elderly gentleman, his gray hair still neatly parted, spoke excitedly and without interruption as his wound—a bullet had grazed his forearm—was being bandaged. No sooner had his arm been swathed in white than he jumped up, seized his rifle, and started back to the rampart of sandbags, which was not, I think, quite bulletproof. How fortunate that a slight faintness brought on by loss of blood forced him to lie down again and take the rest indispensable to an elderly gentleman who has just been wounded. Moreover, the wiry little quinquagenarian, who wore a steel helmet but from whose breast pocket peered the tip of a silk handkerchief, this gentleman with the elegant movements of a knight in government office, the very same Dr. Michon who had sternly questioned Jan Bronski the previous evening, commanded the wounded elderly gentleman to keep quiet in the name of Poland.

The second wounded man lay breathing heavily on a straw tick and showed no further desire for sandbags. At regular intervals he screamed loudly and without shame; he had been shot in the belly.

Still searching, Oskar was about to give the row of men behind the sandbags another inspection when two shells, striking almost simultaneously above and beside the main entrance, set the hall to rattling. The chests that had been moved against the door burst open, releasing piles of bound records, which fluttered aloft, scattered, and landed on the tile floor where they came into contact with slips and tags whose acquaintance they were never intended to make. Needless to say, the rest of the window glass burst asunder, while great chunks and smaller chunks of plaster fell from the walls and ceiling. Another wounded man was carried into the middle of the hall through clouds of plaster and calcimine, but then, by order of the steel-helmeted Dr. Michon, taken upstairs to the first floor.

The wounded postal clerk moaned at every step. Oskar followed him and his carriers. No one called him back, no one asked him where he was going or, as Michon had done a short while before, boxed his ears. It is true that he did his best to keep out of the grown-up post-office defenders' way.

When I reached the second floor behind the slow-moving carriers, my suspicion was confirmed: the wounded man was being taken to the windowless and therefore safe storeroom that I had reserved for myself. No mattresses being available, it was decided that the mail baskets, though rather too short, would provide relatively comfortable resting places for the wounded. Already I regretted having put my drum to bed in one of these movable laundry baskets full of undeliverable mail. Would the blood of these torn and punctured postmen and postal clerks not seep through ten or twenty layers of paper and give my drum a color it had hitherto known only in the form of enamel? What had my drum in common with the blood of Poland? Let them color their records and blotting paper with their life sap! Let them pour the blue out of their inkwells and fill them up again with red! Let them dye their handkerchiefs and starched white shirts half-red and make Polish flags out of them! After all, it was Poland they were concerned with, not my drum! If they insisted that Poland, though lost, must remain white and red, was that any reason why my drum, rendered suspect by the fresh paint job, should be lost too?

Slowly the thought took root in me: it's not Poland they're worried about, it's my drum. Jan had lured me to the post office in order to give his colleagues, for whom Poland wasn't a good enough rallying signal, an inflammatory standard and watchword. That night, as I slept in a laundry basket on rollers, though neither rolling nor dreaming, the waking post office clerks had whispered to one another: A dying toy drum has sought refuge with us. We are Poles, we must protect it, especially since England and France are bound by treaty to defend us.

While these useless and abstract meditations hampered my freedom of movement outside the half-open door of the storeroom for undeliverable mail, machine-gun fire rose up for the first time from the court. As I had foreseen, the Home Guards were making their first attack from the Police Headquarters Building on Schneidermühlen-Gasse. A little later we were all sent sprawling. The Home Guard had managed to blast the door into the package room above the loading ramp. In another minute they were in the package room, and soon, the door to the corridor leading to the main hall was open.

The men who had carried up the wounded man and bedded him in the mail basket where my drum lay rushed off: others followed them. By the noise I judged that they were fighting in the main-floor corridor, then in the package room. The Home Guards were forced to withdraw.

First hesitantly, then with assurance, Oskar entered the storeroom. The wounded man's face was grayish-yellow; he showed his teeth and his eyeballs were working behind closed lids. He spat threads of blood. But since his head hung out over the edge of the mail basket, there was little danger of his soiling the letters. Oskar had to stand on tiptoe to reach into the basket. The man's seat was resting, and resting heavily, exactly where Oskar's drum lay buried. At first Oskar pulled gingerly, taking care not to hurt either the wounded postal clerk or the letters; then he tugged more violently. At length, with a furious ripping and tearing, he managed to remove several dozen envelopes from beneath the groaning man.

Today, it pleases me to relate that my fingers were already touching the rim of my drum when men came storming up the stairs and down the corridor. They were coming back, they had driven the Home Guards

175

from the package room; for the time being they were victorious. I heard them laughing.

Hidden behind one of the mail baskets, I waited near the door until they crowded round the wounded man. At first shouting and gesticulating, then cursing softly, they bandaged him.

Two antitank shells struck the wall of the façade on the level of the ground floor, then two more, then silence. The salvos from the battleships in the Free Port, across from the Westerplatte, rolled along in the distance, an even, good-natured grumbling—you got used to it.

Unnoticed by the bandagers, I slipped out of the storeroom, leaving my drum in the lurch, to resume my search for Jan, my presumptive father and uncle, and also for Kobyella the janitor.

On the third floor was the apartment of Chief Postal Secretary Naczalnik, who had apparently sent his family off to Bromberg or Warsaw in time. First I searched a few storerooms on the court side, and then I found Jan and Kobyella in the nursery of the Naczalnik flat.

It was a light, friendly room with amusing wallpaper, which unfortunately had been gashed here and there by stray bullets. In peaceful times, it must have been pretty nice to look out the windows at the Hevelius-Platz. An unharmed rocking horse, balls of various sizes, a medieval castle full of upset tin soldiers mounted and on foot, an open cardboard box full of rails and miniature freight cars, several more or less tattered dolls, doll's houses with disorderly interiors, in short a superabundance of toys showed that Chief Postal Secretary Naczalnik must have been the father of two very spoiled children, a boy and a girl. How lucky that the brats had been evacuated to Warsaw and that I was spared a meeting with such a pair, the like of which was well known to me from the Bronskis. With a slight sadistic pleasure I reflected how sorry the little boy must have been to leave his tin soldiers. Maybe he had put a few Uhlans in his pants pocket to reinforce the Polish cavalry later on at the battle for the fortress of Modlin.

Oskar has been going on too much about tin soldiers; the truth is that there's a confession he has to make and he may as well get on with it. In this nursery there was a kind of bookcase full of toys, picture books, and games; the top shelf was taken up with miniature musical instruments. A honey-yellow trumpet lay silent beside a set of chimes which followed the hostilities with enthusiasm, that is to say, whenever a shell struck, they went bim-bim. A brightly painted accordion hung down on one side. The parents had been insane enough to give their offspring a real little fiddle with four real strings. And next to the fiddle, showing its white, undamaged roundness, propped on some building blocks to keep it from rolling off the shelf, stood—you'll never believe it!—a toy drum encased in red and white lacquer.

I made no attempt to pull the drum down from the rack by my own resources. Oskar was quite conscious of his limited reach and was not beyond asking grownups for favors in cases where his gnomelike stature resulted in helplessness.

Jan Bronski and Kobyella lay behind a rampart of sandbags filling the lower third of the windows that started at the floor. Jan had the left-hand window. Kobyella's place was on the right. I realized at once that the janitor was not likely to find the time to recover my drum from its hiding place beneath the wounded, blood-spitting post-office defender who was surely crushing it, and repair it. Kobyella was very busy; at regular intervals he fired his rifle through an embrasure in the sandbag rampart at an antitank gun that had been set up on the other side of the Hevelius-Platz, not far from Schneidermühlen-Gasse and the Radaune Bridge.

Jan lay huddled up, hiding his head and trembling. I recognized him only by his fashionable dark-grey suit, though by now it was pretty well covered with plaster and sand. The lace of his right, likewise gray shoe had come open. I bent down and tied it into a bow. As I drew the bow tight, Jan quivered, raised his disconcertingly blue eyes above his sleeve, and gave me an unconscionably blue, watery stare. Although, as Oskar quickly determined, he was not wounded, he was weeping silently. He was afraid. I ignored his whimpering, pointed to young Naczalnik's drum, and asked Jan with transparent gestures to step over to the bookcase, with the utmost caution of course and taking advantage of the dead corner of the nursery, and hand me down the drum. My uncle did not understand me. My presumptive father did not see what I was driving at. My mama's lover was busy with his fear, so full of it that my pleading gestures had no other effect than to add to his fear. Oskar would have liked to scream at him, but was afraid of distracting Kobyella, who seemed to have ears only for his rifle.

And so I lay down beside Jan on the sandbags and pressed close to him, in the hope of communicating a part of my accustomed equanimity to my unfortunate uncle and presumptive father. In a short while he seemed rather calmer. By breathing with exaggerated regularity, I persuaded his pulse to become approximately regular. But when, far too soon I must admit, I tried once more to call Jan's attention to Naczalnik Junior's drum by turning his head slowly and gently but firmly in the direction of the bookcase, he still failed to see what I wanted. Terror invaded him by way of his feet, surged up through him and filled him entirely; then it flowed back down again, but was unable to escape, perhaps because of the inner soles he always wore, and rebounded invading his stomach, his spleen, his liver, rising to his head and expanding so mightily that his blue eyes stood out from their sockets and the whites disclosed a network of blood vessels which Oskar had never before had occasion to observe in his uncle's eyes.

It cost me time and effort to drive my uncle's eyeballs back into place, to make his heart behave a little. But all my esthetic efforts were frustrated when the Home Guards began to fire that field howitzer of theirs and, with an accuracy bearing witness to the high quality of their training, flattened out the iron fence in front of the building by demolishing, one by one, the brick posts to which it was anchored. There must have been from fifteen to twenty of those posts and Jan suffered heart and soul at the demise of each one, as though it were no mere pedestals that were being pounded into dust but with them imaginary statues of imaginary gods, well known to my uncle and necessary to his very existence.

It is only by some such thought that I can account for the scream with which Jan registered each hit of the howitzer, a scream so shrill and piercing that, had it been consciously shaped and aimed, it would, like my own glass-killing creations, have had the virtue of a glass-cutting diamond. There was fervor in Jan's screaming but no plan or system; all it accomplished was at long last to attract Kobyella's attention; slowly the bony, crippled janitor crept toward us, raised his cadaverous, eyelashless bird's head, and surveyed our distress society out of watery gray eyeballs. He shook Jan. Jan whimpered. He opened Jan's shirt and passed his hand quickly over Jan's body, looking for a wound—I could hardly keep from laughing. Failing to detect the slightest scratch, he turned him over on his back, seized him by the jaw, and shook it till the joints cracked, looked him grimly in the eye, swore at him in Polish, spraying his face with saliva in the process, and finally tossed him the rifle which Jan, though provided with his own private embrasure, had thus far left untouched; in fact it was still on safety. The stock struck his kneecap with a dull thud. The brief pain, his first physical pain after so much mental torment, seemed to do him good, for he seized the rifle, took fright when he felt the coldness of the metal parts in his fingers and a moment later in his blood, but then, encouraged by Kobyella, alternately cursing and coaxing, crept to his post.

For all the effeminate lushness of his imagination, my presumptive father took so realistic a view of war that it was hard, in fact impossible, for him to be brave. Instead of surveying his field of vision through his embrasure and picking out a worth-while target, he tilted his rifle so that it pointed upward, over the roofs of the houses on the Hevelius-Platz; quickly and blindly he emptied his magazine and, again empty-handed, crawled back behind the sandbags. The sheepish look with which he implored the janitor's forgiveness made me think of a schoolboy trying to confess that he has not done his homework. Kobyella gnashed his teeth in rage; when he had had enough of that, he burst out laughing as though he never would stop. Then with terrifying suddenness, his laughter broke off, and he gave Bronski, who as postal secretary was supposed to be his superior officer, a furious kick in the shins. His ungainly foot was drawn back for a kick in the ribs, but just then a burst of machine-gun fire shattered what was left of the upper window-panes and scored the ceiling. The orthopedic shoe fell back into place; he threw himself behind his rifle and began to fire with morose haste, as though to make up for the time he had wasted on Jan. At all events, he accounted for a fraction, however infinitesimal, of the ammunition consumed during the Second World War.

Had the janitor failed to notice me? He was ordinarily a gruff kind of man; like many war invalids, he had a way of keeping you at a respectful distance. Why, I wondered, did he tolerate my presence in this drafty room? Could Kobyella have thought: it's a nursery after all, so why shouldn't Oskar stay here and play during lulls in the battle?

I don't know how long we lay flat, I between Jan and the lefthand wall of the room, both of us behind the sandbags, Kobyella behind his rifle, shooting for two. It must have been about ten o'clock when the shooting died down. It grew so still that I could hear the buzzing of flies; I heard voices and shouts of command from the Hevelius-Platz, and occasionally turned an ear to the dull drone of the naval guns in the harbor. A fair to cloudy day in September, the sun spread a coating of old gold, the air was thin, sensitive, and yet hard of hearing. My fifteenth birthday was coming up in the next few days. And as every year in September, I wished for a drum, nothing less than a drum; renouncing all the treasures of the world, my mind was set unswervingly on a tin drum, lacquered red and white.

Jan didn't stir. Kobyella's breathing was so even that Oskar began to think he was asleep, that he was taking advantage of the brief lull in the battle to take a little nap, for do not all men, even heroes, need a refreshing little nap now and then? I alone was wide awake and, with all the uncompromising concentration of my years, intent on that drum. It should not be supposed that I *remembered* young Naczalnik's drum in this moment, as the silence gathered and the buzzing of a fly tuckered out from the summer heat died away. Oh, no. Even during the battle, even amid the tumult, Oskar hadn't taken his eyes off that drum. But it was only now that I saw the golden opportunity which every fiber of my being commanded me to seize.

Slowly Oskar arose, moved slowly, steering clear of the broken glass, but unswerving in purpose and direction, toward the bookcase with the toys; he was already figuring how, by putting the box of building blocks on one of the little nursery chairs, he would build a stand high and solid enough to make him the possessor of a brand-new drum, when Kobyella's voice and immediately thereafter his horny hand held me back. Desperately I pointed at the drum. It was so near. Kobyella pulled me back. With both arms I reached out for the drum. The janitor was weakening; he was just about to reach up and hand me happiness when a burst of machine-gun fire invaded the nursery and several antitank shells exploded in front of the entrance; Kobyella flung me in the corner beside Jan Bronski and resumed his position behind his rifle. I was still looking up at the drum when he started on his second magazine.

There lay Oskar, and Jan Bronski, my sweet blue-eyed uncle, didn't even lift up his nose when the clubfoot with the bird's head and the watery lashless eyes caught me, hard before my goal, and thrust me into the corner behind the sandbags.

Fat, bluish-white, eyeless maggots wriggled and multiplied, looking for a worthwhile corpse. What was Poland to me? Or the Poles for that matter? Didn't they have their cavalry? Let them ride. They were always kissing ladies' hands and never till it was too late did they notice that what they were kissing was not a lady's languid fingers but the unrouged muzzle of a field howitzer. And the daughter of the Krupps proceeded to vent her feelings. She smacked her lips, gave a corny yet convincing imitation of battle noises, the kind you hear in newsreels. She peppered the front door of the post office, burst into the main hall, and tried to take a bite out of the staircase, so that no one would be able to move up or down. Then came her retinue: machine guns and two trim little armored reconnaissance cars with their names painted on them. And what pretty names: *Ostmark* and *Sudetenland*. What fun they were having! Back and forth they drove, rat-tat-tatting from behind their armor and looking things over: two young ladies intent on culture and so eager to visit the castle, but the castle was still closed. Spoiled young things they were, just couldn't wait to get in. Bursting with impatience, they cast pene-trating, lead-grey glances, all of the same caliber, into every visible room in the castle, making things hot, cold, and uncomfortable for the cas-tellans.

One of the reconnaissance cars—I think it was the *Ostmark*—was just rolling back toward us from Rittergasse when Jan, my uncle, who for some time now had seemed totally inanimate, moved his right leg toward the embrasure he was supposed to be shooting through and raised it high in the air, hoping no doubt that somebody would see it and take a shot at it, or that a stray bullet would take pity on him and graze his calf or heel, inflicting the blessed injury that permits a soldier to limp —and what a limp!—off the battlefield.

A difficult position to hold for very long. From time to time Jan was obliged to relax. But then he changed his position. By lying on his back and propping up his leg with both hands, he was able to expose his calf and heel for a very considerable period and vastly improve their prospects of being hit by an aimed or errant bullet.

Great as my sympathy for Jan was and still is, I could easily understand the temper it put Kobyella in to see Postal Secretary Bronski, his superior, in this desperate, not to say ludicrous posture. The janitor leapt to his feet and with a second leap was standing over us. He seized Jan's jacket and Jan with it, lifted the bundle and dashed it down, up down, up down; dropping it for good, he hauled off with his left, hauled off with his right; then, still not satisfied, his two hands met in mid-air and clenched into one great fist that was going to crush my presumptive father when—there came a whirring as of angels' wings, a singing as of the ether singing over the radio. It didn't hit Bronski, no, it hit Kobyella, Lord, what a sense of humor that projectile had: bricks laughed themselves into splinters and splinters into dust, plaster turned to flour, wood found its ax, the whole silly nursery hopped on one foot, Käthe Kruse dolls burst open, the rocking horse ran away—how happy it would have been to have a rider to throw off!—Polish Uhlans occupied all four corners of the room at once, and at last, the toy rack toppled over: the chimes rang in Easter, the accordion screamed, the trumpet blew something or other, the whole orchestra sounded the keynote at once, as though tuning up: screaming, bursting, whinnying, ringing, scraping, chirping, high and shrill but digging down into cavernous foundations. I myself, as befits a three-year-old child, was in the safest spot, directly under the window, as the shell struck, and into my lap, as it were, fell the drum. No holes at all and hardly a crack in the lacquer. Oskar's new drum.

When I looked up from my new possession, I saw that I would have to help my uncle, who was unable by his own resources to get out from under the heavy janitor. At first I supposed that Jan too had been hit, for he was whimpering very realistically. Finally, when we had rolled Kobyella, who was groaning just as realistically, to one side, Jan's injuries proved to be negligible. His right cheek and the back of one hand had been scratched by broken glass, and that was all. A quick comparison showed me that my presumptive father's blood was lighter in color than the janitor's, which was seeping, dark and sticky, through the tops of his trouser legs.

I wondered whether it was Kobyella or the explosion that had ripped and twisted Jan's pretty gray jacket. It hung down in tatters from his shoulders, the lining had come loose, the buttons had fled, the seams had split, and the pockets had been turned inside out.

Don't be too hard on my poor Jan Bronski, who insisted on scraping his belongings together before dragging Kobyella out of the nursery with my help. He found his comb, the photographs of his loved ones—including one of my poor mama; his purse hadn't even come open. He had a hard and not undangerous time of it, for the bulwark of sandbags had been partly swept away, collecting the skat cards that had been scattered all over the room: he wanted all thirty-two of them, and he was downright unhappy when he couldn't find the thirty-second. When Oskar found it between two devastated doll's houses, and handed it to him, Jan smiled, even though it was the seven of spades.

We dragged Kobyella out of the nursery. When we finally had him in the corridor, the janitor found the strength to utter a few words that Jan Bronski was able to make out: "Is it all there?" he asked. Jan reached into Kobyella's trousers, between his old man's legs, found a handful and nodded.

We were all happy: Kobyella had kept his pride, Jan Bronski had found all his skat cards including the seven of spades, and Oskar had a new drum which beat against his knee at every step while Jan and a man whom Jan called Victor carried the janitor, weak from loss of blood, downstairs to the storeroom for undeliverable mail.

The Card House

Though losing more and more blood, the janitor was becoming steadily heavier. Victor Weluhn helped us to carry him. Victor was very near-sighted, but at the time he still had his glasses and was able to negotiate the stone steps without stumbling. Victor's occupation, strange as it may seem for one so nearsighted, was delivering funds sent by money order. Nowadays, as often as Victor's name comes up, I refer to him as poor Victor. Just as my mama became my poor mama as a result of a family excursion to the harbor breakwater, Victor, who carried money for the post office, was transformed into poor Victor by the loss of his glasses, though other considerations played a part.

"Have you ever run into poor Victor?" I ask my friend Vittlar on visiting days. But since that streetcar ride from Flingern to Gerresheim —I shall speak of it later on—Victor Weluhn has been lost to us. It can only be hoped that his persecutors have also been unable to locate him, that he has found his glasses or another suitable pair, and if it isn't too much to ask, that he is carrying money again, if not for the Polish Post Office—that cannot be—then for the Post Office of the Federal Republic, and that, nearsighted but bespectacled, he is once more delivering happiness in the form of multicolored banknotes and hard coins.

"Isn't it awful," said Jan, supporting Kobyella on one side and panting under the weight.

"And the Lord knows how it will end," said Victor, who was holding up the other side, "if the English and the French don't come."

"Oh, they'll come all right. Only yesterday Rydz-Smigly said on the radio: 'We have their pledge,' he said. 'If it comes to war, all France will rise as one man.' " Jan had difficulty in maintaining his assurance until the end of the sentence, for though the sight of his own blood on the back of his hand cast no doubt on the Franco-Polish treaty of mutual defense, it did lead him to fear that he might bleed to death before all France should rise as one man and, faithful to its pledge, overrun the Siegfried Line.

"They must be on their way right now. And this very minute the British fleet must be plowing through the Baltic." Victor Weluhn loved strong, resounding locutions. He paused on the stairs, his right hand was immobilized by the wounded janitor, but he flung its left counterpart aloft to welcome the saviors with all five fingers: "Come, proud Britons!"

While the two of them, slowly, earnestly weighing the relations between Poland and her Western allies, conveyed Kobyella to the emergency hospital, Oskar's thoughts leafed through Gretchen Scheffler's books, looking for relevant passages. Keyser's *History of the City of Danzig*: "During the war of 1870 between Germany and France, on the afternoon of August 21, 1870, four French warships entered Danzig Bay, cruised in the roadstead and were already directing their guns at the harbor and city. The following night, however, the screw corvette *Nymph*, commanded by Corvette Captain Weickhmann, obliged the formation to withdraw."

Shortly before we reached the storeroom for undeliverable mail on the second floor, I formed the opinion, which was later to be confirmed, that in this desperate hour for the Polish Post Office and the whole of Poland, the Home Fleet was lying, nicely sheltered, in some firth in northern Scotland, and, as for the large French Army, that it was still at luncheon, confident that a few reconnaissance patrols in the vicinity of the Maginot Line had squared it with Poland and the Franco-Polish treaty of mutual defense.

Outside the storeroom and emergency hospital, we ran into Dr. Michon; he still had on his steel helmet and his silk handkerchief still peered from his breast pocket; he was talking with one Konrad, the liaison officer sent from Warsaw. Seized with fifty-seven varieties of terror, Jan made it plain that he was seriously wounded. Victor Weluhn, who was unhurt and as long as he had his glasses could reasonably be expected to do his bit with a rifle, was sent down to the main hall. Jan and I were admitted to the windowless room, scantily lit by tallow candles, the municipal power plant having declared and implemented its unwillingness to supply the Polish Post Office with current.

Dr. Michon wasn't exactly taken in by Jan's wounds but on the other hand he had little faith in my uncle's military prowess. Converting the postal secretary and former rifleman into a medic, he commissioned him to care for the wounded and also—at this point the postmaster and commander honored me with a brief and, it seemed to me, despairing pat on the head—to keep an eye on me, lest the poor child get mixed up in the fighting.

The field howitzer scored a hit down below. We took quite a shaking. Michon in his helmet, Konrad, the liaison officer from Warsaw, and Weluhn dashed down to their battle stations. Jan and I found ourselves with seven or eight casualties in a sealed-off room where the sounds of battle were muffled. The candles hardly flickered when the howitzer struck home. It was quiet in spite, or perhaps because, of the moaning around us. With awkward haste Jan wrapped some strips of bed sheet around Kobyella's thighs; then he prepared to treat his own wounds. But his cheek and the back of his hand had stopped bleeding. His cuts had nothing to say for themselves, yet they must have hurt and the pain fed his terror, which had no outlet in the low-ceilinged, stuffy room. Frantically he looked through his pockets and found the complete deck of cards. From then till the bitter end we played skat.

Thirty-two cards were shuffled, cut, dealt, and played. Since all the mail baskets were occupied by wounded men, we sat Kobyella down against a basket. When he kept threatening to keel over, we tied him into position with a pair of suspenders taken from one of the wounded men. We made him sit up straight, we forbade him to drop his cards, for we needed Kobyella. What could we have done without a third? Those fellows in the mail baskets could hardly tell black from red; they had lost all desire to play skat. Actually Kobyella didn't much feel like it either. He would have liked to lie down. Just let things take their course, that was all Kobyella wanted. He just wanted to look on, his janitor's hands inactive for once in his life, to look on through lowered lashless eyelids as the demolition work was completed. But we wouldn't stand for such fatalism, we tied him fast and forced him to play the third hand, while Oskar played the second—and no one was the least bit surprised that Tom Thumb could play skat.

When for the first time I lent my voice to adult speech and bid "Eighteen," Jan, it is true, emerged from his cards, gave me a brief and inconceivably blue look, and nodded. "Twenty?" I asked him. And Jan without hesitation: "Yes, yes." And I: "Two? Three? Twenty-four?" No, Jan couldn't go along. "Pass." And Kobyella? Despite the braces, he was sagging again. But we pulled him up and waited for the noise of a shell that had struck somewhere far from our gaming room to die down. Then Jan hissed into the erupting silence: "Twenty-four, Kobyella. Didn't you hear the boy's bid?"

Who knows from what cavernous depths the janitor awoke. Ever so slowly he jacked up his eyelids. Finally his watery gaze took in the ten cards which Jan had pressed discreetly, conscientiously refraining from looking at them, into his hand.

"Pass," said Kobyella, or rather we read it from his lips, which were too parched for speech.

I played a club single. On the first tricks Jan, who was playing contra, had to roar at Kobyella and poke him good-naturedly in the ribs, before he would pull himself together and remember to play. I started by drawing off all their trumps. I sacrificed the king of clubs, which Jan took with the jack of spades, but having no diamonds, I recovered the lead by trumping Jan's ace of diamonds and drew his ten of hearts with my jack. Kobyella discarded the nine of diamonds, and then I had a sure thing with my chain of hearts. One-play-two-contra-three-schneider-four-times-clubs-is-forty-eight-or twelve-pfennigs. It wasn't until the next hand, when I attempted a more than risky grand without two that things began to get exciting. Kobyella, who had had both jacks but only bid up to thirty-three, took my jack of diamonds with the jack of clubs. Then, as though revived by the trick he had taken, he followed up with the ace of diamonds and I had to follow suit. Jan threw in the ten, Kobyella took the trick and played the king, I should have taken but didn't, instead I discarded the eight of clubs, Jan threw in what he could, he even led once with the ten of spades, I bettered it and I'm damned if Kobyella didn't top the pile with the jack of spades, I'd forgotten that fellow or rather thought Jan had it, but no, Kobyella had it. Naturally he led another spade, I had to discard, Jan played something or other, the rest of the tricks were mine but it was too late: grand-without-two-play-three-makes-sixty-hundred-and-twenty-for-the-loser-makes-thirty-pfennigs. Jan loaned me two gulden in change, and I paid up, but despite the hand he had won, Kobyella had collapsed again, he didn't take his winnings and even the first antitank shell bursting on the stairs didn't mean a thing to the poor janitor, though it was his staircase that he had cleaned and polished relentlessly for years.

Fear regained possession of Jan when the door to our mailroom rattled and the flames of our tallow candles didn't know what had come over them or in which direction to lie down. Then it grew relatively still in the stairwell and the next antitank shell burst far off against the façade. But even so, Jan Bronski shuffled with an insane frenzy and misdealt twice, but I let it pass. As long as there was shooting to be heard, Jan was too overwrought to hear anything I could say, he neglected to follow suit, even forgot to discard the skat, and sometimes sat motionless, his sensory ear attuned to the outer world while we waited impatiently for him to get on with the game. Yet, while Jan's play became more and more distraught, Kobyella kept his mind pretty well on the game though from time to time he needed a poke in the ribs to keep him from sagging.

185

His playing wasn't nearly as bad as the state he seemed to be in. He only collapsed after he had won a hand or had spoiled a grand for Jan or me. He didn't care one bit whether he had won or lost. It was only the game itself that could hold his attention. As we counted up the score, he would sag on the borrowed suspenders, giving no sign of life except for the terrifying spasms of his Adam's apple.

This card game was a great strain on Oskar too. Not that the sounds connected with the siege and defense of the post office bothered him particularly. For me the nerve-racking part of it was that for the first time I had suddenly dropped all disguises—though not, I resolved, for long. Up until then I had been my true unvarnished self only for Master Bebra and his somnambulistic Lady Roswitha. And now I had laid myself bare not only to my uncle and presumptive father but also to an invalid janitor (neither of whom, to be sure, looked much like a future witness) as the fifteen-year-old inscribed in my birth certificate, who, despite his diminutive stature, played a rather foolhardy but not unskillful hand of skat. My will was up to it, but the exertion was too much for my gnomelike proportions. After barely an hour of skat-playing, my limbs and head were aching abominably.

Oskar felt inclined to give up; it would not have been hard for him slip away between two of the shell hits which were shaking the building in quick succession, if a feeling of responsibility, such as he had never before experienced, had not bidden him hold on and counter his presumptive father's terror by the one effective means: skat-playing.

And so we played and refused to let Kobyella die. He just couldn't get around to it, for I took good care that the cards should be in movement at all times. When, after an explosion on the stairs, the candles toppled over and the flames vanished, it was I who had the presence of mind to do the obvious, to take a match from Jan's pocket, and Jan's gold-tipped cigarettes too while I was at it; it was I who restored light to the world, lit a comforting Regatta for Jan, and pierced the night with flame upon flame before Kobyella could take advantage of the darkness to make his getaway.

Oskar stuck two candles on his new drum and set down the cigarettes within reach. He wanted none for himself, but from time to time he would pass Jan a cigarette and put one between Kobyella's distorted lips. That helped; the tobacco appeased and consoled, though it could not prevent Jan Bronski from losing game after game. Jan perspired and, as he had always done when giving his whole heart to the game, tickled his upper lip with the tip of his tongue. He grew so excited that in his enthusiasm he began to call me Alfred or Matzerath and to take Kobyella for my poor mama. When out in the corridor someone screamed: "They've got Konrad!" he looked at me reproachfully and said: "For goodness' sake, Alfred, turn off the radio. A man can't hear himself think in here."

Jan became really irritated when the door was torn open and the lifeless Konrad was dragged in.

"Close that door. You're making a draft!" he protested. There was indeed a draft. The candles flickered alarmingly and came to their senses only when, after dumping Konrad in a corner, the men had closed the door behind them. A strange threesome we made. Striking us from below, the candlelight gave us the look of all-powerful wizards. Kobyella bid his hearts without two; twenty-seven, thirty, he said, or rather gurgled. His eyes had a way of rolling out of sight and there was something in his right shoulder that wanted to come out, that quivered and jumped like mad. It finally stopped, but Kobyella sagged face foremost, setting the mail basket which he was tied to rolling with the dead suspenderless man on top of it. With one blow into which he put all his strength Jan brought Kobyella and the laundry basket to a standstill, whereupon Kobyella, once more prevented from sneaking out on us, finally piped "Hearts." To which Jan hissed "Contra" and Kobyella "Double contra." At this moment it came to Oskar that the defense of the Polish Post Office had been successful, that the assailants, having scarcely begun the war, had already lost it, even if they succeeded in occupying Alaska and Tibet, the Easter Islands and Jerusalem.

The only bad part of it was that Jan was unable to play out his beautiful, sure-thing grand hand with four and a declaration of schneider schwarz.

He led clubs; now he was calling me Agnes while Kobyella had become his rival Matzerath. With an air of false innocence he played the jack of diamonds—I was much happier to be my poor mama for him than to be Matzerath—then the jack of hearts—it didn't appeal to me one bit to be mistaken for Matzerath. Jan waited impatiently for Matzerath, who in reality was a crippled janitor named Kobyella, to play; that took time, but then Jan slammed down the ace of hearts and was absolutely unwilling and unable to understand, the truth is he had never fully understood, he had never been anything but a blue-eyed boy, smelling of cologne and incapable of understanding certain things, and so he simply could not understand why Kobyella suddenly dropped all his cards, tugged at the laundry basket with the letters in it and the dead man on top of the letters, until first the dead man, then a layer of letters, and finally the whole excellently plaited basket toppled over, sending us a wave of letters as though we were the addressees, as though the thing for us to do now was to put aside our playing cards and take to reading our correspondence or collecting stamps. But Jan didn't feel like reading and he didn't feel like collecting, he had collected too much as a child, he wanted to play, he wanted to play out his grand hand to the end, he wanted to win, Jan did, to triumph. He lifted Kobyella up, set the basket back on its wheels, but let the dead man lie and also neglected to put the letters back in the basket. Anyone could see that the basket was too light, yet Jan showed the utmost astonishment when Kobyella, dangling from the light, unstable basket, just wouldn't sit still but sagged lower and lower. Finally Jan shouted at him: "Alfred, I beg of you, don't be a spoilsport. Just this one little game and then we'll go home. Alfred, will you listen to me!"

Oskar arose wearily, fought down the increasing pains in his limbs and head, laid his wiry little drummer's hands on Jan Bronski's shoulders, and forced himself to speak, gently but with authority: "Leave him be, Papa. He can't play any more. He's dead. We can play sixty-six if you like."

Jan, whom I had just addressed as my father, released the janitor's mortal envelope, gave me an overflowing blue stare, and wept nono-nono . . . I patted him, but still he said no. I kissed him meaningly, but still he could think of nothing but his interrupted grand.

"I would have won it, Agnes. It was a sure thing." So he lamented to me in my poor mama's stead, and I—his son—threw myself into the role, yes, he was right, I said, I swore that he would have won, that to all intents and purposes he actually had won, that he simply must believe what his Agnes was telling him. But Jan wouldn't believe; he believed neither me nor my mama. For a time his weeping was loud and articulate; then his plaint subsided into an unmodulated blubbering, and he began to dig skat cards from beneath the cooling Mount Kobyella; some he scraped from between his legs, and the avalanche of mail yielded a few. Jan would not rest before he had recovered all thirty-two. One by one, he cleaned them up, wiping away the sticky blood. When he had done, he shuffled and prepared to deal. Only then did his well-shaped forehead—it would have been unjust to call it low, though it was rather too smooth, rather too impenetrable—admit the thought that there was no third skat hand left in this world.

It grew very still in the storeroom for undeliverable mail. Outside, as well, a protracted minute of silence was dedicated to the memory of the world's last skat hand. To Oskar it seemed, though, that the door was slowly opening. Looking over his shoulder, expecting heaven knows what supernatural apparition, he saw Victor Weluhn's strangely blind empty face. "I've lost my glasses, Jan. Are you still there? We'd better run for it. The French aren't coming or, if they are, they'll be too late. Come with me, Jan. Lead me, I've lost my glasses."

Maybe Victor thought he had got into the wrong room. For when he received no answer and no guiding arm was held out to him, he withdrew his unspectacled face and closed the door. I could still hear Victor's first few steps as, groping his way through the fog, he embarked on his flight.

Heaven knows what comical incident may have transpired in Jan's little head to make him start laughing, first softly and plaintively but then loudly and boisterously, making his fresh, pink little tongue quiver like a bell clapper. He tossed the cards into the air, caught them, and finally, when a Sunday quietness descended on the room with its silent men and silent letters, began, with wary measured movements and bated breath, to build an ever so fragile house of cards. The seven of spades and the queen of clubs provided the foundation. Over them spanned the king of diamonds. The nine of hearts and the ace of spades, spanned by the eight of clubs, became a second foundation adjacent to the first. He then proceeded to join the two with tens and jacks set upright on their edges, using queens and aces as crossbeams, so that one part of the edifice supported another. Then he decided to set a third story upon the second, and did so with the spellbinding hands that my mother must have known in connection with other rituals. And when he leaned the queen of hearts against the king with the red heart, the edifice did not collapse; no, airily it stood, breathing softly, delicately, in that room where the dead breathed no more and the living held their breath. That house of cards made it possible for us to sit back with folded hands, and even the skeptical Oskar, who was quite familiar with the rules of statics governing the construction of card houses, was enabled to forget the acrid smoke and stench that crept, in wisps and coils, through the cracks in the door, making it seem as though the little room with the card house in it were right next door and wall to wall with hell.

They had brought in flame throwers; fearing to make a frontal assault, they had decided to smoke out the last defenders. The operation had been so successful that Dr. Michon resolved to surrender the post office. Removing his helmet, he had picked up a bed sheet and waved it; and when that didn't satisfy him, he had pulled out his silk handkerchief with his other hand and waved that too.

It was some thirty scorched, half-blinded men, arms upraised and hands folded behind their necks, who left the building through the left-hand side door and lined up against the wall of the courtyard where they waited for the slowly advancing Home Guards. Later the story went round that in the brief interval while the Home Guards were coming up, three or four had got away: through the post office garage and the adjoining police garage they had made their way to an evacuated and hence unoccupied house on the Rähm, where they had found clothes, complete with Party insignia. Having washed and dressed, they had vanished singly into thin air. One of them, still according to the story, had gone to an optician's in the Altstädtischer Graben, had himself fitted out with a pair of glasses, his own having been lost in the battle of the post office. Freshly bespectacled, Victor Weluhn—for it was he—allegedly went so far as to have

189

a beer on the Holzmarkt, and then another, for the flame throwers had made him thirsty. Then with his new glasses, which dispersed the environing mists up to a certain point, but not nearly as well as his old ones had done, had started on the flight that continues—such is the doggedness of his pursuers!—to this day.

The others, however—as I have said, there were some thirty of them who couldn't make up their minds to run for it—were standing against the wall across from the side entrance when Jan leaned the queen of hearts against the king of hearts and, thoroughly blissful, took his hands away.

What more shall I say? They found us. They flung the door open, shouting "Come out!" stirred up a wind, and the card house collapsed. They had no feeling for this kind of architecture. Their medium was concrete. They built for eternity. They paid no attention whatever to Postal Secretary Bronski's look of indignation, of bitter injury. They didn't see that before coming out Jan reached into the pile of cards and picked up something, or that I, Oskar, wiped the candle ends from my newly acquired drum, took the drum but spurned the candle ends, for light was no problem with all those flashlights shining in our eyes. They didn't even notice that their flashlights blinded us and made it hard for us to find the door. From behind flashlights and rifles, they shouted: "Come out of there," and they were still shouting "Come out" after Jan and I had reached the corridor. These "come outs" were directed at Kobyella, at Konrad from Warsaw, at Bobek and little Wischnewski, who in his lifetime had kept the telegraph window. The invaders were alarmed at these men's unwillingness to obey. I gave a loud laugh every time the Home Guards shouted "Come out" and after a while they saw they were making fools of themselves, stopped shouting, and said, "Oh!" Then they led us to the thirty in the courtyard with arms upraised and hands folded behind their necks, who were thirsty and having their pictures taken for the newsreels.

The camera had been mounted on top of an automobile. As we were led out through the side door, the photographers swung it around at us and shot the short strip that was later shown in all the movie houses.

I was separated from the thirty defenders by the wall. At this point Oskar remembered his gnomelike stature, he remembered that a three-year-old is not responsible for his comings and goings. Again he felt those disagreeable pains in his head and limbs; he sank to the ground with his drum, began to thrash and flail, and ended up throwing a fit that was half real and half put on, but even during the fit he hung on to his drum. They picked him up and handed him into an official car belonging to the SS Home Guard. As the car drove off, taking him to the City Hospital, Oskar could see Jan, poor Jan, smiling stupidly and blissfully into the air. In his upraised hands he held a few skat cards and with one hand—holding the queen of hearts, I think—he waved to Oskar, his departing son.

He Lies in Saspe

I have just reread the last paragaph. I am not too well satisfied, but Oskar's pen ought to be, for writing tersely and succinctly, it has managed, as terse, succinct accounts so often do, to exaggerate and mislead, if not to lie.

Wishing to stick to the truth, I shall try to circumvent Oskar's pen and make a few corrections: in the first place, Jan's last hand, which he was unhappily prevented from playing out and winning, was not a grand hand, but a diamond hand without two; in the second place, Oskar, as he left the storeroom, picked up not only his new drum but also the old broken one, which had fallen out of the laundry basket with the dead suspenderless man and the letters. Furthermore, there is a little omission that needs filling in: No sooner had Jan and I left the storeroom for undeliverable mail at the behest of the Home Guards with their "Come outs," their flashlights, and their rifles, than Oskar, concerned for his comfort and safety, made up to two Home Guards who struck him as good-natured, uncle-like souls, put on an imitation of pathetic sniveling, and pointed to Jan, his father, with accusing gestures which transformed the poor man into a villain who had dragged off an innocent child to the Polish Post Office to use him, with typically Polish inhumanity, as a buffer for enemy bullets.

Oskar counted on certain benefits for both his drums, and his expectations were not disappointed: the Home Guards kicked Jan in the small of the back and battered him with their rifle stocks, but left me both drums, and one middle-aged Home Guard with the careworn creases of a paterfamilias alongside of his nose and mouth stroked my cheeks, while another, tow-headed fellow, who kept laughing and in laughing screwed up his eyes so you couldn't see them, picked me up in his arms, which was distasteful and embarrassing to Oskar.

Even today, if fills me with shame to think, as I sometimes do, of this disgusting behavior of mine, but I always comfort myself with the thought that Jan didn't notice, for he was still preoccupied with his cards and remained so to the end, that nothing, neither the funniest nor the most fiendish inspiration of the Home Guards, could ever again lure his attention away from those cards. Already Jan had gone off to the eternal realm of card houses and castles in Spain, where men believe in happiness, whereas the Home Guards and I—for at this moment Oskar counted himself among the Home Guards—stood amid brick walls, in stone corridors, beneath ceilings with plaster cornices, all so intricately interlocked with walls and partitions that the worst was to be feared for the day when, in response to one set of circumstances or another, all this patchwork we call architecture would lose its cohesion.

Of course this belated perception cannot justify me, especially when it is remembered that I have never been able to look at a building under construction without fancying this same building in process of being torn down and that I have always regarded card houses as the only dwellings worthy of humankind. And there is still another incriminating factor. That afternoon I felt absolutely certain that Jan Bronski was no mere uncle or presumptive father, but my real father. Which put him ahead of Matzerath then and for all time: for Matzerath was either my father or nothing at all.

September 1, 1939—I assume that you too, on that ill-starred afternoon, recognized Bronski, the blissful builder of card houses, as my father—that date marks the inception of my second great burden of guilt.

Even when I feel most sorry for myself, I cannot deny it: It was my drum, no, it was I myself, Oskar the drummer, who dispatched first my poor mama, then Jan Bronski, my uncle and father, to their graves.

But on days when an importunate feeling of guilt, which nothing can dispel, sits on the very pillows of my hospital bed, I tend, like everyone else, to make allowances for my ignorance—the ignorance which came into style in those years and which even today quite a few of our citizens wear like a jaunty and oh, so becoming little hat.

Oskar, the sly ignoramus, an innocent victim of Polish barbarism, was taken to the City Hospital with brain fever. Matzerath was notified. He had reported my disappearance the night before, although his ownership of me had never been proved.

As for the thirty men with upraised arms and hands folded behind their necks, they—and Jan—after having their pictures taken for the newsreels, were taken first to the evacuated Victoria School, then to Schiesstange Prison. Finally, early in October, they were entrusted to the porous sand behind the wall of the run-down, abandoned old cemetery in Saspe.

How did Oskar come to know all this? I heard it from Leo Schugger. For of course there was never any official announcement to tell us against what wall the thirty-one men were shot and what sand was shoveled over them.

Hedwig Bronski first received a notice to vacate the flat in Ringstrasse, which was taken over by the family of a high-ranking officer in the Luftwaffe. While she was packing with Stephan's help and preparing to move to Ramkau—where she owned a house and a few acres of forest and farmland—she received the communication which made her officially a widow. She gazed at it out of eyes which mirrored but did not penetrate the sorrows of the world, and it was only very slowly, with the help of her son Stephan, that she managed to distil the sense of it.

Here is the communication:

So you see, not a word about Saspe. Out of solicitude for the men's relatives, who would have been crushed by the expense of caring for so large and flower-consuming a mass grave, the authorities assumed full responsibility for maintenance and perhaps even for transplantation. They had the sandy soil leveled and the cartridge cases removed, except for one—one is always overlooked—because cartridge cases are out of place in any respectable cemetery, even an abandoned one.

But this one cartridge case, which is always left behind, the one that concerns us here, was found by Leo Schugger, from whom no burial, however discreet, could be kept secret. He, who knew me from my poor mama's funeral and from that of my scar-covered friend Herbert Truczinski, who assuredly knew where they had buried Sigismund Markus —though I never asked him about it—was delighted, almost beside himself with joy, when late in November, just after I was discharged from the hospital, he found an opportunity to hand me the telltale cartridge case.

But before I guide you in the wake of Leo Schugger to Saspe Cemetery with that slightly oxidized cartridge case, which perhaps had harbored the lead kernel destined for Jan, I must ask you to compare two hospital beds, the one I occupied in the children's section of the Danzig City Hospital, and the one I am lying in now. Both are metal, both are painted with white enamel, yet there is a difference. The bed in the children's section was shorter but higher, if you apply a yardstick to the bars. Although my preference goes to the shorter but higher cage of 1939, I have found peace of mind in my present makeshift bed, intended for grownups, and learned not to be too demanding. Months ago I put in a petition for a higher bed, though I am perfectly satisfied with the metal and the white enamel. But let the management grant my petition or reject it; I await the result with equanimity.

Today I am almost defenseless against my visitors; then, on visiting days in the children's section, a tall fence separated me from Visitor Matzerath, from Visitors Greff (Mr. and Mrs.) and Scheffler (Mr. and Mrs.). And toward the end of my stay at the hospital, the bars of my fence divided the mountain-of-four-skirts named after my grandmother Anna Koljaiczek, into worried, heavily breathing compartments. She came, sighed, raised her great multifarious hands, disclosing her cracked pink palms, then let hands and palms sink in despair. So violent was her despair that they slapped against her thighs, and I can hear that slapping to this day, though I can give only a rough imitation of it on my drum.

On the very first visit she brought along her brother Vincent Bronski, who clutched the bars of my bed and spoke or sang softly but incisively and at great length about the Virgin Mary, Queen of Poland. Oskar was glad when there was a nurse nearby. For those two were my accusers, they turned their unclouded Bronski eyes on me and, quite oblivious of the time I was having with this brain fever I had acquired while playing skat in the Polish Post Office, expected me to comfort them with a kind word, to reassure them about Jan's last hours, spent between terror and card houses. They wanted a confession from me that would put Jan in the clear; as though I had it in my power to clear him, as though my testimony carried any weight.

Supposing I had sent an affidavit to the court-martial of the Eberhardt Group. What would I have said? I, Oskar Matzerath, avow and declare that on the evening of August 31 I waited outside Jan Bronski's home for him to come home and lured him, on the ground that my drum needed repairing, back to the Polish Post Office, which Jan Bronski had left because he did not wish to defend it.

Oskar made no such confession; he did nothing to exculpate his presumptive father. Every time he decided to speak, to tell the old people what had happened, he was seized with such convulsions that at the demand of the head nurse his visiting hours were curtailed and the visits of his grandmother Anna and his presumptive grandfather Vincent were forbidden.

The two old people, who had walked in from Bissau and brought me apples, left the children's ward with the wary, helpless gait of country folk in town. And with each receding step of my grandmother's four skirts and her brother's black Sunday suit, redolent of cow dung, my burden of guilt, my enormous burden of guilt increased.

So much happened at once. While Matzerath, the Greffs, the Schefflers crowded round my bed with fruit and cakes, while my grandmother and Uncle Vincent walked in from Bissau by way of Goldkrug and Brenntau because the railroad line from Karthaus to Langfuhr had not yet been cleared, while nurses, clad in anesthetic white, babbled hospital talk and substituted for angels in the children's ward, Poland was not yet lost, almost lost, and finally, at the end of those famous eighteen days, Poland was lost, although it was soon to turn out that Poland was not yet lost; just as today, despite the efforts of the Silesian and East Prussian patriotic societies, Poland is not yet lost.

O insane cavalry! Picking blueberries on horseback. Bearing lances with red and white pennants. Squadrons of melancholy, squadrons of tradition. Picture-book charges. Racing across the fields before Lodz and Kutno. At Modlin substituting for the fortress. Oh, so brilliantly galloping! Always waiting for the sunset. Both foreground and background must be right before the cavalry can attack, for battles were made to be picturesque and death to be painted, poised in mid-gallop, then falling, nibbling blueberries, the dog roses crackle and break, providing the itch without which the cavalry will not jump. There are the Uhlans, they've got the itch again, amid haystacks—another picture for you—wheeling their horses, they gather round a man, his name in Spain is Don Quixote, but here he is Pan Kichot, a pure-blooded Pole, a noble, mournful figure, who has taught his Uhlans to kiss ladies' hands on horseback, ah, with what aplomb they will kiss the hand of death, as though death were a lady; but first they gather, with the sunset behind them—for color and romance are their reserves—and ahead of them the German tanks, stallions from the studs of the Krupps von Bohlen und Halbach, no nobler steeds in all the world. But Pan Kichot, the eccentric knight in love with death, the talented, too talented knight, half-Spanish half-Polish, lowers his lance with the red-and-white pennant and calls on his men to kiss the lady's hand. The storks clatter white and red on the rooftops, and the sunset spits out pits like cherries, as he cries to his cavalry: "Ye noble Poles on horseback, these are no steel tanks, they are mere windmills or sheep, I summon you to kiss the lady's hand."

So rode the squadrons out against the gray steel foe, adding another dash of red to the sunset glow.

Oskar hopes to be forgiven for the poetic effects. He might have done better to give figures, to enumerate the casualties of the Polish cavalry, to commemorate the so-called Polish Campaign with dry but eloquent statistics. Or another solution might be to let the poem stand but append a footnote.

Up to September 20, I could hear, as I lay in my hospital bed, the roaring of the cannon firing from the heights of the Jeschkental and Oliva forests. Then the last nest of resistance on Hela Peninsula surrendered. The Free Hanseatic City of Danzig celebrated the Anschluss of its brick Gothic to the Greater German Reich and gazed jubilantly into the blue eyes (which had one thing in common with Jan Bronski's blue eyes, namely their success with women) of Adolf Hitler, the Führer and Chancellor, as he stood in his black Mercedes distibuting rectangular salutes.

In mid-October Oskar was discharged from the City Hospital. It was hard for me to take leave of the nurses. When one of them—her name was Berni or maybe Erni, I think—when Sister Erni or Berni gave me my two drums, the battered one that had made me guilty and the whole one that I had conquered during the battle of the Polish Post Office, it came to me that I hadn't thought of my drums for weeks, that there was something else in the world for me beside drums, to wit, nurses.

Matzerath held me by the hand as, still rather shaky on my three-year-old pins, I left the City Hospital with my instruments and my new self-knowledge, for the flat in Labesweg, there to face the tedious weekdays and still more tedious Sundays of the first war year.

One Tuesday late in November, I was allowed to go out for the first time after weeks of convalescence. As he was gloomily drumming through the streets, paying little attention to the cold rain, whom should Oskar run into on the corner of Max-Halbe-Platz and Brösener-Weg but Leo Schugger, the former seminarist.

We stood for some time exchanging embarrassed smiles, and it was not until Leo plucked a pair of kid gloves from the pockets of his morning coat and pulled the yellowish-white, skinlike coverings over his fingers and palms, that I realized whom I had met and what this encounter would bring me. Oskar was afraid.

For a while we examined the windows of Kaiser's grocery store, looked after a few streetcars of lines Number 5 and 9, which crossed on Max-Halbe-Platz, skirted the uniform houses on Brösener-Weg, revolved several times round an advertising pillar, studied a poster telling when and how to exchange Danzig guldens for reichsmarks, scratched a poster advertising Persil soap powder, and found a bit of red under the blue and white but let well enough alone. We were just starting back for Max-Halbe-Platz when suddenly Leo Schugger pushed Oskar with both hands into a doorway, reached under his coat-tails with the gloved fingers of his left hand, poked about in his pants pocket, sifted the contents, found something, studied it for a moment with his fingers, then, satisfied with what he had found, removed his closed fist from his pocket, and let his coat-tail fall back into place. Slowly he thrust forward the gloved fist, forward and still forward, pushing Oskar against the wall of the doorway; longer and longer grew his arm, but the wall did not recede. That arm, I was beginning to think, was going to jump out of its socket, pierce my chest, pass through it, and make off between my shoulder blades and the wall of this musty doorway. I was beginning to fear that Oskar would never see what Leo had in his fist, that the most he would ever learn in this doorway was the text of the house regulations, which were not very different from those in his own house in Labesweg. And then the five-fingered skin opened.

Pressing against one of the anchor buttons on my sailor coat, Leo's glove opened so fast that I could hear his finger joints crack. And there, on the stiff, shiny leather that protected the inside of his hand, lay the cartridge case.

When Leo closed his fist again, I was prepared to follow him. That little scrap of metal had spoken to me directly. We walked side by side down Brösener-Weg; this time no shopwindow, no advertising pillar detained us. We crossed Magdeburger-Strasse, left behind us the last two tall, boxlike buildings on Brösener-Weg, topped at night by warning lights for planes that were taking off or about to land, skirted the fence of the airfield for a time, but then moved over to the asphalt road, where the going was less wet, and followed the rails of the Number 5 streetcar line in the direction of Brösen.

We said not a word, but Leo still held the cartridge case in his glove. The weather was miserably cold and wet, but when I wavered and thought of going back, he opened his fist, made the little piece of metal hop up and down on his palm, and so lured me on, a hundred paces, then another hundred paces, and even resorted to music when, shortly before the city reservation in Saspe, I seriously decided to turn back. He turned on his heel, held the cartridge case with the open end up, pressed the hole like the mouthpiece of a flute against his protruding, slavering lower lip, and projected a new note, now shrill, now muffled as though by the fog, into the mounting whish of the rain. Oskar shivered. It wasn't just the music that made him shiver; the wretched weather, which seemed made to order for the occasion, had more than a little to do with it. So intense was my misery that I hardly bothered to hide my shivering.

What lured me to Brösen? Leo, the pied piper, of course, piping on his cartridge case. But there was more to it than that. From the roadstead and from Neufahrwasser, from behind the November fog, the sirens of the steamships and the hungry howling of a torpedo boat entering or leaving the harbor carried over to us past Schottland, Schellmühl, and Reichskolonie. In short, it was child's play for Leo, supported by foghorns, sirens, and a whistling cartridge case, to draw a frozen Oskar after him.

Not far from the wire fence which turns off in the direction of Pelonken and divides the airfield from the new drill ground, Leo Schugger stopped and stood for a time, his head cocked on one side, his saliva flowing over the cartridge case, observing my trembling little body. He sucked in the cartridge case, held it with his lower lip, then, following a sudden inspiration, flailed wildly with his arms, removed his long-tailed morning coat, and threw the heavy cloth, smelling of moist earth, over my head and shoulders.

We started off again. I don't know whether Oskar was any less cold. Sometimes Leo leapt five steps ahead and then stopped; as he stood there in his rumpled but terrifying white shirt, he seemed to have stepped directly out of a medieval dungeon, perhaps the Stockturm, to illustrate a disquisition on What the Lunatics Will Wear. Whenever Leo turned his eyes on Oskar staggering along in the long coat, he burst out laughing and flapped his wings like a raven. I must indeed have looked like a grotesque bird, a raven or crow, especially with those coat-tails dragging over the asphalt highway like a train or a huge mop and leaving a broad majestic track, which filled Oskar with pride whenever he looked back, and foreshadowed, if it did not synabolize the tragic fate, not yet fully implemented, that slumbered within him.

Even before leaving Max-Halbe-Platz, I had suspected that Leo had no intention of taking me to Brösen or Neufahrwasser. From the very start it was perfectly clear that our destination could only be the cemetery in Saspe, near which a modern rifle range had been laid out for the Security Police.

From September to April the cars serving the seaside resorts ran only every thirty-five minutes. As we were leaving the suburb of Langfuhr, a car without trailer approached from the direction of Brösen and passed us by. A moment later the car that had been waiting on the Magdeburger-Strasse siding came up behind us and passed by. It was not until we had almost reached the cemetery, near which there was a second siding, that another car moved up clanking and tinkling behind us, and soon its companion piece, which we had long seen waiting in the mist up ahead, its yellow light shining wet in the fog, started up and passed us by.

The flat morose face of the motorman was still sharp in Oskar's mind when Leo Schugger led him off the asphalt road. Through loose sand not very different from that of the dunes by the beach. The cemetery was square with a wall running round it. We went in on the south side, through a little gate that was covered with ornamental rust and only supposed to be locked. Most of the tombstones were of black Swedish granite or diorite, rough hewn on the back and sides and polished in front. Some leaned perilously, others had already toppled. Unfortunately Leo left me no time to look at them more closely. The place was poor in trees; five or six gnarled and moth-eaten scrub pines, that was all. Mama in her lifetime had admired this tumble-down graveyard; as she often said it was her favorite among last resting places. And now she lay in Brenntau. There the soil was richer, elms and maples grew.

By way of an open gate that had lost its grating, Leo led me out of the cemetery through the northern wall, before I could attune my thoughts to its romantic decay. Close behind the wall the soil was flat and sandy. Amid the steaming fog, broom, scrub pine, and dog rose stretched out toward the coast. When I looked back toward the cemetery, it struck me at once that a piece of the northern wall had been freshly whitewashed.

Close to this stretch of wall, which gave the impression of being new, as painfully white as Leo's rumpled shirt, Leo became very active. He took great long strides which he appeared to count; at all events, he counted aloud and, as Oskar believes to this day, in Latin. Whatever this litany was, he chanted it as he had no doubt learned to do at the seminary. Leo marked a spot some ten yards from the wall and also set down a piece of wood not far from the whitewashed portion, where, it seemed pretty obvious, the wall had been mended. All this he did with his left hand, for in his right hand he held the cartridge case. Finally, after interminable searching and measuring, he bent down near the piece of wood and there deposited the hollow metallic cylinder, slightly tapered at the front end, which had lodged a lead kernel until someone with a curved forefinger had exerted just enough pressure to evict the lead projectile and start it on its death-dealing change of habitat.

We stood and stood. The spittle flowed from Leo Schugger's mouth and hung down in threads. Wringing his gloves, he chanted for a time in Latin, but stopped after a while as there was no one present who knew the responses. From time to time he turned about and cast a peevish, impatient look over the wall toward the highway, especially when the streetcars, empty for the most part, stopped at the switch and clanged their bells as they passed one another by and moved off in opposite directions. Leo must have been waiting for mourners. But neither on foot nor by car did anyone arrive to whom he could extend a glove in condolence.

Once some planes roared over us, preparing to land. We did not look up, we submitted to the noise without bothering to ascertain that three planes of the Ju-52 type, with blinking lights on their wing tips, were preparing to land.

Shortly after the motors had left us—the stillness was as painful as the wall facing us was white—Leo Schugger reached into his shirt and pulled something out. A moment later he was standing beside me. Tearing his crow costume from Oskar's shoulders, he darted off coastward, into the broom, dog rose, and scrub pine, and in departing dropped something with a calculated gesture suggesting that it was meant to be found.

Only when Leo had vanished for good—for a time he could be seen moving about in the foreground like a spook, until at last he was swallowed up by low-lying pools of milky mist—only when I was all alone with the rain, did I reach out for the object that lay in the sand: it was a skat card, the seven of spades.

A few days after this meeting at Saspe Cemetery, Oskar met his grandmother Anna Koljaiczek at the weekly market in Langfuhr. Now that there was no more borderline at Bissau, she was able once again to bring her eggs, butter, cabbages, and winter apples to market. The people bought plentifully, they had begun to lay in stocks, for food rationing was in the offing. Just as Oskar caught sight of his grandmother sitting behind her wares, he felt the skat card on his bare skin, beneath his coat, sweater, and undershirt. At first, while riding back from Saspe to Max-Halbe-Platz, after a streetcar conductor had invited me to come along free of charge, I had meant to tear up that seven of spades. But Oskar did not tear it up. He gave it to his grandmother. She seemed to take fright behind her cabbages when she saw him. Maybe it passed through her mind that Oskar's presence could bode no good. But then she motioned the three-year-old urchin, half-hiding behind some baskets of fish, to come over. Oskar took his time; first he examined a live codfish nearly a yard long, lying in a bed of moist seaweed, then watched some crabs crawling about in a basket; finally, himself adopting the gait of a crab, he approached his grandmother's stand with the back of his sailor coat and, turning to show her his gold anchor buttons, jostled one of the sawhorses under her display and started the apples rolling.

Schwerdtfeger came over with his hot bricks wrapped in newspaper, shoved them under my grandmother's skirts, removed the cold bricks with his rake as he had done ever since I could remember, made a mark on the slate that hung from his neck, and proceeded to the next stand while my grandmother handed me a shining apple.

What could Oskar give her if she gave him an apple? He gave her first the skat card and then the cartridge case, for he hadn't abandoned that in Saspe either. For quite some time Anna Koljaiczek stared uncomprehending at these two so disparate objects. Then Oskar's mouth approached her aged cartilaginous ear beneath her kerchief and, throwing caution to the winds, I whispered, thinking of Jan's pink, small, but fleshy ear with the long, well-shaped lobes. "He's lying in Saspe," Oskar whispered and ran off, upsetting a basket of cabbages.

Maria

While history, blaring special communiqués at the top of its lungs, sped like a well-greased amphibious vehicle over the roads and waterways of Europe and through the air as well, conquering everything in its path, my own affairs, which were restricted to the belaboring of lacquered toy drums, were in a bad way. While the history-makers were throwing expensive metal out the window with both hands, I, once more, was running out of drums. Yes, yes, Oskar had managed to save a new instrument with scarcely a scratch on it from the Polish Post Office, so lending some significance to the defense of said post office, but what could Naczalnik Junior's drum mean to me, Oskar, who in my least troubled days had taken barely eight weeks to transform a drum into scrap metal?

Distressed over the loss of my nurses, I began to drum furiously soon after my discharge from the City Hospital. That rainy afternoon in Saspe Cemetery did nothing to diminish my drumming; on the contrary, Oskar redoubled his efforts to destroy the last witness to his shameful conduct with the Home Guards, namely, that drum.

But the drum withstood my assaults; as often as I struck it, it struck back accusingly. The strange part of it is that during this pounding, whose sole purpose was to eradicate a very definite segment of my past, Victor Weluhn, the carrier of funds, kept turning up in my mind, although, nearsighted as he was, his testimony against me couldn't have amounted to much. But hadn't he managed to escape despite his nearsightedness? Could it be that the nearsighted see more than others, that Weluhn, whom I usually speak of as poor Victor, had read my gestures like the movements of a black silhouette, that he had seen through my betrayal and that now, on his flight, he would carry Oskar's secret, Oskar's shame, all over the world with him?

It was not until the middle of December that the accusations of the serrated red and white conscience round my neck began to carry less conviction: the lacquer cracked and peeled: the tin grew thin and fragile. Condemned to look on at this death agony, I was eager, as one always is in such cases, to shorten the sufferings of the moribund, to hasten the end. During the last weeks of Advent, Oskar worked so hard that Matzerath and the neighbors held their heads, for he was determined to settle his accounts by Christmas Eve; I felt confident that for Christmas I should receive a new and guiltless drum.

I made it. On the twenty-fourth of December I was able to rid my body and soul of a rusty, dissipated, shapeless something suggestive of a wrecked motor car; by discarding it, I hoped, I should be putting the defense of the Polish Post Office behind me forever.

Never has any human being—if you are willing to accept me as one—known a more disappointing Christmas than Oskar, who found everything imaginable under the Chistmas tree, save only a drum.

There was a set of blocks that I never opened. A rocking swan, viewed by the grownups as the most sensational of presents, was supposed to turn me into Lohengrin. Just to annoy me, no doubt, they had had the nerve to put three or four picture books on the gift table. The only presents that struck me as in some sense serviceable were a pair of gloves, a pair of boots, and a red sweater knitted by Gretchen Scheffler. In consternation Oskar looked from the building blocks to the swan, and stared at a picture in one of the picture books, showing an assortment of teddy bears which were not only too cute for words but, to make matters worse, held all manner of musical instruments in their paws. One of these cute hypocritical beasts even had a drum; he looked as if he knew how to drum, as if he were just about to strike up a drum solo; while as for me, I had a swan but no drum, probably more than a thousand building blocks but not one single drum; I had mittens for bitter-cold winter nights, but between my gloved fists no round, smooth-lacquered, metallic, and ice-cold object that I might carry out into the winter nights, to warm their icy heart.

Oskar thought to himself: Matzerath has hidden the drum. Or Gretchen Scheffler, who has come with her baker to polish off our Christmas goose, is sitting on it. They are determined to enjoy my enjoyment of the swan, the building blocks, the picture books, before disgorging the real treasure. I gave in; I leafed like mad through the picture books, swung myself upon the swan's back and, fighting back my mounting repugnance, rocked for at least half an hour. Despite the overheated apartment I let them try on the sweater; aided by Gretchen Scheffler, I slipped into the shoes. Meanwhile the Greffs had arrived, the goose had been planned for six, and after the goose, stuffed with dried fruit and masterfully prepared by Matzerath, had been consumed, during the dessert, consisting of stewed plums and pears, desperately holding a picture book which Greff had added to my four other picture books; after soup, goose, red cabbage, boiled potatoes, plums, and pears, under the hot breath of a tile stove which had hot breath to spare, we all sang, Oskar too, a Christmas carol and an extra verse, Rejoice, and Ochristmastree, Ochristmastree, green-arethybellstingalingtingelingyearafteryear, and I was good and sick of the whole business; outside the bells had already started in, and I wanted my drum; the alcoholic brass band, to which Meyn the musician had formerly belonged, blew so the icicles outside the window . . . but I wanted my drum, and they wouldn't give it to me, they wouldn't cough it up. Oskar: "Yes!" The others: "No!" Whereupon I screamed, it was a long time since I had screamed, after a long rest period I filed my voice once again into a sharp, glass-cutting instrument; I killed no vases, no beer glasses nor light bulbs, I opened up no showcase nor deprived any spectacles of their power of vision—no, my vocal rancor was directed against all the balls, bells, light refracting silvery soap bubbles that graced the Ochristmas-tree: with a tinkle tinkle and a klingaling, the tree decorations were shattered into dust. Quite superfluously several dustpans full of fir needles detached themselves at the same time. But the candles went on burning, silent and holy, and with it all Oskar got no drum.

Matzerath had no perception. I don't know whether he was trying to wean me away from my instrument or whether it simply didn't occur to him to keep me supplied, amply and punctually, with drums. I was threatened with disaster. And it was only the coincidence that just then the mounting disorder in our shop could no longer be overlooked which brought help, before it was too late, both to me and the shop.

Since Oskar was neither big enough nor in any way inclined to stand behind a counter selling crackers, margarine, and synthetic honey, Matzerath, whom for the sake of simplicity I shall once more call my father, took on Maria Truczinski, my poor friend Herbert's youngest sister, to work in the store.

She wasn't just called Maria; she *was* one. It was not only that she managed, in only a few weeks, to restore the reputation of our shop; quite apart from her firm though friendly business management, to which Matzerath willingly submitted, she showed a definite understanding for my situation.

Even before Maria took her place behind the counter, she had several times offered me an old washbasin as a substitute for the lump of scrap metal with which I had taken to stamping accusingly up and down the more than hundred steps of our stairway. But Oskar wanted no substitute. Steadfastly he refused to drum on the bottom of a washbasin. But no sooner had Maria gained a firm foothold in the shop than she succeeded, Matzerath to the contrary notwithstanding, in fulfilling my desires. It must be admitted that Oskar could not be moved to enter a toystore with her. The inside of one of those emporiums bursting with multi-colored wares would surely have inspired painful comparisons with Sigismund Markus' devastated shop. The soul of kindness, Maria would let me wait outside while she attended to the purchases alone; every four or five weeks, according to my needs, she would bring me a new drum. And during the last years of the war, when even toy drums had grown rare and come to be rationed, she resorted to barter, offering the storekeepers sugar or a sixteenth of a pound of real coffee and receiving my drum under the counter in return. All this she did without sighing, shaking her head, or glancing heavenward, but seriously and attentively and as matter-of-factly as though dressing me in freshly washed, properly mended pants, stockings, and school smocks. Though, in the years that followed, the relations between Maria and me were in constant flux and have not been fully stabilized to this day, the way in which she hands me a drum has remained unchanged, though the prices are a good deal higher than in 1940.

Today Maria subscribes to a fashion magazine. She is becoming more chic from one visiting day to the next. But what of those days?

Was Maria beautiful? She had a round, freshly washed face and the look in her somewhat too prominent gray eyes with their short but abundant lashes and their dark, dense brows that joined over the nose, was cool but not cold. High cheekbones—when it was very cold, the skin over them grew taut and bluish and cracked painfully—gave the planes of which her face was constructed a reassuring balance which was scarcely disturbed by her diminutive but not unbeautiful or comical nose, which though small was very well shaped. Her forehead was small and round, marked very early by thoughtful vertical creases toward the middle. Rising from the temples, her brown, slightly curly hair, which still has the sheen of wet tree trunks, arched tightly over her little round head, which, like Mother Truczinski's, showed little sign of an occiput. When Maria put on her white smock and took her place behind the counter in our store, she still wore braids behind her florid, healthy ears, the lobes of which unfortunately did not hang free but grew directly into the flesh of her lower jaws—there were no ugly creases, but still the effect was degenerate enough to admit of inferences about Maria's character. Later on, Matzerath talked her into a permanent and her ears were hidden. Today, beneath tousled, fashionably short-cropped hair, Maria exhibits only the lobes of her ears; but she hides the flaw in her beauty beneath large clips that are not in very good taste.

Similar in its way to her small head with its full cheeks, prominent cheekbones, and large eyes on either side of her small, almost insignificant nose, Maria's body, which was distinctly on the small side, disclosed shoulders that were rather broad, full breasts swelling upward from her armpits, and an ample pelvis and rear end, which in turn were supported by legs so slender, though quite robust, that you could see between them beneath her pubic hair.

It is possible that Maria was a trifle knock-kneed in those days. Moreover, it seemed to me that in contrast to her figure, which was that of a grown woman, her little red hands were childlike and her fingers reminded me rather of sausages. To this day there is something childlike about those paws of hers. Her feet, however shod at the time in lumpy hiking shoes and a little later in my poor mama's chic, but outmoded high heels, which were scarcely becoming to her, gradually lost their childish redness and drollness in spite of the ill-fitting hand-me-downs they were forced into and gradually adapted themselves to modern shoe fashions of West German and even Italian origin.

Maria did not talk much but liked to sing as she was washing the dishes or filling blue pound and half-pound bags with sugar. When the shop closed and Matzerath busied himself with his accounts, or on Sundays, when she sat down to rest, Maria would play the harmonica that her brother Fritz had given her when he was drafted and sent to Gross-Boschpol.

Maria played just about everything on her harmonica. Scout songs she had learned at meetings of the League of German Girls, operetta tunes, and song hits that she had heard on the radio or learned from her brother Fritz, who came to Danzig for a few days at Easter 1940 on official business. But Maria never took out her "Hohner" during business hours. Even when there were no customers about, she refrained from music and wrote price tags and inventories in a round childlike hand.

Though it was plain for all to see that it was she who ran the store and had won back a part of the clientele that had deserted to our competitors after my poor mama's death, her attitude toward Matzerath was always respectful to the point of servility; but that didn't embarrass Matzerath, who had never lacked faith in his own worth.

"After all," he argued when Greff the greengrocer and Gretchen Scheffler tried to nettle him, "it was me that hired the girl and taught her the business." So simple were the thought processes of this man who, it must be admitted, became more subtle, more sensitive, and in a word more interesting only when engaged in his favorite occupation, cookery. For Oskar must give the devil his due: his Kassler Rippchen with sauerkraut, his pork kidneys in mustard sauce, his Wiener Schnitzel, and, above all, his carp with cream and horse radish, were splendid to look upon and delectable to smell and taste. There was little he could teach Maria in the shop, because the girl had a native business sense whereas Matzerath himself knew little about selling over the counter though he had a certain gift for dealing with the wholesalers, but he did teach Maria to boil, roast, and stew; for though she had spent two years working for a family of civil servants in Schidlitz, she could barely bring water to a boil when she first came to us.

Soon Matzerath's program was very much what it had been in my poor mama's lifetime: he reigned in the kitchen, outdoing himself from Sunday roast to Sunday roast, and spent hours of his time contentedly washing the dishes. In addition, as a sideline so to speak, he attended to the buying and ordering, the accounts with the wholesale houses and the Board of Trade—occupations which became more and more complicated as the war went on—carried on, and not without shrewdness, the necessary correspondence with the fiscal authorities, decorated the showcase with considerable imagination and good taste, and conscientiously performed his so-called Party duties. All in all—while Maria stood imperturbably behind the counter—he was kept very busy.

You may ask: what am I getting at with these preparatory remarks, why have I gone into so much detail about a young girl's cheekbones, eyebrows, ear lobes, hands, and feet? I agree with you perfectly, I too am opposed to this kind of description. Oskar knows perfectly well that he has succeeded at best in distorting Maria's image in your mind, perhaps for good. For this reason I will add one sentence that should make everything clear: If we disregard all the anonymous nurses, Maria was Oskar's first love.

I became aware of this state of affairs one day when, as seldom happened, I listened to my drumming. I could not help noticing the insistent new note of passion which Oskar, despite all his precautions, was communicating to his drum. Maria took this drumming in good part. But I was none too pleased when she set her harmonica to her lips, assumed an unprepossessing frown, and felt called upon to accompany me. Often, though, while darning stockings or filling sugar bags, her quiet eyes would gaze earnestly and attentively at me and my drumsticks and, before resuming her work, she would run her hand slowly and sleepily over my short-cropped hair.

Oskar, who ordinarily could not bear the slightest contact, however affectionately meant, accepted Maria's hand and became so enslaved to this caress that he would often, quite consciously, spend hours drumming the rhythms that brought it on, until at last Maria's hand obeyed and brought him well-being.

After a while Maria began to put me to bed at night. She undressed me, washed me, helped me into my pajamas, advised me to empty my bladder one last time before going to sleep, prayed with me, although she was a Protestant, an Our Father, three Hail Mary's and from time to time a JesusfortheeIlivejesusfortheeIdie, and finally tucked me in with a friendly, drowsy-making face.

Pleasant as were the last minutes before putting out the light—gradually I exchanged Our Father and JesusfortheeIlive for the tenderly allusive StaroftheseaIgreetthee and MaryIlovethee—these daily preparations for bed embarrassed me. They almost shattered my self-control, reducing Oskar—who had always prided himself on his mastery over his features—to the telltale blushes of starry-eyed maidens and tormented young men. Oskar must own that every time Maria undressed me, put me in the zinc tub, scrubbed the dust of a drummer's day off me with washcloth, brush, and soap, every time it was brought home to me that I, almost sixteen, was standing or sitting mother-naked in the presence of a girl somewhat older than myself, I blushed long and loud.

But Maria did not seem to notice my change of color. Could she have thought that washcloth and brush brought such a flush to my cheeks? Or was Maria modest and tactful enough to see through my daily evenglow and yet to overlook it?

I am still subject to this sudden flush, impossible to hide, that may last as much as five minutes or longer. Like my grandfather, Koljaiczek the firebug, who turned flaming red whenever the word "match" was dropped in his hearing, the blood rushes to my head whenever anyone, even a total stranger, speaks in my presence of small children being tubbed and scrubbed before they go to bed at night. Oskar stands there like an Indian; those around me call me eccentric if not vicious; for what can it mean to them that little children should be soaped, scrubbed, and visited with a washcloth in their most secret places?

Maria, on the other hand, was a child of nature: she did the most daring things in my presence without embarrassment. Before scrubbing the living room or bedroom floor, she would hoist her skirt to mid-thigh and take off her stockings, a gift from Matzerath, for fear of soiling them. One Saturday after the shop had closed—Matzerath had business at the local party headquarters—Maria shed her skirt and blouse, stood beside me in a pitiful but clean petticoat, and began to remove some spots from her skirt and artificial silk blouse with gasoline.

What could it have been that gave Maria, whenever she removed her outer garments and as soon as the smell of gasoline had worn off, a pleasantly and naively bewitching smell of vanilla? Did she rub herself with some such extract? Was there a cheap perfume with this sort of smell? Or was this scent as specific to her as, for example, ammonia to Mrs. Kater or rancid butter to my grandmother's skirts? Oskar, who liked to get to the bottom of things, investigated the vanilla: Maria did not anoint herself. Maria just smelled that way. Yes, I am still convinced that she was not even aware of the scent that clung to her; for on Sunday, when, after roast veal with mashed potatoes and cauliflower in brown butter, a vanilla pudding trembled on the table because I was tapping my foot on the table leg, Maria, who was wild about other varieties of pudding, ate but little and with evident distaste, while Oskar to this day is in love with this simplest and perhaps most commonplace of all puddings.

In July, 1940, shortly after the special communiqués announcing the rapid success of the French campaign, the Baltic bathing season opened. While Maria's brother Fritz, now a corporal, was sending the first picture postcards from Paris, Matzerath and Maria decided that Oskar must go to the beach, that the sea air would surely be good for his health. It was decided that Maria should take me at midday—the shop was closed from one to three—to the beach at Brösen, and if she stayed out until four, Matzerath said, it didn't matter; he liked to stand behind the counter from time to time and show himself to the customers.

A blue bathing suit with an anchor sewn on it was purchased for Oskar. Maria already had a green one with red trimmings that her sister Guste had given her as a confirmation present. Into a beach bag from Mama's days were stuffed a white woolen bathrobe of the same vintage and, quite superfluously, a pail and shovel and a set of sand molds. Maria carried the bag, while I carried my drum.

Oskar was apprehensive of the streetcar ride past the cemetery at Saspe. Was it not to be feared that the sight of this silent, yet so eloquent spot would put a crimp in his enthusiasm about bathing, which was no more than moderate to begin with? What, Oskar asked himself, will the ghost of Jan Bronski do when his assassin, dressed for summer, goes jingling past his grave in a streetcar?

The Number 9 car stopped. The conductor announced Saspe. I looked fixedly past Maria in the direction of Brösen, whence the other car crept toward us, growing gradually larger. Mustn't let my eyes wander. What, after all, was there to look at? Scrub pines, rusty ironwork, a maze of tumble-down tombstones with inscriptions that only the thistles and wild oats could read. Under such circumstances, it was better to look out the open window and up into the sky: there they hummed, the fat Ju-52's, as only trimotored planes or enormous flies can hum in a cloudless July sky.

We moved up with a great clanging of bells and the other car cut off our view. The moment we passed the trailer, my head turned of its own accord and I was treated to the whole tumble-down cemetery and also a bit of the north wall; the white patch lay in the shadow, but it was still painfully white . . . .

Then the cemetery was gone, we approached Brösen, and once again I looked at Maria. She had on a light summer dress with a flower pattern. On her round neck with its faintly radiant skin, over her well-upholstered collarbone, she wore a necklace of red wooden cherries, all the same size and simulating bursting ripeness. Was it my imagination or did I really smell it? Maria seemed to be taking her vanilla scent along with her to the Baltic. Oskar leaned slightly forward, took a long whiff of it, and in an instant vanquished the moldering Jan Bronski. The defense of the Polish Post Office had receded into history even before the flesh had fallen from the defenders' bones. Oskar, the survivor, had very different smells in his nostrils than that of his presumptive father, once so elegant a figure, now dust.

In Brösen Maria bought a pound of cherries, took me by the hand —well she knew that only she was permitted to do so—and led me through the pine woods to the bathing establishment. Though I was nearly sixteen—the attendant had no eye for such things—I was allowed into the ladies' section. Water: 65, said the blackboard, air: 80; wind: east; forecast: fair. Beside the blackboard hung a poster, dealing with artificial respiration. The victims all had on striped bathing suits, the rescuers wore mustaches, straw hats floated upon treacherous, turbulent waters.

The barefooted girl attendant went ahead. Around her waist, like a penitent, she wore a cord from which hung the enormous key that opened the cabins. Plank walks. Railings. Alongside the cabins a hard runner of coconut fiber. We had cabin Number 53. The wood of the cabin was warm, dry, and of a natural bluish-white hue that I should call blind. Beside the window hung a mirror that had ceased to take itself seriously.

First Oskar had to undress. This I did with my face to the wall and it was only reluctantly that I let Maria help me. Then Maria turned me round in her sturdy, matter-of-fact way, held out my new bathing suit, and forced me ruthlessly into the tight-fitting wool. No sooner had I buttoned the shoulder straps than she lifted me up on the wooden bench against the back wall of the cabin, put my drum and sticks on my lap, and began, with quick energetic movements, to undress.

First I drummed a little and counted the knotholes in the floorboards. Then I stopped counting and drumming. It was quite beyond me why Maria, with oddly pursed lips, should whistle while removing her shoes, two high notes, two low notes, and while stripping off her socks. Whistling like the driver of a brewery truck, she took off the flowery dress, whistling she hung up her petticoat over her dress, dropped her brassiere, and still without finding a tune, whistled frantically while pulling her panties, which were really gym shorts, down to her knees, letting them slip to the floor, climbing out of the rolled-up pants legs, and kicking the shorts into the corner with one foot.

Maria frightened Oskar with her hairy triangle. Of course he knew from his poor mama that women are not bald down there, but for him Maria was not a woman in the sense in which his mama had shown herself to be a woman in her dealings with Matzerath or Jan Bronski.

And I recognized her at once. Rage, shame, indignation, disappointment, and a nascent half-comical, half-painful stiffening of my watering can under my bathing suit made me forget drum and drumsticks for the sake of the new stick I had developed.

Oskar jumped up and flung himself on Maria. She caught him with her hair. He buried his face in it. It grew between his lips. Maria laughed and tried to pull him away. I drew more and more of her into me, looking for the source of the vanilla smell. Maria was still laughing. She even left me to her vanilla, it seemed to amuse her, for she didn't stop laughing. Only when my feet slipped and I hurt her—for I didn't let go the hair or perhaps it was the hair that didn't let me go—only when the vanilla brought tears to my eyes, only when I began to taste mushrooms or some acrid spice, in any case, something that was not vanilla, only when this earthy smell that Maria concealed behind the vanilla brought me back to the smell of the earth where Jan Bronski lay moldering and contaminated me for all time with the taste of perishability—only then did I let go.

Oskar slipped on the blind-colored boards of the bathhouse cabin and was still crying when Maria, who was laughing once more, picked him up, caressed him, and pressed him to the necklace of wooden cherries which was all she had on.

Shaking her head, she picked her hairs from between my lips and said in a tone of surpise: "What a little rascal you are! You start up and you don't know what's what and then you cry."

Fizz Powder

Does that mean anything to you? Formerly, you could buy it at any time of year in little flat packages. In our shop my mama sold woodruff fizz powder in a nauseatingly green little bag. Another sack that had the color of not-quite-ripe oranges claimed to have an orange flavor. There was also a raspberry flavor, and another variety which, if you poured fresh water over it, hissed, bubbled, and acted excited, and if you drank it before it quieted down, tasted very remotely like lemon, and had a lemon color in the glass, only more so: an artificial yellow masquerading as poison.

What else was on the package except for the flavor? Natural Product, it said. Patented. Protect Against Moisture, and, under a dotted line, Tear Here.

Where else could you buy this fizz powder? Not only in my mama's shop was it for sale, but in all grocery stores, except for Kaiser's and the cooperatives. In the stores and at all refreshment stands a package cost three pfennigs.

Maria and I got ours free of charge. Only when we couldn't wait to get home were we obliged to stop at a grocery store or refreshment stand and pay three pfennigs or even six, because we could never get enough of it and often asked for two packages.

Who started up with the fizz powder? The old old quarrel between lovers. I say Maria started it. Maria never claimed that Oskar started it. She left the question open and the most she would say, if pressed, was: "The fizz powder started it."

Of course everyone will agree with Maria. Only Oskar could not accept this verdict. Never would I have admitted that Oskar was seduced by a little package of fizz powder at three pfennigs. I was sixteen, I wanted to blame myself or Maria if need be, but certainly not a powder demanding to be protected against moisture.

It began a few days after my birthday. According to the calendar, the bathing season was drawing to an end. But the weather would hear nothing of September. After a rainy August, the summer showed its mettle; its belated accomplishment could be read on the bulletin board beside the artificial-respiration poster: air: 84; water: 68; wind: southwest; forecast: generally fair.

While Fritz Truczinski, a corporal in the air corps, sent postcards from Paris, Copenhagen, Oslo, and Brussels—the fellow was always traveling on official business—Maria and I acquired quite a tan. In July we had occupied a place on the family beach. But here Maria had been exposed to the inept horseplay of some boys from the Conradinum and to interminable declarations of love emanating from a student at the Petri School; in mid-August we moved to the beach reserved for ladies, where we found a quiet spot near the water. Buxom ladies panted and puffed as they submerged their varicose veins up to their knees, and naked, misbehaved urchins waged war on fate; that is, they piled up sand into crude castles that kept toppling down.

The ladies' beach: when women are by themselves and think themselves unobserved, a young man—and Oskar was well aware of being a young man beneath the surface—will do well to close his eyes rather than become a witness, however involuntary, to uninhibited womanhood.

We lay in the sand, Maria in her green bathing suit bordered with red, I in my blue one. The sand slept, the sea slept, the shells had been crushed and did not listen. Amber, which allegedly keeps you awake, was elsewhere; the wind, which according to the bulletin board came from the southwest, fell gradually asleep; the whole wide sky, which had surely been overexerting itself, did nothing but yawn; Maria and I were also somewhat tired. We had already bathed and we had eaten after, not before, bathing. Our cherries, reduced to moist pits, lay in the sand beside bleached cherry pits from the previous year.

At the sight of so much transience, Oskar took to picking up handfuls of sand mingled with fresh young cherry pits and others that were one or a thousand years old, and sifting it over his drum; so he impersonated an hourglass and at the same time tried to think himself into the role of death by playing with bones. Under Maria's warm, sleepy flesh I imagined parts of her surely wide-awake skeleton; I relished the view between radius and ulna, played counting games up and down her spine, reached in through her iliac fossae and played with her sternum.

Despite all the fun I was having playing the part of death with my hourglass and my skeleton, Maria moved. Blindly, trusting wholly to her fingers, she reached into the beach bag and looked for something, while I dropped what was left of my sand and cherry pits on the drum, which was almost half-buried. When she failed to find what she was looking for, probably her harmonica, Maria turned the bag inside out: a moment later, something lay on the beach towel; but it was not a harmonica; it was a package of woodruff fizz powder.

Maria affected surprise. Or maybe she really was surprised. As for me, my surprise was real: over and over I asked myself, as I still ask myself: how did this package of fizz powder, this miserable cheap stuff, bought only by the children of dock workers and the unemployed, because they had no money for real pop, how did this unsalable article get into our beach bag?

While Oskar pondered, Maria grew thirsty. And breaking off my meditations, I too, quite against my will, had to confess to an irresistible thirst. We had no cup, and besides it was at least thirty-five paces to the drinking water if Maria went and nearly fifty if I did. To borrow a cup from the attendant and use the tap by the bathhouse, it was necessary to pass over burning sand between mountains of flesh shining with Nivea oil, some lying on their backs, others on their bellies.

We both dreaded the errand and left the package lying on the towel. Finally I picked it up, before Maria showed any sign of picking it up. But Oskar only put it back on the towel in order that Maria might reach out for it. Maria did not reach out. So I reached out and gave it to Maria.

211

Maria gave it back to Oskar. I thanked her and made her a present of it. But she wanted no presents from Oskar. I had to put it back on the towel. There it lay a long while without stirring.

Oskar wishes to make it clear that it was Maria who after an oppressive pause picked up the package again. But that was not all: she tore off a strip of paper exactly on the dotted line where it said to Tear Here. Then she held out the opened package—to me. This time Oskar declined with thanks. Maria managed to be vexed. She resolutely laid the open package down on the towel. What was there for me to do but to pick the package up before sand should get into it, and offer it to Maria.

Oskar wishes to make it clear that it was Maria who made one finger disappear into the opening of the package, who coaxed the finger out again, and held it up vertically for inspection: something bluish-white, fizz powder, was discernible on the fingertip. She offered me the finger. I took it of course. Although it made my nose prickle, my face succeeded in registering pleasure. It was Maria who held out a hollow hand. Oskar could hardly have helped pouring some fizz powder into the pink bowl. What she would do with the little pile of powder, she did not know. This mound in the cup of her hand was something too new, too strange. At this point I leaned forward, summoning up all my spit, and directed it at the powder; I repeated the operation and leaned back only when I was out of saliva.

In Maria's hand a hissing and bubbling set in. The woodruff erupted like a volcano, seethed like the greenish fury of some exotic nation. Something was going on that Maria had never seen and probably never felt, for her hand quivered, trembled, and tried to fly away, for woodruff was biting her, woodruff penetrated her skin, woodruff excited her, gave her a feeling, a feeling, a feeling . . .

The green grew greener, but Maria grew red, raised her hand to her mouth and licked her palm with a long tongue. This she did several times, so frantically that Oskar was very close to supposing that her tongue, far from appeasing the woodruff feeling that so stirred her, raised it to the limit, perhaps beyond the limit, that is appointed to all feeling.

Then the feeling died down. Maria giggled, looked around to make sure there had been no witnesses, and when she saw that the sea cows breathing in bathing suits were motionless, indifferent, and Nivea-brown, she lay down on the towel; against the white background, her blushes died slowly away.

Perhaps the seaside air of that noonday hour might still have sent Oskar off to sleep, if Maria, after only a few minutes, had not sat up again and reached out once more for the package, which was still half-full. I do not know whether she struggled with herself before pouring the rest of the powder into her palm, which was no longer a stranger to the effect of woodruff. For about as long as a man takes to clean his glasses, she held the package on the left and the bowl on the right, motionless and antagonistic. Not that she directed her gaze toward the package or the hollow hand, or looked back and forth between half-full and empty; no, Maria looked between package and hand with a stern scowl. But her sternness was soon to prove weaker than the half-full package. The package approached the hollow hand, the hand came to meet the package, the gaze lost its sternness sprinkled with melancholy, became curious, and then frankly avid. With painstakingly feigned indifference, she piled up the rest of the woodruff fizz powder in her well-upholstered palm, which was dry in spite of the heat, dropped package and indifference, propped up the filled hand on the now empty one, rested her gray eyes on the powder for a time, then looked at me, gave me a gray look, her gray eyes were demanding something of me. It was my saliva she wanted, why didn't she take some of her own, Oskar had hardly any left, she certainly had much more, saliva doesn't replenish itself so quickly, she should kindly take her own, it was just as good, if not better, in any case she surely had more than I, because I couldn't make it so quickly and also because she was bigger than Oskar.

Maria wanted my saliva. From the start it was perfectly plain that only my spit could be considered. She did not avert those demanding eyes from me, and I blamed this cruel obstinacy of hers on those ear lobes which, instead of hanging free, grew straight into her lower jaws. Oskar swallowed; he thought of things which ordinarily made his mouth water, but—it was the fault of the sea air, the salt air, the salty sea air no doubt—my salivary glands were on strike. Goaded by Maria's eyes, I had to get up and start on my way. My labor was to take more than fifty steps through the burning sand, looking neither to left nor right, to climb the still more burning steps to the bathhouse, to turn on the tap, to twist my head and hold my mouth under it, to drink, to rinse, to swallow in order that Oskar might be replenished.

When I had completed the journey, so endless and bordered by such terrible sights, from the bathhouse to our white towel, I found Maria lying on her belly, her head nestling in her arms. Her braids lay lazy on her round back.

I poked her, for Oskar now had saliva. Maria didn't budge. I poked her again. Nothing doing. Cautiously I opened her left hand. She did not resist: the hand was empty, as though it had never seen any woodruff. I straightened the fingers of her right hand: pink was her palm, with moist lines, hot and empty.

Had Maria resorted to her own saliva? Had she been unable to wait? Or had she blown away the fizz powder, stifling that feeling before feeling it; had she rubbed her hand clean on the towel until Maria's familiar little paw reappeared, with its slightly superstitious mound of the moon, its fat Mercury, and its solidly padded girdle of Venus?

Shortly after that we went home, and Oskar will never know whether Maria made the fizz powder fizz for the second time that same day or whether it was not until a few days later that the mixture of fizz powder with my spittle became, through repetition, a vice for herself and for me.

Chance, or if you will a chance pliant to our wishes, brought it about that on the evening of the bathing day just described—we were eating blueberry soup followed by potato pancakes—Matzerath informed Maria and me, ever so circumspectly, that he had joined a little skat club made up of members of the local Party group, that he would meet his new skat partners, who were all unit leaders, two evenings a week at Springer's restaurant, that Sellke, the new local group leader, would attend from time to time, and that that in itself obliged him to be present, which unfortunately meant leaving us alone. The best arrangement, he thought, would be for Oskar to sleep at Mother Truczinski's on skat nights.

Mother Truczinski was agreed, all the more so as this solution appealed to her far more than the proposal which Matzerath, without consulting Maria, had made her the day before, to wit, that instead of my spending the night at Mother Truczinski's, Maria should sleep on our sofa two nights a week.

Up until then Maria had slept in the broad bed where my friend Herbert had formerly laid his scarred back. This extraordinarily heavy piece of furniture stood in the small rear room. Mother Truczinski had her bed in the living room. Guste Truczinski, who still waited on tables at the snack bar in the Hotel Eden, lived at the hotel; she occasionally came home on her day off, but rarely spent the night, and when she did, it was on the couch. When Fritz Truczinski, laden with presents, came home on furlough from distant lands, he slept in Herbert's bed, Maria took Mother Truczinski's bed, while the old woman camped on the couch.

This order of things was disturbed by my demands. Originally I was expected to sleep on the couch. This plan I rejected out of hand. Then Mother Truczinski offered to cede me her bed and take the couch for herself. Here Maria objected, her mother needed her sleep, her mother must not be made uncomfortable. Very simply and directly Maria expressed her willingness to share Herbert's former bed with me. "I'll be all right in the same bed with Oskar," she said. "He's only an eighth of a portion."

And so, twice weekly, beginning a few days later, Maria carried my bedclothes from our ground-floor apartment to the Truczinski dwelling on the second floor and prepared a night lodging for me and my drum on the left side of her bed. On Matzerath's first skat night nothing at all happened. Herbert's bed seemed frightfully big to me. I lay down first, Maria came in later. She had washed herself in the kitchen and entered the bedroom in an old-fashioned, absurdly long and absurdly starched nightgown. Oskar had expected her to be naked and hairy and was disappointed at first, but soon he was perfectly happy, because the heirloom nightgown made pleasant bridges, reminding him of trained nurses and their white draperies.

Standing at the washstand, Maria undid her braids and whistled. Maria always whistled while dressing or undressing, doing or undoing her braids. Even while combing her hair, she never wearied of squeezing out those two notes between her pursed lips, without ever arriving at a tune.

The moment Maria put her comb aside, the whistling stopped. She turned, shook her hair once again, put the washstand in order with a few quick strokes. Order made her frolicsome: she threw a kiss at her photographed, retouched, and mustachioed father in the ebony frame, then with exaggerated gusto jumped into bed and bounced a few times. At the last bounce she pulled up the eiderdown and vanished beneath the mountain as far as her chin. I was lying under my own quilt and she didn't touch me at all; she stretched out a well-rounded arm from under the eiderdown, groped about overhead for the light cord, found it, and switched out the light. Only when it was dark did she say, in much too loud a voice: "Good night!"

Maria was soon breathing evenly. I do not think she was pretending; it is quite likely that she did drop right off to sleep, for the quantities of work she did each day certainly called for corresponding quantities of sleep.

For quite some time, absorbing and sleep-dispelling images passed before Oskar's eyes. For all the dense darkness between the far walls and the blacked-out windows, blonde nurses bent over to examine Herbert's scarred back, from Leo Schugger's white rumpled shirt arose—what else would you expect?—a sea gull, which flew until it dashed itself to pieces against a cemetery wall, which instantly took on a freshly whitewashed look. And so on. Only when the steadily mounting, drowsy-making smell of vanilla made the film flicker before his eyes did Oskar begin to breathe as peacefully as Maria had been doing for heaven knows how long.

Three days later I was treated to the same demure tableau of maidenly going-to-bed. She entered in her nightgown, whistled while undoing her braids, whistled while combing her hair, put the comb down, stopped whistling, put the washstand in order, threw the photo a kiss, made her wild leap, took hold of the eiderdown, and caught sight—I was contemplating her back—caught sight of a little package—I was admiring her lovely long hair—discovered something green on the quilt—I closed my eyes, resolved to wait until she had grown used to the sight of the fizz powder. The bedsprings screamed beneath the weight of a Maria flopping down backward, I heard the sound of a switch, and when I opened my eyes because of the sound, Oskar was able to confirm what he already knew; Maria had put out the light and was breathing irregularly in the darkness; she had been unable to accustom herself to the sight of the fizz powder. However, it seemed not unlikely that the darkness by her ordained had only given the fizz powder an intensified existence, bringing woodruff to bloom and mingling soda bubbles with the night.

I am almost inclined to think that the darkness was on Oskar's side. For after a few minutes—if one can speak of minutes in a pitch-dark room—I became aware of stirrings at the head end of the bed; Maria was fishing for the light cord, the cord bit, and an instant later I was once more admiring the lovely long hair falling over Maria's sitting nightgown. How steady and yellow shone the light bulb behind the pleated lampshade cover! The eiderdown still bulged untouched on the foot end of the bed. The package on top of the mountain hadn't dared to budge in the darkness. Maria's ancestral nightgown rustled, a sleeve rose up with the little hand belonging to it, and Oskar gathered saliva in his mouth. In the course of the weeks that followed, the two of us emptied over a dozen little packages of fizz powder, mostly with woodruff flavoring, then, when the woodruff ran out, lemon or raspberry, according to the very same ritual, making it fizz with my saliva, and so provoking a sensation which Maria came to value more and more. I developed a certain skill in the gathering of saliva, devised tricks that sent the water running quickly and abundantly to my mouth, and was soon able, with the contents of one package, to give Maria the desired sensation three times in quick succession.

Maria was pleased with Oskar; sometimes, after her orgy of fizz powder, she pressed him close and kissed him two or three times, somewhere in the face. Then she would giggle for a moment in the darkness and quickly fall asleep.

It became harder and harder for me to get to sleep. I was sixteen years old; I had an active mind and a sleep-discouraging need to associate my love for Maria with other, still more amazing possibilities than those which lay dormant in the fizz powder and, awakened by my saliva, invariably provoked the same sensation.

Oskar's meditations were not limited to the time after lights out. All day long I pondered behind my drum, leafed through my tattered excerpts from Rasputin, remembered earlier educational orgies between Gretchen Scheffler and my poor mama, consulted Goethe, whose *Elective Affinities* I possessed in excerpts similar to those from Rasputin; from the faith healer I took his elemental drive, tempered it with the great poet's world-encompassing feeling for nature; sometimes I gave Maria the look of the Tsarina or the features of the Grand Duchess Anastasia, selected ladies from among Rasputin's following of eccentric nobles; but soon, repelled by this excess of animal passion, I found Maria in the celestial transparency of an Ottilie or the chaste, controlled passion of a Charlotte. Oskar saw himself by turns as Rasputin in person, as his murderer, often as a captain, more rarely as Charlotte's vacillating husband, and once—I have to own—as a genius with the well-known features of Goethe, hovering over a sleeping Maria.

Strange to say, I expected more inspiration from literature than from real, naked life. Jan Bronski, whom I had often enough seen kneading my mother's flesh, was able to teach me next to nothing. Although I knew that this tangle, consisting by turns of Mama and Jan or Matzerath and Mama, this knot which sighed, exerted itself, moaned with fatigue, and at last fell stickily apart, meant love, Oskar was still unwilling to believe that love was love; love itself made him cast about for some other love, and yet time and time again he came back to tangled love, which he hated until the day when in love he practiced it; then he was obliged to defend it in his own eyes as the only possible love.

Maria took the fizz powder lying on her back. As soon as it bubbled up, her legs began to quiver and thrash and her nightgown, sometimes after the very first sensation, slipped up as far as her thighs. At the second fizz, the nightgown usually managed to climb past her belly and to bunch below her breasts. One night after I had been filling her left hand for weeks, I quite spontaneously—for there was no chance to consult Goethe or Rasputin first—spilled the rest of a package of raspberry powder into the hollow of her navel, and spat on it before she could protest. Once the crater began to seethe, Maria lost track of all the arguments needed to bolster up a protest: for the seething, foaming navel had many advantages over the palm of the hand. It was the same fizz powder, my spit remained my spit, and indeed the sensation was no different, but more intense, much more intense. The sensation rose to such a pitch that Maria could hardly bear it. She leaned forward, as though to quench with her tongue the bubbling raspberries in her navel as she had quenched the woodruff in the hollow of her hand, but her tongue was not long enough; her bellybutton was farther away than Africa or Tierra del Fuego. I, however, was close to Maria's bellybutton; looking for raspberries, I sank my tongue into it and found more and more of them; I wandered far afield, came to places where there was no forester to demand a permit to pick berries; I felt under obligation to cull every last berry, there was nothing but raspberries in my eyes, my mind, my heart, my ears, all I could smell in the world was raspberries, and so intent was I upon raspberries that Oskar said to himself only in passing: Maria is pleased with your assiduity. That's why she has turned off the light. That's why she surrenders so trustingly to sleep and allows you to go on picking; for Maria was rich in raspberries.

And when I found no more, I found, as though by chance, mushrooms in other spots. And because they lay hidden deep down beneath the moss, my tongue gave up and I grew an eleventh finger, for my ten fingers proved inadequate for the purpose. And so Oskar acquired a third drumstick—he was old enough for that. And instead of drumming on tin, I drummed on moss. I no longer knew if it was I who drummed or if it was Maria or if it was my moss or her moss. Do the moss and the eleventh finger belong to someone else and only the mushrooms to me? Did the little gentleman down there have a mind and a will of his own? Who was doing all this: Oskar, he, or I?

And Maria, who was sleeping upstairs and wide awake downstairs, who smelled upstairs of innocent vanilla and under the moss of pungent mushrooms, who wanted fizz powder, but not this little gentleman whom I didn't want either, who had declared his independence, who did just what he was minded to, who did things I hadn't taught him, who stood up when I lay down, who had other dreams than I, who could neither read nor write and nevertheless signed for me, who goes his own way to this very day, who broke with me on the very day I first took notice of him, who is my enemy with whom I am constrained, time and time again, to ally myself, who betrays me and leaves me in the lurch, whom I should like to auction off, whom I am ashamed of, who is sick of me, whom I wash, who befouls me, who sees nothing and flairs everything, who is so much a stranger to me that I should like to call him Sir, who has a very different memory from Oskar: for today when Maria comes into my room and Bruno discreetly slips off into the corridor, he no longer recognizes Maria, he can't, he won't, he sprawls most phlegmatically while Oskar's leaping heart makes my mouth stammer: "Listen to me, Maria, tender suggestions. I might buy a compass and trace a circle around us; with the same compass, I might measure the angle of inclination of your neck while you are reading, sewing, or as now, tinkering with the buttons of my portable radio. Let the radio be, tender suggestions: I might have my eyes vaccinated and find tears again. At the nearest butcher shop Oskar would put his heart through the meat grinder if you would do the same with your soul. We might buy a stuffed animal to have something quiet between us. If I had the worms and you the patience, we might go fishing and be happier. Or the fizz powder of those days? Do you remember? You call me woodruff, I fizz up, you want still more, I give you the rest—Maria, fizz powder, tender suggestions.

"Why do you keep playing with those radio knobs, all you care about nowadays is the radio, as though you were taken with a mad passion for special communiqués."

Special Communiqués

It is hard to experiment on the white disk of my drum. I ought to have known that. My drum always wants the same wood. It wants to be questioned with drumsticks and to beat out stiking answers or, with an easy, conversational roll, leave questions and answers open. So you see, my drum is neither a frying pan which, artificially heated, cooks raw meat to a crisp, nor a dance floor for couples who do not know whether they belong together. Consequently, even in the loneliest hours, Oskar has never strewn fizz powder on his drum, mixed his saliva with it, and put on a show that he has not seen for years and that I miss exceedingly. It is true that Oskar couldn't help trying an experiment with said powder, but he proceeded more directly and left the drum out of it; and in so doing, I exposed myself, for without my drum I am always exposed and helpless.

It was hard to procure the fizz powder. I sent Bruno to every grocery store in Grafenberg, I sent him to Gerresheim by streetcar. I asked him to try in town, but even at refreshment stands of the sort you find at the end of streetcar lines, Bruno could find no fizz powder. Young salesgirls had never heard of it, older shopkeepers remembered loquaciously; thoughtfully—as Bruno reported—they rubbed their foreheads and said: "What is it you want? Fizz powder? That was a long time ago. Under Wilhelm they sold it, and under Adolf just in the beginning. Those were the good old days. But if you'd like a bottle of soda or a Coke?"

My keeper drank several bottles of soda pop or Coke at my expense without obtaining what I wanted, and nevertheless Oskar got his fizz powder in the end: yesterday Bruno brought me a little white package without a label; the laboratory technician of our mental hospital, a certain Miss Klein, had sympathetically agreed to open her drawers, phials, and reference works, to take a few grams of this and a few grams of that, and finally, after several attempts, had mixed up a fizz powder which, as Bruno reported, could fizz, prickle, turn green, and taste very discreetly of woodruff.

And today was visiting day. Maria came. But first came Klepp. We laughed together for three-quarters of an hour about something worth forgetting. I was considerate of Klepp and spared his Leninist feelings, avoided bringing up current events, and said nothing of the special announcement of Stalin's death, which had come to me over my little portable radio—given to me by Maria a few weeks ago. But Klepp seemed to know, for a crepe was sewn incompetently to the sleeve of his brown checked overcoat. Then Klepp arose and Vittlar came in. The two friends seem to have quarreled again, for Vittlar greeted Klepp with a laugh and made horns at him. "Stalin's death surprised me as I was shaving this morning," he said sententiously and helped Klepp into his coat. His broad face coated with unctuous piety, Klepp lifted up the black cloth on his sleeve: "That's why I am in mourning," he sighed and, giving an imitation of Armstrong's trumpet, intoned the first funereal measures of New Orleans Function: trrah trahdaha traah dada dadada—then he slipped through the door.

But Vittlar stayed; he didn't want to sit down, but hopped about in front of the mirror and for a few minutes we exchanged understanding smiles that had no reference to Stalin.

I don't know whether I meant to confide in Vittlar or to drive him away. I motioned him to come close, to incline an ear, and whispered in his great-lobed spoon: "Fizz powder! Does that mean anything to you, Gottfried?" A horrified leap bore Vittlar away from my cage-bed; he thrust out his forefinger and in tones of theatrical passion that came easy to him, declaimed: "Wilt thou seduce me with fizz powder, O Satan? Dost thou not know I am an angel?"

And like an angel, Vittlar, not without a last look at the mirror over the washbasin, fluttered away. The young folks outside the mental hospital are really an odd and affected lot.

And then Maria arrived. She has a new tailor-made spring suit and a stylish mouse-grey hat with a discreet, sophisticated straw-colored trimming. Even in my room she does not remove this *objet d'art*. She gave me a cursory greeting, held out her cheek to be kissed, and at once turned on the portable radio which was, to be sure, a present from her to me, but seems to have been intended for her own use, for it is the function of that execrable plastic box to replace a part of our conversation on visiting days. "Did you hear the news this morning? Isn't it exciting? Or didn't you?" "Yes, Maria," I replied patiently. "They haven't kept Stalin's death secret from me, but please turn off the radio."

Maria obeyed without a word, sat down, still in her hat, and we spoke as usual about little Kurt.

"Just imagine, Oskar, the little rascal don't want to wear long stockings no more, when it's only March and more cold weather coming, they said so on the radio." I ignored the weather report but sided with Kurt about the long stockings. "The boy is twelve, Maria, he's ashamed to go to school in wool stockings, his friends make fun of him."

"Well, as far as I'm concerned, his health comes first; he wears the stockings until Easter."

This date was stated so unequivocally that I tried another tack. "Then you should buy him ski pants, because those long woolen stockings are really ugly. Just think back to when you were his age. In our court in Labesweg. Shorty always had to wear stockings until Easter, you remember what they did to him? Nuchi Eyke, who was killed in Crete, Axel Mischke, who got his in Holland just before the war was over, and Harry Schlager, what did they do to Shorty? They smeared those long woolen stockings of his with tar so they stuck to his skin, and Shorty had to be taken to the hospital."

"That wasn't the fault of the stockings, Susi Kater was to blame," cried Maria furiously. Although Susi had joined the Blitz Girls at the very beginning of the war and was rumored to have married in Bavaria later on, Maria bore Susi, who was several years her senior, a lasting grudge such as women and only women can carry with them, from childhood to a ripe old age. Even so, my allusion to Shorty's tar-daubed stockings produced a certain effect. Maria promised to buy Kurt ski pants. We were able to go on to something else. There was good news about Kurt. The school principal had spoken well of him at the parents' and teachers' meeting. "Just imagine. He's second in his class. And he helps me in the shop, I can't tell you what a help he is to me."

I nodded approval and listened as she described the latest purchases for the delicatessen store. I encouraged Maria to open a branch in Oberkassel. The times were favorable, I said, the wave of prosperity would continue—I had just picked that up on the radio. And then I decided it was time to ring for Bruno. He came in and handed me the little white package containing the fizz powder.

Oskar had worked out his plan. Without explanation I asked Maria for her left hand. She started to give me her right hand, but then corrected herself. Shaking her head and laughing, she offered me the back of her left hand, probably expecting me to kiss it. She showed no surprise until I turned the hand around and poured the powder from the package into a pile between mound of the Moon and mound of Venus. But even then she did not protest. She took fright only when Oskar bent down over her hand and spat copiously on the mound of fizz powder.

"Hey, what is this?" she cried with indignation, moved her hand as far from her as possible, and stared in horror at the frothing green foam. Maria blushed from her forehead down. I was beginning to hope, when three quick steps carried her to the washbasin. She let water, disgusting water, first cold, then hot, flow over the fizz powder. Then she washed her hands with my soap.

"Oskar, you're really impossible. What do you expect Mr. Münsterberg to think of us?" She turned to Bruno, who during my experiment had taken up a position at the foot end of the bed, as though pleading with him to overlook my insane behavior. To spare Maria any further embarrassment, I sent the keeper out of the room, and as soon as he had closed the door behind him, called her back to my bedside: "Don't you remember? Please remember. Fizz powder! Three pfennigs a package. Think back! Woodruff, raspberry, how beautifully it foamed and bubbled, and the sensation, Maria, the way it made you feel."

Maria did not remember. She was taken with an insane fear of me, she hid her left hand, tried frantically to find another topic of conversation, told me once again about Kurt's good work in school, about Stalin's death, the new icebox at Matzerath's delicatessen, the projected new branch in Oberkassel. I, however, remained faithful to the fizz powder, fizz powder, I said, she stood up, fizz powder, I begged, she said a hasty good-by, plucked at her hat, undecided whether to go or stay, and turned on the radio, which began to squeak. But I shouted above it: "Fizz powder, Maria, remember!"

Then she stood in the doorway, wept, shook her head, and left me alone with the squeaking, whistling radio, closing the door as cautiously as though she were leaving me on my deathbed.

And so Maria can't remember the fizz powder. Yet for me, as long as I may breathe and drum, that fizz powder will never cease to fizz and foam; for it was my spittle which in the late summer of 1940 aroused woodruff and raspberry, which awakened feelings, which sent my flesh out questing, which made me a collector of morels, chanterelles, and other edible mushrooms unknown to me, which made me a father, yes indeed, young as I was, a father, from spittle to father, kindler of feelings, gathering and begetting, a father; for by early November, there was no room for doubt, Maria was pregnant, Maria was in her second month and I, Oskar, was the father.

Of that I am convinced to this day, for the business with Matzerath happened much later; two weeks, no, ten days after I had impregnated the sleeping Maria in the bed of her brother Herbert, rich in scars, in plain sight of the postcards sent by her younger brother, the corporal, and then in the dark, between walls and blackout paper, I found Maria, not sleeping this time but actively gasping for air on our sofa; under Matzerath she lay, and on top of her lay Matzerath.

Oskar, who had been meditating in the attic, came in from the hallway with his drum and entered the living room. The two of them didn't notice me. Their heads were turned toward the tile stove. They hadn't even undressed properly. Matzerath's underdrawers were hanging down to his knees. His trousers were piled up on the carpet. Maria's dress and petticoat had rolled up over her brassiere to her armpits. Her panties were dangling round one foot which hung from the sofa on a repulsively twisted leg. Her other leg lay bent back, as though unconcerned, over the head rest. Between her legs Matzerath. With his right hand he turned her head aside, the other hand guided him on his way. Through Matzerath's parted fingers Maria stared at the carpet and seemed to follow the pattern under the table. He had sunk his teeth into a cushion with a velvet cover and only let the velvet go when they talked together. For from time to time they talked, though without interrupting their labors. Only when the clock struck three quarters did the two of them pause till the last stroke, and then, resuming his efforts, he said: "It's a quarter of." Then he wanted to know if she liked it the way he was doing it. She said yes several times and asked him to be careful. He promised. She commanded, no, entreated him to be particularly careful. Then he inquired if it was time. And she said yes, very soon. Then she must have had a cramp in her foot that was hanging down off the sofa, for she kicked it up in the air, but her panties still hung from it. Then he bit into the velvet cushion again and she screamed: go away, and he wanted to go away, but he couldn't, because Oskar was on top of them before he could go away, because I had plunked down my drum on the small of his back and was pounding it with the sticks, because I couldn't stand listening any more to their go away go away, because my drum was louder than their go away, because I wouldn't allow him to go away as Jan Bronski had always gone away from my mother; for Mama had always said go away to Jan and go away to Matzerath, go away, go away. And then they fell apart. But I couldn't bear to see it. After all, I hadn't gone away. That's why I am the father and not this Matzerath who to the last supposed himself to be my father. But my father was Jan Bronski. Jan Bronski got there ahead of Matzerath and didn't go away; he stayed right where he was and deposited everything he had; from Jan Bronski I inherited this quality of getting there ahead of Matzerath and staying put; what emerged was my son, not his son. He never had any son at all. He was no real father. Even if he had married my poor mama ten times over, even if he did marry Maria because she was pregnant. That, he thought, is certainly what the people in the neighborhood think. Of course they thought Matzerath had knocked up Maria and that's why he's marrying her though she's only seventeen and he's going on forty-five. But she's a mighty good worker for her age and as for little Oskar, he can be very glad to have such a stepmother, for Maria doesn't treat the poor child like a stepmother but like a real mother, even if little Oskar isn't quite right in the head and actually belongs in the nuthouse in Silberhammer or Tapiau.

On Gretchen Scheffler's advice, Matzerath decided to marry my sweetheart. If we think of this presumptive father of mine as my father, it follows inevitably that my father married my future wife, called my son Kurt his son Kurt, and expected me to acknowledge his grandson as my half-brother, to accept the presence of my darling vanilla-scented Maria as a stepmother and to tolerate her presence in his bed, which stank of fish roe. But if, more in conformance to the truth, I say: this Matzerath is not even your presumptive father, he is a total stranger to you, deserving neither to be liked nor disliked, who is a good cook, who with his good cooking has thus far been a father of sorts to you, because your poor mother handed him down to you, who now in the eyes of all has purloined the best of women away from you, who compels you to witness his marriage and five months later a baptism, to play the role of guest at two family functions where you should properly have been the host, for *you* should have taken Maria to the City Hall, *you* should have picked the child's godfather and godmother. When I considered the miscasting of this tragedy, I had to despair of the theater, for Oskar, the real lead, had been cast in the role of an extra, that might just as well have been dropped.

Before I give my son the name of Kurt, before I name him as he should never have been named—for I would have named the boy after his great-grandfather Vincent Bronski—before I resign myself to Kurt, Oskar feels obliged to tell you how in the course of Maria's pregnancy he defended himself against the expected event.

On the evening of the very same day on which I surprised the two of them on the sofa, the day when I sat drumming on Matzerath's sweat-bathed back and frustrated the precautions demanded by Maria, I made a desperate attempt to win back my sweetheart.

Matzerath succeeded in shaking me off when it was already too late. As a result, he struck me. Maria took Oskar under her protection and reviled Matzerath for not taking care. Matzerath defended himself like an old man. It was Maria's fault, he protested, she should have been satisfied with once, but she never had enough. Maria wept and said with her things didn't go so quick, in and out before you can say Pilsener beer, he'd better get somebody else, yes, she admitted she was inexperienced but her sister Guste that was at the Eden knew what was what and she said it don't go so quick, Maria had better watch out, some men just wanted to shoot their snot, the sooner the better, and it looked like Matzerath was one of that kind, but he could count her out from now on, her bell had to ring too, like last time. But just the same he should have been careful, he owed her that much consideration. Then she cried some more and stayed sitting on the sofa. And Matzerath in his under-drawers shouted that he couldn't abide her wailing any more; then he was sorry he had lost his temper and blundered again, that is, he tried to pat her bare ass under her dress, and that really threw Maria into a tizzy.

Oskar had never seen her that way. Red spots came out all over her face and her gray eyes got darker and darker. She called Matzerath a mollycoddle, whereupon he picked up his trousers, stepped in, and but-toned up. She screamed for all she was worth: he could clear out for all she cared, he could join his unit leaders, a bunch of quick-squirts the whole lot of them. Matzerath picked up his jacket and gripped the door-knob, there'd be changes, he assured her, he had women up to here; if she was so hot, why didn't she get her hooks on one of the foreign laborers, the Frenchie that brought the beer would surely do it better. To him, Matzerath, love meant something more than piggishness, he was going to shoot some skat, in a skat game at least you knew what to expect.

224

And then I was alone with Maria in the living room. She had stopped crying and was thoughtfully pulling on her panties, whistling, but very sparingly. For a long while she smoothed out her dress that had lain on the sofa. Then she turned on the radio and tried to listen to the announcement of the water level of the Vistula and Nogat. When, after announcing the level of the lower Mottlau, the speaker promised a waltz and his promise was directly kept, she suddenly removed her panties again, went into the kitchen, plunked down a basin, and turned the water on; I heard the puffing of the gas and guessed that Maria had decided to take a sitz bath.

In order to dispel this rather unpleasant image, Oskar concentrated on the strains of the waltz. If I remember aright, I even drummed a few measures of Strauss and enjoyed it. Then the waltz was broken off for a special communiqué. Oskar bet on news from the Atlantic and was not mistaken. Several U-boats had succeeded in sinking seven or eight ships of so and so many thousand tons off the west coast of Ireland. Another group of subs had sent almost as much tonnage to the bottom. A U-boat under Lieutenant Schepke—or it may have been Lieutenant Kretschmar, in any case it was one or the other of them unless it was a third equally famous submarine captain—had especially distinguished itself, sinking not only the most tonnage but also a British destroyer of the XY class.

While I on my drum picked up the ensuing "Sailing against England" and almost turned it into a waltz, Maria came into the living room with a Turkish towel under her arm. In an undertone she said: "Did you hear that, Oskar, another special communiqué. If they keep on like that . . ."

Without letting Oskar know what would happen if they kept on like that, Maria sat down in the chair on which Matzerath customarily hung his jacket. She twisted the wet towel into a sausage and whistled "Sailing against England" along with the radio; she whistled loudly and in tune. She repeated the final chorus once more after it had stopped on the radio, and switched off the radio as soon as the strains of immortal waltz resumed. She left the sausaged towel on the table, sat down, and rested her sweet little hands on her thighs.

A deep silence fell in our living room, only the grandfather clock spoke louder and louder and Maria seemed to be wondering whether it might not be better to turn on the radio again. But then she made another decision. She pressed her face to the sausaged towel on the table, let her arms hang down between her knees to carpetward, and began, steadily and silently, to weep.

Oskar wondered if Maria was ashamed because of the embarrassing situation I had found her in. I decided to cheer her up; I crept out of the living room and in the dark shop, beside the waxed paper and packages of pudding, found a little package which in the corridor, where there was some light, proved to be a package of fizz powder with woodruff flavoring. Oskar was pleased with his blind choice, for at the time it seemed to me that Maria preferred woodruff to all other flavors.

When I entered the living room, Maria's right cheek still lay on the bunched-up towel. Her arms still dangled helplessly between her thighs. Oskar approached her from the left and was disappointed when he saw that her eyes were closed and dry. I waited patiently until her eyelids stickily opened, and held out the package, but she didn't notice the woodruff, she seemed to look through the package and Oskar too.

Her tears must have blinded her, I thought, for I wanted to forgive her; after a moment's deliberation, I decided on a more direct approach. Oskar crawled under the table, and huddled at Maria's feet—the toes were turned slightly inward—took one of her dangling hands, twisted it till I could see the palm, tore open the package with my teeth, strewed half the contents into the inert bowl, and contributed my saliva. Just as the powder began to foam, I received a sharp kick in the chest that sent Oskar sprawling under the table.

In spite of the pain I was on my feet in an instant and out from under the table. Maria stood up too, and we stood face to face, breathing hard. Maria picked up the towel, wiped her hand clean, and flung the towel at my feet; she called me a loathsome pig, a vicious midget, a crazy gnome, that ought to be chucked in the nuthouse. She grabbed hold of me, slapped the back of my head, and reviled my poor mama for having brought a brat like me into the world. When I prepared to scream, having declared war on all the glass in the living room and in the whole world, she stuffed the towel in my mouth; I bit into it and it was tougher than tough boiled beef.

Only when Oskar made himself turn red and blue did she let me go. I might easily have screamed all the glasses and windowpanes in the room to pieces and repeated my childhood assault on the dial of the grandfather clock. I did not scream, I opened the gates of my heart to a hatred so deep-seated that to this day, whenever Maria comes into the room, I feel it between my teeth like that towel.

Capricious as Maria could be, she forgot her anger. She gave a good-natured laugh and with a single flip turned the radio back on again. Whistling the radio waltz, she came toward me, meaning to make up, to stroke my hair. The fact is that I liked her to stroke my hair.

Oskar let her come very close. Then with both fists he landed an uppercut in the exact same spot where she had admitted Matzerath. She caught my fists before I could strike again, whereupon I sank my teeth into the same accursed spot and, still clinging fast, fell with Maria to the sofa. I heard the radio promising another special communiqué, but Oskar had no desire to listen; consequently he cannot tell you who sank what or how much, for a violent fit of tears loosened my jaws and I lay motionless on Maria, who was crying with pain, while Oskar cried from hate and love, which turned to a leaden helplessness but could not die.

How Oskar Took His Helplessness to Mrs. Greff

I didn't like Greff. Greff didn't like me. Even later on, when Greff made me the drumming machine, I didn't like him. Lasting antipathies require a fortitude that Oskar hasn't really got, but I still don't care much for Greff, even now that Greff has gone out of existence.

Greff was a greengrocer. But don't be deceived. He believed neither in potatoes nor in cabbage, yet he knew a great deal about vegetable-raising and liked to think of himself as a gardener, a friend of nature, and a vegetarian. But precisely because Greff ate no meat, he was not an authentic greengrocer. It was impossible for him to talk about vegetables as vegetables. "Will you kindly look at this extraordinary potato," I often heard him say to a customer. "This swelling, bursting vegetable flesh, always devising new forms and yet so chaste. I love a potato because it speaks to me." Obviously, no real greengrocer will embarrass his customers with such talk. Even in the best potato years, my grandmother Anna Koljaiczek, who had grown old in potato fields, would never say anything more than: "Hm, the spuds are a little bigger than last year." Yet Anna Koljaiczek and her brother Vincent Bronski were far more dependent on the potato harvest than Greff, for in his line of business a good plum year could make up for a bad potato year.

Everything about Greff was overdone. Did he absolutely have to wear a green apron in the shop? The presumption of the man! The knowing smile he would put on to explain that this spinach-green rag of his was "God's green gardener's apron." Worst of all, he just couldn't give up boy-scouting. He had been forced to disband his group in '38—his boys had been put into brown shirts or dashing black winter uniforms—but the former scouts, in civilian clothes or in their new uniforms, came regularly to see their former scout leader, to sing morning songs, evening songs, hiking songs, soldier's songs, harvest songs, hymns to the Virgin, and folk songs native and foreign. Since Greff had joined the National Socialist Motorists' Corps before it was too late and from 1941 on termed himself not only greengrocer but air raid warden as well; since, moreover, he had the support of two former scouts who had meanwhile made places for themselves, one as a squad leader, the other as a platoon leader, in the Hitler Youth, the song feasts in Greff's potato cellar were tolerated if not exactly authorized by the district bureau of the Party. Greff was even asked by Löbsack, the district chief of training, to organize song festivals during the training courses at Jenkau Castle. Early in 1940 Greff and a certain schoolteacher were commissioned to compile a young people's songbook for the district of Danzig-West Prussia, under the title: "Sing with Us." The book was quite a success. The greengrocer received a letter from Berlin, signed by the Reich Youth Leader, and was invited to attend a meeting of song leaders in Berlin.

Greff certainly had ability. He knew all the verses of all the songs; he could pitch tents, kindle and quench campfires without provoking forest fires, and find his way in the woods with a compass, he knew the first names of all the visible stars and could reel off no end of stories of both the funny and exciting variety; he knew the legends of the Vistula country and gave lectures on "Danzig and the Hanseatic League." He could list all the grand masters of the Teutonic Knights with the corresponding dates, and even that did not satisfy him; he could talk for hours about the Germanic mission in the territories of the Order, and it was only very rarely that locutions smacking too strongly of boy scout turned up in his lectures.

Greff liked young people. He liked boys more than girls. Actually he didn't like girls at all, just boys. Often he liked boys more than the singing of songs could express. Possibly it was Mrs. Greff, a sloven with greasy brassieres and holes in her underwear, who made him seek a purer measure of love among wiry, clean-cut boys. But perhaps, on the other hand, the tree on whose branches Mrs. Greff's dirty underwear blossomed at every season of the year had another root. Perhaps, that is, Mrs. Greff became a sloven because the greengrocer and air raid warden lacked sufficient appreciation of her carefree and rather stupid *embonpoint*.

Greff liked everything that was hard, taut, muscular. When he said "nature," he meant asceticism. When he said "asceticism," he meant a particular kind of physical culture. Greff was an expert on the subject of his body. He took elaborate care of it, exposing it to heat and, with special inventiveness, to cold. While Oskar sang glass, far and near, to pieces, occasionally thawing the frost flowers on the windowpanes, melting icicles and sending them to the ground with a crash, the greengrocer was a man who attacked ice at close quarters, with hand tools.

Greff made holes in the ice. In December, January, February, he made holes in the ice with an ax. Long before dawn, he would haul his bicycle up from the cellar and wrap his ice ax in an onion sack. Then he would ride via Saspe to Brösen, whence he would take the snow-covered beach promenade in the direction of Glettkau. Between Brösen and Glettkau he would alight. As the day slowly dawned, he would push his bicycle over the icy beach, and then two or three hundred yards out into the frozen Baltic. The scene was immersed in coastal fog. No one could have seen from the beach how Greff laid down the bicycle, unwrapped the ax from the onion sack, and stood for a while in devout silence, listening to the foghorns of the icebound freighters in the roadstead. Then he would throw off his smock, do a bit of gymnastics, and finally begin, with steady, powerful strokes, to dig a circular hole in the Baltic Sea.

Greff needed a good three-quarters of an hour for his hole. Don't ask me, please, how I know. Oskar knew just about everything in those days, including the length of time it took Greff to dig his hole in the ice. Drops of salt sweat formed on his high, bumpy forehead and flew off into the snow. He handled his ax well; its strokes left a deep circular track. When the circle had come full circle, his gloveless hands lifted a disk, perhaps six or seven inches thick, out of the great sheet of ice that extended, it seems safe to say, as far as Hela if not Sweden. The water in the hole was old and gray, shot through with ice-grits. It steamed a bit, though it was not a hot spring. The hole attracted fish. That is, holes in the ice are said to attract fish. Greff might have caught lampreys or a twenty-pound cod. But he did not fish. He began to undress. He took off his clothes and he was soon stark naked, for Greff's nakedness was always stark.

Oskar is not trying to send winter shudders running down your spine. In view of the climate, he prefers to make a long story short: twice a week, during the winter months, Greff the greengrocer bathed in the Baltic. On Wednesday he bathed alone at the crack of dawn. He started off at six, arrived at half-past, and dug until a quarter past seven. Then he tore off his clothes with quick, excessive movements, rubbed himself with snow, jumped into the hole, and, once in it, began to shout. Or sometimes I heard him sing: "Wild geese are flying through the night" or "Oh, how we love the storm . . . ." He sang, shouted, and bathed for two minutes, or three at most. Then with a single leap he was standing, terrifyingly distinct, on the ice: a steaming mass of lobstery flesh, racing round the hole, glowing, and still shouting. In the end, he was dressed once more and departing with his bicycle. Shortly before eight, he was back in Labesweg and his shop opened punctually.

Greff's other weekly bath was taken on Sunday, in the company of several boys, youths, striplings, or young men. This is something Oskar never saw or claimed to have seen. But the word got round. Meyn the musician knew stories about the greengrocer and trumpeted them all over the neighborhood. One of his trumpeter's tales was that every Sunday in the grimmest winter months Greff bathed in the company of several boys. Yet even Meyn never claimed that Greff made the boys jump naked into the hole in the ice like himself. He seems to have been perfectly satisfied if, lithe and sinewy, they tumbled and gamboled about on the ice, half-naked or mostly naked, and rubbed each other with snow. So appealing to Greff were striplings in the snow that he often romped with them before or after his bath, helped them with their reciprocal rubdowns, or allowed the entire horde to rub him down. Meyn the musician claimed that despite the perpetual fog he once saw from the Glettkau beach promenade how an appallingly naked, singing, shouting Greff lifted up two of his naked disciples and, naked laden with naked, a roaring, frenzied troika raced headlong over the solidly frozen surface of the Baltic.

It is easy to guess that Greff was not a fisherman's son, although there were plenty of fishermen named Greff in Brösen and Neufahrwasser. Greff the greengrocer hailed from Tiegenhof, but he had met Lina Greff, née Bartsch, at Praust. There he had helped an enterprising young vicar to run an apprentices' club, and Lina, on the same vicar's account, went to the parish house every Saturday. To judge by a snapshot, which she must have given me, for it is still in my album, Lina, at the age of twenty, was robust, plump, light-headed, and dumb. Her father raised fruit and vegetables on a considerable market garden at Sankt Albrecht. As she later related on every possible occasion, she was quite inexperienced when at the age of twenty-three she married Greff on the vicar's advice. With her father's money they opened the vegetable store in Langfuhr. Since her father provided them with a large part of their vegetables and nearly all their fruit at low prices, the business virtually ran itself and Greff could do little damage.

Without Greff's childish tendency to invent mechanical contrivances, he could easily have made a gold mine of this store, so well situated, so far removed from all competition, in a suburb swarming with children. But when the inspector from the Bureau of Weights and Measures presented himself for the third or fourth time, checked the scales, confiscated the weights, and decreed an assortment of fines, some of Greff's regular customers left him and took to buying at the market. There was nothing wrong with the quality of Greff's vegetables, they said, and his prices were not too high, but the inspectors had been there again, and something fishy must be going on.

Yet I am certain Greff had no intention of cheating anyone. This is what had happened: After Greff had made certain changes in his big potato scales, they weighed to his disadvantage. Consequently, just before the war broke out, he equipped these self-same scales with a set of chimes which struck up a tune after every weighing operation; what tune depended on the weight registered. A customer who bought twenty pounds of potatoes was regaled, as a kind of premium, with "On the Sunny Shores of the Saale"; fifty pounds of potatoes got you "Be True and Upright to the Grave," and a hundredweight of winter potatoes made the chimes intone the naively bewitching strains of "Ännchen von Tharau."

Though I could esily see that these musical fancies might not be to the liking of the Bureau of Weights and Measures, Oskar was all in favor of the greengrocer's little hobbies. Even Lina Greff was indulgent about her husband's eccentricities, because, well, because the essence and content of the Greff marriage was forbearance with each other's foibles. In this light the Greff marriage may be termed a good marriage. Greff did not beat his wife, was never unfaithful to her with other women, and was neither a drinker nor a debauchee; he was a good-humored man who dressed carefully and was well liked for his sociable, helpful ways, not only by lads and striplings but also by those of his customers who went on taking music with their potatoes.

And so Greff looked on calmly and indulgently as his Lina from year to year became an increasingly foul-smelling sloven. I remember seeing him smile when sympathetic friends called a sloven a sloven. Blowing into and rubbing his own hands, which were nicely kept in spite of the potatoes, he would sometimes, in my hearing, say to Matzerath, who had been chiding him over his wife: "Of course you're perfectly right, Alfred. Our good Lina does rather let herself go. But haven't we all got our faults?" If Matzerath persisted, Greff would close the discussion in a firm though friendly tone: "You may be right on certain points, but Lina has a good heart. I know my Lina."

Maybe he did. But she knew next to nothing of him. Like the neighbors and customers, she never saw anything more in Greff's relations with his frequent youthful visitors than the enthusiasm of young men for a devoted, though nonprofessional, friend and educator of the young. As for me, Greff could neither educate me nor fire me with enthusiasm. Actually Oskar was not his type. If I had made up my mind to grow, I might have become his type, for my lean and lank son Kurt is the exact embodiment of Greff's type, though he takes mostly after Maria, bears little resemblance to me, and none whatever to Matzerath.

Greff was one witness to the marriage of Maria Truczinski and Alfred Matzerath; the other was Fritz Truczinski, home on furlough. Since Maria, like the bridegroom, was a Protestant, they only had a civil marriage. That was in the middle of December. Matzerath said "I do" in his Party uniform. Maria was in her third month. The stouter my sweetheart became, the more Oskar's hate mounted. I had no objection to her being pregnant. But that the fruit by me engendered should one day bear the name of Matzerath deprived me of all pleasure in my anticipated son and heir. Maria was in her fifth month when I made my first attempt at abortion, much too late of course. It was in Carnival. Maria was fastening some paper streamers and clown's masks with potato noses to the brass bar over the counter, where the sausage and bacon were hung. Ordinarily the ladder had solid support in the shelves; now it was propped up precariously on the counter. Maria high above with her hands full of streamers, Oskar far below, at the foot of the ladder. Using my drumsticks as levers, helping with my shoulder and firm resolve, I raised the foot of the ladder, then pushed it to one side: amid streamers and masks, Maria let out a faint cry of terror. The ladder tottered, Oskar jumped to one side, and beside him fell Maria, drawing colored paper, sausages, and masks in her wake. It looked worse than it was. She had only turned her ankle, she had to lie down and be careful, but there was no serious injury. Her shape grew worse and worse and she didn't even tell Matzerath who had been responsible for her turned ankle. It was not until May of the following year when, some three weeks before the child was scheduled to be born, I made my second try, that she spoke to Matzerath, her husband, though even then she didn't tell him the whole truth. At table, right in front of me, she said: "Oskar has been awful rough these days. Sometimes he hits me in the belly. Maybe we could leave him with my mother until the baby gets born. She has plenty of room."

Matzerath heard and believed. In reality, a fit of murderous frenzy had brought on a very different sort of encounter between Maria and me.

She had lain down on the sofa after lunch. Matzerath had finished washing the dishes and was in the shop decorating the window. It was quiet in the living room. Maybe the buzzing of a fly, the clock as usual, on the radio a newscast about the exploits of the paratroopers on Crete had been turned low. I perked up an ear only when they put on Max Schmeling, the boxer. As far as I could make out, he had hurt his world's champion's ankle, landing on the stony soil of Crete, and now he had to lie down and take care of himself; just like Maria, who had had to lie down after her fall from the ladder. Schmeling spoke with quiet modesty, when some less illustrious paratroopers spoke, and Oskar stopped listening: it was quiet, maybe the buzzing of a fly, the clock as usual, the radio turned very low.

I sat by the window on my little bench and observed Maria's belly on the sofa. She breathed heavily and kept her eyes closed. From time to time I tapped my drum morosely. She didn't stir, but still she made me breathe in the same room with her belly. The clock was still there, and the fly between windowpane and curtain, and the radio with the stony island of Crete in the background. But quickly all this was submerged; all I could see was that belly; I knew neither in what room that bulging belly was situated, nor to whom it belonged, I hardly remembered who had made it so big. All I knew was that I couldn't bear it: it's got to be suppressed, it's a mistake, it's cutting off your view, you've got to stand up and do something about it. So I stood up. You've got to investigate, to see what can be done. So I approached the belly and took something with me. That's a malignant swelling, needs to be deflated. I lifted the object I had taken with me and looked for a spot between Maria's hands that lay breathing with her belly. Now is the time, Oskar, or Maria will open her eyes. Already I felt that I was being watched, but I just stood gazing at Maria's slightly trembling left hand, though I saw her right hand moving, saw she was planning something with her right hand, and was not greatly surprised when Maria, with her right hand, twisted the scissors out of Oskar's fist. I may have stood there for another few seconds with hand upraised but empty, listening to the clock, the fly, the voice of the radio announcer announcing the end of the Crete program, then I turned about and before the next program—light music from two to three—could begin, left our living room, which in view of that space-filling abdomen had become too small for me.

Two days later Maria bought me a new drum and took me to Mother Truczinski's third-floor flat, smelling of ersatz coffee and fried potatoes. At first I slept on the couch; for fear of lingering vanilla Oskar refused to sleep in Herbert's old bed. A week later old man Heilandt carried my wooden crib up the stairs. I allowed them to set it up beside the bed which had harbored me, Maria, and our fizz powder.

Oskar grew calmer or more resigned at Mother Truczinski's. I was spared the sight of the belly, for Maria feared to climb the stairs. I avoided our apartment, the store, the street, even the court, where rabbits were being raised again as food became harder to come by.

Oskar spent most of his time looking at the postcards that Sergeant Fritz Truczinski had sent or brought with him from Paris. I had my ideas about the city of Paris and when Mother Truczinski brought me a postcard of the Eiffel Tower, I took up the theme and began to drum Paris, to drum a musette though I had never heard one.

On June 12, two weeks too soon according to my calculations, in the sign of Gemini and not as I had reckoned in that of Cancer, my son Kurt was born. The father in a Jupiter year, the son in a Venus year. The father dominated by Mercury in Virgo, which makes for skepticism and ingenuity; the son likewise governed by Mercury but in the sign of Gemini, hence endowed with a cold, ambitious intelligence. What in me was attenuated by the Venus of Libra in the house of the ascendant was aggravated in my son by Aries in the same house; I was to have trouble with his Mars.

With mousy excitement, Mother Truczinski imparted the news: "Just think, Oskar, the stork has brought you a little brother. Just when I was beginning to think if only it isn't a girl that makes so much worry later on." I scarcely interrupted my drumming of the Eiffel Tower and the Arc de Triomphe, which had arrived in the meantime. Even in the guise of Grandma Truczinski, Mother Truczinski seemed to expect no congratulations from me. Though it was Sunday, she decided to put on a little color, rubbed her cheeks with the good old chicory wrapping, and thus freshly painted, went downstairs to give Matzerath, the alleged father, a hand.

As I have said, it was June. A deceptive month. Victories on all fronts—if you choose to lend so high-sounding a term to victories in the

Balkans—but still greater triumphs were imminent on the Eastern Front. An enormous army was moving forward. The railroads were being kept very busy. Fritz Truczinski, who until then had been having so delightful a time of it in Paris, was also compelled to embark on an eastward journey which would prove to be a very long one and could not be mistaken for a trip home on furlough. Oskar, however, sat quietly looking at the shiny postcards, dwelling in the mild Paris springtime, and lightly drumming "Trois jeunes tambours"; having no connection with the Army of Occupation, he had no reason to fear that any partisans would attempt to toss him off the Seine bridges. No, it was clad as a civilian that I climbed the Eiffel Tower with my drum and enjoyed the view just as one is expected to, feeling so good and despite the tempting heights so free from bittersweet thoughts of suicide, that it was only on descending, when I stood three feet high at the foot of the Eiffel Tower, that I remembered the birth of my son.

Voilà, I thought, a son. When he is three years old, he will get a tin drum. We'll see who's the father around here, that Mr. Matzerath or I, Oskar Bronski.

In the heat of August—I believe that the successful conclusion of another battle of encirclement, that of Smolensk, had just been announced—my son Kurt was baptized. But how did my grandmother Anna Koljaiczek and her brother Vincent Bronski come to be invited? Of course if you accept—as I do—the version according to which Jan Bronski was my father and the silent, increasingly eccentric Vincent Bronski my paternal grandfather, there was reason enough for the invitation. After all my grandparents were my son Kurt's great-grandparents.

But it goes without saying that no such reasoning ever occurred to Matzerath, who had sent the invitation. Even in his moments of darkest self-doubt, even after losing a game of skat by six lengths, he regarded himself as twice a progenitor, father, and provider. It was other considerations that gave Oskar the opportunity to see his grandparents. The old folks had been turned into Germans. They were Poles no longer and spoke Kashubian only in their dreams. German Nationals, Group 3, they were called. Moreover, Hedwig Bronski, Jan's widow, had married a Baltic German who was local peasant leader in Ramkau. Petitions were already under way, which, when approved, would entitle Marga and Stephan Bronski to take the name of their stepfather Ehlers. Seventeen-year-old Stephan had volunteered, he was now in the infantry Training Camp at Gross-Boschpol and had good prospects of visiting the war theaters of Europe, while Oskar, who would soon be of military age, was reduced to waiting behind his drum until there should be an opening for a three-year-old drummer in the Army or Navy, or even in the Air Corps.

It was Local Peasant Leader Ehlers who took the first steps. Two weeks before the baptism he drove up to Labesweg with Hedwig beside him on the seat of a carriage and pair. He had bowlegs and stomach trouble and was not to be mentioned in the same breath with Jan Bronski. A good head shorter than Jan, he sat beside cow-eyed Hedwig at our living room table. The looks of the man came as a surprise, even to Matzerath. The conversation refused to get started. They spoke of the weather, observed that all sorts of things were happening in the East, that our troops were getting ahead fine—much faster than in '15, as Matzerath, who had been there in '15, remembered. All took great pains not to speak of Jan Bronski, until I spoiled their game by making a droll infantile pout and crying out loudly and more than once for Oskar's Uncle Jan. Matzerath gave himself a jolt and said something affectionate followed by something thoughtful about his former friend and rival. Ehlers joined in effusively, although he had never laid eyes on his predecessor. Hedwig even produced a few authentic tears that rolled slowly down her cheeks and finally said the words that closed the topic of Jan: "He was a good man. He wouldn't hurt a fly. Who'd have thought he'd come to such an end, a scarecat like him that was scared of his shadow."

These words having been spoken, Matzerath bade Maria, who was standing behind him, to bring in a few bottles of beer and asked Ehlers if he played skat. No, Ehlers was sorry to say he didn't, but Matzerath magnanimously forgave the peasant leader this little shortcoming. He even gave him a tap on the shoulder and assured him, after the beer glasses had been filled, that it didn't matter if he wasn't a skat player, they could still be good friends.

Thus Hedwig Bronski in the guise of Hedwig Ehlers found her way back to our flat and brought with her, to attend the baptism of my son Kurt, not only her local peasant leader but also her former father-in-law Vincent Bronski and his sister Anna. Matzerath gave the old folks a loud, friendly welcome out in the street, beneath the neighbors' windows, and in the living room, when my grandmother reached under her four skirts and brought forth her baptismal gift, a fine fat goose, he said: "You didn't have to do that, Grandma. I'd be glad to have you even if you didn't bring a thing." But this was going too far for my grandmother, who wanted her goose to be appreciated. Smacking the noble bird with the palm of her hand, she protested: "Don't make so much fuss, Alfred. She's no Kashubian goose, she's a German National bird and tastes just like before the war."

With this all problems of nationality were solved and everything went smoothly until it came time for the baby to be baptized and Oskar refused to set foot in the Protestant church. They took my drum out of the taxi and tried to lure me with it, assuring me not once but several times that drums were allowed in Protestant churches. I persevered, however, in the blackest Catholicism; I would rather at that moment have poured a detailed and comprehensive confession into the apostolic ear of

Father Wiehnke than listen to a Protestant baptismal sermon. Matzerath gave in, probably dreading my voice and attendant damage claims. While my son was being baptized, I remained in the taxi, staring at the back of the driver's head, scrutinizing Oskar's features in the rear view mirror, thinking of my own baptism, already far in the past, and of Father Wiehnke's valiant effort to drive Satan out of the infant Oskar.

Afterwards we ate. Two tables had been put together. First came mock turtle soup. The countryfolk lapped. Greff crooked his little finger. Gretchen Scheffler bit into the soup. Guste smiled broadly over her spoon. Ehlers spoke with the spoon in his mouth. Vincent's hands shook as he looked for something that wouldn't come into the spoon. Only the old women, Grandma Anna and Mother Truczinski, were committed heart and soul to their spoons. As for Oskar, he dropped his and slipped away while the others were still spooning and sought out his son's cradle in the bedroom, for he wanted to think about his son, while the others, behind their spoons, shriveled more and more into unthinking, spooned-out emptiness, even though the soup was being spooned, not out of, but into them.

Over the basket on wheels a sky-blue canopy of tulle. The edge of the basket was too high and all I could see at first was a puckered little reddish-bluish head. By laying my drum on the floor and standing on it. I was able to observe my sleeping son, who twitched nervously as he slept. O paternal pride, ever on the lookout for grand words! Gazing upon my infant son, I could think of nothing but the short sentence: When he is three years old, he shall have a drum. My son refused to grant me the slightest insight into his intellectual situation, and I could only hope that he might, like me, belong to the race of clairaudient infants. Quite at a loss, I repeated my promise of a drum for his third birthday, descended from my pedestal, and once more tried my chance with the grownups in the living room.

They were just finishing the mock turtle soup. Maria brought in canned green peas with melted butter. Matzerath, who was responsible for the pork roast, dressed the platter in person; he took his coat off and, standing in his shirtsleeves, cut slice after slice, his features so full of unabashed tenderness over the tender, succulent meat that I had to avert my eyes.

Greff was served separately: he was given canned asparagus, hard-boiled eggs, and black radish with cream, because vegetarians eat no meat. Like the others, he took a dab of mashed potatoes: however, he moistened them not with meat gravy but with brown butter which the attentive Maria brought in from the kitchen in a sizzling frying pan. While the others drank beer, he drank apple juice. The encirclement of Kiev was discussed, the prisoners taken counted on fingers. Ehlers, a native of the Baltic, showed a special aptitude for counting Russian prisoners; at every hundred thousand, a finger shot up; when his two outstreched hands had completed a million, he went right on counting by decapitating one finger after another. When the subject of prisoners, whose mounting numbers made them increasingly useless and uninteresting, was exhausted, Scheffler spoke of the U-boats at Gotenhafen and Matzerath whispered in my grandmother Anna's ear that they were launching two subs a week at Schichau. Thereupon Greff explained to all present why submarines had to be launched sideways instead of stem first. He was determined to make it all very clear and visual; for every operation he had a gesture which those of the guests who were fascinated by U-boats imitated attentively and awkwardly. Trying to impersonate a diving submarine, Vincent Bronski's left hand upset his beer glass. My grandmother started to scold him. But Maria smoothed her down, saying it didn't matter, the tablecloth was due for the laundry anyway, you couldn't celebrate without making spots. Mother Truczinski came in with a cloth and mopped up the pool of beer; in her left hand she carried our large crystal bowl, full of chocolate pudding with crushed almonds.

Ah me, if that chocolate pudding had only had some other sauce or no sauce at all! But it had to be vanilla sauce, rich and yellow and viscous: vanilla sauce! Perhaps there is nothing so joyous and nothing so sad in this world as vanilla sauce. Softly the vanilla scent spread round about, enveloping me more and more in Maria, to the point that I couldn't bear to look at her, root and source of all vanilla, who sat beside Matzerath, holding his hand in hers.

Oskar slipped off his baby chair, clung to the skirts of Lina Greff, lay at her feet as above board she wielded her spoon. For the first time I breathed in the effluvium peculiar to Lina Greff, which instantly outshouted, engulfed, and killed all vanilla.

Acrid as it was to my nostrils, I clung to the new perfume until all recollections connected with vanilla seemed to be dulled. Slowly, without the slightest sound or spasm, I was seized with a redeeming nausea. While the mock turtle soup, the roast pork in chunks, the canned green peas almost intact, and the few spoonfuls I had taken of chocolate pudding with vanilla sauce escaped me, I became fully aware of my helplessness, I wallowed in my helplessness. Oskar's helplessness spread itself out at the feet of Lina Greff—and I decided that from then on and daily I should carry my helplessness to Lina Greff.

165 lbs.

Vyazma and Bryansk; then the mud set in. In the middle of October, 1941, Oskar too began to wallow intensively in mud. I hope I shall be forgiven for drawing a parallel between the muddy triumphs of Army Group Center and my own triumphs in the impassable and equally muddy terrain of Mrs. Lina Greff. Just as tanks and trucks bogged down on the approaches to Moscow, so I too bogged down; just as the wheels went on spinning, churning up the mud of Russia, so I too kept on trying— I feel justified in saying that I churned the Greffian mud into a foaming lather—but neither on the approaches to Moscow nor in the Greff bedroom was any ground gained.

I am not quite ready to drop my military metaphor: just as future strategists would draw a lesson from these unsuccessful operations in the mud, so I too would draw my conclusions from the natural phenomenon named Lina Greff. Our efforts on the home front during the Second World War should not be underestimated. Oskar was only seventeen, and despite his tender years Lina Greff, that endless and insidious infiltration course, made a man of him. But enough of military comparisons. Let us measure Oskar's progress in artistic terms: If Maria, with her naively bewitching clouds of vanilla, taught me to appreciate the small, the delicate; if she taught me the lyricism of fizz powder and mushroom-picking, then Mrs. Greff's acrid vapors, compounded of multiple effluvia, may be said to have given me the epic breadth which enables me today to mention military victories and bedroom triumphs in the same breath. Music! From Maria's childlike, sentimental, and yet so sweet harmonica I was transported, without transition, to the concert hall, and I was the conductor; for Lina Greff offered me an orchestra, so graduated in depth and breadth that you will hardly find its equal in Bayreuth or Salzburg. There I mastered brasses and wood winds, the percussion, the stings, bowed and pizzicato; I mastered harmony and counterpoint, classical and diatonic, the entry of the scherzo and the tempo of the andante; my beat could be hard and precise or soft and fluid; Oskar got the maximum out of his instrument, namely Mrs. Greff, and yet, as befits a true artist, he remained dis- if not un-satisfied.

The Greff vegetable shop was only a few steps across and down the street from our store. A convenient location, much handier for me than the quarters of Alexander Scheffler, the master baker, in Kleinhammer-Weg. Maybe the convenient situation was the main reason why I made rather more progress in female anatomy than in the study of my masters Goethe and Rasputin. But perhaps this discrepancy in my education, which remains flagrant to this day, can be explained and in part justified by the difference between my two teachers. While Lina Greff made no attempt to instruct me but passively and in all simplicity spread out all her riches for me to observe and experiment with, Gretchen Scheffler took her pedagogic vocation far too seriously. She wanted to see results, to hear me read aloud, to see my drummer's finger engaged in penmanship, to establish a friendship between me and fair Grammatica and benefit by it her own self. When Oskar refused to show any visible sign of progress,

Gretchen Scheffler lost patience; shortly after the death of my poor mama—by then, it must be admitted, she had been teaching me for seven years—she reverted to her knitting. From then on her interest in me was expressed only by occasional gifts of hand-knitted sweaters, stockings, and mittens—her marriage was still childless—bestowed for the most part on the principal holidays. We no longer read or spoke of Goethe or Rasputin, and it was only thanks to the excerpts from the works of both masters which I still kept hidden in various places, mostly in the attic of our apartment house, that this branch of Oskar's studies was not wholly forgotten; I educated myself and formed my own opinions.

Moored to her bed, the ailing Lina Greff could neither escape nor leave me, for her ailment, though chronic, was not serious enough to snatch Lina, my teacher Lina, away from me. But since on this planet nothing lasts forever, it was Oskar who left his bedridden teacher the moment it seemed to him that his studies were complete.

You will say: how limited the world to which this young man was reduced for his education! A grocery store, a bakery, and a vegetable shop circumscribed the field in which he was obliged to piece together his equipment for adult life. Yes, I must admit that Oskar gathered his first, all-important impressions in very musty *petit-bourgeois* surroundings. However, I had a third teacher. It was he who would open up the world to Oskar and make him what he is today, a person whom, for want of a better epithet, I can only term cosmopolitan.

I am referring, as the most attentive among you will have noted, to my teacher and master Bebra, direct descendant of Prince Eugene, scion from the tree of Louis XIV, the midget and musical clown Bebra. When I say Bebra, I also, it goes without saying, have in mind the woman at his side, Roswitha Raguna, the great somnambulist and timeless beauty, to whom my thoughts were often drawn in those dark years after Matzerath took my Maria away from me. How old, I wondered, can the signora be? Is she a fresh young girl of nineteen or twenty? Or is she the delicate, the graceful old lady of ninety-nine, who in a hundred years will still indestructibly embody the diminutive format of eternal youth.

If I remember correctly, I met these two, so kindred to me in body and spirit, shortly after the death of my poor mama. We drank mocha together in the Café of the Four Seasons, then our ways parted. There were slight, but not negligible political differences; Bebra was close to the Reich Propaganda Ministry, frequented, as I easily inferred from the hints he dropped, the privy chambers of Messrs. Goebbels and Goering —corrupt behavior which he tried, in all sorts of ways, to explain and justify to me. He would talk about the influence wielded by court jesters in the Middle Ages, and show me reproductions of Spanish paintings respresenting some Philip or Carlos with his retinue; in the midst of these stiff, pompous gatherings, one could distinguish fools about the size of Bebra or even Oskar, in ruffs, goatees, and baggy pantaloons. I liked the pictures—for without exaggeration I can call myself an ardent admirer of Diego Velasquez—but for that very reason I refused to be convinced, and after a while he would drop his comparisons between the position of the jester at the court of Philip IV of Spain and his own position in the entourage of the Rhenish upstart Joseph Goebbels. He would go on to speak of the hard times, of the weak who must temporarily incline, of the resistance that thrives in concealment, in short, the words "inward emigration" cropped up, and for Oskar that was the parting of the ways.

Not that I bore the master a grudge. In the years that followed, I searched vaudeville and circus posters for Bebra's name. Twice I found it, side by side with that of Signora Raguna, yet I did nothing that might have led to a meeting with my friends.

I left it to chance, but chance declined to help, for if Bebra's ways and mine had crossed in the autumn of '42 rather than in the following year, Oskar would never have become the pupil of Lina Greff, but would have become the disciple of Bebra the master. As it was, I crossed Labesweg every day, sometimes early in the morning, entered the vegetable shop, for propriety's sake spent half an hour in the vicinity of the greengrocer, who was becoming more and more crotchety and devoting more and more of his time to his inventions. I looked on as he constructed his weird, tinkling, howling, screaming contraptions, and poked him when customers entered the shop; for Greff had ceased to take much notice of the world around him. What had happened? What was it that made the once so open-hearted, so convivial gardener and friend of the young so silent? What was it that transformed him into a lonely, eccentric, rather unkempt old man?

The young people had stopped coming to see him. The new generation didn't know him. His following from the boy scout days had been dispersed by the war. Letters came from various fronts, then there were only postcards, and one day Greff indirectly received the news that his favorite, Horst Donath, first scout, then squad leader, then lieutenant in the Army, had fallen by the Donets.

From that day Greff began to age, neglected his appearance, and devoted himself exclusively to his inventions, until there were more ringing and howling machines to be seen in his shop than potatoes or cabbage. Of course the general food shortage had something to do with it; deliveries to the shop were few and far between, and Greff was not, like Matzerath, a good buyer with good connections in the wholesale market.

The shop was pitiful to look upon, and one could only be grateful to Greff's silly noise machines for taking up space in their absurd but decorative way. I liked the creations that sprang from Greff's increasingly fuzzy brain. When today I look at the knotted string spooks of Bruno my keeper, I am reminded of Greff's exhibits. And just as Bruno relishes my smiling yet serious interest in his artistic amusements, so Greff, in his distraught way, was glad when I took pleasure in one of his music machines. He who for years had paid no attention to me was visibly disappointed when after half an hour I left his vegetable and work shop to call on his wife, Lina Greff.

What shall I tell you about my visits to the bedridden woman, which generally took from two to two and a half hours? When Oskar entered, she beckoned from the bed: "Ah, it's you, Oskar. Well, come on over, come in under the covers if you feel like it, it's cold and Greff hasn't made much of a fire." So I slipped in with her under the featherbed, left my drum and the two sticks I had just been using outside, and permitted only a third drumstick, a used and rather scrawny one, to accompany me on my visit to Lina.

It should not be supposed that I undressed before getting into bed with Lina. In wool, velvet, and leather, I climbed in. And despite the heat generated by my labors, I climbed out of the rumpled feathers some hours later in the same clothing, scarcely disarranged.

Then, fresh from Lina's bed, her effluvia still clinging to me, I would pay another call on Greff. When this had happened several times, he inaugurated a ritual that I was only too glad to observe. Before I arose from the palace of matrimony, he would come into the room with a basin full of warm water and set it down on a stool. Having disposed soap and towel beside it, he would leave the room without a word or so much as a glance in the direction of the bed.

Quickly Oskar would tear himself out of the warm nest, toddle over to the washbasin, and give himself and his bedtime drumstick a good wash; I could readily understand that even at second hand the smell of his wife was more than Greff could stomach.

Freshly washed, however, I was welcome to the inventor. He would demonstrate his machines and their various sounds, and I find it rather surprising to this day that despite this late intimacy no friendship ever developed between Oskar and Greff, that Greff remained a stranger to me, arousing my interest no doubt, but never my sympathy.

It was in September, 1942—my eighteenth birthday had just gone by without pomp or ceremony, on the radio the Sixth Army was taking Stalingrad—that Greff built the drumming machine. A wooden framework, inside it a pair of scales, evenly balanced with potatoes; when a potato was removed from one pan, the scales were thrown off balance and released a lever which set off the drumming mechanism installed on top of the frame. There followed a rolling as of kettledrums, a booming and clanking, basins struck together, a gong rang out, and the end of it all was a tinkling, transitory, tragically cacophonous finale.

The machine appealed to me. Over and over again I would ask Greff to demonstrate it. For Oskar imagined that the greengrocer had invented and built it for him. Soon my mistake was made clear to me. Greff may have taken an idea or two from me, but the machine was intended for himself; for its finale was his finale.

It was a clear October morning such as only the northwest wind delivers free of charge. I had left Mother Truczinski's flat early and Matzerath was just raising the sliding shutter in front of his shop as I stepped out into the street. I stood beside him as the green slats clanked upward; a whiff of pent-up grocery store smell came out at me, then Matzerath kissed me good morning. Before Maria showed herself, I crossed Labesweg, casting a long westward shadow on the cobblestones, for to the right of me, in the East, the sun rose up over Max-Halbe-Platz by its own power, resorting to the same trick as Baron Münchhausen when he lifted himself out of the swamp by his own pigtail.

Anyone who knew Greff the greengrocer as well as I would have been just as surprised to find the door and showcase of his shop still curtained and closed at that hour, the last few years, it is true, had transformed Greff into more and more of a crank. However, the shop had always opened on time. Maybe he is sick, thought Oskar, but dismissed this notion at once. For how could Greff, who only last winter, though perhaps not as regularly as in former years, had chopped holes in the Baltic Sea to bathe in—how, despite certain signs that he was growing older, could this nature lover suddenly fall sick from one day to the next? The privilege of staying in bed was reserved for his wife, who managed for two; moreover, I knew that Greff despised soft mattresses, preferring to sleep on camp beds and wooden planks. There existed no ailment that could have fastened the greengrocer to his bed.

I took up my position outside the closed shop, looked back toward our store, and ascertained that Matzerath was inside; only then did I roll off a few measures on my drum, hoping to attract Mrs. Greff's sensitive ear. Barely a murmur was needed, already the second window to the right beside the shop door opened. La Greff in her nightgown, her hair full of curlers, shielding her bosom with a pillow, appeared over the window box and its ice plants. "Why, Oskar, come in, come in. What are you waiting for when it's so chilly out?"

I explained by tapping the iron curtain over the shop window with one drumstick.

"Albrecht," she cried. "Albrecht, where are you? What's the matter?"

Still calling her husband, she removed herself from the window. Doors slammed, I heard her rattling round the shop, then she began to scream again. She screamed in the cellar, but I couldn't see why she was screaming, for the cellar transom, through which potatoes were poured on delivery days, but more and more seldom in the war years, was also closed. Pressing an eye to the tarred planks covering the transom, I saw that the light was burning in the cellar. I could also distinguish the top part of the cellar steps, on which lay something white, probably Mrs. Greff's pillow.

She must have dropped the pillow on the stairs, for she was no longer in the cellar but screaming again in the shop and a moment later in the bedroom. She picked up the phone, screamed, and dialed; she screamed into the telephone; but Oskar couldn't tell what it was about, all he could catch was accident and the address, Labesweg 24, which she screamed several times. She hung up, and a moment later, screaming in her night-gown, pillowless but still in curlers, she filled the window frame, pouring the vast bipartite bulk with which I was so familiar into the window box, over the ice plants, and thrusting both her hands into the fleshy, pale-red leaves. She screamed upward, so that the street became narrow and it seemed to Oskar that glass must begin to fly. But not a windowpane broke. Windows were torn open, neighbors appeared, women called out questions, men came running, Laubschad the watchmaker, pulling on his jacket, old man Heilandt, Mr. Reissberg, Libischewski the tailor, Mr. Esch, emerged from the nearest house doors; even Probst, not the barber but the coal dealer, appeared with his son. Matzerath came sailing up in his white smock, while Maria, holding Kurt in her arms, stood in the doorway of our store.

I had no difficulty in submerging myself in the swarm of excited grownups and in evading Matzerath, who was looking for me. He and Laubschad the watchmaker were the first to spring into action. They tried to enter the house through the window. But Mrs. Greff wouldn't let anybody climb up, much less enter. Scratching, flailing, and biting, she still managed to find time to scream louder than ever and in part intel-ligibly. The ambulance men should be first to go in; she had telephoned long ago, there was no need for anyone to telephone again, she knew what had to be done in such cases. They should attend to their own shops, things were already bad enough without their meddling. Curiosity, noth-ing but curiosity, you could see who your friends were when trouble came. In the middle of her lament, she must have caught sight of me outside her window, for she called me and, after shaking off the men, held out her bare arms to me, and someone—Oskar still thinks it was Laubschad the watchmaker—lifted me up, tried, despite Matzerath's opposition, to hand me in. Close by the window box, Matzerath nearly caught me, but then Lina Greff reached out, pressed me to her warm nightgown, and stopped screaming. After that she just gave out a falsetto whimpering and between whimpers gasped for air.

A moment before, Mrs. Greff's screams had lashed the neighbors into a shamelessly gesticulating frenzy; now her high, thin whimpering reduced those pressing round the window box to a silent, scraping, embarrassed mob which seemed almost afraid to look her lamentations in the face and projected all its hope, all its curiosity and sympathy into the moment when the ambulance should arrive.

Oskar too was repelled by Mrs. Greff's whimpering. I tried to slip down a little lower, where I wouldn't be quite so close to the source of her lamentations; I managed to relinquish my hold on her neck and to seat myself partly on the window box. But soon Oskar felt he was being watched; Maria, with the child in her arms, was standing in the doorway of the shop. Again I decided to move, for I was keenly aware of the awkwardness of my situation. But I was thinking only of Maria; I didn't care a hoot for the neighbors. I shoved off from the Greffian coast, which was quaking too much for my taste and reminded me of bed.

Lina Greff was unaware of my flight, or else she lacked the strength to restrain the little body which had so long provided her with compensation. Or perhaps she suspected that Oskar was slipping away from her forever, that with her screams a sound had been born which, on the one hand, would become a wall, a sound barrier between the drummer and the bedridden woman, and on the other hand would shatter the wall that had arisen between Maria and myself.

I stood in the Greff bedroom. My drum hung down askew and insecure. Oskar knew the room well, he could have recited the sap-green wallpaper by heart in any direction. The washbasin with the gray soapsuds from the previous day was still in its place. Everything had its place and yet the furniture in that room, worn with sitting, lying, and bumping, looked fresh to me, or at least refreshed, as though all these objects that stood stiffly on four legs along the walls had needed the screams, followed by the falsetto whimpering of Lina Greff, to give them a new, terrifyingly cold radiance.

The door to the shop stood open. Against his will Oskar let himself be drawn into that room, redolent of dry earth and onions. Seeping in through cracks in the shutters, the daylight designed stripes of luminous dust particles in the air. Most of Greff's noise and music machines were hidden in the half-darkness, the light fell only on a few details, a little bell, a wooden prop, the lower part of the drumming machine, the evenly balanced potatoes.

The trap door which, exactly as in our shop, led down to the cellar, stood open. Nothing supported the plank cover which Mrs. Greff must have opened in her screaming haste: nor had she inserted the hook in its eye affixed to the counter. With a slight push Oskar might have tipped it back and closed the cellar.

Motionless, I stood behind those planks, breathing in their smell of dust and mold and staring at the brightly lit rectangle enclosing a part of the staircase and a piece of concrete cellar floor. Into this rectangle, from the upper right, protruded part of a platform with steps leading up to it, obviously a recent acquisition of Greff's, for I had never seen it on previous visits to the cellar. But Oskar would not have peered so long and intently into the cellar for the sake of a platform; what held his attention was those two woolen stockings and those two black laced shoes which, strangely foreshortened, occupied the upper righthand corner of the picture. Though I could not see the soles, I knew them at once for Greff's hiking shoes. It can't be Greff, I thought, who is standing there in the cellar all ready for a hike for the shoes are not standing but hanging in midair, just over the platform, though it seems possible that the tips of the shoes, pointing sharply downward, are in contact with the boards, not much, but still in contact. For a second I fancied a Greff standing on tiptoes, a comical and strenuous exercise, yet quite conceivable in this athlete and nature lover.

To check this hypothesis, meaning, if it were confirmed, to have a good laugh at the greengrocer's expense, I climbed cautiously down the steep stairs, drumming, if I remember correctly, something or other of a nature to create and dispel fear: "Where's the Witch, black as pitch?"

Only when Oskar stood firmly on the concrete floor did he pursue his investigation—by detours, via bundles of empty onion bags, via piles of empty fruit crates—until, grazing a scaffolding he had never seen before, his eyes approached the spot where Greff's hiking shoes must have been hanging or standing on tiptoes.

Of course I knew Greff was hanging. The shoes hung, consequently the coarsely knitted dark green stockings must also be hanging. Bare adult knees over the edges of the stockings, hairy thighs to the edges of the trousers; at this point a cutting, prickling sensation rose slowly from my private parts, slowly following my rump to my back, which grew suddenly numb, climbed my spinal cord, settled down in the back of my neck, struck me hot and cold, raced down again between my legs, made my scrotum, tiny to begin with, shrivel to nothingness, leapt upward again, over my back, my neck, and shrank—to this day Oskar feels that same gagging, that same knife thrust, when anyone speaks of hanging in his presence, even of hanging out washing. It wasn't just Greff's hiking shoes, his woolen stockings, knees, and knee breeches that were hanging; the whole of Greff hung by the neck, and the strained expression of his face, above the cord, was not entirely free from theatrical affectation.

Surprisingly soon, the cutting, prickling sensation died down. I grew accustomed to the sight of Greff; for basically the posture of a man hanging is just as normal and natural as that of a man walking on his hands or standing on his head, or of a human who puts himself in the truly unfortunate position of mounting a four-legged horse with a view to riding.

Then there was the setting. Only now did Oskar appreciate the trouble Greff had gone to. The frame, the setting in which Greff hung, was studied to the point of extravagance. The greengrocer had aimed at a form of death appropriate to himself, a well-balanced death. He who in his lifetime had had difficulties and unpleasant correspondence with the Bureau of Weights and Measures, whose weights had several times been confiscated, who had had to pay fines for inaccuracy in the weighing of fruit and vegetables, had weighed himself to the last ounce with potatoes.

The faintly shiny rope, soaped I should think, ran, guided by pulleys, over two beams which, for the last day of his life, Greff had fashioned into a scaffolding whose sole purpose it was to serve as his last scaffolding. Obviously the greengrocer had spared no expense, he had used the very best wood. What with the wartime shortage of building materials, those planks and beams must have been hard to come by. Greff must have bartered fruit for wood. The scaffolding was not lacking in superfluous but decorative struts and braces. The platform and the steps leading up to it—Oskar had seen a corner of it from the shop—gave the whole edifice a quality verging on the sublime.

As in the drumming machine, which the inventor may have taken as his model, Greff and his counterweight hung inside a frame. Forming a sharp contrast to the four whitewashed cross-beams, a graceful little green ladder stood between him and the potatoes that counterbalanced him. With an ingenious knot such as scouts know how to tie, he had fastened the potato baskets to the main rope. Since the interior of the scaffolding was illumined by four light bulbs which, though painted white, gave off an intense glow, Oskar was able, without desecrating the platform with his presence, to read the inscription on a cardboard tag fastened with wire to the scout knot over the potato basket: 165 lbs. (less 3 oz.).

Greff hung in the uniform of a boy scout leader. On his last day he had resumed the uniform of the pre-war years. But it was now too tight for him. He had been unable to close the two uppermost trouser buttons and the belt, a jarring note in his otherwise trim costume. In accordance with scout ritual Greff had crossed two fingers of his left hand. Before hanging himself, he had tied his scout hat to his right wrist. He had had to forgo the neckerchief. He had also been unable to button the collar of his shirt, and a bush of curly black hair burst through the opening.

On the steps of the platform lay a few asters, accompanied inappropriately by parsley stalks. Apparently he had run out of flowers to strew on the steps, for he had used most of the asters and a few roses to wreathe

the four little pictures that hung on the four main beams of the scaffolding. Left front, behind glass, hung Baden-Powell, founder of the Boy Scouts. Left rear, unframed, St. George. Right rear, without glass, the head of Michelangelo's David. On the right front post, provided with frame and glass, hung the photo of an expressively handsome boy, aged perhaps sixteen: an early picture of his favorite, Horst Donath, later Lieutenant Donath, who had fallen by the Donets.

Perhaps I should say a word about the four scraps of paper on the platform steps between the asters and the parsley. They were disposed in such a way that they could easily be pieced together. Oskar pieced them together and deciphered a summons to appear in court on a morals charge.

The ambulance siren aroused me from my meditations about the greengrocer's death. A moment later they came hobbling down the cellar stairs, mounted the steps to the platform, and took the dangling Greff in hand. No sooner had they lifted him than the potato baskets making a counterweight fell with a crash, releasing a mechanism similar to that of the drumming machine, housed on top of the scaffolding but discreetly sheathed in plywood. While down below potatoes rolled over the platform or fell directly to the concrete floor, up above clappers pounded upon tin, wood, bronze, and glass, an orchestra of drums was unleashed: Albrecht Greff's grand finale.

Oskar finds it very difficult to reproduce on his drum an echo of that avalanche of potatoes—a windfall, incidentally, to some of the ambulance orderlies—and of the organized din of Greff's drumming machine. And yet, perhaps because my drum accounted in good part for the form Greff imprinted upon his death, I occasionally manage to drum a pretty faithful tone-poem of Greff's death. When friends, or Bruno my keeper, ask me what my piece is called, I tell them the title is "165 Lbs."

Bebra's Theater at the Front

In mid-June, 1942, my son Kurt was one year old. Oskar, the father, attached little importance to this birthday; two years more, he thought to himself. In October, '42, Greff, the greengrocer, hanged himself on a gallows so ingeniously conceived that I, Oskar, have ever since looked upon suicide as one of the noble forms of death. In January, '43, there was a good deal of talk about the city of Stalingrad. But since Matzerath uttered the name of this city very much in the same tone as previously Pearl Harbor, Tobruk, and Dunkirk, I paid no more attention to the happenings there than I had to those in the other cities whose names had been made familiar to me by special communiqués; for Wehrmacht communiqués and newscasts had become Oskar's school of geography. How else would I have learned the situation of the Kuban, Mius, and Don rivers, who could have taught me more about the Aleutian Islands, Atu, Kiska, and Adak than the radio commentaries on the events in the Far East? So it came about that in January, 1943, I learned that the city of Stalingrad is situated on the Volga; but I was far less interested in the fate of the Sixth Army than in Maria, who had a slight case of grippe at the time.

As Mama's grippe drew to a close, the geography lesson went on: to this day, Oskar can locate Rzev and Demyansk instantly and with his eyes shut on any map of Soviet Russia. No sooner was Maria well again than my son Kurt came down with the whooping cough. While I struggled to retain the difficult names of a few hotly disputed Tunisian oases, Kurt's whooping cough, simultaneously with the Afrika Korps, came to an end.

Oh, merry month of May: Maria, Matzerath, and Gretchen Scheffler made preparations for little Kurt's second birthday. Oskar, too, took considerable interest in the impending celebration; for from June 12, 1943 it would be only a brief year. If I had been present, I might have whispered into my son's ear on his second birthday: "Just wait, soon you too will be drumming." But it so happened that on June 12, 1943, Oskar was no longer in Danzig-Langfuhr but in Metz, an ancient city founded by the Romans. My absence was indeed so protracted that Oskar had considerable difficulty in getting back to his native place by June 12, 1943 before the big air raids and in time for Kurt's third birthday.

What business took me abroad? I won't beat around the bush: Outside the Pestalozzi School, which had been turned into an Air Force barracks, I met my master Bebra. But Bebra by himself could not have persuaded me to go out into the world. On Bebra's arm hung Raguna, Signora Roswitha, the great somnambulist.

Oskar was coming from Kleinhammer-Weg. He had paid Gretchen Scheffler a call and had leafed through the *Struggle for Rome*. Even then, even in the days of Belisarius, he had discovered, history had its ups and downs, even then victories and defeats at river crossings and cities were celebrated or deplored with a fine geographical sweep.

I crossed the Fröbelwiese, which in the course of the last few years had been turned into a storehouse for the Organization Todt; I was thinking about Taginae—where in the year 552 Narses defeated Totila —but it was not the victory that attracted my thoughts to Narses, the great Armenian; no, what interested me was the general's build; Narses was a misshapen hunchback, Narses was undersized, a dwarf, a gnome, a midget. Narses, I reflected, was a child's head taller than Oskar. By then I was standing outside the Pestalozzi School. Eager to make comparisons, I looked at the insignia of some Air Force officers who had shot up too quickly. Surely, I said to myself, Narses hadn't worn any insignia, he had no need to. And there, in the main entrance to the school, stood the great general in person; on his arm hung a lady—why shouldn't Narses have had a lady on his arm? As they stepped toward me, they were dwarfed by the Air Force giants, and yet they were the hub and center, round them hung an aura of history and legend, they were old as the hills in the midst of these half-baked heroes of the air—what was this whole barracks full of Totilas and Tejas, full of mast-high Ostrogoths, beside a single Armenian dwarf named Narses? With measured tread Narses approached Oskar; he beckoned and so did the lady on his arm. Respectfully the Air Force moved out of our way as Bebra and Signora Roswitha Raguna greeted me. I moved my lips close to Bebra's ear and whispered: "Beloved master, I took you for Narses the great general; I hold him in far higher esteem than the athlete Belisarius."

Modestly Bebra waved my compliment away. But Raguna was pleased by my comparison. How prettily her lips moved when she spoke: "Why, Bebra, is our young *amico* so mistaken? Does not the blood of prince Eugene flow in your veins? *E Lodovico quattordicesimo?* Is he not your ancestor?"

Bebra took my arm and led me aside, for the Air Force kept admiring us and annoying us with their stares. After a lieutenant and a moment later two sergeants had saluted Bebra—the master bore the stripes of a captain and on his sleeve an armband with the legend "Propaganda Company"—after the fliers had asked Raguna for autographs and obtained them, Bebra motioned the driver of his official car and we got in. As we drove off, there was more applause from the Air Force.

We drove down Pestalozzi-Strasse, Madgeburger-Strasse, Heeresanger. Bebra sat beside the driver. It was in Magdeburger-Strasse that Raguna started in, taking my drum as a springboard: "Still faithful to your drum, dear friend?" she whispered with her Mediterranean voice that I had not heard in so long. "And in general how faithful have you been?" Oskar gave no answer, spared her the narrative of his complicated sex life, but smilingly permitted the great somnambulist to caress first his drum, then his hands, which were clutching the drum rather convulsively, to caress his hands in a more and more meridional way.

As we turned into the Heeresanger and followed the rails of the Number 5 car line, I even responded, that is, I stroked her left hand with mine, while her right hand bestowed tenderness on my right hand. We had passed Max-Halbe-Platz, it was too late for Oskar to get out, when, looking into the rear view mirror, I saw Bebra's shrewd, light-brown, age-old eyes observing our caresses. But Raguna held on to my hands, which, out of consideration for my friend and master, I should have liked to withdraw. Bebra smiled in the rear view mirror, then looked away and struck up a conversation with the driver, while Roswitha for her part, warmly caressing and pressing my hands, embarked in

Mediterranean tones upon a discourse addressed simply and directly to my heart, fluid, lyrical words which, after taking a brief practical turn, became sweeter than ever, paralyzing all my scruples and thoughts of flight. We were at Reichskolonie, heading for the Women's Clinic, when Raguna owned to Oskar that she had never stopped thinking of him all these years, that she still had the glass from the four Seasons Café, upon which I had sung an inscription, that Bebra was an excellent friend and working companion, but marriage was out of the question; Bebra had to live alone, said Raguna, in answer to a question from me; she allowed him complete freedom, and he too, although extremely jealous by nature, had come to understand in the course of the years that Raguna could not be tied, and anyway Bebra, as director of the Theater at the Front, had little time for conjugal duties, but as for the troupe, it was tops, in peacetime it could perfectly well have played at the Wintergarten or the Scala, would I, Oskar, with all my divine talent that was just going to waste, be interested in a trial year, I was certainly old enough, a trial year, she could promise me I would like it, but presumably I, Oskar, had other obligations, *vero?* So much the better, they were leaving today, they had just given their last performance in the military district of Danzig-West Prussia, now they were going to France, there was no danger of being sent to the Eastern Front for the present, they had that behind them, thank goodness, I, Oskar, could be very glad that the East was passé, that I would be going to Paris, yes, they were certainly going to Paris, had I, Oskar, ever been in Paris? Well, then, *amico*, if Raguna cannot seduce your hard drummer's heart, let Paris seduce you, *andiamo!*

As the great somnambulist spoke these last words, the car stopped. Green grew the trees on Hindenburg-Allee, at regular Prussian intervals. We got out, Bebra told the driver to wait. I wasn't in the mood for the Four Seasons, my head was spinning and in need of fresh air. We strolled about the Steffens-Park, Bebra to my right, Roswitha to my left. Bebra explained the nature and purpose of the Propaganda Company. Roswitha related anecdotes from the daily life of the Propaganda Company. Bebra spoke of war artists, war correspondents, and his theater. From Roswitha's Mediterranean lips poured the names of distant cities I had heard of on the radio. Bebra said Copenhagen, Roswitha murmured Palermo. Bebra sang Belgrade; Athens, lamented Roswitha in the tones of a tragedienne. But both of them raved about Paris; even if I never saw those other cities, they assured me, Paris would compensate for my loss. And finally Bebra, speaking as director and captain of a front-line theater, made me what sounded like an official offer: "Join us, young man, drum, sing beer glasses and light bulbs to pieces. The German Army of Occupation in fair France, in Paris the city of eternal youth, will reward you with gratitude and applause."

Purely for the sake of form, Oskar asked for time to think it over. For a good half an hour I walked about in the springtime shrubbery, apart from Raguna, apart from Bebra my friend and master; I gave myself an air of tormented reflection, I rubbed my forehead, I hearkened, as I had never done before, to the little birds in the trees; a little robin would tell me what to do. Suddenly some winged creature was heard to outchirp all the rest, and I said: "Mother Nature in her wisdom and benevolence advises me, revered master, to accept your offer. You may look upon me from this moment on as a member of your troupe."

Then we went to the Four Seasons after all, drank an anemic mocha, and discussed the details of my getaway, but we didn't call it a getaway, we spoke of it rather as a departure.

Outside the café we recapitulated the details of our plan. Then I took my leave of Raguna and Captain Bebra of the Propaganda Company, who insisted on putting his official car at my disposal. While the two of them sauntered up Hindenburg-Allee in the direction of town, the captain's driver, a middle-aged corporal, drove me back to Langfuhr. He let me off at Max-Halbe-Platz, an Oskar driving into Labesweg in an official Wehrmach have attracted far too much attention.

I hadn't too much time ahead of me. A farewell visit to Matzerath and Maria. For a while I stood by the playpen of my son Kurt; if I remember right, I even managed a few paternal thoughts and tried to caress the blond little rascal. Little Kurt rebuffed my caresses, but not so Maria. With some surprise she accepted my fondlings, the first in years, and returned them affectionately. I found it strangely hard to take leave of Matzerath. He was standing in the kitchen cooking kidneys in mustard sauce; utterly at one with his cooking spoon, he may even have been happy. I feared to disturb him. But when he reached behind him and groped blindly for something on the kitchen table, Oskar guessed his intention, picked up the little board with the chopped parsley on it, and handed it to him; to this day, I am convinced that long after I had left the kitchen Matzerath must have stood there surprised and bewildered with his parsley board; for never before had Oskar handed Matzerath anything.

I ate supper with Mother Truczinski; I let her wash me and put me to bed, waited until she had retired and was snoring, each snore followed by a soft whistle. Then I located my slippers, picked up my clothes, and tiptoed through the room where the gray-haired mouse was snoring, whistling, and growing older; in the hallway I had a little trouble with the key, but finally coaxed the bolt out of its groove. Still in my nightgown, I carried my bundle of clothes up the stairs to the attic. Stumbling over the air defense sand pile and the air defense bucket, I came to my hiding place behind piles of roofing tiles and bundles of newspapers, stored there in defiance of air defense regulations. There I unearthed a brand-new drum that I had set aside unbeknownst to Maria. And I also found Oskar's one-volume library: Rasputin and Goethe. Should I take my favourite authors with me?

While slipping into his clothes, adjusting the drum round his neck, stowing his drumsticks under his suspenders, Oskar carried on negotiations with his two gods Dionysus and Apollo. The god of unreflecting drunkenness advised me to take no reading matter at all, or if I absolutely insisted on reading matter, then a little stack of Rasputin would do; Apollo, on the other hand, in his shrewd, sensible way, tried to talk me out of this trip to France altogether, but when he saw that Oskar's mind was made up, insisted on the proper baggage; very well, I would have to take the highly respectable yawn that Goethe had yawned so long ago, but for spite, and also because I knew that *The Elective Affinities* could never solve all my sexual problems, I also took Rasputin and his naked women, naked but for their black stockings. If Apollo strove for harmony and Dionysus for drunkenness and chaos, Oskar was a little demigod whose business it was to harmonize chaos and intoxicate reason. In addition to his mortality, he had one advantage over all the full divinities whose characters and careers had been established in the remote past: Oskar could read what he pleased, whereas the gods censored themselves.

How accustomed one becomes to an apartment house and the kitchen smells of nineteen tenants. I took my leave of every step, every story, every apartment door with its name plate: O Meyn the musician, whom they had sent home as unfit for service, who played the trumpet again, drank gin again, and waited for them to come for him again—and later on they actually did come for him, but this time they didn't let him take his trumpet. O Axel Mischke, for what did you exchange your whip? Mr. and Mrs. Woiwuth, who were always eating kohlrabi. Because Mr. Heinert had stomach trouble, he was working at Schichau instead of serving in the infantry. And next door lived Heinert's parents, who were still called Heimowski. O Mother Truczinski; gently slumbered the mouse behind her apartment door. My ear to the wood, I heard her whistling. Shorty, whose name was really Retzel, had made lieutenant, even though as a child he had always been compelled to wear long woolen stockings. Schlager's son was dead, Eyke's son was dead, Kollin's son was dead. But Laubschad the watchmaker was still alive, waking dead clocks to life. And old man Heilandt was still alive, hammering crooked nails straight. And Mrs. Schwerwinski was sick, and Mr. Schwerwinski was in good health but nevertheless died first. And what of the ground floor? Who lived there? There dwelt Alfred and Maria Matzerath and a little rascal almost two years old, named Kurt. And who was it that left the large, heavily breathing apartment house? It was Oskar, little Kurt's father.

What did he take out with him into the darkened street? He took his drum and a big educational book. Why did he stop still amid all the blacked-out houses, amid all those houses that put their trust in the air-defense regulations, why did he stop outside one of these blacked-out houses? Because there dwelt the widow Greff, to whom he owed not his education but certain delicate skills. Why did he take off his cap outside the black house? Because he was thinking of Greff the greengrocer, who had curly hair and an aquiline nose, who weighed and hanged himself both at the same time, who hanging still had curly hair and an aquiline nose, though his brown eyes, which ordinarily lay thoughtfully in their grottoes, were now strained and protuberant. Why did Oskar put his sailor cap with the flowing ribbons back on again and plod off? Because he had an appointment at the Langfuhr freight station. Did he get there on time? He did.

At the last minute, that is, I reached the railway embankment, not far from the Brünshofer-Weg underpass. No, I did not stop at the nearby office of Dr. Hollatz. In my thoughts I took leave of Sister Inge and sent greetings to the baker couple in Kleinhammer-Weg, but all this I did while walking, and only the Church of the Sacred Heart forced me to pause a moment—a pause that almost made me late. The portal was closed. But only too vividly my mind's eye saw that pink boy Jesus perched on the Virgin Mary's left thigh. My poor mama, there she was again. She knelt in the confessional, pouring her grocery wife's sins into Father Wiehnke's ear very much as she had poured sugar into blue pound and half-pound bags. And Oskar knelt at the left-side altar, trying to teach the boy Jesus how to drum, but the little monster wouldn't drum, wouldn't give me a miracle. Oskar had sworn at the time, and today outside the closed church door he swore again: I'll teach him to drum yet. Sooner or later.

Having a long journey ahead of me, I settled for later and turned a drummer's back on the church door, confident that Jesus would not escape me. Not far from the underpass, I scrambled up the railway embankment, losing a little Goethe and Rasputin in the process, but most of my educational baggage was still with me when I reached the tracks. Then I stumbled on a few yards, over ties and crushed stone, and nearly knocked Bebra over in the darkness.

"If it isn't our virtuoso drummer!" cried the captain and musical clown. Bidding one another to be careful, we groped our way over tracks and intersections, lost our bearings amid a maze of stationary freight cars, and finally found the furlough train, in which a compartment had been assigned to Bebra's troupe.

Oskar had many a streetcar ride behind him, but now he was going to ride in a train. When Bebra pushed me into the compartment, Raguna looked up with a smile from something she was sewing and kissed me on the cheek. Still smiling, but without interrupting her needlework, she introduced the other two members of the troupe: the acrobats Felix and Kitty. Kitty, honey-blonde with a rather gray complexion, was not unattractive and seemed to be about the signora's size. She had a slight Saxon accent that added to her charm. Felix, the acrobat, was no doubt the tallest member of the troupe. He must have measured almost four feet. The poor fellow suffered from his disproportionate stature. The arrival of my trim three feet made him more self-conscious than ever. His profile was rather like that of a highly bred race horse, which led Raguna to call him "Cavallo" or "Felix Cavallo." Like Captain Bebra, the acrobat wore a field-grey Army uniform, though with the insignia of a corporal. The ladies, too, wore field-grey tailored into traveling uniforms which were not very becoming. Raguna's sewing also proved to be field-grey, my future uniform. Felix and Bebra had purchased the cloth, Roswitha and Kitty took turns sewing, snipping away more and more of the material until trousers, jacket, and cap were the right size for me. As to shoes, it would have been useless to search the clothing depots of the Wehrmacht for Oskar's size. I had to content myself with my civilian laced shoes, and I never did get any Army boots.

My papers were forged. Felix the acrobat proved very clever at this delicate work. Sheer courtesy deterred me from protesting when the great somnambulist adopted me as her brother, her elder brother, I might add: Oskarnello Raguna, born on October 21, 1912 in Naples. I have used all sorts of names in my time. Oskarnello Raguna was certainly not the least mellifluous.

The train pulled out. By way of Stolp, Stettin, Berlin, Hanover, and Cologne, it carried us to Metz. Of Berlin I saw next to nothing. We had a five-hour stopover. Naturally there was an air raid. We had to take refuge in the Thomaskeller. The soldiers from the train were packed like sardines in the vaulted rooms. There was quite a to-do as an MP tried to fit us in. A few of the boys who had just come from the Eastern Front knew Bebra and his troupe from earlier performances; they clapped and whistled and Raguna blew kisses. We were asked to perform; in a few minutes something resembling a stage was improvised at one end of the former beer hall. Bebra could hardly say no, especially when an Air Force major requested him amiably and with exaggerated deference to give the men a treat.

For the first time, Oskar was to appear in a real theatical performance. Though not wholly unprepared—in the course of the train trip Bebra had several times rehearsed my number with me—I was stricken with stage fright and Raguna found occasion to soothe me by stroking my hands.

With loathsome alacrity the boys handed in our professional luggage and a moment later Felix and Kitty started their act. They were both made of rubber. They tied themselves into a knot, twined in and out and around it, exchanged arms and legs. The spectacle gave the pushing, wide-eyed soldiers fierce pains in their joints and sore muscles that would plague them for days. While Felix and Kitty were still tying and untying themselves, Bebra embarked on his musical clown number. On beer bottles ranging from full to empty, he played the most popular hits of the war years; he played "Erika" and "Mamatchi, Give Me a Horse"; he made the "Stars of the Homeland" twinkle and resound from the bottle-necks, and when that didn't quite take, fell back on his old standby: "Jimmy the Tiger" raged and roared among the bottles. That appealed to the soldiers and even to Oskar's jaded ear; and when after a few ridiculous but successful tricks of magic Bebra announced Roswitha Raguna the great somnambulist and Oskarnello Raguna the glass-slaying drummer, the audience was nicely warmed up: the success of Roswitha and Oskarnello was assured. I introduced our performance with a light roll on my drum, led up to the climaxes with crescendo rolls, and after each phase invited applause with a loud and accurately timed boom. Raguna would invite a soldier, even an officer or two, to step forward; she would bid a leathery old corporal or a bashfully cocky young ensign sit down beside her. And then she would look into his heart—yes, Raguna saw into the hearts of men. She would reveal not only the data, always correct, out of her subject's paybook, but details of his intimate life as well. Her indiscretions were always full of delicacy and wit. In conclusion she rewarded one of her victims with a bottle of beer and asked him to hold it up high so the audience could see it. Then she gave me, Oskarnello, the signal: my drum rolled crescendo and I lifted up my voice, a voice designed for far more exacting tasks. It was child's play to shatter that beer bottle, not without a resounding explosion: the bewildered, beer-bespattered face of a case-hardened corporal or of a milk-faced ensign— I don't remember which—wrote finis to our act—and then came applause, long and thunderous, mingled with the sounds of a major air raid on the capital.

Our offering was hardly in the international class, but it entertained the men, it made them forget the front and the furlough that was ended, and it made them laugh and laugh; for when the aerial torpedoes landed overhead, shaking and burying the cellar and everything in it, dousing the light and the emergency light, when everything about us was tossed topsy-turvy, laughter still rang through the dark, stifling coffin, accompanied by cries of "Bebra! We want Bebra!" And good old indestructible Bebra spoke up, played the clown in the darkness, wrung volleys of laughter from the buried mob. And when voices demanded Raguna and

255

Oskarnello, he blared out: "Signora Raguna is verrry tired, my dear tin soldiers. And Oskarnello must also take a little nap for the sake of the Greater German Reich and final victory."

She, Roswitha, lay with me and was frightened. Oskar, on the other hand, was not frightened, and yet he lay with Raguna. Her fear and my courage brought our hands together. I felt her fear and she felt my courage. At length I became rather fearful, and she grew courageous. And after I had banished her fear and given her courage, my manly courage raised its head a second time. While my courage was eighteen glorious years old, she, in I know not what year of her life, recumbent for I know not the howmanieth time, fell a prey once more to the fear that aroused my courage. For like her face, her body, sparingly measured but quite complete, showed no trace of time. Timelessly courageous and timelessly fearful, Roswitha offered herself to me. And never will anyone learn whether that midget, who during a major air raid on the capital lost her fear beneath my courage in the buried Thomaskeller until the air-raid wardens dug us out, was nineteen or ninety-nine years old; what makes it all the easier for Oskar to be discreet is that he himself has no idea whether this first embrace truly suited to his physical dimensions was conferred upon him by a courageous old woman or by a young girl made submissive by fear.

Inspection of Concrete, or Barbaric, Mystical, Bored

For three weeks we played every night in the venerable casemates of Metz, long a city of garrisons and once a Roman outpost. We did the same program for two weeks in Nancy. A few words of French had begun to sprout from Oskar's lips. In Reims we had an opportunity to admire damage created by the previous World War. Sickened by humanity, the stone menagerie of the world-famous cathedral spewed water and more water on the cobblestones round about, which is a way of saying that it rained all day in Reims even at night. But Paris gave us a mild and resplendent September. I spent my nineteenth birthday strolling on the *quais* with Roswitha on my arm. Although Paris was well known to me from Sergeant Fritz Truczinski's postcards, I wasn't a bit disappointed. The first time Roswitha and I—she measured three feet three, three inches more than myself—stood arm in arm at the foot of the Eiffel Tower, looking up, we became aware—this too for the first time—of our grandeur and uniqueness. We exchanged kisses wherever we went, but that's nothing new in Paris.

How wonderful it is to rub shoulders with art and history! Still with Roswitha on my arm, I visited the Dôme des Invalides, thinking of the great Emperor and feeling very close to him, because, though great, he was not tall. Recalling how, at the tomb of Frederick the Great, himself no giant, Napoleon had said: "If he were still alive, we should not be standing here," I whispered tenderly into my Roswitha's ear: "If the Corsican were still alive, we should not be standing here, we should not be kissing each other under the bridges, on the *quais, sur le trottoir de Paris*."

In collaboration with other groups, we put on colossal programs at the Salle Pleyel and the Théâtre Sarah Bernhardt, Oskar quickly grew accustomed to the theatrical style of the big city, perfected his repertory, adapted himself to the jaded tastes of the Paris occupation troops: No longer did I waste my vocal prowess on common German beer bottles; here, in the city of light, I shattered graceful, invaluable vases and fruit bowls, immaterial figments of blown glass, taken from French castles. My number was conceived along historical lines. I started in with glassware from the reign of Louis XIV, and continued, like history itself, with the reign of Louis XV. With revolutionary fervor I attacked the crockery of the unfortunate Louis XVI and his headless and heedless Marie Antoinette. Finally, after a sprinkling of Louis-Philippe, I carried my battle to the vitreous fantasies of the Third Republic.

Of course the historical significance of my act was beyond the reach of the field-grey mass in the orchestra and galleries; they applauded my shards as common shards; but now and then there was a staff officer or a newspaperman from the Reich who relished my historical acumen along with the damage. A scholarly character in uniform complimented me on my art when we were introduced to him after a gala performance for the Kommandantur. Oskar was particularly grateful to the correspondent for a leading German newspaper who described himself as an expert on France and discreetly called my attention to a few trifling mistakes, not to say stylistic inconsistencies, in my program.

We spent the whole winter in Paris. They billeted us in first-class hotels, and I shall not deny that all winter long Roswitha joined me in investigating the superior qualities of French beds. Was Oskar happy in Paris? Had he forgotten his dear ones at home, Maria, Matzerath, Gretchen and Alexander Scheffler; had Oskar forgotten his son Kurt and his grandmother Anna Koljaiczek?

Though I had not forgotten them, I missed none of them. I wrote no Army postcards, gave no sign of life, but on the contrary gave the folks at home every opportunity to live a whole year without me; for from the moment of my departure I had been resolved to return, whence it followed that I would have been rather interested to know how they were getting along in my absence. On the street or during performances, I sometimes searched the soldiers' faces for familiar features. Perhaps, Oskar speculated, Fritz Truczinski or Axel Mischke has been transferred here from the Eastern Front, and once or twice he thought he had recognized Maria's handsome brother amid a horde of infantrymen; but it wasn't he; field-gray can be misleading.

Only the Eiffel Tower made me homesick. Don't go supposing that I rode to the top and that remote vistas made me dream of home. Oskar had mounted the Eiffel Tower so often on postcards and in his thoughts that an actual ascension could only have brought him disappointment. As I stood or sat at the foot of the Eiffel Tower, but without Roswitha, alone beneath those towering girders flung upward by the pioneers of steel construction, the great vault, which seems so solidly closed despite spaces on all sides, became for me the sheltering vault of my grandmother Anna: sitting beneath the Eiffel Tower, I was sitting beneath her four skirts, the Champ de Mars was a Kashubian potato field, the Paris October rain slanted endlessly down between Bissau and Ramkau, and on such days all Paris, even the Metro, smelled of slightly rancid butter. I grew silent and thoughtful. Roswitha respected my sorrow and was very kind and considerate on these occasions; she was a sensitive soul.

In April, 1944—from all fronts came communiqués announcing that our lines had been successfully shortened—we were obliged to pack up and leave Paris for a tour of the Atlantic Wall. Our first stop was Le Havre. It seemed to me that Bebra was becoming taciturn and distraught. Though he never lost his grip during performances and still had the laughs on his side, his age-old Narses face turned to stone once the last curtain had fallen. At first I thought he was jealous, or, worse, that he had capitulated in the face of my youthful vigor. In whispers Roswitha dispelled my error; she didn't know exactly what was going on, but she had noticed that certain officers were meeting with Bebra behind closed doors after the show. It looked as though the master were emerging from his inward emigration, as though, inspired by the blood of his ancestor Prince Eugene, he were planning some direct action. His plans had carried him so far away from us, had involved him in preoccupations so vast and far-reaching, that Oskar's intimacy with his former Roswitha could arouse no more than a weary wrinkled smile. One day in Trouville—we were lodged at the Casino—he found us intertwined on the carpet of the dressing room he shared with us. Our impulse was to leap apart, but with a gesture he gave us to understand that there was no need to. Looking into his make-up glass, he said: "Enjoy yourselves, children, hug and kiss, tomorrow we inspect concrete, and the day after tomorrow it's concrete you'll have between your lips. Gather ye rosebuds while ye may."

That was in June, '44. By that time we had done the Atlantic Wall from the Bay of Biscay to Holland, but we spent most of our time inland and saw little of the legendary pillboxes. It wasn't until Trouville that we played directly on the coast. Here we were offered an opportunity to visit the Atlantic Wall. Bebra accepted. After our last show in Trouville, we were driven to the village of Bavent near Caen, three miles behind the shore dunes. We were lodged with peasants. Pasture, hedgerows, apple trees. That is where the apple brandy called calvados is distilled. We had a drink of it and went to bed. Brisk air came in through the window, a frog pond croaked until morning. Some frogs are good drummers. I heard them in my sleep and said to myself: Oskar, you've got to go home, soon your son Kurt will be three years old, you've got to give him his drum, you've promised. Thus admonished, Oskar, the tormented father, awoke each hour, groped about in the darkness, made sure his Roswitha was there, breathed in her smell: Raguna smelled ever so slightly of cinnamon, crushed cloves, and nutmeg; even in summer she had that scent of Christmas, of cake spice.

In the morning an armored personnel carrier drove up to the farm. We stood in the doorway, chatting into the sea wind, all of us shivering a little. It was early and very chilly. We got in: Bebra, Raguna, Felix and Kitty, Oskar, and a Lieutenant Herzog who was taking us to his battery west of Cabourg.

To say Normandy is green is to disregard the spotted brown and white cows which were chewing their cuds on misty meadows, wet with dew, to the right and left of the straight highway, greeted our armored vehicle with such indifference that the armor plate would have turned red with shame had it not previously been daubed with camouflage paint. Poplars, hedgerows, creepers, the first hulking beach hotels, empty, their shutters clattering in the wind. We turned into the beach promenade, got out, and plodded along behind the lieutenant, who showed Captain Bebra a condescending yet properly military respect, across the dunes, against a wind full of sand and surf roar.

This wasn't the mild, bottle-green Baltic, sobbing like a tender-hearted maiden as it waited for me to come in. It was the Atlantic carrying out its immemorial maneuver, pressing forward at high tide, receding at low tide.

And then we had our concrete. We could admire it and even pat it to our heart's content; it didn't budge. "Attention!" cried someone inside the concrete and leapt, tall as a mast, from the pillbox, which was shaped like a flattened-out turtle, lay amid sand dunes, was called "Dora Seven," and looked out upon the shifting tides through gun embrasures, observation slits, and machine-gun barrels. The man's name was Corporal Lankes. He reported to Lieutenant Herzog and at the same time to our Captain Bebra.

LANKES (*saluting*): Dora Seven, one corporal and four men. Nothing special to report.

HERZOG: Thank you. At ease, Corporal Lankes. Did you hear that, Captain? Nothing special to report. That's how it's been for years.

BEBRA: There's still the tide. Ebbing and flowing. Nature's contribution.

HERZOG: That's just what keeps our men busy. That's why we go on building pillboxes one after another. They're already in each other's field of fire. Pretty soon we'll have to demolish a few of them to make room for more concrete.

BEBRA (*knocks on the concrete; the members of his troupe do likewise*): And you have faith in concrete?

HERZOG: Faith is hardly the right word. We haven't much faith in anything any more. What do you say, Lankes?

LANKES: Right, sir. No more faith.

BEBRA: But they keep on mixing and pouring.

HERZOG: Between you and me, Captain, we're getting valuable experience. I'd never built a thing until I came here. I was in school when the war started. Now I've learned a thing or two about cement and I hope to make use of it after the war. The whole of Germany is going to have to be rebuilt. Take a good look at this concrete. (BEBRA *and his troupe poke their noses into the concrete.*) What do you see? Shells. We've got all we need right at the doorstep. Just have to take the stuff and mix. Stones, shells, sand, cement . . . What else can I tell you, Captain, you are an artist, you know how it is. Lankes, tell the captain what we put in our cement.

LANKES: Yes, sir. I'll tell the captain. Puppies, sir. Every one of our pillboxes has a puppy in it. Walled up in the foundation.

BEBRA'S TROUPE: A puppy?

LANKES: Pretty soon there won't be a single puppy left in the whole sector from Caen to Le Havre.

BEBRA'S TROUPE: No more puppies.

LANKES: That's what eager beavers we are.

BEBRA'S TROUPE: What eager beavers!

LANKES: Pretty soon we'll have to use kittens.

BEBRA'S TROUPE: Meow!

LANKES: But cats aren't as good as dogs. That's why we hope there'll be a little action here soon.

BEBRA'S TROUPE: The big show! (*They applaud.*)

LANKES: We've rehearsed enough. And if we run out of puppies . . .

BEBRA'S TROUPE: Oh!

LANKES: . . . we'll have to stop building. Cats are bad luck.

BEBRA'S TROUPE: Meow! Meow!

LANKES: Would you like me to tell you short and sweet why we put in puppies . . .

BEBRA'S TROUPE: Puppies!

LANKES: Personally I think it's the bunk . . .

BEBRA'S TROUPE: For shame!

LANKES: But my buddies, here, are mostly from the country. And in the country when they build a house or a barn or a village church, it's the custom to put something living in the foundations . . . and . . .

HERZOG: That's enough, Lankes. At ease. As you've heard, sir, we're given to superstition here on the Atlantic Wall. Like you theater people who mustn't whistle before an opening night or spit over your shoulders before the curtain goes up . . .

BEBRA'S TROUPE: Toi-toi-toi! (*Spit over each other's shoulders.*)

HERZOG: But joking aside, we've got to let the men have their fun. Recently they've started decorating the entrances to the pillboxes with improvisations in concrete or sea-shell mosaics, and it's tolerated by order from way up. The men like to be kept busy. Those concrete pretzels get on our C.O.'s nerves, but what I tell him is: better pretzels in the concrete, sir, than pretzels in the head. We Germans are no good at sitting idle. That's a fact.

BEBRA: And we, too, do our bit to distract the men who are waiting on the Atlantic Wall . . .

BEBRA'S TROUPE: Bebra's front-line theater sings for you, plays for you, boosts your morale for the final victory.

HERZOG: Yes, you've got the right point of view. But the theater alone isn't enough. Most of the time we have only ourselves to depend on, and we do our best. Am I right, Lankes?

LANKES: Right, sir. We do our best.

HERZOG: There you have it. And if you'll excuse me now, sir, I've got to take a run over to Dora Four and Dora Five. Take your time, have a good look at our concrete. It's worth it. Lankes will show you everything . . .

LANKES: Everything, sir.

> (*Lankes and Bebra exchange salutes. Herzog goes out right, Raguna, Oskar, Felix, and Kitty, who have thus far been standing behind Bebra, jump out. Oskar is holding his drum, Raguna is carrying a basket of provisions. Felix and Kitty climb up on the concrete roof of the pillbox and begin doing acrobatic exercises. Oskar and Raguna play with pails and shovels, make it plain that they are in love, yodel, and tease Felix and Kitty.*)

BEBRA (*wearily, after examining the pillbox from all sides*): Tell me, Corporal, what is your civilian occupation?

LANKES: Painter, sir, but that was a long time ago.

BEBRA: House painter?

LANKES: Houses too, but mostly pictures.

BEBRA: Hear, hear! You mean you emulated the great Rembrandt, or maybe Velasquez?

LANKES: Sort of in between.

BEBRA: Why, good God, man! Why are you mixing, pouring, guarding concrete? You ought to be in the Propaganda Company. Why, a war artist is just what we need!

LANKES: It's not my line, sir. My stuff slants too much for present tastes. But if you've got a cigarette . . .

(BEBRA *hands him a cigarette.*)

BEBRA: Slants? I suppose you mean it's modern?

LANKES: What do you mean by modern? Well, anyway, before they started up with their concrete, slanting was modern for a while.

BEBRA: Oh.

LANKES: Yep.

BEBRA: I guess you lay it on thick. With a trowel maybe?

LANKES: Yeah, I do that too. I stick my thumb in, automatic like, I put in nails and buttons, and before '33 I had a period when I put barbed wire on cinnabar. Got good reviews. A private collector in Switzerland has them now. Makes soap.

BEBRA: Oh, this war! This awful war! And today you're pouring concrete. Hiring out your genius for fortification work. Well, I've got to admit, Leonardo and Michelangelo did the same thing in their day. Designed military machines and fortifications when they didn't have a madonna on order.

LANKES: See! There's always something cockeyed. Every real artist has got to express himself. If you'd like to take a look at the ornaments over the entrance, sir, I did them.

BEBRA (*after a thorough examination of them*): Amazing! What wealth of form. What expressive power!

LANKES: Structural formations I call them.

BEBRA: And your creation, your picture, or should I call it a relief, has it a title?

LANKES: I just told you: Formations, or Oblique Formations if you like that better. It's a new style. Never been done before.

BEBRA: Even so, you ought to give it a title. Just to avoid misunderstandings. It's your work, after all.

LANKES: What for? What good are titles? Except to put in the catalog when you have a show.

BEBRA: You're putting on airs, Lankes. Think of me as an art lover, not as an officer. Cigarette? (LANKES *takes it.*) Well then, what's on your mind?

LANKES: Oh, all right, if you put it that way. This is how I figure it. When this war is over—one way or another, it will be over some day—well, then, when the war is over, the pillboxes will still be here. These things were made to last. And then my time will come. The centuries . . . (*He puts the last cigarette in his pocket.*) Maybe you've got another cigarette, sir? Thank you, sir . . . the centuries start coming and going, one after another like nothing at all. But the pillboxes stay put just like the Pyramids stayed put. And one fine day one of those archaeologist fellows comes along. And he says to himself: what an artistic void there was between the First and the Seventh World Wars! Dull drab concrete; here and there, over a pillbox entrance, you find some clumsy amateurish squiggles in the old-home style. And that's all. Then he discovers Dora Five, Six, Seven; he sees my Structural Oblique Formations, and he says to himself, Say, take a look at that, Very, very interesting, magic, menacing, and yet shot through with spirituality. In these works a genius, perhaps the only genius of the twentieth century, has expressed himself clearly, resolutely, and for all time. I wonder, says our archaeologist to himself, I wonder if it's got a name? A signature to tell us who the master was? Well, sir, if you look closely, sir, and hold your head on a slant, you'll see, between those Oblique Formations . . .

BEBRA: My glasses. Help me, Lankes.

LANKES: All right, here's what it says: Herbert Lankes, anno nineteen hundred and forty-four. Title: BARBARIC, MYSTICAL, BORED.

BEBRA: You have given our century its name.

LANKES: See!

BEBRA: Perhaps when they restore your work in five hundred or a thousand years, they will find a few puppy bones in the concrete.

LANKES: That will only give additional force to my title.

BEBRA (excited): What are the times and what are we, my friend, if our works . . . but take a look at Felix and Kitty, my acrobats. They are performing on the concrete.

(For some time a piece of paper has been passing back and forth between Roswitha and Oskar and Felix and Kitty, each pair writing on it by turns.)

KITTY (with a slight Saxon accent): Mr. Bebra, see what we can do on the concrete. (She walks on her hands.)

FELIX: Nobody ever did a back flip on concrete before. Not even a front flip. (He does both.)

KITTY: We oughta have a stage like this.

FELIX: It's a bit too windy for me.

KITTY: But it's not hot and stinky like the movie houses. (She ties herself into a knot.)

FELIX: And we've just composed a poem up here.

KITTY: What do you mean we? Oskarnello and Roswitha made it up.

FELIX: But we helped out when they were stuck for a rhyme.

KITTY: Just one word is missing, then it'll be done.

263

FELIX: Oskar wants to know what those spikes in the sand are called.

KITTY: 'Cause he needs them for the poem.

FELIX: They're too important to leave out.

KITTY: Won't you tell us, Mr. Corporal? What are they called?

FELIX: Maybe he's not allowed to. On account of enemy ears.

KITTY: We promise not to tell anybody.

FELIX: It's for art.

KITTY: Oskarnello has gone to so much trouble.

FELIX: And how beautifully he writes. In Sütterlin script.

KITTY: I wonder where he learned it.

FELIX: Oh, Oskar's educated. He knows everything, except what those spikes are called.

LANKES: I'll tell you if the captain has no objection.

BEBRA: But maybe it's top secret.

FELIX: But Oskar needs to know.

KITTY: Or the poem will be ruined.

ROSWITHA: And we're all so curious.

BEBRA: You might as well tell us. It's an order.

LANKES: Well, we put them in as a defense against tanks and landing craft. They look like asparagus, don't they? Well, that's why we call them Rommel asparagus.

FELIX: Rommel . . .

KITTY: . . . asparagus? Does it fit, Oskarnello?

OSKAR: It fits! (*He writes the word on the paper, hands the poem to Kitty on top of the pillbox. She knots herself still more and recites the following lines like a schoolchild.*)

KITTY: On the Atlantic Wall

Rommel has sent us steel asparagus
And here we sit, bristling and camouflaged,
Dreaming of the land of carpet slippers,
Of Sunday's roasts and Friday's kippers,
Where everything is soft and snug:
The trend is toward the bourgeois-smug.

We live in concrete and barbed wire,
We bury mines in the latrines.
But then we dream of garden bower
Of frigidaires and happy hours
Bestowed by an electric plug:
The trend is toward the bourgeois-smug.

Though some of us are sure to die
And many a mother's heart must break,

Though death still wears a parachute
And Martian harness on his suit,
The thought of comfort's like a drug:
The trend is toward the bourgeois-smug.

(All applaud, including Lankes.)

LANKES: It's low tide.

ROSWITHA: That's time for breakfast. (She brandishes her big basket, which is decorated with bows and artificial flowers.)

KITTY: Oh, yes, a picnic in the open.

FELIX: Nature has whetted our appetites.

ROSWITHA: Oh, sacred act of belly-filling that will unite the nations as long as men eat breakfast!

BEBRA: Let us feast on the concrete. Let us have human rituals built on solid foundations! (All except for Lankes climb up on the pillbox. Roswitha spreads out a bright flowery tablecloth. From the bottomless basket she produces little cushions with tassels and fringes. A pink and bright green parasol is opened, a tiny gramophone with loudspeaker is set up. Little plates, little spoons, little knives, egg cups, and napkins are distributed.)

FELIX: I'd like some of the pâté de foie gras.

KITTY: Have you still got any of that caviar we rescued from Stalingrad?

OSKAR: You oughtn't to spread the Danish butter so thick, Roswitha.

BEBRA: I'm glad to see you looking out for her figure. That's the right spirit, son.

ROSWITHA: But I like it and it's good for me. Oh! When I think of the cake and whipped cream the Air Force served us in Copenhagen.

BEBRA: The Dutch chocolate in the thermos bottle is still nice and warm.

KITTY: I'm just crazy about these canned American cookies.

ROSWITHA: But they're only good if you spread some of the South African ginger preserve on top.

OSKAR: A little moderation, Roswitha, I beseech you.

ROSWITHA: What about you? Look at the big thick slices of that nasty English corned beef you've been helping yourself to.

BEBRA: What about you, my dear corporal? May I offer you a paper-thin slice of raisin bread with plum jam?

LANKES: If I weren't on duty, sir.

ROSWITHA: He needs an official order.

KITTY: Yes, do give him an order.

BEBRA: Very well. Corporal Lankes, you are hereby ordered to accept a slice of raisin bread with French plum jam, a soft-boiled Danish egg, a spot of Soviet caviar, and a little cup of genuine Dutch chocolate.

LANKES: Yes, sir. (He joins the others on top of the pillbox.)

BEBRA: Haven't we another cushion for the corporal?

OSKAR: He can have mine. I'll sit on my drum.

ROSWITHA: Mustn't catch cold, precious. Concrete is treacherous, and you're not used to it.

KITTY: He can have my cushion too. I'll just knot myself up a little, it helps my digestion anyway.

FELIX: But do eat over the tablecloth or you'll get honey on the concrete. We wouldn't want to damage the defenses! (*All giggle.*)

BEBRA: Ah, the sea air! How fine it makes us feel.

ROSWITHA: Feel!

BEBRA: The breast expands.

ROSWITHA: Expands!

BEBRA: The heart casts off its crust.

ROSWITHA: Crust!

BEBRA: The soul is reborn.

ROSWITHA: Reborn!

BEBRA: The eyes soar aloft.

ROSWITHA: Aloft!

BEBRA: Over the sea, the endless sea . . . I say, Corporal, I see something black down there on the beach. Whatever it is, there's five of them.

KITTY: So do I. With five umbrellas.

FELIX: Six.

KITTY: Five! One, two, three, four, five!

LANKES: It's the nuns from Lisieux. They've been evacuated and shipped over here with their kindergarten.

KITTY: I don't see any children. Just five umbrellas.

LANKES: They leave the children at Bavent. Sometimes they come down here at low tide to pick up the crabs and shellfish that get stuck in the Rommel asparagus.

KITTY: Poor things!

ROSWITHA: Shouldn't we offer them some corned beef and cookies?

OSKAR: I suggest raisin bread with plum jam. It's Friday; nuns aren't allowed to eat corned beef on Friday.

KITTY: They're running now. They seem to be gliding on their umbrellas.

LANKES: They always do that when they've finished picking. Then they begin to play. Especially Agneta, the novice, she's just a kid that doesn't know which way is up. Maybe you could spare another cigarette? Thank you, sir. And the one back there, the fat one that isn't running is Scholastica, the mother superior. She doesn't like them to play on the beach, she thinks it might be against the rule of their order.

(*Nuns with umbrellas are seen running in the background. Roswitha puts on the gramophone: "Sleigh Bells in St. Petersburg." The nuns dance and shout.*)

AGNETA: Yoohoo, Sister Scholastica!

SCHOLASTICA: Agneta, Sister Agneta!

AGNETA: Yoohoo, Sister Scholastica!

SCHOLASTICA: Come back now, child! Sister Agneta!

AGNETA: I can't. It carries me away.

SCHOLASTICA: Then you must pray, sister, for a conversion.

AGNETA: A sorrowful one?

SCHOLASTICA: A merciful one.

AGNETA: A joyful one?

SCHOLASTICA: Just pray, Sister Agneta!

AGNETA: I'm praying to beat the band. But I'm still being carried away.

SCHOLASTICA (*her voice dying away in the distance*): Agneta, Sister Agneta.

AGNETA: Yoohoo, Sister Scholastica!

> (*The nuns disappear, but from time to time their umbrellas appear in the background. The phonograph record runs down. Beside the pillbox entrance the telephone rings. Lankes jumps down and picks up the receiver, the others go on eating.*)

ROSWITHA: Telephones, telephones, wherever you go. Between the sea and the sky, telephones.

LANKES: Dora Seven speaking. Corporal Lankes.

HERZOG (*comes in slowly from the right, holding a telephone and dragging the wire after him. He stops repeatedly and talks into the phone*): Are you asleep, Lankes? There's something moving in front of Dora Seven. I'm sure of it.

LANKES: It's the nuns, sir.

HERZOG: What are nuns doing down there? And suppose they're not nuns.

LANKES: But they are nuns. I can see them plain as day.

HERZOG: Never hear of camouflage? Never hear of the fifth column? The English have been at it for centuries. They come in with their Bibles and before you know what they're up to, boom!

LANKES: They're picking up crabs, sir . . .

HERZOG: I want that beach cleared immediately. Is that clear?

LANKES: Yes, sir, but they're just picking up crabs.

HERZOG: Lankes, I want you to get your ass behind your MG!

LANKES: But suppose they're just looking for crabs, 'cause it's low tide and the children in their kindergarten . . .

HERZOG: That's an official order, Lankes.

LANKES: Yes, sir. (*Lankes disappears into the pillbox. Herzog goes out right with the telephone.*)

OSKAR: Roswitha, stop your ears, there's going to be shooting like in the newsreels.

KITTY: Oh, how awful! I'm going to knot myself still tighter.

BEBRA: I myself am almost inclined to think that we shall soon hear some noise.

FELIX: Let's put on another record. That will help some. (*He puts on the*

267

gramophone: The Platters singing "The Great Pretender." The rat-tat-tat of the machine gun punctuates the slow mournful music. Roswitha holds her ears. Felix stands on his head. In the background five nuns with umbrellas are seen flying heavenward. The record sticks in its groove and repeats. Felix returns to his feet. Kitty unties herself. Roswitha begins to clear the table and repack her basket. Oskar and Bebra help her. They leave the roof of the pillbox. Lankes appears in the entrance.)

LANKES: Captain, sir, if you could spare another cigarette . . .

BEBRA (*his frightened troupe huddle behind him*): You smoke too much, Corporal.

BEBRA'S TROUPE: He smokes too much.

LANKES: That's on account of the concrete, sir.

BEBRA: And suppose some day there's no more concrete?

BEBRA'S TROUPE: No more concrete.

LANKES: Concrete is immortal, sir. Just us and our cigarettes . . .

BEBRA: I know, I know, we vanish like a puff of smoke.

BEBRA'S TROUPE: (*slowly going out*): Smoke!

BEBRA: But in a thousand years they will still be coming to see the concrete.

BEBRA'S TROUPE: In a thousand years!

BEBRA: They'll find puppy bones.

BEBRA'S TROUPE: Puppy bones.

BEBRA: And your Oblique Formations in the concrete.

BEBRA'S TROUPE: BARBARIC, MYSTICAL, BORED!

(*Lankes is left alone, smoking*)

Though Oskar hardly opened his mouth in the course of that breakfast on the concrete, the mere fact that such words should be spoken on the eve of the invasion has impelled me to record them. Moreover, we haven't seen the last of Corporal Lankes, the master of "concrete" art; we shall meet him again when the time comes to speak of the postwar period and the present apotheosis of bourgeois comfort.

On the beach promenade, our armored personnel carrier was still waiting for us. With long strides Lieutenant Herzog returned to his protégés and breathlessly apologized to Bebra for the little incident, adding, however, that the beach was off limits for civilians and "Off limits is off limits." He helped the ladies into the vehicle, gave the driver some instructions, and back we rode to Bavent. We had to hurry, there was no time for lunch, for at two o'clock we had a show at the charming little Norman château nestling among the poplars at the edge of the village.

We had barely half an hour in which to test the lighting; then Oskar raised the curtain with a drum flourish. We were playing to an audience of enlisted men. We laid it on thick and the laughter was hearty and frequent. I sang at a glass chamber pot containing a pair of hot dogs with mustard. Bebra, in white grease paint, wept clown's tears over the broken pot, salvaged the sausages from the shards, and devoured them to the joy of the field-grey mass. Felix and Kitty had taken to appearing in leather shorts and Tyrolian hats, which lent their act a special cachet. Roswitha wore a close-fitting silvery gown and long pale-green gloves; her tiny feet were encased in gold-embroidered sandals. Her half-closed bluish eyelids and drowsy Mediterranean voice produced their usual effect of eerie magic. Oskar—or have I mentioned it before?—required no special costume. I wore my good old sailor hat with S.M.S. *Seydlitz* on the band, my navy-blue shirt, and my jacket with the golden anchor buttons. As the camera eye descended, it registered the bottoms of my knee-pants, rolled stockings, and a very dilapidated pair of boots. From my neck hung my red and white lacquered drum, serene in the knowledge that there were five more like it in my luggage.

That night we repeated the same show for officers and for the Blitz Girls from the Cabourg message center. Roswitha was a trifle nervous. She made no mistakes, but in the middle of her number she put on a pair of sunglasses with blue rims and abruptly changed her tone. Here revelations became more direct; for instance, she informed an anemic-looking Blitz Girl, whose embarrassment made her snippish, that she was having an affair with her commanding officer. This, it seemed to me, was in poor taste, but there were plenty of laughs, for there was an officer sitting beside the Blitz Girl, and there was good reason to suppose . . .

After the show the regimental staff officers, who were billeted in the château, gave a party. Bebra, Kitty, and Felix stayed on, but Raguna and Oskar slipped quietly away and went to bed. It had been a trying day. We dropped off quickly and slept until 5 A.M. when the invasion woke us up.

What shall I tell you about the invasion? Canadians landed in our sector, not far from the mouth of the Orne. Bavent had to be evacuated. Our luggage was already stowed in the truck. We were pulling out with the regimental staff. A motorized field kitchen had stopped in the court of the château Roswitha asked me to get her a cup of coffee. Rather nervous and afraid of missing the truck, I refused. I was even a little rude to her. Thereupon she herself ran over to the field kitchen in her high-heeled shoes, and reached the steaming hot coffee exactly at the same time as a shell from a naval gun.

O Roswitha, I know not how old you were, I know only that you measured three foot three, that the Mediterranean spoke from your lips, that you smelled of cinnamon and nutmeg, and that you could see into the hearts of men; but you couldn't see into your own heart, or else you would have stayed with me instead of running after that coffee, which was much too hot.

In Lisieux Bebra managed to wangle marching orders for Berlin. We

269

waited for him outside the Kommandantur, and it was only when he joined us that he mentioned Roswitha's death for the first time: "We dwarfs and fools have no business dancing on concrete made for giants. If only we had stayed under the rostrums where no one suspected our presence!"

In Berlin I parted from Bebra. "What," he said with a smile as thin as a spiderweb, "will you do in all those air-raid shelters without your Roswitha?" Then he kissed me on the forehead. He made me a present of the five remaining drums and sent Kitty and Felix to Danzig with official travel orders to keep me company. So it was that armed with six drums and my "book," I returned on June 11, 1944, the day before my son's third birthday, to my native city, which was still intact and medieval and which still resounded with bells of every size ringing out the hour from belfries high and low.

The Imitation of Christ

Ah, yes, homecoming! At four minutes after twenty hundred, the furlough train pulled into Danzig station. Felix and Kitty accompanied me as far as Max-Halbe-Platz. Kitty burst into tears as they were saying good-by. Then—it was almost twenty-one hundred—they went on to Propaganda Troop headquarters in Hochstriess, while Oskar toted his luggage down Labesweg.

Homecoming indeed! Nowadays every young man who forges a little check, joins the Foreign Legion, and spins a few yarns when he gets home a few years later, tends to be regarded as a modern Ulysses. Maybe on his way home our young man gets into the wrong train which takes him to Oberhausen instead of Frankfurt, and has some sort of experience on the way—why not?—and the moment he reaches home, he begins to bandy mythological names about: Circe, Penelope, Telemachus.

Oskar was no Ulysses, if only because on his return home he found everything unchanged. Far from being beset by lecherous suitors, his beloved Maria, who, had he been Ulysses, would have had to play the role of Penelope, still had her Matzerath, in whose favor she had decided long before Oskar's departure. And I do hope the more classical-minded among my readers will not, because of her somnambulism, mistake my poor Roswitha for Circe, the enchantress who turned men into beasts. Lastly, my son Kurt didn't raise a finger for his returning father; accordingly, he was no Telemachus, even if he did fail to recognize me.

If comparison there must be—and I can see that homecomers must put up with a comparison or two—I prefer to be looked upon as the Prodigal Son; for Matzerath opened the door and welcomed me like a true, not a presumptive, father. In fact, he managed to be so happy over

Oskar's return, to the point of shedding real, speechless tears, that from that day on I ceased to call myself exclusively Oskar Bronski and called myself Oskar Matzerath as well.

Maria's reception of me was less emotional but not unfriendly. She was sitting at the table, pasting up food stamps for the Board of Trade, having previously piled up a few birthday presents for little Kurt. Practical as she was, she thought first of my physical well-being, undressed me, bathed me as in times gone by, overlooked my blushes, and set me down in my pajamas at the table, Matzerath having meanwhile served up a dish of fried eggs and browned potatoes. I drank milk with my food, and as I ate and drank, the questions began: "Where have you been? We looked all over like mad; we even had to go to the police and swear we hadn't done you in. Well, here you are and thank the Lord for that. But plenty of trouble you made us and there's going to be more, because now we've got to report you back again. I only hope they won't put you in an institution. That's what you deserve. Running away without a word."

Maria was right. There was plenty of bother. A man came from the Ministry of Public Health and spoke to Matzerath in private, but Matzerath shouted so loud you could hear him all over the house: "It's out of the question. I promised my wife on her deathbed. *I'm* his father, not the Board of Health."

So I was not sent to an institution. But every two weeks an official letter came, asking Matzerath for a little signature; Matzerath refused to sign, but his forehead was creased with care.

Oskar has been getting ahead of himself; now he must smooth the creases out of Matzerath's brow, for on the night of my arrival he beamed; he was much less worried than Maria, also asked fewer questions, and was happy just to have me home. All in all, he behaved like a true father. "Won't Kurt be glad to have a little brother again!" he said as they were putting me to bed in the flat of the rather bewildered Mother Truczinski. "And just imagine, tomorrow is Kurt's third birthday."

On his birthday table my son Kurt found a cake with three candles, a crimson sweater knitted by Gretchen Scheffler, to which he paid no attention at all, and various other articles. There was a ghastly yellow ball, which he sat on, rode about on, and finally punctured with a potato knife. From the wound in the rubber he sucked the sickly sweet fluid that gathers inside all air-filled balls, and when he had enough of that began to dismantle and wreck the sailboat. The whistling top and the whip that went with it lay untouched, but frighteningly close at hand.

Oskar, who had long been thinking of this birthday, who had hastened eastward amid one of history's wildest frenzies, determined not to miss the third birthday of his son and heir—Oskar stood aside viewing the little fellow's destructive efforts, admiring his resolution, comparing his own dimensions with those of his son. I had to face the facts. While you were gone, I said to myself in some alarm, Kurt has grown by more than a head. He is already a good inch taller than the three feet you've kept yourself down to ever since your third birthday nearly seventeen years ago; it is time to make a drummer of him and call a halt to that immoderate growth.

I had stored away my drums along with my one-volume library behind the roof tiles in the attic. I picked out a gleaming, brand-new instrument, resolved—since the grownups weren't doing anything about it—to offer my son the same opportunity as my poor mother, faithful to her promise, had offered me on *my* third birthday.

In my own infancy Matzerath had chosen me as his successor in the shop. Now that I had failed him, there was every reason to suppose that he had transferred his designs to Kurt. This, I said to myself, must be prevented at all costs. But I should not like you to see in Oskar a sworn enemy of the retail trade. If my son had been offered the ownership of a factory, or even of a kingdom complete with colonies, I should have felt exactly the same. Oskar had wanted no hand-me-downs for himself and he wanted none for his son. What Oskar wanted—and here was the flaw in my logic—was to make Kurt a permanently three-year-old drummer, as though it were not just as nauseating for a young hopeful to take over a tin drum as to step into a ready-made grocery store.

This is Oskar's present opinion. But at the time he was consumed by one desire: to see a drummer son beside a drummer father, two diminutive drummers looking on at the doings of the grown-up world; to establish a dynasty of drummers, capable of perpetuating itself and of handing down my work, drummed on tin encased in red and white lacquer, from generation to generation.

What a life lay ahead of us! How we might have drummed. Side by side, but also in different rooms, side by side, but also he in Labesweg and I in Luisenstrasse, he in the cellar, I in the attic, Kurt in the kitchen, Oskar in the toilet, father and son, hither and yon but occasionally together; and when we had the chance, the two of us might have slipped under the skirts of Anna Koljaiczek, my grandmother and his great-grandmother, to live and drum and breathe in the smell of slightly rancid butter. Squatting by her portal, I should have said to Kurt: "Look inside, my son. That's where we come from. And if you're a good little boy, we shall be allowed to go back for an hour or more and visit those who are waiting."

And bending low, little Kurt would have peeped in. And ever so politely he would have asked me, his father, for explanations.

And Oskar would have whispered: "The lovely lady sitting there in the middle, playing with her lovely hands, the lovely lady whose sweet oval face brings the tears to my eyes, and yours no doubt as well, is my poor mama, your good grandmother, who died of eating eel soup, or maybe because her heart was too tender."

"Tell me more, Papa, tell me more," little Kurt would have clamored. "Who is the man with the mustache?"

With an air of mystery, I should have lowered my voice: "That's Joseph Koljaiczek, your great-grandfather. Take a good look at those flashing incendiary eyes, at his divine Polish wildness and the practical Kashubian shrewdness of his brow. Observe, if you please, the webs between his toes. In the year 1913, when the *Columbus* ran down the ways, he was hiding under a timber raft. After that he had to swim a long way; he swam and swam till he came to America and became a millionaire. But sometimes he takes to the water, swims back, and dives in here, where the fugitive firebug first found shelter and contributed his part toward my mama."

"But what about the handsome gentleman who has been hiding behind the lady who is my grandmother, who is sitting down now beside her and stroking her hands with his hands? His eyes are just as blue as yours, Papa."

Then I, unnatural son and traitor that I was, should have summoned up all my courage to answer my dear child: "Those are the dreamy blue eyes of the Bronskis that are looking at you, my boy. Your eyes, it is true, are gray. They come to you from your mother. And yet, just like this Jan who is kissing my poor mama's hands, or his father Vincent, for that matter, you too are a Bronski, a dreamer through and through, yet with a practical Kashubian side. One day we will go back there, one day we shall follow the source whence flows that smell of slightly rancid butter. It's something to look forward to."

In those days it seemed to me that true family life was possible only in the interior of my grandmother Koljaiczek, in the grandmotherly butter tub, as I liked to call it. Today many things have changed. With a snap of my fingers I can equal if not surpass God the Father, the only begotten Son, and most important of all, the Holy Ghost. The imitation of Christ has become an occupation with me, that I practice with the same distaste as all my other occupations. And yet, though nothing is farther away from me today than the entrance to my grandmother, it is among my forebears that I picture the most beautiful family scenes.

These fantasies come to me mostly on rainy days: my grandmother sends out invitations and we all meet inside her. Jan Bronski comes with flowers, carnations mostly, in the bullet holes perforating his Polish Post Office defender's breast. Timidly Maria, who at my behest has also received an invitation, approaches my mama; currying favor, she shows her the account books impeccably set up by my mama and impeccably carried on

273

by Maria, and Mama, with her most Kashubian laugh, draws my darling to her, kisses her on the cheek, and says with a twinkle: "Why, child, there's nothing to be ashamed of. Haven't the both of us married a Matzerath and nursed a Bronski?"

I must sternly forbid myself any further reflections along these lines, speculations for example about a son begotten by Jan, deposited by my mama inside Grandma Koljaiczek, and finally born in the butter tub. Such notions would inevitably lead too far. Might it not occur to my half brother Stephan Bronski, who is after all one of us, to cast first a glance, and thereafter heaven knows what else, at my Maria? My imagination prefers to limit itself to an innocent family gathering. Renouncing a third and fourth drummer, I content myself with Oskar and Little Kurt. For the benefit of those present, I drum something or other about that Eiffel Tower which replaced my grandmother for me in a strange land, quite satisfied if the guests and Anna Koljaiczek, our hostess, enjoy our drumming and clap each other on the knees in obedience to the rhythm.

Delightful as it may be to see the world and its relationships unfolding inside my own grandmother, to be profound in a limited area, Oskar must now—since like Matzerath he is only a presumptive father—turn back to the events of June 12, 1944, to Kurt's third birthday.

I repeat: the child had been given a sweater, a ball, a sailboat, a whistling top, and the whip that went with it, and was going to get a drum, lacquered red and white. When he had finished dismantling his sailboat, Oskar approached, the new gift drum hidden behind his back, the battered old one dangling beneath his belly. We stood face to face, only a short step apart: Oskar, the Lilliputian; Kurt, he too a Lilliputian but an inch taller. He had a furious, vicious look on his face, for he was still busy demolishing the sailing vessel. Just as I drew forth the drum and held it up, he cracked the last remaining mast of the *Pamir*, for that was the windjammer's name.

Kurt dropped the wreck, took the drum, and turned it over; he seemed to have calmed down a bit, but his expression was still tense. It was time to hand him the drumsticks. Unfortunately, he misinterpreted my twin movements, felt threatened, and instantly knocked the sticks out of my fingers with the edge of the drum. As I bent down to pick up the sticks, he reached behind himself. I tried again to hand him the sticks, whereupon he hauled off with his birthday present and struck me. It wasn't the top that he whipped but Oskar, not the whistling top, that was meant to be whipped, but his father. Determined to teach his father to spin and to whistle, he whipped me, thinking: just wait, little brother. Thus did Cain whip Abel until Abel began to spin, staggering at first, then faster and with greater precision, until he began to sing at first in a low, disagreeable grumble, then higher and more steadily, till at last he was singing the song of the whistling top. And higher and higher Cain made me sing with his whip; I sang like a tenor singing his morning prayers, like angels forged of silver, like the Vienna Sängerknaben, like a chorus of eunuchs—I sang as Abel may have sung before he collapsed, as I too collapsed under the whip of my son Kurt.

When he saw me lying there, moaning like a run-down top, he lashed at the air as though his arm had not yet exhausted its fury. At length he examined the drum carefully while at the same time keeping a suspicious eye on me. First he chipped off the lacquer against the edge of a chair; then he threw my gift to the floor and armed himself with the massive hull of the erstwhile sailing vessel and began to beat the drum. But the sounds he produced were not drumbeats. Not even the most rudimentary rhythm was discernible. With a look of frantic concentration he hammered ruthlessly at an instrument that had never expected such a drummer, that was made for a light roll, a playful flourish, and not for the blows of a nautical battering ram. The drum buckled, tried to escape by breaking away from its casing, tried to conceal its identity by shedding its red and white lacquer. In the end it was dull-grey tin that sued for mercy. But toward the father's birthday present the son was unrelenting. And when the father tried again to make peace, to cross the carpet to his son in spite of his many aches and pains, the son resorted once more to his whip. The weary top said uncle and ceased to spin, moan, or whistle, and the drum gave up all hope of a sensitive drummer who would wield the sticks with authority but without brutality.

When Maria came in, the drum was ready for the scrap heap. She took me in her arms, kissed my swollen eyes and lacerated ear, licked my blood and the welts on my hands.

Oh, if only Maria had not kissed the maltreated, backward, deplorably abnormal child! If she had recognized the beaten father and in every wound the lover. What a consolation, what a loyal though secret husband I might have been to her during the dark months to come!

The first blow—though it cannot have meant too much to Maria—was the death on the Arctic front of my half brother, Stephan Bronski, or Ehlers, if you will, for by then he had taken his stepfather's name. He had just been promoted to lieutenant, but now his career was cut short forever. Unlike his father, Jan, who, when shot in Saspe Cemetery for defending the Polish Post Office, had borne a skat card under his shirt, the lieutenant was buried with the Iron Cross Second Class, the Infantry Badge, and the so-called Cold Storage Medal.

At the end of June, Mother Truczinski suffered a slight stroke when the mailman brought her bad news. Sergeant Truczinski had fallen for three things at once: Führer, Folk, and Fatherland. This had happened in the Center Sector, and Fritz' belongings—his wallet containing snapshots taken in Heidelberg, Brest, Paris, Bad Kreuznach, and Saloniki, of pretty girls, most of them smiling, the Iron Cross First and Second Class, various medals for various wounds, the bronze close-combat clasp, his two antitank patches, and a few letters—had been sent directly from Headquarters Center Sector to Labesweg, Langfuhr, by a certain Captain Kanauer.

Matzerath helped as much as he could and soon Mother Truczinski felt better, though she never fully recovered. All day she sat in her chair by the window, periodically asking me or Matzerath, who would come up two or three times a day with something to eat or drink, where this "Center Sector" was, whether it was far away, and whether you could go there by train over Sunday.

With all his good intentions Matzerath could tell her nothing. Oskar, however, had learned geography from the special newscasts and Wehrmacht communiqués. I spent many a long afternoon trying with my drum to tell Mother Truczinski, who sat motionless in her chair except for her wagging head, all I could about Center Sector and its increasingly precipitate movements.

Maria had been very fond of her handsome brother. His death made her religious. All through July, she tried the religion she had been raised in; every Sunday she went to hear Pastor Hecht preach at Christ Church; once or twice Matzerath went with her, although she preferred to go alone.

Protestant services failed to satisfy Maria. One weekday—a Thursday or maybe a Friday—Maria entrusted the shop to Matzerath's care, took me, the Catholic, by the hand, and left the house. Starting off in the direction of the Neue Markt, we turned into Elsenstrasse, then took Marienstrasse, past Wohlgemuth's butcher shop, as far as Kleinhammer-Park—we're headed for Langfuhr Station, Oskar was beginning to think, we're going to take a little trip, maybe to Bissau in Kashubia. But then we turned left, waited superstitiously near the underpass for a freight train to go by, and went on through the oozing, dripping tunnel. On the far side, instead of going straight ahead toward the Film-Palast, we turned left along the embankment. Either, I figured, she is dragging me to see Dr. Hollatz in Brunshofer-Weg or else she's going to Sacred Heart to be converted.

The church door faced the railway tracks. Between the embankment and the open door we stopped still. An afternoon in late August, full of humming and buzzing. Behind us some Ukrainian women in white kerchiefs were picking and shoveling on the ballast. We stood there, peering into the cool, shady belly of the church. Far in the distance, ingeniously alluring, a violently inflamed eye: the eternal light. Behind us on the embankment the Ukrainian women stopped their picking and shoveling.

276

A horn blew, a train was coming, there it was, still there, not yet past, gone, the horn tooted, and the women set to work again. Maria was undecided, perhaps uncertain which foot to put forward, and put all the responsibility on me, who by birth and baptism was closer to the only-saving Church; for the first time in years, for the first time since those two weeks full of fizz powder and love, she resigned herself to Oskar's guidance.

We left the embankment and its sounds, August and its buzzing, outside. Rather mournfully, letting my fingertips under my smock play sleepily over my drum, while outwardly a look of indifference settled on my features, I recalled the Masses, pontifical offices, Vespers services and Saturday confessions I had experienced at the side of my mother, who shortly before her death was rendered pious by the intensity of her relations with Jan Bronski, who Saturday after Saturday cast off her burden by confessing, who fortified herself with sacraments on Sunday in order, thus unburdened and fortified, to meet Jan in Tischlergasse the following Thursday. Who was the priest in those days? His name, then as now, for he was still priest of Sacred Heart, was Father Wiehnke, his sermons were pleasantly soft-spoken and unintelligible, his singing of the Credo was so thin and plaintive that even I should have been invaded by something resembling faith in those days if not for that left side-altar with the Virgin, the boy Jesus, and the boy John the Baptist.

And yet it was that altar which impelled me to pull Maria from the sunshine into the doorway and then across the flags into the nave.

Oskar took his time, sat quietly beside Maria in the oak pew, feeling more and more at his ease. Years had passed, and yet it seemed to me that the same people were still leafing through their missals, working out their strategy while waiting for Father Wiehnke's ear. We were sitting slightly to one side of the center aisle. I wanted to let Maria do the choosing, but to make the choice easier for her. On the one hand, the confessional was not so close as to upset her, thus her conversion could be leisurely, unofficial as it were; on the other hand, she was in a position to see how people behaved while preparing to confess and, while looking on, make up her mind. She had not far to go to consult Father Wiehnke in the confessional, to discuss with him the details of her conversion to the only-saving faith. I felt sorry for her; she seemed so little, so awkward as she knelt amid dust, incense, plaster, tortuous angels, refracted light, convulsed saints, as she knelt beneath and amid the sweetness and sorrow, the sorrowful sweetness of Catholicism and for the first time crossed herself the wrong way around. Oskar gave Maria a poke and showed her the right way. She was eager to learn. He showed her where behind her forehead, where deep in her heart, exactly where in the joints of her shoulders Father, Son, and Holy Ghost have their dwelling places, and

277

how you must fold your hands if your amen is to be successful. Maria obeyed, her hands came to rest in amen, and she began to pray.

At first Oskar, too, tried to pray for some of the dead, but while praying to the Lord for his Roswitha, while trying to negotiate peace for her and admission to heavenly joys, he so lost himself in earthly details that in the end peace and heavenly joys settled down in a Paris hotel. Accordingly, I took refuge in the Preface, because here there is nothing much to pin you down; for all eternity I said, *sursum corda, dignum et justum*—it is just and right. Then I let well enough alone and took to watching Maria from the side.

Catholic prayer was becoming to her. She was pretty as a picture in her devotions. Prayer lengthens the lashes, lifts the eyebrows, inflames the cheeks, makes the forehead grave, lends suppleness to the neck, and makes the nostrils quiver. Maria's features, flowering in sorrow, almost beguiled me into a display of affection. But one must not disturb those who are praying, one must neither seduce them nor let oneself be seduced by them, even if it is pleasant for those who pray and conducive to prayer, to know that someone considers them worth watching.

Oskar slipped off the smooth bench and fled from Maria. My hands, under my smock, were still quietly folded over my drum, as we, my drum and I, made our way over the flags, past the stations of the Cross in the left aisle of the nave; we did not stop with St. Anthony—pray for us!—for we had lost neither a purse nor a house key, nor with St. Adalbert of Prague who was slain by the heathen Prussians. We did not halt until, hopping from flag to flag as over a checkerboard, we reached the carpeted steps to the left side-altar.

You will not doubt my word when I tell you that nothing had changed in the Neo-Gothic brick Church of the Sacred Heart or, *a fortiori*, on the left side-altar. The boy Jesus still sat pink and naked on the Virgin's pink thigh—I shall not call her the Virgin Mary for fear of confusion with my Mary, my Maria, then busy with her conversion. Young John the Baptist, scantily clad in the same old shaggy, chocolate-colored pelt, was still pressing against the Virgin's right knee. She herself was still pointing her left forefinger at Jesus, but looking at John.

Yet even after years of absence, Oskar was less interested in the Virgin's maternal pride than in the constitutions of the two boys. Jesus was about the size of my son Kurt on his third birthday, in other words, he was about an inch taller than Oskar. John, who according to the documents was older than the Nazarene, was my size. But both of them had the same precocious expression as I, the eternal three-year-old. Nothing had changed. They had had that same sly look on their faces years before, in the days when I had frequented the Church of the Sacred Heart with my poor mama.

Climbing the carpeted steps, though without saying the Introit, I examined every fold in the drapery; slowly, carefully, I explored the painted plaster exterior of those two little nudists with my drumstick, which had more feeling than all my fingers together; omitting nothing, I covered the thighs, the bellies, the arms, taking in every crease and dimple. Jesus was the spit and image of Oskar, my healthy flesh, my strong, rather plump knees, my short but muscular drummer's arms. And the little rascal's posture was that of a drummer too. He sat on the Virgin's thigh, arms and fists upraised as though he were planning to beat a drum, as though Jesus, not Oskar, were the drummer, as though he were just waiting for my drum, as though this time he seriously intended to imprint some charming rhythm on the drum for the benefit of the Virgin, John and myself. I did what I had done years before; I removed the drum from my belly and put Jesus to the test. Cautiously, careful not to harm the painted plaster, I set Oskar's red and white drum on his pink thighs. This time, however, I was driven by sheer malice, I had lost my idiotic faith in miracles, all I wanted was to show him up. For though he sat there with upraised fists, though he had my dimensions and rugged build, though he was a plaster copy of the three-year-old that I—by dint of what effort, what privations!—had remained, he could not drum, he could only give himself an air of knowing how to drum. If I had one, I could do it, he seemed to be thinking; ha-ha, I said, now you've got one, what are you going to do? Shaking with laughter, I pressed both sticks into his little sausage fingers, ten of them—sweet little plaster Jesus, go on and drum! Oskar steps back, descends three steps; he leaves the carpet for the flags, go on and drum, little boy Jesus. Oskar takes a long step backward for detachment. Oskar begins to laugh himself sick, because all Jesus can do is sit there, unable to drum, though maybe he'd like to. Boredom is beginning to gnaw at me as a mouse gnaws at a side of bacon when—I'm damned if he doesn't begin to drum.

While round us nothing stirred, he started in with his right stick, then a tap or two with the left, then both together. Blessed if he isn't crossing his sticks, say, that roll wasn't bad. He was very much in earnest and there was plenty of variety in his playing. He did some very complicated things but his simple rhythms were just as successful. There was nothing phony about his playing, he steered clear of gimmicks and just played the drum. His style wasn't even religious, and there was no military vulgarity about it. He was a musician through and through, but no snob. He knew all the hits. He played "Everything Passes," which everyone was singing at the time, and, of course, "Lili Marlene." Slowly, a little jerkily perhaps, he turned his curly head with the blue Bronski eyes toward me, smiled, rather arrogantly it seemed to me, and proceeded to weave Oskar's favorites into a potpourri: it began with "Smash a Little

Windowpane" and there was a bare suggestion of "The Schedule"; just like me, the little scoundrel played off Rasputin against Goethe; he climbed up the Stockturm with me, crawled under the rostrum with me, caught eels on the breakwater, walked with me behind the coffin, tapered at the foot end, of my poor mama, and, what flabbergasted me most of all, took refuge again and again beneath the four skirts of my grandmother Anna Koljaiczek.

Oskar stepped closer. Something drew him forward. He wanted to be on the carpet, he didn't want to stand on the flags any more. One stair sent him up the next. I climbed up, though I would rather have had him climb down. "Jesus," I said, summoning up what little voice was left me, "that wasn't our bargain. Give me back my drum this minute. You've got your cross, that should do you." He stopped playing, but gently, without abruptness, crossed the sticks over the drum with ex-aggerated care, and without a word of discussion returned what Oskar had unthinkingly lent him.

I was on the point of racing down the steps without thanks, of running away from Catholicism as fast as my legs would carry me, when a pleasant though imperious voice touched my shoulder: "Dost thou love me, Oskar?" Without turning, I replied: "Not that I know of." Where-upon he, without raising his voice: "Dost thou love me, Oskar?" This time my tone was more biting: "Sorry, old man, I'm afraid not." For the third time he came at me with that irritating voice of his: "Oskar, dost thou love me?" I turned around and looked him full in the face: "You bastard, I hate you, you and all your hocus-pocus."

Strange to say, my hostility, far from getting him down, was his occasion to triumph. Raising his forefinger like a lady schoolteacher, he gave me an assignment: "Thou art Oskar, the rock, and on this rock I will build my Church. Follow thou me!"

You can imagine my indignation. I had gooseflesh with rage. I broke off one of his plaster toes, but he didn't budge. "Say that again," Oskar hissed, "and I'll scratch the paint off you."

After that, not a single word came forth; what came, as always, was the old man who is forever shuffling about all the churches in the world. He cast a glance at the left side-altar but failed to see me, and shuffled on. He had already reached St. Adalbert of Prague when I stumbled down the steps, passed from the carpet to the flags, and, without looking back, crossed the checkerboard pattern to Maria, who just then crossed herself correctly in accordance with my instructions.

I took her by the hand and led her to the holy water font; just before the door, I bade her cross herself again in the direction of the high altar, but I did not join in, and when she wanted to genuflect, I pulled her out into the sunlight.

It was late in the afternoon. The Ukrainian women were gone from the railroad tracks. In their place, a freight train was being shunted about, not far from Langfuhr Station. Clusters of gnats hung in mid-air. From overhead came the sound of bells, mingling with the railroad noises. The gnats still hung in clusters. Maria's face was wet with tears. Oskar would have liked to scream. What was I going to do about Jesus? I felt like loading my voice. What had I to do with his Cross? But I was perfectly well aware that my voice was powerless against the windows of his church. Let him go on building his temple on people called Peter. "Watch out, Oskar, leave those church windows alone," Satan whispered within me. "One of these days that fellow's going to ruin your voice." I cast one solitary glance upward, took the measure of one of those Neo-Gothic windows, and wrenched myself away. I did not sing, I did not follow Him, I just trotted along by Maria's side to the underpass in Bahnhof-strasse. Through the oozing, dripping tunnel, up the hill to Kleinhammer-Park, right turn into Marienstrasse, past Wohlgemuth's butcher shop, left turn into Elsenstrasse, across the Striessbach to the Neuer Markt, where they were building a water tank for the air-raid defense. Labesweg was endless, but then we were home. Leaving Maria, Oskar climbed over a hundred steps to the attic. Bed sheets had been hung up to dry; behind the bed sheets a mound of air-defense sand; behind sand and buckets, behind bundles of newspaper and piles of roofing tiles, were secreted my book and my supply of drums. But there was also a shoe box containing several burned-out, but still pear-shaped light bulbs. Oskar selected one and sang it to pieces; he took another, turned it to pulverized glass, cut a third neatly in two. Upon a fourth his voice inscribed JESUS in Sütterlin script, then pulverized both bulb and inscription. He wanted to do it again, but there were no more bulbs. Exhausted, I sank down on the air-defense sand: Oskar still had his voice. Maybe Jesus had a disciple. As for me, my first disciples were to be the Dusters.

The Dusters

Oskar was not cut out to be a follower of Christ; for one thing, he has no aptitude for enlisting disciples. Nevertheless Christ's "follow thou me" found its way indirectly, circuitously, to my heart and I became his follower though I did not believe in him. But, as they say, he who doubts, believes, and it is the unbeliever who believes longest. Jesus had treated me to a little private miracle in the Church of the Sacred Heart and I was unable to stifle that miracle under my doubts; quite on the contrary, I did all I could to make Jesus put on a repeat performance.

After that Oskar returned to Sacred Heart a number of times without Maria. It was not very difficult to slip away from Mother Truczinski, who was glued to her chair. What had Jesus to offer me? Why did I spend half the night in the left-hand aisle of the nave and let the sacristan lock me in? Why did Oskar stand at the left side-altar until his limbs congealed and his ears were frozen stiff? For with all my crushing humility and no less crushing blasphemies, I never got to hear either my drum or Jesus' voice again.

Miserere. Never in all my life have I heard my teeth chatter as they did in those midnight hours in Sacred Heart. What jester could ever have found a better rattle than Oskar? I sounded like a machine-gun nest, I had a bevy of typists between my upper and lower jaws. My teeth chattered in all directions, calling forth echoes and applause. Pillars shivered, arches had gooseflesh, and when my teeth weren't chattering, I coughed. My cough hopped over the checkerboard pattern of the flags, down the transept, up the nave, hoisted itself into the choir. Multiplied by sixty, it organized a Bach society that did not sing but specialized in coughing, and just as I was beginning to think that Oskar's cough had crawled away into the organ pipes and wouldn't be heard again until the Sunday chorale, a cough rang out in the sacristy, and another from the pulpit, until at length the cough died down, coughed out its soul behind the high altar, not far from the Athlete on the Cross. It is accomplished, said my cough; but nothing was accomplished. The boy Jesus sat there stiff and proud, holding my drumsticks and my drum, but drum he would not, he refused to confirm my mission. For Oskar wanted to have it in writing.

A sorry habit has remained with me from that period. Whenever I visit a church or even a famous cathedral I begin to cough. Even if I am in the best of health. The moment I set foot inside, I embark on a sustained cough which takes on a Gothic, Romanesque, perhaps even a Baroque character according to the style of the church. I feel certain that years hence I shall still be able to give you a drum rendition of Oskar's cough in the Cathedral of Ulm, or of Speyer for that matter. At that time, however, in the days when I was suffering the effects of the most glacial Catholicism in mid-August, there was no opportunity to visit churches in distant lands, unless you happened to be a soldier participating in the planned withdrawals of the Reichswehr, noting perhaps in your diary: "Evacuated Orvieto today; wonderful church, must come back with Monica after the war and look at it properly."

It was easy for me to become a churchgoer, for there was nothing to keep me at home. There was Maria. But Maria had Matzerath. There was my son Kurt. But he was getting more and more insufferable, throwing sand in my eyes and clawing me so ferociously that his fingernails broke off in my parental flesh. Moreover, my son showed me a pair of fists with knuckles so white that the mere sight of them sent the blood gushing from my nose.

Strange to say, Matzerath defended me, awkwardly perhaps but not without tenderness. In his surprise, Oskar would allow this man, who had never meant a thing to him, to pick him up on his lap, hug him, gaze at him, and once even to kiss him. With tears in his eyes Matzerath had said, more to himself than to Maria: "It's impossible. I can't send my own son away. The doctors can say what they like. They don't stop to think. I bet they have no children of their own."

Maria, who was sitting at the table, pasting food stamps in ledgers as she did every evening, looked up: "Take it easy, Alfred. You talk as if I didn't care. But when they say it's the modern way to do, I don't know what to think."

Matzerath pointed at the piano, which had produced no music since the death of my poor mama: "Agnes would never have done that, she'd never have allowed it."

Maria cast a glance at the piano, shrugged her shoulders, and let them drop back into place only when she opened her mouth to speak. "Of course not, she was his mother, she kept hoping he'd get better. But you see how it is: nothing has happened, he's always being pushed around, he don't know how to live and he don't know how to die."

Was it the likeness of Beethoven, who still hung over the piano, glumly mustering the glum Hitler, who gave Matzerath the strength? "No," he shouted. "Never!" and banged his fist on the table and its damp sticky papers. He asked Maria to hand him the letter from the institution, he read it and read it again, then tore it up and scattered the scraps among the bread stamps, fat stamps, food stamps, travel stamps, heavy-labor stamps, extra-heavy-labor stamps, and the stamps for pregnant women and nursing mothers. Though, thanks to Matzerath, Oskar never fell into the hands of those doctors, he beheld a vision, and to this day, whenever he lays eyes on Maria, he beholds a vision of a beautiful clinic situated in the mountain air, of a light, airy, friendly, and modern operating room; outside its padded door, Maria, shy but smiling, hands me over confidently, to a group of first-class physicians, who are smiling too and ever so confidence-inspiring, and holding first-class, confidence-inspiring and immediately effective syringes behind their white, sterile aprons.

The whole world had forsaken me and it was only the shadow of my poor mama, falling across Matzerath's fingers and paralyzing them whenever he thought of signing the authorization form drawn up by the Ministry of Public Health, that kept me alive.

Oskar would not like to seem ungrateful. I still had my drum. I still had my voice, which is of no use to you now that you have heard all about my triumphs with glass and is probably beginning to bore the lovers of novelty among you—but to me Oskar's voice, even more than his drum, was proof of my existence and as such forever new; for as long as I sang glass to pieces, I existed.

In that period, Oskar sang a good deal. He sang with an energy born of desperation. Every time I left the Church of the Sacred Heart at a late hour, I sang something to pieces. I did not go looking for targets of particular interest. On my way home, I would select an attic window that hadn't been properly blacked out or a street lamp painted regulation blue. Each time I went to church, I chose a different way home. One evening Oskar would take Anton-Möller-Weg and Marienstrasse. Another, he would pass by the Conradinum and shatter the glass in the main entrance. One day toward the end of August, I reached the church too late and found the door locked. Wishing to walk off my fury, I picked a particularly circuitous way home. I started off on Bahnhofstrasse, where I demolished every third street lamp, passed the Film-Palast and turned right into Adolf-Hitler-Strasse. I ignored the windows of the infantry barracks, but vented my rage on an almost empty streetcar coming toward me from Oliva, stripping one side of it of all its lugubrious blackout glass.

Brakes screeched, the car stopped, the people got out, cursed a while, and got back in again. A triumph, if you will, but Oskar gave it little thought. He started off in search of a dessert for his rage, a tasty morsel in that period so poor in tasty morsels, and did not stop until, approaching Langfuhr, he saw the Baltic Chocolate Factory spread out in the moonlight between Berendt's carpentry shop and the spacious hangars of the airfield.

By this time, however, my rage had lost some of its intensity. Instead of introducing myself to the factory at once, I took my time and counted the moonlit windows. That done, I was just about ready to introduce myself, but first wanted to find out what the youngsters who had been following me from Hochstriess, and perhaps all the way from Bahnhofstrasse, were up to. Six or seven of them were standing by the shelter at the nearby streetcar stop, and I could make out five more behind the trees on the avenue.

I had already decided to postpone my visit to the chocolate factory, to give them a wide berth and make for home by way of the overpass and the Aktien Brewery, when Oskar heard an exchange of whistle signals. One group was signaling from the overpass. There was no room for doubt: this troop movement was for my benefit.

I had seen my pursuers, but the hunt had not yet begun. In such situations one tends to enumerate the remaining possibilities of escape with great relish and thoroughness: Oskar might have cried out for Mama and Papa. I might have summoned heaven knows whom, a policeman maybe, on my drum. My stature would assuredly have won me grown-up support, but even Oskar had his principles and occasionally stuck to them. And so I resolved to do without the help of any policemen or other adults who might be within earshot. Spurred by curiosity and flattered at so much attention, I decided to let things take their course and did the stupidest thing imaginable: I went looking for a hole in the tarred fence surrounding the chocolate factory. I found none. Slowly and nonchalantly, the young bandits converged: from the car-stop shelter, from under the trees on the avenue, and at length from the overpass. Oskar moved along the fence, still looking for that hole. They gave me just the time I needed to find the place where the plank was missing. But when I squeezed through, tearing my pants in the process, there were four of these characters in windbreakers on the other side, waiting for me with their hands in the pockets of their ski pants.

Recognizing that nothing could be done about my situation, I ran my hands over my pants, looking for the tear. It was in the seat. I measured it with outspread fingers, found it annoyingly large but put on a show of indifference, and before looking up to face the music, waited until all the boys from the car stop, the avenue, and the overpass had climbed over the fence, for they were too big to squeeze through the gap.

This was in the last days of August. From time to time the moon hid behind a cloud. I counted about twenty of these young fellows. The youngest were fourteen, the oldest sixteen, almost seventeen. The summer of '44 was hot and dry. Four of the larger boys had on Air Force Auxiliary uniforms. It was a good cherry year, I remember. They stood round Oskar in small groups, talked in an undertone, using a jargon that I made no effort to understand. They gave each other weird names, only a few of which I bothered to take note of. A little fifteen-year-old with rather misty doe's eyes was addressed, I recall, as Ripper and occasionally as Bouncer. The one beside him was Putty. The smallest, though surely not the youngest, with a protruding upper lip and a lisp, was called Firestealer. One of the Air Force Auxiliaries was addressed as Mister and another, very aptly, as Soup Chicken. There were also historical names such as Lionheart and Bluebeard—Bluebeard had the look of a milksop—and old friends of mine like Totila and Teja. Two of them even had the impudence to call themselves Belisarius and Narses. The leader was a sixteen-year-old named Störtebeker after the celebrated pirate. He had on a genuine velour hat with the crown battered in to look like a duck pond, and a raincoat that was too long for him.

No one paid any attention to Oskar; they were trying to wear him down with suspense. Half-amused and half-annoyed at myself for bothering with these adolescent Romantics, I sat wearily down on my drum, studied the moon, which was just about full, and tried to dispatch a part of my thoughts to the Church of the Sacred Heart.

Just today He might have drummed and said a word or two. And here I was, sitting in the yard of the Baltic Chocolate Factory, wasting my time with cops and robbers. Maybe He was waiting for me, maybe after a brief introduction on the drum, He was planning to open His mouth again, to elaborate on the ways of imitating Christ. Disappointed at my failure to show up, He was probably, at this very moment, lifting His eyebrows in that arrogant way of His. What would Jesus think of these young scamps? What could Oskar, his likeness, his disciple and vicar, be expected to do with this horde? Could he have addressed the words of Jesus: "Suffer little children to come unto me!" to a gang of young hoodlums calling themselves Putty, Bluebeard, Firestealer, and Störtebeker?

Störtebeker approached, accompanied by Firestealer, his right hand. Störtebeker: "Stand up!"

Oskar's eyes were still on the moon, his thoughts by the left side-altar of the Church of the Sacred Heart. He did not stand up, and Firestealer, at a signal from Störtebeker, kicked the drum out from under me.

Rising for want of anything to sit on, I put the drum under my smock to protect it against further damage.

Nice-looking boy, this Störtebeker, Oskar thought. The eyes are a bit too deep-set and close together, but there's life and imagination in the cut of his mouth.

"Where are you from?"

So they were going to question me. Displeased at this overture, I turned back to the moon, thinking to myself—the moon doesn't seem to care what one thinks—that it looked like a drum, and smiled at my harmless megalomania.

"He's got a grin on his face, Störtebeker."

Firestealer looked me over and suggested an activity that he called "dusting." Others in the background, pimple-faced Lionheart, Mister, Bouncer, and Putty were also in favor of dusting.

Still on the moon, I mentally spelled out the word "dusting." A nice word, but it was sure to stand for something unpleasant.

Störtebeker asserted his authority: "I'm the one that says who's going to be dusted around here and when." Then he addressed me: "We've been seeing quite a lot of you in Bahnhofstrasse. How come? Where you been?"

Two questions at once. Oskar would have to give at least one answer if he was to remain master of the situation. I turned away from the moon, faced him with my blue persuasive eyes, and said calmly: "Church."

From behind Störtebeker's raincoat came commentaries on my answer. Firestealer figured out that by church I meant Sacred Heart.

"What's your name?"

An inevitable question, a question that arises wherever man meets man and that plays a vital role in human conversation. It provides the substance of whole plays, even operas—*Lohengrin*, for instance.

I waited for the moon to pass between two clouds, let the sheen in

286

my eyes work on Störtebeker for the time it takes to eat three spoonfuls of soup. Then I spoke, intent on the effect, named myself—what would I have got but a laugh if I had owned to the name of Oskar? "My name is Jesus," I said. A long silence ensued. Finally Firestealer cleared his throat: "We'll have to dust him after all, chief."

This time Firestealer met with no opposition; with a snap of his fingers, Störtebeker gave his permission, and Firestealer seized me, dug his knuckles into my arm just above the elbow, and gouged, producing a hot, painful sensation, until Störtebeker snapped his fingers again as a sign to stop—so that was dusting!

"Well now, what *is* your name?" The chief in the velour hat gave himself an air of boredom, did a little shadow boxing, which made the long sleeves of his raincoat slide up to his elbows, and held up his wristwatch in the moonlight. "You've got one minute to think it over," he whispered. "Then I give the boys the green light."

Oskar had a whole minute in which to study the moon with impunity, to look for a solution among the craters, to reconsider his idea of stepping into Christ's shoes. This green-light talk was not to my liking, and I certainly was not going to let any half-baked hoodlums put me on a schedule. I waited about thirty-five seconds; then Oskar said: "I am Jesus."

What happened next was pretty good, but I can't say I planned it. Immediately after my second announcement that I was Jesus, before Störtebeker could snap his fingers or Firestealer could dust, the air-raid sirens let loose.

". . . Jesus," said Oskar and took a breath. Thereupon my identity was confirmed, successively, by the sirens at the nearby airfield, the siren on the main building of the Hochstriess Infantry Barracks, the siren on the roof of Horst-Wessel High School, the siren on Sternfeld's Department Store, and far in the distance, from the direction of the Hindenburg-Allee, the siren of the Engineering School. It was some time before all the sirens in the suburb, like a choir of iron-lunged, overenthusiastic archangels, took up my glad tidings, made the night rise and fall, made dreams flare up and crash, crept into the ears of the sleeping population, and transformed the cold, disinterested moon into a merciless light that there was no way to black out.

Oskar knew that the alarm was on his side; not so Störtebeker, the sirens made him nervous. For some of his henchmen the alarm was a call to duty. The four Air Force Auxiliaries had to climb the fence, rush back to their batteries between the car barn and the airfield, and help man the 88's. Three others, including Belisarius, were wardens at the Conradinum. Störtebeker managed to keep his hold on the rest, some fifteen of them. Since nothing more was doing in the sky, he went on questioning me:

"Very well, if my ears do not deceive me, you are Jesus. O.K. One more question: that trick of yours with the street lights and windowpanes, how do you do it? You'd better come clean. We know all about it."

Of course they didn't know a thing. They had witnessed one or two of my vocal triumphs and that was that. Oskar told himself that he must not be too severe in his appraisal of these junior hoodlums, or juvenile delinquents as we should call them today. Their way of doing things was amateurish, too eager, too direct, but boys will be boys; I was determined to be patient with them. So these were the notorious Dusters that everybody had been talking about for the last few weeks, the gang that the police and several Hitler Youth patrols had been trying to track down. As it later turned out, they were schoolboys, students at the Conradinum, the Petri and Horst-Wessel High Schools. There was a second group of Dusters in Neufahrwasser, led by high school students but made up chiefly of apprentices at the Schichau shipyards and the railroad car factory. The two groups worked separately, joining forces only for night expeditions to the Steffens-Park and Hindenburg-Allee, where they would waylay leaders of the League of German Girls on their way home after training sessions. Friction between the groups was avoided; their territories were marked out with precision, and Störtebeker looked upon the leader of the Neufahrwasser group more as a friend than a rival. The Dusters were against everything. They raided the offices of the Hitler Youth, attacked soldiers found necking in the parks to strip them of their medals and insignia of rank, and with the help of their members among the Air Force Auxiliaries stole arms, ammunition, and gasoline from the AA batteries. But their main project, which they had been maturing ever since their inception, was an all-out attack on the Rationing Office.

At the time Oskar knew nothing about the Dusters, their organization or plans, but he was feeling low and forsaken, and he thought these young men might give him a sense of security, a sense of belonging somewhere. Despite the difference in our ages—I would soon be twenty—I already considered myself secretly as one of them. Why, I said to myself, shouldn't you give them a sample of your art? The young are always eager to learn. You yourself were fifteen or sixteen once. Set them an example, show them your accomplishments. They will look up to you. Maybe they will choose you as their leader. Now at last you will be able to exert influence, to bring your intelligence and experience to bear; this is your chance to heed your vocation, to gather disciples and walk in the footsteps of Christ.

Perhaps Störtebeker suspected that there was thought behind my thoughtfulness. He gave me time to think, and I was grateful to him for that. A moonlit night toward the end of August. Slightly cloudy. Air-raid alarm. Two or three searchlights on the coast. Maybe a reconnaissance plane. Paris was just being evacuated. Facing me the front, rich in windows, of the Baltic Chocolate Factory. After a long retreat, Army Group Center had dug in on the Vistula. Baltic was no longer working for the retail market, its whole output went to the Air Force. Oskar was having to get used to the idea of General Patton's soldiers strolling beneath the Eiffel Tower in American uniforms. In response to this painful thought —ah, the happy hours with Roswitha!—Oskar lifted a drumstick. Störtebeker noticed my gesture, his eye followed my drumstick to the chocolate factory. While in broad daylight the Japanese were being cleaned out of some Pacific island, on our side of the globe the moon was shining on the windows of a chocolate factory. And to all those who had ears to hear, Oskar said: "The voice of Jesus will now demolish some glass."

Before I had disposed of the first three panes, I heard the buzzing of a fly far above me. While two more panes were surrendering their share of moonlight, I thought: that fly must be dying or it wouldn't buzz so loud. Thereupon I blackened the rest of the windows on the top floor. Awfully pale, those searchlight beams, I said to myself before expelling the reflected lights—probably from the battery near Camp Narvik—from several first- and second-floor windows. The coastal batteries fired, then I finished off the second floor. A moment later the batteries at Altschottland, Pelonken, and Schellmühl let loose. Three ground-floor windows, then the pursuit planes took off and flew low over the factory. Before I had finished off the ground floor, the AA suspended fire to let the pursuit planes take care of a four-motored bomber that was receiving the attentions of three searchlights at once over Oliva.

At first Oskar feared the spectacular efforts of the antiaircraft batteries might distract my new friends' attention. My work done, I was overjoyed to see them all gaping at my alterations in the chocolate factory. Even when applause and cries of "Bravo" rose up from nearby Hohenfriedberger-Weg as from a theater, because the bomber had been hit and could be seen falling in flames over Jeschkenthal Forest, only a few members of the gang, among then Putty, looked away from the unglassed factory. Neither Störtebeker nor Firestealer, and it was they who mattered, showed any interest in the bomber.

Once more the heavens were bare, except for the moon and the small-fry stars. The pursuit planes landed. Far in the distance fire engines could be heard. Störtebeker turned, showing me the contemptuous curve of his mouth, and put up his fists, disengaging his wristwatch from the long sleeve of his raincoat. Taking off the watch, he handed it to me without a word. Then he sighed and tried to say something, but had to wait for the all-clear signal to die down. At last, amid the applause of his henchmen, he got the words out: "O.K., Jesus. If you feel like it, you're in. We're the Dusters if that means anything to you."

Oskar weighed the wristwatch in his hand, a cute little thing with a luminous dial and hands indicating twenty-three minutes after midnight, and handed it to Firestealer. Firestealer cast a questioning look at his boss. Störtebeker nodded his consent. Shifting his drum to a comfortable position for the homeward march, Oskar said: "Jesus will lead you. Follow Him."

The Christmas Play

There was a good deal of talk in those days about secret weapons and final victory. We, the Dusters, discussed neither one, but we had the secret weapon.

Oskar's first move after taking over the leadership of the thirty to forty members of the gang was to have Störtebeker introduce me to the leader of the Neufahrwasser outfit. Moorkähne, a sixteen-year-old with a limp, was the son of an official at the Neufahrwasser pilot office; his physical defect—his right leg was almost an inch shorter than his left— had prevented him from being drafted or taken on as an Air Force Auxiliary. Though a bit ostentatious about his limp, Moorkähne was shy and soft-spoken. There was always an artful smile on his lips, and he was regarded as the best student in the graduating class at the Conradinum. He had every prospect, if the Russian Army should raise no objection, of passing his final examination brilliantly; he was planning to study philosophy.

Like Störtebeker, whose unstinting respect I had won, Moorkähne recognized me as Jesus, first in command of the Dusters. Oskar insisted at once on being shown the storehouse and treasury, for both groups kept their loot in the same place, the spacious cellar of a quiet, fashionable villa on Jeschkenthaler-Weg in Langfuhr. This house, covered with ivy and creepers and separated from the street by a gently sloping meadow, was the abode of Putty's parents, whose name was Von Puttkamer. Mr. von Puttkamer, a nobleman of Pomeranian, Polish, and Prussian descent and a wearer of the Knight's Cross, was off commanding a division in fair France; Mrs. Elisabeth von Puttkamer had been spending the last few months in the Bavarian highlands for reasons of health. Wolfgang von Puttkamer, whom the Dusters called Putty, had been left in charge of the house; as for the elderly, half-deaf maid who ministered to the young gentleman's needs, she never went below the ground floor, and we never saw her, for we entered the cellar through the laundry room.

In the storeroom were piled canned goods, tobacco, and several bolts of parachute silk. From one of the shelves hung two dozen Army watches, which Putty had orders from Störtebeker to keep running and properly set. Another of his duties was to keep the two tommy guns, the rifle, and the pistols clean. I was shown a bazooka, some machine-gun ammunition, and twenty-five hand grenades. All this and an impressive supply of gasoline in jerrycans was intended for the assault on the Rationing Office. Oskar-Jesus' first order was: "Bury the arms and gasoline in the garden. Hand over all bolts and firing pins to Jesus. Our weapons are of a different kind."

When the boys produced a cigar box full of stolen decorations and insignia, I smiled and said they could keep them. But I should have taken away the paratroopers' knives. Later on they made use of the blades which fitted so neatly into their handles, as though just begging to be used.

Then they brought me the treasury. Oskar ordered a counting and checked it over. The Dusters' liquid assets amounted to two thousand four hundred and twenty Reichsmarks. This was at the beginning of September, 1944. When, in mid-January, 1945, Koniev and Zhukov broke through on the Vistula, Putty confessed and we were obliged to hand over our treasury to the authorities. Thirty-six thousand Reichsmarks were counted into piles and bundles on the bench of the District Court.

In keeping with my nature, Oskar remained in the background during operations. In the daytime I would go out alone or with Störtebeker, to find worth-while targets for the Dusters' night expeditions. I let Störtebeker or Moorkähne do the actual organizing. After nightfall I never stirred from Mother Truczinski's apartment. That brings us to the secret weapon. I would stand at my bedroom window and send out my voice, farther than ever before, to demolish windows at the other end of town. I unglassed several Party headquarters, a printshop that turned out ration cards, and once, acceding reluctantly to the request of my comrades-in-arms, shattered the kitchen windows of an apartment belonging to a high school principal who had incurred their displeasure.

That was in November. While V-1 and V-2 rockets were winging their way to England, my voice winged its way over Langfuhr and along the file of trees on Hindenburg-Allee, hopped over the Central Station and the Old City, and sought out the museum in Fleischergasse; my men had orders to look for Niobe, the wooden figurehead.

They did not find her. In the adjoining room Mother Truczinski sat motionless but for the wagging of her head. In a way we had something in common; for while Oskar engaged in long-distance song, she was occupied with long-distance thoughts. She searched God's heaven for her son Herbert and the front lines of Center Sector for her son Fritz. She also had to look far away for her eldest daughter Guste, who early in 1944 had married and gone off to distant Düsseldorf, for it was there that Headwaiter Köster had his home; though he personally was spending most of his time in Courland. A scant two weeks' furlough was all the time Guste had to keep him for herself and get to know him.

Those were peaceful evenings. Oskar sat at Mother Truczinski's feet, improvised a bit on his drum, took a baked apple from the recess in the tile stove, and with this wrinkled fruit meant for old women and little children vanished into the dark bedroom. He would raise the blackout paper and open the window just a crack, letting in a little of the frosty night. Then he would take aim and dispatch his long-distance song. He did not sing at the stars, the Milky Way was not on his route. His song was directed at Winterfeld-Platz, not at the Radio Building but at the boxlike structure across the way, which housed the district headquarters of the Hitler Youth.

In clear weather my work took hardly a minute. Meanwhile my baked apple had cooled a little by the open window. Munching, I returned to Mother Truczinski and my drum, and soon went to bed with every assurance that while Oskar slept the Dusters, in Jesus' name, were looting Party treasuries, stealing food cards, rubber stamps, printed forms, or a membership list of the Hitler Youth Patrol.

Indulgently I allowed Störtebeker and Moorkähne to engage in all sorts of monkey business with forged documents. The gang's main enemy was the Patrol Service. It was all right with me if they chose to kidnap their adversaries, dust them, and—as Firestealer, who had charge of this activity, called it—polish their balls.

Since I remained aloof from these expeditions, which were a mere prologue that can give you no idea of my real plans, I cannot say for sure whether it was the Dusters who in September, 1944, tied up two high officers of the Patrol Service, including the dreaded Helmut Neitberg, and drowned them in the Mottlau, above the Cows' Bridge.

However, I, Oskar-Jesus, who gave the Dusters their orders, feel the need to deny certain stories that gained currency later on: that the Dusters had connections with the Edelweiss Pirates of Cologne or that Polish partisans from Tuchlerheide had exerted an influence on us or even directed our movement. All this is pure legend.

At our trial we were also accused of having ties with the July 20th conspirators, because Putty's father, August von Puttkamer, had been close to Field Marshal Rommel and had committed suicide. Since the beginning of the war, Putty had seen his father no more than five or six times, and then scarcely long enough to get used to his changing insignia of rank. It was not until our trial that he first heard about this officer's foolishness, which, to tell the truth, was a matter of utter indifference to us. When he did hear about it, he cried so shamefully, so shamelessly that Firestealer, who was sitting beside him, had to dust him right in front of the judges.

Only once in the course of our activity did any grownups approach us. Some shipyard workers—with Communist affiliations, as I could tell at a glance—tried to gain influence over us through our apprentices at the Schichau dockyards and turn us into a Red underground movement. The apprentices were not unwilling. But the schoolboys among us rejected all political trends. Mister, an Air Force Auxiliary who was the cynic and theoretician of the gang, stated his views at one of our meetings: "We have nothing to do with parties," he declared. "Our fight is against our parents and all other grownups, regardless of what they may be for or against."

He put it rather too strongly, no doubt, but all the schoolboys agreed; the outcome was a factional split. The shipyard apprentices started a club of their own—I was sorry to lose them, they were good workers. Despite the objections of Störtebeker and Moorkähne, they continued to call themselves Dusters. At the trial—their outfit was caught at the same time as ours—the burning of the training sub in the shipyard basin was pinned on them. Over a hundred U-boat captains and ensigns had met a terrible death in the fire which broke out below decks; the U-boat crews were blocked in their quarters, and when the ensigns, lads of eighteen, tried to escape through portholes, their hips wouldn't pass and the fire caught them from behind. They had hung there screaming and the only way of putting them out of their misery had been to bring a cutter alongside and shoot them.

We had nothing to do with that fire. It may have been the Schichau apprentices and it may have been the Westerland Society. The Dusters were not firebugs though I, their spiritual guide, may have inherited an incendiary gene or two from my grandfather Koljaiczek.

I remember well the mechanic, recently transferred to Schichau from the Deutsche Werke at Kiel, who came to see us in our cellar shortly before the split. Erich and Horst Pietzger, the sons of a longshoreman in Fuchswall, had brought him. He inspected our storehouse with a professional air, deplored the absence of any weapons in working order, but uttered a few grudging words of approval. When he asked to speak to the chief, Störtebeker promptly, and Moorkähne with some hesitation, referred him to me. Thereupon he flew into a gale of laughter so long and so insolent that Oskar came very close to handing him over to the dusters for a dusting.

"What kind of a sawed-off runt do you call that?" he said to Moorkähne, pointing his thumb at me over his shoulder.

Moorkähne smiled in visible embarrassment. Before he could think of anything to say, Störtebeker replied with ominous calm: "He is our Jesus."

That was too much for the mechanic, whose name was Walter; he took it on himself to insult us right there in our own headquarters. "Say, are you revolutionaries or a bunch of choirboys getting ready for a Christmas play?"

The blade of a paratrooper's knife popped out of Störtebeker's sleeve;

he opened the cellar door, gave Firestealer a sign, and said, more to the gang than to the mechanic: "We're choirboys and we're getting ready for a Christmas play."

But nothing drastic happened to the mechanic. He was blindfolded and led away. A few days later this same Walter organized the dockyard apprentices into a club of their own, and I am quite sure it was they who set the training sub on fire.

From my point of view Störtebeker had given the right answer. We were not interested in politics. Once we had so intimidated the Hitler Youth Patrols that they scarcely left their quarters except occasionally to check the papers of flighty young ladies at the railroad stations, we shifted our field of operations to the churches and began, as the Communist mechanic had put it, to occupy ourselves with Christmas plays.

Our first concern was to find replacements for the invaluable Schichau apprentices. At the end of October, Störtebeker swore in the brothers Felix and Paul Rennwand, both choirboys at Sacred Heart. Störtebeker had approached them through their sister Lucy, a girl of sixteen who, over my protest, was allowed to attend the swearing-in ceremony. Setting their left hands on my drum, which the boys, incurable Romantics that they were, liked to think of as some sort of symbol, the Rennwand brothers repeated the oath of allegiance, a text so absurd and full of hocus-pocus that I can no longer remember it.

Oskar watched Lucy during the ceremony. In one hand she held a sandwich that seemed to quiver slightly, she shrugged her shoulders and gnawed at her lower lip. Her triangular fox face was expressionless, and she kept her eyes riveted on Störtebeker's back. Suddenly I had misgivings about the Dusters' future.

We began to redecorate our basement. In close collaboration with the choirboys, I oversaw the acquisition of the required furnishings. From St. Catherine's we took a sixteen-century half-length Joseph who turned out to be authentic, a few candelabra, some chalices, patens, and cruets, and a Corpus Christi banner. A night visit to the Church of the Trinity brought us a wooden, trumpet-blowing angel of no artistic interest, and a colored tapestry, copied from an older original, showing a lady who seemed ever so prim, prissy, and deceitful, and a mythical animal known as a unicorn, who was obviously very much under her influence. The lady's smile, as Störtebeker observed, had the same playful cruelty as that which predominated in Lucy's fox face, and I hoped my lieutenant would not prove as submissive as the unicorn. We hung the tapestry on the rear wall of our cellar, formerly decorated with death's heads, black hands, and other such absurdities, and soon the unicorn motif seemed to dominate all our deliberations. Meanwhile Lucy had made herself at home in our midst, coming and going as she pleased and sniggering behind my back.

Why then, I asked myself, did we have to bring in this second, woven Lucy, who is turning your lieutenants into unicorns, who alive or woven is really out to get you, Oskar, for you alone of the Dusters are truly fabulous and unique, you are the human unicorn.

But then Advent was upon us, and I was mighty glad of it. We began to collect Nativity figures from all the churches in the neighborhood, and soon the tapestry was so well hidden behind them that the fable—or so I thought—was bound to lose its influence. In mid-December Rundstedt opened his offensive in the Ardennes and we completed preparations for our major coup.

Several Sundays running I attended ten o'clock Mass with Maria, who, to Matzerath's chagrin, had become thoroughly immersed in Catholicism. The Dusters, too, at my behest, had become regular churchgoers. This was our way of casing the joint. Finally, on the night of September 18, we broke into the Church of the Sacred Heart. "Broke" is a manner of speaking. Thanks to our choirboys, there was no need to break anything, not even for Oskar to sing at any glass.

It was snowing, but the snow melted as it fell. We stowed the three handcarts behind the sacristy. The younger Rennwand had the key to the main door. Oskar went in first, led the boys one by one to the holy-water font, where at his bidding they genuflected toward the high altar. Then I had them throw a Labor Service blanket over the statue of Jesus bearing his Sacred Heart, lest his blue gaze interfere with our work. Bouncer and Mister carried the tools to the scene of action, the left side-altar. The manger with its Nativity figures and evergreen boughs had to be cleared out of the way. We already had all the shepherds and angels, all the sheep, asses, and cows we needed. Our cellar was full of extras; all that was lacking were the central figures. Belisarius removed the flowers from the altar. Totila and Teja rolled up the carpet. Firestealer unpacked the tools. Oskar, on his knees behind a pew, supervised the operations.

The first to be sawed off was little John the Baptist in his chocolate-colored pelt. Luckily, we had a metal saw, for inside the plaster there were metal rods as thick as your finger connecting the boy Baptist with the cloud. Firestealer did the sawing. He went about it like an intellectual, that is to say, clumsily. Once again the Schichau apprentices were sorely missed. Störtebeker relieved Firestealer. He was somewhat handier and after half an hour's rasping and squeaking we were able to topple the boy Baptist over and wrap him in a woolen blanket. Then for a moment we breathed in the midnight ecclesiastical silence.

It took a little longer to saw off the child Jesus, whose whole rear end rested on the Virgin's thigh. Bouncer, the elder Rennwand, and Lionheart were at work for fully forty minutes. But where, I wondered, was Moorkähne? His idea had been that our movements would attract less attention if he and his men came directly from Neufahrwasser and met us in the church. Störtebeker seemed nervous and irritable. Several times he asked the Rennwand brothers about Moorkähne. When at length, as we all expected, Lucy's name came up, Störtebeker stopped asking questions, wrenched the metal saw out of Lionheart's unpracticed hands, and working feverishly gave the boy Jesus the *coup de grâce*.

As they laid Jesus down, his halo broke off. Störtebeker apologized to me. Controlling myself with some difficulty—for I too was succumbing to the general irritability—I told them to pick up the pieces, which were gathered into two caps. Firestealer thought the halo could be glued together again. Jesus was bedded in cushions and wrapped in blankets.

Our plan was to saw off the Virgin at the waist, making a second cut between the cloud and the soles of her feet. We would leave the cloud where it was and take only the figures, Jesus, the two halves of the Virgin, and the boy Baptist if there was still room in one of the carts. The figures, as we were glad to discover, weighed less than we had expected. The whole group was hollow cast. The walls were no more than an inch thick, and the only heavy part was the iron skeleton.

The boys were exhausted, especially Firestealer and Lionheart. Operations had to be suspended while they rested, for the others, including the Rennwand brothers, could not saw. The gang sat shivering in the pews. Störtebeker stood crumpling his velour hat, which he had removed on entering the church. The atmosphere was not to my liking. Something had to be done. The boys were suffering the effects of the religious architecture, full of night and emptiness. Some were worried about Moorkähne's absence. The Rennwand brothers seemed to be afraid of Störtebeker; they stood to one side, whispering until Störtebeker ordered them to be still.

Slowly, I seem to remember, slowly and with a sigh, I rose from my prayer cushion and went straight up to the Virgin, who was still in her place. Her eyes, which had been turned toward John, were now resting on the altar steps, white with plaster dust. Her right forefinger, hitherto aimed at Jesus, pointed into the void, or rather, the dark left aisle of the nave. I took one step after another, then looked behind me, trying to catch Störtebeker's attention. His deep-set eyes were far away until Firestealer gave him a poke. Then he looked at me, but with a lack of assurance such as I had never seen in him. At first he failed to understand, then he understood, or partly so, and stepped slowly, much too slowly forward. However, he took the altar steps at one bound and then lifted me up on the white, jagged, incompetent saw cut on the Virgin's thigh, which roughly reproduced the imprint of the boy Jesus' behind.

Störtebeker turned back at once and with one step he was back on the flags. He almost fell back into his reverie, but then he gave himself a jolt, and his eyes narrowed. No more than our henchmen in the pews could he conceal his emotion at the sight of me sitting so naturally in Jesus' place, all ready to be worshipped.

He soon saw what I was after and even gave me more than I had bargained for. He ordered Narses and Bluebeard to shine their Army flashlights upon me and the Virgin. When the glare blinded me, he told them to use the red beam. Then he summoned the Rennwand brothers and held a whispered conference with them. They were reluctant to do his bidding; Firestealer stepped over to the group and exhibited his knuckles, all ready for dusting; the brothers gave in and vanished into the sacristy with Firestealer and Mister. Oskar waited calmly, moved his drum into position, and was not even surprised when Mister, who was a tall, gangling fellow, came back attired as a priest, accompanied by the two Rennwand brothers in the red and white raiment of choirboys. Firestealer, wearing some of the vicar's clothing, brought in everything needed for Mass, stowed his equipment on the cloud, and withdrew. The elder Rennwand bore the vestments, Mister gave a fair imitation of Father Wiehnke. At first he performed with a schoolboy's cynicism, but then, letting himself be carried away by the words and gestures, offered us all, and myself in particular, not a silly parody, but a Mass which even at our trial was consistently referred to as a Mass, though a black one to be sure.

The three of them began with the gradual prayers; the boys in the pews and on the flags genuflected, crossed themselves, and Mister, who knew the words up to a point, embarked on the Mass with the expert support of the two choir boys. I began to drum, cautiously in the Introit, but more forcefully in the Kyrie. *Gloria in excelsis Deo*—I praised the Lord on my drum, summoned the congregation to prayer, substituted a drum solo of some length for the Epistle. My Halleluia was particularly successful. In the Credo, I saw that the boys believed in me; for the Offertory, I drummed rather more softly as Mister presented the bread and mixed wine with water. Sharing a whiff of incense with the chalice, I looked on to see how Mister would handle the Lavabo. *Orate, fratres*, I drummed in the red glow of the flashlights, and led up to the Transubstantiation: This is My body. *Oremus*, sang Mister, in response to orders from above —the boys in the pews offered me two different versions of the Lord's Prayer, but Mister managed to reconcile Protestants and Catholics in one Communion. Even before the meal was over, my drum introduced the Confiteor. The Virgin pointed her finger at Oskar, the drummer. I had indeed taken the place of Christ. The Mass was going like clockwork. Mister's voice rose and fell. How splendidly he pronounced the benediction: pardon, absolution, and remission. *"Ite, missa est*—Go, you are dismissed." By the time these words were spoken, every one of us, I

297

believe, had experienced a spiritual liberation. When the secular arm fell, it was upon a band of Dusters confirmed in the faith in Oskar's and Jesus' name.

I had heard the motors during the Mass and Störtebeker too had turned his head. We alone showed no surprise when voices were heard and heavy heels converged on us from the front and side doors and from the sacristy.

Störtebeker wanted to lift me down from the Virgin's thigh. I motioned him away. He understood, nodded, and made the boys keep kneeling. There they remained, waiting for the police. They trembled, a few lost their balance, some dropped on two knees, but they waited in silence until the law, converging in three groups, had surrounded the left side-altar.

The police had flashlights too, but favored a white beam. Störtebeker arose, crossed himself, stepped forward into the light, and handed his velour hat to Firestealer, who was still kneeling. Moving quickly around a bloated shadow without a flashlight—Father Wiehnke—Störtebeker seized a thin figure that thrashed about and tried to defend itself—Lucy Rennwand. He slapped and punched the pinched triangular face under the beret until a blow from one of the policemen sent him rolling among the pews.

Still perched on my Virgin, I heard one of the cops exclaiming: "Good God, Jeschke, that's the boss's kid."

To Oskar it was a source of modest satisfaction to learn that my excellent lieutenant had been the son of the chief of police. I offered no resistance, but stepped automatically into the role of a sniveling three-year-old who had been led astray by gangsters. All I wanted was to be comforted and protected. Father Wiehnke picked me up in his arms.

Everyone was quiet except for the policemen. The boys were led away. Father Wiehnke felt faint and had to sit down, but first he deposited me on the floor not far from our equipment. Behind hammers and crowbars, I found the basket full of sandwiches that Bouncer had made before we started on our expedition.

I took the basket, went over to Lucy, who was shivering in her light coat, and offered her the sandwiches. She picked us both up, Oskar and basket. A moment later she had a sandwich between her teeth. I studied her flaming, battered, swollen face: restless eyes in black slits, a chewing triangle, a doll, a wicked witch devouring sausage and, even as she ate, growing skinnier, hungrier, more triangular, more doll-like. The sight set its stamp on me. Who will efface that triangle from my mind? How long will it live within me, chewing sausage, chewing men, and smiling as only triangles, or lady unicorn-tamers on tapestries, can smile.

As he was led away between two inspectors, Störtebeker turned his blood-smeared face toward Lucy and Oskar. I looked past him. I recognized him no longer. When all my erstwhile followers had left, I too was led away, still in the arms of the sandwich-eating Lucy.

Who stayed behind? Father Wiehnke with our flashlights, still shining red, and the vestments hurriedly shed by Father Mister and his assistants. Chalice and ciborium lay on the steps to the altar. The sawed-off John and the sawed-off Jesus were still there with the Virgin, who was to have formed a counterweight to the lady with the unicorn in our cellar headquarters.

Oskar, however, was carried away to a trial that I still call the second trial of Jesus, a trial that ended with the acquittal of Oskar, hence also of Jesus.

The Ant Trail

Imagine, if you please, a swimming pool lined with azure-blue tiles. Quite a few sunburned, athletic young people in the water, and more sunburned young men and women sitting or reclining on the tiles round the edges. Perhaps a bit of soft music from the loudspeaker. Healthy boredom and a mild, noncommittal sexuality. The tiles are smooth, but no one slips. Only a few signs prohibiting anything; no need of them, the bathers come only for an hour or two and have other places to do what is forbidden. Now and then someone dives from the ten-foot springboard but fails to attract the attention of those in the water, or to lure the eyes of those reclining on the tiles away from their illustrated weeklies. Suddenly a breeze! No, not a breeze, but a young man who slowly, resolutely, reaching from rung to rung, climbs the ladder to the thirty-foot diving tower. Magazines droop, eyes rise, recumbent bodies grow longer, a young woman shades her forehead, someone forgets what he was thinking about, a word remains unspoken, a flirtation, just begun, comes to a sudden end in the middle of the sentence—for there he stands virile and well built, jumps up and down on the platform, leans on the gently curved tubular railing, casts a bored look downward, moves away from the railing with a graceful swing of the haunches, ventures out on the springboard that sways at every step, focuses his eyes on an azure-blue, alarmingly small swimming pool, full of intermingling bathing caps: yellow, green, white, red, yellow, green, white, red, yellow, green. . . . That's where his friends must be sitting, Doris and Erika Schüler, and Jutta Daniels with her boy friend, who isn't right for her. They wave, Jutta waves too. Rather worried about his balance, he waves back. They shout. What can they want? He should go ahead, they shout, dive, cries Jutta. But he had climbed up with no such intention, he had just wanted to see how things looked from up here, and then climb down,

299

slowly, rung by rung. And now they are shouting so everybody can hear: Dive! Go ahead and dive! Go ahead.

This, you will admit, though a diving tower may be a step nearer heaven, is a desperate plight to be in. In January, 1945, the Dusters and I, though it was not the bathing season, found ourselves in a similar situation. We had ventured high up, we were all crowded together on the diving tower, and below, forming a solemn horseshoe round a waterless pool, sat the judges, witnesses, and court clerks.

Störtebeker stepped out on the supple, railingless springboard. "Dive!" cried the judges.

But Störtebeker didn't feel like it.

Then from the witnesses' bench there arose a slender figure with a gray pleated skirt and a little Bavarian-style jacket. A pale but not indistinct face which, I still maintain, formed a triangle, rose up like a target indicator: Lucy Rennwand did not shout. She only whispered: "Jump, Störtebeker, jump!"

Then Störtebeker jumped. Lucy sat down again on the witnesses' bench and pulled down the sleeves of her Bavarian jacket over her fists.

Moorkähne limped onto the springboard. The judges ordered him to dive. But Moorkähne didn't feel like it; smiling in embarrassment at his fingernails, he waited for Lucy to pull up her sleeves, let her fists fall out of the wool, and display the black-framed triangle with the slits for eyes. Then he plunged furiously at the triangle, but missed it.

Even on the way up, Firestealer and Putty hadn't been exactly lovey-dovey; on the springboard they came to blows. Putty was dusted, and even when he plunged, Firestealer wouldn't let him go.

Bouncer, who had long silky eyelashes, closed his deep, sad doe's eyes before taking the leap.

The Air Force Auxiliaries had to take off their uniforms before plunging.

Nor were the Rennwand brothers permitted to take their heavenward plunge attired as choirboys; that would have been quite unacceptable to their sister Lucy, sitting on the witnesses' bench in her jacket of threadbare wartime wool and encouraging young men to dive.

In defiance of history, Belisarius and Narses dove first, then Totila and Teja. Bluebeard plunged, Lionheart plunged, then the rank and file: The Nose, Bushman, Tanker, Piper, Mustard Pot, Yatagan, and Cooper.

The last to jump was Stuchel, a high school student so cross-eyed it made you dizzy to look at him; he had only half belonged to the gang and that by accident. Only Jesus was left on the platform. Addressing him as Oskar Matzerath, the judges asked him to dive, but Jesus did not comply. Lucy, the stern and unbending, Lucy with the scrawny Mozart pigtail hanging between her shoulders, rose from the witnesses' bench, spread her sweater arms, and whispered without visibly moving her compressed lips: "Jump, sweet Jesus, jump." At this moment I understood the fatal lure of a thirty-foot springboard; little gray kittens began to wriggle in my knee joints, hedgehogs mated under the soles of my feet, swallows took wing in my armpits, and at my feet I saw not only Europe but the whole world. Americans and Japanese were doing a torch dance on the island of Luzon, dancing so hard that slant-eyes and round-eyes alike lost the buttons off their uniforms. But at the very same moment a tailor in Stockholm was sewing buttons on a handsome suit of evening clothes. Mountbatten was feeding Burmese elephants shells of every caliber. A widow in Lima was teaching her parrot to say "Caramba." In the middle of the Pacific two enormous aircraft carriers, done up to look like Gothic cathedrals, stood face to face, sent up their planes, and simultaneously sank one another. The planes had no place to land, they hovered helplessly and quite allegorically like angels in mid-air, using up their fuel with a terrible din. This was all one to the streetcar conductor in Haparanda, who had just gone off duty. He was breaking eggs into a frying pan, two for himself and two for his fiancé, whom he was expecting any minute, having planned the whole evening in advance. Obviously the armies of Koniev and Zhukov could be expected to resume their forward drive; while rain fell in Ireland, they broke through on the Vistula, took Warsaw too late and Königsberg too soon, and even so were powerless to prevent a woman in Panama, who had five children and only one husband, from burning the milk she was warming up on her gas range. Inevitably the thread of events wound itself into loops and knots which became known as the fabric of History. I also saw that activities such as thumb-twiddling, frowning, looking up and down, handshaking, making babies, counterfeiting, turning out the light, brushing teeth, shooting people, and changing diapers were being practiced all over the world, though not always with the same skill. My head swimming at the thought of so much purposive movement, I turned back to the trial which was continuing in my honor at the foot of the diving tower. "Jump, sweet Jesus, jump," whispered Lucy Rennwand, the witness and virgin temptress. She was sitting on Satan's lap, and that brought out her virginity. He handed her a sandwich. She bit into it with pleasure, but lost none of her chastity. "Jump, sweet Jesus," she chewed, offering me her triangle, still intact.

I did not jump, and you will never catch me jumping or diving from a diving tower. This was not to be Oskar's last trial. Many attempts have been made, one very recently, to persuade me to jump. At the ring-finger trial—which I prefer to call the third trial of Jesus—there were again plenty of spectators at the edge of the waterless swimming pool. They sat on witnesses' benches, determined to enjoy and survive my trial.

301

But I made an about-face, stifled the fledgling swallows in my armpits, squashed the hedgehogs mating under the soles of my feet, starved the gray kittens out from under my kneecaps. Scorning the exaltation of plunging, I went stiffly to the railing, swung myself onto the ladder, descended, let every rung in the ladder reinforce my conviction that diving towers can not only be climbed but also relinquished without diving.

Down below, Maria and Matzerath were waiting for me. Father Wiehnke gave me his blessing though I hadn't asked for it. Gretchen Scheffler had brought me a little winter coat and some cake. Kurt had grown and refused to recognize me either as a father or as a half brother. My grandmother Koljaiczek held her brother Vincent by the arm. He knew the world and talked incoherent nonsense.

As we were leaving the courthouse, an official in civilian clothes approached Matzerath, handed him a paper, and said: "You really ought to think it over, Mr. Matzerath. You've got to get the child off the streets. You see how helpless and gullible he is, always ready to be taken in by disreputable elements."

Maria wept and gave me my drum, which Father Wiehnke had taken care of during the trial. We went to the streetcar stop by the Central Station. Matzerath carried me the last bit of the way. I looked back over his shoulder, searching the crowd for a triangular face, wondering whether she too had had to climb the tower, whether she had jumped after Störtebeker and Moorkähne, or whether like me she had availed herself of the alternative possibility, of climbing down the ladder.

To this day I have not been able to dispel the habit of looking about in streets and public places for a skinny teen-age girl, neither pretty nor ugly, but always biting men. Even in my bed in the mental hospital I am frightened when Bruno announces an unexpected visitor. My nightmare is that Lucy Rennwand will turn up in the shape of a wicked witch and for the last time bid me to plunge.

For ten days Matzerath pondered whether to sign the letter and send it to the Ministry of Public Health. When on the eleventh day he signed and mailed it, the city was already under artillery fire, and it was doubtful that his letter would cover much ground. Armored spearheads of Marshal Rokossovski's army reached Elbing. The German Second Army, commanded by Weiss, took up positions on the heights surrounding Danzig. Like everyone else, we began to live in the cellar.

As we all know, our cellar was under the shop. You could reach it by way of the cellar door in the hallway across from the toilet; you went down eighteen steps, past Heilandt's cellar and Kater's cellar, but before Schlager's. Old man Heilandt was still in the house. But Mrs. Kater, Laubschad the watchmaker, the Eykes, and the Schlagers had slipped away with a few bundles. Later the story went round that they, and with them Alexander and Gretchen Scheffler, had managed at the last minute to board a Strength through Joy ship which had either reached Stettin or Lübeck or struck a mine; in any case over half of the flats and cellars were empty.

Our cellar had the advantage of a second entrance which, as we also all of us know, consisted of a trap door behind the counter of our shop. Consequently, no one could see what Matzerath put into the cellar or removed from it. Otherwise Matzerath's accumulation of provisions during the war years would never have been tolerated. The warm, dry room was full of dried peas and beans, noodles, sugar, artificial honey, wheat flour, and margarine. Boxes of Swedish bread rested on cases of Crisco. Matzerath was clever with his hands. He himself had put up shelves, which were well stocked with canned fruit and vegetables. Thanks to a few uprights which Matzerath, at Greff's instigation, had wedged between floor and ceiling toward the middle of the war, the storeroom was as safe as a regulation air-raid shelter. On several occasions Matzerath had thought of removing the uprights, for there had been no heavy air raids. But when Greff the air-raid warden was no longer there to remonstrate with him, Maria insisted that he leave the props in place. She demanded safety for little Kurt, and occasionally even for me.

During the first air raids at the end of January, old man Heilandt and Matzerath joined forces to remove Mother Truczinski and her chair to our cellar. Then, perhaps at her request, possibly to avoid the effort of carrying her, they left her in her flat, sitting beside the window. After the big raid on the inner city, Maria and Matzerath found the old woman with her jaw hanging down, squinting as though a sticky little gnat had got caught in her eye.

The door to the bedroom was lifted off its hinges. Old man Heilandt brought his tools and a few boards, mostly disassembled crates. Smoking Derby cigarettes that Matzerath had given him, he took measurements. Oskar helped him with his work. The others vanished into the cellar, for the artillery shelling had started in again.

Old man Heilandt was in a hurry, he had in mind a simple rectangular box. But Oskar insisted on the traditional coffin shape. I held the boards in place, making him saw to my specifications, and the outcome was a coffin tapered at the foot end, such as every human corpse has a right to demand.

It was a fine-looking coffin in the end. Lina Greff washed Mother Truczinski, took a fresh nightgown from the cupboard, cut her fingernails, arranged her bun and propped it up on three knitting needles. In short, she managed to make Mother Truczinski look, even in death, like a gray mouse who had been given to potato pancakes and Postum in her lifetime.

The mouse had stiffened in her chair during the bombing and her knees refused to unbend. Before he could put on the coffin lid, old man Heilandt was obliged, when Mama left the room for a few moments, to break her legs.

Unfortunately there was no black paint, only yellow. Mother Truczinski was carried out of the flat and down the stairs in boards unpainted, but properly tapered at the foot end. Oskar followed with his drum, reading the inscription on the coffin lid: Vitello Margarine—Vitello Margarine—Vitello Margarine: evenly spaced and thrice repeated, these words bore witness to Mother Truczinski's taste in household fat. For indeed she had preferred that good Vitello Margarine, made exclusively from vegetable oils, to the best butter, because margarine stays fresh, is wholesome and nutritious, and makes for good humor.

Old man Heilandt loaded the coffin on the handcart belonging to Greff's vegetable shop, and pulled it through Luisenstrasse, Marienstrasse, down Anton-Möller-Weg, where two houses were burning, toward the Women's Clinic. Little Kurt had remained with the widow Greff in our cellar. Maria and Matzerath pushed, Oskar sat in the cart beside the coffin, he would have liked to climb on top, but was not allowed to. The streets were clogged with refugees from East Prussia and the Delta. It was just about impossible to get through the underpass by the Sports Palace. Matzerath suggested digging a hole in the park of the Conradinum. The idea did not appeal to Maria or to old man Heilandt, who was the same age as Mother Truczinski. I too was opposed to the school park. Still, there was no hope of reaching the city cemetery, for from the Sports Palace on, Hindenburg-Allee was closed to all but military vehicles. And so, unable to bury the mouse beside her son Herbert, we chose a place for her in Steffens-Park, not far from the Maiwiese.

The ground was frozen. While Matzerath and old man Heilandt took turns with the pickax and Maria tried to dig up some ivy beside the stone benches, Oskar slipped away to Hindenburg-Allee. What traffic! Tanks retreating from the heights and the Delta, some being towed. From the trees—lindens if I remember rightly—dangled soldiers and Volkssturm men. To their jackets were affixed cardboard signs identifying them quite legibly as traitors. I looked into the convulsed faces of several of these hanging men and drew comparisons—with other hanged men as such and in general and with Greff the greengrocer in particular. There were also whole clusters of youngsters strung up in uniforms that were too big for them, and several times I thought I recognized Störtebeker —but youngsters at the end of a rope all look alike. Nevertheless, I said to myself: so now they've hanged Störtebeker, I wonder if they've strung up Lucy Rennwand.

That thought gave Oskar wings. He searched the trees to left and right for a skinny, dangling girl, and even crossed the street in between the tanks, but there too he found only soldiers, old men in Volkssturm uniforms, and youngsters who looked like Störtebeker. Disappointed, I trotted along as far as the half-demolished Four Seasons Café, and turned back only reluctantly. As I stood by Mother Truczinski's grave, helping Maria to strew ivy and leaves over the fresh earth, the vision, clear in every detail, of a dangling Lucy was still with me.

We didn't return the cart to the vegetable shop. Matzerath and old man Heilandt took it apart and piled up the pieces by the counter. "Maybe we'll be needing the cart again," said Matzerath. "Here it's fairly safe." Then he gave the old man three packs of Derby cigarettes.

Old man Heilandt said nothing but helped himself to several packages of noodles and two bags of sugar from the near-empty shelves. Then he shuffled off in his felt slippers, which he had worn for the funeral, leaving Matzerath to remove what little remained of his stock from the shelves and carry it down to the cellar.

After that we seldom emerged from our hole. The Russians were said to be in Zigankenberg, Pietzgendorf, and on the outskirts of Schidlitz. There was no doubt that they occupied the heights, for they were firing straight down into the city. Inner City and Outer City, Old City, New City and Old New City, Lower City and Spice City—what had taken seven hundred years to build burned down in three days. Yet this was not the first fire to descend on the city of Danzig. For centuries Pomerellians, Brandenburgers, Teutonic Knights, Poles, Swedes, and a second time Swedes, Frenchmen, Prussians, and Russians, even Saxons, had made history by deciding every few years that the city of Danzig was worth burning. And now it was Russians, Poles, Germans, and Englishmen all at once who were burning the city's Gothic bricks for the hundredth time. Hook Street, Long Street, and Broad Street, Big Weaver Street and Little Weaver Street were in flames; Tobias Street, Hound Street, Old City Ditch, Outer City Ditch, the ramparts and Long Bridge, all were in flames. Built of wood, Crane Gate made a particularly fine blaze. In Breeches-maker Street, the fire had itself measured for several pairs of extra-loud breeches. The Church of St. Mary was burning inside and outside, festive light effects could be seen through its ogival windows. What bells had not been evacuated from St. Catherine, St. John, St. Brigit, Saints Barbara, Elisabeth, Peter, and Paul, from Trinity and Corpus Christi, melted in their belfries and dripped away without pomp or ceremony. In the Big Mill red wheat was milled. Butcher Street smelled of burnt Sunday roast. The Municipal Theater was giving a première, a one-act play entitled The Firebug's Dream. The town fathers decided to raise the firemen's wages retroactively after the fire. Holy Ghost Street was burning in the name of the Holy Ghost. Joyously, the Franciscan

Monastery blazed in the name of St. Francis, who had loved fire and sung hymns to it. Our Lady Street burned for Father and Son at once. Needless to say the Lumber Market, Coal Market, and Haymarket burned to the ground. In Baker Street the ovens burned and the bread and rolls with them. In Milk Pitcher Street the milk boiled over. Only the West Prussian Fire Insurance Building, for purely symbolic reasons, refused to burn down.

Oskar has never been very much interested in fires. I would have stayed in the cellar when Matzerath ran up the stairs for a view of Danzig in flames, if I had not improvidently stored my few, highly inflammable belongings in the attic. I was determined to save the last of the drums Bebra had given me and my volume of Goethe-Rasputin. Between the pages of the book, I had been saving a fan, light as gossamer and delicately painted, that my Roswitha had wielded, so gracefully, so graciously, in her lifetime. Maria remained in the cellar. But little Kurt wanted to go up on the roof with me and Matzerath, to see the fire. Though irritated by my son's uncontrollable enthusiasm, Oskar told himself that Kurt must have inherited his interest in fire from his great-grandfather, my grandfather, Koljaiczek the firebug. Maria kept Kurt downstairs, I was allowed to go up with Matzerath. I took my belongings, cast a glance through the window of the loft, and was amazed to see what a burst of vitality our venerable old city had been able to summon up.

When shells began to land nearby, we went downstairs. Later on, Matzerath wanted to go up again, but Maria wouldn't let him. He gave in and burst into tears while giving a detailed description of the fire to the widow Greff, who had remained below. Once more he returned to the flat and turned on the radio, but nothing came out. You couldn't even hear the crackling flames of the burning radio station, let alone a special newscast.

Matzerath stood there in the middle of the cellar, tugging at his suspenders, as bewildered as a child who can't make up his mind whether to go on believing in Santa Claus, and for the first time expressed doubts about the final victory. On the widow Greff's advice, he removed his Party pin from his lapel, but couldn't figure out what to do with it; for the cellar had a concrete floor, Lina Greff was unwilling to take it, Maria said he should bury it in the winter potatoes, but the potatoes didn't seem safe, and he was afraid to go upstairs, because they were bound to come soon, they were on their way, they had already reached Brenntau and Oliva when he had looked from the attic, and he was sorry now that he hadn't left it up there in the air-defense sand, for it would be a fine kettle of fish if they found him with the thing in his hand. He dropped it on the concrete, meaning to stamp on it, to grind it to powder, but Kurt and I leapt at it both together. I had it first and I kept my hold on it when Kurt began to punch as he always did when he wanted something, but I wouldn't give my son the Party badge for fear of endangering him, because you didn't joke with the Russians. Oskar remembered that from his readings in Rasputin, and I wondered, while Kurt pummeled me and Maria tried to separate us, whether it would be White Russians or Great Russians, Cossacks or Georgians, Kalmucks or Crimean Tartars, Ruthenians or Ukrainians, or maybe even Kirghizes who would find the Party badge on Kurt if Oskar were to give way under his son's blows.

When Maria with the widow Greff's help parted us, I was clutching the pin victoriously in my fist. Matzerath was glad to be rid of it. Maria was busy with Kurt, who was bawling. The open pin pricked my hand. I had never liked the thing much and I still didn't. But just as I was trying to pin it to the back of Matzerath's jacket—what business of mine, after all, was that Party of his?—they were in the shop over our heads and, to judge by the screaming women, in the neighboring cellars as well.

When they lifted the trap door, the pin was still sticking into me. There was nothing to do but sit down by Maria's trembling knees and watch the ants which had laid out a military highway running from the winter potatoes, across the concrete floor, to a sack of sugar. Perfectly normal Russians, slight racial mixture, I said to myself, as six or seven of them appeared on the stairs with big eyes and tommy guns. Amid all the screaming it was reassuring to note that the ants were in no way affected by the arrival of the Russian Army. They still had the same interests—potatoes and sugar—despite the men with the tommy guns who put other conquests first. It struck me as perfectly normal that the grownups should put up their hands. I knew about that from the newsreels, and I had witnessed the same gesture of submission after the fall of the Polish Post Office. But why Kurt should ape the grownups was more than I could see. He should have taken an example from me, his father—or if not from his father, then from the ants. Instantly three of the rectangular uniforms turned their attentions to Lina Greff, and that put some life into the hitherto static ensemble. La Greff, who after her long widowhood and the lean years preceding it, had scarcely expected such sudden popularity, let out a few screams of surprise but soon reaccustomed herself to an occupation she had almost forgotten.

I had read in Rasputin that the Russians are great lovers of children. This, as I was soon to learn, is perfectly true. Maria trembled needlessly. She failed to understand why the four Ivans who were not busy with la Greff left Kurt sitting on her lap instead of taking turns at it themselves; she was amazed to see them fondle him and say dadada, and pat him on the cheeks with an occasional pat for herself.

307

Someone picked up me and my drum from the floor; I could no longer observe the ants and judge the life of my times by their purposeful industry. My drum hung on my belly, and with his thick fingers the big Russian with the dilated pores tapped out a few measures one might have danced to; not bad for a grownup, I thought. Oskar would have liked to show off his own talents, but that was impossible because Matzerath's party pin was still sticking into his hand.

A peaceful atmosphere, one would almost have called it cozy, settled on our cellar. More and more calmly la Greff lay spread out beneath one after another of the three Ivans. When one of them decided to call it a day, my gifted drummer handed Oskar on to a sweating young fellow with slanting eyes, a Kalmuck no doubt. Holding me with his left hand, he buttoned his fly with his right, while his predecessor, the drummer, did the exact opposite. For Matzerath, however, nothing had changed. He was still standing by the shelf full of Leipzig stew with his hands up, clearly displaying their lines; but nobody wanted to read his palms. The women meanwhile showed a remarkable aptitude for adjustment: Maria learned her first words of Russian, her knees stopped shaking, she even laughed, and would have played her harmonica had it been within reach.

Oskar, who was less adaptable, looked about for something to take the place of his ants and discovered a colony of flat grayish-brown insects that were strolling about on the edge of my Kalmuck's collar. I wanted to catch one of them and examine it, for I had read a good deal about lice, not so much in Goethe but all the more in Rasputin. However, it is difficult to chase lice with one hand, so I decided to get rid of the Party pin. Oskar feels that he ought to explain his behavior at this point. Well, this is the best he can do: This pin was sticking me and preventing me from catching lice. The Kalmuck's chest was already covered with medals and insignia. So I held out my loosely closed hand to Matzerath, who was standing beside me.

You may say that I shouldn't have done it. But perhaps I am entitled to reply that Matzerath shouldn't have grasped at my hand.

Anyway, he grasped. I was rid of the thing. Little by little, fear took possession of Matzerath as he felt the emblem of his Party between his fingers. Now that my hands were free, I didn't want to see what Matzerath did with the pin. Too distraught to pursue the lice, Oskar tried to concentrate on the ants, but couldn't help taking in a swift movement of Matzerath's hand. Unable to remember what I thought at the time, I can only say in retrospect that it would have been wiser of him to keep the little colored lozenge in his hand.

But he wanted desperately to get rid of it, and despite the rich imagination he had shown as a cook and window dresser, he could think of no other hiding place than his mouth.

How important a trifling gesture can be! That little move from hand to mouth was enough to startle the two Ivans who had been sitting peacefully to left and right of Maria and make them jump up from the air-defense cot. They thrust their tommy guns at Matzerath's belly, and it was plain for all to see that Matzerath was trying to swallow something.

If only he had first, with an adroit finger maneuver, closed the pin. As it was, he gagged, his face went purple, his eyes stood out of his head, he coughed, cried, laughed, and all this turmoil made it impossible for him to keep his hands up. But on that point the Ivans were firm. They shouted at him, they wanted to see the palms of his hands. Matzerath, however, was preoccupied with his windpipe. He couldn't even cough properly. He began to dance and thrash about with his arms and swept a can of Leipzig stew off the shelf. My Kalmuck, who until then had been quietly looking on, deposited me carefully on the floor, reached behind him, brought something or other into a horizontal position, and shot from the hip. He had emptied a whole magazine before Matzerath finished suffocating.

What strange things one does at the moments when fate puts on its act! While my presumptive father was swallowing the Party and dying, I, involuntarily and unaware of what I was doing, squashed between my fingers a louse I had just caught on the Kalmuck. Matzerath had fallen across the ant highway. The Ivans left the cellar by way of the stairs leading to the shop, taking with them a few packages of artificial honey. My Kalmuck went last, but he took no honey, for he had to change the magazine of his tommy gun. The widow Greff lay disheveled and undone between the margarine crates. Maria clutched little Kurt to her as though to crush him. A phrase from Goethe passed through my mind. The ants found themselves facing a new situation but, undismayed by the detour, soon built a new highway round the doubled-up Matzerath; for the sugar that trickled out of the burst sack had lost none of its sweetness while Marshal Rokossovski was occupying the city of Danzig.

Should I or Shouldn't I?

First came the Rugii, then the Goths and Gepidae, then the Kashubes from whom Oskar is descended in a straight line. A little later the Poles sent in Adalbert of Prague, who came with the Cross and was slain with an ax by the Kashubes or Borussians. This happened in a fishing village called Gyddanycz. Gyddanycz became Danczik, which was turned into Dantzig, later written without the t, and today the city is called Gdansk.

But before this orthographic development and after the arrival of the Kashubes, the dukes of Pomerelia came to Gyddanycz. They bore such names as Subislaus, Sambor, Mestwin, and Swantopolk. The village became a small town. Then came the wild Borussians, intent on pillage and destruction. Then came the distant Brandenburgers, equally given to pillage and destruction. Boleslaw of Poland did his bit in the same spirit and no sooner was the damage repaired than the Teutonic Knights stepped in to carry on the time-honored tradition.

The centuries passed. The city was destroyed and rebuilt in turn by the dukes of Pomerelia, the grand masters of the Teutonic Order, the kings and antikings of Poland, the counts of Brandenburg, and the bishops of Wloclawek. The directors of the building and wrecking enterprises were named Otto and Waldemar, Bogussa, Heinrich von Plotzke—and Dietrich von Altenberg, who built the fortress of the Teutonic Knights on the spot which became the Hevelius-Platz, where in the twentieth century the Polish Post Office was defended.

The Hussites came, made a little fire here and there, and left. The Teutonic Knights were thrown out of the city and the fortress was torn down because the townspeople were sick of having a fortress in their city. The Poles took over and no one was any the worse for it. The king who brought this to pass was Kazimierz, who became known as the Great, son of Wladyslaw the First. Then came Louis of Hungary and after Louis his daughter Jadwiga. She married Jagiello of Lithuania, founder of the Jagellon dynasty. After Wladyslaw II came Wladyslaw III, then another Kazimierz, who lacked the proper enthusiasm and nevertheless, for thirteen long years, squandered the good money of the Danzig merchants making war on the Teutonic Knights. The attentions of John Albert, on the other hand, were more taken up by the Turks. Alexander was followed by Zygmunt Stary, or Sigismund the Elder. After the chapter about Sigismund Augustus comes the one about Stefan Batory, for whom the Poles like to name their ocean liners. He besieged the city and shot cannon balls into it for Lord knows how long (as we may read in our books), but never succeeded in taking it. Then came the Swedes and continued in the same vein. They got so fond of besieging the city that they repeated the performance several times. In the same period, the Gulf of Danzig also became exceedingly popular with the Dutch, Danes, and English, and a number of these foreign sea captains came to be heroes of the sea just by cruising around the Danzig roadstead.

The Peace of Oliva. How sweet and peaceful it sounds! There the great powers noticed for the first time that the land of the Poles lends itself admirably to partition. Swedes, Swedes, and more Swedes—Swedish earthworks, Swedish punch, Swedish gallows. Then came the Russians and Saxons, because Stanislaw Leszczynski, the poor King of Poland, was hidden in the city. On account of this one king, eighteen hundred houses were destroyed, and when poor Leszczynski fled to France because that's where his son-in-law Louis was living, the people of Danzig had to cough up a round million.

Then Poland was divided in three. The Prussians came uninvited and painted the Polish eagle over with their own bird on all the city gates. Johannes Falk, the educator, had just time to write his famous Christmas carol "O Du fröhliche . . ." when the French turned up. Napoleon's general was called Rapp and after a miserable siege the people of Danzig had to rap out twenty million francs to him. The horrors of the French occupation should not necessarily be held in doubt. But it lasted only seven years. Then came the Russians and the Prussians and set the Speicherinsel on fire with their artillery. That was the end of the Free State that Napoleon had dreamed up. Again the Prussians found occasion to paint their bird on all the city gates. Having done so with Prussian thoroughness, they proceeded to establish a garrison consisting of the 4th Regiment of Grenadiers, the 1st Artillery Brigade, the 1st Battalion of Engineers, and the 1st Regiment of Leib-Hussars. The 30th Infantry Regiment, the 18th Infantry Regiment, the 3rd Regiment of Foot Guards, the 44th Infantry Regiment, and the 33rd Regiment of Fusiliers were all at one time or another garrisoned in the city, though none of them for very long. But the famous 128th Infantry Regiment did not leave until 1920. For the sake of completeness it may be worth mentioning that in the course of the Prussian period the First Artillery Brigade was expanded to include the 1st Battalion of Fortress Artillery, the 2nd Infantry Battalion, the 1st East-Prussian Artillery Regiment, and later the 2nd Pomeranian Foot Artillery Regiment, which was subsequently replaced by the 16th West Prussian Foot Artillery Regiment. The 1st Regiment of Leib Hussars was succeeded by the 2nd Regiment of Leib Hussars. The 8th Regiment of Uhlans, on the other hand, spent only a brief time within the city's walls, while the 17th West-Prussian Quartermaster Battalion was stationed outside the walls, in the suburb of Langfuhr.

In the days of Burckhardt, Rauschning, and Greiser, German authority was represented in the Free State only by the green-uniformed security police. This changed in '39 under Forster. The brick barracks filled rapidly with happy lads in uniform, who juggled with every known weapon. We might go on to list all the units that were quartered in Danzig and environs from '39 to '45 or shipped out from Danzig to fight on the Arctic front. This Oskar will spare you and merely say: then, as we have already seen, came Marshal Rokossovski. At the sight of the still intact city, he remembered his great international precursors and set the whole place on fire with his artillery in order that those who came after him might work off their excess energies in rebuilding.

This time, strange to say, no Prussians, Swedes, Saxons, or Frenchmen came after the Russians; this time it was the Poles who arrived.

The Poles came with bag and baggage from Vilna, Bialystok, and

Lwow, all looking for living quarters. To us came a gentleman by the name of Fajngold; he was all alone in the world, but he behaved as though surrounded by a large family that couldn't manage for one minute without his instructions. Mr. Fajngold took over the grocery store at once and proceeded to show his wife Luba, who remained invisible and unresponsive, the scales, the kerosene tank, the brass rod to hang sausages on, the empty cash drawer, and with the utmost enthusiasm, the provisions in the cellar. He engaged Maria as salesgirl and introduced her very verbosely to his imaginary Luba, whereupon Maria showed Mr. Fajngold our Matzerath, who had been lying in the cellar for three days under a square of canvas. We had been unable to bury him because the streets were swarming with Russians avid for bicycles, sewing machines, and women.

When Mr. Fajngold saw the corpse, which we had turned over on his back, he clapped his hands over his head in the same expressive gesture as Oskar had seen Sigismund Markus, his toy dealer, make years before. He called not only Luba his wife, but his whole family into the cellar, and there is no doubt that he saw them all coming, for he called them by name: Luba, Lev, Jakub, Berek, Leon, Mendel, and Sonya. He explained to them all who it was who was lying there dead and went on to tell us that all those he had just summoned as well as his sister-in-law and her other brother-in-law who had five children had lain in the same way, before being taken to the crematoria of Treblinka, and the whole lot of them had been lying there—except for him because he had had to strew lime on them.

Then he helped us to carry Matzerath upstairs to the shop. His family was about him again, and he asked his wife Luba to help Maria wash the corpse. She didn't stir a finger, but Mr. Fajngold didn't notice, for by now he was moving supplies from the cellar up to the shop. This time Lina Greff, who had washed Mother Truczinski, wasn't there to help us; she had a houseful of Russians and we could hear her singing.

Old man Heilandt had found work as a shoemaker. He was busy resoling the boots the Russians had worn out during their rapid advance and was unwilling at first to make us a coffin. But after Mr. Fajngold had drawn him into a business deal—Derby cigarettes from our shop for an electric motor from his shed—he set his boots aside and took up other tools and the last of his boards.

At that time—until we were evicted and Mr. Fajngold turned the cellar over to us—we were living in Mother Truczinski's flat, which had been stripped bare by neighbors and Polish immigrants. Old man Heilandt removed the door between the kitchen and living room from its hinges, for the door between the living room and bedroom had been used for Mother Truczinski's coffin. Down below, in the court, he was smoking Derby cigarettes and throwing the box together. We remained upstairs.

I took the one chair that was left in the flat and pushed open the broken window. It grieved me to see that the old fellow was taking no pains at all with his work and turning out a plain rectangular box without the tapering characteristic of self-respecting coffins.

Oskar didn't see Matzerath again, for when the box was lifted onto the widow Greff's handcart, the Vitello Margarine slats had already been nailed down, although in his lifetime Matzerath, far from eating margarine, had despised it even for cooking.

Maria asked Mr. Fajngold to come with us; she was afraid of the Russian soldiers in the streets. Fajngold, who was squatting on the counter, spooning artificial honey out of a cardboard cup, expressed misgivings at first; he was afraid Luba might object, but then apparently his wife gave him permission to go, for he slipped off the counter, giving me the honey. I passed it on to Kurt, who made short shrift of it, while Maria helped Mr. Fajngold into a long black coat with gray rabbit fur. Before he closed the shop, bidding his wife to open for no one, he put on a top hat, considerably too small for him, which Matzerath had worn at various weddings and funerals.

Old man Heilandt refused to pull the cart as far as the City Cemetery. He hadn't the time, he said, he still had boots to mend. At Max-Halbe-Platz, the ruins of which were still smouldering, he turned left into Brösener-Weg and I guessed he was heading for Saspe. The Russians sat outside the houses in the thin February sun, sorting out wristwatches and pocket watches, polishing silver spoons with sand, experimenting to see how brassieres worked out as ear muffs, and doing stunt bicycle-riding over an obstacle course fashioned of oil paintings, grandfather clocks, bathtubs, radios, and clothes trees. Enthusiastically applauded for their skill, they did figure eights, twists, and spirals, all the while dodging the baby carriages, chandeliers, and such like that were being thrown out of the windows. As we passed, they broke off their sport for a few seconds. A few soldiers with negligees over their uniforms helped us to push and tried to make passes at Maria, but were called to order by Mr. Fajngold, who spoke Russian and had an official pass. A soldier in a lady's hat gave us a birdcage containing a live lovebird on a perch. Kurt, who was hopping along beside the cart, tried to pull out its feathers. Afraid to decline the gift, Maria lifted the cage out of Kurt's reach and handed it up to me on the cart. Oskar, who was in no mood for lovebirds, put the cage down on Matzerath's enlarged margarine crate. I was sitting in the rear end of the cart, dangling my legs and looking into the folds of Mr. Fajngold's face, which bore a look of thoughtful gloom, suggesting a mind at work on a complicated problem that refused to come out.

I beat my drum a little, something sprightly, in an effort to dispel Mr. Fajngold's somber thoughts. But his expression remained unchanged, his eyes were somewhere else, maybe in far-away Galicia; one thing they did not see was my drum. Oskar gave up, and after that there was no sound but Maria's weeping and the rumbling of the wheels.

What a mild winter, I thought when we had left the last houses of Langfuhr behind us; I also took some notice of the lovebird, which was puffing out its feathers in consideration of the afternoon sun hovering over the airfield.

The airfield was guarded, the road to Brösen closed. An officer spoke with Mr. Fajngold, who during the interview held his top hat between his fingers, letting his thin, reddish-blond hair blow in the wind. After tapping for a moment on Matzerath's crate as though to determine its contents and tickling the lovebird with his forefinger, the officer let us pass, but assigned two young fellows, who couldn't have been more than sixteen, with caps that were too little and tommy guns that were too big, to escort us, perhaps for our protection or perhaps to keep an eye on us.

Old man Heilandt pulled, without ever once turning around. He had a trick of lighting his cigarette with one hand, without slowing down. Planes darted about overhead. The engines were so clearly audible because of the season, late February or early March. Only in the vicinity of the sun were there a few clouds which gradually took on color. The bombers were heading for Hela or returning from Hela Peninsula, where what was left of the Second Army was still holding out.

The weather and the droning of the planes made me sad. There is nothing so tedious, nothing that makes for such a feeling of surfeit and disgust, as a cloudless March sky full of airplane motors crescendo and decrescendo. To make matters worse, the two Russian puppies kept trying, quite unsuccessfully, to march in step.

Perhaps some of the boards of the hastily assembled coffin had been jolted loose, first on the cobblestones, then on battered asphalt; we were heading into the wind and, as we have seen, I was sitting in back; in any case, it smelled of dead Matzerath, and Oskar was glad when we reached Saspe Cemetery.

We couldn't take the cart as far as the iron gate, for the road was blocked shortly before the cemetery by the charred wreckage of a T-34. Other tanks, obliged to detour around it on their way to Neufahrwasser, had left their tracks in the sand to the left of the highway and flattened a part of the cemetery wall. Mr. Fajngold asked old man Heilandt to take the rear. They carried the coffin, which sagged slightly in the middle, along the tracks of the tank treads, traversed with some difficulty the stone pile into which the cemetery wall had been transformed, and finally, with their last strength, took a few steps among the tumble-down tombstones. Old man Heilandt tugged avidly at his cigarette and blew out smoke over the coffin. I carried the cage with the lovebird. Maria dragged two shovels behind her. Little Kurt carried or rather brandished a pickax, attacking the gray granite tombstones at the risk of his life, until Maria took it away from him and helped the men to dig.

How fortunate that the soil here is sandy and not frozen, I said to myself, while looking for Jan Bronski's place behind the northern wall. It must be here, I thought, or maybe there. I couldn't be sure, for the changing seasons had turned the telltale fresh whitewash a crumbling gray like all the walls in Saspe.

I came back through the hind gate, looked up at the stunted pines: So now they're burying Matzerath, I thought, for fear of thinking something irrelevant. And I found at least partial meaning in the circumstance that the two skat brothers, Bronski and Matzerath, should lie here in the same sandy ground, even if my poor mama was not here to keep them company.

Funerals always make you think of other funerals.

The sandy soil put up a fight, it probably wanted more experienced gravediggers. Maria paused, leaned panting on her pick, and began to cry again when she saw Kurt throwing stones at the lovebird in its cage. Kurt missed, his stones overshot the mark; Maria wept loudly and in all sincerity, because she had lost Matzerath, because she had seen something in Matzerath which in my opinion wasn't there, but which, as far as she was concerned, was to remain henceforth real and lovable. Mr. Fajngold said a few comforting words, which gave him a chance to rest, for the digging was too much for him. Old man Heilandt wielded his shovel with the regularity of a seeker after gold, tossed the earth behind him, and blew out puffs of smoke, also at measured intervals. The two Russian puppies sat on the cemetery wall a few steps away from us, chatting into the wind. Overhead, airplanes and a sun growing steadily riper.

They may have dug about three feet. Oskar stood idle and perplexed amid the old granite, amid the stunted pines, between Matzerath's widow and a Kurt throwing stones at a lovebird.

Should I or shouldn't I? You are going on twenty-one, Oskar. Should you or shouldn't you? You are an orphan. Actually you should, it's high time. When your poor mama died, you were left half an orphan. That was when you should have made up your mind. Then they laid Jan, your presumptive father, under the crust of the earth. That made you a presumptive full orphan. You stood here on this sand named Saspe, holding a slightly oxidized cartridge case. It was raining and a Ju-52 was getting ready to land. Wasn't this "Should I or shouldn't I?" audible even then, if not in the sound of the rain, then in the roaring of the landing transport plane? You said to yourself: it's the rain, it's the sound of airplanes engines; uninspired interpretations of this sort can be read into any text you please. You wanted everything to be perfectly plain and not just presumptive.

Should I or shouldn't I? Now they are digging a hole for Matzerath, your second presumptive father. As far as you know, you have no more presumptive fathers. Why, then, do you keep juggling with two bottle-green bottles: should I or shouldn't I? Who else is there to question? These stunted pines, themselves so questionable?

I found a slender cast-iron cross with crumbling ornaments and encrusted letters adding up to Mathilde Kunkel—or Runkel. In the sand—should I or shouldn't I?—between thistles and wild oats—should I?—I found—or shouldn't I?—three or four rusty metal wreaths the size of dinner plates—should I?—which once upon a time—or shouldn't I? —were no doubt supposed to look like oak leaves or laurel—or should I after all?—weighed them in my hand, took aim—should I?—the top end of the ironwork cross—or shouldn't I?—had a diameter of—should I?—maybe an inch and a half—or shouldn't I?—I ordered myself to stand six feet away—should I?—tossed—or shouldn't I?—and missed —should I try again?—the cross was too much on a slant—should I?— Mathilde Kunkel or was it Runkel—should I Runkel, should I Kunkel?—that was the sixth throw and I had allowed myself seven, six times I shouldn't and now seven—*should,* the wreath was on the cross— *should*—wreathed Mathilde—*should*—laurel for Miss Kunkel—should I? I asked young Mrs. Runkel—yes, said Mathilde; she had died young, at twenty-seven, and born in '68. As for me, I was going on twenty-one when I made it on the seventh throw, when my problem—should I or shouldn't I?—was simplified, transformed into a demonstrated, wreathed, aimed, and triumphant "I should."

As Oskar, with his new "I should" on his tongue and in his heart, made his way back to the gravediggers, the lovebird let out a squeak and shed several yellow-blue feathers, for one of Kurt's stones had struck home. I wondered what question may have impelled my son to keep throwing stones at a lovebird until at last a hit gave him his answer.

They had moved the crate to the edge of the pit, which was about four feet deep. Old man Heilandt was in a hurry, but had to wait while Maria completed her Catholic prayers, while Mr. Fajngold stood there with his silk hat over his chest and his eyes in Galicia. Kurt, too, came closer. After his bull's-eye he had probably arrived at a decision; he approached the grave for reasons of his own but just as resolutely as Oskar.

The uncertainty was killing me. After all, it was my son who had decided for or against something. Had he decided at last to recognize and love me as his only true father? Had he, now that it was too late, decided to take up the drum? Or was his decision: death to my presumptive father Oskar, who killed my presumptive father Matzerath with a Party pin for no other reason than because he was sick of fathers? Perhaps he, too, could express only by homicide the childlike affection that would seem to be desirable between fathers and sons.

316

While old man Heilandt flung rather than lowered the crate containing Matzerath, the Party pin in Matzerath's windpipe and the magazineful of Russian tommy-gun ammunition in Matzerath's belly, into the grave, Oskar owned to himself that he had killed Matzerath deliberately, because in all likelihood Matzerath was not just his presumptive father, but his real father; and also because he was sick of dragging a father around with him all his life.

And so it was not true that the pin had been open when I picked up the badge from the concrete floor. The pin had been opened within my closed hand. It was a jagged, pointed lozenge that I had passed on to Matzerath, intending that they find the insignia on him, that he put the Party in his mouth and choke on it—on the Party, on me, his son; for this situation couldn't go on forever.

Old man Heilandt began to shovel. Little Kurt helped him clumsily but with alacrity. I had never loved Matzerath. Occasionally I liked him. He took care of me, but more as a cook than as a father. He was a good cook. If today I sometimes miss Matzerath, it is his Königsberg dumplings, his pork kidneys in vinegar sauce, his carp with horseradish and cream, his green eel soup, his Kassler Rippchen with sauerkraut, and all his unforgettable Sunday roasts, which I can still feel on my tongue and between my teeth. They forgot to put a cooking spoon in the coffin of this man who transformed feelings into soups. They also forgot to put a deck of skat cards in his coffin. He was a better cook than skat player. Still, he played better than Jan Bronski and almost as well as my poor mama. Such was his endowment, such was his tragedy. I have never been able to forgive him for taking Maria away from me, although he treated her well, never beat her, and usually gave in when she picked a fight. He hadn't turned me over to the Ministry of Public Health, and had signed the letter only after the mails had stopped running. When I came into the world under the light bulbs, he chose the shop as my career. To avoid standing behind a counter, Oskar had spent more than seventeen years standing behind a hundred or so toy drums, lacquered red and white. Now Matzerath lay flat and could stand no more. Smoking Matzerath's Derby cigarettes, old man Heilandt shoveled him in. Oskar should have taken over the shop. Meanwhile Mr. Fajngold had taken over the shop with his large, invisible family. But I inherited the rest: Maria, Kurt, and the responsibility for them both.

Maria was still crying authentically and praying Catholically. Mr. Fajngold was sojourning in Galicia or solving some knotty reckoning. Kurt was weakening but still shoveling. The Russian puppies sat chatting on the cemetery wall. With morose regularity old man Heilandt shoveled the sand of Saspe over the margarine-crate coffin. Oskar could still read three letters of the word Vitello. At this point he unslung the drum from his neck, no longer saying "Should I or shouldn't I?" but instead: "It must be," and threw the drum where the sand was deep enough to muffle the sound. I tossed in the sticks too. They stuck in the sand. That was my drum from the Duster days, the last of those Bebra had given me. What would the Master have thought of my decision? Jesus had beaten that drum, as had a Russian with large, open pores and built like a bank safe. There wasn't much life left in it. But when a shovelful of sand struck its surface, it sounded. At the second shovelful, it still had something to say. At the third it was silent, only showing a little white lacquer until that too was covered over. The sand piled up on my drum, the sand mounted and grew—and I too began to grow; the first symptom being a violent nosebleed.

Kurt was the first to notice the blood. "He's bleeding, he's bleeding," he shouted, calling Mr. Fajngold back from Galicia, calling Maria from her prayers, and even making the two young Russians, who had been sitting on the wall the whole while, chatting the direction of Brösen, look up in momentary fright.

Old man Heilandt left his shovel in the sand, took the pickax, and rested my neck against the blue-black iron. The cool metal produced the desired effect. The bleeding began to subside. Old man Heilandt returned to his shoveling. There was still a little sand left beside the grave when the bleeding stopped entirely, but the growth continued, as I could tell by the rumbling and cracking and grinding inside me.

When old man Heilandt had finished shoveling, he took a dilapidated wooden cross with no inscription on it from a nearby tomb and thrust it into the fresh mound, approximately between Matzerath's head and my buried drum. "That does it!" said the old man and picked up Oskar, who was unable to walk, in his arms. Carrying me, he led the others, including the Russian puppies with the tommy guns, out of the cemetery, across the crushed wall, along the tank tracks to the handcart on the highway. I looked back over my shoulder toward the cemetery. Maria was carrying the cage with the lovebird, Mr. Fajngold was carrying the tools, Kurt was carrying nothing, the two Russians with the caps that were too small were carrying the tommy guns that were too big for them, and the scrub pines were bent beneath so much carrying.

From the sand to the asphalt highway, still blocked by the burned-out tank. On the tank sat Leo Schugger. High overhead planes coming from Hela, headed for Hela. Leo Schugger was careful not to blacken his gloves on the charred T-34. Surrounded by puffy little clouds, the sun descended on Tower Mountain near Zoppot. Leo Schugger slid off the tank and stood very straight.

The sight of Leo Schugger handed old man Heilandt a laugh. "D'you ever see the like of it? The world comes to an end, but they can't get

Leo Schugger down." In high good humor, he gave the black tailcoat a slap on the back and explained to Mr. Fajngold: "This is our Leo Schugger. He wants to give us sympathy and shake hands with us."

He spoke the truth. Leo Schugger made his gloves flutter and, slavering as usual, expressed his sympathies to all present. "Did you see the Lord?" he asked. "Did you see the Lord?" No one had seen Him. Maria, I don't know why, gave Leo the cage with the lovebird.

When it was the turn of Oskar, whom old man Heilandt had stowed on the handcart, Leo Schugger's face seemed to decompose itself, the winds inflated his garments, and a dance seized hold of his legs. "The Lord, the Lord!" he cried, shaking the lovebird in its cage. "See the Lord! He's growing, he's growing!"

Then he was tossed into the air with the cage, and he ran, flew, danced, staggered, and fled with the screeching bird, himself a bird. Taking flight at last, he fluttered across the fields in the direction of the sewage land and was heard shouting through the voices of the tommy guns: "He's growing, he's growing!" He was still screaming when the two young Russians reloaded. "He's growing!" And even when the tommy guns rang out again, even after Oskar had fallen down a stepless staircase into an expanding, all-engulfing faint, I could hear the bird, the voice, the raven, I could hear Leo proclaiming to all the world: "He's growing, he's growing, he's growing . . ."

Disinfectant

Last night I was beset by hasty dreams. They were like friends on visiting days. One dream after another; one by one they came and went after telling me what dreams find worth telling; preposterous stories full of repetitions, monologues which could not be ignored, because they were declaimed in a voice that demanded attention and with the gestures of incompetent actors. When I tried to tell Bruno the stories at breakfast, I couldn't get rid of them, because I had forgotten everything; Oskar has no talent for dreaming.

While Bruno cleared away the breakfast, I asked him as though in passing: "My dear Bruno, how tall am I exactly?"

Bruno set the little dish of jam on my coffee cup and said in tones of concern: "Why, Mr. Matzerath, you haven't touched your jam."

How well I know those words of reproach. I hear them every day after breakfast. Every morning Bruno brings me this dab of strawberry jam just to make me build a newspaper roof over it. I can't even bear to look at jam, much less eat it. Accordingly I dismissed Bruno's reproach with quiet firmness: "You know how I feel about jam, Bruno. Just tell me how tall I am."

Bruno's eyes took on the expression of an extinct octopod. He always casts this prehistoric gaze up at the ceiling whenever he has to think, and if he has anything to say, it is also the ceiling he addresses. This morning, then, he said to the ceiling: "But it's strawberry jam." Only when after a considerable pause—for by my silence I sustained my question about Oskar's size—Bruno's gaze came down from the ceiling and twined itself round the bars of my bed, was I privileged to hear that I measured four feet one.

"Wouldn't you kindly measure me again, Bruno, just to be sure?"

Without batting an eyelash, Bruno drew a folding rule from his back pants pocket, threw back my covers with a gesture that was almost brutal, pulled down my nightgown, which had bunched up, unfolded the ferociously yellow ruler which had broken off at five feet eleven, placed it alongside me, shifted its position, checked. His hands worked efficiently, but his eyes were still dwelling in the age of dinosaurs. At length the ruler came to rest and he declared, as though reading off his findings: "Still four feet one."

Why did he have to make so much noise folding up his ruler and removing my breakfast tray? Were my measurements not to his liking?

After leaving the room with the breakfast tray, with the egg-yellow ruler beside the revoltingly natural-colored strawberry jam, Bruno cast a last glance back through the peephole in the door—a glance that made me feel as old as the hills. Then at length he left me alone with my four feet and my one inch.

So Oskar is really so tall! Almost too big for a dwarf, a gnome, a midget? What was the altitude of la Raguna's, my Roswitha's, summit? At what height did Master Bebra, who was descended from Prince Eugene, succeed in keeping himself? Today I could look down even on Kitty and Felix. Whereas all those I have just mentioned once looked down with friendly envy upon Oskar, who, until the twenty-first year of his life, had measured a spare three feet.

It was only when that stone hit me at Matzerath's funeral in Saspe Cemetery that I began to grow.

Stone, Oskar has said. I had better fill in my record of the events at the cemetery.

After I had found out, thanks to my little game of quoits, that for me there could be no more "Should I or shouldn't I?" but only an "I should, I must, I will!" I unslung my drum, cast it complete with drumsticks into Matzerath's grave, and made up my mind to grow. At once I felt a buzzing, louder and louder, in my ears. Just then I was struck in the back of the head by a stone about the size of a walnut, which my son Kurt had thrown with all his four-year-old might. Though the blow came as no surprise to me—I had suspected that my son was cooking up something against me—I nevertheless made a dash for my drum in Matzerath's grave. Old man Heilandt pulled me out of the hole with his dry, old man's grip, but left drum and drumsticks where they were. Then when my nose began to bleed, he laid me down with my neck against the iron of the pickax. The nosebleed, as we know, soon subsided, but I continued to grow, though so slowly that only Leo Schugger noticed, whereupon he proclaimed my growth to the world with loud cries and birdlike fluttering.

So much for my addendum, which is actually superfluous; for I had started to grow even before I was hit by the stone and flung myself into Matzerath's grave. But from the very first Maria and Mr. Fajngold saw but one reason for my growth, or sickness as they called it, namely, the stone that had hit me in the head, my leap into the grave. Even before we had left the cemetery, Maria gave Kurt a sound spanking. I was sorry for Kurt. For after all he may have thrown that stone at me to help me, to accelerate my growth. Perhaps he wanted at last to have a real grown-up father, or maybe just a substitute for Matzerath; for to tell the truth, he has never acknowledged or honored the father in me.

In the course of my growth, which went on for nearly a year, there were plenty of doctors of both sexes who confirmed the theory that the stone and my headlong leap into the grave were responsible, who said and wrote in my case history: Oskar Matzerath is a deformed Oskar because a stone hit him in the back of the head, etc. etc.

Here it seems relevant to recall my third birthday. What had the grownups said about the beginning of my biography proper? This is what they had said: At the age of three, Oskar Matzerath fell from the cellar stairs to the concrete floor. This fall put an end to his growth, etc. etc.

In these explanations we find man's understandable desire to find physical justification for all alleged miracles. Oskar must admit that he too examines all alleged miracles with the utmost care before discarding them as irresponsible hokum.

On our return from Saspe Cemetery, we found new tenants in Mother Truczinski's flat. They were nice enough people and offered to take us in until we had found something else, but Mr. Fajngold refused to countenance such overcrowding and said we could have the bedroom of the ground-floor flat, he could manage for the present with the living room. To this arrangement Maria objected, feeling that it would not be right in her recently widowed state to live at such close quarters with a gentleman alone. At the time Fajngold was unaware of being a gentleman alone, but Luba's energetic presence made it easier in a way for him to appreciate Maria's arguments. For Luba's sake as well, they would make a different arrangement, he would turn the cellar over to us. He even helped us to rearrange the storeroom, but he would not let me move into the cellar, for I was sick, a poor sick child, and so a bed was set up for me in the living room, beside my poor mama's piano.

It was hard to find a doctor. Most of the doctors had left with the troops, because in January the medical insurance fund had been evacuated westward and patients had become exceedingly rare. After a long search, Mr. Fajngold managed to scare up a lady doctor from Elbing, who was amputating at the Helene Lange School, where wounded from the Wehrmacht and the Red Army lay side by side. She promised to look in, and four days later she actually did. She sat down by my sickbed, smoked three or four cigarettes in a row while examining me, and on the last cigarette fell asleep.

Mr. Fajngold was afraid to wake her up. Maria gave her a timid poke. But the lady doctor didn't wake up until her cigarette burned down and singed her finger. She stood up and stamped out the butt on the carpet. She spoke tersely in a tone of nervous irritation: "You'll have to excuse me. Haven't closed an eye in three weeks. I was in Käsemark with a trainload of children from East Prussia. Couldn't get the kids on the ferry. Only took troops. Four thousand kids. All blown to pieces." There was the same terseness in the way she stroked my cheek. Thrusting a fresh cigarette into her face, she rolled up her left sleeve and took an ampoule out of her briefcase. While giving herself a shot in the arm, she said to Maria: "I can't tell you what's the matter with the boy. Ought to be in a hospital, but not here. You've got to get away. To the West. The joints of his wrists, knees, and shoulders are swollen. It's bound to attack his brain in the end. Make him cold compresses. I'm leaving you a few pills in case the pain prevents him from sleeping."

I liked this terse lady doctor, who didn't know what was wrong with me and admitted as much. In the few weeks that followed, Maria and Mr. Fajngold made me several hundred cold compresses which soothed me, but didn't prevent my knee, wrist, and shoulder joints, and my head as well, from swelling and aching. What horrified Maria and Mr. Fajngold the most was my swelling head. She gave me the pills, but they were soon gone. He began to plot fever curves, took to experimenting with pencil and ruler, constructed bold fantastic shapes round my temperature, which he took five times a day with a thermometer obtained on the black market in exchange for synthetic honey. My fever chart looked like a mountain range with terrifying chasms—I thought of the Alps, the snowy peaks of the Andes. In reality, there was nothing so fantastic about my temperature: in the morning I usually had a hundred and five-tenths; by evening it had risen to something over a hundred and two and the most I ever had during my period of growth was a hundred and two point seven. I saw and heard all sorts of things in my fever; I was riding a merry-go-round, I wanted to get off but I couldn't. I was one of many little children sitting in fire engines and hollowed-out swans, on dogs, cats, pigs, and stags, riding round and round. I wanted to get off but I wasn't allowed to. All the little children were crying, like me they wanted to get out of the fire engines and hollowed-out swans, down from the backs of the cats, dogs, pigs, and stags, they didn't want to ride on the merry-go-round any more, but they weren't allowed to get off. The Heavenly Father was standing beside the merry-go-round and every time it stopped, he paid for another turn. And we prayed: "Oh, our Father who art in heaven, we know you have lots of loose change, we know you like to treat us to rides on the merry-go-round, we know you like to prove to us that this world is round. Please put your pocket-book away, say stop, finished, *fertig, basta, stoi,* closing time—we poor little children are dizzy, they've brought us, four thousand of us, to Käsemark on the Vistula, but we can't get across, because your merry-go-round, your merry-go-round . . ."

But God our Father, the merry-go-round owner, smiled in his most benevolent manner and another coin came sailing out of his purse to make the merry-go-round keep on turning, carrying four thousand children with Oskar in their midst, in fire engines and hollowed-out swans, on cats, dogs, pigs, and stags, round and round in a ring, and every time my stag—I'm still quite sure it was a stag—carried us past our Father in heaven, the merry-go-round owner, he had a different face: He was Rasputin, laughing and biting the coin for the next ride with his faith healer's teeth; and then he was Goethe, the poet prince, holding a beautifully embroidered purse, and the coins he took out of it were all stamped with his father-in-heaven profile; and then again Rasputin, tipsy, and again Herr von Goethe, sober. A bit of madness with Rasputin and a bit of rationality with Goethe. The extremists with Rasputin, the forces of order with Goethe. The tumultuous masses round Rasputin, calendar mottoes with Goethe . . . until at length the merry-go-round slowed down—not because my fever subsided, but because a soothing presence bent down over my fever, because Mr. Fajngold bent over me and stopped the merry-go-round. He stopped the fire engines, the swan, and the stag, devaluated Rasputin's coins, sent Goethe back to the Mothers, sent four thousand dizzy little children floating off to Käsemark, across the Vistula, to the kingdom of heaven—and picked Oskar up from his sickbed, and lifted him up on a cloud of Lysol, that is to say, he disinfected me.

It started on account of the lice and then became a habit. He first discovered the lice on little Kurt, then on me, Maria, and himself. The lice had probably been left behind by the Kalmuck who had taken Matzerath from Maria. How Mr. Fajngold yelled when he discovered them. He summoned his wife and children; the whole lot of them, he suspected, were infested with vermin. Then, having bartered rolled oats and synthetic honey for different kinds of disinfectant, he took to disinfecting himself, his whole family, Maria, and myself every single day. He rubbed us, sprayed us, and powdered us. And while he sprayed, powdered, and rubbed, my fever blazed, his tongue wagged, and I learned about the whole carloads of carbolic acid, lime, and Lysol that he had sprayed, strewn, and sprinkled when he was disinfector in Treblinka Concentration Camp. Every day at 2 P.M., in his official capacity as Disinfector Mariusz Fajngold, he had sprinkled Lysol on the camp streets, over the barracks, the shower rooms, the cremating furnaces, the bundles of clothing, over those who were waiting to shower, over those who lay recumbent after their showers, over all that came out of the ovens and all who were about to go in. He listed the names, for he knew them all. He told me about Bilauer, who one hot day in August had advised the disinfector to sprinkle the camp streets with kerosene instead of Lysol. Mr. Fajngold had taken his advice. And Bilauer had the match. Old Zev Kurland of the ZOB had administered the oath to the lot of them. And Engineer Galewski had broken into the weapons room. Bilauer had shot Hauptsturmführer Kutner. Sztulbach and Warynski got Zisenis by the throat; the others tackled the guards from Trawniki Camp. Some were electrocuted cutting the high-tension fence. SS Sergeant Schöpke, who had always made little jokes while taking his protégés to the showers, stood by the camp gate shooting. But it didn't help him, they were all on top of him at once: Adek Kave, Motel Levit, and Henoch Lerer; Hersz Rotblat and Letek Zegel were there too, and Tosias Baran with his Deborah. And Lolek Begelmann shouted: "What about Fajngold? Got to get him out of here before the planes come." Mr. Fajngold was waiting for Luba, his wife. But even then she had stopped coming when he called her. So they seized him left and right, Jakub Gelernter on the left side, Mordechaj Szwarcbard on the right. And in front of him ran little Dr. Atlas, who, in the camp at Treblinka and later in the woods round Vilna, had recommended a thorough sprinkling with Lysol and maintained that Lysol is more important than life. This Mr. Fajngold could corroborate, for he had sprinkled the dead, not one corpse but many, why bother with figures; he had sprinkled dead men and dead women with Lysol and that was that. And he knew names, so many that it became tedious, that to me who was also swimming in Lysol the question of the life and death of a hundred thousand names became less important than the question of whether life and, if not life, then death, had been disinfected adequately and on time with Mr. Fajngold's disinfectants.

Gradually my fever left me and it was April. Then the fever went up again, the merry-go-round spun, and Mr. Fajngold sprinkled Lysol on the living and the dead. Then the fever was down again and April was at an end. Early in May, my neck grew shorter and my chest grew broader and higher, so that I could rub Oskar's collarbone with my chin without lowering my head. Again there was fever and Lysol. And I heard Maria whispering words that floated in Lysol: "If only he don't grow crooked! If only he don't get a hump! If only he don't get water on the brain!"

Mr. Fajngold comforted Maria, telling her about people he had known who in spite of humps and dropsy had made a success of life. There was a certain Roman Frydrych, for instance, who had gone to the Argentine with his hump and started a sewing-machine business which got to be big-time and very well known.

The story of Frydrych the successful hunchback failed to comfort Maria but filled the narrator, Mr. Fajngold, with such enthusiasm that he resolved to give our grocery store a new face. In the middle of May, shortly after the war ended, new merchandise made its appearance. He began to sell sewing machines and spare parts for sewing machines, but to facilitate the transition, he still carried groceries for a while. What blissful times. Hardly anything was paid for in cash. Everything was done by barter. Synthetic honey, oat flakes, sugar, flour, margarine, and the last little bags of Dr. Oetker's Baking Powder were transformed into bicycles; the bicycles and bicycle spare parts into electric motors, and these into tools; the tools became furs, and as though by magic Mr. Fajngold turned the furs into sewing machines. Little Kurt made himself useful at this game of swap and swap again; he brought in customers, negotiated deals, and caught on much more quickly than Maria to the new line. It was almost as in Matzerath's days. Maria stood behind the counter, waiting on those of the old customers who were still in town, and trying hard, with her painful Polish, to find out what the new customers wanted. Kurt was a born linguist. Kurt was all over the place. Mr. Fajngold could rely on him. Though not quite five, he became an expert on sewing machines. Amid the hundred-odd middling to miserable models displayed on the black market in Bahnhofstrasse he detected the first-class Singers and Pfaffs at a glance, and Mr. Fajngold valued his knowledge.

At the end of May my grandmother Anna Koljaiczek came to see us and flung herself panting on the sofa. She had walked all the way from Bissau by way of Brenntau. Mr. Fajngold was full of praise for little Kurt and had plenty of good things to say about Maria as well. He told my grandmother the story of my illness at great length, coming back over and over again to the utility of his disinfectant. For Oskar, too, he had words of praise: I had been so quiet and well-behaved and during the whole of my illness hadn't cried once.

My grandmother wanted kerosene because there was no light in Bissau. Mr Fajngold told her about his experience with kerosene in the camp at Treblinka and about his multifarious duties as camp disinfector. He told Maria to fill two quart bottles with kerosene, added a package of synthetic honey and a whole assortment of disinfectants, and listened, nodding absently, as my grandmother listed all the many things that had burned down in Bissau and Bissau Quarry during the fighting. She also described the damage in Viereck, which had been renamed Firoga as in times gone by. And Bissau had again been given its pre-war name of Bysew. As for Ehlers, who had been local peasant leader in Ramkau and very competent, who had married her brother's son's wife, Hedwig, widow of Jan who had lost his life at the post office, the farm laborers had hanged him outside his office. They had come very close to hanging Hedwig for marrying Ehlers when she was the widow of a Polish hero, and also because Stephan had been a lieutenant and Marga had belonged to the League of German Girls.

"Well," said my grandmother, "they couldn't hurt Stephan no more, because he was killed up there in the Arctic. They wanted to take Marga away and put her in a camp. But then Vincent opened his mouth and spoke like he never spoke in all his life. And now Hedwig and Marga are both with us, helping in the fields. But Vincent was knocked out from talking so much and I think maybe he won't last long. As for old Grandma, I've had my share of trouble too; pains all over, in the heart and in the head where some numbskull hit me 'cause he thought it was the right thing to do."

Such were the lamentations of Anna Koljaiczek; holding her head and stroking mine as it grew, she thought things over and came up with the following wisdom: "Yes, Oskar, that's how it is with the Kashubes. They always get hit on the head. You'll be going away where things are better, only Grandma will be left. The Kashubes are no good at moving. Their business is to stay where they are and hold out their heads for everybody else to hit, because we're not real Poles and we're not real Germans, and if you're a Kashube, you're not good enough for the Germans or the Polacks. They want everything full measure."

My grandmother gave a loud laugh, hid the bottle of kerosene, the synthetic honey, and the disinfectant under her four skirts, which despite the most violent military, political, and historical upheavals had never lost their potato color.

She was about to go, but Mr. Fajngold asked her to wait a few moments, he wanted her to meet his wife Luba and the rest of his family. When Luba failed to appear, my grandmother said: "Never mind. I'm always calling people, too: Agnes, I say, Agnes, my daughter, come and help your old mother wring out the wash. And she don't come no more than your Luba. And Vincent, my brother, in the black of night he stands outside the door though he's a sick man and shouldn't and wakes up the neighbors hollering for his son Jan that was in the post office and got killed."

She was already in the doorway, putting on her kerchief, when I called from my bed: "Babka, Babka," which means Grandma, Grandma. She turned around and lifted her skirt a little as though to let me in and take me with her. But then she probably remembered that the haven and refuge was already occupied by kerosene bottles, honey, and disinfectant, and went off without me, without Oskar.

At the beginning of June the first convoys left for the West. Maria said nothing, but I could see that she was taking leave of the furniture, the shop, the house, the tombs on both sides of Hindenburg-Allee, and the mound in Saspe Cemetery.

Sometimes in the evening, before going down in the cellar with Kurt, she would sit beside my bed, at my poor mama's piano, playing the harmonica with her left hand and trying to accompany her little tune on the piano with one finger of her right hand.

The music made Mr. Fajngold unhappy; he asked Maria to stop, and then, when she had taken the harmonica out of her mouth and was going to close the piano, he would ask her to play a little more.

Then he proposed to her. Oskar had seen it coming. Mr. Fajngold called his Luba less and less often, and one summer evening full of humming and buzzing, when he was sure she was gone, he proposed to Maria. He promised to take care of her and both children, Oskar, the sick one, too. He offered her the flat and a partnership in the business.

Maria was twenty-two. The beauty of her younger days, which seemed to have been pieced together by chance, had taken on firmer, perhaps harder contours. The last few months before and after the end of the war had uncurled the permanents Matzerath had paid for. She no longer wore pigtails as in my day; now her hair hung long over her shoulders, giving her the look of a rather solemn, perhaps somewhat soured young girl— and this young girl said no, rejected Mr. Fajngold's proposal. Maria stood on the carpet that had once been ours with Kurt to one side of her and pointed her thumb at the tile stove. Mr Fajngold and Oskar heard her say: "It can't be done. Here the whole place is washed up and finished. We're going to the Rhineland where my sister Guste is. She's married to a headwaiter. His name is Köster and he'll take us in temporarily, all three of us."

Next day she filled out the application and three days later we had our papers. After that Mr. Fajngold was silent. He closed the shop. While Maria was packing, he sat in the dark shop on the counter, beside the scale; he hadn't even the heart to spoon out honey. But when Maria came to say good-by, he slid off the counter, got out the bicycle and trailer, and said he would take us to the station.

Oskar and the baggage—we were allowed fifty pounds each—were loaded on the two-wheeled rubber-tired trailer. Mr. Fajngold pushed the bicycle. Maria held Kurt by the hand and took a last look back as we turned left into Elsenstrasse. I couldn't look back at Labesweg because it hurt me to twist my neck. Oskar's head remained motionless on his shoulders, and it was only with my eyes, which had preserved their mobility, that I took leave of Marienstrasse, Striessbach, Kleinhammer-Park, the underpass, which still oozed as disgustingly as ever, Bahnhof-strasse, my undestroyed Church of the Sacred Heart, and the Langfuhr station—Langfuhr was now called Wrzeszcz, but who can pronounce that?

We had to wait. When a train finally rolled in, it was a freight. There were hordes of people and far too many children. The baggage was inspected and weighed. Soldiers threw a bale of straw into each car. There was no music, but at least it wasn't raining. The weather was partly cloudy with an easterly wind.

We found a place in the fourth car from the end. Mr. Fajngold stood below us on the tracks, his thin, reddish hair blowing in the wind. When the locomotive revealed its arrival with a jolt, he stepped closer, handed Maria three packages of margarine and two of synthetic honey, and when orders in Polish, screaming and wailing, announced that the train was pulling out, he added a package of disinfectant to our provisions—Lysol is more important than life. Then we began to move, leaving Mr. Fajngold behind. He stood there with his reddish hair blowing in the wind, becoming smaller and smaller, as is fitting and proper when trains leave, until nothing was left of him but a waving arm, and soon he had ceased to exist altogether.

Growth in a Freight Car

Those aches and pains are still with me. They have thrown me back on my pillows. I have taken to grinding my teeth to keep from hearing the grinding in my bones and joints. I look at my ten fingers and have to admit that they are swollen. A last attempt to beat my drum has proved to me that Oskar's fingers are not only somewhat swollen but temporarily no good for drumming; they just can't hold the drumsticks.

My fountain pen also refuses my guidance. I shall have to ask Bruno for cold compresses. Then, when my hands, feet, and knees are all wrapped and cool, when Bruno has put a cool cloth on my forehead too, I shall give him paper and pencil; for I don't like lending him my fountain pen. Will Bruno be willing and able to listen properly? Will his record do justice to that journey in a freight car, begun on June 12, 1945? Bruno is sitting at the table under the picture of the anemones. Now he turns his head, showing me the side of it that calls itself face, while with the

328

eyes of a mythical animal he looks past me, one eye to the left, the other to the right of me. He lays the pencil slantwise over his thin, puckered lips. That is his way of impersonating someone who is waiting. But even admitting that he is really waiting for me to speak, waiting for the signal to begin taking down my story, his thoughts are busy with his knotted fantasies. He will knot strings together, whereas Oskar's task will be to disentangle my knotted history with the help of many words. Now Bruno writes:

I, Bruno Münsterberg, of Altena in Sauerland, unmarried and childless, am a male nurse in the private pavilion of the local mental hospital. Mr. Matzerath, who has been here for over a year, is my patient. I have other patients, of whom I cannot speak here. Mr. Matzerath is my most harmless patient. He never gets so wild that I have to call in other nurses. Today, in order to rest his overstrained fingers, he has asked me to write for him and to stop making my knotted figures. However, I have put a supply of string in my pocket and as he tells his story, I shall start on the lower limbs of a figure which, in accordance with Mr. Matzerath's story, I shall call "Refugee from the East." This will not be the first figure I have derived from my patient's stories. So far, I have done his grandmother, whom I call "Potato in Four Skirts," and his grandfather, the raftsman, whose string image I have called, rather pretentiously perhaps, "Columbus"; my strings have turned his poor mama into "The Beautiful Fish Eater," and his two fathers, Matzerath and Jan Bronski, have become "The Two Skat Players." I have also rendered the scarry back of his friend Herbert Truczinski; this piece is entitled "Rough Going." In addition, I have drawn inspiration from such sites and edifices as the Polish Post Office, the Stockturm, the Stadt-Theater, Arsenal Passage, the Maritime Museum, the cellar of Greff's vegetable store, Pestalozzi School, the Brösen bathing establishment, the Church of the Sacred Heart, the Four Seasons Café, the Baltic Chocolate Factory, the pillboxes of the Atlantic Wall, the Eiffel Tower, the Stettin Station in Berlin, Reims Cathedral, and neither last nor least the apartment house where Mr. Matzerath first saw the light of this world. The fences and tombstones of the cemeteries of Saspe and Brenntau suggested ornaments; with knot upon knot, I have made the Vistula and the Seine flow and set the waves of the Baltic and Atlantic dashing against coasts of pure disembodied string. I have shaped pieces of string into Kashubian potato fields and Norman pastures, and peopled the resulting landscape, which I call Europe for short, with such figures as post office defenders, grocers, people on rostrums, people at the foot of the rostrums, schoolboys with cornucopias, expiring museum attendants, juvenile delinquents preparing for Christmas, Polish cavalrymen at sunset, ants that make history, Theater at the Front, standing

men, disinfecting recumbent figures in Treblinka Camp. I have just begun
"Refugee from the East," which will probably develop into a group of
refugees from the East.

On June 12, 1945, at approximately 11 A.M., Mr. Matzerath pulled
out of Danzig, which at the time was already called Gdansk. He was
accompanied by the widow Maria Matzerath, whom my patient refers to
as his former mistress, and by Kurt Matzerath, my patient's alleged son.
In addition, he tells me, there were thirty-two other persons in the freight
car, including four Franciscan nuns, dressed as such, and a young girl
with a kerchief on her head, whom Mr. Oskar Matzerath claims to have
recognized as one Lucy Rennwand. In response to repeated questions, my
patient admits that this young lady's real name was Regina Raeck, but
he continues to speak of a nameless triangular fox face and call it by name,
namely Lucy. All this to the contrary notwithstanding, the young lady's
real name, as I here beg leave to state, was Miss Regina Raeck. She was
traveling with her parents, her grandparents, and a sick uncle who for
his part was accompanied by, in addition to his family, an acute cancer
of the stomach. The sick uncle was a big talker and lost no time in
identifying himself as a former Social Democrat.

As far as my patient can remember, the trip was uneventful as far as
Gdynia, which for four and a half years had borne the name of Gotenhafen.
Two women from Oliva, several children, and an elderly gentleman from
Langfuhr cried until the train had passed Zoppot, while the nuns resorted
to prayer.

In Gdynia the convoy stopped for five hours. Two women with six
children were shown into the car. The Social Democrat, as my patient
tells me, protested on the ground that he was sick and was entitled, as
a prewar Social Democrat, to special treatment. But when he refused to
sit down and hold his tongue, the Polish officer in charge of the convoy
slapped him in the face and gave him to understand in very fluent German
that he, the Polish officer, didn't know what "Social Democrat" meant.
During the war he had paid forced visits to various parts of Germany,
and never had the word Social Democrat been dropped in his hearing.
The Social Democrat with the stomach cancer never did get a chance to
explain the aims, nature, and history of the Social Democratic Party of
Germany to the Polish officer, for the Polish officer left the car, closed
the doors, and bolted them from outside.

I have forgotten to write that everyone was sitting or lying on straw.
When the train started to move late that afternoon, some of the women
screamed: "We're going back to Danzig." But they were mistaken. It
was just some sort of switching maneuver, and soon they were on their
way westward, headed for Stolp. The trip to Stolp, my informant tells
me, took four days; the train was constantly stopped in the open fields

by former partisans and young Polish gangsters. The youngsters opened the sliding doors, letting in a little fresh air, and each time removed part of the travelers' baggage along with the carbon dioxide. Whenever the young bandits occupied Mr. Matzerath's car, the four nuns rose to their feet and held up their crucifixes. The four crucifixes made a profound impression on the young fellows, who never failed to cross themselves before tossing the travelers' suitcases and knapsacks out on the roadbed.

When the Social Democrat held out a paper in which the Polish authorities in Danzig or Gdansk attested that he had been a dues-paying member of the Social Democratic Party from '31 to '37, the boys did not cross themselves, but knocked the paper out of his fingers and took his two suitcases and his wife's knapsack; the fine winter coat with the large checks, on which the Social Democrat had been lying, was also carried out into the fresh Pomeranian air.

Even so, Mr. Matzerath says the boys had seemed well disciplined and in general made a favorable impression on him. This he attributes to the influence of their leader, who despite his tender years, just sixteen of them, had cut quite a figure and reminded Mr. Matzerath, to his pleasure and sorrow, of Störtebeker, commander of the Dusters.

When this young man who so resembled Störtebeker was pulling the knapsack out of Mrs. Maria Matzerath's hands, Mr. Matzerath reached in at the last moment and removed the family photograph album, which was fortunately lying on top. The young bandit was on the point of getting angry. But when my patient opened the album and showed him a picture of his grandmother Koljaiczek, the boy dropped Maria's knapsack, thinking no doubt of his own grandmother. Raising two fingers to his pointed Polish cap in salute, he said *"Do widzenia, good-by,"* in the general direction of the Matzerath family, and taking someone else's suitcase instead of the Matzerath knapsack, left the car with his men.

Apart from a small amount of underwear, this knapsack, which remained in the family's possession thanks to the family photograph album, contained the books, bankbooks, and tax vouchers of the Matzerath grocery enterprise; and a ruby necklace, once the property of Mr. Matzerath's mother, which my patient had hidden in a package of disinfectant; the educational tome, consisting half of excerpts from Rasputin and half of selections from Goethe, also accompanied Mr. Matzerath on his journey westward.

My patient tells me that in the course of the trip he often perused the photo album and occasionally consulted the educational tome and that despite the violent pains in his joints he derived a good many happy though pensive hours from both volumes.

He has also asked me expressly to say that all the shaking and jolting, the switches and intersections, the constant vibration of the front axle on which he was lying, promoted his growth. He ceased to broaden and began to grow lengthwise. His joints, which were swollen but not inflamed, were given an opportunity to relax. Even his ears, nose, and sex organ, I am told, grew perceptibly, aided by the pounding of the rails. As long as the train was in motion, Mr. Matzerath seems to have felt no pain. Only when the train stopped for partisans or juvenile delinquents did he, so he tells me, suffer the shooting, pulling pains which he soothed as best he could with the photograph album.

He tells me that apart from the Polish Störtebeker several other youthful bandits and a middle-aged partisan took an interest in the family photos. The hardened warrior went so far as to sit down, light a cigarette, and leaf thoughtfully through the album, omitting not a single rectangle. He began with the likeness of grandfather Koljaiczek, followed the richly imaged rise of the family, and continued on to the snapshots of Mrs. Maria Matzerath with her one-, two-, three-, four-year-old son Kurt. My patient even saw him smile at some of the family idylls. The partisan took umbrage only at the unmistakable Party insignia on the lapels of the late Mr. Matzerath senior and of Mr. Ehlers, formerly a local peasant leader in Ramkau, who had married the widow of Jan Bronski, the post office defender. My patient tells me that he scratched out the offending insignia with his penknife before the eyes, and to the satisfaction, of his critic.

Mr. Matzerath has just seen fit to inform me that this partisan, unlike so many of them, was an authentic partisan. For—to quote the rest of my patient's lecture—there is no such thing as a part-time partisan. Real partisans are partisans always and as long as they live. They put fallen governments back in power and overthrow governments that have just been put in power with the help of partisans. Mr. Matzerath contended—and his thesis struck me as perfectly plausible—that among all those who go in for politics your incorrigible partisan, who undermines what he has just set up, is closest to the artist because he consistently rejects what he has just created.

My own situation is rather similar. No sooner have I applied the coat of plaster that gives my knot sculptures body than as likely as not I smash them with my fist. In this connection I am reminded of the commission my patient gave me some months ago. He wished me, with plain, ordinary string, to combine Rasputin, the Russian faith healer, and Goethe, the German poet prince, into a single figure which, moreover, should present a striking resemblance to himself. He even knows how many miles of string I have tied into knots, trying to create a valid synthesis of the two extremes. But like the partisan whom Mr. Matzerath so admires, I remain restless and dissatisfied; what I knot with my right hand, I undo with my left, what my left hand creates, my right fist shatters.

But Mr. Matzerath himself is unable to keep his story running in a straight line. Take those four nuns in the freight car. First he refers to them as Franciscans and the next time he calls them Vincentians. But what throws his story out of kilter more than anything else is this young lady with her two names and her one supposedly foxlike face. To be really conscientious, I should have to write two or more separate versions of his journey from East to West. But that kind of thing is not in my line. I prefer to concentrate on the Social Democrat, who managed with one name and, my patient assures me, one story, which he repeated incessantly until shortly before Stolp, to the effect that up to 1937 he had been a kind of partisan, risking his health and sacrificing his free time pasting posters, for he had been one of the few Social Democrats to put up posters even when it was raining.

He told the same story when shortly before Stolp the convoy was stopped for the nth time by a large gang of youthful bandits. Since there was hardly any baggage left, the visitors devoted their attentions to the travelers' clothing. But they took a very reasonable attitude, all they wanted was gentlemen's outer garments. To the Social Democrat, however, their procedure seemed the very opposite of reasonable; he was of the opinion, which he also stated, that a clever tailor could make several excellent suits from the yards and yards of material in which the nuns were draped. The Social Democrat, as he piously proclaimed, was an atheist. The young bandits made no pious proclamations, but their attachment to the only-saving Church could not be held in doubt. Despite the wood fiber that had gone into the material, the atheist's single-breasted suit interested them far more than the nuns' ample woolens. The atheist declined to remove his jacket, vest, and trousers; instead, he told them about his brief but brilliant career as a Social Democratic poster paster, and when he refused either to stop talking or to take off his suit, he received a kick in the stomach with a boot formerly the property of the German Army.

The Social Democrat vomited. His vomiting fit was long and violent and at the end he threw up blood. He vomited without regard for his clothing, and our young delinquents lost all interest in the suit though it could easily have been salvaged with a good dry cleaning. Turning their backs on men's clothing, they removed a light-blue imitation silk blouse from Mrs. Maria Matzerath and a Bavarian-style knitted jacket from the young lady whose name was not Lucy Rennwand but Regina Raeck. Then they closed the car doors, but not entirely, and the train started up, while the Social Democrat began to die.

A mile or two before Stolp the train was switched onto a siding where it remained all night—a clear, starry night but rather cool, my informant tells me, for the month of June.

The Social Democrat, who had set too much store by his single-

333

breasted suit, died that night. He died without dignity, loudly blaspheming God and summoning the working class to struggle. His last words, as in the movies, were "Long live freedom!" Then he expired in a fit of vomiting that filled the whole car with horror.

Afterwards, my patient says, there was no screaming or wailing. A long silence fell, broken only by the chattering teeth of Mrs. Maria Matzerath, who was cold without her blouse and had put all the clothing she had left on her son Kurt and Mr. Matzerath. Toward morning two nuns with stout hearts and strong stomachs took advantage of the open door and swept out quantities of wet straw, the feces of children and grownups, and the Social Democrat's vomit.

In Stolp the train was inspected by Polish officers. Hot soup and a beverage resembling coffee substitute were distributed. The corpse in Mr. Matzerath's car was confiscated because of the danger of contagion, laid on a plank, and carried away by some medical corps men. At the request of the nuns, a superior officer gave the members of the family time for a short prayer. They were also permitted to remove the dead man's shoes, socks, and suit. During the undressing scene—later the body was covered with cement bags—my patient watched the former Social Democrat's niece. Once again, though the young lady's name was Raeck, he was reminded, to his concurrent loathing and fascination, of Lucy Rennwand, whose image in knotted string I have entitled "The Sandwich Eater." The girl in the freight car, it is true, did not reach for a sandwich at the sight of her despoiled uncle, but she did participate in the pillage, appropriating the vest of her uncle's suit, putting it on in place of the knitted jacket that had been taken from her, and studying her not unbecoming new costume in a pocket mirror. And then Mr. Matzerath tells me—he he is still seized with panic when he thinks of it—she captured him in this same mirror and coolly, coldly, observed him out of eyes that were slits in a triangle.

The trip from Stolp to Stettin took two days. There were still plenty of involuntary stops and more visits from juvenile delinquents with tommy guns and paratrooper's knives. But though frequent, the visits became shorter and shorter, because there was very little left to take.

My patient claims that he grew three and a half to four inches between Danzig-Gdansk and Stettin. The stretching was mostly in the legs, there was little change in the chest or head. However, though my patient lay on his back throughout the trip, he could not prevent the emergence of a hump, rather high up and slightly displaced to leftward. Mr. Matzerath also admits that the pain increased after Stettin—meanwhile German railroad men had taken over—and that leafing through the family photograph album didn't help much. Though the screams that escaped him were loud and protracted, they caused no damage in the glass of any of the stations (Matzerath: "my voice had lost its power to demolish glass")

334

but they brought the four nuns scurrying over to his tick of pain, where they began to pray interminably.

A good half of his fellow travelers, including Miss Regina and the other members of the deceased Social Democrat's family, left the convoy at Schwerin. Mr. Matzerath was sorry. He had grown so accustomed to looking at the young girl. The sight of her had indeed become so necessary to him that when she had gone, he was seized with convulsions accompanied by high fever. According to Mrs. Maria Matzerath, he cried out desperately for a certain Lucy, called himself a mythical animal, a unicorn, and seems to have been afraid of falling, but at the same time eager to plunge, from a thirty-foot diving tower.

In Lüneburg Mr. Oskar Matzerath was taken to a hospital. There in his fever he made the acquaintance of several nurses but was soon transferred to the University Clinic in Hanover, where they managed to bring his fever down. For a time Mr. Matzerath saw little of Maria Matzerath and her son Kurt; it was only after she had found work as a cleaning woman in the clinic that she was able to visit him every day. Mrs. Matzerath was not lodged at the clinic; she and her little boy ended up in a refugee camp on the outskirts of the city and she spent at least three hours traveling back and forth, always in overcrowded trains, usually on the running board. Soon she was thoroughly exhausted, and the doctors, despite grave misgivings, granted permission to move the patient to Düsseldorf, where Mrs. Matzerath had a sister. This sister, whose name was Guste, was married to a headwaiter whom she had met during the war. The headwaiter was receiving free board and lodging in Russia at the time, and that enabled her to give Mrs. Matzerath one of her two and a half rooms. Mr. Matzerath was admitted to the Düsseldorf City Hospital.

The apartment was conveniently located. There were several streetcar lines going directly to the City Hospital.

There Mr. Matzerath lay from August, 1945, to May, 1946. For the last hour or more he has been telling me about several nurses at once. Their names are Sister Monica, Sister Helmtrud, Sister Walburga, Sister Ilse, and Sister Gertrude. He remembers all sorts of the most tedious chitchat and seems to be obsessed by nurses' uniforms and the details of their daily life. Not a word about the hospital food, which, if my memory does not mislead me, was unspeakable in those days, or about the freezing-cold rooms. All he can talk about is nurses, he goes on and on about this most boring of all social groups. It seems that Sister Ilse had told the head nurse, in the strictest confidence, whereupon the head nurse had had the gall to inspect the quarters of the nurses in training shortly after lunch hour; something or other had been stolen and some nurse from Dortmund—Gertrude I think he said—was accused unjustly. Then there were the young doctors who were always chasing after the nurses and they wanted just one thing—the nurses' cigarette stamps. On top of all this he sees fit to tell me about a laboratory assistant—not a nurse, for once —who was accused of giving herself an abortion, perhaps abetted by one of the interns. It is beyond me why my patient wastes his time and brains on such trivialities.

Mr. Matzerath has just asked me to describe him. It will be a pleasure. Now I shall be able to omit several dozen of his sententious and interminable stories about nurses.

My patient is four feet one inch tall. He carries his head, which would be too large even for a person of normal proportions, between his shoulders on an almost nonexistent neck. His eyes are blue, brilliant, alive with intelligence; occasionally they take on a dreamy, ecstatic, wide-eyed look. He has dense, slightly wavy, dark-brown hair. He likes to exhibit his arms, which are powerful in comparison with the rest of the body, and his hands, which, as he himself says, are beautiful. Especially when Mr. Matzerath plays the drum—which the management allows for three or at most four hours a day—his fingers move as though of their own accord and seem to belong to another, better proportioned body. Mr. Matzerath has made a fortune on phonograph records and they are still bringing in money. Interesting people come to see him on visiting days. Even before his trial, before he was brought here to us, his name was familiar to me, for Mr. Oskar Matzerath is a well-known performer. I personally believe him to be innocent and am not sure whether he will stay here with us or be let out and resume his successful career. Now he wants me to measure him, though I did so only two days ago.

Without bothering to read over what Bruno my keeper has written, I, Oskar, take up my pen again.

Bruno has just measured me with his folding rule. He has left the rule lying alongside me, and hurried out of the room, loudly proclaiming the result. He even dropped the knot creation he was secretly working on while I was telling him my story. I presume that he has gone to get Dr. (Miss) Hornstetter.

But before she comes in and confirms Bruno's measurements, Oskar will tell you what it is all about: In the three days during which I told my keeper the story of my growth, I grew a whole inch.

And so, as of today, Oskar measures four feet two. He will now relate how he fared after the war when in relatively good health, despite my deformity, writing with difficulty, but fluent at talking and reading, I was discharged from the Düsseldorf City Hospital in the hope that I might embark—as people discharged from hospitals are always expected to do—on a new and adult life.

Book
Three

Firestones and Tombstones

Fat, sleepy, good-natured. There had been no need for Guste Truczinski to change in becoming Guste Köster, especially as her association with Köster had been so very limited: they had been engaged for two weeks when he was shipped out to the Arctic Front; when he came home on furlough, they had married and spent a few nights together, most of them in air-raid shelters. Though there was no news of Köster's whereabouts after the army in Courland surrendered, Guste, when asked about her husband, would reply with assurance, at the same time gesturing toward the kitchen: "Oh, he's a prisoner in Russia. There's going to be some changes around here when he gets back."

The changes she had in mind involved Maria and more particularly little Kurt. Discharged from the hospital, I said good-by to the nurses, promising to come and see them as soon as I had the chance. Then I took the streetcar to Bilk, where the two sisters and my son Kurt were living. The apartment house stopped at the fourth floor; the rest, including the roof, had been destroyed by fire. Entering the third-floor flat, I found Maria and my son busily engaged in black market operations. Kurt, who was six years old, counted on his fingers. Even in the black market Maria remained loyal to her Matzerath. She dealt in synthetic honey. She spooned the stuff from unlabeled pails and weighed out quarter-pounds on the kitchen scales. I had barely time to get my bearings in the cramped flat before she put me to work doing up packages.

Kurt was sitting behind his counter—a soap box. He looked in the direction of his homecoming father, but his chilly gray eyes seemed to be concerned with something of interest that could be seen through me. Before him on his counter lay a sheet of paper on which he was adding up imaginary columns of figures. After just six weeks of schooling in overcrowded, poorly heated classrooms, he had the look of a very busy self-made man.

Guste Köster was drinking coffee, real coffee, as Oskar noticed when she presented me with a cupful. While I busied myself with the honey, she observed my hump with curiosity and a look suggesting commiseration with her sister Maria. It was all she could do to sit still and not caress my hump, for like all women she was convinced that it's good luck to touch, pat, or stroke a hump. To Guste good luck meant the return of Köster, who would change everything. She restrained herself, patted her coffee cup instead, and heaved a sigh, followed by the litany that I was to hear several times a day for several months: "When Köster gets home there's going to be changes around here before you can say Jakob Schmidt. You can bet your bottom taler on that."

Guste frowned on black market activities but was not averse to drinking the real coffee obtained for synthetic honey. When customers came, she left the living room and padded away into the kitchen, where she raised an ostentatious clatter in protest.

There was no shortage of customers. At nine o'clock, right after breakfast, the bell began to ring: short, long, short. At 10 P.M. Guste disconnected the bell, often amid protests from Kurt, whose schooling made distressing inroads on his business day.

"Synthetic honey?" said the visitor.

Maria nodded gently and asked: "A quarter or a half a pound?" But there were other customers who didn't want honey. They would say: "Flints?" Whereupon Kurt, who had school alternately in the morning and afternoon, would emerge from his columns of figures, grope about under his sweater for a little cloth bag, and project his challenging child-like voice into the living room air: "Would you like three or four? My advice is to take five. They'll be up to twenty-four before you know it. Last week they were eighteen, and this morning I had to ask twenty. If you'd come two hours ago, right after school, I could have let you have them for twenty-one."

In a territory six blocks long and four blocks wide, Kurt was the only dealer in flints. He had a "source"; he never told anybody who or what it was, though he never stopped talking about it. Even before going to sleep at night, he would say, instead of his prayers: "I've got a source."

As his father, I claimed that I was entitled to know my son's source. He didn't even trouble to inject a note of mystery into his voice when he said "I've got a source." If his tone conveyed anything at all, it was pride and self-assurance. "Where did you get those flints?" I roared at him. "You will tell me this minute."

Maria's standing remark in that period, whenever I tried to get at the source, was: "Leave the kid alone. In the first place, it's none of your business; in the second place, if anybody's going to ask questions, it's me; in the third place, don't take on like you was his father. A few months ago, you couldn't even say boo."

When I went on too long about Kurt's source, Maria would smack her hand down on the honey pail and, indignant to the elbow, launch into a diatribe against me and also Guste, who sometimes supported

Oskar in his effort to penetrate the source: "A fine lot you are. Trying to ruin the kid's business. Biting the hand that feeds you. When I think of the ten calories Oskar gets for sick relief that he gobbles up in two days, it makes me good and sick, in fact, it makes me laugh."

Oskar can't deny it: I had a monstrous appetite in those days: it was thanks to Kurt and his source, which brought in more than the honey, that Oskar was able to regain his strength after the meager hospital fare.

Oskar was reduced to shamefaced silence; taking the ample pocket money with which little Kurt deigned to provide him, he would leave the flat in Bilk and stay away as much as he could, to avoid having his nose rubbed in his shame.

Today there are plenty of well-heeled critics of the economic miracle who proclaim nostalgically—and the less they remember about the situation in those days the more nostalgic they become—"Ah, those were the days, before the currency reform! Then people were still alive! Their empty stomachs didn't prevent them from waiting in line for theater tickets. And the wonderful parties we used to improvise with two pretzels and a bottle of potato schnaps, so much more fun than the fancy doings today, with all their caviar and champagne."

This is what you might call the romanticism of lost opportunities. I could lament with the best of them if I chose, for in the days when Kurt's "source" was gushing, I developed a sudden interest in adult education and imbibed a certain amount of culture almost free of charge. I took courses at night school, became a steady visitor at the British Center, also known as "Die Brücke," discussed collective guilt with Catholics and Protestants alike, and shared the guilt feelings of all those who said to themselves: "Let's do our stint now; when things begin to look up we'll have it over with and our consciences will be all right."

Be that as it may, it is to night school that I owe what education I possess; I am the first to own that it doesn't amount to much, though there is something rather grandiose about the gaps in it. I began to read avidly, no longer satisfied, now that I had grown, with an oversimplified world evenly divided between Goethe and Rasputin or with the information that could be culled from the 1904-1916 issues of Köhler's *Naval Calendar*. I was always reading, though I don't remember what. I read in the toilet. I read while waiting in line for theater tickets, surrounded by young girls with Mozart pigtails, also reading. I read while Kurt sold his flints and while I myself was packaging synthetic honey. And when the current was shut off, I read by the light of tallow candles also obtained from Kurt's "source."

I am ashamed to say that what I read in those days did not become a part of me, but went in one eye and out the other. I have retained a few turns of phrase, an aphorism or two, and that is about all. And the

341

theater? A few names of actors: Hoppe, Peter Esser, Flickenschildt and her special way of pronouncing the letter r. I recall some drama students in experimental theaters, who tried to improve on Flickenschildt's r's; I remember Gründgens as Tasso, he wore the regulation black, but had discarded the laurel wreath called for in Goethe's text, alleging that the greenery burned his hair. And Gründgens again, still in black, as Hamlet. And la Flickenschildt claiming that Hamlet is fat. Yorick's skull made quite an impression on me because of the impressive remarks it drew from Gründgens. *Draussen vor der Tür* played in unheated theaters to spellbound audiences; to me Beckmann as the man with the broken glasses was Köster, Guste's husband, who would change everything on his return home and stop up my son Kurt's source forever.

Now all that is behind me; today I know that a postwar binge is only a binge and therefore followed by a hangover, and one symptom of this hangover is that the deeds and misdeeds which only yesterday were fresh and alive and real, are reduced to history and explained as such. Today I am able once more to appreciate the instruction Gretchen Scheffler meted out to me amid her travel souvenirs and her knitting: not too much Rasputin, Goethe in moderation, Keyser's *History of the City of Danzig,* the armament of a battleship that has long been lying on the bottom of the sea, the speed (in knots) of all the Japanese torpedo boats that took part in the battle of Tsushima, not to mention Belisarius and Narses, Totila and Teja, as represented in Felix Dahn's *A Struggle for Rome.*

In the spring of '47 I abandoned night school, the British Center, and Pastor Niemöller, and took my leave, from the second balcony, of Gustaf Gründgens, who still figured on the program as Hamlet.

Two years had not passed since at Matzerath's grave I had resolved to grow, and already I had lost interest in grown-up life. I dreamed of my lost three-year-old dimensions. I wanted to be three feet tall again, smaller than my friend Bebra, smaller than the dear departed Roswitha. Oskar missed his drum. I took long walks which often ended up at the City Hospital. In any event I was expected to call once a month on Professor Irdell, who regarded Oskar as an interesting case. At regular intervals Oskar visited the nurses he had known during his illness, and even when they had no time for him, their hurrying white uniforms, betokening recovery or death, gave him a feeling bordering on happiness.

The nurses liked me, they played childish, but not malicious, games with my hump, gave me good things to eat, and told me interminable, pleasantly soporific stories about the complexities of hospital life. I listened, gave advice, and was able even to arbitrate some of their little disputes, for I enjoyed the sympathy of the head nurse. On these days Oskar was the only man among twenty or more young or not so young girls camouflaged beneath nurse's uniforms—and in some strange way he was an object of desire.

As Bruno has already said, Oskar has lovely, expressive hands, fine wavy hair, and those winning, ever so blue, Bronski eyes. Possibly the attractiveness of my hands, eyes, and hair was accentuated by my hump and the shocking proximity of my chin to my narrow, vaulted chest. It was not infrequent, in any case, that as I was sitting in the nurses' room, they would take hold of my hands, play with my fingers, fondle my hair, and say to one another in leaving: "When you look into his eyes, you forget all the rest."

Thus I was superior to my hump and I might well have attempted a conquest in the hospital if I had still had my drum, if I had been able to count on my reliable drummer's potency of former years. As it was, I felt unsure of myself and my physical reactions and I would leave the hospital after these affectionate hors d'oeuvres, fearing to reach out for the main course. I would take the air, go for a walk in the garden or around the wire fence which, with its close-meshed regularity, gave me a peace of mind that I expressed by whistling. I would watch the streetcars headed for Wersten and Benrath or stroll along the park promenade beside the bicycle path, smiling in pleasant boredom at the efforts of nature, which was playing spring and, following the program to a T, making buds burst open almost audibly.

Across the way, our Sunday painter who art in heaven, was each day adding a little more green fresh from the tube to the trees of Wersten Cemetery. Cemeteries have always had a lure for me. They are well kept, free from ambiguity, logical, virile, and alive. In cemeteries you can summon up courage and arrive at decisions, in cemeteries life takes on distinct contours—I am not referring to the borders of the graves—and if you will, a meaning.

Along the northern wall of the cemetery ran a street called Bittweg, occupied by no less than six manufacturers of tombstones. There were two large establishments: C. Schnoog and Julius Wöbel. The rest were small artisans: R. Haydenreich, J. Bois, Kühn & Müller, and P. Korneff. Sheds and workshops with large signs hanging from the roofs, some freshly painted, others barely legible, indicating the name of the firm and the nature of its wares: Tombstones—Mortuary Monuments and Borders—Natural and Artificial Stone—Mortuary Art. Korneff's sign, in such disrepair that I had to spell it out, said: P. Korneff, Stonecutter and Mortuary Sculptor.

Between the workshop and the wire fence enclosing the yard stood neat rows of monuments on simple and double pedestals; they were of different sizes, calculated to adorn anything from a solitary one-man grave to a family vault with room for four. Just behind the fence, reflecting its diamond-shaped pattern in sunny weather, an assortment of tombstones: shell-lime cushions for modest pocketbooks, polished diorite slabs with unpolished palms, standard thirty-inch children's tombstones of slightly

343

cloudy Silesian marble, surrounded by fluting and adorned toward the top with sunken reliefs, most of which represented broken roses. Next came a row of plain, red sandstone slabs taken from the façades of bombed-out banks and department stores. At the center the prize piece was displayed: a monument of bluish-white Tyrolian marble with three pedestals, two sidepieces, and a large richly carved slab featuring what is known in the trade as a corpus. This corpus was beardless; his distinguishing features were: head and knees turned leftward, a crown of thorns, three nails, open hands, and stylized bleeding from the wound in his flank, five drops, I seem to recall.

This was far from being the only mortuary monument in Bittweg showing a corpus turned leftward—sometimes there were as many as ten of them getting ready for the spring season. But Korneff's Jesus Christ had made a particular impression on me, because, well, because he showed a marked resemblance to my Athlete on the Cross, flexing his muscles and expanding his chest over the main altar of the Church of the Sacred Heart. I spent hours by that fence, scraping a stick along the close wire meshes, thinking of everything and nothing and toying perhaps with a wish or two. For a long while Korneff remained in hiding. A stovepipe full of knees and elbows emerged from one of the windows of the shop and jutted over the flat roof. You couldn't get very good coal in those days. Yellow smoke arose in fitful puffs and fell back on the roofing paper. More smoke seeped from the windows, slid down the drainpipe, and lost itself amid tombstones in various stages of completion. Outside the sliding door of the workshop stood a three-wheeled truck under several tarpaulins, as though camouflaged against attack from low-flying planes. Sounds from the shop—wood striking iron, iron chipping stone—bore witness to the stonecutter at work.

In May the canvas was gone from over the three-wheeler, the sliding door stood open. I could see inside the workshop gray on gray, stones on the cutting bench, a polishing machine that looked like a gallows, shelves full of plaster models, and at last Korneff. He walked with a stoop and permanently bent knees, his head thrust rigidly forward. The back of his neck was crisscrossed with grimy, once pink adhesive tape. He stepped out of the shop with a rake and, assuming no doubt that spring had come, began to clean up the grounds. He raked carefully between the tombstones, leaving tracks in the gravel, occasionally stopping to remove dead leaves from one of the monuments. As he was raking between the shell-lime cushions and diorite slabs near the fence, I was suddenly surprised by his voice: "What's the matter, boy; don't they want you at home no more?"

"I'm very fond of your tombstones," I said. "Mustn't say that out loud," he replied. "Bad luck. Talk like that and they'll be putting one on top of you."

Only then did he move his stiff neck, catching me, or rather my hump, in a sidelong glance: "Say, what they done to you? Don't it get in your way for sleeping?"

I let him have his laugh. Then I explained that a hump was not necessarily a drawback, that it didn't get me down, that, believe it or not, some women and even young girls had a special weakness for humps and were only too glad to adapt themselves to the special proportions and possibilities of a hunchback.

Leaning his chin on his rake handle, Korneff pondered: "Maybe so. I've heard tell of it."

He went on to tell me about his days in the basalt quarries when he had had a woman with a wooden leg that could be unbuckled. This, to his way of thinking, was something like my hump, even if my gas meter, as he insisted on calling it, was not removable. The stonecutter's memory was long, broad, and thorough. I waited patiently for him to finish, for his woman to buckle her leg on again. Then I asked if I could visit his shop.

Korneff opened the gate in the fence and pointed his rake in invitation at the open sliding door. Gravel crunched beneath my feet and a moment later I was engulfed in the smell of sulphur, lime, and dampness.

Heavy, pear-shaped wooden mallets with fibrous hollows showing frequent repetition of the same expert blow, rested on roughly hewn slabs of stone. Stippling irons for the embossing mallet, stippling tools with round heads, freshly reforged and still blue from tempering; long, springy etching-chisels and bull chisels for marble, polishing paste drying on four-cornered sawing trestles, and, on wooden rollers, ready to move, an up-ended, polished travertine slab, fatty, yellow, cheesy, porous for a double grave.

"That's a bush hammer, that's a spoon chisel, that's a groove cutter, and that," Korneff lifted a board a hand's breadth wide and three feet long and examined the edge closely, "that's a straight edge; I use it to whack the apprentices with if they don't keep moving."

My question was not one of pure politeness: "You employ apprentices then?"

Korneff told me his troubles: "I could keep five boys busy. But you can't get none. All the young pantywaists wants to learn nowadays is how to turn a crooked penny on the black market." Like me, the stonecutter was opposed to the dark machinations that prevented so many a young hopeful from learning a useful trade. While Korneff was showing me carborundum stones ranging from coarse to fine and their effect on a Solnhof slab, I was playing with a little idea. Pumice stones, chocolate-brown sandstone for rough polishing, tripoli for high polish, and there was my little idea popping up again, but it had taken on a higher, shinier

345

polish. Korneff showed me models of lettering, spoke of raised and sunken inscriptions, and told me about gilding; that it wasn't nearly so expensive as generally supposed, that you could gild a horse and rider with one genuine old taler. This made me think of the equestrian monument of Kaiser Wilhelm on the Heumarkt in Danzig, which the Polish authorities would maybe decide to gild, but neither horse nor rider could make me give up my little idea, which seemed to become shinier and shinier. I continued to toy with it, and went so far as to formulate it while Korneff was explaining the workings of a three-legged stippling machine for sculpture and tapping his knuckles on some plaster models of Christ crucified: "So you're thinking of taking on an apprentice?" This was my first formulation. My little idea gained ground. What I actually said was: "I gather you're looking for an apprentice, or am I mistaken?" Korneff rubbed the adhesive tape covering the boils on his neck. "I mean, would you consider taking me on as an apprentice, other things being equal?" I had put it awkwardly and corrected myself at once: "Don't underestimate my strength, my dear Mr. Korneff. It's just my legs that are underdeveloped. There's plenty of strength in my arms." Delighted with my resolution and determined to go the whole hog, I bared my left arm and asked Korneff to feel my muscle, which was small but tough. When he made no move to feel it, I picked up an embossing chisel that was lying on some shell lime and made the metal bob up and down on my biceps. I continued my demonstration until Korneff turned on the polishing machine; a carborundum disk raced screeching over the travertine pedestal of a slab for a double grave. After a while Korneff, his eyes glued to the machine, shouted above the noise: "Sleep on it, boy. It's hard work. Come back and see me when you've thought it over. I'll take you on if you still feel like it."

Following Korneff's instructions, I slept a whole week on my little idea; I weighed and compared: on the one hand Kurt's fire-stones, on the other, Korneff's tombstones. Maria was always finding fault: "You're a drain on our budget, Oskar. Why don't you start something? Tea or cocoa maybe, or powdered milk." I started nothing; instead, I basked in the approval of Guste, who held up the absent Köster as the example to follow and praised me for my negative attitude toward the black market. What really troubled me was my son Kurt, who sat there writing columns of imaginary figures and overlooking me just as I had managed for years to overlook Matzerath.

We were having our lunch. Guste had disconnected the bell so our customers wouldn't find us eating scrambled eggs with bacon. Maria said: "You see, Oskar, we have nice things to eat. Why? Because we don't sit with our hands folded." Kurt heaved a sigh. Flints had dropped to eighteen. Guste ate heartily and in silence. I too. I savored the eggs, but even

346

while savoring, I felt miserable, perhaps because powdered eggs are not really so very appetizing, and suddenly, while biting into some gristle, experienced a yearning for happiness so intense that it made my cheeks tingle. Against all my better judgment, despite my ingrained skepticism, I wanted happiness. I wanted to be boundlessly happy. While the others were still eating, content with scrambled egg-powder, I left the table and went to the cupboard, as though it contained happiness. Rummaging through my compartment, I found, not happiness, but behind the photograph album, two packages of Mr. Fajngold's disinfectant. From one package I took—no, not happiness, but the thoroughly disinfected ruby necklace which had belonged to my mother, which Jan Bronski years ago, on a winter's night that smelled of more snow to come, had removed from a shopwindow with a circular hole cut out a short while before by Oskar, who in those days was still happy and able to cut glass with his voice. And with that necklace I left the flat. The necklace, I felt, would be my start, my jumping-off place. I took the car to the Central Station, thinking if all goes well . . . and throughout the lengthy negotiations, the same thoughts were with me. But the one-armed man and the Saxon, whom the other called the Assessor, were aware only of my article's material value, they failed to suspect what pathways of happiness they laid out before me when in return for my poor mama's necklace they gave me a real leather briefcase and twelve cartons of "Ami" cigarettes, Lucky Strikes.

That afternoon I was back in Bilk. I unloaded twelve cartons of Lucky Strikes, a fortune. I savored their amazement, thrust the mountain of blond tobacco at them, and said: this is for you. From now on I want you to leave me alone. It's not too much to ask for all these cigarettes. Aside from that I want a lunchbox with lunch in it, beginning tomorrow. I hope you will be happy with your honey and flints, I said without anger or resentment; as for me, I shall practice another art, my happiness will be written, or to put it more professionally, incised on tombstones.

Korneff took me on as his helper for a hundred reichsmarks a month. Not much money, but I worked hard for it just the same. It was clear by the end of the first week that I was not strong enough for the heavy work. I had been given the job of embossing a slab of Belgian granite, fresh from the quarry, for a family vault. In an hour's time I could scarcely hold the chisel and my mallet hand was numb. I also had to leave the blunt chiseling for Korneff, but thanks to my skill, I was able to take over the fine chiseling and scalloping, to square off the slabs, draw the lines for the four blows, and finish the dolomite borders. Sitting on an improvised stool, in my right hand the chisel and in my left, despite the objections of Korneff, who wished to make me right-handed, a pear-shaped wooden mallet or an iron bush hammer; metal rang on stone, the

347

sixty-four teeth of the bush hammer bit simultaneously into the stone to soften it. Here was happiness; not my drum, to be sure, just an ersatz, but there is also such a thing as ersatz happiness, perhaps happiness exists only as an ersatz, perhaps all happiness is an ersatz for happiness. Here I was, then, in a storehouse of ersatz happiness: Marble happiness, sandstone happiness. Hard happiness: Carrara. Cloudy, brittle happiness: alabaster. The happiness of chrome steel cutting into diorite. Dolomite: green happiness; gentle happiness: tufa. Colored happiness from the river Lahn. Porous happiness: basalt. Cold happiness from the Eifel. Like a volcano the happiness erupted and fell in a layer of dust, of grit between my teeth. I proved most talented at cutting inscriptions. I soon outdid Korneff and he entrusted me with all the ornamental work, the acanthus leaves, the broken roses for those who died in their tender years, such Christian symbols as XP or INRI, the flutes and beads, the eggs and anchors, chamfers and double chamfers. Oskar provided tombstones at all prices with all manner of ornaments. And when I had spent eight hours clouding a polished diorite slab with my breath and incising an inscription such as: Here rests in God my beloved husband—new line—Our beloved father, brother, and uncle—new line—Joseph Esser—new line—b. April 3, 1885, d. June 22, 1946—new line—Death is the Gateway to Life—I was conscious, as I reread the text, of an ersatz happiness, that is, I was pleasantly happy. In gratitude to Joseph Esser, who had passed away at the age of sixty-one, and to the little green clouds of diorite raised by my chisel, I took special care with the O's in Esser's epitaph; Oskar was particularly fond of the letter O, and there was always a fine regularity and endlessness about my O's, though they tended to be rather too large.

At the end of May I went to work as a stonecutter's helper; at the beginning of October Korneff developed two new boils, and it was time to set up the travertine slab for Hermann Webknecht and Else Webknecht, née Freytag, in the South Cemetery. Until then Korneff, doubting my strength, had refused to take me with him to the cemetery. When he had a tombstone to haul and set up, he usually borrowed one of Julius Wöbel's helpers, who was almost stone-deaf but otherwise a satisfactory worker. In retun Korneff would give Wöbel—who employed eight men—a hand in emergencies. Time and time again I had offered my services for work at the cemetery; cemeteries had retained their attraction for me, though at the time there were no decisions to be made. Fortunately, the beginning of October was the rush season at Wöbel's, he would need all his men until the frosts set in; Korneff had to fall back on me.

We put the travertine slab on hardwood rollers and rolled it up the ramp onto the back of the three-wheel truck. We set the pedestal beside it, cushioned the edges in empty paper sacks, loaded on tools, cement, sand, gravel, and the rollers and crates for unloading; I shut the tail gate, Korneff got in and started the motor. Then he stuck his head and boil-infested neck out of the cab and shouted: "Come along, boy. Get your lunchbox and pile in."

We drove slowly round the City Hospital. Outside the main gate white clouds of nurses, including one I knew, Sister Gertrude. I waved, she waved back. Lucky seeing her like that, I thought, I ought to ask her out one of these days, even if she has disappeared now that we've turned off toward the Rhine, invite her to do something with me, heading for Kappeshamm; the movies maybe, or to the theater to see Gründgens; ha, there it is, that yellow brick building, but it doesn't necessarily have to be the theater, smoke rising from the crematory over autumnal trees, a change of surroundings might do you good, Sister Gertrude. Another cemetery, other makers of tombstones: Beutz & Kranich, Pottgiesser, natural stones, Bohm, mortuary art, Gockeln, mortuary gardening and landscaping; questions at the entrance, it's not so easy to get into a cemetery: travertine for grave Number 79, Section Eight, Webknecht Hermann. Guard raises two fingers to his cap, leave lunchpails at the crematory to be warmed up, and in front of the ossuary stood Leo Schugger.

"The fellow with the white gloves," I ask Korneff, "isn't that Leo Schugger?"

Korneff, feeling his boils: "No, no, never heard of any Leo Schugger. That's Willem Slobber; he lives here."

How could I have contented myself with this information? I myself, after all, had been in Danzig and now I was in Düsseldorf, but I was still called Oskar: "In Danzig there was a fellow who hung around the cemeteries and looked exactly like this fellow. His name was Leo Schugger; before he was in the cemeteries he was called just plain Leo and he was a student at the seminary."

Korneff, left hand on his boils, right hand turning the wheel as we curved round the crematory: "I don't doubt it. I know a whole raft of them that look the same, that started out at the seminary, and now they're living in cemeteries under different names. This one here is Willem Slobber."

We drove past Willem Slobber. He waved a white glove at us, and I felt at home at the South Cemetery.

October, cemetery paths, the world losing its hair and teeth, which is just another way of saying that yellow leaves kept falling from the trees. Silence, sparrows, people out for a stroll, our three-wheeler chugging along on its way to Section Eight, which is still far off. Here and there old women with watering cans and grandchildren, sun on black Swedish granite, obelisks, truncated columns—symbolic or real war damage—a tarnished green angel behind a yew tree or something that looked like a yew tree. A woman shading her eyes with a marble hand, dazzled by her

349

own marble. Christ in stone sandals blessing the elm trees, and in Section Four another Christ, blessing a birch. Delicious daydreams on the path between Section Four and Section Five: the ocean, for instance. And this ocean casts, among other things, a corpse up on the beach. From the direction of the Zoppot beach promenade, violin music and the bashful beginnings of a fireworks display for the benefit of the war blind. Oskar, aged three, bends down over the flotsam, hoping it will prove to be Maria, or perhaps Sister Gertrude, whom I should ask out some time. But it is fair Lucy, pale Lucy, as I can see by the light of the fireworks, now hurrying toward their climax. Even if I couldn't see her face, I'd recognize her by the knitted Bavarian jacket she always has on when she is planning evil. When I take it off her, the wool is wet. Wet too is the jacket she has on under the jacket. Another little Bavarian jacket. And at the very end, as the fireworks die down and only the violins are left, I find, under wool on wool on wool, her heart wrapped in an athletic jersey marked League of German Girls, her heart, Lucy's heart, a little cold tombstone, on which is written: Here lies Oskar—Here lies Oskar—Here lies Oskar . . .

"Wake up, boy," Korneff interrupted my daydreams, washed ashore by the sea, illumined by the fireworks. We turned left and Section Eight, a new section without trees and with but few tombstones, lay flat and hungry before us. The graves were all alike, too fresh to be decorated, but the last five burials were easily recognizable: moldering mounds of brown wreaths with faded, rain-soaked ribbons.

We quickly found Number 79 at the beginning of the fourth row, adjoining Section Seven, which already had a more settled look with its sprinkling of young, quick-growing trees and its considerable number of tombstones, mostly of Silesian marble, arranged with a certain regularity. We approached 79 from the rear, unloaded the tools, cement, gravel, and the travertine slab with its slightly oily sheen. The three-wheeler gave a jump as we rolled the slab down on the crates waiting to receive it. Korneff removed the temporary cross, bearing the names of H. Webknecht and E. Webknecht, from the head end of the grave; I handed him the drill and he began to dig the two holes—depth five feet three inches, stipulated the cemetery regulations—for the concrete posts, while I brought water from Section Seven and mixed concrete. I had finished just as he, having dug five feet, said he had finished. I began to fill the holes with concrete while Korneff sat catching his breath on the travertine slab, reaching behind him and feeling his boils. "Coming to a head," he said. "I can always feel it when they're ready to bust." My mind just about vacant, I rammed in the concrete. Coming from Section Seven, a Protestant funeral crawled through Section Eight to Section Nine. As they were passing three rows away from us, Korneff slid off the travertine slab and, in compliance with the cemetery regulations, we took our caps off for the procession from the pastor to the next of kin. Immediately after the coffin came, all alone, a lopsided little woman in black. Those who followed her were all much bigger and solidly built.

"Gawd a'mighty," Korneff groaned. "I got a feeling they're going to pop before we can get that slab up."

Meanwhile the funeral party had reached Section Nine, where it arranged itself and poured forth the pastor's voice, rising and falling. The concrete had contracted, and we could have put the pedestal on its foundations. But Korneff lay prone on the travertine slab. He slipped his cap under his forehead and pulled down the collar of his jacket and shirt, baring his neck, while the biography of the dear departed drifted over to us from Section Nine. I had to climb up on the slab and sit on Korneff's back. I took in the situation at a glance; there were two of them almost on top of each other. A straggler with an enormous wreath hurried toward Section Nine and the sermon that was drawing slowly to an end. I tore off the plaster at one tug, wiped away the ichthyol salve with a beech leaf, and examined the two indurations. They were almost the same size, tar-brown shading into yellow. "Let us pray," said the breeze from Section Nine. Taking this as a sign, I turned my head to one side and simultaneously pressed and pulled the beech leaves under my thumbs. "Our Father . . ." Korneff croaked: "Don't squeeze, pull." I pulled. ". . . be Thy name." Korneff managed to join in the prayer: ". . . Thy Kingdom come." Pulling didn't help, so I squeezed again. "Will be done, on as it is in." A miracle that there was no explosion. And once again: "give us this day." And again Korneff caught up the thread: "trespasses and not into temptation . . ." There was more of it than I had expected. "Kingdom and the power and the glory." I squeezed out the last colorful remnant. ". . . and ever, amen." While I give a last squeeze, Korneff: "Amen," and a last pull: "Amen." As the folks over in Section Nine started on their condolences, Korneff said another amen. Still flat on the travertine slab, he heaved a sigh of relief: "Amen," to which he added: "Got some concrete left for under the pedestal?" Yes, I had. And he: "Amen."

I spread the last shovelfuls as a binder between the two posts. Then Korneff slid down off the polished inscription and Oskar showed him the autumnal beech leaves and the similarly colored contents of his boils. We put our caps back on, took hold of the stone, and, as the funeral in Section Nine dispersed, put up the slab that would mark the grave of Hermann Webknecht and Else Webknecht, née Freytag.

Fortuna North

In those days only people who left something valuable behind them on the surface of the earth could afford tombstones. It didn't have to be a diamond or a string of pearls. For five sacks of potatoes, you could get a

351

plain but good-sized stone of Grenzheim shell lime. A Belgian granite monument on three pedestals for a tomb for two brought us material for two three-piece suits. The tailor's widow, who gave us the goods, still had an apprentice working for her; she agreed to make the suits in return for a dolomite border.

One evening after work Korneff and I took the Number 10 car out to Stockum, where we dropped in on the Widow Lennert and had our measurements taken. Absurd as it may sound, Oskar was wearing an armored infantry uniform with alterations by Maria. The buttons on the jacket had been moved, but even so, what with my peculiar build, it was impossible to button them.

The suit which Anton the apprentice proceeded to make me was dark blue with a pin stripe and light gray lining; it was single-breasted, adequately but not misleadingly padded at the shoulders: it did not conceal my hump, but made the most of it, though without exaggeration; cuffs on the trousers but not ostentatiously wide. My model, in matters of dress, was still Master Bebra, hence no loops for a belt but buttons for suspenders; vest shiny in back, subdued in front, lined with old rose. The whole thing took five fittings.

While Anton was still working on Korneff's double-breasted and my single-breasted suit, a trafficker in shoes came to see us about a tombstone for his wife, who had been killed in an air raid in '43. First he tried to palm off ration coupons on us, but we demanded merchandise. For Silesian marble with fancy border plus installation Korneff obtained for himself one pair of dark-brown brown oxfords and one of carpet slippers and for me a pair of high, old-fashioned but wonderfully supple black shoes size five, which supported my weak ankles and, despite their archaic cut, had a pleasingly elegant look.

Laying a bundle of reichsmarks on the honey scales, I asked Maria to buy me two white shirts, one with pin stripes, and two ties, one light gray, the other dark brown. "The rest," I said, "is for Kurt and for you, my dear Maria, who never think of yourself but only of others."

While my giving spree lasted, I gave Guste an umbrella with a real bone handle and a deck of almost new skat cards, for she liked to lay out cards, but it pained her to borrow a deck from the neighbors every time she was curious to know when Köster would come home.

Maria carried out my commission without delay. With the money that was left—and there was quite a lot—she bought herself a raincoat and Kurt a school satchel of imitation leather, which was horrible to look upon but served its purpose for the time. To my shirts and ties she added three pairs of gray socks that I had forgotten to order.

When Korneff and Oskar called for our suits, we were embarrassed at our reflections in the glass, but quite impressed by one another. Korneff

352

hardly dared to turn his ravaged neck. His arms hung forward from drooping shoulders, and he tried to straighten his bent knees. My new clothes gave me a demonic, intellectual look, especially when I folded my arms over my chest, so adding to my upper horizontal dimension, and, supporting my weight on my feeble right leg, held out my left at a nonchalant angle. Smiling at Korneff and his astonishment, I approached the mirror, stood close enough to kiss my reverse image, but was satisfied to cloud myself over with my breath and said as though in passing: "Ho, there, Oskar. You still need a tie pin."

When, one Sunday afternoon a week later, I visited my nurses in the City Hospital and not without vanity displayed my spruce, brand-new self, I was already in possession of a silver tie pin with a pearl in it.

The dear girls were speechless when they saw me sitting in the nurses' room. That was late in the summer of '47. I crossed my arms over my chest in the traditional way and played with my leather gloves. For more than a year now I had been a stonecutter's helper, a master at fluting and grooving. I crossed my legs, careful not to disturb the crease in my trousers. Our good Guste took care of my suit as though it had been made to order for Köster, whose homecoming was going to change everything. Sister Helmtrud wanted to feel the material and of course I let her. In the spring of '47 we celebrated Kurt's seventh birthday with home-mixed egg liqueur and homemade sand cake—take two pounds of butter. Take this, take that—and I gave him a mouse-grey loden coat. Meanwhile Sister Gertrude had joined the other nurses and I passed around some candy which, in addition to twenty pounds of brown sugar, we had been given for a diorite slab. Little Kurt, it seemed to me, was much too fond of school. His teacher, who was young and attractive and in no way resembled la Spollenhauer, spoke well of him; she said he was bright, though a trifle solemn. How gay nurses can be when you bring them candy. When left alone for a moment with Sister Gertrude, I inquired about her free Sundays.

"Well, today for instance, I'm off at five. But," said Sister Gertrude with resignation, "there's nothing doing in town."

I said it was worth trying. Her reaction was: "What's the use?" Her idea was to have her sleep out. I made my invitation more definite, and when she still couldn't make up her mind, concluded mysteriously with the words: "A little gumption, Sister Gertrude. We're only young once. I know someone who's got plenty of cake stamps." I illustrated this last remark with a light, stylized tap on my breast pocket and offered her another piece of candy. Strange to say, I was rather terrified when this strapping Westphalian lass, who was not my type at all, said as though to the medicine chest: "All right, if you feel like it. Let's say six o'clock, but not here, how about Cornelius-Platz?"

353

As though I would ever have expected Sister Gertrude to meet me or anyone else in or near the hospital entrance! At six o'clock I was waiting for her under the Cornelius-Platz clock, which was still feeling the effects of the war and did not tell time. She was punctual, as I could tell by the not very expensive pocket watch I had bought some weeks before. I hardly recognized her; if I had seen her a little sooner, on her descent for instance from the streetcar some fifty paces away, before she could notice me, I should have slipped quietly away; for Sister Gertrude did not come as Sister Gertrude in white with a Red Cross pin, she came in miserably cut civilian dress as Miss Gertrude Wilms from Hamm or Dortmund or one of those towns between Dortmund and Hamm.

She didn't notice my dismay, but told me she had nearly been late because, just to be mean, the head nurse had given her something to do just before five.

"Well, Miss Gertrude, may I offer a few suggestions? Let's first relax a while in a pastry shop and after that whatever you say: we could go to the movies, it's too late to get theater tickets, or how about a little dance?"

"Oh, yes, let's go dancing," she cried with enthusiasm. It was too late when she realized, but then with ill-concealed distress, that despite my finery I was hardly cut out to be her dancing partner.

With a certain malice—why hadn't she come in the nurse's uniform I was so fond of?—I confirmed the arrangements; she, for lack of imagination, soon forgot her fright, and joined me in consuming—I one piece, she three—some cake that must have had cement in it. After I had paid with money and cake stamps, we boarded the Gerresheim car, for if Korneff were to be believed, there was a dance hall below Grafenberg.

We did the last bit of the way slowly on foot, for the car stopped before the uphill stretch. A September evening by the book. Gertrude's wooden sandals, obtainable without coupons, clattered like the mill on the floss. The sound made me feel gay. The people coming downhill turned around to look at us. Miss Gertrude was embarrassed. I was used to it and took no notice. After all it was my cake stamps that had fed her three slices of cement cake at Kürten's Pastry Shop.

The dance hall was called Wedig's and subtitled The Lions' Den. There was tittering before we left the ticket window, and heads turned as we entered. Sister Gertrude was ill at ease in her civilian clothing and would have fallen over a folding chair if a waiter and I hadn't held her up. The waiter showed us a table near the dance floor, and I ordered two iced drinks, adding in an undertone audible only to the waiter: "But toss in a couple of shots, if you please."

The Lions' Den consisted chiefly of a large room that must once have been a riding academy. The rafters and bomb-scarred ceiling had been decorated with streamers and garlands from last year's carnival. Muted

354

colored lights swung in circles, casting reflections on the resolutely slicked hair of the young black marketeers, some of them fashionably dressed, and the taffeta blouses of the girls, who all seemed to know each other.

When the drinks were served, I bought ten American cigarettes from the waiter, offered Sister Gertrude one and gave another to the waiter, who stored it behind his ear. After giving my companion a light, I produced Oskar's amber cigarette holder and smoked half a Camel. The tables around us quieted down. Sister Gertrude dared to look up. When I crushed out my enormous Camel butt in the ash tray and left it there, Sister Gertrude picked it up with a practiced hand and tucked it away in the side pocket of her oilskin handbag.

"For my fiancé in Dortmund," she said. "He smokes like mad."

I was glad I wasn't her fiancé and glad too that the music had started up.

The five-piece band played "Don't Fence Me In." Males in crêpe soles dashed across the dance floor without colliding and appropriated young ladies who as they arose gave their bags to girl friends for safe-keeping.

A few of the couples danced with a smoothness born of long practice. Quantities of gum were being ruminated; now and then a group of young black marketeers would stop dancing for a few measures to confer in Rhenish leavened with American slang while their partners, held vaguely by the arm, bobbed and joggled impatiently. Small objects exchanged hands: a true black marketeer never takes time off.

We sat the first dance out and the next foxtrot as well. Oskar took an occasional look at the men's feet. When the band struck up "Rosa-mund," he asked a bewildered Sister Gertrude to dance.

Remembering Jan Bronski's choreographic arts, I, who was almost two heads shorter than Sister Gertrude, decided to try a *schieber*; I was well aware of the grotesque note we struck and determined to accentuate it. With resignation she let herself be led. I held her firmly by the rear end, thirty percent wool content; cheek to blouse, I pushed her, every pound of her, backward and followed in her footsteps. Sweeping away obstacles with our unbending side arms, we crossed the dance floor from corner to corner. It went better than I had dared to hope. I risked a variation or two. My cheek still clinging to her blouse, my hand still supported by her hips, I danced around her without relinquishing the classical posture of the *schieber*, whose purpose it is to suggest that she is about to fall backward and that he is about to fall on top of her, though because they are such good dancers, they never actually fall.

Soon we had an audience. I heard cries such as: "Didn't I tell you it was Jimmy? Hey, take a look at Jimmy. Hello, Jimmy. Come on, Jimmy. Let's go, Jimmy."

Unfortunately, I couldn't see Sister Gertrude's face and could only

355

hope that she was taking the applause in her stride as a well-meant homage. A nurse, after all, should be used to embarrassing flattery.

When we sat down, those around us were still clapping. The five-piece band did a flourish and another and another; the percussion man outdid himself. There were cries of "Jimmy!" And "Say, did you see those two?" At this point Sister Gertrude arose, mumbled something about going to the ladies' room, took her handbag containing the cigarette butt for her fiancé in Dortmund, and blushing scarlet, shoved her way, colliding with everything in her path, between chairs and tables, toward the ladies' room, which happened to be near the exit.

She never came back. Before leaving, she had drained her drink at one long gulp, a gesture that apparently meant good-by; Sister Gertrude had walked out on me.

And Oskar? An American cigarette in his amber holder, he ordered a straight schnaps from the waiter who was discreetly removing Sister Gertrude's empty glass. He was determined to smile at all costs. His smile may have been a bit sorrowful, but it was still a smile; folding his arms and crossing his legs, he waggled one delicate black shoe, size five, and savored the superiority of the forsaken.

The young habitués of the Lions' Den were very nice; it was a swing number, and they winked at me from the dance floor as they swung by. "Hello," cried the boys and "Take it easy" the girls. With a wave of my cigarette holder I thanked the repositories of true humanity and smirked indulgently as the percussion man gave a sumptuous roll and did a solo number on the drums, cymbals, and triangle, which reminded me of my good old rostrum days. The next dance, he then announced, would be ladies' invitation.

A hot number, "Jimmy the Tiger," meant for me no doubt, though no one at the Lions' Den could have known about my career as a disrupter of mass meetings. A fidgety little thing with a henna mop came over to me and, pausing a moment in her gum chewing, whispered in my ear with a voice husky from smoking: "Jimmy the Tiger." I was the partner of her choice. Conjuring up jungle menaces, we danced Jimmy; the Tiger walked—for about ten minutes—on velvet paws. Again a flourish, applause and another flourish, because my hump was well dressed and I was nimble on my legs and cut a pretty good figure as Jimmy the Tiger. I asked my admirer to my table, and Helma—that was her name—asked if her girl friend Hannelore could come too. Hannelore was silent, sedentary, and hard-drinking. Helma, on the other hand, was addicted to American cigarettes, and I had to ask the waiter for some more.

A fine evening. I danced "Hey Bob A Re Bop," "In the Mood," "Shoeshine Boy," chatted between dances, and entertained the two young ladies, who were not very exacting and told me that they worked in the telephone exchange on Graf-Adolf-Platz and that lots of girls from the exchange came to Wedig's every Saturday and Sunday night. They themselves came regularly when they weren't on duty, and I too promised to come often, because Helma and Hannelore were so nice, and because telephone operators seemed so easy to get along with when there was no telephone—a little joke that they were good enough to laugh at.

It was a long while before I went back to the City Hospital. When I resumed my occasional visits, Sister Gertrude had been transferred to gynecology. I never saw her again except to wave to from a distance. I became a welcome habitué at the Lions' Den. The girls exploited me but not immoderately. Through them I made the acquaintance of several members of the British Army of Occupation and picked up a few dozen words of English, I made friends with a couple of the musicians, but controlled myself, that is, I kept away from the drums and contented myself with the modest happiness of cutting inscriptions at Korneff's.

During the hard winter of 1947 to 1948, I kept up my contact with the telephone girls. At no great expense, I obtained a certain amount of warmth from the silent, sedentary Hannelore, though we never went beyond the noncommittal manual stage.

In the winter the stonecutter took care of his equipment. The tools had to be reforged, a few leftover blocks were trimmed and made ready for their inscriptions. Korneff and I replenished our stores, which had been thinned out during the autumn season, and made a few artificial stones from shell-lime waste. I also tried my hand at some simple sculpture with the stippling machine, did reliefs representing angels' heads, heads of Christ with crowns of thorns, and doves of the Holy Ghost. When snow fell, I shoveled it away, and when there was none, thawed out the water pipe leading to the polishing machine.

At the end of February, '48, soon after Ash Wednesday—I had lost weight during carnival and may have been looking rather ethereal, for some of the girls at the Lions' Den took to calling me Doctor—the first peasants from the left bank of the Rhine came over to look at our offerings. Korneff was absent on his annual rheumatism cure, tending a blast furnace in Duisburg. When he came back two weeks later, parched and boilless, I had already sold three stones, one of them for a tomb for three, on favorable terms. Korneff sold two slabs of Kirchheim shell lime; and early in March we began to set them up. One slab of Silesian marble went to Grevenbroich; the two Kirchheim stones are in a village cemetery near Neuss; the red sandstone with my angels' heads can still be admired in the cemetery at Stomml. At the end of March we loaded the diorite slab with the thorn-crowned Christ and drove slowly, because the three-wheeler was overloaded, in the direction of Kappes-Hamm, meaning to cross the Rhine at Neuss. From Neuss via Grevenbroich to Rommerskirchen, then left on the road to Bergheim Erft. Leaving Rheydt and Niederaussem behind us, we reached Oberaussem without breaking an axle. The cemetery was situated on a hill sloping gently toward the village.

Ah, the view! At our feet the Erftland soft coal country. The eight chimneys of the Fortuna Works, steaming heavenward. The new Fortuna North power plant, hissing as though about to explode. The mountains of slag surmounted by telpher lines. Every three minutes a train empty or full of coke, no larger than a toy, moving to or from the power plant; a larger toy, a toy for giants, was the high-tension line that swept across one corner of the cemetery on its way, three abreast, buzzing with high tension, to Cologne. Other lines hurried horizonward in other directions, to Belgium and Holland: hub of the world. We set up the diorite slab for the Flies family—electricity is generated by . . . The gravedigger with his helper, who substituted for Leo Schugger on this occasion, passed by with their implements. We were standing in a field of tension. Three rows away, they started to dig up a grave preparatory to moving its occupant—war reparations flowing over high-tension wires—the wind carried the smells typical of a premature exhumation—not so bad, it was only March. Amid the coke piles the green fields of spring. The bows of the gravedigger's glasses were mended with string, he was arguing in an undertone with his Leo Schugger, until for exactly one minute the Fortuna siren gave a gasp, leaving us breathless, not to mention the woman whose remains were being moved, only the high-tension lines got on with their work. The siren tipped, fell overboard, and drowned—while from the slate-grey slate roofs of the village rose coils of smoke betokening the lunch hour, followed by the church bells: pray and work, industry and religion, boon companions. Change of shifts at Fortuna. We unwrapped our smoked pork sandwiches, but exhumation suffers no delay and the high-tension current continued without interruption on its way to the victor powers, to light the lamps of Holland, while here the juice was constantly being shut off—but the dead woman saw the light.

While Korneff dug the five-foot holes for the foundation, she was brought up into the fresh air. She hadn't been lying very long down in the darkness, only since the fall, and already she had made progress, keeping pace with the improvements that were everywhere under way. Those who were dismantling industrial plants in the Ruhr and Rhineland had progressed like anything; during the winter that I had frittered away at the Lions' Den, this woman had made serious progress and now, as we were laying on concrete and putting the pedestal in place, it was piece by piece that she had to be persuaded to let herself be dug up. But that's what the zinc casket was for, to prevent anything, even the most negligible part of her, from getting lost. Just as when free coal was distributed at Fortuna, children ran behind the overloaded trucks and picked up the chunks that fell out, because Cardinal Frings had proclaimed from the pulpit: Verily I say unto you, it is not a sin to filch coal. But for this woman there was no longer any need to keep up a fire. I don't think she was cold in the proverbially chilly March air, she had quite a good deal of skin left; to be sure it had sprung leaks and runners; but these were compensated for by vestiges of cloth and hair, the latter still permanently waved, hence the term. The coffin fittings were also worth moving and there were even bits of wood that wanted to go along to the other cemetery, where there would be no peasants or miners from Fortuna, for this next last resting place was in the city where there was always something doing, nineteen movie houses operating all at once. For as the gravedigger told us, she wasn't from around here, she had been evacuated: "She was from Cologne, and now they're taking her to Mülheim on the other side of the Rhine." He would have said more if the siren hadn't gone off again for another minute. Taking advantage of the siren, I approached the grave; tacking against the siren, I wanted to witness this exhumation, and I took something with me which turned out, when I reached the zinc casket, to be my spade, which I put into action, not in order to help but because I happened to have it with me. On the blade I picked up something that had fallen on the ground. This spade had formerly been the property of the Reich Labor Service. And what I picked up on the Reich Labor Service spade was or had been the middle finger and, as I am still convinced, the ring finger of the evacuated woman; they had not fallen off but had been chopped off by the gravedigger, an unfeeling sort. But it seemed to me that they had been beautiful and adroit. Similarly the woman's head, which had already been placed in the casket, had preserved a certain regularity through the winter of '47 to '48, which was a severe one as you surely remember, and it was reasonably possible to speak of beauty, though on the decline. Moreover, this woman's head and fingers were closer to me, more human, than the beauty of Fortuna North. It seems safe to say that I enjoyed the industrial landscape as I had enjoyed Gustaf Gründgens at the theater—a surface beauty which I have always distrusted, though assuredly there was art in it, whereas the effect produced by this evacuee was only too natural. Granted that the high-tension lines, like Goethe, gave me a cosmic feeling, but the woman's fingers touched my heart. They still touched my heart when I began to think of her as a man, because it was more compatible with my thing about making decisions and with the fancy that transformed me into Yorick and the woman—half of her still in the earth, half in the zinc casket—into Hamlet. And I, Yorick, Act V, the fool, "I knew him, Horatio," Scene 1, I who on all the stages of this world—"Alas, poor Yorick!"—lend Hamlet my skull so that some Gründgens or Sir Laurence Olivier in the role of Hamlet may ponder over it: "Where be your gibes now? your gambols?" I held Gründgens' Hamlet fingers on the blade of the Labor Service shovel, stood on the solid ground of the Rhenish soft coal fields, amid the graves of miners, peasants, and their families, and looked down on the slate roofs of the village of Oberaussem. The village cemetery became for me the center of the world, while Fortuna North stood there as the redoubtable demigod, my antagonist. The fields were the fields of Denmark; the Erft was my Belt, whatever rot lay round about was rotten in the state of Denmark—and I was Yorick. Charged with high tension, crackling, the high-tension angels, in lines of three, sang as they made their way to the horizon, to Cologne with its fabulous Gothic monster, heavenly hosts over the beet fields. But the earth yielded up coal and the corpse, not of Yorick but of Hamlet. As to the others, who had no parts in the play, they lay buried for good—"The rest is silence"—weighed down with tombstones just as we were weighing down the Flies family with this ponderous diorite slab. But for me, Oskar Matzerath Bronski Yorick, a new era was dawning, and scarcely aware of it, I took another quick look at Hamlet's worn-out fingers on the blade of my shovel—"He is fat and scant of breath"—I looked on as Gründgens, Act III, Scene 1, labored his dilemma about being or not being, rejected this absurd formulation, and put the question more concretely: "My son and my son's lighter flints, my presumptive earthly and heavenly father, my grandmother's four skirts, the beauty, immortalized in photographs, of my poor mama, the maze of scars on Herbert Truczinski's back, the blood-absorbing mail baskets at the Polish Post Office, America—but what is America compared to Streetcar Number 9 that went to Brösen? I considered Maria's scent of vanilla, still perceptible now and then, and my hallucination of Lucy Rennwand's triangular face; I asked Mr. Fajngold, that disinfector unto death, to search for the Party pin that had disappeared in Matzerath's windpipe. And at last, turning to Korneff, or more to the pylons of the power line, I said—my decision was made, but before coming out with it, I felt the need of a theatrical question that would cast doubt on Hamlet but legitimize me, Yorick, as a citizen—turning, then, to Korneff, who had called me because it was time to join our slab to the pedestal, I, stirred by the desire to become an honest citizen, said, slightly imitating Gründgens, although he could scarcely have played Yorick, said across the shovel blade: "To marry or not to marry, that is the question."

After this crisis at the cemetery facing Fortuna North, I gave up dancing at Wedig's Lions' Den, broke off all connections with the girls at the telephone exchange, whose foremost quality had been their ability to provide connections.

In May I took Maria to the movies. After the show we went to a restaurant and ate relatively well. We had a heart to heart talk. Maria was dreadfully worried because Kurt's source was drying up, because the honey business was falling off, because I, weakling, so she put it, that I was, had been supporting the whole family for several months. I comforted Maria, told her that Oskar was glad to be doing what he could, that Oskar liked nothing better than to bear a heavy responsibility, complimented her on her looks, and finally came out with a proposal.

She asked for time to think it over. For weeks the only answer to my Yorick's question was silence and evasion; in the end it was answered by the currency reform.

Maria gave me innumerable reasons. She caressed my sleeve, called me "dear Oskar," said I was too good for this world, begged me to understand and always be her friend, wished me the best of everything for my future as a stonecutter and otherwise, but when asked more explicitly and urgently, declined to marry me.

And so Yorick did not become a good citizen, but a Hamlet, a fool.

Madonna 49

The currency reform came too soon, it made a fool of me, compelling me in turn to reform Oskar's currency. I was obliged to capitalize, or at least to make a living from, my hump.

Yet I might have been a good citizen. The period following the currency reform, which—it has now become perfectly clear—contained all the seeds of the middle-class paradise we are living in today, might have brought out the bourgeois Oskar. As a husband and family man I should have participated in the reconstruction of Germany, I should now be the owner of a medium-sized sized stonecutting business, giving thirty workers their livelihood and providing office buildings and insurance palaces with the shell-lime and travertine façades that have become so popular: I should be a businessman, a family man, a respected member of society. But Maria turned me down.

It was then that Oskar remembered his hump and fell a victim to art. Before Korneff, whose existence as a maker of tombstones was also threatened by the currency reform, could dismiss me, I walked out. I took to standing on streetcorners when I wasn't twiddling my thumbs in Guste Köster's kitchen-living room; I gradually wore out my tailor-made suit and began to neglect my appearance. There were no fights with Maria, but for fear of fights I would leave the flat in Bilk in the early forenoon. First I went to see the swans in Graf-Adolf-Platz, then I shifted to the swans in the Hofgarten. Small, thoughtful, but not embittered, I would sit on a park bench across the street from the Municipal Employment Agency and the Academy of Art, which are neighbors in Düsseldorf.

It is amazing how long a man can sit on a park bench; he sits till he turns to wood and feels the need of communicating with other wooden figures: old men who come only in good weather, old women gradually reverting to garrulous girlhood, children shouting as they play tag, lovers who will have to part soon, but not yet, not yet. The swans are black, the weather hot, cold, or medium according to the season. Much paper is dropped; the scraps flutter about or lie on the walks until a man in a cap, paid by the city, spears them on a pointed stick.

Oskar was careful in sitting to blouse the knees of his trousers evenly. Of course I noticed the two emaciated young men and the girl in glasses before the girl—she had on a leather overcoat with an ex-Wehrmacht belt—addressed me. The idea seemed to have originated with her companions, who despite their sinister underworldly look were afraid to approach me, the hunchback, for they sensed my hidden greatness. It was the girl who summoned up the courage. She stood before me on firm, widely spaced columns until I asked her to sit down. There was a mist blowing up from the Rhine and her glasses were clouded over; she talked and talked, until I asked her to wipe her glasses and state her business intelligibly. Then she beckoned to her sinister companions. I had no need to question them; they introduced themselves at once as painters in search of a model. I was just what they were looking for, they said with an enthusiasm that was almost frightening. When I rubbed my thumb against my index and middle finger, they told me the Academy paid one mark eighty an hour, or two marks for posing in the nude, but that, said the stout girl, didn't seem very likely.

Why did Oskar say yes? Was it the lure of art? Or of lucre? No need to choose. It was both. I arose, leaving the park bench and the joys and sorrows of park bench existence behind me forever, and followed my new friends—the stout girl marching with determination, the two young men, stooped as though carrying their genius on their backs—past the Employment Agency to the partially demolished Academy of Art.

Professor Kuchen—black beard, coal-black eyes, black soft hat, black fingernails—agreed that I would be an excellent model.

For a time he walked around me, darting coal-black looks, breathing black dust from his nostrils. Throttling an invisible enemy with his black fingers, he declared: "Art is accusation, expression, passion. Art is a fight to the finish between black charcoal and white paper."

Professor Kuchen led me to a studio, lifted me up with his own hands on a revolving platform, and spun it about, not in order to make me dizzy, but to display Oskar's proportions from all sides. Sixteen easels gathered round. The coal-breathing professor gave his disciples a short briefing: What he wanted was expression, always expression, pitch-black, desperate expression. I, Oskar, he maintained, was the shattered image of man, an accusation, a challenge, timeless yet expressing the madness of our century. In conclusion he thundered over the easels: "I don't want you to sketch this cripple, this freak of nature, I want you to slaughter him, crucify him, to nail him to your paper with charcoal!"

This was the signal to begin. Sixteen sticks of charcoal rasped behind sixteen easels; charcoal came to grips with my expression, that is, my hump, blackened it, and put it on paper. Professor Kuchen's students took so black a view of my expression that inevitably they exaggerated the dimensions of my hump; it refused to fit on the paper though they took larger and larger sheets.

Professor Kuchen gave the sixteen charcoal-crushers a piece of good advice: not to begin with the outlines of my hump—which was allegedly so pregnant with expression that no format could contain it—but first to black in my head on the upper fifth of the paper, as far to the left as possible.

My beautiful hair is a glossy chestnut-brown. They made me a scraggly-haired gypsy. Not a one of them ever noticed that Oskar has blue eyes. During an intermission—for every model is entitled to fifteen minutes' rest after posing for three-quarters of an hour—I took a look at the sixteen sketches. On all sides my cadaverous features thundered condemnation, but nowhere did I see the blue radiance of my eyes; where there should have been a clear, winning sparkle, I saw narrow, sinister orbs of crumbling coal-black charcoal.

However, the essence of art is freedom. I took an indulgent view. These sons and daughters of the Muses, I said to myself, have recognized the Rasputin in you; but will they ever discover the Goethe who lies dormant in your soul, will they ever call him to life and put him on paper, not with expressive charcoal but with a sensitive and restrained pencil point? Neither the sixteen students, gifted as they may have been, nor Professor Kuchen with his supposedly unique charcoal stroke, succeeded in turning out an acceptable portrait of Oskar. Still, I made good money and was treated with respect for six hours a day. Facing the clogged washbasin, a screen, or the sky-blue, slightly cloudy studio windows, I posed for six hours a day, displaying an expression valued at one mark and eighty pfennigs an hour.

In a few weeks' time the students produced a number of pleasant little sketches. The "expression" became more moderate, the dimensions of my hump more plausible; sometimes they even managed to get the whole of me into the picture from top to toe, from the jacket buttons over my chest to the hindmost promontory of my hump. Occasionally there was room for a background. Despite the currency reform, these young people had not forgotten the war; behind me they erected ruins with accusing black holes where the windows had been. Or they would represent me as a forlorn, undernourished refugee, amid blasted tree trunks; or their charcoal would imprison me, weave ferociously barbed barbed-wire fences behind me, and build menacing watchtowers above me; they dressed me as a convict and made me hold an empty tin bowl, dungeon windows lent me graphic charm. And all in the name of artistic expression.

But since it was a black-haired gypsy-Oskar who was made to look upon all this misery out of coal-black eyes, and not my true blue-eyed self, I stood (or sat) still and kept my peace though I well knew that barbed wire is no fit subject for drawing. Nevertheless I was glad when the sculptors, who, as everyone knows, have to manage without timely backgrounds, asked me to pose for them in the nude.

This time it was not a student but the master in person who spoke to me. Professor Maruhn was a friend of my charcoal-crusher. One day when I was standing motionless in Kuchen's private studio, a dismal repair full of framed charcoal sketches, letting the black beard with the inimitable black stroke put me on paper, Professor Maruhn dropped in. A short, stocky man in his fifties, whose neat white smock might have suggested a surgeon if a dusty beret hadn't identified him as an artist.

Maruhn, as I could see at a glance, was a lover of classical form. He thoroughly disapproved of my build and began to poke fun at Kuchen: couldn't he be satisfied with the gypsy models who had earned him the nickname of Gypsy Cake? Must he try his hand at freaks? The gypsy period had sold well, there was that to be said for it; did the charcoal-crusher entertain hopes that a midget period would sell still better?

Smarting under his friend's mockery, Professor Kuchen translated it into furious strokes of charcoal: of all his pictures of Oskar this was the blackest. It was all black except for a touch of murky dawn on the cheekbones, nose, forehead, and hands—Kuchen always made my hands enormous, swollen with gout, screaming with expression, and put them in the middle ground of his charcoal orgies. In this drawing, however, which was later admired at exhibitions, my eyes are blue, that is, the usual somber glow has given way to a distinctly light tone. Oskar attributes this anomaly to the influence of Maruhn, who was not a fanatic of coal-black expression but a classicist, alert to the Goethean clarity of my eyes. It can only have been Oskar's eyes that persuaded this lover of classical harmony to select me as a fit model for sculpture, his sculpture.

Maruhn's studio was light, dusty, and bare. It contained not a single piece of finished work. But everywhere there were skeletons for projected sculptures, so perfectly thought out that wire, iron, and bare lead tubing, even without modeling clay, gave promise of future harmony.

I posed in the nude for five hours a day, and he paid me two marks an hour. A chalk mark on the platform showed where my right foot was to take root. An imaginary vertical rising from the instep had to pass directly between my collarbones. The left leg was "free moving". Illusory freedom. I was expected to bend the knee slightly and hold this leg slightly to one side, with an air of negligence, but I was not allowed to move it. It too was rooted in a chalk mark on the platform.

I spent several weeks posing for Maruhn. In all that time he was able to find no set pose for my arms comparable to that of the legs. He made me try everything: left arm drooping, right arm curved over my head; both arms folded over my chest or crossed under my hump; hands on hips; the possibilities were legion and the sculptor tried just about everything, first on me, then on the iron skeleton with the flexible lead joints.

When finally, after a month of strenuous effort, he decided to do me in clay, either with hands folded behind my head or as an armless torso, he was so exhausted from building and rebuilding his skeleton that he could do no more. He would pick up a handful of clay, sometimes he would even move forward to apply it, but then he would drop the dull, unformed clod back in the box. Then he would sit and stare at me and my skeleton, trembling as with fever: the skeleton was too perfect.

He sighed with resignation, said he had a headache, and without resentment toward Oskar gave up. He picked up the humpbacked skeleton, with fixed leg and free-moving leg, with tubular arms and upraised wire fingers joined behind iron neck, and put it in the corner with all his other prematurely finished skeletons. Gently, without mockery, aware of their own futility, the wooden bars, known also as butterflies, which were to have borne the weight of the clay, quivered in the spacious cage that was my hump.

After that we drank tea and chatted for an hour or so, which was counted as posing time. He spoke of former times when, vigorous and uninhibited as a young Michelangelo, he had spread whole wagonloads of clay on skeletons and completed innumerable sculptures, most of which had been destroyed during the war. I told him about Oskar's activity as a stonecutter and engraver of inscriptions. We talked shop a while and then he took me to pose for his students.

If long hair is an indication of sex, six of Professor Maruhn's ten pupils can be designated as girls. Four were homely and talented. Two were pretty, lively, and scatterbrained: real girls. It has never embarrassed me to pose in the nude. On the contrary, Oskar savored the astonishment of the two pretty, scatterbrained sculptresses when they viewed me on the platform for the first time and observed, not without a certain dismay, that Oskar, despite his hump, despite his small size, carried with him a sex organ which could, in a pinch, have borne comparison with just about anyone else's.

The students' trouble was rather different from the master's. The framework was complete in two days; with the frenzy of genius, they would fling clay on the hastily and inexpertly fastened lead tubes, but apparently they hadn't put enough wooden butterflies into my hump. For no sooner was the moist modeling clay in place, representing an Oskar who looked for all the world like a rugged mountain landscape, than this mountain-Oskar, or rather ten of them, would begin to sag. My head fell between my feet, the clay parted from the tubing, my hump drooped nearly to my knees, and I came to appreciate Maruhn, the master, whose skeletons were so perfect that there was no need to hide them beneath vile flesh.

The homely but gifted sculptresses wept when the clay Oskar parted from the skeleton Oskar. The pretty but scatterbrained sculptresses laughed as the perishable flesh fell symbolically from my bones. After several weeks, however, the class managed to turn out a few passable sculptures, first in clay, then in plaster and imitation marble. They were shown at the End of Term Exhibition and I had occasion to draw new comparisons between the homely but gifted sculptresses and the pretty but scatter-brained young ladies. While the homely but not untalented young ladies reproduced my head, limbs, and hump with the utmost care but, seized with a strange diffidence, either ignored my sex organ or stylized it ad absurdum, the pretty young ladies with the big blue eyes, with the shapely but awkward fingers, gave little heed to the articulations and proportions of my body, but reproduced my imposing genitals with the utmost pre-cision. But while I am on this subject, I mustn't forget the four male sculptors: they abstracted me; making use of flat, grooved boards, they slapped me into a cube. As for the object that the homely young ladies neglected and the pretty ones rendered with carnal verism, they, with their masculine intellects, saw it as two cubes of like size, surmounted by an elongated rectangular block: Priapus in terms of solid geometry.

Was it because of my blue eyes or because of the sun-bowl heaters with which the sculptors surrounded the nude Oskar: in any case, some young painters who had come to see the pretty young sculptresses dis-covered a picturesque charm either in the blue of my eyes or in my glowing, irradiated, lobster-red skin and carried me away to the upper floors where the painting classes were held.

At first the painters were too much under the influence of my blue eyes and saw the whole of me as blue. Oskar's fresh complexion, his brown wavy hair, his fresh, pink mouth—all were submerged in macabre blues; here and there, serving only to intensify the putrefaction, a moribund green, a nauseous yellow crept in between the patches of blue flesh.

Oskar did not take on other colors until carnival week, when, in the course of festivities held in the basement of the Academy, he discovered Ulla and brought her to the painters to be their Muse.

366

Was it on Shrove Monday? Yes, it was on Shrove Monday that I decided to join in the festivities, to put on a costume and to add a costumed Oskar to the motley throng.

When Maria saw me at the mirror, she said: "You'd better stay home, Oskar. They'll just step on you." Nevertheless, she helped me with my costume, cutting out patches which her sister Guste, with garrulous needle, joined into a jester costume. My first idea had been one of Velasquez' dwarfs. I should also have liked to appear as Narses or as Prince Eugene. When at length I stood before the big mirror, whose image was slightly distorted by a diagonal crack left over from the war, when the whole motley costume, baggy, slashed, and hung with bells came to light, making my son Kurt laugh so hard that he couldn't stop coughing, I said to myself softly and none too happily: Now, Oskar, you are Yorick, the fool. But where is the king for you to play the fool to?

In the streetcar that took me to Ratinger Tor, near the Academy, I soon noted that Oskar-Yorick did not bring laughter to the populace— all these cowboys and Spanish dancers trying to forget their tawdry daily occupations. No, I frightened them. They edged away from me, so much so that though the car was jammed, I easily found a seat. Outside the Academy, policemen were wielding genuine billics which had no connection with carnival make-believe.

The art students' ball was jam-packed and still there were crowds trying to get in. The resulting forays with the police were more colorful than bloody.

When Oskar made his bells tinkle, the throng parted like the Red Sea, and a policeman, his eye sharpened by his occupation, perceived my true stature. He looked down, saluted, and swinging his billy escorted me to the cellar festivities. When I arrived, the pot was on the fire but hadn't quite come to a boil.

No one should suppose that an artists' ball is an affair at which artists have themselves a ball. Most of the actual artists, looking rather worried and serious through their carnival paint, were standing behind amusingly decorated but very unstable counters, trying to make a little extra money selling beer, schnaps, champagne, and sausages. The merrymakers, for the most part, were workaday citizens who thought it would be fun, just this once, to carouse and fling money about like artists.

After spending an hour or so on staircases, in nooks and corners, under tables, frightening couples who seemed to be investigating the charms of discomfort, I made friends with two Chinese girls from Lesbos, or should I say Lesbians from China? They were very much wrapped up in one another. Though they left no finger unturned in their mutual dealings, they did not trespass on my more critical zones and offered me a spectacle that was entertaining at times. We drank warm champagne together and at length, with my permission, they made use of my hump, which was sharp and horny at the extremity, for experiments which were crowned with success, once more confirming my thesis that a hump is good luck to women.

In the long run, however, these occupations made me more and more morose. Thoughts plagued me, I began to worry about the political situation; I painted the blockade of Berlin on the table top with champagne and sketched out a picture of the air lift. Contemplating these Chinese girls who couldn't get together, I despaired of the reunification of Germany and did something that is very unlike me. Oskar, in the role of Yorick, began to look for the meaning of life.

When my girl friends could think of nothing more to show me, they began to cry, leaving telltale traces in their oriental make-up. Slashed and baggy and powdered, I stood up, ringing my bells. Two-thirds of me wanted to go home, but the remaining third still hoped for some little carnivalesque experience. It was then that I caught sight of Corporal Lankes, that is, he spoke to me.

Do you remember? We met on the Atlantic Wall during the summer of '44. He had guarded concrete and smoked my master Bebra's cigarettes.

A dense crowd sat necking on the stairs. I tried to squeeze through. I had just lighted up when someone poked me and a corporal from the last war spoke: "Hi, buddy, can you spare a butt?"

Quite aside from these familiar words, he was costumed in field gray. Small wonder that I recognized him at once. Even so, I should have made no move to revive our acquaintance if the young lady sitting on the corporal and concrete painter's field-gray lap had not been the Muse in person.

Let me speak with the painter first and describe the Muse afterwards. I not only gave him a cigarette, but even lighted it for him, and said as the first cloud of smoke arose: "Corporal Lankes, do you remember? Bebra's Theater at the Front? Barbaric, mystical, bored?"

A tremor ran through the painter as I addressed him in these terms; he managed to keep a hold on his cigarette, but the Muse fell from his knees. She was hardly more than a child, long-legged and very drunk. I caught her in mid-air and returned her to him. As the two of us, Lankes and Oskar, exchanged reminiscences with a disparaging remark or two for Lieutenant Herzog, whom Lankes called a nut, and a thought for Bebra my master as well as the nuns who had been picking up crabs that day amid the Rommel asparagus, I gazed in amazement at the Muse. She had come as an angel and had on a hat molded from the variety of cardboard that is used for shipping eggs. Despite her drooping wings and far-advanced drunkenness, she still exerted the somewhat artsy-craftsy charm of a dweller in heaven.

368

"This here is Ulla," Lankes informed me. "She studied to be a dressmaker, but now she wants to be an artist, but I say to hell with it, with dressmaking she can bring in some dough."

Oskar, who made a good living on art, offered forthwith to introduce Ulla to the painters at the Academy, who would be sure to take her on as a model and Muse. Lankes was so delighted with my proposal that he helped himself to three cigarettes at once, but in return asked me to come see his studio if I didn't mind paying the taxi fare.

Off we rode, leaving the carnival behind us. I paid the fare, and Lankes, on his alcohol stove, made us some coffee that revived the Muse. Once she had relieved the weight on her stomach with the help of my right forefinger, she seemed almost sober.

Only then did I see the look of wonderment in her light-blue eyes and hear her voice, which was a little birdlike, a little tinny perhaps, but touching in its way and not without charm. Lankes submitted my proposal that she should pose at the Academy, putting it more as an order than as a suggestion. At first she refused; she wished to be neither a Muse nor a model for other painters, but to belong to Lankes alone.

Thereupon he, as talented painters sometimes do, gave her a resounding slap in the face; then he asked her again and chuckled with satisfaction when, weeping just as angels would weep, she professed her willingness to become the well-paid model and maybe even the Muse of the painters at the Academy.

It must be borne in mind that Ulla measures roughly five feet ten; she is exceedingly slender, lithe, and fragile, reminding one of Botticelli, Cranach, or both. We posed together in the nude. Lobster meat has just about the color of her long, smooth flesh, which is covered by a light childlike down. The hair on her head is perhaps a trifle thin, but long and straw-blonde. Her pubic hair is reddish and curly, restricted to a small triangle. Ulla shaves under her arms regularly once a week.

As one might have expected, the run-of-the-mill students couldn't do much with us, they made her arms too long, my head too big, and were unable to squeeze us into any known format. It was only when Ziege and Raskolnikov discovered us that pictures worthy of Oskar and the Muse came into being. She asleep. I startling her awake: faun and nymph.

I sitting; she, with small, always slightly shivering breasts, leaning over me, stroking my hair: Beauty and the beast.

She lying, I between her legs, playing with the mask of a horned horse: The lady with the unicorn.

All this in the style of Ziege or Raskolnikov; color or delicate gray tones laid on with a fine brush (Raskolnikov) or with the impetuous palette knife of genius (Ziege). Some of these paintings carried an intimation of the mystery surrounding Ulla and Oskar; they were the work

369

of Raskolnikov, who, with our help, found his way to surrealism: Oskar's face became a honey-yellow dial like that of our grandfather clock; in my hump bloomed mechanical roses which Ulla picked; Ulla, smiling on one end and long-legged on the other, was cut open in the middle and inside sat Oskar between her spleen and liver, turning over the pages of a picture book. Sometimes they put us in costume, turning Ulla into a Columbine and me into a mournful mime covered with white grease paint. It was Raskolnikov—so nicknamed because he never stopped talking of crime and punishment, guilt and atonement—who turned out the masterpiece: I sitting on Ulla's milk-white, naked thigh, a crippled child—she was the Madonna, while I sat still for Jesus.

This painting, entitled "Madonna 49," was shown at a number of exhibitions; it also proved effective as a poster, which came to the eyes of my ever so respectable Maria and brought on a domestic quarrel. However, it was purchased for a considerable sum by a Rhenish industrialist and today it is hanging in the boardroom of a big business firm, influencing the board of directors.

I was amused by the ingenious monstrosities perpetrated on the basis of my hump and proportions. Ulla and I were in great demand, and received two marks fifty each for posing together. Ulla was delighted with her new career. Now that she was bringing in a regular income, the horny-handed Lankes treated her better and beat her only when his own abstractions demanded an angry mood. He could make no use of her as a model, but for him too she was a kind of Muse, for it was only by boxing her ears that his hand could achieve its true creative power.

I too was fired to acts of violence by Ulla's plaintive fragility, which was actually the indestructibility of an angel; however, I kept myself under control, and whenever the desire to whip her became too strong, I took her out to a pastry shop. Or else, with a certain dandyism inspired by my association with artists, I would exhibit her as a rare plant, highlighted by the contrast with my own proportions, on the busy Königs-Allee, where we would be much gaped at. Or as a last resort I would buy her lavender stockings and pink gloves.

It was a different story with Raskolnikov, who, without ever touching her, kept up the most intimate relations with her. He would have her pose sitting down, her legs far apart. On such occasions he did not paint. He would settle himself on a stool a few steps away, stare at her private parts, and talk, in a hoarse, impassioned whisper, of guilt and atonement. The Muse's private parts became moist and distended, and after a while Raskolnikov, by dint of looking and listening to himself would experience exultation and release. Thereupon, he would jump up from his stool and belabor the "Madonna 49" on his easel with grandiose brushstrokes.

Sometimes Raskolnikov stared at me as well, but for other reasons.

It seemed to him that I lacked something. He spoke of a vacuum between my fingers and kept putting one object after another—what with his surrealist imagination he was never at a loss for an object—into my hands. He armed Oskar with a pistol, made Oskar-Jesus take aim at the Madonna. Or I would hold out an hourglass to her or a mirror which, being convex, would distort her horribly. He made me hold scissors, fishbones, telephone receivers, death's heads, little airplanes, armored cars, steamships, but none of these filled the vacuum. Oskar dreaded the day when the painter would turn up with the object which alone of all objects was made to be held by me. When at length he brought the drum, I cried out: "No!"

Raskolnikov: "Take the drum, Oskar. I have seen through you."

I, trembling: "Never again. All that is ended."

He, darkly: "Nothing is ended, everything returns, guilt, atonement, more guilt."

I, with my last strength: "Oskar has atoned, spare him the drum. I'll hold anything you say, anything but a drum."

I wept when the Muse Ulla bent over me. Blinded with tears, I could not prevent her from kissing me, I could not prevent the Muse from giving me that terrible kiss. All of you who have ever been kissed by the Muse will surely understand that Oskar, once branded by that kiss, was condemned to take back the drum he had rejected years before, the drum he had buried in the sand of Saspe Cemetery.

But I did not drum. I merely posed—but that was plenty—and was painted as Jesus the drummer boy, sitting on the nude left thigh of the Madonna 49.

It was thus that Maria saw me on a poster advertising an art show. Unbeknownst to me, she attended the exhibition and looked at the picture; she must have stood there long and cloud-gathering, for when she spoke of it, she struck me with my son Kurt's school ruler. She, who for some months had been holding down a well-paid job in a luxury delicatessen store, first as a salesgirl, then, thanks to her obvious ability, as cashier, was now an established citizen of West Germany and no longer a black marketing refugee from the East. Thus it was with a certain conviction that she was able to call me a pig, a pimp, a degenerate. She went so far as to shout that she wanted no more of the filthy money I made with my filthy occupations, nor of me either for that matter.

Though Maria soon took back this last remark and only two weeks later was again accepting a considerable share of my modeling fees in return for my board and lodging, I nevertheless decided to stop living with her, her sister Guste, and my son Kurt. My first idea was to go far away, to Hamburg or perhaps to the seashore, but Maria, who had no objection to my moving, persuaded me, with her sister Guste's support, to look for a room not too far away from herself and Kurt, in any case in Düsseldorf.

The Hedgehog

It was only as a subtenant that Oskar learned the art of drumming back the past. It wasn't just the room; the Hedgehog, the coffin warehouse in the court, and Mr. Münzer helped—not to mention Sister Dorothea.

Do you know *Parsifal*? I don't know it very well either. All that has stuck with me is the story about the three drops of blood in the snow. There is truth in that story, because it fits me like a glove. It is probably the story of everyone who has an idea.

I was still a servant of the arts; I let myself be painted in blue, green, and earth tones; I let myself be sketched in charcoal and put in front of backgrounds; in collaboration with the Muse Ulla, I inspired a whole winter semester at the Academy and the following summer semester as well, but already the snow had fallen which was to receive those three drops of blood, the sight of which transfixed me as it had transfixed Parsifal the fool, about whom Oskar the fool knows so little that it costs him no effort at all to identify himself with this same Parsifal.

My image is clumsy but clear enough, I think: the snow is the uniform of a nurse; the red cross, which most nurses, including Sister Dorothea, wear in the middle of the brooch that holds their collar together, was for me the three drops of blood. There I sat and couldn't take my eyes off it.

But before I could sit in the erstwhile bathroom of the Zeidler apartment, I had to go room-hunting. The winter semester was drawing to a close; some of the students, those who were not planning to return after Easter vacation, would be giving up their rooms. My associate, the Muse Ulla, was helpful; she took me to the students' housing office, where they gave me several addresses and a recommendation from the Academy.

Before looking up the addresses, I went to see Korneff the stone-cutter at his shop in Bittweg. It was a long time since I had seen him. I was drawn by my fondness for him, but I was also in search of work during the vacation period; I had a few hours of private posing with or without Ulla, but that could hardly be expected to keep me for the next six weeks, and moreover if I was to take a room, I would have to raise the rent.

I found Korneff unchanged—one boil that had not yet come to a head and two that were nearly healed—over a block of Belgian granite that he had roughed out and was now engaged in polishing. We spoke a while; I began to play suggestively with the lettering chisels and looked round for stones that were already cut and polished, waiting for an inscription. Two stones, one of shell lime, the other of Silesian marble, looked as if Korneff had sold them and they were waiting for an expert cutter of inscriptions. I congratulated Korneff on his success in weathering the hard times after the currency reform. Yet even at the time we had drawn comfort from the thought that a currency reform, however vigorous, vital, and optimistic, cannot deter people from dying and ordering tombstones.

Our prediction had been confirmed. Once more people were dying and buying. In addition, moreover, the currency reform had brought new business: butchers were having their fronts and sometimes even the insides of their shops faced with fancy marble; certain banks and department stores were obliged, in order to recapture their old prestige, to have their damaged sandstone and tufa façades repaired and redecorated.

I complimented Korneff on his industry and asked him if he was able to handle all the work. At first he replied evasively, then he admitted that he had sometimes wished he had four hands, and finally he made me a proposition: I could cut inscriptions for him on a half-time basis; he would pay forty-five pfennigs a letter for hollow lettering in limestone, fifty-five in granite and diorite, while for raised lettering he was prepared to pay sixty and seventy-five.

I started right in on a piece of shell lime. Quickly recovering my knack, I cut out: Aloys Küfer, September 3, 1887—June 10, 1946. I had the thirty-four letters and figures done in just three hours and received fifteen marks and thirty pfennigs on leaving.

This was more than a third of the monthly rent I had decided I could afford. I was determined to pay no more than forty, for Oskar still felt in duty bound to help with the upkeep of the household in Bilk.

The people in the Housing Office had been kind enough to give me four addresses. My first choice was: Zeidler, Jülicher-Strasse 7, because it was near the Academy.

Early in May, a warm, misty day typical of spring in the lower Rhineland, I started out, provided with sufficient cash. Maria had ironed my suit, I looked presentable. Crumbling stucco façade, in front of it a dusty chestnut tree. As Jülicher-Strasse was half in ruins, it would be unrealistic to speak of the house next door or across the street. To the left, a mound of rubble overgrown with grass and dandelions, here and there disclosing part of a rusty T-girder, suggested the previous existence of a four-story building. To the right a partly damaged house had been repaired as far as the third floor. But the builders had apparently run out of funds; the façade of polished, black Swedish granite was cracked in many places and in urgent need of repair. The inscription "Schornemann, Undertaker" lacked several letters, I don't remember which. Fortunately, the two palm branches incised in the mirror-smooth granite were still intact and helped to give the shop a certain air of piety and respectability.

This enterprise had been in existence for seventy-five years. Its coffin warehouse was in the court, across from my window, and I often found it worth looking at. In good weather I watched as the workmen rolled a coffin or two out of the shed and set them up on sawhorses, to refresh their polish. All of these last dwelling places, as I noted with pleasure, were tapered at the foot end in the old familiar way.

It was Zeidler in person who opened at my ring. Short, squat, breathless, and hedgehoggy, he stood in the doorway; he had on thick glasses and the lower half of his face was hidden beneath a dense shaving lather. He held his shaving brush against his cheek, appeared to be an alcoholic, and sounded like a Westphalian.

"If you don't like the room, don't shilly-shally. I'm shaving and after that I've got to wash my feet."

Clearly Zeidler didn't stand on ceremony. I took a look at the room. Of course I didn't like it; it was a decommissioned bathroom, half in turquoise tile, half in wallpaper with a convulsive sort of pattern. However, I kept my feelings to myself. Disregarding Zeidler's drying lather and unwashed feet, I asked if the bathtub could be taken out, especially as it had no drainpipe in the first place.

Smiling, Zeidler shook his gray hedgehog's head, and tried in vain to whip up a lather. That was his reply. Thereupon I expressed my willingness to take the room with bathtub for forty marks a month.

We returned to the dimly lighted, tubular corridor, disclosing several partly glassed doors, painted in various colors, and I asked who else lived in the flat.

"Wife and roomers."

I tapped on a frosted-glass door, hardly a step from the entrance to the flat.

"A nurse," said Zeidler. "But it's no skin off your nose. You'll never see her. She only comes here to sleep and sometimes she doesn't."

I am not going to tell you that Oskar trembled at the word "nurse". He nodded his head, not daring to ask about the other roomers, but noted the situation of his room with bathtub; it was on the right-hand side, at the end of the hall.

Zeidler tapped me on the lapel: "You can cook in your room if you've got an alcohol stove. You can use the kitchen off and on too, for all I care, if the stove isn't too high for you."

That was his first allusion to Oskar's stature. He gave my recommendation from the Academy a cursory glance; it was signed by Professor Reuser, the director, and seemed to impress him favorably. I agreed to all his do's and don'ts, impressed it on my mind that the kitchen was next to my room on the left, and promised to have my laundry done outside; he was afraid the steam would be bad for the bathroom wallpaper. It was a promise I could make with a clear conscience; Maria had agreed to do my washing.

At this point I should have left, announcing that I was going to get my baggage and fill out the police registration forms. But Oskar did nothing of the sort. He couldn't bear to leave that apartment. For no reason at all, he asked his future landlord to show him the toilet. With his thumb mine host pointed to a plywood door reminiscent of the war and postwar years. When something in Oskar's movements suggested a desire to use it—the toilet, that is—Zeidler, his face itching with crumbling shaving soap, turned on the light.

Once within, I was vexed, for Oskar didn't have to go. However, I waited stubbornly for Oskar to make a little water. In view of my insufficient bladder pressure and also because the wooden seat was too close, I had to be very careful not to wet the seat or the tile floor. Even so, I had to daub a few drops off the worn-down seat with my handkerchief and efface a few unfortunate traces on the tiles with the soles of my shoes.

Zeidler had not taken advantage of my absence to wash the hardened soap from his face. He had preferred to wait in the hallway, perhaps because he had sensed the joker in me. "Aren't you the funny guy! Using the toilet before you've even signed your lease."

He approached me with a cold crusty shaving brush, surely planning some silly joke. But he did nothing, just opened the door for me. While Oskar slipped out backward into the stairway, keeping an eye on the Hedgehog as I passed him, observed that the toilet door was situated between the kitchen door and the frosted-glass door behind which a trained nurse sometimes, not always, spent her nights.

When late that afternoon Oskar, with his baggage including the new drum given him by Raskolnikov, the painter of madonnas, returned brandishing the registration form, a freshly shaved Hedgehog, who had meanwhile no doubt washed his feet, led me into the living room.

The living room smelled of cold cigar smoke. Of cigars that had been lighted several times. There was also a smell of carpets, valuable carpets perhaps, which lay in several layers all over the room. It also smelled of old calendars. But I didn't see any calendars, so it must have been the carpets. Strange to say, the comfortable, leather-upholstered chairs had in themselves no smell. This came as a disappointment to me, for Oskar, who had never sat in a leather chair, had so vivid a notion of what leather upholstery must smell like that he suspected this leather of being artificial.

In one of these smooth, unsmelling, and, as I later ascertained, genuine leather chairs, sat Mrs. Zeidler. She had on a gray tailored suit, which fitted her only very approximately. Her skirt had slipped up over her knees, revealing three fingers' breadth of slip. Since she made no move to arrange her clothing and, it seemed to Oskar, had been crying, I did not dare to greet her or to introduce myself in words. My bow was a silent one; in its last stages, it turned back to Zeidler, who had introduced his wife with a motion of his thumb and a slight cough.

The room was large and square. The shadow of the chestnut tree in front of the house made it seem larger and smaller. I left my suitcase and drum near the door and, holding my registration form, approached Zeidler, who was standing near the windows. Oskar did not hear his own steps, for he walked on four carpets—I counted them later—four superimposed carpets of decreasing size which, with their fringed or unfringed edges of different colors, added up to a strange color pattern. The bottommost carpet was reddish-brown and began near the walls; the next, approximately green, was largely hidden by furniture, the heavy sideboard, the china closet filled entirely with liqueur glasses, dozens of them, and the spacious marriage bed. The third carpet was of a blue design and ran from corner to corner. The fourth, a solid claret-color, supported the extensible dining table covered with protective oilcloth, and four leather-upholstered chairs with evenly spaced brass rivets.

Since there were more rugs, hardly intended for that purpose, hanging on the walls, and still others rolled up in the corners, Oskar assumed that the Hedgehog had traded in carpets before the currency reform and been stuck with them afterwards.

The only picture was a glass-covered likeness of Bismarck, hanging on the outer wall between two seemingly oriental rugs. The Hedgehog sat in a leather chair beneath the Iron Chancellor, to whom he showed a certain family resemblance. He took the form from my hand, studied both sides of the official document alertly, critically, and impatiently. His wife asked him in a whisper if anything was wrong. Her question threw him into a fit of rage which made him look still more like the Chancellor. The chair spewed him out. Standing on four carpets, he held the form out to one side and filled himself and his waistcoat with air. With one bound he was on the first and second carpets, looking down on his wife, who had meanwhile taken up her needlework, and pouring forth words on the order of: Whoaskedyoul'dliketoknow? Nobody's-goingtodoanytalkingaroundherebutmeme! Shutthatmouthofyoursand-keepitshut!

Since Mrs. Zeidler kept her peace and attended unflustered to her sewing, the problem for the Hedgehog, as he trod the carpets, was to let his fury rise and fall with an air of plausibility. A single step took him to the china closet, which he opened with such violence as to call forth a general tinkling. Carefully, each outstretched finger a precision mechanism, he picked up eight liqueur glasses, removed them undamaged from the case, tiptoed—like a host planning to divert himself and seven guests with an exercise in dexterity—toward the green tiled stove, and then, suddenly throwing all caution to the winds, hurled his fragile freight at the cold, cast-iron stove door.

The most amazing part of it was that during this performance, which required a certain accuracy of aim, the Hedgehog kept a bespectacled eye on his wife, who had risen and was trying to thread a needle by the right-hand window. Scarcely a second after his annihilation of the glasses, she carried this delicate operation, which required a steady hand, to a successful conclusion. Then she went back to her chair and sat down, and again her skirt slipped up disclosing three fingers' breadth of pink slip. With a malevolent though submissive look, the Hedgehog had followed his wife's movement to the window, her threading of the needle, her return to the chair. No sooner had she resumed her seat than he reached behind the stove, took up dustpan and brush, swept up the fragments, and poured them into a newspaper, which was already half full of shattered liqueur glasses. There would not have been room for a third outburst.

If the reader should suppose that Oskar recognized his old glass-shattering self in the glass-shattering Hedgehog, I can only say that the reader is not entirely mistaken; I too once tended to transform my rage into shattered glass—but never in those days did anyone see me resort to dustpan and brush!

Having removed the traces of his wrath, Zeidler sat down again. Once more Oskar handed him the registration form that the Hedgehog had been obliged to drop in order to have both hands free for the liqueur glasses.

Zeidler signed the form and gave me to understand that he expected order to reign in his flat, where would we be if everyone did as he pleased, he was in a position to know, he had been a salesman for fifteen years, sold hair clippers, was I familiar with this article?

Oskar made certain movements from which Zeidler could infer that I was adequately informed on the subject of hair clippers. Zeidler's well-clipped brush suggested confidence in his merchandise, hence effectiveness as a salesman. After he had explained his work schedule—a week on the road, two days at home—he lost interest in Oskar. More hedgehoggy than ever, he sat rocking himself in the squeaky light-brown leather, his eyeglasses sparkled, and with or without reason he muttered: jajajajaja. It was time for me to go.

First Oskar took leave of Mrs. Zeidler. Her hand was cold, boneless, but dry. The Hedgehog from his chair waved me toward the door where Oskar's baggage stood. I already had my hands full when his voice came to me: "What you got there, tied to your suitcase?"

"That's my drum."

"You expect to play it here?"

"Not necessarily. There was a time when I played quite a lot."

"Go ahead as far as I care. I'm never home anyway."

"It is very unlikely that I shall ever drum again."

"And what made you stay so little?"

"An unfortunate accident hampered my growth."

"Well, I only hope you don't give us any trouble, fits and that kind of thing."

"The state of my health has improved steadily in the last few years. See how nimble I am." Thereupon Oskar, for the benefit of the Zeidlers, did a few flips and semi-acrobatic exercises he had learned in his theatrical period. Mrs. Zeidler tittered while Mr. Zeidler assumed the look of a Hedgehog on the point of slapping his thighs. Then I was in the hallway. Past the nurse's frosted-glass door, the toilet door, and the kitchen door, I carried my belongings, including drum, to my room.

This was in the beginning of May. From that day on I was tempted, possessed, overwhelmed by the mystery of the trained nurse. My feeling for nurses is a kind of sickness. Perhaps it is incurable, for even today, with all that far behind me, I contradict Bruno my keeper when he says that only men can be proper nurses, that a patient's desire to be cared for by lady nurses is just one more symptom of his disease. Whereas, still according to Bruno, your male nurse takes conscientious care of his patient and sometimes cures him, his female counterpart, woman that she is, beguiles the patient, sometimes into recovery, sometimes into a death pleasantly seasoned with eroticism.

So speaks Bruno my keeper. Perhaps he is right, but I should be very reluctant to admit it. One who has been brought back to life every two or three years by lady nurses cannot help being grateful; he is not going to allow any grumpy old male nurse, however likable, to sully my image of my beloved lady nurses, especially as his one and only motive is professional jealousy.

It began with my fall down the cellar steps on the occasion of my third birthday. I think she was called Sister Lotte and came from Praust. Dr. Hollatz' Sister Inge was with me for several years. After the defense of the Polish Post Office, I fell into the hands of several nurses at once. I remember only one of them by name: Sister Erni or Berni. Nameless nurses in Lüneburg, then at the University Clinic in Hanover. Then the nurses at the City Hospital in Düsseldorf, first and foremost Sister Gertrude. And then, without my having to go to any hospital, She came. In the best of health, Oskar succumbed to a nurse who was a roomer in the Zeidler flat. From that day on my world was full of nurses. When I went to work in the early morning, to cut inscriptions at Korneff's, my streetcar stop was named: Marien-Hospital. Outside the brick gateway and in the flower-choked grounds, nurses came and went, on their way to and from work. I often found myself riding in the same trailer car, on the same platform with several of these exhausted, or at least weary-looking nurses. At first I breathed in their scent with repugnance, soon I sought it out, stationed myself as near as possible to their uniforms.

Then Bittweg. In good weather I worked outside amid the display of tombstones and saw them passing arm in arm, two by two, four by four, on their hour off, compelling Oskar to look up from his granite, to neglect his work, for every upward look cost me twenty pfennigs.

Movie posters: the Germans have always been addicted to films about nurses. Maria Schell lured me to the movies. She wore a nurse's uniform, laughed and wept; her days were full of self-sacrifice; smiling and still wearing her nurse's cap, she played somber music. Later on, in a fit of despair, she came very close to tearing her nightgown. But after her attempted suicide, she sacrificed her love—Borsche as the doctor—remained true to her profession, and retained her cap and Red Cross pin. While Oskar's conscious mind laughed and wove an endless chain of obscenities into the film, Oskar's eyes wept tears, I wandered about half-blind in a desert of white-clad anonymous lady Samaritans, searching for Sister Dorothea, who—and that was all I knew about her—rented the room behind the frosted-glass door in the Zeidler flat.

Sometimes I heard her steps as she came home from night duty. I also heard her toward nine o'clock at night, after the day shift. Oskar did not always remain seated in his chair when he heard her in the hall. Quite often he played with his doorknob. Who could have resisted? Who does not look up at the passage of something which is passing perhaps for him? Who can sit still in his chair when every nearby sound seems to serve the sole purpose of making him jump up?.

Still worse is the silence. We have seen the power of silence in connection with the female figurehead, wooden, silent, and passive. There lay the first museum attendant in his blood. And everyone said Niobe had killed him. The director looked for a new attendant, for the museum had to be kept open. When the second attendant was dead, everyone screamed that Niobe had killed him. The museum director had difficulty in finding a third attendant—or was it already the eleventh he was looking for? One day, in any case, this attendant it had been so hard to find was dead. And everyone screamed: Niobe, Niobe of the green paint and amber eyes; wooden Niobe, naked, unbreathing, unsweating, untrembling, suffering neither heat nor cold; Niobe, wormless because, what with her historical value, she had been sprayed against worms. A witch was burned on her account, the woodcarver's hand was cut off, ships sank, but she floated, she survived. Niobe was wooden but fireproof, Niobe killed and remained valuable. Schoolboys, students, an elderly priest, and a bevy of museum attendants all fell prey to her silence. My friend Herbert Truczinski jumped her and died; but Niobe, still dry, only increased in silence.

When the nurse left her room, the hallway, and the Hedgehog's apartment early in the morning, at about six o'clock, it became very still, though when present she had never made any noise. Unable to stand the silence, Oskar had to coax a squeak or two from his bed, move a chair, or roll an apple in the direction of the bathtub.

Toward eight o'clock a rustling. That was the postman dropping letters and postcards through the slit in the outer door. Not only Oskar, but Mrs. Zeidler as well had been waiting for that sound. She was a secretary at the offices of the Mannesmann Company and didn't go to work until nine o'clock. She let me go first; it was Oskar who first looked into the rustling. I moved quietly though I knew she could hear me just the same, and left my room door open in order not to have to switch on the light. I picked up all the mail at once. Regularly once a week there was a letter from Maria, giving a complete account of herself, the child, and her sister Guste. Having secreted it in my pajama pocket, I would look quickly through the rest of the mail. Everything addressed to the Zeidlers or to a certain Mr. Münzer who lived at the end of the hallway, I would replace on the floor. As for Sister Dorothea's mail, I would turn it over, smell it, feel it, and examine the return address.

Sister Dorothea received more mail than I, but not very much. Her full name was Dorothea Köngetter; but I called her only Sister Dorothea and occasionally forgot her last name—what, indeed, does a trained nurse need a last name for? She received letters from her mother in Hildesheim. There were also postcards from all over West Germany, most of them with pictures of ivy-covered hospitals, written by nurses she had known at training school, obviously in reply to Sister Dorothea's halting efforts to keep up with her old friends.

Nearly all these communications, as Oskar soon found out, were quite rapid and unrevealing. Nevertheless, they threw some light on Sister Dorothea's past; she had worked at the Vinzent-Hospital in Cologne, at a private clinic in Aachen, and in Hildesheim, where her mother was still living. It could be inferred either that she was from Lower Saxony or that like Oskar she was a refugee from the East and had settled there after the war. I also found out that Sister Dorothea was working nearby, at the Marien-Hospital, that she had a close friend by the name of Beata, for the postcards were full of references to, and regards for, this Sister Beata.

The existence of a girl friend gave me wild ideas. I composed letters to Beata, in one I asked her to intercede for me, in the next I said nothing about Dorothea, my idea being to approach Beata first and switch to Dorothea later on. I drafted five or six letters and even addressed one or two; several times I started for the mailbox, but none was ever sent.

Yet perhaps, in my madness, I would actually have mailed one of these pleas to Sister Beata had I not—one Monday it was, the day Maria started up with Mr. Stenzel, her boss, an occurrence that left me surprisingly cold—found on the floor, below the letter slot, the missive which transformed my passion from love to jealous love.

The name and address printed on the envelope told me that the letter had been written by a Dr. Erich Werner at the Marien-Hospital. On Tuesday a second letter came. Thursday brought a third. What shall I say of my state of mind on that Thursday? Oskar tottered back to his room, fell on one of the kitchen chairs which helped to turn my bathroom into a place of residence, and drew Maria's weekly letter from his pajama pocket—in spite of her love affair Maria continued to write punctually, neatly, and exhaustively. Oskar even tore open the envelope and gazed at the letter with sightless eyes; he heard Mrs. Zeidler in the hall, calling Mr. Münzer, who did not answer. But Münzer must have been in, for Mrs. Zeidler opened his room door, handed in the mail, and kept on talking to him.

Mrs. Zeidler was still talking but I could no longer hear her. I surrendered myself to the madness of the wallpaper, the vertical, horizontal, diagonal madness, the curved madness, reproduced a thousandfold; I saw myself as Matzerath, eating the alarmingly nutritious bread of cuckolds; and no shame or scruple deterred me from representing my Jan Bronski as a seducer in Satanic make-up, clad by turns in the traditional overcoat with velvet collar, in Dr. Hollatz' white smock, and in the equally white smock of Dr. Werner, in every case seducing, corrupting, desecrating, insulting, scourging, and torturing, in short, doing everything a seducer has to do if he is to be plausible.

Today I can smile when I recall the idea which then turned Oskar as yellow and mad as the wallpaper: I decided to study medicine. I would graduate in no time. I would become a doctor, at the Marien-Hospital, of course. I would expose Dr. Werner, demonstrate his incompetence, nay more, prove that his criminal negligence had been responsible for the death of a patient in the course of a larynx operation. It would turn out that this Mr. Werner had never attended medical school. He had picked up a smattering of medicine while working as an orderly in a field hospital during the war. Off to jail with the charlatan. And Oskar, despite his youth, becomes head physician. A new Professor Sauerbruch, with Sister Dorothea at his side, followed by a white-clad retinue, strides down resounding corridors, visits his patients, decides at the last minute to operate. How fortunate that this film was never made!

In the Clothes Cupboard

It should not be supposed that Oskar's whole life was taken up with nurses. After all, I had my professional occupations. I had to give up cutting inscriptions, the summer semester at the Academy had begun. Once again Ulla and I received good money for sitting still while art students, employing methods old or new, subjected us to their vision or blindness. There were many who destroyed our objective existence, rejected and negated us, covering paper and canvas with lines, rectangles, spirals, producing wallpaper designs which had everything in them but Oskar and Ulla, or mystery and tension if you will, and giving these absurdities high-sounding titles such as: "Plaited Upward," "Hymn above Time," "Red in New Spaces".

This manner was particularly favored by the younger students who had not yet learned to draw. We fared better at the hands of my old friends from the studios of Kuchen and Maruhn, not to mention the prize students Ziege and Raskolnikov.

In her earthly existence the Muse Ulla revealed a marked taste for applied art. Lankes had left her but in her enthusiasm for the new wallpaper designs she soon forgot him and convinced herself that the decorative abstractions of a middle-aged painter named Meitel were sweet, amusing, cute, fantastic, terrific, and even chic. Meitel had a special fondness for forms suggesting sugary-syrupy Easter eggs, but that is hardly worth mentioning; since then she has found many other occasions to become engaged and at the present moment—as she informed me when she came to see me the day before yesterday, with candy for me and Bruno—is on the point of entering upon a serious and lasting relationship, as she has always put it.

At the beginning of the semester, Ulla wanted to pose only for the "new trends"—a flea that Meitel, her Easter egg painter, had put in her ear; his engagement present to her had been a vocabulary which she tried out in conversations with me. She spoke of relationships, constellations, accents, perspectives, granular structures, processes of fusion, phenomena of erosion. She, whose daily fare consisted exclusively of bananas and tomato juice, spoke of proto-cells, color atoms which in their dynamic flat trajectories found their natural positions in their fields of forces, but did not stop there; no, they went on and on . . . This was the tone of her conversation with me during our rest periods or when we went out for an occasional cup of coffee in Ratinger-Strasse. Even when her engagement to the dynamic painter of Easter eggs had ceased to be, even when after a brief episode with a Lesbian she took up with one of Kuchen's students and returned to the objective world, she retained this vocabulary which so strained her little face that two sharp, rather fanatical creases formed on either side of her mouth.

Here I must admit that it was not entirely Raskolnikov's idea to dress the Muse Ulla as a nurse and paint her with Oskar. After the "Madonna 49" he put us into "The Abduction of Europa"—I was the bull. And immediately after the rather controversial "Abduction" came "Fool Heals Nurse".

It was a little word of mine that fired Raskolnikov's imagination. Somber, red-haired, and crafty, he cleaned his brushes and brooded; staring fixedly at Ulla, he began to speak of guilt and atonement. At this

I advised him to picture me as guilt, Ulla as atonement; my guilt, I said, was patent; as for Atonement, why not dress her as a nurse?

If this excellent picture later bore another, misleadingly different title, it was Raskolnikov's doing. I myself should have called it "Temptation," because my right, painted hand was gripping and turning a doorknob, opening the door to a room where The Nurse is standing. Or it might have been called "The Doorknob," for if I were asked to think up a new name for temptation, I should recommend the word "doorknob," because what are these protuberances put on doors for if not to tempt us, because the doorknob on the frosted-glass door of Sister Dorothea's room was to me temptation itself whenever I knew that Hedgehog Zeidler was on the road, Sister Dorothea at the hospital, and Mrs. Zeidler in the office at Mannesmann's.

Oskar would emerge from his room with the drainless bathtub, cross the hallway, approach the nurse's room, and grip the doorknob.

Until about the middle of June—and I made the experiment almost every day—the door had resisted my temptation. I was beginning to think that Sister Dorothea's work had just made her too orderly in her ways, that I might as well give up hope of her ever neglecting to lock it. And that is why, when one day the door opened under my pressure, my dull-witted, mechanical reaction was to close it again.

For several minutes Oskar stood there in a very tight skin, a prey to so many thoughts of the most divergent origins that his heart had difficulty in imposing any sort of arrangement upon them.

It was only after I had transferred my thoughts to another context —Maria and her lover, I thought; Maria has a lover, lover gives her a coffee pot, lover and Maria go to the Apollo on Saturday night, Maria addresses lover as Mr. So-and-So during working hours, he is her boss, owner of the store where she works— only after I had thus considered Maria and her lover from various angles, that I managed to create a little order in my poor brain . . . and opened the frosted-glass door.

I had already figured out that the room must be windowless, for never had the upper, dimly transparent part of the door revealed the slightest trace of daylight. Reaching to the right, exactly as in my own room, I found the switch. The forty-watt bulb was quite sufficient for this cubbyhole which hardly deserved to be called a room. I was rather distressed to find myself face to face with my bust in the mirror. Though his reverse image had nothing to tell him, Oskar did not move away; he was too fascinated by the objects on the dressing table in front of the mirror.

There were blue-black spots in the white enamel of the washbasin. The table top in which the washbasin was sunk almost to the rim also had blemishes. The left corner was missing and the missing piece lay on the table top under the mirror, showing the mirror its veins. Traces of peeling glue on the broken edge bore witness to a bungled attempt to repair the damage. My stonecutter's fingers itched. I thought of Korneff's homemade marble cement, which transformed even the most dilapidated marble into enduring slabs fit to adorn the façades of large butcher stores.

Once these familiar thoughts had diverted me from my cruelly distorted image in the mirror, I was able to give the smell that had struck me the moment I came in a name.

It was vinegar. Later, and again only a few weeks ago, I justified that acrid smell by the assumption that Sister Dorothea must have washed her hair the day before and had put vinegar in the rinse water. However, there was no vinegar bottle on the dressing table. Nor did I detect vinegar in any of the containers otherwise labeled; moreover, I have often said to myself, would Sister Dorothea be likely to heat water in the Zeidler kitchen, for which she would have required Zeidler's permission, and go through the bother of washing her hair in her room, when the hospital is full of the best showers and bathrooms? Yet possibly the head nurse or the hospital management had forbidden the nurses to use certain sanitary installations in the hospital; perhaps Sister Dorothea actually was obliged to wash her hair in this enamel bowl, in front of this deceitful mirror.

Though there was no vinegar bottle on the table, there were plenty of other bottles and jars on the clammy marble. A package of cotton and a half-empty package of sanitary napkins discouraged Oskar from investigating the contents of the little jars. But I am still of the opinion that they contained nothing but routine cosmetics or harmless medicinal ointments.

Sister Dorothea had left her comb in her brush. It cost me a struggle to pull it out and take a good look at it. How fortunate that I did so, for in that instant Oskar made his important discovery; the nurse's hair was blonde, perhaps ashblonde, but one cannot be too suspicious of conclusions drawn from the dead hair that comes out in a comb. Suffice it to say that Sister Dorothea had blonde hair.

In addition, the alarmingly abundant contents of the comb told me that Sister Dorothea suffered from falling hair, an ailment that must have distressed her. It's the fault of her nurse's caps, I said to myself; but I did not condemn them, for how can a hospital be run properly without nurses' caps?

Distasteful as the vinegar smell was to Oskar, the only sentiment aroused in me by the thought that Sister Dorothea was losing her hair was love, seasoned with solicitude and compassion. It is characteristic of the state I was in that I thought of several hair lotions I had heard recommended and resolved to supply Sister Dorothea with one or more of them at the first opportunity. Dreaming of our first meeting, which would take place beneath a warm summer sky, amid fields of waving grain, I plucked the homeless hairs from the comb and arranged them in a bundle, which I secured by tying a knot in it. I blew off some of the dust and dandruff and carefully secreted my treasure in a compartment of my wallet from which I had quickly removed its previous contents.

Having stowed my wallet in my jacket, I picked up the comb, which I had laid down on the table top for want of hands. I held it up to the naked light bulb, making it transparent, examined the two rows of prongs, coarse and fine, and noted that two of the finer prongs were missing. I could not resist the temptation to run the nail of my left forefinger over the tips of the coarse prongs, and while thus playing Oskar was gladdened by the glitter of a few hairs which, to avert suspicion, I had intentionally neglected to remove.

At length I dropped the comb back into the brush and left the dressing table, which, it seemed to me, was giving me an unbalanced picture. On my way to Sister Dorothea's bed I bumped into a chair on which hung a brassiere—much washed, I noted, and faded at the edges.

Oskar had nothing but his fists with which to fill the two concavities. They were inadequate. Too hard, too nervous, they were alien and unhappy in these bowls which in my ignorance of their contents I should gladly have lapped up with a teaspoon day after day; I might have experienced a little nausea now and then, for too much of any fare will unsettle the stomach, but after nausea sweetness, such sweetness as to make nausea desirable, the seal of true love.

I thought of Dr. Werner and took my fists out of the brassiere. But then Dr. Werner vanished and I was able to approach Sister Dorothea's bed. So this was her bed! How often Oskar had tried to visualize it, and now it was the same hideous wooden structure, painted brown, that served as a setting for my own repose and occasional insomnia. What I should have wished for her was a white-enameled metal bed with brass knobs, a light, immaterial frame, and not this cumbersome and loveless object. Immobile, with heavy head, devoid of passion, incapable even of jealousy, I stood for a time gazing at this altar of sleep—the comforter, it seemed to me, must be granite. Then I turned away from the loathsome sight. Never could Oskar have visualized Sister Dorothea and her slumbers in this repulsive tomb.

I started back toward the dressing table, planning perhaps to open the presumed ointment jars. On my way, the clothes cupboard board commanded me to note its dimensions, to qualify its paint as black-brown, to follow the contours of its molding, and at last to open it; for where is the cupboard that does not demand to be opened?.

There was no lock, the doors were held together by a bent nail; I turned it to a vertical position and at once, with no help from me, the doors swung apart with a sigh, offering me so wide a vista that I had to step backward to take it all in. Oskar didn't want to lose himself in details as he had at the dressing table; nor did he wish, as in the case of the bed, to let prejudice pass judgment; no, he was determined to give himself to that cupboard, which opened out its arms to him, with the freshness of the first day of Creation.

Nevertheless Oskar, the incorrigible esthete, could not refrain entirely from criticism: some barbarian had hurriedly sawed off the legs, tearing splinters out of the wood, and set the disfigured cupboard down flat on the floor.

The inside was in the best of order. On the right there were three deep shelves piled with undergarments and blouses; white, pink, and a light blue which Oskar felt certain would not discolor. Two red and green oilcloth bags hung inside the right-hand door, one containing stockings with runs, the other stockings Sister Dorothea had mended. These stockings, it seemed to me, were equal in quality to those that Maria's employer and boy friend had given her, but of closer weave and more durable. To the left hung starched, gleaming white nurse's uniforms. In the hat compartment on top, in beauty and simplicity, sat the fragile nurse's caps, fearing the touch of any unpracticed hand. I cast only a brief glance at the civilian clothes to the left of the undergarments. The cheap, haphazard assortment confirmed my secret hope: Sister Dorothea was not deeply interested in this department of her clothing. And the same impression was conveyed by the three or four pot-shaped hats with imitation flowers, which, tossed negligently in a heap beside the caps, suggested nothing so much as an unsuccessful cake. The hat compartment also contained ten or a dozen books with colored backs, leaning on a shoe box filled with wool left over from knitting.

Oskar had to step closer and tilt his head in order to read the titles. It was with an indulgent smile that my head resumed a vertical position: so our good Sister Dorothea read crime novels. But I have said enough about the civilian section of the cupboard. Lured closer by the books, I did not retreat; quite on the contrary, I stuck my head in the cupboard and ceased to resist my mounting desire to belong to it, to become a part of the clothes cupboard where Sister Dorothea kept a not inappreciable part of her visible presence.

I didn't even have to move the sensible low-heeled shoes that stood on the cupboard floor, meticulously polished and waiting to go out. As though to invite me in, the contents of the cupboard were so arranged that Oskar was able, without crushing a single garment, to take shelter in the middle of it. Full of anticipation, I crawled in and squatted on my heels.

At first, however, my mind was not at rest. Oskar felt himself observed by the furniture and the light bulb. Wishing to make my sojourn in the cupboard more intimate, I tried to pull the doors shut. It was none too easy, the catch was worn out, the doors refused to close properly.

Light still entered, but not enough to disturb me. The smell became more concentrated. An old-fashioned, clean smell, no longer of vinegar, but of some mild moth deterrent; a good smell.

What did Oskar do as he sat in the cupboard? He leaned his forehead against Sister Dorothea's nearest uniform, which opened the door to every aspect of life. My left hand, perhaps in search of something for me to lean on, reached backward, past the civilian clothes, went astray, lost its hold, shot out, gripped something smooth and flexible, and finally—still holding the smoothness—found a horizontal strut, intended to support the rear wall of the cupboard, but willing to do the same for me. My hand was free, I brought it forward and showed myself what I had found behind me.

I saw a black leather belt, but instantly I saw more than the belt because it was so gray in the cupboard that a patent-leather belt could easily be something else. It might just as well have been something different, something just as smooth and long, something I had seen as an incorrigible three-year-old drummer on the harbor breakwater at Neufahrwasser: my poor mama in her light-blue spring coat with the raspberry-colored facings, Matzerath in his brown overcoat, Jan Bronski with his velvet collar, Oskar in his sailor hat with the gold-embroidered inscription "S.M.S. *Seydlitz*"; ulster and velvet collar jumped on ahead of me and Mama, who because of her high heels could not jump from stone to stone as far as the beacon, at the foot of which sat the longshoreman with the clothesline and the potato sack full of salt and movement. At the sight of the sack and clothesline, we asked the man under the beacon why he was fishing with a clothesline, but this fellow from Neufahrwasser or Brösen just laughed and spat out viscous brown juice, which bobbed up and down in the water beside the breakwater and didn't stir from the spot until a seagull carried it away; for a seagull will pick up anything under the sun, it's not one of your picky-and-choosy doves, nor is it by any stretch of the imagination a nurse—wouldn't it be just too simple if you could lump everything white under one head and toss it into a cupboard? And the same goes for black, for in those days I was not yet afraid of the wicked black Witch, I sat fearless in the cupboard and then again not in the cupboard, but equally fearless on the breakwater in Neufahrwasser, in the one case holding a patent-leather belt, in the other something else, which was also black and slippery but not a belt. Because I was in the cupboard, I cast about for a comparison, for cupboards force comparisons, called the wicked black Witch by name, but at that time she meant little to me, I was farther gone on the subject of white, scarcely able to distinguish between a gull and Sister Dorothea. Nevertheless, I expelled doves, pigeons, and all such rot from my thoughts, all the more readily as it wasn't Pentecost but Good Friday when we rode out to Brösen and continued on to the breakwater—besides, there were no pigeons over the breakwater where this fellow from Neufahrwasser was sitting with his clothesline, sitting and spitting. And when the longshoreman from Brösen pulled the line in until the line stopped and showed why it had been so hard to pull it out of the brackish waters of the Mottlau, when my poor mama laid her hand on Jan Bronski's shoulder and velvet collar, because her face was as green as green cheese, because she wanted to go away but had to look on as this longshoreman flung the horse's head down on the stones, as the smaller, sea-green eels fell out of the mane and he pulled the larger, darker ones out of the cadaver. Someone ripped open a featherbed which is just a way of saying that the gulls swooped down and set to, because gulls, when there are three or more of them, can easily finish off a small eel, though they have a bit of trouble with the bigger fellows. The longshoreman wrenched open the horse's mouth, forced a piece of wood between the teeth, which made the horse laugh, and reached in with his hairy arm, groped and reached some more, like me in the cupboard, and extracted, as I in the cupboard had extracted the patent-leather belt, two eels at once. He swung them through the air and dashed them against the stones, until my poor mama's face disgorged her whole breakfast, consisting of café au lait, egg white and egg yolk, a bit of jam, and a few lumps of white bread. So copious was that breakfast that in an instant the gulls had assumed an oblique position, come a story lower, and fallen to—I won't even mention the screams, and that gulls have wicked eyes is generally known. They wouldn't be driven off, not in any case by Jan Bronski, for he was scared stiff of gulls and held both hands before his frantic blue eyes. They wouldn't even pay any attention to my drum, but gobbled, while I with fury, but also with enthusiasm, created many a new rhythm on my drum. But to my poor mama it was all one, she was too busy; she gagged and gagged, but nothing more would come up, she hadn't eaten so very much, for my mama was trying to lose weight and did gymnastics twice a week at the Women's Association, but it didn't help because she kept eating in secret and always found some little loophole in her resolutions. As for the man from Neufahrwasser, when all present thought it was over, there could be no more, he, in defiance of all theory, pulled one last eel out of the horse's ear. It was all full of white porridge, it had been exploring the horse's brains. But the long-shoreman swung it about until the porridge fell off, until the eel showed its varnish and glittered like a patent-leather belt. What I am trying to get at is that Sister Dorothea wore just such a belt when she went out in civvies, without her Red Cross pin.

We started homeward although Matzerath wanted to stay on because a Finnish ship of some eighteen hundred tons was putting into port and making waves. The longshoreman left the horse's head on the breakwater. A moment later the horse turned white and screamed. But he didn't scream like a horse, he screamed more like a cloud that is white and voracious and descends on a horse's head. Which was all to the good, because now the horse was hidden from sight, though one could imagine what was at the bottom of that white frenzy. The Finn diverted us too; he was as rusty as the fence in Saspe Cemetery and was carrying timber. But my poor mama turned to look neither at the Finn nor the gulls. She was done in. Though formerly she had not only played "Fly, little seagull, fly away to Heligoland" on our piano, but sung it as well, she never sang that song again or anything else for that matter; at first she wouldn't eat any more fish, but suddenly she began to eat so much fish, such big fish and fat fish, that one day she couldn't, wouldn't eat any more, that she was sick of it, sick of eels and sick of life, especially of men, perhaps also of Oskar, in any case she, who had never been able to forgo anything, became frugal and abstemious and had herself buried in Brenntau. I have inherited this combination of self-indulgence and frugality. I want everything but there's nothing I cannot do without—except for smoked eels; whatever the price, I can't live without them. And another such exception was Sister Dorothea, whom I had never seen, whose patent-leather belt I was not really wild about—and yet I could not tear myself away from it, it was endless, it multiplied, and with my free hand I unbuttoned my trousers in order to reclarify my image of Sister Dorothea, which had been blurred by the Finnish merchantman and those innumerable varnished eels.

Finally Oskar, with the help of the gulls, managed to shake off his obsession with the breakwater and rediscover Sister Dorothea's world amid her empty, yet winsome uniforms. But when at last I could see her before me and distinguish certain of her features, suddenly, with a screech and a whine, the cupboard doors swung open; the bright light upset me, and it cost me an effort not to soil the smock that hung closest to me.

Only in order to create a transition, to relax the tension of my stay in the cupboard, which had been more strenuous than I had expected, I did something I had not done for years; I drummed a few measures, nothing very brilliant, on the dry rear wall of the cupboard. Then I emerged, checked once more for neatness; I had created no disorder, even the patent-leather belt had preserved its sheen, no, there were a few dull spots that had to be breathed on and rubbed before the belt became once again an object capable of suggesting eels that were caught many years before on the harbor breakwater at Neufahrwasser.

I, Oskar, cut off the current from the forty-watt bulb that had watched me throughout my visit and left Sister Dorothea's room.

Klepp

There I was in the hallway with a bundle of pale blonde hair in my pocket book. For a second I tried to feel the hair through the leather, through the lining of my jacket, through my waistcoat, shirt, and undershirt; but I was too weary, too satisfied in a strangely morose way to look upon my treasure as anything more than leavings found on a comb.

Only then did Oskar own to himself that he had been looking for treasures of a very different kind. What I had really wanted was to demonstrate the presence of Dr. Werner somewhere in Sister Dorothea's room, if only by finding a letter or one of those envelopes I knew so well. I found nothing. Not so much as an envelope, let alone a sheet of paper with writing on it. Oskar owns that he removed the crime novels, one by one, from the hat compartment and opened them, looking for dedications and bookmarks. I was also looking for a picture, for Oskar knew most of the doctors of the Marien-Hospital by sight though not by name—but there was no photograph of Dr. Werner.

Sister Dorothea's room seemed unknown to Dr. Werner, and if he had ever seen it, he had not succeeded in leaving any traces. Oskar had every reason to be pleased. Didn't I have a considerable advantage over the doctor? Wasn't the absence of any trace of him proof positive that the relations between doctor and nurse were confined to the hospital, hence purely professional, and that if there was anything personal about them, it was unilateral?

Nevertheless, Oskar's jealousy clamored for a motive. Though the slightest sign of Dr. Werner would have come as a blow to me, it would at the same time have given me a satisfaction incommensurable with my brief little adventure in the cupboard.

I don't remember how I made my way back to my room, but I do recall hearing a mock cough, calculated to attract attention, behind Mr. Münzer's door at the end of the hall. What was this Mr. Münzer to me? Didn't I have my hands full with Sister Dorothea? Was it any time to burden myself with this Münzer—who knows what the name might conceal? And so Oskar failed to hear the inviting cough, or rather, I failed to understand what was wanted of me, and realized only after I was back in my room that this Mr. Münzer, this total stranger who meant nothing to me, had coughed in order to lure Oskar to his room.

I admit it: for a long while I was sorry I had not reacted to that cough, for my room seemed so cramped and at the same time so enormous that a conversation, even of the most forced and tedious kind, with the coughing Mr. Münzer would have done me good. But I could not summon up the courage to establish a delayed contact—I might, for instance, have gone out into the corridor and given an answering cough—with the gentleman behind the door at the end of the hallway. I surrendered passively to the unyielding angularity of my kitchen chair, grew restless as I always do when sitting in chairs, took up a medical reference book from the bed, dropped the expensive tome I had spent my good money on in a disorderly heap, and picked up Raskolnikov's present, the drum, from the table. I held it, but neither could I take the sticks to it nor was Oskar able to burst into tears that would have fallen on the round white lacquer and brought me a rhythmical relief.

Here I could embark on an essay about lost innocence, a comparison between two Oskars, the permanently three-year-old drummer and the voiceless, tearless, drumless hunchback. But that would be an oversimplification and would not do justice to the facts: even in his drumming days, Oskar lost his innocence more than once and recovered it or waited for it to grow in again; for innocence is comparable to a luxuriant weed —just think of all the innocent grandmothers who were once loathsome, spiteful infants—no, it was not any absurd reflections about innocence and lost innocence that made Oskar jump up from the kitchen chair; no, it was my love for Sister Dorothea that commanded me to replace the drum undrummed, to leave room, hallway, and flat, and hasten to the Academy although my appointment with Professor Kuchen was not until late in the afternoon.

When Oskar left the room with faltering tread, stepped out into the corridor, opened the apartment door as ostentatiously as possible, I listened for a moment in the direction of Mr. Münzer's door. He did not cough. Shamed, revolted, satiated and hungry, sick of living and avid for life, I was on the verge of tears as I left, first the flat, then the house in Jülicher-Strasse.

A few days later I carried out a long-cherished plan, which I had spent so much time rejecting that I had prepared it in every detail. That day I had the whole morning free. Not until three were Oskar and Ulla expected to pose for the ingenious Raskolnikov, I as Ulysses who in homecoming presents Penelope with a hump—something he had grown during his absence no doubt. In vain I tried to talk the artist out of this idea. For some time he had been successfully exploiting the Greek gods and demigods and Ulla felt quite at home in mythology. In the end I gave in and allowed myself to be painted as Vulcan, as Pluto with Proserpina, and finally, that afternoon, as a humpbacked Ulysses. But because I am more concerned with the events of the morning, Oskar will not tell you how the Muse Ulla looked as Penelope, but say instead: all was quiet in the Zeidler flat. The Hedgehog was on the road with his hair clippers, Sister Dorothea was on the day shift and had left the house at six o'clock, and Mrs. Zeidler was still in bed when, shortly after eight, the mail came.

At once I looked it over, found nothing for myself—Maria had written only two days before—but discovered at the very first glance an envelope mailed in town and addressed unmistakably in Dr. Werner's handwriting.

First I put the letter in with the others, addressed to Mr. Münzer and Mrs. Zeidler, went to my room and waited until Mrs. Zeidler had emerged, brought Münzer his letter, gone to the kitchen, then back to the bedroom, and in just ten minutes left the flat, for her work at Mannesmann's began at nine o'clock.

For safety's sake Oskar waited, dressed very slowly, cleaned his fingernails with a show (for his own benefit) of perfect calm, and only then resolved to act. I went to the kitchen, set an aluminum pot half-full of water on the largest of the three gas burners, and turned the flame on full, but reduced it as soon as the water came to a boil. Then, carefully supervising my thoughts, holding them as close as possible to the action in hand, I crossed over to Sister Dorothea's room, took the letter, which Mrs. Zeidler had thrust half under the frosted-glass door, returned to the kitchen, and held the back of the envelope cautiously over the steam until I was able to open it without damage. It goes without saying that Oskar had turned off the gas before venturing to hold Dr. Werner's letter over the pot.

I did not read the doctor's communication in the kitchen, but lying on my bed. At first I was disappointed, for neither the salutation, "Dear Miss Dorothea," nor the closing formula, "Sincerely yours, Erich Werner," threw any light on the relations between doctor and nurse.

Nor in reading the letter did I find one frankly tender word. Werner expressed his regret at not having spoken to Sister Dorothea the previous day, although he had seen her from the doorway of the Men's Private Pavilion. For reasons unknown to Dr. Werner, Sister Dorothea had turned away when she saw him in conference with Sister Beata—Dorothea's friend, as we all remember. Dr. Werner merely requested an explanation. His conversation with Sister Beata, he begged leave to state, had been of a purely professional nature. Sister Beata was rather impetuous, but as she, Sister Dorothea, knew, he had always done his best to keep her at a distance. This was no easy matter, as she, Dorothea, knowing Beata, must surely realize. There were times when Sister Beata made no attempt to conceal her feelings, which he, Dr. Werner, had never reciprocated. The last sentence of the letter ran: "Please believe me that you are free to drop in on me at any time." Despite the formality and coldness bordering on arrogance of these lines, I had no great difficulty in seeing through Dr. E. Werner's epistolary style and recognizing the note for what it was, a passionate love letter.

Mechanically I put the letter back in its envelope. Forgetting the most elementary measures of hygiene, I moistened the flap, which Werner may well have licked, with Oskar's tongue. Then I burst out laughing. Still laughing, I began to slap my forehead and occiput by turns. It was only after this had been going on for some time that I managed to divert my right hand from Oskar's forehead to the doorknob of my room, opened the door, stepped out into the hallway, and slipped the letter half under Sister Dorothea's door.

I was still crouching with one, maybe two fingers on the letter, when I heard Mr. Münzer's voice from the other end of the hall. He spoke slowly and emphatically as though dictating; I could make out every word: "Would you, kind sir, please bring me some water?"

I stood up. It ran through my mind that the man must be sick, but I realized at once that the man behind the door was not sick and that Oskar had hit on this idea only to have an excuse for bringing him water. Never would I have set foot in a total stranger's room in response to any ordinary unmotivated call!

At first I was going to bring him the still tepid water that had helped me to open Dr. Werner's letter. But then I poured the used water into the sink, let fresh water gush into the pot, and carried pot and water to the door behind which dwelt the voice that had cried out for me and water, perhaps only for water.

Oskar knocked, entered, and was hit by the smell that is so very characteristic of Klepp. To call this effluvium acrid would be to overlook its density and sweetness. The air surrounding Klepp had, for example, nothing in common with the vinegary scent of Sister Dorothea's room. To say sweet and sour would also be misleading. This Münzer, or Klepp as I call him today, this corpulent, indolent, yet not inactive, superstitious, readily perspiring, unwashed, but not derelict flutist and jazz clarinettist, had, though something or other was always preventing him from dying, and still has, the smell of a corpse that never stops smoking cigarettes, sucking peppermints, and eating garlic. So smelled he even then, and so smells he and breathes he today when, injecting transience and love of life into the atmosphere along with, and I might say enveloped in, his aroma, he descends upon me on visiting days, compelling Bruno to fling open every available door and window the moment Klepp, after elaborate farewells and promises to come again, has left the room.

Today Oskar is bedridden. Then, in the Zeidler flat, I found Klepp in the leftovers of a bed, cheerfully rotting. Within reaching distance of him, I observed an old-fashioned, extremely baroque-looking alcohol lamp, a dozen or more packages of spaghetti, several cans of olive oil, a few tubes of tomato paste, some damp, lumpy salt wrapped in newspaper, and a case of beer which turned out to be lukewarm. Into the empty beer bottles he urinated lying down, then, as he told me confidentially an hour or so later, he recapped the greenish receptacles, which held about as much as he did and for the most part were full to the brim. These, to avoid any misunderstanding born of sudden thirst, he set aside, careful to segregate them from the beer bottles still properly deserving of the name. Although he had running water in his room—with a little spirit of enterprise he might have urinated in the washbasin—he was too lazy, or rather too busy with himself, to get up, to leave the bed he had taken such pains adjusting to his person, and put fresh water in his spaghetti pot.

Since Klepp, Mr. Münzer I mean, was always careful to cook his spaghetti in the same water and guarded this several times drained-off, increasingly viscous liquid like the apple of his eye, he was often able, aided by his supply of beer bottles, to lie flat on his back for upward of four days at a time. The situation became critical only when his spaghetti water had boiled down to an oversalted, glutinous sludge. On such occasions Klepp might, of course, have let himself starve to death; but in those days he lacked the ideological foundations for that kind of thing, and moreover, his asceticism seemed by its very nature to fall into four- or five-day periods. Otherwise, he might easily have made himself still more independent of the outside world with the help of Mrs. Zeidler, who brought him his mail, or of a larger spaghetti pot.

On the day when Oskar violated the secrecy of the mails, Klepp had been lying independently in bed for five days. The remains of his spaghetti water might have been fine for posting bills. This was his situation when he heard my irresolute step, a step preoccupied with Sister Dorothea and her correspondence, in the corridor. Having observed that Oskar did not react to his mock cough, he threw his voice into the breach on the day when I opened Dr. Werner's coolly passionate love letter, and said: "Would you, kind sir, please bring me some water?"

And I took the pot, poured out the tepid water, turned on the faucet, let the water gush until the little pot was half-full, added a little, and brought him the fresh water. I was the kind sir he had guessed me to be; I introduced myself as Matzerath, stone-cutter and maker of inscriptions.

He, equally courteous, raised the upper part of his body a degree or two, identified himself as Egon Münzer, jazz musician, but asked me to call him Klepp, as his father before him had borne the name of Münzer. I understood this request only too well; it was sheer humility that impelled me to keep the name of Matzerath and it was only on rare occasions that I could make up my mind to call myself Oskar Bronski; I preferred to call myself Koljaiczek or just plain Oskar. Consequently I had no difficulty whatever in calling this corpulent and recumbent young man—I gave him thirty but he proved to be younger—just plain Klepp. He, unable to get his tongue around Koljaiczek, called me Oskar.

We struck up a conversation, taking pains at first to give it an easy flow and sticking to the most frivolous topics. Did he, I asked, believe in predestination? He did. Did he believe that all men were doomed to die? Yes, he felt certain that all men would ultimately have to die, but he was much less sure that all men had to be born; he was convinced that he himself had been born by mistake, and again Oskar felt a strong sense of kinship with him. We both believed in heaven, but when Klepp said "heaven," he gave a nasty little laugh and scratched himself under the bed covers: it was clear that Mr. Klepp, here and now, was hatching out indecent projects that he was planning to carry out in heaven. When the subject of politics came up, he waxed almost passionate; he reeled off the names of some three hundred noble German families to which he wished to hand over the whole of Germany on the spot, all except the Duchy of Hanover, which Klepp magnanimously ceded to the British Empire. When I asked him who was to rule over the erstwhile Free City of Danzig, he said he was sorry, he had never heard of the place, but even so, could offer me one of the counts of Berg, descended, he could assure me, in an almost direct line from Jan Wellem himself. Finally—we had been trying to define the concept of truth and making definite progress—I found out by an adroitly interpolated question or two that Mr. Klepp had been rooming at Zeidler's for the last three years. We expressed our regrets at not having met sooner. I said it was the fault of the Hedgehog, who had not told me nearly enough about his bedridden roomer, just as it had never occurred to him to say anything about Sister Dorothea, except that a nurse was living behind the frosted-glass door.

Oskar didn't wish to start right in burdening Mr. Münzer with his troubles. And so I did not ask for any information about the nurse. Instead, I asked him about himself. "Apropos of nurses," I said, "are you unwell?"

Again Klepp raised his body by one degree, but when it became clear to him that he would never arrive at a right angle, he sank back again and confided his true reason for lying in bed: he was trying to find out whether his health was good, middling, or poor. He hoped in a few weeks to gain the assurance that it was middling.

Then it happened. This was just what I had feared, but hoped that a long and widely ramified conversation might avoid. "Ah, my dear sir, won't you please join me in a plate of spaghetti!" There was no help for it. We ate spaghetti prepared in the fresh water I had brought. I should have liked to give his pasty cooking pot a thorough scouring in the kitchen sink, but I was afraid to say a word. Klepp rolled over on one side and silently, with the assured movements of a somnambulist, attended to his cookery. When the spaghetti was done, he drained off the water into a large empty can, then, without noticeably altering the position of his body, reached under the bed and produced a plate incrusted with grease and tomato paste. After what seemed like a moment's hesitation, he reached again under the bed, fished out a wad of newspaper, wiped the plate with it, and tossed the paper back under the bed. He breathed on the smudged plate as though to blow away a last grain of dust, and finally, with a gesture of noblesse oblige, handed me the most loathsome dish I have ever seen and invited Oskar to help himself.

After you, I said. But nothing doing, he was the perfect host. After providing me with a fork and spoon so greasy they stuck to my fingers, he piled an immense portion of spaghetti on my plate; upon it, with another of his noble gestures, he squeezed a long worm of tomato paste, to which, by deft movements of the tube, he succeeded in lending an ornamental line; finally he poured on a plentiful portion of oil from the can. He himself ate out of the pot. He served himself oil and tomato paste, sprinkled pepper on both helpings, mixed up his share, and motioned me to do likewise. "Ah, dear sir," he said when all was in readiness, "forgive me for having no grated parmesan. Nevertheless, I wish you the best of appetites."

To this day Oskar is at a loss to say how he summoned up the courage to ply his fork and spoon. Strange to say, I enjoyed that spaghetti. In fact, Klepp's spaghetti became for me a culinary ideal, by which from that day on I have measured every menu that is set before me.

In the course of our repast, I managed to take a good look round the bedridden gentleman's room—but without attracting his attention. The main attraction was an open chimney hole, just under the ceiling, through which a black breath invaded the room. There were two windows, and it was windy out. Apparently it was the gusts of wind that sent clouds of soot puffing intermittently from the chimney hole into the room, where the soot settled evenly on the furniture. Since the furniture consisted solely of the bed in the middle of the room and several rolled carpets covered with wrapping paper, it was safe to say that nothing in the room was more blackened than the once-white bed sheet, the pillow slip under Klepp's head, and a towel with which Klepp always covered his face when a gust of wind wafted a soot cloud into the room.

Both windows, like those of the Zeidler living room, looked out on Jülicher-Strasse, or, more precisely, on the green leaves of the chestnut tree that stood in front of the house. The only picture in the room was a color photo of Elizabeth of England, probably cut out of an illustrated weekly. Under the picture bagpipes hung on a hook, the plaid pattern still recognizable beneath the pervading blackness. While I contemplated the colored photo, thinking less of Elizabeth and her Philip than of Sister Dorothea, torn, poor thing, perhaps desperately, between Oskar and Dr. Werner, Klepp informed me that he was a loyal and enthusiastic supporter of the British Royal Family and had consequently taken bagpipe lessons from the pipers of a Scottish regiment in the British Army of Occupation; Elizabeth, it so happened, was colonel of said regiment, which was all the more reason for him to take these particular pipers for his bagpipe teachers; Klepp had seen her in newsreels, wearing a kilt as she reviewed the regiment.

Here, strange to say, the Catholic in me began to stir. I said I doubted whether Elizabeth knew a thing about bagpipe music, tossed in a word or two about the cruel and unjust execution of the Catholic Mary Stuart, and, in short, gave Klepp to understand that in my opinion Elizabeth was tone-deaf.

I had been expecting an outburst of rage on the royalist's part. But he smiled like one graced with superior knowledge and asked me for an explanation: had I any grounds for setting myself up as an authority on music?

For a long while Oskar gazed at Klepp. Unwittingly, he had touched off a spark within me, and from my head that spark leapt to my hump. It was as though all my old, battered, exhausted drums had decided to celebrate a Last Judgment of their own. The thousand drums I had thrown on the scrap heap and the one drum that lay buried in Saspe Cemetery were resurrected, arose again, sound of limb; their resonance filled my whole being. I leapt up from the bed, asked Klepp to excuse me for just one moment, and rushed out of the room. Passing Sister Dorothea's frosted-glass door—half the letter still protruded—I ran to my own room, where I was met by the drum which Raskolnikov had given me while he was painting his "Madonna 49." I seized the drum and the two drumsticks, I turned or was turned, left the room, rushed past the forbidden room, and entered Klepp's spaghetti kitchen as a traveler returns from long wanderings. I sat on the edge of the bed and, without waiting to be asked, put my red and white lacquered cylinder into position. Feeling a little awkward at first, I toyed for a moment with the sticks, made little movements in the air. Then, looking past the astonished Klepp, I let one stick fall on the drum as though at random, and ah, the drum responded to Oskar, and Oskar brought the second stick into play. I began to drum, relating everything in order: in the beginning was the beginning. The moth between the light bulbs drummed in the hour of my birth; I drummed the cellar stairs with their sixteen steps and my fall from those same stairs during the celebration of my legendary third birthday; I drummed the schedule at the Pestalozzi School, I climbed the Stockturm with my drum, sat with it beneath political rostrums, drummed eels and gulls, and carpet-beating on Good Friday. Drumming, I sat on the coffin, tapered at the foot end, of my poor mama; I drummed the saga of Herbert Truczinski's scarry back. As I was drumming out the defense of the Polish Post Office, I noted a movement far away, at the head end of the bed I was sitting on: with half an eye, I saw Klepp sitting up, taking a preposterous wooden flute from under his pillow, setting it to his lips, and bringing forth sounds that were so sweet and unnatural, so perfectly attuned to my drumming that I was able to lead Klepp to the cemetery in Saspe and, after Leo Schugger had finished his dance, Klepp helped me to make the fizz powder of my first love foam up for him; I even led Klepp into the jungles of Mrs. Lina Greff; I made Greff's drumming machine with its 165-pound counterweight play its grand finale and run down; I welcomed Klepp to Bebra's Theater at the Front, made Jesus speak, and drummed Störtebeker and his fellow Dusters off the diving tower—and down below sat Lucy. I let ants and Russians take possession of my drum, but I did not guide Klepp back to the cemetery in Saspe, where I threw my drum into the grave after Matzerath, but struck up my main, never-ending theme: Kashubian potato fields in the October rain, there sits my grandmother in her four skirts; and Oskar's heart nearly turned to stone when I heard the October rain trickling from Klepp's flute, when, beneath the rain and the four skirts, Klepp's flute discovered Joseph Koljaiczek the firebug and celebrated, nay represented, the begetting of my poor mama.

We played for several hours. After a number of variations on my grandfather's flight over the timber rafts, we concluded our concert, happy though exhausted, with a hymn, a song of hope, suggesting that perhaps the vanished arsonist had been miraculously saved.

Before the last tone had quite left his flute, Klepp jumped up from his warm, deep-furrowed bed. Cadaverous smells followed him, but he tore the windows open, stuffed newspaper in the chimney hole, tore the picture of Elizabeth of England to tatters, announced that the royalist era was ended, ran water into the washbasin and washed himself: yes, Klepp washed, there was nothing he feared to wash away. This was no mere washing, it was a purification. And when the purified one turned away from the water and stood before me in his dripping, naked corpulence, his ungainly member hanging down at a slant, and, bursting with vigor, lifted me, lifted me high in the air—for Oskar was and still is a lightweight—when laughter burst out of him and dashed against the ceiling, I understood that Oskar's drum had not been alone in rising from the dead, for Klepp too was as one resurrected. And so we congratulated one another and kissed each other on the cheeks.

That same day—we went out toward evening, drank beer and ate blood sausage with onions—Klepp suggested that we start a jazz band together. I asked for time to think it over, but Oskar had already made up his mind to give up his modeling and stonecutting activities and become percussion man in a jazz band.

On the Fiber Rug

There can be no doubt that on the day just recorded Oskar supplied Klepp with grounds for getting out of bed. He leapt overjoyed from his musty bedclothes; he allowed water to touch him, he was a new man, the kind that says "Terrific" and "The world is my oyster." And yet today, now that it is Oskar who is privileged to lie in bed, here is what I think: Klepp is trying to get even with me, he is trying to throw me out of my bed in this mental hospital, because I made him forsake his bed in the spaghetti kitchen.

Once a week I have to put up with his visits, listen to his tirades about jazz and his musico-Communist manifestoes, for no sooner had I deprived him of his bed and his Elizabeth-of-the-bagpipes than he, who as long as he lay in bed was a royalist, devoted heart and soul to the English royal family, became a dues-paying member of the Communist Party, and Communism has been his illegal hobby ever since: drinking beer, devouring blood sausage, he holds forth to the harmless little men who stand at bars, studying the labels on bottles, about the benefits of collective endeavour, of a jazz band working full time, or a Soviet kolkhoz.

In these times of ours, there isn't very much an awakened dreamer can do. Once alienated from his sheltering bed, Klepp had the possibility of becoming a comrade, and illegally at that, which added to the charm. Jazz was the second religion available to him. Thirdly Klepp, born a Protestant, could have been converted to Catholicism.

You've got to hand it to Klepp: he left the roads to all religions open. Caution, his heavy, glistening flesh, and a sense of humor that lives on applause, enabled him to devise a sly system, combining the teachings of Marx with the myth of jazz. If one day a left-wing priest of the worker-priest type should cross his path, especially if this priest should happen to have a collection of Dixieland records, you will see a Marxist jazz fan starting to take the sacraments on Sunday and mingling his above-mentioned body odor with the scent of a Neo-Gothic Cathedral.

Between me and such a fate stands my bed, from which Klepp tries to lure me with throbbing, life-loving promises. He sends petition after petition to the court and works hand in glove with my lawyer in demanding a new trial: he wants Oskar to be acquitted, set free—he wants them to turn me out of my hospital—and why? Just because he envies me my bed.

Even so, I have no regret that while rooming at Zeidler's I transformed a recumbent friend into a standing, stamping, and occasionally even running friend. Apart from the strenuously thoughtful hours that I devoted to Sister Dorothea, I now had a carefree private life. "Hey, Klepp," I would cry, slapping him on the shoulder, "what about that jazz band?" And he would fondle my hump, which he loved almost as much as his belly. "Oskar and me," he announced to the world, "we're going to start a jazz band. All we need is a good guitarist who can handle the banjo maybe if he has to."

He was right. Drum and flute would not have been enough. A

399

second melodic instrument was needed. A plucked bass wouldn't have been bad, and visually there was certainly something to be said for it, but even then bass players were hard to come by. So we searched frantically for a guitarist. We went to the movies a good deal, had our pictures taken twice a week as you may remember, and over beer, blood sausage, and onions, did all sorts of silly tricks with our passport photos. It was then that Klepp met his redheaded Ilse, thoughtlessly gave her a picture of himself, and just for that had to marry her. But we didn't find a guitarist.

In the course of my life as a model, I had gained some knowledge of the Old City of Düsseldorf, with its bull's-eye windowpanes, its mustard and cheese, its beer fumes and Lower Rhenish coziness, but it was only with Klepp that I became really familiar with it. We looked for a guitarist all around St. Lambert's Church, in all the bars, and most particularly in Ratinger-Strasse, at the Unicorn, because Bobby, who led the dance band, would sometimes let us join in with our flute and toy drum and was enthusiastic about my drumming, though he himself, despite the finger that was missing from his right hand, was no slouch as a percussion man.

We found no guitarist at the Unicorn, but I got a certain amount of practice. What with my wartime theatrical experience, I would have gotten back into the swing of it very quickly if not for Sister Dorothea, who occasionally made me miss my cue.

Half my thoughts were still with her. That would have been all right if the rest had remained entirely on my drum. But as it worked out, my thoughts would start with my drum and end up with Sister Dorothea's Red Cross pin. Klepp was brilliant at bridging over my lapses with his flute; but it worried him to see Oskar so half-immersed in his thoughts. "Are you hungry? I'll order some sausage."

Behind all the sorrows of this world Klepp saw a ravenous hunger; all human suffering, he believed, could be cured by a portion of blood sausage. What quantities of fresh blood sausage with rings of onion, washed down with beer, Oskar consumed in order to make his friend Klepp think his sorrow's name was hunger and not Sister Dorothea.

Usually we left the Zeidler flat early in the morning and took our breakfast in the Old City. I no longer went to the Academy except when we needed money for the movies. The Muse Ulla, who had meanwhile become engaged for the third or fourth time to Lankes, was unavailable, because Lankes was getting his first big industrial commissions. But Oskar didn't like to pose without Ulla, for when I posed alone, they would always distort me horribly and paint me in the blackest colors. And so I gave myself up entirely to my friend Klepp. I could still go to see Maria and little Kurt, but their apartment offered me no peace. Mr. Stenzel, her boss and married lover, was always there.

One day in the early fall of '49, Klepp and I left our rooms and converged in the hallway, not far from the frosted-glass door. We were about to leave the flat with our instruments when Zeidler opened the door of his living room by a crack and called out to us.

He was pushing a bulky roll of narrow carpeting and wanted us to help him lay it—a coconut-fiber runner it proved to be—in the hallway. The runner measured twenty-eight feet, but the hallway came to just twenty-five feet and seven inches; Klepp and I had to cut off the rest. This we did sitting down, for the cutting of coconut fiber proved to be hard work. When we were through, the runner was almost an inch too short, though the width was just right. Next Zeidler, who said he had trouble bending down, asked us to do the tacking. Oskar hit on the idea of stretching the runner as we tacked, and we managed to make up the gap, or very close to it. We used tacks with large, flat heads; small heads wouldn't have held in the coarse weave. Neither Oskar nor Klepp brought the hammer down on his thumb; we did bend a few tacks, though. But it wasn't our fault, it was the quality of the tacks, which were from Zeidler's stock, that is to say, manufactured before the currency reform. When the runner was half in place, we laid down our hammers crosswise and gave the Hedgehog, who was supervising our work, a look which while not insolently demanding must surely have been wistful. He disappeared into his bed-living room and came back with three of his famous liqueur glasses and a bottle of schnaps. We drank to the durability of the carpet; the first glass drained, we remarked—and again our tone was more wistful than demanding—that coconut fiber makes a man thirsty. I feel sure those liqueur glasses must have been glad of the opportunity to hold schnaps several times in a row before being reduced to smithereens by one of the Hedgehog's temper tantrums. When Klepp accidentally dropped an empty glass on the carpet, it did not break or even make a sound. We all sang the praises of the carpet. When Mrs. Zeidler, who was watching our work from the bed-living room, joined us in praising the fiber carpet because it protected falling liqueur glasses from harm, the Hedgehog flew into a rage. He stamped on the part of the runner that had not yet been tacked down, seized the three empty glasses, and vanished into the bed-living room. The china closet rattled—he was taking more glasses, three were not enough—and a moment later Oskar heard the familiar music: to his mind's eye appeared the Zeidler tile stove, eight shattered liqueur glasses beneath its cast-iron door, Zeidler bending down for the dustpan and brush, Zeidler sweeping up all the breakage that the Hedgehog had created. Mrs. Zeidler remained in the doorway while the glasses went tinkle-tinkle and crash-bang behind her. She took a considerable interest in our work; during the Hedgehog's tantrum we had picked up our hammers again. He never came back, but he had left the schnaps bottle. At first Mrs. Zeidler's presence embarrassed us, as

401

alternately we set the bottle to our lips. She gave us a friendly nod. That put us at our ease, but it never occurred to us to pass the bottle and offer her a nip. However, we made a neat job of it, and our tacks were evenly spaced. As Oskar was wielding his hammer outside Sister Dorothea's room, the panes of frosted glass rattled at every stroke. This stirred him to the quick and for an anguished moment he let the hammer drop. But once he had passed the frosted-glass door, he and his hammer felt better.

All things come to an end, and so did that fiber runner. The broad-headed tacks ran from end to end, up to their necks in the floorboards, holding just their heads above the surging, swirling coconut fibers. Well pleased with ourselves, we strode up and down the hallway, enjoying the length of the carpet, complimented ourselves on our work, and intimated just in passing that it was not so easy to lay a carpet before breakfast, on an empty stomach. At last we achieved our end: Mrs. Zeidler ventured out on the brand-new, virgin runner and found her way over it to the kitchen, where she poured out coffee and fried some eggs. We ate in my room; Mrs. Zeidler toddled off, it was time for her to go to the office at Mannesmann's. We left the door open, chewed, savored our fatigue, and contemplated our work, the fiber runner running fibrously toward us.

Why so many words about a cheap carpet which might at most have had a certain barter value before the currency reform? The question is justified. Oskar anticipates it and replies: it was on this fiber runner that Oskar, in the ensuing night, met Sister Dorothea for the first time.

It must have been close to midnight when I came home full of beer and blood sausage. I had left Klepp in the Old City, still looking for the guitarist. I found the keyhole of the Zeidler flat, found the fiber runner in the hallway, found my way past the dark frosted glass to my room, and, having taken my clothes off, found my bed. I did not find my pajamas, they were at Maria's in the wash; instead I found the extra piece of fiber runner we had cut off, laid it down beside my bed, got into bed, but found no sleep.

There is no reason to tell you everything that Oskar thought or revolved unthinking in his head because he could not sleep. Today I believe I have discovered the reason for my insomnia. Before climbing into bed, I had stood barefoot on my new bedside rug, the remnant from the runner. The coconut fibers pierced my bare skin and crept into my bloodstream: long after I had lain down, I was still standing on coconut fibers, and that is why I was unable to sleep; for nothing is more stimulating, more sleep-dispelling, more thought-provoking than standing barefoot on a coconut-fiber mat.

Long after midnight Oskar was still standing on the mat and lying in bed both at once; toward three in the morning he heard a door and another door. That, I thought, must be Klepp coming home without a guitarist but full of blood sausage; yet I knew it was not Klepp who opened first one door and then another. In addition, I thought, as long as you are lying in bed for nothing, with coconut fibers cutting into the soles of your feet, you might as well get out of bed and really, not just in your imagination, stand on the fiber mat beside your bed. Oskar did just this. There were consequences. The moment I set foot on the mat, it reminded me, via the soles of my feet, of its origin and source, the twenty-five-foot-six-inch runner in the hallway. Was it because I felt sorry for the cut-off remnant? Was it because I had heard the doors in the hallway and presumed, without believing, that it was Klepp? In any event, Oskar, who in going to bed had failed to find his pajamas, bent down, picked up one corner of the mat in each hand, moved his legs aside until he was no longer standing on the mat but on the floor, pulled up the thirty-inch mat between his legs and in front of his body, which, as we recall, measured four feet one. His nakedness was decently covered, but from knees to collarbone he was exposed to the influence of the coconut fiber. And that influence was further enhanced when behind his fibrous shield he left his dark room for the dark corridor and set his feet on the runner.

Is it any wonder if I took hurried little steps in order to escape the fibrous influence beneath my feet, if, in my search for salvation and safety, I made for the one place where there was no coconut fiber on the floor—the toilet?

This recess was as dark as the hallway or Oskar's room but was occupied nonetheless, as a muffled feminine scream made clear to me. My fiber pelt collided with the knees of a seated human. When I made no move to leave the toilet—for behind me threatened the coconut fibers—the seated human tried to expel me. "Who are you? what do you want? go away!" said a voice that could not possibly belong to Mrs. Zeidler. There was a certain plaintiveness in that "Who are you?"

"Well, well, Sister Dorothea, just guess." I ventured a little banter which, I hoped, would distract her from the slightly embarrassing circumstances of our meeting. But she wasn't in the mood for guessing; she stood up, reached out for me in the darkness and tried to push me out onto the runner, but she reached too high, into the void over my head. She tried lower down, but this time it wasn't I but my fibrous apron, my coconut pelt that she caught hold of. Again she let out a scream— oh, why do women always have to scream? Sister Dorothea seemed to have mistaken me for somebody, for she began to tremble and whispered: "Oh, heavens, it's the Devil!" I couldn't repress a slight giggle, but it wasn't meant maliciously. She, however, took it as the Devil's sniggering. That word Devil was not to my liking and when she again, but now in a very cowed tone, asked: "Who are you?" Oskar replied: "I am Satan, come to call on Sister Dorothea!" And she: "Oh, heavens, what for?"

Slowly I felt my way into my role, and Satan was my prompter.

"Because Satan is in love with Sister Dorothea!" "No, no, no, I won't have it," she cried. She tried again to escape, but once again encountered the Satanic fibers of my coconut pelt—her nightgown must have been very thin. Her ten fingers also encountered the jungle of seduction, and suddenly she felt faint. She fell forward; I caught her in my pelt, managed to hold her up long enough to arrive at a decision in keeping with my Satanic role. Gently giving way, I let her down on her knees, taking care that they should not touch the cold tiles of the toilet but come to rest on the fiber rug in the hallway. Then I let her slip down backward on the carpet, her head pointing westward in the direction of Klepp's room. The whole dorsal length of her—she must have measured at least five feet four—was in contact with the runner; I covered her over with the same fibrous stuff, but I had only thirty inches available. First I put the top end under her chin, but then the lower edge came down too far over her thighs. I had to move the mat up a couple of inches; now it covered her mouth, but her nose was still free, she could still breathe. She did more than breathe; she heaved and panted as Oskar lay down on his erstwhile mat, setting all its thousand fibers in vibration, for instead of seeking direct contact with Sister Dorothea, he relied on the effects of the coconut fiber. Again he tried to strike up a conversation, but Sister Dorothea was still in a half-faint. She could only gasp "Heavens, heavens!" and ask Oskar over and over who he was and where he was from. There was shuddering and trembling between fiber runner and fiber mat when I said I was Satan, pronounced the name with a Satanic hiss, gave hell as my address, and described it with a picturesque touch or two. I thrashed about vigorously on my bedside mat to keep it in motion, for my ears told me plainly that the fibers gave Sister Dorothea a sensation similar to that which fizz powder had given my beloved Maria years before, the only difference being that the fizz powder had allowed me to hold up my end successfully, nay triumphantly, while here on the fiber mat, I suffered a humiliating failure. I just couldn't throw anchor. My little friend who in the fizz powder days and frequently thereafter had stood erect, full of purpose and ambition, now drooped his head; here on the coconut fiber he remained puny, listless, and unresponsive. Nothing could move him, neither my intellectual arguments nor the heart-rending appeals of Sister Dorothea, who whimpered and moaned: "Come, Satan, come!" I tried to comfort her with promises: "Satan is coming," I said in a Satanic tone, "Satan will be ready in a minute." At the same time I held a dialogue with the Satan who has dwelt within me since my baptism. I scolded: Don't be a kill-joy, Satan. I pleaded: For goodness' sake, Satan, don't disgrace me this way. And cajoled: It's not a bit like you, old boy. Think back, think of Maria, or better still of the widow Greff, or of how you and I used to frolic with my darling Roswitha in gay Paree? Satan's reply was morose and repetitious: I'm not in the mood, Oskar. When Satan's not in the mood, virtue triumphs. Hasn't even Satan a right not to be in the mood once in a while?

With these and similar saws, Satan refused me his support. I kept the fiber mat in motion, scraping poor Sister Dorothea raw, but I was gradually weakening. "Come, Satan," she sighed, "oh, please come." And at length I responded with a desperate, absurd, utterly unmotivated assault beneath the mat: I aimed an unloaded pistol at the bull's-eye. She tried to help her Satan, her arms came out from under the mat, she flung them around me, found my hump, my warm, human, and not at all fibrous skin. But this wasn't the Satan she wanted. There were no more murmurs of "Come, Satan, come." Instead, she cleared her throat and repeated her original question but in a different register: "For heaven's sake who are you, what do you want?" I could only pull in my horns and admit that according to my papers my name was Oskar Matzerath, that I was her neighbor, and that I loved her, Sister Dorothea, with all my heart.

If any malicious soul imagines that Sister Dorothea cursed me and pushed me down on the fiber runner, Oskar must assure him, sadly yet with a certain satisfaction, that Sister Dorothea removed her hands very slowly, thoughtfully as it were, from my hump, with a movement resembling an infinitely sad caress. She began to cry, to sob, but without violence. I hardly noticed it when she wriggled out from under me and the mat, when she slipped away from me and I slipped to the floor. The carpet absorbed the sound of her steps. I heard a door opening and closing, a key turning; then the six squares of the frosted-glass door took on light and reality from within.

Oskar lay there and covered himself with the mat, which still had a little Satanic warmth in it. My eyes were fixed on the illumined squares. From time to time a shadow darted across the frosted glass. Now she is going to the clothes cupboard, I said to myself, and now to the washstand. Oskar attempted a last diabolical venture. Taking my mat with me I crawled over the runner to the door, scratched on the wood, raised myself a little, sent a searching, pleading hand over the two lower panes. Sister Dorothea did not open; she kept moving busily between cupboard and washstand. I knew the truth and admitted as much: Sister Dorothea was packing, preparing to take flight, to take flight from me.

Even the feeble hope that in leaving the room she would show me her electrically illumined face was to be disappointed. First the light went out behind the frosted glass, then I heard the key, the door opened, shoes on the fiber runner—I reached out for her, struck a suitcase, a stockinged leg. She kicked me in the chest with one of those sensible hiking shoes I had seen in the clothes cupboard, and when Oskar pleaded a last time: "Sister Dorothea," the apartment door slammed: a woman had left me.

You and all those who understand my grief will say now: Go to bed, Oskar. What business have you in the hallway after this humiliating episode? It is four in the morning. You are lying naked on a fiber rug, with no cover but a small and scraggly mat. You've scraped the skin off your hands and knees. Your heart bleeds, your member aches, your shame cries out to high heaven. You have waked Mr. Zeidler. He has waked his wife. In another minute they'll get up, open the door of their bed-living room, and see you. Go to bed, Oskar, it will soon strike five.

This was exactly the advice I gave myself as I lay on the fiber runner. But I just shivered and lay still. I tried to call back Sister Dorothea's body. I could feel nothing but coconut fibers, they were everywhere, even between my teeth. Then a band of light fell on Oskar: the door of the Zeidler bed-living room opened a crack. Zeidler's hedgehog-head, above it a head full of metal curlers, Mrs. Zeidler. They stared, he coughed, she giggled, he called me, I gave no reply, she went on giggling, he told her to be still, she asked what was wrong with me, he said this won't do, she said it was a respectable house, he threatened to put me out, but I was silent, for the measure was not yet full. The Zeidlers opened the door, he switched on the light in the hall. They came toward me, making malignant little eyes; he had a good rage up, and it wasn't on any liqueur glasses that he was going to vent it this time. He stood over me, and Oskar awaited the Hedgehog's fury. But Zeidler never did get that tantrum off his chest. A hubbub was heard in the stair well, an uncertain key groped for, and at last found, the keyhole, and Klepp came in, bringing with him someone who was just as drunk as he: Scholle, the long-sought guitarist.

The two of them pacified Zeidler and wife, bent down over Oskar, asked no questions, picked me up, and carried me, me and my Satanic mat, to my room.

Klepp rubbed me warm. The guitarist picked up my clothes. Together they dressed me and dried my tears. Sobs. Daybreak outside the window. Sparrows. Klepp hung my drum round my neck and showed his little wooden flute. Sobs. The guitarist picked up his guitar. Sparrows. Friends surrounded me, took me between them, led the sobbing but unresisting Oskar out of the flat, out of the house in Jülicher-Strasse, toward the sparrows, led him away from the influence of coconut fiber, led me through dawning streets, through the Hofgarten to the planetarium and the banks of the river Rhine, whose gray waters rolled down to Holland, carrying barges with flowing clotheslines.

From six to nine that misty September morning, Klepp the flutist, Scholle the guitarist, and Oskar the percussion man sat on the right bank of the river Rhine. We made music, played ourselves into the groove, drank out of one bottle, peered across at the poplars on the opposite bank, and regaled the steamers that were bucking the current after taking on coal in Duisburg, with hot jazz and sad Mississippi music. Meanwhile we wondered about a name for the jazz band we had just founded.

When a bit of sun colored the morning mist and a craving for breakfast crept into our music, Oskar, who had put his drum between himself and the preceding night, arose, took some money from his coat pocket, by which he meant and they understood breakfast, and announced to his friends the name of the newborn band: We agreed to call ourselves "The Rhine River Three" and went to breakfast.

In the Onion Cellar

We loved the Rhine meadows, and it so happened that Ferdinand Schmuh, the restaurant and night-spot owner, also loved the right bank of the Rhine between Düsseldorf and Kaiserswerth. We did most of our practicing above Stockum. Meanwhile Schmuh, carrying a small-caliber rifle, searched the riverside hedges and bushes for sparrows. That was his hobby, his recreation. When business got on his nerves, Schmuh bade his wife take the wheel of the Mercedes; they would drive along the river and park above Stockum. Slightly flat-footed, his rifle pointing at the ground, he set off across the meadows, followed by his wife, who would rather have stayed in the car. At the end of their cross-country jaunt, he deposited her on a comfortable stone by the riverbank and vanished amid the hedges. While we played our ragtime, he went pop pop in the bushes. While we made music, Schmuh shot sparrows.

When Scholle, who like Klepp knew every bar owner in town, heard shooting in the shrubbery, he announced: "Schmuh is shooting sparrows."

Since Schmuh is no longer living, I may as well put in my obituary right here: Schmuh was a good marksman and perhaps a good man as well; for when Schmuh went sparrow-shooting, he kept ammunition in the left-hand pocket of his coat, but his right-hand pocket was full of bird food, which he distributed among the sparrows with a generous sweeping movement, not before, but after he had done his shooting, and he never shot more than twelve birds in an afternoon.

One cool November morning in 1949, when Schmuh was still among the living and we for our part had been rehearsing for some weeks on the banks of the Rhine, he addressed us in a voice too loud and angry to be taken quite seriously: "How do you expect me to shoot birds when you scare them away with your music?"

"Oh," Klepp apologized, holding out his flute as though presenting arms. "You must be the gentleman with the superb sense of rhythm, whose shooting keeps such perfect time with our melodies. My respects, Mr. Schmuh!"

Schmuh was pleased that Klepp knew him by name, but inquired how so. Klepp, with a show of indignation: Why, everybody knows Schmuh. In the street I can always hear somebody saying: There's Schmuh, there goes Schmuh, did you see Schmuh just now, where is Schmuh today, Schmuh is out shooting sparrows.

Thus transformed into a public figure, Schmuh offered us cigarettes, asked us our names, and requested a piece from our repertory. We obliged with a tiger rag, whereupon he called his wife, who had been sitting in her fur coat on a stone, musing over the waters of the Rhine. Fur-coated, she joined us and again we played; this time it was "High Society," and when we had finished, she said in her fur coat: "Why, Ferdy, that's just what you need for the Cellar." He seemed to be of the same opinion; indeed, he was under the impression that he personally had gone scouting for us and found us. Nevertheless, Schmuh, pondering, maybe calculating, sent several flat stones skipping over the waters of the Rhine before he made his offer: would we play at the Onion Cellar from nine to two, for ten marks an evening apiece, well, let's say twelve? Klepp said seventeen in order that Schmuh might say fifteen; Schmuh said fourteen fifty, and we called it a deal.

Seen from the street, the Onion Cellar looked like many of the newer night clubs which are distinguished from the older bars and cabarets by, among other things, their higher prices. The higher prices were justified by the outlandish decoration of these night spots, many of which termed themselves "Artists' clubs" and also by their names. There was "The Ravioli Room" (discreet and refined), "The Taboo" (mysterious and ex-istentialist), "The Paprika" (spicy and high-spirited). And of course there was "The Onion Cellar".

The words "Onion Cellar" and a poignantly naive likeness of an onion had been painted with deliberate awkwardness on an enamel sign which hung in the old German manner from elaborate wrought-iron gallows in front of the house. The one and only window was glassed with bottle-green bull's-eye panes. The iron door, painted with red lead, had no doubt seen service outside an air-raid shelter in the war years. Outside it stood the doorman in a rustic sheepskin. Not everyone was allowed in the Onion Cellar. Especially on Fridays, when wages turn to beer, it was the doorman's business to turn away certain Old City characters, for whom the Onion Cellar was too expensive in the first place. Behind the red-lead door, those who were allowed in found five concrete steps. You went down, found yourself on a landing some three feet square, to which a poster for a Picasso show lent an original, artistic turn. Four more steps took you to the checkroom. "Please pay later," said a little cardboard sign, and indeed, the young man at the counter, usually an art student with a beard, refused to take money in advance, because the Onion Cellar was not only expensive but also and nevertheless high class.

The owner in person welcomed every single guest with elaborate gestures and mobile, expressive eyebrows, as though initiating him into a secret rite. As we know, the owner's name was Ferdinand Schmuh; he was a man who shot sparrows now and then, and had a keen eye for the society which had sprung up in Düsseldorf (and elsewhere, though not quite so quickly) since the currency reform.

The Onion Cellar—and here we see the note of authenticity essential to a successful night club—was a real cellar; in fact, it was quite damp and chilly under foot. Tubular in shape, it measured roughly thirteen by sixty, and was heated by two authentic cast-iron stoves. Yet in one respect the Cellar wasn't a cellar after all. The ceiling had been taken off, so that the club actually included the former ground-floor apartment. The one and only window was not a real cellar window, but the former window of the ground-floor apartment. However, since one might have looked out of the window if not for its opaque bull's-eye panes; since there was a gallery that one reached by a highly original and highly precipitous staircase, the Onion Cellar can reasonably be termed "authentic," even if it was not a real cellar—and besides, why should it have been?

Oskar has forgotten to tell you that the staircase leading to the gallery was not a real staircase but more like a companionway, because on either side of its dangerously steep steps there were two extremely original clotheslines to hold on to; the staircase swayed a bit, making you think of an ocean voyage and adding to the price.

The Onion Cellar was lighted by acetylene lamps such as miners carry, which broadcast a smell of carbide—again adding to the price—and transported the customer unto the gallery of a mine, a potash mine for instance, three thousand feet below the surface of the earth: cutters bare to the waist hack away at the rock, opening up a vein; the scraper hauls out the salt, the windlass roars as it fills the cars; far behind, where the gallery turns off to Friedrichshall Two, a swaying light; that's the head foreman and here he comes with a cheery hello, swinging a carbide lamp that looks exactly like the carbide lamps that hung from the unadorned, slapdashly whitewashed walls of the Onion Cellar, casting their light and smell, adding to the prices, and creating an original atmosphere.

The customers were uncomfortably seated on common crates covered with onion sacks, yet the plank tables, scrubbed and spotless, recalled the guests from the mine to a peaceful peasant inn such as we sometimes see in the movies.

That was all! But what about the bar? No bar. Waiter, the menu please! Neither waiter nor menu. In fact, there was no one else but ourselves, the Rhine River Three. Klepp, Scholle, and Oskar sat beneath the staircase that was really a companionway. We arrived at nine, unpacked our instruments, and began to play at about ten. But for the present it is only a quarter past nine and I won't be able to speak about

409

us until later. Right now let us keep an eye on Schmuh, who occasionally shot sparrows with a small-caliber rifle.

As soon as the Onion Cellar had filled up—half-full was regarded as full—Schmuh, the host, donned his shawl. This shawl had been specially made for him. It was cobalt-blue silk, printed with a golden-yellow pattern. I mention all this because the donning of the shawl was significant. The pattern printed on the shawl was made up of golden-yellow onions. The Onion Cellar was not really "open" until Schmuh had put on his shawl.

The customers—businessmen, doctors, lawyers, artists, journalists, theater and movie people, well-known figures from the sporting world, officials in the provincial and municipal government, in short, a cross section of the world which nowadays calls itself intellectual—came with wives, mistresses, secretaries, interior decorators, and occasional male mistresses, to sit on crates covered with burlap. Until Schmuh put on his golden-yellow onions, the conversation was subdued, forced, dispirited. These people wanted to talk, to unburden themselves, but they couldn't seem to get started; despite all their efforts, they left the essential unsaid, talked around it. Yet how eager they were to spill their guts, to talk from their hearts, their bowels, their entrails, to forget about their brains just this once, to lay bare the raw, unvarnished truth, the man within. Here and there a stifled remark about a botched career, a broken marriage. One gathers that the gentleman over there with the massive head, the intelligent face and soft, almost delicate hands, is having trouble with his son, who is displeased about his father's past. Those two ladies in mink, who still look quite attractive in the light of the carbide lamp, claim to have lost their faith, but they don't say in what. So far we know nothing about the past of the gentleman with the massive head, nor have we the slightest idea what sort of trouble his son is making for him on account of this unknown past; if you'll forgive Oskar a crude metaphor, it was like laying eggs; you push and push . . .

The pushing in the Onion Cellar brought meager results until Schmuh appeared in his special shawl. Having been welcomed with a joyful "Ah!" for which he thanked his kind guests, he vanished for a few minutes behind a curtain at the end of the Onion Cellar, where the toilets and storeroom were situated.

But why did a still more joyous "Ah," an "Ah" of relief and release, welcome the host on his reappearance? The proprietor of a successful nightclub disappears behind a curtain, takes something from the storeroom, flings a choice selection of insults in an undertone at the washroom attendant who is sitting there reading an illustrated weekly, reappears in front of the curtain, and is welcomed like the Saviour, like the legendary uncle from Australia!

Schmuh came back with a little basket on his arm and moved among the guests. The basket was covered with a blue-and-yellow checkered napkin. On the cloth lay a considerable number of little wooden boards, shaped like pigs or fish. These he handed out to his guests with little bows and compliments which showed, beyond the shadow of a doubt, that he had grown up in Budapest and Vienna; Schmuh's smile was like the smile on a copy of a copy of the supposedly authentic Mona Lisa.

The guests, however, looked very serious as they took their little boards. Some exchanged boards with their neighbors, for some preferred the silhouette of a pig, while others preferred the more mysterious fish. They sniffed at the pieces of wood and moved them about. Schmuh, after serving the customers in the gallery, waited until all the little boards had come to rest.

Then—and every heart was waiting—he removed the napkin, very much in the manner of a magician: beneath it lay still another napkin, upon which, almost unrecognizable at first glance, lay the paring knives.

These too he proceeded to hand out. But this time he made his rounds more quickly, whipping up the tension that permitted him to raise his prices; he paid no more compliments, and left no time for any exchanges of knives; a calculated haste entered into his movements. "On your mark, get set," he shouted. At "Go" he tore the napkin off the basket, reached into the basket, and handed out, dispensed, distributed among the multitude . . . onions—onions such as were represented, golden-yellow and slightly stylized, on his shawl, plain ordinary onions, not tulip bulbs, but onions such as women buy in the market, such as the vegetable woman sells, such as the peasant, the peasant's wife, or the hired girl plants and harvests, onions such as may be seen, more or less faithfully portrayed in the still lifes of the lesser Dutch masters. Such onions, then, Schmuh dispensed among his guests until each had an onion and no sound could be heard but the purring of the stoves and the whistling of the carbide lamps. For the grand distribution of onions was followed by silence. Into which Ferdinand Schmuh cried: "Ladies and gentlemen, help yourselves." And he tossed one end of his shawl over his left shoulder like a skier just before the start. This was the signal.

The guests peeled the onions. Onions are said to have seven skins. The ladies and gentlemen peeled the onions with the paring knives. They removed the first, third, blond, golden-yellow, rust-brown, or better still, onion-colored skin, they peeled until the onion became glassy, green, whitish, damp, and water-sticky, until it smelled, smelled like an onion. Then they cut it as one cuts onions, deftly or clumsily, on the little chopping boards shaped like pigs or fish; they cut in one direction and another until the juice spurted or turned to vapor—the older gentlemen were not very handy with paring knives and had to be careful not to cut their fingers; some cut themselves even so, but didn't notice it—the ladies were more skillful, not all of them, but those at least who were housewives at home, who knew how one cuts up onions for hash-brown potatoes, or for liver with apples and onion rings; but in Schmuh's onion cellar there was neither, there was nothing whatever to eat, and anyone who wanted to eat had to go elsewhere, to the "Fischl," for instance, for at the Onion Cellar onions were only cut. Why all these onions? For one thing, because of the name. The Onion Cellar had its specialty: onions. And moreover, the onion, the cut onion, when you look at it closely . . . but enough of that, Schmuh's guests had stopped looking, they could see nothing more, because their eyes were running over and not because their hearts were so full; for it is not true that when the heart is full the eyes necessarily overflow, some people can never manage it, especially in our century, which in spite of all the suffering and sorrow will surely be known to posterity as the tearless century. It was this drought, this tearlessness that brought those who could afford it to Schmuh's Onion Cellar, where the host handed them a little chopping board—pig or fish—a paring knife for eighty pfennigs, and for twelve marks an ordinary field-, garden-, and kitchen-variety onion, and induced them to cut their onions smaller and smaller until the juice—what did the onion juice do? It did what the world and the sorrows of the world could not do: it brought forth a round, human tear. It made them cry. At last they were able to cry again. To cry properly, without restraint, to cry like mad. The tears flowed and washed everything away. The rain came. The dew. Oskar has a vision of floodgates opening. Of dams bursting in the spring floods. What is the name of that river that overflows every spring and the government does nothing to stop it?

After this cataclysm at twelve marks eighty, human beings who have had a good cry open their mouths to speak. Still hesitant, startled by the nakedness of their own words, the weepers poured out their hearts to their neighbors on the uncomfortable, burlap-covered crates, submitted to questioning, let themselves be turned inside-out like overcoats. But Oskar, who with Klepp and Scholle sat tearless behind the staircase or companionway, will be discreet; from among all the disclosures, self-accusations, confessions that fell on his ears, he will relate only the story of Miss Pioch, who lost her Mr. Vollmer many times over, so acquiring a strong heart and a tearless eye, which necessitated frequent visits to Schmuh's Onion Cellar.

We met, said Miss Pioch when she had finished crying, in the streetcar. I had just come from the store—she owns and operates an excellent bookstore. The car was full and Willy—that's Mr. Vollmer—stepped on my right foot. He stepped so hard that I couldn't stand on it any more, and we loved each other at first sight. I couldn't walk either, so he offered me his arm, escorted, or rather carried, me home, and from that day on he took loving care of the toenail which had turned black and blue under his heel. He loved me, not just my toe, until the toenail came loose from its toe—the right big toe—and there was nothing to prevent a new toenail from growing in. The day the dead toenail fell, his love began to cool. Both of us were miserable about it. It was then that Willy—he still cared for me in a way and, besides, we had so much in common—had his terrible idea. Let me, he pleaded, trample your left big toe until the nail turns a light, then a darker purple. I consented and he trampled. Again he loved me with his whole being, and his love endured until my big toenail, the left one it was, fell away like a withered leaf; and then it was autumn again for our love. Willy wanted to start in again on my right big toe, the nail had meanwhile grown in again. But I wouldn't let him. If your love for me is really so overpowering, I said, it ought to outlast a toenail. He couldn't seem to understand. He left me. Months later, we met at a concert. The seat beside me happened to be unoccupied and after the intermission he sat down in it. They were doing the *Ninth Symphony*. When the chorus started up, I removed the shoe from my right foot and held the foot out in front of him. He stepped on it with might and main, but I didn't do anything to interfere with the concert. Seven weeks later Willy left me again. We had two more brief reprieves; twice more I held out my toe, first the left one, then the right one. Today both my toes are maimed. The nails won't grow in again. From time to time Willy comes to see me; shaken, full of pity for me and for himself, he sits at my feet on the rug and stares, unloving and unweeping, at the two nailless victims of our love. Sometimes I say: Come along Willy, let's go to Schmuh's Onion Cellar and have a good cry. But so far he has refused to come. What the poor soul must suffer without the consolation of tears!

Later—this Oskar relates only to satisfy the curious among you— Mr. Vollmer (he sold radios, I might mention in passing) did come to our Cellar. They cried together and it seems, as Klepp told me yesterday in visiting hour, that they have just been married.

It was from Tuesday to Saturday—the Onion Cellar was closed on Sunday—that the onion brought the more basic tragedies of human existence welling to the surface. But the most violent weeping was done on Mondays, when our cellar was patronized by the younger set. On Monday Schmuh served onions to students at half-price. The most frequent guests were medical and premedical students—of both sexes. Quite a few art students as well. particularly among those who were planning to teach drawing later on, spent a portion of their stipends on onions. But where, I have wondered ever since, did the boys and girls in their last year of high school get the money for onions?

Young people have a different way of crying. They have entirely different problems from their elders, but this doesn't mean that examinations are their only source of anguish. Oh, what conflicts between father and son, mother and daughter, were aired in the Onion Cellar! A good many of the young people felt that they were not understood, but most of them were used to it; nothing to cry about. Oskar was glad to see that love, and not just sexual frustration, could still wring tears from the young folks. Gerhard and Gudrun for instance.

At first they sat downstairs; it was only later that they wept side by side in the gallery. She, large and muscular, a handball player and student of chemistry. She wore her hair over her neck in a big bun. Most of the time she looked straight ahead of her out of gray, motherly eyes, a clean forthright gaze that reminded me of the Women's Association posters during the war.

In spite of her fine forehead, smooth, milky-white, and radiant with health, her face was her misfortune. Her cheeks and her round, firm chin down to her Adam's apple bore the distressing traces of a vigorous growth of beard that the poor thing kept trying in vain to shave off. Her sensitive skin reacted violently to the razor blade. Gudrun wept for her red, cracked, pimply complexion, she wept for the beard that kept growing back in. They had not met in the streetcar like Miss Pioch and Mr. Vollmer, but in the train. He was sitting opposite her, they were both on their way back from their between-semesters vacation. He loved her instantly in spite of the beard. She, because of her beard, was afraid to love him, but was full of admiration for what to him was his misfortune, his chin, which was as smooth and beardless as a baby's bottom, and made him bashful in the presence of girls. Nevertheless, Gerhard spoke to Gudrun, and by the time they left the train at the Düsseldorf station, they were friends at least. After that they saw each other every day. They spoke of this and that, and shared a good part of their thoughts, but never alluded to the beard that was missing or the beard that was all too present. Gerhard was considerate of Gudrun; knowing that her skin was sensitive, he never kissed her. Their love remained chaste, though neither of them set much store by chastity, for she was interested in chemistry while he was studying medicine. When a friend suggested the Onion Cellar, they smiled contemptuously with the skepticism characteristic of chemists and medical men. But finally they went, for purposes of documentation, as they assured each other. Never has Oskar seen young people cry so. They came time and time again; they went without food to save up the six marks forty it cost them, and wept about the beard that was absent and the beard that devastated the soft, maidenly skin. Sometimes they tried to stay away from the Onion Cellar. One Monday they didn't come, but the following Monday they were back again. Rubbing the chopped onion

414

between their fingers, they admitted that they had tried to save the six marks forty; they had tried doing it by themselves in her room with a cheap onion, but it wasn't the same. You needed an audience. It was so much easier to cry in company. It gave you a real sense of brotherhood in sorrow when to the right and left of you and in the gallery overhead your fellow students were all crying their hearts out.

This was another case in which the Onion Cellar bestowed not only tears but also, little by little, a cure. Apparently the tears washed away their inhibitions and brought them, as the saying goes, closer together. He kissed her tortured cheeks, she fondled his smooth chin, and one day they stopped coming to the Onion Cellar; they didn't need it any more. Oskar met them months later in Königs-Allee. He didn't recognize them at first. He, the glabrous Gerhard, sported a waving, reddish-blond beard; she, the prickly Gudrun, had barely a slight dark fuzz on her upper lip, very becoming to her. Her chin and cheeks were smooth, radiant, free from vegetation. Still studying but happily married, a student couple. Oskar can hear them in fifty years talking to their grandchildren. She, Gudrun: "That was long ago, before Grandpa had his beard." And he, Gerhard: "That was in the days when your Grandma was having trouble with her beard and we went to the Onion Cellar every Monday."

But to what purpose, you may ask, are three musicians still sitting under the companionway or staircase? What use had the onion shop, what with all this weeping, wailing, and gnashing of teeth, for a regular, and regularly paid, band?

Once the customers had finished crying and unburdening themselves, we took up our instruments and provided a musical transition to normal, everyday conversation. We made it easy for the guests to leave the Onion Cellar and make room for more guests. Klepp, Scholle, and Oskar were not personally lovers of onions. Besides, there was a clause in our contract forbidding us to "use" onions in the same way as the guests. We had no need of them anyway. Scholle, the guitarist, had no ground for sorrow, he always seemed happy and contented, even when two strings on his banjo snapped at once in the middle of a rag. As to Klepp, the very concepts of crying and laughing are to this day unclear to him. Tears make him laugh; I have never seen anyone laugh as hard as Klepp did at the funeral of the aunt who used to wash his shirts and socks before he got married. But what of Oskar? Oskar had plenty of ground for tears. Mightn't he have used a few tears to wash away Sister Dorothea and that long, futile night spent on a still longer coconut-fiber runner? And my Maria? There is no doubt that she gave me cause enough for grief. Didn't Stenzel, her boss, come and go as he pleased in the flat in Bilk? Hadn't Kurt, my son, taken to calling the grocery-store-owner first "Uncle Stenzel" and then "Papa Stenzel"? And what of those who lay in the faraway sand of Saspe Cemetery or in the clay at Brenntau: my poor mama, the foolish and lovable Jan Bronski, and Matzerath, the cook who knew how to transform feelings into soups? All of them needed to be wept for. But Oskar was one of the fortunate who could still weep without onions. My drum helped me. Just a few very special measures were all it took to make Oskar melt into tears that were no better or worse than the expensive tears of the Onion Cellar.

As for Schmuh, the proprietor, he never touched his onions either. In his case the sparrows he shot out of hedges and bushes in his free time filled the bill. Sometimes, after shooting, Schmuh would line up his twelve dead sparrows on a newspaper, shed tears over the little bundles of feathers before they even had time to grow cold, and, still weeping, strew bird food over the Rhine meadows and the pebbles by the water. In the Cellar he had still another outlet for his sorrow. He had gotten into the habit of giving the washroom attendant a ferocious tongue-lashing once a week, making more and more use of archaic expressions like "slut," "miserable strumpet," "blasted old harridan." "Out of my sight!" we could hear him bellow, "Despicable monster! You're fired!" He would dismiss his victim without notice and hire a new one. But soon he ran into difficulty, there were no washroom attendants left. There was nothing for it but to hire back those he had previously fired. They were only too glad to accept; most of Schmuh's insults didn't mean much to them anyway, and they made good money. The guests at the Onion Cellar— an effect of so much weeping no doubt—made exorbitant use of the facilities, and moreover Homo lacrimans tends to be more generous than his dry-eyed counterpart. Especially the gentlemen, who, after begging leave in voices choked with tears to step out for a minute, could be counted on to reach deep into their purses. Another source of income for the washroom attendant was the sale of the famous onion-print handker-chiefs inscribed with the legend: "In the Onion Cellar." They sold like hotcakes, for when they were no longer needed to wipe the eyes with they made attractive souvenirs and could be worn on the head. They could also be made into pennants which the habitués of the Onion Cellar would hang in the rear windows of their cars, so bearing the fame of Schmuh's Onion Cellar, in vacation time, to Paris, the Côte d'Azur, Rome, Ravenna, Rimini, and even remote Spain.

We musicians and our music had still another function. Occasionally some of the guests would partake of two onions in quick succession; the result was an outbreak that might easily have degenerated into an orgy. Schmuh insisted on a certain restraint; when gentlemen began taking off their ties and ladies undoing their blouses, he would order us to step in with our music and counteract the stirrings of lewdness. However, Schmuh himself was largely responsible for these ticklish situations, what with his insidious habit of serving up a second onion to particularly vulnerable customers.

The most spectacular outburst I can recall was to influence Oskar's whole career, though I shall not go so far as to speak of a crucial turning point. Schmuh's wife, the vivacious Billy, did not come to the Cellar very often, and when she did, it was in the company of friends to whom Schmuh was far from partial. One night she turned up with Woode, the music critic, and Wackerlei, the architect and pipe-smoker. Both of them were regular customers, but their sorrows were of the most boring variety. Woode wept for religious reasons—he was always being converted or reconverted to something or other; as for Wackerlei, the pipe-smoker, he was still bewailing a professorship he had turned down in the twenties for the sake of a little Danish fly-by-night who had gone and married a South American and had six children by him, which was still a source of grief to Wackerlei and made his pipe go out year after year. It was the somewhat malicious Woode who persuaded Madame Schmuh to cut into an onion. She cut, the tears flowed, and she began to spill. She laid Schmuh bare, told stories about him that Oskar will tactfully pass over in silence; it took several of the more powerful customers to prevent Schmuh from flinging himself on his spouse; don't forget that there were paring knives on every table. In any case, Schmuh was forcibly restrained until the indiscreet Billy could slip away with her friends Woode and Wackerlei.

Schmuh was very upset. I could see that by the way his hands flew about arranging and rearranging his onion shawl. Several times he vanished behind the curtain and reviled the washroom attendant. Finally he came back with a full basket and informed his guests in a tone of hysterical glee that he, Schmuh, was in a generous mood and was going to hand out a free round of onions. Which he proceeded to do.

Every human situation, however painful, strikes Klepp as a terrific joke, but on this occasion he was tense and held his flute at the ready. For we knew how dangerous it was to offer these high-strung people a double portion of tears, of the tears that wash away barriers.

Schmuh saw that we were holding our instruments in readiness and forbade us to play. At the tables the paring knives were at work. The beautiful outer skins, colored like rosewood, were thrust heedlessly aside. The knives bit into vitreous onion flesh with pale-green stripes. Oddly enough, the weeping did not begin with the ladies. Gentlemen in their prime—the owner of a large flour mill, a hotel-owner with his slightly rouged young friend, a nobleman high in the councils of an important business firm, a whole tableful of men's clothing manufacturers who were in town for a board meeting, the bald actor who was known in the Cellar as the Gnasher, because he gnashed his teeth when he wept—all were in tears before the ladies joined in. But neither the ladies nor the gentlemen wept the tears of deliverance and release that the first onion had called forth; this was a frantic, convulsive crying jag. The Gnasher gnashed his teeth blood-curdlingly; had he been on the stage, the whole audience would have joined in; the mill-owner hanged his carefully groomed gray head on the table top; the hotel-owner mingled his convulsions with those of his delicate young friend. Schmuh, who stood by the stairs, let his shawl droop and peered with malicious satisfaction at the near-unleashed company. Suddenly, a lady of ripe years tore off her blouse before the eyes of her son-in-law. The hotel-owner's young friend, whose slightly exotic look had already been remarked on, bared his swarthy torso, and leaping from table top to table top performed a dance which exists perhaps somewhere in the Orient. The orgy was under way. But despite the violence with which it began, it was a dull, uninspired affair, hardly worth describing in detail.

Schmuh was disappointed; even Oskar lifted his eyebrows in disgust. One or two cute strip tease acts; men appeared in ladies' underwear, Amazons donned ties and suspenders; a couple or two disappeared under the table; the Gnasher chewed up a brassiere and apparently swallowed some of it.

The hubbub was frightful, wows and yippees with next to nothing behind them. At length Schmuh, disgusted and maybe fearing the police, left his post by the stairs, bent down over us, gave first Klepp, then me a poke, and hissed: "Music! Play something, for God's sake. Make them stop."

But it turned out that Klepp, who was easy to please, was enjoying himself. Shaking with laughter, he couldn't do a thing with his flute. Scholle, who looked on Klepp as his master, imitated everything Klepp did, including his laughter. Only Oskar was left—but Schmuh could rely on me. I pulled my drum from under the bench, nonchalantly lit a cigarette, and began to drum.

Without any notion of what I was going to do, I made myself understood. I forgot all about the usual café concert routine. Nor did Oskar play jazz. For one thing I didn't like to be taken for a percussion maniac. All right, I was a good drummer, but not a hepcat. Sure, I like jazz, but I like Viennese waltzes too. I could play both, but I didn't have to. When Schmuh asked me to step in with my drum, I didn't play anything I had ever learned, I played with my heart. It was a three-year-old Oskar who picked up those drumsticks. I drummed my way back, I drummed up the world as a three-year-old sees it. And the first thing I did to these postwar humans incapable of a real orgy was to put a harness on them: I led them to Posadowski-Weg, to Auntie Kauer's kindergarten. Soon I had their jaws hanging down; they took each other by the hands, turned their toes in, and waited for me, their Pied Piper. I left my post under the staircase and took the lead. "Bake, bake, bake a cake": that was my first sample. When I had registered my success—childlike merriment on every hand—I decided to scare them out of their wits. "Where's the Witch, black as pitch?" I drummed. And I drummed up the wicked black Witch who gave me an occasional fright in my childhood days and in recent years has terrified me more and more; I made her rage through the Onion Cellar in all her gigantic, coal-black frightfulness, so obtaining the results for which Schmuh required onions; the ladies and gentlemen wept great round, childlike tears, the ladies and gentlemen were scared pink and green; their teeth chattered, they begged me to have mercy. And so, to comfort them, and in part to help them back into their outer and undergarments, their silks and satins, I drummed: "Green, green, green is my raiment" and "Red, red, red is my raiment," not to mention "Blue, blue, blue . . ." and "Yellow, yellow, yellow." By the time I had gone through all the more familiar colors, my charges were all properly dressed. Thereupon I formed them into a procession, led them through the Onion Cellar as though it were Jeschkentaler-Weg. I led them up the Erbsberg, round the hideous Gutenberg Monument, and on the Johannis-Wiese grew daisies which they, the ladies and gentlemen, were free to pick in innocent merriment. Then, at last, wishing to give all those present, including Schmuh the head man, something by which to remember their day in kindergarten, I gave them all permission to do number one. We were approaching Devil's Gulch, a sinister place it was, gathering beechnuts, when I said on my drum: now, children, you may go. And they availed themselves of the opportunity. All the ladies and gentlemen, Schmuh the host, even the far-off washroom attendant, all the little children wet themselves, psss, psss they went, they all crouched down and listened to the sound they were making and they all wet their pants. It was only when the music had died down—Oskar had left the infant sound effects to themselves except for a soft distant roll—that I ushered in unrestrained merriment with one loud, emphatic boom. All about me the company roared, tittered, babbled childish nonsense:

Smash a little windowpane
Put sugar in your beer,
Mrs. Biddle plays the fiddle,
Dear, dear, dear.

I led them to the cloakroom, where a bewildered student gave Schmuh's kindergarteners their wraps; then, with the familiar ditty "Hard-working washerwomen scrubbing out the clothes," I drummed them up the concrete steps, past the doorman in the rustic sheepskin. I dismissed the kindergarten beneath the night sky of spring, 1950, a trifle cool perhaps, but studded with fairytale stars, as though made to order for the occasion. Forgetful of home, they continued for quite some time to make childish mischief in the Old City, until at length the police helped them to remember their age, social position, and telephone number.

As for me, I giggled and caressed my drum as I went back to the Onion Cellar, where Schmuh was still clapping his hands, still standing bowlegged and wet beside the staircase, seemingly as happy in Auntie Kauer's kindergarten as on the Rhine meadows when a grown-up Schmuh went shooting sparrows.

On the Atlantic Wall or Concrete Eternal

I had only been trying to help him. But Schmuh, owner and guiding spirit of the Onion Cellar, could not forgive me for my drum solo which had transformed his well-paying guests into babbling, riotously merry children who wet their pants and cried because they had wet their pants, all without benefit of onions.

Oskar tries to understand him. Could he help fearing my competition when his guests began to push aside the traditional onions and cry out for Oskar, for Oskar's drum, for me who on my drum could conjure up the childhood of every one of them, however old and feeble?

Up until then, Schmuh had contented himself with dismissing his washroom attendants without notice. Now it was the whole Rhine River Three that he fired. In our place he took on an ambulatory fiddler who, if you closed an eye or two, might have been taken for a gypsy.

But when, as a result of our dismissal, several of the guests, the most faithful at that, threatened to leave the Onion Cellar for good, Schmuh had to accept a compromise. Three times a week the fiddler fiddled. Three times a week we performed, having demanded and obtained a raise: twenty DM a night. There were good tips too; Oskar started a savings account and rejoiced as the interest accrued.

Only too soon my savings account was to become a friend in need and indeed, for then came Death and carried away our Ferdinand Schmuh, our job, and our earnings.

I have already said that Schmuh shot sparrows. Sometimes he took us along in his Mercedes and let us look on. Despite occasional quarrels about my drum, which involved Klepp and Scholle, because they took my part, relations between Schmuh and his musicians remained friendly until, as I have intimated, death came between us.

We piled in. As usual, Schmuh's wife was at the wheel. Klepp beside her. Between Oskar and Scholle sat Schmuh, holding his rifle over his knees and caressing it from time to time. We stopped just before Kaiserswerth. On both banks of the Rhine lines of trees: the stage was set. Schmuh's wife stayed in the car and unfolded a newspaper. Klepp had bought some raisins which he munched with noteworthy regularity. Scholle, who had been a student of something or other before taking up the guitar in earnest, managed to conjure up from his memory a number of poems about the river Rhine, which had indeed put its poetic foot forward and, apart from the usual barges, was giving us quite a display of swaying autumnal foliage in the direction of Duisburg, though according to the calendar it was still summer. If Schmuh's rifle had not spoken up from time to time, that afternoon below Kaiserswerth might well have been termed peaceful or even serene.

By the time Klepp had finished his raisins and wiped his fingers on the grass, Schmuh too had finished. Beside the eleven cold balls of feathers on the newspaper, he laid a twelfth—still quivering, as he remarked. The marksman was already packing up his "bag"—for some unfathomable reason Schmuh always took his victims home with him—when a sparrow settled on a tree root that the river had washed ashore not far from us. The sparrow was so cocky about it, so gray, such a model specimen of a sparrow, that Schmuh couldn't resist; he who never shot more than twelve sparrows in an afternoon shot a thirteenth—he shouldn't have.

After he had laid the thirteenth beside the twelve, we went back to the black Mercedes and found Madame Schmuh asleep. Scholle and Klepp got into the back seat. I was about to join them but didn't; I felt like a little walk, I said, I'd take the streetcar, no need to bother about me. And so they drove off without Oskar, who had been very wise not to ride with them.

I followed slowly. I didn't have far to go. There was a detour round a stretch of road that was under repair. The detour passed by a gravel pit. And in this gravel pit, some twenty feet below the surface of the road, lay the black Mercedes with its wheels in the air.

Some workmen from the gravel pit had removed the three injured persons and Schmuh's body from the car. The ambulance was on its way. I climbed down into the pit—my shoes were soon full of gravel—and busied myself a little with the injured; in spite of the pain they were in, they asked me questions, but I didn't tell them Schmuh was dead. Stiff and startled, he stared up at the sky, which was mostly cloudy. The newspaper containing his afternoon's bag had been flung out of the car. I counted twelve sparrows but couldn't find the thirteenth; I was still looking for it when they eased the ambulance down into the gravel pit.

Schmuh's wife, Klepp, and Scholle had nothing very serious the matter with them: bruises, a few broken ribs. When I went to see Klepp in the hospital and asked him what had caused the accident, he told me an amazing story: As they were driving past the gravel pit, slowly because of the poor condition of the road, hundreds maybe thousands of sparrows had swarmed out of the hedges, bushes, and fruit trees, casting a great shadow over the Mercedes, crashing against the windshield, and frightening Mrs. Schmuh. By sheer sparrow power, they had brought about the accident and Schmuh's death.

You are free to think what you please of Klepp's story; Oskar is skeptical, especially when he considers that when Schmuh was buried in the South Cemetery, he, Oskar, was able to count no more sparrows than years before when he had come here to set up tombstones. Be that as it may, as I, in a borrowed top hat, was following the coffin with the mourners, I caught a glimpse of Korneff in Section Nine, setting up a diorite slab for a two-place grave, with an assistant unknown to me. As the coffin with Schmuh in it was carried past the stonecutter on its way to the newly laid-out Section Ten, Korneff doffed his cap in accordance with cemetery regulations; perhaps because of the top hat, he failed to recognize me, but he rubbed his neck in token of ripening or over-ripe boils.

Funerals! I have been obliged to take you to so many cemeteries. Somewhere, I went so far as to say that funerals remind one of other funerals. Very well, I will refrain from speaking at length of Schmuh's funeral or of Oskar's retrospective musings at the time. Suffice it to say that Schmuh had a normal, decent burial and that nothing unusual happened. All I really have to tell you is that when they had finished burying Schmuh—the widow was in the hospital, or perhaps a little more decorum would have been maintained—I was approached by a gentleman who introduced himself as Dr. Dösch.

Dr. Dösch ran a concert bureau but the concert bureau did not belong to him. He had been a frequent guest, he told me, at the Onion Cellar. I had never noticed him, but he had been there when I transformed Schmuh's customers into a band of babbling, happy children. Dösch himself, in fact, as he told me in confidence, had returned to childhood bliss under the influence of my drum, and he was dead set on making a big thing out of me and my "terrific stunt," as he called it. He had been authorized to offer me a contract, a terrific contract; why wouldn't I sign it on the spot? Outside the crematorium, where Leo Schugger, who in Düsseldorf bore the name of Willem Slobber, was waiting in his white gloves for the mourners, Dr. Dösch pulled out a paper which, in return for enormous sums of money, committed the undersigned, hereinafter referred to as "Oskar, the drummer," to give solo performances in large theaters, to appear all by myself on the stage before audiences numbering two to three thousand. Dösch was inconsolable when I said I could not sign right away. As my reason, I gave Schmuh's death; Schmuh, I said, had been very close to me, I just couldn't go to work for someone else before he was cold in his grave, I'd have to think the matter over, maybe I'd take a little trip somewhere; I'd look up Dr. Dösch the moment I got back and then perhaps I would sign this paper that he called a contract.

However, though I signed no contract at the cemetery, Oskar's financial situation impelled him to accept an advance which Dr. Dösch handed me discreetly, hidden away in an envelope with his visiting card, outside the cemetery where he had parked his car.

And I did take the trip, I even found a traveling companion. Actually I should have liked Klepp to go with me. But Klepp was in the hospital, Klepp couldn't even laugh, for he had four broken ribs. I should have liked to take Maria. But the summer holidays were still on, little Kurt would have to come with us. And besides, she was still tied up with Stenzel, her boss, who had got Kurt to call him Papa Stenzel.

In the end I set out with Lankes. You remember him no doubt as Corporal Lankes and as the Muse Ulla's sometime fiancé. When, with my advance and my savings book in my pocket, I repaired to Lankes' studio in Sittarder-Strasse, I was hoping to find Ulla, my former partner; I thought I would ask the Muse to come along on my trip.

Ulla was there. Right in the doorway she told me: We're engaged. Been engaged for two weeks. It hadn't worked with Hänschen Krages, she had been obliged to break it off. Did I know Hänschen Krages?

No, said Oskar, to his infinite regret he hadn't known Ulla's former fiancé. Then Oskar made his generous offer but before Ulla could accept, Lankes, emerging from the studio, elected himself Oskar's travel companion and boxed the long-legged Muse on the ear because she didn't want to stay home and had burst into tears in her disappointment.

Why didn't Oskar defend himself? Why, if he wanted the Muse as his traveling companion, didn't he take the Muse's part? Much as I was attracted by the prospect of a journey with Ulla by my side, Ulla so slender, Ulla so fuzzy and blond, I feared too close an intimacy with a Muse. Better keep the Muses at a distance, I said to myself, or the kiss of the Muses will get to be a domestic habit. It will be wiser to travel with Lankes, who gives his Muse a good licking when she tries to kiss him.

There was little discussion about our destination. Normandy, of course, where else? We would visit the fortifications between Caen and Cabourg. For that is where we had met during the war The only difficulty was getting visas. But Oskar isn't one to waste words on visas.

Lankes is a stingy man. The lavishness with which he flings paint —cheap stuff to be sure, and scrounged as often as not—on poorly prepared canvas is equalled only by his tight-fistedness with money, coins as well as paper. A constant smoker, he has never been known to buy a cigarette. Moreover his stinginess is systematic: whenever someone gives him a cigarette, he takes a ten-pfennig piece out of his left pants pocket, raises his cap in a brief gesture of recognition, and drops the coin into his right pants pocket where it takes its place among other coins—how many depends on the time of day. As I have said, he is always smoking, and one day when he was in a good humor, he confided in me: "Every day I make about two marks, just by smoking."

Last year Lankes bought a bombed-out lot in Wersten. He paid for it with the cigarettes of his friends and acquaintances.

This was the Lankes with whom Oskar went to Normandy. We took the train—an express. Lankes would rather have hitchhiked. But since he was my guest and I was paying, he had to give in. We rode past poplars, behind which there were meadows bounded by hedgerows. Brown and white cows gave the countryside the look of an advertisement for milk chocolate, though of course for advertising purposes one would have had to block out the war damage. The villages, including the village of Bavent where I had lost my Roswitha, were still in pretty bad shape.

From Cabourg we walked along the beach toward the mouth of the Orne. It wasn't raining. As we approached Le Home, Lankes said: "We're home again, my boy. Give me a butt." Before he had finished transferring his coin from pocket to pocket, he stretched out his wolf's head toward one of the numerous unharmed pillboxes in the dunes. With one long arm he toted his knapsack, his traveling easel, and his dozen frames; with the other, he pulled me toward the concrete. Oskar's luggage consisted of a suitcase and his drum.

On the third day of our stay on the Atlantic Coast—we had meanwhile cleared the drifted sand out of Dora Seven, removed the distasteful traces of lovers who had found a haven there, and furnished the place with a crate and our sleeping bags—Lankes came up from the beach with a good-sized codfish. Some fishermen had given it to him in return for a picture he had done of their boat.

In view of the fact that we still called the pillbox Dora Seven, it is hardly surprising that Oskar's thoughts, as he cleaned the fish, turned to Sister Dorothea. The liver and milt spurted over both my hands. While scaling, I faced the sun, which gave Lankes a chance to dash off a water color. We sat behind the pillbox, sheltered from the wind. The August sun beat down on the concrete dome. I larded the fish with garlic. The cavity once occupied by the milt, liver, and entrails, I stuffed with onions, cheese, and thyme; but I didn't throw away the milt and liver; I lodged both delicacies between the fish's jaws, which I wedged open with a lemon. Lankes reconnoitred. He disappeared into Dora Four, Dora Three, and so on down the line. Soon he returned with boards and some large cartons. The cartons he kept to paint on; the wood was for the fire.

There was no difficulty in keeping up the fire; the beach was covered with pieces of dry, feather-light driftwood, casting a variety of shadows.

Over the hot coals I laid part of an iron balcony grating which Lankes had torn off a deserted beach villa. I rubbed the fish with olive oil and set it down on the hot grate, which I had also smeared with oil. I squeezed lemon juice over the crackling codfish and let it broil slowly—one should never be in a hurry about cooking fish.

We had made a table by laying a big piece of tarboard over some empty buckets. We had our own forks and tin plates. To divert Lankes —he was circling round the fish like a hungry sea gull—I went to the pillbox and brought out my drum. Bedding it in the sand, I drummed into the wind, variations on the sounds of the surf and the rising tide: Bebra's Theater at the Front had come to inspect the concrete. From Kashubia to Normandy. Felix and Kitty, the two acrobats, tied themselves into knots on top of the pillbox and, just as Oskar was drumming against the wind, recited against the wind a poem the refrain of which, in the very midst of the war, announced the coming of an era of cozy comfort: ". . . The thought of comfort's like a drug: The trend is toward the bourgeois-smug," declaimed Kitty with her Saxon accent; and Bebra, my wise Bebra, captain of the Propaganda Company, nodded; and Roswitha, my Raguna from the Mediterranean, took up the picnic basket and set the table on the concrete, on top of Dora Seven; and Corporal Lankes, too, ate our white bread, drank our chocolate, and smoked Captain Bebra's cigarettes. . . .

"Man!" Lankes called me back from the past. "Man, Oskar! If I could only paint like you drum; give me a butt."

I stopped drumming, gave my traveling companion a cigarette, examined the fish, and saw that it was good: the eyes were white, serene, and liquid. Slowly I squeezed a last lemon, omitting not the slightest patch of the skin, which had cracked in places but was otherwise a beautiful brown.

"I'm hungry," said Lankes. He showed his long yellow fangs and, apelike, beat his breast with both fists through his checkered shirt.

"Head or tail?" I asked, setting the fish down on a sheet of waxed paper, which we had spread over the tarboard in lieu of a tablecloth.

"What's your advice?" Lankes pinched out his cigarette and put away the butt.

"As a friend, I'd say: Take the tail. As a cook, I can only recommend the head. On the other hand, if my mama, who was a big fish-eater, were here now, she'd say: Mr. Lankes, take the tail, then you know what you've got. On the third hand, the doctor used to advise my father . . . "

"I'm not interested in doctors," said Lankes distrustfully.

"Dr. Hollatz advised my father always to eat the head of the codfish."

"Then I'll take the tail. I see you're trying to sell me a bill of goods." Lankes was still suspicious.

"So much the better for Oskar. The head is what I prefer."

"Well, if you're so crazy about it, I'll take the head."

"You're having a tough time, aren't you, Lankes," I said. "All right, the head is yours, I'll take the tail." This, I hoped, would be the end of our dialogue.

"Heh, heh!" said Lankes. "I guess I put one over on you."

Oskar admitted that Lankes had put one over on him, Well I knew that his portion wouldn't taste right unless it were seasoned with the assurance that he had put one over on me. A shrewd article, a lucky bastard, I called him—then we fell to.

He took the head piece, I squeezed what was left of the lemon juice over the white, crumbling flesh of the tail piece, whence, as I picked it up, two or three butter-soft wedges of garlic detached themselves.

Sucking at his bones, Lankes peered over at me and the tail piece: "Give me a taste of your tail." I nodded, he took his taste, and was undecided until Oskar took a taste of his head piece and assured him once again that he, Lankes, had as usual got the better deal.

We drank red Bordeaux with the fish. I felt sorry about that, I should have preferred to see white wine in our coffee cups. Lankes swept my regrets aside; when he was a corporal in Dora Seven, he remembered, they had never drunk anything but red wine. They had still been drinking red wine when the invasion started: "Boy, oh boy, were we liquored up! Kowalski, Scherbach, and little Leuthold didn't even notice anything was wrong. And now they're all in the same cemetery, the other side of Cabourg. Over by Arromanches, it was Tommies, here in our sector, Canadians, millions of them. Before we could get our suspenders up, there they were, saying, 'How are you?' "

A little later, waving his fork and spitting out bones: "Say, who do you think I ran into in Cabourg today? Herzog, Lieutenant Herzog, the nut, you met him on your tour of inspection. You remember him, don't you?"

Of course Oskar remembered Lieutenant Herzog. Lankes went on to tell me over the fish that Herzog returned to Cabourg year in, year out, with maps and surveying instruments, because the thought of these fortifications gave him no sleep. He was planning to drop in at Dora Seven and do a bit of measuring.

We were still on the fish—little by little the contours of the backbone were emerging—when Lieutenant Herzog turned up. Khaki knee breeches, plump calves, tennis shoes; a growth of gray-brown hair emerged from the open neck of his linen shirt. Naturally we kept our seats. Lankes introduced me as Oskar, his peacetime friend and wartime buddy, and addressed Herzog as Reserve Lieutenant Herzog.

The reserve lieutenant began at once to inspect Dora Seven. He began with the outside, and Lankes raised no objection. Herzog filled out charts and examined the land and sea through his binoculars. Then for a moment he caressed the gun embrasures of Dora Six as tenderly as though fondling his wife. When he wished to inspect the inside of Dora Seven, our villa, our summer house, Lankes wouldn't hear of it: "Herzog, man, what's the matter with you? Poking around in concrete. Maybe it was news ten years ago. Now it's passé."

"Passé" is a pet word with Lankes. Everything under the sun is either news or passé. But the reserve lieutenant held that nothing was passé, that the accounts were still unclear, that some of the figures would have to be rectified, that men would always be called upon to give an account of themselves before the judgment seat of history, and that was why he wanted to inspect the inside of Dora Seven: "I hope, Lankes, that I have made myself clear."

Herzog's shadow fell across our table and fish. He meant to pass around us to the pillbox entrance, over which concrete ornaments still bore witness to the creative hand of Corporal Lankes.

But Herzog never got past our table. Rising swiftly, Lankes' fist, still gripping its fork but making no use of it, sent Reserve Lieutenant Herzog sprawling backward on the sand. Shaking his head, deploring the interruption of our meal, Lankes stood up, seized a fistful of the lieutenant's shirt, dragged him to the edge of the dune—the track in the sand was remarkably straight, I recall—and tossed him off. He had vanished from my sight but not, unfortunately, from my hearing. He gathered together his surveying instruments, which Lankes had thrown after him, and went away grumbling and conjuring up all the historical ghosts that Lankes had dismissed as passé.

"He's not so very wrong," said Lankes, "even if he is a nut. If we hadn't been so soused when the shooting started, who knows what would have happened to those Canadians."

I could only nod assent, for just the day before, at low tide, I had found the telltale button of a Canadian uniform in among the empty crab shells. As pleased as though he had found a rare Etruscan coin, Oskar had secreted the button in his wallet.

Brief as it was, Lieutenant Herzog's visit had conjured up memories: "Do you remember, Lankes, when our theatrical group was inspecting your concrete and we had breakfast on top of the pillbox? There was a little breeze just like today. And suddenly there were six or seven nuns, looking for crabs in the Rommel asparagus, and you, Lankes, you had orders to clear the beach; which you did with a murderous machine gun."

Sucking bones, Lankes remembered; he even remembered their names: Sister Scholastica, Sister Agneta . . . he described the novice as a rosy little face with lots of black around it. His portrait of her was so vivid that it partly, but only partly, concealed the image, which never left me, of my trained nurse, my secular Sister Dorothea. A few minutes later— I wasn't surprised enough to put it down as a miracle—a young nun came drifting across the dunes from the direction of Cabourg. Pink little face, with lots of black around it, there was no mistaking her.

She was shielding herself from the sun with a black umbrella such as elderly gentlemen carry. Over her eyes arched a poison-green celluloid shade, suggesting dynamic movie directors in Hollywood. Off in the dunes someone was calling her. There seemed to be more nuns about. "Sister Agneta!" the voice cried, "Sister Agneta, where are you?"

And Sister Agneta, the young thing who could be seen over the backbone of our codfish: "Here I am, Sister Scholastica. There's no wind here."

Lankes grinned and nodded his wolf's head complacently, as though he himself had conjured up this Catholic parade, as though nothing in the world could startle him.

The young nun caught sight of us and stopped still, to one side of the pillbox. "Oh!" gasped her rosy face between slightly protruding but otherwise flawless teeth.

Lankes turned head and neck without stirring his body: "Hiya, Sister, taking a little walk?"

How quickly the answer came: "We always go to the seashore once a year. But for me it's the first time. I never saw the ocean before. It's so big."

There was no denying that. To this day I look upon her description of the ocean as the only accurate one.

Lankes played the host, poked about in my portion of fish and offered her some: "Won't you try a little fish, Sister? It's still warm."

I was amazed at the ease with which he spoke French, and Oskar also tried his hand at the foreign language: "Nothing to worry about. It's Friday anyway."

But even this tactful allusion to the rules of her order could not move the young girl, so cleverly dissimulated in the nun's clothes, to partake of our repast.

"Do you always live here?" her curiosity impelled her to ask. Our pillbox struck her as pretty and a wee bit comical. But then, unfortunately, the mother superior and five other nuns, all with black umbrellas and green visors, entered the picture over the crest of the dune. Agneta whished away. As far as I could understand the flurry of words clipped by the east wind, she was given a good lecture and made to take her place in the group.

Lankes dreamed. He held his fork in his mouth upside down and gazed at the group floating over the dunes. "That ain't no nuns, it's sailboats."

428

"Sailboats are white," I objected.

"It's black sailboats." It wasn't easy to argue with Lankes. "The one out there on the left is the flagship. Agneta's a fast corvette. Good sailing weather. Column formation, jib to sternpost, mainmast, mizzenmast, and foremast, all sails set, off to the horizon and England. Think of it: tomorrow morning the Tommies wake up, look out the window, and what do they see: twenty-five thousand nuns, all decked with flags. And here comes the first broadside . . ."

"A new war of religion," I helped him. The flagship, I suggested, should be called the Mary Stuart or the De Valera or, better still, the Don Juan. A new, more mobile Armada avenges Trafalgar. "Death to all Puritans!" was the battle cry and this time the English had no Nelson on hand. Let the invasion begin. England has ceased to be an island.

The conversation was getting too political for Lankes.

"The nuns are steaming away," he announced.

"Sailing," I corrected.

Whether steaming or sailing, they were floating off in the direction of Cabourg, holding umbrellas between themselves and the sun. Only one lagged behind a little, bent down between steps, picked up something, and dropped something. The rest of the fleet made its way slowly, tacking into the wind, toward the gutted beach hotel in the background.

"Looks like her steering gear is damaged or maybe she can't get her anchor up," said Lankes, running his nautical image into the ground. "Hey, that must be Agneta, the fast corvette."

Frigate or corvette, it was indeed Sister Agneta, the novice, who came toward us, picking up shells and throwing some of them away.

"What are you picking up there, Sister?" Lankes could see perfectly well what she was picking up.

"Shells," she pronounced the word very clearly and bent down.

"You allowed to do that? Ain't they earthly goods?"

I came out for Sister Agneta: "You're wrong, Lankes. There's nothing earthly about sea shells."

"Whether they come from the earth or the sea, in any case they are goods and nuns shouldn't have any. Poverty, poverty, and more poverty, that's what nuns should have. Am I right, Sister?"

Sister Agneta smiled through her protruding teeth: "I only take a few. They are for the kindergarten. The children love to play with them. They have never been to the seashore."

Agneta stood outside the entrance to the pillbox and cast a furtive, nun's glance inside.

"How do you like our little home?" I asked, trying to make friends. Lankes was more direct: "Come in and take a look at our villa. Won't cost you a penny."

Her pointed high shoes fidgeted under her long skirt, stirring sand that the wind picked up and strewed over our fish. Losing some of her self-assurance, she examined us and the table between us out of eyes that were distinctly light brown. "It surely wouldn't be right."

"Come along, Sister," Lankes swept aside all her objections and stood up. "There's a fine view. You can see the whole beach through the gun slits."

Still she hesitated; her shoes, it occurred to me, must be full of sand. Lankes waved in the direction of the entrance. His concrete ornament cast sharp ornamental shadows. "It's tidy inside."

Perhaps it was Lankes' gesture of invitation that decided the nun to go in. "But just a minute!" And she whished into the pillbox ahead of Lankes. He wiped his hands on his trousers—a typical painter's gesture —and flung a threat at me before disappearing: "Careful you don't take none of my fish."

But Oskar had his fill of fish. I moved away from the table, surrendered myself to the sandy wind and the exaggerated bellowing of Strong Man Sea. I pulled my drum close with one foot and tried, by drumming, to find a way out of this concrete landscape, this fortified world, this vegetable called Rommel asparagus.

First, with small success, I tried love; once upon a time I too had loved a sister. Not a nun, to be sure, but Sister Dorothea, a nurse. She lived in the Zeidler flat, behind a frosted-glass door. She was very beautiful, but I never saw her. It was too dark in the Zeidler hallway. A fiber runner came between us.

After following this theme to its abortive end on the fiber rug, I tried to convert my early love for Maria into rhythm and set it down on the concrete like quick-growing creepers. But there was Sister Dorothea again, interfering with my love of Maria. A smell of carbollc acid blew in from the sea, gulls in nurse's uniforms waved at me, the sun insisted on glittering like a Red Cross pin.

Oskar was glad when his drumming was interrupted. Sister Scholastica, the mother superior, was coming back with her five nuns. They looked tired and their umbrellas slanted forlornly: "Have you seen a little nun, our little novice? The child is so young. The child had never seen the ocean before. She must have got lost. Sister Agneta, where are you?"

There was nothing I could do but send the little squadron, now with the wind in their stern, off toward the mouth of the Orne, Arromanches, and Port Winston, where the English had wrested an artificial harbor from the sea. There would hardly have been room for all of them in the pillbox. For a moment, I have to admit, I was tempted to surprise Lankes with their visit, but then friendship, disgust, malice, all in one, bade me hold out my thumb in the direction of the Orne estuary. The nuns obeyed my thumb and gradually turned into six receding, black, wind-blown spots on the crest of the dune; their plaintive "Sister Agneta,

Sister Agneta" came to me more and more diluted with wind, until at last it was swallowed up in the sand.

Lankes was first to come out. Again the typical painter's gesture: he wiped his hands on his trousers, demanded a cigarette, put it into his shirt pocket, and fell upon the cold fish. "It whets the appetite," he said with a leer, pillaging the tail end which was my share. Then he sprawled himself out in the sun.

"She must be unhappy now," I said accusingly, savoring the word "unhappy."

"How so? Got nothing to be unhappy about."

It was inconceivable to Lankes that his version of human relations might make anyone unhappy.

"What's she doing now?" I asked, though I really meant to ask him something else.

"Sewing," said Lankes with his fork. "Ripped her habit a bit, now she's mending it."

The seamstress came out of the pillbox. At once she opened the umbrella and started to babble gaily, yet, it seemed to me, with a certain strain: "The view is really divine. The whole beach and the ocean too."

She stopped by the wreckage of our fish.

"May I?"

Both of us nodded at once.

"The sea air whets the appetite," I encouraged her. Nodding, she dug into our fish with chapped, reddened hands revealing her hard work in the convent, and filled her mouth. She ate gravely, with pensive concentration, as though mulling over, with the fish, something she had had before the fish.

I looked under her coif. She had left her green reporter's eyeshade in the pillbox. Little beads of sweat, all of equal size, lined up on her smooth forehead, which, in its white starched frame, had a madonna-like quality. Lankes asked for another cigarette though he hadn't smoked the previous one. I tossed him the pack. While he stowed three in his shirt pocket and stuck a fourth between his lips, Sister Agneta turned, threw the umbrella away, ran—only then did I see that she was barefoot—up the dune, and vanished in the direction of the surf.

"Let her run," said Lankes in an oracular tone. "She'll be back or maybe she won't."

For an instant I managed to sit still and watch Lankes smoking. Then I climbed on top of the pillbox and looked out at the beach. The tide had risen and very little beach was left.

"Well?" Lankes asked.

"She's undressing." That was all he could get out of me. "Probably means to go swimming. Wants to cool off."

That struck me as dangerous at high tide, especially so soon after

431

eating. Already she was in up to the knees; her back was bent forward and she sank deeper and deeper. The water could not have been exactly warm, but that didn't seem to bother her: she swam, she swam well, practicing several different strokes, and dove through the waves.

"Let her swim, and come down off that pillbox." I looked behind me and saw Lankes sprawling in the sand and puffing away. The smooth backbone of the codfish glistened white in the sun, dominating the table.

As I jumped off the concrete, Lankes opened his painter's eyes and said: "Christ, what a picture! Nuns at High Tide."

"You monster," I shouted. "Supposing she drowns?" Lankes closed his eyes: "Then we'll call it: Nuns Drowning."

"And if she comes back and flings herself at your feet?"

Wide-eyed, the painter declaimed: "Then she and the picture will be called: Fallen Nun."

With him it was always either-or, head or tail, drowned or fallen. He took my cigarettes, threw the lieutenant off the dune, ate my fish, showed the inside of a pillbox to a little girl who was supposed to be the bride of Christ, and while she was still swimming out to sea, drew pictures in the air with his big lumpy foot. He even listed the titles and plotted the formats: Nuns at High Tide, eight by five, Nuns Drowning, Fallen Nuns, Twenty-five Thousand Nuns. Nuns at Trafalgar. Nuns Defeat Lord Nelson. Nuns Bucking the Wind. Nuns Before the Breeze. Nuns Tacking. Black, lots of black; dingy white and cold blue: The Invasion, or Barbaric, Mystical, Bored. And on our return to the Rhineland Lankes actually painted all these pictures, in formats ranging from wide and low to high and narrow. He did whole series of nuns, found a dealer who was wild about nuns, exhibited forty-three of these nunsuch canvases and sold seventeen to collectors, industrialists, museums, and an American; some of the critics even saw fit to compare him, Lankes, to Picasso. It was Lankes' success that persuaded me, Oskar, to dig up the visiting card of Dr. Dösch, the concert manager, for Lankes' art was not alone in clamoring for bread. The time had come to transmute the prewar and wartime experience of Oskar, the three-year-old drummer, into the pure, resounding gold of the postwar period.

The Ring Finger

"So that's it," said Zeidler. "So you've decided not to work any more." It riled him that Klepp and Oskar should spend the whole day sitting either in Klepp's or Oskar's room, doing just about nothing. I had paid the October rent on both rooms out of what was left of Dr. Dösch's advance, but the prospects, financial and otherwise, for November, were bleak.

432

And yet we had plenty of offers. Any number of dance halls or night clubs would have taken us on. But Oskar was sick of playing jazz. That put a strain on my relations with Klepp. Klepp said my new drum style had no connection with jazz. He was right and I didn't deny it. He said I was disloyal to the jazz ideal. Early in November Klepp found a new percussion man, and a good one at that, namely Bobby from the Unicorn, and was able to accept an engagement in the Old City. After that we were friends again, even though Klepp was already beginning to think, or perhaps it would be safer to say talk, along Communist lines.

In the end Dr. Dösch was my only resort. I couldn't have gone back to live with Maria even if I had wanted to; Stenzel was getting a divorce, meaning to convert my Maria into a Maria Stenzel. From time to time I knocked out an inscription for Korneff or dropped in at the Academy to be blackened or abstracted. Quite frequently I went calling, with nothing definite in mind, on Ulla, who had been obliged to break her engagement to Lankes shortly after our trip to the Atlantic Wall, because Lankes wasn't doing anything but nuns and didn't even want to beat Ulla any more.

Dr. Dösch's visiting card lay silently clamoring on my table beside the bathtub. One day, having decided that I wanted none of Dr. Dösch, I tore it up and threw it away. To my horror I discovered that the address and telephone number were graven on my memory. I could read them off like a poem. I not only could but did. This went on for three days; the telephone number kept me awake at night. On the fourth day, I went to the nearest telephone booth. Dösch spoke as though he had been expecting my call from one minute to the next and asked me to drop in at the office that same afternoon; he wanted to introduce me to the boss, in fact the boss was expecting me.

The West Concert Bureau had its offices on the eighth floor of a new office building. Expensive carpeting, quantities of chrome, indirect lighting, soundproofing, crisp, long-legged secretaries, wafting their boss's cigar smoke past me; two seconds more and I would have fled.

Dr. Dösch received me with open arms though he did not actually hug me—a narrow escape, it seemed to Oskar. Beside him a green sweater girl was typing; her machine stopped as I entered, but speeded up almost instantly to make up for lost time. Dösch announced me to the boss. Oskar sat down on the front left sixth of an armchair upholstered in English vermilion. A folding door opened, the typewriter held its breath, a hidden force raised me to my feet, the doors closed behind me, a carpet, flowing through the large, luminous room, led me forward until an enormous oak table top supported by steel tubing said to me: now Oskar is standing in front of the boss's desk, I wonder how much he weighs. I raised my blue eyes, looked for the boss behind the infinitely empty oak

433

surface, and found, in a wheelchair that could be cranked up and tipped like a dentist's chair, my friend and master Bebra, paralyzed, living only with his eyes and fingertips.

He still had his voice though. And Bebra's voice spoke: "So we meet again, Mr. Matzerath. Did I not tell you years ago, when you still chose to face the world as a three-year-old, that our kind can never lose one another? However, I see to my regret that you have altered your proportions, immoderately so, and not at all to your advantage. Did you not measure exactly three feet in those days?"

I nodded, on the verge of tears. The wall behind the master's wheelchair—it was operated by an electric motor which gave off a low, steady hum—had just one picture on it: a life-size bust of Roswitha, the great Raguna, in a baroque frame. Bebra didn't have to follow my eyes to know what I was looking at. His lips, when he spoke, were almost motionless: "Ah, yes, our good Roswitha! How, I wonder, would she have liked the new Oskar? Not too well, I think. It was another Oskar that she cared for, a three-year-old with cheeks like a cherub, but oh, so loving! She worshipped him, as she never wearied of telling me. But one day he was disinclined to bring her a cup of coffee; she herself went for it and lost her life. And if I am not mistaken, that is not the only murder committed by our cherubic little Oskar. Is it not true that he drummed his poor mama into her grave?"

I nodded. I looked up at Roswitha, I was able to cry, thank the Lord. Bebra recoiled for the next blow; "And what of Jan Bronski, the postal secretary, whom three-year-old Oskar liked to call his presumptive father? Oskar handed him over to the centurions who shot him. And now perhaps, Mr. Oskar Matzerath, you who have had the audacity to change your shape, now perhaps you can tell me what became of your second presumptive father, Matzerath the grocer?"

Again I confessed. I admitted that I had murdered Matzerath, because I wanted to be rid of him, and told my judge how I had made him choke to death. I no longer hid behind a Russian tommy gun, but said: "It was I, Master Bebra. I did it; this crime, too, I committed; I am not innocent of this death. Have mercy!"

Bebra laughed, though I don't know what with. His wheelchair trembled, winds ruffled his gnome's hair over the hundred thousand wrinkles that constituted his face.

Again I begged for mercy, charging my voice with a sweetness which I knew to be effective and covering my face with my hands, which I knew to be touchingly beautiful: "Mercy, dear Master Bebra! Have mercy!"

Bebra, who had set himself up as my judge and played the role to perfection, pressed a button on the little ivory-white switchboard that he held between his hands and knees.

The carpet behind me brought in the green sweater girl, carrying a folder. She spread out the contents of the folder on the oak table top, which was roughly on a level with my collarbone, too high for me to see exactly what she was spreading out. Then she handed me a fountain pen: I was to purchase Bebra's mercy with my signature.

Still, I ventured to ask a few questions. I couldn't just sign with my eyes closed.

"The document before you," said Bebra, "is a contract for your professional serices. Your full name is required. We have to know whom we are dealing with. First name and last name: Oskar Matzerath."

The moment I had signed, the hum of the electric motor increased in force. I looked up from the fountain pen just in time to see a wheelchair race across the room and vanish through a side door.

The reader may be tempted to believe that the contract in duplicate to which I affixed my signature provided for the sale of my soul or committed me to some monstrous crime. Nothing of the sort. With the help of Dr. Dösch I studied the contract in the foyer and found no difficulty in understanding that all Oskar had to do was to appear in public all by himself with his drum, to drum as I had drummed as a three-year-old and once again, more recently, in Schmuh's Onion Cellar. The West Concert Bureau undertook to organize tours for me and to provide suitable advance publicity.

I received a second generous advance, on which I lived while the publicity campaign was in progress. From time to time I dropped in at the office and submitted to interviewers and photographers. Dr. Dösch and the sweater girl were always most obliging, but I never saw Master Bebra again.

Even before the first tour I could well have afforded better lodgings. However, I stayed on at Zeidler's for Klepp's sake. Klepp resented my dealings with an agency; I did what I could to placate him but I did not give in, and there were no more expeditions to the Old City to drink beer or eat fresh blood sausage with onions. Instead, to prepare myself for the life of a traveling man, I treated myself to excellent dinners at the railroad station.

Oskar hasn't space enough to describe his success at length. The publicity posters, building me up as a miracle man, a faithhealer, and little short of a Messiah, proved scandalously effective. I made my debut in the cities of the Ruhr Valley in halls with a seating capacity of fifteen hundred to two thousand. The spotlight discovered me in a dinner jacket, all alone against a black velvet curtain. I played the drum, but my following did not consist of youthful jazz addicts. No, those who flocked to hear me were the middle-aged, the elderly, and the doddering. My message was addressed most particularly to the aged, and they responded.

They did not sit silent as I awakened my three-year-old drum to life; they gave vent to their pleasure, though not in the language of their years, but burbling and babbling like three-year-olds. "Rashu, Rashu!" they piped when Oskar drummed up an episode from the miraculous life of the miraculous Rasputin. But most of my listeners were not really up to Rasputin. My biggest triumphs were with numbers evoking not any particular happenings, but stages of infancy and childhood. I gave these numbers such titles as: "Baby's First Teeth," "That Beastly Whooping Cough," "Itchy Stockings," "Dream of Fire and You'll Wet Your Bed."

That appealed to the old folks. They went for it hook, line, and sinker. They cut their first teeth and their gums ached. Two thousand old folks hacked and whooped when I infected them with whooping cough. How they scratched when I put woolen stockings on them! Many an old lady, many an aged gentleman wet his or her underwear, not to mention the upholstery he or she was sitting on, when I made the children dream of a fire. I don't recall whether it was in Wuppertal or in Bochum; no, it was in Recklingshausen: I was playing to a house of aged miners, the performance was sponsored by the union. These old-timers, I said to myself, have been handling black coal all their lives; surely they'll be able to put up with a little black fright. Whereupon Oskar drummed "The Wicked Black Witch" and lo and behold, fifteen hundred crusty old miners, who had lived through cave-ins, explosions, flooded pits, strikes, and unemployment, let out the most bloodcurdling screams I have ever heard. Their screams—and this is why I mention the incident—demolished several windows in spite of the heavy drapes covering them. Indirectly, I had recovered my glass-killing voice. However, I made little use of it; I didn't want to ruin my business.

Yes, business was good. When the tour was over and I reckoned up with Dr. Dösch, it turned out that my tin drum was a gold mine.

I hadn't even asked after Bebra the master and had given up hope of seeing him again. But as Dr. Dösch soon informed me, Bebra was waiting for me.

My second meeting with the master was quite different from the first. This time Oskar was not made to stand in front of the oak table top. Instead, I sat in an electric wheelchair, made to order for Oskar. Dr. Dösch had made tape recordings of my press notices, and Bebra and I sat listening as he ran them off. Bebra seemed pleased. To me the effusions of the newspapers were rather embarrassing. They were building me up into a cult, Oskar and his drum had become healers of the body and soul. And what we cured best of all was loss of memory. The word "Oskarism" made its first appearance, but not, I am sorry to say, its last.

Afterward, the sweater girl brought me tea and put two pills on the master's tongue. We chatted. He had ceased to be my accuser. It was

436

like years before at the Four Seasons Café, except that the Signora, our Roswitha, was missing. When I couldn't help noticing that Master Bebra had fallen asleep over some longwinded story about my past, I spent ten or fifteen minutes playing with my wheelchair, making the motor hum, racing across the floor, circling to left and right. I had difficulty in tearing myself away from this remarkable piece of furniture, which offered all the possibilities of a harmless vice.

My second tour was at Advent. I conceived my program accordingly and was highly praised in the religious press. For I succeeded in turning hardened old sinners into little children, singing Christmas carols in touching watery voices. "Jesus, for thee I live, Jesus, for thee I die," sang two thousand five hundred aged souls, whom no one would have suspected of such childlike innocence or religious zeal.

My third tour coincided with carnival, and again I rearranged my program. No so-called children's carnival could have been merrier or more carefree than those evenings that turned palsied grandmas into Carmens and Indian maidens, while Grampa went bang-bang and led his robbers into battle.

After carnival I signed a contract with a record company. The recording was done in soundproof studios. The sterile atmosphere cramped my style at first, but then I had the walls plastered with enormous photographs of old people such as one sees in homes for the aged and on park benches. By fixing my attention on them, I was able to drum with the same conviction as in concert halls full of human warmth.

The records sold like hotcakes. Oskar was rich. Did that make me give up my miserable sometime bathroom in the Zeidler flat? No. Why not? Because of my friend Klepp and also because of the empty room behind the frosted-glass door, where Sister Dorothea had once lived and breathed. What did Oskar do with all his money? He made Maria, his Maria, a proposition.

This is what I said to Maria: If you give Stenzel his walking papers, if you not only forget about marrying him but throw him out altogether, I'll buy you a modern, up-and-coming delicatessen store. Because after all, my dear Maria, you were born for business and not for any no-good Mr. Stenzel.

I was not mistaken in Maria. She gave up Stenzel and with my financial assistance built up a first-class delicatessen store in Friedrichstrasse. The business prospered and three years later, last week that is— as Maria informed me only yesterday, bursting with joy and not without gratitude—she opened a branch store in Ober-Kassel.

Was it on my return from my seventh or from my eighth tour? In any case it was July and very hot. From the Central Station, where I was besieged by aged autograph hunters, I took a cab straight to the concert bureau and was besieged on alighting by some more aged autograph hunters, who should have been looking after their grandchildren. I sent in my name; the folding doors were open, the carpet still led to the big desk, but behind the desk there was no Bebra and no wheelchair was waiting for me. There was only a smiling Dr. Dösch.

Bebra was dead. He had died several weeks ago. He had not wished them to inform me of his illness. Nothing, not even his death, he had said, must interfere with Oskar's tour. The will was soon read; I inherited a small fortune and the picture of Roswitha that hung over his desk. At the same time I incurred a severe financial loss, for I was in no state to perform. I called off two whole tours—in Southern Germany and Switzerland—on insufficient notice and was sued for breach of contract.

And alas, my loss was more than financial. Bebra's death was a severe blow to me and I did not recover overnight. I locked up my drum and refused to stir from my room. To make matters worse, this was the moment my friend Klepp chose to get married, to take a redheaded cigarette girl as his life companion, and all because he had once given her a photograph of himself. Shortly before the wedding, to which I was not invited, he gave up his room and moved to Stockum. Oskar was left as Zeidler's only roomer.

My relations with the Hedgehog had changed. Now that the papers carried my name in banner headlines, he treated me with respect; in return for a bit of change, he even gave me the key to Sister Dorothea's room. Later I rented the room to prevent anyone else from doing so.

My sorrow had its itinerary. I opened the door of both rooms, dragged myself from my bathtub down the fiber runner to Dorothea's room, gazed into the empty clothes cupboard, faced the ridicule of the washstand mirror, despaired at the sight of the gross, coverless bed, retreated to the hallway, and fled to my room. But there too it was intolerable.

Speculating no doubt on the needs of lonely people, an enterprising East Prussian who had lost his Masurian estates had opened, not far from Jülicher-Strasse, an establishment specializing in the rental of dogs.

There I rented Lux, a rottweiler—glossy black, powerful, a trifle too fat. As the only alternative to racing back and forth between my bathtub and Sister Dorothea's empty clothes cupboard, I began to take walks with Lux.

Lux often led me to the Rhine, where he barked at the ships. He often led me to Rath, to Grafenberg Forest, where he barked at lovers. At the end of July, 1951, he led me to Gerresheim, a suburb which, with the help of a few factories including a large glassworks, is rapidly losing its rural character. Beyond Gerresheim the path winds between kitchen gardens separated by fences from the outlying pastures and grain-fields.

Have I said that it was hot on the day when Lux led me to Gerresheim

438

and past Gerresheim between the grain—rye, it was, I think—and the gardens? When the last houses of the suburb were behind us, I let Lux off the leash. Still he tagged along at my heels; he was a faithful dog, an unusually faithful dog when you consider that in his line of business he had to be faithful to several masters.

The fact is he was too well behaved for my liking, I should rather have seen him run about, and indeed I kicked him to give him the idea. But when he did run off, it was plain that his conscience troubled him; on his return, he would hang his glossy black head and look up at me with those proverbially faithful eyes.

"Run along now, Lux," I demanded. "Get going."

Lux obeyed several times but so briefly that I was delighted when at length he disappeared into the rye field and stayed and stayed. Lux must be after a rabbit, I thought. Or maybe he just feels the need to be alone, to be a dog, just as Oskar would like for a little while to be a human without a dog.

I paid no attention to my surroundings. Neither the gardens nor Gerresheim nor the low-lying city in the mist behind it attracted my eye. I sat down on a rusty iron drum, on which cable had at one time been wound, and hardly had Oskar taken his rusty seat when he began to drum on the cable drum with his knuckles. It was very hot. My suit was too heavy for this kind of weather. Lux was gone and did not come back. Of course no cast-iron cable drum could take the place of my little tin drum, but even so: gradually I slipped back into the past. When I bogged down, when the images of the last few years, full of hospitals and nurses, insisted on recurring, I picked up two dry sticks, and said to myself: Just wait a minute, Oskar. Let's see now who you are and where you're from. And there they glowed, the two sixty-watt bulbs of the hour of my birth. Between them the moth drummed, while the storm moved furniture in the distance. I heard Matzerath speak, and a moment later my mama. He promised me the store, she promised me a toy; at the age of three I would be given a drum, and so Oskar tried to make the three years pass as quickly as possible; I ate, drank, evacuated, put on weight, let them weigh me, swaddle, bathe, brush, powder, vaccinate, and admire me; I let them call me by name, smiled when expected to, laughed when necessary, went to sleep at the proper time, woke up punctually, and in my sleep made the face that grownups call an angel face. I had diarrhea a few times and several colds, caught whooping cough, hung on to it, and relinquished it only when I had mastered its difficult rhythm, when I had it in my wrists forever, for, as we know, "Whooping Cough" is one of the pieces in my repertory, and when Oskar played "Whooping Cough" to an audience of two thousand, two thousand old men and women hacked and whooped.

Lux whimpered at my feet, rubbed against my knees. Oh, this rented

dog that my loneliness had made me rent! There he stood four-legged
and tail-wagging, definitely a dog, with that doggy look and something
or other in his slavering jaws: a stick, a stone, or whatever may seem
desirable to a dog.

Slowly my childhood—the childhood that means so much to me—
slipped away. The pain in my gums, foreshadowing my first teeth, died
down; tired, I leaned back: an adult hunchback, carefully though rather
too warmly dressed, with a wristwatch, identification papers, a bundle
of banknotes in his billfold. I put a cigarette between my lips, set a match
to it, and trusted the tobacco to expel that obsessive taste of childhood
from my oral cavity.

And Lux? Lux rubbed against me. I pushed him away, blew cigarette
smoke at him. He didn't like that but he held his ground and kept on
rubbing. He licked me with his eyes. I searched the nearby telegraph
wires for swallows, a remedy it seemed to me against importunate dogs.
There were no swallows and Lux refused to be driven away. He nuzzled
in between my trouser legs, finding his way to a certain spot with as
much assurance as if his East Prussian employer had trained him for that
kind of thing.

The heel of my shoe struck him twice. He retreated a few feet and
stood there, four-legged and quivering, but continued to offer me his
muzzle with its stick or stone as insistently as if what he was holding
had been not a stick or stone but my wallet which I could feel in my
jacket or my watch that was ticking audibly on my wrist.

What then was he holding? What was so important, so eminently
worth showing me?

I reached out between his warm jaws, I had the thing in my hand,
I knew what I was holding but pretended to be puzzled, as though looking
for a word to name this object that Lux had brought me from the rye
field.

There are parts of the human body which can be examined more
easily and accurately when detached, when alienated from the center. It
was a finger. A woman's finger. A ring finger. A woman's ring finger.
A woman's finger with an attractive ring on it. Between the metacarpus
and the first finger joint, some three-quarters of an inch below the ring,
the finger had allowed itself to be chopped off. The section was neat,
clearly revealing the tendon of the extensor muscle.

It was a beautiful finger, a mobile finger. The stone on the ring was
held in place by six gold claws. I identified it at once—correctly, it later
turned out—as an aquamarine. The ring itself was worn so thin at one
place that I set it down as an heirloom. Despite the line of dirt, or rather
of earth under the nail, as though the finger had been obliged to scratch
or dig earth, the nail seemed to have been carefully manicured. Once I

440

had removed it from the dog's warm muzzle, the finger felt cold and its peculiarly yellowish pallor also suggested coldness.

For several months Oskar had been wearing a silk handkerchief in his breast pocket. He laid the ring finger down on this square of silk and observed that the inside of the finger up to the third joint was marked with lines indicating that this had been a hardworking finger with a relentless sense of duty.

After folding up the finger in the handkerchief, I rose from the cable drum, stroked Lux's neck, and started for home, carrying handkerchief and finger in my right hand. Planning to do this and that with my find, I came to the fence of a nearby garden. It was then that Vittlar, who had been lying in the crook of an apple tree, observing me and the dog, addressed me.

The Last Streetcar
Or Adoration of a Preserving Jar

That voice for one thing, that arrogant, affected whine! Besides, he was lying in the crook of an apple tree. "That's a smart dog you've got there," he whined.

I, rather bewildered: "What are you doing up there?" He stretched languidly: "They are only cooking apples. I assure you. you have nothing to fear."

He was beginning to get on my nerves: "Who cares what kind of apples you've got? And what do you expect me to fear?"

"Oh, well!" His whine was almost a hiss. "You might mistake me for the Snake. There were cooking apples even in those days."

I, angrily: "Allegorical rubbish!"

He, slyly: "I suppose you think only eating apples are worth sinning for?"

I was about to go. I hadn't the slightest desire to discuss the fruit situation in Paradise. Then he tried a more direct approach. Jumping nimbly down from the tree, he stood long and willowy by the fence: "What did your dog find in the rye ?"

I can't imagine why I said: "A stone."

"And you put the stone in your pocket?" Blessed if he wasn't beginning to cross-examine me.

"I like to carry stones in my pocket."

"It looked more like a stick to me."

"That may well be. But I still say it's a stone."

"Aha! So it is a stick?"

"For all I care: stick or stone, cooking apples or eating apples . . ."

"A flexible little stick?"

"The dog wants to go home. I'll have to be leaving."

"A flesh-colored stick?"

"Why don't you attend to your apples? Come along, Lux."

"A flesh-colored, flexible little stick with a ring on it?"

"What do you want of me? I'm just a man taking a walk with this dog I borrowed to take a walk with."

"Splendid. See here, I should like to borrow something too. Won't you let me, just for a second, try on that handsome ring that sparkled on the stick and turned it into a ring finger? My name is Vittlar. Gottfried von Vittlar. I am the last of our line."

So it was that I made Vittlar's acquaintance. Before the day was out, we were friends, and I still call him my friend. Only a few days ago, when he came to see me, I said: "I am so glad, my dear Gottfried, that it was you who turned me in to the police and not some common stranger."

If angels exist, they must look like Vittlar: long, willowy, vivacious, collapsible, more likely to throw their arms around the most barren of lampposts than a soft, eager young girl.

You don't see Vittlar at first. According to his surroundings, he can make himself look like a thread, a scarecrow, a clothestree, or the limb of a tree. That indeed is why I failed to notice him when I sat on the cable drum and he lay in the apple tree. The dog didn't even bark, for dogs can neither see, smell, nor bark at an angel.

"Will you be kind enough, my dear Gottfried," I asked him the day before yesterday, "to send me a copy of the statement you made to the police just about two years ago?" It was this statement that led to my trial and formed the basis of Vittlar's subsequent testimony.

Here is the copy, I shall let him speak as he testified against me in court:

On the day in question, I, Gottfried Vittlar, was lying in the crook of an apple tree that grows at the edge of my mother's garden and bears each year enough apples to fill our seven preserving jars with applesauce. I was lying on my side, my left hip embedded in the bottom of the crook, which is somewhat mossy. My feet were pointing in the direction of the Gerresheim glassworks. What was I looking at? I was looking straight ahead, waiting for something to happen within my field of vision.

The accused, who is today my friend, entered my field of vision. A dog came with him, circling round him, behaving like a dog. His name, as the accused later told me, was Lux, he was a rottweiler, and could be rented at a "dog rental shop" not far from St. Roch's Church.

The accused sat down on the empty cable drum which has been lying ever since the war outside the aforesaid kitchen garden belonging to my mother, Alice von Vittlar. As the court knows, the accused is a small man. Moreover, if we are to be strictly truthful, he is deformed. This fact caught my attention. What struck me even more was his behavior. The small, well-dressed gentleman proceeded to drum on the rusty cable drum, first with his fingers, then with two dry sticks. If you bear in mind that the accused is a drummer by trade and that, as has been established beyond any shadow of a doubt, he practices his trade at all times and places; if you consider, furthermore, that there is something about a cable drum which, as the name suggests, incites people to drum on it, it seems in no wise unreasonable to aver that one sultry summer day the accused Oskar Matzerath sat on a cable drum situated outside the kitchen garden of Mrs. Alice von Vittlar, producing rhythmically arranged sound with the help of two willow sticks of unequal length.

I further testify that the dog Lux vanished for some time into a field of rye; yes, the rye was about ready to mow. If asked exactly how long he was gone, I should be unable to reply, because the moment I lie down in the crook of our apple tree, I lose all sense of time. If I say notwithstanding that the dog disappeared for a considerable time, it means that I missed him, because I liked his black coat and floppy ears.

The accused, however—I feel justified in saying—did not miss the dog.

When the dog Lux came back out of the ripe rye, he was carrying something between his teeth. I thought of a stick, a stone, or perhaps, though even then it did not seem very likely, a tin can or even a tin spoon. Only when the accused removed the corpus delicti from the dog's muzzle did I definitely recognize it for what it was. But between the moment when the dog rubbed his muzzle, still holding the object, against the trouser leg of the accused—the left trouser leg, I should say—to the moment when the accused took possession of it, several minutes passed —exactly how many I should not venture to say.

The dog tried very hard to attract the attention of his temporary master; the accused, however, continued to drum in his monotonous, obsessive, disconcerting, I might say childish way. Only when the dog resorted to indecency, forcing his moist muzzle between the legs of the accused, did he drop the willow sticks and give the dog a kick with his right—yes, of that I am perfectly sure—foot. The dog described a half-circle, came back, trembling like a dog, and once again presented his muzzle and the object it held. Without rising, the accused—with his left hand—reached between the dog's teeth. Relieved of his find, the dog Lux backed away a few feet. The accused remained seated, held the object in his hand, closed his hand, opened it, closed it, and the next time he opened his hand, I could see something sparkle. When the accused had grown accustomed to the sight of the object, he held it up with his thumb and forefinger, approximately at eye level.

Only then did I identify the object as a finger, and a moment later, because of the sparkle, more specifically as a ring finger. Unsuspecting, I had given a name to one of the most interesting criminal cases of the postwar period. And indeed, I, Gottfried Vittlar, have frequently been referred to as the star witness in the Ring Finger Case.

Since the accused remained motionless, I followed suit. In fact, his immobility communicated itself to me. And when the accused wrapped the finger and ring carefully in the handkerchief he had previously worn in his breast pocket, I felt a stirring of sympathy for the man on the cable drum: how neat and methodical he is; now there's a man I'd like to know.

So it was that I called out to him as he was about to leave in the direction of Gerresheim with his rented dog. His first reaction, however, was irritable, almost arrogant. To this day, I cannot understand why, just because I was lying in a tree, he should have taken me for a symbolic snake and even suspected my mother's cooking apples of being the Paradise variety.

It may well be a favorite habit with the Tempter to lie in the crooks of trees. In my case, it was just boredom, a state of mind I come by without effort, that impelled me to assume a recumbent position several times a week in the aforesaid tree. Perhaps boredom is in itself the absolute evil. And now let me ask: What motive drove the accused to Gerresheim in the outskirts of Düsseldorf that sultry day? Loneliness, as he later confessed to me. But are not loneliness and boredom twin sisters? I bring up these points only in order to explain the accused, not in order to confound him. For what made me take a liking to him, speak to him, and finally make friends with him was precisely his particular variety of evil, that drumming of his, which resolved evil into its rhythmical components. Even my denunciation of him, the act which has brought us here, him as the accused, myself as a witness, was a game we invented, a means of diverting and entertaining our boredom and our loneliness.

After some hesitation the accused, in response to my request, slipped the ring off the ring finger—it came off without difficulty—and onto my little finger. It was a good fit and I was extremely pleased. It hardly seems necessary to tell you that I came down out of the tree before trying on the ring. Standing on either side of the fence, we introduced ourselves and chatted a while, touching on various political topics, and then he gave me the ring. He kept the finger, which he handled with great care. We agreed that it was a woman's finger. While I held the ring and let the light play on it, the accused, with his left hand, beat a lively little dance rhythm on the fence. The wooden fence surrounding my mother's garden is in a very dilapidated state: it rattled, clattered, and vibrated in response to the accused's drumming. I do not know how long we stood there, conversing with our eyes. We were engaged in this innocent pastime when we heard airplane engines at a moderate altitude; the plane was probably getting ready to land in Lohhausen. Although both of us were curious to know whether it was going to land on two or four engines, we did not interrupt our exchange of glances nor look up at the plane; later on, when we had occasion to play the game again, we gave it a name: Leo Schugger's asceticism; Leo Schugger, it appears, is the name of a friend with whom the accused had played this game years before, usually in cemeteries.

After the plane had found its landing field—whether on two or four engines I am at a loss to say—I gave back the ring. The accused put it on the ring finger, which he folded up again in the handkerchief, and asked me to go with him some of the way.

That was on July 7, 1951. We walked as far as the streetcar terminus in Gerresheim, but the vehicle we mounted was a cab. Since then the accused has found frequent occasion to treat me with the utmost generosity. We rode into town and had the taxi wait outside the dog rental shop near St. Roch's Church. Having got rid of the dog Lux, we rode across town, through Bilk and Oberbilk to Wersten Cemetery, where Mr. Matzerath had more than twelve marks fare to pay. Then we went to Korneff's stonecutting establishment.

The place was disgustingly filthy and I was glad when the stonecutter had completed my friend's commission—it took about an hour. While my friend lovingly lectured to me about the tools and the various kinds of stone, Mr. Korneff, without a word of comment on the finger, made a plaster cast of it—without the ring. I watched him with only half an eye. First the finger had to be treated; that is, he smeared it with fat and ran a string round the edge. Then he applied the plaster, but before it was quite hard split the mold in two with the string. I am by trade a decorator and the making of plaster molds is nothing new to me; nevertheless, the moment Mr. Korneff had picked up that finger, it took on —or so I thought—an unesthetic quality which it lost only after the cast was finished and the accused had recovered the finger and wiped the grease off it. My friend paid the stonecutter, though at first Mr. Korneff was reluctant to take money, for he regarded Mr. Matzerath as a colleague, and further pointed out that Oskar, as he called Mr. Matzerath, had squeezed out his boils free of charge. When the cast had hardened, the stonecutter opened the mold, gave Mr. Matzerath the cast, and promised to make him a few more in the next few days. Then he saw us out to Bittweg through his display of tombstones.

A second taxi ride took us to the Central Station. There the accused treated me to a copious dinner in the excellent station restaurant. From his familiar tone with the waiters I inferred that he must be a regular customer. We ate boiled beef with fresh horseradish, Rhine salmon, and cheese, the whole topped off with a bottle of champagne. When the conversation drifted back to the finger, I advised him to consider it as someone else's property, to send it in to the Lost and Found, especially as he had a cast of it. To this the accused replied very firmly that he regarded himself as the rightful owner, because he had been promised just such a finger on the occasion of his birth—in code to be sure, the word actually employed being "drumstick"; further, certain finger-length scars on the back of his friend Herbert Truczinski had forecast this ring finger; finally, the cartridge case he had found in Saspe Cemetery had also had the dimensions and implications of a future ring finger.

Though at first I smiled at my new-found friend's arguments, I had to admit that a man of discernment could not fail to see through the sequence: drumstick, scar, cartridge case, ring finger.

A third taxi took me home after dinner. We made an appointment to meet again, and when I visited my friend three days later, he had a surprise for me.

First he showed me his rooms. Originally, he had rented only one, a wretched little place formerly used as a bathroom, but later on, when his drum recitals had brought him wealth and fame, he had undertaken to pay a second rent for a windowless recess which he referred to as Sister Dorothea's room, and ultimately he had rented a third room, formerly occupied by a Mr. Münzer, a musician and associate of the accused. All this cost him a pretty penny, for Mr. Zeidler, the landlord, was well aware of Mr. Matzerath's prosperity and determined to profit by it.

It was in Sister Dorothea's room that the accused had prepared his surprise. On the marble top of a washstand—or perhaps I should call this article of furniture a dressing table because of the mirror behind it —stood a preserving jar about the size of those which my mother, Alice von Vittlar, uses for putting up the applesauce she makes from our cooking apples. This preserving jar, however, contained not applesauce but the ring finger, swimming in alcohol. Proudly the accused showed me several thick scientific books which he had consulted while preserving the finger. I leafed absently through them, pausing only at the illustrations, but admitted that the accused had done an excellent job and that the finger's appearance was unchanged. Speaking as a decorator, I also told him that the glass with its contents looked interestingly decorative at the foot of the mirror.

When the accused saw that I had made friends with the preserving jar, he informed me that he sometimes worshiped it and prayed to it. My curiosity was aroused and I asked him for a sample of his prayers. He asked me a favor in return: providing me with paper and pencil, he asked me to write his prayer down. I could ask questions as he went along; while praying, he would answer to the best of his knowledge.

Here I give in testimony the words of the accused, my questions, his answers: Adoration of a preserving jar: I adore. Who, I? Oskar or I? I, piously; Oskar, with distraction. Devotion, perpetual, never mind about repetitions. I, discerning because without recollections; Oskar, discerning because full of recollections. I, cold, hot, lukewarm. Guilty under examination. Innocent without examination. Guilty because of, succumbed because of, remitted my guilt, unloaded the guilt on, fought through to, kept free of, laughed at and about, wept for, over, without, blasphemed in speech, blasphemed in silence, I speak not, I am not silent, I pray. I adore. What? A glass jar. What kind of a jar? A preserving jar. What is preserved in it? A finger. What sort of finger? A ring finger. Whose finger? Blond. Who's blond? Medium height. Five feet four? Five feet five. Distinguishing marks? A mole. Where? Inside of arm. Left, right? Right. Ring finger where? Left. Engaged? Yes, but not married. Religion? Protestant. Virgin? Virgin. Born? Don't know. Where? Near Hanover. When? December. Sagittarius or Capricorn? Sagittarius. Character? Timid. Good-natured? Conscientious, talkative. Sensible? Economical, matter-of-fact, but cheerful. Shy? Fond of goodies, straightforward, and bigoted. Pale, dreams of traveling, menstruation irregular, lazy, likes to suffer and talk about it, lacks imagination, passive, waits to see what will happen, good listener, nods in agreement, folds her arms, lowers eyelids when speaking, opens eyes wide when spoken to, light-grey with brown close to pupil, ring a present from boss, married man, didn't want to take it at first, took it, terrible experience, fibers, Satan, lots of white, took trip, moved, came back, couldn't stop, jealous, too, but for no reason. Sickness but not, death but not, yes, no, don't know, I can't go on. Picking cornflowers when murderer arrived, no, murderer was with her all along . . . Amen? Amen.

I, Gottfried Vittlar, append this prayer only because, confused as it may seem, the indications contained in it concerning the owner of the ring finger coincide very largely with the testimony regarding the murdered woman, Sister Dorothea Köngetter. However, I am not tryng to cast doubt on the accused's allegation that he did not murder Dorothea Köngetter and never saw her face to face.

It seems to me, in any case, that the extreme devotion with which the accused prayed and drummed—he was kneeling and had wedged his drum between his knees—to that preserving jar argues in his favor.

I had further occasion, in the year or more that followed, to see the accused pray and drum, for he was soon to offer me a generous salary—which I accepted—to accompany him on his tours, which he had interrupted for a considerable period but resumed shortly after finding the ring finger. We visited the whole of Western Germany and had offers to play in the East Zone and even abroad. But Mr. Matzerath preferred to remain within the boundaries of the Federal Republic; as he himself put it, he didn't want to get into the usual international rat race. He never drummed or prayed to the jar before performing. But after his appearance and a long-drawn-out dinner we would repair to his hotel room: then he drummed and prayed, while I asked questions and wrote; afterwards we would compare his prayer with those of the previous days and weeks. The prayers vary in length. Sometimes the words clashed violently, on other days the rhythm was fluid, almost meditative. Yet the prayers I collected, which I herewith submit to the court, contain no more information than my first transcript, which I incorporated in my deposition.

In the course of the year, I became superficially acquainted, between tours, with a few of Mr. Matzerath's friends and relatives. I met his stepmother, Mrs. Maria Matzerath, whom the accused adores, though with a certain restraint. And the same afternoon I made the acquaintance of Kurt Matzerath, the accused's half brother, a well-behaved boy of eleven. Mrs. Augusta Köster, the sister of Mrs. Maria Matzerath, also made a favorable impression on me. As the accused confessed to me, his relations with his family became more than strained during the first postwar years. It was only when Mr. Matzerath helped his stepmother to set up a large delicatessen store, which also carries tropical fruit, and helped financially whenever business difficulties arose, that relations between stepmother and stepson became really friendly.

Mr. Matzerath also introduced me to a number of former colleagues, for the most part jazz musicians. Mr. Münzer, whom the accused calls familiarly Klepp, struck me as a cheerful and amiable sort, but so far I have not had the energy or desire to develop these contacts.

Though, thanks to the generosity of the accused, I had no need to practice my trade during this period, love of my profession led me, between tours, to decorate a showcase or two. The accused took a friendly interest in my work. Often, late at night, he would stand out in the street, looking on as I practiced my modest arts. Occasionally, when the work was done, we would do the town a bit, though we avoided the Old City because the accused, as he himself explained, couldn't stand the sight of any more bull's-eye panes or signs in old-fashioned Gothic lettering. One of these excursions—and I am coming to the end of my deposition—took us through Unterrath to the car barn. It was past midnight.

We stood there at peace with the world and each other, watching the last cars pull in according to schedule. It's quite a sight. The dark city round about. In the distance, because it was Friday, the roaring of a drunken workman. Otherwise silence, because the last cars, even when they ring their bells and squeak on the curves, make no noise. Most of the cars ran straight into the barn. But a few stood outside, facing every which way, empty, but festively lighted. Who had the idea? Both of us, but it was I who said: "Well, my dear friend, what do you say?" Mr. Matzerath nodded, we got in without haste, I took the motorman's place and immediately felt quite at home. I started off gently, but gradually gathered speed. I turned out to be a good motorman. Matzerath—by now the brightly lit barn was behind us—acknowledged my prowess with these words: "You must have been baptized a Catholic, Gottfried, to be able to run a streetcar so well."

Indeed, this unaccustomed occupation gave me great pleasure. At the car barn no one seemed to have noticed our departure, for we were not followed, and they could easily have stopped us by turning off the current. I took the direction of Flingern; after Flingern I thought of turning left at Haniel and going on toward Rath and Ratingen, but Mr. Matzerath asked me to head for Grafenberg and Gerresheim. Though I had misgivings about the hill below the Lions' Den Dance Hall, I acceded to the request of the accused. I made the hill, the dance hall was behind me, but then I had to jam on the brakes because three men were standing on the tracks.

Shortly after Haniel, Mr. Matzerath had gone inside the car to smoke a cigarette. So it was I, the motorman, who had to cry "All aboard!" Two of the men were wearing green hats with black bands; the third, whom they held between them, was hatless. I observed that in getting on this third man missed the running board several times, either because of clumsiness or poor eyesight. His companions or guards helped him, or perhaps it would be more accurate to say that they dragged him brutally, onto my motorman's platform and then into the car.

I had started off again when suddenly from behind me, from inside the car, I heard a pitiful whimpering and a sound as of someone being slapped. But then I was reassured to hear the firm voice of Mr. Matzerath giving the new arrivals a piece of his mind, telling them to stop hitting an injured, half-blind man who had lost his glasses.

"You mind your own business," I heard one of the green hats roar. "This time he's going to get what's coming to him. It's been going on long enough."

While I drove on slowly in the direction of Gerresheim, my friend Matzerath asked what the poor fellow had done, Then the conversation took a strange turn: We were carried back to the days, in fact to the very first day, of the war: September 1, 1939; it seemed that this man, who was so nearsighted as to be almost blind, had participated as an irregular in the defense of some Polish post office. Strange to say, Mr. Matzerath, who could not have been more than fifteen at the time, knew all about it; he even recognized the poor devil as one Victor Weluhn, a nearsighted carrier of money orders, who had lost his glasses in the battle, escaped while the battle was still on, and given his pursuers the slip. But the chase had continued, they had pursued him till the end of the war, and

449

even then they had not given up. They produced a paper issued in 1939, an execution order. At last they had him, cried the one green hat; the other agreed: "And damn glad to get it over with. I've given up all my free time, even my vacations. An order, if you please, is an order, and this one has been hanging fire since '39. You think I've nothing else to do. I've got my work." He was a salesman, it appeared, and his associate had his troubles too, he had lost a good business in the East Zone and been obliged to start up from scratch. "But enough's enough; tonight we carry out that order, and that's an end to the past. Damn lucky we were to catch the last car!"

Thus quite unintentionally I became a motorman on a streetcar carrying two executioners and their intended victim to Gerresheim. The Gerresheim marketplace was deserted and looked rather lopsided; here I turned right, meaning to unload my passengers at the terminus near the glassworks and start home with Mr. Matzerath. Three stations before the terminus, Mr. Matzerath came out on the platform and deposited his briefcase, in which as I knew the preserving jar stood upright, approximately in the place where professional motormen put their lunchboxes.

"We've got to save him. It's Victor, poor Victor!" Mr. Matzerath was very upset.

"He still hasn't found glasses to fit him. He's terribly nearsighted, they'll shoot him and he'll be looking in the wrong direction." The executioners looked unarmed to me. But Mr. Matzerath had noticed the ungainly lumps in their coats.

"He carried money orders at the Polish Post Office. Now he has the same job at the Federal Post Office. But they hound him after working hours; they still have an order to shoot him."

Though I could not entirely follow Mr. Matzerath's explanations, I promised to attend the shooting with him and help him if possible to prevent it.

Behind the glassworks, just before the first gardens—if the moon had been out I could have seen my mother's garden with its apple tree —I put on the brakes and shouted into the car: "Last stop! All out!" And out they came with their green hats and black hatbands. Again poor Victor had trouble with the running board. Then Mr. Matzerath got out, but first he pulled out his drum from under his coat and asked me to take care of his briefcase with the jar in it.

We followed the executioners and their victim. The lights of the car were still on, and looking back we could see it far in the distance.

We passed along garden fences. I was beginning to feel very tired. When the three of them stopped still ahead of us, I saw that my mother's garden had been chosen as the execution site Both of us protested. Paying no attention, they knocked down the board fence, not a very difficult task for it was about to collapse of its own accord, and tied poor Victor to the apple tree just below my crook. When we continued to protest, they turned their flashlight on the crumpled execution order. It was signed by an inspector of courts-martial by the name of Zelewski and dated, if I remember right, Zoppot, October 5, 1939. Even the rubber stamps seemed to be right. The situation looked hopeless. Nevertheless, we talked about the United Nations, collective guilt, Adenauer, and so on; but one of the green hats swept aside all our objections, which were without juridical foundation, he assured us, because the peace treaty had never been signed, or even drawn up. "I vote for Adenauer just the same as you do," he went on. "But this execution order is still valid; we've consulted the highest authorities. We are simply doing our duty and the best thing you can do is to run along."

We did nothing of the sort. When the green hats produced the machine pistols from under their coats, Mr. Matzerath put his drum in place. At that moment the moon—it was almost full, just the slightest bit battered—burst through the clouds. And Mr. Matzerath began to drum . . . desperately.

A strange rhythm, yet it seemed familiar. Over and over again the letter O took form: lost, not yet lost, Poland is not yet lost! But that was the voice of poor Victor, he knew the words to Mr. Matzerath's drumming: While we live, Poland cannot die. The green hats, too, seemed to know that rhythm, I could see them take fright behind their hardware in the moonlight. And well they might. For the march that Mr. Matzerath and poor Victor struck up in my mother's garden awakened the Polish cavalry to life. Maybe the moon helped, or maybe it was the drum, the moon, and poor, nearsighted Victor's cracking voice all together that sent those multitudes of horsemen springing from the ground: stallions whinnied, hoofs thundered, nostrils fumed, spurs jangled, hurrah, hurrah! . . . No, not at all: no thundering, no jangling, whinnying, or shouts of hurrah; silently they glided over the harvested fields outside of Gerreshcim, but beyond any doubt they were a squadron of Polish Uhlans, for red and white like Mr. Matzerath's lacquered drum, the pennants clung to the lances; no, clung is not right, they floated, they glided, and indeed the whole squadron floated beneath the moon, coming perhaps from the moon, floated off, wheeled to the left, toward our garden, floated, seemingly not of flesh and blood, floated like toys fresh out of the box, phantoms, comparable perhaps to the spooklike figures that Mr. Matzerath's keeper makes out of knotted string: Polish cavalry of knotted string, soundless yet thundering, fleshless, bloodless, and yet Polish, down upon us they thundered, and we threw ourselves upon the ground while the moon and Poland's horsemen passed over us and over my mother's garden and all the other carefully tended gardens. But they did not harm

451

the gardens. They merely took along poor Victor and the two executioners and were lost in the open fields under the moon—lost, not yet lost, they galloped off to the east, toward Poland beyond the moon.

Panting, we waited for the night to quiet down, for the heavens to close again and remove the light that alone could have persuaded those riders long dead, long dust, to mount a last charge. I was first to stand up. Though I did not underestimate the influence of the moon, I congratulated Mr. Matzerath on his brilliant performance; a triumph I called it. He waved me aside with a weary, dejected gesture: "Triumph, my dear Gottfried? I have had too many triumphs, too much success in my life. What I would like is to be unsuccessful for once. But that is very difficult and calls for a great deal of work."

This speech was not to my liking, because I am the hardworking, conscientious type and have never met with the least success, let alone a triumph. It seemed to me that Mr. Matzerath showed a lack of gratitude, and I told him as much. "You are being very arrogant, Oskar," I ventured—by then we were calling each other by our first names. "All the papers are full of you. You've made a name for yourself. I'm not thinking of money. But do you suppose that it is easy for me, whom no newspaper has ever so much as mentioned, to live side by side with a darling of fame like you. Oh, how I long to do something big, unique, spectacular like what you have just done, to do it all by myself and get into the newspapers, to appear in print: This was the achievement of Gottfried von Vittlar."

I was offended at Mr. Matzerath's laughter. He lay on his back, rolling his hump in the loose earth, pulling out clumps of grass with both hands, tossing them up in the air, and laughing like an inhuman god who can do anything he pleases: "Nothing could be simpler, my friend. Here, take this briefcase. Luckily, the Polish cavalry hasn't crushed it. I make you a present of it; it contains a jar with a ring finger in it. Take it; run to Gerresheim, the streetcar is still there with all the lights on. Get in, drive to the Fürstenwall, take my present to Police Headquarters. Report me, and tomorrow you'll see your name in all the papers."

At first I rejected his offer; I argued that he wouldn't be able to live without his jar and his finger. But he reassured me; he said he was sick of the whole finger business, besides he had several plaster casts, he had even had a gold cast made. So would I please make up my mind, pick up the briefcase, get in that car, and go to the police.

So off I went. I could long hear Mr. Matzerath laughing behind me. He stayed there, lying on his back, he wanted to savor the charms of the night while I rode off ting-a-ling into town. I didn't go to the police until the following morning, but my report, thanks to Mr. Matzerath's kindness, brought me quite a lot of attention in the papers.

* * *

452

Meanwhile I, the kindly Mr. Matzerath, lay laughing in the night-black grass outside Gerresheim, rolled with laughter within sight of several deadly serious stars, laughed so hard that I worked my hump into the warm earth, and thought: Sleep, Oskar, sleep a little while before the police come and wake you up. Never again will you lie so free beneath the moon.

And when I awoke, I noticed, before noticing that it was broad daylight, that something, someone was licking my face: the quality of the sensation was warm, rough but not very, and moist.

Could that be the police so soon, awakened by Vittlar and now licking you awake? Nevertheless, I was in no hurry to open my eyes, but let myself be licked a while: warmly, moistly, not too roughly, it was quite pleasant. I chose not to care who was licking me: it's either the police, Oskar conjectured, or a cow. Only then did I open my blue eyes.

Spotted black and white, she breathed on me and licked me until I opened my eyes. It was broad daylight, clear to cloudy, and I said to myself: Oskar, don't waste your time on this cow even if there is something divine in her way of looking at you. Don't let that rasping-soothing tongue of hers tranquilize you by shutting off your memory. It is day, the flies are buzzing, you must run for your life. Vittlar is turning you in; consequently, you must flee. You can't have a bona fide denunciation without a bona fide flight. Leave the cow to her mooing and make your getaway. They will catch you either way, but why let that worry you?

And so, licked, washed, and combed by a cow, I fled. After the very first steps of my flight, I burst into a gale of fresh, early-morning laughter. Leaving my drum with the cow, who lay still and mooed, I embarked, laughing, upon my flight.

Thirty

Ah, yes, my flight, my getaway. There's still that to tell you about. I fled in order to enhance the value of Vittlar's denunciation. A getaway, I said to myself, requires first of all a destination. Whither, O Oskar, will you flee? Political obstacles, the so-called Iron Curtain, forbade me to flee eastward. It was not possible to head for my grandmother Anna Koljaiczek's four skirts, which to this day billow protectively in the Kashubian potato fields, although I told myself that if flight there must be, my grandmother's skirts were the only worthwhile destination.

Just in passing: today is my thirtieth birthday. At the age of thirty, one is obliged to discuss serious matters like flight as a man and not as a boy. As she brought in the cake with the thirty candles, Maria said: "You're thirty now, Oskar. It's time you were getting some sense into your head."

Klepp, my friend Klepp, gave me as usual some jazz records and used five matches to light the thirty candles on my cake: "Life begins at thirty!" said Klepp; he is twenty-nine.

Vittlar, however, my friend Gottfried, who is dearest to my heart, gave me sweets, bent down over the bars of my bed and whined: "When Jesus was thirty years of age, he set forth and gathered disciples round him."

Vittlar has always liked to mess things up for me. Just because I am thirty, he wants me to leave my bed and gather disciples. Then my lawyer came, brandishing a paper and trumpeting congratulations. Hanging his nylon hat on my bedpost, he proclaimed to me and all my birthday guests: "What a happy coincidence! Today my client is celebrating his thirtieth birthday; and just today I've received news that the Ring Finger Case is being reopened. A new clue has been found. Sister Beata, her friend, you remember . . . "

Just what I have been dreading for years, ever since my getaway: that they would find the real murderer, reopen the case, acquit me, discharge me from this mental hospital, take away my lovely bed, put me out in the cold street, in the wind and rain, and oblige a thirty-year-old Oskar to gather disciples round himself and his drum.

So apparently it was Sister Beata who murdered my Sister Dorothea out of festering green jealousy.

Perhaps you remember? There was this Dr. Werner who—the situation is only too common in life as it is in the movies—stood between the two nurses. A nasty business: Beata was in love with Dr. Werner. Dr. Werner was in love with Dorothea. And Dorothea wasn't in love with anyone, unless it was secretly, deep down, with little Oskar. Werner fell sick. Dorothea took care of him, because he was put into her section. Sister Beata couldn't bear it. She inveigled Dorothea into taking a walk with her and killed or, if you prefer, did away with her in a rye field near Gerresheim. Now Beata was free to take care of Dr. Werner. But it seems that she took care of him in a special way, so much so that he did not get well; just the opposite. Perhaps the love-crazed nurse said to herself: As long as he is sick, he belongs to me. Did she give him too much medicine? Did she give him the wrong medicine? In any case, Dr. Werner died; but when she testified in court, Sister Beata said nothing about wrong or too much, and not one word about her stroll in the rye fields with Sister Dorothea. And Oskar, who similarly confessed to nothing, but was the owner of an incriminating finger in a preserving jar, was convicted of the crime in the rye field. But esteeming that Oskar was not fully responsible for his actions, they sent me to the mental hospital for observation. Be that as it may, before they convicted him and sent him to the mental hospital, Oskar fled, for I wished, by my disappearance, to heighten the value of my friend Gottfried's denunciation.

454

At the time of my flight, I was twenty-eight. A few hours ago thirty candles were still dripping phlegmatically over my birthday cake. On the day of my flight it was September, just as it is today. I was born in the sign of Virgo. At the moment, though, it's my getaway I'm talking about, not my birth beneath the light bulbs.

As I have said, the eastward escape route, the road to my grandmother, was closed. Accordingly, like everyone else nowadays, I saw myself obliged to flee westward. If, Oskar, I said to myself, the inscrutable ways of politics prevent you from going to your grandmother, why not run to your grandfather, who is living in Buffalo, U.S.A.? Take America as your destination; we'll see how far you get.

This thought of Grandfather Koljaiczek in America came to me while my eyes were still closed and the cow was licking me in the meadow near Gerresheim. It must have been about seven o'clock and I said to myself: the stores open at eight. Laughing, I ran off, leaving my drum with the cow, saying to myself: Gottfried was tired, I doubt if he goes to the police before eight or maybe half-past. Take advantage of your little head start. It took me ten minutes, in the sleepy suburb of Gerresheim, to get a cab by telephone. The cab carried me to the Central Station. On the way I counted my money; several times I had to start counting all over again, because I couldn't help laughing, sending out gales of fresh early-morning laughter. Then I leafed through my passport and found that, thanks to the efforts of the West Concert Bureau, I possessed visas for France as well as the U.S.; Dr. Dösch had always hoped that one day Oskar the Drummer would consent to tour those countries.

Voilà, I said to myself, let us flee to Paris, it looks good and sounds good, it could happen in the movies, with Gabin smoking his pipe and tracking me down, inexorably but with kindness and understanding. But who will play *me*? Chaplin? Picasso? Laughing, stimulated by my thoughts of flight, I was still slapping the thighs of my slightly rumpled trousers when the driver asked me for seven DM. I paid up and had breakfast in the station restaurant. I laid out the timetable beside my soft-boiled egg and found a suitable train. After breakfast I had time to provide myself with foreign exchange and buy a small suitcase of excellent leather. Fearing to show myself in Jülicher-Strasse, I filled the suitcase with expensive but ill-fitting shirts, a pair of pale-green pajamas, toothbrush, toothpaste, and so on. Since there was no need to economize, I bought a first-class ticket, and soon found myself in a comfortable, upholstered first-class window seat, fleeing without physical effort. The cushions helped me to think. When the train pulled out, inaugurating my flight proper, Oskar began casting about for something to be frightened of; for not without reason I said to myself: you can't speak of a flight without fear. But what, Oskar, are you going to fear? What is worth running away from if all the police can wring from you is fresh, early-morning laughter?

455

Today I am thirty; flight and trial are behind me, but the fear I talked myself into during my flight is still with me.

Was it the rhythmic thrusts of the rails, the rattling of the train? Little by little the song took form, and a little before Aachen I was fully conscious of it. Monotonous words. They took possession of me as I sank back in the first-class upholstery. After Aachen—we crossed the border at half-past ten—they were still with me, more and more distinct and terrible, and I was glad when the customs inspectors changed the subject. They showed more interest in my hump than in my name or passport, and I said to myself: Oh, that Vittlar! That lazybones. Here it is almost eleven, and still he hasn't got to the police with that preserving jar under his arm, whereas I, for his sake, have been busy with this getaway since the crack of dawn, working myself up into a state of terror just to create a motive for my flight. Belgium. Oh, what a fright I was in when the rails sang: Where's the Witch, black as pitch? Here's the black, wicked Witch. Ha, ha, ha . . .

Today I am thirty, I shall be given a new trial and presumably be acquitted. I shall be thrown out in the street, and everywhere, in trains and streetcars, those words will ring in my ears: Where's the Witch, black as pitch? Here's the black, wicked Witch.

Still, apart from my dread of the Black Witch whom I expected to turn up at every station, the trip was pleasant enough. I had the whole compartment to myself—but maybe she was in the next one, right behind the partition—I made the acquaintance first of Belgian, then of French customs inspectors, dozed off from time to time, and woke up with a little cry. In an effort to ward off the Witch, I leafed through *Der Spiegel,* which I had bought on the platform in Düsseldorf; how they get around, how well informed they are, I kept saying to myself. I even found a piece about my manager, Dr. Dösch of the West Concert Bureau, confirming what I already knew, namely, that Oskar the Drummer was the mainstay and meal ticket of the Dösch agency—good picture of me too. And Oskar the Mainstay pictured to himself the inevitable collapse of the West Concert Bureau after my arrest.

Never in all my life had I feared the Black Witch. It was not until my flight, when I wanted to be afraid, that she crawled under my skin. And there she has remained to this day, my thirtieth birthday, though most of the time she sleeps. She takes a number of forms. Sometimes, for instance, it is the name "Goethe" that sets me screaming and hiding under the bedclothes. From childhood on I have done my best to study the poet prince and still his Olympian calm gives me the creeps. Even now, when, no longer luminous and classical but disguised as a black witch more sinister by far than any Rasputin, he peers through the bars of my bed and asks me, on the occasion of my thirtieth birthday: "Where's the Witch, black as pitch?"—I am scared stiff.

Ha, ha, ha! said the train carrying Oskar the fugitive to Paris. I was already expecting to see the International Police when we pulled in to the North Station, the Gare du Nord as the French call it. But there was no one waiting for me, only a porter, who smelled so reassuringly of red wine that with the best of intentions I couldn't mistake him for the Black Witch. I gave him my suitcase and let him carry it to within a few feet of the gate. The police and the Witch, I said to myself, probably don't feel like wasting money on a platform ticket, they will accost you and arrest you on the other side of the gate. So you'd better take back your suitcase before you go through. But the police weren't there to relieve me of my suitcase; I had to haul it to the Metro my very own self.

I won't go on about that famous Metro smell. I have recently read somewhere that it has been done into a perfume and that you can spray yourself with it. The Metro also asked about the whereabouts of the Black Witch, though in a rhythm rather different from that of the railroad. And another thing I noticed: the other passengers must have feared her as much as I did, for they were all asweat with terror. My idea was to continue underground to the Porte d'Italie, where I would take a cab to Orly Airport. If I couldn't be arrested at the North Station, it seemed to me that Orly, the world-famous airport—with the Witch done up as an airline hostess—would do very nicely, that it was an interesting place to be arrested in. There was one change of trains, I was glad my suitcase was so light. The Metro carried me southward and I pondered: where, Oskar, are you going to get off? Goodness me, how many things can happen in one day, this morning a cow licked you not far from Gerresheim, you were fearless and gay, and now you are in Paris—where will you get off, where will she come, black and terrible, to meet you? At the Place d'Italie? Or not until the Porte?

I got off at Maison Blanche, the last station before the Porte, thinking: they must think I think they are waiting at the Porte. But She knows what I think and what they think. Besides, I was sick of it all. My getaway and the pains I had taken to keep up my fear had been very tiring. Oskar had lost all desire to go on to the airfield; Maison Blanche, at this point, struck him as more original than Orly. He was right too. Because this particular Metro station has an escalator. An escalator, I said to myself, can be counted on to inspire me with a lofty sentiment or two, and the clatter will be just right for the Witch. "Here's the black, wicked Witch. Ha, ha, ha!"

Oskar is somewhat at a loss. His flight is drawing to an end and with it his story: Will the escalator in the Maison Blanche Metro station be high, steep, and symbolic enough to clank down the curtain suitably upon these recollections?

But there is also my thirtieth birthday. To all those who feel that an escalator makes too much noise and those who are not afraid of the

Black Witch, I offer my thirtieth birthday as an alternate end. For of all birthdays, isn't the thirtieth the most significant? It has the Three in it, and it foreshadows the Sixty, which thus becomes superfluous. As the thirty candles were burning on my birthday cake this morning, I could have wept with joy and exaltation, but I was ashamed in front of Maria: at thirty, you've lost your right to cry.

The moment I trod the first step of the escalator—if an escalator can be said to have a first step—and it began to bear me upward, I burst out laughing. Despite or because of my fear, I laughed. Slowly it mounted the steep incline—and there they were. There was still time for half a cigarette. Two steps above me a couple of lovers were carrying on brazenly. A step below me an old woman, whom I at first, for no good reason, suspected of being the Witch. She had on a hat decorated with fruit. Smoking, I summoned up—I worked hard at it—the kind of thoughts that an escalator should suggest. Oskar was Dante on his way back from hell; up above, at the end of the escalator, those dynamic reporters for *Der Spiegel* were waiting for him. "Well, Dante," they ask, "how was it down there?" Then I was Goethe, the poet prince, and the reporters asked me how I had enjoyed my visit to the Mothers. But then I was sick of poets and I said to myself: it's not any reporters for *Der Spiegel* or detectives with badges in their pockets that are standing up there. It's She, the Witch. "Here's the black, wicked Witch. Ha, ha, ha!"

Alongside the escalator there was a regular stairway, carrying people from the street down into the Metro station. It seemed to be raining outside. The people looked wet. That had me worried; I hadn't had time to buy a raincoat before leaving Düsseldorf. However, I took another look upward, and Oskar saw that the gentlemen with the faces had civilian umbrellas—but that cast no doubt on the existence of the Black Witch.

How shall I address them? I wondered, slowly savoring my cigarette as slowly the escalator aroused lofty feelings in me and enriched my knowledge: one is rejuvenated on an escalator, on an escalator one grows older and older. I had the choice of leaving that escalator as a three-year-old or as a man of sixty, of meeting the Interpol, not to mention the Black Witch, as an infant or as an old man.

It must be getting late. My iron bedstead looks so tired. And Bruno my keeper has twice showed an alarmed brown eye at the peephole. There beneath the water color of the anemones stands my uncut cake with its thirty candles. Perhaps Maria is already asleep. Someone, Maria's sister Guste, I think, wished me luck for the next thirty years. I envy Maria her sound sleep. What did Kurt, the schoolboy, the model pupil, always first in his class, what did my son Kurt wish me for my birthday? When Maria sleeps, the furniture round about her sleeps too. I have it: Kurt wished me a speedy recovery for my thirtieth birthday. But what I wish myself is a slice of Maria's sound sleep, for I am tired and words fail me.

Klepp's young wife made up a silly but well-meant birthday poem addressed to my hump. Prince Eugene was also deformed, but that didn't prevent him from capturing the city and fortress of Belgrade. Prince Eugene also had two fathers. Now I am thirty, but my hump is younger. Louis XIV was Prince Eugene's presumptive father. In years past, beautiful women would touch my hump in the street, they thought it would bring them luck. Prince Eugene was deformed and that's why he died a natural death. If Jesus had had a hump, they would never have nailed him to the Cross. Must I really, just because I am thirty years of age, go out into the world and gather disciples round me?

But that's the kind of idea you get on an escalator. Higher and higher it bore me. Ahead of me and above me the brazen lovers. Behind and below me the woman with the hat. Outside it was raining, and up on top stood the detectives from the Interpol. The escalator steps had slats on them. An escalator ride is a good time to reconsider, to reconsider everything: Where are you from? Where are you going? Who are you? What is your real name? What are you after? Smells assailed me: Maria's youthful vanilla. The sardine oil that my mother warmed up in the can and drank hot until she grew cold and was laid under the earth. In spite of Jan Bronski's lavish use of cologne, the smell of early death had seeped through all his buttonholes. The storage cellar of Greff's vegetable store had smelled of winter potatoes. And once again the smell of the dry sponges that dangled from the slates of the first-graders. And my Roswitha who smelled of cinnamon and nutmeg. I had floated on a cloud of carbolic acid when Mr. Fajngold sprinkled disinfectant on my fever. Ah, and the Catholic smells of the Church of the Sacred Heart, all those vestments that were never aired, the cold dust, and I, at the left side-altar, lending my drum, to whom?

But that's the kind of idea you get on an escalator. Today they want to pin me down, to nail me to the Cross. They say: you are thirty. So you must gather disciples. Remember what you said when they arrested you. Count the candles on your birthday cake, get out of that bed and gather disciples. Yet so many possibilities are open to a man of thirty. I might, for example, should they really throw me out of the hospital, propose to Maria a second time. My chances would be much better today. Oskar has set her up in business, he is famous, he is still making good money with his records, and he has grown older, more mature. At thirty a man should marry. Or I could stay single and marry one of my professions, buy a good shell-lime quarry, hire stonecutters, and deliver directly to the builders. At thirty a man should start a career. Or—in case my business is ruined by prefabricated slabs—I could revive my partnership with the Muse Ulla, side by side we would dispense inspiration to artists. Some day I might even make an honest woman of the Muse, poor thing, with all those blitz engagements. At thirty a man should marry. Or

459

should I grow weary of Europe, I could emigrate: America, Buffalo, my old dream: Off I go, in search of my grandfather, Joe Colchic, formerly Joseph Koljaiczek, the millionaire and sometime firebug. At thirty a man should settle down. Or I could give in and let them nail me to the Cross. Just because I happen to be thirty, I go out and play the Messiah they see in me; against my better judgment I make my drum stand for more than it can, I make a symbol out of it, found a sect, a party, or maybe only a lodge.

This escalator thought came over me in spite of the lovers above me and the woman with hat below me. Have I said that the lovers were two steps, not one, above me, that I put down my suitcase between myself and the lovers? The young people in France are very strange. As the escalator carried us all upward, she unbuttoned his leather jacket, then his shirt, and fondled his bare, eighteen-year-old skin. But so businesslike, so completely unerotic were her movements that a suspicion arose in me: these youngsters are being paid by the government to keep up the reputation of Paris, city of unabashed love. But when they kissed, my suspicion vanished, for he nearly choked on her tongue and was still in the midst of a coughing fit when I snuffed out my cigarette, preferring to meet the detectives as a non-smoker. The old woman below me and her hat—what I am trying to say is that her hat was on a level with my head because the two steps made up for my small stature—did nothing to attract attention, all she did was to mutter and protest a bit all by herself, but lots of old people do that in Paris. The rubber-covered bannister moved up along with us. You could put your hand on it and give your hand a free ride. I should have done so if I had brought gloves along. Each tile on the wall reflected a little drop of electric light. Cream-colored pipes and cables kept us company as we mounted. It should not be thought that this escalator made a fiendish din. Despite its mechanical character, it was a gentle, easygoing contrivance. In spite of the witch jingle, the Maison Blanche Metro station struck me as a pleasant place to be in, almost homelike. I felt quite at home on that escalator; despite my terror, despite the Witch, I should have esteemed myself happy if only the people round me on the escalator had not been total strangers but my friends and relatives, living and dead: my poor mama between Matzerath and Jan Bronski; Mother Truczinski, the gray-haired mouse, with her children Herbert, Guste, Fritz, Maria; Greff the greengrocer and his slovenly Lina; and of course Bebra the master and Roswitha so lithe and graceful—all those who had framed my questionable existence, those who had come to grief on the shoal of my existence. But at the top, where the escalator ended, I should have liked, in place of the Interpol men, to see the exact opposite of the Black Witch: my grandmother Anna Koljaiczek standing there like a mountain, ready to receive me and my retinue, our journey ended, under her skirts, into the heart of the mountain.

Instead there were two gentlemen. wearing not wide skirts, but American-style raincoats. And toward the end of my journey, I had to smile with all ten of my toes and admit to myself that the brazen lovers above me and the muttering woman below me were plain ordinary detectives.

What more shall I say: born under light bulbs, deliberately stopped growing at age of three, given drum, sang glass to pieces, smelled vanilla, coughed in churches, observed ants, decided to grow, buried drum, emigrated to the West, lost the East, learned stonecutter's trade, worked as model, started drumming again, visited concrete, made money, kept finger, gave finger away, fled laughing, rode up escalator, arrested, convicted, sent to mental hospital, soon to be acquitted, celebrating this day my thirtieth birthday and still afraid of the Black Witch.

I threw away my cigarette. It fell in one of the grooves in the escalator step. After riding upward for some distance at an angle of forty-five degrees, he traveled three more steps on the horizontal; then he let the brazen detective lovers and the detective grandmother push him off the escalator onto a stationary platform. When the gentlemen from the Interpol had introduced themselves and called him Matzerath, he replied, in obedience to his escalator idea, first in German: "Ich bin Jesus," then, aware that these were international agents, in French, and finally in English: "I am Jesus."

Nevertheless, I was arrested under the name of Oskar Matzerath. Offering no resistance, I put myself under the protection and, since it was raining on the Avenue d'Italie, the umbrellas, of the Interpol men. But I was still afraid. Several times I looked anxiously around and several times, here and there—yes, that is one of her talents—I saw the terribly placid countenance of the Black Witch among the passers-by on the avenue and then in the crowd that gathered round the paddy wagon.

I am running out of words, and still I cannot help wondering what Oskar is going to do after his inevitable discharge from the mental hospital. Marry? Stay single? Emigrate? Model? Buy a stone quarry? Gather disciples? Found a sect?

All the possibilities that are open nowadays to a man of thirty must be examined, but how examine them if not with my drum? And so I will drum out the little ditty which has become more and more real to me, more and more terrifying; I shall call in the Black Witch and consult her, and then tomorrow morning I shall be able to tell Bruno my keeper what mode of existence the thirty-year-old Oskar is planning to carry on in the shadow of a buggaboo which, though getting blacker and blacker, is the same old friend that used to frighten me on the cellar stairs, that said boo in the coal cellar, so I couldn't help laughing, but it was there just the same, talking with fingers, coughing through the keyhole, moaning in the stove, squeaking in tune with the door, smoking up from

461

chimneys when the ships were blowing their foghorns, when a fly buzzed for hours as it died between the double windows, or when eels clamored for Mama and my poor mama for eels, and when the sun sank behind Tower Mountain but lived on as pure sunlit amber. Whom was Herbert after when he assaulted the wooden statue? And behind the high altar—what would Catholicism be without the Witch who blackens every confessional with her shadow? It was her shadow that fell when Sigismund Markus' toys were smashed to bits. The brats in the court of our building, Axel Mischke and Nuchi Eyke, Susi Kater and Hänschen Kollin, they knew: For what did they sing as they cooked their brick-meal soup: "Where's the Witch, black as pitch? Here's the black wicked Witch. Ha, ha, ha! You're to blame. And you are too, You're most to blame, You! you! you! Where's the Witch, black as pitch? . . ." She had always been there, even in the woodruff fizz powder, bubbling so green and innocent; she was in clothes cupboards, in every clothes cupboard I ever sat in; later on, she borrowed Lucy Rennwand's triangular fox face, ate sausage sandwiches skins and all and sent the Dusters up on the diving tower: Oskar alone remained, he watched the ants, and he knew: it's *her* shadow that has multiplied and is following the sweetness. All words: blessed, sorrowful, full of grace, virgin of virgins . . . and all stones: basalt, tufa, diorite, nests in the shell lime, alabaster so soft . . . and all the shattered glass, glass transparent, glass blown to hair-thinness . . . and all the groceries, all the flour and sugar in blue pound and half-pound bags. Later on four tomcats, one of whom was called Bismarck, the wall that had to be freshly whitewashed, the Poles in the exaltation of death, the special communiqués, who sank what when, potatoes tumbling down from the scales, boxes tapered at the foot end, cemeteries I stood in, flags I knelt on, coconut fibers I lay on . . . the puppies mixed in the concrete, the onion juice that draws tears, the ring on the finger and the cow that licked me . . . Don't ask Oskar who she is! Words fail me. First she was behind me, later she kissed my hump, but now, now and forever, she is in front of me, coming closer.

Always somewhere behind me, the Black Witch.
Now ahead of me, too, facing me, Black.
Black words, black coat, black money.
But if children sing, they sing no longer:
Where's the Witch, black as pitch?
Here's the black, wicked Witch.
Ha! ha! ha!

Glossary

Bollermann and Wullsutski: popular characters, symbolizing German and Polish elements, frequent in Danzig jokes or stories.

Burckhardt, Carl Jacob: Swiss diplomat and historian who served as League of Nations High Commissioner of Danzig, 1937-1939.

Cold Storage Medal: the colloquial name given to the medal for service in the German army on the arctic front.

Currency Reform: the West German monetary policy established in 1948. The introduction of the Deutsche mark to replace the inflated reichsmark had a highly beneficial psychological effect on German businessmen and is considered the turning point in the postwar reconstruction and economic development of West Germany.

Draussen vor der Tür: a drama by Wolfgang Borchert describing the hopeless situation of the returning prisoner of war after World War II.

Edelweiss Pirates of Cologne: the most notorious of the armed bands of youths which appeared in Germany toward the end of World War II.

Forster, Albert: Gauleiter, or Nazi district leader, of Danzig from 1930. On September 1, 1939, Forster declared the Free City Treaty provisions null and void, suspended the constitution, and proclaimed the annexation of Danzing to the German Reich with himself as sole administrator.

Frings, Joseph Cardinal: Cardinal of Cologne, today the official leader of all German Catholics.

Greiser, Arthur: President of the Danzig Senate from 1934 who signed a treaty with the Nazis regularizing Polish-Danzing relations. After World War II he was condemned to death in Poland as a war criminal.

Hartmannsweilerkopf: Vosges Mountain peak fiercely contested by the French and the Germans in World War I.

Hitler Youth Quex and SA-Mann Brand: leading characters in popular books and propaganda films who represent ideal members of the Hitler Youth and the SA and who become martyrs for the Nazi cause. Quex, for example, is murdered by Communists. On his deathbed he converts his father, who is a Communist, to National Socialism.

463

Jan Wellem: popular name for the elector palatine Johann Wilhelm (1679-1716), whose monument still stands today in Düsseldorf.

July 20th conspirators: a group, led by high-ranking German generals, who made an attempt on Hitler's life in 1944.

Kashubes: a Germanized West Slavic people living in the northwestern part of the earlier province of West Prussia and in northeastern Pomerania. Until 1945, some 150,000 people spoke Kashubian as their mother tongue. The language forms a transitional dialect between Polish and West Pomeranian.

Kasperl: a popular puppet character, similar to Punch.

Käthe-Kruse dolls: individually designed, handmade cloth dolls from the workshop of Käthe Kruse, one-time actress.

Kyffhäuser Bund: a right-wing, monarchist, ex-serviceman's association of a paramilitary nature founded in 1900. Its merger with other servicemen's groups after World War I resulted in a combined membership of over four million.

Matka Boska Częstokowska: an icon representing the Virgin Mother which hangs in a monastery church in Częstochowa and is traditionally believed to have been painted by St. Luke. Its miraculous power is said to be responsible for the lifting of a Swedish siege in the seventeenth century. One of the most famous religious and national shrines in Poland; still visited annually by throngs of pilgrims.

Niemoller, Pastor Martin: a Protestant clergyman and the leading figure in the anti-Nazi Confessional Church who spent seven years in a concentration camp.

Organisation Todt: the organization directed by engineer Fritz Todt which conscripted forced labor—often children—for construction work, notably on the fortification of the West Wall in 1938 and the Atlantic Wall in 1940.

Pan Kichot: Polish for Don Quixote.

pay book: unlike American soldiers, who carry no identification but their dogtags, the German soldiers carried a booklet containing full information as to their vital statistics, military history, and pay.

Poland is not yet lost, etc.: in reference to the Polish national anthem (*Jeszcze Polska Nie Zginęla*).

Rauschning, Hermann: President of the Danzig Senate 1933-1934. Rauschning ended his association with Hitler and the National Socialists in 1934 when he became opposed to the policies of the Danzig Gauleiter Forster. He fled from Germany in 1936 and subsequently wrote several books criticizing the Nazi regime.

Rentenmark: the temporary currency established in 1923 to stabilize money during the inflationary period in Germany following World War I.

Sauerbruch, Professor Ferdinand: a famous German surgeon (1875-1951).

Speicherinsel: an island formed by the Mottlau River in the middle of Danzig, so-called because of its famous half-timbered grain warehouses.

Strength through Joy (Kraft durch Freude): a Nazi organization which provided regimented leisure for members of the German working class. It provided theaters, sports, travel, and vacation opportunities at reduced prices. No organized social or recreational group was allowed to function in Germany except under the control of this official, all-embracing organization.

Sütterlin script: the standard German script developed by Ludwig Sütterlin and taught in schools from 1915 to 1945.

Winter Aid (Winterhilfe): the major Nazi charity, set up under the slogan "War on Hunger and Cold," to which the German people made compulsory contributions.

ZOB: Żydowska Organizacja Bojowa, or Jewish Combat Organization, an underground movement formed in the ghetto in 1942-1943.

CAT AND MOUSE

Chapter I

. . . and one day, after Mahlke had learned to swim, we were lying in the grass, in the Schlagball field. I ought to have gone to the dentist, but they wouldn't let me because I was hard to replace on the team. My tooth was howling. A cat sauntered diagonally across the field and no one threw anything at it. A few of the boys were chewing or plucking at blades of grass. The cat belonged to the caretaker and was black. Hotten Sonntag rubbed his bat with a woolen stocking. My tooth marked time. The tournament had been going on for two hours. We had lost hands down and were waiting for the return game. It was a young cat, but no kitten. In the stadium, handball goals were being made thick and fast on both sides. My tooth kept saying one word, over and over again. On the cinder track the sprinters were practicing starts or limbering up. The cat meandered about. A trimotored plane crept across the sky, slow and loud, but couldn't drown out my tooth. Through the stalks of grass the caretaker's black cat showed a white bib. Mahlke was asleep. The wind was from the east, and the crematorium between the United Cemeteries and the Engineering School was operating. Mr. Mallenbrandt, the gym teacher, blew his whistle: Change sides. The cat practiced. Mahlke was asleep or seemed to be. I was next to him with my toothache. Still practicing, the cat came closer. Mahlke's Adam's apple attracted attention because it was large, always in motion, and threw a shadow. Between me and Mahlke the caretaker's black cat tensed for a leap. We formed a triangle. My tooth was silent and stopped marking time: for Mahlke's Adam's apple had become the cat's mouse. It was so young a cat, and Mahlke's whatsis was so active—in any case the cat leaped at Mahlke's throat; or one of us caught the cat and held it up to Mahlke's neck; or I, with or without my toothache, seized the cat and showed it Mahlke's mouse: and Joachim Mahlke let out a yell, but suffered only slight scratches.

And now it is up to me, who called your mouse to the attention of this cat and all cats, to write. Even if we were both invented, I should have to write. Over and over again the fellow who invented us because it's his business to invent people obliges me to take your Adam's apple in my hand and carry it to the spot that saw it win or lose. And so, to begin with, I make the mouse bob up and down above the screwdriver, I fling a multitude of replete sea gulls into the fitful northeast wind, high over Mahlke's head, call the weather summery and persistently fair, assume that the wreck was a former mine sweeper of the *Czaika* class, and give the Baltic the color of thick-glass seltzer bottles. Now that the scene of action has been identified as a point southeast of the Neufahrwasser harbor buoy, I make Mahlke's skin, from which water is still running in rivulets, take on a texture somewhere between fine and coarse-grained. It was not fear, however, that roughened Mahlke's skin, but the shivers customary after long immersion in the sea that seized hold of Mahlke and took the smoothness from his skin.

And yet none of us, as we huddled lean and long-armed between our upthrust knees on the remains of the bridge, had asked Mahlke to dive down again into the fo'c'sle of the sunken mine sweeper and the adjoining engine room amidships, and work something loose with his screwdriver, a screw, a little wheel, or something really special: a brass plate inscribed with the directions in Polish and English for operating some machine. We were sitting on the superstructure, or as much of it as remained above the water, of a former Polish mine sweeper of the *Czaika* class, built in Gdynia and launched in Modlin, which had been sunk the year before southeast of the harbor buoy, well outside the channel so that it did not interfere with shipping.

Since then gull droppings had dried on the rust. In all kinds of weather the gulls flew sleek and smooth, with eyes like glass beads on the sides of their heads, grazing the remains of the pilothouse, then wildly up again, according to some indecipherable plan, squirting their slimy droppings in full flight—and they never fell into the soft sea but always on the rusty superstructure. Hard, dense, calcareous, the droppings clung fast, side by side in innumerable spots, or heaped up in mounds. And always when we sat on the barge, fingernails and toenails tried to chip off the droppings. That's why our nails cracked and not because we bit our fingernails—except for Schilling, who was always chewing at them and had nails like rivets. Only Mahlke had long nails, though they were yellow from all his diving, and he kept them long by neither biting them nor scratching at the gull droppings. And he was the only one who never ate the chips we broke loose—the rest of us, because it was there, chewed the stony, shell-like mess into a foaming slime, which we spat overboard. The stuff tasted like nothing at all or like plaster or like fish meal or like everything imaginable: happiness, girls, God in His heaven. "Do you realize," said Winter, who sang very nicely, "that tenors eat gull droppings every day?" Often the gulls caught our calcareous spittle in full flight, apparently suspecting nothing.

* * *

470

When shortly after the outbreak of the war Joachim Mahlke turned fourteen, he could neither swim nor ride a bicycle; there was nothing striking about his appearance and he lacked the Adam's apple that was later to lure the cat. He had been excused from gymnastics and swimming, because he had presented certificates showing him to be sickly. Even before he learned to ride a bicycle—a ludicrous figure with his deep-red, protuberant ears and his knees thrust sideways as he pedaled—he reported for swimming in the winter season, at the Niederstadt pool, but at first he was admitted only to the "dry swimming" class for eight-to-ten-year-olds. Nor did he make much progress the following summer. The swimming teacher at Brösen Beach, a typical swimming teacher with a torso like a life buoy and thin hairless legs, had to put Mahlke through his paces in the sand and then hold him by a life line. But after we had swum away from him several afternoons in a row and come back telling fantastic stories about the sunken mine sweeper, he was mightily inspired and in less than two weeks he was swimming.

Earnestly and conscientiously he swam back and forth between the pier, the big diving tower, and the bathing beach, and he had no doubt achieved a certain endurance by the time he began to practice diving off the little breakwater outside the pier, first bringing up some common Baltic mussels, then diving for a beer bottle filled with sand, which he threw out pretty far. My guess is that Mahlke soon succeeded in recovering the bottle quite regularly, for when he began to dive with us on the mine sweeper, he was no longer a beginner.

He pleaded with us to let him come along. Six or seven of us were getting ready for our daily swim, elaborately moistening our skins in the shallow water of the family pool, as a precaution against sudden chill. And there was Mahlke on the plank walk: "Please take me with you. I'll make it, I'm positive."

A screwdriver hung around his neck, distracting attention from his Adam's apple.

"OK!" And Mahlke came along. Between the first and second sand bank he passed us, and we didn't bother to catch up with him. "Let him knock himself out."

When Mahlke swam breast stroke, the screwdriver bobbed visibly up and down between his shoulder blades, for it had a wooden handle. When he swam on his back, the wooden handle danced about on his chest, but never entirely covered the horrid piece of cartilage between chin and collarbone, which cut through the water like a dorsal fin, leaving a wake behind it.

And then Mahlke showed us. He dove several times in quick succession with his screwdriver and brought up whatever he was able to unscrew: lids, pieces of sheathing, a part of the generator; he found a rope, and with the help of the decrepit winch hoisted up a genuine fire extinguisher from the fo'c'sle. The thing—made in Germany, I might add—still worked; Mahlke proved it, squirting streams of foam to show us how you extinguish with foam, extinguishing the glass-green sea—from the very first day he was tops.

The flakes still lay in islands and long streaks on the flat, even swell, attracting a few gulls which were soon repelled, settled, and like a big mess of whipped cream turned sour drifted off toward the beach. Then Mahlke called it a day and sat down in the shadow of the pilot-house; and even before the stray tatters of foam on the bridge had time to lose their stiffness and start trembling in the breeze, his skin had taken on that shriveled, coarse-grained look.

Mahlke shivered and his Adam's apple jogged up and down; his screwdriver did dance steps over his quaking collarbones. His back, white in spots, burned lobster-red from the shoulders down, forever peeling with fresh sunburn on both sides of his prominent spinal column, was also covered with gooseflesh and shaken with fitful shudders. His yellowish lips, blue at the edges, bared his chattering teeth. But he tried to bring his body—and his teeth—under control by clasping his knees, which he had bruised on the barnacle-covered bulkheads, with his big waterlogged hands.

Hotten Sonntag—or was it I?—rubbed Mahlke down. "Lord, man, don't go catching something. We've still got to get back." The screwdriver began to calm down.

The way out took us twenty-five minutes from the breakwater, thirty-five from the beach. We needed a good three quarters of an hour to get back. No matter how exhausted he was, he was always standing on the breakwater a good minute ahead of us. He never lost the lead he had taken the first day. Before we reached the barge—as we called the mine sweeper—Mahlke had already been under once, and as soon as we reached out our washerwoman's hands, all of us pretty much at once, for the rust and gull droppings of the bridge or the jutting gun mounts, he silently exhibited a hinge or something or other that had come off easily, and already he was shivering, though after the second or third time he covered himself with a thick, extravagant coat of Nivea cream; for Mahlke had plenty of pocket money.

Mahlke was an only child.

Mahlke was half an orphan.

Mahlke's father was dead.

Winter and summer Mahlke wore old-fashioned high shoes which he must have inherited from his father.

He carried the screwdriver around his neck on a shoelace for high black shoes.

472

It occurs to me only now that, in addition to the screwdriver, Mahlke, for certain reasons, wore something else around his neck; but the screwdriver was more conspicuous.

He wore a little silver chain, from which hung something silver and Catholic: the Blessed Virgin; most likely he had always worn it, but we had never noticed; he certainly had it on ever since the day when he had started to swim in harness and to make figures in the sand while practicing his kick.

Never, not even in gym class, did Mahlke remove the medal from his neck; for no sooner had he taken up dry swimming and swimming in harness in the winter swimming pool at Niederstadt than he turned up in our gymnasium, and never again did he produce any doctor's certificates. Either the silver Virgin disappeared under his white gym shirt or lay just over the red stripe that ran around it at chest level.

Even the parallel bars held no horrors for Mahlke. Only three or four of the best members of the first squad were equal to the horse exercises, but Mahlke was right with them, leaping from the springboard, sailing over the long leather horse, and landing on the mat with Virgin awry, sending up clouds of dust. When he did knee-swings on the horizontal bar his form was miserable, but later he succeeded in doing two more than Hotten Sonntag, our gymnastics champion—well, when Mahlke ground out his thirty-seven knee-swings, the medal tugged out of his gym shirt, and hurtiled thirty-seven times around the squeaking horizontal bar, always in advance of his medium-brown hair. But it never came free from his neck, for the wildly agitated chain was held in place not only by his jutting Adam's apple but also by his protuberant occiput, with its thick growth of hair.

The screwdriver lay over the medal, and in places the shoelace covered the chain. However, the screwdriver did not outshine the medal, especially as the object with the wooden handle was not allowed in the gymnasium. Our gym teacher, a Mr. Mallenbrandt who was also assistant principal and was well known in sports circles because he had written a rulebook to end all rulebooks for the game of Schlagball, forbade Mahlke to wear the screwdriver around his neck in gym class. Mallenbrandt never found any fault with the medal on Mahlke's neck, because in addition to physical culture and geography, he taught religion, and up to the second year of the war guided the remnants of a Catholic workers' gymnastic society over and under the horizontal and parallel bars.

And so the screwdriver had to wait in the dressing room, over his shirt on the hook, while the slightly worn silver Virgin was privileged to hang from Mahlke's neck and succor him amid gymnastic perils.

A common screwdriver it was, cheap and sturdy. Often Mahlke, in order to detach a small plaque no larger than the name plate beside an apartment door, had to dive five or six times, especially when the plate

473

was affixed to metal and the screws were rusted. On the other hand, he sometimes managed, after only two dives, to bring up larger plaques with long texts inscribed on them by using his screwdriver as a jimmy and prying screws and all from the waterlogged wooden sheathing. He was no great collector; he gave many of his plaques to Winter and Jürgen Kupka, who fanatically collected everything removable, including street markers and the signs in public toilets; for himself he took only the few items that particularly struck his fancy.

Mahlke didn't make things easy for himself; while we dozed on the barge, he worked under water. We scratched at the gull droppings and turned brown as cigars; those of us who had blond hair were transformed into towheads. Mahlke at most took on fresh lobster tones. While we followed the ships north of the beacon, he looked unswervingly downward: reddened, slightly inflamed lids with sparse lashes, I think; light-blue eyes which filled with curiosity only under water. Sometimes Mahlke came up without any plaques or other spoils, but with a broken or hopelessly bent screwdriver. That too he would exhibit, and always got an effect. The gesture with which he tossed it over his shoulder into the water, exasperating the gulls, was commanded neither by resigned disappointment nor by aimless rage. Never did Mahlke throw away a broken tool with indifference, real or affected. Even this act of tossing away signified: I'll soon have something more to show you.

. . . and once—a hospital ship with two smokestacks had put into port, and after a brief discussion we had identified it as the *Kaiser* of the East Prussian Maritime Service—Joachim Mahlke went down into the fo'c'sle without a screwdriver and, holding his nose with two fingers, vanished in the open, slate-green, slightly submerged forward hatchway. He went in headfirst—his hair was plastered flat and parted from swimming and diving; he pulled in his back and hips, kicked once at the empty air, but then, bracing both feet against the edge of the hatch, pushed down into the dusky cool aquarium, floodlighted through open portholes: nervous sticklebacks, an immobile school of lampreys, swaying hammocks, still firmly attached at the ends, overgrown with seaweed, a playhouse for baby herring. Rarely a stray cod. Only rumors of eels. We never once saw a flounder.

We clasped our slightly trembling knees, chewed gull droppings into a sludge; half weary, half fascinated, we counted a formation of Navy cutters, followed the stacks of the hospital ship, whence smoke was still rising vertically, exchanged sidelong glances. He stayed down a long while—gulls circled, the swell gurgled over the bow, broke against the forward gun mount—the gun itself had been removed. A splashing as the water flowed back between the ventilators behind the bridge, licking always at the same rivets; lime under fingernails; itching on dry skin, shimmering light, chugging of motors in the wind, private parts half stiff, seventeen poplars between Brösen and Glettkau—and then he came shooting upward: bluish-red around the chin, yellowish over the cheekbones. His hair parted exactly in the middle, he rose like a fountain from the hatch, staggered over the bow through water up to his knees, reached for the jutting gun mount, and fell watery-goggle-eyed to his knees; we had to pull him up on the bridge. But before the water had stopped flowing from his nose and the corner of his mouth, he showed us his find, a steel screwdriver in one piece. Made in England. Stamped on the metal: Sheffield. No scars, no rust, still coated with grease. The water formed into beads and rolled off.

Every day for over a year Mahlke wore this heavy, to all intents and purposes unbreakable screwdriver on a shoelace, even after we had stopped or almost stopped swimming out to the barge. Though he was a good Catholic, it became a kind of cult with him. Before gym class, for instance, he would give the thing to Mr. Mallenbrandt for safekeeping; he was dreadfully afraid it might be stolen, and even took it with him to St. Mary's Chapel; for not only on Sunday, but also on weekdays, he went to early Mass on Marineweg, not far from the Neuschottland co-operative housing development.

He and his English screwdriver didn't have far to go—out of Osterzeile and down Bärenweg. Quantities of two-story houses, villas with gable roofs, porticoes, and espaliered fruit trees. Then two rows of housing developments, plain drab walls ornamented only with water spots. To the right the streetcar line turned off and with it the overhead wires, mostly against a partly cloudy sky. To the left, the sandy, sorry-looking kitchen gardens of the railroad workers: bowers and rabbit hutches built with the black and red boards of abandoned freight cars. Behind the gardens the signals of the railway leading to the Free Port. Silos, movable and stationary cranes. The strange full-colored superstructures of the freighters. The two gray battleships with their old-fashioned turrets were still there, the swimming dock, the Germania bread factory; and silvery sleek, at medium height, a few captive balloons, lurching and bobbing. In the right background, the Gudrun School (the Helen Lange School of former years) blocking out the iron hodgepodge of the Schichau Dockyards as far as the big hammer crane. To this side of it, covered, well-tended athletic fields, freshly painted goal posts, foul lines marked in lime on the short grass: next Sunday Blue-and-Yellow versus Schellmühl 98—no grandstand, but a modern, tall-windowed gymnasium painted in light ocher. The fresh red roof of this edifice, oddly enough, was topped with a tarred wooden cross; for St. Mary's Chapel had formerly been a gymnasium belonging to the Neuschottland Sports Club. It had been found necessary to transform it into an emergency church, because the Church

475

of the Sacred Heart was too far away; for years the people of Neuschottland, Schellmühl, and the housing development between Osterzeile and Westerzeile, mostly shipyard, railroad, or post-office workers, had sent petitions to the bishop in Oliva until, still during the Free State period, this gymnasium had been purchased, remodeled, and consecrated.

Despite the tortuous and colorful pictures and ornaments, some privately donated but for the most part deriving from the cellars and storerooms of just about every church in the diocese, there was no denying or concealing the gymnasium quality of this church—no amount of incense or wax candles could drown out the aroma of the chalk, leather, and sweat of former years and former handball matches. And the chapel never lost a certain air of Protestant parsimony, the fanatical sobriety of a meetinghouse.

In the Neo-Gothic Church of the Sacred Heart, built of bricks at the end of the nineteenth century, not far from the suburban railway station, Joachim Mahlke's steel screwdriver would have seemed strange, ugly, and sacrilegious. In St. Mary's Chapel, on the other hand, he might perfectly well have worn it openly: the little chapel with its well-kept linoleum floor, its rectangular frosted glass windowpanes starting just under the ceiling, the neat iron fixtures that had formerly served to hold the horizontal bar firmly in place, the planking in the coarse-grained concrete ceiling, and beneath it the iron (though whitewashed) crossbeams to which the rings, the trapeze, and half a dozen climbing ropes had formerly been affixed, was so modern, so coldly functional a chapel, despite the painted and gilded plaster which bestowed blessing and consecration on all sides, that the steel screwdriver which Mahlke, in prayer and then in communion, felt it necessary to have dangling from his neck, would never have attracted the attention either of the few devotees of early Mass, or of Father Gusewski and his sleepy altar boy—who often enough was myself.

No, there I'm going too far. It would certainly not have escaped me. As often as I served at the altar, even during the gradual prayers I did my best, for various reasons, to keep an eye on you. And you played safe; you kept your treasure under your shirt, and that was why your shirt had those grease spots vaguely indicating the shape of the screwdriver. Seen from the altar, he knelt in the second pew of the left-hand row, aiming his prayer with open eyes—light gray they were, I think, and usually inflamed from all his swimming and diving—in the direction of the Virgin.

. . . and once—I don't remember which summer it was—was it during the first summer vacation on the barge, shortly after the row in France, or was it the following summer?—one hot and misty day, enormous crowd on the family beach, sagging pennants, overripe flesh, big rush at the refreshments stands, on burning feet over the fiber runners, past locked cabins full of tittering, through a turbulent mob of children engaged in slobbering, tumbling, and cutting their feet; and in the midst of this spawn which would now be twenty-three years old, beneath the solicitous eyes of the grownups, a little brat, who must have been about three, pounded monotonously on a child's tin drum, turning the afternoon into an infernal smithy—whereupon we took to the water and swam out to our barge; from the beach, in the lifeguard's binoculars for instance, we were six diminishing heads in motion; one head in advance of the rest and first to reach the goal.

We threw ourselves on burning though wind-cooled rust and gull droppings and lay motionless. Mahlke had already been under twice. He came up with something in his left hand. He had searched the crew's quarters, in and under the half-rotted hammocks, some tossing limply, others still lashed fast, amid swarms of iridescent sticklebacks, through forests of seaweed where lampreys darted in and out, and in a matted mound, once the sea kit of Seaman Duszynski or Liszinski, he had found a bronze medallion the size of a hand, bearing on one side, below a small embossed Polish eagle, the name of the owner and the date on which it had been conferred, and on the other a relief of a mustachioed general. After a certain amount of rubbing with sand and powdered gull droppings the circular inscription told us that Mahlke had brought to light the portrait of Marshal Pilsudski.

For two weeks Mahlke concentrated on medallions; he also found a kind of tin plate commemorating a regatta in the Gdynia roadstead and amidships, between fo'c'sle and engine room, in the cramped, almost inaccessible officers' mess, a silver medal the size of a mark piece, with a silver ring to pass a chain through; the reverse was flat, worn, and anonymous, but the face, amid a profusion of ornament, bore the Virgin and Child in sharp relief.

A raised inscription identified her as the famous Matka Boska Często-chowska; and when Mahlke on the bridge saw what he had found, we offered him sand, but he did not polish his medal; he preferred the black patina.

The rest of us wanted to see shining silver. But before we had finished arguing, he had knelt down on his knobby knees in the shadow of the pilothouse, shifting his treasure about until it was at the right angle for his gaze, lowered in devotion. We laughed as, bluish and shivering, he crossed himself with his waterlogged fingertips, attempted to move his lips in prayer, and produced a bit of Latin between chattering teeth. I still think it was even then something from his favorite sequence, which normally was spoken only on the Friday before Palm Sunday: "*Virgo virginum praeclara, Mihi iam non sis amara . . .*"

Later, after Dr. Klohse, our principal, had forbidden Mahlke to wear

477

this Polish article openly on his neck during classes—Klohse was a high party official, though he seldom wore his uniform at school—Joachim Mahlke contented himself with wearing his usual little amulet and the steel screwdriver beneath the Adam's apple which a cat had taken for a mouse.

He hung the blackened silver Virgin between Pillsudski's bronze profile and the postcard-size photo of Commodore Bonte, the hero of Narvik.

Chapter II

Was all this praying and worshipping in jest? Your house was on Westerzeile. You had a strange sense of humor, if any. No, your house was on Osterzeile. All the streets in the housing development looked alike. And yet you had only to eat a sandwich and we would laugh, each infecting the other. Every time we had to laugh at you, it came as a surprise to us. But when Dr. Brunies, one of our teachers, asked the boys of our class what profession they were planning to take up and you—you already knew how to swim—said: "I'm going to be a clown and make people laugh," no one laughed in the classroom—and I myself was frightened. For while Mahlke firmly and candidly stated his intention of becoming a clown in a circus or somewhere else, he made so solemn a face that it was really to be feared that he would one day make people laugh themselves sick, if only by publicly praying to the Virgin between the lion tamer and the trapeze act; but that prayer of yours on the barge must have been in earnest—or wasn't it?

He lived on Osterzeile and not on Westerzeile. The one-family house stood beside, between, and opposite similar one-family houses which could be distinguished perhaps by different patterns or folds in the curtains, but hardly by the vegetation of the little gardens out in front. And each garden had its little birdhouse on a pole and its glazed garden ornaments: frogs, mushrooms, or dwarfs. In front of Mahlke's house sat a ceramic frog. But in front of the next house and the next, there were also green ceramic frogs.

In short, it was number twenty-four, and when you approached from Wolfsweg, Mahlke lived in the fourth house on the left side of the street. Like Westerzeile, which ran parallel to it, Osterzeile was perpendicular to Bärenweg, which ran parallel to Wolfsweg. When you went down Westerzeile from Wolfsweg and looked to the left and westward over the red tiled roofs, you saw the west side and front of a tower with a tarnished bulbiform steeple. If you went down Osterzeile in the same direction, you saw over the rooftops the east side and front of the same belfry; for Christ Church lay on the far side of Bärenweg, exactly halfway between Osterzeile and Westerzeile, and with its four dials beneath the green, bulbiform roof, provided the whole neighborhood, from Max-Halbe-Platz to the Catholic and clockless St. Mary's Chapel, from Magdeburger Strasse to Posadowskiweg near Schellmühl, with the time of day, enabling Protestant as well as Catholic factory workers and office workers, salesgirls and schoolboys to reach their schools or places of work with interdenominational punctuality.

From his window Mahlke could see the dial of the east face of the tower. He had his room in the attic; the walls were slightly on a slant, and the rain and hail beat down directly over his head: an attic room full of the usual juvenile bric-à-brac, from the butterfly collection to the postcard photos of movie stars, lavishly decorated pursuit pilots and Panzer generals; but in the midst of all this, an unframed color print of the Sistine Madonna with the two chubby-cheeked angels at the lower edge, the Pilsudski medal, already mentioned, and the consecrated amulet from Częstochowa beside a photograph of the commander of the Narvik destroyers.

The very first time I went to see him, I noticed the stuffed snowy owl. I lived not far away, on Westerzeile; but I'm not going to speak of myself, my story is about Mahlke, or Mahlke and me, but always with the emphasis on Mahlke, for his hair was parted in the middle, he wore high shoes, he always had something or other dangling from his neck to distract the eternal cat from the eternal mouse, he knelt at the altar of the Virgin, he was the diver with the fresh sunburn; though he was always tied up in knots and his form was bad, he always had a bit of a lead on the rest of us, and no sooner had he learned to swim than he made up his mind that someday, after finishing school and all that, he would be a clown in the circus and make people laugh.

The snowy owl had Mahlke's solemn part in the middle and the same suffering, meekly resolute look, as of a redeemer plagued by inner toothache. It was well prepared, only discreetly retouched, and held a birch branch in its claws. The owl had been left him by his father.

I did my best to ignore the snowy owl, the color print of the Madonna, and the silver piece from Częstochowa; for me the center of the room was the phonograph that Mahlke had painstakingly raised from the barge. He had found no records; they must have dissolved. It was a relatively modern contrivance with a crank and a player arm. He had found it in the same officers' mess that had already yielded his silver medal and several other items. The cabin was amidships, hence inaccessible to the rest of us, even Hotten Sonntag. For we went only as far as the fo'c'sle and never ventured through the dark bulkhead, which even the fishes seldom visited, into the engine room and the cramped adjoining cabins.

Shortly before the end of our first summer vacation on the barge,

479

Mahlke brought up the phonograph—German-made it was, like the fire extinguisher—after perhaps a dozen dives. Inch by inch he had moved it forward to the foot of the hatch and finally hoisted it up to us on the bridge with the help of the same rope that had served for the fire extinguisher.

We had to improvise a raft of driftwood and cork to haul the thing ashore; the crank was frozen with rust. We took turns in towing the raft, all of us except Mahlke.

A week later the phonograph was in his room, repaired, oiled, the metal parts freshly plated. The turntable was covered with fresh felt. After winding it in my presence, he set the rich-green turntable to revolving empty. Mahlke stood behind it with folded arms, beside the snowy owl on its birch branch. His mouse was quiet. I stood with my back to the Sistine color print, gazing either at the empty, slightly wobbling turntable, or out the mansard window, over the raw-red roof tiles, at Christ Church, one dial on the front, another on the east side of the bulbiform tower. Before the clock struck six, the phonograph droned to a stop. Mahlke wound the thing up again, demanding that I glve his new rite my unflagging attention: I listened to the assortment of soft and medium sounds characteristic of an antique phonograph left to its own devices. Mahlke had as yet no records.

There were books on a long sagging shelf. He read a good deal, including religious works. In addition to the cactuses on the window sill, to models of a torpedo boat of the *Wolf* class and the dispatch boat *Cricket,* I must also mention a glass of water that always stood on the washstand beside the bowl; the water was cloudy and there was an inch-thick layer of sugar at the bottom. In this glass Mahlke each morning, with sugar and care, stirred up the milky solution designed to hold his thin, limp hair in place; he never removed the sediment of the previous day. Once he offered me the preparation and I combed the sugar water into my hair; it must be admitted that thanks to his fixative, my hairdo preserved a vitreous rigidity until evening: my scalp itched, my hands were sticky, like Mahlke's hands, from passing them over my hair to see how it was doing—but maybe the stickiness of my hands is only an idea that came to me later, maybe they were not sticky at all.

Below him, in three rooms only two of which were used, lived his mother and her elder sister. Both of them quiet as mice when he was there, always worried and proud of the boy, for to judge by his report cards Mahlke was a good student, though not at the head of the class. He was—and this detracted slightly from the merit of his performance —a year older than the rest of us, because his mother and aunt had sent the frail, or as they put it sickly, lad to grade school a year later than usual.

But he was no grind, he studied with moderation, let everyone copy from him, never snitched, showed no particular zeal except in gym class, and had a conspicuous horror of the nasty practical jokes customary in Third. He interfered, for instance, when Hotten Sonntag, having found a condom in Steffenspark, brought it to class mounted on a branch, and stretched it over our classroom doorknob. The intended victim was Dr. Treuge, a dottering half-blind pedant, who ought to have been pensioned years before. A voice called from the corridor: "He's coming," whereupon Mahlke arose, strode without haste to the door, and removed the loathsome object with a sandwich paper.

No one said a word. Once more he had shown us; and today I can say that in everything he did or did not do—in not being a grind, in studying with moderation, in allowing all and sundry to copy from him, in showing no particular zeal except in gym class, in shunning nasty practical jokes—he was always that very special, individual Mahlke, always, with or without effort, gathering applause. After all he was planning to go into the circus later or maybe on the stage; to remove loathsome objects from doorknobs was to practice his clowning; he received murmurs of approval and was almost a clown when he did his knee-swings on the horizontal bar, whirling his silver Virgin through the fetid vapors of the gymnasium. But Mahlke piled up the most applause in summer vacation on the sunken barge, although it would scarcely have occurred to us to consider his frantic diving a circus act. And we never laughed when Mahlke, time and time again, climbed blue and shivering onto the barge, bringing up something or other in order to show us what he had brought up. At most we said with thoughtful admiration: "Man, that's great. I wish I had your nerves. You're a cool dog all right. How'd you ever get ahold of that?"

Applause did him good and quieted the jumping mouse on his neck; applause also embarrassed him and started the selfsame mouse up again. Usually he made a disparaging gesture, which brought him new applause. He wasn't one to brag; never once did you say: "You try it." Or: "I dare one of you guys to try." Or: "Remember the day before yesterday, the way I went down four times in a row, the way I went in amidships as far as the galley and brought up that famous can. . . . None of you ever did that. I bet it came from France, there were frogs' legs in it, tasted something like veal, but you were yellow, you wouldn't even try it after I'd eaten half the can. And damned if I didn't raise a second can, hell, I even found a can opener, but the second can stank, rotten corned beef."

No, Mahlke never spoke like that. He did extraordinary things. One day, for instance, he crawled into the barge's one-time galley and brought up several cans of preserves, which according to the inscriptions stamped in the metal were of English or French origin; he even located an almost serviceable can opener. Without a word he ripped the cans open before our eyes, devoured the alleged frogs' legs, his Adam's apple doing push-ups as he chewed—I forgot to say that Mahlke was by nature an eater—and when the can was half empty, he held out the can to us, invitingly but not overbearingly. We said no thank you, because just from watching, Winter had to crawl between the empty gun mounts and retch at length but in vain in the direction of the harbor mouth.

After this bit of conspicuous consumption, Mahlke naturally received his portion of applause; waving it aside, he fed the putrid corned beef and what was left of the frogs' legs to the gulls, which had been coming steadily closer during his banquet. Finally he bowled the cans and shooed the gulls overboard, and scoured the can opener, which alone struck him as worth keeping. From then on he wore the can opener suspended from his neck by a string like the English screwdriver and his various amulets, but not regularly, only when he was planning to look for canned goods in the galley of a former Polish mine sweeper—his stomach never seemed to mind. On such days he came to school with the can opener under his shirt beside the rest of his hardware; he even wore it to early Mass in St. Mary's Chapel; for whenever Mahlke knelt at the altar rail, tilting his head back and sticking out his tongue for Father Gusewski to lay the host on, the altar boy by the priest's side would peer into Mahlke's shirt collar: and there, dangling from your neck was the can opener, side by side with the Madonna and the grease-coated screwdriver; and I admired you, though you were not trying to arouse my admiration. No, Mahlke was never an eager beaver.

In the autumn of the same year in which he had learned to swim, they threw him out of the Young Folk and into the Hitler Youth, because several Sundays in a row he had refused to lead his squad—he was a squad leader in the Young Folk—to the morning meet in Jeschkental Forest. That too, in our class at least, brought him outspoken admiration. He received our enthusiasm with the usual mixture of coolness and embarrassment and continued, now as a rank-and-file member of the Hitler Youth, to shirk his duty on Sunday mornings; but in this organization, which embraced the whole male population from fourteen to twenty, his remissness attracted less attention, for the Hitler Youth was not as strict as the Young Folk, it was a big, sprawling organization in which fellows like Mahlke could blend with their surroundings. Besides, he wasn't insubordinate in the usual sense; he regularly attended the training sessions during the week, made himself useful in the "special activities" that were scheduled more and more frequently, and was glad to help with the junk collections or stand on street corners with a Winter Aid can, as long as it didn't interfere with his early Mass on Sunday. There was nothing unusual about being transferred from the Young Folk to the Hitler Youth, and Member Mahlke remained a colorless unknown quantity in the official youth organization, while in our school, after the first summer on the barge, his reputation, though neither good nor bad, became legendary.

There is no doubt that unlike the Hitler Youth our gymnasium became for you, in the long run, a source of high hopes which no common gymnasium, with its traditional mixture of rigor and good-fellowship, with its colored school caps and its often invoked school spirit, could possibly fulfill.

"What's the matter with him?"

"I say he's got a tic."

"Maybe it's got something to do with his father's death."

"And what about all that hardware on his neck?"

"And he's always running off to pray."

"And he don't believe in nothing if you ask me."

"Hell no, he's too realistic."

"And what about that thing on his neck?"

"You ask him, you're the one that sicked the cat on him . . ."

We racked our brains and we couldn't understand you. Before you could swim, you were a nobody, who was called on now and then, usually gave correct answers, and was named Joachim Mahlke. And yet I believe that in Sixth or maybe it was later, certainly before your first attempts at swimming, we sat on the same bench; or you sat behind me or in the same row in the middle section, while I sat behind Schilling near the window. Later somebody recollected that you had worn glasses up to Fifth; I never noticed them. I didn't even notice those eternal laced shoes of yours until you had made the grade with your swimming and begun to wear a shoelace for high shoes around your neck. Great events were shaking the world just then, but Mahlke's time reckoning was Before learning to swim and After learning to swim; for when the war broke out all over the place, not all at once but little by little, first on the Westerplatte, then on the radio, then in the newspapers, this schoolboy who could neither swim nor ride a bicycle didn't amount to much; but the mine sweeper of the *Czaika* class, which was later to provide him with his first chance to perform, was already, if only for a few weeks, playing its military role in the Pitziger Wiek, in the Gulf, and in the fishing port of Hela.

The Polish fleet was small but ambitious. We knew its modern ships, for the most part built in England or France, by heart, and could reel off their guns, tonnage, and speed in knots with never a mistake, just as we could recite the names of all Italian light cruisers, or of all the obsolete Brazilian battleships and monitors.

Later Mahlke took the lead also in this branch of knowledge; he learned to pronounce fluently and without hesitation the names of the Jappanese destroyers from the modern *Kasumi* class, built in '38, to the slower craft of the *Asagao* class, modernized in '23: *"Fumizuki, Satsuki, Yuuzuki, Hokaze, Nadakaze,* and *Oite."*

It didn't take very long to rattle off the units of the Polish fleet. There were the two destroyers, the *Blyskawica* and the *Grom,* two thousand tons, thirty-eight knots, but they decommissioned themselves two days before the outbreak of the war, put into English ports, and were incorporated into the British Navy. The *Blyskawica* is still in existence. She has been converted into a floating naval museum in Gdynia and schoolteachers take their classes to see it.

The destroyer *Burza,* fifteen hundred tons, thirty-three knots, took the same trip to England. Of the five Polish submarines, only the *Wilk* and, after an adventurous journey without maps or captain, the elevenhundred-ton *Orzel* succeeded in reaching English ports. The *Rys, Zbik,* and *Semp* allowed themselves to be interned in Sweden.

By the time the war broke out, the ports of Gdynia, Putzig, Heisternest, and Hela were bereft of naval vessels except for an obsolete former French cruiser that served as a training ship and dormitory, the mine layer *Gryf,* built in the Norman dockyards of Le Havre, a heavily armed vessel of two thousand tons, carrying three hundred mines. Otherwise there were a lone destroyer, the *Wicher,* a few former German torpedo boats, and the six mine sweepers of the *Czaika* class, which also laid mines. These last had a speed of eighteen knots; their armament consisted of a 75-millimeter forward gun and four machine guns on revolving mounts; they carried, so the official handbooks say, a complement of twenty mines.

And one of these one-hundred-and-eighty-five-ton vessels had been built specially for Mahlke.

The naval battle in the Gulf of Danzig lasted from the first of September to the second of October. The score, after the capitulation on Hela Peninsula, was as follows: The Polish units *Gryf, Wicher, Baltyk,* as well as the three mine sweepers of the *Czaika* class, the *Mewa,* the *Jaskolka,* and the *Czapala,* had been destroyed by fire and sunk in their ports; the German destroyer *Leberecht* had been damaged by artillery fire, the mine sweeper *M 85* ran into a Polish antisubmarine mine north of Heisternest ternest and lost a third of its crew.

Only the remaining, slightly damaged vessels of the *Czaika* class were captured. The *Zuraw* and the *Czaika* were soon commissioned under the names of *Oxthöft* and *Westerplatte*; as the third, the *Rybitwa,* was being towed from Hela to Neufahrwasser, it began to leak, settle, and wait for Joachim Mahlke; for it was he who in the following summer raised brass plaques on which the name *Rybitwa* had been engraved. Later, it was said that a Polish officer and a bosun's mate, obliged to man the rudder under

German guard, had flooded the barge in accordance with the well-known Scapa Flow recipe.

For some reason or other it sank to one side of the channel, not far from the Neufahrwasser harbor buoy and, though it lay conveniently on one of the many sandbanks, was not salvaged, but spent the rest of the war right there, with only its bridge, the remains of its rail, its battered ventilators, and the forward gun mount (the gun itself had been removed) emerging from the water—a strange sight at first, but soon a familiar one. It provided you, Joachim Mahlke, with a goal in life; just as the battleship *Gneisenau,* which was sunk in February '45 just outside of Gdynia harbor, became a goal for Polish schoolboys; though I can only wonder whether, among the Polish boys who dove and looted the *Gneisenau,* there was any who took to the water with the same fanaticism as Mahlke.

Chapter III

He was not a thing of beauty. He could have had his Adam's apple repaired. Possibly that piece of cartilage was the whole trouble.

But it went with the rest of him. Besides, you can't prove everything by proportions. And as for his soul, it was never introduced to me. I never heard what he thought. In the end, all I really had to go by was his neck and its numerous counterweights. It is true that he took enormous bundles of margarine sandwiches to school and to the beach with him and would devour quantities of them just before going into the water. But this can only be taken as one more reminder of his mouse, for the mouse chewed insatiably.

There were also his devotions at the altar of the Virgin. He took no particular interest in the Crucified One. It struck me that though the bobbing on his neck did not cease when he joined his fingertips in prayer, he swallowed in slow motion on these occasions and contrived, by arranging his hands in an exaggeratedly stylized pose, to distract attention from that elevator above his shirt collar and his pendants on strings, shoelaces, and chains—which never stopped running.

Apart from the Virgin he didn't have much truck with girls. Maybe if he had had a sister? My girl cousins weren't much use to him either. His relations with Tulla Pokriefke don't count, they were an anomaly and would not have been bad as a circus act—remember, he was planning to become a clown—for Tulla, a spindly little thing with legs like toothpicks, might just as well have been a boy. In any case, this scrawny girl child, who swam along with us when she felt like it during our second summer on the barge, was never the least embarrassed when we decided to give our swimming trunks a rest and sprawled naked on the rusty bridge, with very little idea what to do with ourselves.

You can draw a good likeness of Tulla's face with the most familiar

485

punctuation marks. The way she glided through the water, she might have had webs between her toes. Always, even on the barge, despite seaweed, gulls, and the sour smell of the rust, she stank of carpenter's glue, because her father worked with glue in her uncle's carpenter's shop. She was all skin, bones, and curiosity. Calmly, her chin in the cup of her hand, Tulla would look on when Winter or Esch, unable to contain himself, produced his modest offering. Hunching over so that the bones of her spine stuck out, she would gaze at Winter, who was always slow in getting there, and mutter: "Man, that's taking a long time!"

But when, finally, the stuff came and splashed on the rust, she would begin to fidget and squirm, she would throw herself down on her belly, make little rat's eyes and look and look, trying to discover heaven-knows-what, turn over, sit up, rise to her knees and her feet, stand slightly knock-kneed over the mess, and begin to stir it with a supple big toe, until it foamed rust-red: "Boy! That's the berries! Now you do it, Atze."

Tulla never wearied of this little game—yes, game, the whole thing was all perfectly innocent. "Aw, you do it," she would plead in that whining voice of hers. "Who hasn't done it yet? It's your turn."

She always found some good-natured fool who would get to work even if he wasn't at all in the mood, just to give her something to goggle at. The only one who wouldn't give until Tulla found the right words of encouragement—and that is why I am narrating these heroic deeds— was the great swimmer and diver Joachim Mahlke. While all the rest of us were engaging in this time-honored, nay Biblical, pursuit, either one at a time or—as the manual puts it—with others, Mahlke kept his trunks on and gazed fixedly in the direction of Hela. We felt certain that at home, in his room between snowy owl and Sistine Madonna, he indulged in the same sport.

He had just come up, shivering as usual, and he had nothing to show. Schilling had just been working for Tulla. A coaster was entering the harbor under its own power. "Do it again," Tulla begged, for Schilling was the most prolific of all. Not a single ship in the roadstead. "Not after swimming. I'll do it again tomorrow," Schilling consoled her. Tulla turned on her heel and stood with outspread toes facing Mahlke, who as usual was shivering in the shadow of the pilothouse and hadn't sat down yet. A high-seas tug with a forward gun was putting out to sea.

"Won't you? Aw, do it just once. Or can't you? Don't you want to? Or aren't you allowed to?"

Mahlke stepped half out of the shadow and slapped Tulla's compressed little face left right with his palm and the back of his hand. His mouse went wild. So did the screwdriver. Tulla, of course, didn't shed one single tear, but gave a bleating laugh with her mouth closed; shaking with laughter, she arched her india-rubber frame effortlessly into a bridge, and peered through her spindly legs at Mahlke until he—he was back in the shade again and the tug was veering off to northwestward—said: "OK. Just so you'll shut your yap."

Tulla came out of her contortion and squatted down normally with her legs folded under her, as Mahlke stripped his trunks down to his knees. The children at the Punch-and-Judy show gaped in amazement: a few deft movements emanating from his right wrist, and his pecker loomed so large that the tip emerged from the shadow of the pilothouse and the sun fell on it. Only when we had all formed a semicircle did Mahlke's jumping Jim return to the shadow.

"Won't you let me just for a second?" Tulla's mouth hung open. Mahlke nodded and dropped his right hand, though without uncurving his fingers. Tulla's hands, scratched and bruised as they always were, approached the monster, which expanded under her questioning fingertips; the veins stood out and the glans protruded.

"Measure it!" cried Jürgen Kupka. Tulla spread the fingers of her left hand. One full span and another almost. Somebody and then somebody else whispered: "At least twelve inches!" That was an exaggeration of course. Schilling, who otherwise had the longest, had to take his out, make it stand up, and hold it beside Mahlke's: Mahlke's was first of all a size thicker, second a matchbox longer, and third looked much more grownup, dangerous, and worthy to be worshiped.

He had shown us again, and then a second time he showed us by producing not one but two mighty streams in quick succession. With his knees not quite together, Mahlke stood by the twisted rail beside the pilothouse, staring out in the direction of the harbor buoy, a little to the rear of the low-lying smoke of the vanishing high-seas tug; a torpedo boat of the *Gull* class was just emerging from the harbor, but he didn't let it distract him. Thus he stood, showing his profile, from the toes extending just over the edge to the watershed in the middle of his hair: strangely enough, the length of his sexual part made up for the otherwise shocking protuberance of his Adam's apple, lending his body an odd, but in its way perfect, harmony.

No sooner had Mahlke finished squirting the first load over the rail than he started in all over again. Winter timed him with his waterproof wrist watch; Mahlke's performance continued for approximately as many seconds as it took the torpedo boat to pass from the tip of the breakwater to the buoy; then, while the torpedo boat was rounding the buoy, he unloaded the same amount again; the foaming bubbles lurched in the smooth, only occasionally rippling swell, and we laughed for joy as the gulls swooped down, screaming for more.

Joachim Mahlke was never obliged to repeat or better this performance, for none of us ever touched his record, certainly not when exhausted from swimming and diving; sportsmen in everything we did, we respected the rules.

For a while Tulla Pokriefke, for whom his prowess must have had the most direct appeal, courted him in her way; she would always be sitting by the pilothouse, staring at Mahlke's swimming trunks. A few times she pleaded with him, but he always refused, though good-naturedly.

"Do you have to confess these things?"

Mahlke nodded, and played with his dangling screwdriver to divert her gaze.

"Will you take me down sometime? By myself I'm scared. I bet there's still a stiff down there."

For educational purposes, no doubt, Mahlke took Tulla down into the fo'c'sle. He kept her under much too long. When they came up, she had turned a grayish yellow and sagged in his arms. We had to stand her light, curveless body on its head.

After that Tulla Pokriefke didn't join us very often and, though she was more regular than other girls of her age, she got increasingly on our nerves with her drivel about the dead sailor in the barge. She was always going on about him. "The one that brings him up," she promised, "can you-know-what."

It is perfectly possible that without admitting it to ourselves we all searched, Mahlke in the engine room, the rest of us in the fo'c'sle, for a half-decomposed Polish sailor; not because we really wanted to lay this unfinished little number, but just so.

Yet even Mahlke found nothing except for a few half-rotted pieces of clothing, from which fishes darted until the gulls saw that something was stirring and began to say grace.

No, he didn't set much store by Tulla, though they say there was something between them later. He didn't go for girls, not even for Schilling's sister. And all my cousins from Berlin got out of him was a fishy stare. If he had any tender feelings at all, it was for boys; by which I don't mean to suggest that Mahlke was queer; in those years spent between the beach and the sunken barge, we none of us knew exactly whether we were male or female. Though later there may have been rumors and tangible evidence to the contrary, the fact is that the only woman Mahlke cared about was the Catholic Virgin Mary. It was for her sake alone that he dragged everything that can be worn and displayed on the human neck to St. Mary's Chapel. Whatever he did, from diving to his subsequent military accomplishments, was done for her or else—yes, I know, I'm contradicting myself again—to distract attention from his Adam's apple. And perhaps, in addition to Virgin and mouse, there was yet a third

motive: Our school, that musty edifice that defied ventilation, and particularly the auditorium, meant a great deal to Joachim Mahlke; it was
the school that drove you, later on, to your supreme effort.

And now it is time to say something about Mahlke's face. A few of us
have survived the war; we live in small small towns and large small towns,
we've gained weight and lost hair, and we more or less earn our living.
I saw Schilling in Duisburg and Jürgen Kupka in Braunschweig shortly
before he emigrated to Canada. Both of them started right in about the
Adam's apple. "Man, wasn't that something he had on his neck! And
remember that time with the cat. Wasn't it you that sicked the cat on
him . . ." and I had to interrupt: "That's not what I'm after; it's his face
I'm interested in."

We agreed as a starter that he had gray or gray-blue eyes, bright
but not shining, anyway that they were not brown. The face thin and
rather elongated, muscular around the cheekbones. The nose not strikingly
large, but fleshy, quickly reddening in cold weather. His overhanging
occiput has already been mentioned. We had difficulty in coming to an
agreement about Mahlke's upper lip. Jürgen Kupka was of my opinion
that it curled up and never wholly covered his two upper incisors, which
in turn were not vertical but stuck out like tusks—except of course when
he was diving. But then we began to have our doubts; we remembered
that the little Pokriefke girl also had a curled-up lip and always visible
incisors. In the end we weren't sure whether we hadn't mixed up Mahlke
and Tulla, though just in connection with the upper lip. Maybe it was
only she whose lip was that way, for hers was, that much is certain. In
Duisburg Schilling—we met in the station restaurant, because his wife
had some objection to unannounced visitors—reminded me of the caricature that had created an uproar in our class for several days. In '41 I
think it was, a big, tall character turned up in our class, who had been
evacuated from Latvia with his family. In spite of his cracked voice, he
was a fluent talker; an aristocrat, always fashionably dressed, knew Greek,
lectured like a book, his father was a baron, wore a fur cap in the winter,
what *was* his name?—well, anyway, his first name was Karel. And he
could draw, very quickly, with or without models: sleighs surrounded by
wolves, drunken Cossacks, Jews suggesting *Der Stürmer,* naked girls riding
on lions, in general lots of naked girls with long porcelainlike legs, but
never smutty, Bolsheviks devouring babies, Hitler disguised as Charlemagne, racing cars driven by ladies with long flowing scarves; and he was
especially clever at drawing caricatures of his teachers or fellow students
with pen, brush, or crayon on every available scrap of paper or with chalk
on the blackboard; well, he didn't do Mahlke on paper, but with rasping
chalk on the blackboard.

He drew him full face. At that time Mahlke already had his ridiculous part in the middle, fixated with sugar water. He represented the face as a triangle with one corner at the chin. The mouth was puckered and peevish. No trace of any visible incisors that might have been mistaken for tusks. The eyes, piercing points under sorrowfully uplifted eyebrows. The neck sinuous, half in profile, with a monstrous Adam's apple. And behind the head and sorrowful features a halo: a perfect likeness of Mahlke the Redeemer. The effect was immediate.

We snorted and whinnied on our benches and only recovered our senses when someone hauled off at the handsome Karel So-and-So, first with his bare fist, then, just before we managed to separate them, with a steel screwdriver.

It was I who sponged your Redeemer's countenance off the blackboard.

Chapter IV

With and without irony: maybe you wouldn't have become a clown but some sort of creator of fashions; for it was Mahlke who during the winter after the second summer on the barge created the pompoms: two little woolen spheres the size of ping-pong balls, in solid or mixed colors, attached to a plaited woolen cord that was worn under the collar like a necktie and tied into a bow so that the two pompoms hung at an angle, more or less like a bow tie. I have checked and am able to state authoritatively that beginning in the third winter of the war, the pompoms came to be worn almost all over Germany, but mostly in northern and eastern Germany, particularly by high-school students. It was Mahlke who introduced them to our school. He might have invented them. And maybe he actually did. He had several pair made according to his specifications by his Aunt Susi, mostly out of the frayed yarn unraveled from his dead father's much-darned socks. Then he wore the first pair to school and they were very very conspicuous on his neck.

Ten days later they were in the dry-goods stores, at first in cardboard boxes bashfully tucked away by the cash register, but soon attractively displayed in the showcases. An important factor in their success was that they could be had without coupons. From Langfuhr they spread triumphantly through eastern and northern Germany; they were worn—I have witnesses to bear me out—even in Leipzig, in Pirna, and months later, after Mahlke had discarded his own, a few isolated pairs made their appearance as far west as the Rhineland and the Palatinate. I remember the exact day when Mahlke removed his invention from his neck and will speak of it in due time.

He wore the pompoms for several months, toward the end as a protest, after Dr. Klohse, our principal, had branded this article of apparel as effeminate and unworthy of a German young man, and forbidden us to wear pompoms inside the school building or even in the recreation yard. Klohse's order was read in all the classrooms, but there were many who complied only during actual classes. The pompoms remind me of Papa Brunies, a pensioned teacher who had been recalled to his post during the war; he was delighted with the merry little things; once or twice, after Mahlke had given them up, he even tied a pair of them around his own stand-up collar, and thus attired declaimed Eichendorff: "Weathered gables, lofty windows . . ." or maybe it was something else, but in any case it was Eichendorff, his favorite poet. Oswald Brunies had a sweet tooth and later, ostensibly because he had eaten some vitamin tablets that were supposed to be distributed among the students, but probably for political reasons—Brunies was a Freemason—he was arrested at school. Some of the students were questioned. I hope I didn't testify against him. His adoptive daughter, a doll-like creature who took ballet lessons, wore mourning in public; they took him to Stutthof, and there he stayed—a dismal, complicated story, which deserves to be written, but somewhere else, not by me, and certainly not in connection with Mahlke.

Let's get back to the pompoms. Of course Mahlke had invented them to make things easier for his Adam's apple. For a time they quieted the unruly jumping jack, but when the pompoms came into style all over the place, even in Sixth, they ceased to attract attention on their inventor's neck. I can still see Mahlke during the winter of '42—which must have been hard for him because diving was out and the pompoms had lost their efficacy—always in monumental solitude, striding in his high, black laced shoes, down Osterzeile and up Bärenweg to St. Mary's Chapel, over crunching cinder-strewn snow. Hatless. Ears red, brittle, and prominent. Hair stiff with sugar water and frost, parted in the middle from crown to forehead. Brows knitted in anguish. Horror-stricken, watery-blue eyes that see more than is there. Turned-up coat collar. The coat had also come down to him from his late father. A gray woolen scarf, crossed under his tapering to scrawny chin, was held in place, as could be seen from a distance, by a safety pin. Every twenty paces his right hand rises from his coat pocket to feel whether his scarf is still in place, properly protecting his neck—I have seen clowns, Grock in the circus, Charlie Chaplin in the movies, working with the same gigantic safety pin. Mahlke is practicing: men, women, soldiers on furlough, children, singly and in groups, grow toward him over the snow. Their breath, Mahlke's too, puffs up white from their mouths and vanishes over their shoulders. And the eyes of all who approach him are focused, Mahlke is probably thinking, on that comical, very comical, excruciatingly comical safety pin.

In the same dry, hard winter I arranged an expedition over the frozen sea to the ice-bound mine sweeper with my two girl cousins, who had come from Berlin for Christmas vacation, and Schilling to make things come out even. The girls were pretty, sleek, tousled blonde, and spoiled from living in Berlin. We thought we would show off some and impress them with our barge. The girls were awfully ladylike in the streetcar and even on the beach, but out there we were hoping to do something really wild with them, we didn't know what.

Mahlke ruined our afternoon. In opening up the harbor channel, the icebreakers had pushed great boulders of ice toward the barge; jammed together, they piled up into a fissured wall, which sang as the wind blew over it and hid part of the barge from view. We caught sight of Mahlke only when we had mounted the ice barrier, which was about as tall as we were, and had pulled the girls up after us. The bridge, the pilothouse, the ventilators aft of the bridge, and whatever else had remained above water formed a single chunk of glazed, bluish-white candy, licked ineffectually by a congealed sun. No gulls. They were farther out, over the garbage of some ice-bound freighters in the roadstead.

Of course Mahlke had turned up his coat collar and tied his scarf, with the safety pin out in front, under his chin. No hat, but round, black ear muffs, such as those worn by garbage men and the drivers of brewery trucks, covered his otherwise protruding ears, joined by a strip of metal at right angles to the part in his hair.

He was so hard at work on the sheet of ice over the bow that he didn't notice us; he even seemed to be keeping warm. He was trying with a small ax to cut through the ice at a point which he presumed to be directly over the open forward hatch. With quick short strokes he was making a circular groove, about the size of a manhole cover. Schilling and I jumped from the wall, caught the girls, and introduced them to him. No gloves to take off; he merely shifted the ax to his left hand. Each of us in turn received a prickly-hot right hand, and a moment later he was chopping again. Both girls had their mouths slightly open. Little teeth grew cold. Frosty breath beat against their scarves and frosty-eyed they stared at his ice-cutting operations. Schilling and I were through. But though furious with him, we began to tell about his summertime accomplishments as a diver: "Metal plates, absolutely, and a fire extinguisher, and tin cans, he opened them right up and guess what was in them—human flesh! And when he brought up the phonograph something came crawling out of it, and one time he . . ."

The girls didn't quite follow, they asked stupid questions, and addressed Mahlke as Mister. He kept right on hacking. He shook his head and ear muffs as we shouted his diving prowess over the ice, but never forgot to feel for his muffler and safety pin with his free hand. When we could think of nothing more to say and were just standing there shivering, he would stop for a moment every twenty strokes or so, though without ever standing up quite straight, and fill the pause with simple, modest explanations. Embarrassed, but at the same time self-assured, he dwelt on his lesser exploits and passed over the more daring feats, speaking more of his work than of adventures in the moist interior of the sunken mine sweeper. In the meantime he drove his groove deeper and deeper into the ice. I wouldn't say that my cousins were exactly fascinated by Mahlke; no, he wasn't witty enough for that and his choice of words was too commonplace. Besides, such little ladies would never have gone all out for anybody wearing black ear muffs like a granddaddy. Nevertheless, we were through. He turned us into shivering little boys with running noses, standing there definitely on the edge of things; and even on the way back the girls treated us with condescension.

Mahlke stayed on; he wanted to finish cutting his hole, to prove to himself that he had correctly figured the spot over the hatch. He didn't ask us to wait till he had finished, but he did delay our departure for a good five minutes when we were already on top of the wall, by dispensing a series of words in an undertone, not at us, more in the direction of the ice-bound freighters in the roadstead.

Still chopping, he asked us to help him. Or was it an order, politely spoken? In any case he wanted us to make water in the wedge-shaped groove, so as to melt or at least soften the ice with warm urine. Before Schilling or I could say: "No dice," or "We just did," my little cousins piped up joyfully: "Oh yes, we'd love to. But you must turn your backs, and you too, Mr. Mahlke."

After Mahlke had explained where they should squat—the whole stream, he said, has to fall in the same place or it won't do any good—he climbed up on the wall and turned toward the beach. While amid whispering and tittering the sprinkler duet went on behind us, we concentrated on the swarms of black ants near Brösen and on the icy pier. The seventeen poplars on the Beach Promenade were coated with sugar. The golden globe at the tip of the Soldiers' Monument, an obelisk towering over Brösen Park, blinked at us excitedly, Sunday all over.

When the girls' ski pants had been pulled up again and we stood around the groove with the tips of our shoes, the circle was still steaming, especially in the two places where Mahlke had cut crosses with his ax. The water stood pale yellow in the ditch and seeped away with a crackling sound. The edges of the groove were tinged a golden green. The ice sang plaintively. A pungent smell persisted because there were no other smells to counteract it, growing stronger as Mahlke chopped some more at the groove and scraped away about as much slush as a common bucket might have held. Especially in the two marked spots, he succeeded in drilling shafts, in gaining depth.

The soft ice was piled up to one side and began at once to crust over im the cold. Then he marked two new places. When the girls had turned away, we unbuttoned and helped Mahlke by thawing an inch or two more of the ice and boring two fresh holes. But they were still not deep enough. He himself did not pass water, and we didn't ask him to; on the contrary we were afraid the girls might try to encourage him.

As soon as we had finished and before my cousins could say a word, Mahlke sent us away. We looked back from the wall; he had pushed up muffler and safety pin over his chin and nose; his neck was still covered but now his pompoms, white sprinkled red, were taking the air between muffler and coat collar. He was hacking again at his groove, which was whispering something or other about the girls and us—a bowed form barely discernible through floating veils of sun-stirred laundry steam.

On the way back to Brösen, the conversation was all about him. Alternately or both at once, my cousins asked questions. We didn't always have the answer. But when the younger one wanted to know why Mahlke wore his muffler so high up and the other one started in on the muffler too, Schilling seized on the opportunity and described Mahlke's Adam's apple, giving it all the qualities of a goiter. He made exaggerated swallowing motions, imitated Mahlke chewing, took off his ski cap, gave his hair a kind of part in the middle with his fingers, and finally succeeded in making the girls laugh at Mahlke; they even said he was an odd-ball and not quite right in the head.

But despite this little triumph at your expense—I put in my two cents' worth too, mimicking your relations with the Virgin Mary—we made no headway with my cousins beyond the usual necking in the movies. And a week later they returned to Berlin.

Here I am bound to report that the following day I rode out to Brösen bright and early; I ran across the ice through a dense coastal fog, almost missing the barge, and found the hole over the fo'c'sle completed. During the night a fresh crust of ice had formed; with considerable difficulty, I broke through it with the heel of my shoe and an iron-tipped cane belonging to my father, which I had brought along for that very purpose. Then I poked the cane around through the cracked ice in the gray-black hole. It disappeared almost to the handle, water splashed my glove; and then the tip struck the deck, no, not the deck, it jutted into empty space. It was only when I moved the cane sideways along the edge of the hole that it met resistance. And I passed iron over iron: the hole was directly over the open forward hatch. Exactly like one plate under another in a pile of plates, the hatch was right under the hole in the ice—well, no, that's an exaggeration, not *exactly,* there's no such thing: either the hatch was a little bigger or the hole was a little bigger; but the fit was pretty good, and my pride in Joachim Mahlke was as sweet as chocolate creams. I'd have liked to glve you my wrist watch.

I stayed there a good ten minutes; I sat on the circular mound of ice—it must have been all of eighteen inches high. The lower third was marked with a pale-yellow ring of urine from the day before. It had been our privilege to help him. But even without our help Mahlke would have finished his hole. Was it possible that he could manage without an audience? Were there shows he put on only for himself? For not even the gulls would have admired your hole in the ice over the forward hatch, if I hadn't gone out there to admire you.

He always had an audience. When I say that always, even while cutting his circular groove over the ice-bound barge, he had the Virgin Mary behind or before him, that she looked with enthusiasm upon his little ax, the Church shouldn't really object; but even if the Church refuses to put up with the idea of a Virgin Mary forever engaged in admiring Mahlke's exploits, the fact remains that she always watched him attentively: I know. For I was an altar boy, first under Father Wiehnke at the Church of the Sacred Heart, then under Gusewski at St. Mary's Chapel. I kept on assisting him at Mass long after I had lost my faith in the magic of the altar, a process which approximately coincided with my growing up. The comings and goings amused me. I took pains too. I didn't shuffle like most altar boys. The truth is, I was never sure, and to this day I am not sure, whether there might not after all be something behind or in front of the altar or in the tabernacle. . . . At any rate Father Gusewski was always glad to have me as one of his two altar boys, because I never swapped cigarette pictures between offering and consecration, never rang the bells too loud or too long, or made a business of selling the sacramental wine. For altar boys are holy terrors: not only do they spread out the usual juvenile trinkets on the altar steps; not only do they lay bets, payable in coins or worn-out ball bearings—Oh no. Even during the gradual prayers they discuss the technical details of the world's warships, sunk or afloat, and substitute snatches of such lore for the words of the Mass, or smuggle them in between Latin and Latin: "*Introibo ad altare Dei*— Say, when was the cruiser *Eritrea* launched?—Thirty-six. Special features? —*Ad Deum, qui laetificat juventutem meam.*—Only Italian cruiser in East African waters. Displacement?—*Deus fortitudo mea*—Twenty-one hundred and seventy-two tons. Speed?—*Et introibo ad altare Dei*—Search me. Armament?—*Sicut erat in principio*—Six hundred-and-fifty-millimeter guns, four seventy-fives. . . . Wrong!—*et nunc et semper*—No, it's right. Names of the German artillery training ships?—*et in saecula saeculorum, Amen.*— *Brummer* and *Bremse*."

Later on I stopped serving regularly at St. Mary's and came only when Gusewski sent for me because his boys were busy with Sunday hikes or collecting funds for Winter Aid.

I'm telling you all this only to explain my presence at the main altar, for from there I was able to observe Mahlke as he knelt at the altar

495

of the Virgln. My, how he could pray! That calflike look. His eyes would grow steadily glassier. His mouth peevish, perpetually moving without punctuation. Fishes tossed up on the beach gasp for air with the same regularity. I shall try to give you an idea of how relentlessly Mahlke could pray. Father Gusewski was distributing communion. When he came to Mahlke, who always, seen from the altar, knelt at the outer left, this particular kneeler was one who had forgotten all caution, allowing his muffler and gigantic safety pin to shift for themselves, whose eyes had congealed, whose head and parted hair were tilted backward, who allowed his tongue to hang out, and who, in this attitude, left an agitated mouse so exposed and defenseless that I might have caught it in my hand. But perhaps Joachim Mahlke realized that his cynosure was convulsed and exposed. Perhaps he intentionally accentuated its frenzy with exaggerated swallowing, in order to attract the glass eyes of the Virgin standing to one side of him; for I cannot and will not believe that you ever did anything whatsoever without an audience.

Chapter V

I never saw him with pompoms at St. Mary's Chapel. Although the style was just beginning to take hold, he wore them less and less. Sometimes when three of us were standing in the recreation yard, always under the same chestnut tree, all talking at once over our woolen doodads, Mahlke removed his pompoms from his neck; then, after the second bell had rung, he would tie them on again, irresolutely, for lack of a better counterweight.

When for the first time a graduate of our school returned from the front, a special bell signal called us to the auditorium though classes were still in progress. On the return journey he had stopped briefly at the Führer's Headquarters, and now he had the coveted lozenge on his neck. He stood, not behind but beside the old-brown pulpit, at the end of the hall, against a background of three tall windows, a row of potted leafy plants, and the faculty gathered in a semicircle. Lozenge on neck, red rosebud mouth, he projected his voice into the space over our heads and made little explanatory gestures. Mahlke was sitting in the row ahead of me and Schilling. I saw his ears turn a flaming transparent red; he leaned back stiffly, and I saw him, left right, fiddling with something on his neck, tugging, gagging, and at length tossing something under his bench: something woolen, pompoms, a green and red mixture I think they were. The young fellow, a lieutenant in the Air Force, started off hesitantly and rather too softly, with an appealing awkwardness; he even blushed once or twice, though there was nothing in what he was saying to warrant it: ". . . well, boys, don't get the idea that life in the Air Force is like

496

a rabbit hunt, all action and never a dull moment. Sometimes nothing happens for whole weeks. But when they sent us to the Channel, I says to myself, if things don't start popping now, they never will. And I was right. On the very first mission a formation with a fighter escort came straight at us, and believe me, it was some merry-go-round. In and out of the clouds, winding and circling the whole time. I try to gain altitude, down below me there's three Spitfires circling, trying to hide in the clouds. I says to myself, it's just too bad if I can't . . . I dive, I've got him in my sights, bam, he's trailing smoke. Just time to turn over on my left wing tip when there's a second Spitfire coming toward me in my sights, I go straight for his nose, it's him or me; well, as you can see, it's him that went into the drink, and I says to myself, as long as you've got two, why not try the third and so on, as long as your gas holds out. So I see seven of them down below me, they've broken formation and they're trying to get away. I pick out one of them, I've got a good sun well in back of me. He gets his, I repeat the number, turns out OK, I pull back the stick as far as she'll go, and there's the third in my line of fire: he goes into a spin, I must have got him, instinctively I trail him, lose him, clouds, got him again, give another burst, he drops into the pond, but so do I pretty near; I honestly can't tell you how I got my crate upstairs again. Anyway, when I come home flapping my wings—as you probably know, you must have seen it in the newsreels, we come in flapping our wings if we've bagged anything—I can't get the landing gear down. Jammed. So I had to make my first crash landing. Later in the officers' club they tell me I've been marked up for a certain six, it's news to me; as you can imagine, I'd been too excited to count. I was mighty happy, but about four o'clock we've got to go up again. Well, to make a long story short, it was pretty much the same as in the old days when we played handball in our good old recreation yard—'cause the stadium hadn't been built yet. Maybe Mr. Mallenbrandt remembers: either I didn't shoot a single goal or I'd shoot nine in a row; that's how it was that day: six that morning and three more in the afternoon. That was my ninth to seventeenth; but it wasn't until a good six months later, when I had my full forty, that I was commended by our CO, and by the time I was decorated at the Führer's Headquarters I had forty-four under my belt; 'cause we guys up at the Channel just about lived in our crates. The ground crews got relieved, not us. There were some that couldn't take it. Well, now I'll tell you something funny for relief. In every airfield there's a squadron dog. One day it was beautiful weather and we decided to take Alex, our dog . . ."

Such, approximately, were the words of the gloriously decorated lieutenant. In between two air battles, as an interlude, he told the story of Alex, the squadron dog, who had been compelled to learn parachute jumping. There was also the little anecdote about the corporal who was always too slow in getting up when the alert was sounded and was obliged to fly several missions in his pajamas.

The lieutenant laughed with his audience; even the graduating class laughed, and some of the teachers indulged in a chuckle. He had graduated from our school in '33 and was shot down over the Ruhr in '43. His hair was dark brown, unparted, combed rigorously back; he wasn't very big, looked rather like a dapper little waiter in a night club. While speaking he kept one hand in his pocket, but took it out whenever he needed two hands to illustrate an air battle with. His use of his outspread palms was subtle and masterful; with a twist of his shoulders, he could make you see his plane banking as it circled in quest of victims, and he had no need of long, explanatory sentences. His chopped phrases were more like cues for his pantomime. At the height of his act he roared out englne noises or stuttered when an engine was in trouble. It was safe to assume that he had practiced his number at his airfield officers' club, especially as the term "officers' club" kept cropping up in his narrative: "We were sitting peacefully in the officers' club . . . I was just heading for the officers' club 'cause I wanted to . . . In our officers' club there's a . . ." But even aside from his mime's hands and his realistic sound effects, he knew how to appeal to his audience; he managed, for instance, to get in a few cracks at some of our teachers, who still had the same nicknames as in his day. But he was always pleasant, full of harmless mischief. And no boaster. He never claimed credit for the difficult things he had done, but put everything down to his luck: "I've always been lucky, even in school, when I think of some of my report cards . . ." And in the middle of a schoolboy's joke he suddenly remembered three of his former classmates who, as he said, shall not have died in vain. He concluded his talk not with the names of the three dead comrades, but with this naïve, heartfelt admission: "Boys, let me tell you this: every last one of us who's out there fighting likes to think back on his school days and, believe me, we often do."

We clapped, roared, and stamped at great length. Only when my hands were hot and burning did I observe that Mahlke was holding back and contributing no applause.

Up front Dr. Klohse shook both his former student's hands demonstratively as long as the applause went on. Then, after gripping the frail figure for a moment by the shoulders, he turned abruptly away, and took up his stance behind the pulpit, while the lieutenant quickly sat down.

The principal's speech went on and on. Boredom spread from the lush green plants to the oil painting on the rear wall of the auditorium, a portrait of Baron von Conradi, the founder of our school. Even the lieutenant, a slender figure between Brunies and Mallenbrandt, kept looking at his fingernails. In this lofty hall Klohse's cool peppermint breath, which suffused all his mathematics classes, substituting for the odor of pure science, wasn't much of a help. From up front his words barely carried to the middle of the auditorium: "Thosewhocomeafterus — Andinthishour — whenthetravelerreturns — butthistimethehomeland — andletusnever — pureofheart — asIsaidbefore — pureofheart — andifanyonedisagreeslet — andinthishour — keepclean — toconclude withthewordsofSchiller — ifyourlifeyoudonotstake — thelaurelneverwill youtake — Andnowbacktowork!"

Dismissed, we formed two clusters at the narrow exits. I pushed in behind Mahlke. He was sweating and his sugar-water hair stood up in sticky blades around his ravaged part. Never, not even in gym, had I seen Mahlke perspire. The stench of three hundred schoolboys stuck like corks in the exits. Beads of sweat stood out on Mahlke's flushed anxiety cords, those two bundles of sinew running from the seventh vertebra of his neck to the base of his jutting occiput. In the colonnade outside the folding doors, amid the hubbub of the little Sixths, who had resumed their perpetual game of tag, I caught up with him. I questioned him head on: "Well, what do you say?"

Mahlke stared straight ahead. I tried not to look at his neck. Between two columns stood a plaster bust of Lessing: but Mahlke's neck won out. Calmly and mournfully, as though speaking of his aunt's chronic ailments, his voice said: "Now they need a bag of forty if they want the medal. At the beginning and after they were through in France and in the north, it only took twenty—if it keeps on like this . . ."

I guess the lieutenant's talk didn't agree with you. Or you wouldn't have resorted to such cheap compensations. In those days lumimous buttons and round, oval, or open-work plaques were on display in the windows of stationery and dry-goods stores. They glowed milky-green in the darkness, some disclosing the contours of a fish, others of a flying gull. These little plaques were purchased mostly by elderly gentlemen and fragile old ladies, who wore them on their coat collars for fear of collisions in the blacked-out streets; there were also canes with luminous stripes.

You were not afraid of the blackout, and yet you fastened five or six plaques, a luminous school of fish, a flock of gliding gulls, several bouquets of phosphorescent flowers, first on the lapels of your coat, then on your muffler; you had your aunt sew half a dozen luminous buttons from top to bottom of your coat; you turned yourself into a clown. In the winter twilight, through slanting snowflakes or well-nigh uniform darkness, I saw you, I still see you and always will, striding toward me down Bärenweg, enumerable from top to bottom and back, with one two three four five six coat buttons glowing moldy-green: a pathetic sort of ghost, capable at most of scaring children and grandmothers—trying to distract

499

attention from an affliction which no one could have seen in the pitch-darkness. But you said to yourself, no doubt: No blackness can engulf this overdeveloped fruit; everyone sees, suspects, feels it, wants to grab hold of it, for it juts out ready to be grabbed; if only this winter were over, so I could dive again and be under water.

Chapter VI

But when the summer came with strawberries, special communiqués, and bathing weather, Mahlke didn't want to swim. On the first of June we swam out to the barge for the first time. We weren't really in the mood. We were annoyed at the Thirds who swam with us and ahead of us, who sat on the bridge in swarms, dived, and brought up the last hinge that could be unscrewed. "Let me come with you, I can swim now," Mahlke had once pleaded. And now it was Schilling, Winter, and myself who pestered him: "Aw, come along. It's no fun without you. We can sun ourselves on the barge. Maybe you'll find something interesting down below."

Reluctantly, after waving us away several times, Mahlke stepped into the tepid soup between the beach and the first sandbank. He swam without his screwdriver, stayed between us, two arms' lengths behind Hotten Sonntag, and for the first time I saw him swim calmly, without excitement or splashing. On the bridge he sat huddled in the shadow of the pilothouse and no one could persuade him to dive. He didn't even turn his neck when the Thirds vanished into the fo'c'sle and came up with trinkets. Yet Mahlke could have taught them a thing or two. Some of them even asked him for pointers—but he scarcely answered. The whole time he looked out through puckered eyes over the open sea in the direction of the harbor mouth buoy, but neither inbound freighters, nor outbound cutters, nor a formation of torpedo boats could divert him. Maybe the submarines got a slight rise out of him. Sometimes, far out at sea, the periscope of a submerged U-boat could be seen cutting a distinct stripe of foam. The 750-ton vessels, built in series at the Schichau Dockyards, were given trial runs in the Gulf or behind Hela; surfacing in the deep channel, they put in toward the harbor and dispelled our boredom. Looked good as they rose to the surface, periscope first. The moment the conning tower emerged, it spat out one or two figures. In dull-white streams the water receded from the gun, ran off the bow and then the stern. Men scrambled out of the hatches, we shouted and waved—I'm not sure whether they answered us, though I still see the motion of waving in every detail and can still feel it in my shoulders. Whether or not they waved back, the surfacing of a submarine strikes the heart, still does—but Mahlke never waved.

500

. . . and once—it was the end of June, summer vacation hadn't started yet and the lieutenant commander hadn't yet delivered his lecture in our school auditorium—Mahlke left his place in the shade because a Third had gone down into the fo'c'sle of the mine sweeper and hadn't come up. Mahlke went down the hatch and brought the kid up. He had wedged himself in amidships, but he hadn't got as far as the engine room. Mahlke found him under the deck between pipes and bundles of cable. For two hours Schilling and Hotten Sonntag took turns working on the kid according to Mahlke's directions. Gradually, the color came back into his face, but when we swam ashore we had to tow him.

The next day Mahlke was diving again with his usual enthusiasm, but without a screwdriver. He swam across at his usual speed, leaving us all behind; he had already been under once when we climbed up on the bridge.

The preceding winter's ice and February storms had carried away the last bit of rail, both gun mounts, and the top of the pilothouse. Only the encrusted gull droppings had come through in good shape and, if anything, had multiplied. Mahlke brought up nothing and didn't answer the questions we kept thinking up. But late in the afternoon, after he had been down ten or twelve times and we were starting to limber up for the swim back, he went down and didn't come up, We were all of us out of our minds.

When I speak of a five-minute intermission, it doesn't mean a thing; but after five minutes as long as years, which we occupied with swallowing until our tongues lay thick and dry in dry hollows, we dove down into the barge one by one: in the fo'c'sle there was nothing but a few baby herring. Behind Hotten Sonntag I ventured through the bulkhead for the first time, and looked superficially about the former officers' mess. Then I had to come up, shot out of the hatch just before I would have burst, went down again, shoved my way twice more through the bulkhead, and didn't give up until a good half hour later. Seven or eight of us lay flat on the bridge, panting. The gulls circled closer and closer; must have noticed something.

Luckily, there were no Thirds on the barge. We were all silent or all talking at once. The gulls flew off to one side and came back again. We cooked up stories for the lifeguard, for Mahlke's mother and aunt, and for Klohse, because there was sure to be an investigation at school. Because I was Mahlke's neighbor, they saddled me with the visit to his mother on Osterzeile. Schilling was to tell our story to the lifeguard and in school.

"If they don't find him, we'll have to swim out here with a wreath and have a ceremony."

"We'll chip in. We'll each contribute at least fifty pfennigs."

"We can throw him overboard from here, or maybe just lower him into the fo'c'sle."

"We'll have to sing something," said Kupka. But the hollow tinkling laughter that followed this suggestion did not originate with any of us: it came from inside the bridge. We all gaped at some unknown point, waiting for the laughter to start up again, but when it did, it was a perfectly normal kind of laughter, had lost its hollowness, and came from the fo'c'sle. The waters parting at his watershed, Mahlke pushed out of the hatch, breathing scarcely harder than usual, and rubbed the fresh sunburn on his neck and shoulders. His bleating was more good-natured than scornful. "Well," he said, "have you got that funeral oration ready?"

Before we swam ashore, Mahlke went down again. Winter was having an attack of the weeping jitters and we were trying to pacify him. Fifteen minutes later Winter was still bawling, and Mahlke was back on the bridge, wearing a set of radio operator's earphones which from the outside at least looked undamaged, almost new; for amidships Mahlke had found the way into a room that was situated inside the command bridge, above the surface of the water; the former radio shack. The place was bone-dry, he said, though somewhat clammy. After considerable stalling he admitted that he had discovered the entrance while disentangling the young Third from the pipes and cables. "I've camouflaged it. Nobody'll ever find it. But it was plenty of work. It's my private property now, in case you have any doubts. Cozy little joint. Good place to hide if things get hot. Lots of apparatus, transmitter and so on. Might try to put it in working order one of these days."

But that was beyond Mahlke's abilities and I doubt if he ever tried. Or if he did tinker some without letting on, I'm sure his efforts were unsuccessful. He was very handy and knew all there was to know about making ship models, but he was hardly a radio technician. Besides, if Mahlke had ever got the transmitter working and started broadcasting witty sayings, the Navy or the harbor police would have picked us up.

In actual fact, he removed all the apparatus from the cabin and gave it to Kupka, Esch, and the Thirds; all he kept for himself was the earphones. He wore them a whole week, and it was only when he began systematically to refurnish the radio shack that he threw them overboard.

The first thing he moved in was books—I don't remember exactly what they were. My guess is that they included *Tsushima, The Story of a Naval Battle,* a volume or two of Dwinger, and some religious stuff. He wrapped them first in old woolen blankets, then in oilcloth, and calked the seams with pitch or tar or wax. The bundle was carried out to the barge on a driftwood raft which he, with occasional help from us, towed behind him as he swam. He claimed that the books and blankets had reached their destination almost dry. The next shipment consisted of candles, an alcohol burner, fuel, an aluminum pot, tea, oat flakes, and dehydrated vegetables. Often he was gone for as much as an hour; we would begin to pound frantically, but he never answered. Of course we admired him. But Mahlke ignored our admiration and grew more and more monosyllabic; in the end he wouldn't even let us help him with his moving. However, it was in our presence that he rolled up the color print of the Sistine Madonna, known to me from his room on Osterzeile, and stuffed it inside a hollow curtain rod, packing the open ends with modeling clay. Madonna and curtain rod were towed to the barge and maneuvered into the cabin. At last I knew why he was knocking himself out, for whom he was furnishing the former radio shack.

My guess is that the print was damaged in diving, or perhaps that the moisture in the airless cabin (it had no portholes or communication with the ventilators, which were all flooded in the first place) did not agree with it, for a few days later Mahlke was wearing somethimg on his neck again, appended to a black shoelace: not a screwdriver, but the bronze medallion with the so-called Black Madonna of Częstochowa in low relief. Our eyebrows shot up knowingly; ah-ha, we thought, there's the Madonna routine again. Before we had time to settle ourselves on the bridge, Mahlke disappeared down the forward hatch. He was back again in no more than fifteen minutes, without shoelace and medallion, and he seemed pleased as he resumed his place behind the pilothouse.

He was whistling. That was the first time I heard Mahlke whistle. Of course he wasn't whistling for the first time, but it was the first time I noticed his whistling, which is tantamount to saying that he was really pursing his lips for the first tirne. I alone—being the only other Catholic on the barge—knew what the whistling was about: he whistled one hymn to the Virgin after another. Leaning on a vestige of the rail, he began with aggressive good humor to beat time on the rickety side of the bridge with his dangling feet; then over the muffled din, he reeled off the whole Pentecost sequence *"Veni, Sancte Spiritus"* and after that—I had been expecting it—the sequence for the Friday before Palm Sunday. All ten stanzas of the *Stabat Mater dolorosa,* including *Paradisi Gloria* and *Amen,* were rattled off without a hitch. I myself, who had once been Father Gusewski's most devoted altar boy but whose attendance had become very irregular of late, could barely have recollected the first lines.

Mahlke, however, served Latin to the gulls with the utmost ease, and the others, Schilling, Kupka, Esch, Hotten Sonntag, and whoever else was there, listened eagerly with a "Boyohboy" and "Ittakesyour-breathaway." They even asked Mahlke to repeat the *Stabat Mater,* though nothing could have been more remote from their interests than Latin or liturgical texts.

* * *

Still, I don't think you were planning to turn the radio shack into a chapel for the Virgin. Most of the rubbish that found its way there had nothing to do with her. Though I never inspected your hideout—we simply couldn't make it—I see it as a miniature edition of your attic room on Osterzeile. Only the geraniums and cactuses, which your aunt, often against your will, lodged on the window sill and the four-story cactus racks, had no counterpart in the former radio shack; otherwise your moving was a perfect job.

After the books and cooking utensils, Mahlke's ship models, the dispatch boat *Cricket* and the torpedo boat of the *Wolf* class, scale 1:1250, were moved below decks. Ink, several pens, a ruler, a school compass, his butterfly collection, and the stuffed snowy owl were also obliged to take the dive. I presume that Mahlke's furnishings gradually began to look pretty sick in this room where water vapor could do nothing but condense. Especially the butterflies in their glassed-over cigar boxes, accustomed as they were to dry attic air, must have suffered from the dampness.

But what we admired most about this game of moving man, which went on for days, was precisely its absurdity and deliberate destructiveness. And the zeal with which Joachim Mahlke gradually returned to the former Polish mine sweeper so many of the objects which he had painstakingly removed two summers before—good old Pilsudski, the plates with the instructions for operating this or that machine, and so on—enabled us, despite the irritating Thirds, to spend an entertaining, I might even say exciting, summer on that barge for which the war had lasted only four weeks.

To give you an example of our pleasures: Mahlke offered us music. You will remember that in the summer of 1940, after he had swum out to the barge with us perhaps six or seven times, he had slowly and painstakingly salvaged a phonograph from the fo'c'sle or the officers' mess, that he had taken it home, repaired it, and put on a new turntable covered with felt. This same phonograph, along with ten or a dozen records, was one of the last items to find their way back again. The moving took two days, during which time he couldn't resist the temptation to wear the crank around his neck, suspended from his trusty shoelace.

Phonograph and records must have come through the trip through the flooded fo'c'sle and the bulkhead in good shape, for that same afternoon he surprised us with music, a hollow tinkling whose source seemed to shift eerily about but was always somewhere inside the barge. I shouldn't be surprised if it shook loose the rivets and sheathing. Though the sun was far down in the sky, we were still getting some of it on the bridge, but even so that sound gave us gooseflesh. Of course we would shout: "Stop it. No. Go on! Play another!" I remember a well-known *Ave Maria,* as long-lasting as a wad of chewing gum, which smoothed the choppy sea; he just couldn't manage without the Virgin.

There were also arias, overtures, and suchlike—have I told you that Mahlke was gone on serious music? From the inside out Mahlke regaled us with something passionate from *Tosca,* something enchanted from Humperdinck, and part of a symphony beginning with dadada daaah, known to us from popular concerts.

Schilling and Kupka shouted for something hot, but that he didn't have. It was Zarah who produced the most startling effects. Her underwater voice laid us out flat on the rust and bumpy gull droppings. I don't remember what she sang in that first record. It was always the same Zarah. In one, though, she sang something from an opera with which we had been familiarized by a movie called *Homeland.* "Alaslhavelosther," she moaned. "Thewindsangmeasong," she sighed. "Onedayamiraclewillhappen," she prophesied. She could sound organ tones and conjure the elements, or she could dispense moments of languor and tenderness. Winter hardly bothered to stifle his sobs and in general our eyelashes were kept pretty busy.

And over it all the gulls. They were always getting frantic over nothing, but when Zarah revolved on the turntable down below, they went completely out of their heads. Their glass-cutting screams, emanating no doubt from the souls of departed tenors, rose high over the much-imitated and yet inimitable, dungeon-deep plaint of this tear-jerking movie star gifted with a voice, who in the war years earned an immense popularity on every front including the home front.

Mahlke treated us several times to this concert until the records were so worn that nothing emerged but a tortured gurgling and scratching. To this day no music has given me greater pleasure, though I seldom miss a concert at Robert Schumann Hall and whenever I am in funds purchase long-playing records ranging from Monteverdi to Bartók. Silent and insatiable, we huddled over the phonograph, which we called the Ventriloquist. We had run out of praises. Of course we admired Mahlke; but in the eerie din our admiration shifted into its opposite, and we thought him so repulsive we couldn't look at him. Then as a low-flying freighter hove into view, we felt moderately sorry for him. We were also afraid of Mahlke; he bullied us. And I was ashamed to be seen on the street with him. And I was proud when Hotten Sonntag's sister or the little Pokriefke girl met the two of us together outside the Art Cinema or on Heeresanger. You were our theme song. We would lay bets: "What's he going to do now? I bet you he's got a sore throat again. I'm taking all bets: Someday he's going to hang himself, or he'll get to be something real big, or invent something terrific."

And Schilling said to Hotten Sonntag: "Tell me the honest truth; if your sister went out with Mahlke, to the movies and all, tell me the honest truth; what would you do?"

Chapter VII

The appearance of the lieutenant commander and much-decorated U-boat captain in the auditorium of our school put an end to the concerts from within the former Polish mine sweeper *Rybitwa*. Even if he had not turned up, the records and the phonograph couldn't have held out for more than another three or four days. But he did turn up, and without having to pay a visit to our barge he turned off the underwater music and gave all our conversations about Mahlke a new, though not fundamentally new, turn.

The lieutenant commander must have graduated in about '34. It was said that before volunteering for the Navy he had studied some at the university: theology and German literature. I can't help it, I am obliged to call his eyes fiery. His hair was thick and kinky, maybe wiry would be the word, and there was something of the old Roman about his head. No submariner's beard, but aggressive eyebrows that suggested an overhanging roof. His forehead was that of a philosopher-saint, hence no horizontal wrinkles, but two vertical lines, beginning at the bridge of the nose and rising in search of God. The light played on the uppermost point of the bold vault. Nose small and sharp. The mouth he opened for us was a delicately curved orator's mouth. The auditorium was overcrowded with people and morning sun. We were forced to huddle in the window niches. Whose idea had it been to invite the two upper classes of the Gudrun School? The girls occupied the front rows of benches; they should have worn brassières, but didn't.

When the proctor called us to the lecture, Mahlke hadn't wanted to attend. Flairing some possible gain in prestige for myself, I took him by the sleeve. Beside me, in the window niche—behind us the window-panes and the motionless chestnut trees in the recreation yard—Mahlke began to tremble before the lieutenant commander had even opened his mouth. Mahlke's hands clutched Mahlke's knees, but the trembling continued. The teachers, including two lady teachers from the Gudrun School, occupied a semicircle of oak chairs with high backs and leather cushions, which the proctor had set up with remarkable precision. Dr. Moeller clapped his hands, and little by little the audience quieted down for Dr. Klohse, our principal. Behind the twin braids and pony tails of the upperclass girls sat Fourths with pocketknives; braids were quickly shifted from back to front. Only the pony tails remained within reach of the Fourths and their knives. This time there was an introduction. Klohse spoke of all those who are out there fighting for us, on land, on the sea, and in

506

the air, spoke at length and with little inflection of himself and the students at Langemarck, and on the Isle of Ösel fell Walter Flex. Quotation: Maturebutpure—the manly virtues. Then some Fichte or Arndt. Quotation: Onyoualoneandwhatyoudo. Recollection of an excellent paper on Fichte or Arndt that the lieutenant commander had written in Second: "One of us, from our midst, a product of our school and its spirit, and in this spirit let us . . ."

Need I say how zealously notes were passed back and forth between us in the window niches and the girls from Upper Second. Of course the Fourths mixed in a few obscenities of their own. I wrote a note saying Godknowswhat either to Vera Plötz or to Hildchen Matull, but got no answer from either. Mahlke's hands were still clutching Mahlke's knees. The trembling died down. The lieutenant commander on the platform sat slightly crushed between old Dr. Brunies, who as usual was calmly sucking hard candy, and Dr. Stachnitz, our Latin teacher. As the introduction droned to an end, as our notes passed back and forth, as the Fourths with pocketknives, as the eyes of the Führer's photograph met those of the oil-painted Baron von Conradi, as the morning sun slipped out of the auditorium, the lieutenant commander moistened his delicately curved orator's mouth and stared morosely at the audience, making a heroic effort to exclude the girl students from his field of vision. Cap perched with dignity on his parallel knees. Under the cap his gloves. Dress uniform. The hardware on his neck plainly discernible against an inconceivably white shirt. Sudden movement of his head, half followed by his decoration, toward the lateral windows: Mahlke trembled, feeling no doubt that he had been recognized, but he hadn't. Through the window in whose niche we huddled the U-boat captain gazed at dusty, motionless chestnut trees; what, I thought then or think now, what can he be thinking, what can Mahlke be thinking, or Klohse while speaking, or Brunies while sucking, or Vera Plötz while your note, or Hildchen Matull, what can he he he be thinking, Mahlke or the fellow with the orator's mouth? For it would have been illuminating to know what a U-boat captain thinks while obliged to listen, while his gaze roams free without crosswires and dancing horizon, until Joachim Mahlke feels singled out; but actually he was staring over schoolboys' heads, through double windowpanes, at the dry greenness of the poker-faced trees in the recreation yard, giving his orator's mouth one last moistening with his bright-red tongue, for Klohse was trying, with words on peppermint breath, to send a last sentence out past the middle of the auditorium: "And today it beseems us in the homeland to give our full attention to what you sons of our nation have to report from the front, from every front."

The orator's mouth had deceived us. The lieutenant commander started out with a very colorless survey such as one might have found in any naval manual: the function of the submarine. German submarines in the First World War: Weddigen and the *U 9*, submarine plays decisive role in Dardanelles campaign, sinking a total of thirteen million gross register tons. Our first 250-ton subs, electric when submerged, diesel on the surface, the name of Prien was dropped, Prien and the *U 47*, and Lieutenant Commander Prien sent the *Royal Oak* to the bottom—hell, we knew all that—as well as the *Repulse,* and Schuhart sank the *Courageous,* and so on and so on. And then all the old saws: "The crew is a body of men who have sworn to stand together in life and death, for far from home, terrible nervous strain, you can imagine, living in a sardine can in the middle of the Atlantic or the Arctic, cramped humid hot, men obliged to sleep on spare torpedoes, nothing stirring for days on end, empty horizon, then suddenly a convoy, heavily guarded, everything has to go like clockwork, not an unnecessary syllable; when we bagged our first tanker, the *Arndale,* 17,200 tons, with two fish amidships, believe it or not, I thought of you, my dear Dr. Stachnitz, and began to recite out loud, without turning off the intercom, *qui quae quod, cuius cuius cuius* . . . until our exec called back: Good work, skipper, you may take the rest of the day off. But a submarine mission isn't all shooting and tube one fire and tube two fire; for days on end it's the same monotonous sea, the rolling and pounding of the boat, and overhead the sky, a sky to make your head reel, I tell you, and sunsets . . ."

Although the lieutenant commander with the hardware on his neck had sunk 250,000 gross register tons, a light cruiser of the *Despatch* class and a heavy destroyer of the *Tribal* class, the details of his exploits took up much less space in his talk than verbose descriptions of nature. No metaphor was too daring. For instance: ". . . swaying like a train of priceless, dazzlingly white lace, the foaming wake follows the boat which, swathed like a bride in festive veils of spray, strides onward to the marriage of death."

The tittering wasn't limited to the pigtail contingent; but in the ensuing metaphor the bride was obliterated: "A submarine is like a whale with a hump, but what of its bow wave? It is like the twirling, many times twirled mustache of a hussar."

The lieutenant commander also had a way of intoning dry technical terms as if they had been dark words of legend. Probably his lecture was addressed more to Papa Brunies, his former German teacher, known as a lover of Eichendorff, than to us. Klohse had mentioned the eloquence of his school themes, and perhaps he wished to show that his tongue had lost none of its cunning. Such words as "bilge pump" and "helmsman" were uttered in a mysterious whisper. He must have thought he was offering us a revelation when he said "master compass" or "repeater compass." Good Lord, we had known all this stuff for years. He saw himself as the kindly grandmother telling fairy tales. The voice in which he spoke of a dog-watch or a watertight door or even something as commonplace as a "choppy cross sea"! It was like listening to dear old Andersen or the Brothers Grimm telling a spooky tale about "sonar impulses."

When he started brushing in sunsets, it got really embarrassing: "And before the Atlantic night descends on us like a flock of ravens transformed by enchantment into a black shroud, the sky takes on colors we never see at home. An orange flares up, fleshy and unnatural, then airy and weightless, bejeweled at the edges as in the paintings of old masters; and in between, feathery clouds; and oh what a strange light over the rolling full-blooded sea!"

Standing there with his sugar candy on his neck, he sounded the color organ, rising to a roar, descending to a whisper, from watery blue to cold-glazed lemon yellow to brownish purple. Poppies blazed in the sky, and in their midst clouds, first silver, then suffused with red: "So must it be," these were his actual words, "when birds and angels bleed to death." And suddenly from out of this sky, so daringly described, from out of bucolic little clouds, he conjured up a seaplane of the *Sunderland* type. It came buzzing toward his U-boat but accomplished nothing. Then with the same orator's mouth but without metaphors, he opened the second part of his lecture. Chopped, dry, matter-of-fact: "I'm sitting in the periscope seat. Just scored a hit. Probably a refrigerator ship. Sinks stern first. We take the boat down at one one zero. Destroyer comes in on one seven zero. We come left ten degrees. New course: one two zero, steady on one two zero. Propeller sounds fade, increase, come in at one eight zero, ash cans: six . . . seven . . . eight . . . eleven: lights go out; pitch-darkness, then the emergency lighting comes on, and one after another the stations report all clear. Destroyer has stopped. Last bearing one six zero, we come left ten degrees. New course four five . . ."

Unfortunately, this really exciting fillet was followed by more prose poems: "The Atlantic winter" or "Phosphorescence in the Mediterranean," and a genre painting: "Christmas on a submarine," with the inevitable broom transformed into a Christmas tree. In conclusion he rose to mythical heights: the homecoming after a successful mission, Ulysses, and at long last: "The first sea gulls tell us that the port is near."

I don't know whether Dr. Klohse ended the session with the familiar words "And now back to work," or whether we sang "Welovethestorms." I seem, rather, to recall muffled but respectful applause, disorganized movements of getting up, begun by girls and pigtails. When I turned around toward Mahlke, he was gone; I saw his hair with the part in the middle bob up several times by the right-hand exit, but one of my legs had fallen asleep during the lecture and for a few moments I was unable to jump from the window niche to the waxed floor.

It wasn't until I reached the dressing room by the gymnasium that

I ran into Mahlke; but I could think of nothing to start a conversation with. While we were still changing, rumors were heard and soon confirmed. We were being honored: the lieutenant commander had asked Mallenbrandt, his former gym teacher, for leave to participate in the good old gym class, though he was out of shape. In the course of the two hours which as usual on Saturday closed the school day, he showed us what he could do. In the second hour, we were joined by the Firsters.

Squat, well built, with a luxuriant growth of black hair on his chest. From Mallenbrandt he had borrowed the traditional red gym pants, the white shirt with the red stripe at chest level, and the black C embedded in the stripe. A cluster of students formed around him while he was dressing. Lots of questions: ". . . may I look at it close up? How long does it take? And what if? But a friend of my brother's in the mosquito boats says . . ." He answered patiently. Sometimes he laughed for no reason but contagiously. The dressing room whinnied; and the only reason why Mahlke caught my attention just then was that he didn't join in the laughter; he was busy folding and hanging up his clothes.

The trill of Mallenbrandt's whistle called us to the gymnasium, where we gathered around the horizontal bar. The lieutenant commander, discreetly seconded by Mallenbrandt, directed the class. Which meant that we were not kept very busy, because he was determined to perform for us, among other things, the giant swing ending in a split. Aside from Hotten Sonntag only Mahlke could compete, but so execrable were his swing and split—his knees were bent and he was all tensed up—that none of us could bear to watch him. When the lieutenant commander began to lead us in a series of free and carefully graduated ground exercises, Mahlke's Adam's apple was still dancing about like a stuck pig. In the vault over seven men, he landed askew on the mat and apparently turned his ankle. After that he sat on a ladder off to one side and must have slipped away when the Firsters joined us at the beginning of the second hour. However, he was back again for the basketball game against the First; he even made three or four baskets, but we lost just the same.

Our Neo-Gothic gymnasium preserved its air of solemnity just as St. Mary's Chapel in Neuschottland, regardless of all the painted plaster and ecclesiastical trappings Father Gusewski could assemble in the bright gymnastic light of its broad window fronts, never lost the feel of the modern gymnasium it had formerly been. While there clarity prevailed over all mysteries, we trained our muscles in a mysterious twilight: our gymnasium had ogival windows, their panes broken up by rosettes and flamboyant tracery. In the glaring light of St. Mary's Chapel, offering, transubstantiation, and communion were disenchanted motions that might have been performed in a factory; instead of wafers, one might just as well have handed out hammers, saws, or window frames, or for that matter gymnastic apparatus, bats and relay sticks, as in former days. While in the mystical light of our gymnasium the simple act of choosing the two basketball teams, whose ten minutes of play was to wind up the session, seemed solemnly moving like an ordination or confirmation ceremony. And when the chosen ones stepped aside into the dim background, it was with the humility of those performing a sacred rite. Especially on bright mornings, when a few rays of sun found their way through the foliage in the yard and the ogival windows, the oblique beams, falling on the moving figures of athletes performing on the trapeze or rings, produced strange, romantic effects. If I concentrate, I can still see the squat little lieutenant commander in altar-boy-red gym pants, executing airy, fluid movements on the flying trapeze, I can see his flawlessly pointed feet—he performed barefoot—diving into a golden sunbeam, and I can see his hands—for all at once he was hanging by his knees—reach out for a shaft of agitated golden dust. Yes, our gymnasium was marvelously old-fashioned; why, even the dressing room obtained its light through ogival windows; that was why we called it the Sacristy.

Mallenbrandt blew his whistle; after the basketball game both classes had to line up and sing "Tothemountainswegointheearlydewfallera"; then we were dismissed. In the dressing room there was again a huddle around the lieutenant commander. Only the Firsters hung back a little. After carefully washing his hands and armpits over the one and only washbasin—there were no showers—the lieutenant commander put on his underwear and stripped off his borrowed gym togs so deftly that we didn't see a thing. Meanwhile he was subjected to more questions, which he answered with good-natured, not too condescending laughter. Then, between two questions, his good humor left him. His hands groped uncertainly. Covertly at first, then openly, he was looking for something. He even looked under the bench. "Just a minute, boys, I'll be back on deck in a second," and in navy-blue shorts, white shirt, socks but no shoes, he picked his way through students, benches, and zoo smell: Pavilion for Small Carnivores. His collar stood open and raised, ready to receive his tie and the ribbon bearing the decoration whose name I dare not utter. On the door of Mallenbrandt's office hung the weekly gymnasium schedule. The lieutenant commander knocked and went right in.

Who didn't think of Mahlke as I did? I'm not sure I thought of him right away, I should have, but the one thing I am sure of is that I didn't sing out: "Hey, where's Mahlke?" Nor did Schilling nor Hotten Sonntag, nor Winter Kupka Esch. Nobody sang out; instead we all ganged up on sickly little Buschmann, a poor devil who had come into the world with a grin that he couldn't wipe off his face even after it had been slapped a dozen times.

The half-dressed lieutenant commander came back with Mallenbrandt in a terry-cloth bathrobe. "Whowasit?" Mallenbrandt roared. "Lethimstepforward!" And we sacrificed Buschmann to his wrath. I too shouted Buschmann; I even succeeded in telling myself as though I really believed it: Yes, it must have been Buschmann, who else could it be.

But while Mallenbrandt, the lieutenant commander, and the upperclass monitor were flinging questions at Buschmann all together, I began to have pins and needles, superficially at first, on the back of my neck. The sensation grew stronger when Buschmann got his first slap, when he was slapped because even under questioning he couldn't get the grin off his face. While my eyes and ears waited for a clear confession from Buschmann, the certainty crawled upward from the back of my neck: Say, I wonder if it wasn't a certain So-and-So!

My confidence seeped away; no, the grinning Buschmann was not going to confess; even Mallenbrandt must have suspected as much or he would not have been so liberal with his slaps. He had stopped talking about the missing object and only roared between one slap and the next: "Wipe that grin off your face. Stop it, I say. I'll teach you to grin."

I may say, in passing, that Mallenbrandt did not achieve his aim. I don't know whether Buschmann is still in existence; but if there should be a dentist, veterinary, or physician by the narne of Buschmann—Heini Buschmann was planning to study medicine—it is certainly a grinning Dr. Buschmann; for that kind of thing is not so easily got rid of, it is long-lived, survives wars and currency reforms, and even then, in the presence of a lieutenant commander with an empty collar, waiting for an investigation to produce results, it proved superior to the blows of Mr. Mallenbrandt.

Discreetly, though all eyes were on Buschmann, I looked for Mahlke, but there was no need to search; I could tell by a feeling in my neck where he was inwardly singing his hymns to the Virgin. Fully dressed, not far away but removed from the crowd, he was buttoning the top button of a shirt which to judge by the cut and stripes must have been still another hand-me-down from his father. He was having trouble getting his distinguishing mark in under the button.

Apart from his struggles with his shirt button and the accompanying efforts of his jaw muscles, he gave an impression of calm. When he realized that the button wouldn't close over his Adam's apple, he reached into the breast pocket of his coat, which was still hanging up, and produced a rumpled necktie. No one in our class wore a tie. In the upper classes there were a few fops who affected ridiculous bow ties. Two hours before, while the lieutenant was still regaling the auditorium about the beauties of nature, he had worn his shirt collar open; but already the tie was in his breast pocket, awaiting the great occasion.

This was Mahlke's maiden voyage as a necktie wearer. There was only one mirror in the dressing room and even so it was covered with spots. Standing before it, but only for the sake of form, for he didn't step close enough to see anything much, he tied on his rag—it had bright polka dots and was in very bad taste, I am convinced today—turned down his collar, and gave the enormous knot one last tug. Then he spoke up, not in a very loud voice but with sufficient emphasis that his words could be distinguished from the sounds of the investigation that was still in progress and the slaps which Mallenbrandt, over the lieutenant commander's objections, was still tirelessly meting out. "I'm willing to bet," Mahlke said, "that Buschmann didn't do it. But has anybody searched his clothing?"

Though he had spoken to the mirror, Mahlke found ready listeners. His necktie, his new act, was noticed only later, and then not very much. Mallenbrandt personally searched Buschmann's clothes and soon found reason to strike another blow at the grin: in both coat pockets he found several opened packages of condoms, with which Buschmann carried on a retail trade in the upper classes; his father was a druggist. Otherwise Mallenbrandt found nothing, and the lieutenant commander cheerfully gave up, knotted his officer's tie, turned his collar down, and, tapping at the spot which had previously been so eminently decorated, suggested to Mallenbrandt that there was no need to take the incident too seriously: "It's easily replaced. It's not the end of the world. Just a silly boyish prank."

But Mallenbrandt had the doors of the gymnasium and dressing room locked and with the help of two Firsters searched our pockets as well as every corner of the room that might have been used as a hiding place. At first the lieutenant commander was amused and even helped, but after a while he grew impatient and did something that no one had ever dared to do in our dressing room: he began to chain smoke, stamping out the butts on the linoleum floor. His mood soured visibly after Mallenbrandt had silently pushed up a spittoon that for years had been gathering dust beside the washbowl and had already been searched as a possible hiding place.

The lieutenant commander blushed like a schoolboy, tore the cigarette he had just begun from his delicately curved orator's mouth, and stopped smoking. At first he just stood there with his arms folded; then he began to look nervously at the time, demonstrating his impatience by the sharp left hook with which he shook his wrist watch out of his sleeve.

He took his leave by the door with gloved fingers, giving it to be understood that he could not approve of the way this investigation was being handled, that he would put the whole irritating business into the hands of the principal, for he had no intention of letting his leave be spoiled by a bunch of ill-behaved brats.

513

Mallenbrandt tossed the key to one of the Firsters, who created an embarrassing pause by his clumsiness in unlocking the dressing-room door.

Chapter VIII

The investigation dragged on, ruining our Saturday afternoon and bringing no results. I remember few details and those are hardly worth talking about, for I had to keep an eye on Mahlke and his necktie, whose knot he periodically tried to push up higher; but for Mahlke's purposes a hook would have been needed. No, you were beyond help.

But what of the lieutenant commander? The question seems hardly worth asking, but it can be answered in few words. He was not present at the afternoon investigation, and it may well have been true, as unconfirmed rumors had it, that he spent the afternoon with his fiancée, looking through the city's three or four medal shops. Somebody in our class claimed to have seen him on Sunday at the Four Seasons Café, sitting with his fiancée and her parents, and allegedly nothing was missing between his collarbones: the visitors to the café may have noticed, with a certain awe, who was sitting there in their midst, trying his well-mannered best to cut the recalcitrant cake of the third war year with a fork.

I didn't go to the café that Sunday. I had promised Father Gusewski to serve as his altar boy at early Mass. Shortly after seven Mahlke came in with his bright necktie and was unable, despite the aid of the usual five little old women, to dispel the emptiness of the former gymnasium. He received communion as usual on the outer left. The previous evening, immediately after the investigation at school, he must have come to St. Mary's Chapel and confessed; or perhaps, for one reason or another, you whispered into Father Wiehnke's ear at the Church of the Sacred Heart.

Gusewski kept me, inquired after my brother, who was fighting in Russia, or maybe he had stopped fighting, for there had been no news of him for several weeks. Once again I had ironed and starched all the altar covers and the alb, and it is perfectly possible that he gave me a roll or two of raspberry drops; what I know for sure is that Mahlke was gone when I left the sacristy. He must have been one car ahead of me. On Max-Halbe-Platz I boarded the trailer of a No. 9 car. Schilling jumped on at Magdeburger Strasse after the car had gathered considerable speed. We spoke of something entirely different. Maybe I offered him some of Father Gusewski's raspberry drops. Between Saspe Manor and Saspe Cemetery, we overtook Hotten Sonntag. He was riding a lady's bicycle and carrying the little Pokriefke girl astraddle on the baggage rack. The spindly little thing's thighs were still as smooth as frogs' legs, but she

514

was no longer flat all over. The wind showed that her hair had grown longer.

We had to wait at the Saspe siding for the car coming from the opposite direction, and Hotten Sonntag and Tulla passed us. At the Brösen stop the two of them were waiting. The bicycle was leaning against a wastepaper basket provided by the beach administration. They were playing brother and sister, standing there with their little fingers linked. Tulla's dress was blue blue washing blue, and in every way too short too tight too blue. Hotten Sonntag was carrying the bundle of bathrobes etc. We managed to exchange a few silent glances, and to catch each other's meaning. At length words fell from the supercharged silence: "Of course it was Mahlke, who else could it have been? What a guy!"

Tulla wanted details, squirmed up to us, and wheedled with a pointed forefinger. But neither of us called the object by name. She got no more out of us than a terse "WhoelsebutMahlke" and an "It'sasclearasday." But Schilling, no, it was I, dreamed up a new title. Into the gap between Hotten Sonntag's head and Tulla's head I inserted the words: "The Great Mahlke. The Great Mahlke did it, only the Great Mahlke can do such things."

And the title stuck. All previous attempts to fasten nicknames on Mahlke had been short-lived. I remember "Soup Chicken"; and when he stood aloof, we had called him "Swallower" or "The Swallower." But the first title to prove viable was my spontaneous cry: "The Great Mahlke!" And in these papers I shall speak now and then of "The Great Mahlke."

At the cashier's window we got rid of Tulla. She disappeared into the ladies' cabins, stretching her dress with her shoulder blades. Before the verandalike structure in front of the men's bathhouse lay the sea, pale and shaded by fair-weather clouds, blowing across the sky in dispersed order. Water: 65. Without having to search, the three of us caught sight, behind the second sandbank, of somebody swimming frantically on his back, splashing and foaming as he headed for the superstructure of the mine sweeper. We agreed that only one of us should swim after him. Schilling and I suggested Hotten Sonntag, but he preferred to lie with Tulla Pokriefke behind the sun screen on the family beach and sprinkle sand on frogs' legs. Schilling claimed to have eaten too much breakfast: "Eggs and all. My grandma from Krampitz has chickens and some Sundays she brings in two or three dozen eggs."

I could think of no excuse. I rarely observed the rule about fasting before communion and I had eaten breakfast very early. Besides, it was neither Schilling nor Hotten Sonntag who had said "The Great Mahlke," but I. So I swam after him, in no particular hurry.

Tulla Pokriefke wanted to swim along with me, and we almost came to blows on the pier between the ladies' beach and the family beach. All

515

arms and legs, she was sitting on the railing. Summer after summer she had been wearing that same mouse-gray, grossly darned child's bathing suit; what little bosom she had was crushed, elastic cut into her thighs, and between her legs the threadbare wool molded itself in an intimate dimple. Curling her nose and spreading her toes, she screamed at me. When in return for some present or other—Hotten Sonntag was whispering in her ear—she agreed to withdraw, three or four little Thirds, good swimmers, whom I had often seen on the barge, came climbing over the railing; they must have caught some of our conversation, for they wanted to swim to the barge though they didn't admit it. "Oh no," they protested, "we're going somewhere else. Out to the breakwater. Or just to take a look." Hotten Sonntag attended to them: "Anybody that swims after him gets his balls polished."

After a shallow dive from the pier I started off, changing my stroke frequently and taking my time. As I swam and as I write, I tried and I try to think of Tulla Pokriefke, for I didn't and still don't want to think of Mahlke. That's why I swam breast stroke, and that's why I write that I swam breast stroke. That was the only way I could see Tulla Pokriefke sitting on the railing, a bag of bones in mouse-gray wool; and as I thought of her, she became smaller, crazier, more painful; for Tulla was a thorn in our flesh—but when I had the second sandbank behind me, she was gone, thorn and dimple had passed the vanishing point, I was no longer swimming away from Tulla, but swimming toward Mahlke, and it is toward you that I write: I swam breast stroke and I didn't hurry.

I may as well tell you between two strokes—the water will hold me up—that this was the last Sunday before summer vacation. What was going on at the time? They had occupied the Crimea, and Rommel was advancing again in North Africa. Since Easter we had been in Upper Second. Esch and Hotten Sonntag had volunteered, both for the Air Force, but later on, just like me who kept hesitating whether to go into the Navy or not, they were sent to the Panzer Grenadiers, a kind of high-class infantry. Mahlke didn't volunteer; as usual, he was the exception. "You must be nuts," he said. However, he was a year older, and there was every likelihood that he would be taken before we were; but a writer mustn't get ahead of himself.

I swam the last couple of hundred yards all in breast stroke, but still more slowly in order to save my breath. The Great Mahlke was sitting as usual in the shadow of the pilothouse. Only his knees were getting some sun. He must have been under once. The gargling remnants of an overture wavered in the fitful breeze and came out to meet me with the ripples. That was his way: dove down into his den, cranked up the phonograph, put on a record, came up with dripping watershed, sat down in the shade, and listened to his music while above him the screams of the gulls substantiated the doctrine of transmigration.

516

No, not yet. Once again, before it is too late, let me turn over on my back and contemplate the great clouds shaped like potato sacks, which rose from Putziger Wiek and passed over our barge in endless procession, providing changes of light and a cloud-long coolness. Never since—except at the exhibition of our local children's painting which Father Alban organized two years ago at our settlement house with my help, have I seen such beautiful, potato-sack-shaped clouds. And so once again, before the battered rust of the barge comes within reach, I ask: Why me? Why not Hotten Sonntag or Schilling? I might have sent the Thirds, or Tulla with Hotten Sonntag. Or the whole lot of them including Tulla, for the Thirds, especially one of them who seems to have been related to her, were always chasing after the little bag of bones. But no, bidding Schilling to make sure that no one followed me, I swam alone. And took my time.

I, Pilenz—what has my first name got to do with it?—formerly an altar boy dreaming of every imaginable future, now secretary at the Parish Settlement House, just can't let magic alone; I read Bloy, the Gnostics, Böll, Friedrich Heer, and often with profound emotion the *Confessions* of good old St. Augustine. Over tea brewed much too black, I spend whole nights discussing the blood of Christ, the Trinity, and the sacrament of penance with the Franciscan Father Alban, who is an open-minded man though more or less a believer. I tell him about Mahlke and Mahlke's Virgin, Mahlke's neck and Mahlke's aunt, Mahlke's sugar water, the part in the middle of his hair, his phonograph, snowy owl, screwdriver, woolen pompoms, luminous buttons, about cat and mouse and *mea culpa*. I tell him how the Great Mahlke sat on the barge and I, taking my time, swam out to him alternating between breast stroke and back stroke; for I alone could be termed his friend, if it was possible to be friends with Mahlke. Anyway I made every effort. But why speak of effort? To me it was perfectly natural to trot along beside him and his changing attributes. If Mahlke had said: "Do this and that," I would have done this and that and then some. But Mahlke said nothing. I ran after him, I went out of my way to pick him up on Osterzeile for the privilege of going to school by his side. And he merely put up with my presence without a word or a sign. When he introduced the pompom vogue, I was the first to take it up and wear pompoms on my neck. For a while, though only at home, I even wore a screwdriver on a shoelace. And if I continued to gratify Gusewski with my services as an altar boy, it was only in order to gaze at Mahlke's neck during holy communion. When in 1942, after Easter vacation—aircraft carriers were battling in the Coral Sea—the Great Mahlke shaved for the first time, I too began to scrape my chin, though no sign of a beard was discernible. And if after the submarine captain's speech Mahlke had said to me: "Pilenz, go swipe that business on the ribbon," I would have taken medal and ribbon off the hook and kept it for you.

But Mahlke attended to his own affairs. And now he was sitting in the shadow of the pilothouse, listening to the tortured remains of his underwater music: *Cavalleria Rusticana*—gulls overhead—the sea now smooth now ruffled now stirred by short-winded waves—two fat ships in the roadstead—scurrying cloud shadows—over toward Putzig a formation of speedboats: six bow waves, a few trawlers in between—I can already hear the gurgling of the barge, I swim slowly, breast stroke, look away, look beyond, in between the vestiges of the ventilators—I can't remember exactly how many—and before my hands grip the rust, I see you, as I've been seeing you for a good fifteen years: You! I swim, I grip the rust, I see You: the Great Mahlke sits impassive in the shadow, the phonograph record in the cellar catches, in love with a certain passage which it repeats till its breath fails; the gulls fly off; and there you are with the ribbon and *it* on your neck.

It was very funny-looking, because he had nothing else on. He sat huddled, naked and bony in the shade with his eternal sunburn. Only the knees glared. His long, semi-relaxed pecker and his testicles lay flat on the rust. His hands clutching his knees. His hair plastered in strands over his ears but still parted in the middle. And that face, that Redeemer's countenance! And below it, motionless, his one and only article of clothing, the large, the enormous medal a hand's breadth below his collarbone.

For the first time the Adam's apple, which, as I still believe—though he had auxiliary motors—was Mahlke's motor and brake, had found its exact counterweight. Quietly it slumbered beneath his skin. For a time it had no need to move, for the harmonious cross that soothed it had a long history; it had been designed in the year 1813, when iron was worth its weight in gold, by good old Schinkel, who knew how to capture the eye with classical forms: slight changes in 1871, slight changes in 1914-18, and now again slight changes. But it bore no resemblance to the *Pour le Mérite,* a development of the Maltese Cross, although now for the first time Schinkel's brain child moved from chest to neck, proclaiming symmetry as a Credo.

"Hey, Pilenz! What do you think of my trinket? Not bad, eh?"

"Terrific! Let me touch it."

"You'll admit I earned it."

"I knew right away that you'd pulled the job."

"Job nothing. It was conferred on me only yesterday for sinking five ships on the Murmansk run plus a cruiser of the *Southampton* class. . . ."

Both of us determined to make a show of lightheartedness; we grew very silly, bawled out every single verse of "We're sailing against England," made up new verses, in which neither tankers nor troop transports were torpedoed amidships, but certain girls and teachers from the Gudrun School; forming megaphones of our hands, we blared out special com-

muniqués, announcing our sinkings in terms both high-flown and obscene, and drummed on the deck with our fists and heels. The barge
groaned and rattled, dry gull droppings were shaken loose, gulls returned,
speedboats passed in the distance, beautiful white clouds drifted over us,
light as trails of smoke, comings and goings, happiness, shimmering
light, not a fish leaped out of the water, friendly weather; the jumping
jack started up again, not because of any crisis in the throat, but because
he was alive all over and for the first time a little giddy, gone the
Redeemer's countenance. Wild with glee, he removed the article from
his neck and held the ends of the ribbon over his hip bones with a mincing
little gesture. While with his legs, shoulders, and twisted head he performed a fairly comical imitation of a girl, but no particular girl, the
great iron cookie dangled in front of his private parts, concealed no more
than a third of his pecker.

In between—your circus number was beginning to get on my
nerves—I asked him if he meant to keep the thing; it might be best, I
suggested, to store it in his basement under the bridge, along with the
snowy owl, phonograph, and Pilsudski.

The Great Mahlke had other plans and carried them out. For if Mahlke
had stowed the object below decks; or better still, if I had never been
friends with Mahlke; or still better, both at once: the object safe in the
radio shack and I only vaguely interested in Mahlke, out of curiosity or
because he was a classmate—then I should not have to write now and I
should not have to say to Father Alban: "Was it my fault if Mahlke later
. . ." As it is, I can't help writing, for you can't keep such things to
yourself. Of course it is pleasant to pirouette on white paper—but what
help are white clouds, soft breezes, speedboats coming in on schedule,
and a flock of gulls doing the work of a Greek chorus; what good can
any magical effects of syntax do me; even if I drop capitals and punctuation,
I shall still have to say that Mahlke did not stow his bauble in the former
radio shack of the former Polish mine sweeper *Rybitwa,* that he did not
hang it between Marshal Pilsudski and the Black Madonna, over the
moribund phonograph and the decomposing snowy owl, that he went
down under with his trinket on his neck, but stayed barely half an hour,
while I counted sea gulls, preening himself—I can swear to that—with
his prize piece for the Virgin's benefit. I shall have to say that he brought
it up again through the fo'c'sle hatch and was wearing it as he slipped
on his trunks and swam back to the bathhouse with me at a good steady
pace, that holding his treasure in his clenched fist, he smuggled it past
Schilling, Hotten Sonntag, Tulla Pokriefke, and the Thirds, into his
cabin in the gentlemen's section.

I was in no mood for talking and gave Tulla and her entourage only half an idea of what was up before vanishing into my cabin. I dressed quickly and caught Mahlke at the No. 9 car stop. Throughout the ride I tried to persuade him, if it had to be, to return the medal personally to the lieutenant commander, whose address it would have been easy to find out.

I don't think he was listening. We stood on the rear platform, wedged in among the late Sunday morning crowd. From one stop to the next he opened his hand between his shirt and mine, and we both looked down at the severe dark metal with the rumpled, still wet ribbon. When we reached Saspe Manor, Mahlke held the medal over the knot of his tie, and tried to use the platform window as a mirror. As long as the car stood motionless, waiting for the car in the opposite direction to pass, I looked out over one of his ears, over the tumbledown Saspe Cemetery toward the airfield. I was in luck: a large trimotored Ju 52 was circling cautiously to a landing. That helped me.

Yet it was doubtful whether the Sunday crowd in the car had eyes to spare for the Great Mahlke's exhibition. Amid benches and bundles of beach equipment, they were kept busy struggling with small children worn out from bathing. The whining and blubbering of children, rising, falling, rising, squelched, and ebbing off into sleep, echoed from the front to the rear platform and back—not to mention smells that would have turned the sweetest milk sour.

At the terminus on Brunshöferweg we got out and Mahlke said over his shoulder that he was planning to disturb the noonday repose of Dr. Waldemar Klohse, our principal, that he was going in alone and there was no point in my waiting for him.

Klohse—as we all knew—lived on Baumbachallee. I accompanied the Great Mahlke through the tiled underpass, then I let him go his way; he did not hurry, I would even say that he zigzagged slightly. He held the ends of the ribbon between thumb and forefinger of his left hand; the medal twirled, serving as a propeller on his course to Baumbachallee.

An infernal idea! And why did he have to carry it out! If you had only thrown the damn thing up into the linden trees: in that residential quarter full of shade-dispensing foliage there were plenty of magpies that would have carried it off to their secret store, and tucked it away with the silver teaspoon, the ring and the brooch and the kit and boodle.

Mahlke was absent on Monday. The room was full of rumors. Dr. Brunies conducted his German class, incorrigibly sucking the Cebion tablets he should have distributed to his pupils. Eichendorff lay open before him. Sweet and sticky, his old man's mumble came to us from the desk: a few pages from the *Scamp,* then poems: *The Mill Wheel, The Little Ring, The Troubadour*— Two hearty journeymen went forth— If there's a fawn you love the best— The song that slumbers in all things— Mild blows the breeze and blue. Not a word about Mahlke.

It was not until Tuesday that Klohse came in with a gray portfolio, and took his stance beside Dr. Erdmann, who rubbed his hands in embarrassment. Over our heads resounded Klohse's cool breath: a disgraceful thing had happened, and in these fateful times when we must all pull together. The student in question—Klohse did not mention the name —had already been removed from the establishment. It had been decided, however, that other authorities, the district bureau for example, would not be notified. In the interests of the school the students were urged to observe a manly silence, which alone could minimize the effects of such scandalous behavior. Such was the desire of a distinguished alumnus, the lieutenant commander and U-boat captain, bearer of the and so on . . .

And so Mahlke was expelled, but—during the war scarcely anyone was thrown out of secondary school for good—transferred to the Horst Wessel School, where his story was kept very quiet.

Chapter IX

The Horst Wessel School, which before the war had been called the Crown Prince Wilhelm School, was characterized by the same dusty smell as our Conradinum. The building, built in 1912, I think, seemed friendlier than our brick edifice, but only on the outside. It was situated on the southern edge of the suburb, at the foot of Jeschkental Forest; consequently Mahlke's way to school and my way to school did not intersect at any point when school resumed in the autumn.

But there was no sign of him during the summer vacation either— a summer without Mahlke!—the story was that he had signed up for a premilitary training camp offering courses in radio operation. He displayed his sunburn neither in Brösen nor at Glettkau Beach. Since there was no point in looking for him at St. Mary's Chapel, Father Gusewski was deprived of one of his most reliable altar boys. Altar Boy Pilenz said to himself: No Mahlke, no Mass.

The rest of us lounged about the barge from time to time, but without enthusiasm. Hotten Sonntag tried in vain to find the way into the radio shack. Even the Thirds had heard rumors of an amazing and amazingly furnished hideaway inside the bridge. A character with eyes very close together, whom the infants submissively addressed as Störtebeker, dove indefatigably. Tulla Pokriefke's cousin, a rather sickly little fellow, came out to the barge once or twice, but never dove. Either in my thoughts or in reality I try to strike up a conversation with him about Tulla; I was interested in her. But she had ensnared her cousin as she had me—what with, I wonder? With her threadbare wool, with her ineradicable smell of carpenter's glue? "It's none of your God-damn business!" That's what the cousin said to me—or might have.

Tulla didn't swim out to the barge; she stayed on the beach, but she had given up Hotten Sonntag. I took her to the movies twice, but even so I had no luck; she'd go to the movies with anybody. It was said that she had fallen for Störtebeker, but if so her love was unrequited, for Störtebeker had fallen for our barge and was looking for the entrance to Mahlke's hideout. As the vacation drew to an end there was a good deal of whispering to the effect that his diving had been successful. But there was never any proof: he produced neither a waterlogged phonograph record nor a decaying owl feather. Still, the rumors persisted; and when, two and a half years later, the so-called Dusters, a somewhat mysterious gang supposedly led by Störtebeker, were arrested, our barge and the hiding place under the bridge appear to have been mentioned. But by then I was in the Army; all I heard was a line or two in letters—for until the end, or rather as long as the mails were running, Father Gusewski wrote me letters ranging from pastoral to friendly. In one of the last, written in January '45—as the Russian armies were approaching Elbing—there was something about a scandalous assault of the Dusters on the Church of the Sacred Heart, where Father Wiehnke officiated. In this letter Störtebeker was referred to by his real name; and it also seems to me that I read something about a three-year-old child whom the gang had cherished as a kind of mascot. I am pretty certain, though sometimes I have my doubts, that in his last or next to last letter—I lost the whole packet and my diary as well near Cottbus—there was some mention of the barge which had its big day before the onset of the summer vacation of '42, but whose glory paled in the course of the summer; for to this day that summer has a flat taste in my mouth—what was summer without Mahlke?

Not that we were really unhappy about his absence. I myself was glad to be rid of him, so I didn't have to chase after him the whole time; but why, I wonder, did I report to Father Gusewski as soon as school began again, offering my services at the altar? The reverend father's eyes crinkled with delight behind his rimless glasses and grew smooth and solemn behind the self-same glasses only when—we were sitting in the sacristy and I was brushing his cassock—I asked, as though in passing, about Joachim Mahlke. Calmly, raising one hand to his glasses, he declared: "Yes, yes, he is still one of the most faithful members of my congregation; never misses a Sunday Mass. You know, I presume, that he was away for four weeks, at a so-called premilitary training camp; but I shouldn't like to think that you're coming back to us only on Mahlke's account. Speak up, Pilenz!"

Exactly two weeks earlier, we had received news that my brother Klaus, a sergeant in the Army, had fallen in the Kuban. I spoke of his death as my reason for wishing to resume my duties as an altar boy. Father Gusewski seemed to believe me; at any rate he tried to believe in me and in my renewed piety.

I don't recollect the particulars of Winter's or Hotten Sonntag's face. But Father Gusewski had thick wavy hair, black with the barest sprinkling of gray, which could be counted on to sprinkle his cassock with dandruff. Meticulously tonsured, the crown of his head had a bluish glint. He gave off an aroma compounded of hair tonic and Palmolive soap. Sometimes he smoked Turkish cigarettes in an ornately carved amber holder. He enjoyed a reputation for progressiveness and played ping-pong in the sacristy with the altar boys and those preparing for their first communion. He liked the ecclesiastical linen, the humeral and the alb, to be immoderately starched, a chore attended to by a certain Mrs. Tolkmit or, when the old lady was ailing, by a handy altar boy, often myself. He himself appended sachets of lavender to every maniple, every stole, to all the Mass vestments, whether they lay in chests or hung in closets. Once when I was about thirteen, he ran his small, hairless hand down my back under my shirt from my neck to the waist of my gym shorts, but stopped there because my shorts had no elastic band and I tied them in front with tapes. I didn't give the incident much thought, for Father Gusewski had won my sympathy with his friendly, often boyish ways. I can still remember his ironic benevolence; so not another word about the occasional wanderings of his hand; all perfectly harmless, it was really my Catholic soul he was looking for. All in all, he was a priest like hundreds of others; he maintained a well-selected library for a working-class congregation that read little; his zeal was not excessive, his belief had its limits—in regard to the Assumption, for instance—and he always spoke, whether over the corporal about the blood of Christ or in the sacristy about ping-pong, in the same tone of unctuous serenity. It did strike me as silly when early in 1940 he put in a petition to have his name changed—less than a year later he called himself, and had others call him, Father Gusewing. But the fashion for Germanizing Polish sounding names ending in *ki* or *ke* or *a*—like Formella—was taken up by lots of people in those days: Lewandowski became Lengnisch; Mr. Olczewski, our butcher, had himself metamorphosed into a Mr. Ohlwein; Jürgen Kupka's parents wanted to take the East Prussian name of Kupkat, but their petition, heaven knows why, was rejected. Perhaps in emulation of one Saul who became Paul, a certain Gusewski wished to become Gusewing—but in these papers Father Gusewski will continue to be Gusewski; for you, Joachim Mahlke, did not change your name.

When for the first time after summer vacation I served early Mass at the altar, I saw him again and anew. Immediately after the prayers at the foot of the altar—Father Gusewski stood on the Epistle side and was busy with the Introit—I sighted him in the second pew, before the altar of Our Lady. But it was only between the reading of the Epistle and the gradual, and more freely during the Gospel reading, that I found time to examine his appearance. His hair was still parted in the middle and still held in place with the usual sugar water; but he wore it a good inch longer. Stiff and candied, it fell over his two ears like the two sides of a steep-pointed roof: he would have made a satisfactory Jesus the way he held up his joined hands on a level with his forehead without propping his elbows; beneath them I perceived a bare, unguarded neck that concealed none of its secrets; for he was wearing his shirt collar open and folded over his jacket collar in the manner hallowed by Schiller: no tie, no pompoms, no pendants, no screwdriver, nor any other item from his copious arsenal. The only heraldic beast in an otherwise vacant field was the restless mouse which he harbored under his skin in place of a larynx, which had once attracted a cat and had tempted me to put the cat on his neck. The area between Adam's apple and chin was still marked with a few crusty razor cuts. At the Sanctus I almost came in too late with the bell.

At the communion rail Mahlke's attitude was less affected. His joined hands dropped down below his collarbone and his mouth smelled as though a pot of cabbage were simmering on a small flame within him. Once he had his wafer, another daring innovation captured my attention: in former days Mahlke, like every other communicant, had returned directly from the communion rail to his place in the second row of pews; now he prolonged and interrupted this silent itinerary, first striding slowly and stiffly to the middle of the altar of Our Lady, then falling on both knees, not on the linoleum floor but on a shaggy carpet which began shortly before the altar steps. Then he raised his joined hands until they were level with his eyes, with the part in his hair, and higher still he held them out in supplication and yearning to the over-life-size plaster figure which stood childless, a virgin among virgins, on a silver-plated crescent moon, draped from shoulders to ankles in a Prussian-blue starry mantle, her long-fingered hands folded over her flat bosom, gazing with slightly protuberant glass eyes at the ceiling of the former gymnasium. When Mahlke arose knee after knee and reassembled his hands in front of his Schiller collar, the carpet had imprinted a coarse, bright-red pattern on his kneecaps.

Father Gusewski had also observed certain aspects of Mahlke's new style. Not that I asked questions. Quite of his own accord, as though wishing to throw off or to share a burden, he began immediately after Mass to speak of Mahlke's excessive zeal, of his dangerous attachment to outward forms. Yes, Father Gusewski was worried; it had seemed to him for some time that regardless of what inner affliction brought Mahlke to the altar, his cult of the Virgin bordered on pagan idolatry.

He was waiting for me at the door of the sacristy. I was so frightened I almost ran back in again, but at once he took my arm, laughed in a free and easy way that was completely new, and talked and talked. He who had formerly been so monosyllabic spoke about the weather—Indian summer, threads of gold in the air. And then abruptly, but in the same conversational tone and without even lowering his voice: "I've volunteered. I can't understand it. You know how I feel about all that stuff: militarism, playing soldier, the current overemphasis on martial virtues. Guess what branch of service. Don't make me laugh. The Air Force is all washed up. Paratroopers? Wrong again! Why wouldn't you think of the submarines? Well, at last! That's the only branch that still has a chance. Though of course I'll feel like an ass in one of those things and I'd rather do something useful or funny. You remember I wanted to be a clown. Lord, what ideas a kid will get!

"I still think it's a pretty good idea. Otherwise things aren't so bad. Hell, school is school. What fool ideas I used to have. Do you remember? Just couldn't get used to this bump. I thought it was some kind of disease. But it's perfectly normal. I've known people, or at least I've seen some, with still bigger ones; they don't get upset. The whole thing started that day with the cat. You remember. We were lying in Heinrich Ehlers Field. A Schlagball tournament was going on. I was sleeping or daydreaming, and that gray beast, or was it black, saw my neck and jumped, or one of you, Schilling I think, it's the kind of thing he would do, took the cat . . . Well, that's ancient history. No, I haven't been back to the barge. Störtebeker? Never heard of him. Let him, let him. I don't own the barge, do I? Come and see us soon."

It was not until the third Sunday of Advent—all that autumn Mahlke had made me a model altar boy—that I accepted his invitation. Until Advent I had been obliged to serve all by myself. Father Gusewski had been unable to find a second altar boy. Actually I had wanted to visit Mahlke on the first Sunday of Advent and bring him a candle, but the shipment came too late and it was not until the second Sunday that Mahlke was able to place the consecrated candle on the altar of Our Lady. "Can you scare up some?" he had asked me. "Gusewski won't give me any." I said that I'd do what I could, and actually succeeded in procuring one of those long candles, pale as potato shoots, that are so rare in wartime; for my brother's death entitled my family to a candle. I went on foot to the rationing office and they gave me a coupon after I had submitted the death certificate. Then I took the streetcar to the religious-articles shop in Oliva, but they were out of candles. I had to go back again and then

525

a second time, and so it was only on the second Sunday of Advent that I was able to give you your candle and see you kneel with it at the altar of Our Lady, as I had long dreamed of seeing you. Gusewski and I wore violet for Advent. But your neck sprouted from a white Schiller collar which was not obscured by the reversed and remodeled overcoat you had inherited from an engine driver killed in an accident, for you no longer —another innovation!—wore a muffler fastened with a large safety pin.

And Mahlke knelt stiffly and at length on the coarse carpet on the second Sunday of Advent and again on the third, the day I decided to take him at his word and drop in on him in the afternoon. His glassy unquivering gaze—or if it quivered, it was when I was busy at the altar—was aimed over the candle at the belly of the Mother of God. His hands formed a steep roof over his forehead and its thoughts, but he did not touch his forehead with his crossed thumbs.

And I thought: Today I'll go. I'll go and take a look at him. I'll study him. Yes, so I will. There must be something behind all that. Besides, he had invited me.

Osterzeile was a short street: and yet the one-family houses with their empty trellises against house fronts scrubbed till they were sore, the uniform trees along the sidewalks—the lindens had lost their poles within the last year but still required props—discouraged and wearied me, although our Westerzeile was identical, or perhaps it was because our Westerzeile had the same smell and celebrated the seasons with the same Lilliputian garden plots. Even today when, as rarely happens, I leave the settlement house to visit friends or acquaintances in Stockum or Lohhausen, between the airfield and the North Cemetery, and have to pass through streets of housing development which repeat themselves just as wearisomely and dishearteningly from house number to house number, from linden to linden, I am still on the way to visit Mahlke's mother and Mahlke's aunt and you, the Great Mahlke; the bell is fastened to a garden gate that I might have stepped over without effort, just by stretching my legs a little. Steps through the wintry but snowless front garden with its top-heavy rosebushes wrapped for the winter. The flowerless flower beds are decorated with Baltic sea shells broken and intact. The ceramic tree frog the size of a rabbit is seated on a slab of rough marble embedded in crusty garden soil that has crumbled over it in places. And in the flower bed on the other side of the narrow path which, while I think of it, guides me from the garden gate to the three brick steps before the ocher-stained, round-arched door, stands, just across from the tree frog, an almost vertical pole some five feet high, topped with a birdhouse in the Alpine manner. The sparrows go on eating as I negotiate the seven or eight paces between flower bed and flower bed. It might be supposed that the development smells fresh, clean, sandy, and seasonal—but Osterzeile, Westerzeile, Bärenweg, no, the whole of Langfuhr, West Prussia, or Germany for that matter, smelled in those war years of onions, onions stewing in margarine; I won't try to determine what else was stewing, but one thing that could always be identified was freshly chopped onions, although onions were scarce and hard to come by, although jokes about the onion shortage, in connection with Field Marshal Göring, who had said something or other about short onions on the radio, were going the rounds in Langfuhr, in West Prussia, and all over Germany. Perhaps if I rubbed my typewriter superficially with onion juice, it might communicate an intimation of the onion smell which in those years contaminated all Germany, West Prussia and Langfuhr, Osterzeile as well as Westerzeile, preventing the smell of corpses from taking over completely.

I took the three brick steps at one stride, and my curved hand was preparing to grasp the door handle when the door was opened from within—by Mahlke in Schiller collar and felt slippers. He must have refurbished the part in his hair a short while before. Neither light nor dark, in rigid, freshly combed strands, it slanted backward in both directions from the part. Still impeccably neat; but when I left an hour later, it had begun to quiver as he spoke and droop over his large, flamboyant ears.

We sat in the rear of the house, in the living room, which received its light from the jutting glass veranda. There was cake made from some war recipe, potato cake; the predominant taste was rose water, which was supposed to awaken memories of marchpane. Afterward preserved plums, which had a normal taste and had ripened during the fall in Mahlke's garden—the tree, leafless and with whitewashed trunk, could be seen in the left-hand pane of the veranda. My chair was assigned to me: I was at the narrow end of the table, looking out, while Mahlke, opposite me at the other end, had the veranda behind him. To the left of me, illumined from the side so that gray hair curled silvery, Mahlke's aunt; to the right, her right side illumined, but less glittering because combed more tightly, Mahlke's mother. Although the room was overheated, it was a cold wintry light that outlined the fuzzy edges of her ears and a few trembling wisps of loose hair. The wide Schiller collar gleamed whiter than white at the top, blending into gray lower down: Mahlke's neck lay flat in the shadow.

The two women were rawboned, born and raised in the country. They were at a loss what to do with their hands and spoke profusely, never at the same time, but always in the direction of Joachim Mahlke even when they were addressing me and asking about my mother's health. They both spoke to me through him, who acted as our interpreter: "So now your brother Klaus is dead. I knew him only by sight, but what a handsome boy!"

Mahlke was a mild but firm chairman. When the questions became

527

too personal—while my father was sending APO letters from Greece, my mother was indulging in intimate relations, mostly with noncoms—well, Mahlke warded off questions in that direction: "Never mind about that, Auntie. Who can afford to judge in times like this when everything is topsy-turvy? Besides, it's really no business of yours, Mamma. If Papa were still alive, he wouldn't like it, he wouldn't let you speak like that."

Both women obeyed him or else they obeyed the departed engine driver whom he quietly conjured up whenever his aunt or mother began to gossip. When they spoke of the situation at the front—confusing the battlefields of Russia with those of North Africa, saying El Alamein when they meant the Sea of Azov—Mahlke managed quietly, without irritation, to guide the conversation into the right geographical channels: "No, Auntie, that naval battle was at Guadalcanal, not in Karelia."

Nevertheless, his aunt had given the cue and we lost ourselves in conjectures about the Japanese and American aircraft carriers that might have been sunk off Guadalcanal. Mahlke believed that the carriers *Hornet* and *Wasp*, the keels of which had been laid only in 1939, as well as the *Ranger*, had been completed in time to take part in the battle, for either the *Saratoga* or the *Lexington*, perhaps both, had meanwhile been sunk. We were still more in the dark about the two big Japanese carriers, the *Akagi* and the *Kaga*, which was decidedly too slow to be effective. Mahlke expressed daring opinions: only aircraft carriers, he said, would figure in the naval battles of the future, there was no longer any point in building battleships, it was the small, fast craft and the carriers that counted. He went into details. When he rattled off the names of the Italian *esploratori*, both women gaped in amazement and Mahlke's aunt clapped her bony hands resoundingly; there was something girlish about her enthusiasm, and in the silence that followed her clapping, she fiddled with her hair in embarrassment.

Not a word fell about the Horst Wessel School. I almost seem to remember that, as I was getting up to go, Mahlke laughingly mentioned his old nonsense about his neck, as he put it, and even went so far—his mother and aunt joined in the laughter—as to tell the story about the cat: this time it was Jürgen Kupka who put the cat on his throat; if only I knew who made up the story, he or I, or who is writing this in the first place!

In any case—this much is certain—his mother found some wrapping paper and packed up two little pieces of potato cake for me as I was taking my leave. In the hall, beside the staircase leading to the upper story and his attic, Mahlke pointed out a photograph hanging beside the brush bag. The whole width of the photograph was taken up with a rather modern-looking locomotive with tender, belonging to the Polish railways—the letters PKP could be clearly distinguished in two places. In front of the engine stood two men, tiny but imposing, with folded arms. The Great Mahlke said: "My father and Labuda the fireman, shortly before they were killed in an accident near Dirschau in '34. But my father managed to prevent the whole train from being wrecked; they awarded him a medal posthumously."

Chapter X

Early in the new year I thought I would take violin lessons—my brother had left a violin—but we were enrolled as Air Force auxiliaries and today it is probably too late although Father Alban keeps telling me that I ought to. And it was he who encouraged me to write about Cat and Mouse: "Just sit yourself down, my dear Pilenz, and start writing. Yes, yes, there was too much Kafka in your first poetic efforts and short stories, but even so, you've got a style of your own: if you won't take up the fiddle, you can get it off your chest by writing—the good Lord knew what He was doing when He gave you talent."

So we were enrolled in the Brösen-Glettkau shore battery, or training battery if you will, behind the gravel-strewn beach promenade, amid dunes and blowing beach grass, in buildings that smelled of tar, socks, and the beach grass used to stuff our mattresses. There might be lots of things to say about the daily life of an Air Force auxiliary, a schoolboy in uniform, subjected in the morning to gray-haired teachers and the traditional methods of education and in the afternoon obliged to memorize gunnery instructions and the secrets of ballistics; but this is not the place to tell my story, or the story of Hotten Sonntag's simple-minded vigor, or to recount the utterly commonplace adventures of Schilling—here I am speaking only of you; and Joachim Mahlke never became an Air Force auxiliary.

Just in passing and without trying to tell a coherent story beginning with cat and mouse, some students from the Horst Wessel School, who were also being trained in the Brösen-Glettkau shore battery, contributed a certain amount of new material: "Just after Christmas they drafted him into the Reich Labor Service. Oh yes, he graduated, they gave him the special wartime diploma. Hell, examinations were never any problem for him, he was quite a bit older than the rest of us. They say his battalion is out on Tuchler Heath. Cutting peat maybe. They say things are happening up there. Partisans and so on."

In February I went to see Esch at the Air Force hospital in Oliva. He was lying there with a fractured collarbone and wanted cigarettes. I gave him some and he treated me to some sticky liqueur. I didn't stay long. On the way to the streetcar bound for Glettkau I made a detour through the Castle Park. I wanted to see whether the good old whispering grotto was still there. It was: some convalescent alpine troops were trying it out with the nurses, whispering at the porous stone from both sides, tittering, whispering, tittering. I had no one to whisper with and went off, with some plan or other in mind, down a birdless, perhaps brambly path which led straight from the castle pond and whispering grotto to the Zoppot highway. It was rather like a tunnel because of the bare branches that joined overhead and it kept growing frighteningly narrower. I passed two nurses leading a hobbling, laughing, hobbling lieutenant, then two grandmothers and a little boy who might have been three years old, didn't want to be connected with the grandmothers, and was carrying but not beating a child's drum. Then out of the February-gray tunnel of brambles, something else approached and grew larger: Mahlke.

We were both ill at ease. There was something eerie, almost awesome, about a meeting on such a path without forks or byways, cut off even from the sky: it was fate or the rococo fantasy of a French landscape architect that had brought us together—and to this day I avoid inextricable castle parks designed in the manner of good old Le Nôtre.

Of course a conversation started up, but I couldn't help staring transfixed at his head covering; for the Labor Service cap, even when worn by others than Mahlke, was unequaled for ugliness: a crown of disproportionate height sagged forward over the visor; the whole was saturated with the color of dried excrement; the crown was creased in the middle in the manner of a civilian hat, but the bulges were closer together, so close as to produce the plastic furrow which explains why the Labor Service head covering was commonly referred to as "an ass with a handle." On Mahlke's head this hat made a particularly painful impression, for it seemed to accentuate the very same part in the middle that the Labor Service had forced him to give up. We were both of us on edge as we stood facing one another between and beneath the brambles. And then the little boy came back without the grandmothers, pounding his tin drum, circumnavigated us in a semicircle with magical overtones, and at last vanished down the tapering path with his noise.

We exchanged a hasty good-by after Mahlke had tersely and morosely answered my questions about fighting with partisans on Tuchler Heath, about the food in the Labor Service, and as to whether any Labor Service Maidens were stationed near them. I also wanted to know what he was doing in Oliva and whether he had been to see Father Gusewski. I learned that the food was tolerable, but that he had seen no sign of any Labor Service Maidens. He thought the rumors about fighting with partisans to be exaggerated but not entirely unfounded. His commander had sent him to Oliva for some spare parts: official business, justifying a two days' absence. "I spoke to Gusewski this morning, right after early Mass." Then a disparaging wave of the hand: "Hell can freeze over, he'll always be the same!" and the distance between us increased, because we were taking steps.

No, I didn't look after him. Unbelievable, you think? But if I say "Mahlke didn't turn around in my direction," you won't doubt me. Several times I had to look behind me because there was no one, not even the little boy with his noise box, coming toward me to help.

Then as I figure it, I didn't see you for a whole year; but not to see you was not, and still is not, to forget you and your fearful symmetry. Besides, there were reminders: if I saw a cat, whether gray or black or pepper-and-salt, the mouse ran into my field of vision forthwith; but still I hesitated, undecided whether the mouse should be protected or the cat goaded into catching it.

Until summer we lived at the shore battery, played endless games of handball, and on visiting Sundays rollicked to the best of our ability in the beach thistles, always with the same girls or their sisters; I alone accomplished nothing at all. Hesitation was my trouble; I haven't got over it yet, and this weakness of mine still inspires me with the same ironical reflections. What else occupied our days? Distributions of peppermint drops, lectures about venereal diseases; in the morning *Hermann and Dorothea*, in the afternoon the 98-K rifle, mail, four-fruit jam, singing contests. In our hours off duty we sometimes swam out to our barge, where we regularly found swarms of the little Thirds who were coming up after us and who irritated us no end, and as we swam back we couldn't for the life of us understand what for three summers had so attached us to that mass of rust encrusted with gull droppings. Later we were transferred to the 88-millimeter battery in Pelonken and then to the Zigankenberg battery. There were three or four alerts and our battery helped to shoot down a four-motor bomber. For weeks several orderly rooms submitted rival claims to the accidental hit—and through it all, peppermint drops, *Hermann and Dorothea*, and lots of saluting.

Because they had volunteered for the Army, Hotten Sonntag and Esch were sent to the Labor Service even sooner than I. Hesitating as usual, unable to make up my mind which branch of service I favored, I had missed the deadline for volunteering. In February 1944, with a good half of our class, I took and passed the final examinations—which differed little from the usual peacetime variety—and promptly received notice to report for Labor Service. Discharged from the Air Force Auxiliaries, I had a good two weeks ahead of me and was determined to do something conclusive in addition to winning my diploma. Whom did I light on but Tulla Pokriefke, who was sixteen or over and very accessible, but I had no luck and didn't get anywhere with Hotten Sonntag's sister either. In this situation and state of mind—I was comforted to some extent by letters from one of my cousins; the whole family had been evacuated to Silesia after an air raid had left their house a total loss—I made a farewell visit to Father Gusewski, promised to help at the altar during the furloughs I hoped I would get, and was given a new Missal and a handy metal crucifix, specially manufactured for Catholic recruits. Then at the corner of Bärenweg and Osterzeile on my way home, I ran into Mahlke's aunt, who wore thick glasses when she went out and was not to be avoided.

Before we had even exchanged greetings, she began to talk, at a good clip in spite of her rural drawl. When people came by, she gripped my shoulder and pulled until one of my ears approached her mouth. Hot, moist sentences. She began with irrelevant chit-chat. The shopping situation: "You can't even get what you've got coupons for." I learned that onions were not to be found, but that brown sugar and barley grits were obtainable at Matzerath's and that Ohlwein, the butcher, was expecting some canned pork. Finally, with no cue from me, she came to the point: "The boy is better now, though he don't exactly say so in his letters. But he's never been one to complain, he's just like his father, who was my brother-in-law. And now they've put him in the tanks. He'll be safer than in the infantry and dry when it rains."

Then whispers crept into my ear and I learned of Mahlke's new eccentricities, of the infantile pictures he drew under the signature of his letters.

"The funny part of it is that he never drew when he was little, except for the water colors he had to make in school. But here's his last letter in my pocketbook. Dear, how rumpled it is! Oh, Mr. Pilenz, there's so many people want to see how the boy is doing."

And Mahlke's aunt showed me Mahlke's letter. "Go ahead and read it." But I didn't read. Paper between gloveless fingers. A dry, sharp wind came circling down from Max-Halbe-Platz and nothing could stop it. Battered my heart with the heel of its boot ahd tried to kick the door in. Seven brothers spoke within me, but none of them followed the writing. There was snow in the wind but I could still see the letter paper distinctly, though it was grayish brown, poor quality. Today I may say that I understood immediately, but I just stared, wishing neither to look nor to understand; for even before the paper crackled close to my eyes, I had realized that Mahlke was starting up again: squiggly line drawings under neat Sütterlin script. In a row which he had taken great pains to make straight, but which was nevertheless crooked because the paper was unlined, eight, twelve, thirteen, fourteen unequally flattened circles and on every kidney a wartlike knob, and from each wart a bar the length of a thumbnail, projecting beyond the lopsided boiler toward the left edge of the paper. And on each of these tanks—for clumsy as the drawings were, I recognized the Russian T-34—there was a mark, mostly between

532

turret and boiler, a cross indicating a hit. And in addition—evidently the artist didn't expect the viewers of his work to be very bright—all fourteen of the T-34s—yes, I'm pretty sure there were fourteen of them—were canceled very emphatically with large crosses in blue pencil.

Quite pleased with myself, I explained to Mahlke's aunt that the drawings obviously represented tanks that Joachim had knocked out. But Mahlke's aunt didn't show the least surprise, plenty of people had already told her that, but what she couldn't understand was why there were sometimes more, sometimes fewer of them, once only eight and, in the letter before last, twenty-seven.

"Maybe it's because the mails are so irregular. But now, Mr. Pilenz, you must read what our Joachim writes. He mentions you too, in connection with candles, but we've already got some." I barely skimmed through the letter: Mahlke was thoughtful, inquiring about all his aunt's and mother's major and minor ailments—the letter was addressed to both of them—varicose veins, pains in the back, and so on. He asked for news of the garden: "Did the plum tree bear well this year? How are my cactuses doing?" Only a few words about his duties, which he called fatiguing and responsible: "Of course we have our losses. But the Blessed Virgin will protect me as in the past." Would his mother and aunt kindly give Father Gusewski one or if possible two candles for the altar of Our Lady? And then: "Maybe Pilenz can get you some; they have coupons." He furthermore asked them to offer prayers to St. Judas Thaddaeus—a nephew twice-removed of the Virgin Mary, Mahlke knew his Holy Family—and also have a Mass said for his late lamented father, who "left us without receiving the sacraments." At the end of the letter, more trifles and some pale landscape painting: "You can't imagine how run-down everything is here, how wretched the people are and all the many children. No electricity or running water. Sometimes I begin to wonder what it's all for, but I suppose it has to be. And someday if you feel like it and the weather is good, take the car out to Brösen—but dress warmly— and look out to the left of the harbor mouth, but not so far out, to see whether the superstructure of a sunken ship is still there. There used to be an old wreck there. You can see it with the naked eye, and Auntie has her glasses—it would interest me to know if it's still . . ."

I said to Mahlke's aunt: "You can spare yourself the ride. The barge is still in the same place. And give Joachim my best when you write. He can set his mind at rest, nothing changes around here, and nobody's likely to walk off with the barge."

And even if the Schichau Dockyards had walked off with it, that is, raised it, scrapped or refitted it, would it have done you any good? Would you have stopped scribbling Russian tanks with childish precision on your letters and crossing them off with blue pencil? And who could have scrapped the Virgin? And who could have bewitched our good old school and turned it into birdseed? And the cat and the mouse? Are there stories that can cease to be?

Chapter XI

With Mahlke's scribbled testimonials before my eyes, I had to live through three more days at home. My mother was devoting her attentions to a construction foreman from the Organisation Todt—or maybe she was still cooking the saltless-diet dishes that found the way to Lieutenant Stiewe's heart—one of these gentlemen at any rate had made himself at home in our apartment and, apparently unaware of the symbolism of the thing, was wearing the slippers my father had broken in. In an atmosphere of cozy comfort that might have been cut out of a woman's magazine, my mother bustled from one room to the next in mourning; black was becoming to her, she wore it to go out and she wore it to stay in. On the sideboard she had erected a kind of altar for my fallen brother: first in a black frame and under glass a passport photo enlarged past recognition, showing him as a sergeant but without the visor cap; second, similarly framed and covered with glass, the death notices from the *Vorposten* and the *Neueste Nachrichten*: third, she had tied up a packet of his letters in a black silk ribbon; to which, fourth, she had appended the Iron Crosses, first and second class, and the Crimean Medal, and placed the bundle to the left of the photographs; while fifth and on the right, my brother's violin and bow, resting on some music paper with notes on it—my brother had tried his hand at composing violin sonatas—formed a counterweight to the letters.

If today I occasionally miss my elder brother Klaus, whom I scarcely knew, what I felt at the time was mostly jealousy on account of that altar; I visualized my own enlarged photo thus framed in black, felt slighted, and often chewed my fingernails when I was alone in our living room with my brother's altar, which refused to be ignored.

One fine morning as the lieutenant lay on the couch preoccupied with his stomach and my mother in the kitchen cooked saltless gruel, I would certainly have smashed that altar—photo, death notices, and perhaps the fiddle as well; my fist would have lost its temper without consulting me. But before that could happen, my departure date came, depriving me of a scene that would still be stageworthy: so well had death in the Kuban, my mother by the sideboard, and I, the great procrastinator, prepared the script. Instead, I marched off with my imitation-leather suitcase, and took the train to Konitz via Berent. For three months between Osche and Reetz, I had occasion to familiarize myself with Tuchler Heath. Everywhere wind and sand. Spring days to gladden the

534

hearts of insect lovers. Rolling, round juniper berries. Wherever you turned, bushes and things to take aim at: the idea was to hit the two cardboard soldiers behind the fourth bush on the left. Over the birches and butterflies beautiful clouds with no place to go. In the bogs, circular, shiny-dark ponds where you could fish with hand grenades for perch and moss-covered carp. Nature wherever you looked. And movies in Tuchel.

Nevertheless and in spite of birches, clouds, and perch, I can give only a rough sketch, as in a sandbox, of this Labor Service battalion with its compound of shacks nestling in a copse, its flagpole, garbage pits, and off to one side of the school shack, its latrine. My only justification for telling you even this much is that a year before me, before Winter, Jürgen Kupka, and Bansemer, the Great Mahlke had worn denims and clodhoppers in the same compound, and literally left his name behind him: in the latrine, a roofless wooden box plunked down amid the broom and the overhead murmuring of the scrub pines. Here the two syllables —no first name—were carved, or rather chipped, into a pine board across from the throne, and below the name, in flawless Latin, but in an unrounded, runic sort of script, the beginning of his favorite sequence: *Stabat Mater dolorosa . . .* The Franciscan monk Jacopone da Todi would have been ever so pleased, but all it meant to me was that even in the Labor Service I couldn't get rid of Mahlke. For while I relieved myself, while the maggot-ridden dross of my age group accumulated behind me and under me, you gave me and my eyes no peace: loudly and in breathless repetition, a painstakingly incised text called attention to Mahlke, whatever I might decide to whistle in opposition.

And yet I am sure that Mahlke had had no intention of joking. Mahlke couldn't joke. He sometimes tried. But everything he did, touched, or said became solemn, significant, monumental; so also his runic inscription in the pine wood of a Reich Labor Service latrine named Tuchel-North, between Osche and Reetz. Digestive aphorisms, lines from lewd songs, crude or stylized anatomy—nothing helped. Mahlke's text drowned out all the more or less wittily formulated obscenities which, carved or scribbled from top to bottom of the latrine wall, gave tongues to wooden boards.

What with the accuracy of the quotation and the awesome secrecy of the place, I might almost have got religion in the course of time. And then this gloomy conscience of mine wouldn't be driving me to do underpaid social work in a settlement house, I wouldn't spend my time trying to discover early Communism in Nazareth or late Christianity in Ukrainian kolkhozes. I should at last be delivered from these all-night discussions with Father Alban, from trying to determine, in the course of endless investigations, to what extent blasphemy can take the place of prayer. I should be able to believe, to believe something, no matter what, perhaps even to believe in the resurrection of the flesh. But one day after

535

I had been chopping kindling in the battalion kitchen, I took the ax and hacked Mahlke's favorite sequence out of the board and eradicated your name.

It was the old story of the spot that found no takers, kind of grisly-moral and transcendent; for the empty patch of wood with its fresh fibers spoke more eloquently than the chipped inscription. Besides, your message must have spread with the shavings, for in the barracks, between kitchen, guardroom, and dressing room, stories as tall as a house began to go around, especially on Sundays when boredom took to counting flies. The stories were always the same, varying only in minor detail. About a Labor Service man named Mahlke, who had served a good year before in Tuchel-North battalion and must have done some mighty sensational things. Two truck drivers, the cook, and the room orderly had been there the whole time, every shipment had passed them by. Without significantly contradicting one another, they spoke roughly as follows: "This is how he looked the first day. Hair down to here. Well, they sent him to the barber. Don't make me laugh. He needed more than a barber: ears like an egg beater and a neck, a neck, what a neck! He also had . . . and once when . . . and for instance when he . . . but the most amazing thing about him was when I sent the whole pack of new recruits to Tuchel to be deloused because as room orderly I . . . When they were all under the shower, I says to myself, my eyes are playing tricks on me, so I look again, and I says to myself, mustn't get envious now, but that dick of his, take it from me, a monster, when he got excited it would stand up to or maybe more, anyway he made good use of it with the commander's wife, a strapping piece of in her forties, because the damn-fool commander—he's been transferred to France, a nut—sent him over to his house, the second from the left in Officers' Row, to build a rabbit hutch. At first Mahlke, that was his name, refused, no he didn't fly off the handle, he just quietly quoted chapter and verse from the Service regulations. That didn't do him a bit of good. The chief personally chewed his ass out till he could hardly and for the next two days he was shoveling shit in the latrine. I hosed him off from a respectful distance, because the boys wouldn't let him into the washroom. Finally he gave in and went toddling over with tools and boards. All that fuss over rabbits! He must have really screwed that old lady! Every day for more than a week she sent for him to work in the garden; every morning Mahlke toddled off and was back again for roll call. But that rabbit hutch wasn't making any headway at all, so finally it dawned on the chief. I don't know if he caught them bare ass, maybe on the kitchen table or maybe between the sheets like mamma and papa, anyway, he must have been struck speechless when he saw Mahlke's, anyway he never said one word about it here in

536

the barracks: it's not hard to see why. And he sent Mahlke off on official trips whenever he could to Oliva and Oxhöft for spare parts, just to get that stud and his nuts out of the battalion. Because the chief's old lady must have had mighty hot pants to judge by the size of his you know. We still get rumors from the orderly room: they correspond. Seems there was more to it than sex. You never know the whole story. And the very same Mahlke—I was there—smoked out a partisan ammunition dump single-handed near Gross-Bislaw. It's a wild story. A plain ordinary pond like there's so many around here. We were out there partly for work, partly for field training. We'd been lying beside this pond for half an hour, and Mahlke keeps looking and looking, and finally he says: Wait a minute, there's something fishy down there. The platoon leader, can't remember his name, grinned, so did we, but he said to go ahead. Before you could say boo, Mahlke has his clothes off and dives into the muck. And what do you know: the fourth time under, but not two feet below the surface, he finds the entrance to an ultra-modern ammunition dump with a hydraulic loading system. All we had to do was carry the stuff away, four truckloads, and the chief had to commend him in front of the whole battalion. In spite of the business with his old lady, they say he even put him in for a medal. He was in the Army when it came, but they sent it on. He was going into the tanks if they took him."

I restrained myself at first. The same with Winter, Jürgen Kupka, and Bansemer; we all clammed up when the conversation came around to Mahlke. When we chanced to pass Officers' Row—on hikes or on our way to the supply room—we would exchange furtive smiles of connivance, for the second house on the left still had no rabbit hutch. Or a meaningful glance would pass between us because a cat lurked motionless in the gently waving grass. We became a kind of secret clan, though I wasn't very fond of Winter and Kupka, and still less of Bansemer.

Four weeks before the end of our stint, the rumors began to creep in. Partisans had been active in the region; we were on twenty-four-hour alert, never out of our clothes, though we never caught anybody and we ourselves suffered no losses. The same room orderly who had issued Mahlke his uniform and taken him to be deloused brought the news from the office: "In the first place there's a letter from Mahlke to the former commander's wife. It's being forwarded to France. In the second place, there's a letter from way up, full of questions about Mahlke. They're still working on it. I always knew that Mahlke had it in him. But he certainly hasn't let any grass grow under his feet. In the old days you had to be an officer if you wanted something nice to wrap around your neck, no matter how badly it ached. Nowadays every enlisted man gets his chance. He must be just about the youngest. Lord, when I think of him with those ears . . ."

537

At that point words began to roll out of my mouth. Then Winter spoke up. And Jürgen Kupka and Bansemer had their own two cents' worth to put in.

"Oh, Mahlke. We've known him for years."

"We had him in school."

"He had a weakness for neckwear when he was only fourteen."

"Christ, yes. Remember when he swiped that lieutenant commander's thingamajig off the hook in gym class. Here's how it . . . "

"Naw, you gotta begin with the phonograph."

"What about the canned goods? I suppose that was nothing. Right in the beginning he always wore a screwdriver . . ."

"Wait a minute! If you want to begin at the beginning, you'll have to go back to the Schlagball match in Heinrich Ehlers Field. Here's how it was: We're lying on the ground and Mahlke's asleep. So a gray cat comes creeping across the field, heading straight for Mahlke. And when the cat sees that neck bobbing up and down, she says to herself, my word, that's a mouse. And she jumps . . ."

"That's the bunk. Pilenz picked up the cat and put it . . . You going to tell me different?"

Two days later we had official confirmation. It was announced at morning roll call: A former Labor Service man from Tuchel-North battalion, serving first as a simple machine-gunner, then as a sergeant and tank commander, always in the thick of battle, strategically important position, so and so many Russian tanks, and furthermore, etcetera etcetera.

Our replacements were expected and we were beginning to turn in our rags when I received a clipping that my mother had cut out of the *Vorposten.* There it was printed in black and white: A son of our city, always in the thick of battle, first as a simple machine-gunner, later as a tank commander, and so on and so on.

Chapter XII

Marl, sand, glittering bogs, bushes, slanting groups of pines, ponds, hand grenades, carp, clouds over birches, partisans behind the broom, juniper juniper (good old Löns, the naturalist, had come from around there), the movie house in Tuchel—all were left behind. I took nothing with me but my cardboard suitcase and a little bunch of tired heather. Even during the trip I began irrationally but stubbornly to look for Mahlke, while throwing the heather between the tracks after Karthaus, in every suburban station and finally in Central Station, outside the ticket windows, in the crowds of soldiers who had poured out of the furlough trains, in the doorway of the control office, and in the streetcar to Langfuhr. I felt ridiculous in my outgrown civilian-schoolboy clothes and convinced that everyone could read my mind. I didn't go home—what had I to hope for at home?—but got out near our school, at the Sports Palace car stop.

I left my suitcase with the caretaker, but asked him no questions. Sure of what to expect, I raced up the big granite stairway, taking three or more steps at a time. Not that I expected to catch him in the auditorium—both doors stood open, but inside there were only cleaning women, upending the benches and scrubbing them—for whom? I turned off to the left: squat granite pillars good for cooling feverish foreheads. The marble memorial tablet for the dead of both wars: still quite a lot of room to spare. Lessing in his niche. Classes were in session, for the corridors were empty, except for one spindle-legged Fourth carrying a rolled map through the all-pervading octagonal stench. 3a—3b—art room—5a—glass case for stuffed mammals—what was in it now? A cat, of course. But where was the delirious mouse? Past the conference room. And there at the end of the corridor, with the bright front window at his back, between the secretariat and the principal's office, stood the Great Mahlke, mouseless—for from his neck hung that very special article, the abracadabra, the magnet, the exact opposite of an onion, the galvanized four-leaf clover, good old Schinkel's brain child, the trinket, the all-day sucker, the thingamajig, the Iwillnotutterit.

And the mouse? It was asleep, hibernating in June. Slumbering beneath a heavy blanket, for Mahlke had put on weight, Not that anyone, fate or an author, had erased or obliterated it, as Racine obliterated the rat from his escutcheon, tolerating only the swan. Mahlke's heraldic animal was still the mouse, which acted up in its dreams when Mahlke swallowed; for from time to time the Great Mahlke, notwithstanding his glorious decoration, had to swallow.

How he looked? I have said that he had filled out in action, not too much, about two thicknesses of blotting paper. You were half leaning, half sitting on the white enameled window sill. You were wearing the banditlike combination of black and field-gray, common to all those who served in the Tank Corps: gray bloused pants concealed the shafts of black, highly polished combat boots. The black, tight-fitting tanker's jacket bunched up under the arms, making them stand out like handles, but it was becoming even so and made you look frail in spite of the few pounds you had gained. No decorations on the jacket. And yet you had both Crosses and some other thing, but no wound insignia: the Virgin had made you invulnerable. It was perfectly understandable that there should be nothing on the chest to distract attention from the new eye-catcher. Around your waist a worn and negligently polished pistol belt, and below it only a hand's breadth of goods, for the tanker's jacket was very short, which is why it was sometimes called a monkey jacket. Sagging from the weight of the pistol, which hung down nearly to your ass, the belt relieved

539

the stiffness of your attitude and gave you a lopsided, jaunty look. But your gray field cap sat straight and severe without the then as now customary tilt; a rectilinear crease down the middle recalled your old love of symmetry and the part that divided your hair in your schoolboy and diving days, when you planned, or so you said, to become a clown. Nevertheless, the Redeemer's hairdo was gone. Even before curing your chronic throat trouble with a piece of metal, they must have given you the ludicrous brush cut which was then characteristic of recruits and today gives some of our pipe-smoking intellectuals their air of functional asceticism. But the countenance was still that of a redeemer: the eagle on your inflexibly vertical cap spread its wings over your brow like the dove of the Holy Ghost. Thin skin, sensitive to the light. Blackheads on fleshy nose. Lowered eyelids traversed by fine red veins. And when I stood breathless between you and the stuffed cat, your eyes scarcely widened.

A little joke: "Greetings, Sergeant Mahlke!"

My joke fell flat. "I'm waiting for Klohse. He's giving a math class somewhere."

"He'll be mighty pleased."

"I want to speak to him about the lecture."

"Have you been in the auditorium?"

"My lecture's ready, every word of it."

"Have you seen the cleaning women? They're scrubbing down the benches."

"I'll look in later with Klohse. We'll have to discuss the seating arrangement on the platform."

"He'll be mighty pleased."

"I'm going to suggest that they limit the audience to students from the lower Third up."

"Does Klohse know you're waiting?"

"Miss Hersching from the secretariat has gone in to tell him."

"Well, he'll be mighty pleased."

"My lecture will be short but full of action."

"I should think so. Good Lord, man, how did you swing it so quick?"

"Have a little patience, my dear Pilenz: all the circumstances will be discussed in my lecture."

"My, won't Klohse be pleased!"

"I'm going to ask him not to introduce me."

"Mallenbrandt maybe?"

"The proctor can announce the lecture. That's enough."

"Well, he'll be mighty . . ."

The bell signal leaped from floor to floor, announcing that classes were at an end. Only then did Mahlke open both eyes wide. Short, sparse lashes. His bearing was meant to be free and easy, but he was tensed to leap. Disturbed by something behind my back, I turned half toward the glass case: the cat wasn't gray, more on the black side. It crept unerringly toward us, disclosing a white bib. Stuffed cats are able to creep more convincingly than live ones. "The Domestic Cat," said a calligraphed cardboard sign. The bell stopped, an aggressive stillness set in; the mouse woke up and the cat took on more and more meaning. Consequently I cracked a little joke and another little joke in the direction of the window; I said something about his mother and his aunt; I talked, in order to give him courage, about his father, his father's locomotive, his father's death near Dirschau, and his father's posthumous award for bravery: "How happy your father would be if he were still alive!"

But before I had finished conjuring up Mahlke's father and persuading the mouse that there was no need to fear the cat, Dr. Waldemar Klohse, our principal, stepped between us with his high, smooth voice. Klohse uttered no congratulations, he didn't address Mahlke as Sergeant or Bearer of the Thingamajig, nor did he say, Mr. Mahlke, I am sincerely pleased. After envincing a pointed interest in my experience in the Labor Service and in the natural beauties of Tuchler Heath—"you will remember that Löns grew up there"—he sent a trim column of words marching over Mahlke's field cap: "So you see, Mahlke, you've made it after all. Have you been to the Horst Wessel School? My esteemed colleague, Dr. Wendt, will certainly be glad to see you. I feel sure that you will wish to deliver a little lecture for the benefit of your former schoolmates, to reinforce their confidence in our armed forces. Would you please step into my office for a moment?"

And the Great Mahlke, his arms raised like handles, followed Dr. Klohse into the principal's office and in the doorway whisked his cap off his stubblehead. Oh, that bumpy dome! A schoolboy in uniform on his way to a solemn conference, the outcome of which I did not wait for, although I was curious to know what the already wide-awake and enterprising mouse would say, after the interview, to that cat which though stuffed had never ceased to creep.

Nasty little triumph! Once again I enjoyed my moment of superiority. Just wait and see! He can't won't can't give in. I'll help him. I'll speak to Klohse. I'll find words to touch his heart. Too bad they've taken Papa Brunies to Stutthof. He'd come out with his good old Eichendorff in his pocket and extend a helping hand.

But no one could help Mahlke. Perhaps if I had spoken to Klohse. But I did speak to him; for half an hour I let him blow peppermint breath in my face. I was crushed, and my answer was very feeble: "By all reasonable standards, sir, you are probably right. But couldn't you in view of, I mean, in this particular case? On the one hand, I understand you perfectly. Yes, it can't be denied, a school has to have discipline. What's done can't be undone, but on the other hand, and because he was so young when he lost his father . . ."

And I spoke to Father Gusewski, and to Tulla, whom I asked to speak to Störtebeker and his gang. I went to see my former group leader in the Young Folk. He had a wooden leg from Crete and was sitting behind a desk in the section headquarters on Winterplatz. He was delighted with my proposal and cursed all schoolmasters: "Sure thing, we'll do it. Bring him over. I dimly remember him. Wasn't there some sort of trouble? Forget it. I'll drum up the biggest crowd I can. Even the League of German Girls and the Women's Association. I can get a hall across from the postal administration, seats three hundred and fifty . . ."

Father Gusewski wanted to gather his old ladies and a dozen Catholic workers in the sacristy, for the public meeting halls were not available to him.

"Perhaps, to bring his talk into line with the concerns of the Church," Father Gusewski suggested, "your friend could say something about St. George to begin with and conclude with a word or two about the power of prayer in times of great distress." He was eagerly looking forward to the lecture.

The young delinquents associated with Störtebeker and Tulla Pokriefke thought they had a cellar that would fill the bill. A youngster by the name of Rennwand, whom I knew slightly—he served as an altar boy in the Church of the Sacred Heart—spoke of the place in the most mysterious terms: Mahlke would need a safe-conduct and would have to surrender his pistol. "Of course we'll have to blindfold him on the way. And he'll have to sign a pledge not to tell a living soul, but that's a mere formality. Of course we'll pay well, either in cash or in Army watches. We don't do anything for nothing and we don't expect him to."

But Mahlke accepted none of these possibilities, and he was not interested in pay. I tried to prod him: "What do you want anyway? Nothing's good enough for you. Why don't you go out to Tuchel-North? There's a new batch of recruits. The room orderly and the cook remember you. I'm sure they'd be pleased as Punch to have you make a speech."

Mahlke listened calmly to all my suggestions, smiling in places, nodded assent, asked practical questions about organizing the meeting in question, and once the obstacles were disposed of, tersely and morosely rejected every single proposition, even an invitation from the regional party headquarters, for from the start he had but one aim in mind: the auditorium of our school. He wanted to stand in the dust-swarming light that trickled through Neo-Gothic ogival windows. He wanted to address the stench of three hundred schoolboys, farting high and farting low. He wanted the whetted scalps of his former teachers around him and behind him. He wanted to face the oil painting at the end of the auditorium, showing Baron von Conradi, founder of the school, caseous and immortal beneath heavy varnish. He wanted to enter the auditorium through one of the old-brown folding doors and after a brief, perhaps pointed speech, to leave through the other; but Klohse, in knickers with small checks, stood barring both doors at once: "As a soldier, Mahlke, you ought to realize. No, the cleaning women were scrubbing the benches for no particular reason, not for you, not for your lecture. Your plan may have been excellently conceived, but it cannot be executed. Remember this, Mahlke: There are many mortals who love expensive carpets but are condemned to die on plain floorboards. You must learn renunciation, Mahlke."

Klohse compromised just a little. He called a meeting of the faculties of both schools, which decided that "Disciplinary considerations make it imperative . . ."

And the Board of Education confirmed Klohse's report to the effect that a former student, whose past history, even though he, but particularly in view of the troubled and momentous times, though without wishing to exaggerate the importance of an offense which, it must be admitted, was none too recent, nevertheless and because the case is unique of its kind, the faculty of both schools has agreed that . . .

And Klohse wrote a purely personal letter. And Mahlke read that Klohse was not free to act as his heart desired. Unfortunately, the times and circumstances were such that an experienced schoolmaster, conscious of his professional responsibilities, could not follow the simple, paternal dictates of his heart; in the interests of the school, he must request manly co-operation in conformity to the old Conradinian spirit; he would gladly attend the lecture which Mahlke, soon, he hoped, and without bitterness, would deliver at the Horst Wessel School; unless he preferred, like a true hero, to choose the better part of speech and remain silent.

But the Great Mahlke had started down a path resembling that tunnel-like, overgrown, thorny, and birdless path in Oliva Castle Park, which had no forks or byways but was nonetheless a labyrinth. In the daytime he slept, played backgammon with his aunt, or sat listless and inactive, apparently waiting for his furlough to be over. But at night he crept with me—I behind him, never ahead of him, seldom by his side —through the Langfuhr night. Our wanderings were not aimless: we concentrated on Baumbachallee, a quiet, genteel, conscientiously blacked-out lane, where nightingales sang and Dr. Klohse lived. I weary behind his uniformed back: "Don't be an ass. You can see it's impossible. And what difference does it make? The few days' furlough you've got left. Good Lord, man, don't be an ass. . . ."

But the Great Mahlke wasn't interested in my tedious appeals to reason. He had a different melody in his protuberant ears. Until two in the morning we besieged Baumbachallee and its two nightingales. Twice

543

he was not alone, and we had to let him pass. But when after four nights of vigilance, at about eleven o'clock, Dr. Klohse turned in from Schwarzer Weg alone, tall and thin in knickers but without hat or coat, for the air was balmy, and came striding up Baumbachallee, the Great Mahlke's left hand shot out and seized Klohse's shirt collar with its civilian tie. He pushed the schoolman against the forged-iron fence, behind which bloomed roses whose fragrance—because it was so dark—was overpowering, louder even than the voices of the nightingales. And taking the advice Klohse had given him in his letter, Mahlke chose the better part of speech, heroic silence; without a word he struck the school principal's smooth-shaven face left right with the back and palm of his hand. Both men stiff and formal. Only the sound of the slaps alive and eloquent; for Klohse too kept his small mouth closed, not wishing to mix peppermint breath with the scent of the roses.

That happened on a Thursday and took less than a minute. We left Klohse standing by the iron fence. That is to say, Mahlke about-faced and strode in his combat boots across the gravel-strewn sidewalk beneath the red maple tree, which was not red at night but formed a black screen between us and the sky. I tried to give Klohse something resembling an apology, for Mahlke—and for myself. The slapped man waved me away; he no longer looked slapped but stood stiff as a ramrod, his dark silhouette, sustained by roses and the voices of rare birds, embodying the school, its founder, the Conradinian spirit, the Conradinum; for that was the name of our school.

After that we raced through lifeless suburban streets, and from that moment on neither of us had a word to spare for Klohse. Mahlke talked and talked, with exaggerated coolness, of problems that seemed to trouble him at that age—and myself, too, to some extent. Such as: Is there a life after death? Or: Do you believe in transmigration? "I've been reading quite a bit of Kierkegaard lately," he informed me. And "you must be sure to read Dostoevski. Later, when you're in Russia. It will help you to understand all sorts of things, the mentality and so on."

Several times we stood on bridges across the Striessbach, a rivulet full of horse leeches. It was pleasant to lean over the railing and wait for rats. Each bridge made the conversation shift from schoolboy banalities —erudition, for instance, about the armor plate, firepower, and speed of the world's battleships—to religion and the so-called last questions. On the little Neuschottland bridge we gazed for a long while at the star-studded June sky and then—each for himself—into the stream. Mahlke in an undertone, while below us the shallow outlet of Aktien Pond, carrying away the yeasty vapors of Aktien Brewery, broke over shoals of tin cans: "Of course I don't believe in God. He's just a swindle to stultify the people. The only thing I believe in is the Virgin Mary. That's why I'm never going to get married."

There was a sentence succinct and insane enough to be spoken on a bridge. It has stayed with me. Whenever a brook or canal is spanned by a small bridge, whenever there is a gurgling down below and water breaking against the rubbish which disorderly people the world over throw from bridges into rivulets and canals, Mahlke stands beside me in combat boots and tanker's monkey jacket, leaning over the rail so that the big thingamajig on his neck hangs down vertical, a solemn clown triumphing over cat and mouse with his irrefutable faith: "Of course not in God. A swindle to stultify the people. There's only Mary. I'll never get married."

And he uttered a good many more words which fell into the Striessbach. Possibly we circled Max-Halbe-Platz ten times, raced twelve times up and down Heeresanger. Stood undecided at the terminus of Line No. 5. Looked on, not without hunger, as the streetcar conductors and marcelled conductorettes, sitting in the blued-out trailer, bit into sandwiches and drank out of thermos bottles.

. . . and then came a car—or should have—in which the conductorette under the cocked cap was Tulla Pokriefke, who had been drafted as a wartime helper several weeks before. We'd have spoken to her and I would certainly have made a date with her if she had been working on Line No. 5. But as it was, we saw only her little profile behind the dark-blue glass and we were not sure.

I said: "You ought to give it a try with her."

Mahlke, tormented: "I just told you that I'm never going to get married."

I: "It would cheer you up."

He: "And who's going to cheer me up afterward?"

I tried to joke: "The Virgin Mary of course."

He had misgivings: "What if she's offended?"

I offered my help. "If you want me to, I'll be Gusewski's altar boy tomorrow morning."

I was amazed at the alacrity with which he said: "It's a deal!" And he went off toward the trailer which still held out the promise of Tulla Pokriefke's profile in a conductor's cap. Before he got in, I called out: "Say, how much more furlough have you got left?"

And from the door of the trailer the Great Mahlke said: "My train left four and a half hours ago. If nothing has gone wrong, it must be pulling into Modlin."

Chapter XIII

"Misereatur vestri omnipotens Deus, et, dimissis peccatis vestris . . ." The words issued light as a soap bubble from Father Gusewski's pursed lips, glittered in all the colors of the rainbow, swayed hesitantly, broke loose from the hidden reed, and rose at last, mirroring windows, the altar, the Virgin,

mirroring you me everything—and burst painlessly, struck by the bubbles of the absolution: *"Indulgentiam, absolutionem et remissionem peccatorum vestrorum . . ."* and the moment these new bubbles of spirit were pricked in their turn by the Amen of the seven or eight faithful, Gusewski elevated the host and began with full-rounded lips to blow the big bubble, the bubble of bubbles. For a moment it trembled terror-stricken in the draft; then with the bright-red tip of his tongue, he sent it aloft; and it rose and rose until at length it fell and passed away, close to the second pew facing the altar of Our Lady: *"Ecce Agnus Dei . . ."*

Of those taking communion, Mahlke was first to kneel. He knelt before the "LordIamnotworthythatthoushouldstenterundermyroof" had been repeated three times. Even before I steered Gusewski down the altar steps to the communicants' rail, he leaned his head back, so that his face, peaked after a sleepless night, lay parallel to the whitewashed concrete ceiling, and parted his lips with his tongue. A moment's wait, while over his head the priest makes a small quick sign of the Cross with the wafer intended for this communicant. Sweat oozed from Mahlke's pores and formed glistening beads which quickly broke, punctured by the stubble of his beard. His eyes stood out as though boiled. Possibly the blackness of his tanker's jacket enhanced the pallor of his face. Despite the wooliness of his tongue, he did not swallow. In humble self-effacement the iron object that had rewarded his childish scribbling and crossing-out of so and so many Russian tanks, crossed itself and lay motionless over his top collar button. It was only when Father Gusewski laid the host on Mahlke's tongue and Mahlke partook of the light pastry, that you swallowed; and then the thingamajig joined in.

Let us all three celebrate the sacrament, once more and forever: You kneel, I stand behind dry skin. Sweat distends your pores. The reverend father deposits the host on your coated tongue. All three of us have just ended on the same syllable, whereupon a mechanism pulls your tongue back in. Lips stick together. Propagation of sobs, the big thingamajig trembles, and I know that the Great Mahlke will leave St. Mary's Chapel fortified, his sweat will dry; if immediately afterward drops of moisture glistened on his face, they were raindrops. It was drizzling.

In the dry sacristy Gusewski said: "He must be waiting outside. Maybe we should call him in, but . . ."

I said: "Don't worry, Father. I'll take care of him."

Gusewski, his hands busy with the sachets of lavender in the closet: "You don't think he'll do anything rash?"

For once I made no move to help him out of his vestments: "You'd better keep out of it, Father." But to Mahlke, when he stood before me wet in his uniform, I said: "You damn fool, what are you hanging around here for? Get down to the assembly point on Hochstriess. Tell them some story about missing your train. I refuse to have anything to do with it."

With those words I should have left him, but I stayed and got wet. Rain is a binder. I tried to reason with him: "They won't bite your head off if you're quick about it. Tell them something was wrong with your mother or your aunt."

Mahlke nodded when I made a point, let his lower jaw sag from time to time, and laughed for no reason. Then suddenly he bubbled over: "It was wonderful last night with the Pokriefke kid. I wouldn't have thought it. She's not the way she puts on. All right, I'll tell you the honest truth: it's because of her that I don't want to go back. Seems to me that I've done my bit—wouldn't you say so? I'm going to put in a petition. They can ship me out to Gross-Boschpol as an instructor. Let other people be brave. It's not that I'm scared, I've just had enough. Can you understand that?"

I refused to fall for his nonsense; I pinned him down. "Oho, so it's all on account of the Pokriefke kid. Hell, that wasn't her. She works on the No. 2 Line to Oliva, not on the No. 5. Everybody knows that. You're scared shitless, that's all. I can see how you feel."

He was determined that there should be something between them. "You can take my word for it about Tulla. The fact is she took me home with her, lives on Elsenstrasse. Her mother doesn't mind. But you're right, I've had my bellyful. Maybe I'm scared too. I was scared before Mass. It's better now."

"I thought you didn't believe in God and all that stuff."

"That's got nothing to do with it."

"OK, forget it. And now what?"

"Maybe Störtebeker and the boys could . . . You know them pretty well, don't you?"

"No dice. I'm having no further dealings with those characters. It's not healthy. You should have asked the Pokriefke kid in case you really . . ."

"Wise up. I can't show my face on Osterzeile. If they're not there already, it won't be long say, could I hide in your cellar, just for a few days?"

That too struck me as unhealthy. "You've got other places to hide. What about your relatives in the country? Or in Tulla's uncle's woodshed. . . . Or on the barge."

For a while the word hung in mid-air. "In this filthy weather?" Mahlke said. But the thing was already decided; and though I refused stubbornly and prolixly to go with him, though I too spoke of the filthy weather, it gradually became apparent that I would have to go: rain is a binder.

We spent a good hour tramping from Neuschottland to Schellmühl and back, and then down the endless Posedowskiweg. We took shelter in the lee of at least two advertising pillars, bearing always the same

547

posters warning the public against those sinister and unpatriotic figures Coalthief and Spendthrift, and then we resumed our tramp. From the main entrance of the Women's Hospital we saw the familiar backdrop: behind the railroad embankment, the gable roof and spire of the sturdy old Conradinum; but he wasn't looking or he saw something else. Then we stood for half an hour in the shelter of the Reichskolonie car stop, under the echoing tin roof with three or four grade-school boys. At first they spent the time roughhousing and pushing each other off the bench. Mahlke had his back turned to them, but it didn't help. Two of them came up with open copybooks and said something in broad dialect. "Aren't you supposed to be in school?" I asked.

"Not until nine. In case we decide to go."

"Well, hand them over, but make it fast."

Mahlke wrote his name and rank in the upper left-hand corner of the last page of both copybooks. They were not satisfied, they wanted the exact number of tanks he had knocked out—and Mahlke gave in; as though filling out a money order blank, he wrote the number first in figures, then in letters. Then he had to write his piece in two more copybooks. I was about to take back my fountain pen when one of the kids asked: "Where'd you knock 'em off, in Bjälgerott [Byelgorod] or Schietemier [Zhitomir]?"

Mahlke ought just to have nodded and they would have subsided. But he whispered in a hoarse voice: "No, most of them around Kovel, Brody, and Brzezany. And in April when we knocked out the First Armored Corps at Buczacz."

The youngsters wanted it all in writing and again I had to unscrew the fountain pen. They called two more of their contemporaries in out of the rain. It was always the same back that held still for the others to write on. He wanted to stretch, he would have liked to hold out his own copybook; they wouldn't let him: there's always one fall guy. Mahlke had to write Kovel and Brody-Brzezany, Cherkassy and Buczacz. His hand shook more and more, and again the sweat oozed from his pores. Questions spurted from their grubby faces: "Was ya in Kriewäurock [Krivoi Rog] too?" Every mouth open. In every mouth teeth missing. Paternal grandfather's eyes. Ears from the mother's side. And each one had nostrils: "And where dya think they'll send ya next?"

"He ain't allowed to tell. What's the use of asking?"

"I bet he's gonna be in the invasion."

"They're keepin 'im for after the war."

"Ask him if he's been at the Führer's HQ?"

"How about it, Uncle?"

"Can't you see he's a sergeant?"

"You gotta picture?"

"'Cause we collect 'em."

"How much more furlough time ya got?"

"Yeah, whenner ya leavin?"

"Ya still be here tomorrow?"

"Yeah, when's yer time up?"

Mahlke fought his way out, stumbling over satchels. My fountain pen stayed in the shelter. Marathon through crosshatching. Side by side through puddles: rain is a binder. It was only after we passed the stadium that the boys fell back. But still they shouted after us; they had no intention of going to school. To this day they want to return my fountain pen.

When we reached the kitchen gardens outside Neuschottland, we stopped to catch our breath. I had a rage inside me and my rage was getting kittens. I thrust an accusing forefinger at the accursed thingamajig and Mahlke quickly removed it from his neck. Like the screwdriver years before, it was attached to a shoelace. Mahlke wanted to give it to me, but I shook my head. "Hell, no, but thanks for nothing."

But he didn't toss the scrap metal into the wet bushes; he had a back pocket.

How am I going to get out of here? The gooseberries behind the makeshift fences were unripe: Mahlke began to pick with both hands. My pretext cast about for words. He gobbled and spat out skins. "Wait for me here, I'll be back in half an hour. You've got to have something to eat or you won't last long on the barge."

If Mahlke had said "Be sure you come back," I would have lit out for good. He scarcely nodded as I left; with all ten fingers he was reaching through the fence laths at the bushes; his mouth full of berries, he compelled loyalty: rain is a binder.

Mahlke's aunt opened the door. Good that his mother wasn't home. I could have taken some edibles from our house, but I thought: What's he got his family for? Besides, I was curious about his aunt. I was disappointed. She stood there in her kitchen apron and asked no questions. Through open doors came the smell of something that makes teeth squeak: rhubarb was being cooked at the Mahlkes'.

"We're giving a little party for Joachim. We've got plenty of stuff to drink, but in case we get hungry . . ."

Without a word she went to the kitchen and came back with two two-pound cans of pork. She also had a can opener, but it wasn't the same one that Mahlke had brought up from the barge when he found the canned frogs' legs in the galley. While she was out wondering what to give me—the Mahlkes always had their cupboards full, relatives in the country—I stood restless in the hallway, gazing at the photograph of Mahlke's father and Fireman Labuda. The locomotive had no steam up.

The aunt came back with a shopping net and some newspaper to wrap the cans and can opener in. "Before you eat the pork," she said, "you'll have to warm it up some. If you don't, it'll be too heavy; it'll sit on your stomach."

If I asked before leaving whether anyone had been around asking for Joachim, the answer was no. But I didn't ask, I just turned around in the doorway and said: "Joachim sends you his love," though Mahlke hadn't sent anything at all, not even to his mother.

He wasn't curious either when I reappeared between the gardens in the same rain, hung the net on a fence lath, and stood rubbing my strangled fingers. He was still gobbling unripe gooseberries, compelling me, like his aunt, to worry about his physical well-being: "You're going to upset your stomach. Let's get going." But even then he stripped three handfuls from the dripping bushes and filled his pants pockets. As we looped around Neuschottland and the housing development between Wolfsweg and Bärenweg, he was still spitting out hard gooseberry skins. As we stood on the rear platform of the streetcar trailer and the rainy airfield passed by to the left of us, he was still pouring them in.

He was getting on my nerves with his gooseberries. Besides, the rain was letting up. The gray turned milky; made me feel like getting out and leaving him alone with his gooseberries. But I only said: "They've already come asking about you. Two plain-clothes men."

"Really?" He spat out the skins on the platform floor. "What about my mother? Does she know?"

"Your mother wasn't there. Only your aunt."

"Must have been shopping."

"I doubt it."

"Then she was over at the Schielkes' helping with the ironing."

"I'm sorry to say she wasn't there either."

"Like some gooseberries?"

"She's been taken down to the military district. I wasn't going to tell you."

We were almost in Brösen before Mahlke ran out of gooseberries. But as we crossed the beach, in which the rain had cut its pattern, he was still searching his sopping pockets for more. And when the Great Mahlke heard the sea slapping against the beach and his eyes saw the Baltic, the barge as a far-off backdrop, and the shadows of a few ships in the roadstead, he said: "I can't swim." Though I had already taken off my shoes and pants. The horizon drew a line through both his pupils.

"Is this a time to make jokes?"

"No kidding. I've got a bellyache. Damn gooseberries."

At this I swore and looked through my pockets and swore some more and found a mark and a little change. I ran to Brösen and rented a boat for two hours from old man Kreft. It wasn't as easy as it looks on paper, though Kreft didn't ask very many questions and helped me to launch the boat. When I pulled up on the beach, Mahlke lay writhing in the sand, uniform and all. I had to kick him to make him get up. He shivered, sweated, dug both fists into the pit of his stomach; but even today I can't make myself believe in that bellyache in spite of unripe gooseberries on an empty stomach.

"Why don't you go behind the dunes? Go ahead. On the double!" He walked hunched over, making curved tracks, and disappeared behind the beach grass. Maybe I could have seen his cap, but though nothing was moving in or out, I kept my eyes on the breakwater. When he came back, he was still hunched over but he helped me to shove off. I sat him down in the stern, stowed the net with the cans in it on his knees, and put the wrapped can opener in his hands. When the water darkened behind the second sandbank I said: "Now *you* can take a few strokes."

The Great Mahlke didn't even shake his head; he sat doubled up, clutching the wrapped can opener and looking through me; for we were sitting face to face.

Although I have never again to this day set foot in a rowboat, we are still sitting face to face: and his fingers are fidgeting. His neck is bare, but his cap straight. Sand trickling from the folds in his uniform. No rain, but forehead dripping. Every muscle tense. Eyes popping out of his head. With whom has he exchanged noses? Both knees wobbling. No cat offshore. But the mouse scurrying.

Yet it wasn't cold. Only when the clouds parted and the sun burst through the seams did spots of gooseflesh pass over the scarcely breathing surface of the water and assail our boat. "Take a few strokes, it'll warm you up." The answer was a chattering of teeth from the stern. And from intermittent groans chopped words were born into the world: ". . . fat lot of good did me. Might have guessed. Fuss for a lot of nonsense. Too bad. It would have been a good lecture. Would have started in with explanations, the sights, armor-piercing shells, Maybach engines, and so on. When I was a loader, I had to come up all the time to tighten up bolts, even under fire. But I wasn't going to talk about myself the whole time. My father and Labuda, the fireman. A few words about the accident near Dirschau. How my father by his courage and self-sacrifice. The way I always thought of my father as I sat there at the sights. Hadn't even received the sacraments when he. Thanks for the candles that time. O thou, most pure. Mother inviolate. Through whose intercession partake. Most amiable. Full of grace. It's the honest truth. My first battle north of Kursk proved it. And in the tangle outside Orel when they counter-attacked. And in August by the Vorskla the way the Mother of God. They all laughed and put the division chaplain on my tail. Sure, but then we stabilized the front. Unfortunately, I was transferred to Center Sector, or they wouldn't have broken through so quick at Kharkov. She appeared to me again near Korosten when the 59th Corps. She never had the child, it was always the picture she was holding. Yes, Dr. Klohse, it's hanging in our hall beside the brush bag. And she didn't hold it over her breast, no, lower down. I had the locomotive in my sights, plain as day. Just had to hold steady between my father and Labuda. Four hundred. Direct hit. See that, Pilenz? I always aim between turret and boiler. Gives them a good airing. No, Dr. Klohse, she didn't speak. But to tell you the honest truth, she doesn't have to speak to me. Proofs? She held the picture, I tell you. Or in mathematics. Suppose you're teaching math. You assume that parallel lines meet at infinity. You'll admit that adds up to something like transcendence. That's how it was that time in the second line east of Kazan. It was the third day of Christmas. She came in from the left and headed for a clump of woods at convoy speed, twenty miles an hour. Just had to keep her in my sights. Hey, Pilenz, two strokes on the left, we're missing the barge."

At first Mahlke's outline of his lecture was little more than a chattering of teeth, but then he had them under control. Through it all he kept an eye on our course. The rhythm at which he spoke made me row so fast that the sweat poured from my forehead, while his pores dried and called it a day. Not for a single stroke was I sure whether or not he saw anything more over the expanding bridge than the customary gulls.

Before we hove alongside, he sat relaxed in the stern playing negligently with the can opener, which he had taken out of its paper. He no longer complained of bellyache. He stood before me on the barge, and when I had tied up, his hands busied themselves on his neck: the big thingamajig from his rear pocket was in place again. Rubbed his hands, the sun broke through, stretched his legs: Mahlke paced the deck as though taking possession, hummed a snatch of litany, waved up at the gulls, and played the cheery uncle who turns up for a visit after years of adventurous absence, bringing himself as a present. O happy reunion! "Hello, boys and girls, you haven't changed a bit!"

I found it hard to join in the game: "Get a move on. Old man Kreft only gave me the boat for an hour and a half. At first he said only an hour."

Mahlke calmed down: "OK, never detain a busy man. Say, do you see that bucket, the one next to the tanker, she's lying pretty low. I'll bet she's a Swede. Just for your information, we're going to row out there as soon as it gets dark. I want you back here at nine o'clock. I've a right to ask that much of you—or haven't I?"

The visibility was poor and of course it was impossible to make out the nationality of the freighter in the roadstead. Mahlke began to undress elaborately, meanwhile spouting a lot of incoherent nonsense. A few words about Tulla Pokriefke: "A hot number, take it from me." Gossip about Father Gusewski: "They say he sold goods on the black market. Altar cloths too. Or rather the coupons for the stuff." A couple of funny stories about his aunt: "But you've got to give her credit for one thing, she always got along with my father, even when they were both kids in the country." More about the locomotive: "Say, you might drop back at our house and get the picture, with or without the frame. No, better let it go. Just weigh me down."

He stood there in red gym pants, a vestige of our school tradition. He had carefully folded his uniform into the regulation bundle and stowed it away in his old-accustomed place behind the pilothouse. His boots looked like bedtime. "You got everything?" I asked. "Don't forget the opener." He shifted the medal from left to right and chattered schoolboy nonsense as if he hadn't a care in the world: "Tonnage of the Argentine battleship *Moreno*? Speed in knots? How much armor plate at the water-line? Year built? When remodeled? How many hundred-and-fifty-mil-limeter guns on the *Vittorio Veneto*?"

I answered sluggishly, but I was pleased to find that I still had the dope. "Are you going to take both cans at once?"

"I'll see."

"Don't forget the can opener. There it is."

"You're looking out for me like a mother."

"Well, if I were you, I'd start going downstairs."

"Right you are. The place must be in a pretty sad state."

"You're not supposed to spend the winter there."

"The main thing is I hope the lighter works. There's plenty of alcohol."

"I wouldn't throw that thing away. Maybe you can sell it as a souvenir someplace. You never can tell."

Mahlke tossed the object from hand to hand. He slipped off the bridge and started looking step by step for the hatch, holding out his hands like a tightrope walker, though one arm was weighed down by the net with the two cans in it. His knees made bow waves. The sun broke through again for a moment and his backbone and the sinews in his neck cast a shadow to leftward.

"Must be half past ten. Maybe later."

"It's not as cold as I expected."

"It's always that way after the rain."

"My guess is water sixty-five, air sixty-eight."

There was a dredger in the channel, not far from the harbor-mouth buoy. Signs of activity on board, but the sounds were pure imagination, the wind was in the wrong direction. Mahlke's mouse was imaginary too, for even after his groping feet had found the rim of the hatch, he showed me only his back.

Over and over the same custom-made question dins into my ears: Did he say anything else before he went down? The only thing I am halfway sure of is that angular glance up at the bridge, over his left shoulder. He crouched down a moment to moisten himself, darkening the flag-red gym pants, and with his right hand improved his grip on the net with the tin cans—but what about the all-day sucker? It wasn't hanging from his neck. Had he thrown it away without my noticing? Where is the fish that will bring it to me? Did he say something more over his shoulder? Up at the gulls? Or toward the beach or the ships in the roadstead? Did he curse all rodents? I don't think I heard you say: "Well, see you tonight." Headfirst and weighed down with two cans of pork, he dove: the rounded back and the rear end followed the neck. A white foot kicked into the void. The water over the hatch resumed its usual rippling play.

Then I took my foot off the can opener. The can opener and I remained behind. If only I had got right into the boat, cast off and away: "Hell, he'll manage without it." But I stayed, counting the seconds. I let the dredger with its rising and falling chain buckets count for me, and frantically followed its count: thirty-two, thirty-three rusty seconds. Thirty-six, thirty-seven mud-heaving seconds. For forty-one, forty-two badly oiled seconds, forty-seven, forty-eight, forty-nine seconds, the dredger with its rising, falling, dipping buckets did what it could: deepened the Neufahrwasser harbor channel and helped me measure the time: Mahlke, with his cans of pork but no can opener, with or without the black candy whose sweetness had bitterness for a twin, must by then have moved into the erstwhile radio shack of the Polish mine sweeper *Rybitwa*.

Though we had not arranged for any signals, you might have knocked. Once again and again once again, I let the dredger count thirty seconds for me. By all calculable odds, or whatever the expression is, he must have . . . The gulls, cutting out patterns between barge and sky, were getting on my nerves. But when for no apparent reason the gulls suddenly veered away, the absence of gulls got on my nerves. I began, first with my heels, then with Mahlke's boots, to belabor the deck of the bridge: flakes of rust went flying, crumbs of gull dropping danced at every blow. Can opener in hammering fist, Pilenz shouted: "Come up! You've forgotten the can opener, the can opener. . . ." Wild, then rhythmic shouting and hammering. Then a pause. Unfortunately, I didn't know Morse code. Two-three two-three, I hammered. Shouted myself hoarse: "Can o-pen-er! Can open-er!"

Ever since that Friday I've known what silence is. Silence sets in when gulls veer away. Nothing can make more silence than a dredger at work when the wind carries away its iron noises. But it was Joachim

Mahlke who made the greatest silence of all by not responding to my noise.

So then I rowed back. But before rowing back, I threw the can opener in the direction of the dredger, but didn't hit it.

So then I threw away the can opener and rowed back, returned old man Kreft's boat, had to pay an extra thirty pfennigs, and said: "Maybe I'll be back again this evening. Maybe I'll want the boat again."

So then I threw away, rowed back, returned, paid extra, said I'd be, sat down in the streetcar and rode, as they say, home.

So then I didn't go straight home after all, but rang the doorbell on Osterzeile, I asked no questions, just got them to give me the locomotive and frame, for hadn't I said to Mahlke and to old man Kreft too for that matter: "Maybe I'll be back again this evening. . . ."

So my mother had just finished making lunch when I came home with the photograph. One of the heads of the labor police at the railroad car factory was eating with us. There was no fish, and beside my plate there was a letter for me from the military district.

So then I read and read my draft notice. My mother began to cry, which embarrassed the company. "I won't be leaving until Sunday night," I said, and then, paying no attention to our visitor: "Do you know what's become of Papa's binoculars?"

So then, with binoculars and photograph, I rode out to Brösen on Saturday morning, and not that same evening as agreed—the fog would have spoiled the visibility, and it was raining again. I picked out the highest spot on the wooded dunes, in front of the Soldiers' Monument. I stood on the top step of the platform—above me towered the obelisk crowned with its golden ball, sheenless in the rain—and for half if not three quarters of an hour I held the binoculars to my eyes. It was only when everything turned to a blur that I lowered the glasses and looked into the dog-rose bushes.

So nothing was moving on the barge. Two empty combat boots were clearly distinguishable. Gulls still hovered over the rust, then gulls settled like powder on deck and shoes. In the roadstead the same ships as the day before. But no Swede among them, no neutral ship of any kind. The dredger had scarcely moved. The weather seemed to be on the mend. Once again I rode, as they say, home. My mother helped me to pack my cardboard suitcase.

So then I packed: I had removed the photograph from the frame and, since you hadn't claimed it, packed it at the bottom. On top of your father, on top of Fireman Labuda and your father's locomotive that had no steam up, I piled my underwear, the usual rubbish, and the diary which was lost near Cottbus along with the photograph and my letters.

* * *

555

Who will supply me with a good ending? For what began with cat and mouse torments me today in the form of crested terns on ponds bordered with rushes. Though I avoid nature, educational films show me these clever aquatic birds. Or the newsreels make me watch attempts to raise sunken freight barges in the Rhine or underwater operations in Hamburg harbor: it seems they are blasting the fortifications near the Howald Shipyard and salvaging aerial mines. Men go down with flashing, slightly battered helmets, men rise to the surface. Arms are held out toward them, the helmet is unscrewed, removed: but never does the Great Mahlke light a cigarette on the flickering screen; it's always somebody else who lights up.

When a circus comes to town, it can count on me as a customer. I know them all, or just about; I've spoken with any number of clowns in private, out behind the trailers; but usually they have no sense of humor, and if they've ever heard of a colleague named Mahlke, they won't admit it.

I may as well add that in October 1959 I went to Regensburg to a meeting of those survivors of the war who, like you, had made Knight's Cross. They wouldn't admit me to the hall. Inside, a Bundeswehr band was playing, or resting between pieces. During one such imtermission, I had the lieutenant in charge of the order squad page you from the music platform: "Sergeant Mahlke is wanted at the entrance." But you didn't show up. You didn't surface.

DOG YEARS

Walter Henn
IN MEMORIAM

Book
One

Morning Shifts

First Morning Shift

You tell. No, you. Or you. Should the actor begin? Or the scarecrows, all at cross purposes? Or should we wait until the eight planets have collected in the sign of Aquarius? You begin, please. After all it was your dog. But before my dog, your dog and the dog descended from the dog. One of us has to begin: You or he or you or I . . . Many many sunsets ago, long before we existed, the Vistula flowed day in day out without reflecting us, and emptied forever and ever.

The present writer bears the name of Brauxel at the moment and runs a mine which produces neither potash, iron, nor coal, yet employs, from one shift to the next, a hundred and thirty-four workers and office help in galleries and drifts, in stalls and crosscuts, in the payroll office and packing house.

In former days the Vistula flowed dangerously, without regulation. And so a thousand day laborers were taken on, and in the year 1895 they dug the so-called cut, running northward from Einlage between Schiewenhorst and Nickelswalde, the two villages on the delta bar. By giving the Vistula a new estuary, straight as a die, this diminished the danger of floods.

The present writer usually writes Brauksel in the form of Castrop-Rauxel and occasionally of Häksel. When he's in the mood, Brauxel writes his name as Weichsel, the river which the Romans called the Vistula. There is no contradiction between playfulness and pedantry; the one brings on the other.

The Vistula dikes ran from horizon to horizon; under the supervision of the Dike Commission in Marienwerder, it was their business to withstand the spring floods, not to mention the St. Dominic's Day floods. And woe betide if there were mice in the dikes.

The present writer, who runs a mine and writes his name in various ways, has mapped out the course of the Vistula before and after regulation on an empty desk top: tobacco crumbs and powdery ashes indicate the river and its three mouths; burnt matches are the dikes that hold it on its course.

Many many sunsets ago; here comes the Dike Commissioner on his way from the district of Kulm, where the dike burst in '55 near Kokotzko, not far from the Mennonite cemetery—weeks later the coffins were still hanging in the trees—but he, on foot, on horseback, or in a boat, in his morning coat and never without his bottle of arrack in his wide pocket, he, Wilhelm Ehrenthal, who in classical yet humorous verses had written that "Epistle on the Contemplation of Dikes," a copy of which, soon after publication, was sent with an amiable dedication to all dike keepers, village mayors, and Mennonite preachers, he, here named never to be named again, inspects the dike tops, the enrockment and the groins, and drives off the pigs, because according to the Rural Police Regulations of November 1848, Clause 8, all animals, furred and feathered, are forbidden to graze and burrow on the dike.

The sun goes down on the left. Brauxel breaks a match into pieces: the second mouth of the Vistula came into being without the help of diggers on February 2, 1840, when in consequence of an ice jam the river broke through the delta bar below Plehnendorf, swept away two villages, and made it possible to establish two new fishing villages, East Neufähr and West Neufähr. Yet rich as the two Neufährs may be in tales, gossip, and startling events, we are concerned chiefly with the villages to the east and west of the first, though most recent, mouth: Schiewenhorst and Nickelswalde were, or are, the last villages with ferry service to the right and left of the Vistula cut; for five hundred yards downstream the sea still mingles its 1.8 percent saline solution with the often ash-gray, usually mud-yellow excretion of the far-flung republic of Poland.

Brauxel mutters conjuring words: "The Vistula is a broad stream, growing constantly broader in memory, navigable in spite of its many sandbanks . . ."—moves a piece of eraser in guise of a ferry back and forth across his desk top, which has been transformed into a graphic Vistula delta, and, now that the morning shift has been lowered, now that the sparrow-strident day has begun, puts the nine-year-old Walter Matern—accent on the last syllable—down on top of the Nickelswalde dike across from the setting sun; he is grinding his teeth.

What happens when the nine-year-old son of a miller stands on a dike, watching the river, exposed to the setting sun, grinding his teeth against the wind? He has inherited that from his grandmother, who sat riveted to her chair for nine years, able to move only her eyeballs.

All sorts of things rush by in the river and Walter Matern sees them. Flood from Montau to Käsemark. Here, just before the mouth, the sea helps. They say there were mice in the dike. Whenever a dike bursts, there's talk of mice in the dike. The Mennonites say that Catholics from the Polish country put mice in the dike during the night. Others claim to have seen the dike keeper on his white horse. But the insurance company refuses to believe either in burrowing mice or in the dike keeper from

Güttland. When the mice made the dike burst, the white horse, so the legend has it, leapt into the rising waters with the dike keeper, but it didn't help much: for the Vistula took all the dike keepers. And the Vistula took the Catholic mice from the Polish country. And it took the rough Mennonites with hooks and eyes but without pockets, took the more refined Mennonites with buttons, buttonholes, and diabolical pockets, it also took Güttland's three Protestants and the teacher, the Socialist. It took Güttland's lowing cattle and Güttland's carved cradles, it took all Güttland: Güttland's beds and Güttland's cupboards, Güttland's clocks and Güttland's canaries, it took Güttland's preacher—he was a rough man with hooks and eyes; it also took the preacher's daughter, and she is said to have been beautiful.

All that and more rushed by. What does a river like the Vistula carry away with it? Everything that goes to pieces: wood, glass, pencils, pacts between Brauxel and Brauchsel, chairs, bones, and sunsets too. What had long been forgotten rose to memory, floating on its back or stomach, with the help of the Vistula: Pomeranian princes. Adalbert came. Adalbert comes on foot and dies by the ax. But Duke Swantopolk allowed himself to be baptized. What will become of Mestwin's daughters? Is one of them running away barefoot? Who will carry her off? The giant Miligedo with his lead club? Or one of the ancient gods? The fiery-red Perkunos? The pale Pikollos, who is always looking up from below? The boy Potrimpos laughs and chews at his ear of wheat. Sacred oaks are felled. Grinding teeth— And Duke Kynstute's young daughter, who entered a convent: twelve headless knights and twelve headless nuns are dancing in the mill: the mill turns slow, the mill turns faster, it grinds the little souls to plaster; the mill turns slow, the mill speeds up, she has drunk with twelve knights from the selfsame cup; the mill turns slow, the mill speeds up, twelve knights twelve nuns in the cellar sup; the mill turns slow, the mill turns faster, they're feasting Candlemas with farting and laughter: the mill turns slow, the mill turns faster . . . but when the mill was burning inside and out and coaches for headless knights and headless nuns drove up, when much later—sunsets—St. Bruno passed through the fire and Bobrowski the robber with his crony Materna, with whom it all began, set fires in houses that had been previously notched —sunsets, sunsets—Napoleon before and after: then the city was ingeniously besieged, for several times they tried out Congreve rockets, with varying success: but in the city and on the walls, on Wolf, Bear, and Bay Horse Bastions, on Renegade, Maidenhole, and Rabbit Bastions, the French under Rapp coughed, the Poles under their Prince Radziwil spat, the corps of the one-armed Capitaine de Chambure hawked. But on the fifth of August came the St. Dominic's Flood, climbed Bay Horse, Rabbit, and Renegade Bastions without a ladder, wet the powder, made the

563

Congreve rockets fizzle out, and carried a good deal of fish, mostly pike, into the streets and kitchens: everyone was miraculously replenished, although the granaries along Hopfengasse had long since burned down —sunsets. Amazing how many things are becoming to the Vistula, how many things color a river like the Vistula: sunsets, blood, mud, and ashes. Actually the wind ought to have them. Orders are not always carried out; rivers that set out for heaven empty into the Vistula.

Second Morning Shift

Here, on Brauxel's desk top and over the Schiewenhorst dike, she rolls, day after day. And on Nickelswalde dike stands Walter Matern with grinding teeth; for the sun is setting. Swept bare, the dikes taper away in the distance. Only the sails of the windmills, blunt steeples, and poplars—Napoleon had those planted for his artillery—stick to the tops of the dikes. He alone is standing. Except maybe for the dog. But he's gone off, now here now there. Behind him, vanishing in the shadow and below the surface of the river, lies the Island, smelling of butter, curds, diaries, a wholesome, nauseatingly milky smell. Nine years old, legs apart, with red and blue March knees, stands Walter Matern, spreads his ten fingers, narrows his eyes to slits, lets the scars of his close-cropped head—bearing witness to falls, fights, and barbed wire—swell, take on profile, grinds his teeth from left to right—he has that from his grandmother—and looks for a stone.

There aren't any stones on the dike. But he looks. He finds dry sticks. But you can't throw a dry stick against the wind. And he wants to got to wants to throw something. He could whistle for Senta, here one second gone the next, but he does no such thing, all he does is grind—that blunts the wind—and feel like throwing something. He could catch Amsel's eye at the foot of the dike with a hey and a ho, but his mouth is full of grinding and not of hey and ho—nevertheless he wants to got to wants to, but there's no stone in his pockets either; usually he has a couple in one pocket or the other.

In these parts stones are called *zellacken*. The Protestants say *zellacken*, the few Catholics *zellacken*. The rough Mennonites say *zellacken*, the refined ones *zellacken*. Even Amsel, who likes to be different, says *zellack* when he means a stone; and Senta goes for a stone when someone says: Senta, go get a *zellack*. Kriwe says *zellacken*, Kornelius Kabrun, Beister, Folchert, August Sponagel, and Frau von Ankum, the major's wife, all say *zellacken;* and Pastor Daniel Kliewer from Pasewark says to his congregation, rough and refined alike: "Then little David picked up a *zellack* and flung it at the giant Goliath . . ." For a *zellack* is a handy little stone, the size of a pigeon's egg.

But Walter Matern couldn't find one in either pocket. In the right pocket there was nothing but crumbs and sunflower seeds, in the left pocket, in among pieces of string and the crackling remains of grasshoppers—while up above it grinds, while the sun has gone, while the Vistula flows, taking with it something from Güttland, something from Mantau, Amsel hunched over and the whole time clouds, while Senta upwind, the gulls downwind, the dikes bare to the horizon, while the sun is gone gone gone—he finds his pocketknife. Sunsets last longer in eastern than in western regions; any child knows that. There flows the Vistula from sky to opposite sky. The steam ferry puts out from the Schiewenhorst dock and bucks the current, slantwise and bumptious, carrying two narrow-gauge freight cars to Nickelswalde, where it will put them down on the Stutthof spur. The chunk of leather known as Kriwe has just turned his cowhide face to leeward and is pattering eye-lashless along the opposite dike top: a few moving sails and poplars to count. A fixed stare, no bending over, but a hand in his pocket. And the eye slides down from the embankment: a curious round something, down below, that bends over, looks as if it wants to swipe something from the Vistula. That's Amsel, looking for old rags. What for? Any child knows that.

But Leather Kriwe doesn't know what Walter Matern, who has been looking for a *zellack* in his pocket, has found in his pocket. While Kriwe pulls his face out of the wind, the pocketknife grows warmer in Walter Matern's hand. Amsel had given it to him. It has three blades, a corkscrew, a saw, and a leather punch. Amsel plump, pink, and comical when crying. Amsel pokes about in the muck on the ledge, for though falling fast the Vistula is up to the dike top because there's a flood between Montau and Käsemark, and has things in it that used to be in Palschau.

Gone. Down yonder behind the dike, leaving behind a spreading red glow. In his pocket Walter Matern—as only Brauxel can know—clenches the knife in his fist. Amsel is a little younger than Walter Matern. Senta, far away looking for mice, is just about as black as the sky, upward from the Schiewenhorst dike, is red. A drifting cat is caught in the driftwood. Gulls multiply in flight: torn tissue paper crackles, is smoothed, is spread out wide; and the glass pinhead eyes see everything that drifts, hangs, runs, stands, or is just there, such as Amsel's two thousand freckles; also that he is wearing a helmet like those worn at Verdun. And the helmet slips forward, is pushed back over the neck, and slips again, while Amsel fishes fence laths and beanpoles, and also heavy, sodden rags out of the mud: the cat comes loose, spins downward, falls to the gulls. The mice in the dike begin to stir again. And the ferry is still coming closer. A dead yellow dog comes drifting and turns over. Senta is facing into the wind. Slantwise and bumptious the ferry transports its two freight cars. Down drifts a calf—dead. The wind falters but does not turn. The gulls stop still in mid-air, hesitating. Now Walter Matern—while the ferry, the wind and the calf and the sun behind the dike and the mice in the dike and the motionless gulls—has pulled his fist out of his pocket with the knife in it. While the Vistula flows, he holds it out in front of his sweater and makes his knucles chalky white against the deepening red glow.

Third Morning Shift

Every child between Hildesheim and Sarstedt knows what is mined in Brauksel's mine, situated between Hildesheim and Sarstedt.

Every child knows why the Hundred and Twentieth Infantry Regiment had to abandon in Bohnsack the steel helmet Amsel is wearing, as well as other steel helmets, a stock of fatigue uniforms, and several field kitchens, when it pulled out by train in '20.

The cat is back again. Every child knows that it's not the same cat, but the mice don't know and the gulls don't know. The cat is wet wet wet. Now something drifts by that is neither a dog nor a sheep. It's a clothes cupboard. The cupboard does not collide with the ferry. And as Amsel pulls a beanpole out of the mud and Walter Matern's fist begins to quiver around the knife, a cat finds freedom: it drifts out toward the open sea that reaches as far as the sky. The gulls grow fewer, the mice in the dike scamper, the Vistula flows, the fist around the knife quivers, the wind's name is Northwest, the dikes taper away, the open sea resists the river with everything it's got, still and for evermore the sun goes down, still and for evermore the ferry and two freight cars move closer: the ferry does not capsize, the dikes do not burst, the mice are not afraid, the sun has no intention of turning back, the Vistula has no intention of turning back, the ferry has no intention of turning back, the cat has no, the gulls have no, nor the clouds nor the infantry regiment, Senta has no intention of going back to the wolves, but merrily merrily . . . And Walter Matern has no intention of letting the pocketknife given him by Amsel short fat round return to his pocket; on the contrary, his fist around the knife manages to turn a shade chalkier. And up above teeth grind from left to right. While it flows approaches sinks drifts whirls rises and falls, the fist relaxes around the knife, so that all the expelled blood rushes back into the now loosely closed hand: Walter Matern thrusts the fist holding the now thoroughly warmed object behind him, stands on one leg, foot, ball of foot, on five toes in a high shoe, lifts his weight sockless in the shoe, lets his entire weight slip into the hand behind him, takes no aim, almost stops grinding; and in that flowing drifting setting lost moment—for even Brauchsel cannot save it, because he has forgotten,

566

forgotten something—while Amsel looks up from the mud at the foot of the dike, with his left hand and a portion of his two thousand freckles pushes his steel helmet back, revealing another portion of his two thousand freckles, Walter Matern's hand is way out in front, empty and light, and discloses only the pressure marks of a pocketknife that had three blades, a corkscrew, a saw, and a leather punch; in the handle of which sea sand, powdered tree bark, a bit of jam, pine needles, and a vestige of mole's blood had become incrusted; whose barter value would have been a new bicycle bell; which no one had stolen, which Amsel had bought in his mother's shop with money he himself had earned, and then given his friend Walter Matern; which last summer had pinned a butterfly to Folchert's barn door, which under the dock of Kriwe's ferry had in one day speared four rats, had almost speared a rabbit in the dunes, and two weeks ago had pegged a mole before Senta could catch it. The inner surface of the hand still shows pressure marks made by the selfsame knife, with which Walter Matern and Eduard Amsel, when they were eight years old and intent on blood brotherhood, had scored their arms, because Kornelius Kabrun, who had been in German Southwest Africa and knew about Hottentots, had told them how it was done.

Fourth Morning Shift

Meanwhile—for while Brauxel lays bare the past of a pocketknife and the same knife, turned missile, follows a trajectory determined by propulsive force, gravitation, and wind resistance, there is still time enough, from morning shift to morning shift, to write off a working day and meanwhile to say—meanwhile, then, Amsel with the back of his hand had pushed back his steel helmet. With one glance he swept the dike embankment, with the same glance took in the thrower, then sent his glance in pursuit of the thrown object; and the pocketknife, Brauxel maintains, has meanwhile reached the ultimate point allotted to every upward-striving object, while the Vistula flows, the car drifts, the gull screams, the ferry approaches, while the bitch Senta is black, and the sun never ceases to set.

Meanwhile—for when a missile has reached that infinitesimal point after which descent begins, it hesitates for a moment, and pretends to stand still—while then the pocketknife stands still at its zenith, Amsel tears his gaze away from the object that has reached this infinitesimal point and once more—the object is already falling quickly fitfully, because now more exposed to the head wind, riverward—has his eye on his friend Matern who is still teetering on the ball of his foot and his toes sockless in high shoe, holding his right hand high and far from his body, while his left arm steers and tries to keep him in balance.

Meanwhile—for while Walter Matern teeters on one leg, concerned

567

with his balance, while Vistula and cat, mice and ferry, dog and sun, while the pocketknife falls riverward, the morning shift has been lowered into Brauchsel's mine, the night shift has been raised and has ridden away on bicycles, the changehouse attendant has locked the changehouse, the sparrows in every gutter have begun the day . . . At this point Amsel succeeded, with a brief glance and a directly ensuing cry, in throwing Walter Matern off his precarious balance. The boy on the top of the Nickelswalde dike did not fall, but he began to stagger and stumble so furiously that he lost sight of his pocketknife before it touched the flowing Vistula and became invisible.

"Hey, Grinder!" Amsel cries. "Is that all you can do? Grind your teeth and throw things?"

Walter Matern, here addressed as Grinder, is again standing stiff-kneed with parted legs, rubbing the palm of his left hand, which still bears the glowing negative imprint of a pocketknife.

"You saw me. I had to throw. What's the use of asking questions?"

"But you didn't throw no *zellack*."

"How could I when there ain't no *zellacks* up here?"

"So what do you throw when you ain't got no *zellack*?"

"Well, if I'd had a *zellack* I'd of thrown the *zellack*."

"If you'd sent Senta, she'd of brought you a *zellack*."

"If I'd sent Senta. Anybody can say that. You try and send a dog anyplace when she's chasing mice."

"So what did you throw if you didn't have no *zellack*?"

"Why do you keep asking questions? I threw some dingbat. You saw me."

"You threw my knife."

"It was my knife. Don't be an Indian giver. If I'd had a *zellack*, I wouldn't of thrown the knife, I'd thrown the *zellack*."

"Whyn't you tell me? Couldn't you tell me you couldn't find a *zellack*, I'd have tossed you one, there's plenty of them down here."

"What's the good of talking so much when it's gone?"

"Maybe I'll get a new knife for Ascension."

"I don't want no new knife."

"If I gave you one, you'd take it."

"You want to bet I wouldn't?"

"You want to bet you would?"

"Is it a bet?"

"It's a bet."

They shake hands on it: tin soldiers against magnifying glass. Amsel reaches his hand with its many freckles up the dike, Walter Matern reaches his hand with the pressure marks left by the pocketknife down the dike and with the handshake pulls Amsel up on the dike top.

568

Amsel is still friendly. "You're exactly like your grandma in the mill. All she does is grind the coupla teeth she's still got the whole time. Except she don't throw things. Only hits people with her spoon."

Amsel on the dike is a little shorter than Walter Matern. As he speaks, his thumb points over his shoulder to the spot where behind the dike lies the village of Nickelswalde and the Materns' postmill. Up the side of the dike Amsel pulls a bundle of roof laths, beanpoles, and wrung-out rags. He keeps having to push up the front rim of his steel helmet with the back of his hand. The ferry has tied up at the Nickelswalde dock. The two freight cars can be heard. Senta grows larger, smaller, larger, approaches black. More small farm animals drift by. Broad-shouldered flows the Vistula. Walter Matern wraps his right hand in the lower frayed edge of his sweater. Senta stands on four legs between the two of them. Her tongue hangs out to leftward and twitches. She keeps looking at Walter Matern, because his teeth. He has that from his grandmother who was riveted to her chair for nine years and only her eyeballs.

Now they have taken off: one taller, one smaller on the dike top against the ferry landing. The dog black. Half a pace ahead: Amsel. Half a pace behind: Walter Matern. He is dragging Amsel's rags. Behind the bundle, as the three grow smaller on the dike, the grass gradually straightens up again.

Fifth Morning Shift

And so Brauksel, as planned, sits bent over his paper and, while the other chroniclers bend likewise and punctually over the past and begin recording, has let the Vistula flow. It still amuses him to recall every detail: Many many years ago, when the child had been born but was not yet able to grind his teeth because like all babies he had been born toothless, Grandma Matern was sitting riveted to her chair in the overhang room, unable as she had been for the last nine years to move anything except her eyeballs, capable only of bubbling and drooling.

The overhang room jutted out over the kitchen, it had one window looking out on the kitchen, from which the maids could be observed at work, and another window in back, facing the Matern windmill, which sat there on its jack, with its tailpole pivoting on its post and was accordingly a genuine postmill; as it had been for a hundred years. The Materns had built it in 1815, shortly after the city and fortress of Danzig had been taken by the victorious Russian and Prussian armies; for August Matern, the grandfather of our grandmother sitting there riveted to her chair, had managed, during the long-drawn-out and listlessly conducted siege, to carry on a lucrative trade with both sides; on the one hand, he began in the spring to supply scaling ladders in exchange for good convention talers; on the other hand, he arranged, in return for Laubtalers and even more substantial Brabant currency, to smuggle little notes in to General Count d'Heudelet, calling his attention to the odd conduct of the Russians who were having quantities of ladders made, though it was only spring and the apples were in no shape to be picked.

When at length the governor, Count Rapp, signed the capitulation of the fortress, August Matern in out-of-the-way Nickelswalde counted the Danish specie and two-thirds pieces, the quickly rising rubles, the Hamburg mark pieces, the Laubtalers and convention talers, the little bags of Dutch gulden and the newly issued Danzig paper money; he found himself nicely off and abandoned himself to the joys of reconstruction: he had the old mill, where the fugitive Queen Louise is said to have spent the night after the defeat of Prussia, the historical mill whose sails had been damaged first on the occasion of the Danish attack from the sea, then of the night skirmish resulting from a sortie on the part of Capitaine de Chambure and his volunteer corps, torn down except for the jack which was still in good condition, and on the old jack built the new mill which was still sitting there with its pole on its jack when Grandmother Matern was reduced to sitting riveted and motionless in her chair. At this point Brauxel wishes, before it is too late, to concede that with his money, some hard, some easy-earned, August Matern not only built the new postmill, but also endowed the little chapel in Steegen, which numbered a few Catholics, with a Madonna, who, though not wanting in gold leaf, neither attracted any pilgrimages worth mentioning nor performed any miracles.

The Catholicism of the Matern family, as one might expect of a family of millers, was dependent on the wind, and since there was always a profitable breeze on the Island, the Matern mill ran year in year out, deterring them from the excessive churchgoing that would have antagonized the Mennonites. Only baptisms and funerals, marriages and the more important holidays sent part of the family to Steegen; and once a year on Corpus Christi, when the Catholics of Steegen put on a procession through the countryside, the mill, with its jack and all its dowels, with its mill post, its oak lever, and its meal bin, but most of all with its sails, came in for its share of blessing and holy water; a luxury which the Materns could never have afforded in such rough-Mennonite villages as Junkeracker and Pasewark. The Mennonites of Nickelswalde, who all raised wheat on rich Island soil and were dependent on the Catholic mill, proved to be the more refined type of Mennonites, in other words, they had buttons, buttonholes, and normal pockets that it was possible to put something into. Only Simon Beister, fisherman and small holder, was a genuine hook-and-eye Mennonite, rough and pocketless; over his boatshed hung a painted wooden sign with the ornate inscription:

Wear hooks and eyes,
Dear Jesus will save you.
Wear buttons and pockets,
The Devil will have you.

But Simon Beister was and remained the only inhabitant of Nickelswalde to have his wheat milled in Pasewark and not in the Catholic mill. Even so, it was not necessarily he who in '13, shortly before the outbreak of the Great War, incited a degenerate farmhand to haul kindling of all sorts to the Matern postmill and set it on fire. The flames were already creeping under jack and pole when Perkun, the young shepherd dog belonging to Pawel the miller's man, whom everyone called Paulchen, began, black and with tail straight back, to describe narrowing circles around hummock, jack, and mill, and brought miller's man and miller running out of the house with his staccato barks.

Pawel or Paul had brought the animal with him from Lithuania and on request exhibited a kind of pedigree, which made it clear to whom it may concern that Perkun's grandmother on her father's side had been a Lithuanian, Russian, or Polish she-wolf.

And Perkun sired Senta; and Senta whelped Harras; and Harras sired Prinz; and Prinz made history . . . But for the present Grandma Matern is still sitting riveted to her chair, able to move only her eyeballs. She is obliged to look on inactive as her daughter-in-law carries on in the house, her son in the mill, and her daughter Lorchen with the miller's man. But the war took the miller's man and Lorchen went out of her mind: after that, in the house, in the kitchen garden, on the dikes, in the nettles behind Folchert's barn, on the near side and far side of the dunes, barefoot on the beach and in among the blueberry bushes in the nearby woods, she goes looking for her Paulchen, and never will she know whether it was the Prussians or the Russians who sent him crawling underground. The gentle old maid's only companion is the dog Perkun, whose master had been her master.

Sixth Morning Shift

Long long ago—Brauxel counts on his fingers—when the world was in the third year of the war, when Paulchen had been left behind in Masuria, Lorchen was roaming about with the dog, but miller Matern was permitted to go on toting bags of flour, because he was hard of hearing on both sides, Grandma Matern sat one sunny day, while a child was being baptized—the pocketknife-throwing youngster of earlier morning shifts was receiving the name Walter—riveted to her chair, rolling her eyeballs, bubbling and drooling but unable to compose one word.

571

She sat in the overhang room and was assailed by mad shadows. She flared up, faded in the half-darkness, sat bright, sat somber. Pieces of furniture as well, the headpiece of the tall carved cupboard, the embossed cover of the chest, and the red, for nine years unused, velvet of the *prie-dieu* flared up, faded, disclosed silhouettes, resumed their massive gloom: glittering dust, dustless shadow over grandmother and her furniture. Her bonnet and the glass-blue drinking cup on the cupboard. The frayed sleeves of her bedjacket. The floor scrubbed lusterless, over which the turtle, roughly size of a man's hand, given to her by Paul the miller's man, moved from corner to corner, glittered and survived the miller's man by nibbling little scallops out of the edges of lettuce leaves. And all the lettuce leaves scattered about the room with their turtle-scallops were struck bright bright bright; for outside, behind the house, the Matern postmill, in a wind blowing thirty-nine feet a second, was grinding wheat into flour, blotting out the sun with its four sails four times in three-and-a-half seconds.

Concurrently with these demonic dazzling-dark goings-on in Grandma's room, the child was being driven to Steegen by way of Pasewark and Junkeracker to be baptized, the sunflowers by the fence separating the Matern kitchen garden from the road grew larger and larger, worshiped one another and were glorified without interruption by the very same sun which was blotted out four times in three-and-a-half seconds by the sails of the windmill; for the mill had not thrust itself between sun and sunflowers, but only, and this in the forenoon, between the riveted grandmother and a sun which shone not always but often on the Island.

How many years had Grandma been sitting motionless?
Nine years in the overhang room.
How long behind asters, ice flowers, sweet peas, or convolvulus?
Nine years bright dark bright to one side of the windmill.
Who had riveted her so solidly to her chair?
Her daughter-in-law Ernestine, née Stange.
How could such a thing come to pass?

This Protestant woman from Junkeracker had first expelled Tilde Matern, who was not yet a grandmother, but more on the strapping loud-mouthed side, from the kitchen; then she had appropriated the living room and taken to washing windows on Corpus Christi. When Stine drove her mother-in-law out of the barn, they came to blows for the first time. The two of them went at each other with feed pans in among the chickens, who lost quite a few feathers on the occasion.

This, Brauxel counts back, must have happened in 1905; for when two years later Stine Matern, née Stange, still failed to clamor for green apples and sour pickles and continued inexorably to come around in accordance with the calendar, Tilde Matern spoke to her daughter-in-law, who stood facing her with folded arms in the overhang room, in the following terms: "It's just like I always thought, Protestant women got the Devil's mouse in their hole. It nibbles everything away so nothing can come out. All it does is stink!"

These words unleashed a war of religion, fought with wooden cooking spoons and ultimately reducing the Catholic party to the chair: for the oaken armchair, which stood before the window between tile stove and *prie-dieu*, received a Tilde Matern felled by a stroke. For nine years now she had been sitting in this chair except when Lorchen and the maids, for reasons of cleanliness, lifted her out just long enough to minister to her needs.

When the nine years were past and it had developed that the wombs of Protestant women do not harbor a diabolical mouse that nibbles everything away and won't let anything germinate, when, on the contrary, something came full term, was born as a son, and had his umbilical cord cut, Grandmother sat, was still sitting, while the christening was proceeding in Steegen under favorable weather conditions, still and forever riveted, in the overhang room. Below the room, in the kitchen, a goose lay in the oven, sizzling in its own fat. This the goose did in the third year of the Great War, when geese had become so rare that the goose was looked upon as a species close to extinction. Lorchen Matern with her birthmark, her flat bosom, her curly hair, Lorchen, who had never got a husband—because Paulchen had crawled into the earth, leaving nothing but his black dog behind—Lorchen, who was supposed to be looking after the goose in the oven, was not in the kitchen, didn't baste the goose at all, neglected to turn it, to say the proper charms over it, but stood in a row with the sunflowers behind the fence—which the new miller's man had freshly whitewashed that spring—and spoke first in a friendly, then in an anxious tone, two sentences angrily, then lovingly, to someone who was not standing behind the fence, who was not passing by in greased yet squeaky shoes, who wore no baggy trousers, and who was nevertheless addressed as Paul or Paulchen and expected to return to her, Lorchen Matern with the watery eyes, something he had taken from her. But Paul did not give it back, although the time of day was favorable—plenty of silence, or at any rate buzzing—and the wind blowing at a velocity of twenty-six feet a second had boots big enough to kick the mill on its jack in such a way that it turned a mite faster than the wind and was able in one uninterrupted session to transform Miehlke's —for it was his milling day—wheat into Miehlke's flour.

For even though a miller's son was being baptized in Steegen's wooden chapel, Matern's mill did not stand still. If a milling wind was blowing, there had to be milling. A windmill knows only days with and days without milling wind. Lorchen Matern knew only days when Paulchen passed by and days when nothing passed by and no one stopped at the fence. Because the mill was milling, Paulchen came by and stopped. Perkun barked. Far behind Napoleon's poplars, behind Folchert's, Miehlke's, Kabrun's, Beister's, Mombert's, and Kriwe's farmhouses, behind the flat-roofed school, and Lührmann's taproom and milk pool, the cows lowed by turns. And Lorchen said lovingly "Paulchen," several times "Paulchen," and while the goose in the oven, unbasted, unspoken-to, and never turned, grew steadily crisper and more dominical, she said: "Aw, give it back. Aw, don't be like that. Aw, don't act like that. Aw, give it back, 'cause I need it. Aw, give it, and don't be, not giving it to me . . ."

No one gave anything back. The dog Perkun turned his head on his neck and whimpering softly looked after the departing Paulchen. Under the cows, milk accumulated. The windmill sat with pole on jack and milled. Sunflowers recited sunflower prayers to each other. The air buzzed. And the goose in the oven began to burn, first slowly, then so fast and pungently that Grandmother Matern in her overhang room above the kitchen set her eyeballs spinning faster than the sails of the windmill were able to. While in Steegen the baptismal chapel was forsaken, while in the overhang room the turtle, hand-size, moved from one scrubbed plank to the next, she, because of the burnt goose fumes rising to the overhang room, began bright dark bright to drivel and drool and wheeze. First she blew hairs, such as all grandmothers have in their noses, out through nostrils, but when bitter fumes quivered bright through the whole room, making the turtle pause bewildered and the lettuce leaves shrivel, what issued from her nostrils was no longer hairs but steam. Nine years of grandmotherly indignation were discharged: the grandmotherly locomotive started up. Vesuvius and Etna. The Devil's favorite element, fire, made the unleashed grandmother quiver, contribute dragonlike to the chiaroscuro, and attempt, amid changing light after nine years, a dry grinding of the teeth; and she succeeded: from left to right, set on edge by the acrid smell, her last remaining stumps rubbed against each other; and in the end a cracking and splintering mingled with the dragon's fuming, the expulsion of steam, the spewing of fire, the grinding of teeth: the oaken chair, fashioned in pre-Napoleonic times, the chair which had sustained the grandmother for nine years except for brief interruptions in behalf of cleanliness, gave up and disintegrated just as the turtle leapt high from the floor and landed on its back. At the same time several stove tiles sprung netlike cracks. Down below the goose burst open, letting the stuffing gush out. The chair disintegrated into powdery wood meal, rose up in a cloud which proliferated, a sumptuously illuminated monument to transience, and settled on Grandmother Matern, who had not, as might be supposed, taken her cue from the chair and turned to grandmotherly dust. What lay on shriveled salad leaves, on the turtle turned turtle, on furniture and floor, was merely the dust of pulverized oakwood; she, the terrible one, did not lie, but stood crackling and electric, struck bright, struck dark by the play of the windmill sails, upright amid dust and decay, ground her teeth from left to right, and grinding took the first step: stepped from bright to dark, stepped bright, stepped dark, stepped over the turtle, who was getting ready to give up the ghost, whose belly was a beautiful sulphur-yellow, after nine years of sitting still took purposive steps, did not slip on lettuce leaves, kicked open the door of the overhang room, descended, a paragon of grandmotherhood, the kitchen stairs in felt shoes, and standing now on stone flags and sawdust took something from a shelf with both hands, and attempted, with grandmotherly cooking stratagems, to save the acridly burning baptismal goose. And she did manage to save a little by scratching away the charred part, dousing the flames, and turning the goose over. But everyone who had ears in Nickelswalde could hear Grandmother Matern, still engaged in her rescue operations, screaming with terrifying distinctness out of a well-rested throat: "You hussy! Lorchen, you hussy! I'll cook your, you hussy. Damn hussy! Hussy, you hussy!"

Wielding a hardwood spoon, she was already out of the burnt-smelling kitchen and in the middle of the buzzing garden, with the mill behind her. To the left she stepped in the strawberries, to the right in the cauliflowers, for the first time in years she was back again among the broad beans, but an instant later behind and between the sunflowers, raising her right arm high and bringing it down, supported in every movement by the regular turning of the windmill sails, on poor Lorchen, also on the sunflowers, but not on Perkun, who leapt away black between the bean trellises.

In spite of the blows and though quite without Paulchen, poor Lorchen whimpered in his direction: "Oh help me please, Paulchen, oh do help me, Paulchen . . ." but all that came her way was wooden blows and the song of the unleashed grandmother: "You hussy! You hussy you! You damn hussy!"

Seventh Morning Shift

Brauxel wonders whether he may not have put too much diabolical display into his account of Grandmother Matern's resurrection. Wouldn't it have been miracle enough if the good woman had simply and somewhat stiffly stood up and gone down to the kitchen to rescue the goose? Was it necessary to have her puff steam and spit fire? Did stove tiles have to crack and lettuce leaves shrivel? Did he need the moribund turtle and the pulverized armchair?

If nevertheless Brauksel, today a sober-minded man at home in a free-market economy, replies in the affirmative and insists on fire and steam, he will have to give his reasons. There was and remains only one reason for his elaborate staging of the grandmotherly resurrection scene: the Materns, especially the teeth-grinding branch of the family, descended from the medieval robber Materna, by way of Grandma, who was a genuine Matern—she had married her cousin—down to the baptizand Walter Matern, had an innate feeling for grandiose, nay operatic scenes; and the truth of the matter is that in May 1917, Grandmother Matern did not just go down quietly to rescue the goose as a matter of course, but began by setting off the above-described fireworks.

It must furthermore be said that while Grandmother Matern was trying to save the goose and immediately thereafter belaboring poor Lorchen with a cooking spoon, the three two-horse carriages bearing the hungry christening party were rolling past Junkeracker and Pasewark on their way from Steegen. And much as Brauxel may be tempted to record the ensuing christening dinner—because the goose didn't yield enough, preserved giblets and pickled pork were brought up from the cellar—he must nevertheless let the christening party sit down to dinner without witnesses. No one will ever learn how the Romeikes and the Kabruns, how Miehlke and the widow Stange stuffed themselves full of burnt goose, preserved giblets, pickled pork, and squash in vinegar in the midst of the third war year. Brauxel is especially sorry to miss the unleashed and newly nimble Grandmother Matern's great scene; it is the widow Amsel, and she alone, whom he is permitted at this point to excerpt from the village idyl, for she is the mother of our plumpish Eduard Amsel, who in the course of the first to fourth morning shifts fished beanpoles, roofing laths, and heavy, waterlogged rags from the rising Vistula and is now, like Walter Matern, about to be baptized.

Eighth Morning Shift

Many many years ago—for Brauksel tells nothing more gladly than fairy tales—there dwelt in Schiewenhorst, a fishing village to the left of the mouth of the Vistula, a merchant by the name of Albrecht Amsel. He sold kerosene, sailcloth, canisters for fresh water, rope, nets, fish traps, eel baskets, fishing tackle of all kinds, tar, paint, sandpaper, yarn, oilcloth, pitch, and tallow, but also carried tools, from axes to pocketknives, and had small carpenter's benches, grindstones, inner tubes for bicycles, carbide lamps, pulleys, winches, and vises in stock. Ship's biscuit was piled up beside cork jackets; a life preserver all ready to have a boat's name written on it embraced a large jar full of cough drops; a schnapps known as "Brotchen" was poured from a stout green bottle encased in basketry; he sold yard goods and remnants, but also new and used clothing, flatirons, secondhand sewing machines, and mothballs. And in spite of the mothballs, in spite of pitch and kerosene, shellack and carbide, Albrecht Amsel's store, a spacious wooden structure resting on a concrete foundation and painted dark green every seven years, smelled first and foremost of cologne and next, before the question of mothballs could even come up, of smoked fish; for side by side with all this retail trade, Albrecht Amsel was known as a wholesale purchaser of fresh-water fish as well as deep-sea fish: chests of the lightest pinewood, golden yellow and packed full of smoked flounder, smoked eel, sprats both loose and bundled, lampreys, codfish roe, and strongly or subtly smoked Vistula salmon, with the inscription: A. Amsel—Fresh Fish—Smoked Fish—Schiewenhorst—Great Island—burned into their front panels, were broken open with medium-sized chisels in the Danzig Market, a brick edifice situated between Lawendelgasse and Junkergasse, between the Dominican church and the Altstädtischer Graben. The top came open with a crisp crackling; nails were drawn squeaking from the sides. And from Neo-Gothic ogival windows market light fell on freshly smoked fish.

In addition, this farsighted merchant, deeply concerned with the future of the fish-smoking industry on the Vistula delta and the harbor-mouth bar, employed a stonemason specializing in chimney construction, who was kept busy from Plehnendorf to Einlage, that is, in all the villages bordering the Dead Vistula, which villages with their smokehouse chimneys had the appearance of fantastic ruins: here he would fix a chimney that was drawing badly, elsewhere he would have to build one of those enormous smokehouse chimneys that towered over lilac bushes and squat fishermen's huts; all this in the name of Albrecht Amsel, who not without reason was said to be wealthy. The rich Amsel, people said—or: "Amsel the Jew." Of course Amsel was not a Jew. Though he was also no Mennonite, he called himself a good Protestant, possessed a permanent pew, which he occupied every Sunday, in the Fishermen's Church in Bohnsack, and married Lottchen Tiede, a reddish-blonde peasant girl inclined to stoutness from Gross-Zünder; which should be taken to mean: how could Albrecht Amsel be a Jew, when Tiede, the wealthy peasant, who never went from Gross-Zünder to Käsemark otherwise than in a coach-and-four and patent-leather shoes, who was a frequent caller at the District President's, who had put his sons in the Cavalry, or to be more precise, in the rather expensive Langfuhr Hussars, gave him his daughter Lottchen for his wife.

Later a good many people are said to have said that old man Tiede had given the Jew Amsel his Lottchen only because he, like many peasants, merchants, fishermen, millers—including miller Matern from Nickelswalde—was deep in debt, dangerously so for the survival of his coach-and-four, to Albrecht Amsel. In the intention of proving something it

577

was also said that speaking before the Provincial Market Regulation Commission, Albrecht Amsel had expressed strong opposition to the undue encouragement of hog raising.

For the present Brauksel, who is a know-it-all, prefers to have done with conjectures: for regardless of whether it was love or debentures that brought Lottchen Tiede into his house, and regardless of whether he sat in the Fishermen's Church in Bohnsack on Sundays as a baptized Jew or a baptized Christian, Albrecht Amsel, the dynamic merchant of the lower Vistula, who, it might be added, was also the broad-shouldered cofounder of the Bohnsack Athletic Club reg. 1905, a mighty-voiced baritone in the church choir, rose to be a multiply-decorated reserve lieutenant by the banks of the Somme and Marne, and fell in 1917, not far from the fortress of Verdun, just two months before the birth of his son Eduard.

Ninth Morning Shift

Butted by the Ram, Walter Matern first saw the light of day in April. The Fishes of March drew Eduard Amsel, restless and gifted, from the maternal cavern. In May, when the goose burned and Grandmother Matern rose again, the miller's son was baptized. The proceedings were Catholic. As early as the end of April the son of the late merchant Albrecht Amsel was already sprinkled in good Protestant style in the Fishermen's Church in Bohnsack, half, as was there customary, with Vistula water and half with water taken from the Baltic.

Whatever the other chroniclers, who have been vying with Brauksel for nine morning shifts, may record that is at variance with Brauksel's opinion, they will have to take my word for it in matters concerning the baptizand from Schiewenhorst: among all the characters intended to breathe life into this anniversary volume—Brauchsel's mine has been producing neither coal, nor iron ores, nor potash for almost ten years—Eduard Amsel, or Eddi Amsel, Haseloff, Goldmouth, and so on, is the most restless hero, except for Brauxel.

From the very start it was his vocation to invent scarecrows. Yet he had nothing against birds; on the other hand, birds, regardless of plumage and characteristics of flight, had plenty against him and his scarecrow-inventing mind. Immediately after the christening ceremony—the bells hadn't even stopped ringing—they knew him for what he was. Eduard Amsel, however, lay plump and rosy on a tight baptismal cushion, and if birds meant anything to him he didn't show it. His godmother was named Gertrud Karweise, later she took to knitting him woolen socks, year in year out, punctually for Christmas. In her robust arms the newly baptized child was presented to the large christening party, which had been invited to an interminable christening dinner. The widow Amsel, née Tiede, who had stayed home, was supervising the setting of the table, issuing last-minute instructions in the kitchen, and tasting sauces. But all the Tiedes from Gross-Zünder, except for the four sons who were living dangerously in the Cavalry—the second youngest was later killed—trudged along in their Sunday best behind the baptismal cushion. Along the Dead Vistula marched: Christian Glomme the Schiewenhorst fisherman and his wife Martha Glomme, née Liedke; Herbert Kienast and his wife Johanna, née Probst; Carl Jakob Ayke, whose son Daniel Ayke had met his death on Dogger Bank in the service of the Imperial Navy; the fisherman's widow Brigitte Kabus, whose boat was operated by her brother Jakob Nilenz; between Ernst Wilhelm Tiede's daughters-in-law, who tripped along city fashion in pink, pea-green, and violet-blue, strode, brushed gleaming black, the aged Pastor Blech—a descendant of the famous Deacon A. F. Blech, who, while Pastor of St. Mary's, had written a chronicle of the City of Danzig from 1807 to 1814, the years of the French occupation. Friedrich Bollhagen, owner of a large smoking establishment, walked behind the retired Captain Bronsard, who had found wartime occupation as a volunteer sluice operator in Plehnendorf. August Sponagel, innkeeper at Wesslinken, walked beside Frau Major von Ankum, who towered over him by a head. In view of the fact that Dirk Heinrich von Ankum, landowner in Klein-Zünder, had gone out of existence early in 1915, Sponagel held the Frau Major's rigidly-rectangularly offered arm. The rear guard, behind Herr and Frau Busenitz, who had a coal business in Bohnsack, consisted of Erich Lau, the disabled Schiewenhorst village mayor, and his superlatively pregnant Margarete who, as daughter of the Nickelswalde village mayor Momber, had not married below her station. Being on duty, Dike Inspector Haberland had been obliged to take his leave outside the church door. Quite likely the procession also included a bevy of children, all too blond and all to dressed up.

Over sandy paths which only sparsely covered the straggling roots of the scrub pines, they made their way along the right bank of the river to the waiting landaus, to old man Tiede's four-in-hand, which he had managed to hold on to in spite of the war and the shortage of horses. Shoes full of sand. Captain Bronsard laughed loud and breathless, then coughed at length. Conversation waited until after dinner. The woods along the shore had a Prussian smell. Almost motionless the river, a dead arm of the Vistula, which acquired a certain amount of current only farther down when the Mottlau flowed into it. The sun shone cautiously on holiday finery. Tiede's daughters-in-law shivered pink pea-green violet-blue and would have been glad to have the widows' shawls. Quite likely so much widow's black, the gigantic Frau Major, and the disabled veteran's monumental limp contributed to the coming of an event which had been in the making from the start: scarcely had the company left the Bohnsack

Fishermen's Church when the ordinarily undisplaceable gulls clouded up from the square. Not pigeons, for fishermen's churches harbor gulls and not pigeons. Now in a steep slant bitterns, sea swallows, and teals rise from the rushes and duckweed. Up go the crested terns. Crows rise from the scrub pines. Starlings and blackbirds abandon the cemetery and the gardens of whitewashed fishermen's houses. From lilac and hawthorn come wagtails and titmice, robins, finches, and thrushes, every bird in the song; clouds of sparrows from eaves and telegraph wires; swallows from barns and crannies in masonry; whatever called itself bird shot up, exploded, flashed like an arrow as soon as the baptismal cushion hove into sight, and was carried across the river by the sea wind, to form a black-torn cloud, in which birds that normally avoid one another mingled promiscuously, all spurred by the same dread: gulls and crows; a pair of hawks amid dappled songbirds; magpies with magpies!

And five hundred birds, not counting sparrows, fled in mass between the sun and the christening party. And five hundred birds cast their ominous shadow upon christening party, baptismal cushion, and baptized child.

And five hundred birds—who wants to count sparrows?—induced the christening party, from Lau, the disabled village mayor, to the Tiedes, to cluster together and first in silence, then muttering and exchanging stiff glances, to press from back to front and hurry their pace. August Sponagel stumbles over pine roots. Between Bronsard and Pastor Blech, who makes only the barest stab at raising his arms in pastoral appeasement, the gigantic Frau Major storms forward, gathering her skirts as in a rainstorm, and carries all in her wake: the Glommes and Kienast with wife, Ayke and the Kabus, Bollhagen and the Busenitzes; even the disabled Lau and his superlatively pregnant wife, who however did not suffer from shock and was delivered of a normal girl child, keep pace, panting heavily—only the godmother, bearing child and topsy-turvy cushion in her strong arms, drops back and is last to reach the waiting landaus and the Tiedes' four-in-hand amid the first poplars on the road to Schiewenhorst.

Did the baptizand cry? Not a whimper, but he didn't sleep either. Did the cloud of five hundred birds and uncounted sparrows disperse immediately after the hasty and not at all festive departure of the carriages? For a long while the cloud over the lazy river found no rest: for a time it hovered over Bohnsack, for a time it hung long and narrow over the woods and dunes, then broad and fluid over the opposite shore, dropping an old crow into a marshy meadow, where it stood out gray and stiff. Only when landaus and four-in-hand drove into Schiewenhorst did the cloud disperse into its various species, which found their way back to the square outside the church, to cemetery, gardens, barns, rushes, lilac bushes, and pines; but until evening, when the christening party, having eaten and drunk its fill, sat weighing down the long table with elbows, anguish darkened numerous bird hearts of varying sizes; for as Eduard lay on his baptismal cushion, his scarecrow-inventing spirit had made itself known to all the birds. From that moment on they knew all about him.

Tenth Morning Shift

Who can tell whether Albrecht Amsel, merchant and reserve lieutenant, wasn't a Jew after all? The people of Schiewenhorst, Einlage, and Neufähr would hardly have called him a rich Jew for no reason at all. And what about the name? Isn't it typical? You say he's of Dutch descent, because in the early Middle Ages Dutch settlers drained the Vistula delta, having brought with them linguistic peculiarities, windmills, and their names?

Now that Brauksel has insisted in the course of past morning shifts that A. Amsel is not a Jew and declared in so many words: "Of course Amsel was not a Jew," he can now, with equal justification—for all origins are what we choose to make of them—try to convince you that of course Albrecht Amsel was a Jew. He came of a family of tailors long resident in Preussisch-Stargard and had been obliged—because his father's house was full of children—to leave Preussisch-Stargard at the age of sixteen for Schneidemühl, Frankfurt on the Oder, and Berlin. Fourteen years later he had come—metamorphosed, Protestant, and wealthy—to the Vistula estuary by way of Schneidemühl, Neustadt, and Dirschau. The cut which had made Schiewenhorst a village on the river was not yet a year old when Albrecht Amsel purchased his property on favorable terms.

And so he went into business. What else should he have gone into? And so he sang in the church choir. Why shouldn't he, a baritone, have sung in the church choir? And so he helped to found an athletic club, and among all the inhabitants of the village it was he who most staunchly believed that he Albrecht Amsel was not a Jew, that the name of Amsel came from Holland: lots of people go by the name of Specht (woodpecker), a famous African explorer was even called Nachtigal (nightingale), only Adler (eagle) is a typically Jewish name, and certainly not Amsel (blackbird). The tailor's son had devoted fourteen years to forgetting his origins and only as a sideline, though with equal success, to amassing a good-Protestant fortune.

And then in 1903 a precocious young man by the name of Otto Weininger wrote a book. This extraordinary book was named *Sex and Character;* published in Vienna and Leipzig, it labored for six hundred pages to demonstrate that women have no soul. Because the topic proved timely in those years of feminist agitation, and particularly because the thirteenth chapter, entitled "The Jewish Character," showed that the Jews, being a feminine race, also have no soul, the extraordinary book ran into an incredible number of editions and found its way into households where otherwise only the Bible was read. And so Weininger's brain child was also taken into the house of Albrecht Amsel.

Perhaps the merchant would not have opened the thick book if he had known that a certain Herr Pfennig was engaged in denouncing Otto Weininger as a plagiarist. In 1906 there appeared a vicious pamphlet attacking the late Weininger—the young man had meanwhile taken his own life—in the crudest terms. Much as he deplored the tone of the vicious pamphlet, even S. Freud, who had called the deceased Weininger an extremely gifted young man, could not overlook the well-documented fact that Weininger's central idea—bisexuality—was not original with him, but had first occurred to a certain Herr Fliess. And so Albrecht Amsel opened the book all unsuspecting and read in Weininger—who in a footnote had introduced himself as a Jew: The Jew has no soul. The Jew does not sing. The Jew does not engage in sports. The Jew must surmount the Jewishness within him . . . And Albrecht Amsel surmounted by singing in the church choir, by not only founding the Bohnsack Athletic Club reg. 1905, but also by coming out for the squad in appropriate attire, by doing his part on the horse and horizontal bar, by high jumping, broad jumping, participating in relay races, and finally, despite opposition—here again a founder and pioneer—by introducing schlagball, a relatively new sport, in the territory to the right and left of all three mouths of the Vistula.

Like the villagers of the Island, Brauksel, who is recording these matters to the best of his ability, would know nothing of the town of Preussisch-Stargard and Eduard Amsel's tailor grandfather, if Lottchen Amsel, née Tiede, had kept silence. Many years after the fatal day in Verdun she opened her mouth.

Young Amsel, of whom we shall be speaking, though with interruptions, from now on, had hastened from the city to his mother's deathbed and she, who was succumbing to diabetes, had whispered feverishly in his ear: "Ah, son. Forgive your poor mother. Amsel, you never knew him but he was your very own father, was one of the circumcised as they say. I only hope they don't catch you now the laws are so strict."

At the time of the strict laws—which, however, were not yet in force in the Danzig Free State—Eduard Amsel inherited the business, the property, and the house with everything in it, including a shelf of books: *The Kings of Prussia, Prussia's Great Men, Frederick the Great, Count Schlieffen, The Battle of Leuthen, Frederick and Katte, Frederick the Great and La Barbarina,* and Otto Weininger's extraordinary book which Amsel henceforth kept about him, whereas the other books were gradually lost. In his own way he read in it, he even read the marginal notes which his singing, athletic father had jotted down. He saved the book down through hard times, and it is thanks to him that the book is now lying on Brauxel's desk, where it can be consulted today and at all times: Weininger has grafted quite a few ideas onto the present writer. The scarecrow is created in man's image.

Eleventh Morning Shift

Brauchsel's hair is growing. As he writes or manages the mine, it grows. As he dines, walks, slumbers, breathes, or holds his breath, as the morning shift is lowered, the night shift raised, and sparrows inaugurate the day, it grows. In fact, while with cold fingers the barber shortens Brauksel's hair at his request because the year is drawing to a close, it grows back under his scissors. One day Brauksel, like Weininger, will be dead, but his hair, toenails, and fingernails will survive him for a time—just as this handbook on the construction of effective scarecrows will be read long after the writer has gone out of existence.

Yesterday mention was made of strict laws. But at the present point in our story, which is just beginning, the laws are still mild, they do not punish Amsel's origin in any way; Lottchen Amsel, née Tiede, knows nothing about the horrors of diabetes; "naturally" Albrecht Amsel was not a Jew; Eduard Amsel is also a good Protestant and has his mother's quickly growing reddish-blond hair; plump, already in possession of all his freckles, he spends his time amid drying fishnets and his favorite way of viewing the world is: filtered through fishnets; small wonder that the world soon takes on for him a netlike pattern, obstructed by beanpoles.

Scarecrows! Here it is contended that at first little Eduard Amsel—he was five and a half when he built his first scarecrow deserving of the name—had no intention of building anything of the sort. But people from the village and salesmen on their way around the Island with fire insurance and seed samples, peasants on their way home from the notary's, in short, all those who watched him as he set up his fluttering figures on the dike near the Schiewenhorst dock, thought along those lines. And Kriwe said to Herbert Kienast: "Look what Amsel's kid has been making: honest-to-goodness scarecrows." As on the day of his christening, Eduard Amsel still had nothing against birds; but all those creatures to left and right of the Vistula that let themselves be carried birdlike by the wind had something against his products, namely scarecrows. He built one every day, and they were never alike. What the day before it had taken him three hours to make from striped pants, a jacketlike rag with bold checks, a brimless hat, and, with the help of an incomplete and ramshackle ladder, an armful of freshly cut willow switches, he tore down the following morning, to construct from the same materials an oddity of a very different race and faith, but which like its predecessor commanded birds to keep their distance.

Though all these transitory edifices revealed industry and imagination on the part of the architect, it was Eduard Amsel's keen sense of reality in all its innumerable forms, the curious eye surmounting his plump cheek, which provided his products with closely observed detail, which made them functional and crow-repellent. They differed not only in form but also in effect from the local scarecrows that stood wavering in the fields and gardens round about; whereas the run-of-the-mill article registered small success with the feathered folk, a *succès d'estime* at best, his creatures, though built for no purpose and with no enemy in view, had the power to instill panic in birds.

They seemed to be alive, and if you looked at them long enough, even in process of construction or when they were being torn down and nothing remained but the torso, they were alive in every way: they sprinted along the dike, running figures beckoned, threatened, attacked, thrashed, waved from shore to shore, let themselves be carried by the wind, engaged in conversation with the sun, blessed the river and its fish, counted the poplars, overtook the clouds, broke off the tips of steeples, tried to ascend to heaven, to board or pursue the ferry, to take flight, they were never anonymous, but signified Johann Lickfett the fisherman, Pastor Blech, time and time again Kriwe the ferryman, who stood with his mouth open and his head to one side, Captain Bronsard, Inspector Haberland, or whomever else those lowlands had to offer. Thus, although the rawboned Frau Major von Ankum had her small homestead in Klein-Zünder and seldom posed at the ferry landing, she made herself at home on the Schiewenhorst dike in the form of a giantess terrifying to birds and children alike, and remained there for three days.

A little later, when school began for Eduard Amsel, it was Herr Olschewski, the young schoolmaster in Nickelswade—for Schiewenhorst did not maintain a school—who was obliged to stand still when his freckliest pupil planted him, insubstantial as a scarecrow, on the great dune to the right of the river mouth. Amid the wind-bowed pines on the crest of the dune Amsel planted the schoolmaster's double and before his canvas-shod feet laid out the griddle-flat Island from the Vistula to the Nogat, the plain as far as the towers of Danzig, the hills and woods beyond the city, the river from mouth to horizon, and the open sea reaching out toward an intimation of Hela Peninsula, including the ships anchored in the roadstead.

Twelfth Morning Shift

The year is running out. It is ending in an odd kind of way, because what with the Berlin crisis, New Year's Eve is to be celebrated not with noisy fireworks but only with the luminous kind. And still another reason for not celebrating New Year's Eve with the usual noise makers here in

Lower Saxony is that Hinrich Kopf, a faithful likeness of a chief of state, has just been carried to his grave. As a precaution Brauxel, after consulting the shop committee, has put up a notice in the surface installations, in the administration building, in the gangways, and on the fill level, so worded: The workers and staff of Brauxel and Co.—Exporters and Importers—are requested to celebrate New Year's Eve quietly, in a manner befitting the troubled times. In addition the present writer, who could not resist the temptation to quote himself, has had his little motto—"The scarecrow is created in man's image"—printed on deckle-edged cards and sent to customers and business friends as a New Year's greeting.

The first school year brought Eduard Amsel a variety of surprises. Displayed each day ludicrously round and freckle-faced to the eyes of two villages, he became a whipping boy. Whatever games the children happened to be playing, he had to join in, or rather, he was joined in. Of course young Amsel cried when the gang dragged him into the nettles behind Folchert's barn or tied him to a post with rotten ropes that stank of tar and painfully if not imaginatively tortured him; but through the tears which, as everyone knows, confer a blurred but uncommonly precise vision, his greenish-gray, fat-encased little eyes never ceased to observe, to appraise, and to analyze typical movements. Two or three days after one of these beatings—and it was quite possible that in between blows, along with other insults and nicknames the word "Sheeny" would be uttered accidentally on purpose—the very same torture scene would be reproduced in the form of a single many-armed scarecrow between dunes or directly on the beach, licked by the sea.

Walter Matern put an end to these beatings and to the ensuing replicas of beatings. One day, perhaps because he had discovered on the beach a tattered but furiously flailing scarecrow, which far from looking unlike him looked like nine of him, he who for quite some time had taken an active part in beatings, who had even accidentally on purpose introduced the word "Sheeny," dropped his fists in midaction, allowed both fists to reflect as it were for the time it would have taken to deal out five punches, and then went on punching: but from that time on it was no longer young Amsel who had to submit quietly when Walter Matern's fists declared their independence; instead, Matern attacked Amsel's tormentors, and this with so much dedication and rhythmic grinding of his teeth that he was still boxing at the soft summer air behind Folchert's barn long after all but the blinking Amsel had vanished.

As we all know from breathtaking movies, friendships concluded during or after beatings are often and breathtakingly put to the test. In the course of this book—and this in itself will make it kind of long—it will be necessary to subject the Matern-Amsel friendship to many more trials. From the very start Walter Matern's fists—luckily for the new friendship—were kept busy, because the local yokels, progeny of fishermen and peasants, were unable to digest this pact of friendship that had been so suddenly concluded; no sooner was school out than, succumbing to old habit, they dragged the struggling Amsel off behind Folchert's barn. For slowly flowed the Vistula, slowly the dikes tapered off, slowly the seasons changed, slowly clouds drifted, slowly the ferry labored, slowly the denizens of the lowlands changed over from oil lamps to electric light, and only slowly did the children in the villages to the right and left of the Vistula get it through their heads that anyone who wanted to pick a bone with young Amsel would have Walter Matern to reckon with. The mystery of friendship began gradually to work wonders. A unique scene, representative of the many colorful situations that youthful friendship could involve in a rural district amid the unchanging embodiments of country life—peasant, farmhand, pastor, schoolmaster, postmaster, peddler, cheesemaker, dairy co-operative inspector, apprentice forester, and village idiot—perpetuated itself for many years without being photographed: somewhere in the dunes, with his back to the woods and their aisles, Amsel is at work. Garments of various cut are spread out in such a way that the artist can find what he needs at a glance. No one style is predominant. Driftwood and small sand heaps weigh down the cotton twill of the defunct Prussian Army and the checkered, stiff-dry yield of the latest flood, inhibiting their tendency to flutter away: nightgowns, morning coats, pants without seats, kitchen rags, jerkins, shriveled dress uniforms, curtains with peepholes, camisoles, pinafores, coachmen's coats, trusses, chest bandages, chewed-up carpets, the bowels of neckties, pennants from a shooting match, and a dowry of table linen stink and attract flies. A many-segmented caterpillar of felt and velours hats, caps, helmets, bonnets, nightcaps, garrison caps, low-crowned caps, and straw hats squirms, tries to bite its tail, clearly exhibits each one of its segments, lies there embroidered with flies, and waits to be used. The sun impels all the fence laths implanted in the sand, not to mention the fragments of ladders, the beanpoles, the smooth canes and knotted canes, and the common sticks washed ashore by sea and river, to cast moving shadows of varying lengths, which carry time along with them in their passage. Further: a mountain of string, wire, half-rotted rope, crumbling leather articles, matted veils, entangled woolens, and bundles of straw blackened with mildew, dislodged from the disintegrating roofs of barns. Potbellied bottles, bottomless milking pails, chamber pots, and soup tureens form a pile by themselves. And amid all this accumulated stock, astonishingly nimble: Eduard Amsel. Sweating, stepping on beach thistles with his bare feet but taking no notice, he groans, grunts, giggles some, plants a beanpole, tosses a roofing lath against it slantwise, throws some wire after it—he doesn't tie things together, just tosses, and they stay in place miraculously—makes a reddish-brown silver-threaded curtain climb three-and-a-half times around beanpole and roofing lath, allows matted bundles of straw to turn into a head around a mustard pot, selects a visor cap, exchanges the student cap for a Quaker's hat, mixes up the caterpillar of hats and the bright-colored sand flies as well, favors a nightcap for a time, but finally appoints a coffee cozy stiffened by the last flood to function as a summit. At the last moment he realizes that the whole lacks a vest and more specifically a vest that is shiny in back, chooses from among the mildewed tatterdemalion tatters, and, half over his shoulder and without really looking, tosses a vest on his creature under the coffee cozy. Already he is planting a tired little ladder to the left, crossing two man-size logs to the right, twisting a triple-width section of garden fence into a screwlike arabesque. He aims briefly, throws stiff army twill and hits, joins with creaking belts, and with the help of the tangled woolens gives this figure, the outrider of his group, a certain military authority. An instant later, laden with rags, hung with leather, entwined in rope, seven times hatted, and surrounded by jubilant flies, he is in front, to one side, to southeast and to starboard of his derelict junkpile, which is little by little metamorphosed into a crow-repellent group; for from the dunes, the lyme grass, the pine woods rise common and—ornithologically speaking—rare birds. Cause and effect: they coagulate into a cloud high above Eduard Amsel's place of work. They write their terror in a birdscript that grows steadily steeper, narrower, and more jumbled. The root sound of this text is *crah,* which with the help of the wood pigeons puts forth the branch *mah-roo-croo.* The text ends when it does end with *pee,* but it also has its inner ferment comprising a great deal of *uebü,* a great deal of *ek,* the *ra-atch* of the teals, and the oxlike roar of the bitterns. Inspired by Amsel's creations, every conceivable kind of terror found expression. But who made his rounds over the rippling crests of the dunes, ensuring the peace necessary to his friend's bird-repellent labors?

Those fists belong to Walter Matern. Seven years old, he gazes gray-eyed over the sea as though it belonged to him. Senta, his young she-dog, barks at the short-winded Baltic waves. Perkun is gone, carried away by one of many canine diseases. Senta of Perkun's line will whelp Harras. Harras of Perkun's line will sire Prinz. Prinz of the Perkun-Senta-Harras line—and at the very beginning the bark of a Lithuanian she-wolf—will make history . . . but for the present Senta is barking at the helpless Baltic. And he stands barefoot in the sand. By sheer force of will and a slight vibration from his knees to the soles of his feet, he is able to dig deeper and deeper into the dune. Soon the sand will reach his rolled-up corduroy trousers stiffened with sea water: but now Walter Matern leaps out of the sand, flinging sand into the wind, and is gone from the dune.

Senta forsakes the short-winded waves, both of them must have flaired something, they hurl themselves, he brown and green in corduroy and wool, she black and elongated, over the crest of the next dune into the beach grass, and—after the sluggish sea has slapped the beach six times—reappear, having gradually grown bored, in an entirely different place. It seems to have been nothing. Air dumplings. Wind soup. Not even a rabbit.

But up above, where from Putzig Bay clouds of roughly equal size against blue drape drift in the direction of the Haff, the birds persist in giving Amsel's near-finished scarecrows the shrill and raucous recognition that any fully finished scarecrow would be proud of.

Thirteenth Morning Shift

Fortunately the year ended peacefully at the mine. From the head-frame the apprentices, under the supervision of Wernicke the head foreman, launched a few fine-looking rockets, which formed the company emblem, the well-known bird motif. Unfortunately the clouds hung so low that a good deal of the magic was lost.

This making of figures; this game played in the dunes, on top of the dike, or in a clearing rich in blueberries amid the scrub pine, took on new meaning late one afternoon when Kriwe the ferryman—the ferry had stopped for the day—took the Schiewenhorst village major with red-and-white-checked daughter to the edge of the woods where Eduard Amsel, guarded as usual by his friend Walter Matern and the dog Senta, had lined up six or seven of his most recent creations against the steeply rising wooded dunes, but not in military formation.

The sun let itself down behind Schiewenhorst. The friends cast long-drawn-out shadows. If Amsel's shadow was nevertheless more rotund, it was because the drooping sun bore witness to the little rascal's extraordinary fatness; he would grow still fatter in time to come.

Neither of them stirred a muscle when the lopsided Leather Kriwe and Lau, the disabled peasant, approached with a daughter in tow and two or three shadows. Senta adopted an attitude of wait and see, and uttered a short growl. The two boys gazed blankly—they had had lots of practice—from the top of the dune over the row of scarecrows, over the sloping meadow where moles had their dwellings, toward the Matern windmill. There it stood with pole on jack, raised windward by a little round hummock, but not running.

And who stood at the foot of the hummock with a sack bent over his right shoulder? The man beneath the sack was Matern, the white miller. He, too, like the sails of the mill, like the two boys on the crest of the dune, like Senta, stood motionless, though for different reasons.

Slowly Kriwe stretched out his left arm and a gnarled, leatherbrown finger. Hedwig Lau, wearing her Sunday best on a weekday, dug a black and buckled patent-leather shoe into the sand. Kriwe's index finger pointed to Amsel's exhibition. "There you are, friend. See what I mean." And his finger pointed with slow thoroughness from scarecrow to scarecrow. Lau's approximately octagonal head followed the leathery finger, remaining two scarecrows behind—there were seven scarecrows—to the very end of the show.

"Them's fine scarecrows, friend; you won't have no more birds to worry about."

Because the patent-leather shoe was digging, its movement was transmitted to the hem of the little girl's dress and to her hair ribbons of like material. Lau scratched himself under his cap and once again, now slowly and solemnly, passed the seven scarecrows in review, this time in reverse order. Amsel and Walter Matern sat on the crest of the dune, dangling their legs unevenly, and kept their eyes on the motionless sails of the windmill. The elastic of Amsel's knee socks cut into his plump calves below the knee, leaving a bulge of doll-like pink flesh. The white miller remained frozen at the foot of the hummock, his right shoulder digging into the hundredweight sack. The miller was in plain sight, but far away. "If you want me to, I can ask the kid what one of them scarecrows costs if it costs anything." No one will ever nod more slowly than Erich Lau, the peasant and village mayor, nodded. For his little daughter every day was Sunday. Head cocked to one side, Senta followed every movement but usually got there first, for she was so young she couldn't help getting ahead of unhurried intimations. When Amsel was baptized and the birds gave the first sign, Hedwig Lau had still been swimming in amniotic fluid. Sea sand is bad for patent-leather shoes. Kriwe in wooden shoes made a half turn toward the crest of the dune and from the corner of his mouth spat brown juice that formed a ball in the sand: "Listen, kid, we'd like to know what one of them scarecrows would cost for the garden if it costs something."

The distant white miller with the bent sack did not drop the sack, Hedwig Lau did not remove her buckled patent-leather shoe from the sand, but Senta gave a short, dust-scattering leap as Eduard Amsel let himself drop from the crest of the dune. Twice he rolled. A moment later, propelled by the two rolls, he stood between the two men in woolen jackets, not far from Hedwig Lau's digging patent-leather shoe.

Step by step, the white miller began to climb the hummock. The patent-leather shoe stopped digging and a giggle dry as bread crumbs began to stir the red-and-white-checked dress and the red-and-white-checked hair ribbons. A deal was in the making. Amsel pointed an inverted thumb at the patent-leather shoes. A stubborn shaking of Lau's head made the shoes into a commodity that was not for sale, leastways not for the present. In response to the offer of barter, hard currency was jingled. While Amsel and Kriwe, but only infrequently Erich Lau the village mayor, figured and in so doing pressed fingers down and let them rise again, Walter Matern was still sitting on the crest of the dune. To judge by the sound his teeth were making, he harbored objections to the negotiations, which he later described as "haggling."

Kriwe and Eduard Amsel arrived at an agreement more quickly than Lau could nod. The daughter was digging again with her shoe. The price of a scarecrow was set at fifty pfennigs. The miller was gone. The mill was milling. Senta was heeling. For three scarecrows Amsel was asking one gulden. In addition and not without reason, for he was planning to expand his business, three rags per scarecrow and as a special premium Hedwig Lau's buckled patent-leather shoes as soon as they could be qualified as worn out.

Oh sober solemn day when a first deal is closed! Next morning the village mayor had the three scarecrows ferried across the river to Schiewenhorst and planted in his wheat behind the railroad. Since Lau, like many peasants on the Island, grew either the Epp or the Kujave variety, both beardless and consequently an easy prey for birds, the scarecrows had ample opportunity to prove their worth. With their coffee cozies, straw-bundle helmets, and crossed straps, they may well have passed for the last three grenadiers of the First Guards Regiment at the battle of Torgau, which, as Schlieffen tells us, was murderous. Already Amsel had given form to his penchant for Prussian precision; in any event the three soldiers were effective; a deathly stillness prevailed amid the ripening summer wheat, over the previously bird-winged and vociferously pillaged field.

Word got around. Soon peasants came from both shores, from Junkeracker and Pasewark, from Einlage and Schnakenburg, from deep in the interior of the Island: from Jungfer, Scharpau, and Ladekopp. Kriwe acted as go-between; but for the present Amsel did not raise his prices and, after remonstrances on the part of Walter Matern, took to accepting only every second and later every third offer. To himself and all his customers he said that he didn't want to botch his work and could turn out only one scarecrow a day, or two at the very most. He declined assistance. Only Walter Matern was permitted to help, to bring raw materials from both banks of the river and to continue guarding the artist and his work with two fists and a black dog.

Brauxel might also relate how Amsel soon had the wherewithal to rent Folchert's decrepit but still lockable barn for a small fee. In this wooden shelter, which had a reputation for spookiness because someone for some reason had hanged himself from one of its rafters, under a roof which would accordingly have inspired any artist, Amsel stored the materials that would subsequently come to life as scarecrows. In rainy weather the barn became his workshop. It was a regular shop, for Amsel let his capital work for him and had purchased in his mother's store, hence at cost price, hammers, two handsaws, drills, pliers, chisels, and the pocket-knife equipped with three blades, a leather punch, a corkscrew, and a saw. This last article he gave to Walter Matern. And two years later, when he couldn't find a stone on the Nickelswalde dike, Walter Matern had thrown it, in place of a stone, into the rising Vistula. We have heard about that.

Fourteenth Morning Shift

Those characters ought to take Amsel's diary as an example and learn to keep their books properly. How many times has Brauchsel described the working method to both coauthors? Two trips at the expense of the firm brought us together and, at a time when those eminent citizens were leading a pampered existence, gave them an opportunity to take notes and to draw up a work plan as well as a few diagrams. Instead, they keep checking back: When does the manuscript have to be delivered? Should a manuscript page have thirty or thirty-four lines? Are you really satisfied with the letter form, or wouldn't something more modern be preferable, along the lines of the new French school, for instance? Is it sufficient for me to describe the Striessbach as a brook between Hochstriess and Langstriess? Or should historical references, such as the boundary dispute between the city of Danzig and the Cistercian monastery in Oliva, be brought in? And what about the letter of ratification written in 1235 by Duke Swantopolk, grandson of Subislaw I, who had founded the monastery? In it the Striessbach is mentioned in connection with Saspe Lake, *"Lacum Saspi usque in rivulum Strieza . . ."* Or the ratifying document issued by Mestwin II in 1283, in which the Striessbach, which constituted the border, is spelled as follows: *"Praefatum rivulum Striesz usque in Vislam . . ."*? Or the letter of 1291 confirming the monasteries of Oliva and Sarnowitz in all their possessions? Here Striessbach is written "Stricze" in one place, while elsewhere we read: *". . . praefatum fluuium Strycze cum utroque littore a lacu Colpin unde scaturit descendendo in Wislam . . ."*

The other coauthor is no more backward about checking back and seasons all his letters with requests for an advance: *". . . perhaps be permitted to point out that according to our verbal agreement each coauthor, on starting work on his manuscript, was to receive . . ."* That's the actor. All right, let him have his advance. But let Amsel's diary, a photostat if not the original, be his Bible.

The log must have inspired him. A log has to be kept on all ships, even a ferry. Kriwe: a cracked, lean chunk of leather with March-gray, lashless, and slightly crossed eyes, which nevertheless permitted him to guide the steam ferry diagonally, or it might be more apt to say crosswise, against the current from landing to landing. Vehicles, fisherwomen with flounder baskets, the pastor, schoolchildren, travelers in transit, salesmen with sample cases, the coaches and freight cars of the Island narrow-gauge railway, cattle for slaughter or breeding, weddings and funerals with coffins and wreaths were squinted across the river by ferryman Kriwe, who entered all happenings in his log. So snugly and unjoltingly did Kriwe put in to his berth that a pfennig could not have been inserted between the sheet metal sheathing on the bow of his ferryboat and the piles of the landing. Moreover he had long served the friends Walter Matern and Eduard Amsel as the most reliable of business agents, asking no commission for the deals he transacted and barely accepting tobacco. When the ferry wasn't operating, he took the two of them to places known only to Kriwe. He urged Amsel to study the terror-inspiring qualities of a willow tree, for the artistic theories of Kriwe and Amsel, which were later recorded in the diary, amounted to this: "Models should be taken primarily from nature." Years later, under the name of Haseloff, Amsel, in the same diary, amplified this dictum as follows: "Everything that can be stuffed should be classified as nature: dolls, for instance."

But the hollow willow tree to which Kriwe led the friends shook itself and had not yet been stuffed. Flat in the background, the mill milled. Slowly the last narrow-gauge train rounded the bend, ringing faster than it ran. Butter melted away. Milk turned sour. Four bare feet, two oiled boots. First grass and nettles, then clover. Over two fences, through three open stiles, then another fence to climb. On both sides of the brook the willows took a step forward, a step back, turned, had hips, navels; and one willow—for even among willows there is the one willow—was hollow hollow hollow, until three days later Amsel filled it in: squats there plump and friendly on both heels, studies the inside of a willow, because Kriwe said . . . and out of the willow in which he is sitting with his curiosity, he attentively examines the willows to the right and left of the brook; as a model Amsel especially prizes a three-headed one that has one foot on dry land but is cooling the other in the brook because the giant Miligedo, the one with the lead club, stepped on its willow foot long long ago. And the willow tree holds still, though to all appearances it would like to run away, especially as the ground fog—for it is very early, a century before school time—is creeping across the meadows from the river and eating away the trunks of the willows by the brook: soon only the three-headed head of the posing willow will be floating on the fog, carrying on a dialogue.

Amsel leaves his niche, but he doesn't feel like going home to his mother, who is mulling over her account books in her sleep, rechecking all her figures. He wants to witness the milk-drinking hour that Kriwe had been telling about. Walter Matern has the same idea. Senta isn't with them, because Kriwe had said: "Don't take the hound, boy; she's likely to whine and get scared when it starts."

So no dog. Between them a hole with four legs and a tail. Barefoot they creep over gray meadows, looking back over the eddying steam. They're on the point of whistling: Here, Senta! Heel! Heel! But they remain soundless, because Kriwe said . . . Ahead of them monuments: cows in the swirling soup. Not far from the cows, exactly between Beister's flax and the willows to either side of the brook, they lie in the dew and wait. From the dikes and the scrub pines graduated tones of gray. Above the steam and the poplars of the highway leading to Pasewark, Steegen, and Stutthof the cross pattern of the sails of the Matern windmill. Flat fretwork. No miller grinds wheat into flour so early in the morning. So far no cocks, but soon. Shadowy and suddenly close the nine scrub pines on the great dune, uniformly bent from northwest to southeast in obedience to the prevailing wind. Toads—or is it oxen?—toads or oxen are roaring. The frogs, slimmer, are praying. Gnats all in the same register. Something, but not a lapwing, calls: an invitation? or is it only announcing its presence? Still no cock. Islands in the steam, the cows breathe. Amsel's heart scurries across a tin roof. Walter Matern's heart kicks a door in. A cow moos warmly. Cozy warm belly-mooing from the other cows. What a noise in the fog; hearts on tin against doors, what is calling whom, nine cows, toads oxen gnats . . . And suddenly—for no sign has been given—silence. Frogs gone, toads oxen gnats gone, nothing calls hears answers anyone, cows lie down, and Amsel and friend, almost without heartbeat, press their ears into the dew, into the clover: they are coming! From the brook a shuffling. A sobbing as of dishcloths, but regular, without crescendo, ploof ploof, pshish—ploof ploof pshish. Ghosts of the hanged? Headless nuns? Gypsies goblins elves? Who's there? Balderle Ashmodai Beng? Sir Peege Peegood? Bobrowski the incendiary and his crony Materna with whom it all began? Kynstute's daughter, whose name was Tulla?—Then they glisten: covered with bottom muck, eleven fifteen seventeen brown river eels have come to bathe in the dew, this is their hour, they slide slither whip through the clover and flow in the direction of. The clover remains bowed in their slimy track. The throats of the toads oxen gnats are still benumbed. Nothing calls and nothing answers. Warm lie the cows on black-and-white flanks. Udders advertise themselves: pale yellow matutinal full to bursting: nine cows, thirty-six teats, eighteen eels. They arrive and suck themselves fast. Brownish-black extensions to pink-spotted teats. Sucking lapping glugging thirst. At first the eels quiver. Pleasure who giving whom? Then one after another the cows let their heavy-heavy heads droop in the clover. Milk flows. Eels swell. The toads are roaring again. The gnats start up. The slim frogs. Still no cock, but Walter Matern has a swollen voice. He'd like to go over and grab. It would be easy, child's play. But Amsel's against it, he has something else in mind and is already planning it out. The eels flow back to the brook. The cows sigh. The first cock. The mill turns slowly. The train rings as it rounds the bend. Amsel decides to build a new scarecrow.

And it took form: a pig's bladder was to be had for nothing because the Lickfetts had just slaughtered. It provided the taut udder. The smoked skin of real eels was stuffed with straw and coiled wire, sewed up and attached to the pig's bladder—upside down, so that the eels twined and twisted like thick hair and stood on their heads on the udder. The Gorgon's head was raised over Karweise's wheat on two forked sticks.

And in his diary Amsel sketched the new scarecrow just as Karweise would buy it—later the tattered hide of a dead cow was thrown over the forked sticks like an overcoat. In the sketch it is overcoatless and more striking, a finished product with its own ragged hide.

Fifteenth Morning Shift

Our friend the actor is creating difficulties. Whereas Brauxel and the young man write day after day—the one about Amsel's diary, the other about and to his cousin—he has come down with a light case of January flu. Has to suspend operations, isn't getting proper care, has always been kind of delicate at this time of year, begs leave once again to remind me of the promised advance. It's been sent, my friend. Quarantine yourself, my friend; your manuscript will benefit by it. Oh sober joy of conscientious effort: There is a diary in which Amsel in beautiful newly learned Sütterlin script noted his expenses in connection with the fashioning of scarecrows for field and garden. The pig's bladder was free. Kriwe procured the worthless cowhide for two sticks of chewing tobacco.

Oh credit balance, what lovely round words: There is a diary in which Amsel, with figures plump and figures angular, entered his receipts from the sale of various scarecrows for garden and field—eels on udder netted him a whole gulden.

Eduard Amsel kept this diary for about two years, drew lines vertical and horizontal, painted Sütterlin pointed, Sütterlin rich in loops, put down blueprints and color studies for various scarecrows, immortalized almost every scarecrow he had sold, and gave himself and his products marks in red ink. Later, as a high school student, he wrapped the several times folded little notebook in cracked black oilcloth, and years later, when he had to hurry from the city to the Vistula to bury his mother,

594

found it in a chest used for a bench. The diary lay among the books left by his father, side by side with those about the battles and heroes of Prussia and underneath Otto Weininger's thick volume, and had a dozen or more empty pages which Amsel later, under the names of Haseloff and Goldmouth, filled in with sententious utterances at irregular intervals separated by years of silence.

Today Brauxel, whose books are kept by an office manager and seven clerks, owns the touching little notebook wrapped in scraps of oilcloth. Not that he uses the fragile original as a prop to his memory! It is stowed away in his safe along with contracts, securities, patents, and essential business secrets, while a photostatic copy of the diary lies between his well-filled ash tray and his cup of lukewarm morning coffee and serves him as work material.

The first page of the notebook is wholly taken up by the sentence, more painted than written: "Scarecrows made and sold by Eduard Heinrich Amsel."

Underneath, undated and painted in smaller letters, a kind of motto: "Began at Easter because I shouldn't forget anything. Kriwe said so the other day."

Brauksel holds that there isn't much point in reproducing here the broad Island idiom written by Eduard Amsel as an eight-year-old schoolboy; in the present narrative it will be possible at most to record in direct discourse the charms of this language, which will soon die out with the refugees' associations and once dead may prove to be of interest to science in very much the same way as Latin. Only when Amsel, his friend Walter, Kriwe, or Grandma Matern open their mouths in the Island dialect, will Brauchsel's pen follow suit. But since in his opinion the value of the diary is to be sought, not in the schoolboy's adventurous spelling but in his early and resolute efforts in behalf of scarecrow development, Eduard's village schoolboy idiom will be reproduced only in a stylized form, halfway between the Island brogue and the literary language. For example: "Today after milking received anuther gulden for scarciu what stands on one legg and holds the uther croocked Wilhelm Ledwormer tuk it. Throo in a Ulan's helmet and a peece of lining what uset to be a gote."

Brauksel will make a more serious attempt to describe the sketch that accompanies this entry: The scarecrow "what stands on one legg and holds the uther croocked" is not a preliminary study but was sketched after completion with all sorts of crayons, brown cinnabar lavender pea-green Prussian-blue, which, however, never reveal their tonality in pure strokes but are laid on in superimposed strata bearing witness to the transience of worn-out clothing. The actual construction sketch, tossed off in a few black lines and still fresh today, is startling when compared to this crayon drawing: the position "what stands on one legg . . ." is suggested by a slightly inclined ladder lacking two rungs; the position "and holds the uther croocked" must be that pole which tries to posture by inclining dancerlike at an angle of forty-five degrees to the middle of the ladder, while the ladder leans slightly to the left. Especially the construction sketch, but the ex post facto crayon drawing as well, suggested a dancer tightly clad in the late reflected splendor of a uniform worn by the musketeers of the Prince of Anhalt-Dessau Infantry Regiment at the battle of Liegnitz.

To come right out with it: Amsel's diary teems with uniformed scarecrows: here a grenadier of the Third Guards Battalion is storming Leuthen cemetery; the Poor Man of Toggenburg appears in the Itzenplitz Infantry Regiment; a Belling hussar capitulates at Maxen; blue and white Natzmer uhlans and Schorlem dragoons battle on foot; blue with red lining, a fusilier of the Baron de La Motte-Fouqué's regiment lives on; in short, just about everybody who for seven years and even earlier had frequented the battlefields of Bohemia and Saxony, Silesia and Pomerania, had escaped at Mollwitz, lost his tobacco pouch at Katholisch-Hennersdorf, sworn allegiance to Fritz in Pirna, deserted to the enemy at Kolin, and achieved sudden fame at Rossbach, came to life under Amsel's hands, though what it was their duty to disperse was no longer a motley Imperial Army, but the birds of the Vistula delta. Whereas Seydlitz was under orders to chase Hildburghausen—". . . *voilà au moins mon martyre est fini* . . ."—to the Main via Weimar, Erfurt, and Saalfeld, the peasants Lickfett, Mommsen, Beister, Folchert, and Karweise were quite satisfied if the scarecrows itemized in Amsel's diary chased the birds of the Vistula delta from beardless Epp wheat to chestnut trees, willows, alders, and scrub pines.

Sixteenth Morning Shift

He acknowledges by phone. The call, it goes without saying, is collect and goes on for a good seven minutes: the money has come, he's beginning to feel better, the crisis is past, his flu is clearing up, tomorrow or at latest the day after he'll be back at his typewriter; yes, unfortunately he has to write directly on the machine, for he is unable to read his own handwriting; but excellent ideas had come to him during his spell of flu . . . As though ideas fostered by fever ever looked like ideas when your temperature was back to normal. My actor friend doesn't think so much of double-entry bookkeeping, even though Brauxel, after years of reckoning up scrupulous accounts, has helped him to achieve a scrupulous credit balance.

It may be that Amsel learned the habit of bookkeeping not only from Kriwe's log but also from his mother, who sat up into the wee hours moaning over her books while her gifted son learned by looking on: conceivably he helped her to order, to file, and to check her accounts.

Despite the economic difficulties of the postwar years, Lottchen Amsel née Tiede managed to keep the firm of A. Amsel afloat and even to reorganize and expand the business—a risk her late husband would never have taken in times of crisis. She began to deal in cutters, some fresh from the Klawitter shipyard, others secondhand, which she had overhauled in Strohdeich, and in outboard motors. She sold the cutters or—as was more profitable—rented them to young fishermen who had just set up housekeeping.

Although Eduard's filial piety never permitted him to fashion even a remote likeness of his mother as a scarecrow, he had no inhibitions whatever, from the age of seven on, about copying her business practices: if she rented out fishing cutters, he rented out extra-stable scarecrows, made expressly for rental. Several pages of the diary show how often and to whom scarecrows were rented. In a steep column Brauxel has added up roughly what they netted him with their scaring: a tidy little sum. Here we shall be able to mention only one rental scarecrow which, though the fees it commanded were nothing out of the ordinary, played an illuminating part in the plot of our story and consequently in the history of scarecrows.

After the above-mentioned study of willows by the brook, after Amsel had built and sold a scarecrow featuring the milk-drinking eels motif, he devised a model revealing on the one hand the proportions of a three-headed willow tree and on the other hand commemorating the spoon-swinging and teeth-grinding Grandmother Matern; it too left its trace in Amsel's diary; but beside the preliminary sketch stood a brief sentence which distinguished this product from all its fellows: "Have to smash it up today, cause Kriwe says it just makes trouble."

Max Folchert, who had it in for the Matern family, had rented the scarecrow, half willow half grandmother, from Amsel and set it up beside the fence of his garden, which bordered the Stutthof highway and faced the Matern vegetable garden. It soon became evident that this rented scarecrow not only drove away birds, but also made horses shy and run off in a shower of sparks. Cows on the way to the barn dispersed as soon as the spoon-swinging willow cast its shadow. The bewildered farm animals were joined by poor Lorchen of the curly hair, who had her daily cross to bear with the real spoon-swinging grandmother. Now she was so terrified and beset by an additional grandmother, who to make matters worse had three heads and was disguised as a willow, that she would wander, frantically wind-blown and disheveled, through fields and scrub pines, over dunes and dikes, through house and garden, and might almost have tangled with the moving sails of the Matern windmill if Lorchen's brother, miller Matern, hadn't grabbed her by the apron. On Kriwe's advice and against the will of old man Folchert, who afterward promptly demanded the refund of part of the rental fee, Walter Matern and Eduard Amsel destroyed the scarecrow during the night. Thus it was brought home to an artist for the first time that, when his works embodied a close enough study of nature, they had power not only over the birds of heaven, but over horses and cows as well and were also capable of disorganizing the tranquil rural gait of Lorchen, a human being. To this insight Amsel sacrificed one of his most successful scarecrows. Moreover, he never again took a willow tree for a model, though he occasionally, in times of ground fog, found a niche in a hollow willow or deemed the thirsty eels on their way from the brook to the recumbent cows worthy of his attention. He avoided mating human and tree, and with self-imposed discipline limited his choice of models to the Island peasants, who, stolid and unoffending as they might be, were effective enough as scarecrows. He made the country folk, disguised as the King of Prussia's grenadiers, fusiliers, corporals, standard bearers, and officers, hover over vegetable gardens, wheat, and rye. He quietly perfected his rental system and, though he never suffered the consequences, became guilty of bribery by persuading a conductor on the Island railway, with the help of carefully wrapped gifts, to transport Amsel's rental scarecrows—or Prussian history put to profitable use—free of charge in the freight car of the narrow-gauge line.

Seventeenth Morning Shift

The actor is protesting. His waning flu, so he says, has not prevented him from carefully studying Brauxel's work schedule, which has been sent to both coauthors. It doesn't suit him that a monument should be erected to miller Matern in the course of this morning shift. Such a monument, he feels, is his affair. Brauksel, who fears for the cohesion of his literary consortium, has abandoned the sweeping portrait he was planning, but must insist on mirroring that aspect of the miller which had already cast its reflected splendor on Amsel's diary.

Though the eight-year-old was especially given to combing the battle-fields of Prussia for ownerless uniforms, there was nonetheless a model, the above-mentioned miller Matern, who was portrayed directly, without Prussian trappings, but with his flour sack over his shoulder.

The result was a lopsided scarecrow, because the miller was an extremely lopsided man. Because he carried his sacks of grain and flour over his right shoulder, this shoulder was a hand's breadth broader, so that all who looked upon miller Matern full face had to fight down a strong temptation to seize the miller's head in both hands and straighten it out. Since neither his work smock nor his Sunday clothes were made to order, every one of his jackets, smocks, or overcoats looked twisted, formed wrinkles around the neck, was too short in the right sleeve, and had permanently burst seams. He was always screwing up his right eye. On the same side of his face, even when there was no hundredweight sack bent over his right shoulder, something tugged the corner of his mouth upward. His nose went along with the movement. Finally—and this is why the present portrait is being drawn—his right ear, for many years subjected to the lateral pressure of thousands of hundredweight, lay creased and flattened against his head, while contrastingly his left ear protruded mightily in pursuit of its natural bent. Seen in front view, the miller had only one ear; but the ear that was missing or discernible only in relief was the more significant of the two.

Though not in a class with poor Lorchen, the miller was not exactly made for this world. The gossip of several villages had it that Grandma Matern had corrected him too freely with her cooking spoon in his childhood. The worst of the Matern family's oddities were traced back to Materna, the medieval robber and incendiary, who had ended up in the Stockturm with his companion in crime. The Mennonites, both rough and refined, exchanged winks, and Simon Beister, the rough, pocketless Mennonite, maintained that Catholicism had done the Materns no good, that there was certainly some Catholic deviltry in the way the brat, who was always prowling around with the tubby Amsel kid from over yonder, gnashed his teeth; and just take a look at their dog, eternal damnation could be no blacker. Yet miller Matern was of rather a gentle disposition and—like poor Lorchen—he had few if any enemies in the villages round about, though there were many who made fun of him.

The miller's ear—and when mention is made of the miller's ear, it is always the right flattened one, pressed down by flour sacks, that is meant—the miller's ear, then, is worth mentioning for two reasons: first, because in a scarecrow, the blueprint of which found its way into his diary, Amsel daringly omitted it, and secondly, because this miller's ear, though deaf to all ordinary sounds, such as coughing talking preaching, the singing of hymns, the tinkling of cowbells, the forging of horshoes, the barking of dogs, the singing of birds, the chirping of crickets, was endowed with the most sensitive understanding for everything down to the slightest whispers, murmurs, and hush-hush revelations that transpired inside a sack of grain or flour. Whether beardless wheat or the bearded variety that was seldom grown on the Island; whether threshed from tough or brittle ears; whether intended for brewing, for baking, for the making of semolina, noodles, or starch, whether vitreous, semivitreous, or mealy, the miller's otherwise deaf ear had the faculty of distinguishing exactly what percentage of vetch seed and mildewed or even sprouting grain it contained. It could also identify a sample, sight unseen, as pale-yellow Frankenstein, varicolored Kujave, reddish Probstein, red flower wheat, which grown in loamy soil yields a good brewer's mash, English club wheat, or as either of two varieties that were grown experimentally on the Island, Urtoba, a hard Siberian winter variety, and Schliephacke's white wheat, No. 5.

The miller's otherwise deaf ear was even more clairaudient when it came to flour. While as an earwitness he was able to tell how many wheat beetles, including pupas and doodlebugs, how many ichneumon flies and flour beetles resided in it, he was able with his ear to the sack to indicate the exact number of mealworms—*Tenebrio molitor*—present in a hundredweight of wheat flour. Moreover—and this is indeed astonishing—he knew, thanks to his flat ear, either instantly or after some minutes of clairaudient listening, how many dead mealworms the living mealworms in a sack had to deplore, because as he slyly revealed with puckered right eye, right corner of his mouth upward and nose acceding to the movement, the sound made by living worms indicated the number of their dead.

The Babylonians, Herodotus tells us, grew wheat with grains the size of peas; but who can lend credence to Herodotus?

Anton Matern the miller made detailed statements about grain and flour; was miller Matern believed?

In Lührmann's taproom, between Folchert's farm and Lührmann's dairy, he was put to the test. The taproom was an ideal testing ground and past tests had left visible traces. From the bar, first of all, there protruded an inch length of nail, allegedly belonging to a two-inch nail, which as a test Erich Block, master brewer in Tiegenhof, had driven into the plank with a single blow of his bare fist; secondly, the whitewashed ceiling of the taproom offered evidence of a different kind: ten or a dozen foot or rather shoe prints, suggesting that someone of succubine origin had been strolling about on the ceiling with his head down. Actually they bear witness to a perfectly human display of strength. When a certain fire insurance salesman expressed doubts about Karweise's muscular prowess, Karweise tossed him up at the ceiling head down and the soles of his shoes heavenward. This he did several times, always catching him in midair, careful that the man should incur no harm but live to corroborate the material evidence of an Island test of strength, namely, the prints of his salesman's shoes on a taproom ceiling.

When Anton Matern was put to the test, the atmosphere wasn't athletic—Matern seemed frail—but more on the spooky and mysterious side. It is Sunday. Door and windows closed. The summer is shut out. Four strips of flypaper, vociferous and variously pitched, are the only reminders of the season. In the bar the inch length of nail, shoe prints on gray, once whitewashed ceiling. The usual photographs of shooting matches and the usual prizes awarded at shooting matches. On the shelf only a few green glass bottles, contents distilled from grain. Competing smells are tobacco, shoe polish, and whey, but alcoholic breath, which had got off to a good start on Saturday, wins by a hair's breadth. They talk chew bet. Karweise, Momber, and young Folchert put up a keg of Neuteich bock beer. Silent over a little glass of goldwater—which only city people drink in these parts—miller Matern puts up an identical keg. From behind the bar Lührmann passes the twenty-pound sack and stands in readiness with the flour sieve for the control test. First a moment's contemplation as the sack rests on the hands of the utterly lopsided miller, then he beds the cushion against his flat ear. At once, because no one is chewing, talking broad brogue, or hardly even breathing alcohol fumes any longer, the flypaper becomes more audible: what is the song of dying swans in the theater beside the death song of iridescent flies in the lowlands!

Lührmann has slipped a slate with pencil attached under the miller's free hand. It lists, for inventory is to be taken: 1. mealworms; 2. pupas; 3. beetles. The miller is still listening. The flies drone. Whey and shoe polish predominate, because hardly anyone dares to expel any alcohol fumes. And now the awkward hand, for the miller's right hand is lightly supporting the sack, creeps across the bar to the slate: after mealworms the pencil grates a stiff 17. Twenty-two pupas it squeaks. These the sponge obliterates and as the wet spot dries, it becomes increasingly clear that there are only nineteen pupas. Eight living beetles are alleged to reside in the sack. And as an extra feature, for the rules of the bet do not demand it, the miller announces on strident slate: "Five dead beetles in the sack." Immediately thereafter alcohol fumes recapture the lead over shoe polish and whey. Someone has turned down the swan song of the flies. The spotlight is on Lührmann with his flour sieve.

To make a long story short, the predicted debit of parchment-hard worms, of soft pupae, horny only at the tip, and of grown beetles, otherwise known as flour beetles, was perfectly accurate. Only one dead beetle of the five dead flour beetles announced was missing; perhaps or undoubtedly its desiccated fragments had passed through the flour sieve.

And so miller Anton Matern received his keg of Neuteich bock beer and gave all those present, especially Karweise, Momber, and young Folchert who had staked the beer, a prophecy as a consolation and premium to take home with them. While setting the keg on his shoulder where the interrogated sack of flour had lain only a moment before, the miller with the flat ear told them, quite incidentally, as though relaying gossip he had just heard, how several mealworms—he couldn't say exactly how many, because they had all been talking at once—had been discussing the prospects for the next harvest—he had heard them distinctly with his flat ear while the twenty pounds had been lying beside it. Well, in the opinion of the mealworms, it would be advisable to mow the Epp variety a week before Seven Brothers and the Kujave wheat as well as Schliephacke's No. 5 two days after Seven Brothers.

Years before Amsel fashioned a scarecrow after the clairaudient miller, the miller had become part of a familiar formula of greeting: "Good morning to you, friend. I wonder what Matern's little mealworm is telling him today."

Skeptical or not, many of the peasants questioned the miller, meaning that he should question a well-filled sack capable of providing information as to when winter wheat or summer wheat should be sowed and knowing pretty well when the wheat should be mowed and when the sheaves should be brought in. And even before he was constructed as a scarecrow and put down in Amsel's diary as a preliminary sketch, the miller issued other predictions, more on the gloomy than on the bright side, which have always been borne out, even to this day when the actor in Düsseldorf has ideas about making the miller into a monument.

For he saw not only the threat of poisonous ergot in the grain, hailstorms warranting insurance benefits, and multitudes of field mice in the near future, but predicted to the day when prices would take a dive on the Berlin or Budapest grain exchange, bank crashes in the early thirties, Hindenburg's death, the devaluation of the Danzig gulden in May 1935. And the mealworms also gave him advance notice of the day when the guns would begin to speak.

It goes without saying that thanks to his flat ear, he also knew more about the dog Senta, mother of Harras, than the dog, who stood black beside the white miller, revealed to the naked eye.

But after the war when the miller with his "A" refugee certificate was living between Krefeld and Düren, he was still able, with the help of a twenty-pound sack that had lived through the flight from the east and the turmoil of war, to prophesy how in the future . . . But as the authors' consortium has decided, not Brauxel but our friend the actor will be privileged to tell about that.

Eighteenth Morning Shift

Crows in the snow—what a subject! The snow puts caps on the rusty scoops and windlasses of potash-mining days. Brauxel is going to have that snow burnt, for who can bear such a sight: crows in the snow, which, if you keep looking, turn into nuns in the snow: the snow must go. Before the night shift pile into the changehouse, let them put in an hour of paid overtime; or else Brauxel will have the new models, which have already been tested—Perkunos, Pikollos, Potrimpos—brought up from the twenty-five-hundred-foot floor and put to work on the snow, then those crows and nuns will see what becomes of them and the snow won't have to be burnt. Unsprinkled, it will lie outside Brauxel's window and lend itself to description: And the Vistula flows, and the mill mills, and the narrow-gauge railway runs, and the butter melts, and the milk thickens—put a little sugar on top—and the spoon stands upright, and the ferry comes over, and the sun is gone, and the sun returns, and the sea sand passes, and the sea licks sand . . . Barefoot run the children and find blueberries and look for amber and step on thistles and dig up mice and climb barefoot into hollow willows . . . But he who looks for amber, steps on the thistle, jumps into the willow, and digs up the mouse will find in the dike a dead and mummified maiden: Tulla Tulla, that's Duke Swantopolk's little daughter Tulla, who was always shoveling about for mice in the sand, bit into things with two incisor teeth, and never wore shoes or stockings: Barefoot run the children, and the willows shake themselves, and the Vistula flows for evermore, and the sun now gone now back again, and the ferry comes or goes or lies groaning in its berth, while the milk thickens until the spoon stands upright, and slowly runs the narrow-gauge train, ringing fast on the bend. And the mill creaks when the wind at a rate of twenty-five feet a second. And the miller hears what the mealworm says. And teeth grind when Walter Matern grinds his teeth from left to right. Same with his grandmother: all around the garden she chases poor Lorchen. Black and big with young, Senta crashes through a trellis of broad beans. For terrible she approaches, raising an angular arm: and in the hand on the arm the wooden spoon casts its shadow on curly-headed Lorchen and grows bigger and bigger, fatter and fatter, more and more . . . Also Eduard Amsel, who is always watching and forgets nothing because his diary stores it all up, has raised his prices some; now he is asking one gulden twenty for a single scarecrow.

This is because. Ever since Herr Olschewski in the low-ceilinged schoolhouse began to speak of all the gods there used to be, who still exist and who existed once upon a time, Amsel has devoted himself to mythology.

It began when a schnapps distiller's shepherd dog took the train with his master from Stutthof to Nickelswalde. The animal's name was Pluto, he had a flawless pedigree, and he came to cover Senta, which took effect. Amsel in the low-ceilinged room wished to know what Pluto was and meant. From that day on Herr Olschewski, a young teacher with ideas about the school system and glad to be inspired by questioning pupils, occupied hours which the schedule assigned to local geography and folklore with long-drawn-out stories revolving first around Wotan, Baldur, Hera, Fafnir, and later around Zeus, Juno, Pluto, Apollo, Mercury, and the Egyptian Isis. He waxed especially eloquent when making old Prussian gods—Perkunos, Pikollos, and Potrimpos—lodge in the branches of creaking oak trees.

Naturally Amsel not only listened but, as the sketches in his diary show, he also transmuted, and most ingeniously: he brought the fiery red Perkunos to life with decrepit red ticking obtained from houses where people had died. A split oak log became Perkunos' head; to right and left Amsel wedged superannuated horseshoes into it, and in the cracks he stuck the tail feathers of slaughtered roosters. Glowing, all fire god, the scarecrow was only briefly exhibited on the dike, then it was sold for one gulden twenty and moved to the interior of the Island, to Ladekopp.

The pale Pikollos, who was said to have looked up from below and for that reason had handled the affairs of the dead in pagan times, was not, as one might imagine, fashioned from the bedsheets of the deceased, young or old, for to costume the god of death in shrouds would have been much too unimaginative, but—Amsel procured his accessories in a house from which some peasants had just moved—was adorned in a fusty-yellow and crumbling bridal dress smelling of lavender, musk, and mouse droppings. This attire draped over his manly form made Pikollos imposing and terrible; when the mortuary-nuptial scarecrow was sold for use on a large farm in Schusterkrug, the god brought in two whole gulden.

But bright and gay as Amsel made him, Potrimpos, the forever laughing youth with the ear of wheat between his teeth, brought in only a single gulden, although Potrimpos protects summer and winter seed against corn cockle, charlock, and wild mustard, against couchgrass, vetches, spurry, and ergot. For over a week the youthful scarecrow, a hazlenut bush shirted in silver paper and skirted in cats' skins, stood exposed on the dike, tinkling invitingly with saffroncolored eggshells. Only then was he purchased by a peasant from Fischer-Babke. His wife, who was pregnant and for that reason more inclined than most to mythology, thought the fruit-promising scarecrow cute and giggly-comical: some weeks later she was delivered of twins.

But Senta too had come in for a portion of the boy Potrimpos' blessing: exactly sixty-four days later, under the jack of the Matern windmill, she whelped six blind but, in keeping with their pedigree, black puppies. All six were registered and gradually sold; among them a male, Harras, who will be spoken of frequently in the next book; for a Herr Liebenau bought Harras as a watchdog for his carpenter shop. In answer to an ad that miller Matern had put in the *Neueste Nachrichten,* the carpenter had taken the train to Nickelswalde and closed the deal.

In the obscure beginnings there is said to have been, there was, in Lithuania a she-wolf, whose grandson, the black dog Perkun, sired the bitch Senta; and Pluto covered Senta; and Senta whelped six puppies, among them the male Harras; and Harras sired Prinz; and Prinz will make history in books that Brauxel does not have to write.

But Amsel never designed a scarecrow in the image of a dog, not even of Senta, who ambled about between him and Walter Matern. All the scarecrows in his diary, except for the one with the milkdrinking eels and the other—half grandmother, half three-headed willow—are likenesses of men or gods.

The lore that Herr Olschewski dispensed to dozing pupils through the summery droning of flies was reflected, out of school hours, in a series of bird-repellent creations modeled, when not on gods, on the grand masters of the order of Teutonic Knights from Hermann Balke via Konrad von Wallenrod down to von Jungingen: there was a considerable clanking of rusty corrugated iron, and black crosses were cut out of white waxed paper with spiked barrel staves. Various members of the Jagello family, the great Kasimir, the notorious robber Bobrowski, Beneke, Martin Bardewiek, and the unfortunate Lesczynski were obliged to pose in the company of Kniprode, Letzkau, and von Plauen. Amsel couldn't get enough of the history of Brandenburg-Prussia; he pottered through the centuries from Albrecht Achilles to Zieten and from the lees of eastern European history harvested scarecrows to disperse the birds of the heavens.

Soon after the carpenter, Harry Liebenau's father, bought the dog Harras from miller Anton Matern, but at a time when the world had not yet registered the presence either of Harry Liebenau or of his cousin Tulla, the *Neueste Nachrichten* offered all those who could read an article dealing lengthily and poetically with the Island. The region and its people were knowledgeably described. The author did not forget the anomalies of the storks' nests or the special features of the farmhouses, those old porch posts, for example. And in the middle section of this article, which Brauksel has had photostated in the East German newspaper archives, one could, and still can, read approximately the following knowledgeable lines: "Though in other respects everything runs its accustomed course on Great Island and the technology that is changing our whole world has not yet made its triumphant entry, an astonishing transformation is becoming discernible in what is, if you will, a secondary domain: The scarecrows in the far-billowing wheatfields of these magnificent plains— which only a few years ago were commonplace and merely useful or at most a trifle ludicrous and sad, but in any event closely resembled the scarecrows of other provinces and regions—now reveal, in the vicinity of Einlage, Jungfer, and Ladekopp, but also as far upstream as Käsemark and Montau and occasionally even in the region of the south of Neuteich, a new and richly variegated aspect: elements of fantasy mingle with immemorial folk ways; delightful figures, but gruesome ones as well, may be seen standing in surging fields and in gardens blessed with abundance; might it not even now be time to call the attention of the local folklore museums or of the provincial Museum to these treasures of naïve, yet formally mature folk art? For we have the impression that in the very midst of a civilization that is leveling everything in its path, the Nordic heritage is here flowering afresh and anew: the spirit of the Vikings and Christian simplicity in an East-German symbiosis. Especially a group of three figures in a far-billowing wheatfield between Scharpau and Bärwalde, which with its striking simplicity suggests the Crucifixion group on the mount of Calvary, the Lord and the two thieves, is marked by a simple piety which goes straight to the heart of the traveler wending his way amid these blessed far-billowing fields—and he does not know why."

Now let no one suppose that Amsel fashioned this group with its childlike piety—only one thief was sketched in the diary—with a view to divine reward: according to the diary, it brought in two gulden twenty.

What became of all the money that the peasants of the Great Island district spontaneously or after brief bargaining counted out into Amsel's palm? Walter Matern kept this mounting wealth in a small leather pouch. He guarded it with a dark frown and not without grinding of the teeth. Slung around his wrist he carried the pouch full of Free State silver currency between the poplars on the highway and through the windy clearings in the scrub pine forest; with it he had himself ferried across the river; he swung it, struck it against garden fences or slapped it challengingly against his own knee, and opened it ceremoniously when a peasant became a customer.

Amsel did not take payment. While Amsel made a show of indifference, Walter Matern had to state the price, seal the bargain with a handshake after the manner of cattle dealers, and pocket or pouch the coins. In addition Walter Matern was responsible for the transportation of sold or rented scarecrows. Amsel made him his flunky. Now and then he rebelled and tried to regain his freedom, but never for very long. The incident with the pocketknife was a feeble attempt of this kind; for Amsel, rolling through the world plump on short legs, was always ahead of him. When the two ran along the dike, the miller's son, after the manner of body servants, remained half a step behind the untiring builder of scarecrows. The servant also carried his master's materials: beanpoles and wet rags and whatever the Vistula had washed ashore.

Nineteenth Morning Shift

"Flunky, flunky!" blasphemed the children when Walter Matern flunkied for his friend Eduard Amsel. Many who blaspheme God are punished; but who is going to bring down the law on all the rancid little stinkpots who daily blaspheme the Devil? Like God and the Devil the two of them—Brauksel is now referring to the miller's son and little fatso from over yonder—were so smitten with each other that the blaspheming of the village youth was if anything incense to them. Moreover, the two of them, like Devil and God, had scored each other with the same knife.

606

Thus at one—for the occasional flunkying was an act of love—the two friends often sat in the overhang room, whose illumination was determined by the sun and the sails of the Matern windmill. They sat side by side on footstools at Grandmother Matern's feet. Outside it was late afternoon. The wood worms were silent. The shadows of the mill were falling somewhere else. The poultry yard was turned down very low, because the window was closed. Only on the flypaper a fly was dying of too much sweetness and couldn't stop. Far below the fly, grumpily, as though no ear were good enough for her yarns, Grandma was telling stories, always the same ones. With her bony grandmother's hands, which indicated all the dimensions that occurred in her tales, she dealt out stories about floods, stories about bewitched cows, the usual stories about eels, the one-eyed blacksmith, the three-legged horse, or how Duke Kynstute's young daughter went out to dig for mice, and the story about the enormous dolphin that a storm had washed ashore in the exact same year as Napoleon marched into Russia.

But decoyed by Amsel with adroit questions, she always ended up —though the detours could be very long—in the dark passageways and dungeons of the endless tale, endless because it has not been concluded to this day, about the twelve headless nuns and the twelve knights with their heads and helmets under their arms, who in four coaches—two drawn by white, two drawn by black horses—drove through Tiegenhof over resounding cobbles, stopped outside a deserted inn, and twelve and twelve went in: Music broke loose. Woodwinds brasses plucked strings. Tongues fluttered and voices twanged expertly. Sinful songs with sinful refrains from male throats—the heads and helmets under the sharply bent arms of the knights—alternated with the watery litanies of pious women. Then it was the turn of the headless nuns. From heads held out in hands a part song poured forth, obscene words to an obscene tune, and there was dancing and stamping and squealing and reeling. And in between, a humble shuffling procession cast headless shadows twelve and twelve through the windows of the inn and out on the paving stones, until once again leching and retching, roaring and stamping loosened the mortar and the dowels of the house. Finally toward morning, just before cock-crow, the four coaches with black horses and white horses drove up without coachmen. And twelve clanking knights, giving off clouds of rust, veils billowing on top, left the inn at Tiegenhof with maggot-pale nuns' faces. And twelve nuns, wearing knights' helmets with closed visors over their habits, left the inn. Into the four coaches, white horses black horses, they mounted six and six and six and six, but not mixed—they had already exchanged heads—and rode through the cowed village, and again the cobblestones resounded. To this day, said Grandma Matern, before spinning the story out some more, directing the coaches to other places and

607

making them draw up outside chapels and castles—they say that to this day pious hymns and blasphemous prayers can be heard farting from the fireplace of that weird inn, where nobody is willing to live.

Thereupon the two friends would gladly have gone to Tiegenhof. But though they started out a number of times, they never got any farther than Steegen or at the farthest Ladekopp. Only in the following winter, which for a builder of scarecrows was naturally bound to be the quiet, truly creative season, did Eduard Amsel find occasion to take the measurements of those headless people: and that was how he came to build his first mechanical scarecrows, an undertaking that used up an appreciable part of the fortune in Matern's leather pouch.

Twentieth Morning Shift

This thaw is drilling a hole in Brauxel's head. The water is dripping on the zinc ledge outside his window. Since there are windowless rooms available in the administration building, Brauksel could easily avoid this therapy; but Brauchsel stays put and welcomes the hole in his head: celluloid, celluloid—if you've got to be a doll, you may as well be a doll with little holes in your dry celluloid forehead. For Brauxel once lived through a thaw and underwent a transformation beneath the water dripping from a dwindling snow man; but before that, many many thaws ago, the Vistula flowed under a thick sheet of ice traversed by horse-drawn sleighs. The young people of the nearby fishing villages tried their hand at sailing on curved skates known as *Schlaifjen*. Two by two—a bedsheet nailed to roofing laths would fill with wind and send them whipping over the ice. Every mouth steamed. Snow was in the way and had to be shoveled. Behind the dunes, barren and fertile land was topped with the same snow. Snow on both dikes. The snow on the beach blended into the snow on the ice sheet that covered the rimless sea and its fish. Under a crooked snow cap, for the snow was falling from the east, the Matern windmill stood splay-footed on its round white hummock amid white fields distinguishable only by their unyielding fences, and milled. Napoleon's poplars sugar-coated. A Sunday painter had covered the scrub pines with white sizing fresh from the tube. When the snow turned gray, the mill was stopped for the day and turned out of the wind. Miller and miller's man went home. The lopsided miller stepped in the miller's man's footsteps. Senta the black dog, nervous since her puppies had been sold, was following trails of her own and biting into the snow. Across from the mill, on a fence that they had previously kicked clear of snow with the heels of their boots, sat Walter Matern and Eduard Amsel muffled and mittened.

For a while they were silent straight ahead. Then they conversed in obscure technical terms. They talked about mills with runners and chasers, Dutch "smock" mills, without jack or tailpole but with three sets of runners and an extra set of burrs. They talked about vanes and sails and stabilizers which adjust themselves to the wind velocity. There were worm drives and rollers and oak levers and rods. There were relationships between drum and brake. Only children sing unwittingly: The mill turns slow, the mill turns faster. Amsel and Walter Matern did not sing, but knew why and when a mill: The mill turns slow and the mill turns faster when the brake puts slight or heavy pressure on the wheel shaft. Even when snow was falling, the mill turned evenly amid the fitful snow squalls, provided the wind kept up a good twenty-five feet a second. Nothing looks quite like a mill turning in a snowfall; not even a fire engine called upon to extinguish a burning water tower in the rain.

But when the mill was stopped for the day and the sails stood silhouetted in the falling snow, it turned out—but only because Amsel screwed up his eyes—that the mill was not yet slated for a rest. Silently the snow, now gray now white now black, drove across from the great dune. The poplars on the highway floated. In Lührmann's taproom light was burning egg-yellow. No train ringing on the bend. The wind grew biting. Bushes whimpered. Amsel glowed. His friend dozed. Amsel saw something. His friend saw nothing. Amsel's little fingers rubbed each other in his mittens, slipped out, looked for the right patent-leather shoe in the left-hand pocket of his jacket and found it: He was cooking with gas. Not a single snowflake kept its identity on Amsel's skin. His lips pursed and into his screwed-up eyes passed more than can be said in one breath: One after the other they drive up. Without coachmen. And the mill motionless. Four sleighs, two with white horses—blending; two with black horses—contrasting—and they help each other out: twelve and twelve, all headless. And a headless knight leads a headless nun into the mill. Altogether twelve headless knights lead twelve nuns without heads into the mill—but knights and nuns alike are carrying their heads under their arms or out in front of them. But on the trampled path things are getting complicated, for despite the likeness of veil and veil, armor and armor, they are still chewing on quarrels dating from the day when they broke up camp in Ragnit. The first nun isn't speaking to the fourth knight. But both are glad to chat with the knight Fitzwater, who knows Lithuania like the holes in his coat of mail. In May the ninth nun should have been delivered of a child, but wasn't, because the eighth knight— Engelhard Rabe his name—had cut off the heads and veils not only of the ninth but also of the sixth nun, who had overindulged in cherries summer after summer, with the sword of the tenth knight, the fat one, who was sitting on a beam and gnawing the meat from the bones of a chicken behind closed visor. And all because the embroidery on the banner of St. George wasn't finished and the River Szeszupe was conveniently frozen over. While the remaining nuns embroidered all the faster—the last red field was almost full—the third waxen nun, who was always following the eleventh knight in the shadows, came bringing the basin to put under the blood. Thereupon the seventh, second, fourth, and fifth nuns laughed, tossed their embroidery behind them, and held out their heads and veils to the eighth knight, the black Engelhard Rabe. He, nothing loath, turned first to the tenth knight, who was relieving himself still squatting on the beam with his chicken behind his visor, and cut off his head, chicken, and helmet with visor, then passed him his sword: and the fat, headless, but nevertheless chewing tenth knight helped the eighth, black knight, helped the second nun, the third waxen nun who had always remained in the shadow, and likewise the fourth and fifth nuns to dispose of their heads and veils and Engelhard Rabe's head. Laughing, they passed the basin from one to the other. Only a few nuns were embroidering on the banner of St. George, although the Szeszupe was conveniently frozen, although the English under Lancaster were already in the camp, although reports on the state of the roads had come in, although Prince Witold preferred to stand aside and Wallenrod was already summoning the company to table. But now the basin was full and running over. The tenth nun, the fat one—for just as there was a fat knight, there was also a fat nun—had to come waddling; and she was privileged to bring the basin three more times, the last time when the Szeszupe was already free of ice and Ursula, the eighth nun, whom everyone called Tulla affectionately and for short, had to kneel, showing the down on her neck. She had taken her vow only the preceding March and had already broken it twelve times. But she didn't know with whom or in what order, because the visors had all been closed; and now the English under Henry Derby; freshly arrived in the camp, but already in a dreadful hurry. There was also a Percy among them, but it was Thomas Percy, not Henry. For him Tulla had cunningly embroidered an individual banner, although Wallenrod had forbidden individual banners. Jacob Doutremer and Pege Peegott were planning to follow Percy. In the end Wallenrod bearded Lancaster. He put Thomas Percy's pocket-sized banner to flight, bade Hattenstein bear the just-finished banner of St. George across the ice-free river, and ordered the eighth nun, known as Tulla, to kneel down while the bridge was being built, in the course of which operation four horses and a squire were drowned. She sang more beautifully than the eleventh and twelfth nuns had sung before her. She was able to twang, to chirp, and at the same time to make her bright-red tongue flutter in the dark-red cavern of her mouth. Lancaster wept behind his visor, for he would rather have stayed home, but he had had a falling out with his family, though he later became king notwithstanding. Suddenly and because no one wanted to cross the Szeszupe any more and all were whimpering to go home, the youngest of the knights jumped out of a tree in which he had been sleeping and took springy little steps toward the down on the neck. He had come all the way from Mörs in the lower Rhineland in the hope of coverting the Barts. But the Barts had all been converted, and Bartenstein had already been founded. There was nothing left but Lithuania, but first the down on Tulla's neck. He smote it above the last vertebra, then tossed his sword in the air and caught it with his own neck. Such was the dexterity of the sixth and youngest knight. The fourth knight, who never spoke to the first nun, tried to imitate him, but had no luck and at the first attempt severed the head of the tenth nun, the fat one, and at the second attempt the sleek stern head of the stern first nun. Thereupon the third knight, who never changed his coat of mail and enjoyed a reputation for wisdom, had to bring the basin, because there wasn't a single nun left.

Followed by the bannerless English, by Hattenstein with banner and men-at-arms, the remaining knights with heads took a short trip into trackless Lithuania. Duke Kynstute gurgled in the bogs. Beneath giant ferns his daughter bleated. Croaking on all sides. Horses floundered. In the end Potrimpos was still unburied; Perkunos still had no inclination to burn; and unblinded Pikollos continued to look up from below. Ah! They should have made a movie. Plenty of extras and nature galore. Twelve hundred pair of greaves, crossbows, breastplates, rotting boots, chewed-up harnesses, seventy bolts of stiff linen, twelve inkwells, twenty thousand torches, tallow lamps, currycombs, balls of twine, sticks of licorice wood—the chewing gum of the fourteenth century—sooty armorers, packs of hounds, Teutonic Knights playing drafts, harpists jugglers muleteers, gallons of barley beer, bundles of pennants, arrows, lances, and smokejacks for Simon Bache, Erik Cruse, Claus Schone, Richard Westrall, Spannerle, Tylman, and Robert Wendell in the bridge-building scene, in the bridge-crossing scene, in ambush, in the pouring rain: sheaves of lightning, splintered oak trees, horses shy, owls blink, foxes track, arrows whir: the Teutonic Knights are getting nervous; and in the alder thicket the blind seeress cries out: "Wela! Wela!" Back back . . . but not until the following July were they again to see that little river which to this day the poet Bobrowski darkly sings. Clear flowed the Szeszupe, tinkling over the pebbles along the shore. Old friends in the crowd: there sat the twelve headless nuns, with their left hands holding their heads and veils and with their right hands pouring the water of the Szeszupe on overheated faces. In the background the headless knights stood sullen, refusing to cool themselves off. Thereupon the remaining knights decided to make common cause with those who were already headless. Near Ragnit they lifted off each other's heads and helmets in unison, harnessed their horses to four crude wagons, and set off with white horses and black horses through territories converted and unconverted. They exalted Potrimpos, dropped Christ, once again blinded Pikollos, but to no avail, and took up the Cross again. They stopped at inns, chapels, and mills and lived it up down through the centuries, terrifying Poles, Hussites, and Swedes. They were at Zorndorf when Seydlitz crossed Saverne Hollow with his squadrons, and when the Corsican had to hurry home, they found four ownerless coaches in his wake. For these they exchanged their crusaders' wagons, and so it was in carriages with comfortable springs that they witnessed the second battle of Tannenberg, which was not fought at Tannenberg any more than the first. In the van of Budenny's ferocious cavalry, they had barely time to turn back when, aided by the Virgin Mary, Pilsudski carried the day in a loop of the Vistula. In the years when Amsel was building and selling scarecrows, they had shuttled restlessly back and forth between Tapiau and Neuteich. Twelve and twelve, they were planning to go right on being restless until redemption should come their way and each one of them, or perhaps one should say each neck, should be enabled to carry his, her, or its own individual head.

Most recently they had been seen in Scharpau and Fischer-Babke. The first nun had taken to wearing the fourth knight's face now and then, but she still wouldn't speak to him. There they came riding through the fields between the dunes and the Stutthof highway; they stopped—only Amsel saw them—outside the Matern mill and alit. It happens to be the second of February, Feast of the Purification of the Virgin Mary, and they are going to celebrate it. They help each other out of the carriages, up the hummock, and into the windmill. A moment later flour loft and sack loft are full of buzzing, quick chatter, sharp screams, witch-sabbath oaths, and prayers said backwards. A chirping is heard and the sound of whistling on iron, while snow falls from the direction of the dune, possibly from the sky. Amsel glows and rubs the patent-leather shoe deep in his pocket, but his friend, aloof and turned inward, is dozing. Time out, for inside they are wallowing in flour, riding the mill post, wedging their fingers between drum and brake, and because it is Candlemas, turning the mill into the wind: slowly it turns, fitfully at first; then twelve heads strike up the sweet sequence: *Stabat mater dolorosa*—O Perkollos, seven of twelve are still so cold, seven frozen sevenfold—*juxta crucem lacrimosa*—O Perkunos, all twelve aflame; when I'm burned to ashes, eleven remain—*Dum pendebat filius*—O Potrimpos, all whitened with flour, we'll mourn Christ's blood in this white hour . . . Then at last, while the millstones jumble the head and helmet of the eighth, black knight with the fat friendly head of the tenth nun, the Matern postmill begins to turn faster and faster, although there is no wind at all. And the youngest, the knight from the lower Rhine, tosses his singing head with wide-open visor to the eighth nun. She affects ignorance, withholds recognition, calls herself Ursula and not Tulla, is quite sufficient to herself, and is riding the cotter that stops the wheel shaft. It begins to quake: The mill turns slow, the mill turns faster; the heads in the hopper howl off-key; staccato gasps on the wooden cotter; crows in the flour, the rafters groan and the bolts wrench loose; upstairs and down, headless forms; from sack loft to flour loft a transubstantiation is under way: amid lecherous grunts and crystalline prayer the old Matern postmill becomes young again and turns—only Amsel with his patent-leather shoe sees it—into a knight with pole on jack, flailing about him and smiting the snowfall; becomes—as only Amsel with his shoe understands—a nun in ample habit, bloated with beans and ecstasy, circling her arms: windmill knight windmill nun: poverty poverty poverty. But fermented mare's milk is guzzled. Corn cockle juice is distilled. Incisor teeth gnaw at fox bones, while the headless bodies go on starving: Poverty. Sweet simpering. And then nevertheless pulling over, pushing under, heads laid aside; and from the crosswise recumbents rise the pure sounds of ascetic discipline, renunciation limpid as water, the Song of Songs pleasing to God: windmill knight brandishes windmill scourge; windmill scourge strikes windmill nun—Amen—or not yet amen; for while silent and without passion snow falls from the sky, while Amsel with narrowed eyes sits on the fence, feels Hedwig Lau's right patent-leather shoe in the left-hand pocket of his jacket and is already hatching his little plan, the little flame that slumbers in every windmill has awakened.

And after heads had promiscuously found their way to bodies, they left the mill, which was now turning sluggishly, scarcely turning at all. And while they entered four carriages and glided away toward the dunes, it began to burn from the inside outward. Then Amsel slipped off the fence, pulling his friend along with him. "Fire, fire!" they shouted in the direction of the village: but the mill was beyond saving.

Twenty-first Morning Shift

Finally the drawings have come. Brauksel had them glassed and hung at once. Medium formats: "Concentration of nuns between Cologne cathedral and railroad station. Eucharistic congress in Munich. Nuns and crows and crows and nuns." Then the large items: DIN A 1, India ink, partly inked in: A Novice Takes the Veil; Large Abbess; Squatting Abbess—excellent. The artist is asking 500 marks. A fair price, absolutely fair. We'll put it right into the construction office. We'll use quiet electric motors: windmill nun brandishes windmill scourge . . .

For while the police were still investigating the scene of the fire, because arson was suspected, Eduard Amsel built his first, and in the ensuing spring when all snow had lost its meaning and it turned out that the Mennonite Simon Beister had set the Catholic postmill on fire on religious grounds, his second, mechanical scarecrow. He put a lot of money into it, the money from the little leather pouch. From sketches in his diary he fashioned a windmill knight and a windmill nun, made both of them, properly costumed in sails, sit on the jack and obey the wind; but though they soon found purchasers, neither windmill knight nor windmill nun did justice to the vision that snowy Candlemas night had given Eduard Amsel: the artist was dissatisfied; and it also seems unlikely that the firm of Brauxel & Co. will be able to complete its experimental series of mobiles and put them into mass production before mid-October.

Twenty-second Morning Shift

After the mill had burned down, the ferry, followed by the Island narrow-gauge railway, brought the pocket and buttonless, in other words rough Mennonite Simon Beister, fisherman and small holder who had made a fire on religious grounds, to the city and then to the municipal prison of Schiesstange, situated in Neugarten at the foot of the Hagelsberg, which became Simon Beister's place of residence for the next few years.

Senta of Perkun's line, Senta who had whelped six puppies and whose blackness had always contrasted so strikingly with the white miller, showed signs of canine nervousness once the puppies were sold, and after the mill burned down went so destructively haywire—tearing a sheep limb from limb like a wolf and attacking an agent from the fire insurance company—that miller Matern was obliged to send his son Walter to see Erich Lau, mayor of Schiewenhorst, for Hedwig Lau's father owned a rifle.

The fire in the mill also brought the friends a certain amount of change. Destiny, or rather the village teacher, widow Amsel, and miller Matern, not to mention Dr. Battke the high school principal, transformed the ten-year-old Walter Matern and the ten-year-old Eduard Amsel into two high school students, who succeeded in being assigned to the same bench. While the new Matern windmill was still being built—the project of a Dutch mill of masonry with a rotating cap had to be abandoned for fear of marring the historical profile of the mill where Queen Louise had passed the night—Easter came around, accompanied by a moderate rise in the river, the first signs of a plague of mice, and a sudden bursting of pussy willows. Soon afterward Walter Matern and Eduard Amsel donned the green velvet caps of Sankt Johann High School. Their heads were the same size. They wore the same size shoes, but Amsel was much stouter, much much stouter. In addition Amsel had only one whorl in his hair. Walter Matern had two, which is said to betoken an early death.

The distance from the mouth of the Vistula to Sankt Johann High School made the friends into commuting schoolboys. Commuting schoolboys are rich in experience and great liars. Commuting schoolboys can sleep sitting up. Commuting schoolboys are students who do their homework in the train and so acquire a trembling script. Even in later years when there is no more homework to be done, their handwriting becomes hardly less cramped, at best it stops trembling. That is why the actor has to write his story directly on the machine; as a former commuting schoolboy, he still writes a cramped, illegible hand, jolted by imaginary joints in the rails.

The narrow-gauge train left from the Island station, which the city people call "Niederstadt Station." By way of Knüppelkrug and Gottswalde, it made its way to Schusterkrug, where it was ferried across the Dead Vistula, and Schiewenhorst, whence the steam ferry carried it across the so-called cut to Nickelswalde. Amsel got out in Schiewenhorst and Walter Matern in Nickelswalde. As soon as the locomotive had pulled each of the four cars separately up the dike, the train continued on to Pasewark, Junkeracker, Steegen, and Stutthof, which was the terminus of the narrow-gauge line.

All the commuting scholars took the first car, right behind the locomotive. Peter Illing and Arnold Mathrey were from Einlage. Gregor Knessin and Joachim Bertulek got on in Schusterkrug. In Schiewenhorst Hedwig Lau's mother brought her to the station on schooldays. Often the child had tonsillitis and didn't come. Was it not unseemly that the narrow-chested narrow-gauge locomotive should chug away regardless of Hedwig Lau's absence? Like Walter Matern and Eduard Amsel, the village mayor's daughter went into sixth after Easter. Later on, beginning in fourth, her health improved, her tonsils stopped acting up; and now that there was no further reason to fear for her days, she became such a bore that Brauxel will soon find it unnecessary to go on mentioning her in these papers. But at the time Amsel still had a glance or two to spare for a quiet to sluggish, pretty little girl, or perhaps she was pretty only by coastwise standards. She sat across from him with hair that was somewhat too blond, eyes that were somewhat too blue, an unreasonably fresh complexion, and an open English book.

Hedwig Lau wears braids. Even as the train pulls in to the city, she smells of butter and whey. Amsel screws up his eyes and lets the coastwise blondness of her braids shimmer. Outside, the first frame saws come into view after Klein-Plehnendorf, and the timber port begins: swallows are replaced by gulls, the telegraph poles go on. Amsel opens his diary. Hedwig Lau's braids hang down, swaying gently just above the open English book. Amsel draws a sketch in his diary: lovely, lovely. From the loose braids which he rejects on formal grounds, he develops two spirals to cover the flaming redness of her ears. He doesn't say: Fix it this

615

way, braids are dumb, you gotta wear spirals. Of course not, but while Kneipab passes outside, he thrusts his diary without a word over her open English book, and Hedwig Lau looks. Then with her eyelashes she nods in assent, almost obedience, although Amsel doesn't look like a boy whom schoolgirls would tend to obey.

Twenty-third Morning Shift

Brauxel has an unblunting distaste for unused razor blades. A handyman who formerly, in the days of the Burbach Potash Co. Inc., worked in the mine and opened up rich salt deposits, breaks in Brauksel's razor blades and delivers them to him after using them once. Thus Brauksel has no need to overcome a revulsion which, though not directed against razor blades, was equally innate and equally strong in Eduard Amsel. He had a thing about new, new-smelling clothes. The smell of fresh underwear compelled him to fight down incipient nausea. As long as he attended the village school, natural limits were imposed on his allergy, for the apparel in which the small fry of Schiewenhorst as well as Nickelswalde weighed down the school benches was baggy, worn, and much mended. Sankt Johann High School had higher vestimentary standards. His mother obliged him to put on new and new-smelling clothes: the green velvet cap has already been mentioned, in addition there were polo shirts, sand-gray knee breeches of expensive material, a blue blazer with mother-of-pearl buttons, and—possibly at Amsel's request—patent-leather shoes with buckles; for Amsel had no objection to buckles or patent leather, he had no objection to mother-of-pearl buttons or blazer, it was only the prospect of all these new things actually touching his skin, the skin, it should not be forgotten, of a scarecrow builder, that gave him the creeps, especially as Amsel reacted to fresh underwear and unworn clothes with an itching rash; just as Brauxel, if he shaves with a fresh blade, must fear the onset of the dread barber's itch.

Fortunately Walter Matern was in a position to help his friend. His school clothes were made of turned cloth, his high shoes had already been twice to the shoemaker's, Walter Matern's thrifty mother had bought his high school cap secondhand. And so for a good two weeks the trip in the narrow-gauge railway began with the same ceremony: in one of the freight cars, amid unsuspecting cattle on their way to the slaughterhouse, the friends changed clothes. The shoes and cap presented no problem, but though Walter Matern was hardly emaciated, his jacket, knee breeches, and shirt were too tight for his friend. Yet uncomfortable as they were, they were a blessed relief, because they had been worn and turned, because they smelled old and not new. Needless to say, Amsel's new clothes hung down limp and loose on his friend's frame, and patent leather and buckles,

616

mother-of-pearl buttons, and the ridiculous blazer looked odd on him. Amsel, with his scarecrow builder's feet in rough, deeply furrowed clod-hoppers, was nevertheless delighted at the sight of his patent-leather shoes on Walter Matern's feet. Walter Matern had to break them in until Amsel pronounced them worn and found them just as cracked as the cracked patent-leather shoe that lay in his school satchel and meant something.

To anticipate, this exchange of clothing was for years a component, though not the cement, of the friendship between Walter Matern and Eduard Amsel. Even handkerchiefs, which his mother had slipped lovingly into his pocket, fresh and folded hem to hem, had to be initiated by his friend, and the same went for socks and stockings. And the exchange didn't stop at clothing; Amsel betrayed similar feelings about new pencils and pens: Walter Matern had to sharpen his pencils, take the shape off his new erasers, break in his Sütterlin pens—he would assuredly, like Brauksel's handyman, have had to initiate Amsel's new razor blades if reddish down had already ripened on Amsel's freckleface.

Twenty-fourth Morning Shift

Who, having relieved himself after breakfast, is standing here contemplating his excrement? A thoughtful, anxious man in search of the past. Why keep ogling a smooth and weightless death's-head? Theatrical ambiance, Hamletlike maunderings, histrionic gestures! Brauxel, the present writer, raises his eyes and pulls the chain; while contemplating, he has remembered a situation that gave the two friends, Amsel rather matter-of-factly, Walter Matern histrionically, an opportunity to meditate and to conjure up a theatrical ambiance.

The layout of the high school on Fleischergasse was a fantastic jumble—the building had formerly been a Franciscan monastery. This prehistory made it an ideal establishment for the two friends, for the former monastery contained any number of passageways and hiding places known neither to the teachers nor to the caretaker.

Brauksel, who is running a mine that produces neither potash nor iron nor coal but is nevertheless functioning down to the twenty-five-hundred-foot floor, would also have taken pleasure in that subterranean confusion, for under all the classrooms, under the gymnasium and the urinals, under the auditorium, even under the board room there were low narrow corridors which, if you followed them, led to dungeons and shafts, but also in circles and astray. When school began after Easter, Amsel was first to enter the ground-floor classroom. Short-legged and wearing Walter Matern's shoes, he took little steps over oiled flooring and sniffed a little with pink nostrils—musty cellar air, theatrical ambiance—stopped still, interlocked his plump little fingers, took a bounce or two on the tips of

617

his toes, and after bouncing and sniffing here and there, drew a cross on one of the floorboards with the tip of his right-hand shoe. When there was no whistle of understanding in response to his mark, he looked behind him with a rotation of his well-padded neck: there stood Walter Matern in Amsel's patent-leather shoes, presenting an obstinately uncommunicative face, but then he caught on from the bridge of his nose up and finally whistled understandingly through his teeth. Because there was a hollow spooky sound under the floorboards, they both felt immediately at home in this classroom assigned to the sixth, even though there was no Vistula flowing broad-shouldered between dikes outside the windows.

But after a week of high school, the two of them, who, as it happened, had rivers in their blood, found access to a little river, to take the place, however inadequately, of the Vistula. A lid had to be lifted in the locker room of the gymnasium, which in Franciscan days had been a library. The cracks around the small rectangle were caulked with the sweepings of many years, but for Amsel's eye that was no camouflage. Walter Matern lifted the lid: musty cellar air, theatrical ambiance! They had found the entrance to a dry musty passageway, which was distinguished from the other passageways beneath other classrooms by the fact that it led to the municipal sewage system and by way of the sewers to the Radaune. The little river with the mysterious name had its source in the Radaune Lakes in the district of Berent, flowed, rich in fish and prawns, past Petershagen, and entered the city to one side of the New Market. Sometimes visible, sometimes underground, it twined its way through the Old City, often bridged over and made picturesque by swans and weeping willows, and emptied into the Mottlau between Karpfenseigen and Barbank, shortly before the confluence of the Mottlau and the Dead Vistula.

As soon as the locker room emptied of witnesses, Amsel and his friend were able to lift the rectangle out of the floorboards—and so they did—, crawl through a low passageway—they crawled—, climb down —making use of the climbing irons inserted in the masonry at regular intervals—into a shaft that couldn't have been far from the urinal— Walter Matern went down first—, easily open a rusty iron door at the bottom of the shaft—Walter Matern opened it —, and pass through a dry, foul-smelling sewer alive with rats—each in the other's shoes they passed through it. To be precise, the sewer led under the Wiebenwall, under the Karrenwall, where stood the Provincial Insurance Company building, under the city park, and under the railroad tracks between Petershagen and the Main Station, and then into the Radaune. Across from Sankt Salvator cemetery, which was situated between Grenadiergasse and the Mennonite church at the foot of the Bischofsberg, the sewer fanned out and emptied. To one side of the opening more climbing irons led up a steeply sloping masonry wall to an ornate wrought-iron railing.

Behind them lay a view known to Brauxel from numerous engravings: out of the fresh, spring-green park rises brick-red the panorama of the city: from Oliva Gate to Leege Gate, from St. Catherine's to St. Peter's on the Poggenpfuhl, the divergent height and girth of numerous towers bear witness to the fact that they are not of the same age.

Two or three times the friends took this excursion through the sewer. The second time they emerged over the Radaune, they were seen by some old folks who were passing the time of day in the park, but not reported. The possibilities seemed exhausted—for the Radaune is not the Vistula—when under the gymnasium, but before the shaft leading to the municipal sewers, they came across a second bifurcation, crudely stopped up with bricks. Amsel's flashlight discovered it. They crawled through the new passageway. It sloped downward. The man-high sewer to which it led was not part of the municipal sewage system, but led crumbling dripping medieval under the hundred-percent Gothic Church of the Trinity. Sankt Trinitatis was next to the museum, not a hundred paces from the high school. One Saturday, when after four hours of school the two friends were free to leave, two hours before train time, they made the above-mentioned discovery which is recorded here not only because medieval passageways are fun to describe, but also because the discovery proved to be of interest to Eduard Amsel and gave Walter Matern an opportunity for play-acting and teeth grinding. Moreover Brauxel, who operates a mine, is able to express himself with particular virtuosity below ground.

So the Grinder—Amsel invented the name, fellow students have taken it up—so the Grinder goes first. In his left hand he holds an army flashlight, while in his right he holds a stick intended to frighten away or, as the case may be, destroy rats. There aren't many rats. The masonry is rough crumbly dry to the touch. The air cool but not glacial, more on the drafty side, though it is not clear where the draft is blowing from. Their steps do not echo as in the municipal sewers. Like the passageway leading to it, this man-high corridor slopes steeply downward. Walter Matern is wearing his own shoes, for Amsel's patent-leather shoes had suffered enough as they were crawling through the low passageways. So that's where the draft and ventilation were coming from: from that hole! They might almost have missed it if Amsel hadn't. It was on the left. Through the gap, seven bricks high, five bricks wide, Amsel pushes the Grinder. Amsel himself has a harder time of it. Holding his flashlight between his teeth, the Grinder tugs Amsel through the hole, helping to transform Amsel's almost new school clothes into the customary school rags. Both stand there for a moment panting. They are on the spacious floor of a round shaft. Their eyes are drawn upward, for a watery light is trickling down from above: the pierced, artfully forged grating on top of the shaft is inserted in the stone floor of the Church of the Trinity: they will investigate that another time. Four eyes follow the diminishing light back down the shaft, and at the bottom—the flashlight points it out to them—what lies in front of the tips of four shoes but a skeleton!

It lies doubled up, incomplete, with interchanged or telescoped details. The right shoulder blade has stove in four ribs. The sternum is driven into the right ribs. The left collarbone is missing. The spinal column is bent above the first lumbar vertebra. The arrangement of the arms and legs is exceedingly informal: a fallen man.

The Grinder stands rigid and allows himself to be relieved of the flashlight. Amsel begins to throw light on the skeleton. Without any intention on Amsel's part, effects of light and shadow are produced. With the tip of one patent-leather shoe—soon Brauxel will have no need to speak of patent leather—he draws a circle through the dry, only superficially crusted dust, circumscribing all the fallen members, moves back, lets the cone of electric light follow the line, screws up his eyes as he always does when he sees something likely to serve as a model, tilts his head, waggles his tongue, covers one eye, turns around, looks behind him over his shoulder, conjures up a pocket mirror from somewhere, juggles with light, skeleton, and mirror image, directs the flashlight behind him under a sharply bent arm, tips the mirror slightly, stands briefly on tiptoes in order to lengthen the radius, then squats by way of comparison, stands again facing his model without mirror, corrects the line here and there, exaggerates the fallen man's pose with sketching shoe, still with his shoe erases and draws new lines to undo the exaggeration, harmonizes, sharpens, softens, strives for dynamic balance ecstasy, concentrates all his powers on sketching the skeleton, preserving the sketch in his memory, and perpetuating it at home in his diary. Small wonder that after all his preliminary studies are concluded, Amsel is taken with the desire to pick up the skull from between the skeleton's incomplete collarbones, and quietly put it into his school satchel with his books and notebooks and Hedwig Lau's crumbling shoe. He wants to carry the skull to the Vistula and put it on one of his scarecrows that are still in the framework stage, or if possible on the scarecrow that he has just sketched in the dust. His hand with its five pudgy, ludicrously spread fingers is already hovering over the vestiges of collarbone; it is about to reach into the eye sockets, the safest way to lift a skull, when the Grinder, who has long stood rigid, giving little sign of his presence, begins to grind several of his teeth. In his usual way: from left to right. But the acoustics of the shaft magnify and multiply the sound so forebodingly that Amsel stops in the middle of his skulduggery, looks behind him over his rounded back, and turns the flashlight on his friend.

The Grinder says nothing. His grinding is plain enough. It means:

620

Amsel should not spread his little fingers. Amsel shouldn't take anything away. The skull is not to be removed. Don't disturb it. Don't touch it. Place of skulls. Golgotha. Barrow. Gnashing of teeth.

But Amsel, who is always at a loss for meaningful props and accessories, who is always short on what he needs most, is again preparing to dispatch his hand skullward and again—for it isn't every day that you find a skull—outspread fingers can be discerned amid the shimmering dust of the flashlight beam. At this point the stick which thus far had struck nothing but rats descends on him, once maybe twice. And the acoustics of the shaft amplify a word uttered between blow and blow: "Sheeny!" Walter Matern calls his friend "Sheeny!" and strikes. Amsel falls sideways beside the skeleton. Dust rises and takes its time about settling. Amsel picks himself up. Who can cry such fat, convulsively rolling tears? But even as the tears roll from both his eyes and turn to beads of dust on the floor of the shaft, Amsel manages to say with a grin somewhere between good-natured and mocking: *"Walter is a very silly boy."* Imitating the teacher's voice, he several times repeats this sentence from his first-year English book; for always, even when tears are flowing, he has to imitate somebody, himself if need be: *"Walter is a very silly boy."* And then in the idiom of the Island: "This here is my head. Didn't I find it? I just wanna try it out. Then I'll bring it back."

But the Grinder is in no mood to be spoken to. The sight of the haphazardly disposed bones makes his face shrink toward the inside corners of his eyebrows. He folds his arms, leans on his stick, freezes in contemplation. Whenever he sees anything dead: a drowned cat, rats he has slain with his own hand, gulls slit open with a throw of his knife, when he sees a bloated fish rolled in the sand by the lapping of the waves, or when he sees a skeleton which Amsel wants to deprive of its skull, his teeth start in from left to right. His bullish young face twists into a grimace. His gaze, ordinarily dull to stupid, becomes piercing, darkens, gives an intimation of directionless hatred: theatrical ambiance in the passages, dungeons, and shafts beneath the Gothic Church of the Trinity. Twice the Grinder pounds his own forehead with his fist, bends down, reaches out, raises the skull to himself and his thoughts, and contemplates it while Eduard Amsel squats down to one side.

Who is squatting there, obliged to relieve himself? Who is standing there, holding a stranger's skull far out in front of him? Who looks behind him with curiosity, examining his excrement? Who stares at a smooth skull, trying to recognize himself? Who has no worms, but did once from salad? Who holds the light skull and sees worms that will one day be his? Who, who? Two human beings, pensive and troubled. Each has his reasons. They are friends. Walter Matern puts the skull back down where he found it. Amsel is scratching again in the dirt with his shoe, looking and looking. Walter Matern declaims high-sounding words into the void: "Let's be going now. This is the kingdom of the dead. Maybe that's Jan Bobrowski or Materna that our family comes from." Amsel has no ear for words of conjecture. He is unable to believe that Bobrowski the great robber, or Materna, robber, incendiary, and ancestor, ever gave flesh to this skeleton. He picks up something metallic, scratches at it, spits on it, rubs it off, and exhibits a metal button, which he confidently identifies as the button of one of Napoleon's dragoons. He dates the button from the second siege and puts it in his pocket. The Grinder does not protest, he has scarcely been listening, he is still with the robber Bobrowski or his ancestor Materna. The cooling feces drive the friends through the hole in the wall. Walter Matern goes first. Amsel squeezes through the hole backwards, his flashlight turned upon the death's-head.

Twenty-fifth Morning Shift

Change of shifts at Brauxel & Co.: The friends had to hurry on the way back. The train in Niederstadt station never waited more than ten minutes.

Change of shifts at Brauxel & Co.: Today we are celebrating the two-hundred-fiftieth birthday of Frederick the Great; it might be a good idea for Brauxel to fill one of the stalls with relics from Frederick's times: a kingdom of Prussia below ground!

Change of shifts at Brauxel & Co.: In the locker room of the gymnasium in the Sankt Johann High School Walter Matern fitted the rectangular lid back into the floorboards. They beat the dust from each other's clothes.

Change of shifts at Brauxel & Co.: What will the great conjunction of February 4-5 bring us? In the sign of Aquarius Uranus will enter into opposition, but not exactly, while Neptune completes the square. Two critical aspects, more than critical!—Shall we, will Brauxel, come through the Great Conjunction unscathed? Will it be possible to carry this book, dealing with Walter Matern, the dog Senta, the Vistula, Eduard Amsel, and his scarecrows, to a conclusion? Despite the critical aspects Brauksel, the present writer, wishes to avoid an apocalyptic tone and record the following events with equanimity, even though there is every reason to expect an auto-da-fé of the lesser apocalypse.

Change of shifts at Brauxel & Co.: After Walter Matern and Eduard Amsel had beaten the medieval dust from one another, they started out: down Katergasse, up the Lastadie. They follow Ankerschmiedgasse. Behind the Postal Savings Bank lies the new boathouse of the school oarsmen's association: boats are being put up on chocks. They wait for the open Cow's Bridge to close and crossing it spit several times into the

Mottlau. Cries of gulls. Horse-drawn vehicles over wooden planks. Beer barrels are rolled. A drunken longshoreman is supporting himself on a sober longshoreman, he has designs on a salt herring, skin, bones, and . . . "You want to bet? You want to bet?" Across the Speicherinsel: Erich Karkutsch, flour, seed, dried peas, and beans; Fischer & Nickel—conveyor belts, asbestos goods; across the railroad tracks, shreds of cabbage, flocks of kapok. They stop outside the establishment of Eugen Flakowski, saddlers' and upholsterers' supplies: bales of seaweed, hemp, jute, horsehair, reels of awning string, porcelain rings and tassels, notions, notions! Through the puddles of horse piss in Münchengasse, across the New Mottlau. Up Mattenbuden. Then climb into the trailer of the Heubude streetcar, but only ride as far as Langgart Gate, and arrive at the station on time for the narrow-gauge train, which smells of butter and whey, which rings fast as it slowly rounds the bend, and which goes to the Island. Eduard Amsel is still holding Napoleon's dragoon's button hot in his pocket.

The friends—and they remain inseparable blood brothers in spite of the death's-head and the word "Sheeny"—spoke no more of the skeleton under the Church of the Trinity. Only once, on Milchkannengasse, between Deutschendorff's sporting goods store and a branch of the Valtinat dairy chain, outside a window displaying stuffed squirrels, martens, and owls, displaying mountain cocks and a stuffed eagle with outspread wings and a lamb in its claws, outside a window with shelves in the form of a grandstand that stopped just before the plate-glass pane, in the presence of rat traps, fox traps, packages of insect powder, little bags of moth flakes, in the presence of gnat bane, roaches' nemesis, and rough-on-rats, in the presence of exterminator's equipment, bird food, dog biscuit, empty fish bowls, tins full of dehydrated flies and waterbugs, in the presence of frogs, salamanders, and snakes in jars and alcohol, of incredible butterflies under glass, of beetles with antlers, hairy spiders, and the usual sea horses, in the presence of the human skeleton—to the right beside the shelf— in the presence of the chimpanzee's skeleton—to the left beside the grandstand—and the skeleton of a running cat at the feet of the smaller chimpanzee, in the presence of the uppermost shelf of the grandstand, upon which stood instructively the skulls of man, woman, aged person, child, premature infant, and abortions, outside this world-embracing shop window—inside the store you could buy puppies or have kittens drowned by an officially licensed hand—, outside glass polished twice weekly, Walter Matern abruptly suggested to his friend that with the rest of the money in the leather pouch they might buy one or another of these skulls and use it in the construction of a scarecrow. Amsel made a negative gesture and said tersely, not with the terseness of one who is offended but with a lofty kind of terseness, that though the topic of death's-heads was not exactly dead or superseded, it was not urgent enough to justify

623

a purchase with their last remaining funds; if they were going to buy anything, they could buy goose, duck, and chicken feathers of inferior quality cheap and by the pound from the peasants and poultry farmers of the Island; he, Amsel, was planning something paradoxical: he was going to create a scarecrow in the form of a giant bird—the shop window on Milchkannengasse full of stuffed zoological items had inspired him, especially the eagle above the lamb.

Sacred ludicrous moment of inspiration: angel taps on forehead. Muses with frayed rosebud mouths. Planets in Aquarius. A brick falls. The egg has two yolks. The ash tray is running over. Dripping from the roof: celluloid. Short circuit. Hatboxes. What turns the corner: a patent-leather shoe. What enters without knocking: La Barbarina, the Snow Queen, snow men. What lends itself to being stuffed: God, eels, and birds. What is extracted from mines: coal, iron, potash, scarecrows, the past.

This scarecrow comes into being soon thereafter. It is Amsel's last for many a year. For under the no doubt ironically intended title "The Great Cuckoo Bird"—suggested, as a note informs us, not by Amsel but by Kriwe the ferryman—this creation, handed down both in a preliminary sketch and in a color study, is the last recorded in the diary which is today still relatively safe in Brauxel's safe.

Rags—as the diary tells us in its own words—have first to be coated with pitch or tar. Rags coated with tar or pitch have to be studded on the outside with large and small feathers and on the inside as well if enough of them are available. But in an unnatural, not a natural, way.

And indeed, when the completed Great Cuckoo Bird, tarred, feathered, and superman-high, was set out on the dike to the amazement of all who approached, its feathers stood unnaturally on end. It looked altogether spooky. The most hardened fisherwomen fled, convinced that looking at the monster could induce goiter, swivel eye, or miscarriage. The men stood their ground stiff and stolid, but let their pipes grow cold. Johann Lickfett said: "Friend, I wouldn't want that thing for a present."

It was hard to find a purchaser. And yet for all the tar and feathers the price was not high. In the forenoon it stood alone on the Nickelswalde dike, silhouetted against the sky. Only when the commuting school-children returned from the city did a few come strolling out as though by chance, but stopped at a safe distance, appraised it, expressed opinions, and were disinclined to buy. Not a gull in the cloudless sky. The mice in the dike looked for other lodgings. The Vistula was unable to make a loop or it would have. Everywhere cockchafers, not in Nickelswalde. When with a laugh that was much too loud Herr Olschewski, the school-teacher who was by nature rather high-strung, expressed interest, more for the fun of it than to protect his sixty square feet of front garden—

the Great Cuckoo Bird had to be unloaded far below the price originally set. It was moved in Olschewski's rack wagon.

For two weeks the monster stood in the front garden, casting its shadow upon the teacher's flat-roofed, whitewashed cottage. No bird dared to let out a peep. The sea wind ruffled tarry feathers. Cats grew hysterical and shunned the village. Schoolchildren made detours, dreamt wet at night, and woke up screaming, with white fingertips. In Schiewenhorst Hedwig Lau came down with a bad case of tonsillitis, complicated by sudden nosebleeds. While old man Folchert was chopping wood, a chip flew into his eye, which for a long time refused to heal. When Grandma Matern passed out in the middle of the poultry yard, there were many who blamed the Great Cuckoo Bird; however, both hens and rooster had been carrying straw around in their beaks for the last month: which has always been a presage of death. Everyone in the miller's house, beginning with poor Lorchen, had heard the woodworm, the deathwatch. Grandma Matern took note of all these omens and sent for the sacraments. Once they had been administered, she lay down and died in the midst of straw-toting chickens. In her coffin she looked surprisingly peaceful. Gloved in white, she was holding a lavender-scented lace handkerchief between her crookedly folded hands. It smelled just right. Unfortunately they forgot to take out her hairpins before the coffin was closed and relegated to Catholically consecrated earth. This omission was no doubt responsible for the shooting headaches that assailed Frau Matern née Stange immediately after the funeral and from then on left her no peace.

When the body was laid out in the overhang room, when the villagers all stiff and starched stood crowded together in the kitchen and on the stairs leading to the overhang room, while they muttered their "Now she's gone!," their "Now she don't need to scold no more," and their "Now her troubles are over, now she's earned eternal rest" over the body, Kriwe the ferryman asked leave to touch the dead woman's right index finger to one of his few teeth, which had been aching and suppurating for several days. Standing between window and armchair, the miller, an unfamiliar figure in black without sack or mealworm, struck by no changing light, for the new mill was not yet running, nodded slowly: gently Grandmother Matern's right glove was removed, and Kriwe conveyed his bad tooth to the tip of her crooked index finger: sacred ludicrous moment of miraculous healing: angel taps, lays on hands, strokes against the grain, and crosses fingers. Toad's blood, crow's eyes, mare's milk. In each of the Twelve Nights thrice over left shoulder, seven times eastward. Hairpins. Pubic hair. Neck fuzz. Exhume, scatter to the winds, drink of the corpse's bath water, pour it across the threshold alone at night before cockcrow on St. Matthew's Day. Poison made from cockles. Fat of a newborn babe. Sweat of the dead. Sheets of the dead. Fingers of the dead: for the truth of the matter is that the suppuration at the base of Kriwe's tooth was said to have subsided after contact with the deceased Grandmother Matern's crooked index finger and, in strict accordance with the superstitious belief that a dead person's finger cures toothache, the pain was also said to have eased and gone away.

When the coffin had been carried out of the house and was swaying first past Folchert's farm, then past the teacher's cottage, one of the pallbearers stumbled, because the Great Cuckoo Bird was still standing hideous and gruesome in the teacher's garden. Stumbling means something. Stumbling is an omen. The pallbearer's stumbling was the last straw: the peasants and fishermen of several villages submitted a petition to Herr Olschewski and threatened to send an even more strongly worded one to the school board.

The following Monday, when Amsel and Walter Matern came home from school, Herr Olschewski was waiting for them at the Schiewenhorst ferry landing. He was standing beneath a straw hat. He was standing in knickers, a sports jacket with large checks, and canvas shoes. While the train was being run onto the ferry, the schoolteacher, seconded by Kriwe the ferryman, remonstrated with the two boys. This just couldn't go on, he declared, a number of parents had complained and were planning to write the school board, they had already got wind of it in Tiegenhof, people *were* superstitious, of course that had something to do with it, even the unfortunate death of Grandmother Matern—a fine woman!— was being attributed—all this in our enlightened twentieth century, but no one, especially here in the villages of the Vistula delta, could swim against the stream, realities were realities: beautiful as the scarecrow was, it was more than village people, especially here on the Island, could stomach.

Literally, Herr Olschewski spoke as follows to Eduard Amsel, his former pupil: "My boy, you're going to high school now, you've taken quite a step out into the wide world. From now on, the village will be too small for you. Let us hope that your zeal, your artistic nature, that gift of God as they say, will find new fields to conquer out there in the world. But here let well enough alone. You know I'm saying this for your own good."

The following day was marked by mildly apocalyptic doings: Amsel broke up shop in Folchert's barn. In other words, Matern opened the padlock and an amazing number of volunteer helpers carried the milliner's—as Amsel was called in the villages—building materials into the open: four scarecrows in process of construction, bundles of roofing laths and flower stakes. Kapok was shredded. Mattresses vomited seaweed. Horsehair exploded from sofa cushions. The helmet, the beautiful full-bottomed wig from Krampitz, the shako, the poke bonnets, the plumed hats, the butterfly bonnets, the felt-straw-velours hats, the sombrero and the Wellington hat donated by the Tiedes of Gross-Zünder, everything that can shelter a human crown passed from head to head, from the twilight of the barn to honey-yellow sunshine: "Milliner milliner!" Amsel's chest, which would have driven a hundred order-loving barracks orderlies out of their minds, poured forth ruffles, sequins, rhinestone beads, braid, clouds of lace, upholstery cord, and carnation-scented silk pompons. Everybody got into the act, pitched in to help the milliner, put things on, took them off, and threw them on the pile: jumpers and jackets, breeches and the frog-green litewka. A traveling agent for a dairy concern had given Amsel the zouave's jacket and a plum-blue vest. Hey, the corset, the corset! Two wrapped themselves in the Blücher overcoat. Brides dancing furiously in bridal dresses fragrant with lavender. Sack races in leggings. Pea-green screamed the shift. Muff equals ball. Young mice in the cape. Jagged holes. Shirts without collars. Roman collars and mustache holders, cloth violets, wax tulips, paper roses, shooting match medals, dogtags and pansies, beauty spots, tinsel. "Milliner milliner!" Whom the shoe fitted and whom it did not fit slipped or struggled into galoshes, top boots, knee boots, laced boots, strode in pointed shoes through tobacco-brown curtains, leapt shoeless but in gaiters through the curtains of a countess, princess, or even queen. Prussian, West Prussian, and Free City wares fell on the pile: What a shindig in the nettles behind Folchert's barn: "Milliner milliner!" And uppermost on the pyre, whence moths were still escaping, stood, supported by beanpoles, the public scandal, the bugaboo, Baal tarred and feathered, the Great Cuckoo Bird.

The sun shines down almost vertically. Kindled by Kriwe's hand with Kriwe's lighter, the fire spreads rapidly. All take a few steps backward, but stay on, eager to witness the great holocaust. While Walter Matern, as he always did at official functions, makes big noises, trying to drown out the crackling by sheer grinding of the teeth, Eduard Amsel, known as "the milliner" and occasionally—the merry bonfire is another such occasion—called "Sheeny," stands negligently on freckled legs, rubs his upholstered palms strenuously together, screws up his eyes and sees something. No green-yellow smoke, no stewing leather goods, no glittering flight of sparks and moths compels him to transform round eyes into oblique slits: no, it is the bird, spouting innumerable tongues of flame, the bird going up in smoke that falls to the ground and creeps over the nettles, which makes him a present of brisk ideas and suchlike flimflam. For as the burning beast, creature of rags, tar, and feathers, sizzling and showering sparks and very much alive, makes a last stab at flying, then collapses into dust, Amsel has resolved in his heart and diary that later, one day when he is big, he will revive the idea of the Great Cuckoo Bird: he will build a giant bird which will burn, spark, and blaze everlastingly, yet never be consumed, but continue in all eternity, forever and ever, by its very nature, apocalypse and ornament in one, to burn, spark, and blaze.

Twenty-sixth Morning Shift

A few days before the fourth of February, before the critical constellation of the heavenly luminaries calls this world into question, Brauxel decides to add an item to his stock or pandemonium: the burning *perpetuum mobile* in the form of a bird, inspired by Amsel—he will have it built. The world is not so rich in ideas that he should abjectly forgo one of the finest inspirations even if the world were coming to an end within the next few morning shifts; especially as Eduard Amsel, after the auto-da-fé behind Folchert's barn, offered an example of stoical fortitude by helping to put out the fire that flying sparks had kindled in Folchert's barn.

A few weeks after the public burning of Amsel's stock and his latest crow-scaring model, after a fire which, as we shall see, kindled all sorts of kindling in Amsel's little head and produced a fire that was never again to be quenched, the widow Lottchen Amsel, née Tiede, and Herr Anton Matern, miller in Nickelswalde, received blue letters, from which it could be gathered that Dr. Battke, principal of Sankt Johann High School, wished to see them in his office on a certain day and hour.

Widow Amsel and miller Matern took one and the same train to the city—they sat facing one another, each in a seat by the window. At Langgart Gate they took the streetcar as far as Milchkannen Bridge. Because they were early, they were able to attend to a few business matters. She had to call on Hahn & Löchel, then on Haubold & Lanser; he had to drop in on the construction firm of Prochnow on Adebargasse in connection with the new mill. They met in the Long Market, stopped at Springer's for a drink, and then—although they might have walked—took a taxi and reached Fleischergasse ahead of time.

To speak in round numbers, they had to wait for ten minutes in Dr. Rasmus Battke's waiting room, before the principal, in light gray shoes and the sports clothes they implied, appeared, imposing and without glasses, in the waiting room. With a small hand on a short arm, he motioned them into his office, and when the country folk hesitated to sit down in the club chairs, he cried out airily: "No formalities, please. I am sincerely delighted to meet the parents of two such promising students."

Two walls of books, one wall of windows. His pipe tobacco smelled English. Schopenhauer glowered between bookshelves, because Schopenhauer . . . Water glass, water pitcher, pipe cleaners on heavy red desk with green felt cover. Four embarrassed hands on upholstered leather arms. Miller Matern showed the principal his protruding ear, not the one that hearkened to mealworms. Widow Amsel nodded after every subordinate clause uttered by the fluent principal. The subjects of his discourse were: First, the economic situation in the countryside, hence the impending regulation of the market necessitated by the Polish customs laws, and the problems of the cheese producers on Great Island. Secondly, Great Island in general, and in particular the wind-swept far-billowing wheatfields; the advantages of the Epp variety and of the winter-resistant Siberian variety; the campaign against corn cockle—"but what a fertile blessed region, yes indeed . . ." Thirdly, Dr. Rasmus Battke had the following to say: Two such gifted students, though of course their gifts lay in very different directions—everything came so easily to little Eduard—two students bound by so productive a friendship—how touching it was to see little Matern defending his friend against the teasing, quite devoid of malice you may rest assured, of his fellow students—in short, two students so deserving of benevolent encouragement as Eduard Amsel, but in no less degree Walter Matern, were to say the least deterred by the long trip in the dreadful, though of course highly entertaining narrow-gauge railroad, from devoting their maximum energies to their work; he, the principal of the establishment, an old hand, as you may well imagine, at problems connected with schooling, who had learned a thing or two from his years of experience with commuting students, wished accordingly to suggest that even before the summer holidays broke upon the land, next Monday in fact, both boys should transfer to a different school. The Conradinum in Langfuhr, whose principal, an old friend, had already been consulted and supported his views wholeheartedly, had an in-student plan, or in plain German, a dormitory where a considerable number of students were provided with board and lodging—for a reasonable fee— thanks to the ample endowment from which the Conradinum benefited; in a word, they would both be well taken care of, it was an arrangement which he as principal of the Sankt Johann High School could only recommend.

And so on the following Monday Eduard Amsel and Walter Matern exchanged the green velvet caps of Sankt Johann for the red caps of the Conradinum. With the help of the narrow-gauge railway they and their suitcases left the Vistula estuary, Great Island, the dikes from horizon to horizon, Napoleon's poplars, the fish-smoking establishments, Kriwe's ferry, the new postmill, the eels between willows and cows, father and mother, poor Lorchen, the Mennonites rough and refined, Folchert, Kabrun, Lickfett, Lührmann, Karweise, schoolmaster Olschewski, and Grandmother Matern's ghost, which was haunting the house because they had forgotten to pour the water in which the corpse had been washed over the threshold in cross form.

Twenty-seventh Morning Shift

The sons of rich peasants, the sons of landowners, the sons of West Prussian, slightly indebted country gentry, the sons of Kashubian brickworks owners, the son of the Neuteich druggist, the son of the pastor in

Hohenstein, the son of the district president in Stüblau, Heini Kadlubek from Otroschken, little Probst from Schönwarling, the Dyck brothers from Ladekopp, Bobbe Ehlers from Quatschin, Rudi Kiesau from Straschin, Waldemar Burau from Prangschin, and Dirk Heinrich von Pelz-Stilowski from Kladau on the Kladau—in short, the sons of rich man, poor man, beggar man, chief, not to mention the pastor, became, not all at once, but most of them shortly after Easter, boarders at the dormitory attached to the Conradinum. For many years the Conradinum had managed to keep afloat as a private institution thanks to an endowment, but by the time Walter Matern and Eduard Amsel became Conradinians, the city was making considerable contributions to its budget. Accordingly the Conradinum was looked upon as part of the municipal school system. Only the in-student facilities were not municipal, but still the private prerogative of the Conradinum and subject to an extra charge.

The sleeping quarters for students of sixth, fifth, and fourth, also called the small sleeping quarters, were situated on the ground floor, with their windows looking out on the school garden, that is to say, on gooseberries. There was always one bedwetter. The place smelled of him and seaweed mattresses. The two friends slept bed to bed under an oleograph showing the Crane Gate, the observatory, and the Long Bridge in winter with ice floes. The two friends never or seldom wet their beds. An attempt to initiate the newcomers, that is, to blacken Amsel's backside with shoe polish, was averted by Walter Matern before anybody could say Jack Robinson. In recreation period the two of them stood aloof under the same chestnut tree. At most little Probst and Heini Kadlubek, the son of a coal dealer, were privileged to listen while Walter Matern maintained a long dark staring silence and Eduard Amsel developed his secret language, giving new names to the new surroundings.

"I tnod ekil eht sdrib ereh."

I don't like the birds here.

"Sworraps ni eht ytic tnera sworraps ni eht yrtnuoc."

Sparrows in the city aren't sparrows in the country. "Draude Lesma sklat sdrawkcab."

With fluent ease he stood long and short sentences word for word on their heads and was even able to speak the new backward language with the broad accent of the Island: Dootendeetz (death's-head) became Zteednetood. With the help of a tongue molded to the Low German language, he smoothed out an awkward c, an unpronounceable ps, the difficult sch, and a tongue-twisting nr, and rendered "Liebärchen" (my friend) by the simplified "Nahkräbeil." Walter Matern caught his meaning and gave brief, equally reversed, and usually correct answers: "Good idea—doog aedi." And impatient of shillyshallying: "Sey ro on?" Little Probst was flabbergasted. But Heini Kadlubek, known as "Kebuldak," proved to be not at all backward at learning to talk backward.

630

Many inventions on a level with Amsel's linguistic arts have been made in the playgrounds of this world; subsequently forgotten, they have ultimately been unearthed and perfected by childish old people in city parks, which were conceived as extensions of school playgrounds. When God was a schoolboy, it occurred to him in the heavenly playground, along with young Satan, his school friend, who was as bright as a button, to create the world. On the fourth of February of this year, as Brauxel has read in a number of newspaper articles, this world is expected to end; another decision arrived at in playgrounds.

Playgrounds, it might also be noted, have something in common with poultry yards: the strutting of the officiating rooster resembles the strutting of the teacher in charge. Roosters also stride about with their hands behind their backs, turn unexpectedly, and cast menacing looks about them.

Dr. Oswald Brunies, who is supervising at the moment—the authors' consortium is planning to build him a monument—does his best to oblige the inventor of the poultry-yard simile: every nine paces he scratches with the tip of his left shoe in the gravel of the school yard; moreover, he crooks his professorial leg—a habit not without significance. Dr. Brunies is looking for something: not for gold, not for a heart or for happiness God fame; he is looking for unusual pebbles. The playground is asparkle with pebbles.

Small wonder if singly, or sometimes two at a time, students come up to him and call his attention, in earnest or animated by the usual schoolboy whimsy, to perfectly ordinary pebbles they have just picked up. But Dr. Oswald Brunies takes each one, even the most contemptible run of the millstream, between the thumb and forefinger of his left hand, holds it away from, then up to light, takes a magnifying glass secured by an elastic band from the breast pocket of his peat-brown and partly threadbare jacket, moves the glass on stretching elastic slowly and expertly into place between pebble and eye, then, elegantly and with full confidence in the elastic, lets the glass spring back into his breast pocket. An instant later he has the pebble in the cup of his left hand, lets it roll about in a small radius at first, then circle more boldly as far as the rim of the cup, and finally rejects it by tapping his left hand with his free right hand. "Pretty but superfluous!" says Dr. Brunies and digs the same hand into a bag which, always and as often as we shall speak of Oswald Brunies here, juts brown and rumpled from his side pocket. By ornamental detours, such as those made by priests in the course of Mass, he guides a cough drop from the bag to his mouth: celebrates, licks, sucks, diminishes, swirls juice between tobacco-stained teeth, shifts lump from cheek to cheek, while the intermission dwindles, while dread of intermission's end mounts in the muddled interiors of many children, while sparrows in chestnut trees yearn for the end of recreation, while he struts, scratches

631

in the gravel of the playground, and causes the cough drop to become smaller and more vitreous.

Short intermission, long intermission. Intermission games, whisperings, sandwiches, and distress: anxiety, says Brauxel: in a moment the bell . . .

Empty playgrounds that belong to the sparrows. A thousand times seen and filmed, as the wind blows a sandwich paper through a deserted, melancholy, Prussian, humanistic, gravel-strewn playground.

The playground of the Conradinum consisted of a small rectangular playground, shaded irregularly by chestnut trees, and to the left of it with no fence intervening, an elongated Big Playground framed by young linden trees propped on poles and standing at regular intervals. The Neo-Gothic gymnasium, the Neo-Gothic urinal, and the Neo-Gothic old-brick-red, ivy-covered school building with its bell-less belfry bounded the Small Playground on three sides and sheltered it from the winds, which sent funnels of dust over the Big Playground from its southeast corner; for here nothing stood up to the wind but the low-lying school garden with its close-meshed wire fence and the two-storied, likewise Neo-Gothic dormitory. Until later, when a modern athletic field with cinder track and turf was laid out beneath the southern gable of the gymnasium, the Big Playground had to serve as an athletic field during gym classes. Also worth mentioning is a tarred wooden shed, some fifty feet in length, which stood between the young lindens and the school garden. Bicycles could be stored in it, front wheel upward. A little game: as soon as the upended front wheels were set in motion with strokes of the flat hand, the gravel that had stuck to the tires after the short ride through the Big Playground flew off and rained down on the gooseberry bushes in the school garden behind the wire network fence.

Anyone who has ever been obliged to play handball, football, völkerball, or faustball, let alone schlagball, in a field strewn with gravel will always, whenever he steps on gravel in later life, be forced to remember all the scraped knees, all those bruises which take forever to heal, which develop crusty scabs, and which transform all gravel-strewn playgrounds into blood-soaked playgrounds. Few things in the world make so lasting an impression as gravel.

But to him, the cock-of-the-playground, Dr. Oswald Brunies, the strutting, candy-sucking teacher—a monument will be erected to him —to him with magnifying glass on elastic, with sticky bag in sticky coat pocket, to him who collected big stones and little stones, rare pebbles, preferably mica gneiss—muscovy biotite—quartz, feldspar, and hornblende, who picked up pebbles, examined them, rejected or kept them, to him the Big Playground of the Conradinum was not an abrasive stumblingblock but a lasting invitation to scratch about with the tip of his shoe after nine rooster steps. For Oswald Brunies, who taught just about everything—geography, history, German, Latin, and when necessary religion—was not one of your universally dreaded gym teachers with shaggy black chest, bristling black legs, a policeman's whistle, and the key to the equipment room. Never did Brunies make a boy tremble under the horizontal bar, suffer on the parallel bars, or weep on hot climbing ropes. Never did he ask Amsel to do a front vault, not to mention a side vault over the long horse that is always too long. Never did he drive Amsel's fleshy knees across mordant gravel.

A man in his fifties with a cigar-singed mustache. The tip of every hair in his mustache sweet from ever-renewed cough drops. On his round head a gray felt hat, to which, often for a whole morning, clung burrs tossed on by his charges. From both ears swirling clumps of hair. A face seamed with wrinkles produced by laughing, giggling, grinning. Romantic poetry nestled in his tousled eyebrows. Schubert songs revolved around never-resting nostrils. Only in the corners of his mouth and on the bridge of his nose, a few blackheads: Heine's pungent *Winter's Tale* and Raabe's abrasive novel *Stopfkuchen*. Well liked and not taken seriously. A bachelor with a Bismarck hat and class director of the sixth, including Walter Matern and Eduard Amsel, the friends from the Vistula delta. By now the two of them smell only mildly of cow barn, curdled milk, and smoked fish; gone too is the smell of fire that clung to their hair and clothing after the public burning behind Folchert's barn.

Twenty-eighth Morning Shift

After a punctual change of shifts, and business worries—the Brussels agricultural agreements are going to create marketing difficulties for the firm of Brauxel & Co.—back to the gravel in the playground. School life promised to be gay for the two friends. Scarcely had they been moved from Sankt Johann to the Conradinum, scarcely had they grown accustomed to the musty dormitory with its smell of nasty little boys—who doesn't know a few stories about dormitories?—scarcely had the gravel in the Big Playground impressed itself upon them, when word went around that in a few days the sixth would be going to Saskoschin for two weeks. They would be supervised by Dr. Brunies and by Dr. Mallenbrand the gym teacher.

Saskoschin! What a tender word!

The country school annex was situated in Saskoschin Forest. The nearest village was called Meisterswalde. Thither the class and two teachers were conveyed by bus via Schüddelkau, Straschin-Prengschin, and Gross-Salau. A village built around a market. The sandy market place big enough for a cattle fair, consequently surrounded by wooden stakes with worn

633

iron rings. Shining puddles, ruffled by every gust of wind: there had been a violent shower shortly before the bus arrived. No cow dung or horse droppings, but several bevies of sparrows, which kept regrouping and raised their hubbub to the third power when Amsel alit from the bus. The market place was bordered by low peasant houses with small windows, some roofed with thatch. There was one new, unfinished two-story structure, Hirsch's emporium. Brand-new plows, harrows, tedders were asking to be bought. Wagon shafts rose skyward. Directly across the way a brick-red factory, deserted, with boarded-up windows. Not until the end of October would the sugar-beet harvest bring life, stench, and profit. The inevitable branch of the Danzig Savings Bank, two churches, the milk pool, a spot of color: the mailbox. And outside the barbershop a second spot of color: the honey-yellow brass disk hung slantwise, sending out light signals as the clouds shifted. A cold treeless village.

Like the entire region to the south of the city, Meisterswalde was part of the Danzig Heights district. Compared to the marshland of the Vistula estuary, the soil was wretched. Beets, potatoes, Polish beardless oats, vitreous stunted rye. At every step the foot struck a stone. Peasants crossing their fields would bend down between steps, pick up one out of a nation of many, and hurl it in a blind rage: it would fall on someone else's field. Such gestures even on Sunday: holding umbrellas in their left hands, peasants in black caps with shiny patent-leather visors walk through the beet fields, bend down, pick things up, throw them in every direction. The stones fall: petrified sparrows, and no one, not even Eduard Amsel, could devise any kind of scarestone.

That was Meisterswalde: black humped backs, umbrella tips menacing the heavens, stones picked up and stones thrown, and an explanation for so many stones: It seems that the Devil, when refused what the peasants had solemnly sworn to give him, had punished them for their breach of faith by driving around the countryside all one night, vomiting up the damned souls that had accumulated in his stomach and scattering them over the fields and meadows. And the souls of the damned turned out to be stones, which there was no way to get rid of, let the peasants pick up and throw till they were old and bent.

The class was obliged to hike in loose formation for two miles, with Dr. Brunies at the head and Dr. Mallenbrand bringing up the rear, first over hilly country where the road was bordered on both sides by stunted, half-grown rye standing amid stone souls, then through the edge of Saskoschin Forest, until whitewashed walls behind beech trees announced the country annex.

Thin, thin! Brauxel, the present writer, suffers from inability to describe unpeopled landscapes. He knows how to begin; but once he has brushed in a rolling hill, rich green, and behind it innumerable graduated hills á la Stifter, ending in the distant gray-blue of the horizon, and gone on to scatter the stones inevitable in the region around Meisterswalde, as the Devil did in his time, through his still unformed foreground; once he has put in the bushes that consolidate the foreground—the moment he says: juniper, hazelnut, broom glossy-green, underbrush, bushes, spherical conical bushy up hill and down dale: withered bushes, thornbushes, bushes in the wind, whispering bushes—for in this region the wind is always blowing—he always itches to blow life into Stifter's wilderness. Brauksel says: And behind the third bush counting from the left, just a little above the one and one-half acres of feed beets, no, not the hazelnut bush—Oh, these wretched bushes!—there there there, below that lovely moss-covered stone, well anyway behind the third bush on the left, in the midst of this unpeopled landscape, a man is hidden.

Not a sower. Not the plowman so often seen in oil paintings. A man in his middle forties. Pale brown black impudent, hidden behind the bush. Hook-nosed rabbit-eared toothless. This *more*, this man, has an *angustri*, a ring, on his little finger and in the course of future morning shifts, while the schoolboys are playing schlagball and Brunies is sucking his cough drop, he will take on importance, because he has a little bundle with him. What is in the bundle? Who is the man?

He is Bidandengero the Gypsy, and the bundle whimpers.

Twenty-ninth Morning Shift

Schlagball was the school sport in those days. In the gravel-strewn Big Playground at the Conradinum a fly had once been hit so high that while the ball was piercing the heavens and leathernly falling, a part of the team responsible for this feat had been able to run in fan formation to both goal posts, unmolested, and run back and collect points—an achievement compared to which twenty-five knee swings or skinning the cat seventeen times in a row were everyday occurrences. At the Saskoschin country annex schlagball was played morning and afternoon. A very moderate amount of class work was done before and after. Walter Matern, his friend Eduard Amsel, and Dr. Mallenbrand looked upon this game with three different sets of eyes.

For Mallenbrand the game of schlagball was a way of life, a philosophy. Walter Mattern was a master of the high fly. He hit them and caught them openhanded, and when he caught one, he threw the ball directly from the catching position to a teammate: which brought in points.

Eduard Amsel, on the other hand, waddled about the schlagball field as though waddling through Purgatory. Stout and short-legged, he was perfect for blocking out and bouncing the ball off of. He was the team's weak spot. He was tracked and hunted down. Hedging him round, four players would execute a dance in which a leather ball figured prominently. Delectable feints would be practiced over his dead body until he rolled whimpering in the grass, smarting under the taut leather before it even reached him.

The ball spared Amsel only when his friend hit a fly; and the truth of the matter is that Walter Matern hit flies only to let Amsel make his way over the field in peace, under the protection of the soaring ball. But the flies didn't always remain in the air long enough: after a few days of philosophy played according to the rules, several black-and-blue moons blossomed on Amsel's freckled flesh—blooms that were long in fading.

A change of shift even then: after Amsel had enjoyed a gentle childhood to the right and left of the Visula, Amsel's torments began far from the Vistula. They will go on for some time. For Dr. Mallenbrand passed as an expert and had written a book, or a chapter in a book, about German field games. In it he discussed the game of schlagball with succinct thoroughness. In the preface he expressed the opinion that the national character of schlagball was brought out most strikingly by a comparison with the international game of soccer. Then he went on to formulate the rules, point for point. A single blast of the whistle means: The ball is dead. A goal that counts is registered by the referee with two blasts of the whistle. A player is not allowed to run with the ball. There were many different kinds of ball: high-flying, known as flies, long balls, flat, corner, short balls, popflies, rollers, grounders, dribblers, goal balls, and triple-run balls. The ball was propelled by vertical blows, long blows, thrusts, or swings, by flat blows with underarm swing and by the two-hand blow, in which the ball must first be thrown to shoulder height. In catching a high-flying ball, a so-called fly—so spake Mallenbrand—the catcher's eye, his catching hand, and the falling ball must form a straight line. Moreover, and this was his title to fame, the field was lengthened from fifty to fifty-five yards at his suggestion. This feature which—as Amsel could testify—made the game more arduous was adopted by nearly every high school in eastern and northern Germany. He was the declared enemy of soccer and many regarded him as a strict Catholic. From his neck and alongside his hairy chest hung his metal referee's whistle. One blast meant: The ball is dead. Two blasts meant: Score obtained by hitting Eduard Amsel with the ball. Often enough he blew for flies that Walter Matern had struck for his friend: Out of bounds!

But his next fly is a good one. And the one after that. The following fly goes wrong: the hitter is out of position, the ball leaves the field and comes down with a whish and a tearing of foliage into the woods bordering the playground. In response to Mallenbrand's whistle—The ball is dead! —Walter Matern races to the fence, he's over and looks around in the moss and bushes at the edge of the forest: a hazelnut bush tosses him the ball.

He catches it and looks up: from a tangle of leaves grow the head and torso of a man. On his ear, the left one, a brass ring jiggles, because he is laughing soundlessly. Dark pale brown. Hasn't a tooth in his mouth. Bidandengero, that means the toothless. Under his arm he has a whimpering bundle. Holding the ball in both hands, Walter Matern moves backward out of the woods. He doesn't tell anyone, not even Amsel, about the soundless laughter behind the bush. The very next morning, or at any rate no later than the afternoon, Walter Matern intentionally hit an oblique fly that came down in the woods. Even before Mallenbrand could blow, he raced across ball field and fence. No bush and no underbrush threw him the ball. He found one ball under the ferns after a long search; as for the next one, the ants must have hauled it away.

Thirtieth Morning Shift

Diligent pencil strokes and sparrows: shading and open areas; breeding and explosions.

Diligent bees, diligent ants, diligent leghorns: diligent Saxons and diligent washerwomen.

Morning shifts, love letters, Materniads: Brauxel and his co-authors have taken an example from someone who worked diligently all his life —on laquered tin.

And the eight planets? Sun Moon Mars Mercury Jupiter Venus Saturn Uranus, to which, such is the awesome rumor spread by the astrological calendars, the secret moon Lilith might be added. Can it be that they have orbited diligently for twenty thousand years solely in order to bring off that evil conjunction day after tomorrow in the sign of Aquarius?

Not every attempted fly was successful. Consequently the hitting of flies, as well as the hitting of oblique, intentionally off-center flies, had to be practiced diligently.

The meadow was bounded on the north side by a long wooden shed, the so-called rest porch. Forty-five wooden cots, forty-five shaggy, sour-smelling blankets neatly folded on the foot ends of the cots stood in readiness each day for the noonday rest period of the sixths. And after the noonday rest period Walter Matern practiced hitting flies to the east of the porch.

The country annex, the rest porch, the schlagball field, and the chickenwire fence running from end to end were surrounded on all sides by the dense, silent, or rustling Saskoschin Forest, a mixed woodland containing wild boar, badgers, adders, and a boundary line that cut across it. For the forest began in Poland, started out with pines and low-lying

637

bushes on Tuchler Heath, acquired an admixture of birches and beeches on the mounds and ridges of Koshnavia, and continued northward into the milder coastal climate: the boulder glaze nurtured a mixed forest, which became purely deciduous as it approached the sea.

Sometimes forest Gypsies slipped back and forth across the border. They were regarded as harmless and lived on rabbits and hedgehogs, and by tinkering. They provided the school annex with wild mushrooms. The forester also needed their help when wasps and hornets nested in hollow tree trunks near the forest roads and made the horses of the timber wagons shy. They called themselves Gakkos, addressed one another as *More,* and were generally called *Mängische,* but sometimes *Ziganken.*

And once a Gakko tossed a high school student a schlagball after an unsuccessful fly had landed in the forest. *More* laughed soundlessly.

The student began to practice hitting out-of-bounds flies whereas previously he had only practiced regular flies.

The student succeeded in hitting two out-of-bounds flies that fell in the woods, but no Gypsy tossed him a ball.

Where did Walter Matern practice hitting good and no-good flies? At the east end of the rest porch there was a swimming pool, roughly twenty-five feet square, in which no one could swim, for it was out of order, clogged, and leaky. At the best rain water lay evaporating in the square of cracked concrete. Although no schoolboys were able to swim in the pool, it always had visitors: cool and active little frogs no bigger than a cough drop hopped about diligently as though practicing the art of hopping—less frequently, big heavily breathing toads—but always frogs, a congress of frogs, a playground of frogs, a ballet of frogs, a ball field of frogs; frogs you could blow up with blades of straw; frogs you could put down somebody's collar; frogs to stamp on; frogs to put in people's shoes; frogs that could be mixed with the always slightly burned pea soup; frogs in beds, frogs in inkwells, frogs in envelopes; frogs to practice flies with.

Every day Walter Matern practiced in the dry swimming pool. He picked slippery frogs out of the inexhaustible supply. If he hit thirty, thirty gray-blue frogs lost their cool young lives. As a rule, only twenty-seven brownish-black frogs were sacrificed to Walter Matern's dedicated devotions. It was not his purpose to send the green-gray frogs high in the air, higher than the trees of the rustling or silent forest. Nor did he practice hitting a common frog with just any portion of his bat. He had no wish to perfect himself in the hitting of long-distance balls, grounders, or treacherous bunts—besides, Heini Kadlubek was a past master at long-distance balls. What Walter Matern wanted was to hit the variously tinted frogs with that part of the bat which, when the bat was correctly raised alongside the body, gave promise of an exemplary, strictly vertical fly that would waver only slightly in the wind. If instead of the variously tinted frogs the dull-brown leather schlagball, shiny only at the seams, had offered resistance to the thick end of the bat, Walter Matern would have succeeded in half a midday hour in turning out twelve extra-special and fifteen to sixteen passable flies. In fairness it must be added that despite all this diligent fly swatting the frogs in the waterless swimming pool grew no fewer: merrily they hopped unequal heights and unequal distances while Walter Matern stood among them dealing death to frogs. They failed to understand, or else—like sparrows in this respect—they were so conscious of their numbers that there was never any possibility of a frog panic in the swimming pool.

In wet weather there were also newts, fire salamanders; and plain lizards in the death-shadowed pool. But these agile little creatures had no need to fear the bat; for the sixths developed a game, the rules of which only cost newts and salamanders their tails.

Courage was tested. The point was to take the twitching, wildly wriggling tail ends that newts and salamanders shed when you grab them with your hand—you can also knock them off with the flip of a hard finger—and swallow these living fragments in their mobile state. If possible, several tails should be swallowed successively as they leap from the concrete. The one who does it is a hero. Moreover, the three to five animated tails must go down unflushed by water and unpushed by crusts of bread. But even if the hero harbors three to five indefatigable tails, newt, salamander, or lizard, in his innards, he is also forbidden to make the slightest grimace. Amsel can do it. Harried and tormented on the schlagball field, Amsel understands and avails himself of the opportunity offered by the swallowing of salamander tails: not only does he successively incorporate seven vivacious tails into his round short-legged body, but he is also able, in return for a promise to set him free from the impending afternoon schlagball game and have him assigned to potato peeling in the kitchen, to withstand a counter-ordeal. One minute after his sevenfold swallowing and without putting his finger down his throat, he manages, thanks to sheer will power and even more to his abject terror of the leather schlagball, to yield up the seven tails: and lo and behold, they are still twitching, though with rather less abandon because inhibited by the mucus that has come up with them, on the concrete floor of the swimming pool, amid hopping frogs that have grown no fewer although Walter Matern, shortly before Amsel's feat of salamander swallowing and the ensuing counter-ordeal, was practicing flies.

The sixths are impressed. Over and over again they count the seven resurrected tails, slap Amsel on his round freckly back, and promise that if Mallenbrand has no objection they will dispense with his services as the afternoon schlagball victim. And in case Mallenbrand should take exception to Amsel's k.p., they will only pretend to victimize him with the schlagball.

Numerous frogs overhear this bargain. The seven swallowed and vomited salamander tails fall gradually asleep. Walter Matern stands by the chickenwire fence, leaning on his schlagball bat and staring into the bushes of the towering, enveloping Saskoschin Forest. Is he looking for something?

Thirty-first Morning Shift

What is in store for us? Tomorrow, on account of the many stars that are forming a clustering ferment above us, Brauksel is going to ride down with the morning shift and spend the day in the archives on the twenty-five-hundred-foot level—the powdermen used to keep their explosives there—concluding his record and endeavoring to the last to write with equanimity.

The first vacation week in the Saskoschin country annex passes amid schlagball games, well-regulated hikes, and moderate scholastic activities. On the one hand, steady consumption of frogs and, the weather permitting, an occasional swallowing of salamander tails; on the other, singing while gathered around the campfire in the evening—cold backs, over-heated faces. Someone gashes his knee. Two have sore throats. First little Probst has a sty, then Jochen Witulski has a sty. A fountain pen is stolen, or Horst Behlau has lost it: tedious investigations. Bobbe Ehlers, a first-class goal player, has to go back to Quatschin ahead of time, because his mother is seriously ill. While one of the Syck brothers who had been a bedwetter back in the dormitory is able to report a dry bed in the Saskoschin country annex, his brother, hitherto dry, begins to wet his country annex bed regularly and his cot on the porch as well. Half-waking afternoon nap on the porch. Unplayed on, the schlagball field gleams in the sunlight. Amsel's slumbers raise beads on his smooth forehead. Back and forth, Walter Matern's eyes prod the distant chickenwire fence and the woods behind it. Nothing. With a little patience you can see hills growing out of the schlagball field: moles go on burrowing even in the midday rest period. At twelve there were peas with smoked pork—as usual slightly burnt. For supper supposedly sautéed mushrooms, followed by blueberry soup and farina pudding, actually there will be something else. And after supper postcards are written home.

No campfire. A few play Monopoly, others morris or checkers. In the dining hall the dry laborious sound of table tennis tries to make itself heard above the roar of the night-dark forest. In his room Dr. Brunies, while a cough drop grows smaller, classifies the yield of a collector's day: the region is rich in biotite and muscovite: they rub together gneissly.

A silvery glimmer when gneisses grind; no silvery glimmer when Walter Matern's teeth grind.

At the edge of the night-dark schlagball field he sits on the concrete rim of the swimming pool rich in frogs and poor in water. Beside him Amsel: "Sti krad ni eht sdoow."

Walter Matern stares at the great black wall—near and coming nearer—of Saskoschin Forest.

Amsel rubs places where the schlagball has hit him that afternoon. Behind what bush? Is he laughing soundlessly? And is the little bundle? Is Bidandengero?

No mica gneiss; Walter Matern grinds from left to right. Heavily breathing toads answer. The forest with its birds groans. No Vistula opening out into sea.

Thirty-second Morning Shift

Brauxel is writing below ground: Hoo, how dark it is in the German forest! Barbale, the ghost that is neither man nor woman, is afoot. Light-handed goblins sprinkle one another. Hoo, how dark it is in the Polish forest! Gakkos are crossing, tinkers. Ashmodai! Ashmodai! Or Beng Dirach Beelzebub, whom the peasants call Old Clootie. Servant girls' fingers that were once too curious, now spook candles, sleeping lights: so many sleeping lights, so many sleepers. Balderle steps on moss: Efta times efta is forty-nine.—Hoo! But it's darkest in the German-Polish forest. Beng is crouching there, Balderle flies upward, sleeping lights flit, ants crawl, trees copulate, Gypsies track through the woods: Leopold's bibi and Bibi the aunt and Estersweh's bibi and Hite's bibi, Gashpari's bibi, all all all strike fulminantes, make light until she shows herself: the immaculate Mashari showing the carpenter's baby where the milk pours from her goose-white crock. Green and resinous it flows and gathers the snakes, forty-nine of them, efta times efta.

Through the ferns the border runs on one leg. This side and that side: white, red-rimmed mushrooms battle black, white, and red ants. Estersweh, Estersweh! Who is looking for his little sister? Acorns fall in the moss. Ketterle calls because something glitters: gneiss lies beside granite and rubs. Glittering spray. Slate grinds. But who can hear it?

Romno, the man behind the bush. Bidandengero, toothless but keen of hearing: Acorns roll, slate slips, high shoe strikes the ground, hush little bundle, high shoe is coming, mushrooms ooze, the snake slithers away into the next century, blueberries burst, ferns tremble—for fear of whom? Light squeezes through the keyhole, steps downstairs into the mixed forest, Ketterle is the magpie—Por, its feather, flies. High shoes creak unpaid. Tittering comes the scrag, the schoolie, the brain buster,

641

the teacher—Brunies, Brunies! Oswald Brunies!—tittering because as they rub, glitter sprays: gneissy slaty grainy scaly knotty: double spar, feldspar, and quartz. Rare, extremely rare, he says, and thrusts his high shoe forward, pulls out his magnifying glass on elastic band, and titters under his Bismarck hat.

He also picks up a beauty, beauty, a piece of reddish mica granite, turns it under the mixed forest into the sun that's on its way downstairs, until all the tiny mirrors say peep. This one he doesn't reject, he holds it out into the light, joins it in prayer, and does not turn around. He walks along, mumbling to himself. He lifts his mica granite into the next light and the next one and the next to next one, to let the thousand mirrors say peep again, one after another and only a few simultaneously. With his high shoe he steps close to the bush. Behind it sits Bidandengero, toothless and very still. And the bundle hushes too. No longer is Romno the magpie. Ketterle calls no more. Por, its feather, flies no more. Because nearby the scrag, the schoolie, the brain buster, the teacher Oswald Brunies.

Deep in the woods, he laughs under his hat, for in the deepest part of the German-Polish Saskoschin Forest he has found a piece of extremely rare flesh-colored mica granite. But because the thousand mirrors refuse to suspend their polyphonic peeping, Dr. Oswald Brunies begins to have a bitter dry taste in his mouth. Brushwood and pine cones have to be gathered. With three big stones that glitter only moderately he has to build a stove. Fulminantes from Swedish boxes have to strike a flame, deep in the woods; so that immediately afterward Ketterle calls again: Por—the magpie loses a feather.

The schoolmaster has a pan in his bag. It is oily, black, covered with tiny mica mirrors, because in his musette he keeps not only the pan, but also pieces of mica gneiss and mica granite and even his rare specimens of double spar. But in addition to pan and mica rock, the teacher's musette yields up several little brown and blue paper bags of varying sizes. As well as a bottle without a label and a tin can with a screw top. The little flame crackles dry. Resin boils. Mica mirrors leap in the hot pan. The pan sizzles when he pours something into it from the bottle. The fire crackles between three stones. Six heaping teaspoonfuls from the tin can. Moderate quantities shaken from the large blue and the pointed brown bag. He takes a spoon-handleful from the small blue, a pinch from the small brown bag. Then he stirs counterclockwise and with his left hand shakes powder from a tiny sprinkler can. Stirs clockwise while again the magpie, while far away beyond the border Estersweh is still being looked for, although there is no wind to carry.

He bends down on schoolmaster's knees and blows until it flares to a blaze. He has to keep stirring until the mash slowly boils down, becomes stickier and more sluggish. Back and forth over the steaming bubbling pan he moves a schoolmaster's nose with long hairs protruding from both nostrils: drops hang from his singed mustache, candy, and grow vitreous as he stirs the mash. From all directions come ants. Undecided, the smoke creeps over the moss, tangles with the ferns. Under a shifting oblique light the great mound of mica stones—who can have made it?—cries aloud in polyphonic confusion: peep peep peep! The mash over the flame begins to burn, but the recipe says it has to burn. Brown has to rise from the bottom. Wax paper is spread out and greased. Two hands lift the pan: a thick weary dough flows brown bubbly lavalike over the greased paper, immediately takes on a glassy skin, wrinkles from the sudden coolness, and darkens. Quickly, before it grows cold, a knife in the schoolmaster's hand divides the flat cake into candy-sized squares; for what Dr. Oswald Brunies has brewed in the dark German-Polish woods under the trees of Saskoschin Forest, between Estersweh and Ketterle's cry, is cough drops.

Because he is lusting for sweets. Because his supply of sweetness was exhausted. Because his musette is always full of little bags and tins. Because in the bags, tins, and bottle, malt and sugar, ginger, anise, and salt of hartshorn, honey and beer, pepper and mutton suet are always in readiness. Because with tiny sprinkler can—that is his secret—he dusts the hardening mash with crushed cloves: now the forest is fragrant and the fragrance of mushrooms, blueberries, moss, decades-old shrubbery, ferns, and resin abandons the competition. Ants run wild. The snakes in the moss are candied. Ketterle's cry changes. Por, its feather, sticks. How is Estersweh to be looked for? The sweet way or the sour way? And who weeps behind the bush and snuffles behind the bush because he has been sitting in the acrid smoke? Had the little bundle been given poppy to be so still while the schoolmaster, hearing nothing, pried the cooled remnants of lava out of the pan with shrill spoon handle?

Dr. Oswald Brunies picks up what splinters have not fallen into the moss or jumped in among the mica stones and guides them beneath his oversweet mustache: sucks, draws juice, lets them melt away. With sticky fingers, kept busy crushing ants between them, he sits beside the fire, which has collapsed and is smoking only feebly, and breaks the hard, glassy-brown cake on the greased paper into some fifty previously scored squares. Along with fragments and candied ants he stuffs the sweet concoction into a large blue sack which before his candymaking had been full of sugar. Everything—the pan, the rumpled bags, the bag with the newly acquired supply of candy, the tin can, the empty bottle, and the tiny sprinkler can—finds its way back to the mica gneiss in the musette bag. Now he is standing, holding the brown-crusted spoon in his schoolmaster's mouth. Now he is striding over the moss in high shoes under

Bismarck hat. He leaves nothing behind him except for tiny splinters and the greased paper. And now the schoolboys come loudly through the blueberries between the tree trunks. Little Probst is crying because of an encounter with wasps. Six have stung him. Four boys have to carry him. Dr. Oswald Brunies greets his colleague Dr. Mallenbrand.

When the class moved on, was no longer there, when nothing remained of it but calls, laughter, screams, and the voices of the scrags, schoolies, brain busters, in short, teachers, the magpie called three times. Por: its feather flew again. Then Bidandengero left his bush. And the other Gakkos as well: Gashpari, Hite, and Leopold disengaged themselves from the bushes, glided from the trees. Near the greased paper that had contained candy lava, they met. Black with ants, the paper moved in the direction of Poland. The Gakkos followed the ants: Hite, Gashpari, Leopold, and Bidandengero whished silently over moss and through ferns in a southerly direction. Bidandengero was the last to grow smaller amid the tree trunks. Along with him went a thin whimpering as though his little bundle, a toothless snugglebunny, a hungry mite, as though Estersweh were crying.

But the border was near, permitting a quick passage back and forth. Two days after the candymaking deep in the woods, Walter Matern, standing solidly planted in the striking zone, struck, quite contrary to his habit and only because Heini Kadlubek had said he could only hit flies but not long-distance balls, a long-distance ball that passed over both goals, over the whole field, and over the swimming pool rich in frogs and destitute of water. Walter Matern sent the schlagball into the woods. Before Mallenbrand came to count the balls, he had to go after it, hell bent for leather, over the chickenwire fence and into the mixed woods.

But he did not find the ball and kept looking where there was none. He lifted every fan of ferns. Outside a half-ruined foxhole, which he knew to be uninhabited, he went down on his knees. He poked about with a branch in the trickling hole. He was about to lie down on his belly and reach a long arm into the foxhole when the magpie screamed, the feather flew, the leather struck him: what bush had thrown it?

The bush was the man. The little bundle kept still. The brass ring in the man's ear jiggled, because the man was laughing soundlessly. His tongue fluttered bright red in his toothless mouth. A frayed string cut into his coat over his left shoulder. In front three hedgehogs dangled on the string, bleeding from pointed snouts. When the man turned slightly, a small bag hung down behind him, forming a counterweight to the hedgehogs. The man had braided the black oiled hair over his temples into short, stiffly protruding pigtails. Zieten's hussars had done the same.

"Are you a hussar?"

"Part hussar, part tinker."

"What's your name, anyway?"

"Bi-dan-den-gero. Have no tooth left."

"And the hedgehogs?"

"To cook in clay."

"And the bundle up front?"

"Estersweh, little Estersweh."

"And the bundle in back? And what are you looking for here? And how do you catch the hedgehogs? And where do you live? And have you really got such a funny name? And suppose the forester catches you? And is it true that the Gypsies? And the ring on your little finger? And the bundle up front?"

Por—that was the magpie calling from deep within the mixed forest. Bidandengero was in a hurry. He had, so he said, to go to the factory without windows. The schoolmaster was there. He was waiting for wild honey for his candy. He also wanted to bring the schoolmaster sparklers, and another little present too.

Walter Matern stood with the ball and didn't know what to do, in what direction. Finally he decided to climb back across the fence to the schlagball field—for the game was proceeding—when Amsel came rolling out of the bushes, asked no questions, had heard everything, and knew of only one direction: Bidandengero . . . He pulled his friend after him. They followed the man with the dead hedgehogs, and when they lost him, they found bright hedgehog blood from three hedgehog snouts on the ferns. They read the trace. And when the hedgehogs on Bidandengero's string were dry and silent, the magpie screamed in their stead: Por— Ketterle's feather—flew ahead. The forest grew denser, more crowded. Branches struck Amsel's face. Walter Matern stepped on the white and red mushroom, fell in the moss, and bit into the cushion. Trees made faces. A fox froze. Faces through spiderwebs. Fingers full of resin. Bark tasted sour. The woods thinned out. Downstairs went the sun as far as the teacher's mound of stones. Afternoon concert: gneisses, some augite, hornblende, slate, mica, Mozart, twittering eunuchs from the *Kyrie* to the chorale *Dona nobis:* polyphonic peeping—but no sign of a teacher under a Bismarck hat.

Only the cold fireplace. Gone was the greased paper. And only when the beeches came together again behind the clearing and screened off the sun, did they overtake the paper: it was black with ants and on its way. Like Bidandengero with his hedgehogs, the ants wished to make off across the border with their prey. They marched in single file, just as Walter Matern and his friend trotted along in single file, following the magpie's lure: here here here. Through knee-high ferns. Through neatly ordered beech trees. Through green church light. Swallowed up again, far away, here again: Bidandengero. But no longer alone. Ketterle had called the

645

Gakkos. Gashpari and Hite, Leopold and Hite's bibi, Aunt Bibi and Leopold's bibi, all the Gypsies, tinkers, and forest hussars had gathered under beech trees in the hushed ferns around Bidandengero. Gashpari's bibi was pulling Bartmann, the goat.

And when the forest thinned out again, eight or nine Gakkos left the woods with Bartmann the goat. Until they reached the trees on the other side, they were hidden by the tall grass of the trough-shaped treeless meadow spreading southward: and in the open meadow stands the factory, shimmering.

An elongated one-story building, gutted. Untrimmed brick, empty window holes blackened with soot. From the ground to mid-height the chimney yawns, a brick maw with teeth missing. All the same it stands upright, probably just topping the beeches huddled close at the far end of the clearing. But it isn't the chimney of a brickworks, although there are plenty of those in the region. Formerly it evacuated the smoke of a distillery, and now that the factory is dead and the chimney cold, it houses a jutting stork's nest. But the nest too is dead. Blackish rotting straw covers the cracked chimney and shimmers emptily.

They approach the factory in fan formation. No more magpie calling. Gakkos swimming in the tall grass. Butterflies staggering over the meadow. Amsel and Walter Matern reach the edge of the woods, lie flat, peer out over the trembling spikes, and see all the Gakkos climbing simultaneously but through different window holes into the dead factory. Gashpari's bibi has tied Bartmann to a hook in the wall.

A white long-haired goat. The factory is not alone in shimmering; the blackish straw on the cracked chimney and the meadow shimmer too, and Bartmann is dissolved in light. It's dangerous to watch staggering butterflies. They have a plan but it has no meaning.

Amsel isn't sure whether or not this is Polish territory. Walter Matern thinks he has recognized Bidandengero's head in a window hole: oily braids hussar style, brass in ear, gone again.

Amsel thinks he has seen the Bismarck hat first in one, then briefly in the next window hole.

Neither of them sees the border. Only bantering white butterflies. And above the variously pitched bumbling of the bumblebees a rising and falling garble. Not a distinct howling, cursing, or screaming. More like a crescendo of blubbering and squeaking. Bartmann the goat bleats two three volleys heavenward.

Then from the fourth window hole on the left leaps the first Gakko: Hite with Hite's bibi in tow. She unties Bartmann. Then another, and then two more in dappled Gypsy tatters: Gashpari and Leopold, his bibi, in numerous skirts. None through the open door, all the Gypsies through window holes, head-first, last of all Bidandengero.

For all Gypsies have sworn by the Virgin Mashari: never through doors, only through windows.

Fanwise as they have come, the Gakkos swim through the quaking grass to the woods that swallow them up. Once again the white goat. Ketterle does not call. Por, her feather, does not fly. Silence, until the clearing begins to buzz again: bantering butterflies. Bumblebees like double deckers, dragonflies pray, sumptuous flies, wasps, and suchlike vagabonds.

And who shut the picture book? Who dripped lemon on homemade June clouds? Who let the milk clabber? How did Amsel's skin and Walter Matern's skin get that porous look, as though bombarded with sleet?

The little bundle. The snugglebunny. The toothless mite. From the dead factory Estersweh screamed over the living meadow. Not the dark window holes but the black gate spat the Bismarck hat into the open air. The scrag, schoolie, brain buster, teacher, Oswald Brunies, stood under the sun with the screaming bundle and didn't know how to hold it. "Bidandengero," he called, "Bidandengero!" But the woods didn't answer. Neither Amsel nor Walter Matern, who were picked up by the outcry and tugged step by step through the hissing grass to the factory, neither Dr. Brunies with the strident little bundle nor the picture-book meadow showed surprise when again something miraculous happened: from the south, from Poland, storks came flying over the meadow with measured wingbeat. Two of them described ceremonious loops and dropped, first one, then the other, into the blackened and disheveled nest on the cracked chimney.

Instantly they began to clatter. All eyes, the schoolmaster's under the Bismarck hat and the schoolboys' eyes as well, climbed up the chimney. The snugglebunny broke off its cries. Adebar Adebar the Stork. Oswald Brunies found a piece of mica gneiss, or was it double spar, in his pocket. Let the baby have it to play with. Adebar Adebar the Stork. Walter Matern wanted to give the little bundle the leather schlagball which had come with them so far, with which the whole thing had started. Adebar Adebar the Stork. But the six-months-old baby girl already has something to finger and play with: Angustri, Bidandengero's silver ring.

Quite possibly Jenny Brunies is wearing it to this day.

Last Morning Shift

It seems to have been nothing. No world has come discernibly to an end. Brauxel can write above ground again. Still, the date, February 4, has had something to show for itself: all three manuscripts have been punctually delivered, Brauchsel is able to set young Harry Liebenau's love letters down on his package of morning shifts; and on "morning shifts"

647

and "love letters" he will pile the actor's confessions. Should a postscript seem desirable, Brauksel will write it, because he is in charge both of the mine and of the author's consortium, it is he who pays out the advances, sets the delivery dates, and will read the proof.

What happened when young Harry Liebenau came to us and applied for the job of authoring the second book? Brauxel examined him. To date he had written and published lyric poetry. His radio plays have all been on the air. He was able to show flattering and encouraging reviews. His style was termed gripping, refreshing, and uneven. Brauchsel began by questioning him about Danzig: "What, young man, were the names of the streets connecting Hopfengasse with the New Mottlau?"

Harry Liebenau rattled them off: "Kiebitzgasse, Stützengasse, Mausegasse, Brandgasse, Adebargasse, Münchengasse, Judengasse, Milchkannengasse, Schleifengasse, Turmgasse, and Leitergasse."

"How, young man," Brauksel inquired, "will you kindly explain, did Portechaisengasse get its delightful name?"

Harry Liebenau explained rather pedantically that it had taken its name from the litters, the taxis of the day, which had stood there in the eighteenth century and in which patricians and their ladies could be carried through muck and pestilence without fear for their costly attire.

In response to Brauxel's question as to who in the year 1936 had introduced the modern Italian rubber truncheon in the Danzig police force, Harry Liebenau spoke up like a recruit: "That was done by Police President Friboess!" But I was not yet satisfied: "Who, my young friend—I doubt if you remember—was the last chairman of the Center Party in Danzig? What was the honorable man's name?" Harry Liebenau had boned up very thoroughly, even Brauxel learned a thing or two: "Richard Stachnik, D.D., clergyman and schoolteacher, became chairman of the Center Party and member of the provincial diet in 1933. In 1937, after dissolution of the Center Party, he was imprisoned for six months: in 1944 he was deported to Stutthof concentration camp, but soon released. All his life Dr. Stachnik was active in behalf of the canonization of the Blessed Dorothea of Montau, who in the year 1392 had caused herself to be immured beside the cathedral of Marienwerder."

I still had a raft of tricky questions on hand. I asked him the course of the Striessbach, the names of all the chocolate factories in Langfuhr, the altitude of the Erbsberg in Jäschkental Forest, and obtained satisfactory answers. When in answer to the question: What well-known actors began their careers at the Danzig Stadttheater?—Harry Liebenau replied without hesitation Renate Müller, who died young, and Hans Söhnker, the movie star, I, in my easy chair, gave him to understand that the examination was over and that he had passed.

And so, after three work sessions, we agreed to link up Brauxel's "morning shifts" and Harry Liebenau's "love letters" with a transitional passage. Here it is:

Tulla Pokriefke was born on June 11, 1927.

When Tulla was born, the weather was variable, mostly cloudy, with a possibility of showers. Light gyratory winds fluttered the chestnut trees in Kleinhammer Park.

When Tulla was born, Dr. Luther, the former chancellor, coming from Königsberg and on his way to Berlin, landed at the Danzig-Langfuhr airfield. In Königsberg he had spoken at a meeting of former German colonials; in Langfuhr he took a snack at the airport restaurant.

When Tulla was born, the Danzig police band, conducted by chief bandmaster Ernst Stieberitz, gave a concert in the gardens of the Zoppot casino.

When Tulla was born, Lindbergh, the transatlantic flier, boarded the cruiser *Memphis*.

When Tulla was born, the police, as their records for the eleventh of the month inform us, arrested seventeen persons.

When Tulla was born, the Danzig delegation to the forty-fifth session of the League of Nations council arrived in Geneva.

When Tulla was born, the Berlin stock exchange reported foreign buying of rayon and electrical industry stocks. Prices were generally firmer: Essen Anthracite: four and one-half points; Ilse and Stolberger Zinc: three points. Certain special securities also advanced. Glanzstoff opened at four points, Bemberg at two points above previous quotations.

When Tulla was born, the Odeon Cinema was showing *His Biggest Bluff* with Harry Piel in his dual and most brilliant role.

When Tulla was born, the NSDAP, Gau Danzig, called a monster mass meeting in the Sankt Josephshaus on Töpfergasse from five to eight. Party Comrade Heinz Haake of Cologne was to speak on the topic of "German workers of brawn and brain, unite!" On the day following Tulla's birth the meeting was to be repeated in the Red Room of the Zoppot casino under the motto: "Nation in distress: who will save it?" The poster was signed by a Herr Hohenfeld, member of the provincial diet, who called upon his fellow citizens to "Come in droves!"

When Tulla was born, the rediscount rate of the Bank of Danzig was unchanged at five and one-half per cent. At the grain exchange rye debentures brought nine gulden sixty a hundredweight: money.

When Tulla was born, the book *Being and Time* had not yet appeared, but had been written and announced.

When Tulla was born, Dr. Citron still had his practice in Langfuhr; later he was obliged to take refuge in Sweden.

When Tulla was born, the chimes in the City Hall tower played "Glory alone to God on high" when even hours were to be struck and

"Heavenly Host of Angels" for the odd hours. The chimes of St. Catherine's played "Lord Jesus Christ, hear our prayer" every half hour.

When Tulla was born, the Swedish steamer *Oddewold* put in to Danzig empty, coming from Oxelösund.

When Tulla was born, the Danish steamer *Sophie* left for Grimsby with a cargo of timber.

When Tulla was born, a child's rep dress cost two gulden fifty at Sternfeld's department store. Girls' "princess" slips two gulden sixty-five. A pail and shovel cost eighty-five gulden pfennigs. Watering cans one gulden twenty-five. And tin drums lacquered, with accessories, were on sale for one gulden and seventy-five pfennigs.

When Tulla was born, it was Saturday.

When Tulla was born, the sun rose at three eleven.

When Tulla was born, the sun set at eight eighteen.

When Tulla was born, her cousin Harry Liebenau was one month and four days old.

When Tulla was born, Dr. Oswald Brunies adopted a foundling, aged six months, who was cutting her milk teeth.

When Tulla was born, Harras, her uncle's watchdog, was one year and two months old.

Book
Two

Love Letters

Dear Cousin Tulla:

I am advised to put you and your Christian name at the beginning, to address you, because you were, are, and will be matter everywhere, informally, as though this were the beginning of a letter. Yet I am telling my story to myself, only and incurably to myself; or can it be that I am telling you that I am telling it to myself? Your family, the Pokriefkes and the Damses, came from Koshnavia.

Dear Cousin:

since every one of my words to you is lost, since all my words, even if I speak obstinately to myself, have only you in mind, let us at last make peace on paper and cement a frail foundation for my livelihood and pastime: I speak to you. You don't listen. And the salutation—as though I were writing you one or a hundred letters—will be my formal crutch, which even now I would like to throw away, which I shall often and with fury in my arm throw into the Striessbach, into the sea, into Aktien Pond: but the dog, black on four legs, will bring it back as he has been trained to do.

Dear Tulla:

like all the Pokriefkes, my mother, a Pokriefke by birth and sister to your father August Pokriefke, hailed from Koshnavia. On the seventh of May, when Jenny Brunies was about six months old, I was normally and properly born. Seventeen years later somebody picked me up with two fingers and put me into a life-size tank as an ammunition loader. In the middle of Silesia, a region which is not as familiar to me as Koshnavia south of Konitz, the tank went into position and backed up, for purposes of camouflage, into a wooden shed which some Silesian glass blowers had filled with their products. Whereas hitherto I had never stopped searching for a word that would rhyme with you, Tulla, that tank backing into position and those screaming glasses showed your Cousin Harry the way to a rhymeless language: from then on I wrote simple sentences, and now that a certain Herr Brauxel has advised me to write a novel, I am writing a normal rhymeless novel.

653

Dear Cousin Tulla:

about Lake Constance and the girls around there I don't know a thing; but about you and Koshnavia I know everything. The geographical co-ordinates of Koshnavia are north latitude fifty-three twenty, east longitude thirty-five. You weighed four pounds and ten ounces at birth. Koshnavia proper consists of seven villages: Frankenhagen, Petztin, Deutsch-Cekzin, Granau, Lichtnau, Schlangenthin, and Osterwick. Your two elder brothers Siegesmund and Alexander were born in Koshnavia; Tulla and her brother Konrad were registered in Langfuhr. The name of Pokriefke is to be found even earlier than 1772 in the parish register of Osterwick. The Damses, your mother's family, are mentioned years after the partitions of Poland, first in Frankenhagen, then in Schlangenthin; probably immigrants from Prussian Pomerania, for I am inclined to doubt that "Dams" is derived from the archbishopric of Damerau, especially in view of the fact that Damerau, along with Obkass and Gross Zirkwitz, was donated to the Archbishop of Gnesen as early as 1275. Damerau was then called Louisseva Dambrova, occasionally Dubrawa; it is not properly a part of Koshnavia: the Damses are outsiders.

Dear Cousin:

you first saw the light of day in Elsenstrasse. We lived in the same apartment house. It belonged to my father, master carpenter Liebenau. Diagonally across the street, in the so-called Aktienhaus, lived my future teacher, Dr. Oswald Brunies. He had adopted a baby girl, whom he called Jenny, although in our region no one had ever borne the name of Jenny. The black shepherd dog in our yard was called Harras. You were baptized Ursula, but called Tulla from the start, a nickname probably derived from Thula the Koshnavian water nymph, who lived in Osterwick Lake and was written in various ways: Duller, Tolle, Tullatsch, Thula or Dul, Tul, Thul. When the Pokriefkes were still living in Osterwick, they were tenants on Mosbrauch Hill near the lake, on the Konitz highway. From the middle of the fourteenth century to the time of Tulla's birth in 1927, Osterwick was written as follows: Ostirwig, Ostirwich, Osterwigh, Osterwig, Osterwyk, Ostrowit, Ostrowite, Osterwieck, Ostrowitte, Ostrów. The Koshnavians said: Oustewitsch. The Polish root of the village name Osterwick, the word *ostrów,* means an island in a river or lake; for originally, in the fourteenth century that is, the village of Osterwick was situated on the island in Osterwick Lake. Alders and birches surrounded this body of water, which was rich in carp. In addition to carp and crucians, roaches, and the compulsory pike, the lake contained a red-blazed calf that could talk on St. John's Day, a legendary leather bridge, two sacks full of yellow gold from the days of the Hussite incursions, and a capricious water nymph: Thula Duller Tul.

654

Dear Tulla:

my father the carpenter liked to say and often did: "The Pokriefkes will never get anywhere around here. They should have stayed where they came from, with their cabbages."

The allusions to Koshnavian cabbage were for the benefit of my mother, a Pokriefke by birth; for it was she who had lured her brother with his wife and two children from sandy Koshnavia to the city suburb. At her behest carpenter Liebenau had taken on the cottager and farmhand August Pokriefke as an assistant in his shop. My mother had persuaded my father to rent the two-and-a-half-room apartment that had become vacant on the floor above us to the family of four—Erna Pokriefke was already pregnant with Tulla—at a low price.

For all these benefits your mother gave my father little thanks. On the contrary. Whenever there was a family scene, she blamed him and his carpenter shop for the deafness of her deaf-mute son Konrad. She maintained that our buzz saw, which roared from morning to closing time and only rarely fell silent, which made all the dogs in the neighborhood including our Harras howl themselves hoarse in accompaniment, had withered and deafened Konrad's tiny ears while he was still in the womb.

The carpenter listened to Erna Pokriefke with serenity, for she fulminated in the Koshnavian manner. Who could understand it? Who could pronounce it? The inhabitants of Koshnavia said *"Tchatchhoff"* for *Kirchhof* (churchyard). *Bäsch* was *Berg* (mountain)—*Wäsch* was *Weg* (way, path). The *"Preistewäs"* was the meadow (*Wiese*), some two acres in size, belonging to the priest in Osterwick.

You'll have to admit, Tulla,

that your father was a rotten helper. The machinist couldn't even use him on the buzz saw. The drive belt would keep slipping off, and he ruined the most expensive blades on nail-studded sheathing which he converted into kindling for his own use. There was only one job that he performed punctually and to the satisfaction of all: the gluepot on the cast-iron stove upstairs from the machine room was always hot and in readiness for five journeymen carpenters at five carpenter's benches. The glue ejected bubbles, blubbered sulkily, managed to turn honey-yellow or muddy-cloudy, succeeded in thickening to pea soup and forming elephant hide. In part cold and crusty, in part sluggishly flowing, the glue climbed over the rim of the pot, formed noses upon noses, leaving not so much as a speck of enamel uncovered and making it impossible to recognize the gluepot as an erstwhile cookpot. The boiling glue was stirred with a section of roofing lath. But the wood also put on skin over skin, swelled bumpy leathery crinkly, weighed heavier and heavier in August

655

Pokriefke's hand and, when the five journeymen called the horny monster an elephant's trunk, had to be exchanged for a fresh section of always the same, positively endless roofing lath.

Bone glue, carpenter's glue! The brown, grooved cakes of glue were piled on a crooked shelf amid a finger-thick layer of dust. From the third to the seventeenth year of my life I faithfully carried a chunk of carpenter's glue in my pants pocket; to me glue was that sacred; I called your father a glue god; for not only had the glue god thoroughly gluey fingers which crackled brittlely whenever he moved, but in addition he invariably gave off a smell that followed him wherever he went. Your two-and-a-half-room apartment, your mother, your brothers smelled of it. But most generously he garnished his daughter with his aroma. He patted her with gluey fingers. He sprayed the child with particles of glue whenever he conjured up finger bunnies for her benefit. In short, the glue god metamorphosed Tulla into a glue maiden; for wherever Tulla went stood ran, wherever she had stood, wherever she had gone, whatever space she had traversed at a run, whatever Tulla took hold of, threw away, touched briefly or at length, whatever she wrapped clothed hid herself in, whatever she played with: shavings nails hinges, every place and object that Tulla had encountered retained a faint to infernal and in no wise to be quenched smell of bone glue. Your Cousin Harry stuck to you too: for quite a few years we clung together and smelled in unison.

Dear Tulla:

when we were four years old, they said you had a calcium deficiency. The same contention was made concerning the marly soil of Koshnavia. The marl dating from the diluvian times, when the ground moraines formed, contains, as we know, calcium carbonate. But the weather-beaten, rain-washed layers of marl in the Koshnavian fields were poor in calcium. No fertilizer helped and no state subsidies. No amount of processions— the Koshnavians were Catholic to a man—could inject calcium into the fields; but Dr. Hollatz gave you calcium tablets: and soon, at the age of five, your calcium deficiency was overcome. None of your milk teeth wobbled. Your incisors protruded slightly: they were soon to become a source of dread to Jenny Brunies, the foundling from across the street.

Tulla and I never believed

that Gypsies and storks had anything to do with the finding of Jenny. A typical Papa Brunies story: with him nothing happened naturally, everywhere he sniffed out hidden forces, he always managed to dwell in an eerie eccentric light. Whether feeding his mania for mica gneiss with ever new and often magnificent specimens—there were similar cranks in cranky Germany with whom he corresponded—or, on the street, in the playground, or in his classroom, carrying on like an Old Celtic druid, a Prussian oak-tree god, or Zoroaster—he was generally thought to be a Freemason—he invariably displayed the qualities that we all of us love in our eccentrics. But it was Jenny, his association with the doll-like infant, that first made Dr. Brunies into an eccentric who acquired a standing not only within the precinct of the high school but also in Elsenstrasse and the streets intersecting or running parallel to it in the big little suburb of Langfuhr.

Jenny was a fat child. Even when Eddi Amsel was roaming around Jenny and Brunies, she seemed no slimmer. Amsel and his friend Walter Matern—they were both Dr. Brunies' students—were said to have witnessed the miraculous finding of Jenny. In any case Amsel and Matern made up half of the group which elicited smiles in our Elsenstrasse and in all Langfuhr.

For Tulla I am going to paint an early picture:

I want to show you an elderly gentleman with a bulbous nose, innumerable wrinkles, and a broad-brimmed soft hat on ice-gray matted hair. He is striding along in a green loden cape. To the left and right of him two schoolboys are trying to keep up with him. Eddi Amsel is what is commonly known as a fatty. His clothes are full to bursting. His knees are marked with little dimples. Wherever his flesh is visible, a crop of freckles burgeons. The general impression is one of boneless waddling. Not so his friend: rawboned and masterful, he stands beside Brunies, looking as though the teacher, Eddi Amsel, and plump little Jenny were under his protection. At the age of five and a half the little girl is still lying in a large baby carriage, because she has walking difficulties. Brunies is pushing. Sometimes Eddi Amsel pushes, rarely the Grinder. And at the foot end lies a half-open crumpled brown paper bag. Half the kids in the neighborhood are following the baby carriage; they are out for candy, which they call "blubblubs."

But only when we reached the Aktienhaus, across the street from where we lived, did Dr. Brunies bring the high-wheeled carriage to a halt and distribute a handful from the brown bag to Tulla, myself, and the other children, on which occasion he never forgot to help himself as well, even if he hadn't quite finished the vitreous remnant in his mumbling elderly mouth. Sometimes Eddi Amsel sucked a candy to keep him company. I never saw Walter Matern accept a candy. But Jenny's fingers were as tenaciously sticky with rectangular cough drops as Tulla's fingers with the bone glue which she rolled into marbles and played with.

Dear Cousin,

just as I am trying to gain clarity about you and your carpenter's glue, so I am determined to get things straight about the Koshnavians, or Koschneiders as they are also called. It would be absurd to accept an allegedly historical but thus far undocumented explanation of the term "Koshnavian." This so-called explanation is that during the Polish uprisings the Koshnavians had been stirred to acts of violence against the Germans, so that the collective noun "Koschneider" derives from the collective noun *"Kopfschneider"* (head cutter). Though I have good reason to adopt this exegesis—you, the scrawny Koshnavian maiden, had every aptitude for the head cutter's trade—I shall nevertheless content myself with the unimaginative but reasonable explanation that in the year 1484 a starosty official in Tuchel, Kosznewski by name, signed a document officially defining the rights and obligations of all the villages in the region, and that these villages later came to be known as Kosznew or Koshnavian villages after him. A vestige of uncertainty remains. The names of towns and districts may lend themselves to pedantry of this kind, but Kosznewski, the methodical starosty official, is no help in deciphering Tulla, more a something than a girl.

Tulla,
tautly encased in white skin, could hang head downward from the carpet-beating rack—for half an hour—all the while singing through her nose. Bones bruised black and blue, muscles uncushioned and unimpeded by fat made Tulla into a perpetually running, jumping, climbing, in a word, flying something. Since Tulla had her mother's deep-set, small-cut, narrow-placed eyes, her nostrils were the biggest thing in her face. When Tulla grew angry—and several times a day she became hard, rigid, and angry—she rolled her eyes so far back that her optical slits revealed nothing but white shot through with blood vessels. Her angry revulsed eyes looked like blinded eyes, the eyes of beggars and mountebanks who pass themselves off as blind beggars. When she went rigid and began to tremble, we used to say: "Tulla's bashed in her windows again."

From the first I was always running after my cousin, or more precisely, I was always two steps behind you and your smell of glue, trying to follow you. Your brothers Siegesmund and Alexander were already of school age and went their own ways. Only Konrad the deaf-mute curlyhead went with us. You and he; I, tolerated. We sat in the woodshed under the tar roof. The planks smelled and I was turned into a deaf-mute; for you and he could talk with your hands. The pushing down or crossing of certain fingers meant something and aroused my suspicions. You and he told each other stories that made you giggle and him shake silently. You and he hatched plans, of which I was mostly the victim. If you loved anyone at all, it was he, the little curlyhead; meanwhile the two of you persuaded me to put my hand under your dress. It was under the tar roof in the woodshed. Acrid was the smell of the wood. Salty was the taste of my hand. I couldn't get away, I was stuck; your bone glue. Outside sang the buzz saw, droned the power plane, howled the finishing machine. Outside whimpered Harras, our watchdog.

Listen Tulla,

that was him: a long-drawn-out black shepherd with erect ears and a long tail. Not a long-haired Belgian Groenendael, but a short-haired German shepherd. Shortly before we were born, my father the carpenter had bought him as a puppy, in Nickelswalde, a village on the Vistula delta. The owner, who also owned Queen Louise's mill in Nickelswalde, asked thirty gulden. Harras had a powerful muzzle with dry, tight lips. Dark eyes set a little obliquely followed our steps. Neck firm, free from dewlap or throatiness. Barrel length two inches in excess of shoulder height: I measured it. Harras could bear scrutiny from all sides: legs always straight and parallel. Toes well closed. Pads thick and hard. Long, slightly sloping croup. Shoulders buttocks knuckles: powerful, well muscled. And every single hair straight, close to the body, harsh and black. Undercoat likewise black. No wolf colors, dark on a gray or yellow ground. No, all over him, even inside the erect slightly forward-tilted ears, on his deep crinkled chest, along his moderately coated hocks, his hair glistened black, umbrella-black, priest-black, widow-black, SS-black, blackboard-black, Falange-black, blackbird-black, Othello-black, dysentery-black, violet-black, tomato-black, lemon-black, flour-black, milk-black, snow-black.

Harras searched, found, pointed, retrieved, and did trail work with his nose to the ground. In a herding contest on the Bürgerwiesen he proved a failure. He was a stud dog with his name in the studbook. Unsatisfactory on the leash: he pulled. Good at barking at intruders but only average at following strange tracks. My father had had him trained by the police in Hochstriess. They thrashed him till he stopped eating his dirt: a nasty habit with puppies. The number 517 was stamped on his dog tag: sum of digits thirteen.

All over Langfuhr, in Schellmühl, in the Schichau housing development, from Saspe to Brösen, up Jäschkentaler Weg, down Heiligenbrunn, all around the Heinrich Ehlers Athletic Field, behind the crematory, outside Sternfeld's department store, along the shores of Aktien Pond, in the trenches of the municipal police, on certain trees of Uphagen Park, on certain lindens of the Hindenburgallee, on the bases of advertising pillars, on the flagpoles of the demonstration-hungry athletic field, on the still unblacked-out lampposts of the suburb of Langfuhr, Harras left his scent marks: he remained true to them for many dog years.

Up to the withers Harras measured twenty-five inches. Five-year-old Tulla measured three foot six. Her cousin Harry was an inch and a half taller. His father, the imposingly built carpenter, stood six foot two

in the morning and an inch less at closing time. As for August and Erna
Pokriefke, as well as Johanna Liebenau, née Pokriefke, none of them was
more than five foot five: the Koshnavians are a short race.

Dear Cousin Tulla,

what would I care about Koshnavia if you, the Pokriefkes, were not
from there? But as it is, I know that from 1237 to 1308 the villages of
Koshnavia belonged to the dukes of Pomerelia. After they died out, the
Koshnavians paid taxes to the Teutonic Knights until 1466. Until 1772
the kingdom of Poland absorbed them. In the course of the European
auction Koshnavia fell to the Prussians. They kept order until 1920. As
of February 1920 the villages of Koshnavia became villages of the Polish
Republic, until the autumn of 1933 when they were incorporated into
the Greater German Reich as part of the Province of West Prussia-Danzig:
Violence. Bent safety pins. Pennants in the wind. Billeting: Swedes Hussites Waffen-SS. Andifyoudon't. Rootandbranch. Asoffourfortyfivethis-
morning. Circles described with compasses on military maps. Schlangenthin
taken in counterattack. Antitank spearheads on the road to Damerau. Our
troops resist heavy pressure northwest of Osterwick. Diversionary attacks
of the twelfth division of airborne infantry thrown back south of Konitz.
In line with the decision to straighten the front, the so-called territory
of Koshnavia is evacuated. Last-ditch fighters take up positions south
of Danzig. Panicmakers, bogeymen, terrible jokesters are shaking the
paperweight again, the fist . . .

Oh Tulla,

how can I tell you about Koshnavia, about Harras and his scent
marks, about bone glue, cough drops, and the baby carriage, when I have
this compulsion to stare at my fist!—Yet roll it must. Once upon a time
there rolled a baby carriage. Many many years ago there rolled a baby
carriage on four high wheels. On four old-fashioned high wheels it rolled,
enameled black and hooded with cracking oil-cloth. Dull-gray spots where
the chromium-plated spokes of the wheels, the springs, the handle to
push it by, had peeled. From day to day the spots grew imperceptibly
larger: Past: Once upon a time. When in the summer of '33: in the days
in the days when I was a boy of five, when the Olympic Games were
being held in Los Angeles, fists were already being moved swift, dry,
down to earth; and yet, as though unaware of the draft that was blowing,
millions of baby carriages on wheels high and low were being propelled
into the sunlight, into the shade.

On four old-fashioned high wheels there rolled, in the summer of
1932, a black-enameled, slightly decrepit baby carriage which Eddi Amsel
the high school student, who knew all the junkshops, had negotiated in

Tagnetergasse. He, Dr. Oswald Brunies, and Walter Matern took turns at pushing the vehicle. The tarred, oiled, and yet dry boards on which the baby carriage was being pushed were the boards of the Brösen pier. The friendly seaside resort—where sea baths were taken as early as 1823—with its low-lying fishing village and dome-surmounted casino, its medium-high dunes and scrub pine forest, with its fishing boats, its hundred and fifty feet of pier, and its tripartite bathhouse, with the watchtower of the German Lifesaving Society, was situated exactly halfway between Neufahrwasser and Glettkau on the shores of the Gulf of Danzig. The Brösen pier had two levels and branched off to the right into a short breakwater designed to resist the waves of the Baltic Sea. Sunday in Sunday out: the Brösen pier floated twelve flags on twelve flagpoles: at first only the flags of the Baltic cities—gradually more and more swastika flags.

Under flags and over boards rolls the baby carriage. Dressed much too black and shaded by his soft hat, Dr. Brunies is pushing now and will be relieved by Amsel the fat or Matern the bullish. In the carriage sits Jenny, who will soon be six years old and is not allowed to walk.

"Couldn't we let Jenny walk a little? Please, sir. Just for a try. We'll hold her on both sides."

Jenny Brunies mustn't. "Do we want the child to get lost? To be pushed about in the Sunday crowd?" People come and go, meet separate bow, or take no notice of each other. They wave, take each other's arms, point to the big breakwater, to Adlerhorst, feed gulls with food brought from home, greet, remind, are vexed. And all so well dressed: large flower patterns for the special occasion. The sleeveless get-ups of the season. Tennis dress and sailing togs. Neckties in the east wind. Insatiable cameras. Straw hats with new sweatbands. Toothpaste-white canvas shoes. High heels dread the cracks between the boards. Pseudo captains aiming spyglasses. Or hands shading far-seeing eyes. So many sailor suits. So many children running, playing, hiding, and scaring each other. I see something you do not see. Eenymeenyminymo. Sour herring one two three. There's Herr Anglicker from Neuer Markt with his twins. They're wearing sailor ties and one as slowly as the other licking raspberry ice with pale tongues. Herr Koschnick from Hertastrasse with his wife and a visitor from Germany. Herr Sellke allows his sons, first one, then the other, to look through his spyglass: smoke trail, superstructure, the *Kaiser* is rising above the horizon. Herr and Frau Behrendt have used up their sea gull biscuit. Frau Grunau, who owns the laundry on Heeresanger, with her three apprentice girls. Scheffler the baker from Kleinhammerweg with giggling wife. Heini Pilenz and Hotten Sonntag without parents. And there's Herr Pokriefke with his gluey fingers. Hanging on his arm, his shriveled little wife, who can't stop moving her head this way and that with ratlike swiftness. "Tulla!" she can't help crying. And "Come here, Alexander." And "Siegesmund, keep an eye on Konrad!" For on the pier the Koshnavians don't talk like Koshnavians, although Herr Liebenau and his wife are not present. On Sunday morning he has to stay in his shop, drawing up a work schedule, so the machinist will know on Monday what goes into the buzz saw. She doesn't go out without her husband. But his son is there because Tulla is there. Though younger than Jenny, both are allowed to walk. Allowed to hop skip jump behind Dr. right up to where it ends in a sharp wind-swept triangle. Allowed down the steps, right left, to the lower story, where the fishermen Brunies and his mildly embarrassed students. Allowed on the pier, squat catching sticklebacks. Allowed to run sandal-swift along narrow runways and to dwell secretly in the framework of the pier, beneath five hundred pairs of Sunday shoes, beneath the gentle tapping of canes and umbrellas. It's cool shady greenish down there. The water smells of salt and is transparent all the way down to the shells and bottles rolling about on the bottom. On the piles supporting the pier and the people on the pier beards of seaweed wave fitfully: back and forth sticklebacks busy silvery common-place. Cigarette butts fall from the top deck, disintegrate brownish, attract finger-length fishes, repel them. Schools react spasmodically, dart forward, hesitate, turn, regather a floor lower, and emigrate someplace where other seaweed waves. A cork bobs up and down. A sandwich paper grows heavy, twists and turns. Between tarred beams Tulla Pokriefke hikes up her Sunday dress, it already has tar spots on it. Her cousin is expected to hold his open hand underneath. But he doesn't feel like it and looks away. Then she can't, doesn't have to any more and jumps from crossed beams to the ramp and runs with clattering sandals, making pigtails fly and fishermen wake up, she's already on the stairs to the pier, the stairs to the twelve flags, stairs to the Sunday forenoon; and her cousin Harry follows her glue smell, which uproariously drowns out the smell of the seaweed, the smell of the tarred and yet rotting beams, the smell of the wind-dry runways, the smell of the sea air.

And you Tulla
 said one Sunday morning: "Aw let her. I want to see how she walks."
 Wonder of wonders, Dr. Brunies nods and Jenny is allowed to walk on the boards of the Brösen pier. Some laugh, many smile, because Jenny is so fat and walks over the boards on two pillars of fat encased in white, bulge-surmounted knee socks and in buckled patent-leather shoes.
 "Amsel!" says Brunies under his black felt hat. "When you were little, say at the age of six, did you suffer from your, well, to put it bluntly, your corpulence?"
 "Not especially, sir. Matern always looked out for me. Only I had trouble sitting down in school, because the seat was too narrow."

Brunies offers candy. The empty baby carriage stands off to one side. Matern guides Jenny awkwardly carefully. The flags all strain in the same direction. Tulla wants to guide Jenny. If only the baby carriage doesn't roll away. Brunies sucks cough drops. Jenny doesn't want to go with Tulla, is on the verge of tears, but Matern is there, and Eddi Amsel quickly and accurately imitates a barnyard. Tulla turns on her heels. At the pointed pier end a crowd is gathering: there's going to be singing. Tulla's face turns triangular and so small that fury gains the upper hand. They are singing on the end of the pier. Tulla rolls her eyes back: bashed-in windows. Up front Hitler Cubs are standing in a semicircle. Scrawny Koshnavian rage: Dul Dul, Tuller. The boys aren't all in uniform, but all join in the singing, and many listen and nod in approval: "Welove-thestorms . . ." they all sing; the only nonsinger strains to hold a black triangular pennant with runic writing straight up in the air. Empty and forsaken stands the baby carriage. Now they sing: "Andtheearlymorn-ingthatisthetimeforus." Then something gay: "Amanwhocalledhimself-Columbus." A fifteen-year-old curlyhead, who is wearing his right arm in a sling, possibly because he has really hurt it, invites the audience in a tone half of command, half of embarrassment, to join in singing the Columbus song, at least the refrain. Young girls who have taken their boy friends' arms and enterprising husbands, among them Herr Pokriefke, Herr Berendt, and Matzerath the grocer, join in the chorus. The northeast wind aligns the flags and smooths out the false notes in the merry song. Anyone who listens closely can hear, now below now above the singing, a child's tin drum. That must be the grocer's son. He isn't quite right in the head. "Gloriaviktoria" and "Wiedewiedewittjuchheirassa" is the refrain of the well-nigh interminable song. Little by little it becomes imperative to join in: "Why isn't *he* singing?" Sidelong glances: Herr and Frau Ropinski are singing too. Even old Sawatzki is with us, and he's an out-and-out Socialist. So come on! Chin up! Aren't Herr Zureck and Postal Secretary Bronski singing, though they both work at the Polish Post Office? "Wiedewiedewittbumbum." And what about Dr. Brunies? Couldn't he at least stop sucking that eternal cough drop and pretend? "Gloriaviktoria!" To one side and empty stands the baby carriage on four high wheels. It glitters black and decrepit. "Wiedewiedewittjuchheir-assa!" Papa Brunies want to pick up Jenny in his arms and unburden her pillars of fat in patent-leather shoes. But his students—"Gloria-viktoria!"—especially Walter Matern, advise him against it. Eddi Amsel joins in the singing: "Wiedewiedewittjuchheirassa!" Because he is an obese child, he has a lovely velvety boy soprano voice, which at certain points in the refrain, in the "juchheirassaaah" for instance, is a silvery bubbling. That's known as descant singing. A number of people look around, curious to know where the spring is gushing.

Now, because contrary to all expectation the Columbus song has a last verse, they are singing a harvest song: "I'veloadedmywagonfull." Now, although such things are best sung in the evening: "Nolovelierlandatthishour." Eddi Amsel lets his fat-boy soprano stand on its head. Brunies sucks ostentatiously and turns on irony lights. Matern darkens under a cloudless sky. The baby carriage casts a solitary shadow . . .

Where is Tulla?

Her cousin has joined in six stanzas of the Columbus song. During the seventh stanza he has erased himself. Only sea air, no more glue smell; for August Pokriefke is standing with his wife and the deaf-mute Konrad on the west side of the triangle at the end of the pier, and the wind has shifted from northeast to east. The Pokriefkes have their backs turned to the sea. They are singing. Even Konrad is opening his mouth in the right places, pursing his lips soundlessly, and he doesn't miss an entrance when the canon Meisterjakobmeisterjakob is attempted with little luck.

Where is Tulla?

Her brothers Siegesmund and Alexander have beat it. Their cousin Harry sees them both on the breakwater. They are diving. Siegesmund is practicing flips and handstand dives. The brothers' clothes are lying, weighted down by shoes, on the windy spur of the pier. Tulla isn't with them. From the direction of the Glettkau pier—even the big Zoppot pier can be made out in the distance—the excursion steamer is approaching on schedule. It is white with a big black smoke trail, like the steamers in children's drawings. Those who wish to take the steamer from Brösen to Neufahrwasser are crowding onto the left side of the pier end. Where is Tulla? The Cubs are still singing, but no one is listening any more, because the steamer is getting bigger and bigger. Eddi Amsel has also withdrawn his high soprano. The tin drum has abandoned the song rhythm and succumbed to the pounding of the engine. It's the *Pike*. But the *Swan* looks exactly the same. Only the side-wheeler, the *Paul Beneke*, looks different. In the first place it has side wheels; in the second place it is bigger, much bigger; and in the third place its run is from Danzig-Langebrücke to Zoppot, Gdingen, and Hela and back—it doesn't come to Glettkau and Brösen at all. Where is Tulla? At first it looks as if the *Pike* had no intention of putting in to the Brösen pier, then she heaves to and is alongside quicker than anyone expected. She churns up foam and not only at bow and stern. She hesitates, marks time, and whips up the sea. Lines are cast: bollards grind. Tobacco-brown cushions on the starboard side muffle the shock. All the children and some of the women are scared because the *Pike* is going to toot in a minute. Children stop their ears, open their mouths, tremble in advance: there she toots with the dark voice that goes hoarse at the end, and is made fast. Ice-cream cones are being licked again, but a few children on board the steamer and on the pier are crying, still stopping their ears and staring at the smokestack, because they know that before casting off the *Pike* will toot again and let off white steam that smells of rotten eggs.

Where is Tulla?

A white steamer is lovely if it has no rust spots. The *Pike* hasn't a single one, though the Danzig Free State flag at the stern and the pennant of the "Vistula" shipyard are washed out and frayed. Some land—some go aboard. Tulla? Her cousin looks behind him: on the right side of the pier stands solely and eternally the baby carriage on four high wheels. It casts a crooked eleven-o'clock shadow, which merges seamlessly with the shadow of the pier railing. A thin unramified shadow approaches this tangle of shadows: Tulla coming up from below. She had been with the waving beards of seaweed, the spellbound fishermen, the exercising stick-lebacks. Bony in short dress, she mounts the steps. Her knees kick against the crocheted hem. From the top of the stairs she heads directly for the carriage. The last passengers go aboard the *Pike*. A few children are still crying or have started up again. Tulla has hooked her arms behind her back. Although her skin is bluish-white in the winter, she turns quickly brown. A dry yellow-brown, the carpenter's glue has missed her vaccination marks: one two three four cherry-size islands on her left arm remain conspicuously ashen. Every steamer brings gulls with it—takes gulls away. The starboard side of the steamer exchanges words with the left side of the pier end: "And drop in again. And take the film to be developed, we can't wait. And give everybody our best regards, hear?" Tulla stands beside the empty baby carriage. The steamer toots high low and its voice cracks. Tulla doesn't stop her ears. Her cousin would like to stop his ears but doesn't. The deaf-mute Konrad, between Erna and August Pokriefke, watches the steamer's wake and holds both ears. The bag lies rumpled wrapping-paper brown at the foot end. Tulla doesn't take a candy. On the breakwater two boys are fighting with one boy: two fall in the water, reappear: all three laugh. Dr. Brunies has picked up Jenny after all. Jenny doesn't know whether she should cry because the steamer has tooted. The teacher and his pupils advise her not to cry. Eddi Amsel has made four knots in his handkerchief and pulled the head covering thus produced over his flaming red hair. Because he looks comical to begin with, the knotted handkerchief makes him look no more comical. Walter Matern stares darkly at the white steamer as it detaches itself trembling from the pier. On board men, women, children, Hitler Cubs with their black pennant wave laugh shout. The gulls circle, fall, rise, and ogle out of heads screwed slantwise. Tulla Pokriefke gives the right hind wheel of

665

the baby carriage a gentle kick: the carriage shadow is scarcely moved. Men, women, and children move slowly away from the left flank of the pier end. The *Pike* sends up a scrawl of black smoke, stamps, puts about, and, growing quickly smaller, takes a course for the Neufahrwasser harbor mouth. Through the calm sea she digs a foaming furrow which is quickly effaced. Not all the gulls follow her. Tulla acts; she throws back her head with its pigtails, lets it snap forward, and spits. Her cousin blushes to kingdom come. He looks around to see if anyone was looking when Tulla spat into the baby carriage. By the left-hand rail of the pier stands a three-year-old in a sailor suit. His sailor cap is encased in a silk ribbon with a gold-embroidered inscription: "HMS Seydlitz." The ends of the ribbon flutter in the northeast wind. At his side hangs a child's tin drum. From his fists grow battered wooden drumsticks. He doesn't drum, has blue eyes, and watches as Tulla spits a second time into the empty baby carriage. A multitude of summer shoes, canvas shoes, sandals, canes, and parasols approach from the end of the pier as Tulla takes aim a third time.

I don't know whether there was any other witness besides me and the grocer's son when my cousin spat three times in quick succession into Jenny's empty baby carriage and then shuffled off skinny angry slowly in the direction of the casino.

Dear Cousin,

I still can't stop putting you on the shimmering boards of the Brösen pier: One Sunday in the following year, but in the same month, to wit, the stormy month of August crawling with jellyfish, when once again men, women, and children with beach bags and rubber animals left the dusty suburb of Langfuhr and rode to Brösen, for the most part to station themselves on the free beach and in the bathing establishment, in lesser part to promenade on the pier, on a day when eight flags of Baltic cities and four swastika flags flapped sluggishly on twelve flagpoles, when out at sea a storm was piling up over Oxhöft, when the red jellyfish were stinging and the nonstinging bluish-white jellyfish were blossoming in the lukewarm sea—one Sunday, then, in August Jenny got lost.

Dr. Brunies had nodded assent. Walter Matern had picked Jenny up out of the baby carriage and Eddi Amsel had failed to take notice when Jenny wandered off in the dominically attired throng. The storm over Oxhöft put on an extra story. Walter Matern didn't find Jenny. Eddi Amsel didn't. I found her, because I was looking for my cousin Tulla: I was always looking for you and found mostly Jenny Brunies.

That time, as the storm built up from the west, I found both of them, and Tulla was holding our Harras, whom I had taken along with my father's permission, by the collar.

On one of the runways that ran lengthwise and crosswise under the pier, at the end of a blind runway, or alley if you will, I found them both. Concealed by beams and struts, huddled in a white dress in green changing light traversed by shadow—above her the scraping of light summer shoes, below her, licking lapping glugging sighing—Jenny Brunies, plump dismayed tearful. Tulla was scaring her. Tulla commanded our Harras to lick Jenny's face. And Harras obeyed Tulla.

"Say shit," said Tulla, and Jenny said it.

"Say: my father farts all the time," said Tulla, and Jenny admitted what Dr. Brunies sometimes did.

"Say: my brother is always swiping things," said Tulla.

But Jenny said: "I haven't got any brother, honest I haven't."

Thereupon Tulla fished under the runway with a long arm and brought up a wobbling nonstinging jellyfish. It took both her hands to hold the whitish glassy pudding, in whose soft center violet-blue veins and knots converged.

"You're going to eat it till there's nothing left," Tulla commanded. "It hasn't any taste, go ahead." Jenny remained frozen and Tulla showed her how you eat jellyfish. She sucked in two soupspoonfuls, swished the gelatinous mass between her teeth, and from the gap between her two upper incisors spat a jet of gook that barely missed Jenny's face. High over the pier the storm front had begun to nibble at the sun.

"You saw me do it. Now do it yourself."

Jenny's face was getting ready to cry. Tulla threatened: "Should I tell the dog?" Before Tulla could sick our Harras on Jenny—I'm sure he wouldn't have hurt her—I whistled Harras to heel. He didn't obey right away, but he turned his head and collar toward me. I had him. But up above, though still at a distance, it was thundering. Tulla, right next to me, smacked the rest of the jellyfish against my shirt, pushed by, and was gone. Harras wanted to follow her. Twice I had to call: "Stay!" With my left hand I held the dog, with my right I took Jenny's hand and led her up to the storm-anticipating pier, where Dr. Brunies and his students were looking for Jenny amid the scurrying bathers, crying "Jenny!" and fearing the worst.

Even before the first gust of wind the caretakers brought in eight different and four identical flags. Papa Brunies held the baby carriage by the handle: the carriage trembled. The first drops broke loose overhead. Walter Matern lifted Jenny into the baby carriage: the trembling did not subside. Even when we had taken shelter and Dr. Brunies with trembling fingers had given me three cough drops, the baby carriage was still trembling. The storm, a traveling theater, passed quickly by with a great to-do.

My Cousin Tulla

had to scream at the top of her lungs on the same pier. By then we were able to write our names. Jenny was no longer being wheeled in a

667

baby carriage, but like us went step by little step to the Pestalozzi School. Punctually vacation came with special fares for schoolchildren, bathing weather, and ever new Brösen pier. On the twelve flagpoles of the pier there now blew, when it was windy, six Free State flags and six swastika flags, which were no longer the property of the resort management, but of the Brösen Party group. And before vacation was over, one morning shortly after eleven o'clock, Konrad Pokriefke drowned.

Your brother, the curlyhead. Who laughed soundlessly, joined in the singing, understood everything. Never again to talk with hands, elbows, forehead, lower eyelid, fingers crossed beside right ear, two fingers cheek to cheek: Tulla and Konrad. Now one small finger pressed down, because under the breakwater . . .

The winter was to blame. With ice, thaws, pack ice, and February storms it had severly battered the pier. The management, to be sure, had had the pier repaired more or less; painted white and equipped with new flagpoles, it had the right holiday sparkle, but some of the old piles, which pack ice and heavy breakers had broken off deep under the surface of the water, still protruded treacherously from the bottom, spelling disaster for Tulla's little brother.

Although bathing off the breakwater was forbidden that year, there were plenty of kids who, starting from the free beach, swam out to the breakwater and used it as a diving board. Siegesmund and Alexander Pokriefke hadn't taken their brother with them; he swam after them dog paddle, arms and legs flailing, and managed to swim, though not in any recognized style. All three together dove perhaps fifty times from the breakwater and came up fifty times. Then they dove together another seventeen times and came up together only sixteen times. No one would have noticed so quickly that Konrad had failed to come up if our Harras hadn't acted like he'd gone crazy. From the pier he had joined in their counting and now he ran up and down the breakwater, yelping uncertainly here and there, and finally stood still, keening at the high heavens.

The steamer *Swan* was just docking; but all the people crowded onto the right side of the pier. Only the ice-cream vendor, who never caught on to anything, continued to call out his flavors: "Vanilla, lemon, woodruff, strawberry, vanilla, lemon . . ."

Walter Matern slipped off only his shoes and dove head-first from the rail of the pier. He dove exactly across from the spot which our Harras indicated, first whimpering, then scratching with both forepaws. Eddi Amsel held his friend's shoes. He came up, but dove again. Fortunately Jenny didn't have to watch this: Dr. Brunies and she were sitting under the trees in the casino park. Only when Siegesmund Pokriefke and a man, who however was not a lifeguard, took turns in helping, was the deaf-mute Konrad, whose head had been wedged between two poles that had snapped close to the bottom, finally dislodged.

668

They had scarcely laid him on the runway when the lifesaving team came with the oxygen apparatus. The steamer *Swan* whistled a second time and resumed its circuit of beach resorts. No one turned off the ice-cream vendor: "Vanilla, lemon, woodruff . . ." Konrad's face had turned blue. His hands and feet, like those of all the drowned, were yellow. The lobe of one ear had been torn between the piles: bright red blood dripped on the boards. His eyes refused to close. His curly hair had remained curly under water. Around him, who looked even tinier drowned than alive, a puddle grew. During the efforts to revive him — they applied the oxygen apparatus as the regulations prescribed—I held Tulla's mouth closed. When they removed the apparatus, she bit into my hand and screamed above the voice of the ice-cream vendor to high heaven, because she could no longer talk silently with Konrad for hours, with fingers, cheek to cheek, with the sign on the forehead and the sign for love: hidden in the woodshed, cool under the pier, secretly in the trenches, or quite openly and yet secretly on busy Elsenstrasse.

Dear Tulla,

your scream was to be long-lived: to this day it nests in my ear and holds that one heaven-high tone.

The following summer and the one after that nothing could move our Harras to go out on the breakwater. He remained with Tulla, who also avoided the pier. Their solidarity had a story behind it:

In the summer of the same year, but shortly before the deaf-mute Konrad drowned while bathing, Harras was summoned for mating purposes. The police were acquainted with the dog's pedigree and once or twice a year sent a letter signed by a Police Lieutenant Mirchau. My father never said no to these letters which were framed more or less as commands. As a master carpenter he wished in the first place to avoid trouble with the police; in the second place stud service, when performed by a male of Harras' parts, brought in a tidy little sum; in the third place my father took manifest pride in his shepherd: when the two of them set out for the profitable mating ceremony, an onlooker could easily have been led to believe that the police had called not upon Harras but upon my father to mate.

For the first time I was allowed to go along: unenlightened, but not ignorant. My father despite the heat wearing a suit, which he otherwise put on only when the carpenter's guild had a meeting. A respectable charcoal with belly-spanning vest. Under his velours hat he held a fifteen-pfennig cigar—he was in the habit of buying seconds. No sooner was Harras out of his kennel and muzzled into inoffensiveness—because we were going to the police—than he lit out and was up to his old trick, pulling on the leash: to judge by the ample remains of the cigar, we were in Hochstriess sooner than anyone would have thought possible.

669

Hochstriess was the name of the street that ran southward from the Main Street of Langfuhr. Past two-family houses where police officers lived with their families; on the right, the gloomy brick barracks built for Mackensen's Hussars, now inhabited by the police. At the Pelonker Weg entrance, which was little used and had no sentry box but only a barrier and a guardroom, my father, without removing his hat, produced Lieutenant Mirchau's letter. Although my father knew the way, a policeman escorted us across gravelstrewn barracks yards where policemen in light-gray twill were drilling or standing in a semicircle around a superior. All the recruits stood at ease with their hands behind their backs and gave the impression of listening to a lecture. The offshore wind sent dust cones whirling through the hole between the police garages and the police gymnasium. Along the endless stables of the mounted police, recruits were hurrying over the obstacle course, hurdling walls and ditches, bars and barbed-wire entanglements. All the barracks yards were framed by evenly spaced young lindens about the thickness of a child's arm, supported by props. At that point it became advisable to hold our Harras close. In a small square—to the left and right windowless storerooms, in the background a flat-roofed building—police dogs, perhaps nine of them, were obliged to heel, to point, to retrieve, to bark, to hurdle walls like the recruits, and finally, after complicated trail work with nose to the ground, attack a policeman who, disguised as a thief and protected by padding, was acting out a classical attempt at a getaway. Well-kept beasts, but none like Harras. All of them iron-gray, ash-gray with white markings, dull yellow with black saddle or dark-brindled on light-brown undercoat. The yard resounded with commands and with the commanded barking of the dogs.

In the orderly room of the police kennels we had to wait. Lieutenant Mirchau wore his very straight part on the left side. Lieutenant Mirchau exchanged such words with my father as a carpenter exchanges with a police lieutenant when they are seated in a room for a short while. Then Mirchau lowered his head. His part moved back and forth over his work—he was probably looking through reports. The room had two windows to the left and right of the door. The drilling police dogs would have been visible if the windows hadn't been painted opaque except for the upper third. On the whitewashed wall across from the window front hung two dozen photographs in narrow black frames. All were of the same format; in two pyramidal groups—six photographs at the bottom, then four, and at the top two—they flanked a picture of large upright format, which though broader was also framed in black. Each of the twenty-four of the pyramidally ordered photographs represented a shepherd heeling for a policeman. The large ceremoniously flanked picture presented the face of an elderly man in a spiked helmet, with tired eyes under heavy eyelids. Much too loudly I asked the man's name. Lieutenant Mirchau replied, without raising head or part, that this was a picture of the Reichspräsident, and that the signature at the bottom had been affixed by the old gentleman in person. There were also ink tracks crowded in under the photographs of dogs and policemen: probably the names of the dogs, references to their pedigrees, the names and ranks of the policemen, possibly, since these were obviously police dogs, allusions to actions performed in line of duty by the dogs and dog-leading policemen, for instance, the names of the burglars, smugglers, and murderers who had been apprehended with the help of the dog in question.

Behind the desk and Lieutenant Mirchau's back hung, again symmetrically echeloned, six framed and glassed paper rectangles, illegible from where I was sitting. To judge by the type and sizes of the lettering, they must have been certificates in Gothic print with gold embossing, seals, and raised stamps. Probably dogs, who had served with the police, who had been drilled in the Langfuhr-Hochstriess police kennels, had won first, second, or even third prize at interregional police dog meets. On the desk, to the right of the inclined part, slowly moving back and forth over the lieutenant's work, stood in tense posture a bronze, or perhaps only plaster shepherd about the height of a dachshund, who, as any dog fancier could see at a glance, was cow-hocked and let his croup, to the onset of the tail, slope much too steeply.

Despite all this emphasis on cynology, the orderly room of the Langfuhr-Hochstriess police kennels didn't smell of dogs, but rather of lime; for the room had been freshly whitewashed—and the six or seven potted dwarf lindens that adorned both window sills gave off a dry acrid smell: my father was obliged to sneeze loudly several times, which embarrassed me.

After a good half hour Harras was brought back. He didn't look any different. My father received twenty-five gulden of stud money and the bright-blue stud certificate, the text of which indicated the circumstances of the covering, such as the male's immediate readiness to mate, and the numbers of two entries in the studbook. To help me preserve it in my memory to this day, Lieutenant Mirchau spat into a white-enameled spittoon, which stood by the left hind leg of his desk, and said they would send word whether it had taken. If the desired result should materialize, he would see to it that the balance of the stud fee was sent as usual.

Harras had his muzzle on again, my father had put away the stud certificate and the five five-gulden pieces, we were already on our way to the door when Mirchau resurfaced from his reports: "You've got to keep that animal more in check. His habits on the leash are deplorable. His pedigree makes it quite clear that the animal came from Lithuania three

671

generations back. Suddenly, from one day to the next, a mutation can set in. We've seen all sorts of things. Moreover breeder Matern should have had the mating of the bitch Senta of Queen Louise's mill with the stud dog Pluto supervised and confirmed by the local dog club in Neuteich." He shot a finger at me: "And don't leave the dog with children too often. He shows signs of reverting to wildness. It's all the same to us, but you'll have trouble later on."

It wasn't you,

but me the lieutenant's finger was aimed at. But it was you who demoralized Harras.

Tulla, skinny bony. Through the cracks in every fence. Under the stairs a tangle; a tangle down the banister.

Tulla's face, in which the overly large, usually crusted nostrils—she talked through her nose—outweighed everything, even the narrow-set eyes, in importance.

Tulla's scraped, scab-forming, healing, newly scraped knees.

Tulla's aroma of bone glue, her carpenter's glue dolls and her wigs of wood shavings, which one of the carpenters had to plane specially for her from long boards.

Tulla could do what she liked with Harras; and she did with Harras everything that entered her head. Our dog and her deaf-mute brother were for a long time her real retinue, whereas I, who wanted passionately to belong, was always just tagging around after the three of them, and yet obliged to do my breathing at a distance from Tulla's aroma of bone glue when I finally caught up with them by the Striessbach, on Aktien Pond, on the Fröbelwiese, in the coconut pile of the Amada margarine factory, or in the police trenches; for when my cousin had wheedled my father long enough—which Tulla was very good at doing—Harras was allowed to go along. Tulla led our Harras to Oliva Forest, to Saspe and across the sewage fields, through the lumber yards behind the New City or to the Brösen pier, until the deaf-mute Konrad drowned while swimming.

Tulla screamed for five hours,

then played deaf and dumb. For two days, until Konrad lay beneath the ground in the Consolidated Cemeteries beside Hindenburgallee, she lay stiff in bed, beside the bed, under the bed, tried to waste away completely, and on the fourth day after Konrad's death moved into the kennel by the front wall of the lumber and plywood shed, which was properly intended only for Harras.

But it turned out that both found room in the kennel. They lay side by side. Or Tulla lay alone in the kennel and Harras lay across the entrance.

This never went on for long, then they were back again, lying flank to flank in the kennel. When it became necessary to bark and growl briefly at a delivery man, bringing door frames or blades for the buzz saw, Harras left the kennel; and when he was drawn to his dinner plate or drinking bowl, Harras left Tulla for a short while, only to push hurriedly and backwards—for in the cramped kennel he had difficulty in turning around—back into the warm hole. He let his superimposed paws, she her thin braids tied up in string, hang out over the threshold of the kennel. Either the sun shone on the tar paper of the kennel roof or they heard the rain on the tar-paper roof; or they didn't hear the rain, heard perhaps the lathe, the finishing machine, the booming planing machine, and the agitated, tranquillized, freshly and more furiously agitated buzz saw, which went its arduous ways when the rain was beating down on the yard, forming always the same puddles.

They lay on shavings. On the first day my father came out, and Dreesen the machinist, who called my father by his first name and vice versa after work hours. August Pokriefke came out in wooden shoes. Erna Pokriefke came out in felt slippers. My mother didn't come out. They all said: "Now come on out of there and get up and stop that." But Tulla didn't come out, didn't get up, and didn't stop. Anyone attempting to set foot in the vicinity of the kennel quailed after the first step; for the kennel—and Harras had no need to take one paw off the other—emitted a growling that meant something. Born Koshnavians, long-time residents of Langfuhr, the tenants of the two-and-a-half-room apartments exchanged the opinion from floor to floor: "She'll come when she's had enough and when she sees she can't bring little Konrad back to life by going on that way."

But Tulla didn't see,

didn't come out, and didn't have enough on the evening of her first dog-kennel day. Two lay on wood shavings. They were renewed every day. August Pokriefke had been doing that for years; and Harras attached importance to the renewal of the shavings. Consequently, of all those who were concerned over Tulla, only old man Pokriefke was allowed to approach the kennel with a basket of crisp shavings. In addition he had a broom and shovel wedged under his arm. As soon as August Pokriefke came padding along thus laden, Harras left the kennel unasked, tugged a little, then harder at Tulla's dress, until she dragged herself out into the daylight and crouched down beside the kennel. As she crouched, her eyes, quite sightless, rolled back so that only the whites shimmered; with "bashed-in windows," she passed water. Not defiantly, indifferently would be more accurate, she waited until August Pokriefke had renewed the shavings and come out with the little speech that was bound to occur to him as a father: "Come on up now. You're still on vacation now, but pretty soon you'll have to go to school. D'you think you're the only one? D'you think we didn't love the boy? And don't act like you was nuts. They'll come and get you and put you in an institution where they swat you from morning to night. They'll think you're crazy. So come up now. It'll be dark soon. Mama's making potato pancakes. Come along now or they'll take you away."

Tulla's first dog-kennel day ended like this:

she stayed in the kennel. August Pokriefke took Harras off the chain. With different keys he locked the lumber shed, the plywood shed, the machine room, and the office where the varnishes and frames, the saw blades and the cakes of bone glue were kept, left the yard, also locked the door to the yard; and no sooner had he locked up than it grew darker and darker. It grew so dark that I, looking out between the curtains of our kitchen window, could no longer distinguish the tar paper of the dog kennel from the ordinarily lighter front wall of the lumber shed.

On the second dog-kennel day,

a Tuesday, Harras no longer had to tug when August Pokriefke wanted to renew the shavings. Tulla began to take food, that is, she ate with Harras out of his dish, after Harras had dragged a boneless chunk of dog meat into the kennel and whetted her appetite by nuzzling the meat with his cold nose.

Now this dog meat really wasn't bad. Usually it was stringy cow meat and was cooked in large quantities on our kitchen stove, always in the same rust-brown enamel pot. We had all of us, Tulla and her brothers and myself as well, eaten this meat in our bare hands, without bread to push it down. It tasted best when cold and hard. We cut it into cubes with our pocketknives. It was cooked twice a week and was compact, gray-brown, traversed by pale-blue little veins, sinews, and sweating strips of fat. It smelled sweetish soapy forbidden. Long after gulping down the marbled cubes of meat—often while playing we had both pockets full of them—our palates were still deadened and tallowy. We even spoke differently when we had eaten of those meat cubes: our speech became palatal metamorphosed four-legged: we barked at each other. We preferred this dish to many that were served at the family board. We called it dog meat. When it wasn't cow meat, it was never anything worse than horse meat or the mutton from a forced slaughtering. My mother threw coarse-grained salt—a handful—into the enamel pot, piled up the foot-long tatters of meat in the boiling salt water, let the water boil up again for a moment, put in marjoram, because marjoram is supposed to be good for a dog's sense of smell, turned the gas down, covered the pot, and didn't touch it for a whole hour; for that was the time required by cow-horse-sheep meat to turn into the dog meat which Harras and we ate and which, thanks to the marjoram cooked with it, provided us all, Harras and the rest of us, with sensitive olfactories. It was a Koshnavian recipe. Between Osterwick and Schlangenthin they said: Marjoram is good for your looks. Marjoram makes money go further. Against Devil and hell strew marjoram over the threshold. The squat long-haired Koshnavian sheep dogs were celebrated for their marjoram-favored keenness of smell.

Rarely, when there was no meat displayed on the low-price counter, the pot was filled with innards: knotted fatty beef hearts, pissy, because unsoaked, pig's kidneys, also small lamb kidneys which my mother had to detach from a finger-thick coat of fat lined with crackling parchment: the kidneys went into the dog pot, the suet was rendered in a cast-iron frying pan and used in the family cooking, because mutton suet wards off tuberculosis. Sometimes, too, a piece of dark spleen, halfway between purple and violet, went into the pot, or a chunk of sinewy beef liver. But because lung took longer to cook, required a larger cooking pot, and when you come right down to it doesn't yield much meat, it almost never went into the enamel pot, in actual fact only during the occasional summer meat shortages brought on by the cattle plague that sometimes came to Kashubia as well as Koshnavia. We never ate the boiled innards. Only Tulla, unbeknownst to the grownups, but before our eyes as we looked on with a tightening of the throat, took long avid gulps of the brownish-gray broth in which the coagulated excretion of the kidneys floated sleet-like and mingled with blackish marjoram to form islands.

On the fourth dog-kennel day

—on the advice of the neighbors and of the doctor who came in when there was an accident in the shop, Tulla was given her way—I brought her—no one was up yet, even the machinist, who was always first at work, hadn't arrived yet—a bowlful of heart, kidney, spleen, and liver broth. The broth in the bowl was cold, for Tulla preferred to drink her broth cold. A layer of fat, a mixture of beef tallow and mutton tallow, covered the bowl like an icecap. The cloudy liquid emerged only at the edges, and drops of it rolled over the layer of tallow. I tiptoed cautiously in my pajamas. I had taken the key to the yard from the big key rack without jangling the other keys. Very early and very late all staircases creak. On the flat roof of the woodshed the sparrows were starting up. In the kennel no sign of life. But varicolored flies on tar paper already touched by slanting sun. I ventured as far as the semicircular earthworks and foot-deep ditch which marked the range of the dog's chain. Inside the kennel: peace, darkness, and not a single varicolored fly. Then there awakened in the darkness: Tulla's hair mixed with shavings. Harras held his head on his paws. Lips pressed tight. Ears scarcely playing, but playing. Several times I called, but there was sleep in my throat and I didn't do very well, swallowed, and called louder: "Tulla!" I also stated my name: "It's Harry and I've brought you something." I tried to lure her with the broth in the bowl, attempted lip-smacking sounds, whistled softly and hissingly, as though trying to lure not Tulla but Harras to the edge of the semicircle.

When there was no life or sign of life but flies, a little oblique sun, and sparrow chatter, at the most dog ears—and once Harras yawned at length but kept his eyes shut—I set down the bowl at the edge of the semicircle, or more precisely, in the ditch dug by the dog's forepaws, left it, and without turning went back into the house. Behind my back: sparrows, varicolored flies, climbing sun, and the kennel.

The machinist was just pushing his bicycle through the passage. He asked, but I didn't answer. In our apartment the windows were still shuttered. My father's sleep was peaceful, confident in the alarm clock. I pushed a stool up to the kitchen window, grabbed a big chunk of dry bread and the pot of plum butter, pushed the curtains to left and right, dipped the bread into the plum butter, and was already gnawing and tugging when Tulla crawled out of the kennel. Even when Tulla had the threshold of the kennel behind her, she stayed on all fours, shook herself limply, shed wood shavings, crawled sluggish and wobbly toward the semicircle described by the dog's chain, reached ditch and earthworks right next to the door to plywood shed, hove to with a sharp twist of the hips, shook off more shavings—her light blue cotton dress was gradually developing blue and white checks—yawned in the direction of the yard —there in the shade, only his cap struck by the oblique rays of the sun, stood the machinist beside his bicycle, rolling himself a cigarette and looking toward the kennel; while I with bread and plum butter looked down on Tulla, ignored the kennel, and aimed only at her, her and her back. And Tulla with sluggish sleepy movements crawled along the semi-circle, letting her head and matted hair hang down, and stopped only, but still behind lowered head, when she reached the glazed brown earthenware bowl, whose contents were covered by an unbroken layer of tallow.

As long as I upstairs forgot to chew, as long as the machinist, whose cap was growing more and more into the sun, used both hands to light his conical handmade cigarette—three times his lighter failed to light— Tulla held her face rigid against the sand, then turned slowly but again from the hips, without raising her head with its hair and shavings. When her face was over the bowl and would have been mirrored if the layer of tallow had been a round pocket mirror, all movement was suspended. And I too, up above, was still not chewing. Almost imperceptibly Tulla's weight was shifted from two supporting arms to her left supporting arm, until seen from the kitchen window her left open palm disappeared under her body. And then, though I couldn't see her free arm coming, she had her right hand on the basin, while I dipped my chunk of bread in the plum butter.

The machinist smoked rhythmically and let his cigarette cling to his lower lip as he blew out smoke till the still-horizontal sun struck it. Strained with propping, Tulla's left shoulder blade stretched the blue-and-white gingham of her dress. Harras, head on paws, raised his eyelids one more slowly than the other and looked toward Tulla: she extended the little finger of her right hand; he slowly and successively lowered his lids. Now, because the sun disclosed the dog's ears, flies flared up and were extinguished in the kennel.

While the sun climbed and a cock crowed nearby—there were roosters in the neighborhood—Tulla stuck the extended little finger of her right hand vertically into the middle of the layer of tallow, and began cautiously but tenaciously to bore a hole in the tallow. I put the bread aside. The machinist shifted to the other leg and let his face slip out of the sunlight. That was something I wanted to see, how Tulla's little finger would bore through the layer of tallow, penetrate to the broth, and break open the layer several times more; but I didn't see how Tulla's little finger reached into the broth, and the layer of tallow didn't break into floes, but was picked up from the basin, round and in one piece, by Tulla's little finger. High over shoulder, hair, and shavings she raises the disk the size of a beer mug mat into the early seven-o'clock sky, offers a glimpse of her screwed-up face, and then hurls the disk with a snap of her wrist into the yard, in the direction of the machinist: in the sand it broke forever, the shards rolled in the sand; and a few fragments of tallow, transformed into tallowy balls of sand, grew after the manner of snowballs and rolled down close to the smoking machinist and his bicycle with its new bell.

As I then looked back from the shattered disk of tallow to Tulla, she was kneeling bony and steep, but still cool, under the sun. She spreads the fingers of her left, overstrained hand five times sideways, folds them over three joints and then back over the same joints. Cupping the bowl in her right hand, which rests on the ground, she slowly guides her mouth and the edge of the bowl together. She laps, sips, wastes nothing. In one breath, without removing the bowl from her lips, Tulla drinks the fatless spleen-heart-kidney-liver broth with all its granular delicacies and surprises, with the tiny bits of cartilage at the bottom, with Koshnavian marjoram and coagulated urea. Tulla drinks to the dregs: her chin raises the bowl. The bowl raises the hand beneath the bowl into the beam of the oblique sun. A neck is exposed and grows steadily longer. A head with hair and shavings leans back and beds itself on shoulders. Two

677

narrow-set eyes remain closed. Skinny, sinewy, and pale, Tulla's childlike neck labors until the bowl lies on top of her face and she is able to lift her hand from the bowl and move it away between the bottom of the bowl and the side-slipping sun. The overturned bowl conceals the screwed-up eyes, the crusty nostrils, the mouth that has had enough.

I think I was happy in my pajamas behind our kitchen window. Plum butter had set my teeth on edge. In my parent's bedroom the alarm clock put an end to my father's slumbers. Down below the machinist was obliged to light up again. Harras raised eyelids. Tulla let the bowl tip off her face. The bowl fell in the sand. It did not break. Tulla fell slowly onto both palms. A few shavings, which the lathe may have spat out, crumbled off her. She executed a ninety-degree turn from the hip, crawled slow sated sluggish first into the oblique sun, then carried sun along with her on her back to the kennel door, pivoted outside the hole, and pushed herself backwards, with hanging head and hair, charged with horizontal sun that made both hair and shavings shimmer, across the threshold into the kennel.

Then Harras closed his eyes again. Varicolored flies returned. My edgy teeth. Beyond his collar his black neck which no illumination could make lighter. My father's getting-up sounds. Sparrows strewn around the empty bowl. A patch of material: blue-and-white checks. Wisps of hair, shimmering light, shavings, paws, flies, ears, sleep, morning sun: tar paper grew soft and smelled.

Dreesen the machinist pushed his bicycle toward the half-glass door to the machine shop. Slowly and in step he shook his head from left to right and right to left. In the machine shop the buzz saw, the band saw, the lathe, the finishing machine, and the planing machine were still cold but hungry. My father coughed solemnly in the toilet. I slipped down off the kitchen stool.

Toward evening of the fifth dog-kennel day,

a Friday, the carpenter tried to reason with Tulla. His fifteen-pfennig cigar formed a right angle to his well-cut face and made his paunch—he was standing in side view—look less protuberant. The imposing-looking man spoke sensibly. Kindness as bait. Then he spoke more force-fully, let the ash break prematurely from his teetering cigar, and took on a more protuberant paunch. Prospect of punishment held out. When he crossed the semicircle, whose radius was measured by the dog's chain, Harras, accompanied by wood shavings, stormed out of the kennel and hurled his blackness and both forepaws against the carpenter's chest. My father staggered back and went red and blue in the face, his cigar still clung to his lips, though the angle had lost its precision. He seized a roofing lath from one of the piles propped up on sawhorses, but did not strike out at Harras, who tense and unbarking was testing the strength of his chain. Arm and lath were lowered, and it was not until half an hour later that he thrashed the apprentice Hotten Scherwinski with his bare hands, because according to the machinist, Hotten Scherwinski had neglected to clean and oil the lathe, and moreover, the apprentice had allegedly made off with some door mountings and a couple of pounds of one-inch nails.

Tulla's next dog-kennel day,

the sixth, was a Saturday. August Pokriefke in wooden shoes moved the sawhorses out of the way, cleaned up Harras' droppings, swept and raked the yard, grooving the sand with patterns that were not even ugly, but more on the strong, simple side. Desperately and over and over again, while the sand grew steadily darker and wetter, he raked in the vicinity of the dangerous semicircle. Tulla was not to be seen. She peed, when she had to pee—and Tulla had to make water regularly every hour—in shavings which August Pokriefke had to change in the evening. But on the evening of the sixth dog-kennel day he did not dare to renew the couch of shavings. As soon as he took venturesome steps with clumsy wooden shoes, with shovel and broom, with his basket of curly shavings from the lathe and finishing machine, and thrust himself and his evening chore across the clawed-up ditch of the semicircle, mumbling "good boy, good boy, be a good boy," the kennel emitted a growling which was not exactly malignant but more in the nature of a warning.

On Saturday the shavings in the kennel were not renewed; and August Pokriefke did not let the dog Harras off the chain. With watchdog fierce but chained the shop lay unguarded beneath a thin moon. But no burglars called.

Sunday,

Tulla's seventh dog-kennel day brought Erna Pokriefke into the picture. In the early afternoon she came out, drawing behind her on the left a chair, whose fourth leg cut a sharp track across the patterns of her yard-raking husband. On the right she carried the dog's dish full of knotty beef kidney and halved lamb's hearts: all the heart chambers lay wide open, revealing their tubes, ligaments, sinews, and smooth inner walls. Near the door of the plywood shed she put down the dish full of innards. A respectful step back from the center of the semicircle, directly across from the kennel door, she set up the chair, and finally sat huddled and askew in her black Sunday dress, with her rat's eyes and her bobbed hair that seemed more chewed than cut. She pulled her knitting out of her front-buttoned taffeta and knitted in the direction of kennel, Harras, and daughter Tulla.

We, that is, the carpenter, my mother, August Pokriefke, as well as his sons Alexander and Siegesmund, spent the whole afternoon standing

679

at the kitchen window, looking, bunched together or singly, out into the yard. At the windows of the other apartments on the court stood and sat neighbors and their children; or else a spinster, such as Fräulein Dobslaff, stood at the window of her ground-floor apartment, looking out into the yard.

I declined to be relieved and stood steadfast the whole time. No game of Monopoly and no Sunday crumb cake could lure me away. It was a balmy August day and on the following day school was to begin. At Erna Pokriefke's request we had had to close the lower double windows. The square upper windows, also double, were open a crack, admitting air, flies, and the crowing of the neighborhood cocks to our kitchen. Sounds came and went, including the trumpet notes emitted by a man who Sunday after Sunday practiced the trumpet in the attic of a house on Labesweg. But all the while a breathless whispering, babbling, chattering, burbling, and twanging: the penetrating nasal clamor of Koshnavian alders in the sandy wind, quantities of lace, a rosary, beads, crumpled paper smoothing out of its own accord, the mouse is cleaning house, straw grows to bundles: not only did Mother Pokriefke knit in the direction of the dog kennel, she whispered, murmured, muttered, smacked her lips, chirped, and whistled luringly in the same direction. I saw her lips in profile, her twitching, grinding, hammering chin, receding and darting forward, her seventeen fingers and four dancing needles, under which something light blue grew in her taffeta lap, something intended for Tulla, and later Tulla actually wore it.

The dog kennel with its inhabitants gave no sign. At the beginning of the knitting and while a lament refused to die down, Harras had come out of the kennel lazily and unseeing. After yawning with cracking jaws and after stretching exercises, he had found his way to his dish, on his way going into a convulsive crouch to expel his knotty sausage and also lifting a leg. He moved the dish over in front of the kennel, where jerkily, with dancing hocks, he bolted the beef kidney and the lamb's hearts with all their wide-open chambers, but covered the kennel door with his bulk, making it impossible to tell whether Tulla like himself was eating of the kidney and the hearts.

Toward evening Erna Pokriefke went back into the house with an almost finished light-blue knitted jacket. She said nothing. We were afraid to ask questions. The Monopoly game had to be put away. There was crumb cake left over. After supper my father pulled himself up to his full height, stared grimly at the oil painting of the Kurish elk, and said that this had been going on too long and something had to be done.

On Monday morning:
    the carpenter made ready to go to the police; Erna Pokriefke, her legs firmly planted in our kitchen, reviled him in an amplified voice,

calling him a no-good dumbhead; I alone, already harnessed with my school satchel, looking out the kitchen window. And then Tulla tottering, bony, followed by Harras with hanging head, left the kennel. At first she crawled on all fours, then stood up like a normal human and, without interference from Harras, crossed the semicircle with fragile steps. On two legs, grimy, gray, licked shiny in places by a long dog's tongue, she found the yard door.

Harras howled after her only once, but his howl cut through the screaming of the buzz saw.

While for Tulla and me,

for Jenny and all the other schoolchildren school began again, Harras resumed his dog's life, a varied routine which was not even interrupted by the arrival, exactly three weeks later, of the news that the stud dog Harras had once again earned twenty-five gulden for my father. Brief as it had been, his visit to the kennels of the Langfuhr-Hochstriess police barracks had produced the desired effect. After an appropriate lapse of time we were informed by a card specially printed for the correspondence of the police kennels that the shepherd dam Thekla of Schüddelkau, breeder: Albrecht Leeb, registration no. 4356, had whelped five puppies. And then, several months later, after the Sundays of Advent, after Christmas, after New Year's, after snow, thaw, more snow, long-lasting snow, after the beginning of spring and the distribution of Easter report cards —everybody was promoted—after a period in which nothing happened —unless I should mention the accident in the machine shop: the apprentice Hotten Scherwinski lost the middle finger and index finger of his left hand to the buzz saw—came the registered letter announcing, over the signature of Gauleiter Forster, that the shepherd puppy Prinz of the litter Falko, Kastor, Bodo, Mira, Prinz—out of Thekla of Schüddelkau, breeder A. Leeb, Danzig-Ohra, by Harras of Queen Louise's mill, breeder and owner Friedrich Liebenau, master carpenter in Danzig-Langfuhr, had been purchased from the police kennels in Langfuhr-Hochstriess and that it had been decided in the name of the Party and the German population of the German city of Danzig, to present the shepherd Prinz to the Führer and Chancellor through a delegation on the occasion of his forty-sixth birthday. The Führer and Chancellor, so the communication went on, had graciously accepted the gift of the Gau of Danzig and declared his intention of keeping the shepherd Prinz along with his other dogs.

Enclosed in the registered letter was a postcard-size photograph of the Führer, signed by his own hand. In the picture he wore the costume of an Upper Bavarian villager, except that the jacket was more fashionably cut. At his feet, with his tongue hanging out, a gray-clouded shepherd

681

dog with light, probably yellow markings on his chest and over his stop. Mountains towered in the distance. The Führer was laughing in the direction of someone who was not in the picture.

Letter and picture of the Führer—both were immediately placed under glass and framed in our own shop—went on long excursions in the neighborhood. As a result, first my father, then August Pokriefke, and finally quite a few of the neighbors joined the Party, while Gustav Mielawske—for over fifteen years a journeyman in our shop and a quiet Social Democrat—gave notice and did not return to his bench until two months later, after a good deal of coaxing by the master carpenter.

Tulla received a new school satchel from my father. I was given a complete Hitler Cub uniform. Harras was presented with a new collar, but couldn't be given better care because he was well taken care of as it was.

Dear Tulla,

did our dog Harras' sudden career have consequences for us? To me Harras brought schoolboy fame. I had to step up to the blackboard and tell the class all about it. Of course I was not allowed to speak about breeding and mating, about the stud certificate and the stud money, about Harras' prowess at stud as noted in the studbook, or about the heat of the bitch Thekla. I was obliged and permitted to babble in baby talk about Papa Harras and Mama Thekla, about their babies Falko, Kastor, Bodo, Mira, and Prinz. Fräulein Spollenhauer wanted to know all about it: "Why did the Herr Gauleiter make our Führer a present of the little dog Prinz?"

"Because it was the Führer's birthday and he'd always wanted a little dog from our city."

"And why is the little dog Prinz so happy on the Obersalzberg that he isn't the least bit homesick for his mama?"

"Because our Führer loves dogs and is always kind to dogs."

"And why should we be glad that Prinz is with the Führer?"

"Because Harry Liebenau is a member of our class."

"Because Harras belongs to his father."

"Because Harras is the little dog Prinz's father."

"And because it is a great honor for our class and our school and our beautiful city."

Were you there, Tulla,

when Fräulein Spollenhauer with me and the whole class paid a visit to our carpenter shop? You were not there, you were in school.

The class stood in a semicircle around the semicircle that Harras had described around his domain. Once again I had to repeat my lecture, then Fräulein Spollenhauer asked my father to say a few words to the children. Assuming that the class had been apprised of the dog's political career, the carpenter obliged with a few sidelights on our Harras' pedigree. He spoke of a she-dog named Senta and of a male by the name of Pluto, both of them just as black as Harras or little Prinz for that matter. They had been Harras' parents. The she-dog Senta had belonged to a miller in Nickelswalde in the Vistula estuary—"Have you ever been in Nickelswalde, children? I went there years ago on the narrow-gauge railway, and the mill there is a place of historical importance, because Queen Louise of Prussia spent the night there when she was fleeing before the French." Under the jack of the mill, said the carpenter, he had found six whelps —"That's what they call dog babies"—and he had bought one baby dog from the miller. "That was our Harras, who has always been such a joy to us, especially lately."

Where were you, Tulla,
    when I, under the machinist's supervision, was allowed to show our class through the machine shop? You were in school, unable to see or hear me naming all the machines to my classmates and Fräulein Spollenhauer: The lathe. The finishing machine. The band saw. The planing machine. The buzz saw.
    Then Herr Dreesen explained the different kinds of wood to the children. He drew a distinction between cross-grained wood and long-grained, knocked on elm, pine, pear wood, oak, maple, beech, and soft linden wood, chatted about rare woods and the annual rings in trees.
    Then we had to stand out in the yard and sing a song that Harras didn't want to listen to.

Where was Tulla
    when Hauptbannführer Göpfert accompanied by Jungbannführer Wendt and several lesser leaders visited our shop? We were both in school and not present when the decision was made to name a newly formed squad of Cubs after our Harras.

And Tulla and Harry were absent
    when after the Röhm putsch and the death of the old gentleman at Neudeck a get-together was arranged on the Obersalzberg behind bright rustic cotton curtains in a low-ceilinged imitation of a peasants' living room; but Frau Raubal, Rudolf Hess, Herr Hanfstaengl, Danzig SA leader Linsmayer, Rauschning, Forster, August Wilhelm of Prussia, called "Auwi" for short, Beanpole Brückner, and Reich Peasant Leader Darré listened to the Führer—and Prinz was there. Prinz out of our Harras, whom Senta had whelped, and Perkun sired Senta.

They ate apple tart that Frau Raubal had baked and spoke of branch and root, of Strasser, Schleicher, Röhm, root and branch. Then they discussed Spengler, Gobineau, and the Protocols of the Elders of Zion. Then Hermann Rauschning mistakenly called Prinz the shepherd pup a "magnificent black wolfhound." Later on all the historians unthinkingly followed him. Yet every cynologist will agree with me that the only real wolfhound is the Irish wolfhound, which differs significantly from the German shepherd. With his long finedrawn head he is related to the degenerate greyhound. He measures thirty-two inches at the withers or seven inches more than our Harras. The Irish wolfhound has long hair. And small, soft ears which do not stand erect but topple. A decorative luxury dog, which the Führer would never have had in his kennels; whereby it is proved for all time that Rauschning was mistaken: no Irish wolfhound weaved nervously around the legs of the cake-eating company; Prinz, our Prinz, listened to conversations and worried about his master with canine fidelity. For the Führer feared for his life. Artful plots might well have been baked into every piece of cake. Fearfully he drank his soda water and often had to vomit for no reason.

But Tulla was present
    when the newspapermen and photographers came. Not only did the *Vorposten* and the *Neueste Nachrichten* send their reporters. Gentlemen as well as ladies in sports clothes came from Elbing, Königsberg, Schneidemühl, Stettin, and even from the national capital. Only Brost, editor of the *Volksstimme,* soon to be suppressed, refused to interview our Harras. Instead, he commented on the hubbub in the newspapers under the title: "Gone to the Dogs." On the other hand, denominational newspapers and specialized journals sent reporters. The organ of the German Shepherd Dog Association sent a cynologist, whom my father was obliged to turn out of the house. For this dog expert began at once to carp at our Harras' pedigree. The names, he declared, were revolting and alien to the breed; there were no data about the bitch that had whelped Senta; the animal itself was not bad, but it would be his duty to inveigh against such methods of dog raising; precisely because this was a historical dog, a sense of responsibility was in order.
    In a word, whether inveighingly or in terms of uncritical praise, Harras was described, printed and photographed. The carpenter shop with machinist, journeymen, helpers, and apprentices also broke into print. Statements by my father, such as: "We are simple artisans with our noses to the grindstone, but all the same we are glad that our Harras . . ."— in brief, the unvarnished utterances of a carpenter were quoted verbatim, often as photograph captions.
    My guess would be that eight solo pictures of Harras were printed in the papers. Three times, I'd say, he appeared with my father, once in

a group picture with the entire personnel of the shop, never with me; but exactly twelve times Tulla found her way with our Harras into German language and international newspapers: slender, on fragile pins, she held still beside our Harras.

Dear Cousin,

and yet you helped him when he moved in. You carried his music, pile after pile, and the porcelain ballerina. For though fourteen tenants went on living in our apartment house, Fräulein Dobslaff moved out of the apartment on the ground floor left, whose windows could be opened on the court. With her remnants of dress material and her numbered photograph albums, with furniture from which wood meal trickled, she went to live with her sister in Schönwarling; and Herr Felsner-Imbs the piano teacher, with his piano and his yellowish stacks of music, his goldfish and his hourglass, his countless photographs of once famous artists, and his procelain figurine in a porcelain tutu, immobilized on pointed porcelain slipper in a perfect arabesque, moved into the empty apartment, without changing the faded wallpaper in the living room or the large flower pattern that covered the walls of the bedroom. To make matters worse, the erstwhile Dobslaffian rooms were dark by nature, because, not seven paces from the windows of both rooms, the gable end of the carpenter shop with its outside staircase reached up to the second floor of the apartment house and cast shadow. And between apartment house and carpenter shop there were two lilac bushes, which did their duty spring after spring. With my father's permission Fräulein Dobslaff had had a garden fence put up around the two bushes, which did not prevent Harras from depositing his scent marks in her garden. Still, it was not because of the dog droppings or the darkness of the apartment that Fräulein Dobslaff moved, but because she wished to die in Schönwarling, where she had come from.

Felsner-Imbs had to burn electric light surrounded by a greenish glass-head lamp shade when pupils called in the morning or afternoon while the sunshine was putting on an orgy outside. To the left of the house entrance he had had an enamel sign put up: Felix Felsner-Imbs— concert pianist and licensed piano teacher. The wobbly old gentleman had not been living in our house for two weeks when the first pupils came, bringing with them the price of a lesson and Damm's *Piano Method,* and were obliged by lamplight to pound out scales and études with right hand, with left hand, with both hands, and once again, until the big hourglass on the piano harbored not a single grain of sand in its upper compartment, so demonstrating in its medieval way that the piano lesson was over.

Felsner-Imbs didn't wear a velvet tam. But flowing blowing hair, snow-white and powdered to boot, hung down over his Schiller collar.

Between little boy's lesson and little girl's lesson he brushed his artist's mane. And when on the treeless Neuer Markt a gust of wind had ruffled his mane he reached for the little brush in the ample pocket of his jacket and, while publicly dressing his astonishing hair, quickly acquired an audience: housewives, schoolchildren, ourselves. As he brushed his hair, an expression of unadulterated pride moved into his eyes. Light blue and lashless, they looked out upon concert halls in which an imaginary public refused to stop applauding him, Felsner-Imbs the concert pianist. Beneath the glass-bead lamp shade a greenish glow fell on the part in his hair: seated on a solidly built piano stool, an Oberon, masterful interpreter of the piano pieces drawn from the opera of that name, metamorphosed boy pupils and girl pupils into water sprites.

The pupils who sat facing the open *Piano Method* at Herr Felsner-Imbs' piano must have been keen of hearing, for from the omnipresent all-day arias of the buzz saw and the lathe, from the modulations of the finishing machine and planing machine, and the ingenuous singsong of the band saw, only a remarkable ear could have hoped to pluck, neatly and note by note, the scales that had to be pounded out beneath the lashless gaze of Felsner-Imbs. Because this concert of machines buried even a fortissimo run of the pupil's hand fathoms deep, the green drawing room behind the lilac bushes resembled an aquarium, silent but full of movement. The piano teacher's goldfish in its bowl on the little lacquered stand was not needed to confirm this impression; it was an accessory too many.

Felsner-Imbs attached particular importance to a correct position of the hands. With a little luck wrong notes could be submerged by the replete yet all-devouring soprano of the buzz saw, but if in playing an étude a pupil let the balls of his hands sink down upon the black wood of the altogether black piano in the course of an ascending or descending scale, if the backs of his hands departed from the desired horizontal position, no amount of carpenter's din could make this obvious lapse in technique unseen. Moreover Felsner-Imbs had made it a feature of his teaching method to lay a pencil across any pupil's hand condemned to execute scales. The hand that failed the test by slumping on the wood in quest of repose sent the control pencil hurtling downward.

Jenny Brunies, the schoolteacher's adoptive daughter from across the street, also had to ride a control pencil on her pudgy right and left hands for the duration of many scales; for, a month after the piano teacher moved in, she became one of his pupils.

You and I

watched Jenny from the little lilac garden. We pressed our faces flat against the windowpanes of the seaweed-green aquarium and saw her sitting on the piano stool: plump and doll-like in brown corduroy. An enormous pinwheel bow performed the function of a brimstone butterfly—in reality the bow was white—on her smoothly falling, approximately medium-brown hair, which was cut to shoulder length. Whereas other pupils frequently enough received a quick painful smack on the back of their hand with the previously fallen pencil, Jenny, although her pencil too fell occasionally on the polar bear skin under the piano stool, never had to fear the punishing blow; at the worst she came in for a look of concern from Felsner-Imbs.

Possibly Jenny was extremely musical—with the buzz saw and the lathe behind us, we, Tulla and I, outside the windowpanes, seldom heard the faintest note; besides, we were not equipped by nature to distinguish winged, accomplished scales from painfully climbed scales —in any case the pudgy little creature from across the street was permitted to ply the keys with both hands sooner than other pupils; moreover, the pencil toppled more and more infrequently and in the end the writing instrument and sword of Damocles was set aside altogether. Through the screaming and squeaking of the daily sawing, planing, and falsetto singing of the carpenter's opera, one could, by trying very hard, more surmise than hear the thin melodies of Damm's *Piano Method:* "Winter Adieu"—"A Hunter from the Palatinate"—"I graze by the Neckar, I graze by the Rhine" . . .

Tulla and I,

we remember that Jenny was favored. Whereas the lessons of the other pupils sometimes came to an abrupt end in the middle of "With Bow and Arrow," because the last grain of sand in the medieval hourglass had said amen to the piano, no hourglass hour struck for either teacher or pupil when Jenny's doll flesh submitted to instruction on the piano stool. And when plump Eddi Amsel got into the habit of escorting plump Jenny Brunies to her piano lesson—Amsel was Dr. Brunies' favorite student and came and went as he pleased across the street—it was perfectly possible that the next pupil would have to wait his turn for an hourglass quarter of an hour on the lumpy sofa in the dusky background of the music room; for Eddi Amsel, who seems to have taken piano lessons at the Conradinum, liked to sit beside the green-maned Felsner-Imbs, playing "Prussia's Glory," the "Finnish Cavalry March," and "Old Comrades" with four-handed gusto.

Amsel also sang. Not only in the high school chorus did his high soprano triumph; Amsel also sang in St. Mary's choir in the venerable Church of St. Mary, whose nave once every month resounded full and round with Bach cantatas and Mozart Masses. Eddi Amsel's high soprano was discovered when the choir decided to do Mozart's early work, the *Missa Brevis.* Every school chorus in town was scoured for a boy soprano. The esteemed conductor of St. Mary's choir surged up to Amsel and assailed him with his enthusiasm: "Truly, my son, you will sing the *Benedictus* more sweetly than Antonio Cesarelli, the celebrated eunuch, who lent his voice when the Mass was first performed. I can hear you rise to such heights of jubilation in the *Dona nobis* that everyone will think: Verily, St. Mary's is too small for that voice."

The story is that although Mr. Lester still represented the League of Nations in the Danzig Free State and all racial laws were constrained to halt at the borders of the diminutive state, Amsel expressed misgivings: "But, sir, they say I'm a half-Jew."

The conductor's answer: "Nonsense, you're a soprano, I expect you to introduce the *Kyrie!*" This succinct reply proved to be long-lived and is said to have been cited with respect many years later in conservative resistance circles.

In any case the chosen boy soprano practiced the difficult passages of the *Missa Brevis* in Felsner-Imbs' green music room. The two of us, Tulla and I, once heard his voice when buzz saw and lathe both had to catch their breath at once: He mined silver. Little knives ground thin as angel's breath quartered the air. Nails melted. Sparrows were ashamed. Apartment houses grew pious, for a corpulent angel sang *Dona nobis* over and over again.

Dear Cousin Tulla,

the only reason for this long and scaly introduction is that Eddi Amsel took to frequenting our apartment house. At first he came only with Jenny, then he brought his bullish friend. Walter Matern might have been regarded as our relation, because his father's shepherd bitch Senta had whelped our Harras. Often my father, as soon as he saw the boy, asked him questions about how the miller was getting along and the economic situation on Great Island. As a rule Eddi Amsel, who was well versed in economics, answered prolixly and with facts which made the employment-promoting plan of the Party and Senate seem unrealistic. He recommended closer relations with the sterling bloc, for want of which he predicted an appreciable devaluation of the gulden. Eddi Amsel even cited figures: the devaluation would have to come to roughly 42 per cent; goods imported from Poland could expect to cost 70 per cent more; even now the devaluation could be predicted for the first days in May; he had all these facts and figures from Matern's father, the miller, who always knew everything in advance. Needless to say, the miller's predictions were confirmed on May 2, 1935.

Amsel and his friend were then in first, working moderately toward their final exams. Both wore real suits with long pants, drank Aktien beer at the Sports Palace or on Zinglers Höhe, and Walter Matern, who smoked Regatta and Artus cigarettes, was said to have seduced a girl in second from the Helene Lange School in Oliva Forest the previous year. No one would have thought of imputing such achievements to the copious Eddi Amsel. Fellow students and girls who were occasionally invited to hear the school choir regarded him as something which they daringly designated as a eunuch. Others expressed themselves more cautiously, saying that Eddi was still rather infantile, more in the neuter gender. As far as I know from hearsay, Walter Matern long put up with this calumny in silence, until one day in the presence of several schoolboys and some girls who were more or less members of the group, he made a speech of some length showing his friend in his true light. Amsel, he said approximately, was far in advance of all the boys present as far as girls etcetera were concerned. He called quite regularly on the whores in Tischlergasse across the street from Adler's Beer Hall. But he did not limit his calls to the usual five minutes, he was a respected guest, because the girls regarded him as an artist. With India ink, brush and pen, at first with pencil as well, he had done a whole pile of portraits and nudes, which were not in the least obscene and not half bad as art. For with a portfolio full of such drawings Eddi Amsel had gone unannounced to see Pfuhle, the celebrated teacher and painter of horses, who taught the architects drawing at the Engineering School, and submitted his drawings. And Pfuhle, who was known as a hard man to approach, had recognized his talent and promised to help him.

After this speech, which I can repeat only in substance, Amsel, or so I heard, was almost exempted from teasing. On several occasions classmates came to see him and wanted to be taken along to Tischlergasse, a request which he, amiably and with Matern's support, turned down. One day, however, when Eddi Amsel—as I was later told—asked his friend to accompany him to Tischlergasse, he met with a rebuff. He, said Walter Matern with precocious assurance, had no wish to disappoint the poor girls. The professional aspect of the thing repelled him. He'd never be able to get a hard on. That would only make him behave like a brute, which in the end would be embarrassing for both parties. It had to be admitted that love was indispensable, or at least passion.

Amsel had no doubt listened to his friend's firm utterances with a shake of the head and, taking his portfolio and an attractive box of assorted candies, gone by himself to call on the girls across the street from Adler's Beer Hall. And yet—if I am correctly informed—he succeeded one wretched day in December in persuading his friend to celebrate the second or third Sunday of Advent with him and the girls. It was only on the fourth Sunday that Matern screwed up the courage. It turned out, however, that the professional aspect of the thing repelled him so attractively that despite his prognosis he did get a hard on, which he was able to lodge securely and discharge at student's prices with a girl of few words by the name of Elisabeth. Yet, I was told, the kindness that had been shown him did not prevent him on the way home, up Altstädtischer Graben and down Pfefferstadt, from grinding his teeth malignantly and lapsing into dark meditations about venal womanhood.

Dear Cousin,

with exactly the same chocolate-brown and egg-yellow tiger-striped portfolio that had made his visits to the ill-famed Tischlergasse into legitimate artistic excursions, Eddi Amsel, accompanied by Walter Matern, came to our apartment house. In Felsner-Imbs' music room we both saw him breathing sketches of the porcelain ballerina onto paper. And one brightly decked day in May I saw him step up to my father, point to his tiger-striped portfolio, and open the portfolio forthwith in an attempt to let his drawings speak for him. But my father, without further ado, gave him permission to draw our watchdog Harras. Only he advised him to station himself and his equipment outside the semicircle which demonstrated with ditch and wall the range of the dog's chain. "The dog is ferocious and I'm sure he doesn't think much of artists," said my father.

From the very first day our Harras heeded Eddi Amsel's slightest word. Amsel made Harras into a canine model. Amsel did not, for instance, say "Sit, Harras!" as Tulla said "Harras, sit!" when Harras was supposed to sit down. From the very first day Amsel ignored the name Harras and said to our dog when he wanted a change of pose: "Now, Pluto, would you kindly first stand on all four legs, then raise the right foreleg and bend it slightly, but make it relaxed, a little more relaxed. And now would you be so kind as to turn your noble shepherd's head half left, like that, that's good, now, Pluto, if you please, stay that way."

And Harras hearkened to the name of Pluto as if he had always been a hound of hell. The ungainly Amsel almost burst his gray-checked sports suit. His head was covered by a white linen visor cap, that gave him somewhat the look of an English reporter. But his clothes were not new: everything Eddi Amsel wore on his body made an impression of second-handness and was indeed secondhand; for the story was that, although he received a fabulous allowance, he purchased only worn clothes, either from the pawnshop or from the junkshops on Tagnetergasse. His shoes must have belonged previously to a postman. He sat with broad posterior on a preposterous little camp chair, which proved however to be inexplicably stable. While on his left bulging thigh he supported the stiff cardboard to which his drawing paper was clamped and with his right hand, with remarkable ease, guided an always rich-black brush, which covered the drawing paper from the upper left to the lower right-hand corner with daintily skimming sketches, some unsuccessful, others excellent and strikingly fresh, of the watchdog Harras or the hellhound Pluto, our yard became each day a little more—and Eddi Amsel spent about six afternoons drawing in our yard—the scene of various tensions.

There stood Walter Matern in the background. Disreputably dressed; a costumed proletarian in a problem play, who has learned social indictments by heart, who in the third act will become an agitator and ringleader, and who nevertheless fell a victim to our buzz saw. Like our Harras, who time and time again, under certain weather conditions, accompanied the song of the buzz saw—never that of the lathe—with a rising and falling howl out of a vertically held head, so the gloomy young man from Nickelswalde reacted directly to the buzz saw. He did not, to be sure, move his head into a vertical position, he did not stammer anarchist manifestoes, but in his old familiar way underscored the sound of work with a dry grinding of the teeth.

This grinding had its effect on Harras: it drew his lips above his scissors bite. He drooled at the lips. The holes on either side of his nose dilated. The bridge of his nose puckered up to the stop. The noted shepherd ears, erect but pointing slightly forward, became uncertain, tilted. Harras drew in his tail, rounded his back from withers to crown to cringing hump, in short he cringed like a dog. And several times Eddi Amsel produced a painful likeness of these shameful positions with dashing rich-black brush, with scratching spread-foot pen, with gushing and gifted bamboo quill. Our buzz saw, Walter Matern's grinding teeth, and our Harras, whom the buzz saw and the grinding teeth turned into a mongrel, played into the artist's hand of Eddi Amsel; taken together, the buzz saw, Matern, the dog, and Amsel formed as productive a work team as Herr Brauxel's authors' consortium: he, I, and yet another are writing simultaneously and are supposed to be finished when the applesauce with the stars begins on the fourth of February.

But my cousin Tulla,

who stood by, more furious from day to day, refused to stand aside any longer. Amsel's power over Pluto the hellhound became for her a loss of power over our Harras. Not that the dog stopped obeying her—just as before he sat when Tulla said "Harras, sit!"—but he carried out her commands, which she snapped out more and more sternly, in a manner so absent and mechanical that neither could Tulla conceal it from herself nor I from myself and Tulla that this Amsel was ruining our dog.

Tulla,

blind with rage, started out by throwing pebbles, and several times hit Amsel's round back and the blubbery back of his head. He, however, gave it to be understood by a graceful shrug of the shoulders and a lazy turn of the head though aware of the blow, he did not acknowledge it.

691

Tulla,

with tiny white face, tipped over his bottle of India ink. A black
puddle with a metallic sheen stood on the sand in our yard and took a
long time to seep away. Amsel took a fresh bottle of India ink from his
coat pocket and nonchalantly showed that he had a third bottle in reserve.

When Tulla,

storming up from behind, threw a handful of sawdust that settled
in the drive belt casing of the buzz saw at an almost finished, still damp
and freshly glistening picture, Eddi Amsel, only briefly astonished, gave
a partly annoyed, partly good-natured laugh, sedately shook a sausagelike
forefinger at Tulla, who watched the effect of her performance from a
distance, and then began, more and more interested in the new technique,
to work the sawdust clinging to the paper and to give the drawing what
is nowadays known as structure. He developed the amusing but short-
lived method of making capital of chance. Reaching into the drive belt
casing of the buzz saw, he made a mixture in his handkerchief of sawdust,
of the knotty shavings from the lathe, the short curls of the power plane,
the fine-grained droppings of the band saw, and with his own hand and
no need of an assault from Tulla gave his brush drawings a pimply relief,
the charm of which was further enhanced when a part of the superficially
blackened wood particles fell off, revealing the white paper ground in
mysterious islands. Once—probably dissatisfied with his overly conscious
strewings and sawdust groundings—he asked Tulla to storm up from
behind and to fling sawdust, shavings, or even sand as though at random.
He expected a good deal from Tulla's collaboration; but Tulla declined
and made "bashed-in windows."

My cousin Tulla was unable

to get the better of Eddi Amsel, artist and dog tamer. It took August
Pokriefke to trip him up. Several times, laden with sawhorses, he stood
beside the artist, accompanied words of criticism or praise with crackling
glue fingers, spoke in eloborate detail about a painter who had used to
come to Koshnavia summer after summer and had painted Osterwick
Lake, the church at Schlangenthin, made oil portraits of a few Koshnavian
types, such as Joseph Butt from Annafeld, Musolf the tailor from Damerau, and the widow Wanda Jentak. He too had been painted while
cutting peat and then been exhibited in Konitz as a peat cutter. Eddi
Amsel expressed interest in his colleague but did not interrupt his deft
sketching. August Pokriefke left Koshnavia and began to speak about our
watchdog's political career. He explained in great detail how the Führer
on the Obersalzberg had come by the shepherd Prinz. He told about the
signed photograph that hung in our parlor over a pear-wood miniature

692

and figured up how often his daughter Tulla had been snapshot and printed in the papers with or in between long articles about Harras. Amsel voiced gratification at Tulla's early triumphs and began to sketch a seated Harras or Pluto. August Pokriefke expressed the opinion that the Führer would set everything to rights, you could bank on that, he knew more than all the rest of them lumped together, and he could draw too. What was more, the Führer wasn't one of those people who always want to act big. "When the Führer rides in a car, he sits next to the driver and not in back like a bigshot." Amsel found words of praise for the Führer's home-spun modesty and made the hellhound's ears stand exaggeratedly erect on his paper. August Pokriefke asked whether Amsel was still in the Hitler Youth or already a Party member; for he, Amsel—that was his name, wasn't it?—must be in the movement somewhere.

At this point Amsel slowly let his hand and brush drop, glanced once again with tilted head at the drawing of the seated Harras or Pluto, then turned his full, shining, and freckle-strewn face toward the inquirer, and answered with alacrity that, he was sorry to say, he was a member of neither nor, that this was the first time he had heard of the man—what was his name again?—but that he would be glad to inquire who the gentleman was, where he came from, and what plans he had for the future.

Tulla

made Eddi Amsel pay for his ignorance the following afternoon. No sooner was he seated on his stable camp chair, no sooner was he holding cardboard and drawing paper on his bursting left thigh, no sooner had Harras as Pluto taken up his new pose, lying with outstretched forepaws and sharply alert neck, no sooner had Amsel's brush steeped itself in India ink, than the door to the yard spat out first August Pokriefke, the glue cook, then the glue stirrer's daughter.

He stands with Tulla in the doorway, whispers, casts sidelong glances at the heavily laden camp chair, vaccinates his daughter with orders, and there she comes, first lazily and by sauntering detours, holding thin arms interlocked across the back of her dirndl dress, flings bare legs aimlessly, then describes quick, narrowing semicircles around the brush-guiding Eddi Amsel, is now to the left, now to the right of him: "Hey!" and then from the left: "Hey, you!" again from the left: "What are you doing around here anyway?" Spoken from the left: "I'm asking you what you're doing around here" and from the right: "You got no business here!" Spoken from the left: " 'Cause you're . . ." and from close up on the right: "Do you know what you are?" Then from the left into his ear: "Want me to tell you?" Now, threaded into the right ear: "You're a sheeny. A sheeny. That's right, a sheeny. Or if you're not a sheeny, what do you come around here for drawing pictures of our dog if you're not a sheeny?" Amsel's brush stops. Tulla at a distance but inexorably: "Sheeny." Eddi Amsel with rigid brush. Tulla: "Sheeny." The word flung into the yard, first only for Amsel, then loud enough to make Matern withdraw his ear from the buzz saw that is just starting up. He reaches out for the thing that's screaming sheeny. Matern fails to catch Tulla: "Sheeny!" The cardboard with the first still moist India ink entries has fallen, sketch down, into the sand. "Sheeny!" Upstairs, on the fourth, fifth, then the second floor, windows were thrust open: Housewives cool their faces. From Tulla's mouth: "Sheeny!" Above the sound of the buzz saw. Matern grabs but misses. Tulla's tongue. Swift legs. Amsel stands beside the camp chair. The word. Matern picks up cardboard and drawing. Tulla bounces up and down on planks laid over sawhorses: "Sheeny, sheeny!" Matern screws the top on the India ink bottle. Tulla bounces off the plank— "Sheeny!"—rolls in the sand: "Sheeny!" Now all windows occupied and carpenters at the windows on the second floor. The word, three times in succession the word. Amsel's face, overheated while he was sketching, cools off. A smile refuses to fade. Sweat, but now cold and clammy, runs over fat and freckles. Matern lays his hand on Amsel's shoulder. Freckles turn gray. The word. Always the same one word. Matern's hand is heavy. Now from the stairs leading to the second floor. Tulla giddily jumping about: "Sheenysheenysheeny!" On his right Matern leads Amsel by the arm. Eddi Amsel is trembling. To the left, Matern, already charged with the portfolio, picks up the camp chair. Released from constraint, Harras relinquishes his pose. He sniffs, understands. Already his chain is taut: The dog's voice. Tulla's voice. The buzz saw bites into a sixteen-foot plank. The finishing machine is still silent. Now it too. Now the lathe. Long twenty-seven steps to the yard door. Harras tries to move the lumber shed to which he is chained. Tulla, dancing wildly, over and over again the word. And by the yard door, where August Pokriefke with crackling fingers stands in wooden shoes, the smell of glue battles with the smell from the little garden outside the piano teacher's windows: the scent of lilacs strikes and wins. It's the month of May after all. The word stops coming but it's still in the air. August Pokriefke wants to spit out what he's been storing up in the hollow of his mouth for some minutes. But he doesn't spit, because Matern is looking at him with clamoring teeth.

Dear Cousin Tulla,

I skip: Eddi Amsel and Walter Matern were turned out of our yard. Nothing was done to you. Because Amsel had spoiled Harras, Harras was sent to the trainer's twice a week. You like me had to learn reading, writing, and 'rithmetic. Amsel and Matern had their oral and written examinations behind them. Harras was trained to bark at strangers and to refuse food from strange hands; but Amsel had already spoiled him too radically. You had trouble with writing, I with arithmetic. We both liked school. Amsel and his friend passed their examinations—the former with distinction, the latter with a certain amount of luck. Turning point. Life began or was supposed to begin: After the devaluation of the gulden the economic situation improved slightly. Orders came in. My father was able to rehire a journeyman whom he had discharged four weeks before devaluation. After their final exams Eddi Amsel and Walter Matern began to play faustball.

Dear Tulla,

faustball is a ball game played by two teams of five in two adjacent fields with a ball that is roughly the size of a football but somewhat lighter. Like schlagball it is a German game, even though Plautus in the third century B.C. mentions a *follis pugilatorius*. In corroboration of the strictly German character of the game—for Plautus was assuredly speaking of faustball-playing Germanic slaves—it is worth recalling that during the First World War fifty teams were engaged in playing faustball in the Vladivostok PW camp; in the PW camp at Oswestry—England—more than seventy teams participated in faustball tournaments which were lost or won without bloodshed.

The game does not involve too much running and can consequently be played by sexagenarians and even by excessively corpulent men and women: Amsel became a faustball player. Who would have thought it? That soft little fist, that fistling, good for concealing a private laugh, that fist that never pounded a table. At the most he could have weighed down letters with his fistling, prevented them from flying away. It was no fist at all, more like a meat ball, two little meat balls, two rosy pompons swinging from abbreviated arms. Not a worker's fist, not a proletarian's fist, not a Red Front salute, for the air was harder than his fist. Little fists for guessing: which one? The law of the fist pronounced him guilty; fist fights made him into a punching bag; and only in the game of faustball did Amsel's fistling triumph; for that reason it will be related here, in chronological order, how Eddi Amsel became a player of faustball, in other words, an athlete who with closed fists—to stick out the thumb was forbidden—punched the faustball from below, from above, from the side.

Tulla and I had been promoted;

a well-earned vacation took Amsel and his friend to the Vistula estuary. The fishermen looked on as Amsel brushed in fishing boots and nets. The ferryman looked over Eddi Amsel's shoulder as he sketched the steam ferry. He visited the Materns on the other side, exchanged oracles about the future with miller Matern and sketched the Matern postmill from all sides. Eddi Amsel also attempted a chat with the village schoolteacher; but the village schoolteacher was said to have snubbed his former pupil. I wonder why. Similarly a Schiewenhorst village beauty seems to have given Amsel a saucy rebuff when he wished to draw her picture on the beach with the wind in her hair and her dress on the beach in the wind. Nevertheless Amsel filled his portfolio and went back to the city with a full portfolio. He had, to be sure, promised his mother to study something serious—engineering—but for the present he frequented Professor Pfuhle, the painter of horses, and like Walter Matern, who was supposed to study economics but much preferred to declaim into the wind in the role of Franz or Karl Moor, couldn't make up his mind to embark on his studies.

Then a telegram came: his mother called him back to Schiewenhorst to her deathbed. The cause of her death seems to have been diabetes. From the dead face of his mother, Eddi Amsel first did a pen-and-ink drawing, then a red crayon drawing. During the funeral in Bohnsack he was said to have wept. Only a few people were at the grave. I wonder why. After the funeral Amsel began to liquidate the widow's household. He sold everything: the house, the business, the fishing boats, the outboard motors, the dragnets, the smokehouses, and the store with its pulleys, tool boxes, and variously smelling miscellaneous wares. In the end Eddi Amsel was looked upon as a wealthy young man. He deposited a part of his fortune in the Agricultural Bank of the City of Danzig, but managed to invest the greater part on profitable terms in Switzerland: for years it worked quietly and did not diminish.

Amsel took but a few tangible possessions with him from Schiewenhorst. Two photograph albums, hardly any letters, his father's war decorations—he had died a reserve lieutenant in the First World War—the family Bible, a school diary full of drawings from his days as a village schoolboy, some old books about Frederick the Great and his generals, and Otto Weininger's *Sex and Character* rode away with Eddi Amsel on the Island narrow-gauge railway.

This last standard work had meant a great deal to his father. Weininger attempted, in twelve long chapters, to prove that woman has no soul, and went on, in the thirteenth chapter entitled "Judaism," to develop his theory that the Jews were a feminine race and therefore soulless, that only if the Jew overcame the Jewishness within him could the world hope to be redeemed from the Jews. Amsel's father had underlined memorable sentences with a red pencil, with the frequent marginal comment: "Very true!" Reserve Lieutenant Albrecht Amsel had found the following very true on p. 408: "The Jews, like women, like to stick together, but they have no social intercourse with each other . . ." On p. 413 he had entered three exclamation marks: "Men who are middlemen always have Jewish blood . . ." On p. 434 he had several times underlined the tail end of a sentence and written "God help us!" in the margin: ". . . things that will forever be beyond the reach of the authentic Jew: spontaneous being, divine right, the oak tree, the trumpet, the Siegfried motif, self-creation, the words: 'I am.' "

Two passages endorsed by his father in red pencil took on meaning for the son as well. Because it was said in the standard work that the Jew does not sing and does not engage in sports, Albrecht Amsel, by way of disproving at least these theses, had founded an athletic club in Bohnsack and lent his baritone to the church choir. In regard to music, Eddi Amsel played the piano in a smooth and dashing manner, let his boy soprano, which even after graduation refused to come down from the upper story, jubilate in Mozart Masses and short arias, and in regard to sports threw himself body and soul into the game of faustball.

He who for years had been the victim of school schlagball slipped of his own free will into the chrome-green gym pants of the Young Prussia Athletic Club and moved his friend, who had hitherto played field hockey at the Danzig Hockey Club, to join with him the Young Prussians. With the permission of the head of his club and after pledging himself to support his hockey club at least twice a week in the Niederstadt field, Walter Matern signed up for handball and light athletics; for the leisurely game of faustball would not in itself have made sufficient demands on the young man's physique.

Tulla and I knew the Heinrich Ehlers Athletic Field
situated between the Municipal Hospitals and the Heiligenbrunn Home for the Blind. Good turf, but run-down wooden grandstand and locker room, through whose cracks the wind found its way. The large field and the two small subsidiary fields were used by players of handball, schlagball, and faustball. Sometimes football players and track men came too, until the sumptuous Albert Forster Stadium was built not far from the crematory and Heinrich Ehlers Field was thought fit only for school sports.

Because Walter Matern had won the shot-put and the three-thousand-meter run at the interschool track meet the preceding year, so earning the reputation of a promising athlete, he was able to gain admission for Eddi Amsel and make him into a Young Prussian. At first they wished to use him only as a handyman. The field manager handed him a broom: locker rooms must be kept spotlessly clean. He also had to keep the balls greased and sprinkle the foul lines of the handball field with lime. Only when Walter Matern protested was Eddi Amsel assigned to a faustball team. Horst Plötz and Siegi Lewand were the guards. Willi

Dobbeck played left forward. And Walter Matern served as line player in a team that soon came to be feared and was to become first in the league. For Eddi Amsel directed, he was the heart and switchboard of the team: a born play maker. What Horst Plötz and Siegi Lewand picked up in the rear and conveyed to the center of the field, he deftly, with supple forearm, dispatched to the line: there stood Walter Matern, the smasher and line player. He received the ball from the air and seldom hit it dead center, but put a twist on it. While Amsel knew how to receive treacherously dealt balls and turn them into neat passes, Matern was unstoppable, piling up points with balls that had been harmlessly roaming around: for when a ball lands without spin, it rebounds at exactly the same angle, it is predictable; but Matern's balls, hit on the lower third of the ball, took on backspin and bounced back the moment they landed. Amsel's specialty was the seemingly simple forearm shot, which however he handled with unusual precision. He picked up low balls. When the opposing team laid down smashes at his feet, he saved them from dropping dead with backhand shots. He recognized spin balls at once, tapped them up with the edge of his little finger, or slammed them with a swift forehand. Often he ironed out balls that his own guards had bungled and, Weininger's assertions to the contrary notwithstanding, was a smiled-at, but respectfully smiled-at non-Aryan faustball player, Young Prussian, and sportsman.

Tulla and I were witnesses

as Eddi Amsel succeeded in taking off a few pounds, a loss which, apart from us, was observed only by Jenny Brunies, the little dumpling who had meanwhile turned ten. She too noticed that Amsel's gelatinous chin was turning into a firm, full-rounded pediment. His chest too lost its tremulous teats and, as his thorax filled out, slipped back into low relief. Yet quite conceivably Eddi Amsel didn't lose a single pound, but only distributed his fat more evenly, his athletically developed muscles lending athletic structure to his previously structureless layer of fat. His torso, formerly a shapeless sack stuffed with down, took on the contours of a barrel. He began to look like a Chinese idol or the tutelary deity of all faustball players. No, Eddi Amsel didn't lose so much as half a pound while playing center; it seems more likely that he gained two and a half pounds; but he sublimated the gain after the manner of an athlete: to what speculations the relativity of a man's weight will lend itself!

In any event Amsel's juggling with his hundred and ninety-eight pounds, in which no one would have discerned his two hundred and three pounds, may have moved Dr. Brunies to prescribe physical exercise for his doll-like Jenny as well. Dr. Brunies and Felsner-Imbs the piano teacher decided to send Jenny to a ballet school three times a week. In the suburb of Oliva there was a street named Rosengasse, which began at the market and zigzagged its way into Oliva Forest. On it stood a modest early-nineteenth-century villa, to whose sand-yellow stucco clung, half concealed by red-blowing hawthorn, the enamel sign of the ballet school. Like Amsel's admission to the Young Prussia Athletic Club, Jenny's admission to the ballet school was obtained through pull: for many years Felix Felsner-Imbs had been the ballet school pianist. No one was so expert at accompanying bar exercises: Every *demi-plié*, from the first to the fifth position, hearkened to his adagio. He sprinkled the *port de bras*. His exemplary rhythm for *battement dégagé* and his sweat-raising rhythm for the *petits battements sur le cou-de-pied*. Besides, he had millions of stories. One had the impression that he had seen Marius Petipa and Preobrajenska, the tragic Nijinsky and the miraculous Massine, Fanny Elssler and la Barbarina all dance simultaneously and in person. No one doubted that this was an eyewitness to historical performances: thus he must have been present when, in the early-romantic days of the last century, la Taglioni, la Grisi, Fanny Cerito, and Lucile Grahn danced the famous *Grand Pas de Quatre* and were showered with roses. He had had difficulty in obtaining a seat on Olympus for the first performance of the ballet *Coppélia*. It went without saying that so accomplished a ballet pianist was able to render the scores of the entire repertory, from the melancholy *Giselle* to the evanescent *Sylphides*, on the piano; and on his recommendation Madame Lara began to make an Ulanova of Jenny.

It was not long before Eddi Amsel became a persevering onlooker. Sitting by the piano equipped with his sketching pad, extracting mana from soft lead, he followed the bar exercises with swift eyes and was soon able to transfer the various positions to paper more pleasingly than the boys and girls, some of them members of the child ballet at the Stadttheater, could perform them at the bar. Often Madame Lara took advantage of Amsel's skill and explained a regulation *plié* to her pupils with the help of his sketches.

Jenny on the dancing floor cut a half-miserable, half-endearingly ludicrous figure. Conscientiously the child learned all the combinations —how diligently she reversed her little feet in the *pas de bourrée*, how touchingly her roly-poly *petit changement de pieds* stood out against the *changements* of the practiced *rats de ballet*, how brightly, when Madame Lara practiced *Little Swans* with the children's class, shone Jenny's dust- and time-dispelling gaze, which the austere Madame called her "Swan Lake look"—and yet, for all the glamour that inevitably attaches to a ballerina, Jenny looked like a little pink pig trying to turn into a weightless *sylphide*.

Why did Amsel, over and over again, take Jenny's lamentable arabesque, Jenny's heart-rending *tour à la seconde* as an occasion for lightly tossed-off sketches? Because his pencil, without flattering the plumpness away, discerned the dancer's line behind all the fat, proving to Madame Lara that within the fat a diminutive star was preparing to rise in the heaven of ballet dancers; it would only be necessary to render the tallow and lard, to increase the heat under the pan until a crisp and slender Terpsichorean rind should be able to execute the famous thirty-two *fouettés en tournant* in the crackling flame.

Dear Tulla,

just as Eddi Amsel became Jenny's audience, so Jenny Brunies looked on from the lawn terraces in the late afternoon as Amsel helped his faustball team to victory. Even when Amsel was practicing, while he was making a light faustball hop on his broad forearm for the time it takes to say three rosaries, wonderment gaped from Jenny's open buttonhole mouth. The two of them with their total of three hundred and twenty pounds came to be a familiar sight throughout the suburb if not the city; everybody in the suburb of Langfuhr knew about Jenny and Eddi, just as they all knew about a tiny little fellow with a tin drum. Except that the dwarf, whom everybody called Oskar, was reputed to be an incorrigible lone wolf.

We all of us,

Tulla, I, and Tulla's brothers, met Amsel, roly-poly Jenny, and Walter Matern, the smasher, on the athletic field. Other nine-year-olds, Hänschen Matull, Horst Kanuth, George Ziehm, Helmut Lewandowski, Heini Pilenz, and the Rennwand brothers met there as well. We were in the same Cub squad, and over the protests of many athletic clubs our squad leader Heini Wasmuth had obtained permission for us to practice relay racing on the cinder track and to drill in uniform and street shoes on the turf of the athletic field. Once Walter Matern gave our squad leader a piece of his mind. They bellowed at each other. Heini Wasmuth showed official orders and a permit issued by the field management, but Matern, who openly threatened violence, managed to put through a new policy, making the cinder track and the turf of the athletic field out of bounds to persons in uniform and street shoes. From then on we drilled on the Johanneswiese and went to Heinrich Ehlers Field only privately and in gym shoes. There the sun fell obliquely because it was afternoon. Activity on all the fields. Variously pitched referees' whistles put the ball into or took it out of play in a wide variety of games. Goals were tossed, sides changed, flies struck, announcements roared. Balls were passed, opponents thrown off; fake-outs, block plays, encirclement; teams were outplayed, contestants played out, games lost and won. Painful cinders in gym shoes. Players dozed while waiting for the return game. The smell from the crematory indicated the direction of the wind. Bats were rubbed, balls greased, foul lines drawn, scores kept, and victors cheered. Lots of laughing, constant yelling, some crying, and frequent irritation over the field manager's cat. Everyone obeyed my cousin Tulla. Everyone was afraid of Walter Matern. Some covertly threw pebbles at Eddi Amsel. Many made a detour around our Harras. The last one out had to lock the locker room and leave the key with the caretaker; Tulla never did that, I did it sometimes.

And once—

Tulla and I were there—Jenny Brunies cried because somebody had burned a hole in her brand-new spring-green dress with a magnifying glass.

Years later—Tulla and I were absent—some high school boys, who were putting on a schlagball tournament, were said to have put the field manager's cat on the neck of a dozing fellow student.

Another time—Jenny, Amsel, and Matern were absent because Jenny was having her ballet lesson—Tulla swiped two schlagball balls for us, and a kid from the Athletic and Fencing Club was suspected.

And once after the faustball game—Walter Matern, Eddi Amsel, and Jenny Brunies were lying on the terrace wall to one side of the small ball field—something really happened and it was marvelous:

We park ourselves a few steps to one side. Tulla, Harras, and I can't take our eyes off the group. The whole time the setting sun is peeping into the athletic fields from Jäschkental Forest. The uncut grass on the edge of the cinder track casts long shadows. We aren't even giving a thought to the smoke that rises up vertically from the chimney of the crematory. Now and then Eddi Amsel's high laugh comes over to us. Harras lets out a brief bark and I have to grab him by the collar. Tulla is pulling up grass with both hands. She isn't listening to me. Over yonder Walter Matern is miming some part in a play. They say he's studying to be an actor. Once Jenny waves to us in her white dress that probably has grass spots on it. I wave cautiously back until Tulla turns toward me with her nostrils and incisor teeth. Butterflies go about their business. Nature crawls aimlessly, bumblebees bumble . . . no, not bumblebees; what we first see, then hear on a late summer afternoon in the 1936, as we sit in separate groups on Heinrich Ehlers Field, on an early summer evening when the last teams have been whistled off and the broadjump pit is being raked, is the airship *Graf Zeppelin*.

We've been expecting it. The newspapers had said it was coming. First Harras gets restless, then we too—Tulla first—hear the sound. It swells, although the zeppelin is supposed to come from the west, from all directions at once. And then suddenly there it is in mid-air, over Oliva

Forest. Of course the sun just happens to be setting. Accordingly, the zeppelin isn't silvery but pink. Now that the sun is slipping behind the Karlsberg and the airship is heading toward the open sea, pink gives way to silver. All stand shading their eyes. Choral singing is wafted over to us from the vocational and home economics school. Polyphonically the girls sing at the zeppelin. On Zinglers Höhe a brass band attempts something along the same lines with the "Hohenfriedberger March." Matern looks hard in a different direction. He has something against the zeppelin. Eddi Amsel applauds with small hands on short arms. Jenny too is jubilant. "Zeppelin, zeppelin!" she cries and bounces like a ball. Even Tulla distends her nostrils, trying to suck up the zeppelin. All Harras' restlessness has gone into his tail. It's so silvery a magpie would want to steal it. While on Zinglers Höhe the "Badenweiler March" follows the "Hohenfriedberger March," while the vocational girls interminably sing "Scared Fatherland," while the zeppelin out toward Hela grows smaller, yet more silvery, smoke—I'm positive—rises imperturbably and vertically from the chimney of the municipal crematory. Matern, who doesn't believe in the zeppelin, watches the Protestant smog.

My cousin Tulla,

otherwise invariably guilty, or at least an accomplice, was not to blame for the scandal at Heinrich Ehlers Field. Walter Matern did something. What he did was recounted in three versions: Either he distributed leaflets in the locker room; or he pasted leaflets on the grandstand benches shortly before the handball game between Schellmühl 98 and the Athletic and Fencing Club; or, while all the fields were busy with games or practice, he secretly stuck leaflets into the hanging pants and jackets of the junior and senior athletes in the locker room; and the manager caught him in the act. It doesn't matter much which version is accredited, for the leaflets, whether openly distributed, pasted, or secretly stuck in pockets, were all identically red.

But since the Danzig senate, first under Rauschning, then under Greiser, had dissolved the Communist Party in '34 and the Social Democratic Party in '36—the Center Party, under its chairman Dr. Stachnik, dissolved itself in October 1937—the propagandist activities of the student Walter Matern—he still wasn't studying but doing something connected with dramatics—could only be regarded as illegal.

Nevertheless, no one wanted to create a disturbance. After brief proceedings in the manager's house, amid loving cups, photographs of athletes, and framed certificates—Koschnik, the field manager, had made a name for himself as a track man in the early twenties—Walter Matern was expelled from the Young Prussians. Eddi Amsel, who, it appears, had been closely and critically examining the bronze statue of a javelin thrower during the proceedings, was also urgently advised, though no reasons were stated, to resign from the club. The two erstwhile Young Prussians were given handwritten documents commemorating the victory of Amsel's faustball team in the last tournament and hands were shaken in a spirit of sportsmanship. All the Young Prussians and the field manager as well took leave of Eddi Amsel and Walter Matern with guarded words of regret and a promise to make no report to the Athletic Association.

Walter Matern remained an esteemed member of the Hockey Club and even joined up for a course in gliding. Near Kahlberg on the Frische Nehrung he is said to have made a number of twelve-minute glider flights and to have photographed the lagoon from the air. But Eddi Amsel had had his fill of sports: he took another fling at the fine arts, and my cousin Tulla helped him.

Listen, Tulla:

sometimes, and it doesn't even have to be quiet in the street outside, I hear my hair growing. I don't hear my fingernails, I don't hear any toenails growing, only my hair. Because you once reached into my hair, because you left your hand for a second and eternity in my hair—we were sitting in the lumber shed amid your collection of extra-long shavings that were wavy like my hair—because afterward, but still in the lumber shed you said: "But that's the only thing that's any good about you." Because you recognized this one and only quality in me, my hair made itself independent, it doesn't really belong to me, it belongs to you. Our Harras belonged to you. The lumber shed belonged to you. All the gluepots and beautiful curly wood shavings belonged to you. It's you I'm writing to, even if I'm writing for Brauxel.

But no sooner had Tulla withdrawn her hand from my hair and said something about my hair than she was gone, over resinous planks, between tall sections of plywood. She was outside in the yard and I, with still electric hair, was too slow in following to prevent her assault on the piano teacher and ballet pianist.

Felsner-Imbs had entered the yard. Stooped, he strode stiffly to the machine shop and inquired of the machinist when the buzz saw and lathe were planning to take a fairly protracted intermission, because he, the ballet pianist and former concert pianist, wished to practice, very softly, something complicated, a so-called adagio. Once or twice a week Felsner-Imbs asked this favor of our machinist or of my father, and it was always granted, though not always immediately. No sooner had the machinist nodded and, pointing a thumb at the buzz saw, said that he just had to run through two more planks; no sooner had Felsner-Imbs, after elaborate bows that looked perilous so near the buzz saw, left the machine shop; scarcely had he covered half the distance to the yard door—I was just crawling out of the lumber shed—when my cousin Tulla let Harras, our watchdog, off the chain.

At first Harras didn't know quite what to do with his sudden freedom, for ordinarily he was put right on the leash when released from his chain; but then he, who a moment before had stood distrustful, with head cocked, bounded into the air with all four legs, landed, shot diagonally across the yard, turned just before the lilac bushes, hurdled a sawhorse with neck outstretched, and went leaping frolicsomely around the pianist who had frozen into a statue: playful barking, a harmless snap, dancing hindquarters; and only when Felsner-Imbs sought safety in flight and Tulla from in front of the kennel—she was still holding the snap of the chain—had sicked our Harras on the game with an inflammatory skiss-skiss-skiss, did Harras pursue the pianist and catch him by his flowing swallowtails; for Felsner-Imbs, who during piano lessons wore only a velvet artist's jacket, slipped, as soon as he had to practice a difficult concert piece or play to an imaginary or actually present audience, into the swallowtails of a concert performer.

The coat was done for and my father had to replace it. Otherwise the pianist had suffered no injury, for the machinist and the master carpenter had managed to pull Harras, who as a matter of fact was only playing, away from the festive cloth.

Tulla was supposed to be spanked. But Tulla had turned to unpunishable air. I got a licking instead, for I had failed to restrain Tulla, I had stood by inactive and as the boss's son I was responsible. My father smacked me with a piece of roofing lath until Felsner-Imbs, whom Dreesen the machinist had put back on his legs, interceded. While with a hairbrush, which in the inside pocket of his swallowtail coat had survived Harras' onslaught, he first brushed his artist's mane against the grain— a sight that made Harras growl—then curried it into his usual leonine hairdo, he remarked that actually not I, but Tulla or the dog was deserving of punishment. But where Tulla had been standing there was only a hole; and my father never laid a hand on our Harras.

Listen, Tulla:

half an hour later buzz saw, lathe, and finishing machine fell silent, as arranged, the band saw was soundless, Harras lay once more lazily on his chain, the deep booming of the planing machine ceased, and from Felsner-Imbs' music room delicate, elaborately slow sounds, now solemn, now sad, detached themselves. Fragilely they strutted across the yard, climbed the façade of the apartment house as far as the third story, then fell headlong, gathered together, and dispersed: Imbs was practicing his complicated piece, the so-called adagio, and the machinist, with a manipulation of the black switch box, had turned off all the machines for the time required to go through the piece three times.

Tulla, I presumed, was sitting deep within the lumber shed, under the tar-paper roof with her long-curled wood shavings. She could probably hear the melody, but she didn't run after it. I was lured by the pianist's concert piece. I climbed the fence around the lilac garden and pressed my face to the windowpanes: a cone of glass-green light in the music room. Inside the cone of electric light two conjuring hands and a snow-white but green-glowing head: Felsner-Imbs at conjured keyboard, with his music. The big hourglass silent and hard at work. The porcelain ballerina also thrusts her horizontal leg, frozen in its arabesque, into the cone of green light. Eddi Amsel and Jenny Brunies huddle mustily on the sofa in the background. Jenny is filling a lemon-yellow dress. Amsel isn't drawing. A sickly pallor coats the ordinarily healthy and apple-glowing faces of the listeners. Jenny has clasped her ten sausage fingers, which the submarine light has transformed into fleshy algae. Amsel builds his hands into a flat roof under his chin. Several times and with relish Felsner repeats a particularly sad passage—Hail and farewell: lapping of waves, army of clouds, birds in flight, love potion, idyl in the woods, early death—then once again, while far in the rear of the room, on the little lacquered stand, the goldfish quivers in its bowl, he plays the whole soft and gentle piece—weary unto death, transition, serene joy—and listens to the last chord with all ten fingers in green air until the half-hour intermission arranged for the lathe and finishing machine, the buzz saw and band saw all at once is at an end.

The congealed group in the Imbs music room began to move again: Jenny's fingers unlocked themselves; Amsel's finger roof collapsed; Felsner removed his fingers from the cone of green light and only then showed his guests his swallowtails, tattered on the sides and in back. The ill-fated garment passed back and forth and finally came to rest with Amsel.

And Amsel lifted it up, counted the remaining fabric-covered buttons, tested every rent with parted fingers, demonstrated what a shepherd's incited fangs can do, and after this instructive Introit, proceeded to the Mass: he ogled through jagged holes, peered through slits, widened burst seams with two malignant fingers, was wind under coattails, finally crawled in, became entirely one with the festive tatter, transubstantiated himself and the cloth, and treated the audience to a performance featuring a disabled swallowtail coat: Amsel looked terrifying; Amsel aroused pity; Amsel the hobbler; Amsel the dodderer; Amsel in the wind and rain, on sheet ice; the merchant on the flying carpet; roc, the fabled bird; the caliph turned stork; the crow, the owl, the woodpecker; the sparrow at its morning bath, behind the horse, with the dog; many sparrows meet, scold each other, take counsel, entertain, and thank the audience for applauding. Then came Amsel's swallowtail divertimenti: the unleashed grandmother; the ferryman has a toothache; the parson fights the wind; Leo Schugger at the cemetery gate; teachers in playgrounds. But let it

705

not be supposed that all were fat, with the build of a lifeguard. Once inside the coat, he conjured up towering beanpoles and windmills, he was Balderle and Ashmodai, the cross by the wayside, and the evil number efta. A dancing, pathetically withered spook seized the porcelain ballerina, abducted her from the piano, courted her with bat's wings, ravished her heart-rendingly, made her vanish ruthlessly, as though forever, in Harras-black cloth that grew longer and longer, reappear safe and thank goodness sound, and return to her native piano. Pressed for encores, he wound up with a few more numbers; still in love with his masquerade, he transformed himself, confident of applause, into this and that, and was grateful to our Harras, for his scissors bite had, he thanked Tulla far away in the lumber shed, for Tulla had sicked, and Harras had beset, and Felsner-Imb's swallowtail coat had released catches deep within Eddi Amsel, unearthed wells, tossed pennies in, and fostered the growth of a whole crop of ideas, which, sowed during Amsel's childhood, gave promise of a barn-bursting harvest.

Hardly a moment after Eddi Amsel had unwrapped himself from black cloth viscera, disclosing the easygoing and old-familiar Amsel in the flowing green light of the music room, he neatly folded his equipment, took the half-frightened, half-amused Jenny by her plump little hand, and, carrying away the Imbsian swallowtails, left the pianist and his goldfish.

Tulla and I

naturally thought Amsel had carried away the hopelessly tattered garment with the intention of taking it to the tailor's. But no tailor received work because our Harras had leapt. My allowance was cut in half because my father had to provide a brand-new coat. The carpenter might have exacted the rag in return, perhaps for use in the machine shop—where wiping rags were always needed—but my father paid, exacted nothing, and even apologized, as carpenters tend to apologize, with embarrassed condescension and a clearing of the throat, and Amsel remained the usufructuary of the garment which, though fragmentary, was susceptible of transformation. From then on he ceased to devote his talents exclusively to drawing and watercoloring; from then on, though he had no intention of scaring crows, Eddi Amsel built life-size scarecrows.

Here it is contended that Eddi Amsel had no special knowledge of birds. Neither was Tulla's cousin a cynologist nor could Eddi Amsel be termed an ornithologist because of his scarecrows. Just about anybody can distinguish sparrows from swallows, an owl from a woodpecker. Even Eddi Amsel did not believe starlings and magpies to be equally thieving; but as far as he was concerned, robin and bullfinch, titmouse and chaffinch were all indifferently songbirds. He was not up to question games such as "What kind of bird is that?" No one had ever seen him leafing through

Brehm's *Life of the Birds.* When I once asked him: "Which is bigger, an eagle or a wren?" he dodged the question with a twinkle: "The Angel Gabriel naturally." But he had a keen eye for sparrows. What no bird expert can do, Amsel could: he was able to distinguish as individuals the members of a crowd bevy congress of sparrows, whom everybody believes to be equally colorless. He took a statistical view of all those who bathed in roof gutters, clamored behind horse-drawn vehicles, and descended on playgrounds after the last bell: in his opinion they were all individualists that had camouflaged themselves as a mass society. And to his eyes blackbirds were never, not even in snow-covered gardens, identically black and yellow-billed.

Nevertheless Eddi Amsel built no scarecrows to ward off the sparrows and magpies with which he was familiar; he built with no adversary in mind, on formal grounds. At the most he wished to convince a dangerously productive environment of his own productivity.

Tulla and I

knew where Eddi Amsel designed and built his scarecrows, though he didn't call them scarecrows but figures. He had rented a spacious villa on Steffensweg. Amsel's inheritance was considerable and the ground floor of the villa was said to be paneled in oak. Steffensweg was situated in the southwestern part of the suburb of Langfuhr. Below Jäschkental Forest it branched off from Jäschkentaler Weg and proceeded in the direction of the Almshouse and Orphanage along the grounds of the Langfuhr fire department. One villa after another. A few consulates: the Latvian and the Argentine. French gardens behind wrought-iron fences, none of them wanting for ornament. Boxwoods, yew trees, and red-flowering hawthorn. Expensive English lawns that had to be sprinkled in the summer and in winter lay gratis beneath the snow. Weeping willows and silver firs flanked, overtowered, and shaded the villas. Espaliered fruit gave a good deal of trouble. Fountains required frequent repairs. Gardeners gave notice. The watch-and-ward society provided burglary insurance. Two consuls and the wife of a chocolate manufacturer put in a petition for a fire alarm, which was immediately granted, although the fire department was right behind the Orphanage and its training tower overlooked all the silver firs, promising the ivy on white house fronts and all the many cornices and porticoes that knew Schinkel from hearsay to dispatch two fire brigades within twenty-seven seconds. At night but few windows were lit up, unless the owner of the Anglas chocolate factory happened to be giving a reception. Footfalls between lampposts could long be heard coming and going. In a word, a quiet genteel neighborhood, where in ten years only two murders and one attempted murder had become audible, that is to say, known.

Soon Walter Matern, who had previously lived in a furnished room in the Old City, on Karpfenseigen, moved into Amsel's villa, where he occupied two oak-paneled rooms. Sometimes an actress or two lived with him for a week at a time, for he still hadn't made up his mind to start studying economics. Instead he had found a place among the supers of the Stadttheater on Kohlenmarkt. As a member of a large crowd, as a soldier among soldiers, as one of six candle-bearing servants, as a drunkard among drunken mercenaries, as a grumbler among grumbling peasants, as a masked Venetian, as a mutinous soldier, and as one among six gentlemen who with six ladies had to provide a birthday party in the first act, a garden party in the second act, a funeral in the third act, and a merry reading of the will in the last act with numbers and with a chatting, joking, mourning, and joyfully animated background, Walter Matern, though not yet privileged to utter two consecutive sentences, was acquiring his first experience of the stage. At the same time, having decided to broaden the original foundation of his histrionic gift, his gruesome grinding of the teeth, he took two lessons a week in comedy with Gustav Nord, a comedian of city-wide reputation; for Matern was convinced that a talent for tragedy had come to him with his mother's milk and that if there were still rough edges, it was only in comedy.

While two oak-paneled rooms of Amsel's villa were constrained to hear Walter Matern in the role of Florian Geyer, the third and largest room, oak-paneled like the actor's, became the witness of Amsel's working methods. Scantily furnished. Crude meathooks in the solid oak ceiling. Chains on trolleys. Close under the paneling, they were hanging big as life. A similar principle is observed in miners' changehouses: air and freedom on the floor; under the ceiling, congestion. Still, there was one piece of furniture, a writing desk, a genuine Renaissance desk. Lying open upon it: the standard work, a work of six hundred pages, a work without equal, a diabolical work, Weininger's work, the unappreciated overestimated best-selling misunderstood too-well-understood stroke of genius, provided with marginal notes by Amsel's father and footnotes by Weininger: *Sex and Character,* Chapter 13, p. 405: ". . . and perhaps, provisionally speaking, the world-historical significance and enormous achievement of Jewry consists solely in this: in having continually brought the Aryan to consciousness of his self, in having reminded him of himself ["of himself" in bold-face type]. It is for this that the Aryan owes the Jew a debt of gratitude; thanks to him, he knows what to guard against: against Jewishness as a possibility in himself."

These and similar sentences, as well as sentences that said the exact opposite or were in themselves paradoxical, Amsel declaimed with a preacher's pathos to already-finished figures dangling from the oak ceiling and to the many wooden and wire frames that occupied the polished floor and peopled the oak-paneled room with an amorphous yet eagerly debating company: and in the course of an easy informal discussion Eddi Amsel, their knowledgeable, sophistical, always original, objective, when necessary subjective, urbane, omnipresent, never offended Olympian host, explained the true nature of women and Jews: "Must we say with Weininger that women and Jews have no soul or does it suffice to say that this applies only to women or only to Jews, and are the Jews, from an anthropological point of view, for in an empirical sense, the tenets of faith argue to the contrary? The Chosen People, begging your pardon. But, and only for the sake of argument, don't we often observe Jewish characteristics in rabid anti-Semites: Wagner, for example, although *Parsifal* will always be incomprehensible to an authentic Jew, and in the same way we can distinguish between Aryan socialism and typically Jewish socialism, for Marx, as we all know, was. That is why women and Jews are equally deficient in Kantian reason, and even Zionism doesn't. The Jews, you see, prefer movable goods. The same with the English. Exactly, exactly, what are we discussing: the Jew lacks, he is fundamentally, no, not only a foreign body in the state, but. But what can you expect when in the Middle Ages and down to the nineteenth century and again today: the Christians are to blame, begging your pardon. Quite the contrary, my dear girl: see here, you know your Bible, don't you, well then, what did Jacob do to his dying father? He lied to Isaac ha-ha-ha, and he swindled Esau, if you please, and Laban didn't come off any better. But such things happen everywhere. Speaking in terms of percentages, the Aryans take the lead in crime and not. Which proves if it proves anything that the Jew has no knowledge either of good or evil, that's why the Jews lack the very concept of angel, not to mention the Devil. May I call your attention to Belial and the Garden of Eden? Still, I think we can agree that the highest ethical elevation and the profoundest moral degradation are equally unknown to him: hence the few crimes of violence, and the same goes for women, which proves again that he lacks stature in every respect, or can you offhand name a saint who. Very clever! That's why I say: we're talking about species, not individuals. Even his proverbial feeling for the family serves only the one purpose of multiplying, that's right, that's why they're such panders: the Jewish pander in antithesis to the aristocrat. But doesn't Weininger say distinctly that he neither nor, that he has no desire whatever to play into the hands of the mob, neither boycott nor expulsion, after all he was one. But he wasn't for Zionism either. And when he quotes Chamberlain. After all, he himself says that the parallel with women doesn't always. But he says both are without a soul. Yes, yes, but only in a platonic sense, so to speak. You forget. I forget nothing, my friend. He states cold facts. For instance: Take your time, with facts anything . . . A quotation from Lenin, eh? You see what I mean? Look here. Darwinism found most of its supporters, because the ape theory: so it's no accident if chemistry is still in the hands, like the Arabs in the past, a related race after all, hence the purely chemical tendency in medicine, whereas naturopathy, in the end it all boils down to the question of the organic and the inorganic as such: it was not without reason that Goethe identified the effort to make a homunculus not with Faust but with Wagner his famulus, because Wagner, it is safe to assume, represents the typically Jewish element, whereas Faust: because one thing is certain, they are without genius of any kind. What about Spinoza? You've taken the word out of my mouth. Because if he hadn't been Goethe's favorite author. Not to mention Heine. The same with the English who also haven't, because if I'm not mistaken Swift and Sterne were. And about Shakespeare we're still insufficiently informed. Able empiricists. Yes, I agree, practical politicians, psychologists, but never. Just the same there's—no, no, let me have my say, my dear, I'm referring to English humor, which the Jew will never, but at the very most clever mockery, exactly like women, but humor? Never! And I'll tell you why, because they believe in nothing, because they *are* nothing and for that very reason they can become anything they please, because with their inclination for abstraction, hence jurisprudence, and because to them nothing, absolutely nothing is inviolable or sacred, because they drag everything into the, because they refuse to respect either a Christian's Christianity or a Jew's baptism, because they are utterly without piety or any true enthusiasm, because they can neither search nor doubt, I'm speaking of authentic doubt, because they are irreligious, because they are neither sunlike nor demonic, because they are neither fearful nor brave, because they are unheroic and never anything but ironic, because like Heine, because they have no ground under their feet, because all they can do is undermine, yes, that they can do all right and never, because they don't even despair, because they are not creative, because they have no song, because they never identify themselves with any cause or idea, because they lack simplicity, shame, dignity, awe, because they never experience wonderment or shattering emotion, only the material side, because they are without honor or profound erotic impulse, because grace, love, humor, yes, that's right, humor I say, and grace and honor and song and faith, the oak tree, the Siegfried motif, the trumpet, and spontaneous being, I say, are forever beyond their grasp, yes, grasp, let me finish: grasp grasp!"

Thereupon Eddi Amsel detaches himself nimbly from the genuine Renaissance writing desk, but nevertheless, as the cocktail party amid the oak paneling turns to other topics, such as the Olympiad and its side effects, does not close Otto Weininger's standard work. He merely takes his distance and appraises the figures which, though possessed of only a framework existence, swagger and express opinions all the same. He

710

reaches behind him into boxes, but not haphazardly, grasps, rejects, selects, and begins to dress up the motley company on the floor in very much the same way as he has done with the company hanging on chains and meathooks under the oak ceiling. Eddi Amsel covers them with old newspapers and vestiges of wallpaper obtained from renovated apartments. Discarded scraps of banners formerly belonging to the seaside resort fleet, rolls of toilet paper, empty tin cans, bicycle spokes, lamp shades, cast-off notions, and Christmas tree decorations set the style. With an ample pot of paste, with moth-eaten odds and ends picked up at auctions or simply picked up, he performs magic. But it has to be admitted that for all their aesthetic harmony, for all their refinement of detail and morbid elegance of line, these scarecrows or, as Amsel said, figures, were less impressive than the scarecrows which Eddi Amsel the village schoolboy seems to have built for many years in his native Schiewenhorst, exhibited on the Vistula dikes, and sold at a profit.

Amsel was the first to notice this loss of substance. Later, when Walter Matern left his own oak paneling and his pocket-sized paperbacks of dramatic works, he too, though remarking on Amsel's amazing talent, called attention to the undeniable absence of the old creative fury.

Amsel tried to show that his friend was mistaken; he placed one of his splendidly bedizened figures on the terrace outside the paneled room, shaded by the beech trees of Jäschkental Forest. The figure enjoyed a modicum of success, for the good old faithful sparrows shut their eyes to the artistic aspect and as usual allowed themselves to be scared a little; but no one could have said that a cloud of feathered beasts, thrown into panic by the sight, had risen screaming from the treetops and re-enacted a scene from Amsel's village childhood over the forest. His art was stagnant. Weininger's text remained paper. Perfection proved tedious. Sparrows were unmoved. Crows yawned. Wood pigeons refused to believe. Chaffinches, sparrows, crows, and wood pigeons took turns in sitting on Amsel's artistic figure—a paradoxical sight which Eddi Amsel bore with a smile. But we, in the bushes behind the fence, heard him sigh.

Neither Tulla nor I could help him;

nature helped: in October Walter Matern had a fist fight with the platoon leader of a platoon of Hitler Cubs, who were putting on so-called war games in the nearby forest. A squad of uniformed Cubs moved into Amsel's garden with the pennant around which the operation revolved. From the open window Walter Matern dove head-first into the wet foliage; and undoubtedly I too would have come in for a licking if I like my squad leader had tried to stand by Heini Wasmuth our group leader.

The following night we were ordered to throw stones at the villa from the woods: we heard several windowpanes crash. That would have been the end of the affair if Amsel, who had remained on the terrace while blows were falling in the garden, had contented himself with looking on: but he sketched his observations on cheap paper and built models the size of upright cigar boxes: wrestling groups, a muddled shapeless free-for-all of scrawny Cubs, short-panted, knee-socked, shoulder-strapped, brown-tattered, pennant-maddened, rune-bepatched, dagger belts askew, Führer-vaccinated and hoarse with triumph—the living image of our Cub squad fighting over the pennant in Amsel's garden. Amsel had found his way back to reality; from that day on he stopped wasting his talent on fashion plates, hothouse plants, studio art; avid with curiosity, he went out into the street.

He developed a mania for uniforms, especially black and brown ones, which were taking on a larger and larger part in the street scene. In a junkshop on Tagnetergasse he managed to scare up an old SA uniform dating back to the heroic period before the seizure of power. But one did not satisfy his needs. With considerable effort he abstained from putting an ad in the *Vorposten* under his own name: "Wanted: Old SA uniforms." In the stores specializing in iniforms the Party rig was obtainable only on presentation of a Party card. Because it was impossible for Eddi Amsel to join the Party or any of its organizations, Eddi Amsel set about, with coaxing, blasphemous, comical, and always adroit words, persuading his friend Walter Matern, who, though he had stopped distributing Communist leaflets, had a photograph of Rosa Luxemburg pinned to his oak paneling, to do what Amsel would have liked to do for the sake of the uniforms he needed, but couldn't.

Out of friendship—the two of them were said to have been blood brothers—half for the hell of it and half out of curiosity, but especially in order that Amsel might obtain those intensely brown uniforms for which he and the skeletons of future scarecrows were thirsting, Walter Matern, step by little step, gave in: he put aside his pocket-sized paperbacks and filled out an application in which he made no secret of the fact that he had been a member of the Red Falcons and later of the C.P.

Laughing, shaking his head, grinning, no longer outwardly but deep within, every tooth in his head, he joined a Langfuhr SA sturm, whose headquarters and meeting place was the Kleinhammerpark Beer Hall, a spacious establishment with a park by the same name, with dance hall, bowling alley, and home cooking, situated between the Aktien Brewery and the Langfuhr railroad station.

Students from the engineering school made up the bulk of this largely petit-bourgeois sturm. At demonstrations on the Maiwiese beside the Sports Place the sturm performed guard duty. For years its main function was to start fights on Heeresanger, near the Polish student house, with members of the "Bratnia Pomoc" student organization, and to wreck the Polish clubhouse. At first Walter Matern had difficulties, because his Red

712

past and even the leaflet incident were known. But since he was not the only former Communist in SA Sturm 84, Langfuhr-North, and since the former Communists began to exchange Red Front salutes as soon as they had a few drinks under their belts, he soon felt at home, especially as the group leader took him under his wing: before '33 Sturmführer Jochen Sawatzki had made speeches as a Red Front Fighter and had read strike proclamations to the shipyard workers in the Schichau housing development: Sawatzki was loyal to his past and said when making his brief and popular speeches in the Kleinhammerpark: "Take it from me, boys, if I know anything about the Führer, he'd get a bigger kick about one Communist that joins the SA than about ten Center Party big shots, that only join the Party because they're scared shitless and not because they realize the new day has dawned, yep, believe you me, she's dawned all right. And the only ones that haven't caught on is the big shots, because all they do is saw wood."

When early in November a delegation from the trusty sturm was sent to the Party congress in Munich and consequently put into new uniforms, Walter Matern succeeded in diverting the old rags that had weathered full many a beer-hall battle, to Steffensweg. Actually Matern, whom Sturmführer Sawatzki had soon appointed squad leader, should have taken the whole kit and boodle including boots and harness to Tiegenhof, where they were just organizing a new SA sturm, which was short on funds. But Eddi Amsel gave his friend a check that had zeroes enough on it to put twenty men into new-smelling togs. Between Amsel's oak panels brown tatters piled up: beer spots, grease spots, blood spots, tar and sweat spots gave the rags additional value in his eyes. He began at once to take measurements. He sorted, counted, piled, took his distance, dreamed of marching columns, let them march by, salute, march by, salute, looked on with screwed-up eyes: beer-hall battles, movement, tumult, men against men, bones and table edges, eyes and thumbs, beer bottles and teeth, screams, crashing pianos, potted plants, chandeliers, and more than two hundred and fifty well-tempered knives; and yet, apart from the piled-up rags there was no one between the oak panels but Walter Matern. He was drinking a bottle of seltzer and didn't see what Eddi Amsel saw.

My cousin Tulla,

of whom I am writing, to whom I am writing, although if Brauxel had his way, I should be writing of nothing but Eddi Amsel, Tulla arranged for our watchdog Harras to attack Felsner-Imbs, the piano teacher and ballet pianist, a second time. On the open street, on Kastanienweg, Tulla let the dog off the leash. Imbs and Jenny—she in a yellowish fluffy coat—were probably on their way from the ballet school, for the laces of her ballet slippers were dangling pink and silky out of a gym bag that

713

Jenny was carrying. Tulla let Harras loose, and the rain was slanting down from all sides because the wind kept shifting. Over rilled and bubbling puddles leapt Harras, whom Tulla had let loose. Felsner-Imbs was holding an umbrella over himself and Jenny. Harras made no detours and knew whom Tulla meant when she released him. This time it was the pianist's umbrella my father had to replace, for Imbs defended himself when the black beast, rain-smooth and distended, sprang at him and his pupil, withdrawing the umbrella from its rain-combating function and wielding it, transformed into a shield with a point in the middle, against the dog. Naturally the umbrella gave way. But the metal stays, radiating toward the star-shaped edge of the umbrella, remained. A few of them bent and broke through the cloth; but they confronted our Harras with a painful obstacle. Both his forepaws became entangled in the forbidding spokes; a couple of passers-by and a butcher, who dashed out of his shop in spotted apron, were able to hold him in check. The umbrella was done for. Harras panted. Tulla wouldn't let me run for it. The butcher and the pianist got wet. Harras was put on the leash. The pianist's inspired mane was reduced to matted strands: diluted hair powder dripped on dark cloth. Jenny, the roly-poly, lay in a gutter which gushed Novemberly, gurgled, and secreted gray bubbles.

The butcher didn't go back to his blood sausage; exactly as he had dashed out of his shop, as bald and hatless and porcine as a heel of bologna, he delivered me and Harras to the master carpenter. He described the incident in terms unfavorable to me, representing Tulla as a timid little girl who had run away in terror when I had been unable to hold the dog on the leash; when the truth of the matter is that Tulla had looked on to the end and beaten it only after I had taken the leash away from her.

The butcher took his leave with a shake of a large hairy hand. I got my licking, this time not with a rectangular roofing lath but with a flat woodworking hand. My father promised Dr. Brunies to pay for cleaning the fluffy yellowish coat: fortunately Jenny's gym bag with the pink silk ballet slippers hadn't been carried away in the gutter, for the gutter flowed into the Striessbach, and the Striessbach flowed into Aktien Pond, and the Striessbach flowed out the other end of Aktien Pond and made its way through the whole of Langfuhr, under Elsenstrasse, Hertastrasse, Luisenstrasse, past Neuschottland, up Leegstriess, and emptied near Broschkenweg, opposite Weichselmünde, into the Dead Vistula, whence, mingled with Vistula water and Mottlau water, it passed through the harbor channel between Neufahrwasser and Westerplatte to merge with the Baltic Sea.

Tulla and I were present
    when in the first week of Advent, at 13 Marienstrasse, in Langfuhr's largest and finest garden restaurant, the Kleinhammerpark, Manager Au-

gust Koschinski, Tel. 41-09-04—fresh waffles every Tuesday—one thing and another led to a brawl that was quelled only an hour and a half later by the police detachment which during Party meetings was always on stand-by duty in the small Hunt Room: Sergeant Burau put in a call for reinforcements: One one eight, whereupon sixteen policemen drove up and restored order with beauty doctors.

The meeting, held under the motto "Home to the Reich—Down with the tyranny of Versailles!," was well attended. Two hundred and fifty people had crowded into the Green Room.

According to the agenda one speaker followed another at the speaker's desk between the potted plants: first Sturmführer Jochen Sawatzki spoke tersely huskily vigorously. Then Local Group Leader Sellke spoke of his impressions at the Reich Party Congress in Nuremberg. The spades of the Labor Service, thousands upon thousands, had particularly impressed him, because sunshine had kissed the blades of Labor Service spades: "I can only tell you, dear citizens of Langfuhr, who have turned out in such gratifying numbers, that was unique, absolutely unique. It's something a man won't forget as long as he lives, how they glittered, thousands upon thousands of them. A shout went up as from thousands upon thousands of throats: our hearts were full to overflowing, dear citizens of Langfuhr, and many a hardened fighter had tears in his eyes. But that's nothing to be ashamed of, not on such an occasion. And I thought to myself, dear citizens of Langfuhr, when I go home, I'll tell all those who could not be present what it's like when thousands upon thousands of Reich Labor Service spades . . ." Then Kreisleiter Kampe spoke of his impressions at the harvest thanksgiving festival in Bückeburg and of the projected new apartments in the projected Albert Forster Housing Development. The SA Sturmführer Sawatzki, supported by two hundred and fifty citizens of Langfuhr, shouted a triple *Siegheil* for the Führer and Chancellor. Both anthems, one too slow and one too fast, were sung too low by the men, too high by the women, and by the children off-key and out of time. This concluded the official part of the program and Local Group Leader Sellke informed the citizens of Langfuhr that the second part would now begin, a friendly informal get-together in the course of which useful and tasty products would be raffled off for the benefit of Winter Aid. The prizes had been donated by: Valtinat Dairy Products, Amada Margarine, Anglas Chocolates, Kanold Candies, Kiesau Wines, Haubold & Lanser Wholesalers, the Kühne Mustard Co., the Danzig Glass Works, and the Aktien Brewery of Langfuhr, which had donated beer, two cases to be raffled off and an extra keg "for SA Sturm 84, Langfuhr-North; for the boys of Langfuhr SA Sturm 84; for our storm troopers, of whom we are proud; a triple hip-hip-hurray for our storm troopers of Sturm 84—hurray, hurray!"

And then came the tangle which could be disentangled only after a phone call to the police—one one eight—and with the help of beauty doctors. It should not be supposed that the peace was disturbed by Communists or Socialists. By that time they were all washed up. What set off the battle at the Kleinhammerpark was booze, the barrel fever that rises up from within to hit the eyeballs from behind. For, as is only natural after long speeches that have had to be made and listened to, liquid nourishment was drunk, guzzled, lushed, slushed, and sopped up; sitting or standing, one good thing led to another; some ran from table to table, growing damper all the while; many leaned on the bar, pouring it in with both hands; few stood upright and gargled headless, for a dense cloud of smoke cut the hall, which was low to begin with, off at shoulder height. Those whose euphoria had made the longest strides struck up a part song as they drank: Knowyoutheforestallshottobits; Inacoolvalley; Ohheadboweddownwithbloodandwounds.

A family affair, everybody was there, all old friends: Alfons Bublitz with Lotte and Fränzchen Wollschläger: "You 'member the time in Höhne Park. Along the Radaune on the way to Ohra, who do we run into but Dulleck and his brother, and there he is, stewed to the gills."

And in a row at the bar stood beer-assed the SA men Bruno Dulleck, Willy Eggers, Paule Hoppe, Walter Matern, and Otto Warnke. "And one time at the Café Derra! You're nuts, man, that was in Zinglers Höhe, they beat Brill up. And then another time, only a coupla days ago. Where was that? By the dam in Straschin-Prangschin. I hear they chucked him into the basin. But he climbed out. Not like Wichmann in Klein-Katz, they gave it to him good, with gun butts: shoilem boil 'em! They say he's gone to Spain. That's what you think! They done him in and stuffed the pieces in a sack. I remember him from the Sharpshooters' Club, before they elected him to the Diet with Brost and Kruppke. They got away, slipped across the border near Goldkrug. Say, would you look at Dau. The guy's a walking bank. One time in Müggenwinkel he said . . ."

Gustav Dau came ambling over, arm in arm with Lothar Budzinski. Wherever he went, he stood a couple of rounds and then another round. Tulla and I sat at a table with the Pokriefkes. My father had left immediately after the speeches. There weren't many children left. Tulla looked at the toilet door: MEN. She drank nothing, said nothing, just looked. August Pokriefke was stewed. He was explaining the railroad connections in Koshnavia to a Herr Mikoteit. Tulla was trying to nail the toilet door closed by just looking: but it swung, moved by full and emptied bladders. The express line Berlin, Schneidemühl, Dirschau passed through Koshnavia. But the express didn't stop. Tulla looked at the door of the ladies' toilet: she saw Walter Matern, disappearing into the men's toilet. Mikoteit worked for the Polish railroad, but that didn't prevent August Pokriefke from listing every single local station on the Konitz-

Laskowitz run. Every five sips of beer Erna Pokriefke said: "Now go on home to beddy-bye, children, it's time." But Tulla kept her grip on the fluttering toilet door: every exit and entrance was snapshot by her slit-eyes. Now August Pokriefke was rattling off the stations on the third Koshnavian run—Nakel-Konitz: Gersdorf, Obkass, Schlangenthin . . . Chances were being sold for the Winter Aid raffle. First prize: a dessert set for twelve, including wine glasses; all crystal, pure crystal! Tulla was allowed to draw three lots, because one time, last year, she had drawn an eleven-pound goose. From the all but full SA cap she drew, without removing her eyes from the toilet door: first, a bar of Anglas chocolate; and then, with small scratched hand, she draws the second lot: blank! but none the less the first prize, the crystal: the door to the men's toilet is slammed and wrenched open. Where pants are being unbuttoned or dropped, things are starting up. Quick on the draw, out come the knives. Stabbing each other and slicing each other's jackets, because Tulla is drawing the lot: China against Japan. Shoilem boil 'em.

And kick and clout and turn over and lay out flat and bellow: "Shut up your trap! You crazy loon! You lousy bastard! You stinking ape! Not so rough!" And all the drunks at the bar: Willy Eggers, Paule Hoppe, Alfons Bublitz, the younger Dulleck, and Otto Warnke pull out their clasp knives: "Shoilem boil 'em!" A brawny-armed chorus, stewed to the gills, take their pick of fruit plates, behead glasses, and oil the toilet door. Because Tulla has pulled a blank, they brawl around and tickle each other with knives hooks chivies. Chair and bone, here and now, nobody's yellow, gimme room, plunk on the head, artifacts crack, Willy stands, self-point totters, beer and blood, exaltation. For all ten are champs and have no need to catch their breath. Each looking for each. Who's crawling down there? Whose ink is running out? What are them plug-uglies hollering about? How are toilet doors lifted off their hinges? Who drew the lot? Blank. Uppercut. Tackle. Inside-out. Squirting brains. Telephone: one one eight. Police, shoilem boil 'em! Sneaky and under-handed. Never never. *Existenz.* Green Room. Chandelier crashes. Being and Time. Fuse blows. No lights. Darkness: for in the Black Room the black beauty doctors of the Black Maria look for pitch-black round heads, until brains, black under black chandelier, and the black women scream: "Light! Where's the light? Oh, my, the police! Shoilem boil 'em."

Only when Tulla in the darkness drew a third lot from the SA cap that had stayed with us between her knees, only when my cousin had drawn and unrolled the third lot—it won her a pail of dill pickles from the Kühne Mustard Co.—did the lights go on again. The four stand-by policemen under Sergeant Burau and the sixteen reinforcements under Police Lieutenant Sausin moved in: from the bar and the swinging door to the cloakroom: green, loved, and feared. All twenty-two cops had police whistles between their lips and warbled down on the crowd. They worked with the new night sticks, introduced from Italy by Police President Froboess, there termed *manganelli,* here beauty doctors. The new billies had the advantage over the old ones that they left no open wounds, but operated dryly, almost silently. After one blow with the new police truncheon, each victim turned two and a half times in patent consternation on his own axis and then, but still in corkscrew fashion, collasped to the floor. Near the toilet door August Pokriefke also submitted to the authority of the article imported from Mussolini's Italy. Without open wounds he was laid up for a week. Not counting him, the final count was three seriously injured and seventeen slightly injured, including four cops. SA men Willy Eggers and Fränzchen Wollschläger, Gustav Dau, the mason, and Lothar Budzinski, the coal dealer, were taken to police headquarters but released the following morning. Herr Koschinski, manager of the Kleinhammerpark, reported one thousand two hundred gulden worth of damages to the insurance company: glass, chairs, the chandelier, the demolished toilet door, the mirror in the toilet, the potted plants around the speaker's stand, the first prize: crystal crystal!—and so on. A police investigation revealed that there had been a short circuit, that someone—I know who!—had unscrewed the fuses.

But nobody suspected that by drawing the blank lot my cousin Tulla had given the signal, had unleashed the beer-hall battle.

Dear Tulla,

all that was within your power. You had the eye and the finger. But what is important for this story is not your beer-hall battle—although you had a part in it, it was a commonplace affair, indistinguishable from other beer-hall battles—the significant item is that Eddi Amsel, owner of a villa on Steffensweg, was able to take delivery of a beer-sour bundle of battle-scarred and blood-encrusted uniforms: Walter Matern was the slightly injured donor.

This time the loot wasn't limited to SA uniforms. It included the togs of plain Party members. But everything was brown: not the brown of summer oxfords; not hazelnut-brown or witch-brown; no brown Africa; no grated tree bark, no furniture, brown with age; no medium-brown or sand-brown; neither young soft coal nor old peat, dug with a peat spade; no breakfast chocolate, no morning coffee enriched with cream; tobacco, so many varieties, but none so brown as; neither the roebuck brown that so deceives the eye nor the suntan-lotion brown of a two weeks' vacation; no autumn spat on the palette when this brown: shit brown, at best clay brown, sodden, pasty, Party brown, SA brown, the brown of all Brown Books, Brown Houses, Braunau brown, Eva Braun, uniform brown, a far cry from khaki brown, the brown shat on white plates by a thousand pimply asses, brown derived from split peas and sausages; no, no, ye gentle witch-brown, hazelnut-brown brunettes, you were not the godmothers when this brown was boiled, born, and dyed, when this dungheap brown—I'm still being polite about it—lay before Eddi Amsel.

Amsel sorted out the brown, took the big scissors from Solingen and made them twitter experimentally. Amsel began to cut into the indescribable brown. A new implement stood voluted beside the genuine Renaissance writing desk supporting Weininger's always open standard work: the tailor's horse, the tailor's organ, the tailor's confessional: a Singer sewing machine. How the kitten purred when from coarse burlap, onion sacks, and other permeable material Eddi Amsel sewed shirtlike undergarments. And the puffed-up Amsel behind the slender little machine: were they not one? Might not the two of them, born, baptized, vaccinated, educated as they were, have borne witness to the same identical development? And with big stitches and little stitches, he sewed scraps of the horrible brown on the burlap shirts like beauty spots. But he also fragmented the armband-red and the sunstroke-maddened bellyache of the swastika. He stuffed with kapok and sawdust. In illustrated magazines and yearbooks he looked for and found faces, a coarse-grained photograph of Gerhard Hauptmann or a glossy black-and-white print of a popular actor of those years: Birgel or Jannings. He fastened Schmeling and Pacelli, the bruiser and the ascetic, under the visors of the brown caps. He turned the League of Nations High Commissioner into an SA man Brand. Undaunted, he snipped at reproductions of old engravings and played God with Solingen scissors until Schiller's bold profile or the dandyface of the young Goethe gave its features to one or another of the movement's martyrs, Herbert Norkus or Horst Wessel. Amsel dismembered, speculated, cross-bred, and gave the centuries a chance to kiss each other under SA caps.

From page 4 of his copy he cut the head of the full-length photograph of the slender, boyish Otto Weininger, author of the standard work, who had committed suicide while still a young man, had the section enlarged to life size at Sönnker's and then proceeded to work at length but always with unsatisfactory results, on "SA man Weininger."

Eddi Amsel's self-portrait was more successful. In addition to the Renaissance desk and the Singer sewing machine, his equipment included a tall, narrow mirror, reaching up to the ceiling paneling, of the kind to be found in tailor shops and ballet schools. Before this responsive glass he sat in a self-tailored Party uniform—among the SA uniforms he had found none capable of containing him—and hung his full-figure likeness on a naked skeleton which, in the middle, as a sort of solar plexus, lodged a winding mechanism. In the end the authentic Amsel sat Buddhalike tailor fashion, appraising the constructed and still more authentic Party

Comrade Amsel. He stood blown up to capacity in burlap and Party brown. The shoulder strap circumscribed him like a tropic. Insignia of rank on his collar made him into a modest section chief. A pig's bladder, daringly simplified and daubed only with a few suggestive black strokes, supported, an excellent likeness, the section chief's cap. And then in the Party comrade's solar plexus the winding mechanism began to operate: the breeches came to attention. Starting at the belt buckle, the right rubber glove, full to bursting, moved jerkily, by remote control, to chest, then to shoulder level, presented first the straight-arm, then the bent-arm Party salute, returned sluggishly, just barely in time, for the mechanism was running down, to the belt buckle, gave a senile tremor or two and fell asleep. Eddi Amsel was in love with his new creation. At the narrow studio mirror he imitated the salute of his life-size facsimile: the Amsel quartet. Water Matern, to whom Amsel displayed himself and the figure on the floor as well as the mirror images of himself and the figure, laughed, at first overloudly and then with embarrassment. Then he just stared in silence at Amsel, at the scarecrow, and at the mirror by turns. He stood in civilian clothes among four figures in uniform. The sight provoked the inborn grinding of his teeth. And grinding he gave it to be understood that he could take a joke but that too much was enough; Amsel should stop harping on one and the same theme; after all there were plenty of people in the SA and the Party as well who were seriously striving for an ideal, good guys and not just bastards.

Amsel replied that precisely this had been his artistic purpose, that he hadn't intended criticism of any kind, but merely wished, through his art, to create a hodgepodge of good guys and bastards, after the manner of life itself.

Thereupon he tinkered with a prefabricated frame until he had turned out a bullish-looking good guy: SA man Walter Matern. Tulla and I, who were peering from the night-black garden into the electrically lit up and oak-paneled studio, saw with round eyes how Walter Matern's uniformed likeness—blood spots still bore witness to the brawl at the Kleinhammerpark—bared the teeth of his photographed face with the help of a built-in mechanism and ground its mechanically moved teeth: yes, we only saw it—but anyone who saw Walter Matern's teeth heard them too.

Tulla and I saw
    how Walter Matern, who with his SA sturm had to do guard duty at a monster mass meeting on the snow-covered Maiwiese, caught sight of the uniformed Eddi Amsel in the crowd. Löbsack spoke. Greiser and Forster spoke. Snow was falling in big flakes, and the crowd shouted Heil so long that snowflakes slipped into the open mouths of the Heil -shouters. Party Comrade Eddi Amsel also shouted Heil and snapped after particularly

720

large snowflakes, until SA man Walter Matern fished him out of the crowd and pushed him off the slushy field into Hindenburgallee. There he gave him hell and we thought in another minute he was going to slug him.

Tulla and I saw

Eddi Amsel in uniform collecting money for the Winter Aid in the Langfuhr market. He jiggled his can, distributed his little jokes among the populace, and took in more coins than the genuine Party comrades; and we thought: if Matern should turn up now and see this, well . . .

Tulla and I

surprised Eddi Amsel and the grocer's son in a snow squall on Fröbelwiese. We were huddled under a trailer that was wintering on the Fröbelwiese. Amsel and the gnome were silhouetted like shadows against the snow flurries. No shadows could have been more different than those shadows. The gnome shadow held out his shadow drum into the snowfall. The Amsel shadow bent down. Both shadows held their ears to the drum as though listening to the sound of December snow on white-lacquered tin. Because we had never seen anything so silent, we too kept still, with frost-red ears: but all we could hear was the snow, we couldn't hear the tin.

Tulla and I

kept an eye peeled for Eddi Amsel when between Christmas and New Year's Day our families went for a walk in Oliva Forest; but he was somewhere else and not in Freudental. There we drank coffee with milk and ate potato pancakes under deer antlers. There wasn't much doing in the outdoor zoo, because in cold weather the monkeys were kept warm in the basement of the forestry house. We shouldn't have taken Harras with us. But my father, the master carpenter, said: "The dog needs a run."

Freudental was a popular place for excursions. We took the Number 2 streetcar to Friedensschluss and then walked through the woods, between trees with red markings, until the valley opened and the forestry house and the outdoor zoo lay before us. As a carpenter, my father was unable to look at any good-sized tree, whether beech or pine, without estimating its utility in cubic feet. This put my mother, who looked upon nature and hence trees more as the adornment of the world, into a bad humor, which was dispelled only by the potato pancakes and coffee. Herr Kamin, the concessionaire of the forestry house and inn, took a seat between August Pokriefke and my mother. Whenever guests appeared, he told the story of how the zoo had come into being. And so Tulla and I heard for the tenth time how a Herr Pikuritz from Zoppot had donated the male bison. The zoo hadn't started with the bison, though, but with a pair of red deer, given by the director of the railroad car factory. Next came the wild boar and the fallow deer. Somebody contributed a monkey, somebody else two monkeys. Nikolai, head of the forestry commission, had provided the foxes and the beavers. A Canadian consul had furnished the raccoons. And the wolves? Who gave the wolves? Wolves that later broke out of the enclosure, tore a berry-picking child to pieces, and, once shot, had their picture in the papers? Who gave the wolves?

Before Herr Kamin can tell us that the Breslau zoo had donated the two wolves, we are outside with Harras. Past Jack, the bison bull. Around the frozen pond. Chestnuts and acorns for wild boar. Brief barking at the foxes. The wolves' den barred. Harras turned to stone. The wolves restless behind iron bars. Pace longer than Harras'. But the chest not so well developed, the stop not so clearly marked, eyes set at a slant, smaller, more protected. Head more thickset, trunk barrel-shaped, height to the withers: less than Harras, coat stiff, light gray with black clouds, on yellow undercoat. A hoarse whining Harras. The wolves pace restlessly. One day the guardian will forget to close . . . Snow falls in plaques from firs. For the time it takes to glance, the wolves stop still behind bars: six eyes, quivering flews. Three noses curl. Breath steams from fangs. Gray wolves—black shepherd. Black as a result of consistent breeding. Oversaturation of the pigment cells, from Perkun by way of Senta and Pluto to Harras of Queen Louise's mill, gives our dog his stiff, unclouded, unbrindled, unmarked black. My father whistles and August Pokriefke claps his hands. Tulla's family and my parents standing outside the forestry house in winter coats. Restless wolves stay behind. But for us and Harras the Sunday walk isn't over yet. In every mouth an aftertaste of potato pancakes.

My father led us all to Oliva. There we took the streetcar to Glettkau. The Baltic was frozen as far as the misty horizon. Sheathed in ice, the Glettkau pier glistened strangely. Consequently my father had to take his camera out of its leather case and we had to group ourselves around Harras against the fantastic sugar candy. It took my father a long while to get focused. Six times we were told to hold still, which Harras did with ease—he was used to having his picture taken from the days when the press photographers had courted him. Of the six pictures my father took, four turned out to be overexposed: the ice shed extra light.

From Glettkau we walked across the crunching sea to Brösen. Black dots as far as the ice-bound steamers in the roadstead. A good many people had had the same idea. No need for the gulls to go hungry. Two days later four schoolboys on their way to Hela across the ice got lost in the fog and, despite a search with private planes, were never seen again.

Shortly before the Brösen pier, which was also wildly ice-covered—we were meaning to turn off toward the fishing village and the street-car stop, because the Pokriefkes, especially Tulla, had a horror of the Brösen pier, where years before the little deaf-mute Konrad—after my father with flat woodworking hand had indicated the new line of march, at approximately four in the afternoon, shortly before New Year's, 1937, on December 28, 1936, Harras, whom my father had been holding on the leash because there were so many other dogs about, broke loose, leash and all, took ten long flat leaps over the ice, disappeared in the screaming crowd and, by the time we caught up to him, had merged with a fluttering overcoat to form a black snow-spewing bundle.

Without a word from Tulla, Felsner-Imbs, the pianist and piano teacher, who with Dr. Brunies and ten-year-old Jenny had come out for a Sunday excurison like ourselves, was attacked a third time by our Harras. This time the damage was not confined to a swallowtail coat or umbrella that had to be replaced. My father had every reason to call the unfortunate episode an expensive joke. Felsner's right thigh had been badly mangled. He had to spend three weeks in Deaconesses' Hospital, over and above which he demanded exemplary damages.

Tulla,

it's snowing. Then and now it snowed and is snowing. Snow drifted, is drifting. Fell, is falling. Came down, is coming down. Swirled, is swirling. Flakes floated, are floating. Powdered, is powdering. Tons of snow on Jäschkental Forest, on the Grunewald; on Hindenburgallee, on Clay-Allee; on Langfuhr Market and on Berka Market in Smaragdendorf; on the Baltic and on the lakes of the Havel; on Oliva, on Spandau; on Danzig-Schidlitz, on Berlin-Lichterfelde; on Emmaus and Moabit; Neufahrwasser and Prenzlauer Berg; on Saspe and Brösen, on Babelsberg and Steinstücken; on the brick wall around the Westerplatte and the rapidly built wall between the two Berlins, snow is falling and lies on the ground, snow was falling and lay on the ground.

For Tulla and me,

who were waiting for snow with sleds, snow fell for two days and remained on the ground. Occasionally the snowfall was slanting, resolute, hard-working, then for a time the flakes were large and aimless—in this light, toothpaste-white with jagged edges; against the light, gray to black: a damp sticky snow, on top of which more resolute slanting snow came powdering down from the east. Through the night the moderate cold remained gray and spongy, so that in the morning all the fences were freshly laden and overloaded branches snapped. Countless janitors, columns of unemployed, the Emergency Technical Aid, and every available municipal vehicle were needed before streets, car tracks, and sidewalks were again discernible. Mountain chains of snow, crusty and lumpy, lined both sides of Elsenstrasse, concealing Harras completely and my father up to his chest. Tulla's woolen cap was two fingers' breadths of blue when there was a slight dip in the ridge. Sand, ashes, and red rock salt were strewn. With long poles men pushed the snow off the fruit trees in the Reichskolonie kitchen gardens and behind Abbot's Mill. And as they shoveled, strewed, and relieved branches, new snow kept falling. Children were amazed. Old people thought back: When had so much snow fallen? Janitors grumbled and said to one another: Who's going to pay for all this? There won't be any sand, ashes, rock salt left. And if it doesn't stop snowing. And if the snow thaws—and thaw it will as sure as we're janitors—it'll all flow into the cellars and the children will get the flu, and so will the grownups, like in '17.

When it's snowing, you can look out of the window and try to count. That's what your cousin Harry is doing, though he's not really supposed to be counting, he's supposed to be writing you letters. When the snow is coming down in big flakes, you can run out in the snow and hold up your open mouth. I'd love to, but I can't, because Brauxel says I've got to write you. If you're a black shepherd, you can run out of your white-capped kennel and bite into the snow. If your name is Eddi Amsel and you've built scarecrows from childhood up, you can build birdhouses for the birds at times when the snow falls breathlessly, and perform acts of mercy with bird food. While white snow is falling on a brown SA cap, you can grind your teeth. If your name is Tulla and you're very light, you can run through and over the snow and leave no trace. As long as vacation lasts and the sky keeps coming down, you can sit in a warm study and sort out your mica gneiss, your double spar, your mica granite and mica slate, and at the same time be a schoolteacher and suck candy. If you're paid for working in a carpentry shop, you can try to earn extra money on days when suddenly a pile of snow is falling, by making snow pushers out of the wood in the carpentry shop. If you have to make water, you can piss into the snow, engrave your name with a yellowish steaming stroke; but it has to be a short name: I wrote Harry in the snow in this manner; whereupon Tulla grew jealous and destroyed my signature with her shoes. If you have long eyelashes, you can catch the falling snow with long eyelashes; but they don't have to be long, thick eyelashes will do; Jenny had that kind in her doll face; when she stood still and gaped in amazement, she was soon looking out sea-blue from under white, snow-covered roofs. If you stand motionless in the falling snow, you can close your eyes and hear the snow fall; I often did so and heard plenty. You can see the likeness of a shroud in the snow; but you don't have to. If you're a roly-poly founding who's been given a sled for Christmas, you may want to go coasting; but nobody wants to take the foundling along. You can cry in the middle of the snowfall and nobody notice, except for Tulla with her big nostrils who notices everything and says to Jenny: "Do you want to go coasting with us?"

We all went coasting and took Jenny along, because the snow was lying there for all children. The snow had blanketed memories from the days when the rain was pelting down and Jenny lay in the gutter: several times over. Jenny's joy at Tulla's offer was almost frightening. Her phiz was radiant, while Tulla's face revealed nothing. Perhaps Tulla had made the offer only because Jenny's sled was new and modern. The Pokriefkes' intricate iron frame was gone with Tulla's brothers; and Tulla didn't like to sit on my sled, because I always had to hold on to her and that impaired my coasting technique. Our Harras wasn't allowed to come along, because the dog behaved like a lunatic in the snow; and yet he was no longer young: a ten-year-old dog corresponds to a man of seventy.

We pulled our empty sleds through Langfuhr as far as the Johanneswiese. Only Tulla let herself be pulled, sometimes by me, sometimes by Jenny. Jenny liked to pull Tulla and often offered to pull. But Tulla let herself be pulled only when she felt like it and not when somebody offered. We coasted on Zinglers Höhe, on Albrechtshöhe, or on the big sled run on the Johannesberg, which was maintained by the city. The sled run was regarded as dangerous and I, a rather scary child, preferred to coast on the gently sloping Johanneswiese, at the foot of the sled run. Often when the city slopes were too crowded, we went coasting in the part of the forest that began to the right of Jäschkentaler Weg and merged with Oliva Forest behind Hochstriess. The hill we coasted on was called the Erbsberg. From its top a sled run led directly to Eddi Amsel's garden on Steffensweg. We lay on our bellies on our sleds, peering through snow-bearing hazelnut bushes and through gorse that gave off a sharp smell even in winter.

Amsel often worked in the open. He was wearing a traffic-light-red sweater. Knitted tights, also red, disappeared into rubber boots. A white muffler, crossed over the chest of his sweater, was held together in back by a conspicuously large safety pin. Red again and for the third time, a fuzzy cap with a white pompon stretched over his head: we felt like laughing, but we couldn't, because the snow would have fallen off the hazelnut bushes. He was pottering with five figures that looked like the orphans from the Almshouse and Orphanage. Sometimes as we lurked behind snow-covered gorse and black gorse pods, a few orphans with a lady supervisor came into Amsel's garden. In blue-gray smocks under blue-gray caps, with mouse-gray earmuffs and black woolen mufflers, they posed parentless and shivering until Amsel dismissed them with little bags of candy.

Tulla and I knew
that Amsel was filling an order at the time. The stage manager of the Stadttheater, to whom Walter Matern had introduced his friend, had examined a portfolio full of sketches and designs submitted by Eddi Amsel, stage and costume designer. Amsel's stage sets and figurines had

appealed to the stage manager, who had commissioned him to design the scenery and costumes for a patriotic play. Since during the last act—the scene was laid in the days of Napoleon: the city was being besieged by Prussians and Russians—orphans had to run back and forth between the advance lines and sing before the duke of Württemberg, Amsel conceived the Amselian idea of putting not real orphans but mechanical orphans on the stage, because, so he maintained, nothing tugs at the heartstrings so much as a quavering mechanical toy; think of the touching music boxes of bygone times. And so Amsel invited the Almshouse children to his garden and dispensed charitable gifts in exchange. He had them pose and sing chorales. "Lord on high, we praise Thee!" sang the Protestant orphans. We, behind the bushes, suppressed our laughter and were all of us glad to have father and mother.

When Eddi Amsel was working in his studio, we couldn't make out what he was working on: the windows behind the terrace with the busily visited birdhouses reflected nothing but Jäschkental Forest. The other children thought he must be pottering with the same kind of thing as outside, comical orphans or cotton and toilet paper brides; only Tulla and I knew he was making SA men who could march and salute, because they had a mechanism in their tummies. Sometimes we thought we could hear the mechanism. We felt our own bellies, looking for the mechanism inside us: Tulla had one.

Tulla and I

didn't stick it out very long behind the bushes. In the first place it was getting too cold; in the second place it was too much of a struggle to keep from laughing; in the third place we wanted to coast.

While one sled run led down Philosophenweg and the second carried our sleds down to Amsel's garden, the third sled run deposited us near the Gutenberg monument. You never saw many children in that clearing, because all the children, except for Tulla, were afraid of Gutenberg. I didn't like to get too close to the Gutenberg monument either. No one knew how the monument had got into the forest; probably the monument builders had been unable to find a suitable place in town; or else they chose the forest, because Jäschkental Forest was a beech woods and Gutenberg, before casting metal type, had carved the letters he printed his books with out of beech wood. Tulla made us coast down to the Gutenberg monument from the Erbsberg, because she wanted to scare us.

For in the middle of the white clearing stood a soot-black cast-iron temple. Seven cast-iron columns supported the embossed cast-iron mushroom roof. Between the columns hung cold cast-iron chains held by cast-iron lion jaws. Blue granite steps, five of them, surrounded the temple, giving it elevation. And in the middle of the iron temple, amidst the seven columns, stood a cast-iron man: a curly iron beard flowed down over his cast-iron printer's apron. On the left he held a black iron book wedged against apron and beard. With the iron index finger of his iron right hand he pointed at the letters of the iron book. You could have read in the book if you had climbed the five granite steps and stood by the iron chain. But we never dared to take those few paces. Only Tulla, the feather-light exception, hopped, as we stood by with bated breath, up the steps to the chain, stood slim and tiny in front of the temple without touching the chain, sat between two iron columns on an iron garland, swung wildly, then more calmly, slipped off the still swinging chain, was in the temple, danced around the gloomy Gutenberg, and climbed up on his left cast-iron knee. It provided support, because he had set his left cast-iron foot with its cast-iron sandal sole on the upper edge of a cast-iron memorial tablet with the informative inscription: Here stands Johannes Gutenberg. To get an idea of how black the man reigned in the Harras-black temple, you have to remember that in front of, above, and behind the temple snow was falling, now in big, now in little flakes: the cast-iron mushroom roof of the temple was wearing a snowcap. While the snow fell, while the chain, set in motion by Tulla, came slowly to rest, while Tulla sat on the iron man's left thigh, Tulla's white index finger—she never wore gloves—spelled out the selfsame iron letters that Gutenberg was pointing at with his iron finger.

When Tulla came back—we had been standing motionless and were snowed in—she asked if we'd like to know what was written in the iron book. We didn't want to know and shook our heads violently, without a word. Tulla claimed the letters were changed from day to day, that every day you could read new but always terrible words in the iron book. This time they were especially terrible: "D'yuh wanna or don'tcha wanna?" We didn't. Then one of the Esch brothers wanted to know. Hänschen Matull and Rudi Ziegler wanted to know. Heini Pilenz and Georg Ziehm still didn't want to know and then they did want to know. Finally Jenny Brunies also wanted to know what was written in Johannes Gutenberg's iron book.

We were frozen to the spot and Tulla danced around us. Our sleds had thick pillows on them. Around the Gutenberg monument the forest cleared, letting the inexhaustible sky down on us. Tulla's bare finger pointed at Hänschen Matull: "You!" His lips became uncertain. "No, you!" Tulla's finger meant me. I'd surely have burst into tears if a moment later Tulla hadn't tapped little Esch and then reached into Jenny's fluffy duffel coat: "You you you! it says. You! You gotta go up or he's coming down and getcha."

The snow melted on our caps. "Kuddenpech said you. He said you. He wants Jenny, nobody else." Repetitions poured out of Tulla, more and more close-knit. As she described witch's circles in the snow around Jenny, the cast-iron Kuddenpech looked gloomily over our heads out of his cast-iron temple.

We began to confer. What, we asked, did Kuddenpech want of Jenny? Does he want to eat her or turn her into an iron chain? Does he want to stick her under his apron or press her flat in his iron book? Tulla knew what Kuddenpech wanted of Jenny. "She's gotta dance for Kuddenpech, 'cause she's always doing ballet with Imbs."

Jenny stood rigid, a doll-like ball in a teddy-bear fur, clutching the rope of her sled. The two snow roofs fell from her long, thick eyelashes: "NonoIdon'twanttoIdon'twantto!" she whispered, probably meaning to scream. But because she had no mouth for screaming, she ran away with her sled: floundered, rolled over, picked herself up, rolled into the beech woods in the direction of Johanneswiese.

Tulla and I let Jenny run;
     we knew she couldn't get away from Kuddenpech. If it was written in Kuddenpech's iron book: "It's Jenny's turn!"—then she'd just have to dance for Kuddenpech the way she was taught to at ballet school.

The next day, when we gathered our sleds on the hard-stamped snow of Elsenstrasse after lunch, Jenny didn't come out, although we whistled up at Dr. Brunies' windows, with fingers and without fingers. We didn't wait long: she was bound to come sooner or later.

Jenny Brunies came the day after. Without a word she fell into line, as usual filling her fluffy yellowish coat.

Tulla and I had no way of knowing
     that Eddi Amsel stepped out into his garden at the same time. As usual he had on his knottily knitted traffic-light-red tights. Red again was his fluffy sweater. His matted white muffler was held together in back by a safety pin. He had had all his woolens knitted from unraveled wool: he never wore anything new. A lead-gray afternoon. It has stopped snowing; but there's a smell of snow that wants to fall. Amsel carries a figure over his shoulder into the garden. He puts it down man-high in the snow. Purse-lipped, he whistles his way across the terrace and into the house, and comes back laden with another figure. He plants the second beside the first. With the march—"We are the guard . . ."—he whistles his way back into the studio and sweats round beads as he totes the third figure to join the two that are waiting in the garden. But he has to whistle the march all over again from the beginning: a path is gradually beaten through the knee-high snow until nine full-grown figures stand lined up in the garden, waiting for his orders. Burlap faced with dry brown. Chin strap under pig's bladder chin. Shined and polished and ready for duty:

one-dish-devouring Spartans, nine against Thebes, at Leuthen, in Teutoburg Forest, the nine loyal stalwarts, the nine Swabians, nine brown swans, the last levy, the lost platoon, the rear guard, the advance guard, nine alliterated Burgundian noses: this is the sorrow of the Nibelungs in Eddi Etzel's snow-covered garden.

Tulla, I, and the others
    had meanwhile left Jäschkentaler Weg behind us. Single file: sled track in sled track. Good crunchy snow. Imprints in the snow: many variously outlined rubber heels and hobnailed soles, with two, five, or no hobnails missing. Jenny stepped in Tulla's tracks; I in Jenny's tracks; Hänschen Matull in my tracks; obediently, little Esch and all who followed. Silently, without shouting or arguing, we trotted along behind Tulla. Only the little sleigh bells tinkled brightly. We were not, as might be supposed, going to cross the Johanneswiese to the top of the big sled run; shortly before the forester's house Tulla hove to: under the beeches we grew tiny. At first we met other children with sleds or on barrel staves. When there was no one left but us, the cast-iron monument had to be near. With short steps we entered Kuddenpech's realm.

While we crept stealthily, still stealthily,
    Eddi Amsel was still whistling merrily merrily, still merrily. From one SS man he hurried to the next. Into the left pants pocket of nine storm troopers he reached: and then he released the mechanism inherent in all of them. They still sat fast on their central axes—metal pipes affixed to broad feet, rather like umbrella stands—and nevertheless, but without gaining ground, they fling eighteen twilightofthegodsy booted legs a hand's breadth above the snow. Nine creakyboned marchers that have to be taught to march in time. This Amsel does to two of the marchers with the old faithful thrust into their left pockets: now they're in order, functioning, marching calmly firmly resolutely forward onward across toward upon and past, first in march step, then in goose step, as required in parades; all nine of them. And nine times the chin-strapped pig's bladders under SA visor caps snap almost simultaneously to the right: eyes right. They all look at him, for Eddi Amsel has pasted pig's bladder faces on all of them. Reproductions from paintings by Schnorr von Carolsfeld, who, as everyone should know, painted the sorrow of the Nibelungs, provide the features: the gloomy SA man Hagen of Tronje; the SA men, father and son, Hildebrand and Hadubrand; the luminous SA Sturmführer Siegfried of Xanten; the sensitive Obersturmführer Gunther; the evermerry Volker Baumann; and three doughty heroes who had capitalized on the sorrows of the Nibelungs: the noble Hebbel of Wesselburen, Richard the Wagoner, and the painter who with subdued Nazarene palette

729

had portrayed the sorrows of the Nibelungs. And as they, all nine of them, are still looking rigidly to the right, their arms, which only a moment before were swinging in march time, rise up jerkily and yet with a remarkable steadiness: slowly but conscientiously right arms climb to the regulation height for the German salute, while left arms bend stiffly until blackened rubber gloves stop near belt buckles. But who is being saluted? To whom are the eyes right addressed? What is the name of the Führer who is expected to look into all their pasted eyes? Who looks, returns the salute, and passes them in review?

In the manner of the Reich Chancellor, with arm bent at an angle, Eddi Amsel answers the salute of the parading storm troopers. For his own benefit and that of his nine mobile men, he whistles a march, this time the Badenweiler.

What Tulla didn't know:

while Eddi Amsel was still whistling, Gutenberg cast his terrible cast-iron gaze over the little group who, with sleds of various sizes, were crowding into his sphere of influence yet remaining at a respectful distance, and who finally excreted one little individual: doll-like fluffy condemned. Step by step, Jenny plodded in the direction of the cast iron. New snow on old snow stuck to rubber soles: Jenny grew a good inch. Believe it or not, crows rose from the white beeches of Jäschkental Forest. Snowy burdens tumbled from branches. Subdued terror lifted Jenny's chubby hands. She grew another half inch because she was again, step by step, approaching the iron temple; while overhead the crows creaked unoiled, while nine black holes glided over the Erbsberg and fell into the beeches bordering the forest and Amsel's garden.

What Tulla couldn't know:

when the crows moved, Eddi Amsel and his nine parading storm troopers were not alone in Amsel's garden; five, six, or more figures with mechanisms built in not by Amsel but by Our Father who art in Heaven, are trampling down the snow. It's not Amsel's studio that has spat them out. They've come in from outside, over the fence: masked disguised shady. With their pulled-down civilian caps, with wide loden capes and black rags slit at eye level, they seem scarecrowy and invented, but it's not scarecrows, it's warm-blooded men who climb over the fence the moment the mechanism in Amsel's figures begins running down: nine saluting right cudgels fall with a jerk; rubber gloves slide away from belt buckles; goose step simplifies itself into marchstep funeral-march drag-step, halt; tinkling, the mechanism runs down; at this point Amsel unpurses his lips; the pig's snout has stopped whistling; cocking his fat head so that his fuzzy cap dangles, he is intrigued by his uninvited guests.

730

While his nine invented creatures stand at attention as commanded, while gradually their overheated mechanism cools off, the nine masked figures move according to plan: they form a semicircle, breathe warm breath through black masks into the January air, and approaching step by step, transform the semicircle around Eddi Amsel into a circle around Eddi Amsel. Soon he will be able to smell them.

Then Tulla called the crows back:

she called the cacophonous birds from across the Erbsberg into the beeches around the Gutenberg monument. The crows saw Jenny stiffen at the foot of the granite steps leading to Kuddenpech's iron temple and look back with her round face: Jenny saw Tulla, saw me, little Esch, Hänschen Matull, Rudi Ziegler, she saw the lot of them far in the distance. Did she count? Did the nine crows count: seven eight nine children in a cluster and one child alone? It wasn't cold. A smell of wet snow and cast iron. "Gwan dance around, dance around him!" Tulla yelled. The forest had an echo. We yelled too and echoed, to make her start dancing, to get the fool dancing over with. All the crows in the beeches, Kuddenpech under his iron mushroom roof, and we saw Jenny pull her right shoe, into which a knitted pants leg disappeared, out of the snow and with her right suggest something in the nature of a *battement développé: passer la jambe.* A plaque of snow fell from her shoe sole just before she sank the right shoe into the snow again and pulled out the left one. She repeated the awkward angle, stood on her right foot, lifted her left, ventured a cautious *rond de jambe en l'air,* went into fifth position, left her hands lying on the air in the *port de bras,* embarked on an *attitude croisée devant,* wobbled an *attitude éffacée,* and took her first fall when her *attitude croisée derrière* went wrong. When she emerged, her coat was no longer yellowish but dusted with white. Under a topsy-turvy woolen cap short leaps were now supposed to continue the dance in Kuddenpech's honor: from the fifth position into the *demi-plié: petit changement de pieds.* The ensuing figure was probably supposed to be the difficult *pas assemblé,* but Jenny took a second fall; and when, in an attempt to shine with a daring *pas de chat,* she took a third fall, tumbling when she should have been floating on air, when instead of weightlessly rejoicing the iron Kuddenpech's heart she flopped like a sack of potatoes into the snow, the crows rose up out of the beeches and squawked their heads off.

Tulla dismissed the crows:

on the north side of the Erbsberg they saw that the masked men had not only closed their circle around Eddi Amsel but had narrowed it. Nine loden capes trying to rub shoulders. Jerkily Amsel turns his glistening face from one to the next. He picks up his feet but makes no headway. His wool bunches up and has barbs. He conjures sweat from his smooth forehead. He gives a high-pitched laugh and wonders with nervous tongue between his lips: "What can I do for the gentlemen?" Pitiful ideas come to him: "Would you like me to make you some coffee? There may be some cake in the house. Or how about a little story? Do you know the one about the milk-drinking eels; or the one about the miller and the talking mealworms; or the one about the twelve headless nuns and the twelve headless knights?" The nine black rags with eighteen eye slits seem to have taken a vow of silence. But when, possibly in order to put on water for coffee, he concentrates his spherical energies and tries to break through the circle of loden capes and pulled-down caps, he receives an answer: a bare, dry, unmasked fist: he falls back with his matted wool, pops quickly up again, begins to brush off the snow that is clinging to him. Then a second fist strikes and the crows rise up from the beeches.

Tulla had called them

because Jenny had had enough. After the second and third tumble she crawled over to us, a whimpering snowball. But Tulla wasn't through. While we stayed where we were, she darted swift and trackless over the snow: toward the snowball Jenny. And when Jenny tried to get up, Tulla pushed her back. No sooner did Jenny stand than she was lying down again. Who would have supposed that she was wearing a fluffy coat under the snow? We retreated toward the edge of the forest and from there saw Tulla at work. Above us the crows were enthusiastic. The Gutenberg monument was as black as Jenny was white. Tulla sent a bleating laugh with echo across the clearing and motioned us to come over. We stayed under the beeches while Jenny was being rolled in the snow. In utter silence she grew fatter and fatter. When Jenny had no legs left to get up with, the crows had done enough spying and projected themselves over the Erbsberg.

Tulla had an easy time of it with Jenny;

but Eddi Amsel, as the crows can bear witness, has to be answered with fists as long as he asks questions. All the fists that answer him are mute except for one. As this fist strikes him, it grinds its teeth behind a black rag. From Amsel's red-foaming mouth, a question blows bubbles: "Is it you? Si ti uoy?" But the grinding fist doesn't speak, it only punches. The other fists are taking a rest. Only the grinding one is working, bending over Amsel because Amsel refuses to get up any more. Several times, with downward thrust, it rams the red-gushing mouth. Possibly the mouth still wants to form the question: Isityou?—but all it can come up with is small, well-shaped pearly teeth: warm blood in cold snow, tin drums, Poles, cherries with whipped cream: blood in the snow. Now they're rolling him as Tulla rolled the girl Jenny.

But Tulla was finished with her snow man first.

With the flat of her hands she beat him firm all around, set him upright, gave him a nose modeled with a few swift strokes, looked around, found Jenny's woolen cap, stretched the cap over the snow man's pumpkin-round head, scratched in the snow with the tips of her shoes until she found leaves, hollow beechnuts, and dry branches, stuck two branches left right into the snow man, gave the snow man beechnut eyes, and stepped back to survey her work from a distance.

Tulla might have drawn comparisons,

for behind the Erbsberg, in Amsel's garden, another snow man is standing. Tulla did not compare, but the crows compared. In the middle of the garden he reigns, while nine scarecrows, hung with brown-tattered burlap, stand dimly in the background. The snow man in Amsel's garden has no nose. No one has put beechnut eyes in his face. There's no woolen cap over his head. He cannot salute, wave, despair with fagot arms. But to make up for all that he has a red mouth that grows larger and larger.

The nine men in loden capes are in more of a hurry than Tulla. Over the fence they climb and vanish into the woods, while we, with Tulla, are still standing by our sleds at the edge of the woods, staring at the snow man in Jenny's woolen cap. Again the crows descend on the clearing, but instead of stopping in the beeches, they circle cacophonously unoiled over Gutenberg's iron temple, then over the snow man. Kuddenpech breathes on us coolly. The crows in the snow are black holes. The sky is darkening on both sides of the Erbsberg. We run away with our sleds. We're hot in our winter clothes.

Dear Cousin Tulla,

you hadn't thought of that: with evening came a thaw. A thaw is said to set in. All right: a thaw set in. The air became pliant. The beeches sweated. The branches gave up burdens of snow. Thudding sounds were heard in the woods. A warm breeze helped. Holes dripped into the snow. A hole dripped into my head, for I had stayed among the beeches. But even if I had gone home with the others and their sleds, a hole would have dripped into my head. No one, regardless of whether he stays or goes home, can get away from a thaw.

The snow men were still standing—the one in Kuddenpech's domain, the one in Amsel's garden—motionless. The gathering dusk excepted a dim whiteness. The crows were somewhere else, telling about what they had seen somewhere else. The snowcap slipped off the cast-iron mushroom roof of the Gutenberg monument. Not only were the beeches sweating, so was I. Johannes Gutenberg, normally a dull cast iron, exuded damply and glittered amid shimmering columns. Above the clearing and also where the forest ends and borders on the gardens of villas, over Langfuhr, the sky moved several stories higher. Hurrying clouds drove in slovenly ranks toward the sea. Through holes the night sky dotted stars. And finally a puffed-up thawtide moon came out and shone with intermissions. It showed me, now through a good-sized hole, now with half its disk, now nibbled, now behind a brittle veil, what had changed in the clearing, in Kuddenpech's domain, now that a thaw had set in.

Gutenberg glistened alive, but stayed in his temple. At first it looked as though the forest were going to take a step forward; but then in the broad light it stepped back; stepped forward on a solid front as soon as the moon was shut off; stepped back again, couldn't make up its mind, and with so much coming and going lost all the snow it had caught in its branches during the days of snow. Thus unburdened and with the help of the mild wind, it began to murmur. In league with the shivery moon, the agitated Jäschkental Forest and the cast-iron Johannes Gutenberg inspired me, Harry-in-the-Woods, with a sopping wet fear. I fled: Away from here! I stumbled up the Erbsberg. Two hundred and seventy-five feet above sea level.

I slid down the Erbsberg with moving snow, I wanted to get away away away, but landed outside Amsel's garden. I peered in through dripping hazelnut bushes and tart-smelling gorse under an absent moon. With thumb and forefinger, as soon as the moon permitted, I took the measure of the snow man in Amsel's garden: he was shrinking but still sizable.

Then I was seized with ambition to measure another snow man on the other side of the Erbsberg. Slipping time and again, I struggled up and in coasting down took care that no accompanying avalanche should carry me into the clearing, into Kuddenpech's realm. A jump to one side saved me: I hugged a sweating beech tree. I let water run down over burning fingers. Now to the right, now to the left of the trunk, I peered into the clearing and, as soon as the moon took the measure of the clearing, took measuring fingers to the snow man outside Gutenberg's temple: Tulla's snow man was shrinking no faster than the snow man to Amselward of the Erbsberg; but he gave clearer indications: his fagot arms were drooping. His nose was falling off. It seemed to Harry-in-the-Woods that the beechnut eyes had come closer together, giving him a crafty expression.

And once again, if I was to keep abreast of developments, I had to climb the shifting Erbsberg and coast down, braking, into the gorse: parched pods rustled. The scent of the gorse tried to make me sleepy.

But gorse pods woke me up and compelled me, with thumb and forefinger, to keep faith with shrinking snow men. After a few more of my ups and downs both of them fell haltingly to their knees, which is meant to mean that they grew thinner up above, swelled into a mealy mass below the belt line, and stood on spreading feet.

And once, to Amselward, a snow man slanted to one side, as though too short a right leg had made him slant. Once, in Kuddenpech's realm, a snow man stuck out his belly and disclosed in profile a rachitic incurving of the spine.

Another time—I was checking Amsel's garden—the snow man's right leg had grown back; that deplorable slant had straightened itself out.

And once—I had just come back from Amsel's garden and was clinging, wet-hot and wool-sticky, to my dripping beech tree—Gutenberg's iron temple, as the moonlight proved, was empty: Horror! briefly the moon flared up: temple's empty. And under the blacked-out moon: the temple an eerie shadow, and Kuddenpech at large: sweating, glittering cast iron with a curly iron beard. With open iron book, with angular iron script he was looking for me among the beeches, fixing to grab me with the book, to press me flat in the iron book, he was after me, Harry-in-the-Woods. And that rustling sound: was it the woods, was it Gutenberg with his rustling beard, whishing between beech trunks, whishing through bushes? Had he opened his book—a hungry maw—where Harry was standing? Now he's going to. What is Harry looking for? Shouldn't he go home to supper? Punishment. *Poena.* Cast iron. And one more demonstration of how terrifyingly deceptive the moonlight can be: when the clouds granted the deceiver a good-sized hole, the iron man was immutably in his house, emitting thawtide glitter.

How glad I was not to be pasted in Gutenberg's album. Exhausted, I slipped down along my dripping beech tree. I forced my tired, terror-popping eyes to be conscientious and go on watching the snow man. But they closed and opened, unfastened window shutters, at every gust of wind. Maybe they rattled. And in between I admonished myself, obsessed by the job I had taken upon myself: You mustn't sleep, Harry. You've got to go up the Erbsberg and down the Erbsberg. The summit is two hundred and seventy-five feet above sea level. You've got to go into the gorse, through the parched pods. You've got to register any alterations the snow man in Amsel's garden may have thought up. Arise, Harry. Ascend!

But I stuck to the dripping beech and would surely, if not for the loud crows, have missed the moment when the snow man in Gutenberg's realm fell apart. As they had done in the afternoon, so in the thickening night they announced the unusual by suddenly erupting and creaking unoiled. Quickly the snow of the snow man collapsed. The crows winged their way, as though for them only one direction existed, across the Erbsberg, Amselward: there too, no doubt, the snow was rapidly collapsing.

Who does not rub his eyes when he looks on at transmutations, but is unable to believe either his eyes or the snow miracle? Is it not strange that the bells always have to ring when snow men collapse: first the Church of the Sacred Heart, then Luther Church on Hermannshöfer Weg. Seven strokes. At home dinner was on the table. And my parents in among the heavy carved and polished furniture—sideboard, buffet, glass cabinet—looked at my empty carved chair: Harry, where are you? What are you doing? What are you looking at? You're going to make your eyes sore with all that rubbing.—There in the slushy, porous gray snow stood no Jenny Brunies, no frozen roly-poly, no ice dumpling, no pudding on legs, there stood a frail line, on which Jenny's yellowish fluffy coat hung loose, as though shrunk after improper washing. And the line had a tiny doll-like face, just as Jenny's face had been doll-like. But there stood a very different doll, thin, so thin you could easily have looked past her, and didn't budge.

Already the crows were returning loudly, plummeting down on the black forest. Assuredly they too had had to rub their eyes on the other side of the Erbsberg. There too wool had assuredly shrunk. A force drew me up the Erbsberg. Certainty seized me though I was reeling yet never slipped. Who had stretched a dry cable to pull me up? Who cabled me down without falling?

His arms folded over his chest, well balanced on supporting leg and unweighted leg, a young man stood in the dingy snow. Skin-tight the woolen sweater: pink; many washings ago it must have been traffic-light red. A white, coarsely knitted muffler, such as Eddi Amsel had owned, was thrown negligently over his left shoulder, not crossed and held together by a safety pin in back. Gentlemen in fashion magazines tend to wear their mufflers thus asymmetrically. Hamlet and Dorian Gray were posing jointly. Mimosa and carnations mingled their aromas. And the pain around the mouth cleverly enhanced the pose, gave it counterweight, and raised the price. And indeed the young man's first movement had to do with the painful mouth. Spasmodically, as though in obedience to an inadequately lubricated mechanism, the right hand climbed and fingered sunken lips; the left hand followed and poked around in the mouth: had the young man boiled-beef fibers between his teeth?

What was he doing when he stopped poking and bent straight-kneed from the hips? Was the young man with his very long fingers looking for something in the snow? Beechnuts? A key? A five-gulden piece? Was he looking for goods of another, intangible kind? The past in the snow? Happiness in the snow? Was he looking in the snow for the meaning of

736

existence, hell's victory, death's sting? Was he looking for God in Eddi Amsel's thawing garden?

And then the young man with the painful mouth found something, found something else, found four times, seven times, found behind before beside him. And as soon as he had found, he held his find out into the moonlight with two long fingers: it glistened, it shimmered, white as sea foam.

Then I was drawn back up the Erbsberg. While he was looking, finding, and holding out into the moonlight, I coasted safely downhill, found my beech tree, and hoped to find the old familiar roly-poly Jenny in Gutenberg's clearing. But still it was the whippety line, hung with Jenny's shrunken coat, that cast a narrow shadow as soon as moonlight broke against it. But the line had meanwhile moved its arms sideways and turned out its feet, heel to heel. In other words, the line stood in the ballet dancer's first position and embarked forthwith, though without any visible exercise bar, on a difficult bar exercise: *grand plié—demie-pointe—équilibre, bras en couronne,* twice each in the first, second, and fifth positions. Next eight *dégagés* outstretched and eight *dégagés en l'air* with closed *plié*. Sixteen *battements dégagés* limbered the line up. In the *rond de jambes á la seconde,* ending in *équilibre en attitude fermée,* and in the *grand port de bras en avant, puis en arriére,* the line showed suppleness. Softer and softer grew the line. Marionettelike arm movements changed to fluid arm movements: already Jenny's coat slipped from shoulders no broader than a hand. Exercise under lateral floodlight: eight *grands battements en croix*: long legs, not quite enough instep, but a line as if Victor Gsovsky had dreamed the line and the line's line: *Finir en arabesque croisée!*

When again I was drawn up the Erbsberg, the hard-working line was reeling off *petits battements sur le cou-de-pied*: fine sweeping arm movements that sprinkled innumerable classical dots on the soft thawing air.

And the other side of the Erbsberg? With the moon looking on for a moment, I was ready to believe that the young man in Amsel's garden not only had Amsel's white muffler, but also Amsel's red hair. But it didn't stand up in flaming stubbles, it lay flat. Now he was standing to one side of a crumbling pile of snow. He had his back turned to the scarecrow group in burlap and brown rags, standing in the shadow of the woods: broad shoulders, narrow hips. Who had given him such ideal proportions? In the hollow of his right hand, held out to one side, lay something that was worth looking at. Supporting leg at a slant. Unweighted leg negligent. Bent neck line, part line, dotted line between eyes and the hollow of his hand: spellbound, ecstatic, photographed: Narcissus! I was already thinking of going up the mountain to watch the low *pliés* of the hard-working line, for nothing worth looking at was shown me in the hollow hand, when the young man acted: what he threw behind him glistened perhaps twenty or thirty-two times in the moonlight before raining down in the hazelnut bushes, in my gorse. I groped for it, especially as he had hit me with something that felt like pebbles. I found two teeth: small, well cared for, with healthy roots; worth saving. Human teeth cast away with a gesture. He didn't look behind him but strode springily across the garden. He took the steps to the terrace in one jump: gone with the moon. But a moment later a small light bulb, possibly veiled in cloth, showed him bustling about Amsel's villa. A glimmer of light in one window, then in the next. Swift comings and goings. Something being carried, something else: the young man was packing Amsel's suitcase and was in a hurry.

I too in a hurry, climbing the Erbsberg for the last time. O everlasting two hundred and seventy-five feet above sea level. For to this day every third dream, I need only have eaten something heavy for dinner, makes me climb the Erbsberg over and over again until I wake: painfully up, wildly down, and then again, for ever and ever.

From my beech tree I saw the line dancing. No more bar exercises, but a soundless adagio: solemnly arms are moved, rest on the air. Steps secure on insecure ground. One leg is enough, the other has been given away. Scales that tip slightly and go back to sleep, weightless. Turning, but not fast, in slow motion, a pencil could follow. It's not the clearing that's turning, but the line, turning two neat pirouttes. No lifting, no balloon flights through the air; Gutenberg should come out of his temple and play the partner. But he as I: audience, while lightfoot the line measures the clearing. Speechless the crows. The beeches weep. *Pas de bourrée, pas de bourrée*. Changing feet. Allegro now, because an allegro has to follow an adagio. Swift little feet. *Échappé échappé*. And out of the *demi-plié* burgeon the *pas assemblés*. What Jenny couldn't quite manage: the merry *pas de chat*; the line wouldn't want to stop on that, it leaps, lingers in the air and manages, while persevering in weightlessness, to bend its knees and touch toe to toe. Is it Gutenberg who, after the bright allegro, whistles an adagio as a finale? What a tender line. The line keeps listening. An accommodating line. Line can grow longer or shorter. A dash, drawn in one line. Line can do a curtsy. Applause. That's the crows, the beeches, the thawtide wind.

And after the final curtain—the moon rang it down—line began with tiny little steps to look for something in the dance-furrowed clearing. But it wasn't looking for lost teeth, its mouth wasn't drawn with pain like the young man's to Amelsward of the Erbsberg, but rather with the ghost of a frozen smile, which didn't expand or grow warmer when the line found what it was looking for: with Jenny's new sled the line moved across the clearing, no longer a dancer but a somewhat hesitant child, picked up Jenny's fallen fuzzy coat, threw it over its shoulders, and—

Gutenberg raised no objection—vanished in the woods, in the direction of Jäschkentaler Weg.

Instantly, now that the clearing was deserted, terror was back again with cast iron and murmuring trees. Turning my back on the deserted clearing, I hurried through the beeches, and when the woods stopped and the street-lamp-studded Jäschkentaler Weg welcomed me, my hopping and hurrying did not abate. I didn't stop till I was on Hauptstrasse, outside Sternfeld's department store.

Across the square the clock outside the optician's indicated a few minutes after eight. The street was full of people. Moviegoers were hurrying into the movie house. A picture with Luis Trenker was being shown, I think. And then, probably after the picture had started, the young man came along, ambling and yet tense, with a suitcase. It couldn't have held much. Which of Amsel's spacious garments could the young man have taken with him? The streetcar came from Oliva, meaning to continue toward the main railroad station. He got into the trailer and stayed on the platform. When the car began to move, he lighted a cigarette. Sorrowfully sunken lips had to hold the cigarette. I'd never seen Eddi Amsel smoke.

And no sooner was he gone than primly, step by little step, the line came along with Jenny's sled. I followed it down Baumbachallee. We were going the same way. Behind the Church of the Sacred Heart I speeded up till I was beside the line, keeping step. I spoke more or less as follows: "Good evening, Jenny."

The line wasn't surprised: "Good evening, Harry."

I, to be saying something: "Have you been coasting?"

The line nodded: "You can pull my sled if you like."

"You're late getting home."

"I'm good and tired, too."

"Have you seen Tulla?"

"Tulla and the others left before seven."

The new Jenny had just as long eyelashes as the other: "I left a little before seven too. But I didn't see you." Jenny informed me politely: "I can see why you didn't see me. I was inside a snow man."

Elsenstrasse grew shorter and shorter: "What was it like in there?"

On the bridge over the Striessbach the new Jenny said: "It was awfully hot in there."

My solicitude, I think, was sincere: "I hope you didn't catch cold in there."

Outside the Aktienhaus, where Dr. Brunies lived with Jenny, the new Jenny said: "Before I go to bed, I'll take a hot lemonade as a precaution."

Many more questions occurred to me: "How did you get out of the snow man?"

The new Jenny said good-by in the entrance: "It began to thaw. But now I'm tired. Because I danced a little. For the first time I did two successful pirouettes. Cross my heart. Good night, Harry."

And then the door closed. I was hungry. I hoped there was something left in the kitchen. It seems, incidentally, that the young man took the train at ten o'clock. He and Amsel's suitcase rode away. It seems that they crossed both borders without any trouble.

Dear Tulla,

Jenny didn't catch cold inside the snow man but on the way home: the ballet in the clearing must have overheated her. She had to stay in bed for a week.

Dear Tulla,

you already know that a young man slipped out of the corpulent Amsel. With a light step, carrying Amsel's suitcase, he hurried through the station and took the train to Berlin. What you don't know yet: in his suitcase the lightfooted young man has a passport, and it's forged. A certain "Hütchen," a piano maker by trade, manufactured the passport some weeks before the double miracle in the snow. The forger's hand thought of everything: for strange to say, the passport is graced with a photograph reproducing the tense, somewhat rigid features of the young man with the painful lips. Moreover, Herr Huth didn't issue this passport in the name of Eduard Amsel: he named the owner of the passport Hermann Haseloff, born in Riga on February 24, 1917.

Dear Tulla,

when Jenny was well again, I showed her the two teeth that the young man had flung into my gorse.

Jenny was delighted. "Oh," she said, "why, those are Herr Amsel's teeth. Will you give me one?" I kept the other tooth and still carry it on me; for Herr Brauxel, who could claim the tooth, leaves it in my purse.

Dear Tulla,

what did Herr Haseloff do when he arrived in Berlin-Stettin Station? He moved into a hotel room and went next day to a dental clinic where he had his sunken mouth filled with gold in exchange for good, erstwhile Amselian, now Haseloffian money. In the new passport Herr Huth had to note, after "Distinguishing Marks": "Artificial denture. Gold crowns." Henceforth when Herr Haseloff laughs, he will be seen laughing with thirty-two gold teeth; but Haseloff seldom laughs.

740

Dear Tulla,

those gold teeth became famous; they still are. Yesterday as I was sitting in Paul's Taproom with some associates, I made an experiment to prove that Haseloff's gold teeth are not a myth. This bar on Augsburger Strasse is frequented mostly by wrestlers, shippers, and unaccompanied ladies. The upholstered bench around our table—the one we always occupied—offered the possibility of arguing hard on a soft foundation. We talked about things people talk about in Berlin. The wall behind us was papered helter-skelter with the photographs of famous boxers, six-day bicycle racers, and track stars. Signatures and dedications offered reading matter; but we weren't reading, we were pondering, as we often do between eleven and twelve o'clock at night, where we could go when we had to leave. Then we joked about the impending fourth of February. The end of the world over beer and gin. I told them about Herr Brauxel, my eccentric employer; and that brought us to Haseloff and his gold teeth, which I called genuine whereas my colleagues refused to believe they were anything more than a myth.

So I called over to the bar: "Hannchen, have you seen Herr Haseloff lately?"

Over her rinsing of glasses Hannchen called back: "Naw. When Goldmouth's in town, he's been going someplace else lately, he's been going to Diener's."

Dear Tulla,

so it's true about the false teeth. Haseloff was and is known as Goldmouth; and the new Jenny, when she was allowed to get up after her bad cold, was given a pair of toe-dancing slippers covered with glittering silvery silk. Dr. Brunies wanted to see her standing on silver points. From then on she danced in Madame Lara's ballet room: Little Swans. The pianist Felsner-Imbs, whose dog bite was healing, poured out Chopin. And I, at Herr Brauxel's request, dismiss Goldmouth and listen to the scraping of silvery exercising ballet slippers: Jenny is holding the bar, embarking on a career.

Dear Tulla,

at that time we were all transferred to different schools: I was sent to the Conradinum; you and Jenny became pupils at the Helene Lange School, which soon had its name changed to the Gudrun School. My father, the master carpenter, had suggested sending you to high school: "The child is bright but unsteady. Why not give it a try?"

From sixth on Dr. Brunies signed our report cards. He taught us German and history. From the start I was conscientious but no grind and nevertheless first in my class: I allowed others to copy from me. Brunies

741

was a lenient teacher. It was easy to divert him from strict insistence on his actual subject: someone only had to bring a piece of mica gneiss to class and ask him to talk about this kind of gneiss or all kinds of gneiss, about his collection of mica gneiss specimens, and instantly Brunies would drop the Cimbri and the Teutons to lecture about his science. But he didn't restrict himself to his hobby; he reeled off his whole litany of minerals: plutonite and pyroxenite; amorphous and crystalline rocks; it is from him that I have the words: multifaceted, tabular, and needle-shaped; the colors: leek-green, air-blue, pea-yellow, silver-white, clove-brown, smoke-gray, iron-black, and dawn-red are from his palette; he taught me tender words: rose quartz, moonstone, lapis lazuli; I adopted little words of reproach: "You tufahead, you hornblender, you nagelfluh!" But even now I couldn't distinguish agate from opal, malachite from labradorite, biotite from muscovite.

When we were unable to distract him with minerals from teaching according to the curriculum, his adoptive daughter Jenny had to fill the bill. The class speaker politely requested permission to speak and asked Dr. Brunies to tell us about Jenny's progress as a ballet dancer. The class, he said, would be pleased. Everyone was eager to know what had happened at the ballet school since the day before yesterday. And just as regularly as the key word "mica gneiss," the key word "Jenny" was able to lead Dr. Brunies astray: he broke off the migrations, let Ostrogoths and Visigoths rot by the Black Sea, and shifted to the new topic. He no longer sat motionless behind his desk: like a dancing bear he hopped about between bookcase and blackboard, seized the sponge and effaced the just outlined itineraries of the Goths. And over a still wet ground he made chalk squeak swiftly: not until a good minute later—he was still writing in the lower lefthand corner—did the wetness begin to dry at the upper right:

"First position, second position, third position, fourth position." That is what was written on the blackboard when Dr. Oswald Brunies began his theoretical instruction in ballet dancing with the words: "As is customary throughout the world, we shall begin with the basic positions and then turn our attention to the bar exercises." The schoolmaster invoked the authority of Arbeau, the first theoretician of the dance. According to Arbeau and Brunies there were five basic positions, all based on the princple of turned-out toes. During my first years in high school the word "turned-out" acquired more weight than the word "spelling." To this day a glance at a ballet dancer's feet tells me whether they are turned out enough; but spelling—with or without an *h,* for instance, or how many *r's* in porridge—is still a puzzle to me.

We uncertain spellers, five or six ballet fans, sat in the gallery of the Stadttheater and looked on critically at the recital that the ballet master had ventured to stage with the help of Madame Lara. The program consisted of *Polovetsian Dances, Sleeping Beauty* with Petipa's ambitious choreography, and the *Valse Triste,* which Madame Lara had rehearsed.

My opinion: "La Petrich has plenty of sparkle in the *adagio,* but she's not turned out enough."

Little Pioch blasphemed: "Man, take a look at la Reinerl: those lopsided pirouettes, and her turnout is just plain embarrassing." Herbert Penzoldt shook his head. "If Irma Leuwelt can't develop a better instep, she won't hold on as first soloist very long, even if her turnout is terrific."

In addition to the word "step" and the word "turnout" the word "sparkle" took on importance. So-and-so "may have plenty of technique, but there's no sparkle." Or a certain superannuated male dancer at the Stadttheater, who had to start in the wings when venturing a *grand jeté,* but then described a magnificent slow arc, received a magnanimous testimonial from the gallery: "With his sparkle, Brake can do what he likes, it's true that he only does three turns but they've got something."

A fourth word that was fashionable during my days in sixth was "balloon." In the *entrechat six de volée,* in the *grand jeté,* in every variety of leap, a dancer either had "balloon" or he didn't have balloon. Which meant either that in leaping he was able to hover weightlessly in air, or that he did not succeed in calling the laws of gravity into question. In fifth I coined the expression: "The new first soloist leaps so slowly a pencil could follow." That is what I still call leaps that are skillfully delayed: leaps that a pencil could follow. If only I could do that: follow leaps with a pencil.

Dear Cousin,

my class teacher, Dr. Brunies, did not content himself with teaching the ABC of ballet as a substitute for a ballad with seventeen stanzas and a regular joggle; he also taught us exactly what stands on tips when a ballet dancer succeeds in remaining faultlessly and effortlessly on her toes for the length of a single pirouette.

One day I don't remember whether we were still on the Ostrogoths or whether the Vandals were already on their way to Rome—he brought Jenny's silver ballet slippers to class with him. At first he acted mysterious, huddled behind his desk, and hid his potato face with all its little creases behind the silvery pair. Then, without showing his hands, he set both slippers on their tips. His old-man's voice intoned a bit of the *Nutcracker Suite*: and between the inkwell and the tin box with his ten-o'clock sandwiches he made the slippers practice all the positions: *petits battements sur le cou-de-pied.*

When the show was over, he whispered, flanked by the silver slippers, that on the one hand the ballet slipper was a still-modern instrument of torture; while on the other hand, a ballet slipper must be regarded as the only kind of shoe in which a young girl can go to heaven in her lifetime.

743

Then he let Jenny's ballet slippers, accompanied by the class monitor, pass down the rows from desk to desk: Jenny's silver slippers meant something to us. Not that we kissed them. We barely caressed them, we gazed upon their frayed silver glitter, tapped their hard unsilvered tips, played absently with silver ribbons, and all of us attributed magical power to the slippers: out of the poor roly-poly they had been able to make something ethereal which, thanks to ballet slippers, was capable, day in day out, of going to heaven on foot. We dreamed sorrowfully of ballet slippers. Boys who suffered from exaggerated love for their mothers saw her enter their room at night dancing on her toes. Those who had fallen in love with a movie poster dreamt of seeing a film with a toe-dancing Lil Dagover. The Catholics among us waited at altars of Our Lady to see whether the Virgin might not deign to exchange the customary sandals for Jenny's ballet slippers.

I alone knew that it wasn't the ballet slippers that had metamorphosed Jenny. I had been a witness: with the help of plain snow Jenny Brunies had been miraculously alleviated, and so had Eddi Amsel—it all came out in the same wash.

Dear Cousin,

our families and all the neighbors were surprised at the obvious change in the child who was not yet eleven. But with an oddly smug wagging of the head as though they had all had a presentiment of Jenny's metamorphosis and prayed for it in common, they expressed their approval of what the snow had brought to pass. Punctually every afternoon at a quarter after four Jenny left the Aktienhaus across the street from us and walked primly, with a small head on a long neck, up Elsenstrasse. She propelled herself entirely with her legs and scarely moved her body. Many neighbors pasted themselves to their streetside windowpanes every day at this hour. As soon as Jenny hove in sight, they said over geraniums and cactuses: "Now Jenny's going to balley."

When my mother missed Jenny's entrance by a minute for housewifely reasons or because she had been gossiping in the hallway, I heard her complaining: "Now I've gone and missed Brunies' Jenny. Well, tomorrow I'll set the alarm clock for a quarter after four, or maybe a little earlier."

The sight of Jenny had the power to move my mother: "What a string bean she's got to be, what a little broomstick." Yet Tulla was just as thin, but thin in a different way. Tulla's wiry figure frightened people. Jenny's figure made them pensive.

Dear Cousin

our walk to school shaped itself into a strange procession. The girls of the Helene-Lange School and I went the same way as far as Neuschottland. At Max-Halbe-Platz I had to turn off to the right, whereas the girls took Bärenweg in the direction of Christ Church. Because Tulla waited in the half-darkness of our entranceway and made me wait until Jenny had left the Aktienhaus, Jenny had a head start: she walked fifteen, sometimes only ten paces ahead of us. All three of us took pains to maintain the interval. When one of Jenny's shoelaces came undone, Tulla had to retie a shoelace. Before I turned off to the right, I stopped behind the advertising pillar on Max-Halbe-Platz and followed the two of them with my eyes: Tulla was still behind Jenny. But one never had the picture of a dogged chase. On the contrary, it became clear that Tulla was running after Jenny without wishing to overtake the girl with the stiff, artificial gait. Sometimes when the morning sun was halfway up and Jenny cast her shadow, long and as wide as a telegraph pole, behind her, Tulla, prolonging Jenny's shadow with her shadow, stepped pace for pace on Jenny's shadow head.

Tulla made it her business to follow in Jenny's wake, and not only on the way to school. Also at a quarter after four, when the neighbors said: "Now Jenny's going to balley," she slipped out of the stair well and dogged her steps.

At first Tulla kept her distance only as far as the streetcar stop and turned back as soon as the car bound for Oliva clanged away. Then she began to spend money for the car, taking my pfennigs. Tulla never borrowed money, she took it. She reached into Mother Pokriefke's kitchen cupboard without asking. She rode in the same trailer as Jenny, but Tulla stood on the rear, Jenny on the front platform. Along the Oliva Castle Park Tulla followed in Jenny's trace at the usual distance, which was slightly diminished only in narrow Rosengasse. And beside the enamel sign "Lara Bock-Fedorova, Ballet School," Tulla stood for a whole hour and no amount of stray cats could distract her attention. After the ballet lesson, she stood with locked-up face, letting the bevy of chattering ballet rats pass with their swinging gym bags. All the girls walked slightly pigeon-toed and carried overly small heads on stem-necks that seemed to need props. For the time it takes to draw a breath Rosengasse smelled, although it was May, of chalk and sour jerseys. Only when Jenny stepped through the garden gate beside the pianist Felsner-Imbs, did Tulla, once the two had a suitable head start, set herself in motion.

What a trio! Always in the lead the stooped Felsner-Imbs in spats and the child with the ash-blond pigtail down her neck; Tulla following at a distance. Once Felsner-Imbs looks around. Jenny doesn't look around. Tulla stands up to the pianist's gaze.

Once Imbs slows down and without stopping plucks a sprig of hawthorn. He puts it in Jenny's hair. Then Tulla likewise breaks off a sprig of hawthorn, but doesn't stick it in her hair, she throws it, after rectifying the interval with rapid steps, into a garden where no hawthorn grows.

Once Felsner-Imbs stops: Jenny stops. Tulla stops. While Jenny and Tulla stand still, the pianist turns about with frightening determination, takes ten paces toward Tulla, raises his right arm, shakes his artist's mane, and points an outstretched finger in the direction of the Castle Park: "Can't you stop molesting us? Haven't you any homework to do? Get along! Go away! We've seen enough of you!" Again and with desperate rashness he turns about, for Tulla neither answers nor obeys the index finger recommending the Castle Park. Imbs is at Jenny's right again. The procession doesn't start moving yet, for while he was sermoning Tulla the pianist's hair has got mussed and has to be brushed. Now it is billowing properly again. Felsner-Imbs takes steps. Jenny takes pigeon steps with feet turned out. Tulla keeps her distance. All three approach the streetcar stop across from the entrance to the Castle Park.

Dear Cousin,

the sight of you exerted a discipline. Passers-by carefully avoided entering the gap between Jenny and Tulla. In busy streets the effect of the two children was amazing. By merely walking in dispersed Indian file they succeeded in creating a moving hole in the crowd.

Tulla never took our Harras with her when she was following Jenny. But I attached myself to them and, as in going to school, left the house with Tulla and walked up Elsenstrasse beside her: the Mozart pigtail ahead of us belonged to Jenny. In June the sun shines with particular beauty between old apartment houses. On the bridge across the Striessbach I detached myself from Tulla and with quick steps moved up to Jenny's left side. It was a cockchafer year. They hung excitedly in the air and scrambled wildly on sidewalks. Some had been stepped on, we stepped on others. The dry remnants of belated cockchafers were always sticking to the soles of our shoes. By Jenny's side—she took pains not to step on any bugs—I offered to carry her gym bag. She handed it to me: air-blue cloth in which the tips of the ballet slippers marked their contours. Behind Kleinhammerpark—clusters of cockchafers buzzed between chestnut trees—I slackened my pace until with Jenny's gym bag I was keeping step beside Tulla. After the railroad underpass, between the empty market booths of the weekly market, on wet pavement and in among the singing brooms of the street sweepers, Tulla asked me for Jenny's bag. Since Jenny never looked around, I allowed Tulla to carry Jenny's bag as far as Haupt-strasse. Outside the moviehouse Jenny was looking at pictures, in which a movie actress had broad cheekbones and was wearing a white doctor's smock. We looked at pictures in another case. Next week: A little actor smirked six times. Shortly before the streetcar stop I took the gym bag back and climbed with Jenny and Jenny's bag into the trailer of the Oliva car. In the course of the ride cockchafers crackled against the windowpanes

746

of the front platform. After the "White Lamb" stop, I, still carrying the bag, left Jenny and visited Tulla on the rear platform but didn't give her the bag. I paid her fare, for at that time I had learned how to earn pocket money, selling firewood from my father's carpenter shop. After the Friedensschluss stop, when I was visiting with Jenny again, I would have paid for her too, but Jenny presented her monthly pass.

Dear Cousin,

before summer vacation was over, it became known that Herr Sterneck, the ballet master of the Stadttheater, had admitted Jenny to the children's ballet. I heard she was going to dance in the Christmas play, that rehearsals had already begun. The play this year, I learned, was called *The Snow Queen* and Jenny, as one could read in the *Vorposten* and the *Neueste Nachrichten* as well, would be playing the part of the Snow Queen, for the Snow Queen was not a speaking part but a dancing part.

In addition to taking the Number 2 to Oliva, Jenny now took the Number 5 to Kohlenmarkt three times a week; there stood the Stadttheater, as Herr Matzerath, who looked down on it from the Stockturm, described it in his book.

I had to cut a lot of firewood and sell it in secret to raise the carfare for Tulla and myself. My father had strictly forbidden this business, but the machinist stood by me. Once—I was late and made my heels clatter on the cobbles of Labesweg—I caught up with the two girls just before Max-Halbe-Platz. Someone had usurped my place: sturdy and diminutive, the grocer's son was marching along, now beside Tulla, now beside Jenny. Occasionally he did what no one else ever dared to do: he thrust himself into the empty gap. Whether he was beside Tulla, beside Jenny, or between them, his tin drum hung down over his belly. And he pounded the drum louder than necessary to provide two slender girls with march time. His mother, so they said, had died recently. Of fish poisoning. A beautiful woman.

Dear Cousin,

it wasn't until late summer that I heard you talk to Jenny. All spring and summer dialogue had been replaced by Jenny's gym bag, passing from hand to hand. Or by cockchafers, avoided by Jenny, stepped on by you. Or in a pinch Felsner-Imbs or I would toss back a word or carry one to and fro.

When Jenny left the Aktienhaus, Tulla was standing in her path and said, more past Jenny than to Jenny: "May I carry your bag with the silver shoes in it?" Without a word Jenny gave Tulla the bag but looked just as far past Tulla as Tulla had spoken past Jenny. Tulla carried the bag. Not that she walked beside Jenny as she carried it; she kept her distance as before, and when we took the Number 2 to Oliva, she stood on the rear platform with Jenny's bag. I was allowed to pay and was superfluous just the same. Not until we were outside the ballet school in Rosengasse did Tulla return the bag with the word "thanks" to Jenny.

So it continued into the fall. I never saw her carry Jenny's school satchel, only her bag. Every afternoon she stood ready in knee socks. Through me she found out when Jenny had rehearsal, when she had ballet school. She stood outside the Aktienhaus, no longer asked, held out her hand without a word, thrust her hand into the loop of the string, carried the bag after Jenny, and observed an unchanging distance.

Jenny possessed several gym bags: leek-green, dawn-red, air-blue, clove-brown, and pea-yellow. She changed colors without method. As Jenny was leaving the ballet school one October afternoon, Tulla, without looking past her, said to Jenny: "I'd like to look at the ballet slippers, to see if they're really silver." Felsner-Imbs was against, but Jenny nodded and pushed the pianist's hand aside with a gentle look. Tulla removed the slippers, which had been neatly packaged with the help of their silk ribbons, from the pea-yellow bag. She didn't open the package, she held it up to eye level on the palms of her hands, let her narrow-set eyes move along the slippers from the heels to the hard tips, tested the slippers for silver content and, though they were worn down and shabby-looking, found them silvery enough. Jenny held the bag open and Tulla let the ballet slippers vanish inside the yellow cloth.

At the end of November, three days before the first night, Jenny spoke to Tulla for the first time. In a gray loden coat she stepped out of the stage entrance of the Stadttheater, and Imbs was not escorting her. Right in front of Tulla she stopped; and while reaching into her leek-green gym bag, she said, without looking very far past Tulla: "Now I know what the iron man in Jäschkental Forest is called."

"His book said something different than what I said."

Jenny had to come out with her knowledge: "His name isn't Kuddenpech, it's Johannes Gutenberg."

"The book said that someday you're going to balley something terrific for thousands of people."

Jenny nodded: "That's very likely, but Johannes Gutenberg invented the printing press in the city of Mainz."

"Sure. That's what I was trying to tell you. He knows everything."

Jenny knows even more: "And he died in fourteen hundred and sixty-eight."

Tulla wanted to know: "Say, what's your weight?"

Jenny gave a precise answer: "Two days ago I weighed seventy-five pounds and two ounces. What's yours?"

Tulla lied: "Seventy-four pounds and eight ounces."

Jenny: "With your shoes on?"

Tulla: "In gym shoes."

Jenny: "Me without shoes, only in my jersey."

Tulla: "Then we're the same weight."

Jenny was delighted: "Very nearly. And I'm not afraid of Gutenberg any more. And here are two tickets for the first night, for Harry and you, if you'd like to come."

Tulla took the tickets. The car arrived. Jenny as usual gets on in front. Tulla gets on in front too. I too of course. At Max-Halbe-Platz Jenny gets out first, then Tulla, I last. Down Labesweg the two of them keep no interval, they walk side by side, looking like friends. I am allowed to carry the green gym bag behind them.

Dear Cousin,

you have to admit that as far as Jenny was concerned that first night was terrific. She turned two neat pirouettes and wasn't afraid to do the *grand pas de basque,* which makes even experienced ballet dancers tremble. She was marvelously turned out. Her "sparkle" made the stage too narrow. When she leapt, she leapt so slowly a pencil could follow, she had "balloon." And it was hardly noticable that Jenny didn't have enough instep.

As the Snow Queen she wore a silver jersey, an icy silvery crown, and a veil that was supposed to symbolize the frost: everything Snow Queen Jenny touched froze fast instantly. With her came the winter. Icicle music announced her entrances. The *corps de ballet,* snowflakes, and three funny-looking snow men obeyed her frost-chattering commands.

I don't remember the plot. But in all three acts there was a talking reindeer. He had to pull a sleigh full of mirrors, and in it, on snow cushions, sat the Snow Queen. The reindeer spoke in verse, ran faster than the wind, and rang silver bells off stage, announcing the Snow Queen's arrival.

This reindeer, as you could read in the program, was played by Walter Matern. It was his first part of any length. Shortly afterward, I heard, he obtained an engagement at the municipal theater in Schwerin. He did the reindeer very nicely and had a benevolent press next day. But the real discovery proclaimed in both papers was Jenny Brunies. One critic expressed the opinion that if Jenny had wanted to, the Snow Queen could have turned the orchestra and both balconies to ice for a thousand years.

My hands were hot from clapping. Tulla didn't clap when the performance was over. She had folded up the program very small and eaten it during the last act. Dr. Brunies, who was sitting between me and the other ballet fans in our class, sucked a whole bag of cough drops empty in the course of the three acts and the intermission after the second act.

After seventeen curtain calls Felsner-Imbs, Dr. Brunies, and I waited outside Jenny's dressing room. Tulla had already gone.

Dear Tulla,

the actor who played the reindeer and who could hit a schlagball into a fly and put a treacherous backspin on a faustball, that actor and athlete who played field hockey and was able to stay up for twelve minutes in a glider, that actor and glider pilot who always had a different lady on his arm—they all looked ailing and afflicted—that actor and lover, who had distributed red leaflets, who systematically read advertising prospectuses, mysteries, and introductions to metaphysics all in a jumble, whose father was a miller with the power of prophecy, whose medieval ancestors had gone by the name of Materna and been terrifying rebels, that well-built, moody, thick-set, tragic, short-haired, unmusical, poetry-loving, lonely, and healthy actor and SA man, that SA squad leader who after an action in January had been promoted platoon leader, that actor, athlete, lover, metaphysician, and platoon leader who on and without occasion could grind his teeth, that is, delve penetratingly and inescapably into last things, that grinder who would have liked to play Othello but had to play the reindeer when Jenny danced the Snow Queen, for one reason or another that SA man, grinder, and actor, even before leaving for the Schwerin Stadttheater where he had been engaged as *jeune premier,* took to drink.

Eddi Amsel, who went into the snow man and left it as Hermann Haseloff, did not become an alcoholic: he began to smoke.

Do you know why he called himself Haseloff and not Thrush, Finch, or Starling? For a whole year, while the two of you, Jenny and you, were keeping your distance, this question plagued me hermeneutically and even in my sleep. Before I suspected that Amsel now had another name, I paid perhaps a real, in any event an imagined visit to the empty villa on Steffensweg, which is conceivably still standing empty for Amsel on the strength of a long lease. Possibly Walter Matern, his faithful—one would think—subtenant, had just left the house—he probably had a show—when I made my way, let us suppose, from the garden across the terrace into Amsel's former studio. I pushed in approximately two windowpanes. In all likelihood I owned a flashlight. What I was looking for I could only find, and actually did find, in the Renaissance desk: important papers. Above me Amsel's scarecrow production of the previous year was still hanging. As I know myself, I wasn't afraid of weird shadows, or only tolerably afraid. The papers were slips of foolscap covered, in big letters, with chains of association and names, as though put there expressly for me. On one scrap of paper Amsel had tried to work himself up a name out of Steppenhuhn (moor hen): Stephun, Steppuh, Steputat, Stepius,

Steppat, Stopoteit, Stappanowski, Stoppka, Steffen. When he dropped Steppenhuhn because it had brought him back so quickly and treacherously to the vicinity of the hastily abandoned Steffensweg, he tried the birds Sperling, Specht, and Sperber (sparrow, woodpecker, sparrow hawk) in combination: Sperla, Sperlinski, Sperluch, Spekun, Sperballa, Spercherling, Spechling. This unsuccessful series was followed by an original development on Sonntag, the Sabbath day: Sonntau, Sonntowski, Sonatowski, Sopalla, Sorau, Sosath, Sowert, Sorge. He abandoned it. He carried the series Rosin, Rossinna, Rosenoth no further. Probably he was looking for a counterpart to the *A* in Amsel when he began with Zoch, wrote Zocholl after Zuchel, squeezed Zuphat from Zuber, and lost interest with the attractive name of Zylinski; for outcries such as "New names and teeth are worth their weight in gold" or "A name is as good as teeth" told me, the at least conceivable spy, how hard a time he had finding a name that was different and yet right. Finally, between two half-developed series deriving from Krisun-Krisin and Krupat-Krupkat, I found a name all by itself and underlined. No series had spawned it. It had sprung from the air and landed on paper. It stood there meaningless and self-evident. Original and yet to be found in every telephone directory. More readily traceable to the circuitous rabbit than to the lunging hawk. The double *f* justified a Russian, or if need be Baltic, twitter. An artist's name. A secret agent's name. An alias. Names cling. Names are worn. Everybody has a name.

I left Eddi Amsel's oak-paneled studio with the name of Haseloff in my heart. I am willing to swear that no one had got wind of it before I came and pushed windowpanes in. All the scarecrows under the ceiling must have had moth balls in their pockets. Had Walter Matern played the housewife and insured Amsel's legacy against decay?

I ought to have taken some papers with me as proof for later.

Dear Tulla,

that actor who even in school and later consistently in his SA sturm was referred to as the "Grinder"—"Where's the Grinder? I want the Grinder to take three men and guard the Feldstrasse car stop, while we comb Mirchauerweg on the other side of the synagogue. I want the Grinder to give three loud grinds as soon as he leaves the town hall"—that enormously busy Grinder was to perfect the art of tooth-grinding very considerably when he took to boozing not off and on but regularly: he barely took time to pour the stuff into a glass; his breakfast began with juniper juice.

Thereupon he was thrown out of the SA. But they didn't bounce him out for drinking—they all tippled—they threw him out because he had stolen when drunk. At first Sturmführer Sawatzki covered him, for

751

the two of them were close friends, they stood shoulder to shoulder at the bar, soaking themselves in the same liquid. It was only when SA Sturm 84 became restive that Sawatzki set up a court of honor. The seven men, all experienced platoon leaders, proved that Matern—only once—had dipped into the Section treasury. Witnesses reported that he had boasted about it when sozzled. The sum spoken of was fifty-three gulden. Matern had spent it buying rounds of gin. Sawatzki argued that the bilge people talked under the influence couldn't be accepted as proof. Matern protested vehemently: weren't they satisfied with him?—"Without me you'd never have caught Brill in Kahlbude."—What was more, he took full responsibility for whatever he had done—"Besides, you all helped me sop it up, every man jack of you. That's not stealing, it's boosting morale."

Then Jochen Sawatzki had to make one of his terse speeches. He is reported to have wept while settling Matern's hash. Intermittently he spoke of friendship: "But I won't put up with any rats in my sturm. None of us wants to throw his best buddy to the dogs. But stealing from your comrades is the worst kind. That's something no Lux or Ivory Soap can wash clean." The story was that he laid his hand on Walter Matern's shoulder and advised him in a voice choked with tears to disappear as quietly as possible. He could go to the Reich and join the SS: "You're through in my sturm, but not with me!"

After that they—nine men in civilian clothing—seem to have paid a visit to the Kleinhammerpark. Undisguised and without loden capes, they occupied the bar. They poured in beer and schnapps and ate blood sausage. They intoned: *"Ich hatt' einen Kameraden. . . ."* Matern was said to have snarled obscene poems and croaked something about the essence of the ground. One of the nine was always in the toilet. But there was no Tulla sitting on a high stool, growing thinner and thinner like a tear-off calendar. No Tulla kept her eye on the toilet door: no beer-hall battle took place.

Dear Tulla,

Walter Matern didn't go to the Reich: the theatrical season continued; *The Snow Queen* was on the program until mid-February; and *The Snow Queen* needed a reindeer. Nor did Matern become a member of the SS, he became what he had forgotten but had been since baptism: a Catholic. In that, alcohol helped him. In May '38—they were doing Billinger's play, *The Giant*; Matern, who played the son of Donata Opferkuch, was fined a number of times for coming to rehearsals drunk—as the theatrical season was drawing to an end, he spent a good deal of his time knocking around the Holm, the waterfront suburb, and Strohdeich. To see him was to hear him. Not only did he perform his usual grinding act on docks and between warehouses, he also quoted with storm and bluster. Only lately, since I have been able to look things up in books, have I begun to unscramble the anthology of quotations that Matern had cooked up: he mixed liturgical texts, the phenomenology of a stockingcap, and abstrusely secular lyrical poetry into a stew seasoned with the cheapest gin. The poetry especially—I sometimes chased after him—formed marbles that stuck in my ears: expressionist poems. Lemurs were sitting on a raft. There was talk of rubble and bacchanalias. How I, a boy plagued by curiosity, puzzled my head over the word "gillyflower-wave." Matern writes finis. The longshoremen, good-natured when they didn't have to unload plywood with the wind in their beam, listened: ". . . it is late." The stevedores nodded. "O soul, rotted through and through . . ." They patted him on the shoulder and he thanked them: "What brotherly joy round Cain and Abel, for whom God journeyed through the clouds—causal-genetic, *haïssable*: the late I."

At that time I only dimly suspected who was meant by Cain and Abel. I padded along behind him, as he reeled—his mouth full of morgue, thrownness, and *Dies irae, dies illa*—between the loading cranes in Strohdeich. And as he sat there with the Klawitter shipyard behind him and the breath of the Mottlau upon him, the Virgin Mary appeared to him.

He is sitting on a bollard and has already sent me home several times. But I don't want any supper. To his bollard and to the others that no one is sitting on, a medium-sized Swedish freighter is made fast. It's a night beneath hasty clouds, for the freighter is sleeping fitfully and the Mottlau is pulling and pushing. All the hawsers by which the Swede is clinging to the bollards are grinding. But he wants to drown them out. He has already spat out the late I, all his thrownness, and the Sequence for the Dead, now he starts competing with the hawsers. In windbreaker and knickers he sticks fast to his bollard, he grinds, before attacking the bottle, goes on grinding the same song as soon as the bottle neck is released, and keeps on blunting his teeth. At the far end of Strohdeich he sits: by Polish Hook, at the confluence of the Mottlau and the Dead Vistula. A good place for tooth grinding. The ferry from Milchpeter had brought him, me, and the longshoremen across. He had started up with his teeth on the ferry, no, already on Fuchswall and Jakobswall, after the gasworks, but it's only on the bollard that he's started drinking and grinding himself into a state: *"Tuba mirum spargens sonum . . ."* The low-lying Swede helps. The Mottlau pushes, pulls, and mixes with the sluggish waters of the Dead Vistula. The shipyards help, they're working the night shift: Klawitter behind him; the shipyard on the other side of Milchpeter; farther off the Schichau shipyard and the railroad car factory. The clouds devouring each other help him too. And I help, because he needs an audience.

That has always been my forte: to pad along behind, to be curious, to listen.

Now that the riveters fall silent and briefly, in all the shipyards, at once, hold their breath, there's nothing left but Matern's teeth and the sullen Swede, until the wind blows around from Kielgraben: there, on Englischer Damm, cattle are being driven into the slaughterhouse. The Germania bread factory is quiet, though all three floors are lit up. Matern has finished his bottle. The Swede slips away. I wide awake in a freight-car shed. With its hangars, grain elevators, ramps, and cranes Strohdeich stretches out as far as Bay Horse Bastion, where the ferryboat with lights on is chugging across to the Brabank pier. His grinding has dwindled to leftovers and he has stopped listening to hawsers. What can he hear when he hears no riveters? Hoarse cattle and sensitive hogs? Does he hear angels? *Liber scriptus proferetur.* Is he reading masthead lights, port and starboard lights line for line? Is he plotting nihilation or writing finis: last rose's dying, raft of lemurs, boulders of the east, barcaroles, Hades rises, morgue, Inca tablets, castle of the moon? This last of course is still at large, still sharp after a second shaving. Over the lead foundry and the pumping station it is licking at the municipal salt elevator, pissing sideways along silhouetted backdrop—Altstadt, Pfefferstadt, Jungstadt, that is to say, the churches of St. John, St. Catherine, St. Bartholomew, St. Mary; until with moon-inflated shift She appears. She must have come on the ferry from Brabank. From lamppost to lamppost She saunters up Strohdeich, disappears behind bird-necked cranes on the waterfront, hovers between shunting tracks, blossoms up again under a street lamp; and closer and closer he grinds her over to his bollard: "Hail, Mary!" But as she stands billowing before him, sheltering a little lamp under her shift, he doesn't get up but sticks fast and sulks: "Say, you. What should I do? Thou'rt weary and footsore from seeking me . . . So see here, Mary: do you know where he's taken himself? Hail, Mary, O.K., but now tell me, could I help it, it was that cynical streak I couldn't stomach: nothing was sacred to him. That's why. Actually we only wanted to teach him a little lesson: *Confutatis maledictis . . .* and now he's gone, he's left me his rags. I've mothproofed them, can you imagine, mothproofed, the whole damn lot! Come sit down, Mary. The thing with the money out of the cash drawer, O.K., I did it, but what about him, where is he? Has he run off to Sweden? Or to Switzerland where his dough is stashed away? Or to Paris?—that's where he belongs. Or Holland? Or overseas? Come on, sit down for God's sake. Bathed in tears, the day will dawn . . . Even as a kid—good Lord, was he fat!—he was always overdoing it: once he wanted a skull from under the Church of the Trinity. To him everything was funny, and always Weininger, that's why we. Where is he? I've got to. Tell me. Blessed art Thou among . . . But only if you. The Germania bread factory is working the night shift. See? Who's going to eat all that bread? Tell me. That's not riveters, it's. Sit down. Where?"

But the illuminated shift doesn't want to sit down. Standing, two hands' breadths above the pavement, She has prepared a little piece: "*Dona eis requiem:* things will be better soon. You will live in the true faith and be an actor in Schwerin. But before you depart for Schwerin, a dog will stand in your path. Fear not."

He on the bollard wants details: "A black dog?"

She with "balloon" in her shift: "A hound of hell."

He nailed to the bollard: "Does he belong to a carpenter?"

She enlightens him: "How can the dog belong to a carpenter when he is dedicated to hell and trained to serve Satan?"

He remembers: "Eddi called him Pluto, but only as a joke."

She with raised index finger: "He will stand in your path."

He tries to worm out of it: "Send him the distemper."

She counsels him: "Poison is obtainable in every drugstore."

He tries to blackmail her: "But first you've got to tell me where Eddi . . ."

Her last word: "Amen!"

I in the freight-car shed know more than both of them put together: he smokes cigarettes and has an entirely different name.

Dear Tulla,

on her way home the Virgin Mary probably took the ferry to Milchpeter beside the gasworks; and Walter Matern crossed with me at Brabank. One thing is certain, that he became even more Catholic than before: he even drank cheap vermouth, because schnapps and gin didn't do the trick any more. His teeth on edge from sugared sweet wine, he may have ground the Virgin to within speaking distance two or three times more: on the Holm, between the lumberyards on either side of Breitenbach Bridge or, as usual, at Strohdeich. It's doubtful whether they discussed anything new. He wanted to know where someone had taken himself to; she no doubt sicked him on the dog: "Formerly people used crow's eyes, but nowadays Grönke, the pharmacist, has a pharmacy on Neuer Markt that carries everything, corrosive, narcotic, and septic poisons. For instance:

As_2O_3—a white vitreous powder extracted from ores, a simple arsenic salt, in a word, rat poison, but if you don't stint, it can do for a dog too."

So it happened that Walter Matern, after long absence, reappeared in our apartment house. Of course he didn't stagger straight into our yard and start caterwauling up at the eaves; he knocked at Felsner-Imbs' door and plumped himself down on the decrepit divan. The pianist brewed tea and kept his patience when Matern began to question him: "Where is he? Man, don't be like that. You know where he is. He can't just have evaporated. If anybody knows, it's you. So speak up!"

Behind windows left ajar I wasn't sure whether the pianist knew any more than I did. Matern threatened. From the divan he worked with his teeth and Imbs clutched a pile of music. Matern reeled in the electric-green music room. Once he reached into the goldfish bowl and threw a handful of water at the flowered wallpaper, unaware that he had thrown only water. But he hit the porcelain ballerina when he tried to smash the big hourglass with his shag pipe. The horizontal arabesque leg fell, after a clean break, on soft sheet music. Matern apologized and promised to pay for the damage, but Imbs mended the figure himself with a glue called "Omnistick." Walter Matern wanted to help but the pianist stood there stooped over and unapproachable. He poured more tea and gave Matern photographs to look at: in a stiff tutu stood Jenny doing an arabesque, like the porcelain ballerina except that her leg was all in one piece. Apparently Matern saw more than the picture, for he muttered things that didn't stand on their toes in silver slippers. The usual questions: "Where? He can't just have. Clears out without even leaving a message. Pushes off without. I've asked all over, even in Tischlergasse and in Schiewenhorst. Hedwig Lau has married in the meantime and broken off all relations with him, she says, broken off . . ."

Walter Matern pushed the music-room window wide open, slipped over the sill, and shoved me into the lilac bushes. By the time I had scrambled to my feet, he was approaching the ravaged semicircle indicating the reach of the chain that attached Harras to the lumber shed in the daytime.

Harras was still keen and black. Only above the eyes he had two little ice-gray islands. And the lips were no longer quite tight. The moment Walter Matern left the lilac garden, Harras was out of his kennel, straining his chain as far as the semicircle. Matern ventured to within two or three feet. Harras panted and Matern looked for a word. But the buzz saw interfered, or the lathe. And to our black shepherd Walter Matern, when he had found the word between buzz saw and lathe, when he had coughed it up and chewed it over, when it lay indigestible between his teeth, said "Nazi!"; to our Harras he said: "Nazi!"

Dear Tulla,

these visits went on for a week or more. Matern brought the word with him; and Harras stood straining forward, for to him was attached the lumber shed where we lodged: you and I and sometimes Jenny, who didn't take up much room. We knelt narrow-eyed behind peepholes. Outside, Matern went down on his knees and assumed the attitude of the dog. Human cranium versus dog's skull, with a child's head's worth of air in between. On one side growling: rising, falling, yet restrained; on the other side a grinding more of sea sand than of gravel, and then in rapid fire the word: "Nazi Nazi Nazi Nazi!"

Lucky that no one, except for us in the shed, heard the snapped word. Yet the windows on the court were chock-full. "The actor's here again," said the neighbors from window to window when Walter Matern came calling on our dog Harras. August Pokriefke ought to have turned him out of his yard, but the machinist said this was none of his business.

And so my father had to cross the yard. He kept one hand in his pocket, and I am sure he was holding a chisel warm. He stopped behind Matern and laid his free hand momentously on Matern's shoulder. In a loud voice, meant to be heard by all the occupied windows of the apartment house and by the journeymen in the second-floor windows of the shop, he said: "Leave the dog alone. Right away. And get out of here. You're drunk. You ought to be ashamed of yourself."

Matern, whom my father had raised to his feet with his carpenter's grip, couldn't resist the temptation to look him menacingly, ominously in the eye in the worst ham actor tradition. My father had very blue, firmly rounded eyes, which blunted Matern's stare. "It won't do you any good to make eyes. There's the door." But Matern chose the route through the lilac garden to Felsner-Imbs' music room.

And once, when Matern did not leave our yard through the pianist's apartment, he said to my father from the doorway of the yard: "Your dog has distemper, hadn't you noticed?" My father with the chisel in his pocket: "Let me worry about that. And the dog hasn't got distemper, but you're stewed and you'd better not show your face around here any more."

The journeymen made menacing noises behind him and brandished drills and spirit levels. Nevertheless my father sent for the veterinary: Harras didn't have distemper. No mucous discharge from his eyes or nose, no drowsy look, no vomiting after feeding. Even so, brewer's yeast was spooned into him: "You never can tell."

Dear Tulla,

then the theatrical season of 1937 to 1938 was over, and Jenny told us: "Now he's in the theater in Schwerin." He didn't stay in Schwerin long but went, this too we heard from Jenny, to Düsseldorf on the Rhine. But because he had been fired without notice in Schwerin, he was unable to find work in any other theater, either in Düsseldorf or elsewhere. "Those things get around," said Jenny. As one might have expected, the next letter informed us that he was working on the radio, lending his voice to children's programs; the letter said he had become engaged but it wouldn't last long; that he still didn't know where Eddi Amsel was keeping himself, but he was sure he must be; that liquor was plaguing him less, he had gone back to sports: field hockey and even faustball, as in happier days; that he had a number of friends, all of them ex-Communists, who like him had their bellies full; but that Catholicism was a lot of shit, he'd got to know a few priests in Neuss and Maria Laach, they were revolting specimens; there'd probably be war soon; and Walter Matern wanted to know whether the beastly black dog was still alive—but Felsner-Imbs didn't answer.

Dear Tulla,

then Matern in person took the train and turned up in Langfuhr to see whether our Harras was still alive. As if it were the most natural thing in the world, as if months hadn't passed since his last visit, he was suddenly standing in our yard, dressed fit to kill: English cloth, red carnation in buttonhole, short-haired, and stewed to the gills. He had left all caution in the train or somewhere else, he no longer went down on his knees in front of Harras, no longer hissed and ground the word, but bellowed it into the yard. He didn't mean only our Harras; the neighbors in the windows, our journeymen, the machinist, and my father were all sick. The word. The neighbors all vanished into their two-and-a-half-room apartments. The journeymen fastened hinges. The machinist unleashed the buzz saw. My father manned the lathe. Nobody wanted to have heard that. August Pokriefke stirred carpenter's glue.

For to our Harras who alone remained available Walter Matern was saying: "You black Catholic hog!" Hymnally he spewed up his guts: "You Catholic Nazi hog! I'm going to grind you up into dog-balls. Dominican! Christian dog! I'm twenty-two dog years old, and I still haven't done anything to earn immortality . . . just wait!"

Felsner-Imbs took the raving young man, who was breathless from roaring against lathe and buzz saw, by the sleeve and led him into the music room, where he served him tea.

In many apartments, on the second floor of our shop and in the machine shop, denunciations to the police were formulated; but no one turned him in.

Dear Tulla,

from May '39 to June 7, '39, Walter Matern was held for questioning in the cellar of police headquarters in Düsseldorf.

This was no theater gossip, passed on to us by Jenny; I sleuthed it out from the records.

For two weeks he was in the Marien Hospital in Düsseldorf, because they had cracked a few of his ribs in the cellar of police headquarters. For a long while he had to wear a bandage and wasn't allowed to laugh, which wasn't very hard on him. No teeth were knocked out.

I had no need to sleuth out these details, they were written black on white—though without mention of the police cellar—on a picture postcard, the picture side of which disclosed the Church of St. Lambert in Düsseldorf. The addressee was not the pianist Felsner-Imbs but Dr. Oswald Brunies.

Who had sent Walter Matern to the police cellar? The director of the Schwerin Stadttheater had not reported him. He had not been dismissed for political unreliability; it was because of continuous drunkenness that he was no longer allowed to act in Schwerin. This information didn't fall in my lap, it had to be painstakingly sleuthed out.

But why did Walter Matern remain in custody for only five weeks? Why only a few ribs and no teeth? He would not have been released from the police cellar if he had not volunteered for the Army: his Free City of Danzig passport saved him. In civilian clothes but with an induction order over still painful ribs he was sent to his home city. There he reported to the Langfuhr-Hochstriess police barracks. Until they were permitted to don uniforms, Walter Matern and several hundred civilians from the Reich had to spoon up one-dish meals for a good eight weeks: the war wasn't quite ripe.

Dear Tulla,

in August 1939—the two battleships had already anchored off the Westerplatte; in our carpentry shop finished parts for army barracks and double- and triple-decker beds were being hammered together—on the twenty-seventh of August our Harras breathed his last.

Somebody poisoned him; for Harras did not have distemper. Walter Matern, who had said: "The dog has distemper," gave him As_2O_3: rat poison.

Dear Tulla,

you and I could have testified against him.

It was a Saturday night: we're sitting in the lumber shed, in your hiding place. How did you arrange, what with the constant coming and going of logs, planks, and plywood, to have your nest spared?

Probably August Pokriefke knows his daughter's hiding place. When shipments of lumber come in, he alone sits in the shed, directs the piling of the planks, and sees to it that Tulla's hiding place is not buried. No one, not even he, dares to touch the furnishings of her hide-out. No one puts on her wood-shaving wigs, lies in her wood-shaving bed, and covers himself with plaited shavings.

After supper we removed to the shed. Actually we wanted to take

Jenny with us, but Jenny was tired; and we understand: after an afternoon of ballet practice and rehearsal, she has to go to bed early, for she has a rehearsal even on Sunday: they are working up *The Bartered Bride,* with all those Bohemian dances.

So the two of us are huddled in the dark, playing silence. Tulla wins four times. Outside, August Pokriefke lets Harras off his chain. For a long while he scratches at the shed walls, whimpers softly, and wants to come in with us: but we want to be alone. Tulla lights a candle and puts on one of her wood-shaving wigs. Her hands around the flame are parchment. She sits behind the candle tailor fashion and moves her head with its dangling fringe of wood shavings over the flame. Several times I say "Cut it out, Tulla!" so she can continue her little tinder-dry game. Once a crisp shaving crackles, but no lumber shed goes up sky-high in flames, contributing an item to the local papers: Langfuhr carpenter shop a total loss.

Now Tulla removes the wig with both hands and I have to lie down in the wood-shaving bed. With the plaited blanket—extra-long shavings that journeyman carpenter Wischnewski planes from long planks—she covers me up. I am the patient and have to feel sick. Actually I'm too old for this game. But Tulla likes to be a doctor and sometimes I get fun out of being sick. I speak in a hoarse voice: "Doctor, I feel sick."

"I don't believe you."

"Oh yes, Doctor, all over."

"All over where?"

"All over, Doctor, all over."

"Maybe it's the spleen this time."

"The spleen, the heart, and the kidneys."

Tulla with her hand under the wood-shaving blanket: "Then you've got diabetes."

Now I have to say: "And I've got hose fever too."

She pinches my watering can. "Is that it? Is that where it hurts?"

In accordance with the rules and because it really hurts, I let out a scream. Now we play the game again, the other way around. Tulla crawls under the wood shavings and I, because she is sick, have to take her temperature with my little finger in her aperture. That too comes to an end. Twice we play stare and don't blink. Tulla wins again. Then, because we can't think of any other game, we play silence again. Once Tulla wins, and then I win, because in the middle of her silence Tulla explodes: out of her frozen face lit up from below, she hisses through ten bright-red paper fingers: "Somebody's crawling on the roof, d'you hear?"

She blows out the candle. I hear the crackling of the tar paper on the roof of the lumber shed. Somebody, possibly with rubber soles, is taking steps, pausing in between. Harras has started to growl. The rubber soles follow the tar paper to the end of the roof. We, Tulla in the lead, creep over the logs in the same direction. He's standing right over the dog kennel. Under him there's barely room for us between roof and piled logs. He's sitting down, with his legs dangling over the gutter. Harras keeps growling, always in the same low register. We peer through the ventilation slit between the roof and the edge of the shed. Tulla's little hand could slip through the slit if she liked and pinch him in either leg. Now he whispers: "Good boy, Harras, good boy." We can't see whoever is whispering "Good boy, Harras" and "Mum's the word," all we can see is his pants; but I bet the shadow he casts on the yard with the half-moon behind him is Walter Matern's shadow.

And what Matern throws into the yard is meat. I breathe in Tulla's ear: "It's poisoned for sure." But Tulla doesn't stir. Now Harras is nuzzling the chunk of meat while Matern on the roof encourages him: "Go on, eat. Eat, will you?" Harras tugs at the chunk of meat, tosses it up in the air. He doesn't feel like eating, he wants to play, although he's an old dog: thirteen dog years and a few months.

Then Tulla says, not even quietly, but with just about her usual voice: "Harras!" through the slit between the roof and the wall of the shed: "Take it, Harras, take it." And our Harras first tilts his head, then devours the meat, scrap by scrap.

Above us rubber soles squeak hastily over the tar paper: heading for adjoining yards. I bet it's him. Today I know it was he.

Dear Tulla,

we let ourselves into the house with your key. Harras was still busy with the meat and didn't come bounding after us, as he usually did. In the stair well I brushed the sawdust and shavings off my clothes and asked you urgently: "Why did you let Harras eat it, why?"

You were up the stairs before me: "Well, he wouldn't have done it for him, would he?"

I, ten steps behind you: "And suppose there was poison in it?"

You, a landing higher: "Well, then he'll kick off."

I over the rising banister: "But why?"

"Because!" Tulla laughed through her nose and was gone.

Dear Tulla,

next morning—I slept heartlessly without any particular dreams—my father woke me. He was really crying and he said: "Our good Harras is dead." And I was able to cry and dressed quickly. The vet came and wrote out a certificate: "The dog would certainly have lived another three years. Too bad."

My mother said it: "I wonder if it wasn't the actor, that used to be a Communist and that's always hollering in the yard." Of course she was crying too. Somebody suspected Felsner-Imbs.

Harras was buried in the police cemetery for dogs between Pelonken and Brennau, and his grave received regular visits. My father filed a complaint. He mentioned Walter Matern and the pianist. Imbs was questioned, but he had spent the evening playing chess with Dr. Brunies, looking at mica stones and drinking two bottles of Moselle. The proceedings against Walter Matern, who also had an alibi handy, bogged down: two days later the war began in Danzig, in Langfuhr, and in other localities as well. Walter Matern marched into Poland.

Not you, Tulla,

but I almost got to see the Führer. He announced his coming with crashing and pounding. On the first of September cannon were firing in just about every direction. Two of the carpenters took me up on the roof of our house. They had borrowed a spyglass from Semrau the optician: the war looked phony and disappointing. All I could ever see was shells being fired—Oliva Forest sent up little cottony clouds—I never saw them landing. Only when the dive bombers began to do acrobatics over Neufahrwasser, showing the spyglass luxuriant smoke trails where the Westerplatte must have been, did I believe that they weren't playing. But as soon as I peered down from the roof into Elsenstrasse and on all ten fingers counted out housewives shopping and loafing kids and cats in the sunshine, I wasn't so sure: Maybe they're only playing and school will start again tomorrow.

But the noise was tremendous. The dive bombers, the twelve knock-kneed howlers, would certainly have made our Harras bark himself hoarse; but our Harras was dead. Not of distemper; someone poisoned our shepherd with poisoned meat. My father wept manly tears and let his cigar dangle cold in is face. Forlorn he stood at his drawing table with inactive carpenter's pencil, and the German troops marching into town couldn't comfort him. Even the news on the radio that Dirschau, Konitz, and Tuchel—all Koshnava—were in German hands, brought him no consolation, although his wife and the Pokriefkes, all born Koshnavians, trumpeted the news across the yard: "Now they've occupied Petzin, and they've taken Schlangenthin, and Lichtnau and Granau. Did you hear that, Friedrich, they marched into Osterwick a few hours ago."

True consolation came to the carpenter only on September 3, in the form of a motorcyclist in uniform. The courier's letter announced that the Füher and Chancellor was sojouring in the liberated city of Danzig and wished to make the acquaintance of deserving citizens, one of these being Friedrich Liebenau, whose shepherd dog Harras had sired the Führer's shepherd dog Prinz. The shepherd dog Prinz was also sojourning in the city. Master carpenter Liebenau was requested to be at the Zoppot casino at such and such a time and report to SS Sturmbannführer So-and-so, the duty adjutant. It would not be necessary to bring the dog Harras, but a member of the family, preferably a child, would be admitted. Required: identification papers. Attire: uniform or well-pressed street clothes.

My father selected his Sunday suit. I, the requisite member of the family, hadn't been wearing anything but my Hitler Cub uniform for the last three days anyway, because something was always going on. My mother brushed my hair until my scalp tingled. Not a button was missing from father or son. When we left the house, the entrance was cramped with neighbors. Only Tulla was absent: she was collecting shell fragments in Neufahrwasser. But outside, every window was occupied with curiosity and admiration. Across the street in the Aktienhaus, a window was open in the Brunies apartment: wispy Jenny was waving to me excitedly; but Dr. Brunies didn't show himself. I long missed his potato face: when we were seated in the open official car behind the uniformed driver, when Elsenstrasse ended, when we had Marienstrasse, Kleinhammerpark, and Kastanienweg behind us, when we were speeding first down Haupstrasse, then down Zoppoter Chaussee in the direction of Zoppot, I still missed the face with the thousand wrinkles.

Not counting the bus, this was my first real ride in an automobile. During the ride my father leaned over and shouted in my ear: "This is a big moment in your life. Open your eyes wide, take it all in, so you can tell about it later on."

I opened my eyes so wide that the wind made them water; and even now as, quite in keeping with my father's, not to mention Herr Brauxel's wishes, I relate what I took in through wide-open eyes and stored up in my memory, my eyes grow strained and moist: at the time I feared that I might look upon the Führer through eyes blinded by tears, and today I have to make an effort to prevent the tears from blurring anything which was then angular, uniformed, beflagged, sunlit, world-shatteringly important, sweat-drenched, and real.

The Zoppot casino and Grand Hotel made us very small as we climbed out of the official car. The casino gardens were cordoned off; the—the population! —were standing outside and were already hoarse. There were two sentries on the broad driveway leading to the entrance. The driver had to stop three times and wave a pass. I have forgotten to speak of the flags in the street. Even in our neighborhood, on Elsenstrasse, there were swastika flags of varying lengths. Poor or thrifty people, who couldn't or wouldn't afford a proper flag, had stuck little paper pennants in their flowerpots. One flagpole was empty, cast doubt upon all the occupied flagpoles, and belonged to Dr. Brunies. But in Zoppot, I believe, the whole population had put out flags; or at least so it seemed. From the round window in the gable of the Grand Hotel a flagpole grew at

763

right angles to the façade. The swastika flag hung down over four stories stopping above the main entrance. The flag looked very new and scarcely stirred, for that side of the hotel was sheltered from the wind. If I had had a monkey on my shoulder, the monkey could have climbed up the flag four stories high, until the flag had to give up.

In the lobby of the hotel, a giant in uniform under visor cap that was much too small and squashed down on one side, took us in charge. Across a carpet that made me weak in the knees he led us diagonally through the lobby. Bustle: figures came, went, relieved one another, announced one another, delivered, took reception: oodles of victories, numbers of prisoners with lots of zeroes. A stairway led down into the cellar. An iron door opened for us on the right: in the air-raid shelter of the Grand Hotel several deserving citizens were already waiting. We were searched for weapons. I was allowed, after a telephonic inquiry, to keep my Hitler Cub knife. My father had to deposit the pretty little penknife with which he cut off the tips of his cigars. All the deserving citizens, among them Herr Leeb of Ohra, to whom the meanwhile deceased Thekla of Schüddelkau had belonged—Thekla and Harras parented Prinz—well, then, my father, Herr Leeb, a few gentlemen with gold Party badges, four of five young whippersnappers in uniform but older than I, we all stood in silence, steeling ourselves. Several times the telephone rang. "Yes, sir. Yes, Sturmführer, I'll take care of it." Some ten minutes after my father had given up his penknife, it was returned to him. With an "All listen please!" the giant and duty adjutant began his explanation: "The Führer cannot receive anyone at the moment. Great tasks, decisive tasks require his attention. At such a time we can only stand back in silence, for on every front weapons are speaking for us all, and that means you and you and you."

Immediately and with a conspicuously practiced hand, he began to distribute postcard-size photographs of the Führer. The Führer's personal signature made them valuable. We already had one such signed postcard; but the second postcard, which we glassed and framed like the first, showed a more earnest Führer: he was wearing field gray and not any Upper Bavarian peasant jacket.

Half relieved, half disappointed, the deserving citizens were crowding through the door of the air-raid shelter, when my father addressed the duty adjutant. I admired his spunk; but he was known for that: in the Carpenters' Guild and in the Chamber of Commerce. He held out the ancient letter from the gauleiter's office, written in the days when Harras was still eager to mate, gave the adjutant a brief and factual account of the events leading up to and following the letter, reeled off Harras' pedigree—Perkun, Senta, Pluto, Harras, Prinz. The adjutant showed interest. My father concluded: "Since the shepherd dog Prinz is now in Zoppot, I request permission to see him." Permission was granted; and

Herr Leeb, who had been standing diffidently to one side, was also given permission. In the lobby the duty adjutant motioned to another colossus in uniform and gave him instructions. The second giant had the face of a mountain climber and said to us: "Follow me." We followed. We crossed a room in which twelve typewriters were rattling and even more telephones were being used. A corridor showed no sign of ending. Doors opened. People streaming in our direction. Folders under arms. We stepped aside. Herr Leeb greeted everyone. In a vestibule six oval-backed chairs stood around a heavy oak table. The carpenter's eyes appraised the furniture. Veneers and inlays. Three walls crowded with heavily framed assortments of fruit, hunt still lifes, peasant scenes—and the fourth wall is glazed and sky-bright. We see the Grand Hotel winter garden: insane incredible forbidden dangerous plants: they must be fragrant, but we smell nothing through the glass.

And in the middle of the winter garden, drowsy perhaps from the emanations of the plants, sits a man in uniform, a little man compared to our giant. At his feet a full-grown shepherd is playing with a medium-sized flowerpot. The plant, something pale green and fibrous, is lying off to one side with its roots and compact soil. The shepherd rolls the flowerpot. We seem to hear the rolling. The giant beside us taps on the glass wall with his knuckles. Instantly the dog stands alert. The guard turns his head without moving his body, grins like an old friend, stands up, apparently meaning to come over to us, then sits down again. The outer glass front of the winter garden offers an expensive view: the terrace of the casino park, the big fountain—turned off—the pier, broad at the beginning, tapering down, fatter again at the end: many flags of the same kind, but no people except for the sentries. The Baltic can't make up its mind: now green, now gray, it tries in vain to glitter blue. But the dog is black. He stands on four legs, his head cocked. The spit and image of our Harras when he was young.

"Like our Harras," says my father.

I say: "The spittin' image of our Harras."

Herr Leeb remarks: "But he could have got his long croup from my Thekla."

My father and I: "Harras had that too: a long, gently sloping croup."

Herr Leeb admiringly: "How tight and dry the lips are —like my Thekla."

Father and son: "Our Harras was tight too. And the toes. And the way he holds his ears. The spittin' image."

Herr Leeb sees only his Thekla: "I guess—of course I can be mistaken—that the Führer's dog's tail is the same length as Thekla's was."

I put in for my father: "And I'm willing to bet the Führer's dog measures sixty-four centimeters to the withers, exactly like our Harras."

My father knocks on the pane. The Führer's dog barks briefly; Harras would have given tongue in exactly the same way.

My father inquires through the pane: "Excuse me. Could you tell us how many centimeters Prinz measures to the withers?" "Centimeters?" "Yes, to the withers."

The man in the winter garden has no objection to telling us the Führer's dog's height to the withers: six times he shows ten fingers, once his right hand shows only four fingers. My father gives Herr Leeb a good-natured tap on the shoulder: "He's a male after all. They come four or five centimeters taller."

All three of us agree about the coat of the dog in the winter garden: short-haired, every hair straight, every hair smooth, harsh, and black.

My father and I: "Like our Harras."

Herr Leeb undaunted: "Like my Thekla."

Our giant in uniform says: "Come off it, don't make such a much. Shepherds all look pretty much the same. The Führer has a whole kennel full of them in the mountains. This trip he took this one. Sometimes he takes different ones, it all depends."

My father wants to give him a lecture about our Harras and his ancestry, but the giant motions him to desist and angles his watch arm.

The Führer's dog is playing with the empty flowerpot again as I, in leaving, venture to tap on the pane: he doesn't even raise his head. And the man in the winter garden prefers to look at the Baltic.

Our withdrawal over soft carpets, past fruit still lifes, peasant scenes, hunt still lifes: pointers licking at dead rabbits and wild boars, no shepherd dogs have been painted. My father caresses furniture. The room full of typewriters and telephones. A dense crowd in the lobby. My father takes me by the hand. Actually he ought to take Herr Leeb's hand too: he's always being jostled. Motorcyclists with dust-gray coats and helmets stagger in among the correct uniforms. Dispatch riders with victory dispatches in their bags. Has Modlin fallen yet? The dispatch riders hand in their bags and drop into wide armchairs. Officers give them a light and stop to chat. Our giant pushes us through the entrance under the four-story flag. I still have no monkey on my shoulder that wants to climb up. We are escorted through all the roadblocks, then dismissed. The population behind the fence wants to know if we've seen the Führer. My father shakes his head: "No, folks, not the Führer, but we've seen his dog, and let me tell you, he's black, just like our Harras."

Dear Cousin Tulla,

no official car carried us back to Langfuhr. My father, Herr Leeb, and I took the suburban railway. We got out first. Herr Leeb stayed in the train and promised to come and see us. I felt humiliated at our having to pass through Elsenstrasse on foot. All the same it had been a wonderful day, and the essay I had, at Father's suggestion, to write the day after our visit to Zoppot and submit to Dr. Brunies, was entitled: "My most wonderful day."

While returning my essay with his corrections, Dr. Brunies looked down from his desk and said: "Very well observed, excellently, in fact. There are, indeed, a number of hunt still lifes, fruit still lifes, and hearty peasant scenes hanging in the Grand Hotel, mostly Dutch masters of the seventeenth century."

I was not allowed to read my essay aloud. Dr. Brunies dwelt at some length on the hunt still lifes and peasant scenes, spoke about genre painting and Adriaen Brouwer, his favorite painter. Then he came back to the Grand Hotel and casino—"The Red Room is especially fine and festive. And in that Red Room Jenny is going to dance." He whispered mysteriously: "As soon as the momentarily reigning warrior caste leaves, as soon they have taken their clanking sabers and shouts of victory to other watering places, the director of the casino, in collaboration with the manager of the Stadttheater, is going to stage an unpretentious but distinguished ballet program."

"Can we come and see it?" asked forty pupils.

"It's to be a charity benefit. The proceeds are going to the Winter Aid." Brunies shared our dismay that Jenny would be dancing for a restricted audience: "She is going to make two appearances. She is actually going to do the famous *Pas de Quatre;* in a simplified version for children, to be sure, but even so."

I returned to my desk with my exercise book. "My most wonderful day" was far behind me.

Neither Tulla nor I

saw Jenny balley. But she must have been good, for someone from Berlin wished to engage her immediately. The performance took place shortly before Christmas. The audience consisted of the usual Party bigwigs, but also of scientists, artists, high Navy and Air Force officers, even diplomats. Brunies told us that immediately after the applause had died down at the end, a fashionably dressed gentleman had appeared, had kissed Jenny on both cheeks, and asked to take her away with him. Brunies, he had shown his card and identified himself as the first ballet master of the German Ballet, the former Strength-through-Joy Ballet.

But Dr. Brunies had declined and had put the ballet master off until some later date: Jenny was still an immature child. She still needed a few more years in her familiar environment: school and home, the good old Stadttheater, Madame Lara.

I went up to Dr. Oswald Brunies in the playground. As usual he is sucking his cough drops, left and right, left and right.

"Dr. Brunies," I ask, "What was that ballet master's name?"

"He didn't tell me, my boy."

"But didn't you say he showed you some kind of a visiting card?"

Dr. Brunies claps his hands. "Right you are, a visiting card. But what on earth was on it? I've forgotten, my boy, forgotten."

Then I begin to guess: "Was he called Steppuhn, or Stepoteit, or Steppanowski?"

Brunies sucks merrily at his cough drop: "Far from it, my boy."

I try other birds: "Was he called Sperla or Sperlinski or Sperballa?"

Brunies titters: "Wrong, my boy, wrong."

I pause for breath: "Then his name was Sorius. Or it was Zuchel, Zocholl, Zylinski. Well, if it wasn't one of those and it wasn't Krisin or Krupkat, I've only got one name left."

Dr. Brunies hops from one leg to the other. His cough drop hops with him: "And what would that last name be?" I whisper in his ear and he stops hopping. I repeat the name softly, and under his matted eyebrows he makes frightened eyes. Then I mollify him, saying: "I asked the clerk at the Grand Hotel and he told me." The bell rings and the recreation period is up. Dr. Brunies wants to go on merrily sucking, but he fails to find the cough drop in his mouth. He fishes a fresh one from his jacket pocket and says, while giving me one too: "You're very curious, my boy, mighty curious."

Dear Cousin Tulla,

then we celebrated Jenny's thirteenth birthday. It was Dr. Brunies who had picked the foundling's birthday: we celebrated it on January 18th—King of Prussia proclaimed Emperor of Germany. It was winter outside, but Jenny had asked for a *bombe*. Dr. Brunies, who knew how to cook candy, had made the ice-cream mold at Koschnick's bakery according to a recipe of his own. That was Jenny's unvarying desire. If anyone said: "Would you like something to eat? What can I bring you? What would you like for Christmas, for your birthday, to celebrate your first night?" she always wanted ice cream, ice cream to lick, ice cream to eat.

We too liked to lick ice cream, but we had other desires. Tulla, for instance, who was a good six months younger than Jenny, was beginning to want a child. Both Jenny and Tulla, in the period after the Polish campaign, had the barest intimations of breasts. It was not until the following summer, during the French campaign and in the weeks after Dunkirk, that a change set in. They would feel each other in the lumber shed: it was as if they had been stung first by wasps, then by hornets. The swellings had come to stay; they were carried about by Tulla with sophistication, by Jenny with wonderment.

Gradually I had to make up my mind. Actually I preferred to be with Tulla; but the minute we were alone in the lumber shed, Tulla wanted a child by me. So I attached myself to Jenny, who at most demanded a ten-pfennig ice-cream cone or a thirty-five-pfennig dish at Toskani's, an ice-cream parlor of repute. What gave her the greatest pleasure was to be taken to the icehouse between the Kleinhammerpark and Aktien Pond; it belonged to the Aktien Brewery, but was situated outside the brick wall spiked with broken glass, which encircled all three of the brewery buildings.

The icehouse was cubical, Aktien Pond was round. Willows stood with their feet in the water. Coming from Hochstriess, the Striessbach flowed into it, through it, and out of it, divided the suburb of Langfuhr into two halves, left Langfuhr at Leegstriess, and emptied, near Broschkescher Weg, into the Dead Vistula. The earliest record of the Striessbach, *"Fluuium Strycze,"* occurs in a document dated 1299, in which it is identified as a brook forming the boundary between the lands of Oliva monastery and those of the township. The Striessbach was neither wide nor deep, but it was rich in leeches. Aktien Pond was also alive with leeches, frogs, and tadpoles. As for the fish in Aktien Pond, we shall get around to them. Over the usually smooth water gnats sustained a single high note, dragonflies hovered transparent and precarious. When Tulla was with us, we had to collect leeches from the inlet in a tin can. A rotting, tumble-down swan house stood crookedly in the muck along the shore. Some years before, there had been swans in Aktien Pond for a single season, then they had died; only the swan house remained. Year in year out, regardless of changes in government, long editorials and indignant letters from readers kept up a stir over Aktien Pond, all demanding, in view of the gnats and the demise of the swans, that it be filled in. But then the Aktien Brewery made a contribution toward a municipal old people's home, and the pond wasn't filled in. During the war the pond was out of danger. It obtained a subtitle, it wasn't just plain Aktien Pond any more, but also the "Kleinhammerpark Firefighting Pond." The air-raid defense people had discovered it and entered it in their operations maps. But the swan house belonged neither to the brewery nor to the air-raid defense; the swan house, somewhat larger than our Harras' kennel, belonged to Tulla. In it she spent whole afternoons, and we handed the cans with the leeches in to her. She undid her clothing and applied them; on the belly and the legs. The leeches swelled up, turned blue-black like blood blisters, trembled slightly and ever more slightly, and as soon as they were full and easily detachable, Tulla, now green about the gills, tossed them into a second tin can.

We too had to apply leeches: I three, Jenny one, on the forearm and not on the legs, because she had to dance. With finely chopped nettles and water from Aktien Pond, Tulla cooked her leeches and ours over a small wood fire until they were done; then they burst, and despite the nettles cooked up with them, colored the soup a brownish black. We had to drink the muddy broth; for to Tulla the cooking of leeches was sacred. If we didn't want to drink, she said: "The sheeny and his friend were blood brothers too, the sheeny told me one time." We drank to the lees and all felt akin.

But one time Tulla almost spoiled the fun. When her cookery was done, she frightened Jenny: "If we drink now, we'll both get a baby and it'll be from him." But I didn't want to be a father. And Jenny said it was too soon for her, she wanted to dance first, in Berlin and all over.

And once when there was already a certain amount of friction between me and Tulla about the baby routine, Tulla forced Jenny in the swan house to put on nine leeches: "If you don't do it this minute, my oldest brother that's fighting in France will bleed to death this minute." Jenny applied all nine leeches all over her, went white, and then fainted. Tulla evaporated and I pulled off the leeches with both hands. They stuck because they weren't full yet. Some of them burst and I had to wash Jenny off. The water brought her to, but she was still livid. The first thing she wanted to know was whether Siegesmund Pokriefke, Tulla's brother in France, was safe now.

"Sure thing," I said, "for the present."

The self-sacrificing Jenny said: "Then we'll have to do it every few months."

I enlightened Jenny. "Now they have blood banks all over. I've read about it."

"Oh!" said Jenny and was a little disappointed. We sat down in the sun beside the swan house. The broad front of the icehouse building was reflected in the smooth surface of Aktien Pond.

Tulla,

I'm telling you what you already know: the icehouse was a box with a flat roof. From corner to corner they had covered it with tar paper. Its door was a tar-paper door. Windows it had none. A black die without white dots. We couldn't stop staring at it. It had nothing to do with Kuddenpech; but Kuddenpech might have put it there, although it wasn't made of cast iron but of tar paper, but Jenny wasn't afraid of Kuddenpech any more and always wanted to go inside the icehouse. If Tulla said: "Now I want a baby, right away," Jenny said: "I'd awfully like to see the icehouse on the inside, will you come with me?" I wanted neither nor; I still don't.

The icehouse smelled like the empty kennel in our yard. Only the dog kennel didn't have a flat roof and actually, in spite of the tar paper, it smelled entirely different: it still smelled of Harras. On the one hand my father didn't want to get another dog, but on the other hand he still didn't wish to chop the kennel into kindling but often, as the journeymen were working at their benches and the machines were biting into wood, stood in front of the kennel for five minutes, staring at it.

The icehouse was reflected in Aktien Pond and darkened the water. Nevertheless, there were fish in Aktien Pond. Old men, with chewing tobacco behind sunken lips, fished from the Kleinhammerpark shore and toward evening caught hand-size roaches. Either they tossed the roaches back or they gave them to us. For they weren't really fit to eat. They were putrid through and through and even when washed in clean water lost none of their living corruption. On two occasions corpses were fished out of Aktien Pond. By the outlet an iron grating collected driftwood. The corpses drifted into it: one was an old man, the other a housewife from Pelonken. Both times I got there too late to see the corpses. For as fervently as Jenny longed to penetrate into the icehouse and Tulla to be with child, I wanted to see an honest-to-goodness corpse; but when relatives died in Koshnavia—my mother had aunts and cousins there— the coffin was always closed by the time we reached Osterwick. Tulla claimed there were little children on the bottom of Aktien Pond, weighted down with stones. In any event Aktien Pond was a convenient place for drowning kittens and puppies. Sometimes there were also elderly cats, floating aimless and bloated; in the end they got caught in the grating and were fished out with a hooked pole by the municipal park guard— his name was Ohnesorge like the Reich Postmaster General. But that is not why Aktien Pond stank, it stank because the waste from the brewery flowed into it. "Bathing prohibited," said a wooden sign. Not we, only the kids from Indian Village went swimming regardless, and always, even in winter, smelled of Aktien beer.

That was what everyone called the housing development which extended from behind the pond, all the way to the airfield. In the development lived longshoremen with large families, widowed grandmothers, and retired bricklayers. I incline to a political explanation of the name "Indian Village." Once upon a time, long before the war, many Socialists and Communists had lived there, and "Red Village" may well have become metamorphosed into "Indian Village." In any case, when Walter Matern was still an SA man, a worker at the Schichau Shipyard was murdered in Indian Village. "Murder in Indian Village," said the headline in the *Vorposten*. But the murderers—possibly nine masked men in loden capes—were never caught.

Neither Tulla's

stories about Aktien Pond nor mine—I'm full of them and have to hold myself back—can outdo certain stories revolving around the icehouse. One of them was that the murderers of the Schichau Shipyard worker had taken refuge in the icehouse and had been sitting ever since, eight or nine frozen murderers, in the iciest part of the icehouse. Many also presumed Eddi Amsel, who had disappeared without trace, to be in the icehouse, but not I. Mothers threatened children who didn't want to finish their soup with the black windowless cube. And it was rumored that because little Matzerath hadn't wanted to eat, his mother had punished him by shutting him up in the icehouse for several hours, and since then he hadn't grown so much as a fraction of an inch.

For there was something mysterious inside that icehouse. As long as the ice trucks were standing out in front and resonant ice blocks were being loaded on, the tar-paper door stood open. When to prove our courage we leaped past the open door, the icehouse breathed on us, and we had to stand in the sun. Especially Tulla, who was unable to pass an open door, was afraid of the icehouse and hid when she saw the broad swaying men who wore black leather aprons and had purple faces. When the icemen pulled the blocks out of the icehouse with iron hooks, Jenny went up to the men and asked if she could touch a block of ice. Sometimes they let her. Then she held one hand on the block until a cubical man pulled her hand away: "That's enough now. You want to get stuck?"

Later there were Frenchmen among the ice haulers. They shouldered the blocks in exactly the same way as the native ice haulers, were exactly as cubical, and had the same purple faces. They were called "foreign workers," and we didn't know whether we were allowed to talk to them. But Jenny, who was learning French in school, accosted one of the Frenchmen: "*Bonjour, Monsieur.*"

He, very courteous: "*Bonjour, Mademoiselle.*"

Jenny curtsied: "*Pardon, Monsieur, vous permettez, Monsieur, que j'entre pour quelques minutes?*"

The Frenchman with a gracious gesture: "*Avec plaisir, Mademoiselle.*"

Jenny curtsied again: "*Merci, Monsieur,*" and let her hand disappear in the hand of the French ice hauler. The two of them, hand in hand, were swallowed up by the icehouse. The other ice haulers laughed and cracked jokes.

We didn't laugh but began to count slowly: twenty-four, twenty-five . . . If she isn't out by two hundred, we'll shout for help.

They came out at a hundred and ninety-two, still hand in hand, In the left she held a chunk of ice, curtsied once again to her ice hauler, and then withdrew into the sun with us. We were shivering. Jenny licked the ice with a pale tongue and offered Tulla the ice to lick. Tulla didn't feel like it. I licked: that's how cold iron tastes.

Dear Cousin Tulla,

after the incident with your leeches and Jenny's fainting, when we were on the outs over that, and because you kept wanting to have a child by me, when you had just about stopped coming to Aktien Pond with us and we, Jenny and I, didn't feel like crawling into the lumber shed with you, when the summer was over and school had begun, Jenny and I took to sitting either in the dill outside the garden fences of Indian Village or beside the swan house, and I helped Jenny by fastening my eyes to the icehouse, for Jenny had eyes only for the black, windowless cube. That is why the icehouse is clearer in my memory than the buildings of the Aktien Brewery behind the chestnut trees. Possibly the compound rose like a turreted castle behind the gloomy brick wall. Definitely, the high church windows of the machine house were framed in smooth Dutch brick. The chimney was squat but nevertheless, regardless of what direction you looked from, dominated the whole of Langfuhr. I could swear that the Aktien chimney wore a complicated helmet, a knight's helmet. Regulated by the wind, it gave off churning black smoke and had to be cleaned twice a year. New and dressed in bright brick-red, the administration building, when I screw up my eyes, looks at me over the glass-spiked wall. Regularly, I assume, trucks drawn by two horses left the yard of the brewery. Stout short-tailed Belgains. Behind leather aprons, under leather caps, with rigid purple faces: the driver and his helper. The whip in the holder. Order book and money pouch under the apron. Wads of tobacco for the day's work. Harness studed with metal buttons. The jolting and clanking of beer cases as front and hind wheels stumble over the iron threshold of the exit. Iron letters on the arch over the portal: D.A.B. Wet sounds: bottlewashing plant. At half past twelve the whistle blows. At one the whistle repeats itself. The xylophone notes of the bottle washers: the score has been lost, but the smell is still with me.

When the east wind turned the helmet on the brewery chimney and rolled black smoke over the chestnut trees, across Aktien Pond, the icehouse, and Indian Village in the direction of the airfield, a sour smell came down: surface-fermented yeast out of copper kettles: Bock Pils Malt Barley March-Beer Urquell. Not to mention the waste. Despite persistent claims that it drained somewhere else, the discharge from Aktien Brewery mixed with the pond, turned it sour and fetid. Accordingly, when we drank Tulla's leech soup, we drank a bitter beer soup. Anyone who trampled a toad was *ipso facto* opening a bottle of bock beer. When one of the tobacco ruminants threw me a hand-size roach and I cleaned the roach beside the swan house, the liver, the milt, and the rest were overdone malt candy. And when I browned it over a crackling little fire, it rose for Jenny like yeast dough, bubbled, and tasted—I had stuffed it full of fresh dill—like last year's pickling fluid. Jenny ate little of the fish.

But when the wind came from the airfield and blew the vapors of the pond and the smoke from the brewery chimney against Kleinhammerpark and the Langfuhr railroad station, Jenny stood up, withdrew her gaze from the ice-filled tar-paper cube, and described numbered steps in the dill. Light to begin with, she weighed only half as much when she balleyed. With a little leap and a graceful curtsy she concluded her act, and I had to applaud as in the theater. Occassionally I gave her a nosegay of dill, having drawn the stems through a rubber beer-bottle washer. These never-fading, ever-red flowers floated by the hundreds on Aktien Pond, formed islands, and were collected: Between the Polish campaign and the taking of the island of Crete, I accumulated over two thousand beer-bottle washers, and felt rich as I counted them. Once I made Jenny a chain out of rubber washers. She wore it like a real necklace, and I was embarrassed for her: "You don't have to wear those things on the street, only by the pond or at home."

But to Jenny the necklace was not without value: "I'm fond of it, because you made it. It seems so personal, you know."

The necklace wasn't bad-looking. Actually I had strung it for Tulla. But Tulla would have thrown it away. When Jenny danced in the dill, the necklace actually looked very nice. After the dance she always said: "But now I'm tired," and looked past the icehouse: "I still have homework to do. And tomorrow we rehearse and the day after tomorrow too."

With the icehouse behind me I made a try: "Have you heard any more from the ballet master in Berlin?"

Jenny supplied information: "Not long ago Herr Haseloff wrote us a postcard from Paris. He says I have to exercise my instep."

I burrowed: "What does this Haseloff look like?"

Jenny's indulgent reproach: "But you've asked me that a dozen times. He's very slim and elegant. He's always smoking long cigarettes. He never laughs or at most with his eyes."

I systematically repeated myself: "But when he does laugh with his mouth for a change and when he speaks?"

Jenny came out with it: "It looks funny but also a little spooky, because when he talks, he has a mouth full of gold teeth."

I: "Real gold?"

Jenny: "I don't know."

I: "Ask him sometime."

Jenny: "I wouldn't like to do that. Maybe they're not real gold."

I: "After all your necklace is only made out of beer-bottle washers."

Jenny: "All right, then I'll write and ask him."

I: "Tonight?"

Jenny: "Tonight I'll be too tired."

I: "Then tomorrow."

Jenny: "But how should I put it?"

I dictated: "Just write: Herr Haseloff, there's something I've been wanting to ask you. Are your teeth real gold? Did you have different teeth before? And if so, what became of them?"

Jenny wrote the letter and Herr Haseloff answered by return mail that the gold was genuine, that he had formerly had white teeth, thirty-two of them; that he had thrown them behind him into the bushes and had bought himself new ones, gold ones; that they had been more expensive than thirty-two pair of ballet slippers.

I said to Jenny: "Now count how many bottle washers there are in your necklace."

Jenny counted and didn't understand: "What a coincidence, exactly thirty-two."

Dear Tulla,

it was inevitable that you should come around again with your scratched-up legs.

At the end of September—the dill went to seed and turned yellow, and the choppy waves of Aktien Pond made a soapy wreath of foam along the shore—at the end of September came Tulla.

Indian Village spat her out, and seven or eight boys. One was smoking a pipe. He stood behind Tulla, using her for a windbreak, and handed her the boiler. Speechlessly she smoked. Slowly, by a calculated detour, they approached, stood looking in the air, looked past us, turned back and were gone: behind the fences and whitewashed cottages of Indian Village.

And once toward evening—we had the sun behind us, the helmet of the brewery chimney sat on the bleeding head of a bleeding knight—they appeared to one side of the icehouse and came goose-stepping through the nettles along the front tar-paper wall. In the dill they spread out, Tulla handed the pipe to the left and said to the gnats: "They've forgotten to close up. Wouldn't you like to go in, Jenny, and see what it's like?"

Jenny was so friendly and always polite: "Oh no, it's late and I'm rather tired. We have English tomorrow, you know, and I have to be rested for my dancing lesson."

Tulla had the pipe again: "O.K., if you don't want to. Then we'll go tell the caretaker to lock up."

But Jenny was already on her feet and I had to stand up: "You can't go, Jenny, it's out of the question. Anyway, you're tired, you just said so." Jenny wasn't tired any more and wanted to look in just for a second: "It's very interesting in there, please, Harry."

I stuck by her side and got into the nettles. Tulla in the lead, the others behind us. Tulla's thumb pointed at the tar-paper door: it was open just a crack and scarcely breathed. Then I had to say: "But I won't let you go alone." And Jenny, slender in the door jamb, said ever so politely: "That's awfully nice of you, Harry."

Who else but Tulla

pushed me through the doorway behind Jenny. And I had forgotten to disarm you and the boys outside with a crossyourheartandhopetodie.

775

As the breath of the icehouse took us in tow—Jenny's little finger hooked itself into my little finger—as icy lungs drew us in, I knew: now Tulla, alone or with that young thug, is going to the caretaker and getting the key, or she's getting the caretaker with the key: and the gang are palavering in nine voices so the caretaker won't hear us while he's locking up.

For that reason or because Jenny had me by the finger, I didn't succeed in calling for help. She led me sure-footedly through the black crackling windpipe. From all sides, from the top and bottom too, breath made us light until there was no ground under our feet. We passed over trestles and stairways that were marked with red position lights. And Jenny said in a perfectly normal voice: "Watch out, please, Harry: we'll be going downstairs now, twelve steps."

But hard as I tried to find ground from step to step, I sank, breathed in by a suction coming from below. And when Jenny said: "Now we're in the first basement, we've got to keep to the left, that's where the entrance to the second basement is supposed to be," I would gladly, though busy with a skin itch, have stayed in the first basement. That was the nettles from before; but what was beating down on my skin was the breath coming from all sides. And every direction creaked, no, crackled, no, crunched: piled blocks, complete sets of teeth rubbed against each other till the enamel splintered, and the breath of iron was yeasty stale stomach-sour furry clammy. The barest touch of tar paper. Yeast rose. Vinegar evaporated. Mushrooms sprouted. "Careful, a step," said Jenny. In whose malt-bitter maw? The second basement of what hell had left pickles uncovered to spoil? What devil had stoked the furnace to subzero?

I wanted to scream and whispered: "They'll lock us in if we don't . . . "

But Jenny was still her methodical self: "They always lock up at seven."

"Where are we?"

"Now we're in the second basement. Some of these blocks are many years old."

My hand wanted to know exactly: "How many years?" and reached out to the left, looked for resistance, found it, and stuck fast on prehistoric giant's teeth: "I'm stuck, Jenny! I'm stuck!"

Then Jenny rests her hand on my sticking hand: instantly I am able to remove my fingers from the giant tooth, but I keep hold of Jenny's arm, arm lovely from dancing, arm that can lie and sleep on air, the other one too. And both rubbed hot by breath in blocks. In the armpits: August. Jenny titters: "You mustn't tickle me, Harry."

But I just want "to hold tight, Jenny."

She lets me and is again "a little tired, Harry."

776

I don't think "there's a bench here, Jenny."

She is not of little faith: "Why shouldn't there be a bench here, Harry?" And because she says so, there is one, an iron bench. But because Jenny sits down, the iron bench turns, the longer she sits on it, into a cozy well-worn wooden bench. Now Jenny, precociously motherly, says to me in the second basement of the icehouse: "You mustn't shiver any more, Harry. You know, once I was hidden inside a snow man. And I learned a great deal in there. So if you can't stop shivering, you must hold me tight. And then if you're still cold, because you weren't ever in a snow man, you must kiss me, that helps, you know. I could give you my dress too, I don't need it, I'm positive. You mustn't be embarrassed. We're all alone. And I'm perfectly at home here. You can throw it around your neck like a muffler. Later on I'll sleep a little, because I have to go to Madame Lara's tomorrow, and the day after tomorrow I have to practice again. Besides, I really am a little tired, you know."

And so we sat through the night on the iron wooden bench. I held Jenny tight. Her dry lips were tasteless. I threw her cotton dress—if I only knew whether it had dots, stripes, or checks—I threw her short-sleeve summer dress over my shoulders and around my neck. Dressless but in her slip, she lay in my arms, which didn't tire, because Jenny was light even when she slept. I didn't sleep, for fear she'd slip away from me. For I'd never been inside a snow man, and without her dry lips, without her cotton dress, without her weightless weight in my arms, without Jenny, I'd have been lost. Surrounded by crackling, sighing, and crunching, in the breath of the ice blocks, breathed on breathed in: the ice would have held me in its clutches to this day.

But as it was, we lived to see the next day. The morning rumbled in the basement above us. That was the icemen in the leather aprons. Jenny in her dress wanted to know: "Did you sleep a little too?"

"Of course not. Somebody had to be on the lookout."

"Imagine, I dreamt my instep had improved and in the end I was able to do the thirty-two *fouettés*: and Herr Haseloff laughed."

"With his gold teeth?"

"Every single one of them, while I turned and turned."

Without difficulty, amid whispering and interpretation of dreams, we made our way to the first basement and then up some more steps. The red position lights showed the path between piled ice blocks to the exit, the rectangular light. But Jenny held me back. We mustn't let anybody see us, because "If they catch us," said Jenny, "they'll never let us in again."

When the glaring rectangle disclosed no more men in leather aprons, when the hefty Belgian horses pulled up and the ice truck rolled away on rubber tires, we dashed through the door before the next ice truck

drove up. The sun slanted down from chestnut trees. We slipped along
tar-paper walls. Everything smelled different from the day before. My
legs were in the nettles again. On Kleinhammerweg, while Jenny was
saying her irregular English verbs, I began to dread the carpenter's hand
waiting for me at home.

You know,

that night we spent in the icehouse had several consequences: I got
a licking; the police, notified by Dr. Brunies, asked questions; we had
grown older and left Aktien Pond with its smells to the twelve-year-olds.
I got rid of my collection of bottle washers the next time the junkman
came around. Whether Jenny stopped wearing her bottle-washer necklace,
I don't know: We elaborately went out of each other's way. Jenny blushed
when we couldn't avoid each other on Elsenstrasse; and I went red in the
face every time Tulla met me on the stairs or in our kitchen, when she
came in for salt or to borrow a saucepan.

Is your memory any good?

There are at least five months, with Christmas in the middle, that
I can't piece together. During this period, in the gap between the French
campaign and the Balkan campaign, more and more of our workmen were
drafted and later, when the war had started in the East, replaced by
Ukrainian helpers and one French carpenter. Wischnewski fell in Greece;
Arthur Kuleise, another of our carpenters, fell right in the beginning at
Lemberg; and then my cousin, Tulla's brother Alexander Pokriefke, fell
—that is, he didn't fall, he was drowned in a submarine: the battle of
the Atlantic had started. Not only the Pokriefkes, but the master carpenter
and his wife as well, each wore crape. I too wore crape and was very
proud of it. Whenever anyone asked me why I was in mourning, I said:
"A cousin of mine, who was very close to me, was on duty in the Caribbean
Sea in a submarine and he didn't come home." Actually I hardly knew
Alexander Pokriefke, and the Caribbean Sea was hokum too.

Did something else happen?

My father received big orders. His shop was turning out nothing
but doors and windows for Navy barracks in Putzig. Suddenly and for
no apparent reason he began to drink, and once, of a Sunday morning,
beat my mother because she was standing where he wanted to stand. But
he never neglected his work and went on smoking his seconds, which he
obtained on the black market in exchange for door frames.

What else happened?

They made your father a cell leader. August Pokriefke threw himself
body and soul into his Party claptrap. He got a certificate of disability

778

from a Party doctor—the usual knee injury—and decided to give in-doctrination lectures in our machine shop. But my father wouldn't allow it. Old family quarrels were dug up. Something about two acres of pasture land left by my grandparents in Osterwick. My mother's dowry was itemized on fingers. My father argued to the contrary that he was paying for Tulla's schooling. August Pokriefke pounded the table: the Party would advance the money for Tulla's school, you bet they will! And he, August Pokriefke, would deliver his indoctrination lectures come hell and high water, after hours if necessary.

And where were you that summer?

Off in Brösen with the thirds. If anyone went looking for you, he found you on the hulk of a Polish mine sweeper, which lay on the bottom not far from the harbor mouth. The thirds dived down into the mine sweeper and brought stuff up. I was a poor swimmer and never dared to open my eyes under water. Consequently I went looking for you in other places and never on the barge. Besides, I had Jenny; and you always wanted the same old thing: a baby. Did they make you one on the mine sweeper?

You showed no sign of it. Or the kids in Indian Village? They left you no reminders. The two Ukrainians in our shop with their perpetually frightened potato faces? Neither of them took you into the shed, and nevertheless my father was always grilling them. And August Pokriefke knocked one of them, Kleba was his name, cold with a spirit level between finishing machine and lathe, because he was always begging for bread. Whereupon my father threw your father out of the shop. Your father threatened to put in a report; but it was my father, who enjoyed a certain standing with the Chamber of Commerce and with the Party as well, who did the reporting. A court of honor of sorts was held. August Pokriefke and master carpenter Liebenau were instructed to make up; the Ukrainians were exchanged for two other Ukrainians—there were plenty of them—and the first two, so we heard, were sent to Stutthof.

Stutthof: on your account!

That little word took on more and more meaning. "Hey, you! You got a yen for Stutthof?"—"If you don't keep that trap of yours shut, you'll end up in Stutthof." A sinister word had moved into apartment houses, went upstairs and downstairs, sat at kitchen tables, was supposed to be a joke, and some actually laughed: "They're making soap in Stutthof now, it makes you want to stop washing."

You and I were never in Stutthof.

Tulla didn't even know Nickelswalde; a Hitler Cub camp took me to Steegen; but Herr Brauxel, who pays me my advances and calls my

779

letters to Tulla important, is familiar with the region between the Vistula and Frisches Haff. In his day Stutthof was a rich village, larger than Schiewenhorst and Nickelswalde and smaller than Neuteich, the county seat. Stutthof had 2698 inhabitants. They made money when soon after the outbreak of the war a concentration camp was built near the village and had to be enlarged again and again. Railroad tracks were even laid in the camp. The tracks connected with the Island narrow-gauge railway from Danzig-Niederstadt. Everybody knew that, and those who have forgotten may as well remember: Stutthof: Danzig-Lowlands County, Reich Province of Danzig-West Prussia, judicial District of Danzig, known for its fine timber-frame church, popular as a quiet seaside resort, an early German settlement. In the fourteenth century the Teutonic Knights drained the flats; in the sixteenth century hard-working Mennonites moved in from Holland; in the seventeenth century the Swedes several times pillaged the Island; in 1813 Napoleon's retreat route ran straight across the flats; and between 1939 and 1945, in Stutthof Concentration Camp, Danzig-Lowlands County, people died, I don't know how many.

Not you but we,
     the thirds at the Conradinum, were taken out to Nickelswalde near Stutthof by our school. The Party had acquired the old Saskoschin country annex and turned it into a staff school. A piece of land between Queen Louise's mill in Nickelswalde and the scrub pine forest was purchased half from miller Matern, half from the village of Nickelswalde, and on it was erected a one-story building with a tall brick roof. As in Saskoschin we played schlagball in Nickelswalde. In every class there were crack players who could hit flies sky-high and whipping boys who were encircled with hard leather balls and made into mincemeat. In the morning the flat was raised; in the evening it was taken down. The food was bad; nevertheless we gained weight; the air on the Island was nourishing.

     Often between games I watched miller Matern. He stood between mill and house. On the left a sack of flour pressed against his ear. He listened to the mealworms and saw the future.

     Let us assume that I carried on a conversation with the lopsided miller. Maybe I said in a loud voice, for he was hard of hearing: "What's new, Herr Matern?"

     He definitely answered: "In Russia the winter will set in too early."

     Possibly I wanted to know more: "Will we get to Moscow?"

     He oracularly: "Many of us will get as far as Siberia."

     Then I may have changed the subject: "Do you know a man by the name of Haseloff, who lives mostly in Berlin?"

     No doubt he listened at length to his flour sack: "I only hear about somebody who had a different name before. The birds were afraid of him."

I'd have had reason enough to be curious: "Has he gold in his mouth and does he never laugh?"

The miller's mealworms never spoke directly: "He smokes a lot of cigarettes, one after another, though he's always hoarse because he caught cold once."

I'm sure I concluded: "Then it's him."

The miller saw the future with precision: "It always will be."

Since there was no Tulla and no Jenny in Nickelswalde,

it cannot be my job to write about the adventures of the thirds in Nickelswalde; anyway the summer was drawing to an end.

The fall brought changes in the school system. The Gudrun School, formerly the Helene Lange School, was turned into an Air Force barracks. All the girls' classes moved to our Conradinum with its stench of boys. The school was operated in shifts: girls in the morning, boys in the afternoon, or vice versa. Some of our teachers, among them Dr. Brunies, also had to teach girls' classes. He taught Tulla's and Jenny's class history.

We no longer saw each other at all. Because we went to school in shifts, we had no difficulty in avoiding each other: Jenny no longer had to blush; I ceased to go red in the face; exceptions are memorable:

for once, around noon—I had left home early and was carrying my school satchel in my right hand—Jenny Brunies came toward me under the hazelnut bushes on Uphagenweg. She must have had five periods that morning and stayed on at the Conradinum for reasons unknown to me. In any case she was coming from school and also carrying her satchel in her right hand. Green hazelnuts and a few pale brownish ones were already lying on the ground, because a wind had been blowing the day before. Jenny in a dark blue woolen dress with white cuffs and a dark blue hat, but not a beret, something more like a tam, Jenny blushed and shifted her satchel from right to left when she was still five hazelnut bushes away from me.

The villas on either side of Uphagenweg seemed to be uninhabited. Everywhere silver firs and weeping willows, red maples and birches, dropping leaf after leaf. We were fourteen years old and walked toward each other. Jenny seemed thinner than I remembered her.

Her toes turned out from all the balleying. Why was she wearing blue when she could have said to herself: I'll turn red if he comes along.

Because I was early and because she flushed to the edge of her tam, because she had shifted her satchel, I stopped, also shifted my satchel, and held out my hand. She briefly let a dry anxious hand slip into mine. We stood amid unripe nuts. Some had been stepped on or were hollow. When a bird in a maple tree had finished, I began: "Hi there, Jenny, why so late? Have you tried the nuts? Want me to crack you a few? They

781

haven't any taste, but after all they're the first. And what have you been doing with yourself? Your old man is still mighty chipper. Only the other day he had his pocket full of sparklers again: must have been ten pounds of them, or at least eight, not bad. And all that tramping around at his age, but what I wanted to ask you: how's the ballet going? How many pirouettes can you do? And how's the instep, improving? I wish I could get to the old Coffee Mill one of these days. How's the first soloist, the one you got from Vienna? I heard you're in *The Masked Ball*. Unfortunately I haven't been able to, because I. But they say you're good, I'm mighty glad. And have you been back to the icehouse? Don't be like that. It was only a joke. But I remember well because when I got home my father. Have you still got the necklace, the one made of bottle washers? And what about Berlin? Have you heard any more from those people?"

I chatted stammered repeated myself. I cracked hazelnuts with my heel, picked half-crushed kernels from splintered shells with nimble fingers, gave some took some; and Jenny amiably ate soapy nuts that dulled the teeth. My fingers were sticky. She stood stiffly, still kept all her blood in her head, and replied slowly monotonously compliantly. Her eyes had agoraphobia. They clung to the birches, weeping willows, silver firs: "Yes, thank you, my father is very well. Except he's been teaching too much. Sometimes I have to help him correct papers. And he smokes too much. Yes, I'm still with Madame Lara. She's really an excellent teacher and widely recognized. Soloists come to her from Dresden and even from Berlin for a little extra workout. You see, she's had the Russian style in her bones ever since she was a child. She learned all sorts of things from watching Preobrajensky and Trefilova. Even if she does seem dreadfully pedantic, always correcting and fussing over something, she never loses sight of the dance, and we learn something more than technique. There's really no need for you to see *The Masked Ball*. Our standards here aren't really the highest. Yes, Harry, of course I remember. But I've never gone back. I read somewhere that you can't or shouldn't repeat certain things, or they disappear entirely. But I wear your necklace sometimes. Yes, Herr Haseloff has written again. To Papa of course. He's really a funny man and writes about thousands of little things other people wouldn't notice. But Papa says he's a great success in Berlin. He's been doing all sorts of things, stage designs too. He's said to be a very strict teacher, but a good one. He goes on the road with Neroda, who really directs the ballet: Paris, Belgrade, Salonika. They don't only dance for soldiers. But Papa says I'm not ready for it yet."

Then there were no nuts left on the ground. And a few schoolboys had passed by. I knew one of them; he grinned. Jenny hurriedly let her right hand disappear in my right hand. I turned her hand over for a moment: five smooth light fingers; and on the ring finger she was wearing a tarnished, primitively wrought silver ring. I took it off without asking.

Jenny with empty ring finger: "That's Angustri, that's its name."

I rub the ring: "Angustri? How come?"

"That's Gypsy language and it means ring."

"Have you always had it?"

"But you mustn't tell anybody. It was on my pillow when I was found."

"And how do you know its name?"

Jenny's blush rises, falls: "That's what the man who left me there called the ring."

I: "A Gypsy?"

Jenny: "His name was Bidandengero."

I: "Then maybe you're one too."

Jenny: "Certainly not, Harry. They have black hair."

I clinch it: "But they can all dance!"

I told Tulla all about it:

she, I, and a lot of other people were crazy about the ring. We thought there was some hocus-pocus in the silver, and when the conversation revolved around Jenny, we called her not Jenny but Angustri. Undoubtedly those of my fellow pupils who had fallen in love with Jenny's ballet slippers from the start were now pining for Angustri. I alone remained calm-to-curious toward Jenny and Angustri. We had been through too much together. And from the very start I had been contaminated by Tulla. Even as a high school student, in relatively clean clothes, she still had her smell of bone glue; and I stuck fast with hardly a struggle.

When Tulla said: "Swipe the ring next time," I said no, and when I waylaid Jenny in Uphagenweg I only half meant to pull the silver off her finger. Twice in one week she blushed, because I crossed her path. Both times she had no Angustri on her, but was wearing the silly bottle-washer necklace.

But Tulla, who was in mourning for her brother Alexander,

soon arranged nevertheless for Jenny to wear mourning. By the late fall of 1941—the special dispatches about victories in the East had stopped—the Conradinum boasted twenty-two fallen Conradinians. The marble tablet with the names, dates, and ranks hung in the main entrance between Schopenhauer and Copernicus. The fallen included one holder of the Knight's Cross. Two holders of the Knight's Cross were still alive and when they had leave regularly visited their old school. Sometimes they made terse or long-winded speeches in the auditorium. We sat spellbound and the teachers nodded approval. After the lectures questions were permitted. The students wanted to know how many Spitfires you had to shoot down, how many gross register tons you had to sink. For we were all determined to win the Knight's Cross later on. The teachers either asked practical questions—were replacements still coming in all right?—or they indulged in high-sounding periods about sticking it out and final victory. Dr. Brunies asked a holder of the Knight's Cross—I think it was the one from the Air Force—what his thoughts had been on first seeing a dead soldier, friend or foe. The fighter pilot's answer has slipped my mind.

Brunies asked the same question of Sergeant Walter Matern, who, because he wasn't a holder of the Knight's Cross, was only entitled to deliver a lecture from the teacher's desk in our classroom on the "Role of Ground Forces Anti-Aircraft in the East." I've also forgotten the answer of the sergeant with the Iron Cross first and second class. All I see is that field-gray, at once haggard and bullish, he clutches the desk top with both hands and stares over our heads at an oleograph on the rear wall of the classroom: the spinach-green Thoma landscape. Wherever he breathes, the air becomes rarefied. We want to know something about the Caucasus, but he talks unswervingly about the Nothing.

A few days after his lecture Walter was sent back to Russia, where he came by a wound which made him unfit for combat in the Ground Forces AA: with a slight limp he was assigned to the home front AA, first in Königsberg, then in Danzig. In the Brösen-Glettkau shore battery and the Kaiserhafen battery he trained Air Force auxiliaries.

He was liked and feared by all, and to me became a shining ideal; only Dr. Brunies, when Matern came for a visit and stood behind the desk, questioned his sergeant's existence by turning on irony lights and asking Matern, instead of delivering a lecture about the fighting at Orel, to read us a poem by Eichendorff, perhaps: "Dark gables, lofty windows . . ."

I can't recall that Dr. Brunies seriously taught us anything. A few subjects for compositions come to mind: "Preparations for marriage among the Zulus." Or: "The destinies of a tin can." Or: "When I was a cough drop, growing smaller and smaller in a little girl's mouth." Apparently his idea was to feed our imaginations, and since out of forty students two can reasonably be expected to have an imagination, thirty-eight thirds were permitted to doze while two—another and myself—unrolled the destinies of the tin can, thought up original marriage customs for the Zulus, and spied on a cough drop growing smaller in a little girl's mouth.

This topic kept me, my classmate, and Dr. Brunies busy for two weeks or more. Tuberous and leathery-crinkly, he sat huddled behind his worn desk top and, by way of inspiring us, gave an imitation of sucking, nibbling, and drawing juice. He made an imaginary cough drop move from one cheek to the other, almost swallowed it, diminished it with closed eyes, let the cough drop speak, narrate; in short, at a time when sweets were rare and rationed, Dr. Brunies' addiction to candy redoubled:

784

if he had none in his pocket, he would invent some. And we wrote on the same topic.

Beginning roughly in the fall of '41, vitamin tablets were distributed to all our students. They were called Cebion tablets and kept in large brown-glass apothecary jars. In the conference room, where previously Meyers Konversations Lexikon had stood back beside back, there now stood a row of labeled jars—sixth to first. Each day they were carried by the class teachers into the classrooms for the vitamin-deficient schoolboys of the third war year.

Of course it did not escape our notice that Dr. Brunies was already sucking and that there was sweet enjoyment around his old man's mouth when he entered the class with the apothecary jar under his arm. The distribution of the Cebion tablets took up a good half of the period, for Brunies did not let the glass pass from seat to seat: in alphabetical order, in strict accordance with the class roster, he let the students step forward one by one, reached elaborately into the glass jar, acted as if he was fishing for something very special, and then, with triumph in every wrinkle, brought out one of the perhaps five hundred Cebion tablets, displayed it as the outcome of a difficult magician's act, and handed it to the student.

We all knew that Dr. Brunies' coat pockets were full of Cebion tablets. They had a sweet-sour taste: a little like lemon, a little like grape sugar, a little like a hospital. Since we liked to suck Cebion tablets, Brunies, who was wild about everything sweet, had good reason to fill his coat pockets. Every day, on his way from the conference room to our classroom, he would stop in the teachers' toilet with the brown apothecary jar and a moment later would be back in the corridor, sucking his way forward; his pocket flaps would be powdered with Cebion dust.

I would like to say that Brunies knew that we knew. Often he vanished behind the blackboard during the class, victualed up, and showed us his busy mouth: "I assume that you haven't seen anything; and if you have seen something, you've seen wrong."

Like other teachers Oswald Brunies had to sneeze often and sonorously; like his colleagues he pulled out a big handkerchief on such occasions; but unlike his colleagues he sent Cebion tablets, whole or broken, tumbling from his pockets along with his snot rag. Those that went rolling on the waxed floor we rescued. A cluster of bowed, zealously collecting schoolboys handed Dr. Brunies half and quarter tablets. We said—the words became a stock phrase —: "Dr. Brunies, you've dropped some of your sparkling stones."

Brunies answered gravely: "If they are common mica gneiss, you may keep them; but if you have found one or several pieces of double spar, I should like you to return them."

We, and that was our tacit agreement, found only pieces of double

785

spar which Brunies caused to disappear between brownish tooth stumps and tested by letting them travel from cheek to cheek until he had attianed certainty: "Indeed, you have discovered several pieces of extremely rare double spar; how gratifying to have found them."

Later Dr. Brunies dropped the detours; he stopped going behind the blackboard and never again referred to lost pieces of double spar. On his way from the conference room to our classroom he gave up visiting the teachers' toilet with his apothecary jar, but avidly and openly helped himself to our Cebion tablets during class. The trembling of his hands was pitiful. It overcame him in the middle of a sentence, between two stanzas of Eichendorff: he didn't pick out a solitary tablet; with three bony fingers he seized five tablets, tossed all five into his insatiable mouth, and smacked his lips so shamelessly that we had to look away.

No, Tulla,

we didn't report him. Several reports were turned in; but none came from our class. A few members of my class, it is true, and I was one of them, were later called into the confernce room to testify; but we were extremely reserved, all we said was yes, Dr. Brunies had eaten candy during class, but not Cebion tablets, only ordinary cough drops. This, we said, was a habit he had always had, even when we were in sixth and fifth; and in those days no one had even heard of Cebion tablets.

Our testimony didn't help much; when Brunies was arrested, Cebion dust was found in the linings of his pockets.

At first it was rumored that Dr. Klohse, our principal, had reported him; some said it was Lingenberg, a mathematics teacher; then word got around that certain pupils in the Gudrun School, some of the girls in Brunies' history class, had turned him in. Before I had time to think: It must have been Tulla, Tulla Pokriefke's name came up.

You did it!

Why? Because. Two weeks later—Dr. Brunies had been obliged to hand our class over to Dr. Hoffmann; he was suspended from teaching but not yet under arrest; he was at home on Elsenstrasse with his sparkling stones—two weeks later we saw the old gentleman once again. Two of my classmates and I were called to the conference room. Two seconds and five girls from the Gudrun School were already waiting; among them: Tulla. We put on a strained grin, and the sun grazed all the brown apothecary jars on the shelf. We stood on a soft carpet and were not allowed to sit down. The classical authors on the walls exchanged disparaging looks. Over the green velvet on the long conference table sunlight wallowed in dust. The door was oiled: Dr. Brunies was led in by a man in civilian clothes, who however was not a teacher but a plain-clothes man. Dr. Klohse came in after them. Brunies gave us a friendly, absent-minded nod, rubbed his brown bony hands, turned on irony lights as though eager to get down to business and tell us about the marriage preparations of the Zulus, the destinies of a tin can, or the cough drop in the mouth of a little girl. But it was the man in civilian clothes who did the speaking. He termed the meeting in the conference room a necessary confrontation. In a drawling voice he asked Dr. Brunies the familiar questions. They dealt with Cebion and the removal of Cebion tablets from jars. Regretfully and headshakingly, Brunies answered all questions in the negative. The seconds were questioned, then we. He was inculpated exculpated. Contradictory stammerings: "No, I didn't see anything, only hearsay. We always thought. We knew he was fond of candy, so we supposed. In my presence, no. But it's true that he . . ."

I don't believe it was I who finally said: "It's true that Dr. Brunies dipped into the Cebion tablets, three or at the very most four times. But we couldn't begrudge him his little pleasure. We knew he was fond of sweets, always had been."

During the questioning and answering I noticed how absurdly and helplessly Dr. Brunies was rummaging left right left through his coat pockets. In so doing he moistened his lips excitedly. The man in civilian clothes ignored this rummaging through pockets and licking of lips. First he spoke, beside the tall window, with Dr. Klohse, then he motioned Tulla over to the window: she was wearing a black pleated skirt. If Brunies had only had his pipe; but he had left it in his overcoat. The plain-clothes man whispered obscenely in Tulla's ear. The soles of my feet burned on the soft carpet. Dr. Brunies' restless hands and the perpetual motion of his tongue. Now Tulla is taking steps in her black pleated skirt. The goods rustles until she comes to a stop. With both hands she takes hold of a brown apothecary jar half full of Cebion tablets. She lifts it down from the shelf and no one stops her. Around the unoccupied green conference table she moves, step by step, in her pleated skirt, her eyes small and narrowed. All look after her and Brunies sees her coming. She stops an arm's length from Dr. Brunies, draws the jar to her bosom, holds it with her left hand, and with her right hand removes the glass cover. Brunies wipes his hands dry on his jacket. She puts the glass cover down to one side: the sunlight strikes it on the green felt of the conference table. Dr. Brunies' tongue has stopped moving but is still between his lips. Again she holds the jar with both hands, lifts it higher, stands on tiptoes in her pleated skirt. Tulla says: "Won't you have some, Dr. Brunies?"

Brunies offered no resistance. He did not hide his hands in his pockets. He did not avert his head and his mouth full of brown tooth stumps. No one heard: "What is the meaning of this nonsense?" Dr.

787

Brunies grabbed, he hastily put his whole hand in. When his three fingers emerged from the jar, they raised six or seven Cebion tablets; two fell back into the jar; one dropped on the light-brown plush carpet and rolled under the conference table; what he had managed to keep between his fingers he stuffed into his mouth. But then he felt badly about the one Cebion tablet that had been lost under the table. He went down on his knees. In front of us, the principal, the man in civilian clothes, and Tulla, he went down on both knees, searched with groping hands beside and under the table; he would have found the tablet and raised it to his sweets-craving mouth, if they hadn't interfered: the principal and the man in civilian clothes. To right and left they picked him up by the arms and set him on his feet. A second opened the oiled door. "Good gracious, Herr Colleague!" said Dr. Klohse. "Really!" Tulla bent down to pick up the tablet under the conference table.

Later we were questioned once again. One after another, we entered the conference room. The business with the Cebion tablets hadn't proved sufficient. The seconds had written down some of Dr. Brunies' utterances. They sounded subversive and negative. All of a sudden everybody said: He was a Freemason. Though none of us knew what a Freemason was. I hung back, as my father had advised me to do. Maybe I shouldn't have said anything about Dr. Brunies' perpetually ungarnished flagpole, but after all he was our neighbor, and everyone saw that he never put out a flag when everybody was putting out flags. The man in civilian clothes knew all about it and nodded impatiently when I said: "Well, for instance on the Führer's birthday, when they all put out flags, Dr. Brunies never hangs out a flag, though he owns one."

Jenny's foster father was placed under arrest. I heard that they let him return home for a few days and then took him away for good. Felsner-Imbs the pianist, who came to the apartment in the Aktienhaus every day and looked after Jenny, said to my father: "Now they've taken the old gentleman to Stutthof. If only he lives through it!"

The Pokriefkes and the Liebenaus,
your family and mine, put off their mourning because your brother Alexander had been dead for a full year; Jenny had her clothes dyed. Once a week a social worker visited the house across the street; Jenny received her in black. At first we heard that Jenny was going to be sent to a welfare home; the Brunies apartment was being vacated. But black-clad Jenny found people to intercede for her. Felsner-Imbs wrote letters; the principal of the Gudrun School put in a petition; the manager of the Stadttheater appealed to the gauleiter's office; and Madame Lara Bock-Fedorova had connections. And so Jenny, though in black, kept on going to school, to ballet classes and rehearsals, wearing a soft black tam and a black coat

that was too big for her, advancing step by step in black cotton stockings. But in the street her face showed no sign of tears. A trifle pale, but that may have been the effect of her black clothing, rigid from the waist up, her shoes turned outward as befits a ballet dancer, she carried her school satchel—which was brown, of artificial leather—to school and her leek-green, dawn-red, and air-blue gym bags, dyed black, to Oliva or to the theater, and returned punctually and pigeon-toed, more well behaved than rebellious, to Elsenstrasse.

Yet there were voices that interpreted Jenny's daily black as a re-bellious color: in those days you were allowed to wear mourning only if you could produce a stamped and certified reason. You were allowed to mourn for fallen sons and deceased grandmothers; but the terse notification of the Danzig-Neugarten police that it had been necessary to place Dr. Oswald Brunies under arrest for unseemly conduct and crimes against the national welfare was not a document acceptable to the rationing office; for there alone, in the clothing section, were purchase permits for mourn-ing garments obtainable.

"What's the matter with her? He's still alive, isn't he? An old man like him, they wouldn't. She's certainly not helping him any, on the contrary. Somebody ought to tell her she's not doing any good, only making a spectacle of herself."

The neighbors and the social worker spoke to Felsner-Imbs. The pianist tried to persuade Jenny to stop wearing her mourning. He said it wasn't the externals that counted. If there was mourning in her heart, that was quite sufficient. His grief was hardly less, for he had lost a friend, his only friend.

But Jenny Brunies stuck to her external black and continued to wear it in accusation all over Langfuhr and on Elsenstrasse. Once at the car stop of the Number 2 to Oliva I spoke to her. Of course she turned red, framed in black. If I had to paint her portrait from memory, she would have light-gray eyes, shadow-casting lashes, brown hair parted in the middle, flowing smooth and lusterless in two tired curves from her fore-head down over her cheeks and ears, and plaited into a stiff pigtail behind. I would paint her long slender face ivory-pale, for her blush was an exception. A face made for mourning: Giselle in the cemetery scene. Her inconspicuous mouth spoke only when asked.

At the streetcar stop I said: "Must you wear mourning the whole time, Jenny? Why, Papa Brunies may be home again any minute."

"My feeling is that he's dead, even if they haven't notified me."

I cast about for a subject, because the car wasn't coming: "Are you always home alone in the evening?"

"Herr Imbs often comes to see me. We sort out the stones and label them. He left lots of unsorted stones, you know."

I wanted to shove off, but the car didn't come: "I suppose you never go to the movies, or do you?"

"When Papa was still alive, we sometimes went to the Ufa-Palast on Sunday morning. He liked educational films best."

I was more interested in the feature: "Wouldn't you like to go to the movies with me sometime?"

Jenny's car approached, straw-yellow: "I'd be glad to if you feel like it." People in winter coats got out: "It wouldn't have to be a funny picture, we could go to a serious one, couldn't we?"

Jenny got in: "They're playing *Liberated Hands* at the Filmpalast. Young people of sixteen and over are admitted."

If Tulla had said:

"One in the orchestra," the cashier would certainly have asked for Tulla's identification; but we didn't have to prove we were sixteen, because Jenny was in mourning. We kept our coats on, because the movie house was poorly heated. No acquaintances in sight. We didn't have to talk, because they kept playing potpourris. Simultaneously the curtain purred up, a fanfare introduced the newsreel, and the lights went out. Only then did I put my arm around Jenny's shoulder. It didn't stay there long, because for at least thirty seconds heavy artillery shelled Leningrad. As an English bomber was downed by our fighter planes, Jenny didn't want to see and buried her forehead in my overcoat. I let my arm wander again, but my eyes pursued the fighter planes, counted Rommel's tanks advancing in Cyrenaica, followed the foaming track of a torpedo, I saw the tanker rocking in the sights, quivered when the torpedo struck, and transferred the flickering and quivering of the disintegrating tanker to Jenny. When the newsreel camera visited the Führer's headquarters, I whispered: "Jenny, look, the Führer is coming on in a second, maybe he'll have the dog with him." We were both disappointed when only Keitel, Jodl, and somebody else were standing around him amid trees on gravel paths.

When the lights went on again, Jenny took her coat off, I didn't. The educational film was about deer which have to be fed in the winter, because otherwise they would starve. Without her coat Jenny was even thinner. The deer were not shy. The pine trees in the mountains were laden with snow. In the movie house everybody's clothes were black, not only Jenny's mourning sweater.

Actually I wanted to during the educational film, but I didn't until the feature had started. *Liberated Hands* wasn't a crime thriller with shooting and handcuffing. The hands belonged to a sculptress, who was nuts about the sculptor who was her teacher, and her real name was Brigitte Horney. Just about every time she did it on the screen, I did it to Jenny in the movie house. She closed her eyes; I could see her. On the screen hands were always kneading lumps of clay into naked figures and frolicking foals. Jenny's skin was cool and dry. She had her thighs pressed together and I was of the opinion she ought to relax. She complied at once but kept her eyes on the feature. Her hole was even smaller than Tulla's; that's what I'd wanted to know. When I inserted a second finger, Jenny turned her head away from the feature: "Please, Harry. You're hurting me." I stopped right away, but left my other arm with her. Horney's sultry, brittle voice filled the sparsely attended movie house. Shortly before the end I smelled my fingers: they smelled like the unripe hazelnuts on our way to school: bitter soapy insipid.

On the way home I became impersonal. Along Bahnhofstrasse I chattered away to the effect that the feature had been tops but the newsreels were always the same old stuff; the thing with the deer had been pretty boring; and tomorrow back to that stupid school; surely it would all come out all right with Papa Brunies: "What do they say about it in Berlin? Have you written Haseloff all about it?" Jenny also thought the feature had been good; Horney was really a great artist; she too hoped it would come out all right with Papa Brunies, though she felt in her bones that he; but Herr Haseloff had written twice since then; he was coming soon to take her away: "He says Langfuhr isn't the right place for me any more. Herr Imbs thinks so too. Will you write me sometimes when I'm in Berlin with the ballet?"

Jenny's information cheered me up. The prospect of soon having her and her mourning black far away from me inspired friendly words. I took her good-naturedly by the shoulder, made detours through dark side streets, stopped with her in February or March under blue blackout lamps, propelled her along to the next lamp-post, pressed her against wrought-iron garden fences, and encouraged her to go to Berlin with Haseloff. Over and over again I promised to write not just now and then but regularly. In the end I commanded her to leave Langfuhr, for Jenny transferred the full responsibility to me: "If you don't want me to leave you, I'll stay with you; but if you think Herr Hascloff is right, I'll go."

I invoked someone who had been taken to Stutthof: "I'll bet that if Papa Brunies were here, he'd say exactly the same as me: Off to Berlin with you! It's the best thing that could happen to you."

On Elsenstrasse Jenny thanked me for the movies. I kissed her again quickly dryly. Her concluding words as usual: "But now I'm a little tired and besides I have English to do for tomorrow."

I was glad she didn't ask me up to Dr. Brunies' empty apartment. What could I have done with her amid crates full of assorted mica gneiss, amid uncleaned pipes, and with desires in my head that asked nothing of Jenny but a good deal of Tulla.

Dear Cousin,

then, shortly before Easter, snow fell. It soon melted away. At the same time you started carrying on with soldiers on furlough, but didn't contract a child. Then shortly after Easter there was an air-raid alarm; but no bombs fell around our way. And early in May Haseloff came and took Jenny away.

He drove up in a black Mercedes with a chauffeur and got out: slender smooth strange. A much too spacious overcoat with strikingly large checks hung loosely over his shoulders. He rubbed white-gloved hands, inspected the front of the Aktienhaus, appraised our house, every floor: I, half behind the curtains, stepped back into the room to the edge of the carpet. My mother had called me to the window: "Say, would you take a look at him!"

I knew him. I was first to see him when he was still new. He threw me a tooth into the hazelnut bush. He went off in the train soon after being reborn. He began to smoke and still smokes—with white gloves. I have his tooth in my change purse. He went away with a sunken mouth. He comes back with a mug full of gold: for he's laughing, he trots down Elsenstrasse a little way and back a little way, laughs, trots, and takes it all in. The houses on both sides, house numbers, odd and even, little stips of garden, pansies. Can't look enough, and breaks into open laughter, showing all the windows Haseloff's mouth full of gold. With thirty-two gold teeth he spits soundless laughter, as though in all this egg-shaped world there were no better reason for showing one's teeth than our Elsenstrasse. But then Felsner-Imbs comes out of our house, respectfully. And then the curtain falls on too much gold on a sunny day in May. Foreshortened as seen from my curtain, the two men greet each other with four hands, as though celebrating a reunion. The chauffeur is stretching his legs beside the Mercedes and takes no interest. But all the windows are loges. The eternally sprouting younger generation form a circle around the reunion. I and the sparrows on the eaves understand: he's back again, takes the pianist by the arm, breaks through the eternally sprouting circle, pushes the pianist into the Aktienhaus, respectfully holds the door open for him, and follows him without looking back.

Jenny had her two suitcases ready, for in less than half an hour she left the Aktienhaus with Felsner-Imbs and Haseloff. She left in mourning. She left with Angustri on her finger and without my bottler-washer necklace; it was in with her underwear in one of the two suitcases that Imbs and Haseloff handed to the chauffeur. The kids drew little men in the dust on the black Mercedes. Jenny stood undecided. The chauffeur took off his cap. Haseloff was about to push Jenny gently into the interior of the car. He had turned up his coat collar, he no longer showed Elsenstrasse his face, he was in a hurry. But Jenny didn't want to get into the car just yet, she pointed at our curtains, and before Imbs and Haseloff could hold her back, she had vanished into our house.

To my mother, who always did what I wanted, I, behind curtains, said: "Don't open if she rings. What on earth can she want?"

Four times the bell rang. Our bell wasn't the kind you press, it was the kind you turn. Our turnbell didn't just scream, it snarled four times, but my mother and I didn't stir from our place behind the curtains.

What our bell repeated four times will stay in my ears.

"Now they're gone," said my mother; but I looked at the miniature chests of walnut, pearwood, and oak in our dining room.

The diminishing engine sound of a receding car has also stayed with me and will probably stay forever.

Dear Cousin Tulla,

a week later a letter came from Berlin; Jenny had written it with her fountain pen. The letter made me as happy as if Tulla had written it with her own hand. But Tulla's hand was writing to a sailor. I ran about with Jenny's letter, telling everybody it was from my girl friend in Berlin, from Jenny Brunies or Jenny Angustri, as she now called herself, for Haseloff her ballet master and Madame Neroda, the managing director of the Strength-through-Joy Ballet, now the German Ballet, had advised her to take a stage name. Her ballet school had already started, and in addition they were rehearsing country dances to early German music which Madame Neroda, who was actually an Englishwoman, had unearthed. This Madame Neroda seemed to be an unusual woman. For instance: "When she goes out, to make calls or even to attend a formal reception, she wears an expensive fur coat but no dress under it, only her dancing tights. But she can afford to do such things. And she has a dog, a Scotty, with eyes exactly like hers. Some people think she's a spy. But I don't believe it and neither does my girl friend."

At intervals of a few days I wrote Jenny a string of love letters very repetitious and full of overt desires. I had to write every letter twice, because the first version was always crawling with slips. Any number of times I wrote: "Believe me, Tulla," wrote: "Why, Tulla? This morning, Tulla. If you want to, Tulla. I want you, Tulla. I dreamed Tulla. Eating Tulla up, holding her tight, loving her, making Tulla a baby."

Jenny answered me promptly in a small tidy hand. Evenly but respecting the margins, she filled two sheets of blue writing paper—both sides—with replies to my propositions and descriptions of her new surroundings. To everything I wanted of Tulla Jenny said yes; except for having babies, it was rather too soon for that— I had myself to consider too; first we must get ahead in our work, she on the stage and I as a historian; that's what I wanted to be.

793

About Neroda she wrote that this extraordinary woman owned the world's largest collection of books on the dance, that she even had an original manuscript from the hand of the great Noverre. She spoke of Herr Haseloff as a rather weird but occasionally comical eccentric, who, once he was through with his strict but imaginatively conducted ballet exercises, cooked up strangely human machines in his cellar workshop. Jenny wrote: "Actually he doesn't think too much of the classical ballet, for often, when the exercises aren't going quite as he would wish, he cracks rather nasty jokes. 'Tomorrow,' he says, 'I'm going to fire you jumping jacks, the whole lot of you. They can put you to work in the munitions factories. If you can't turn a single piroutte as neatly as my little machines, you'll be better off turning out shells.' He claims that his figures in the cellar go into positions lovely enough to give you religion; he says his figures are always well turned out; that he's planning to put one of them up in front of the class, at the bar: 'It'll make you green with envy. Then you'll realize what classical ballet can be, you little holes and stoppers.' "

That's what Herr Haseloff called girl and boy dancers. In one of the next letters Jenny wrote me at Elsenstrasse I found a P.S. in which one such mechanical figure was described and summarily sketched. It stood at the bar, displaying a regulation *port de bras* for the benefit of the little holes and stoppers.

Jenny wrote: "You wouldn't believe it, but I've learned a lot from the mechanical figure, which, incidentally, is neither a hole nor a stopper. Especially, I've learned to carry my back properly, and the little dots in the *port de bras*—Madame Lara neglected that—have become quite clear to me. Whatever I do, whether I'm polishing my shoes or picking up a glass of milk, I always make dots in the air. And even when I yawn— because when the day is over we're all frankly tired—and cover my mouth with my hand, I always watch the dots. But now I must close. I'll love you and hold you tight as I fall asleep and tomorrow morning, too, when I wake up. And please don't read too much or you'll ruin your eyes.— As ever, Your Jenny."

Dear Tulla:

with one of these Jenny letters I tried to strike a bridge: to you. We ran into each other in the stair well of our apartment house, and I made no attempt to dispel the usual blush: "Look, Jenny's written me again. You interested? It's pretty funny, the stuff she writes about love and all that. If you feel like a laugh, you ought to read the stuff she writes. Now she calls herself Angustri like the ring, and pretty soon she's going on tour with the troupe."

I held out the letter as if it were something unimportant and mildly amusing. Tulla flipped the paper with one finger: "You really ought to get some sense into you and stop coming around all the time with the same old applesauce and ballet rubbish."

Tulla wore her hair loose, mustard-brown, shoulder-length, and stringy. There were still faint signs of a permanent wave that the sailor from Putzig had treated her to. A strand of hair hung down over her left eye. With a mechanical movement—Haseloff's figure couldn't have done anything more mechanical—she pushed back the strand of hair with a contemptuous expulsion of breath, and with a shrug of her bony shoulders sent it back down over the same eye. But she wasn't wearing make-up yet. By the time the Hitler-Youth patrol caught her in the railroad station after midnight and then on a bench in Uphagenpark with an ensign from the Neuschottland Naval Training School, she wore make-up all over.

She was kicked out of school. My father spoke of money thrown out the window. To the principal of the Gudrun School, who despite the report of the patrol service wanted to give Tulla another chance, Tulla was said to have said: "Never mind, ma'am, go ahead and throw me out. I've got the joint up to here anyway. What I want is to have a baby by somebody, just to get a little action around here."

Why did you want a baby? Because!—Tulla was thrown out but didn't get a baby. In the daytime she sat home listening to the radio, after supper she went out. Once she brought home six yards of the best Navy serge for herself and her mother. Once she came home with a fox fur from the Arctic front. Once her loot was a bolt of parachute silk. She and her mother wore underthings from all over Europe. When somebody came from the Labor Office and wanted to put her to work in the power plant, she had Dr. Hollatz make out a certificate of poor health: anemia and a shadow on her lung. Tulla obtained extra food tickets and a sick benefit, but not much.

When Felsner-Imbs moved to Berlin with hourglass, porcelain ballerina, goldfish, stacks of music, and faded photographs—Haseloff had engaged him as pianist for the ballet—Tulla gave him a letter to take with him: for Jenny. I have never been able to find out what Tulla wrote with her fountain pen, for all Jenny said in her next to next letter was that Felsner-Imbs had arrived safely, that she had received a very nice letter from Tulla, and that she sent Tulla her very best regards.

There I was on the outside again, and the two of them had something in common. When I ran into Tulla, I didn't turn red any more but chalky. Yes, I still stuck to you, but I gradually learned to hate you and your glue; and hatred—a disease of the soul with which one can live to a ripe old age—made it easier for me to get along with Tulla: amiably and condescendingly, I gave her good advice. My hatred never made me violent, for in the first place I watched myself even in my sleep, in the

795

second place I read too much, in the third place I was a conscientious student, almost a grind, with no time to vent my hatred, and in the fourth place I built myself an altar, on which stood Jenny turned out in her tutu, her arms opened for second position; or more accurately, I piled up Jenny's letters and resolved to become engaged to her.

My darling Tulla,

Jenny could be awfully prim and boring when you sat facing her or walked beside her, but she could be very entertaining with her witty saucy letters. Seen from without, her eyes were silly under melancholy lashes; appraised from within, they had the gift of seeing things dryly and sharply etched, even things that stood on the tips of silver slippers and in stage lighting signified a dying swan.

Thus she described for my benefit a ballet class that Haseloff had given his little holes and stoppers. They were rehearsing a ballet that was going to be called *Scarecrows* or *The Scarecrows* or *The Gardener and the Scarecrows*.

And everything—at the bar on the floor—went wrong. Felsner-Imbs sat with endlessly bowed back and repeated the bit of Chopin to no avail. In the rain outside the windows stood pine trees full of squirrels and the Prussian past. In the morning there had been an air-raid alarm and practice in the furnace room. Now the little holes in leotards were wilting on the long practice bar. Injected with cod-liver oil, the stoppers flapped their eyelashes until Haseloff with a tensing of his knees jumped up on the piano, an occurrence quite familiar to Felsner-Imbs and not at all harmful to the piano, for Haseloff was able, from a standing position, to make high, slow, and long leaps and land delicately on the brown piano lid without jolting the innards of the hard-tuned instrument. At this the holes and stoppers should have come to life, for they all knew perfectly well what Haseloff's rage-propelled leap to the piano meant and boded.

From aloft, not directly but into the big mirror that turned the front wall into a spy, Haseloff spoke warningly to the holes and stoppers: "Do you want my brush to show you how to dance? Haven't you any *joie de vivre*? Do you want rats to bite the swans from underneath? Must Haseloff take out his bag of pepper?"

Once again he built up his notorious bar exercise: "*Grand plié*— twice each in the first, second, and fifth position; eight slow *dégagés* and sixteen quick ones in the second position; eight *petits battements dégagés*, dabbed on the floor with the accent on the outside." But only the holes put the accent on the outside and dabbed in the dot; as for the stoppers, neither the threatened bag of pepper nor Chopin in league with Felsner-Imbs could give them *joie de vivre* or a tidy *plié*: batter on a spoon, mayonnaise, Turkish honey make threads: so streched the boys, or stoppers—Wolf, Marcel, Schmitt, Serge, Gotti, Eberhard, and Bastian. They fluttered their eyelashes, sighed a little between *battements tendus* on half-toe, in the *rond de jambes à la seconde* they twisted their necks like swans just before feeding, and waited in resignation, seven sleep-warm stoppers, for Haseloff's second leap, which, on the occasion of the *grand battement,* was not long in coming.

Haseloff's second leap also started from the standing position: from the piano lid it carried him, with straight knees and amazingly high instep, over the pianist's snow-white hair into the middle of the room, in front of the mirror. And concealing nothing from the mirror, he produced the announced bag, miraculously. The pointed bag, the cone-shaped bag, feared, familiar, the bag, powder-soft, doesaworldofgood butinmoderation, he drew the two-ounce bag from his special breast pocket and ordered all the girls or holes to desist from the bar. He sent them into the corner beside the sizzling, glow-cheeked pot-bellied stove. There they crowded together twittering, turned toward the wall, covering their eyes with pale fingers. And Felsner-Imbs also covered his leonine head with his silk scarf.

For while eyes were covered and a head modestly veiled, Haseloff commanded: *"Face à la barre!"* Seven boys or stoppers excitedly peeled black, pink, egg-yellow, and spring-green leotards from each other's boyish flesh. *"Préparation!"* cried Haseloff with a dry snap of the fingers: their faces to the wall, they lined up along the bar with their indefatigable eyelashes and with fourteen hands clutched the worn wood. Supported by blindly played Chopin, seven trunks bent forward with straight arms and knees, making one and the same soft-skinned boyish bottom jut sevenfold into the well-heated room.

Then Haseloff went into first position alongside the first bottom; in his left hand he held the little conical bag; in the right, as though conjured out of the air, he had a paint brush between his fingers. He dipped the badger-hair brush, expensive and durable, into the little bag and, sustained by Felsner-Imbs, began to whistle merrily the time-honored polonaise as he shifted nimbly, always sure of the mirror, from boy-bottom to stopper-bottom.

In so doing—and this is what all the fuss was about—he made the powder-charged badger brush emerge seven times from the bag and vanish seven times powder-charged in the young men's rear ends, the stopper-bottoms, abracadabra.

No foot powder this. Nor was sleeping powder injected. Nor reducing powder, nor anti-lion powder, nor baking powder, nor insect powder, nor milk powder; neither cocoa nor powdered sugar, nor flour to bake buns with, nor face powder nor tooth powder; it was pepper, black, finely ground pepper, that Haseloff discharged seven times unflaggingly with his brush. Finally, only a hair's breadth from the mirror, he concluded his educational performance with a slow pirouette, stood, his mouth full of gold teeth, facing the room and trumpeted: *"Alors, mes enfants!* Stoppers first, then holes. *Première position: Grand plié, bras en couronne."*

And scarcely had Imbs, no longer blind, flung his Chopin-laden fingers at the keys, than quick as a flash and as though self-propelled, colored leotards rolled over seven peppered stopper-bottoms. An exercise got a wiggle on: swift feet, long legs, graceful arm movements. Eyelashes fell silent, lines awakened, beauty perspired; and Haseloff made his badger brush disappear—somewhere. Such was the long-lasting effect of the pepper that after a successful exercise the holes without pepper and the pepper-animated stoppers could be summoned to a rehearsal of the scare-crow ballet: Third Act, Destruction of the garden by the massed scare-crows, culminating in a *pas de deux.*

Because subsequently the big scene, danced to traditional Prussian military music, was so spicily successful — a precise chaos *sur pointes*— Haseloff called it a day with thirty-two gold teeth, waved his towel, bade Felsner-Imbs close the piano and bury Chopin and Prussia's marches in his brief case, and distributed compliments: "Bravo Wölfchen, bravo Schmittchen, bravo all holes and stoppers! A special bravo for Marcel and Jenny. Hang around, the two of you. We'll do the gardener's daughter and the Prince, first act, without music *en demie-pointe.* The rest of you, go right to bed and no gallivanting around. Tomorrow morning, the whole *corps de ballet,* adduction of the gardener's daughter and grand finale."

Dear Tulla,

in the Jenny letter whose contents I have tried to reproduce, as in all other Jenny letters, it was written how very much she loved me now and forever, even though Haseloff was making up to her—with restraint and ever so ironically. But I mustn't worry about that. Incidentally, she would be coming to Langfuhr, though only for two days: "The apartment after all has to be vacated. And so we've decided to move the furniture and the stone collection to a safe place. You can imagine all the red tape it took to get permission to move the things. But Haseloff knows how to handle people. But he thinks the furniture will be safer in Langfuhr, because Berlin is being bombed more and more. Just the same he wants to move the mica stones to Lower Saxony, where he knows some peasants and the manager of a mine."

Dear Tulla,

first a moving van drove up across the street. Fifteen families occupied the windows of our house. Then, soundlessly, the Mercedes pulled up behind the moving van, but left room for loading. The chauffeur stood promptly at the door with lifted cap: in a black fur coat, possibly mole, her face ensconced in the turned-up collar, Jenny stood on the sidewalk, and raised her eyes for a moment to our windows: a lady who isn't allowed to catch cold. In a black ulster with a brown fur collar, nutria, Haseloff took Jenny's arm. The switchman, the great impresario, half a head shorter than Jenny: Hermann Haseloff, his mouth full of gold teeth. But he didn't laugh, didn't look at our house. Elsenstrasse didn't exist.

My father said from behind his newspaper: "There's no reason why you shouldn't help with the moving as long as you're always writing each other."

I almost missed Jenny's hand in the wide sleeve of her fur coat. She introduced me. Haseloff had only an eighth of a glance available. "Hm," he said, and "Nice-looking stopper." Then he directed the moving men like a *corps de ballet*. I wasn't allowed to help or even to go up to the apartment. The loading of the furniture, heavy pieces, dark brown for the most part, all oak, was exciting, because under Haseloff's direction a bookcase as wide as a wall became weightless. When Jenny's room left the Aktienhaus—Biedermeier in light birch—the pieces hovered over the cubical men and had "balloon." Between the coat rack and the Flemish chest Haseloff half turned to me. Without leaving the movers to their own strength he invited Jenny and me to dinner at the Hotel Eden by the Main Station, where they were staying. Heavy open crates were piled on the sidewalk in among the last kitchen chairs. I accepted: "At half past seven." All at once, as though Haseloff had staged it, the sun broke through up above, awakening sparkle in open crates. The smell of the absent teacher revived too: cold pipe smoke joined in the moving; but some of the mica gneiss had to stay behind. Eight or nine crates walled up the moving van, for two there was no room. That gave me my entrance in Haseloff's moving-man's ballet, for I offered to make room in our cellar for mica gneiss and mica granite, for biotite and muscovite.

My father, whom I asked for permission in the machine room, surprised me by calmly consenting: "That's a good idea, my son. There's plenty of room in the second cellar next to the window frames. Put Dr. Brunies' crates in there. If the old gentleman collected stones all his life, he must have had his reasons."

Dear Tulla,

the crates were moved to our cellar and in the evening I sat beside Jenny, across from Haseloff, in the dining room of the Hotel Eden. Allegedly you had met Jenny in town that afternoon, without Haseloff. Why? Because. We hardly spoke, and Haseloff looked between Jenny and me. You had met, so I heard, at the Café Weitzke on Wollwebergasse. What did you have to talk about? All sorts of things! Jenny's little finger had meanwhile hooked itself to my little finger under the table. I'm sure

799

Haseloff noticed. What had there been to eat at the Café Weitzke? Bad cake and watery ice cream for Jenny. At the Hotel Eden there was turtle soup, breaded veal cutlet with canned asparagus, and for dessert, at Jenny's request, frozen pudding. Maybe I rode after you as far as Kohlenmarkt and saw you in the Café Weitzke: sitting, talking, laughing, saying nothing, crying. Why? Because. After dinner I noticed a thousand and more ice-gray freckles on Haseloff's tense or rigid face. Eddi Amsel, when he still existed, had fewer but larger freckles in his fat face, brownish and genuine. You spent at least two hours chattering away in the Café Weitzke. At half past nine I had to speak: "I used to know somebody who looked like you, but he had a different name."

Haseloff summoned the waiter: "A glass of hot lemonade, please."

I had my lines ready: "First he was called Stephuhn, then he was called Sperballa, then Sperlinski. Do you know him?"

Haseloff, who had a cold, received his hot lemonade: "Thank you. Check please."

Behind me the waiter added up the bill: "For a few minutes the man I knew was even called Zocholl. Then he was called Zylinski. And then he found a name that he still goes by. Would you like to know what it is, or would you, Jenny?"

Haseloff let two white tablets dissolve in a teaspoon and paid with bank notes hidden under the check: "Keep the change."

When I wanted to tell them the man's name, Haseloff swallowed the tablets and took a long drink from the lemonade glass. Then it was too late. And Jenny was tired. Only in the hotel lobby, after Jenny had been allowed to give me a kiss, Haseloff showed a few of his gold teeth and said in a hoarse voice: "You're talented. You know lots of names. I'll help you, today or the day after tomorrow, and now let me tell you one more name: Brauxel written with an x; or Brauksel written like Häksel; or Brauchsel, written like Weichsel. Remember that name and the three ways of spelling it."

Then they both, elegantly and with unnatural slowness, climbed the stairs. Jenny looked round and round and round; even when I wasn't in the hotel lobby any more with three times Brauxel in my head.

Dear Tulla,

he exists. I found him while I was looking for you. He tells me how to write when I write to you. He sends me money so I can write you without having to worry. He owns a mine between Hildesheim and Sarstedt. Or maybe he only manages it. Or holds the biggest block of shares. Or maybe the whole thing is sculduggery camouflage fifth column, even if his name is Brauxel Brauksel Brauchsel. Brauksel's mine produces no ore, no salt, no coal. Brauksel's mine produces something else. I am not allowed to name it. All I am allowed and ordered to say is Tulla, over and over again. And I have to keep the deadline, the fourth of February. And I have to heap up the pile of bones. And I have to start on the last story, for Brauchsel has sent me an urgent telegram: "Aquarius conjunction approaching stop heap up bone pile stop start miscarriage stop let dog loose and finish on time."

There was once a girl, her name was Tulla,

and she had the pure forehead of a child. But nothing is pure. Not even the snow is pure. No virgin is pure. Even a pig isn't pure. The Devil never entirely pure. No note rises pure. Every violin knows that. Every star chimes that. Every knife peels it: even a potato isn't pure: it has eyes, they have to be scooped out.

But what about salt? Salt is pure! Nothing, not even salt, is pure. It's only on boxes that it says: Salt is pure. After all, it keeps. What keeps with it? But it's washed. Nothing can be washed clean. But the elements: pure? They are sterile but not pure. The idea? Isn't it always pure? Even in the beginning not pure. Jesus Christ not pure. Marx Engels not pure. Ashes not pure. And the host not pure. No idea stays pure. Even the flowering of art isn't pure. And the sun has spots. All geniuses menstruate. On sorrow floats laughter. In the heart of roaring lurks silence. In angles lean compasses.—But the circle, the circle is pure!

No closing of the circle is pure. For if the circle is pure, then the snow is pure, the virgin is, the pigs are, Jesus Christ, Marx and Engels, white ashes, all sorrows, laughter, to the left roaring, to the right silence, ideas immaculate, wafers no longer bleeders and geniuses without efflux, all angles pure angles, piously compasses would describe circles: pure and human, dirty, salty, diabolical, Christian and Marxist, laughing and roaring, ruminant, silent, holy, round pure angular. And the bones, white mounds that were recently heaped up, would grow immaculately without crows: pyramids of glory. But the crows, which are not pure, were creaking unoiled, even yesterday. nothing is pure, no circle, no bone. And piles of bones, heaped up for the sake of purity, will melt cook boil in order that soap, pure and cheap; but even soap cannot wash pure.

There was once a girl, her name was Tulla,

and she let numerous pimples, big and little, bloom and fade on her childlike forehead. Her cousin Harry long combated pimples of his own. Tulla never tried tinctures and remedies. Neither ground almonds nor stinky sulphur nor cucumber milk nor zinc ointment found a place on her forehead. Untroubled, she strode through the world pimples first, for she still had the jutting forehead of a child, and dragged sergeants and ensigns into night-black parks: for she wanted to have a baby, but didn't.

After Tulla had vainly tried every rank and branch of service, Harry advised her to try uniformed high school students. He had lately been wearing attractive Air Force blue and living no longer in Elsenstrasse but, in tiptop bathing weather, in the barracks of the Brösen-Glettkau shore battery, a large battery strung out behind the dunes, equipped with twelve 88-millimeter guns and a whole raft of 40-millimeter AA-guns.

At the very start Harry was assigned as Number 6 to an 88-millimeter gun with outriggers. The Number 6 had to adjust the fuze setter with the aid of two cranks. This Harry did throughout his term as an Air Force auxiliary. A priviledged job, for the Number 6 alone of nine cannoneers was entitled to sit on a little stool attached to the gun; when the gun was rotated quickly, he traveled along free of charge and didn't bash his shins against the iron of the outriggers. During gunnery practice Harry sat with his back to the muzzle of the cannon and while with his cranks he made two mechanical pointers hurry after two electrical pointers, he pondered back and forth between Tulla and Jenny. This he did rather adroitly: the mechanical pointer chased the electrical pointer, Tulla chased Jenny, and as far as Harry Liebenau was concerned, the fuze setter was operated to the complete satisfaction of the tech sergeant in charge of training.

Once there was a tech sergeant,
    who could grind his teeth loudly. Along with other decorations he wore the silver wound insignia. Accordingly he limped slightly but obviously between the shacks of the Brösen-Glettkau shore battery. He was looked upon as strict but fair, admired, and superficially imitated. When he went out to the dunes to hunt dune rabbits, he chose as his companion an Air Force auxiliary whom the others called Störtebeker. While hunting dune rabbits the tech sergeant either didn't say a single word or he uttered quotations, interspersed by ponderous pauses, from one and the same philosopher. Störtebeker repeated his quotations and created a philosophical schoolboy language that was soon prattled by many, with varying success.

    Störtebeker prefixed most of his sentences with "I, as a pre-Socratic." Anyone who looked on as he mounted guard could see him drawing in the sand with a stick. With a superiorly guided stick he plotted the advent of the still unuttered essence of unconcealment, or to put it more bluntly, of Being. But if Harry said: "Being," Störtebeker corrected him impatiently: "There you go again. What you really mean is essents—things that are."

    Even in everyday matters philosophical tongues made pre-Socratic leaps, appraising every commonplace incident or object with the tech sergeant's painstakingly acquired knowledge. Underdone potatoes in their

jackets—the kitchen was poorly supplied and even more poorly run—
were called "spuds forgetful of Being." If someone reminded someone of
something that had been borrowed, promised, or asserted days before,
the answer came prompt and absolute: "Who thinks about thoughts any
more," or, analogically, about the borrowed, the promised, or the asserted? The daily facts of life in an AA battery, such as semi-serious
disciplinary drill, tedious practice alerts, or greasy-messy rifle cleaning,
were disposed of with an expression overheard from the tech sergeant:
"After all, the essence of being-there is its existence."

The word "existence" and its collaterals met all requirements: "Would
you exist me a cigarette? Who feels like existing a movie with me? Shut
your trap or I'll exist you one."

To go on sick call was to plug for a sack existence. And anybody
who had hooked a girl—as Störtebeker had hooked Harry's cousin
Tulla—boasted after taps how often he had bucked the girl's existence.

And existence itself—Störtebeker tried to draw it in the sand with
a stick: it looked different each time.

There was once an Air Force auxiliary

named Störtebeker, who was supposed to get Harry's cousin with
child and probably did his best. On Sundays when the Brösen-Glettkau
battery was open to visitors, Tulla came out in high-heeled shoes and
took her nostrils and pimply forehead for a stroll amid 88-millimeter
guns. Or she hobbled into the dunes between the tech sergeant and Air
Force auxiliary Störtebeker, in the hope that they would both make her
a baby; but tech sergeant and Air Force auxiliary preferred to indulge in
other proofs of existence: they shot dune rabbits.

There was once a cousin,

his name was Harry Liebenau and all he was good for was looking
on and saying what he'd heard other people say. There he lay flat with
half-closed eyes in the sand amid wind flattened beach grass and made
himself still flatter when three figures appeared on the crest of the dune.
The foursquare staff sergeant, with the sun behind him, held a heavy
protective arm around Tulla's shoulder. Tulla was carrying her high-
heeled shoes in her right hand and with the left clutched the hind paws
of a bleeding dune rabbit. To the right of Tulla—but without touching
her—Störtebeker held his carbine, barrel down. The three figures didn't
notice Harry. For an eternity they stood motionlessly silhouetted, because
the sun was still behind them, on the crest of the dune. Tulla reached
up to the tech sergeant's chest. She carried his arm like a crossbeam.
Störtebeker to one side and yet belonging, rigid and on the lookout for
Being. A handsome and precise picture that grieved the flat-lying Harry,

for he had less rapport than the bleeding rabbit with the three figures against the drooping sun.

There was once a picture,

painful at sunset; Air Force auxiliary Harry Liebenau was never to see it again, for suddenly one day he had to pack. Inscrutable decree transferred him, Störtebeker, thirty other Air Force auxiliaries, and the tech sergeant to another battery. No more dunes gently-wavy. No Baltic Sea, smoothly virginal. Beach flexibly musical. No longer did twelve eighty-eights jut somberly into the balmy bugle-call sky. Never again the reminders of home in the background: Brösen's wooden church, Brösen's black and white fishermen's cows, Brösen's fishnets hung on poles to be dried or photographed. Never again did the sun set for them behind rabbits sitting on their haunches and worshipping the departing sun with erect ears.

In the Kaiserhafen battery there were no such pious animals, only rats; and rats worship fixed stars.

The way to the battery led from Troyl, a harbor quarter between the Lower City and the Holm, for three quarters of an hour over sand roads through sparse woods in the direction of Weichselmünde. Left behind: the widely scattered repair shops of the German Railways, the lumber sheds behind the Wojahn shipyard; and here projected into the area between the Troyl streetcar stop and the Kaiserhafen battery, the water rats held uncontested sway.

But the smell that hung over the battery and didn't budge a step even in a violent west wind, didn't come from rats.

The first night after Harry moved into the battery, his gym shoes were gnawed, both of them. The regulations prohibited getting out of bed with bare feet. Everywhere they sat and grew fatter; on what? They were reviled as the grounds of the ground; but to this name they did not answer. The battery was equipped with metal ratproof lockers. Many were slain, unsystematically. It didn't help much. Then the tech sergeant, who performed the functions of top sergeant in his battery and every morning reported to his Captain Hufnagel how many corporals and sergeants, how many Air Force auxiliaries and Ukrainian volunteers had fallen in, issued an order of the day whereby the water rats were appreciably diminished; but the smell that hung over the battery did not diminish: it didn't come from the grounds of the ground.

There was once an order of the day;

it promised premiums for slain rodents. The Pfc.'s and corporals, all matured in the service, received a cigarette for three rats. The Ukrainian volunteers were illicitly given a package of machorka if they could produce eighteen. The Air Force auxiliaries received a roll of raspberry drops for five rats. Some of the corporals gave us three cigarettes for two rolls of raspberry drops. We didn't smoke machorka. In accordance with the order of the day, the battery split up into hunt groups. Harry belonged to a group that staked out its territory in the washroom, which had only one door and no window. First the washroom door was left open and leftovers of food were deposited in the washtroughs. Then both drains were plugged up. Thereupon we waited behind the windows of the school shack until it began to grow dark. Soon we saw the long shadows pouring past the shack toward the washroom door with a single monotone whistle. No flute strains lured; the suction of an open door. And yet nothing was there but cold grits and kohlrabi stalks. Strewn across the threshold, beef bones ten times boiled and two handfuls of moldy oat flakes—contributed by the kitchen—were expected to lure rats. They would have come even without the oats.

When the washroom promised sufficient game, the school shack spat out five men in high rubber boots, armed with clubs, whose tips were armed with hooks. The washroom swallowed up the five. The last slammed the door. Obliged to remain outside: belated rats, forgetful of Being; the smell grounded on the battery; the moon in case it should nihilate; stars in so far as they were thrown; the radio, blaring from world-related noncoms' barracks; the ontic voices of ships. For inside rose up a music *sui generis*. No longer monotone, but leaping over octaves: grit-shrill kohlrabi-soft bony tinny plucked nasal inauthentic. And, as rehearsed, suddenly illumination came-to-be: five left-handed flashlights part the darkness. For the space of two sighs, silence. Now they rise up lead-gray in the light, slide on their bellies over tin-sheathed washtroughs, smack halfpoundly on the tile flooring, crowd around the drains plugged with oakum, try to climb up the concrete pillar and get at the brown wood. Claw themselves fast, scurry away. Unwilling to leave the grits and stalks. Eager to save beef bones and not their own skins: smooth, waxed, water-proof, sound, lovely, precious, vulnerable, currycombed for thousands of years, upon which the hooks descend without regard: No, rat blood is not green but. Are stripped off with boots and nothing else. Are spitted, two with the same hook: Being-beside—Being-with. Are caught in mid-air: music! The same old song since the days of Noah. Rat stories, true and made up. World-relation attitude irruption: grain ships gnawed bare. Hollowed-out granaries. The Nothing acknowledged. Egypt's lean years. And when Paris was besieged. And when the rat sat in the tabernacle. And when thought forsook metaphysics. And when help was most needed. And when the rats left the ship. And when the rats came back. When they attacked even infants and old people riveted to their chairs. When they negated the newborn babe away from the young mother's breast.

When they attacked the cats and nothing was left of the rat-terriers but bare teeth, which sparkle to this day, lined up in the museum. And when they carried the plague back and forth and pierced the pink flesh of the pigs. When they devoured the Bible and multiplied in accordance with its instructions. When they disemboweled the clocks and confuted time. When they were sanctified in Hamelin. And when someone invented the poison that struck their fancy. When rattail knotted with rattail to make the rope that plumbed the well. When they grew wise, as long as poems, and appeared on the stage. When they channelized transcendence and crowded into the light. When they nibbled away the rainbow. When they announced the beginning of the world and made leaks in hell. When rats went to heaven and sweetened St. Cecilia's organ. When rats squeaked in the ether and were resettled on stars, ratless stars. When rats existed self-grounded. When an order of the day became known, which offered rewards for rats, slain ones: coarse tobacco, hand-rolled cigarettes, sweet-and-sour raspberry drops. Rat stories rat stories: They collect in the corners. If it doesn't hit them, it hits concrete. They pile up. Stringtails. Curly noses. Fleeing forward. Vulnerable, they attack. Club must help club. Flashlights fall soft, roll hard, are rolled; but buried crosswise, they still glare through, and when dug up they point again to something bounding from a mound that lay still, already written off. For each club counts as it goes along: seventeen, eighteen, thirty-one. But the thirty-second runs, is gone, back again, two hooks too late, a club pounces too soon, whereupon it bites its way through and through and through and topples Harry over: the soles of his rubber boots slip on terror-wet tiles. He falls back soft and screams loud; from the other clubs constrained laughter. On blood-soaked furs, on prey, on quivering layers, on gluttonous generations, on never-ending rat history, on consumed grits, on stalks, Harry screams: "I've been bitten. Been bitten. Bitten . . ." But no rat had. Only fear when he fell, when he fell not hard but soft.

Then all grew still within the washroom walls. Anyone who had an ear available heard the world-related radio blaring from the noncoms' barracks. A few clubs kept aiming dispiritedly and struck what was quivering-to-an-end. Perhaps clubs couldn't cease-to-exist from one second to the next just because there was silence. The clubs still hold a vestige of life; it had to emerge and carry on a vestigial existence. But even when on top of the silence club-peace set in, the rat story wasn't over; for Harry Liebenau filled in this existential pause. Because he had fallen soft, he was obliged to throw up at length inot an empty bowl that had contained grits. He couldn't empty his stomach on the rats. They had to be counted, lined up, and tied by their tails to a wire. There were four heavily tenanted lengths of wire, which the tech sergeant, aided by the company clerk who kept the tally, was able to count at morning roll call: A hundred and fifty-eight rats, rounded out on the friendly side, yielded thirty-two rolls of raspberry drops, half of which Harry's hunt group exchanged for cigarettes.

The strung-up rats—that same morning they had to be buried behind the latrine—smelled damp, earthy, with an overtone of sourness, like an open potato cellar. The smell over the battery had greater density: no rat exhaled it.

There was once a battery —

it was near Kaiserhafen and for that reason was called the Kaiserhafen battery. Conjointly with the Brösen-Glettkau battery, the Heubude, Pelonken, Zigankenberg, Camp Narvik, and Altschottland batteries, it guarded the air space over Danzig and its harbor.

During Harry's term of service in the Kaiserhafen battery, there were only two air-raid alerts; but rats were hunted every day. When once a four-engine bomber was shot down over Oliva Forest, the Pelonken and Altschottland batteries shared the credit; the Kaiserhafen battery came off empty-handed, but could point to increasing success in purging the battery area of water rats.

Ah yes, this being-in-the-midst-of surpassed itself, attaining the dimension of a world-project! And Harry's hunt group was among the most successful. But all the groups, even the volunteer auxiliaries who worked behind the latrine, were outdone by Störtebeker, who joined no group.

He withdrew rats in broad daylight and always had an audience. As a rule he lay on his belly in front of the kitchen shack, right next to the drain cover. He grounded with long arm in a drain which provided Störtebeker with overarching withdrawal from the sewer that ran from Troyl to the drainage fields.

O manifold why! Why thus and not otherwise? Why water rats and not other essents? Why anything at all rather than nothing? These questions in themselves contained the first last primordial answer to all questioning: "The essence of the rat is the transcendentally originating threefold dispersion of the rat in the world-project or in the sewage system."

You couldn't help admiring Störtebeker, although a heavy leather glove, such as welders wear, protected his right hand that lurked open in the drain. To tell the truth, we all waited to see rats, four or five of them, chew up his glove and lacerate his bare hand. But Störtebeker lay serenely with barely open eyes, sucking his raspberry drop—he didn't smoke—and every two minutes with suddenly rising leather glove smacked down a water rat with rat head on the corrugated edge of the drain cover. Between rat death and rat death he whispered in his own tongue, which however had been infected with obscurity by the tech sergeant's language, rat propositions and ontological rat truths, which, so we all believed, lured the prey within reach of his glove and made possible his overarching withdrawal. Imperturbably, while he harvested below and piled up above, his discourse ran its course: "The rat withdraws itself by unconcealing itself into the ratty. So the rat errates the ratty, illuminating it with errancy. For the ratty has come-to-be in the errancy where the rat errs and so fosters error. That is the essential area of all history."

Sometimes he called not-yet-withdrawn rats "latecomers." He referred to the piled-up rats as "foretimely" or as "essents." When, his work accomplished, Störtebeker surveyed his ordered prey, he spoke almost tenderly and with a mild didacticism: "The rat can endure without the ratty, but never can there be rattiness without the rat." In an hour he produced as many as twenty-five water rats and could have withdrawn more if he had wanted to. Störtebeker used the same wire as we did for stringing up water rats. This tail-knotted and enumerable demonstration, repeated every morning, he termed his being-there-relatedness. With it he earned quantities of raspberry drops. Sometimes he gave Harry's cousin a roll. Often, as though to appease the ratty, he tossed three separate drops ceremonially into the open drain outside the kitchen shack. Concepts gave rise to a controversy among schoolboys. We were never sure whether the sewer should be termed world-project or errancy.

But the smell that grounded on the battery came neither from world-project nor from errancy, as Störtebeker called his multirelational drain.

There was once a battery,

over which, from first gray to last gray, there flew busy, never-resting crows. Not gulls but crows. There were gulls over Kaiserhafen proper, over the lumber warehouses, but not over the battery. If gulls ever invaded the area, a furious cloud immediately darkened brief happening. Crows do not tolerate gulls.

But the smell that hung over the battery came neither from crows nor from gulls, which weren't there anyway. While Pfc.'s, corporals, Ukrainian volunteer auxiliaries, and Air Force auxiliaries slew rats for reward, the ranks from sergeant to Captain Hufnagel had a different distraction: shooting—though not for promised rewards, but only to fire and hit something—individual crows out of the agglomeration of crows over the battery. Yet the crows remained and became no fewer.

But the smell which hung over the battery, which stood between barracks and gun positions, between the computer and the shrapnel trenches, and scarcely moved its supporting leg, the smell which, as Harry and everyone else knew, was projected neither by rats nor by crows, which arose from no drain and hence from no errancy, this smell was wafted, regardless of whether the wind was working from Putzig or Dirschau, from the harbor-mouth bar or from the open sea, by a whitish mound blocked off by barbed wire and situated to the south of the battery. This mound stood in front of, and half hid, a brick-red factory, which from squat chimney discharged self-involved smoke, which probably dropped its fallout on Troyl or the Lower City. Between mound and factory ended railroad tracks leading to the Island Station. The mound, neatly conical, rose just a little higher than a rusty shaking-conveyor similar to those used in coal yards and potash mines for piling waste. At the foot of the mound tip cars stood motionless on a movable track. The mound shimmered faintly when struck by the sun. It stood out, sharply silhouetted, when the sky hung low and touched it. If you disregarded the crows that inhabited it, the mound was clean; but it has been written at the beginning of this concluding tale, that nothing is pure. And thus, for all its whiteness, the mound to one side of the Kaiserhafen battery was not pure; it was a pile of bones, and its components, even after processing in the factory, were still overgrown with remnants; and the crows couldn't stop living there, restlessly black. So it came about that a smell, which hovered over the battery like the bell that didn't feel like going to Rome, injected into every mouth, Harry's too, a taste which, even after the immoderate consumption of raspberry drops, lost none of its heavy sweetness.

No one talked about the pile of bones. But everybody saw smelled tasted it. Anyone who stepped out of a barracks whose doors opened southward had the cone-shaped mound in his field of vision. Anyone who like Harry, the Number 6, sat upraised beside a gun and who, in gunnery practice, was swung around with gun fuze setter in accordance with instructions given by the computer, was time and time again, as though computer and bone-pile were engaged in conversation, confronted with a picture: a whitish mountain beside a smoke-spewing factory, an idle shaking-conveyor, motionless tip cars, and a moving blanket of crows. Nobody spoke of the picture. Anyone who dreamed teeming images of the mound remarked over his morning coffee that he had had a funny dream: about climbing stairs or about school. At the most, a phrase which had been used emptily until then took on, in the usual conversations, a vague weightiness that may have come from the unnamed mound. Words occur to Harry: placedness—instandingness—nihilation; for in the daytime workers never moved tip cars to diminish the placedness, although the factory was under steam. No freight cars rolled on tracks and came from the Island Station. In the daytime the shaking-conveyor gave instandingness nothing to chew on. But once during a night maneuver—for one hour the eighty-eight had to chase a target plane caught in four searchlights—Harry and everybody else heard work sounds for the first time. The factory was still blacked out, but lanterns red and white were waved on the railroad tracks. Freight cars bumped each other. A monotonous clanking started up; the shaking-conveyor. Rust against rust: the tip cars. Voices, commands, laughter: for an hour activity prevailed in the nihilation area, while the target plane flew over the city again from the sea side, slipped away from the searchlights, and, caught again, became a Platonic target: The Number 6 manned the fuze setter, trying with cranks to make two mechanical pointers coincide with two electrical pointers and unflinchingly nihilating the evasive essent.

The next day placedness took on a quality of growth, for Harry and all those who had been disregarding the mound. The crows had received visitors. The smell remained unchanged. But no one inquired after its meaning, although Harry and everyone else had it on their tongues.

There was once a pile of bones —

so it was called, ever since Harry's cousin Tulla had spat out the words in the direction of the mound.

"That's a pile o' bones," she said, helping with her thumb. Harry and many others contradicted, but didn't state exactly what was piled up to the south of the battery.

"Bet you it's bones. And what's more, human bones. Everybody knows that." Tulla offered to bet with Störtebeker rather than her cousin. All three and others were sucking raspberry drops.

Though freshly uttered, Störtebeker's answer had been ready for weeks: "We must conceive of pildupedness in the openness of Being, the divulgation of care, and endurance to death as the consummate essence of existence."

Tulla demanded greater precision: "And I'm telling you they come straight from Stutthof, want to bet?"

Störtebeker refused to be pinned down geographically. He declined the bet and became impatient: "Will you stop chewing my ear off with your threadbare scientific concepts. The most we can say is that here Being has come into unconcealment."

But when Tulla kept harping on Stutthof and called unconcealment by its name, Störtebeker evaded the proffered bet with a grandiose gesture of blessing which took in the battery and the mound of bones: "There lies the essence-ground of all history."

Rats went on being slain after duty hours and even during policing-and-mending period. The ranks from sergeant up shot crows. The smell clung to the battery, no relief showed up. And Tulla said, not to Störtebeker, who was standing aside, drawing figures in the sand, but to the tech sergeant, who had twice exhausted the magazine of his carbine: "Want to bet that they're not honest-to-God human bones, a whole pile of them?"

It was Sunday, visitors' day. But only a few visitors, mostly parents, stood strange in civilian clothes beside their sons who had shot up too fast. Harry's parents hadn't come. November was dragging on, and rain hovered the whole time between low clouds and the earth with its barracks. Harry was standing with the group around Tulla and the tech sergeant, who was loading his carbine for the third time.

"Want to bet that . . ." said Tulla and held out a small white hand ready to shake on it. Nobody wanted to. The hand remained alone. Störtebeker's stick projected the world in the sand. On Tulla's forehead pimples crumbled. Harry's hand played with pieces of bone glue in pants pockets. And then the tech sergeant said: "I bet they're not . . ." and shook on it, without looking at Tulla.

Instantly, as though in possession of a complete plan, Tulla turned on her heels and took the broad strip of weeds between two gun positions as her path. Despite the damp cold she had on only a sweater and a pleated skirt. She strode along on bare spindly legs, arms locked behind back, hair stringy, colorless, and far removed from her last permanent. She grew smaller as she walked, but remained distinct in the damp air.

At first Harry and everybody thought: Moving so unswervingly, she'll pass straight through the barbed-wire fence; but just before the barbs, she dropped to the ground, lifted the bottommost strand of the fence between battery area and factory area, rolled under without difficulty, stood again knee-deep in withered-brown weeds, and strode again, but now as though bucking resistance, toward the crow-inhabited mound.

Harry and everybody looked after Tulla and forgot the raspberry drops on their palates. Störtebeker's stick hesitated in the sand. A grinding gathered strength: somebody had grit between his teeth. And only when Tulla stood tiny in front of the mound, when crows lazily rose up, when Tulla stooped down—bending in the middle—only when Tulla about-faced and came back, more quickly than everybody and Harry had feared, the grinding between the tech sergeant's teeth ebbed away; whereupon silence broke out, the silence that scoops out the ears.

She didn't come back empty-handed. What she carried between two hands rolled under the wire of the barbed-wire fence with her into the battery area. Between two 88-millimeter guns, which in line with the last order of the computer pointed to northwest at exactly the same angle as the other two guns, Tulla grew larger. A short intermission takes as long as Tulla's trip there and back. For five minutes she shrank to toy size and then expanded: almost grown up. Her forehead was still pimpleless, but what she carried in front of her already meant something. Störtebeker started a new world-project. Again the tech sergeant ground gravel, coarse gravel this time, between his teeth. The silence was hatch-marked with self-grounded sounds.

When Tulla stood in front of everybody and to one side of her cousin with her gift, she said without special emphasis: "See? Do I win or don't I?"

The tech sergeant's flat hand struck the left side of her face from the temple over the ear to the chin. Her ear didn't fall off. Tulla's head grew hardly smaller. But she dropped the skull, the one she had brought back, on the spot.

With two clammy yellow hands Tulla rubbed her struck cheek, but didn't run away. On her forehead crumbled exactly as many pimples as before. The skull was a human skull and didn't break when Tulla dropped it, but bounced twice in the weeds. The tech sergeant seemed to see more than the skull. A few looked away over barracks roofs. Harry was unable to pry his eyes away. A piece of the skull's lower jaw was missing. Mister and little Thrasher cracked jokes. Quite a few laughed gratefully in the right places. Störtebeker tried to make the oncoming manifest itself in the sand. His narrow-set eyes saw the essent which clings to itself in its fate, whereupon, suddenly and unexpectedly, world came-to-be; for the tech sergeant shouted with his carbine on safety: "You bastards! Get moving! To your barracks! Policing-and-mending time!"

All moved lethargically and made detours. Jokes congealed. Between the shacks Harry turned his head on shoulders that didn't want to join in the turning: the tech sergeant stood rigid and rectangular with dangling carbine, self-conscious as on the stage. Behind him held geometrically still: placedness, instandingness, nihilation, the essence-ground of history, the difference between Being and the essent—the ontological difference.

But the volunteer auxiliaries were batting the breeze as they peeled potatoes in the kitchen shack. The noncoms' radio was dishing out a request concert. The Sunday visitors took their leave in an undertone. Tulla was standing right next to her cousin, rubbing the struck side of her face. Her mouth, distorted by her massaging hand, muttered past Harry: "Is this the way to treat me when I'm pregnant?"

Naturally Harry had to say: "By whom?"

But she didn't care about that: "Want to bet I'm not?"

Harry didn't want to, because Tulla won all bets. Outside the washroom he pointed his thumb at the half-open door: "In that case, you'd better wash your hands right away, with soap."

Tulla obeyed.—Nothing is pure.

There was once a city —

in addition to the suburbs of Ohra, Schidlitz, Oliva, Emmaus, Praust, Sankt Albrecht, Schellmühl, and the seaport suburb of Neufahrwasser, it had a suburb named Langfuhr. Langfuhr was so big and so little that whatever happens or could happen in this world, also happened or could have happened in Langfuhr.

In this suburb, with its kitchen gardens, drill grounds, drainage fields, slightly sloping cemeteries, shipyards, athletic fields, and military compounds, in Langfuhr, which harbored roughly 72,000 registered inhabitants, which possessed three churches and a chapel, four high schools, a vocational and home-economics school, at all times too few elementary schools, but a brewery with Aktien Pond and icehouse, in Langfuhr, which derived prestige from the Baltic Chocolate Factory, the municipal airfield, the railroad station, the celebrated Engineering School, two movie houses of unequal size, a car barn, the always overcrowded Stadium, and a burned-out synagogue; in the well-known suburb of Langfuhr, whose authorities operated a municipal poorhouse-and-orphanage and a home for the blind, picturesquely situated near Heiligenbrunn, in Langfuhr, incorporated in 1854, a pleasant residential section on the fringe of Jäschkental Forest where the Gutenberg monument was located, in Langfuhr, whose streetcar lines went to Brösen, the seaside resort, Oliva, the episcopal seat, and the city of Danzig—in Danzig-Langfuhr, then, a suburb made famous by the Mackensen Hussars and the last Crown Prince, a suburb traversed from end to end by the Striessbach, there lived a girl by the name of Tulla Pokriefke, who was pregnant but didn't know by whom.

In the same suburb, actually in the same apartment house on Elsenstrasse, which like Hertastrasse and Luisenstrasse connects Labesweg with Marienstrasse, lived Tulla's cousin; his name was Harry Liebenau, he was serving as an Air Force auxiliary in the Kaiserhafen AA battery and was not one of those who might have impregnated Tulla. For Harry merely cogitated in his little head what others actually did. A sixteen-year-old who suffered from cold feet and always stood slightly to one side. A knowledgeable young man, who read a hodgepodge of books on history and philosophy and took care of his handsomely wavy medium-brown hair A bundle of curiosity who mirrored everything with his gray, but not cold-gray eyes and had a fragile, porous feeling about his smooth but not sickly body An always cautious Harry, who believed not in God but in the Nothing, yet did not want to have his sensitive tonsils removed. A melancholic, who liked honey cake, poppy-seed cake, and shredded coconut, and though not a good swimmer had volunteered for the Navy. A young man of inaction, who tried to murder his father by means of long poems in school copybooks and referred to his mother as the cook. A hypersensitive boy, who, standing and lying, broke out in sweat over his cousin and unswervingly though secretly thought of a black shepherd dog. A fetishist, who for reasons carried a pearl-white incisor tooth in his purse. A visonary, who lied a good deal, spoke softly, turned red when, believed this and that, and regarded the never-ending war as an extension of his schooling. A boy, a young man, a uniformed high school student, who venerated the Führer, Ulrich von Hutten, General Rommel, the historian Heinrich von Treitschke, for brief moments Napoleon, the panting movie actor Emil Jannings, for a while Savonarola, then again Luther, and of late the philosopher Martin Heidegger. With the help of these models he succeeded in burying a real mound made of human bones under medieval allegories. The pile of bones, which in reality cried out to high heaven between Troyl and Kaiserhafen, was mentioned in his diary as a place of sacrifice, erected in order that purity might come-to-be in the luminous, which transluminates purity and so fosters light.

In addition to the diary Harry Liebenau kept up an often languishing and then for a time lively correpondence with a girl friend, who under the stage name of Jenny Angustri danced in the German Ballet in Berlin and who in the capital and on tours of the occupied regions appeared first as a member of the *corps de ballet,* later as a soloist.

When Air Force auxiliary Harry Liebenau had a pass, he went to the movies and took the pregnant Tulla Pokriefke. Before Tulla was pregnant, Harry had tried several times in vain to persuade her to attend the movies by his side. Now that she was telling all Langfuhr: "Somebody's knocked me up"—though there were still no visible signs—she was more indulgent and said to Harry: "It's O.K. with me if you'll pay."

They let several films flicker past them in Langfuhr's two movie houses. The Art Cinema ran first the newsreel, then the educational film, then the feature. Harry was in uniform; Tulla was sitting there in a much too spacious coat of Navy serge, which she had had tailored especially for her condition. While grapes were being harvested on rainy screen and peasant girls, festooned with grapes, wreathed with vine-leaves, and forced into corsets, were smiling, Harry tried to clinch with his cousin. But Tulla disengaged herself with the mild reproach: "Cut that out, Harry. There's no sense in it now. You should have come around sooner."

In the movies Harry always had a supply of raspberry drops on him, which were paid out in his battery every time you had laid low a specific number of water rats. Accordingly, they were known as rat drops. In the darkness, while up front the newsreel started up with a din, Harry peeled paper and tin foil from a roll of raspberry drops, thrust his thumbnail between the first and the second drop, and offered Tulla the roll. Tulla lifted off the raspberry drop with two fingers, clung to the newsreel with both pupils, sucked audibly, and whispered while up front the muddy season was setting in in Center Sector: "Everything stinks in that battery of yours, even the raspberry drops, of that whatchacallit behind the fence. You ought to ask for a transfer."

But Harry had other desires, which were fulfilled in the movies: Gone: the muddy season. No more Christmas preparations on the Arctic front. Counted: the gutted T-34 tanks. Docked: the U-boat after a suc-

cessful expedition. Taken off: our fighter planes to attack the terror bombers. Different music. Different cameraman: a quiet pebble-strewn afternoon,
sunlight sprinkling through autumn leaves: the Führer's headquarters.
"Hey, look. There he runs stands wags his tail. Between him and the
aviator. Sure thing, that's him: our dog. Our dog's dog, I mean; it's him
all over. Prinz, that's Prinz, that our Harras . . ."

For a good minute, while the Führer and Chancellor under low-
pulled visor cap, behind anchored hands, chats with an Air Force
officer—was it Rudel?—and walks back and forth among the trees at the
Führer's headquarters, an obviously black shepherd is privileged to stand
beside his boots, rub against the Führer's boots, let the side of his neck
be patted—for once the Führer unlocks his anchored hands, only to
recouple them as soon as the newsreel has captured the cordiality prevailing
between master and dog.

Before Harray took the last streetcar to Troyl—he had to change at
the Main Station for the Heubude train—he took Tulla home. They
talked by turns: neither listened: she about the feature; he about the
newsreel. In Tulla's picture a girl was raped while picking mushrooms
and consequently—something Tulla refused to understand—jumped in
the river; Harry tried, in Störtebeker's philosophical language, to keep
the newsreel alive and at the same time define it: "The way I see it, dog-
being—the very fact of it—implies that an essent dog is thrown into his
there. His being-in-the-world is the dog-there, regardless of whether his
there is a carpenter's yard or the Führer's headquarters or some realm
removed from vulgar time. For future dog-being is not later than the
dog-there of having-beenness, which in turn is not anterior to being-held-
out-into the dog-now."

Nevertheless, Tulla said outside the Pokriefkes' door: "Beginning
next week I'll be in my second month, and by Christmas you're sure to
see something."

Harry dropped in at his parent's apartment for fifteen minutes,
meaning to take some fresh underwear and edibles. His father, the carpenter, had swollen feet because he had been on them all day: from one
building site to another. Consequently he was soaking his feet in the
kitchen. Large and gnarled, they moved sadly in the basin. You couldn't
tell from the carpenter's sighs whether it was the well-being bestowed by
his footbath or tangled memories that made him sigh. Harry's mother
was already holding the towel. She was kneeling and had taken off her
reading glasses. Harry pulled a chair over from the table and sat down
between father and mother: "Want me to tell you a terrific story?"

As his father took one foot out of the basin and his mother expertly
received the foot in the Turkish towel, Harry began: "There was once a
dog, his name was Perkun. Perkun sired the bitch Senta. And Senta

whelped Harras. And the stud dog Harras sired Prinz. And do you know where I just saw our Prinz? In the newsreel. At the Führer's headquarters. Between the Führer and Rudel. Plain as day, out of doors. Might have been our Harras. You've got to go see it, Papa. You can leave before the feature if you've had enough. I'm definitely going again, maybe twice."

With one dry but still steaming foot, the carpenter nodded absently. He said of course he was glad to hear it and would go see the newsreel if he could find time. He was too tired to be pleased aloud though he tried hard, and later, with two dry feet, actually did put his pleasure into words: "You don't say, our Harras' Prinz. And the Führer patted him in the newsreel. And Rudel was there too. You don't say."

There was once a newsreel;

it showed the muddy season in Center Sector, Christmas preparations on the Arctic front, the aftermath of a tank battle, laughing workers in a munitions plant, wild geese in Norway, Hitler Cubs collecting junk, sentries on the Atlantic Wall, and a visit to the Führer's headquarters. All this and more could be seen not only in the two movie houses of the suburb of Langfuhr, but in Salonika as well. For from there came a letter written to Harry Liebenau by Jenny Brunies, who under the stage name of Jenny Angustri was performing for German and Italian soldiers.

"Just imagine," Jenny wrote, "what a small world it is: last night —for once we weren't playing—I went to the movies with Herr Haseloff. And whom did I see in the newsreel? I couldn't have been mistaken. And Herr Haseloff also thought the black shepherd, who was there for at least a minute in the headquarters scene, could only be Prinz, your Harras' Prinz.

"The funny part of it is that Herr Haseloff can't possibly have seen your Harras except in the photographs I've shown him. But he has tremendous imagination, and not only in artistic matters. And he always wants to know about things down to the slightest details. That's probably why he has sent in a request to the propaganda unit here. He wants a copy of the newsreel for purposes of documentation. He'll probably get it, for Herr Haseloff has connections all over, and it's unusual for anyone to refuse him anything. Oh, Harry, then we'll be able to look at the newsreel together, any time we please, later, when the war is over. And someday when we have children, we'll be able to show them on the screen how things used to be.

"It's stupid here. I haven't seen a bit of Greece, just rain. Unfortunately we had to leave our good Felsner-Imbs in Berlin. The school goes on even when we're on tour.

"But just imagine—but of course you know all about it—Tulla is expecting a baby. She told me about it on an open postcard. I'm glad for her, though I sometimes think she's going to have a hard time of it, all alone without a husband to take care of her or any real profession . . ."

Jenny did not conclude her letter without pointing out how very much the unaccustomed climate fatigued her and how very much—even in far-off Salonika—she loved her Harry. In a postscript she asked Harry to look out for his cousin as much as possible. "In her condition, you know, she needs a prop, especially as her home isn't exactly what you would call well regulated. I'm going to send her a package with Greek honey in it. Besides, I've unraveled two practically new sweaters I was recently able to buy in Amsterdam. One light-blue, the other pale-pink. I'll be able to knit her at least four pairs of rompers and two little jackets. We have so much time between rehearsals and even during performances."

There was once a baby,

which, although rompers were already being knitted for him, was not to be born. Not that Tulla didn't want the baby. She still showed no sign, but she represented herself, with a sweetness verging on the maudlin, as an expectant mother. Nor was there any father growling with averted face: I don't want a child! for all the fathers that might have come into consideration were absorbed from morning till night in their own affairs. To mention only the tech sergeant from the Kaiserhafen battery and Air Force auxiliary Störtebeker: the tech sergeant shot crows with his carbine and ground his teeth whenever he made a bull's-eye: Störtebeker soundlessly drew in the sand what his tongue whispered: errancy, the ontological difference, the world-project in all its variations. How, with such existential occupations, could the two of them find time to think of a baby that suffused Tulla Pokriefka with sweetness though it did not yet round out her expressly tailored coat?

Only Harry, the receiver of letters, the writer of letters, said: "How are you feeling? Are you sick to your stomach before breakfast? What does Dr. Hollatz say? Don't strain yourself. You really ought to stop smoking. Should I get you some malt beer? Matzerath will give me dill pickles for food tickets. Don't worry. I'll take care of the child later on."

And sometimes, as though to replace the two plausible but persistently absent fathers in the expectant mother's eyes, he stared gloomily at two imaginary points, ground inexperienced teeth in the tech sergeant's manner, drew Störtebeker's symbols in the sand with a stick, and prattled with Störtebeker's philosophical tongue, which, with slight variations, might also have been the tech sergeant's tongue: "Listen to me, Tulla, I'll explain. The fact is that the average everydayness of child-being can be defined as thrown, projected being-in-the-child-world, which in its child-being-in-the-world and its child-being-with-others involves the very core of child-being capacity —Understand? No? Let's try again . . ."

But it was not only his innate imitativeness that inspired Harry with such sayings; in the becoming uniform of an Air Force auxiliary he occasionally took up his stance in the middle of the Pokriefkes' kitchen and delivered self-assured lectures to Tulla's grumbling father, a dyspeptic Koshnavian from the region between Konitz and Tuchel. He made no profession of fatherhood, but took everything on himself. He even offered—"I know what I'm doing"—to become his pregnant cousin's future husband, yet was relieved when, instead of taking him up, August Pokriefke found troubles of his own to chew on: August Pokriefke had been drafted. Near Oxhöft—he had been declared fit only for home-front duty—he had to guard military installations, an occupation which enabled him, in the course of long weekend furloughs, to tell the whole family —the master carpenter and his wife were also obliged to lend their ears —interminable stories about partisans; for in the winter of '43 the Poles began to extend their field of operations: whereas previously they had made only Tuchler Heath insecure, now partisan activity was also reported in Koshnavia. Even in the wooded country inland from the Gulf of Danzig and extending to the foot of Hela Peninsula, they were making raids and imperiling August Pokriefke.

But Tulla, with flat hands on still-flat tummy, had other things to think about besides guerrillas stealthy and insidious, and guerrilla-fighter groups. Often she stood up in the middle of a night attack west of Heisternest and left the kitchen so noticeably that August Pokriefke was unable to bring in his two prisoners and save his motor pool from plunder.

When Tulla left the kitchen, she went to the lumber shed. What could her cousin do but follow her as in the years when he had been permitted to carry the school satchel on his back. Tulla's hiding place was still there among the timber. The logs were still piled in such a way as to leave an empty space just big enough for Tulla and Harry.

There sit an expectant sixteen-year-old mother and an Air Force auxiliary who has enlisted in the Army and is looking forward to his induction, in a children's hiding place: Harry had to lay a hand on Tulla and say: "I can feel something. Plain as day. There it is again." Tulla potters with tiny wood-shaving wigs, weaves woodshaving dolls from soft linden shavings, and as ever disseminates her aroma of bone glue. Unquestionably the baby, as soon as emerged, will distill his mother's unbanishable smell; but only months later, when sufficient milk teeth are present, and still later at the sandbox age, will it become apparent whether the child often and significantly grinds his teeth or whether he prefers to draw little men and world-projects in the sand.

Neither bone-glue aroma nor grinding tech sergeant nor sign-setting Störtebeker. The baby didn't feel like it; and on the occasion of an outing—Tulla obeyed Harry, who, putting on the airs of a father, said an expectant mother needed plenty of fresh air—under the open sky, the infant gave it to be understood that it had no desire to disseminate the aroma of bone glue after the manner of its mother, or to perpetuate the paternal habits of teeth-grinding or world-projecting.

Harry had a weekend pass: an existential pause. Because the air was so Decemberly, cousin and cousin decided to go out to Oliva Forest, and if it wasn't too much for Tulla, to walk as far as the Schwedenschanze. The streetcar, Line Number 2, was crowded, and Tulla was furious because nobody stood up for her. Several times she poked Harry, but the sometimes bashful Air Force auxiliary was disinclined to speak up and demand a seat for Tulla. In front of her, with rounded knees, sat a dozing infantry Pfc. Tulla fumed at him: couldn't he see she was expecting? Instantly the Pfc. transformed his rounded sitting knees into neatly pressed standing knees. Tulla sat down, and on all sides total strangers exchanged glances of complicity. Harry was ashamed not to have demanded a seat and ashamed a second time that Tulla had asked for a seat so loudly.

The car had already passed the big bend on Hohenfriedberger Weg and was jogging from stop to stop on a stretch that was straight as a die. They had agreed to get out at "White Lamb." Right after "Friedens-schluss," Tulla stood up and directly behind Harry pushed her way through winter coats to the rear platform. Even before the trailer reached the traffic island at "White Lamb"—so called after an inn favored by excursionists—Tulla was standing on the bottommost running board, screwing up her eyes in the head wind.

"Don't be a fool," said Harry above her.

Tulla had always liked to jump off streetcars.

"Wait till it stops," Harry had to say from above.

From way back, jumping on and off had been Tulla's favorite sport.

"Don't do it, Tulla, watch out, be careful!" But Harry didn't hold her back.

Beginning roughly in her eighth year, Tulla had jumped from moving streetcars. She had never fallen. Never, as stupid, foolhardy people do, had she risked jumping against the motion of the car; and now, on the trailer of the Number 2, which had been running between Main Station and the suburb of Oliva since the turn of the century, she did not jump from the front platform, but from the rear platform. Nimbly and light as a cat, she jumped with the motion of the car and landed with an easy flexing of the knees and gravel-scraping soles.

Tulla said to Harry, who had jumped off right behind her: "Watcha always nagging for? You think I'm dumb?"

They took a dirt road to one side of the White Lamb Inn. Turning off through the fields at right angles to the rectilinear streetcar line, it led toward the dark forest, huddled on hills. The sun was shining with spinsterish caution. Rifle practice somewhere near Saspe punctuated the afternoon with irregular dots. The White Lamb, haven of excursionists, was closed, shuttered, boarded. The owner, it seemed, had been jailed for economic subversion—buying canned fish on the black market. The furrows of the field and the frozen ruts of the road were filled with wind-blown snow. Ahead of them hooded crows were shifting from stone to stone. Small, under a sky too high and too blue, Tulla clutched her belly first over, then under, the material of her coat. For all the fresh December air, her face couldn't produce a healthy color: two nostrils dilated with fright in a shrinking, chalky phiz. Luckily Tulla was wearing ski pants.

"Something's gone wrong."

"What's wrong? I don't get it. You feel sick? You want to sit down? Or can you make it to the woods? What is it, anyway?"

Harry was frightfully excited, knew nothing, understood nothing, half suspected and didn't want to know. Tulla's nose crinkled, the bridge sprouted beads of sweat that didn't want to fall off. He dragged her to the nearest stone—the crows abandoned it—then to a farm roller, its shaft spitting the December air. Then at the edge of the woods, after crows had had to move another few times, Harry leaned his cousin against the trunk of a beech tree. Her breath flew white. Harry's breath too came in puffs of white steam. Distant rifle practice was still putting sharp pencil points on nearby paper. From crumbly furrows ending just before the woods, crows peered out with cocked heads. "It's good I got pants on, or I wouldn't have made it this far. It's all running off!"

Their breath at the edge of the woods rose up and blew away. Undecided. "Should I?" First Tulla let her Navy serge coat slip off. Harry folded it neatly. She herself undid her waistband, Harry did the rest with horrified curiosity: the finger-size two-months-old fetus lay there in her panties. Made manifest: there. Sponge in gelatin: there. In bloody and in colorless fluids: there. Through world onset: there. A small handful: unkept, beforelike, partly there. Dismal in sharp December air. Grounding as fostering steamed and cooled off quickly. Grounding as taking root, and Tulla's handkerchief as well. Unconcealed into what? By whom attuned? Space-taking never without world-disclosure. Therefore: panties off. Ski pants up, no child, but. What a vision of essence! Lay there warm, then cold: Withdrawal provides the commitment of the enduring project with a hole at the edge of Oliva Forest: "Don't stand there! Do something. Dig a hole. Not there, that's a better place." Ah, are we ourselves ever, is mine ever, now under the leaves, in the ground, not deeply frozen; for higher than reality is potentiality: here manifested: what primarily and ordinarily does not show itself, what is hidden but at the same time is an essential part of what does primarily and ordinarily show itself, namely, its meaning and ground, which is not frozen but loosened with heels of shoes from the Air Force supply room, in order that the baby may come into its there. There into its there. But only project there. Shorn of its essence: there. A mere neuter, a mere impersonal pronoun

—and the impersonal pronoun not there in the same sense as the there in general. And happening-to-be-present confronts being-there with the facticity of its there and without disgust sets it down with bare fingers, unprotected by gloves: Ah, the ecstatic-horizontal structure! There only toward death, which means: tossed in layers, with a few leaves and hollow beechnuts on top, lest the crows, or if foxes should come, the forester, diviners, vultures, treasure seekers, witches, if there are any, gather fetuses, make tallow candles out of them or powder to strew across thresholds, ointments for everything and nothing. And so: fieldstone on it. Grounding in the ground. Placedness and abortion. Matter and work. Mother and child. Being and time. Tulla and Harry. Jumps off the streetcar into her there, without stumbling. Jumps shortly before Christmas, nimbly but too overarchingly: pushed in two moons ago, out through the same hole. Bankrupt! The nihilating Nothing. Lousy luck. Come-to-be in errancy. Spitting cunt. Not even transcendental but vulgar ontic unconcealed ungrinded unstörtebekert. Washed up. Error fostered. Empty egg. Wasn't a pre-Socratic. A bit of care. Bullshit. Was a latecomer. Vaporized, evaporated, cleared out, "You shut your trap. Stinking luck. Why did it have to happen to me? Beans. I was going to call him Konrad or after *him*. After who? After him. Come on, Tulla. Let's go. Yes, come on, let's go."

And cousin and cousin left after securing the site with one large and several small stones against crows, foresters, foxes, treasure seekers, and witches.

A little lighter, they left; and at first Harry was allowed to support Tulla's arm. Distant practice shots continued irregularly to punctuate the written-off afternoon. Their mouths were fuzzy. But Harry had a roll of raspberry drops in his breast pocket.

When they were standing at the "White Lamb" car stop and the car coming from Oliva grew yellow and larger, Tulla said out of gray face into his rosy face: "We'll wait till it starts to move. Then you jump in front and me on the rear platform."

There was once an abortion
    named Konrad, and no one heard about him, not even Jenny Brunies, who, under the name of Jenny Angustri, was dancing in Salonika, Athens, Belgrade, and Budapest in pointed slippers for sound and convalescent soldiers and knitting little things from unraveled wool, pink and blue, intended for a girl friend's baby who was supposed to be named Konrad, the name by which they had called the girl friend's little brother before he drowned while swimming.

In every letter that came fluttering Harry Liebenau's way—four in January, in February only three—Jenny wrote something about slowly growing woolies: "In between I've been working hard. Rehearsals drag out dreadfully, because there's always something wrong with the lighting and the stage hands here act as if they didn't understand a word. Sometimes, when they take forever to shift scenes, one's tempted to think of sabotage. At any rate the routine here leaves me lots of time for knitting. One pair of rompers is done and I've finished the first jacket except for crocheting the scallops on the collar. You can't imagine how I enjoy doing it. Once when Herr Haseloff caught me in the dressing room with an almost finished pair of rompers, he had a terrible scare, and I've kept him on the hook by not telling him whom I was knitting for.

"He certainly thinks I'm expecting. In ballet practice, for instance, he sometime stares at me for minutes on end, in the weirdest way. But otherwise he's nice and ever so considerate. For my birthday he gave me a pair of fur-lined gloves, though I never wear anything on my fingers, no matter how cold it is. And about other things, too, he's as kind as he could be: for instance, he often talks about Papa Brunies, in the most natural way, as if we were expecting him back any minute. When we both know perfectly well that it will never be."

Every week Jenny filled a letter with her babbling. And in the middle of February she announced, apart from the completion of the third pair of rompers and the second jacket, the death of Papa Brunies. Matter-of-factly and without making a new paragraph, Jenny wrote: "The official notice has finally come. He died in Stutthof Camp on November 12, 1943. Stated cause of death: heart failure."

The signature, the unvarying "As ever, your faithful and somewhat tired Jenny," was followed by a postscript with a bit of special news for Harry: "Incidentally, the newsreel came, the one with the Führer's Headquarters and your Harras' pup in it. Herr Haseloff ran the scene off at least ten times, even in slow motion, so as to sketch the dog. Twice was as much as I could bear. Don't be cross with me, but the news of Papa's death—the announcement was so awfully official—has affected me quite a lot. Sometimes I feel like crying the whole time, but I can't."

There was once a dog,
his name was Perkun, and he belonged to a Lithuanian miller's man who had found work on the Vistula delta. Perkun survived the miller's man and sired Senta. The bitch Senta, who belonged to a miller in Nickelswalde, whelped Harras. The stud dog, who belonged to a carpenter in Danzig-Langfuhr, covered the bitch Thekla, who belonged to a Herr Leeb, who died early in 1942, shortly after the bitch Thekla. But the dog Prinz, sired by the shepherd male Harras and whelped by the shepherd bitch Thekla, made history: he was given to the Führer and Chancellor for his birthday and, because he was the Führer's favorite dog, shown in the newsreels.

When dog breeder Leeb was buried, the carpenter attended his funeral. When Perkun died, a normal canine ailment was entered on the studbook. Senta had to be shot because she grew hysterical and did damage. According to an entry in the studbook, the bitch Thekla died of old age. But Harras, who had sired the Führer's favorite dog Prinz, was poisoned on political grounds with poisoned meat, and buried in the dog cemetery. An empty kennel was left behind.

There was once a kennel

which had been inhabited by a black shepherd by the name of Harras until he was poisoned. Since then the kennel had stood empty in the yard of the carpenter shop, for carpenter Liebenau had no desire to acquire a new dog; as far as he was concerned, Harras had been the one and only.

Often on his way to the machine shop, the imposing man could be seen to hesitate outside the kennel, long enough to draw a few puffs from his cigar or even longer. The wall of earth which Harras, on taut chain, had thrown up with his two forepaws had been leveled by the rain and the apprentices' wooden shoes. But the open kennel still gave off the smell of a dog who, in love with his own smell, had deposited his scent marks in the yard and all over Langfuhr. Especially under the piercing August sun or in the damp spring air, the kennel smelled pungently of Harras and attracted flies. Not a suitable ornament for an active carpenter shop. The tar paper of the kennel roof had begun to fray around roofing nails, which seemed to be coming loose. A sad sight, empty and full of memories: once when Harras still lay keen and chained, the carpenter's little niece had lived beside him in the kennel for a whole week. Later, photographers and newspapermen came, snapped the dog's picture and described him. Numerous papers termed the yard of the carpenter shop a historical site because of the celebrated kennel. Celebrities, even foreigners, came and tarried as much as five minutes on the memorable spot. Later a fatso by the name of Amsel spent hours drawing the dog with pen and brush. He didn't call Harras by his right name, he called him Pluto; the carpenter's little niece didn't call Amsel by his right name, but reviled him as "Sheeny." Then Amsel was turned out of the yard. And once a disaster was barely averted. But an article of clothing belonging to a piano teacher, who lived in the right-hand rear apartment on the ground floor, was badly ripped and had to be paid for. And once, or several times, somebody came around reeling drunk and insulted Harras in political terms, louder than buzz saw and lathe could scream to high heaven. And one time somebody who was good at grinding his teeth tossed poisoned meat from the roof of the lumber shed and it landed right in front of the kennel. The meat was not left lying.

Memories. But let no one try to read the thoughts of a carpenter who hesitates in front of an empty kennel and stops in his tracks. Maybe he's thinking back. Maybe he's thinking about lumber prices. Maybe he isn't thinking about anything in particular, but losing himself, while smoking his fifteen-pfennig cigar, between memories and lumber prices. And this for half an hour until the machinist cautiously calls him back: time to cut panels for prefabricated Navy barracks. Empty and full of memories, the kennel doesn't run away.

No, the dog had never been sick, only black: coat and undercoat. Short-haired like the five other members of his litter, who were doing well in police work. The lips closed dry. Neck taut and without dewlap. Croup long and gently sloping. Ears always erect and slightly tilted. And once again now: every single Harras hair straight, smooth, harsh, and black.

The carpenter finds a few stray hairs, now dull and brittle, between the floorboards of the kennel. Sometimes, after closing time, he bends down and pokes about in the moldy warm hole, paying no attention to the tenants hanging out the windows.

But when one day the carpenter lost his purse, containing aside from change a bundle of faded dog hairs; but when the carpenter went to see the Führer's favorite dog, whom Harras had sired, in the newsreel, but next week's newsreel unrolled before his eyes without the Führer's dog; but when news came that a fourth former journeyman of the Liebenau carpenter shop had met a soldier's death; when heavy oak buffets, walnut sideboards, extensible dining-room tables on richly carved legs could no longer be turned out at the carpenter's workbenches, and the only operation permitted was the nailing together of numbered pine boards: parts for Army barracks; when the year 1944 was in its fourth month; when people said: "Now they've done old Herr Brunies in too"; when Odessa was evacuated and Tarnopol was encircled and had to surrender; when the bell rang for the next-to-last round; when food tickets stopped keeping their promises; when carpenter Liebenau heard that his only son had volunteered for the Navy; when all this—the lost purse and the flickering newsreel, the fallen journeyman and the lousy barracks parts, Odessa evacuated and the lying food tickets, old Herr Brunies and his enlisted son—when all this added up to a round sum demanding to be written off, carpenter Friedrich Liebenau walked out of his office, picked up an ax that was new and still coated with grease, crossed the yard on April 20, 1944, at two in the afternoon, planted himself with parted legs in front of the empty kennel of the poisoned shepherd Harras, and with steady overhead strokes, lonely and speechless, smashed the edifice into kindling.

But because the fifty-fifth birthday of the selfsame Führer and Chancellor, to whom the young shepherd dog Prinz of Harras' line had been presented ten years before, was celebrated on April 20th, everybody at the apartment house windows and at the workbenches in the shop understood that more had been smashed than rotting wood and torn tar paper.

After this deed the carpenter had to stay in bed for a good two weeks. He had overtaxed himself.

There was once a carpenter,

who with practiced overhead strokes chopped into kindling a dog kennel that stood for a good many things.

There was once an assassin, who packed a bomb, experimentally, in his brief case.

There was once an Air Force auxiliary who was waiting impatiently to be inducted into the Navy; he wanted to submerge and to sink enemy ships.

There was once a ballet dancer who, in Budapest, Vienna, and Copenhagen, was knitting rompers and jackets for a baby that had long lain buried at the edge of Oliva Forest, weighted down with stones.

There was once an expectant mother who liked to jump off moving streetcars and in so doing, although she had jumped nimbly and not against the motion of the car, lost her two-months child. Thereupon the expectant mother, again a flat young girl, went to work: Tulla Pokriefke became—as one might have expected—a streetcar conductress.

There was once a police president whose son, generally known as Störtebeker, who intended to study philosophy later on, who might almost have become a father, and who, after projecting the world in sand, founded a teen-agers' gang, which later became famous under the name of the Dusters. He stopped drawing symbols in the sand; instead, he drew the rationing office, the Church of the Sacred Heart, the Post Office Administration Building: all angular buildings into which he later, and at night, led the self-grounded Dusters. The conductorette Tulla Pokriefke belonged halfway to the gang. Her cousin didn't belong at all. At the most he stood lookout when the gang met in the storage sheds of the Baltic Chocolate Factory. A permanent possession of the gang appears to have been a three-year-old child, their mascot, who was addressed as Jesus and survived the gang.

There was once a tech sergeant who trained Air Force auxiliaries as AA gunners and quasi-philosophers, who limped slightly, had a way of grinding his teeth, and might almost have become a father, but was tried, first by a special, then by a general court-martial, was broken of his rank and transferred to a punitive battalion, because, while in a state of drunkenness between the barracks of the Kaiserhafen battery, he had insulted the Führer and Chancellor in sentences marked by such locutions as:

forgetful of Being, mound of bones, structure of care, Stutthof, Todtnau, and concentration camp. As they were taking him away—in broad daylight—he bawled mysteriously: "You ontic dog! Alemannic dog! You dog with stocking cap and buckled shoes! What did you do to little Husserl? What did you do to tubby Amsel? You pre-Socratic Nazi dog!" On account of this unrhymed hymn, he was compelled, in spite of his bad leg, to dig up mines on the steadily advancing Eastern front and later, when the invasion had begun, in the West; but the demoted tech sergeant was lucky and wasn't blown sky-high.

There was once a black shepherd, his name was Prinz. He was transferred, along with the Führer's headquarters, to Rastenburg in East Prussia. He was lucky, he didn't step on any mines; but the wild rabbit he was chasing jumped on a mine and could be retrieved only very partially.

Like "Camp Werewolf" northeast of Vinnitsa, the Führer's Headquarters in East Prussia bordered on mined woods. The Führer and his favorite dog lived a secluded life in Zone A of the "Wolf's Lair." To give Prinz exercise, the officer in charge of dogs, an SS captain, who had owned a well-known dog kennel before the war, took him for walks in Zones I and II; but the Führer had to stay in his constricted Zone A, because he was always busy with staff conferences.

Life was tedious at the Führer's headquarters. Always the same barracks, where the Führer Escort Battalion, the Army Chiefs of Staff, or guests come to comment on the situation, were lodged. Some distraction was provided by the goings-on at the gate of Zone II.

It was there that a rabbit ran between the sentries on the perimeter of the Zone, was shooed away amid hoots of laughter, and made a black shepherd forget the lessons learned in his school days at the police kennel: Prinz broke loose, bounded through the gate, past the still laughing sentries, crossed with dragging leash the road leading to the camp—rabbits pucker up their noses, which is something no dog can stand—resolved to follow a pucker-nosed rabbit which luckily had a good head start; for when the rabbit lit out into the mined woods and disintegrated on an exploding mine, the dog incurred little danger, although he had taken a bound or two into the mined area. Cautiously, step by step, the officer in charge of dogs led him back.

When the report was drawn up and had found its way through channels—first SS Major Fegelein appended comments, then it was submitted to the Führer—the officer in charge of dogs was broken to private and assigned to the very same punitive battalion as the demoted tech sergeant reduced to clearing mines.

The onetime officer in charge of dogs took an unlucky step east of Mogilev; but when the battalion was transferred to the West, the tech sergeant, with limping yet lucky leg, deserted to the Allies. He was

826

moved from one PW camp to the next and finally found peace in an English camp for antifascist prisoners, for along with the usual guardhouse peccadilloes the reason for his demotion was noted in his paybook. Shortly after, at a time when the *Götterdämmerung* recording was all ready to be put on, he and some like-minded companions organized a camp theater. On an improvised stage he, a professional actor, played leading roles in plays by German classical authors; a slightly limping Nathan the Wise and a teeth-grinding Götz.

But the would-be assassin, who months before had concluded his experiments with bomb and brief case, couldn't get himself admitted to a camp for antifascist prisoners of war. His attempt at assassination was also a failure, because he wasn't a professional assassin, because in his inexperience he neglected to go the whole hog, because he decamped before his bomb had plainly said yes, and tried to save himself for great tasks after a successful assassination.

There he stands between General Warlimont and Navy Captain Assmann as the Führer's staff conference drags on, and can't figure out where to put his brief case. A liaison officer of the Field Economic Office concludes his talk on the fuel question. Materials in short supply, such as rubber, nickel, bauxite, manganese, and wolfram are listed. The ball-bearing shortage is general. Somebody from the Foreign Office—is it Ambassador Hewel?—speculates on the situation in Japan now that the Tojo cabinet has resigned. Still the brief case has found no satisfactory resting place. The new alignment of the Tenth Army after the evacuation of Ancona, the fighting strength of the Fourteenth Army after the fall of Livorno are discussed. General Schmundt asks for the floor, but He does all the talking. Where to put the brief case? A freshly arrived report creates animation in the group around the card table: the Americans have entered Saint-Lô! Hastily, before the Eastern front, the position around Bialystok for instance, can come up, action is taken: haphazardly the assassin puts the brief case with contents under the card table, on which lie the general staff maps with their complicated markings, around which Messrs. Jodl, Scherff, Schmundt, and Warlimont stand calmly or bob up and down on booted toes, around which the Führer's black shepherd rambles restlessly, because his master, likewise restless, wants to stand now here now there, rejecting this, demanding that with hard knuckle, talking constantly, about those defective 152-millimeter howitzers, then a moment later about the excellent 210-millimeter Skoda howitzer. "Had all-round firing capacity; with the trailer mount removed, just the thing for coastal fortifications, Saint-Lô, for instance." What a memory! Names, figures, distances pell-mell, and moving about the whole time, always with the dog at heel, all over the place except in the vicinity of the brief case at the feet of Generals Schmundt and Warlimont.

To sum it up, the assassin was a dud; but the bomb wasn't a dud, it went off punctually, cut off several officers' careers, but removed neither the Führer nor the Führer's favorite dog from the world. For Prinz, to whom as to all dogs the region under the table belonged, had sniffed at the abandoned brief case and possibly heard an uncanny ticking: in any event, his cursory sniffing commanded him to transact a piece of business that well-trained dogs transact only out of doors.

An attentive adjutant, standing by the shack door, saw what the dog wanted, opened the door a crack—wide enough for Prinz—and closed it without disturbing noise. But his solicitude brought him no reward; for when the bomb said Now!, when it said Time's up! Pickupthechips! Endoftheline!, when the bomb in the brief case of the assassin who had meanwhile run for it said Amen, the adjutant among others was hit by several splinters, but not a one touched the Führer or his favorite dog.

Air Force auxiliary Harry Liebenau—to get back to the suburb of Langfuhr from the great world of assassins, general staff maps, and the unscathed Führer's figure—heard about the unsuccessful attempt on the Führer's life on the turned-up radio. The names of the assassin and his fellow conspirators were given. Thereupon Harry began to worry about the dog Prinz, descended from the dog Harras; for no special communiqué, not a line in the papers, not so much as a whispered word revealed whether the dog was among the victims or whether Providence had spared him as well as his master.

It wasn't until the next newsreel—Harry had his induction order in his pocket, was no longer wearing the uniform of an Air Force auxiliary, was making good-by calls, and going often, because there were seven more days to kill, to the movies—that the German Movietone News had something to say, quite marginally, about the dog Prinz.

The Führer's headquarters with demolished shack and living Führer was shown in the distance. And against the boots of the Führer, whose face under low-pulled cap seemed slightly swollen but otherwise unchanged, rubbed, black with erect ears, a male shepherd whom Harry identified without difficulty as the carpenter's dog's dog.

The bungling assassin, however, was taken to the gallows.

There was once a little girl,

whom forest Gypsies palmed off on a high school teacher who was sorting mica stones in an abandoned factory and was named Oswald Brunies. The girl was baptized with the name Jenny, grew up, and became fatter and fatter. Jenny looked unnaturally roly-poly and had to put up with a good deal. At an early age, the plump little girl took piano lessons from a piano teacher by the name of Felsner-Imbs. Imbs had billowing snow-white hair, which demanded to be brushed for a good hour every day. On his advice, Jenny, by way of keeping her weight in check, was sent to a ballet school to learn ballet dancing.

But Jenny went on swelling and promised to become as fat as Eddi Amsel, Dr. Brunies' favorite pupil. Amsel often came with his friend to look at the teacher's collection of mica stones and was also present when Jenny tinkled out scales. Eddi Amsel had many freckles, weighed 203 pounds, had ready wit, knew how to draw good likenesses quick as a flash, and in addition could sing clear as a bell—even in church.

One winter afternoon when snow lay all about and new snow kept falling on top of it, Jenny was transformed behind the Erbsberg, near the gloomy Gutenberg monument, into a snow man by playing children.

At the same hour, as chance would have it, fat funny Amsel, on the opposite side of the Erbsberg, was likewise transformed into a snow man; but those who transformed him were not playing children.

But suddenly and from all sides a thaw set in. Both snow men melted away and discharged: near the Gutenberg monument a dancing line; on the other side of the mountain, a slender young man, who looked for his teeth in the snow and found them. Whereupon he made them rain down on the bushes.

The dancing line went home, represented herself when she got there as Jenny Brunies, fell slightly ill, soon recovered, and embarked on the arduous career of a successful ballet dancer.

The slender youth, however, packed Eddi Amsel's suitcase and in the guise of a Herr Haseloff took the train from Danzig via Schneidemühl to Berlin. There he had his mouth filled with new teeth and tried to cure a violent cold he had caught in the snow man; but his chronic hoarseness was there to stay.

The dancing line had to keep on going to school and working hard at ballet exercises. When the Stadttheater's children's ballet took part in the Christmas play, *The Snow Queen,* Jenny danced the role of the Snow Queen and was praised by the critics.

Then came the war. But nothing changed, or at most the ballet audience: Jenny danced in the Red Room of the Zoppot casino before high-ranking officers, Party leaders, artists, and scientists. The chronically hoarse Herr Haseloff, who had escaped from the Amselian snow man, had meanwhile become a ballet master in Berlin. As a prominent member of the ballet world, he had been invited to the Red Room, and now he said to himself over the long-lasting final applause: "What amazing sparkle! What heavenly arm movements! That line in the adagio! Somewhat lacking in warmth but classical to the finger tips. Clean technique, still rather self-conscious. Instep not high enough. Definitely talented. It would be a good thing to work with the child, work and bring out everything she's got."

Only after Dr. Brunies had been questioned by the police in connection with an embarrassing affair—he had diverted vitamin tablets intended for his pupils to his own mouth—arrested by the Gestapo, and sent to Stutthof concentration camp, did ballet master Haseloff find an opportunity to carry Jenny off to Berlin.

It was hard for her to part from the suburb of Langfuhr. She wore mourning and had fallen in love with a high school student by the name of Harry Liebenau. She wrote him many letters. Her tidy script told of a mysterious Madame Neroda, who headed the ballet, of the pianist Felsner-Imbs, who had followed her to Berlin, of little Fenchel, her partner in the *pas de deux,* and of ballet master Haseloff, who, chronically hoarse and always rather weird, directed exercises and rehearsals.

Jenny wrote of progress and minor setbacks. All in all she was getting ahead; there was only one trouble and there was no help for it. For all the praise Jenny earned with her *entrechats,* her instep was still flat and feeble, a source of dismay to the ballet master and to the dancer, because every true ballerina—ever since the days of Louis XIV—has had to have a fine high instep.

Several ballets, including some early German country dances and the usual bravura pieces from the venerable Petipa's repertory, were rehearsed and performed for the soldiers who had occupied half Europe. Long trips took Jenny all over. And from all over Jenny wrote her friend Harry, who answered now and then. Between rehearsals and during performances Jenny didn't sit there like a bonehead leafing through illustrated magazines; diligently she knitted baby clothes for a school friend who was expecting a baby.

When the ballet group returned from France in the summer of '44—taken unawares by the invasion, it had lost several sets and a number of costumes—ballet master Haseloff decided to work up a ballet in three acts, with which he had been fiddling ever since his childhood. Now, after the washout in France, he was in a hurry to put his childhood dream on its feet. He decided to call it *The Scarecrows* or *The Revolt of the Scarecrows,* or *The Gardener's Daughter and the Scarecrows,* and expected it to open in August.

Since there were no suitable composers available, he had Felsner-Imbs arrange a blend of Scarlatti and Handel. The costumes that had been wrecked or badly damaged in France fitted nicely into the new ballet. The survivors of a group of midgets, who had belonged to Haseloff's propaganda unit and had also suffered losses at the beginning of the invasion, were taken on as acrobatic extras. This ballet was intended to tell a story with the help of masks, twittering machines, mobile automata, and a large illusionist stage.

Jenny wrote to Harry: "The curtain rises on the wicked old gardener's colorful garden, which is being looted by dancing birds. Half in league with the birds, the gardener's daughter—that's me—is teasing the wicked old gardener. As the birds whirl about him, he does a frantically funny solo dance and fastens a sign to the garden fence: 'Scarecrow wanted!' Instantly, jumping over the fence with a *grand jeté*, a young man in picturesque rags appears and offers his services as a scarecrow. After a choreographic discussion—*pas battus, entrechats, and brisés dessus-dessous*— the wicked old gardener agrees, exits left, and the young man scares away—*pas chassé*, and *glissades* in all directions—all the birds, the last being a particularly impudent blackbird—*tours en l'air*. Of course the pretty young gardener's daughter—that's me—falls in love with the bouncing scarecrow—*pas de deux* in among the wicked old gardener's rhubarb stalks—sweet adagio: *attitude en promenade*. With a show of timidity, the gardener's daughter shrinks back, then surrenders and is led away over the fence, another *grand jeté*. The two of us—little Fenchel plays the young man—exit right.

"In the second act—as you'll soon see—the young man's true nature comes out. He is the prefect of all scarecrows and rules over their underground realm, where scarecrows of every variety have to spin around ceaselessly. Here they engage in leaping processions, there they assemble for a scarecrow mass and sacrifice to an old hat. Our midgets, with old Bebra in the lead, combine to form a midget scarecrow, sometimes short, sometimes long, but always closely knotted. They weave picturesquely through history: shaggy Germani, baggy-panted lansquenets, imperial couriers, moth-eaten mendicant friars, mechanical headless knights, bloated nuns possessed of epilepsy, General Zieten emerging from the woods, and Lützow's intrepid band. Many-armed clothes trees are on the march. Cupboards vomit forth whole dynasties with court dwarfs. Then they all turn into windmills: the monks, the knights, nuns, couriers and lansquenets, the Prussian grenadiers and Natzmer uhlans, the Merovingians and Carolingians, and in between, popping like weasels, our midgets. Air is moved with wild wings but no grain is milled. Yet the big mill hopper is filled with rag entrails, lace clouds, flag salad. Hat pyramids and pants porridge mix into a cake, which all the scarecrows noisily devour. Growling rattling howling. A whistling of keys. A stifled moaning. Ten abbots belch. Farting of the nuns. Goats and midgets bleat. Rattling, scraping, guzzling, neighing. Silk sings. Velvet buzzes. On one leg. Two in one skirt. Wedded in pants. Sailing in a hat. They fall out of pockets, they multiply in potato sacks. Arias tangled in curtains. Yellow light bursts through seams. Trunkless heads. A jumping luminous button. Mobile baptism. And gods too: Potrimpos, Pikollos, Perkunos —among them a black dog. And right in the middle of this exercising, acrobatic, complexly ordered confusion—unclassical vibrati alternate with richly varied *pas de bourrée*—the prefect of all scarecrows, little Fenchel in other words, deposits the kidnaped gardener's daughter. And I, the gardener's daughter, am scared on frantic slippers. For all my love for

831

the young man and prefect—only on the stage, mind you—I'm awfully frightened. After the nasty scarecrows have hung a moth-clouded bridal dress on me and crowned me with a rattling nutshell crown, I dance a terrified regal solo—the midgets carry my train—to solemnly tinkling court music; and with my dancing I, that is to say, the crowned gardener's daughter, succeed in dancing to sleep all the scarecrows, some standing singly, others in groups, one after the other: last of all, little Fenchel, that is, the prefect. Only the shaggy black dog, who is a member of the prefect's retinue, tosses restlessly about among sprinkled midgets, but is unable to stand on his twelve diabolical legs. Then, out of a perfect arabesque, I as the gardener's daughter bend down over the sleeping prefect, blow a sorrowful ballerina's kiss—without ever touching little Fenchel—and run away. Too late the black dog howls. Too late the midgets squeal. Too late the scarecrow mechanisms start up. And much too late the prefect wakes up. The second act ends with a furious finale: leaps and acrobatics. Music warlike enough to chase away Turkish armies. The hectically excited scarecrows scatter, boding trouble in the third act.

"The scene is the wicked old gardener's garden again. Sad and defenseless against the birds, he twists and turns in vain. Then shamefacedly—I have to play it half repentant, half defiant—the wicked old gardener's young daughter comes back in raggedy bridal dress and sinks down at her gardener father's feet. She clasps his knees and wants to be lifted up: *pas de deux,* father and daughter. A choreographic conflict, with lifts and promenades. In the end the old man's evil nature comes out: he rejects me, his daughter. I'm sick of living and I can't die. A roaring from behind: scarecrows and birds in strange alliance. A fluttering, chirping, whirring, squeaking, hissing monster rolls across the stage, holding up an enormous empty bird cage supported by the claws of innumerable scarecrows, bulldozes the garden, and catches the gardener's daughter with nimble midgets. The prefect shouts for joy when he sees me in the cage. Black, the shaggy dog describes swift circles. Triumph in every joint, the thousand-voiced monster rattles and squeaks away, taking me with it. Leaving the ruined garden behind. Leaving behind a limping figure in rags: the wicked old gardener. The teasing birds come back again—*pas de chat, pas de basque*—and encircle the old man. Wearily and as though to defend himself, he lifts his arms wrapped in tatters: and lo and behold, the very first movement frightens the birds, scares them away. He has turned into a scarecrow, forever after he will be gardener and scarecrow in one. On his macabre scarecrow solo—Herr Haseloff is toying with the idea of dancing this role—the final curtain falls."

This ballet, so sympathetically described by Jenny to her friend Harry, this ballet in three acts, so meticulously rehearsed, this sumptuously staged ballet—Haseloff in person had designed noise-making

832

mechanisms and button-spitting automata—this scarecrow ballet was never to open. Two gentlemen from the Reich Propaganda Ministry, who attended the dress rehearsal, found the first act charming and promising, cleared their throats for the first time in the second act, and stood up right after the final curtain. In general, they thought the latter part of the story too sinister and allusive. The life-affirming element was absent, and the two gentlemen declared in unison: "Soldiers at the front want something gay, not some gloomy rumbling underworld."

Negotiations were carried on. Madame Neroda brought her connections to bear. The top authorities were showing signs of approving a new version when, before Haseloff had time to tack on a happy ending consonant with the situation at the front, a bomb hit demolished the costumes and sets. And the ensemble also suffered losses.

Though the rehearsal ought to have been interrupted during an air-raid alert, they kept right on: the gardener's daughter is dancing the scarecrows, the hellhound, all the midgets, and the prefect to sleep—Jenny was doing admirably, except that her instep still wasn't high enough and left the impression of a slight but disturbing blemish—Haseloff was just about to arrange the new and positive plot—Jenny was supposed to handcuff all the scarecrows and the prefect, after which she would put them to work for the benefit of the upper world, in other words, the formerly wicked gardener, who was now so good butter wouldn't melt in his mouth—just as Jenny, laden with cumbersome handcuffs, was standing alone on the stage, uncertain because of the changes that had been made, the bomb, meant for the radio tower next door, fell on the exhibition hall, which had been rigged up as a theater workshop.

The storeroom containing the sensitive mechanisms, flimsy costumes, and movable sets sank to its knees, never to rise again; Felsner-Imbs the pianist, who had accompanied all the rehearsals with ten fingers, was flattened against the keyboard for all time. Four little holes, two stoppers, the midget Kitty, and three stage hands were injured, only slightly thank heavens. But ballet master Haseloff came off with a sound skin and, as soon as the smoke and dust had settled, went looking for Jenny with hoarse cries.

He found her recumbent and had to extricate her feet from under a beam. At first they feared the worst, a ballerina's death. Actually the beam had only crushed her right as well as her left foot. Her ballet slippers had grown too tight for her swelling feet, and at long last Jenny Angustri appeared to have the perfect high instep that every ballerina ought to have.—Float hither, ye airy *slyphides*. Approach like brides, Giselle and Coppélia, or weep from enamel eyes. Grisi and Taglioni, Lucile Grahn and Fanny Cerito, come and weave your *Pas de Quatre* and strew roses on pitiful feet. Palais Garnier, burst into all your lights that the stones of the pyramid may join in the *grand défilé:* the first and second quadrille, the hopeful *coryphées,* the *petits sujets* and the *grands sujets,* the *premiers danseurs,* and, as embittered as they are unattainable, the Stars: Leap, Gaetano Vestris! Far-famed Camargo, still in command of the *entrechats huit.* Vaslav Nijinsky, slowly leaping god and specter of the rose, have done with butterflies and black spiders. Restless Noverre, break off your journey and make a halt here. Turn off the suspension machine, that moonbeams light as *sylphides* may cast their coolness. Wicked Diaghilev, lay your magical hand upon her. Anna Pavlova, for the time of this sorrow forget your millions. Chopin, once again, by candlelight, spit your blood upon the keys. Turn away, Bellastriga and Archisposa. Once again let the dying swan swoon away. And now, Petrushka, lie down beside her. The last position. *Grand plié.*

And yet Jenny went on living: a dismal life, never again on toes. The toes—how hard a thing to write!—of both feet had to be amputated. Shoes, ungainly things, were made for the stumps. And Harry Liebenau, whom Jenny had loved until then, received a matter-of-factly typewritten letter, the last. He too, Jenny asked, should write no more. All that was over. He should try to forget everthing, almost everything. "I too will try hard not to think of us."

Some days later—Harry Liebenau was packing his bags, he was off to the wars—a package came with melancholy contents. In packets tied with silk ribbon: Harry's half-true letters; knitted jackets and rompers, finished, pink and blue. He found a necklace made of bottle washers. Harry had given it to Jenny when they were children playing by Aktien Pond, on whose surface floated bottle washers and no lotus blossoms.

There was once a streetcar —

it ran from Heeresanger in Langfuhr to Weidengasse in the Lower City and belonged to Line Number 5. Like all cars that ran between Langfuhr and Danzig, the Number 5 also stopped at the Main Station. The motorman of this particular car, concerning which it has been said: there was once a streetcar, was named Lemke; the conductor in the lead car was named Erich Wentzeck; and the conductorette in the trailer of this particular car was named Tulla Pokriefke. No longer was she working on the Number 2 Line to Oliva. Every day for nine hours she rode back and forth on the Number 5: quick, as though born to the trade, somewhat foolhardy; for in the evening rush hour when the car was overcrowded and it was impossible to get through inside, she jumped, with the car running at moderate speed, off the front platform and onto the rear platform. When Tulla Pokriefke collected fares, all those who rode with her coughed up their money: even her cousin Harry had to pay.

Two minutes after Tulla Pokriefke had rung the bell as a sign that this particular car, concerning which it has been said: there was once a streetcar, namely, the 10:05 P.M. car, due at the Main Station at 10:17, could and should push off from the Heeresanger terminus, a boy of seventeen got on at Max-Halbe-Platz, pushed a cardboard suitcase reinforced with leather corners onto the rear platform of the trailer, and lit a cigarette.

The car was empty and remained relatively empty. At "Reichskolonie" stop an elderly couple got on, and they got out at the Sporthalle. At "Halbe-Allee" four Red Cross nurses got into the trailer and asked for transfers to Heubude. The lead car was busier.

While on the rear platform of the trailer conductorette Tulla Pokriefke made entries in her trip book, the seventeen-year-old smoked awkwardly beside his lurching cardboard suitcase. It is only because the two of them, she with her trip book, he with the unaccustomed cigarette, knew each other—as a matter of fact they were related, cousins—only because the two of them were about to part for life, that this car on Line Number 5 was a special car; in other respects it was running normally on schedule.

When Tulla had rung the bell at "Women's Clinic," she closed her trip book and said: "Leaving town?" Harry Liebenau, with his induction order in the breast pocket of his jacket, replied quite in the spirit of the indispensable leavetaking scene: "The farther the better."

Tulla's trip book, a prosaic prop, was encased in worn wooden covers: "Don'tcha like our town any more?"

Because Harry knew Tulla was no longer working on the Number 2 Line, he had decided in favor of a last trip on the Number 5: "I'm off to the Prussians. They're stymied without me."

Tulla jiggled the wooden covers: "I thought you were joining the Navy."

Harry offered Tulla a cigarette: "Nothing doing out there any more."

Tulla put the Juno away in the pigeonhole where the trip book was kept: "Watch out or they'll putcha in the infantry. It's no skin off their ass."

This dialogue drunk with parting was beheaded by Harry: "Maybe so. It's all one to me. So long as I get out of this lousy burg."

The particular car with trailer lurched down the avenue. Cars whished by in the opposite direction. Neither of them could look out, because all the windows in the trailer were blinded with blackout paint. So they had to keep looking at each other; but no one will ever find out how Tulla saw her cousin Harry when he stared at her as if to store up a supply: Tulla Tulla Tulla! The pimples on her forehead had dried out. But she had a fresh permanent, paid for with her own earnings. If you're not pretty, you've got to fix yourself up. But still and for the last time the

835

smell of bone glue, carpenter's glue, rode back and forth with her between Heeresanger und Weidengasse. The four Red Cross nurses inside the car were all talking at once in an undertone. Harry had his mouth full of artistically turned phrases. But no delicate phrase wanted to start out. After "Four Seasons," he put himself to the torture: "How's your father?" But Tulla replied with a shrug of the shoulders and the usual counter-question: "How's yours?"

At this Harry too had only a shrug of the shoulders to spare, although his father wasn't very well. Swollen feet had deterred the carpenter from taking his son to the station; and Harry's mother never went out without Harry's father.

Even so, a member of the family witnessed Harry's departure: the streetcar uniform was becoming to his cousin. The uniform skiff clung tilting to permanent waves. Shortly before "Oliva Gate," she removed two empty ticket pads from her ticket box: "D'you wanna ticket pad?"

The parting gift! Harry received two cardboard covers to which metal clasps fastened a finger-thick wad of ticket stubs. Instantly his fingers became childlike and made the thin paper purr. Tulla gave a bleating and almost good-natured laugh. But then she remembered something that had been forgotten amid protracted leavetaking: Her cousin hadn't paid his fare. Harry was playing with the empty ticket pads and hadn't provided himself with a valid ticket. Tulla pointed at the pads and at Harry's smugly playing fingers: "You can keep 'em, but you gotta pay your fare all the same. One to the station with baggage."

After Harry had let his purse slip back into his back pocket, he found a colorless slit in the blackout paint on the platform window; somebody had scratched with his fingernail in order that Harry might stop staring at his cousin and capture in one eye the panorama of the approaching city. Moonlight for his express benefit. He counted the towers. Not a one was missing. All grew toward him. What a silhouette! Brick Gothic strained his eye till it moistened: tears? Only one. For already Tulla was calling out his stop: "Main Station!"—and Harry let two empty ticket pads slip into his pocket.

When he clutched his cardboard suitcase by the handle, Tulla held out a little hand; a red rubber finger was supposed to protect the thumb and make it reliable at counting change. Tulla's other hand waited by the bellpull: "Take care of yourself, don't let 'em shoot off your nose, hear."

Tulla's cousin nodded obediently again and again, even after Tulla had rung for the car to push off and he for her and she for him—he on the sidewalk outside the station, she on the departing Number 5—were growing smaller and smaller.

No wonder that when Harry Liebenau was sitting on his suitcase in the express, playing with empty ticket pads from Danzig to Berlin, he had a Koshnavian ditty in his ears, which ran to the rhythm of the joints in the tracks: "Duller Duller, Tulla. Dul Dul Dul, Tulla. Tulla, Tulla, Dul."

There was once a ditty;
 it was about love, it was short, easy to remember, and so strikingly rhythmical that armored infantryman Harry Liebenau, who had gone off with two purring ticket pads to learn what fear was, had it between his teeth, kneeling standing lying, in his sleep, over his pea soup, while cleaning his rifle, crawling hopping snoozing, under his gas mask, while tossing real hand grenades, when falling in for guard duty, weeping sweating miserable, on foot blisters, under his steel helmet, on his ass in the latrine, while taking the oath to the flag in Fallingbostel, kneeling without support, looking for the bead in the notch, in other words, shooting swearing shitting, and similarly while shining his shoes and lining up for coffee: so persistent and universally appropriate was the ditty. For when he hammered a nail in his locker to hang up a framed photograph—Führer with black shepherd—hammerhead and nailhead spoke up: Dul Dul, Tulla. When for the first time bayonets were fixed in three steps, his three steps were called: Tulla Tulla Dul! When he had to mount guard at night behind Meat Depot 2, and drowsiness hit him behind the knees with the flat of its hand, he awakened himself rhythmically: Duller Duller, Tulla! He worked the universally appropriate Tulla text into every marching song, regardless of whether it featured Erika, Rosemarie, or Anushka, or dark-brown hazelnuts. When he picked his lice and night after night—until the company was deloused in Münster —searched the seams of his drawers and undershirts with lice-cracking fingernails, he didn't crush two and thirty lice, but subjugated Tulla two and thirty times. Even when he had a chance to stay out until reveille, to insert his member for the first time and very briefly into an honest-to-goodness girl, he didn't pick an Air Force auxiliary or a nurse, but screwed, in Lüneburg's autumnal park, a Lüneburg streetcar conductress; her name was Ortrud but he, meanwhile and during, called her Tulla Tulla Tulla! Which appealed to her only moderately.
 And all this—Tulla song, oath to the flag, lice and Lüneburg—was recorded in love letters, three a week, to Tulla. History was made in January February March; but he searches for timeless words for Tulla. Between Lake Balaton and the Danube the Fourth Cavalry Brigade is fighting off counterattacks; but he describes the bucolic beauty of Lüneburg Heath to his cousin. The relief offensive never reaches Budapest but comes to a standstill near Pressburg; he, indefatigably, compares Lüneburg Heath with Tuchler Heath. Slight gains in the Bastogne sector; and he

sends Tulla a little bag of juniper berries done up with violet greetings. South of Bologna the 362nd Infantry Division parries armored attacks by pulling back the main line of battle; but he writes a poem—for whom, I wonder?—in which heather, at the beginning of January, is still in bloom: purple, purple! From dawn to dusk a thousand American bombers attack targets in the Paderborn, Bielefeld, Koblenz, Mannheim area; he, unmoved, reads Löns, who molds his epistolary style and lends a purple coloration to the Tulla poem he has begun. Full-scale offensive near Baranov; he, without looking up, paints the one word, not blue, not red, with his fountain pen. The Tarnow bridgehead is evacuated—breakthrough to the Inster; but armored infantryman Harry Liebenau, who has completed his training, is looking for a rhyme to conjure up Tulla. Thrusts toward Leslau by way of Kutno—breakthrough at Hohensalza; but the armored infantryman of Münster-North Company has still found no suitable rhyme for his cousin. Enemy armored spearheads in Gumbinnen and across the Rominte. At this point armored infantryman Harry Liebenau, with marching orders and marching rations but without the vital word, is set in motion in the direction of Kattowitz, where he is supposed to make contact with the 18th Armored Division, which is being transferred just then from the northern Danube front to upper Silesia. Gleiwitz and Oppeln fall—he never gets to Kattowitz, for new marching orders accompanied by extra rations project armored infantryman Harry Liebenau to Vienna, where he has a chance of finding the 11th Air Force Division that has retreated from the southeast, and perhaps also the cover that fits the pot named Tulla. The main line of battle is now twelve miles east of Königsberg; in Vienna armored infantryman Harry Liebenau climbs to the top of St. Stephen's and searches under the half-clouded sky. For what? Enemy armored spearheads reach the Oder and establish a bridgehead near Steinau; Harry sends rhymeless picture postcards and fails to find the headquarters of the Air Force division that had been promised him. The battle of the Ardennes is over. Budapest is still holding out. In Italy not much fighting. Colonel-General Schörner takes over Center Sector. The barrier at Lötzen is forced. Near Glogau successful defensive action. Enemy spearheads in Prussian Holland. Geography! Bielitz—Pless—Ratibor. Who knows where Zielenzig is located? For it is to Zielenzig, northwest of Küstrin, that new marching orders are supposed to propel armored infantryman Harry Liebenau, who has just been issued fresh rations; but he only gets as far as Pirna; there he is rounded up and attached to a nameless replacement battalion, which is expected to wait in an evacuated school building until the 21st Armored Division has been transferred from Küstrin to the area north of Breslau. Combat reserves. Harry finds a dictionary in the basement of the school, but refuses to rhyme such names as Sulla and Abdullah, which yield no meaning, with

Tulla. The promised armored division fails to materialize. But Budapest falls. Glogau is cut off. The combat reserve, including armored infantryman Harry Liebenau, is set in motion in no particular direction. And every day, punctually, there is a smidgin of four-fruit jam, a third of a loaf of army bread, the sixteenth part of a two-pound can of fat pork, and three cigarettes. Orders from Schörner's Hq.: new combat unit set up. Spring breaks through. Buds burst between Troppau and Leobschütz. Near Schwarzwasser four spring poems sprout. In Sagan, shortly before crossing the Bober north of the city, Harry Liebenau makes the acquaintance of a Silesian girl; her name is Ulla and she darns two pairs of his socks. In Lauban he is swallowed up by the 25th Armored Infantry Division, which has been pulled back from the Western front and sent to Silesia.

Now at last he knows where he belongs. No more marching orders sending him to units that cannot be found. Pondering and looking for rhymes, he sits huddled with five other armored infantrymen on a self-propelled gun that is being moved back and forth between Lauban and Sagan, but always behind the lines. He receives no mail. But that doesn't prevent him from writing to his cousin Tulla, who, when she is not cut off in Danzig-Langfuhr with elements of the Vistula Army Group, goes on working as a streetcar conductress; for the streetcar runs till the bitter end.

There was once a self-propelled gun,
    Panzer IV, old model, which was supposed to move up behind the main line of battle in mountainous Silesia. It weighed over forty tons, and to avoid being spotted from the air it backed up on two caterpillar treads into a woodshed secured only by a padlock.
    But because this shed belonged to a Silesian glassblower, it contained, on shelves and bedded in straw, more than five hundred products of the glassblower's art.
    The encounter between the self-propelled gun, backing on caterpillar treads, and the Silesian glass had two consequences. In the first place, the armored vehicle damaged quite a lot of glass; in the second place, the effect of the glass, breaking in several different keys, on Harry Liebenau, who, as a member of the infantry team assigned to the self-propelled gun, was standing outside the screaming glass shed, was a change of idiom. From this moment on, no more purple melancholy. Never again will he search for a rhyme to the name of Tulla. No more poems written with adolescent sperm and heart's blood. Once the screaming of that shed has splattered his ears like birdshot, his diary is restricted to simple sentences: The gun backs into the glass shed. War is more boring than school. Everybody's waiting for miracle weapons. After the war I'm going to see

lots of movies. Yesterday I saw my first dead man. I've filled my gas mask container with strawberry jam. We are due for transfer. I haven't seen a Russian yet. Sometimes I stop thinking of Tulla. Our field kitchen is gone. I always read one and the same thing. The roads are clogged with fugitives, who have lost all faith. Löns and Heidegger are wrong about lots of things. In Bunzlau there were five soldiers and two officers hanging on seven trees. This morning we fired on a wooded area. Couldn't write for two days because of contact with the enemy. Many are dead. After the war I'm going to write a book. We are to be moved to Berlin. There the Führer is fighting. I've been assigned to the Wenck combat team. They want us to save the capital. Tomorrow is the Führer's birthday. I wonder if he's got the dog with him.

Once there was a Führer and Chancellor,
  who on April 20, 1945, celebrated his fifty-sixth birthday. Since the center of the capital, including the government quarter and the Chancellery, was under intermittent artillery fire that day, the modest celebration was held in the Führer's air-raid shelter.
  Celebrities, several of whom were normally on hand for staff conferences—evening situation, noon situation—had come to offer their congratulations: Field Marshal General Keitel, Colonel General von John, Naval Commander Lüdde-Neurath, Admirals Voss and Wagner, Generals Krebs and Burgdorf, Colonel von Below, Reichsleiter Bormann, Ambassador Hewel of the Foreign Office, Frülein Braun, Dr. Herrgesell, the Field Headquarters stenographer, SS Hauptsturmführer Günsche, Dr. Morell, SS Obergruppenführer Fegelein, and Herr and Frau Goebbels with all their six children.
  After the congratulants had presented their best wishes, the Führer and Chancellor cast a searching look around him, as though missing a last and indispensable congratulant: "Where is the dog?"
  The birthday company began at once to look for the Führer's favorite dog. Cries of "Prinz!" "Here Prinz!" SS Hauptsturmführer Günsche, the Führer's personal adjutant, combed the garden of the Chancellery, although the area was not infrequently marked by artillery hits. Inside the shelter a number of absurd hypotheses were formulated. Everybody had some suggestion to make. Only SS Obergruppenführer Fegelein had a clear grasp of the situation. Seconded by Colonel von Below, he rushed to the telephones connecting the Führer's bomb shelter with all the staff offices and with the MP battalion guarding the Chancellery: "Attention everybody! Attention everybody! Führer's dog missing. Answers to the name of Prinz. Stud dog. Black German shepherd Prinz. Connect me with Zossen. Attention everybody: the Führer's dog is missing."
  In the course of the ensuing staff conference—report confirmed: enemy armored spearheads have advanced south of Cottbus and entered

Calau—"Operation Wolftrap" is set up and all plans for the defense of the capital are co-ordinated with it. The Fourth Armored Corps postpones counterattack south of Spremberg indefinitely and secures Spremberg-Senftenburg highway against deserting Führerdog. Similarly the Steiner Group transforms the deployment zone for the relief offensive scheduled to move southward from the Eberswalde sector, into a deeply echeloned dogcapture zone. The operation proceeds according to plan. All available planes of the Sixth Air Fleet fly ground reconnaissance missions for the purpose of determining Führerdogescaperoute. Pursuant to "Wolftrap," the main battle line is pulled back behind the Havel. Führerdogsearch-groups are set up from combat reserves. They receive orders to maintain walkie-talkie contact with Führerdogcapturegroups consisting of motor-cycle and bicycle companies. The Holste Corps digs in. But the Twelfth Army under General Wenck launches a relief offensive from the southwest and cuts off Führerdogescaperoute, for presumably Führerdog is planning to desert to Westenemy. To make Operation Wolftrap viable, the Seventh Army has to disengage itself from the Ninth and First American Armies and seal off the Western front between Elbe and Mulde. On the Jüterbog-Torgau line, projected antitank trenches are replaced by Führerdogtrap-trenches. The Twelfth Army, the Blumentritt Army Group, the Thirty-eighth Armored Corps are placed under the direct orders of the Army High Command, which as of now is transferred from Zossen to Wannsee, where under General Burgdorf it sets up a "Wolftrap Command Staff" —WCS.

But despite all this vigorous regrouping the only dispatches to come in are the usual situation reports—Soviet spearheads reach Treuenbrietzen-Königswusterhausen line—and no information about Führerdogescape-route. At one nine four o hours, during the evening situation report, Field Marshal Keitel has a telephone conversation with Chief of Staff Steiner: "As per Führerorder, 25th Armored Infantry Division will close frontline gap at Cottbus and secure area against Führerdogbreakthrough."

Reply of Hq. Steiner Group: "As per instructions date one seven four, 25th Armored Infantry Division withdrawn Bautzen area and attached Twelfth Army. Available remaining units alerted against Füh-rerdogbreakthrough."

Finally, in the early morning hours of April 20, not far from the bitterly contested Fürstenwalde-Strausberg-Bernau line, shots are fired at a black shepherd, who, however, when brought to the Führer's Head-quarters and carefully examined by Dr. Morell, proves to be an impostor.

Thereupon, as per WCS instructions, all units in the Greater Berlin area are briefed on Führerdogdimensions.

The concentration between Lübben and Baruth receives support from Soviet armored spearheads pursuing identical aim. Forest fires spread despite drizzle and constitute natural dogbarrier.

On April 22 enemy armor pushes across the Lichtenberg-Niederschönhausen-Frohnau line and enters outer defenses of the capital. Two reports of dogcapture in the Königswusterhausen area prove inaccurate, since neither captured object can be identified as a male.

Dessau and Bitterfeld are lost. American armored force attempts Elbe crossing near Wittenberge.

On April 23, Dr. Goebbels, gauleiter and Reich Defense Commissioner, issues the following statement: "The Führer is at his post in the capital and has assumed supreme command of all forces engaged in finishfight. As of now, Führerdogsearchgroups will obey only Führerinstructions."

WCS communique: "Köpenick railroad station retaken in counterattack. Enemy infiltration blocked by Tenth Führerdogcapturegroup, guarding area bordering Prenzlauer Allee. Two Soviet dogcapture appliances captured, proving that Eastenemy has intelligence of Operation Wolftrap." Due to sensation-mongering misrepresentation of Führerdogloss by enemy radio and press, WCS, as of April 25, transmits Führerinstructions in new, pre-established code—minuted by Dr. Herrgesell: "To what is the manifestness of the studdog Prinz attuned?"

"The original manifestness of the Führerdog is attuned to distantiality."

"What is the Führerdog attuned to distantiality acknowledged as?"

"The Führerdog attuned to distantiality is acknowledged as the Nothing."

Thereupon exlocution to all: "What is the Nothing attuned to distantiality acknowledged as?"

To which Hq. Steiner Group replies from combat position in Liebenwerda: "The Nothing attuned to distantiality is acknowledged as the Nothing in Steiner Group sector."

Whereupon Führerexlocution to all: "Is the Nothing attuned to distantiality an object or more generally an essent?"

Immediate reply from Command Staff Wenck Group: "The Nothing attuned to distantiality is a hole. The Nothing is a hole in the Twelfth Army. The Nothing is a black hole that just ran by. The Nothing is a black running hole in the Twelfth Army."

Whereupon Führerexlocution to all: "The Nothing attuned to distantiality runs. The Nothing is a hole attuned to distantiality. It is acknowledged and can be investigated. A black running hole attuned to distantiality manifests the Nothing in its original manifestation."

Whereupon supplementary WCS exlocutions: "First and foremost, modes of encounter between Nothing attuned to distantiality and Twelfth Army will be investigated for their encounter-structure. Primarily and a priori, penetration areas in Köngswusterhausen sector will be investigated for their what-content. Manipulation-utilization of relation-inducing

842

Wolftrap I equipment and supplementary Wolfpoint equipment will un-conceal Nothing attuned to distantiality. The digressiveness of the not-at-hand will provisionally be passed over with a view to establishing authentic at-handness of bitches in heat, since the Nothing attuned to distantiality is fundamentally and at all times coexistence-oriented."

An urgent dispatch from contested Neubabelsberg-Zehlendorf-Neu-kölln line—"The Nothing is coming-to-be between enemy armor and our own spearheads. The Nothing is running on four legs"—is imme-diately followed by Führerexlocution: "The Nothing will be after-accom-plished on the double. Each and every activity of the Nothing attuned to distantiality will be substantivized in view of final victory so that later, sculptured in marble or shell-lime, it may be at-hand in a state of to-be-viewedness."

Not until April 25 did General Wenck, Twelfth Army, reply from the Nauen-Ketzin sector: "Nothing being after-accomplished on double and substantivized. The Nothing attuned to distantiality discloses dread in every sector of the front. Dread is-there. We are speechless with dread. Out."

After the accomplishment reports of the Holster and Steiner combat teams have disclosed similar dread, a WCS exlocution of April 26 goes out, as per Führerinstructions, to all: "Dread impedes apprehension of the Nothing. As of now, dread will be surmounted by speeches or singing. Negation of Nothing attuned to distantiality prohibited. Never must the Reichcapital in its locus-wholeness be infirmed by dread."

When accomplishment reports of all combat teams continue to show openness to dread, a supplement to Führerinstructions of April 26 goes out to all: "Twelfth Army will manifest counter-tonality to fusty atonality of Reichcapital. Unburdenings of Being in Steglitz and southern edge of Tempelhof Airfield will project advanced selfpoint. The final struggle of the German people will be conducted with regard to the Nothing attuned to distantiality."

In response to additional instructions from Burgdorf WCS staff to Air Fleet 6—"Between Tegel and Siemensstadt elucidate running Noth-ing in advance of enemy armored spearheads"—Air Fleet 6 reports after the all-clear: "Running Nothing sighted between Silesian and Görlitz stations. The Nothing is neither an object nor any essent, hence also no dog."

Thereupon, in accordance with Führerinstructions with new key, a direct exlocution signed Colonel von Below goes out to Air Fleet 6: "Jutting out into the Nothing, the dog has surpassed the essent and will as of now be referred to as Transcendence."

On the twenty-seventh Brandenburg falls. The Twelfth Army reaches Beelitz. After numerous dispatches from all sectors have reported increasing negation of the fugitive Führerdog Prinz and his code names "Nothing" and "Transcendence," a Führerorder to all goes out at one four one two hours: "Negative attitude toward running Transcendence will as of now be considered a court-martial offense."

When no accomplishment reports come in and openness-to-dread is registered even in the government quarter, drastic measures are taken, followed by an exlocution: "The prevailing negative attitude toward Transcendence attuned to distantiality is manifested primarily and decisively by the having-beenness of the following officers." (Names and ranks follow.) Only now, after repeated Führerinquiry—"Where are Wenck's spearheads? Where are Wenck's spearheads? Where is Wenck?"—command staff Wenck, Twelfth Army, replies on April 28: "Bogged down south Lake Schwielow. Joint missions with Air Fleet 6 reveal weather conditions bar visibility Transcendence. Out."

Nihilating reports come in from Halle Gate, from the Silesian Station, and from the Tempelhof Airfield. Space is split up into loci. Alexanderplatz dogcapturepost claims to have investigated twelve-legged Transcendence in advance of enemy armored spearheads. A conflicting dispatch reports three-headed Transcendence sighted in Prenzlau area. At the same time a message Twelfth Army is received at Führerheadquarters: "Slightly wounded armored infantryman claims to have seen and fed dog untranscendent in garden of villa on Lake Schwielow, and to have addressed him by the name of Prinz."

Whereupon inquiry direct from Führer: "Name of the armored infantryman?"

Twelfth Army: "Armored infantryman Harry Liebenau, slightly wounded on chowline."

Führer direct: "Armored infantryman Liebenau's present whereabouts?"

Twelfth Army: "Armored infantryman Liebenau in need of hospitalization removed westward."

Führer direct: "Terminate removal. Fly armored infantryman to garden area Reichchancellery per Air Fleet 6."

Whereupon General Wenck, Twelfth Army, to Führer direct: "Escape-permitting relegation to sinking locus-wholeness Greater Berlin to the point of finite transcending utilization lays bare end structure."

The following Führerexlocution—"The question of the dog is a metaphysical question, calling the entire German nation into question" —is followed by the famous Führerdeclaration: "Berlin is German. Vienna will be German. And never will the dog be negated."

Whereupon an urgent report comes in: "Enemy armor entering Malchin." Followed by radio message, uncoded, to Reichchancellery: "Enemy radio reports dog sighted east bank Elbe."

Whereupon Soviet leaflets, secured in the contested Kreuzberg and

Schöneberg sectors, announce that fugitive Führerdog has been captured by Eastenemy.

Situation report of April 29: "In the course of bitter house-to-house battle on Potsdamer Strasse and Belle-Alliance-Platz, Führerdog-search-groups disbanding without orders. Morale increasingly impaired by Soviet loudspeakeraction with genuine amplified dogbarking. Beelitz retaken by enemy. No news of Ninth Army. Twelfth Army still trying to exert pressure on Potsdam, consequent to rumors of dogdeath on historical site. Reports of English dogcapture positions near Elbe bridgehead in Lauenburg and of American dogcapture in Fichtel Mountains unconfirmed." In the light of which, final Führerinstructions to all, with new code: "The dog itself—as such—was-there, is-there, and will remain-there."

Whereupon General Krebs to Colonel General Jodl: "Request prospective orientation on Führersuccession eventuality death."

Whereupon, in accordance with the situation report of April 30 command staff Operation Wolftrap is disbanded. Dogcapture operations in Transcendence and on historical site having met with no success, the Army High Command withdraws the Twelfth Army from the Potsdam-Beelitz area.

Whereupon radio message signed Bormann to Grand Admiral Dönitz: "The Führer appoints you successor former Reichmarshal Göring. Written appointment and pedigree Führerdog on way."

Whereupon Führerdesign presentifies overclimb. Whereupon unofficial Swedish report to effect that Führerdog has been sent to Argentine by submarine is not denied. The Soviet announcement—"Tattered fur of twelve-legged black dog found in destroyed ballet storeroom"—is contradicted by accomplishment report of the Bavarian Liberation Committee on the Erding radio: "Black dogcorpse secured outside Feldherrnhalle, Munich." Simultaneously, reports come in to the effect that Führerdog corpses have been washed ashore: first, in the Gulf of Bothnia; second, on the east coast of Ireland; third, on the Atlantic coast of Spain. Ultimate Führerintimations, recorded by General Burgdorf and in Führertestament: "Dog Prinz will try to reach Vatican City. If Pacelli raises claims, protest immediately and invoke codicil to will."

Thereupon world twilight. Over the ruins of the artifact-world climbs world-time. Situation report May 1: "In the center of the Reichcapital the brave garrison is fighting in narrowed space, reinforced by disbanded Führerdogsearchgroups."

Thereupon at-handness takes its leave in the not-noticeableness of the inutilizable, giving rise to top secret message, Reichsleiter Bormann to Grand Admiral Dönitz: "Führer passed away yesterday one five three o hours. Testament in force and on way. As per instructions April 29,

845

Führer's favorite dog Prinz, black, short-haired shepherd, is Führer's gift to the German people. Acknowledge receipt."

Whereupon the last radio stations play *Götterdämmerung*. Grounded on him. Whereupon there is no time for a minute of silence grounded on him. Whereupon the remnants of the Vistula Army Group, the remnants of the Twelfth and Ninth Armies, the remnants of the Holste and Steiner combat teams, try to reach English- and American-held territory west of the Dömitz-Wismar line.

Whereupon radio silence settles over the government quarter of the Reichcapital. Locus-wholeness, nihilation, open-to-dread, and together-pieceable. Greatness. Entirety. The madeness of Berlin. Made finite. The end.

But the heavens did not darken over the structure of the end.

There was once a dog;

he belonged to the Führer and Chancellor and was his favorite dog. One day this dog ran away from the Führer. Why would he run away?

Ordinarily this dog cannot speak, but here, questioned as to the great why, he speaks and says why: "Sick of moving all over the place. No fixed dog-here, dog-there, dog-now. Bones buried everywhere and never found again. No allowed-to-run-loose. Always being-in-restricted-zone. Moving around for dog years, from operation to operation, and for every operation code names: Operation White goes on for eighteen days. While Weser maneuvers are in progress in the north, they have to start up Operation Hartmut to protect Weser maneuvers. Operation Yellow against neutral countries develops into Operation Red all the way to the Spanish border. And then Autumn Journey is arranged with a view to organizing Operation Sea Lion that will force perfidious Albion to its knees. It's called off. Instead, Marita rolls up the Balkans. Oh, what poet has he in his pay? Who writes his poetry for him? Christmastree against the Swiss; nothing comes of it. Barbarossa and Silverfox against subhumans; plenty comes of them. Operation Siegfried leads from Kharkov to Stalingrad. Thunderbolt and Blizzard don't help the Sixth Army one bit. A last try is made: Fridericus I and Fridericus II. Autumn Crocus soon fades. Landbridge to Demnyansk collapses. Typhoon has to straighten out the fronts. Operation Buffalo degenerates into stampede back to the stable. Home sweet home! In such a situation even a dog is fed up, but waits, faithful as a dog, to see if the newly planned bastion near Kursk will hold out, and to see what comes of Knight's-move against convoys headed for Murmansk. But alas! Gone are the happy days when Sunflower was transplanted to North Africa, when Mercury did business on Crete, when Mouse burrowed deep into the Caucasus. Nothing doing now but Spring Storm, Ball Lightning, and Poundcake against Tito's partisans. Oaktree is supposed to put Il Duce back in the saddle. But Westenemies

Gustav, Ludwig, and Marten II land and provoke Sunrise at Nettuno. Enemy flowers blossom in Normandy. Griffin, Autumn Mist, and Sentinel try in vain to pluck them in the Ardennes. Before that the bomb goes off in rabbitless Wolf's Redoubt. It doesn't hurt the dog, but it blunts his enthusiasm: Fed up! Always being dragged this way and that way. Special trains. Special food, but no freedom, with juicy nature for miles around.

"Oh dog of many travels! From Berghof to Felsennest. From the Zoppot Winter Garden to the Tannenburg. From the Black Forest to Wolf's Lair I. Never did get to see anything of France and in Berghof nothing but clouds. Northwest of Vinnitsa, in a little forest allegedly full of foxes, lies Werewolf Camp. Shuttling back and forth between Ukraine and East Prussia. From Wolf's Redoubt propelled to Wolf's Lair II. One day's stay in the Eyrie, then down into the hole for good. Down into the Führer's air-raid shelter. Day after day: nothing but air-raid shelters. After Eagle, Wolf, and again Wolf, air-raid shelters day in day out. After Cloudview and Crowsnest, after Tannenburg and the air of the Black Forest, nothing but a stuffy old air-raid shelter.

When things come to such a pass, a dog has his belly full. After the failure of Dentist and the fumbling of Baseplate, he decides to migrate with the Visigoths. To escape. To be-in-space. To give up being-faithful-as-a-dog. When things come to such a pass, a dog, who ordinarily and as a rule cannot talk, says: "I disengage myself."

While the birthday preparations in the Führer's shelter were going on, he slipped innocently across the inner courtyard of the Chancellery. Just as the Reichmarshal was driving in, he passed the sentry post and, having gathered from the situation reports that there was a gap in the front near Cottbus, started off in a southwesterly direction; but wide and attractive as the gap seemed to be, the dog, sighting Soviet armored spearheads, reversed his direction east of Jüterbog, abandoned the route of the Ostrogoths, and hurried toward the Westenemy: over the ruins of the inner city, around the government quarter, close call on the Alexanderplatz, guided through the Tiergarten by two bitches in heat, and damn near captured near the Zoological Gardens air-raid shelter, where gigantic mousetraps were waiting for him, but he seven times circumambulated the Victory Column, shot down the Siegesalle, counseled by dog instinct, that wise old saw, joined a gang of civilian moving men, who were moving theater accessories from the exhibition pavilion by the radio tower to Nikolassee. But German loudspeakers as well as the far-carrying loudspeakers of the Eastenemy—alluring voices promising him rabbits —aroused his suspicion of residential suburbs like Wannsee and Nikolassee: not far enough west!—and he set himself a goal for the first leg of his journey: the Elbe bridge at Magdeburg-Burg.

South of Lake Schwielow he passed without incident the advance elements of the Twelfth Army that were supposed to relieve the pressure on the capital. After he had taken a short rest in the overgrown garden of a villa, an armored infantryman fed him still-warm pea soup and, without taking an offical tone, called him by his name. Immediately thereafter enemy artillery subjected the villa area to harassing fire, slightly wounded the armored infantryman, but missed the dog; for what you see there, running with steady, reliable haunches, following the pre-established Visigothic migration route, is still one and the same self-grounded black German shepherd.

Panting between rippled lakes on a windy day in May. The ether teeming with weighty happening. Snapping at his goal, westward over the Prussian sand into which pine trees claw. A horizontal tail, fangs far in advance, waving tongue cut down the distance on sixteen times four legs: dog's leap in successive part movements. Everything in sixteenths: landscape, spring, air, freedom, tufty trees, beautiful clouds, first butterflies, singing of birds, buzzing of insects, kitchen gardens bursting into green, musical lath fences. Furrows spit out rabbits, partridges flush, nature without scale, no more sandbox but horizons, smells you could spread on bread, slowly drying sunsets, boneless dawns, now and then a wrecked tank, romantic against the five-o'clock-in-the-morning sky, moon and dog, dog in the moon, dog eats moon, dog close-up, evaporating dog, dog project, dog deserter, get-out-of-here dog, count-me-out dog, dog-thrownness, genealogicals: And Perkun sired Senta; and Senta whelped Harras; and Harras sired Prinz . . . Dog greatness, ontic and scientific, dog deserter with the wind in his sails; for the wind too, like everybody else, is headed west: The Twelfth Army, the remains of the Ninth Army, what is left of the Steiner and Holste combat teams, the weary Löhr, Schörner, and Rendulic army groups, unsuccessfully the East Prussia and Kurland army groups from the ports of Libau and Windau, the garrison of Rügen Island, whoever is able to get away from Hela and the Vistula delta, in short, the remains of the Second Army; everybody who has a nose to smell with runs, swims, drags himself away: away from the Eastenemy toward the Westenemy; civilians on foot, on horseback, packed into former cruise steamers, hobble in stocking feet, drown wrapped in paper money, crawl with too little gas and too much baggage; behold the miller with his twenty-pound sack of flour, the carpenter, laden with doorframes and bone glue, relatives and in-laws, Party members, active and passive, children with dolls and grandmothers with photograph albums, the imaginary and the real, all all all see the sun rising in the west and take their bearings from the dog.

Left behind: mounds of bones, mass graves, card files, flagpoles, Party books, love letters, homes, church pews, and pianos difficult to transport.

Unpaid: taxes, mortgage payments, back rent, bills, debts, and guilt.

All are eager to start out fresh with living, saving, letter writing, in church pews, at pianos, in card files and homes of their own.

All are eager to forget the mounds of bones and the mass graves, the flagpoles and Party books, the debts and the guilt.

There was once a dog,

who left his master and traveled a long way. Only rabbits pucker up their noses; but let no one who can read suppose that the dog didn't get there.

On May 8, 1945, at 4:45 A.M., he swam across the Elbe above Magdeburg almost unseen and went looking for a new master on the west side of the river.

Book
Three

Materniads

First Materniad

The dog stands central. Between him and the dog runs barbed wire, old and new, from corner to corner of the camp. While the dog stands, Matern scratches tin out of an empty tin can. He has a spoon but no memory. Everybody and everything are trying to give him one: the central dog; the tin can filled with air; the English questionnaire; and now Brauxel is sending advances and setting deadlines determined by the entrances and exists of certain planets: he wants Matern to shoot the shit about those days.

To begin is to select. What about this double row of barbed wire between dog and tin can: deprivation of freedom, prison camp jitters, all very graphic though the current has been turned off. Or stick to the dog, then you'll be central. Pour soup, noodled with names, into the tin can for him, expelling the air. Because you can always find scraps—dog food: the twenty-nine potato years. Memory soup. Remembrance dumplings. All those unseasoned lies. Theatrical roles and life. Matern's dehydrated vegetables. Gritty guilt: that's the salt.

To cook is to select. Which takes longer to cook, barley grits or barbed wire? Grits are spooned up, and yet underdone barbed wire between him and the dog induces grinding of the teeth. Matern could never abide wire and fences. Even his ancestor, who still called himself Materna, carried subversive grinding of the teeth with him to the Stockturm, the windowless tower.

To remember is to select. This, that, or the other dog? Every dog is central. What will drive a dog away? There aren't that many stones in the world; and Camp Munster—who doesn't remember it from the old days?—was built on sand and has scarcely changed. Barracks burned down, Nissen huts went up. The camp movie house, a few stray pines, the inevitable mess hall, and the whole enclosed in old wire, enriched by new wire: Matern, whom an English antifascist camp had spewed out, is spooning up barley grits behind the new barbed wire surrounding a discharge camp.

Twice a day he laps soup from a clattering tin can and follows his footprints in the sand along the double row of wire. Don't look around, the Grinder's around. Twice a day the selfsame dog refuses to eat stones: "Beat it! Clear out! Go out back where you came from!"

For tomorrow or the day after the papers will be ready for somebody who wants to be alone, without a dog.

"Where will you go when you get your discharge?"

"Let's see, Mr. Brooks, let's say Cologne or Neuss."

"Date and place of birth?"

"April 1917, just a minute: the nineteenth, to be exact, in Nickelswalde, Danzig Lowlands District."

"Education and special training?"

"Well, first the usual: public school in the village, then high school. After graduating I was supposed to study economics, but I took up acting instead, under good old Gustav Nord, played Shakespeare marvelously, but he did Shaw, too, *Saint Joan* . . ."

"Then you're an actor by profession?"

"That's right, Mr. Broox. Played everything that came along. Karl and Franz Moor: Slavish wisdom, slavish fears! And once, in our good old Coffee Mill, when I was still a beginner, I even took the part of a talking reindeer. Those were the days, Mr. . . ."

"Ever a member of the C.P.? During what period?"

"Well, I graduated in '35. I must have started in with the Red Falcons at the beginning of second. Pretty soon I joined the Communist Party and stayed in until it was suppressed in Danzig, that was in '34. I worked illegally for a while after that, handing out leaflets and putting up posters, it was no use."

"Have you ever been a member of the National Socialist Party or any of its organizations?"

"A few months in the SA, for the hell of it. Sort of snooping around to see what was going on, and partly because a friend of mine . . ."

"During what period?"

"I just told you, Mr. Braux, a couple of months. From late summer '37 to spring '38. Then they threw me out. My sturm had me up for trial for insubordination."

"What sturm?"

"If I could only remember! You see, I wasn't in very long. The whole thing was on account of this good friend of mine, who was a half-Jew. I was trying to protect him from the pack . . . All right, it was SA Sturm 84, Langfuhr-North. Belonged to Standarte 128 SA Brigade 6, Danzig."

"What was your friend's name?"

"Amsel. Eduard Amsel. He was an artist. We grew up together, so to speak. He could be awfully funny. Made stage sets, mechanical things. For instance, he wouldn't put on a suit or a pair of shoes until they'd

854

been worn by somebody else. He was terribly fat but he had a good singing voice. A wonderful guy, really."

"What became of Amsel?"

"No idea. Had to leave town, because they'd kicked me out of the SA. I asked all over, for instance, I went to see Brunies, our former German teacher . . ."

"Where's the teacher now?"

"Brunies. He must be dead. Sent to a concentration camp in '34."

"Which one?"

"Stutthof. Near Danzig."

"Your last and next-to-last military unit?"

"Up to November, '43, 22nd AA Regiment, Kaiserhafen battery. Then I was court-martialed for insulting the Führer and undermining Army morale. They broke me from tech sergeant to private and sent me to the Fourth Punitive Battalion to clear mines. On January 23, '45, I deserted to the 28th American Infantry Division in the Vosges."

"Any other trouble with the authorities?"

"Plenty, Mr. Brooks. Well, first the business with my SA sturm. Then, just a year later—I'd gone to Schwerin to work in the theater— I was dismissed without notice for insulting the Führer and so on. Then I went to Düsseldorf. I did odd jobs on children's radio programs and played faustball on the side with the Unterrath Sports Club. A couple of the club members turned me in: I was held for questioning at the Kavalleriestrasse police headquarters, if that means anything to you. When they got through with me, I was ready for the hospital, and if the war hadn't broken out in the nick of time . . . Oh yes, I almost forgot the business with the dog. That was in midsummer 1939 . . ."

"In Düsseldorf?"

"No, Mr. Broox, that was back in Danzig. I'd had to volunteer or they'd have cooked me. So I was stationed in the former police barracks in Hochstriess, and during that time, maybe because I was mad or maybe just because I was against, I poisoned a dog, a shepherd."

"What was this shepherd's name?"

"Harras, and he belonged to a carpenter."

"Anything special about the dog?"

"He was a stud dog, as they say. And in '35 or '36 this Harras had sired a dog by the name of Prinz, honest to God, as true as I'm standing here, that was given to Hitler for his birthday and was supposed—there must be witnesses—to have been his favorite dog. In addition—and here, Mr. Braux, the story gets personal—Senta, our Senta, had been Harras' mother. In Nickelswalde—that's in the Vistula estuary—she whelped Harras and a couple of other pups under the jack of our windmill when

I was just ten. Then it burned down. This windmill of ours was a very special mill . . ."

"In what way?"

"Well, it was known as the historical mill of Nickelswalde, because on her flight from Napoleon Queen Louise of Prussia spent the night in our mill. It was a fine German postmill. My great-grandfather built it, that was August Matern. He was a lineal descendant of Simon Materna, the famous hero of Polish independence, who in 1516 was arrested by Hans Nimptsch, the city captain, and beheaded in the Danzig Stockturm; but by 1524 his cousin, the journeyman barber Gregor Materna, was sounding the call for another uprising, and on August 14, while the St. Dominic's Day market was going on, he in turn, because that's the way we Materns are, we can't button up, we're always shooting our traps off, even my father, Anton Matern, the miller, who could predict the future, because the mealworms . . ."

"Thank you, Mr. Matern. You've given us sufficient information. Your discharge papers will be issued tomorrow morning. Here's your pass. You may go."

Through this door on two hinges, to give the sun outside a chance to show what it can do: on the camp grounds POW Matern, barracks, Nissen huts, the remaining pines, the crowded bulletin board, the double row of barbed wire, and the patient dog outside the fence cast shadows, all in the same direction. Remember! How many rivers empty into the Vistula? How many teeth has a man? What were the names of the ancient Prussian gods? How many dogs? Were there eight or nine muffled figures? How many names are still alive? How many women have you . . . ? How long did your grandmother sit riveted to her chair? What did your father's mealworms whisper when the miller's son asked him how somebody was getting along and what he was doing? He whispered, remember, that this somebody was hoarse as a grater and nevertheless chain-smoked all day long. And when did we do Billinger's *The Giant* at the Stadttheater? Who played the part of Donata Opferkuch, and who did her son? What did Strohmenger the critic write in the *Vorposten*? Here's what it said, remember: "The gifted young Matern distinguished himself as the son of Donata Opferkuch, who, it should be added, was played sloppily but powerfully by Maria Bargheer; son and mother, two interesting, ambivalent figures . . ." *Chien . . . cane . . . dog . . . kyon*! I've been discharged. In my windbreaker I've got papers, six hundred reichsmarks and traveler's food tickets! My barracks bag contains two pairs of drawers, three undershirts, four pairs of socks, a pair of American combat boots with rubber soles, two almost new Ami shirts, dyed black, a German officer's overcoat, undyed, a real civilian hat from Cornwall, gentlemanlike, two packages of K-rations, a pound can of English pipe tobacco, fourteen packs of

856

Camels, about twenty paperbacks—mostly Shakespeare Grabbe Schiller —a complete edition of *Being and Time*—still containing the dedication of Husserl—five cakes of first-class soap and three cans of corned beef . . . *Chien*, I'm rich! *Cane*, where is thy victory? Beat it, dog! Get thee behind me, *kyon*!

On foot, with his barracks bag over his shoulder, Matern takes steps on sand which outside the camp isn't trampled as hard as inside the camp. No more social life, that was the main thing! Accordingly, shank's mare and no trains for the present. The dog shrinks back and refuses to understand. A real or simulated throwing of stones drives him into plowed fields or up the path. Empty throwing motions make him tense; real stones he retrieves: *zellacken*.

With ineluctable dog Matern covers three sandy miles in the direction of Fallingbostel. Since the good dirt road is not like himself headed southwest, he drives the critter across the fields. Anyone who has noticed that Matern is striding normally on the right side will have to admit that on the left side he has a barely perceptible limp. All this was once a military terrain and will remain so for all eternity: damage to crops. A brown heath starts up and merges into young woods. A felling makes him a present of a club: "Beat it, dog. Faithfulasadog. You no-good bastard, beat it!"

I can't take him with me, can I? To live for once without admirers. Haven't I been hounded enough? What can I do with this flea bag? Rat poison, cuckoo clocks, doves of peace, sharks, Christian dogs, Jewish swine, domestic animals, domestic animals . . . Beat it, dog."

This from morning to night till he was almost hoarse. From Ostenholz to Essel his mouth full of self-defense and names aimed not only at the dog but at the whole environing world. In his cold homeland *zellacken* and not stones were picked up from the fields whenever there was somebody to be stoned. These, and clods of earth and the club as well, are meant to hit the critter and just about everything else. Never has a dog, unwilling to leave his self-chosen master, had an opportunity to learn so much about the dog's function in mythology: is there any underworld he doesn't have to guard; any river of the dead whose waters some dog doesn't lap up? Lethe Lethe, how do we get rid of memories? No hell but has its hellhound!

Never has a dog unwilling to leave his self-chosen master been sent to so many countries and cities at once: Go where the pepper grows. To Buxtehude, Jericho, Todtnau. What multitudes of people this dog is told to nuzzle up to! Names names—but he doesn't go to hell, doesn't go to Pepper City, doesn't kiss the ass of strangers, but follows, faithfulasadog, his self-chosen master.

Don't look around, here comes the hound.

Then Matern gives a peasant a piece of advice in Mandelsloh—that makes him a Lower Saxon peasant, they had been following the River Leine together. In exchange for four Camels the peasant has let him sleep in a real bed, white in and out. Over steaming fried potatoes Matern suggests: "Couldn't you use a dog? He's a stray, he's been after me all day. I can't get rid of him. Not a bad mutt, only kind of run down."

But the following day from Mandelsloh to Rothenuffeln isn't dogless for a single step, though in the peasant's opinion the dog wasn't bad, only neglected, he'd sleep on it and tell him in the morning. At breakfast the peasant was willing, but not the dog, his mind was made up.

The Steinhuder Sea sees them coupled; a load off Matern's feet between Rothenuffeln and Brackwede when a three-wheeled cart picks him up whereas the dog has to shake a leg; and in Westphalia, when their day's destination goes by the name of Rinkerode, the couple is still undivided: not a dog more, not a dog less. And as they are hiking from Rinkerode past Othmarsbocholt to Ermen, he begins to share with him: rye bread and corned beef. But while the dog bolts scraps, a club that has come along from Lower Saxony thuds dully on matted fur.

On which account he scrubs him next day—after the two of them have maintained a moderate distance from Ermen via Olfen to Eversum —in the River Stever, until he glistens black: coat and undercoat. A pipeful of tobacco is traded for an old dog comb. Matern receives an attestation: "He's a purebred." He can see that for himself, he knows a thing or two about dogs. "You're not telling me anything new, man. I grew up with a dog. Take a look at the legs. He's not cow-hocked or bowlegged. And the line from croup to withers: no sign of lumpiness, just that he isn't as young as he used to be. Take a look at the lips, they don't close tight. And those two gray spots over the stop. But his teeth will be good for years."

Appraisal and shoptalk with English tobacco in their pipes:

"How old would he be? Ten is my guess."

Matern is more exact: "More likely eleven. But that breed keeps lively up to seventeen. With proper care, mind you."

After lunch a few words about the world situation and the atom bomb. Then Westphalian dog stories: "In Bechtrup there was a male shepherd one time, long before the war, that quietly passed away at the age of twenty, which, I always say, makes a hundred and forty human years. And my grandfather used to tell about a dog from Rechede, raised in the Dülmen kennels, that lived to be twenty-two, even if he was half blind, which makes a hundred and fifty-four. Next to him your dog, with his eleven dog years, which makes seventy-seven human years, is still a youngster."

His dog, whom he doesn't send away with stones and hoarseness, but keeps close to him as a nameless possession. "What's he called anyway?"

"He isn't called anything yet."

"Are you looking for a name for the dog?"

"Don't look for names or you'll find names."

"Well, why don't you call him Fido or Towser, or Falko or Hasso, or Castor or Wotan . . . I once knew a male shepherd, believe it or not, his name was Jasomir."

Oh lousy shit! Who has squatted here in the open fields, expelled a hard sausage, and is now contemplating his excrement? Someone who doesn't want to eat it, yet recognizes himself in it: Matern, Walter Matern, who is good at grinding his teeth: gravel in the dung; who is always looking for God and finding at best excrement; who kicks his dog: shit! But across the same field, cutting across the furrows, he whimpers back, and still has no name. Shit shit! Should Matern call his dog Shit?

Nameless, they make their way across the Lippe-Seiten Canal into the Haard, a moderately hilly forest. He really means to cut across the mixed forest to Marl with the nameless dog—should his name be Kuno or Thor?—but then they turn off on a path to the left—Audifax?—and, emerging from the woods, come across the railroad: Dülmen-Haltern-Recklinghausen. And here there are coal mines with names that would do perfectly well for dogs: Hannibal, Regent, Prosper?—In Speckhorn master and nameless dog find a bed.

Consult the books, draw up lists. Chiseled in granite and marble. Names names. History is made of them. Can should may a dog bear the name of Totila, Attila, or Kaspar Hauser? What was the first of the long line called? Maybe the other gods could supply a name: Potrimpos or Pikollos?

Who tosses and turns, unable to sleep, because names, now private ones unfit for any dog, are gouging his spine? In the early morning, through ground fog, the two of them stick to the railroad embankment, walk on ballast, step aside to let overcrowded morning trains pass by. Silhouetted ruins: that's Recklinghausen or, later on, Herne, to the right Wanne, to the left Eickel. Emergency bridges cross the Emscher Canal and the Rhine-Herne Canal. Nameless figures pick up coal in the mist. On headframes windlays turn or are silent over nameless mines. No noise. Everything bedded in cotton. At most the ballast speaks, or crows in their usual way: namelessly. Until something branches off to the right and has a name. Rails, single-tracked, come from Eickel and don't want to go to Hüllen. Over an open entrance, on a weatherbeaten sign, big letters: PLUTO BRANCH LINE.

That does it: "Here Pluto. Sit Pluto. Heel Pluto. Fetch it Pluto. Nice Pluto. Down, fetch it, eat, Pluto. Quick Pluto. Seek Pluto. My pipe Pluto." Godfather is Pluton, bestower of grain and shekels, who, like Hades—or old Pikollos—attends to the business of the underworld, shady business, templeless business, invisible business, underground business, the big pension, the elevator to the fill level, where they let you in but not out, he can't be bribed, you're there to stay, each and all go to Pluto, whom nobody worships. Only Matern and the Elians pile the altar: with heart, spleen, and kidneys for Pluto!

They follow the branch line. Weeds between the tracks mean there hasn't been a train here in a long time, and the rails are dull with rust. Matern tries the new name, loudly and softly. Now that he's taken possession of the dog, his hoarseness has been letting up. The name works. Surprise at first, then zealous obedience. That dog has had training sometime. He's no bum. When whistled, Pluto stands and lies down in the middle of the coal fields. Halfway between Dortmund and Oberhausen Pluto shows what he has learned and not forgotten, but only repressed a little because of the troubled, masterless times. Tricks. The mist has begun to curdle and swallow itself up. Around half past four, there's even a sun in these parts.

This mania for taking your bearings once a day: Where are we anyway? A memorable spot! To the left Schalke-North with Wilhelmine-Victoria Mine, to the right Wanne without Eickel, past the Emscher marshes Gelsenkirchen stops, and here, which is where the branch line with its rusty rails and weeds was headed, there lies, silenced and half destroyed by bombs beneath an old-fashioned knock-kneed headframe, that Pluto Mine which has given Pluto, the black shepherd male, his name.

What a war can do: everything closed down. Nettles and buttercups grow faster than the world can imagine. Crumpled walls that were expected to stand forever. T-girders and radiators twisted into iron belly-aches. Wreckage shouldn't be described but turned into cash; and so junk dealers will come and bend the scrap-iron question marks straight. Just as bluebells ring in the summer, so junk dealers will strike peaceful notes from scrap iron and announce the great smelting process. O ye unshaven angels of peace, spread your wings, bestir your battered mudguards and settle in places like this: Pluto Mine, between Schalke and Wanne.

The environment appeals to both of them: Matern and his four-legged buddy. Why not a little training right away? A nice piece of wall, about four feet three inches high, is still standing. Go to it, Pluto. It won't be hard, not with those long withers and perfectly angulated forelegs, not with that comparatively short but powerful back, not with those efficient hindquarters. Jump, Pluto. Black bow-wow, without spots or markings on straight back: speed, staying power, willingness to jump. Go to it, doggy, I'll put a little something on top. Those two hocks will bring home the bacon. Away from the earthly. A little trip through the

Rhenish-Westphalian air. Land softly, it's easier on the joints. Gooddog modeldog: shipshape Pluto!

Pants here, sniffs there. Nose to the ground, he collects scent marks: antiques. In a burned-out headframe he barks at dangling chain hoists and hooks, though second sight is needed to glimpse what's left of the rags of the last morning shift. Echo. It's fun to make a racket in abandoned ruins; but the master whistles his dog into the sun, out into the playground. In a wrecked shunting engine a fireman's cap is found. You can throw it up in the air or put it on. Fireman Matern: "All this belongs to us. We've got the headframe. Now let's occupy the offices. The proletariat seizes the means of production."

But there wasn't a single rubber stamp in the thoroughly ventilated offices. And if not for the—"Say, there's a hole in the floor!"—they would have had every reason to go back to the sunlit playground. "Say, there's a way down!" an almost complete staircase. "But watch your step!" there might be a mine lying around from the day before yesterday. But there are no mines in the furnace room. "Let's take a look in here." Step by little step: "Where is my candle and what about my good old lighter? Picked it up in Dunkirk, it's seen Piraeus, Odessa, and Novgorod, and lighted my way home; it's always done its stuff, why not here?"

Every dark place knows why. All secrets are ticklish. Every treasure seeker has expected more. There they stand on six feet in the full-to-bursting cellar. No crates to break open; no little bottles to glug out of; neither displaced Persian carpets nor silver spoons; no church treasure nor castle valuables: nothing but paper. Not naked white paper, that might still have been good business. Or a correspondence between great men on handmade ragpaper. This paper was printed, in four colors: forty thousand posters still smelled fresh. One as smooth as the next. On each one He with low-pulled visor cap: solemn rigid Führergaze: As of four forty-five today. Providence has saved. When long ago I decided. Innumerable. Ignominious. Pitiful. If need be. To the very last. In the end. Remains, will again, never. Contemptible traitors. In this hour the whole world. The turning point. I call upon you. We will join ranks. I have. I will. I am well aware. I . . .

And every poster that Matern brushes from the pile with two fingers hovers for a time in midair and then settles in front of Pluto's forepaws. Only a few fall on the face. For the most part He stares at the furnace pipes on the ceiling: solemn rigid Führergaze. Matern's two fingers are indefatigable, as though he had reason to expect a different gaze from the next or next-to-next poster. Where there's life . . .

Then a siren swells in the pin-drop cellar. The Führergaze has set off this aria in the dog's heart. The dog croons and Matern can't turn him off. "Quiet Pluto. Lie down Pluto."

But the whimpering dog tips his erect ears, all four legs go limp, and his tail sags. Rising to the concrete ceiling, the sound threads its way into burst pipes, and Matern has nothing to oppose it with but a dry grinding of the teeth. Ineffectual, the grinding breaks off, and he spits: phlegm on a picture portrait taken before the attempt on his life; oysters into the solemn rigid Führergaze; lung butter loops the loop and strikes: him him him. But it doesn't lie for long, for the dog has a tongue, which licks, long and colorful, the Führer's flatlying face: snot from his cheek. No longer does spittle cloud the gaze. Laps saliva from the little square mustache: faithfulasadog.

Thereupon counteraction. Matern has ten fingers which crumple radically what smoothly records a four-tone face, what lies on the floor, what lies in piles, what looks up at the ceiling: He He He. No! says the dog. Growling in crescendo. Pluto's iron jaws: No! A dog says no: Stop that, stop it this minute! The fist over Matern's head relaxes: "O.K. Pluto. Sit Pluto. Come come. I didn't mean it that way, Pluto. Why don't we take a little nap and save the candle? Sleep and be nice to each other again? Nice Pluto, nice Pluto."

Matern blows out the candle. On piled-up Führergaze lie master and dog. Panting heavily in the darkness. Each breathes by himself. God in His heaven looks on.

Second Materniad

They are no longer walking on six feet, one of which seems to be defective and has to be dragged; they are riding in a packjammed train from Essen via Duisburg to Neuss, for a man must have some goal or other: a doctor's degree or a sharpshooter's medal, the kingdom of heaven or a home of his own, on his way to Robinson Crusoe's island, world-record, Cologne on the Rhine.

The trip is hard and long. Lots of people, if not the whole population, are on the move with sacks of potatoes or sugarbeets. Accordingly—if sugarbeets are to be trusted—they are not riding into the spring but toward St. Martin's Day. And so, for Novemberly reasons, life, for all the crush of smelly overcoats, is more tolerable inside the packjammed car than on the rounded roof, on the jangling bumpers, or on running boards that have to be reconquered at every station. For not all the travelers have the same destination.

Even before the train pulls out of Essen, Matern gets Pluto settled. Inside the car an acrid smell mingles with the effluvia of late potatoes, earth-damp sugarbeets, and sweating humanity.

Out in the wind Matern smells only the locomotive. In league with his barracks bag, he holds the running board against enemy onslaughts at the Grossenbaum and Kalkum stations. It would be pointless to grind his teeth against the wind. In the old days, when he challenged the buzz saw with his jaws—the story was that he could grind his teeth even under water—in the old days his teeth would have spoken up even in the train wind. Silently, then, but his head full of dramatic parts, he speeds through the unmoving landscape. In Derendorf Matern makes room on the running board for a bilious watchmaker, who might also be a professor, by up-ending his barracks bag. The watchmaker is trying to convey eight bri-quettes to Küppersteg. At Düsseldorf Central Station Matern manages to save him, but in Benrath he is swallowed up by the mob along with his briquettes. Simply to be fair, Matern forces the character who in the watchmaker's place is determined to transport his kitchen scales to Co-logne, to change in Leverkusen. Glances over his shoulder reassure him: Inside the car a dog is still standing on four paws and keeping an eye, faithfulasadog, on the window: "Good dog, good dog, just a little longer. That pile of bricks for instance promises to be Mülheim. We don't stop in Kalk. But from Deutz we can see the double prongs, the Devil's Gothic horns, the cathedral. And where the cathedral is, its secular counterpart, the Central Station, can't be far off. They go together like Scylla and Charybdis, throne and altar, Being and Time, master and dog."

So that's what they call the Rhine! Matern grew up by the Vistula. In recollection, every Vistula is wider than every Rhine. And it's only because the Materns must always live by rivers—the everlasting parade of water gives them a sense of being alive—that we've undertaken this crusade to Cologne. But also because Mathern has been here before. And because his forebears, the brothers Simon and Gregor Materna, always came back mostly to wreak vengeance with fire and sword: that was how Drehergasse and Petersiliengasse went up in flames, how Langgarten and St. Barbara's burned down in the east wind; well, in this place others have had ample opportunity to try out their lighters. There's not much kindling left. "I come to judge with a black dog and a list of names incised in my heart, spleen, and kidneys. THAT DEMAND TO BE CROSSED OFF."

O acrid unglassed drafty holy Catholic Central Station of Cologne! Nations with suitcases and knapsacks come to see and smell you, disperse throughout the world, and can never again forget you: you and the double stone monstrosity across the way. Anyone who wants to understand hu-manity must kneel down in your waiting rooms; for here all are pious and confess to one another over watery beer. Whatever they do, whether they sleep with open jaws, embrace their pathetic baggage, quote earthly prices for heavenly lighter flints and cigarettes, whatever they may omit and pass over in silence, whatever they may add and repeat, they are working on the great confession. At the ticket windows, in the paper-blown station hall—two overcoats a plot, three overcoats in cahoots a riot!—and similarly down below in the tiled toilets, where the beer flows off again, warmed. Men unbutton, stand silently as though deep in thought in white-enameled bays, whisper with prematurely worn-out cocks, seldom in a straight line, usually with a slight but calculated elevation. Urine comes-to-be. Pissing stallions stand for eternities with arched back on two legs in pants, forming a roof over their excrescences with right hands, mostly married, prop their hips with their left hands, look ahead with mournful eyes, and decipher inscriptions, dedications, confessions, prayers, outcries, rhymes, and names, scribbled in blue pencil scratched with nail scissors, leather punch, or nail.

So too Matern. Except that he doesn't prop his hip with his left hand, but holds behind him a leather leash, which cost two Camels in Essen and in Cologne joins him with Pluto. All men stand for eternities, but Matern's eternity is longer, even after his water has stopped leaning on enamel. Already he is fingering button after button, with pauses the length of a paternoster in between, into the corresponding buttonhole, his back no longer arched, but rather humped like that of a reader. Nearsighted people hold their eyes that close to printed matter or script. Thirst for knowledge. Reading room atmosphere. The student of Scripture. Don't disturb the reader. Knowledge is power. An angel passes through the enormous tiled warm sweetandpungentsmelling holy Catholic men's toilet of Cologne Central Station.

There it is written: "Deadhead, watch out." Recorded for all time: "Dobshe dobshe trallala—Schnapps is good for cholera." A Lutheran nail has scratched: "And though the world were full of devils . . ." Hard to decipher: "Germany awaken!" Perpetuated in capitals: "ALL WOMEN ARE SLUTS." A poet has written: "In ice and flame—we're still the same." And someone has stated tersely: "The Führer is alive." But another handwriting knew more and added: "Right, in Argentina." Brief ejaculations such as: "No! Count me out! Chin up!" are frequent. So are drawings, which over and over again have as their subject the indestructible Vienna roll with its hairy halo, as well as recumbent women viewed as Mantegna viewed the recumbent Christ, that is, by an eye situated between the soles of their feet. Finally, wedged in between the cry of rejoicing: "Happy New Year '46!" and the obsolete warning: "Caution! Enemy ears are listening!," Matern, buttoned below, open on top, reads a name and address without rhymed or prose commentary: "Jochen Sawatzki—Fliesteden—Bergheimer Strasse 32."

Instantly Matern—with heart, spleen, and kidneys already on his way to Fliesteden—has a nail in his pocket that wants to write. Significantly cutting across dedications, confessions, and prayers, across the strangely hairy Vienna rolls and the recumbent Mantegna ladies, the nail scratches the child's jingle: "DON'T TURN AROUND, THE GRINDER'S AROUND."

864

It's a village lined up along the highway between Cologne and Erft. The bus from the main post office to Grevenbroich by way of Müngersdorf, Lövenich, Brauweiler, stops there before Büsdorf, where it turns off to Stommeln. Matern finds his way without having to ask. Sawatzki in rubber boots opens: "Man, Walter, you still alive? Ain't that a surprise? Come on in, or wasn't it us you was coming to see?"

Inside it smells of boiling sugarbeets. Up from the cellar, head in kerchief, comes a doll who smells no better. "See, we're cooking syrup. Then we peddle it. It's rough work, but it pays. This here's my little wife. Her name's Inge, she's a native of Frechen. Inge, this here's a friend of mine, a buddy, kind of. We were in the same sturm for a while. My, oh my, haven't we been screwed: Shoilem boil 'em! remember, the two of us in the Kleinhammerpark, lights out—knives out! Get in there and fight. Christ, what a brawl! You remember Gustav Dau and Lothar Budczinski? Fränzchen Wollschläger and the Dulleck brothers? And Willy Eggers, man! And Otto Warnke, hell, and little Bublitz? Rough customers one and all, but good as gold, except they drank too much and you can say that again.—So there you are again. Man, I'm kind of scared of that mutt. Couldn't you lock him up in the other room?—All right, let him stay here. So give: where did you run off to at exactly the right time? Because once you left the sturm, we were through. Oh, it's easy to say when it's all over that we were damn fools to throw you out for nothing. It didn't amount to a hill of beans. But that's how they wanted it, especially the Dulleck brothers and Wollschläger too: Court of honor! An SA man don't steal! Robbing his comrades!—I really cried—honest to God, Inge—when he had to go. Well, here you are. You can take it easy in here or come into the laundry where the beets are cooking. You can flop in the deck chair and watch. Man, you old rascal. You can't lose a bad penny is what I always say to Inge, eh, Inge? I'm mighty glad."

In the cozy laundry room the sugarbeets cook away, spreading sweetness. Matern sprawls in the deck chair and has something between his teeth that can't come out because the two of them are so pleased and besides they're cooking syrup with four hands. She stirs the washtub with a shovel handle: pretty strong, though she's only a handful; he keeps the fire burning evenly: they have piles of briquettes, black gold. She's a regular Rhenish type: doll face with googoo eyes and can't stop googooing; he has hardly changed, maybe a little stouter. She just makes eyes and doesn't say boo; he bullshits about old times: "The storm troops march with firm and tranquil tread . . . Remember? Shoilem, boil 'em!" Why can't she stop making eyes? The bone I have to pick is with him, not with Ingewife. Cooking. What a racket! Out in the fields at night, stealing beets, peeling them, cutting them up, and so on. You won't see the last of Walter Matern so soon, because Walter has come to judge you with a black dog and a list of names incised in his heart, spleen, and kidneys, one of them exhibited for all to read in the Cologne Central Station, in the pisswarm part with the tiled floor and the cozy enameled bays: Sturmführer Jochen Sawatzki led the popular and notorious 84th SA Sturm, Langfuhr-North, through hell and high water. His terse but spirited speeches. His boyish charm when he spoke of the Führer and Germany's future. His favorite songs and favorite liquor: The Argonne Forest at midnight and for steady drinking gin with or without a plum. A good worker all the same. Energetic and trustworthy. Thoroughly disillusioned with the Commies, which is what made him so staunch a believer in the new idea. His operations against the Sozis Brill and Wichmann; the brawl at the Café Woike, the Polish student hangout; the eight-man action on Steffensweg . . .

"Say," says Matern across the dog reclining at his feet and through the sugarbeet mist. "What ever became of Amsel? You know whom I mean. The guy that made the funny figures. The one you beat up on Steffensweg, remember, that's where he lived."

This gets no rise out of the dog, but provokes a brief lull in the beet corner. "Man, whatcha asking me for? That little visit was your idea. I never could get it straight, seeing he was a friend of yours, wasn't he."

The deck chair answers through the steam: "There were certain reasons, private reasons that I won't go into. But this is what I want to know: What did you do with him afterwards, I mean after the eight of you on Steffensweg . . ."

Ingewife makes googoo eyes and stirs. Sawatzki doesn't forget to put briquettes on the fire: "Whassat? We didn't do nothing else. And whatcha asking questions for anyway, when there wasn't eight of us but nine, including you. And you were the one that really pasted him so there wasn't much left. Anyway, he wasn't the worst. Too bad we never caught Dr. Citron. He cleared out for Sweden. What am I saying, too bad? To hell with the final solution and final victory routine. It's finished and good riddance. Forget it. Forget all that crap, and don't try to put the finger on me or I'll get mad. Because, sonny boy, you and I were tarred with the same brush, and neither of us if is any cleaner than the other, right?"

The deck chair grumbles. The dog Pluto looks up, faithfulasadog. Chunks of sugarbeet boil unthinking: Don't cook beets, or you'll smell of beets. Too late, by this time all smell in unison: Fireman Sawatzki, Ingewife with eyes in her head, the inactive Matern—even the dog has ceased to smell of dog alone. The washtub has begun to glug heavily: Syrup syrup thick and sweet is—flies are dying of diabetes. Ingewife's stirring shovel handle meets with resistance: Never when syrup is being stirred, stir up the past with a single word. Sawatzki puts on the last briquettes: Sugarbeets need husbandry—God has sugar in his pee!

Then Sawatzki decides it's done and sets up a double row of pot-bellied two-quart bottles. Matern wants to help but they won't let him: "No, my boy. When the bottles are full, we'll go upstairs and pour a little something under our belts. An occasion like this needs to be celebrated, whatcha say, Ingemouse?"

They do it with potato schnapps. Eggnog liqueur is on hand for Ingemouse. Considering their circumstances, the Sawatzkis have set themselves up pretty nicely. A large oil painting, "Goats," two grand-father clocks, three club chairs, a Persian carpet under their feet, the "people's radio" turned down low, and a glassed-in heavy-oak bookcase, containing an encyclopedia in thirty-two volumes: *A* as in "Afterbirth."—Aw, don't cry, maybe you'll get another sometime. *B* as in "Beerhouse brawl."—I've been through maybe fifty of them, ten for the Commies and at least twenty for the Nazis, but do you think I can even keep the places straight, Ohra Riding Academy, Café Derra, Bürgerwiese, Kleinhammerpark. *C* as in "Cuckold."—Hell no, nobody's jealous around here. *D* as in "Danzig."—In the East it was nicer, but in the West it's better. *E* as in "Eau de Cologne."—Believe you me. The Russians used to lap it up like water. *F* in "Father"—They sent mine down with the *Gustlow*. What about yours?—*G* as in "Gunsight."—I took a bead on him, ping ping. Out like a light. *H* as in "Hard feelings."—Aw, stop stirring up the old shit. *I* as in "Inge."—Go on, give us a little dance, something oriental. *J* as in "Jacket"—Take your coat off, man. *K* as in "*Kabale und Liebe*." —You used to be an actor, whyn't you do something for us? *L* as in "Laughing gas."—Cut the giggling, Inge. He's doing Franz Moor. *M* as in "Merriment."—If you ask me, we should crack another bottle. *N* as in "Neutral." Matern's steam has subsided. *O* as in "Oasis."—Here let us settle down. *P* as in "Palestine."—That's where they should of sent them, or Madagascar. *Q* as in "Question mark."—What's on your mind, man? *R* as in "Rabbit."—And he wrote on the paper that I'd treated him decently. His name was Dr. Weiss and he lived at Mattenbuden 25. *S* as in "Square."—Take it from me, there is more fun than four. *T* as in "Tobacco."—For twelve Lucky Streeks we got the whole dinner set with the cups thrown in. *U* as in "U-boat."—A hell of a lot of good they did us. *V* as in "Victory," as in—Well, that's for the birds. *W* as in "Walter."—So go sit on his lap instead of wearing your eyes out. *X* as in "Xanthippe."—That was a dame for you, but I'll settle for Ingemouse. *Y* as in "Yankee."—No Ami ever got his mitts on her, or any Tommy either. *Z* as in "Zero hour."—And now let's all go beddy-by together. Bottoms up! The night is young. Me on the right, you on the left, and Ingemouse snug as a bug in a rug in the middle. But not the dog. He can stay in the kitchen. We'll give him something to eat to make it nice for him too. If you feel like washing, Walter boy, here's the soap."

And after drinking potato schnapps and eggnog liqueur out of coffee cups, after Ingemouse has done a solo dance and Matern some solo acting and Sawatzki has told them both stories from times past and present, after making up a bed for the dog in the kitchen and washing themselves sketchily but with soap, three lie in the broad seaworthy marriage bed, which the Sawatzkis call their marriage fortress, purchase price: seven two-quart bottles of syrup brewed from sugarbeets. NEVER SLEEP THREE IN A BED—OR YOU'LL WAKE UP THREE IN A BED.

Matern prefers to lie on the left. As host Sawatzki contents himself with the right. To Inge belongs the middle. Oh, ancient friendship, grown cold after two and thirty beerhouse brawls, now rewarmed in lurching marriage fortress. Matern, who came with black dog to judge, explores Ingepussy with affectionate finger: there he meets his friend's goodnatured husbandfinger; and both, friendly affectionate goodnatured, as long ago on the Bürgerwiese, at the Ohra Riding Academy or the Kleinhammerpark bar, join forces, find a cozy nook, and take turns. She's having a fine time: so much choice and variety; and emulation spurs the friends on—for potato schnapps makes a body sleepy. A race is run in friendly competition: neck and neck. O night of open doors, when Ingemouse lies on her side, so the friend in front, with the husband politely following up from the rear: so spacious, though slight and Rhenish-maidenly, Ingepussy offers shelter and comfort. If only there weren't this restlessness. O friendship, so complex! Each the other's phenotype. Intentions, leitmotives, murder motives, the difference in education, the yearning for intricate harmony: so many arms and legs! Who's kissing whom around here? Did you—did I? Who in such a case can stand on possession? Who pinches himself to make his counterpart yell? Who has come here to judge with names incised in his heart, spleen, and kidneys? Let us be fair! Each wants to crawl across to the sunny side. Each wants a chance at the buttered side. Three in a bed always need a referee: Ah, life is so rich: nine and sixty positions has heaven designed, has hell granted us: the knot, the loop, the parallelogram, the seesaw, the anvil, the preposterous rondo, the scales, the hop-skip-jump, the hermitage; and names kindled by Ingepussy: Ingeknee—Suckinge—Ingescream—Snapinge Ingefish Yesinge Spreadumslegsinge, Blowinge Biteinge Inge-tired Ingeclosed Ingeintermission—Wakeupinge Openupinge Visitors-inge Bringingcodliveringe Twofriendsinge Yourlegmyarminge Don'tfallasleepinge Turnaroundinge Itwassolovelyinge It'slateinge She'sworkedhardtodayinge: Sugarbeetsinge—Syrupinge—Dogtiredinge —Goodnightinge—Godinhisheaven'swatchinginge!

Now they are lying in the black, formerly square room, breathing unevenly. No one has lost. All have won: Three victors in one bed. Inge holds her pillow in her arms. The men sleep with open mouths. It sounds roughly as if they were sawing tree trunks. They are felling the whole

Jäschkental Forest, round about the Gutenberg monument: beech after beech. Already the Erbsberg is bare. Soon Steffensweg can be seen: villa after villa. And in one of these Steffensweg villas lives Eddi Amsel in oak-paneled rooms, building life-sized scarecrows: one represents a sleeping SA man; the second represents a sleeping SA Sturmführer; the third signifies a girl, splattered from top to toe with sugarbeet syrup which attracts ants. While the plain SA man grinds his teeth in his sleep, the SA Sturmführer snores normally. Only the syrup girl emits no sound, but thrashes her arms and legs, because everywhere ants. While outside the beautiful smooth beeches of Jäschkental Forest continue to be felled one by one—to make matters worse, it would have been a good beechnut year—Eddi Amsel in his villa on Steffensweg builds the fourth life-size scarecrow: a black mobile twelve-legged dog. To enable the dog to bark, Eddi Amsel builds in a barking mechanism. And then he barks and wakes up the snorer, the grinder, the ant-maddened syrupfigure.

It's Pluto in the kitchen. He demands to be heard. The three of them roll out of bed without saying good morning. "Never sleep three in a bed—or you'll wake up three in a bed."

For breakfast there's coffee with milk and bread spread with syrup. Each chews by himself. All syrup is too sweet. Every cloud has shed rain. Every room is too square. Every forehead is against. Every child has two fathers. Every head is somewhere else. Every witch burns better. And that for three weeks, breakfast for breakfast: Each chewing by himself. The triangle play is still on the program. Secret and semi-overt designs to turn the farce into a one-man play: Jochen Sawatzki soliloquizes as he cooks sugarbeets. Into a whispering twosome: Walterkins and Ingemouse sell a dog, grow rich and happy; but Matern doesn't want to sell and turn into a whispering twosome, he'd rather be alone with the dog. Sick of rubbing shoulders.

Meanwhile, outside the square bedroom-livingroom, that is to say, between Fliesteden and Büsdorf, between Ingendorf and Glessen, and similarly between Rommerskirchen, Pulheim, and Quadrath-Ichendorf, a hard postwar winter has set in. Snow is falling for reasons of de-Nazification: everybody is putting objects and facts out into the severe wintry countryside to be snowed under.

Matern and Sawatzki have made a little birdhouse for the innocent birds, who aren't to blame. They are planning to set it up in the garden so they can watch it from the kitchen window. Sawatzki reminisces: "I've never seen so much snow piled up except once. That was in '37-'38, the time we paid Fatso a visit on Steffensweg. It was snowing like today, it just went on snowing and snowing."

Later on, he's down in the laundry room, corking two-quart bottles. Meanwhile the stay-at-home couple have counted all the outdoor sparrows. By that time their love needs an airing. They and the dog make tracks in the famous triangle: Fliesteden-Büsdorf-Stommeln, but see none of those villages, because of the snow drifting and steaming round about. Along the Büdorf-Stommeln highway, only the telegraph poles coming from Bergheim-Erft and running toward Woringen on the Rhine, remind Walterkins and Ingemouse that this winter is numbered, that the snow is earthly, and that under the snow sugarbeets once grew, on whose coveted substance they are still living; all four of them, for, says he, the dog needs proper care; whereas she says we ought to sell it, it's a revolting mutt, she doesn't love anybody but him him him: "If it weren't so cold, I'd do it with you right here in the open, day and night, under the open sky, in the bosom of nature—but the dog has to go, see? He gets on my nerves."

Pluto is still black. The snow becomes him. Ingemouse wants to cry, but it's too cold. Matern is patient and speaks, between onesidedly snow-laden telegraph poles, about parting, which must always be anticipated. He also pours forth his favorite poet. Self-immortelle, says the leavetaker, and: Last rose's dying. However, he doesn't lose himself in the causal-genetic, but transfers in the nick of time to the ontic. Ingemouse loves it when, snapping snowflakes, he roars, grinds, hisses, and squeezes out strange words: "I exist self-grounded! World never is, but worldeth. Freedom is freedom to the I. I essent. The projecting I as projecting midst. I, localized and encompassed. I, worldproject! I, source of grounding! I, possibility—soil—identification! I, GROUND, GROUNDING IN THE GROUNDLESS!"

Ingemouse learns the meaning of these obscure words shortly before Christmas. Though she has got together any number of attractive and useful little presents, he leaves. He shoves off—"Take me with you!"— He wants to celebrate Christmas, I I I, alone with the dog—"Take me with you!"—Consequently, lamentations in the snow shortly before Stommeln: "Me with you!" But thinly as she threads her little voice into his hairy masculine ear: Every train pulls in. Every train pulls out. Ingemouse stays behind.

He who had come to judge, with a black dog and with names incised in his heart, spleen, and kidneys, leaves the sugarbeet environment and takes the train, after crossing off the names of Jochen Sawatzki and wife, to Cologne on the Rhine. In the holy Central Station, in view of the avenging double finger, master and dog stand once again centrally on six feet.

Third to Eighty-fourth Materniad

This was Matern's idea: We, Pluto and I, will celebrate Christmas all alone with sausage and beer in the big silent drafty holy Catholic waiting room in Cologne. We will think, alone, in the midst of humanity, about

Ingemouse and Ingepussy, about ourselves and the Glad Tidings. But things turn out differently, they always do: There in Cologne's tiled men's toilet a message has been scratched on the wall in the sixth enameled bay from the right. Amid the usual meaningless outcries and proverbs Matern reads, after buttoning up, the significant entry: Captain Erich Hufnagel, Altena, Lenneweg 4.

And so they celebrate Christmas Eve not in Cologne's Central Station, but with a family in the Sauerland. A hilly wooded Christmas countryside, where for the rest of the year it mostly rains. A wretched climate that induces specifically regional ailments: isolated forest Westphalians succumb to melancholy and work and drink too-much too-quickly too-cheap.

To avoid too much sitting, master and dog leave the train in Hohenlimburg and start uphill early in the Holy Night. An arduous climb, for here too snow has fallen abundantly and gratis. Across Hohbräcker Rücken and on toward Wibblingswerde, Matern recites himself and Pluto through a forest made for robbers: by turns Franz and Karl Moor invoke fate, Amalie, and the gods: "Another complainant against God!—Continue." Step by step. Snow grinds, stars grind, Franz Moor grinds, virgin branches grind, nature grinds: "Do I hear you hissing, adders of the abyss?"—but from the sparkling valley of the Lenne Altena's unsmelted bells ring in the second postwar Christmas.

Lenneweg leads from homeofmyown to homeofmyown. Every homeofmyown has already lighted its Christmas tree candles. All Christmas angels lisp. All doors can be opened: Captain Hufnagel, wearing bedroom slippers, opens in person.

This time it doesn't smell of sugarbeets but instantly and overpoweringly of gingerbread. The slippers are new. The Hufnagels have already distributed their Christmas gifts. Master and dog are requested to wipe their six feet on the doormat. Without effort it becomes manifest that Frau Dorothea Hufnagel has been made happy with an immersion heater. The thirteen-year-old Hans-Ulrich in turn is immersed in a book on submarine warfare, and Elke, the gorgeous daughter, is trying out, on Christmas wrapping paper which in her mother's opinion really ought to be smoothed out and put away for next Christmas, a genuine Pelikan fountain pen. In capitals she writes: ELKE ELKE ELKE.

Without moving his shoulders, Matern looks round and round. Familiar environment. So here we are. Don't bother. Won't be staying long. No time for visitors, especially the visitor who has come on Christmas Eve to judge: "Well, Captain Hufnagel? Memory need refreshing? You look bewildered. Glad to help you: 22nd AA Regiment, Kaiserhafen battery. Magnificent country: lumber piles, water rats, Air Force auxiliaries, volunteers, crow shooting, pile of bones across the way, stank whichever way the wind was blowing, I initiated operation raspberry drop, I was your first sergeant: Matern, Tech Sergeant Matern reporting.

The fact is that once, in the area of your excellent battery, I shouted something about Reich, nation, Führer, mound of bones. Unfortunately my poem didn't appeal to you. But that didn't prevent you from writing it down with a fountain pen. It was a Pelikan too, just like the young lady's. And then you sent in a report: court-martial, demotion, punitive battalion, mine removal, suicide team. All that because you with your Pelikan fountain pen . . ."

However, it's not the indicted wartime fountain pen, but a blameless postwar fountain pen that Matern grabs out of warm Elkefingers and crushes, smearing his fingers with ink. Phooey!

Captain Hufnagel grasps the situation in a flash. Frau Hufnagel doesn't grasp anything at all, but does the right thing: presuming the intruder in her fragile Christmas room to be a slave laborer from the East, now masterless, she holds out, with bravely trembling hands, the brand-new immersion heater, expecting the brute to blow off steam by demolishing this household utensil. But Matern, misjudged on account of his outspread inky fingers, declines to be fed the first thing that comes to mind. In a pinch he might find the Christmas tree to his taste, or maybe the chairs, or the whole kit and boodle: How much cozy comfort can you stand?

Fortunately Captain Hufnagel, who has a position in the civilian administration of the Canadian occupation authorities and is able to treat himself and his family to a genuine peacetime Christmas—he's even managed to scare up some nut butter!—takes a different and more civilized view: "On the one hand—and on the other hand. After all, there are two sides to every question. But meanwhile, Matern, won't you be seated. Very well, stand if you prefer. Well then, on the one hand, of course, you're perfectly; but on the other hand—whatever injustice you've—it was I who saved you from. Perhaps you are unaware that in your case the death penalty, and if my testimony hadn't led the court-martial to remove your case from the jurisdiction of the special court . . . Very well, you won't believe me, you've been through too much. I don't expect you to. However—and I'm saying this tonight, on Christmas Eve, in full consciousness—if not for me you wouldn't be standing here playing the raving Beckmann. Excellent play, incidentally. Took the whole family to see it in Hagen, pathetic little theater. Goes straight to the heart. Weren't you a professional actor? What a part that would be for you. That Borchert hits the nail on the head. Haven't we all of us been through it, myself too? Didn't we all become strangers to ourselves and our loved ones while we were out there at the front? I came back four months ago. French prison camp. Take it from me! Bad Kreuznach, if that rings a bell. But even that's better than. That's what we had coming to us if we hadn't cleared out of the Vistula sector before. Anyway, there I stood empty-handed with nothingness literally staring me in the face. My business gone, my little house occupied by Canadians, wife and children evacuated to Espei in the mountains, no coal, nothing but trouble with the authorities, in short, a Beckmann situation straight out of *Outside the Door*! And so, my dear Matern—won't you please be seated—I am doubly, triply, aware how you. After all I knew you in the 22nd AA Regiment as a serious young man, who liked to get to the bottom of things. I trust and hope you haven't changed. And so let us be Christians and treat this holy night as it deserves. My dear Herr Matern, from the bottom of my heart and in the name of my cherished family, I wish you a merry and a blessed Christmas."

And in this spirit the evening passes: Matern cleans up his fingers in the kitchen with pumice stone, sits down freshly combed at the family board, allows Hans-Ulrich to pet Pluto, cracks, in the absence of a proper nutcracker, walnuts with his hands for the whole Hufnagel family, receives a present of some socks, washed only once, from Frau Dorothea, promises the gorgeous Elkedaughter a new Pelikan fountain pen, tells stories about his medieval forebears, robbers and heroes of independence, until weariness sets in, sleeps with the dog in the attic, has dinner with the family on the first day of Christmas: sauerbraten with mashed potatoes; on the second day of Christmas barters two packs of Camels on Altena's black market for an almost new Mont-Blanc fountain pen, in the evening tells the assembled family the rest of his stories about the Vistula estuary and the heroes of independence Simon and Gregor Materna, plans, at a late hour when every weary head lies elsewhere, to deposit stocking-footed the Mont-Blanc fountain pen outside Elke's bedroom door; but instead of co-operating, the boards creak, whereupon a soft "Come in" threads its way through the keyhole. Not every room is barred. And so in his stocking feet he enters Elke's bedchamber to bestow. But he's welcome there and able to take vengeance on the father by: Elkeblood flows demonstrably: "You're the first that ever. On Christmas Eve the moment you, and wouldn't even take your hat off. And now do you think I'm a bad girl? It's not the way I usually, and my girl friend always says. Are you as happy as I am now, without any other desire, except only. Do you know what? When I'm through with school, I'm going to travel, travel the whole time! Say, what's that? Is it a scar, and this one here too. Oh, that awful war! It didn't spare anybody. And now what? Are you going to stay here? It can be awfully nice around here when it's not raining: the woods, the animals, the mountains, the Lenne, the High Sondern, and all the dams, and Lüdenschied is an awfully pretty place, and wherever you look, woods and mountains and lakes and rivers and deer and dams and woods and mountains, oh, please stay!"

Nevertheless Matern, stocking-footed with black dog, goes his way.

873

He even carries the almost new Mont-Blanc fountain pen away to Cologne on the Rhine; for he hadn't gone to the Sauerland to make presents, but to judge the father by dishonoring: Only God in His heaven looked on, this time framed and glassed above the bookshelf.

And so justice pursues its course. Cologne's station toilet, that warm Catholic place, speaks of a Sergeant Leblich, resident in Bielefeld, where underwear blooms and a children's choir sings. Accordingly, a long trip on rails with return ticket in pocket, up three flights, second door on the right, straight into the environment without knocking: but Erwin Leblich, through no fault of his own, has had an accident at work and is lying in bed with a high-hoisted plaster leg and an angular plaster arm, but with powers of speech unimpaired. "All right, do anything you please with me, let your dog eat plaster. All right. I chewed you out and made you doubletime with your gas mask on; but two years before that somebody chewed me out and made me doubletime with my gas mask on; and the same thing happened to him: running and singing with his gas mask on. So what the hell do you want?"

Questioned about his wishes, Matern looks around and wants Leblich's wife; but Veronika Leblich had died in '44 in the air-raid shelter. Whereupon Matern asks for Leblich's daughter; but the six-year-old child has recently started school and gone to live with her grandmother in Lemgo. But Matern is determined to build a monument to his vengeance at any price; he kills the Leblichs' canary, who has managed to come through the war in good shape, despite strafing and saturation bombing.

When Erwin Leblich asks him to bring him a glass of water from the kitchen, he leaves the sickroom, picks up a glass in the kitchen with his left hand, fills it under the faucet, and on the way back, quickly in passing, reaches into the bird cage with his right hand: except for the dripping faucet, only God in His heaven looks upon Matern's fingers.

The same onlooker sees Matern in Göttingen. There, without the help of the dog, he wrings the neck of some chickens—five of them—belonging to Paul Wesseling, an unmarried postman: because Wesseling, when still an MP, had picked him up in a brawl in Le Havre. The consequence had been three days in solitary; in addition Matern, who was to be rewarded with a transfer to Officers Training School for his resolute conduct during the French campaign, was prevented by this blot on his record from becoming a lieutenant.

The following day, between Cologne's cathedral and Cologne's Central Station, he sells the neck-wrung chickens unplucked for two hundred and eighty reichsmarks. His treasury is in need of replenishment; for the trip from Cologne to Stade near Hamburg, first class with dog and return, costs a tidy sum.

There behind the Elbe dike lives Wilhelm Dimke with dim wife and deaf father. Dimke, the assistant magistrate who had served as associate judge on the special court in Danzig-Neugarten while a case of undermining military discipline and insulting the Führer was being tried, had threatened Matern with the death penalty until, on the advice of Matern's former battery commander, the case was transferred to the competent court-martial. From Stargard, where he had last participated in the deliberations of a special court, Associate Judge Dimke had succeeded in rescuing a large stamp collection, possibly of considerable value. On the table, between half-emptied coffee cups, lie the albums: the Dimkes are engaged in cataloguing their possessions. Environmental studies? Matern has no time. Since Dimke remembers lots of cases on which he has deliberated, but not Matern's, Matern, by way of refreshing Dimke's memory, tosses album after album into the blazing pot-bellied stove, concluding with the colorful and exotic colonial issues: the stove is delighted, warmth spreads through the overcrowded fugitives' room; in the end, he even tosses in the stock of adhesive corners and the tweezers; but Wilhelm Dimke still can't remember. His dim wife is in tears. Dimke's deaf father utters the word: "Vandalism." On top of the cupboard lie shriveled winter apples. No one offers Matern any. Matern, who had come to judge, feels unappreciated and leaves the Dimke family with a dog who has shown little interest, but without saying good-by.

O eternal tiled men's toilet of Cologne Central Station. It has a memory. It doesn't lose a name: for as previously in the ninth and twelfth bays the name of the MP and the associate judge were inscribed, so now the name and address of Alfred Lüxenich, sometime special judge, are etched legibly and precisely in the enamel of the second bay from the left: Aachen, Karolingerstrasse 112.

There Matern finds himself in musical surroundings. District Magistrate Lüxenich is of the opinion that music, the great consoler, can help us to live through hard and troubled times. He advises Matern, who has come to judge the former special judge, to listen first to the second movement of a Schubert trio: Lüxenich is a violin virtuoso; a Herr Petersen is no mean hand at the piano; Fräulein Oelling plies the cello, and Matern, with restless dog, listens resignedly, though his heart, his spleen, his kidneys are good and sick of it and are beginning in their introverted way to cough. Then Matern's dog and Matern's three sensitive organs are treated to the third movement of the same trio. Whereupon District Magistrate Lüxenich is not quite satisfied with himself or with Fräulein Oelling's cello playing: "My goodness! Let's have the third movement again; and then our Herr Petersen, who, it may interest you to know, teaches mathematics at the local high school, will play you the Kreutzer Sonata; I for my part should like to conclude the evening, before we enjoy a glass of Moselle together, with a Bach violin sonata. Now there's a piece for connoisseurs!"

All music begins. Unmusical from the waist up, Matern falls under the sway of classical rhythm. All music feeds comparisons. He and the cello between Fräulein Oelling's knees. All music opens up abysses. It tugs and pulls and supplies the background for silent films. The Great Masters. Imperishable heritage. Leitmotives and murder motives. God's Pious Minstrel. If in doubt, Beethoven. A prey to harmony. It's lucky nobody's singing; for he sang silvery bubbling: *Donna nobis.* Voice always in the upper story. A *Kyrie* that could pull your teeth. An *Agnus Dei* that melted like butter. Like a cutting torch: a boy soprano. For in every fat man a thin man is hidden, who wants to come out and sing higher than buzz saw and band saw. The Jews do not sing; he sang. Tears roll down over the letter scales, heavy tears. Only the truly unmusical can cry over serious classical German music. Hitler cried when his mother died and in 1918 when Germany collapsed; and Matern, who has come to judge with black dog, sheds tears while Dr. Petersen, the schoolteacher, plays the genius's piano sonata note for note. While District Magistrate Lüxenich bows the Bach violin sonata note for note on an instrument that has come through the war safe and sound, he is unable to dam the rising torrent.

Who is ashamed of manly tears? Who still has hatred in his heart as St. Cecilia glides through the music room? Who is not thankful to Fräulein Oelling when, all-understanding, she seeks Matern out, lets her woman's gaze strike roots, lays her well-manicured but clawlike cellist's fingers on his hand, and with whispered words plows Matern's soul? "Open your heart, dear friend. Please. You must have a great sorrow. May we share it? Ah, what can be going on inside you? When you came in with that dog, I felt as if a world were crashing down on me, a world torn by grief, lashed by storms, filled with despair. But now that I see you are a man, a human being, who has come among us—a stranger, yet somehow close to us—now that we have been privileged to help him with the modest means at our disposal, I find faith again, and courage. Courage to lift you from despair. For you too, my friend, ought to. What was it that moved you so deeply? Memories? Dark days rising up before your mind's eye? Is it some loved one, long dead, who holds your soul in thrall?"

Then Matern speaks bit by bit. He sets building blocks one on another. But the building he has in mind isn't the Danzig-Neugarten Courthouse with the Special Court on the fourth floor; rather, it is the thickset Church of St. Mary, which he erects Gothically, brick by brick. And in that acoustically superb vaulted church—cornerstone laid on March 28, 1343—a fat boy, supported by the main organ and the echo organ, sings a slender Credo. "Yes, I loved him. And they took him away from me. As a boy, I defended him with my fists, for we Materns, all my ancestors, Simon Materna, Gregor Materna, have always protected the

876

weak. But the others were stronger, and I could only look on helplessly as terror broke that voice. Eddi, my Eddi! Since then a lot of things have broken inside me incurably: dissonance, ostracism, shards, fragments of myself, that can never be put together again."

At this point Fräulein Oelling disagrees and Herren Lüxenich and Petersen, sympathizing over sparkling Moselle, side with her: "Dear friend, it's never too late. Time heals wounds. Music heals wounds. Faith heals wounds. Art heals wounds. Especially love heals wounds!" Omnistickum. Gum arabic. The glue with the iron grip. Spittle.

Still incredulous, Matern is willing to make a try. At a late hour, when both gentlemen are beginning to doze over their Moselle, he offers Fräulein Oelling his strong arm and the powerful jaws of his dog Pluto as an escort home through the nocturnal Aachen. Since their path takes them into no park and past no riverside meadows, Matern sits Fräulein Oelling—she's heavier than she sounded—down on a garbage can. She expresses no objection to offal and stench. Yes says she to the fermenting refuse, demanding only that love be stronger than the ugliness of this world: "Throw me, roll shove carry me wherever you please, into the gutter, into the foulest of places, down into cellars unspeakable; as long as it's you who do the throwing, rolling, shoving, and carrying."

Of this there can be no doubt: she rides the garbage can but doesn't make an inch of headway, because Matern, who had come to judge, is leaning against it three-legged; an uncomfortable position which only the desperate can profitably maintain for any length of time.

This time—it isn't raining snowing moonshining—someone besides God in His heaven is looking on: Pluto on four legs. He is guarding the garbage-can horse, the garbage-can equestrienne, the horse trainer, and a cello full of all-healing music.

Matern spends six weeks in Fräulein Oelling's care. He learns that her first name is Christine and that she doesn't like to be called Christel. They live in her attic room, where it smells of environment, rosin, and gum arabic. This is rough on Herren Lüxenich and Petersen. The district magistrate and his friend have to do without their trios. Matern punishes a former special court judge by forcing him to practice duets from February to early April; and when Matern leaves Aachen with dog and three freshly ironed shirts—Cologne has called him and he responds—a district magistrate and a schoolteacher have to find many comforting, pieces-mending, and faith-restoring words, before Fräulein Oelling is in any condition to round out the trio with her well-nigh flawless cello playing.

All music stops sooner or later, but the tiled men's toilet in Cologne Central Station will never for all eternity stop whispering names that are incised in the inner organs of railway traveler Walter Matern: now he has to pay a visit to former Kreisleiter Sellke in Oldenburg. Suddenly he realizes how big Germany still is; for from Oldenburg, where there are still honest-to-goodness court barbers and court pastry cooks, he must hurry via Cologne to Munich. There, according to the station toilet, lives his good old friend Otto Warnke, with whom he has to wind up certain discussions begun long ago at the bar of the Kleinhammerpark. The city on the Isar proves a disappointment—two days are more than enough; but he becomes very familiar with the hills of the upper Weser, for in Witzenhausen, as Matern can't help finding out in Cologne, Bruno Dulleck and Egon Dulleck, the so-called Dulleck brothers, have holed up. For a good two weeks, for all three soon run out of topics of conversation, he plays skat with them, after which he turns to further visitations. Next comes the city of Saarbrücken, where he enters the sphere of Willy Eggers, whom he tells about Jochen Sawatzki, Otto Warnke, Bruno and Egon Dulleck, all old friends: thanks to Matern, they are able to write each other postcards with greetings from buddies.

But even Matern doesn't travel for nothing. As souvenirs or spoils of the chase—for Matern is traveling with dog, to judge—he brings back to Cologne: a tightly knitted winter muffler, donated by former Kreisleiter Sellke's secretary; a Bavarian loden coat, for Otto Warnke's cleaning-woman possessed a supply of warm outer garments; and from Saarbrücken, where Willy Eggers briefs him on the frontier traffic between Gross-Rosseln and Klein-Rosseln, he brings, because the Dulleck brothers in the hills of the upper Weser had nothing to offer him but country air and three-handed skat, a good case of urban and French-occupied gonorrhea.

DON'T TURN AROUND—THE CLAP'S GOING AROUND. With pistol thus loaded, with barbed scourge of love, with serum-maddened hypodermic, Matern with dog visits the cities of Bückeburg and Celle, the lonely Hunsrück, the smiling Bergstrasse, Upper Franconia including the Fichtel Mountains, even Weimar in the Russian occupation zone—where he stops at the Hotel Elephant—and the Bavarian Forest, an underdeveloped region.

Wherever the two of them, master and dog, set their six feet, whether on the rugged Alb, on East Frisian marshland, or in the destitute villages of the Westerwald, everywhere the clap has a different name: here they say dripping Johnny, there they warn against lovesnot; here they count candledrops, there they tell of snipe honey; goldenrod and his lordship's cold, widow's tears and pistachio oil are pithy regional terms, as are cavalryman and runner; Matern calls it "the milk of vengeance."

Equipped with this product, he visits all four occupation zones and the quartered remains of the former national capital. Here Pluto is taken with nervous jitters, which subside only when they are west of the Elbe again, still delivering the milk of vengeance, which is nothing other than sweat gathered from the dripping forehead of blind Justitia.

Don't turn around, the clap's going around. And faster and faster, because Matern's avenging apparatus gives the avenger no rest and, leaping ahead of vengeance just inflicted, is off to a new start: on to Freudenstadt; around the corner, as it were, to Rendsburg; from Passau to Kleve; Matern doesn't shrink back from changing trains four times and even makes his way straddle-legged on foot.

Anyone who takes a look at the statistics on venereal disease in Germany during the first postwar years will be struck by a sudden increase in this benign but troublesome venereal ailment beginning in May '47. The curve attains its apogee at the end of October in the same year, then falls rapidly, and finally flattens off at its springtime level. The determining factors in the minor fluctuations that occur from then on appear to be demographic shifts and changes in the stations of the occupation troops, and no longer Matern who, privately and without a license, journeyed through the land to cross off names with a gonococcus-loaded syringe and to de-Nazify a large circle of acquaintances. Accordingly Matern, when postwar adventures are being retailed among friends, refers to his six-months case of gonorrhea as antifascist gonorrhea; and indeed, Matern was able to subject the female relations of former Party mediumshots to an influence which can be described, by extension, as salutary.

But who will cure him? Who will draw the pain from the root of him who has put the plague into circulation? Physician, heal thyself.

Now after forays through Teutoburg Forest and a brief stay in Detmold, he is in a little village near Camp Munster, where the rolling stone started rolling. Figures back and compares with his memo book: all around him heather in bloom and goldenrod as well, for in among the heath sheep and the heath peasants Matern finds any number of old friends; among others, Hauptbannführer Uli Göpfert who, in co-operation with Jungbannführer Wendt, had year after year directed the popular tent camps in Poggenkrug Forest near Oliva. He is living here in Elmke without Otto Wendt, but attached to a knot of long hair that formerly had been leading German girls, in two rooms which actually have electric light.

Pluto has plenty of freedom. Göpfert on the other hand sits fettered near the stove, putting on peat that he cut in the spring, grumbling at himself and the world, cussing out swine whom he never calls by name, and pondering: What now? Should he emigrate? Should he join the Christian Democrats, the Social Democrats, or the lost squadron of olden days? Later, after ups and downs, he will join the Liberals and carve out a career for himself in North Rhenish Westphalia as a so-called Free Democrat; but for the present—and here in Elmke—he is obliged to doctor himself without results for a case of gonorrhea brought into the house by a sick friend with a healthy dog.

Sometimes, when Frau Vera Göpfert is teaching school and her bun

879

isn't there to tempt dripping Johnny, Göpfert and Matern sit peaceably by the warm stove, making each other soothing peat poultices, doctoring the selfsame misery in the manner of the health peasants, and cussing out swine, some of them nameless and others who have made quite a name for themselves.

"How those bastards screwed us!" laments the former Hauptbann-führer. "And we believed and hoped and trusted implicitly, we went along blindly, and now, what now?"

Matern reels off names from Sawatzki to Göpfert. So far he has been able to cross off some eighty entries in his heart, spleen, and kidneys. No end of common acquaintances. Göpfert remembers, for instance, the band leader of SA Brigade 6, Erwin Bukolt was his name: "That, my boy, wasn't in '36, but exactly on April 20th, '38, because believe it or not, you were there on monitor duty. At ten A.M. in Jäschkental Forest. Führerweather. Stage set up in the woods. Young people's Eastland celebration with a cantata by Baumann: 'Call from the East.' A chorus of a hundred and twenty boys and a hundred and eighty girls. All first-rate voices. Parade on three terraces. Out of the woods in measured tread over beechnuts from the year before. The girls were all doing their year of farm duty. I can still see them: full blouses, red and blue aprons and kerchiefs. That rhythmic marching flow. The merging of the choruses. On the main terrace stands the small boys' chorus, and after I have made a brief introductory speech, they ask the fateful questions. Two large boys' choruses and two large girls' choruses give the answers slowly and word for word. In between—do you remember?—a cuckoo called from the Gutenberg clearing. Regularly in the pauses between fateful questions and fateful answers: Cuckoo! But it doesn't upset those four boys, the solo speakers on the second terrace, raised above the choruses. On the third terrace stands the brass band. You fellows from the Langfuhr-North SA Sturm are standing at the lower left held in reserve behind Bukolt's band, because when it's over you'll have to organize the homeward march. Man, that was good! Jäschkental Forest has amazing echoes: they come back from the Gutenberg clearing, where the cuckoo goes on and on, from the Erbsberg, and from Friedrichshöhe. The cantata is about the destiny of the East. A horseman rides through German lands, proclaiming: 'the Reich is bigger than its borders.' The choruses and the four main questioners ask questions which the horseman answers as though hammering on metal: 'Yours to hold the fort and the gate to the East.' Slowly the questions and answers culminate in a single ardent profession of faith. Finally the cantata rises to a mighty close with a hymn to the Greater Germany. Echo effects. It was a beech forest. First-rate voices. The cuckoo didn't bother anybody. Führerweather. You were there too, my boy. Don't kid yourself. In 1938. On April 20th. Lousy shit. We wanted to set out for the Eastland with Hölderlin and Heidegger in our knapsacks. Now we're sitting here in the West with the clap."

Thereupon Matern grinds his teeth, rubbing East against West. He's fed up on avenging nettle juice, on the milk of vengeance, on love pearls and candledrops. Low and peat-warm is the peasants' room where he stands straddle-legged after four and eighty Materniads. Enough enough! cries his pain-inhabited root.

Enough is never enough! admonish other names incised in heart, spleen, and kidneys.

"Two shots of cement and every hour a fresh peat poultice," laments former Hauptbannführer Göpfert, "and still no improvement. Penicillin's out of sight and even belladonna's very scarce."

Thereupon Matern with pants wide open strides toward a whitewashed wall that bounds the room on the east. This festive hour will have to get along without cuckoo and brass bands. Nevertheless he raises his honey-sweating penis to eastward. "The Reich is bigger than its borders!" Nine million refugees' identity cards pile up westward of Matern: "Yours to hold the fort and the gate to the East!" A horseman rides through German lands, but in the east he looks not for a door but for a simple wall socket. And between the socket and his penis contact is established. Matern, to put it plainly, pisses into the socket and obtains—thanks to an unbroken stream of water—a powerful, electric, skyhigh-sending, and salutary shock; for as soon as he can stand up again, pale and trembling under hair aghast, all the honey drains. The milk of vengeance curdles. The love pearls roll into cracks in the floor. The goldenrod withers. Dripping Johnny breathes again. Runner marks time. The widow's tears dry up. His lordship's cold has been cured by an electric shock. The physician has healed himself. Pluto has looked on. Former Hauptbannführer Göpfert has also looked on. And naturally God in His heaven has looked on too. Only Frau Vera Göpfert has seen nothing; for when she comes home from the village school with ample bun, all she finds of Matern is rumors and undarned woolen socks: Cured but unredeemed, master and dog leave the withered Lüneberg Heath. From this moment on, the clap is on the decline in Germany. Every pestilence purifies. Every plague has its day. Every joy is the last.

The Philosophical Eighty-fifth and the Confessed Eighty-sixth Materniad

What does Brauxel want? He's pestering the life out of Matern. As if it weren't bad enough vomiting up his guts for pages on end for a measly advance, now he has to send in a report every week: "How many pages today? How many tomorrow? Will the episode with Sawatzki and wife have consequences? Was snow falling when he began to shuttle back and forth between Freiburg im Breisgau and the ski slopes of Todtnau? In which bay of the men's toilet in Cologne Central Station did he find his travel order to the Black Forest? Written or scratched?"

O.K., Brauxel, here it is. Matern's excretion amounts to: Seven pages today. Seven pages tomorrow. Seven pages yesterday. Every day seven pages. Every episode has consequences. Snow wasn't falling between Todtnau and Freiburg. It is falling. In the twelfth bay from the left it wasn't written, it is written. Matern writes in the present: All Holzwege, all woodcutter's tracks, lead astray.

Crowds at every bay. The damp cold fills the men's toilet, for the cathedral is unheated. Matern doesn't shove, but when at long last he has occupied his bay, the twelfth from the left, he's in no hurry to leave it: Man is entitled to a resting place on earth. But already they're jostling behind him. All right, so he isn't entitled. "Hurry up, buddy. We gotta go too, buddy. He ain't pissing no more, he's just looking. What's so interesting to look at, buddy? Tell us about it."

Fortunately Pluto assures the reading Matern of privacy and leisure. Seven times he is able to lap up the delicate inscription that seems to have been breathed on the wall with silver point. After so much lust and pestilence he is comforted by spiritual fare. The passed water of all men in this world steams. But Matern stands alone and copies the subtle trace of the silver point in heart, spleen, and kidneys. The steaming Catholic men's toilet is a steaming Catholic kitchen. Behind Matern push cooks bent on cooking: "Hurry up, buddy. You're not the only pebble on the beach, buddy! Love your neighbor, buddy!"

But Matern stands central. The large ruminant ruminates every word in the twelfth bay from the left: "The Alemannic Stockingcap is capping between Todtnau and Freiburg."

Thus edified, Matern turns away. "At last!" He holds Pluto to heel. "Think it over, dog, but not with reason! He was with me when I flew gliders and played chess. With him—soul in soul, arm in arm—I roamed the streets and the waterfront. Eddi passed him on to me as a joke. Words that read like soft butter. He was good for headache and warded off thought when Eddi ratiocinated about sparrows. Think back, dog, but without reason. I read him aloud to Langfuhr SA Sturm 84. They were doubled up at the bar, I had them whinnying out of *Being and Time*. He wears a stockingcap that's longer than any march forward or backward. I took him with me in my musette bag from Warsaw to Dunkirk, from Salonika to Odessa, from the Mius front to Kaiserhafen battery, from police headquarters to Kurland, and from there—those are long distances—to the Ardennes; with him I deserted all the way to southern England, I dragged him to Camp Munster, Eddi bought him secondhand

882

in Tagnetergasse: a copy of the first edition, published in 1927, dedicated to little Husserl, whom he later with his stockingcap . . . Get this straight, dog: he was born in Messkirch. That's near Braunau on the Inn. He and the Other had their umbilical cords cut in the same stockingcap year. He and the Other Guy invented each other. One day He and the Other will stand on the same pedestal. He is calling me, he is always calling me. Think it over, dog, but without reason! Where will the train take us this very day?"

They get out in Freiburg im Breisgau and drop in at the university. The environment is still ringing with the turgid speech he delivered in '33—"Our own selves: that is our goal!"—but there's no stockingcap hanging in any of the lecture halls. "He isn't allowed to any more, because he . . ."

Master and dog ask their way and find a villa with wrought-iron garden gate in front of it. They bellow and bark in the quiet residential quarter: "Open up, Stockingcap! Matern is here, manifesting himself as the call of care. Open up!"

The villa remains wintry still. No window is yellowed by electric light. But a note stuck to the mailbox beside the iron gate yields information: "The cap is capping on the ski slopes."

And so master and dog have to climb on six feet in the shadow of the Feldberg. Above Todtnau the snowstorm buffets them. Philosopher's weather—insight weather! Swirls in swirls, grounding. And no Black Forest fir to give information. If not for the dog without reason, they would be lost in errancy. Nose to the ground, he finds the ski hut, shelter from the wind. And instantly big words and dog's barking are clipped by the storm: "Open up, Stockingcap! Matern is here, manifesting revenge! We who have come here to enact our Being in Materniads and make visible Simon Materna, the hero of independence. He forced the cities of Danzig, Dirschau, and Elbing to their knees, sent Drehergasse and Petersiliengasse up in flames; that's what's going to happen to your cap, you skiing Nothing—open up."

Though the hut remains barred, doweled, chinkless, and inhospitable, there is a note, snow-powdered and barely legible, stuck on barkless Black Forest wood: "Stockingcap has to read Plato in the valley."

Downhill. This is no Erbsberg, it's the Feldberg. Without map through Todtnau and Cry-of-Anguish—such are the names of the places around here—to Care, Overclimb, Nihilation. For that very reason Plato fouled up. Why shouldn't *he*? What Syracuse was to the one philosopher, a rectoral address was to the other. Therefore settle down in the sticks. Why do we stay in the sticks? Because Stockingcap sticks to them. When he's not skiing up top, he's reading Plato down below. That is the subtle provincial distinction. A little game among philosophers: Peekaboo, here

I am. Peekaboo, I fooled you: up down—down up. Applesauce! O Matern, seven times down the Feldberg without ever overtaking himself! Cap, capping, uncapped, cappedness: always ahead of oneself, never being-with, never being-already-in, no present-at-hand togetherness, always away-from-oneself-toward, neither curable nor incurable, hopelessly surrounded by fir environment, exceptionless. Once again Matern plummets from lofty attunedness to rockbottom contingency without at-handness; for in the valley, on the little square note beside the garden door, an already familiar script whispers: "Stockingcap, like all greatness, is out in the storm." And up above, storm-ventilated, he reads: "Stockingcap has to rake the field path below."

What hard work is the execution of vengeance! Rage snaps at snowflakes. Hatred sabers icicles. But the firs nihilate and guard the riddle of the enduring: if he isn't erring below, he's enacting his Being up above; if he isn't coming-to-be up top, he's grounding on a slip of paper beside the iron gate: "The amplitude of all the Black Forest firs that dwell around Stockingcap confers world and powder snow." Skiingweather skiingweather! O Matern, what will you do when after seven times up and down the Feldberg you haven't overtaken yourself, when seven times you have had to read down below: "Stockingcap up top" and seven times up top the words have flickered before your eyes: "Down below Stockingcap manifests Nothing."

Then in the quiet residential quarter master and dog stand panting outside a particular villa: exhausted duped fir-crazed, hatred and rage try to piss into a mailbox. Shouting climbs iron fences, larded with pauses: "Say, where can I catch you, Cap? What book is bookmarked with your cap?—In what cap have you hidden the lime-sprinkled forgetful of Being?—How long was the stockingcap you strangled little Husserl with? How many of your teeth do I have to pull to turn thrownness into essent stockingcapped Being?"

That's a lot of questions, but don't let it worry you. Matern answers them all by himself. He's in the habit. The questions of one who always stands central—phenotype, selfpoint-possessed—are never at a loss for answers. Matern doesn't formulate, he acts with two paws. First the iron gate outside the garden of a certain villa is shaken and cursed. But no more Alemannic stockingcap language; Matern's vituperation is down-to-earth and autonomously idiomatic: "C'mon out, ya louse! I'll show ya, ya clunk! Ya slimy gazoop! Ya big beezack! Ya—hatrack. I'm gonna kick ya in the slats and cut yer bleeding heart out. I'm gonna unravel you like an old sock. I'm gonna make hamburger out of ya and feed ya to the dog in little pieces. We're fed up on thrownness and existence-into-nuttin. Matern's gonna getcha. Matern's gonna getcha. C'mon out, philosopher! Matern's a philosopher too: Shoilem boil 'em."

These words and Matern's claws do the trick: not that the philosopher follows the friendly invitation and steps out of the villa with Alemannic stolidness, in stockingcap and buckled shoes; instead, Matern lifts the wrought-iron garden gate off its hinges. He brandishes it, and Pluto falls speechless, for several times Matern succeeds in shaking it at the sky. And when the sky, black and smelling of snow, won't relieve him of the gate, he hurls it into the garden: an amazing distance.

The wrecker brushes off his hands: "That's that!" The hero looks around for witnesses: "Did you see? That's the way Matern does it. Phenomenal!" The avenger savors the aftertaste of accomplished revenge: "He's got his. Now we're quits." But aside from the dog, no one can testify that it happened thus and not otherwise; unless God, despite the snow in the air, was eavesdropping from upstairs: nihilating essentiating catching-cold.

And the police have no objections when Matern with dog wants to leave the city of Freiburg im Breisgau. He has to travel third class because the ups and downs have exhausted his treasury: he has had to spend one night in Todtnau, two in Cry-of-Anguish, and once each in Nihilation and Overclimb; that's the price of associating with philosophers—and were it nor for charitable women and tender-hearted young girls, master and dog would hunger thirst perish.

But they journey after him, eager to cool a brow overheated by philosophical disputation, eager to win a man who has narrowly escaped being shanghaied by Transcendence back to earth and its double beds: cello-playing Fräulein Oelling, Captain Hufnagel's gorgeous daughter, the brown-haired secretary from Oldenburg, Warnke's curly black-haired cleaningwoman, as well as Gerda, who gave him the dripping Johnny between Völklingen and Saarbrücken, all whom he enriched with and without goldenrod now want him and only him: Ebeling's daughter-in-law from Celle; Grete Diering from Bückeburg; Budczinski's sister leaves lonely Hunsrück; Irma Jaeger the flowering Bergstrasse; Klingenberg's Upper Franconian daughters Christa and Gisela, from the Soviet zone comes Hildchen Wollschläger without Franz Wollschläger; Johanna Tietz is sick of living with her Tietz in the Bavarian Forest; in search of him go: a Princess von Lippe with her girl friend, daughter of an East Frisian hotelkeeper, women from Berlin and maidens from the Rhine. German women grope for Matern with the help of newspaper ads and detective agencies. They bait their hooks with rewards. An iron will lurks in wait with a dissyllabic goal. They chase find corner him, try to strangle him with Vera Göpfert's copious hair. They snap at him with Irmapussies, Gretetraps, cleaningwomen's chasms, garbage-can covers, Elkecracks, housewives' shopping bags, Berlin rolls, princessquiffs, fishcakes, and Silesian meat pudding. In compensation they bring with them: tobacco, socks, silver spoons, wedding rings, Wollschläger's pocket watch, Bud-czinski's gold cuff links, Otto Warnke's shaving soap, their brother-in-law's microscope, their husband's savings, the special judge's violin, the captain's Canadian currency, and hearts souls love.

Matern isn't always able to evade these riches. They wait, touching to look upon, between Cologne's Central Station and Cologne's immovable cathedral. Treasures demand to be admired in air-raid-shelter hotels and one-night hotels, on Rhine meadows and pine needles. They've also brought sausage skins for the dog, lest counter-part payments be disturbed by demanding dog muzzle: "Don't do the same thing twice, or you'll be doing the same thing twice."

And whenever he sets out to visit the quiet men's toilet alone with dog, to meditate and practice detachment, demanding girlfingers house-wifefingers princessfingers touch him in the bustling station hall: "Come. I know where. I know a janitor who rents. A girl friend of mine has gone away for a few days. I know a gravel pit they're not using any more. I've taken a place for us in. Only a little while. Time enough to unburden our hearts. Wollschläger sent me. I had no choice. Afterwards I'll go away, I promise. Come!"

As a result of all this solicitude, Matern goes to the dogs and Pluto gets fat. O recoiling vengeance! Rage bites cotton. Hate excretes love. The boomerang strikes when he thinks he has struck five and eighty times: DON'T DO THE SAME THING TWICE—IT'S NEVER THE SAME. For with the best of fare he loses weight: Göpfert's shirts have begun to fit him; cool and soothing as Otto Warnke's bird tonic is to his scalp, Matern's hair is falling. Bankrupt! And who should turn up as the receiver but his old friend dripping Johnny; for what he thought he had got rid of in the Bavarian Forest or in the District of Arich, reinfects him in Upper Franconia, the Soviet zone, the backwoods. Leitmotives and murder motives: six times, on dripping Johnny's account, he has to piss into wall sockets. It knocks him cold. It flattens him. Horse medicine cures him. Gonococci infect him. Electricity sends Matern for the count. Double beds transform a traveling avenger into a leaky Don Juan. Already he presents the sat-urated look. Already he talks glibly and seductively about love and death. He can turn on the tenderness without even looking. He's begun to fondle his clap like the favorite child of genius. Minor madness has dropped its visiting card. Soon he'll be wanting to emasculate himself after shaving, to throw his lopped-off phenotype to Leporello, to the dog.

Who will save Matern? For what is all presumptuous philosophy compared to a single bounceback man without reason! What is the seven-fold stockingcap-maddened ascent of the Feldberg compared to six contact-crazed light sockets! And to make matters worse, the blubbering: "Make me a baby. Spill me one. Knock me up. Be careful, don't waste any.

Pump me full. Curette me. Clean me out. Ovaries!" Who saves Matern, combs away the dead hair, and buttons up his pants till the next time? Who is kind to him, selfless? Who puts himself between Matern and the hairy soggy Vienna rolls?

At most the dog. Pluto manages to avert the worst: He chases Otto Warnke's cleaningwoman and Göpfert's Vera, the one in April, the other in May, across the Rhine meadows out of a gravel pit where they've been trying to suck Matern's spinal fluid and bite off his testicles. And Pluto manages to sniff about and make it known when one of them turns up with dripping Johnny's love pearls in her purse. He barks, growls, gets between, and with butting nose indicates the treacherous focus of pestilence. By unmasking Hildchen Wollschläger and the princess's girl friend, the servant spares his master two additional electric shocks; but even he cannot save Matern.

Cologne's double prongs see him thus: broken, carvern-eyed, bald at the temples, with Pluto, faithfulasadog, frolicking around him. And this picture of misery, so close to the footlights, starts out again, makes his way through the bustle of Central Station, resolved to descend to quiet regions, tiled, Catholic, and whispering; for Matern still senses the presence of names, painfully incised in internal organs and demanding to be crossed off—be it with trembling hand.

And step by step with knotted stick he almost makes it. Thus she sees him: man and stick with dog. The picture moves her. Without hesitation she, the sugarbeet woman with whom all his vengeance began, comes toward him: compassionate charitable motherly. Inge Sawatzki pushes a baby carriage, in which dwells a Novemberly sugarbeet bunny, who came into the world syrupsweet a year ago next July and since then has been called Walli, for Walburga; for such is Inge Sawatzki's certainty that little Walli's father answers to a name beginning with *W*, such as Walter—although Willibald and Wunibald, the saintly brothers of the great witch-banishing saint, makers to this day of Walburga Oil, a product still in demand, are closer to her from a Catholic point of view.

Matern stares darkly into the occupied baby carriage. Inge Sawatzki curtails the usual period of silent admiration. "Pretty baby, isn't she? You're not looking at all well. She'll be walking any day now. Don't worry. I don't want anything of you. But Jochen would be pleased. You look all worn out. Really, we're both so fond of you. Besides, it's sweet the way he takes care of the baby. An easy confinement. We were lucky. Was supposed to be in Cancer, but she turned out to be a Leo girl, with Libra in the ascendant. They have an easy time of it later on: usually pretty, domestic, adaptable, versatile, affectionate, and with all that, strong-willed. We're living over in Mülheim now. We can take the ferry if you like, sailing, sailing over the bounding main. You really need rest and care. Jochen's working in Leverkusen. I advised against it, because wherever he goes he gets mixed up in politics, and he swears by Reimann. My goodness, you look tired. We could take the train too, but I like the ferry. Oh, well, Jochen must know what he's doing. He says a man has to show his colors. After all you were in there too. Is that where you met or was it in the SA sturm? You're not saying a word. I really don't want anything of you. If you feel like it, we'll baby you for a couple of weeks. You need a rest. A homey place. We've got two and a half rooms. You'll have the attic room all to yourself. I'll leave you alone, honest. I love you. But in a perfectly peaceful way. Walli just smiled at you. Did you see? She's doing it again. Does the dog like babies? They say shepherds love children. I love you and the dog. And I wanted to sell him, remember, I was dumb in those days. You've got to do something to save your hair."

They go on board: mother and child—master and dog. The well-fed sun cooks Mülheim's ruins and Mülheim's meagerly fed consumers in the same pot. Never has Germany been so beautiful. Never has Germany been so healthy. Never have there been more expressive faces in Germany than in the days of the thousand and thirty-two calories. But Inge Sawatzki declares while the Mülheim ferry is docking: "We'll be getting new money pretty soon. Goldmouth even knows when. What, you don't know him? Everybody that knows which way is up around here knows him. Take my word for it, he's got a finger in everything. The whole black market, from Trankgasse to the Amis in Bremerhaven, takes its cue from Goldmouth. But he says it's on the way out. He says we should reconvert. The new money won't be worthless paper; it'll be rare and precious, you'll have to work for it. He came to the christening. Hardly anybody knows his real name. Jochen says he's not a pure Aryan. I couldn't care less. Anyway he didn't come into the church, but gave us two sets of baby clothes and piles of gin. He himself doesn't touch it, he only smokes. My goodness, he doesn't smoke them, he eats them. Right now he's out of town. They say he has his headquarters near Düren. Other people say it's somewhere near Hanover. But with Goldmouth you never know. This is where we live. You get used to the view."

Staying with good old friends, Matern witnesses X-Day, the currency reform. This is the time to take stock of the situation. Sawatzki walks straight out of the C.P. For his money it stinks anyway. Everybody gets his quota. They don't drink it up. Certainly not: "This here is our investment capital. We'll live on our reserves. The syrup'll do us for twelve months at least. By the time we've worn out all the shirts and underwear, Walli will be going to school. 'Cause we haven't been sitting on our stocks, we saw what was coming, we unloaded. That was Goldmouth's advice. A tip like that is worth its weight in gold. He let Inge in on a way of getting CARE packages, just to be obliging, because he likes us. He's always asking about you, because we told him about you. Where you been keeping yourself all this time?"

With leaden pauses in between, Matern, who is slowly regaining his strength, lists German countrysides: East Frisia, the rugged Alb, Upper Franconia, charming Bergstrasse, Sauerland, the Hunsrück, the Eifel, the Saar, Lüneburg Heath, Thuringia or the green heart of Germany. He describes the Black Forest where it is highest and blackest. And his vivid geography lesson is enriched with the names of cities: "On my way from Celle to Bückeburg. Aachen, the ancient city founded by the Romans, where the Holy Roman emperors were crowned. Passau, where the Inn and the Ilz flow into the Danube. Of course I went to see the Goethe house in Weimar. Munich was a disappointment but Stade, the country behind the Elbe dikes, is a highly developed fruit-growing region."

Sawatzki's question "AND NOW WHAT?" ought to be embroidered, given a border, and hung up over the couch. Matern wants to sleep, eat, read the paper, sleep, look out the window, commune with himself, and look at Matern in the shaving mirror: Gone the bleary eyes. The hollows under the cheekbones excellently filled in. But there's no holding the hair, it's emigrating. His forehead grows, lengthening his character-actor's phiz, molded by thirty-one dog years. "And what now?" Eat humble pie? Go dogless into business now that things are starting up? Go back to acting, leave the dog in the checkroom? Grind teeth no longer on the open hunting ground, but only on the stage? Franz Moor? Danton? Faust in Oberhausen? Sergeant Beckmann in Trier? Hamlet in the experimental theater? No. Never! Not yet. His accounts aren't settled yet. Matern's X-Day hasn't dawned yet. Matern wants to pay his debts in the old currency, that's why he raises hell in Sawatzki's two-and-a-half-room apartment. With heavy hand he crushes a celluloid rattle and expresses doubts that Walli stems from the stem of Walter. Matern also wipes all the sure-fire tips grown in Goldmouth's garden off the breakfast table with the sugar bowl. He takes his cue from himself, from his heart, spleen, and kidneys. He and Sawatzki aren't calling each other by their first names any more, but denounce each other, according to mood and time of day, as "Trotzkyite, Nazi, you traitor, you crumby little fellow traveler!" But only when Matern boxes Inge's ears in the middle of the living room—let the reason lie buried in Matern's attic room—does Jochen Sawatzki throw his guest with dog out of the two-and-a-half-room apartment. Instantly Inge wants to be thrown out too with child. But Sawatzki brings a flat hand down on the oilclothed tabletop: "The kid stays here with me. She ain't going to be mixed up in this. Go where you please, go to the dogs. But not with the kid, I'll take care of her."

So without child but with dog and little of the new currency. Matern still has Wollschläger's pocket watch, Budczinski's gold cuff links, and two Canadian dollars. Between Cologne's cathedral and Cologne's Central Station they make merry on the proceeds of the watch. There's just enough left over for a week in a hotel in Benrath, offering a view of the castle with round pond and square garden.

"And what now?" she says.

He massages his scalp at the wardrobe mirror.

She points her thumb in the direction of the curtains: "It seems to me if you want work the Henkel works are over there, and over there on the right Demag is starting up again. We could look for a place to live in Wersten or right in Düsseldorf."

But at the mirror and later, out in the wet cold, Matern doesn't feel like working; he wants to wander. After all, he comes of a miller's family, and millers, says the poet, delight in wandering. Besides, the dog needs exercise. And before he raises a finger for those capitalist swine, he'll . . . "Henkel, Demag, Mannesmann! Don't make me laugh!"

Two with dog along the Trippelsberg, across the Rhine meadows to Himmelgeist. There they find an inn that has a room available and doesn't bother about marriage certificates and manandwife. A restless night, for from Mülheim Inge Sawatzki has brought not hiking shoes but an ornamental coverlet with the embroidered question, "And what now?" Won't let him sleep. Always in the same groove. Pillowwhispering: "Do something. Anything. Goldmouth says: invest, invest, and invest some more, it'll pay off in three years at the latest. Sawatzki, for instance, is going to quit his job in Leverkusen and go into business for himself in some small town. Goldmouth suggested men's coats and suits. Wouldn't you like to try something, anything? You're educated, after all, as you're always saying. A consultant's bureau, for instance, or a horoscope magazine, something serious-looking. Goldmouth says there's a future in that kind of thing. People have simply stopped believing in the old baloney. They want something different, really reliable information about what's written in the stars . . . You're Capricorn, for instance, and I'm Cancer. You can do whatever you please with me."

Obligingly Matern does for her next day. They have barely enough money left for the Rhine ferry from Himmelgeist to Üdesheim. The rain is free of charge. O wet cold bondage! In sopping shoes they hike in single file, the dog in the lead, to Grimlinghausen. There hunger is waiting but nothing to eat. They can't even change sides and ferry to Volmerswerth on the right bank. He does for her on the left bank of the Rhine, under the eyes of St. Quirinus, who was burned in Moscow under the name of Kuhlmann and nevertheless was powerless to protect the city of Neuss from bombs.

Where do you sleep without a penny to your name, but with a pious sinful heart? You get yourself locked up in a church, more precisely in an only true, unheated, namely, Catholic church. Familiar environment. Restless night. For a long time they lie, each in his own pew, until only she is lying and he with dog and dragging leg is roaming about the nave: everywhere scaffoldings and pails of whitewash. A cockeyed kind of place. A little of everything. Typical Transition style. Romanesquely begun when it was already too late, later pasted over with baroque, the dome for example. Damp plaster steams. With floating plaster dust is mingled the smell of elaborate pontifical offices from the dog years of the thirties. Still hovering indecisively and refusing to settle. Matern has been here before, in the days when he carried on conversations with the Virgin Mary. Today Ingewife does the talking: "And what now?" is her ever-ready question. "It's cold," she says. And: "Can't you sit down?" And: "Should we get a rug?" And: "If it weren't a church, I'd say come on, would you like to too?" And then in the somnolent three-quarters darkness: "Say, look. There's a confessional. You think it's closed?"

It isn't closed but ready at all times. In a confessional he does for her. Something new for a change. In there it's a safe bet that nobody ever. So the dog has to go in where ordinarily the priest has his ear. For Pluto joins in the game. Matern with her enters the adjacent cubicle. And as she kneels, he bucks her uncomfortably from behind, while she has to blabber through the grating behind which Pluto is playing the father confessor. And he presses her fuckedout doll's face against the sinfully ornate wooden grille: baroque, masterly, Rhenish woodcarving outlives the centuries, doesn't break, but squashes the doll face's nose. Every sin counts. Works of penance are imposed. A prayer for intercession is offered up. Not, St. Quirinus, help! But: "Sawatzki, come and help me. Oh oh oh!"

Well, when it's all over, the confessional is undamaged. But she lies for a long while on cold flags and lets her nose bleed in the dusk. He goes roaming again, dog at heel, wordless. And back again at the indestructible confessional after two lonely echoing rounds, he snaps open his good old lighter with a view to lighting a comforting pipe, the lighter accomplishes more than he expected: first, it helps the pipe, second it proves that Inge's nose blood is red, and third it lights up a little card pinned to the confessional, and on the card something is written: a name in black and white: Joseph Knopf. Without further address, for at the moment the name is residing right here and has no need, like other names, to indicate street and number in Cologne's holy men's toilet; daily, for half an hour, from nine forty-five to ten fifteen this Knopf inhabits the indestructible confessional, making his certified ear available to each and all. O leit- and murder motives! O revenge, syrup-sweet! O justice plying the rails in all directions! O names crossed off and still to be crossed off: Joseph Knopf—or the Eighty-sixth Materniad!

Matern crosses him off on the dot of ten, solo and in person. Meanwhile he has tied Pluto—parting is sweet sorrow—to a bicycle stand still intact amid the ruins of Neuss. Still weeping, Inge slips away without a word shortly before early Mass and with squashed nose tramps back in the direction of Cologne. Some truck will pick her up—but he stays; on Batteriestrasse, almost exactly halfway between Münsterplatz and the industrial port, he doesn't seek but finds ten pfennings in one piece. Wealth! St. Quirinus has put it there especially for him; with it you can buy a butt; or the *Rheinische Post,* fresh of press; it's the price of a box of matches or a stick of chewing gum; you could put it in a slot and, if you stood on the scales, out into the world would come a little card: your weight! But Matern smokes a pipe and when necessary snaps open his lighter. Matern reads newspapers in showcases. Matern has plenty to chew on. Matern doesn't need to be weighed. For ten found pfennigs Matern buys a beautiful long smooth chaste knitting needle—for what?

Don't turn around, knitting needle's going round.

This knitting needle is for the priest's ear and is intended to enter the ear of Joseph Knopf. With malice aforethought Matern, at nine forty-five, walks into the asymmetrical church of St. Quirinus to judge with a long knitting needle alienated from its function.

Ahead of him two old women confess briefly and meagerly. Now in the somnolent church night he kneels down in the very place where Inge, having been put into position, was going to confess to the dog. Anyone looking for evidence could probably find Ingeblood on the wooden grille and bear witness to a case of martyrdom. He takes aim and whispers. Joseph Knopf's ear is large and fleshy and doesn't quiver. There's room for the whole confession, sins checked off on fingers, and bang in the midst of it an old story that happened in the dog years of the late thirties, involving a former SA man, then a Neo-Catholic, and a professional Old-Catholic who, on the strength of the so-called resolutions of Maria Laach, advised the Neo-Catholic to get back into a regular SA sturm in spite of everything and with the help of the Blessed Virgin to reinforce the Catholic wing of the inherently godless SA. A complicated story that turns cart-wheels on thin ice. But the priest's ear doesn't quiver. Matern whispers names, dates, and quotations. He breathes: his name was Soandso, the other one's name was Soandso. No fly molests the priest's ear. Matern is still as busy as a bee: And the one whose name was Soandso said to the other one after devotions, that was in May of the year . . . The priest's ear is still hewn of marble. And from time to time substantial words issue from the other side: "My son, do you repent with all your heart? You know that Jesus Christ, who died for us on the cross, knows of every sin, even the most venial, and is watching us, whatever we do. Be contrite. Keep nothing back, my son."

Such precisely were Matern's intentions. Once again he reels off the whole story. From an ingenious music box emerge the carved figures: Kaas, the prelate, Pacelli, the nunzio, the former SA man, the repentant Neo-Catholic, the crafty Old-Catholic, and the representative of the Catholic wing of the SA. All, lastly the merciful Virgin Mary, do their little dance and exit; but Matern still hasn't unreeled the whole of his whispered spool: "And it was you, you and no one else, who said that, get back into the SA. A lot of rubbish about the concordat and anecdotes from Maria Laach. They even secretly blessed a banner and whined out prayers for the Führer. You Dominican! You black shitbag. And to me, Matern, you said: My son, resume the brown garment of honor. Jesus Christ, who died on the cross and watches us in all our works, has sent us the Führer to stamp out the seed of the godless with your help and mine. That's right. Stamp out!" But the priest's ear, mentioned several times by name, is still the ingenious product of a Gothic stonecutter. When the knitting needle, retail price ten pfennings, is put in motion, when the instrument of vengeance rests on the ornate grille of the confessional and is aimed knittingneedle-sharp at the priest's ear, nothing quivers in alarm for the eardrum; only the old man's voice, thinking the penitent has finished, drones out wearily and with routine mildness the everlasting words: *"Ego te absolvo a peccatis tuis in nomine Patris et Filii et Spiritus Sancti. Amen."* The penance imposed consists of nine Paternosters and thirty-two Ave Marias.

Then Matern, who has come to judge with a ten-pfenning knitting needle, lets his instrument recoil: this priest is lending his ear only symbolically. He is invulnerable. You can tell him your whole story twice a day, all he hears is the wind in the trees or not even. Joseph Knopf. Deaf-as-a-button Knopf. Deaf-as-a-button priest absolves me in the name of this one and that one, and in the name of the dove. Behind the grille stonedeaf Joseph makes monkeysigns for me to leave. Clear out, Matern! Other people have things to confide in my deaf ear. Get thee behind me. All your sins are remitted. O.K., get a move on, cleaner can't be did. Mingle with the penitents: Maria Laach is near Neviges. Find yourself some nice little Canossa. Take the knitting needle back to the store. Maybe they'll take it back and return your ten pfennigs. For that you can get matches or chewing gum. That's the price of the *Rheinische Post*. For ten pfennings you can see how much you weigh after alleviating confession. Or buy your dog some sausage skins. Pluto has to be kept in form.

The Eighty-seventh Worm-eaten Materniad

Everybody has at least two fathers. They aren't necessarily acquainted with each other. Some fathers don't even know. Sometimes fathers get lost. Speaking of uncertain fathers, Matern possesses one who is particularly deserving of a monument, but doesn't know where he; or suspect what he; in whom he hopes. But he doesn't look for him.

Instead, and even in his dreams, whose work consists in felling a murmuring beech forest trunk by trunk, he gropes for Goldmouth, concerning whom mysterious things are being said on all sides. Yet, painstakingly as he searches every bay in the men's toilet of Cologne Central Station for hints about Goldmouth, no pointing arrow starts him on a dogtrot; but he reads—and this lesson puts him on the track of his father Anton Matern—a maxim freshly engraved in defective enamel: "Don't listen to the worm. There's a worm in the worm."

Without striking his search for Goldmouth and his dream job of felling beeches from his program, Matern sets out in a fatherly direction.

The miller with the flat ear. Standing beside the historical postmill in Nickelswalde, situated to the east of the Vistula estuary and surrounded by Siberian frost-resistant Urtoba wheat, he shouldered a hundredweight sack until the mill, with turning sails, burned down from the jack via the flour loft to the sack loft. Thereupon the miller evaded the clutches of war, which was approaching from Tiegenhof by way of Scharpau. Laden with a twenty-pound sack of wheat flour—milled from the Epp variety —he, along with his wife and sister, found room on a ferry barge which had operated for years between the Vistula villages of Nickelswalde and Schiewenhorst. The convoy included the ferryboat *Rothebude,* the railroad ferry *Einlage,* the tugboat *Future,* and a bevy of fishing launches. Northeast of Rügen the ferry barge *Schiewenhorst* had to be unloaded because of engine trouble and taken in tow by the Rothebude-Käsemark ferry. The miller, the twenty-pound sack of white flour, and the miller's family were allowed to board a torpedo boat. This vessel, overloaded with sea-sickness and children's screams, struck a mine west of Bornholm, and sank instantly, taking with it screams and collywobbles, not to mention the miller's wife and sister; he, however, managed to find standing room for himself and his sack of flour on the excursion steamer *Swan,* which had put out from Danzig-Neufahrwasser, destination Lübeck. Without further change of ship, miller Anton Matern, with flat ear and still-dry twenty-pound sack, reached the port of Travemünde, *terra firma,* the continent.

In the course of the following months—history goes right on: peace breaks out!—the miller is obliged to defend his shouldered refugee property often and craftily, for around him there are many who would like to eat cake but have no flour. He himself is often tempted to diminish the twenty pounds by a handful and cook himself a creamy wheat soup; but whenever his stomach prods him, his left hand gives his right-hand fingers, toying with the sack strings, a sharp smack. And it is thus that creeping misery, now engaged in environmental studies, finds him: lopsided, silent, and abstemious in waiting rooms, lodged in refugee barracks, squeezed into Nissen huts. The one ear protrudes enormously, while the flat ear is pressed by the undiminished twenty-pound sack. There the sack lies safe and—to an outside observer—as still as a mouse.

When, between the Hanover railroad station and the perforated but still long-tailed equestrian monument, miller Matern is caught in a police raid, taken to headquarters, and—because of the flour-filled sack—threatened with prosecution for black marketing, King Ernest Augustus, the Hanoverian, does not dismount from his charger to save him; a German official employed by the Allied military government takes his part, defends him and the twenty pounds with a fluent speech, and little by little in the course of his half-hour plea allows two and thirty gold teeth to glitter: Goldmouth vouches for miller Matern and takes the lopsided man and his sack of flour under his protection, nay more: in consideration of the miller's professional aptitudes, he buys him a slightly damaged postmill on the plains between Düren and Krefeld, and has the roof fixed, though he has no intention of having the tattered sails mended and turned into the wind.

For at Goldmouth's behest, the miller is to live a contemplative life on two stories: upstairs, under the main shaft and the dust-matted gears, in the so-called sack loft, he sleeps. Though cluttered with the big bed-stone, the hopper, and the counterwheel which projects between the rafters, this loft, where formerly grist was piled, provides ample space for a bed, which, what with the proximity of the border, is an almost Dutch bed. The stone serves as a table. The damsel over the hopper contains shirts, underwear, and other belongings. Bats evacuate the counterwheel and lantern, arbor and windlay drive, to make room for Goldmouth's little presents: the radio, the lamp—he had electricity put in—the illustrated magazines, and the few utensils required by an old man who knows how to conjure up the smell of fried potatoes from a camp stove. The steps leading down are equipped with a new banister. For the spacious flour loft, marked in the center by the mill post, yields the miller's parlor and soon his consultation room. Under the iron plank and the overhung rail, under the inextricable clutter of machinery which formerly served to adjust the burrs, Goldmouth, who translates the miller's every whim into suggestions, places an imposing newly upholstered wing chair. Because one of its wings get in the way of the shouldered twenty-pound bag, it ultimately has to be exchanged for a wingless easy chair. The mill creaks even on windless days. When the wind blows outside, dust still clouds up from the meal bin through the chute into the tattered bolter that hangs crooked in its frame. Easterly winds make the pot-bellied stove smoke. But usually the clouds, coming from the canal, scud low over the Rhenish Lowlands. Once, right after he has moved in, the miller oils the cotter that holds the oak lever in place and retightens the keys in the tenons to do justice to the occasion: a miller has moved into a mill. After that he lives in felt slippers and dark denims, sleeps until nine, eats breakfast alone or with Goldmouth when he happens to be visting, and leafs through wartime or post-wartime numbers of *Life*. He signs his contract right away, immediately after the momentous tightening of the keys in the tenons. Goldmouth doesn't demand much: with the exception of Thursday, the miller with his flat ear has to give consultations from ten to twelve every morning. In the afternoon, except for Thursday, which sees him hard at work from three to five, he is free. Then he sits with protruding ear by the radio, or goes to the movies in Viersen, or plays skat with two officers of the Refugee Party, to which he also gives his vote, because he holds that the cemeteries to the left and right of the Vistula estuary, especially the one in Steegen, are richer in ivy than any of the cemeteries between Krefeld and Erkelenz.

But who comes to consult the lopsided miller with the flat ear in the morning and Thursday afternoon office hours? At first the nearby peasants come to see him and pay in produce such as butter and asparagus; later on, small manufacturers from Düren and Gladbach come, bringing finished products with barter value; early in '46, he is discovered by the press.

What attracts these visitors, at first few and far between, then swelling to a stream that can hardly be regulated? For the benefit of anyone who is still in the dark: miller Anton Matern listens to the future with his flat ear. The lopsided miller knows important dates in advance. His recumbent ear, which seems to be deaf to everyday sounds, hears pointers with the help of which the future can be manipulated. No table tipping, laying out of cards, stirring of coffee grounds. Nor does he, from the sack loft, point a telescope at the stars. Nor unravel meaningful lines in hands. No poking around in hedgehog hearts and fox spleens or in the kidneys of a red-spotted calf. For the benefit of anyone who is still in the dark: it's the twenty-pound sack that knows so much. More specifically, mealworms, which in the flour milled from wheat of the Epp variety have survived the trip on the ferry barge, the swift sinking of the torpedo boat, in short, the turmoil of the war and the postwar period, at first with God's, later with Goldmouth's help, whisper predictions; the miller's flat ear—ten thousand and more hundredweight sacks of Urtoba wheat, of Epp wheat, of wheat flour milled from Schliephacke No. 5, have made it so flat, deaf and clairaudient—hears what the future has to offer and the miller's voice passes the mealworms' pointers on to those in quest of advice. For a reasonable fee, miller Anton Matern, abetted by East German worms, helps in no small degree to guide the destinies of West Germany; for when, after peasants and small manufacturers, Hamburg's future press moguls sit down facing his easy chair and write their questions on a small

896

slate, he begins to wield influence: showing the way, molding opinion, influencing world politics, speaking the universal language of pictures, of reversed mirror images.

After handing out advice for many years in his native Nickelswalde, after guiding wheat production between Neuteich and Bohnsack with mealworm pointers and making it profitable, after predicting, with flat ear against mealworm-inhabited sack, plagues of mice, hailstorms, the devaluation of the Free City gulden, the collapse of the grain exchange, the date of the Reichspresident's death, and the ill-omened visit of the fleet to Danzig harbor, he now succeeds, with Goldmouth's support, in leaping from provincial obscurity to world fame throughout West Germany: three gentlemen drive up in a jeep belonging to the occupation authorities. Young and hence blameless, they take the stairs to the flour loft in two and a half steps, bringing with them noise, talent, and ignorance, pound on the mill post, potter with the windlay drive, and are determined to climb up to the sack loft and dirty their fingers in the mill machinery. But the "Private" sign on the banister of the sack-loft stairs enables them to show good breeding; they quiet down like schoolboys as they face miller Matern, who points to the slate and slate pencil, in order that wishes may be formulated and opened to fulfillment.

What the mealworms have to say to the three gentlemen may sound prosaic: the handsomest of the three is advised to insist, in his negotiations with the British authorities, on newspaper license No. 67, in order that, under the name of *Hör zu* (Tune In), it may run up a circulation and—just in passing—provide miller Matern with a free subscription; for the miller is wild about illustrated magazines and gone on the radio. License No. 6, titled *Die Zeit* (Time) at the worms' suggestion, is the advice given to the most agile of the three gentlemen. But to the smallest and most distinguished of the young gentlemen, who is bashfully chewing his fingernails and doesn't even dare to step forward, the mealworms whisper by way of the miller that he should have a try with license No. 123 and drop his unsuccessful experiment, known as *Die Woche* (The Week).

The smooth Springer taps the unworldly Rudi on the shoulder: "Ask Grampa what name to give your baby."

Instantly the blind mealworms send their message through the lopsided miller: *Der Spiegel* (The Mirror), which finds the pimple on the smoothest forehead, has its place in every modern household, but the mirror has to be concave; what's easily read can easily be forgotten and yet quoted; the truth isn't always essential, but the house number has to be right; in short, a good card index, ten thousand or more well-filled file drawers, take the place of thought; "people," so say the mealworms, "don't want to be made to think, they want to be accurately informed."

By right the consultation is over, but Springer sulks and sticks at

897

the mealworm prognoses, because in his heart he doesn't want to start a radio magazine for the great masses, but is more inclined toward a radically pacifist weekly. "I want to stir people up, stir them up." At this the mealworms via miller Matern comfort him and forecast, for June 1952, the birth of an institution conducive to the general welfare: "Every morning three million reading illiterates will breakfast over an illustrated daily."

Quickly, before the miller can spring open his pocket watch a second time, the gentleman who only a moment before was as cheerful as a senator and whose manners Axel Springer and little Augstein are trying to copy, owns to perplexity bordering on despair, and pleads for help. At night, so he confesses on the slate, he has Social-democratic dreams, by day he dines with Christian heavy industry, but his heart is with avant-garde literature, in short, he can't make up his mind. Whereupon the mealworm informs him that this mixture—left by night, right by day, and avant-garde at heart—is characteristic and timely: wholesome, honorable, liberal, prudently courageous, pedagogic, and lucrative.

Question after question comes bubbling out. "Advertising rates? Who's going to be the vetoing minority in the house of Ullstein?"—but the mealworms, represented by miller Matern, decline to reply. Before they politely take their leave, all three gentlemen are permitted to carve their names in the mill post—which the miller exhibits to this day: the handsome Springer, the weltschmerz-tormented Rudi, and Herr Bucerius, whose family tree has its roots in the medieval enlightenment.

After a quiet week—a carpet is laid under miller Matern's feet; the lever, which formerly started or stopped the shaking movement of the hopper, serves as a temporary support for the glassed photograph of the aged President Hindenburg—; after a week of trifling domestic changes and of organizational initiative—Goldmouth has the path leading to the idle windmill widened and a sign put up on the highway between Viersen and Dülken—after a week, then, of quiet preparation, a number of big businessmen or their agents with decartelization troubles drive in over the freshly graveled driveway; and in a twinkling the mealworms, rested and communicative, cure the headaches of the tangled Flick group. On a hard stool sits Otto-Ernst Flick in person, representing his father and needful of advice. Not that the miller knows who is sitting there, crossing leg and leg, each time in a different way; with benign indifference he leafs through his worn illustrated magazines, while the slate fills up with urgent questions. The Allied decartelization law demands that Flick Senior should drop either iron or coal. The mealworm proclaims: "Unload your coal mines." So it happens that the holding company whose merger with Mannesmann has been dissolved takes over the majority of Essen Anthracite AG and later, as the mealworm advises, rejoins Mannesmann.

Nine years later, or five years after his anticipated and mealworm-dated release from a term at hard labor, Flick Senior manages to get back into Harpener Coal, this time as a majority stockholder.

In the same year, incidentally, Dr. Ernst Schneider, who calls at the windmill shortly after Flick Junior, joins the Trinkhaus Bank; and with him the whole Michel group comes aboard: soft coal, soft coal!—and the carbon dioxide industry, whose chairman he is, thanks to the mealworm; for with a tongue as broad as the Vistula the miller hands out positions which shortly before were filled by the mealworms. Thus, for example, a retired cavalry captain, soon to be the key figure of the burgeoning German economy, is promised twenty-two board memberships including six chairmanships, because if Herr von Bülow-Schwante is to remain in the saddle, he will have to lead the entire Stumm Corporation over high and crowded hurdles that the Allies have put in his path.

Coming and going. Gentlemen exchange greetings on the stairs leading to the flour loft and to miller Matern. Resounding names begin to fill up the mill post, for nearly everyone wants to immortalize himself, Hoesch, or the Bochum Association in this famous place. Krupp sends Beitz, and Beitz learns how, with the fickle times working in Krupp's favor, decartelization is to be sidestepped. At an early date the mealworms also pave the way for the crucial interview between Messrs. Beitz and R. Murphy, U.S. Undersecretary of State. The mealworms speak, as Beitz and Murphy will do later on, of long-term credits to underdeveloped countries; but it is not the government that should open its moneybags, let Krupp pour out riches privately and with careful aim: iron foundries in India are projected by mealworms who, if they had been permitted to live in Nickelswalde to the right of the Vistula estuary, would have devised projects for the People's Republic of Poland; but the Poles refused to be helped by the East German mealworm.

Accordingly Siemens & Halske; Klöckner and Humboldt; Petroleum and Potash, wherever rocksalt flourishes. This honor is accorded miller Matern on a rainy Wednesday morning. Dr. Quandt comes in person and finds out how Wintershall AG is going to obtain a majority interest in the Burbach Potash Works. A deal is being arranged, in which Gold-mouth, who has an interest in a shut-down potash mine between Sarstedt and Hildesheim, blandly participates.

But when on the ensuing free Thursday morning—it is still raining—which miller Matern spends driving nails into props and hanging the great President's picture now here, now there, Goldmouth, who to tell the truth had dropped in only to leave a pile of illustrated magazines for the miller, is gone again. Next day, however—the persistent downpour hasn't been able to discourage them—the IG-successors call in a body. Although decartelized, Baden Aniline, Bayer, and Hoechst come together and let the mealworm vote their policy for the ensuing years: "Don't pay dividends, increase your capital." But this mealworm slogan isn't restricted to the chemical industry; whoever calls, Feldmühle AG or Esso, the Haniels or North German Lloyd, all the big banks and insurance companies—the chorus of mealworms repeats emphatically: "No dividends. Increase your capital!" And concurrently the usual chickenfeed: How can the old-established Hertie Corporation, associated with the still-older-established firm of Tietz, transform itself into the Karg Family Foundation? Should Brenninkmeyer introduce customers' credit? What will the men's suit of the future look like—this refers to the doublebreasted number responding to revived consumer demand—which Peek & Cloppenburg will soon be putting on the market?

The mealworm answers all questions after advance payment at fixed rates. He refurbishes the Mercedes star, forecasts the rise and fall of Borgward, disposes of Marshall Plan funds, is present when the Ruhr Authority meets, dismisses the Constitution before it is approved by the Parliamentary Council, fixes the date of the currency reform, counts votes before the first Bundestag elections are held, builds the imminent Korean crisis into the shipbuilding program of the Howaldt Work of Kiel and Hamburg, arranges the Petersberg Agreement, picks a certain Dr. Nordhoff as the future pacemaker in the setting of prices, and, when it suits him and his ilk, exerts terrifying pressure on the stock market.

But by and large the trend is favorable, though the Thyssen ladies do not shun the path to the converted windmill. Is the mill a mill of youth? Are wrinkles smoothed, calves upholstered? Is the mealworm a matchmaker? An elderly Stahlhelm veteran who comes to attention at the sight of President von Hindenburg—who has meanwhile moved from the sack loft to the flour loft—and gives him an ingratiating salute, this gentleman, still hale and hearty, is advised to establish cordial family relations with the key figure Bülow-Schwante, as an encouragement to the construction industry: "*Tu, felix* Portland Cement, *nube!*"—for family enterprises are favored by the mealworm.

Of course anyone who is on his way to the mealworm has to carry humility and childlike faith in his baggage. This is something the indestructible Hjalmar Schacht, the imp with the stand-up collar, can't get through his head, although he often shares the opinion of the mealworms. Both the worms and Schacht warn against overexpansion of the export trade, overaccumulation of dollars, overincrease of currency volume, and rising prices. But only the mealworms reveal the solution to future problems. Consulted separately by Schäffer, the future Minister of Finance, and Vocke, the future President of the Reichsbank—future pillars of the state, they will go down in history!—the mealworms advise them to loosen up: let the minister stop hoarding enormous reserves; let the bank president lend wings to his piles of gold. Once again, as in the mealworm-arranged Krupp-Beitz-Murphy conversations, the watchword is: "Dollar credits to underdeveloped countries."

A first boom. Wool markets strengthened by orders from Latin America. Bremen jute picks up. Warning against weakening Canadian dollar. A breathing spell, wisely ordered by the mealworms with a view to consolidation, prevents the market from running wild. The trend remains favorable. Goldmouth has the driveways surfaced with asphalt. The miller's crazy notion of getting married—a widow from Viersen seems to have been under consideration—comes to nothing, because it would have meant giving up a pension. Still alone but not lonely, the miller leafs through the illustrated magazines: *Quick* and *Kristall, Stern* and *Revue,* all supplied in gratitude and gratis: the *Frankfurter* and the *Münchner Illustrierte, Tune In,* now in its third year. And all who have been loyal to him from the very first, and those who have only belatedly found their way to the right faith, call regularly or bashfully for the first time, carve or reinforce their names in and on the imposing mill post, attentively bring little gifts, and cough when the stove smokes in the east wind: the gentlemen who have risen from the ranks: Münnemann and Schlieker, Neckermann and Grundig; the old foxes Reemtsma and Brinkmann; potential leaders such as Abs, Forberg, and Pferdmenges; the erstwhile future, then present Erhard comes regularly and is allowed to swallow a surplus mealworm: which lives to this day, miraculously miracle-working, in the exemplary paunch—expansion expansion! The freemarket economy is run by the mealworm. From the very first the worm's been inside the father of the economic miracle, miraculously miracle-working. "Don't listen to the worm, there's a worm in the worm!"

So cackles the opposition, which doesn't come calling, doesn't pay, doesn't cough in the east wind, and doesn't consult miller Matern. In line with a decision of the Socialist Party in Bundestag, it refuses to have any truck with medieval hocus-pocus. Certain trade union leaders secretly take the path to the mill notwithstanding. But although their mealworm-formulated directives have had a good deal to do with the present powerful position of the German Trade Union League, they are sooner or later exposed. For all Social Democrats brand the miller and his mealworm-counseled clientele as heretics. The lawyer Arndt harvests nothing but laughter when in the course of a question period in the Bundestag he tries to prove that association with, and taking counsel of, mealworms constitute an offense against Article 2 of the Constitution, because the rising mealworm cult represents a threat to the free development of the individual personality. Cynical worm jokes are hatched in the Bonn Socialist Party headquarters and when publicized as election slogans deprive the party of critically needed votes. Herr Schumacher and—as of August

1952—Herr Ollenhauer have not made a single election speech without heaping scorn and contempt on the consultations in the converted windmill. Party officals speak of the "capitalistic worm cure" and are sitting —small wonder!—on the opposition benches.

But the clergy comes. Not, to be sure, in vestments, not with Cardinals Frings and Faulhaber at the head of field processions; those who come to the windmill that gives directives are for the most part anonymous Dominicans, seldom motorized, usually on foot, occasionally on bicycles.

More tolerated than favored, they sit outside the mill with open breviary and wait humbly until a Dr. Oetker of Bielefeld had received his personal order of the day: "Bake fleet of ships with Oetker's baking powder. Stir Oetker's pudding mix, bring it to boil, let it cool, spill it carefully into all seven seas—and behold: Dr. Oetker's tankers are afloat." Later, after Oetker has immortalized himself on the mill post and left, Father Rochus is obliged to breathe on his spectacles in wild surprise, for as soon as he has quoted the catechism with shrill slate pencil: "Lord, send us Thy spirit and everything will be created anew . . ." the mealworms speak up as vicars: working through the Christian government party, the true Church must strive little by little to restore the ways of life of the Gothic and late Romanesque periods; Charlemagne's empire must be renewed, if necessary with Latin help; better lay off the torture and witch burning as a starter, because heretics like Gerstenmaier and Dibelius will eat out of the blessed Virgin's hand unasked: "Mary, virgin with the child, give us all thy blessing mild."

Overwhelmed with gifts, pious fathers return home on foot and on bicycles. Once the wind even blows six Franciscan nuns from the Convent of Our Lady in Aachen directly and decoratively to the mill. Though Sister Alfons-Maria, the mistress of novices, spends half an hour asking the miller for information, what the mealworms have to say to the nuns is a secret that no one must ever spill; only this much is certain: Catholic mealworms—miller Anton Müller is a Catholic—drafted pastoral letters for every conceivable situation; they whisper the name of a rising minister; *nomen est omen*—he will be Würmeling and, with the help of Catholic families, will create a state within the state; mealworms submit bills; mealworms demand measures in favor of denominational schools; for religious reasons Catholic mealworms oppose reunification; mealworms govern West Germany—for the East German government sends its planning expert too late.

Before the miller with his twenty-pound sack of wheat flour, which, it should be mentioned in passing, has had to be replenished with a few pounds of the Epp variety, obtained with difficulty from the now Polish Vistula delta—before miller Matern with his well-fed mealworms has a chance to participate in the planning of the Stalinstadt steel combine in the Oder marshes, in the building of the Black Pump power combine, in the uranium– and wolfram-mining operations of the notorious Wismuth AG, before he can help to organize socialist brigades, plain-clothes men are sent in to guard the area surrounding the speaking mealworms; for if Herren Leuschner and Mewis—and Ulbricht went so far as to send Nuschke—had been able in those days to slip two, three, or several times through the cordon set up by a general and his men, the German Democratic Republic would have a different look today, would have potatoes galore and paperclips to burn—while as things stand, it hasn't even enough barbed wire.

Equally slow in getting started, certain critics of the economic miracle, whose oratorical potshots at the symbolic Erhard are consistently wide of the mark, have also missed the bus to Düren. Herr Kuby and all the cabaret wits would have poisoned arrows, arguments, and biting satirical songs fit to shake an empire if they had only dropped in on miller Matern. For it is a mistake to suppose that partisan worms were always behind the one and only Konrad. Not at all! Early visitors to the mealworms, the gentlemen of the press and those with decartelization troubles, will testify that the dominant sentiment in the twenty-pound bag was strongly anti-Adenauer from the very start; it was not the mealworms who put forward the incompetent mayor as the first chancellor; why, he only visited the windmill four times, and then with nothing but questions of foreign policy on his mind. No, their vote was not for him, actually they cried out unanimously: "The man for us is Hans Globke, the modest resistance fighter who worked in the background."

It was not to be. But if mealworm-trained supporters, mindful of the mealworm's words, had not made a shadow chancellor of Dr. Hans Globke, so obtaining a hearing for the mealworm party in the Bundestag and for certain undersecretaries in the most important ministries, a great deal, everything perhaps, would have gone wrong.

And miller Matern? What honors was he accorded? Was a free subscription to this and that illustrated weekly, were the New Year's presents—calendars of corporations from Auto Union to Hanover-Hannibal Mines—his only profit? Did appointments, decorations, or blocks of shares come his way? Did the miller grow rich?

His son, who drops in with black shepherd in March 1949, doesn't get to see a red cent at first. Outside, the west wind is tugging at the idle sails. Neckarsulm Motors and United Boiler Works have just roared down the driveway. Visiting hours are over. The twenty-pound sack is resting in the safe. This article of furniture—donated by Krauss-Maffei, which has belonged to the Flick syndicate since Buderus acquired a majority interest—was installed by Goldmouth, who thought it unsafe just to leave the sack lying in the hopper. Other noteworthy acquisitions are nonutilitarian: in a spacious bird cage—the gift of Wintershall AG—bill and coo two parakeets—a gift of the Gerling Corporation. But father and son sit facing one another in silence, unless importance is attached to such exclamations as "Hmm" or "Well, well." The son politely opens the conversation: "Well, Pa, what's the mealworm been saying?"

The father waves the question aside. "What's he been saying? Just spinning yarns."

Then the son, as is fitting and proper, has to inquire after his mother and his aunt: "And Ma? And Auntie Lorrchen? Ain't they with you?"

The miller points his thumb up toward the flour loft: "They was all drownded on the way."

It occurs to the son to ask about old acquaintances: "And Kriwe? Lührmann? Karweise? What became of the Kabruns? Old Folchert and Lau's Hedwig from the Schiewenhorst side?"

Again the miller's thumb points at the ceiling timbers: "Drownded. They was all drownded on the way."

Even if mother, aunt, and all the neighbors have been swallowed up by the Baltic, there's no harm in asking about his father's mill. And again the miller has to announce a loss: "She burned down in broad daylight."

The son has to shout when he wants information of his father. At first cautiously, then directly, he comes out with his business. But the miller understands neither with his flat nor with his protruding ear. Accordingly, the son writes wishes on the slate. He asks for money. "Dough, dough!"—for he's as flat as the Vistula delta: "Hard luck, broke!" The millerfather nods understandingly and advises his son to go to work either in the coalfields or for him. "Make yourself useful around here. You can always find something to do. And we'll need to be doing some building pretty soon."

But before Matern, the son with black dog, makes up his mind to give his father a hand, he wants to know, just in passing, whether the miller knows a man, a heavy smoker, called Goldmouth, and whether it mightn't be possible to locate this Goldmouth with the help of the mealworms: "Whyn't you ask them?"

At this the miller turns to stone. The mealworms are silent in their safe: Krauss-Maffei. Only the parakeets—Gerling Corp.—go on chatting in their cage—Wintershall AG. Nevertheless, Matern Jr. stays on and hammers together a kennel for Pluto under the jack of the idle windmill. If there were a Vistula here and Vistula dikes from horizon to horizon, the village over yonder would be Schiewenhorst and here, where every morning except Thursday the coke barons and trustees drive up, would be Nickelswalde. Consequently the place will soon be called New Nickelswalde.

Matern Jr. makes himself at home. Father and son sign a contract in due form. From this day on, it will be the duty of the dog Pluto to guard the mill with contents and announce business visitors by barking. One of the son's duties will be to regulate the outward flow of the worm-guided economic process. As a superintendent receiving more than regulation wages, he arranges for a parking lot at the foot of the mill hummock, but refuses to have an Esso service station installed. While the gasoline pumps are relegated to the intersection of the driveway and the Düren highway, he allows the Federal Post Office department and Blatzheim Enterprises to build right here on the parking lot, flanking it on three sides, but only with one-story buildings, for he holds that the windmill—which has meanwhile become a national symbol, popularized in the form of lapel pins—must tower appropriately over the flourishing bustle down below. The telephone exchange and offices communicate and formulate worm instructions and worm logic. The main building harbors a relatively low-priced restaurant and provides twelve single and six double rooms for wormthinkers in need of sleep. The basement is the natural place for the bar, where in the late afternoon worm technocrats—nowadays they are called potential leaders—fasten themselves to bar stools. Over cold drinks, nibbling salted almonds, they develop the wormpromoted trend toward monopoly, discuss the worm-eaten competitive system, sell, pay dividends, support for the time being, mark time, fluctuate, depress, quote, record, rise sharply, and smile at a poster which Matern, the super, has hung up, white on red background, in the cellar bar:

THE WHEELS WON'T GO—WHEN THE MEALWORM SAYS NO.

For Matern Jr. joins in the conversation. Many of his sentences begin with the unvarying formula: "Marxism-Leninism has proved . . ." or: "On the wings of socialism the . . ."

The worm technocrats—for they never became leaders—wince on their bar stools when super Matern points with Lenin's famous gesture at the red-and-white poster and speaks of the mealworm collectivity, of the wormstructure of victorious socialism, and of history as a dialectical worm-process. While upstairs in the converted windmill the lopsided miller, with the twenty-pound sack to his ear, helps the German postwar economy to gain world prestige—it is to his collaboration and tolerance that we owe the pioneering work by the economist W. Eucken: "The Tasks of Public-spirited Mealworms in a Constitutional State"—down below his son, the super, is lambasting monopolistic mealworm exploiters. Quotations crawl with worms. There are class-conscious and classless worms. Some practice collective self-eduction, others keep a brigade diary. Pioneering worms build the house of socialism. Under modified social conditions the capitalistic worm is converted to. They purge themselves, cast out, triumph. In the course of interminable conversations in the bar—upstairs Matern Sr. has long been asleep, dreaming of ivy-clogged cemeteries to the left and right of the Vistula estuary—Matern Jr., over gin and whisky, disseminates Marx-fed worm myths, which are made to sustain the theory of necessary development: "For there are worm planners and worm brigades, which on the wings of socialism have embarked on the path from the I to the We."

Matern, the super, isn't a bad talker. In the smoke-filled bar, his head on the way to baldness directly under the ceiling light, he clutches his whisky glass, brandishes his tinkling drink, points with oft-painted Lenin finger at the future, and performs didactic plays for a theater-loving public. For those who huddle on stools, the worm technocrats Abs and Pferdmenges, the Thyssen ladies and Axel Springer, Blessing, the business leader, and Stein, the trustee, the associates with unlimited liability, and the chairmen of seven boards of directors—all play along, because each one of them—"That's basic"—has a different opinion, which demands to be aired. Moreover, every one of them once upon a time in his youth—"cross my heart and hope to die!"—was somewhere on the left. After all, we're among friends: "Krauss-Maffei and Röchling-Buderus!" You old ruffians: "Lübbert and Bülow-Schwante, Alfred's witnesses and Hugo's heirs!" All in all, decides Matern the super, these people are open-minded—after midnight. They aren't rolling in clover. Every one of them, even the widow Siemens, has his cross to bear. Every one of them, even the Gutehoffnung Foundry, had to start at the bottom of the ladder. Not a one of them, not even Phoenix-Rheinrohr, was built in a day. "But let's get one thing straight, you reinsurance and hail-insurance companies, you coal-tar wizards and steel manufacturers, you widely ramified and well-connected moguls, you Krupps, Flicks, Stumms, and Stinneses: Socialism will triumph! Bottoms up! Let the mealworm provide! Prost, Vicco! Outlook favorable. You're a good guy even if you were an SS leader. That's water under the bridge. Weren't we all? Each in his own way. Call me Walter!"

But only at midnight are all men brothers beneath the converted windmill; in the daytime, while the parking lot is overcrowded, the telephone exchange overloaded, and consultations at their peak, ideological guerrilla warfare prevails. No mysterious wirepullers finance the super; out of his own pocket he has leaflets printed, which serve a purpose thanks to their novel style.

On the left side quotations from Marx alternate with data from the family history of the Materns; on the right, quickly reacting pencils note the predicted annual capacity of the projected Rourkela Plant in Orissa, India.

On the left, class-struggle fighters Luxemburg and Liebknecht shower exclamation marks; on the right, a colon followed by the announcement that in a few years Opel will pay a superdividend of 66%.

On the left, the bandits Simon and Gregor Materna found—in the sixteenth century, mind you!—brigades consecrated to collective endeavor; on the right, the Mining Union is formulated.

On the left, anyone who is so inclined can read how the super's great-grandfather, who believed in Napoleon but sold scaling ladders to the Russians, acquired, thanks precisely to this ambivalence, money that had previously belonged to militarists and capitalists; on the right are listed the investments and write-offs of the Baden Aniline and Soda works for the still remote year 1955.

In short: while on the left side of his all-red leaflets super Matern makes himself known as someone who wishes to hasten the end of the decadent Western social order, the unprinted part of the same leaflets is filled with: graphs of costs, stock-market quotations, antitrust regulations—what a visual anticipation of present-day coexistence!

What gratuitous pleasure it would be, while this chronicle pauses for breath on its way to conclusion, to toss in an intermezzo or two; for who, in this day and age, hasn't got anecdotes up his sleeve? What happened to the movie industry, for instance, which sent its agents to New Nickelswalde too late? Who hasn't a lament to offer? About agriculture, for instance. Ah, what sins of omission, despite the fact that the mealworms, inspired by their environment, never cease to herald the impending agricultural crises. And who couldn't compile an almanac of social gossip? The Hamburg alliances, for instance: Rosenthal-China-Rowohlt-Publishers. Springer's grounds for divorce; tedious social criticism. We prefer to skip all this and to state succinctly: from March 1949 to summer 1953 Walter Matern, who had come to judge with black dog, serves as superintendent and insubordinate son to his father Anton Matern, who came to give advice with a whispering twenty-pound sack. This period has become generally known as the springtime of the economic miracle, whose germ-cell was New Nickelswalde. A good deal of what went on—rumors of wirepulling and international involvements—must and will remain in the dark. Matern, the super, for instance, never lays eyes on Goldmouth, though everybody knows who he and nobody knows where he—not even the mealworms. But they do leak the news of Stalin's death before it is officially announced. A few weeks later Pluto, the watchdog, who is allowed to run loose at night, announces: Fire under the mill! The fire is quickly checked. Only four small struts in the jack frame have to be changed. The damage to the saddle and to the corner beams of the flour loft is insignificant. The Düsseldorf police president drives up. Definitely a case of arson. But all attempts to establish a connection between this incident and the undoubtedly successful assault on the mill which occurred shortly thereafter amount to pure imagination;

for to this day proofs are still lacking. Similarly, all those who suspect a link on the one hand between Stalin's death and the unsuccessful attempt at arson, or on the other hand between the successful assault and the workers' revolts in the Soviet-occupied zone, are indulging in unadulterated speculation. Nevertheless, Communists are still generally regarded as incendiaries and kidnapers.

And so miller Matern's son must submit to questioning over a period of weeks. But he knows the tune from the old days. He has always enjoyed games of question-and-answer. Every answer, he supposes, will bring him applause.

"Trained for what trade?"

"Acting."

"Present occupation?"

"Up to the time of the assault on my father's property, I was serving as superintendent."

"Where were you on the night in question?"

"In the basement bar."

"Who can testify to that effect?"

"Herr Vicco von Bülow-Schwante, chairman of the board of the Stumm Corporation; Herr Dr. Lübbert, partner in the firm of Dyckerhoff & Widmann; and Herr Gustav Stein, chief executive of the German Manufacturers' Association."

"What were you discussing with the witnesses?"

"First the tradition of the Uhlan regiment in which Herr von Bülow-Schwante served; then the part played by the firms of Lenz-Bau AG and Wayss & Freytag in the reconstruction of West Germany; finally, Herr von Stein explained to me the many characteristics that cultural leaders and business leaders have in common."

But obstinately as the guilty parties avoid the public eye, the fact remains: in spite of the Gehlen Organization and the triple cordon, persons unknown succeed, in the night of June 15, 1953, in abducting miller Anton Matern from his residence in a shut-down mill at New Nickelswalde. In addition to the miller, the following objects are found missing from the windmill on the morning of June 16: in the sack loft: a framed and glassed picture of former President von Hindenburg and a Grundig radio. In the flour loft: issues, covering a period of five years, of the radio magazine *Tune In,* two parakeets with cage, and a twenty-pound bag of wheat flour, which had been locked in a safe that the criminals—it is assumed that there was more than one—succeeded in opening without resorting to force.

But since the abducted twenty-pound sack is a sack in which are living mealworms of East German origin and since by their central guidance these mealworms have ushered in a flowering of the West German

908

economy, which, even now that its end is in sight, is still stimulating the market with its late bloom, the loss of the sack and of the miller who goes with it provokes extreme alarm. In the basement bar and on the parking lot, gentlemen who are not permitted to leave New Nickelswalde for the duration of the preliminary investigations, cast about for comparable disasters in the history of Germany and the Western world. The words Cannae, Waterloo, and Stalingrad are heard. With dark foreboding observers recall the dismissal of Bismarck as recorded in an English caricature of the time: "The pilot leaves the ship." Those who feel that this caption doesn't do justice to the situation intercalate an ominous adjective borrowed from a well-known adage about rats: "The pilot leaves the sinking ship!"

But the public is not permitted to share the anguish of the business leadership. Although no one orders a news blackout on the occurrence in New Nickelswalde, not a single newspaper, not even the *Bild-Zeitung*, runs alarmist headlines: Mealworms leave Federal Republic." "Soviet Blow Against West German Economic Center!" "Germany's Star on the Wane."

Not a word in *Die Welt*. Whatever calls itself a newspaper between Hamburg and Munich devotes its columns to the spreading revolt of the Berlin construction workers; but Ulbricht, supported by the sound of tanks, stays—while miller Matern vanishes without musical accompaniment.

Whereupon all those who have been living by his dialect-tinged mealworm utterances, the Krupps, Flicks, Stumms, and Stinneses; all those who continue to sail a mealworm-plotted course, the Deutsche Länder-Bank and Bahlsen's Cookies; whereupon all who stood in line outside a converted windmill, holding companies and chambers of commerce, savings banks and govenment associations; whereupon all those who have listened respectfully to the worm, dismiss the consultations in miller Matern's mill from their minds. Henceforth, at inaugurations cornerstonelayings shiplaunchings, the word is no longer: "This prosperity was inspired by mealworm whispers. What we posses we owe to the miller and his public-spirited twenty-pound sack. Long live miller Matern!" Instead, former worm technocrats, now vainglorious public speakers, who in calm or windy weather sound off about German Ability. About the industrious German People. About the Phoenix risen from the ashes. About Germany's miraculous rebirth. Or at best about the Grace of God, without which all effort is vain.

One man alone has been thrown off by the miller's departure. Matern, the former superintendent, grinds his way unemployed with black dog through the countryside. Every wave of prosperity ebbs in time. Every miracle can be explained. Every crisis has had its warning: "Don't listen to the worm—there's a worm in the worm."

909

The Eighty-eighth Sterile Materniad

Trend dull: meanwhile bald up top, sullenly grimly on the move, but strict with the dog. Pluto obeys and isn't as young as he used to be. How strenuous to grow older; for every railroad station has bad things to say of the next. On every meadow others are already grazing. In every church the same God: *Ecce Homo!* Behold me: baldheaded inside and out. An empty closet full of uniforms of every color. I was red, put on brown, wore black, dyed myself red. Spit on me: clothing for every kind of weather, adjustable suspenders, bounceback man walks on leaden soles, bald on top, hollow within, outside bedecked with remnants: red brown black—spit on me! But Brauxel doesn't spit, he sends advances, gives advice, speaks at random of export-import and the impending end of the world, while I grind: a bald-head demands justice. This is a question of teeth, thirty-two of them. So far no dentist has made a nickel on mine. Every tooth counts.

Trend dull. Even the Cologne Central Station isn't what it used to be. Christ, who can multiply loaves and turn off drafts, has had it glassed in. Christ, who has forgiven us all, has also had the bays of the men's toilet freshly enameled. No more names charged with guilt, no more treacherous addresses. Everybody wants to be left alone and eat new potatoes every day; only Matern still feels drafts and painful names incised in heart, spleen, and kidneys, demanding to be crossed off, every last one of them. A beer in the waiting room. Once with dog around the cathedral, so he can piss on all thirty-two of its corners. Then another beer across the street. Conversations with bums who take Matern for a bum. Then a last try at the men's toilet. The smell is still the same, although the beer used to be poorer and thinner. How absurd to buy condoms. With arched back and stallion-long: drainage and absolution in thirty-two bays, all nameless. Matern buys rubbers, ten packs. He decides to visit friends in Mülheim. "The Sawatzkis? They moved out long ago. Started a little business in Bedburg. Men's suits and coats. Then they bought into the garment industry. I hear they've just opened a big fancy place in Düsseldorf. Two stories."

So far he had always managed to steer clear of this pesthole. Gone through on the train, never got out. Cologne? Sure. And Neuss with knitting needle. A week in Benrath. The coalfields, from Dortmund to Duisburg. Two days in Kaiserswerth one time. Aachen, a pleasant memory. A few nights in Büderich, but never at Hans' Flophouse. Christmas in the Sauerland, but not at the Acrobats' Hostel. Never in Düsseldorf. Krefeld, Düren, Gladbach, the country between Viersen and Dülken, where Papa worked wonders with mealworms, all that was bad enough, but nothing compared to this abscess taped over with bull's-eye panes, this insult to a nonexistent God, this half-dried blob of mustard between Düssel and Rhine, this stories-high tub of stale, bitter beer, this monster that had come into the world after Jan Wellem straddled the Lorelei. City of art, they call it, city of expositions, city of gardens. Petit-bourgeois Babel. Fogbowl of the Lower Rhine and provincial capital. Godfather to the city of Danzig. Here Grabbe suffered and struggled. "He put up with the place. That makes us even. But in the end he cleared out." For even Christian Dietrich Grabbe refused to conk out in this hole, and preferred Detmold. Grabbe laughter: "I could laugh Rome to death, why not Düsseldorf!" Grabbe tears. Hannibal's ancient eye complaint: "It will do you good to cry, ye *aficionados*! At the most convenient time, when you've won all there is to win!" But without laugh-itch or bugs in his eyes, sober with black dog at heel, Matern comes to haunt the fair city of Düsseldorf, which at carnival time is governed by the blue-and-white Prince's guard, where money burgeons, beer blooms, art foams, a city good to live in from cradle to grave: merry merry!

But even at the Sawatzkis' the trend is dull. Inge says: "Boy, are you bald!" They live on Schadowstrasse over the store, in five rooms at once, furnished in style. Standing beside the medium-sized built-in aquarium, Jochen speaks correct German now, isn't it amazing? From the good old days in Mülheim—"Do you remember, Walter?"—they still have the encyclopedia in thirty-two volumes, which way back in Fliesteden the three of them never wearied of leafing through: *A* as in "Army."— They don't want you guys. *B* as in "Business."—We started small in Bedburg, but then. *C* as in "Currency."—Nowadays the mark isn't worth fifty pfennigs. *D* as in "Dinner."—Why don't you have a bite with us? No trouble. We'll just open a few cans. *E* as in "Easter."—Just think of it. Walli will be going to school after Easter. It's been a long time. *F* as in "Fanatic."—Like you. They never get anywhere in life. *G* as in "Goods."—Just feel it. No, it's not Scotch. We make it ourselves. That's why we can sell cheaper than. *H* as in "Harpsichord."—This one's Italian-made. We picked it up in Amsterdam. Pretty good buy. *I* as in "Igloo."—We're as snug as a bug in a rug. *J* as in "Journey."—Last year we went to Austria. Burgenland. You need a change now and then. It's dirt cheap and still so unspoiled. *K* as in "Kennel."—When are you going to get rid of that dog? *L* as in "Life."—This is the only one we've got. *M* as in "Maid."—The one before last got fresh before the first week was out. *N* as in "Nature."—The grounds include two acres of woods and a duck pond. *O* as in "Oskar."—He's from Danzig, too, he was putting on a show in the Onion Cellar for a while. *P* as in "Pearls."— Jochen gave me these for our anniversary. *Q* as in "Qualm."—At first the Chamber of Commerce had qualms about us, but when Jochen showed them our credentials. *R* as in "Raspberries."—Raspberry jelly and yoghurt,

911

that's what we eat for breakfast now. *T* as in "Textiles."—Goldmouth tipped us off. *U* as in "Underground."—No, no idea where he is. *V* as in "Vanished."—Oh well, maybe he'll turn up one of these days. *W* as in "Walli."—She's our child, Walter. Don't go making any claims. *X* as in "Xylophone."—Or cymbal, that's what they play at the Czikos. Should we drop in for a little while? *Y* as in "Yucatán."—That's another place we could go. Just been opened. *Z* as in "Zombie."—No, that's no good any more. Let's go to the Morgue. You've really got to see it. It'll shake you. Absolutely wild. The limit. Downright crazy. You'll love it. Well, anyway it's fun. You'lllaughyourselfsick. Medicalsotospeak. Nakednoofcoursenot. Everythingontop. Andsohighclass. Cutthroughthemiddle. Makesyouwanttothrowup. Sadistic bestial weird. Theyoughttocloseitdown. Buttheydon't. We've been there millionsoftimes. Theygiveyouyamstoeat. It'sJochen'streat.

Inge's idea is that Pluto should stay with the maid in the five-room apartment to guard the sleeping Walli, but Matern insists that Pluto come along to the Morgue. Sawatzki suggests: "Hadn't we better go to the Czikos?" But Inge is dead set on the Morgue. The three of them with dog push off. Up Flingerstrasse, down Bolkertstrasse. Naturally the Morgue, like all authentic Düsseldorf nightclubs, is in the Old City. Who owns the place is uncertain. Some speak of F. Schmuh, owner of the Onion Cellar. Otto Schuster of the Czikos is also mentioned. Right now Film-Mattner, owner of the Choo-Choo and the Dacha, which they had first wanted to call the "Troika," is the coming man; just recently he opened a new joint, the Fleamarket. But at the time when Matern went out on the town with dog and Sawatzkis, he was only starting out. Along Mertenstrasse, before they venture into the Morgue, Inge Sawatzki racks her brains behind her doll's face that has grown five years older: "I really wonder who hit on the idea. Somebody had to think of it, didn't they? Goldmouth used to say such funny things sometimes. Of course we never believed the line he spills. In business matters you can trust him, but in other things? For instance, he tried to make us believe that he'd owned a whole ballet. And all that tripe about the Front Line Theater during the war and so on. And he's certainly not a pure Aryan. They'd have noticed that in those days. I asked him a couple of times: Tell me, Goldmouth, where do you actually come from? Once he said Riga, another time: They call it Swibno today. What it was called before he didn't say. But there must be some truth in the ballet business. Maybe they really didn't notice. They say Schmuh's one too. He's the one with the Onion Cellar. They say he was some kind of an air-raid warden the whole time. But they're the only ones I. And they're both typical. That's why I say that an idea like the Morgue could only have been thought up by somebody like Goldmouth who. You'll see. I'm not exaggerating. Am I, Jochen? It's right after Andreasgasse, across from the Magistrate's Court.

There it is—in white letters on a black tombstone: THE MORGUE. And yet, if you don't look too closely, it could be a plain funeral parlor. In the window there's even an ivory-colored child's coffin—empty. And the usual: wax lilies and unusually attractive coffin mountings. Pedestals fitted with white velvet support photographs of first-class funerals. Wreaths as round as life preservers lean against them. In the foreground stands an impressive stone urn of the bronze age, found, as a small plaque informs one, in Coesfeld near Münster.

Inside, the guests find equally gentle reminders of human transience. Although they have made no reservations, the Sawatzskis, with Matern and dog, are shown to a table not far from the Swedish movie actress killed in an automobile accident and now lying in state. She is under glass and naturally made of wax. A white quilt, showing no contours, the welted edges attenuated by clouds of lace, covers the actress to the navel; but from the softly wavy black hair to the waist, the left half of her, the cheek, the chin, the gently sloping neck, the barely delineated collarbone, the steeply rising bosom are of waxen, yet pink-and-yellow-skinned flesh; to the right, however, as seen by Matern and the Sawatzkis, the illusion is created that a surgeon's scalpel has laid her bare; also modeled in wax, but true to life: heart, spleen, and the left kidney. The prize package is the heart, which beats exactly as it should, and a few of the Morgue's customers are always standing around the glass case, trying to see how it works.

Hesitantly, Inge Sawatzki last, they sit down. In indirectly lighted wall niches the roving eye distinguishes various parts of the human skeleton, the arm with radius and ulna, the inevitable death's-head, but also clearly displayed in large labeled flasks, as though for purposes of instruction, the lobe of a lung, a cerebrum, a cerebellum, and a placenta. There is even a library offering book after book, not glassed in but ready at hand: volumes on general physiology, richly illustrated, and more exacting works for the specialist—an account, for example, of experiments in the grafting of organs and a two-volume study of the pituitary gland. And between the niches, all of the same format and framed in good taste, photographs and engravings of celebrated physicians: Paracelsus, Virchow, Sauerbruch, and the Greek god of medicine leaning on a snake-entwined staff watch the guests at dinner.

The menu is nothing unusual: wiener schnitzel, beef brisket with horseradish, calves' brains on toast, beef tongue in Madeira, lamb kidneys flambé, even common pig's knuckles, and the usual roast chicken with French-fried potatoes. At most the cutlery and china are deserving of mention: Matern and the Sawatzkis eat calves' knuckles with sterile dissecting instruments; around the plates runs the inscription: "Academy of Medicine—Autopsy"; the beer, common Düsseldorf brew, foams in Erlenmeyer flasks; but otherwise there is no exaggeration. The average restaurant owner or proponent of the Düsseldorf modern style, the now-prominent Film-Mattner and his interior decorators, for instance, would have made too much of a good thing. They might, for example, have run off tape recordings of operating-room sounds: the slow, chewinggum-sluggish counting before the anesthetic takes effect, whispered or sharp instructions, metal touches metal, a saw functions, something buzzes on one note, something else pumps more and more slowly, then faster, staccato instructions, heart sounds, heart sounds . . . Nothing of the kind. Not even muffled dinner music fills the Morgue with irrelevant sound. Softly the dissecting instruments tinkle over the main course. Evenly sprinkled conversation at every table; but the tables again, apart from the damask tablecloths, are authentic: operating-room tables, elongated, on rollers, adjustable, are not mercilessly illuminated by powerful operating-room lamps, but watched over and bathed in a warm, personal light by charmingly old-fashioned, definitely Biedermeier lampshades. Nor are the guests doctors in civilian clothes, but, like the Sawatzkis and Matern, business people with friends, an occasional member of the provincial diet, a sprinkling of foreigners whose hosts want to show them something special, rarely young couples, and in every case consumers who wish to spend money on their evening out; for the Morgue—originally it was to be called the "Mortuary"—isn't exactly cheap, and besides, it's full of temptations. At the bar sit none of the usual hostesses, encouraging liquor consumption, no such sexy tactics as at the Rififi or the Taboo; instead, conservatively dressed young men, in a word, graduate physicians, are prepared, over a glass of champagne, well, perhaps not to provide final diagnoses, but to tell instructive and yet generally intelligible tales out of school. Here, far from his overkindly family doctor, many a guest has been made aware for the first time that his ailment bears this or that name, arteriosclerosis, for instance. Deposits of a fatty substance, cholesterol for example, have caused a hardening of the blood vessels. Amiably, but without the familiarity characteristic of most barroom conversation, the learned employee of the Morgue calls attention to possible consequences, coronary thrombosis, apoplexy, or what have you, then beckons a colleague, sitting nearby over a drink, to come over: The colleague, a biochemist and authority on the metabolism of fats, enlightens the guest—they stick to champagne—about animal fats and vegetable fats: "You needn't worry, the only fats used in our establishment are those containing acids that reduce cholesterol: our calves' brains on toast are prepared with pure corn oil. We also use sunflower oil and, you may be surprised to learn, even whale oil, but never lard or butter."

The Sawatzkis, especially Inge Sawatzki, try to persuade Matern, who has been troubled by kidney stones of late, to join one of the "B-doctors," as Inge calls them, at the bar. But Matern dislikes the idea of crossing the room, and so Sawatzki with a gesture summons one of the young men, who introduces himself as a urologist. No sooner has the word "kidney stones" been dropped than the young man insists on ordering the juice of two lemons: "You see, we used to be glad if we could eliminate small stones with a long and troublesome treatment; our lemon cure brings better results and all in all it's less expensive. We simply dissolve the stones, but only the so-called urate stones, I have to admit. Generally speaking, our guests' urine is normal at the end of two months. On one condition, I'm sorry to say: absolutely no liquor."

Matern puts down the beer he has just picked up. Not wishing to outstay his welcome, the urologist—it has come out that he studied under big men in Berlin and Vienna—takes his leave: "Against oxalate stones —you can see them over there, in the second case from the left—we are still powerless. But our lemon cure—perhaps you'd like me to leave you a prospectus—is the simplest thing in the world. Herodotus tells us that the Babylonians were curing kidney stones with lemon juice more than two thousand years ago; of course when he speaks of stones the size of an infant's head, we have to bear in mind that Herodotus was sometimes given to exaggeration."

Matern has a rough time with his double lemon juice. Good-natured cracks from the Sawatzkis. Leafing through the Morgue's prospectus. Why, they've got everything: specialists for the diseases of the thorax and the thyroid. A neurologist. A special prostate man. Pluto is well behaved under the operating table. Sawatzki says hello to a radio dealer acquaintance and companion at another table. Business is going strong at the bar. The B-doctors aren't being stingy with their knowledge. The calves' knuckles were excellent. Now what? Cheese or something sweet? The waiters come unbidden.

Ah yes, the waiters! They, too, are true to life. White linen tunics, buttoned up to the neck and showing only discreet reminders of the operating room, white surgeon's caps, and a white mask over nose and mouth, making them anonymous sterile soundless. Naturally they don't carry the platters of beef brisket or pork tenderloin *en croûte* in their bare hands, but wear rubber gloves in accordance with professional standards. That's going too far. It is not Inge Sawatzki but Matern who finds the gloves exaggerated: "You've got to draw the line somewhere. But that's typical again: from one extreme to the other, always wanting to drive out the Devil with. Honest shopkeepers if you will, but so stupid and so infernally smug. And they never learn from their history, they always think everyone else is to. Determined to let well enough alone and never to tilt against. Wherever they can make themselves heard, they want to cure the world of what ails it. Salomé of nothingness. Over corpses to Neverneverland. Always missed their calling. Always wanting to be brothers with everybody, to embrace the millions. Always coming around in the dead of night with their categorical thingamajig. Any thought of change scares them. Luck was never on their side. Freedom always dwells in mountains that are too high—geographically speaking, of course. Wedged into a narrow, overcrowded. Revolutions only in music, but never want to foul their own. The best infantrymen all the same, though when it comes to artillery the French. Lots of great composers and inventors have been. Copernicus for instance wasn't a Pole but. Even Marx felt himself to be. But they always have to carry things to. Like those rubber gloves. Of course they're supposed to mean something. I wonder what the owner. Assuming him to be one. Because nowadays Italian and Greek, Spanish and Hungarian joints are springing up like mushrooms. And in every dive somebody has thought up some idea. Cutting onions in the Onion Cellar, laughing gas in the Grabbe Room—and here it's this waiter's rubber gloves. Say, I know that guy! Why, it's. If he'd just take that white rag off his face. Then! Then! His name was. What was it anyway? Got to leaf back, names names, in heart, spleen, and . . . " Matern came to judge with black dog.

But the waiter-surgeon doesn't remove the cloth from nose and mouth. Nameless, with discreetly downcast eyes, he clears the dissected remains of calves' knuckles from the damask-clothed operating table. He will come again and serve the dessert with the same rubber gloves. Meanwhile we can reach into kidney-shaped bowls and chew yams. They're supposed to be good for the memory. Matern has a respite, which he spends chewing on gnarled roots: Why, that was. It must be that bastard who. You've got him and the others to thank if you. I've got a little bone to. He was—I'm not seeing things—Number 4 when the nine of us came out of the woods and climbed the. I'll give his memory a jolt. Sawatzki doesn't notice? Or he knows and he isn't saying. But I'll settle his hash all by. Coming around here with rubber gloves and a white rag on his mug. If it were black at least like at Zorro's or like the time when we. It was a curtain. We cut it up with scissors into nine triangles: one for Willy Eggers, one for Otto Warnke, one and then another for the Dulleck brothers, one for Paule Hoppe, one for somebody else, one for Wollschläger, one for Sawatzki, there he sits like a hypocrite, or maybe he really hasn't noticed, and the ninth for that guy, just wait. So we climbed the fence into the grounds of the villa on Steffensweg. The same fence day in day out for dog years. Behind nine black cloths over the fence. But not tied the same way as this character. Completely covering the eyes, with slits to look out of. While this guy: you know those eyes all right. Snow lay heavy as lead. He was a waiter even then, in Zoppot and later at the Eden. Here he comes with the pudding. Bublitz. Of course. I'll tear that rag off his. Alfons Bublitz. O.K., friend, just wait.

But Matern, who has come to judge and to tear a rag from a face, doesn't tear and doesn't judge, but stares at the pudding, served in plexiglass bowls such as those used by dentists. With art and precision a pastry cook—there's no limit to what those fellows can do—has reproduced the human dentition in two colors: curved pink gums holding shimmering pearly evenly spaced teeth together: the human dentition numbers thirty-two teeth, to wit, above, below, and on either side, two incisors, one canine, five molars—coated with enamel. At first Grabbe laughter, which, as everyone knows, had the power to laugh Rome to pieces, tries to surge up in Matern and wreck the joint; but as Inge and Jochen Sawatzki, his hosts to left and right of him, apply spatula-shaped dental instruments to their pudding teeth, the Grabbe laughter that has been building up languishes deep within, Rome and the Morgue are not laid waste, but inside him as he stores up breath for a grandiose and seldom enacted scene, dissected calf's knuckle says no to more food, especially sweets. Slowly he slips off his round stool. With difficulty he casts off from the white-covered operating table. He has to prop himself against the glass case where the heart of the Swedish movie actress beats imperturbably. Pilotless, he drifts between occupied tables, at which dinner jackets and muchtoomuchjewelry are eating liver *en brochette* and breaded sweetbreads. Voices in the fog. Chatting B-doctors. Position lights over the bar. Followed by Pluto, he lurches past the blurred pictures of the benefactors Asclepius, Sauerbruch, Paracelsus, and Virchow. And reaches port: which, except for the reproduction of Rembrandt's famous *Anatomy Lesson,* is a perfectly normal toilet. He vomits thoroughly and for years. No one looks on but God in His heaven, for Pluto has to stay outside with the attendant. Reunited with his dog, he washes his hands and face.

When he's through, Matern has no change on him and gives the attendant a two-mark piece. "It's not so bad," she says. "A lot of people get that way the first time." She gives him advice for the homeward voyage: "Take some strong coffee and a slug of schnapps and you'll be all right."

Matern complies: from a clinical porcelain cup he sips black coffee; from cylindrical test tubes he pours down a first—drink one more schnapps, or you'll be short one schnapps—then—why not?—a second drink of framboise.

Inge Sawatzki is concerned: "What's the matter with you? Can't you hold it any more? Should we call back the urologist or maybe another one that specializes in this sort of thing?"

It's the same waiter who, after calves' knuckles, yams, and pudding teeth, serves the coffee and schnapps; but Matern has lost all desire to cross off a first or last name that keeps itself sterile behind a white surgeon's mask.

During a chance lull, Sawatzki says: "Check please, waiter, or should

917

I say doctor, or professor, hahaha!" On a printed "death certificate" form, the disguised waiter serves up the check with rubber stamp, date, and illegible signature—doctor's scrawl—for the tax people: "It's deductible. Business expenses. Where'd we be if we couldn't regularly. If the tax collectors had their way, they'd. Don't worry, the government won't go hungry."

The costumed waiter pantomimes thanks and sees the Sawatzkis and their guest with black shepherd to the door. From there Inge Sawatzki, but not Matern, casts a last backward glance. She waves "so-long" to one of the B-doctors, probably the biochemist, quite inappropriately, especially as it's an authentic hospital double door. First leather, then white enamel, runs on rails. But you don't have to push, it responds to electrical pressure. The sterile waiter presses the button.

Helping each other into their coats in a normal cloakroom, they look behind them; over the double door a red light is shining: "PLEASE DO NOT DISTURB. OPERATION IN PROGRESS!"

"Christ!" Jochen Sawatzki draws a deep breath of fresh air. "I wouldn't want to eat there every night. Every two weeks at the most, what do you say?"

Matern breathes deeply, as though to suck in piece by piece the whole Old City with its leaded panes and pewter dishes, with its crooked St. Lambert's steeple and its antiquated wrought iron. Every breath can be the last.

The Sawatzkis are worried about their friend: "You ought to take up athletics, Walter, or you'll go to pieces one of these days."

The Eighty-ninth Athletic and the Ninetieth Stale Beer Materniad

Been am sick. Got had the grippe. But I didn't put my fever to bed, I took it to the Choo-Choo, and propped it against the bar. What a joint. Latest Lower-Rhenish railroad style, all mahogany and brass like a club car. Sitting between this one and that one until four forty-five, the whole time clutching the same brand of whisky, watching the ice getting smaller and smaller in the glass, holding forth for the benefit of all seven bartenders. Chit-chat with phonies and floozies about the first Cologne football club, about the speed limit in towns and villages, about the end of the world on the fourth of next month, about poppycock and the negotiations over Berlin. Then all of a sudden Mattner gives me hell, because I've been scratching the fancy varnish off the wall with a pipe cleaner: the whole thing is phony! I got to see what's behind it, don't I? And all these people jammed into a club car. Squeezed into dinner jackets, with celluloid cunts in tow: crispy, crunchy, cute. But no place for a first-class act. The most I can do is to work off my manly play instinct: wind it up slowly and let it unroll fast. Out comes *Eine Kleine Nachtmusik.* In the end it was rich and schmaltzy. It seems that Mattner treated to a round of drinks, whereupon Franz Moor hollered, Act Five, Scene 1: "Slavish wisdom, slavish fears!—It's still a moot question whether the past is dead or whether there's an eye above.—Hum, hum! What whispered voice? Is there an avenger up there? Is there an avenger up there?—No, no!—Yes, yes! That awful whispering around me: Someone above. This very night I'll go to meet the avenger above. No! I say. Miserable subterfuge behind which. It's empty, lonely, deaf up there above.—And yet if there isn't! I command it: there isn't."

They applauded with hands as big as office folders and snapped at Matern with powder boxes, encore: "Command it: there isn't."

What does an avenger do when his victims pat him familiarly on the back: "It's all right, boy. We get you: When you command, it isn't. Let bygones be bygones. Put on a new record. Weren't you a glider flier one time?—Sure, sure, you're perfectly right. You're an A-1 antifascist and we're lousy little Nazis, the whole lot of us, O.K.? But weren't you once, and didn't you once, and somebody told me you used to play faustball, a lineman, the captain . . ."

Bronze, silver, and gold. Every athlete refurbishes his past. Every athlete was better once upon a time. Every day both Sawatzkis, before and after dinner: "You've got to get some exercise, Walter. Go hiking in the woods, or goswimmingintheRhine. Think of your kidney stones. Do something about them. Take our bicycle out of the cellar or buy a punching bag and charge it to me."

Nothing can tickle Matern out of his chair. He sits, hands planted on both knees, as fused with the furniture as if he were planning to sit it out for nine years like his grandmother, old grandma Matern, who sat riveted to her chair for nine years, only rolling her eyeballs. And yet, what riches Düsseldorf and the world have to offer: thirty-two movie houses, Gründgens' Theater, up and down the Königsstrasse, tart Düsseldorf beer, the Rhine famed in song, the reconstructed Old City, the swan-mirroring castle gardens, Bach Society, Art Society, Schumann Hall, men's fashion shows, the carnival bells that ring in the carnival, athletic fields athletic fields; the Sawatzkis list them all: "Why don't you go out to Flingern and have a look at the Fortuna Stadium? There's all sorts of things going on there, not just football." But none of these sports—and Sawatzki lists more than he has fingers—can lift Matern off his chair. And then by chance—his friends have already given up—the word "faustball" is dropped. It makes no difference who whispered it, Inge or Jochen, or maybe little Walli, mighty cute. In any event, no sooner has the word fallen than he is on his feet. Just as Düsseldorf and the world are about to write him off, Matern takes short steps on the pocket-book-thick carpet. Little limbering-up movements. Startled cracking of joints. Sudden loquacity: "Boy, it's been a long time. Faustball. '35 and '36 on Heinrich Ehlers Field. The Engineering School on the right, the crematory on the left. We won every tournament, crushed them all: the Athletic and Fencing Club, the Danzig Touring Club, Schellmühl 98, even the police. Played lineman for the Young Prussians. We had a marvelous center. He teased every ball up in the air for me and served with dauntless calm. His calm was Olympian, I'm telling you; with machinelike underhand shots he hit one ball after another down to the line, and I just pounced: sharp forehand shots and long shots that the opposing team couldn't. Just before the war, I played here for a while with the Unterrath Athletic Club, until they. Well, better not talk about that."

It's not far, you take the Number 12 from Schadowplatz to Ratingen, up Grafenberger Allee to the Haniel and Lueg plant, then turn off to the left through vegetable gardens, through Mörsenbroich and the Municipal Forest, to the Rath Stadium, a medium-sized setup at the foot of Aap Forest. A fine flourishing piece of woods, with a view through the nearby gardens down to the city immersed in the usual mist: churches and factories alternate significantly. Empty lots, fenced-in building sites, and, massive on the other side, the Mannesheim Corporation. Here and there: activity on every field. They're always laying out fresh cinders somewhere. Junior handball teams, sloppy playing, three-thousand-meter runners trying to better their time; and on a small field off to one side and surrounded by Lower-Rhenish poplars, the Unterrath Seniors are playing the Derendorf Seniors. Seems to be an unscheduled game. The field is sheltered from the wind, but Unterrath is losing. Matern with dog can see that at a glance. He can also see why: the lineman is no good and doesn't coordinate with the center, who under different circumstances wouldn't be bad.

Overhead return shots are all right for the backs, but not for the man on the line. The left forward is pretty good, but they're not using him enough. Actually the team hasn't got a playmaker, the center—he looks mighty familiar to Matern, but that could be because of the gym suit, and as a rule a lot too many look familiar to him—well, all the center does is to bounce the ball high, so anybody at all can come running up: both backs, the lineman; naturally the Derendorfers, who aren't really so hot, get in close and pile up points by smashing. Only the left forward—he too looks as if Matern had seen him somewhere sometime —stays put and manages, mostly with backhand shots, to save the honor of the Unterrath Seniors. The return game also ends with a defeat for the home team. They've switched the lineman and the right back; but up to the final whistle the new lineman exhibits no prowess capable of saving the day.

Matern with dog stands at the entrance to the field: anyone heading for the locker rooms has to pass by him and his inquiring gaze; the moment they come in sight with their gym suits over their shoulders, he's sure. His heart hops. Something presses against his spleen. Painful kidneys. It's them. Once Unterrath Juniors like himself: Fritz Ankenrieb and Heini Tolksdorf. Even then, so and so many dog years ago, Fritz played center and Heini played left forward, while Matern was lineman: what forwards! What a team altogether, the backs—what were their names anyway—were class too. They even beat the stuffings out of a Cologne University team and the boys from the Düsseldorf SS, but then the team suddenly went to pot, because . . . I'll ask the boys if they remember why, and who it was that turned, if it wasn't a certain Ankenrieb that, and even Heini Tolksdorf agreed that I . . .

But before Matern has a chance to confront them: I've come with a black dog . . . Ankenrieb starts jawing at him from one side: "Christ, is it possible? Is it you or . . . Take a look, Heini, who's been watching our lousy playing. I said to myself before, when we were changing sides: You know that guy. Look at that posture, the same old. Hasn't changed a bit, except on top. Well, none of us can claim that his looks are improving. Once we were the hope of Unterrath, today we get one drubbing after another. Christ, those were the days, remember the police meet in Wuppertal. And you on the line. The whole time right under the nose of that cop from Herne. You've got to come to our bar, we still have all the pictures and scrolls. As long as we had you for a lineman, nobody could, after that, am I right, Heini, we went downhill fast. We never did recover. Lousy politics!".

A group of three, with a black dog frolicking around them. They've put him in the middle, they talk about victories and defeats, they blurt it out quite frankly, yes, they were the ones who went to the club manager, so he'd. "You just couldn't keep your trap shut, though of course you were right about a good many things." A few whispered remarks in the locker room had done it. "If you'd said that to me at home or somewhere else, I'd have listened, maybe even agreed with you, but that's how it is. Politics and sports have never mixed. They still don't."

Matern quotes: "This is what you said, Ankenrieb: We can do without a lineman who spreads Jewish-Bolshevist propaganda. Is that right?"

Heini Tolksdorf comes to the rescue: "We were brainwashed, the whole lot of us. You yourself didn't always say the same things. They threw dust in our eyes for years. We had to foot the bill. Our backs, do you remember, little Rielinger and Wölfchen Schmelter, never came back from Russia. Christ! And what for?"

The club's hangout is where it always was, on Dorotheenplatz in Flingern. With four five old friends, Matern is affably constrained to remember the game in Gladbach, the quarter finals in Wattenscheid, and the unforgettable end game in Dortmund. The corner reserved for the Unterrath Club isn't lacking in decoration. He has a chance to admire himself, the lineman, in twelve photographs of the team, all framed and glassed. From late fall '38 to early summer '39 Matern played, here he has it in black and white, on the Unterrath team. Barely seven months, and what relics of victory! What thick rebellious hair he had! Always serious. Always the center of attraction, even when he was standing on the right wing. And the scrolls. Brown calligraphy under the eagle emblem of those days. "You really should have stuck something over that. I just can't stand the sight of the animal. Memories well and good, but not under that bankrupt gallows bird."

That's a suggestion worth discussing. At a late hour—the drinks are beer and gin—they patch up an exemplary compromise: Heini Tolksdorf borrows a tube of paste from the owner and, encouraged by cheers, sticks common beer mats, Schwaben-Bräu, over the offensive emblem on all the honor scrolls. In return, Matern makes a solemn promise—all the club members rise to their feet—never again to waste a word on the stupid old incident and to play lineman again—shake hands on it—for the Unterrath Seniors.

"Good will is the main thing. We'll make out. What comes between us shall be forgotten, what unites us shall be held in honor. If everybody makes a concession or two, strife and dissension will be things of the past. For true democracy is unthinkable without readiness to compromise. We're all sinners, we've all. Who will cast the first? Who can say, I am without? Who can claim to be infallible? Therefore let us. We of Unterrath have always. And so let us first, in honor of our comrades who in Russian soil. And then to the health of our good old, who is with us today, and lastly to the old and the new comradeship among athletes. I raise my glass!"—Every toast is the toast before last. Every round has no end. Every man is merriest among men.—Under the table Pluto licks spilled beer.

So things seem to be on the mend. Inge and Jochen Sawatzki are delighted when Walter Matern parades his brand-new gym suit: "Boy, has he got a figure!" But the figure is deceptive. Of course you have to get back into the feel of the game. It would be dumb to put him on the line right off. But for the present he's too slow for a back—a back has to get away fast—and he proves a failure at center because he wants to cover the whole field and can't manage to maneuver the ball effectively from the backfield to the line. He plays neither to the left forward nor to the lineman. He takes everything that comes up from the backs as intended for him personally, cuts the ball off from his own men, and then half the time proceeds to lose it. A solo artist, who hands the opposing team set-up shots on a platter, just asking to be smashed. Where can they put him if it's too soon to put him on the line?

"He's got to be on the line."

"And I'm telling you he has to get back into shape first."

"His type can only be used on the line."

"His reactions aren't quick enough."

"Anyway, he's big enough for a lineman."

"He's got to taste blood, then he'll perk up."

"Too ambitious for a center."

"All right, put him up front, we'll see."

But playing right forward, all he can manage is an occasional trick serve that drops square in front of the opposition's feet. Only seldom does he surprise the Oberkassel or Derendorf Seniors with tricky backspins; but then, when the ball takes a sharp, flat, and unpredicatable bounce in enemy territory, one gets an inkling of the lineman that Matern once was. Ankenrieb and Tolksdorf exchange wistful nods: "Man, what a champ he used to be! Too bad." And keep their patience. They give him good passes, they keep the ball up high for him, and he shoots it down the drain. He's hopeless. "But we've got to be sporting about this. How can you expect him to be in form after all these years? And besides, there's his leg injury. It's hardly noticeable, but just the same. Why don't you make him a reasonable proposition, Heini? Something like this: 'See here, Walter, it seems to me you've lost some of the old zip. I can understand that. God knows there are more important things than being a lineman for the Unterrath Athletic Club, but couldn't you referee the next game or two, just until you get the feel of the thing?' "

Team members try to make things easy for Matern. "Sure! Why not? There's nothing I'd like better. I'm only glad you're still willing to. Whatever you like: line watcher, scorekeeper, referee. Like me to make you a cup of coffee or bring you a coke? Can I have a real referee's whistle?" That's something Matern has always longed for. His true calling: to make decisions. "Foul ball. The score is now nineteen to twelve in favor of Wersten. You're wrong. I know all the rules. When I was knee-high to a grasshopper, at home on Heinrich Ehlers Field. Man, what a center we had. A fat kid with freckles, but light on his feet like lots of tubbies, and, boy, was he calm! Nothing could rattle him. And always cheerful. Like me, he knew all the rules: The player who puts the ball into play must have both feet behind the line of play. At the moment of hitting the ball and putting it into play, he must have at least one foot on the ground. The open hand or a fist with disengaged thumb may not be used in putting the ball into play. Any one player may only once, and in general three times is the limit. The ball may strike the ground only once between strokes, neither the goalpost nor the line must be, only arm and fist may be—Ah, if only I could play again with Eddi, he in midfield, I on the line!—any infringement turns the ball into a foul ball, the whistle is blown twice, which means: The ball is dead!" Who would have thought it: Matern, who had come with black dog to judge, makes out fine as a referee and trains his mutt to be a line judge: Pluto barks at every foul; Matern, who had always been hot on the heels of an enemy, knows no opponent, but only teams which are all, without exception, subject to the same rules and regulations.

His old faustball friends, Fritz Ankenrieb and Heini Tolksdorf, admire him. They talk Matern up at meetings of the club's officers, and especially to the Juniors. "You can take an example from him. When he saw that his form wasn't what it used to be, he gave up his position on the line without a single bitter word and unselfishly offered his services as referee. He'd be a swell coach for you, what a guy! Went through the whole war. Wounded three times. Always ready for a suicide mission. When he begins to tell stories, your eyes pop out of your head."

Who would have thought it: Matern, who had come to judge the Seniors Ankenrieb and Tolksdorf, turns into an unbiased referee, declines when someone, in a well-meant attempt at subornation, offers him a half-time job at Mannesmann's, which would keep master and dog in style, and stands incorruptible, with dog at heel, among the Juniors of the Unterrath Athletic Club. The boys in the blue gym suits form a loose semicircle, and he in crimson gym suit explains his raised striking fist, showing the surfaces employed in the backhand shot and the inside shot. While he demonstrates his lowered fist, showing the surfaces used in the forehand shot and the snap shot, the Sunday morning sun does a headstand on his hairless dome: how it glitters. The boys can hardly wait to apply what Matern has drummed into them: his horizontal fist shows the surface employed in the backhand shot and the risky roundhouse shot. And then, after a lively practice game and the starting exercises for the backs—his own idea—he tells the boys stories from wartime and peacetime. Seated, the dark-blue gym suits around him, the crimson-clad coach, form a loose but tense semicircle. At last somebody who knows how to get at the youngsters. No question falls unanswered on the turf of the faustball field. He knows about everything. Matern knows how it happened; how things came to such a pass; what an undivided Germany was and could be; who is to blame for all this; what jobs the old-time murderers are holding down again; and how to make sure it will never happen again. He has the right tone for the youngsters. He makes what was jellyfish-soft wood-cut-clear. His leitmotives unmask murder motives. He simplifies laby-rinths into straight broad highways. When coach Matern says: "And that is our still unconquered past!," every Unterrath youngster looks upon him as the one and only true conqueror of the past. After all, he has set

924

an example, not once but many times: "For instance, when I stepped up to that member of the special court and a little later to the judge himself, those bastards crawled, crawled I'm telling you, and Local Group Leader Sellke in Oldenburg, who used to talk so big, began to snivel when I and the dog . . ." In general, allusions to Pluto, who is never absent when past and present are being clarified in the loose semicircle, are the refrain of Matern's long didactic poem: "And when I went to the Upper Weser country with the dog. The dog was there when in Altena-Sauerland. The dog is a witness that in Passau I." The boys applaud whenever Matern tumbles one of the old-time bigshots. They are carried away. Model and coach in one. But throughout these pleasurable Nazi funerals Matern unfortunately can't refrain—and not just in subordinate clauses—from making socialism triumph.

"What business has Marx on an athletic field?" asks the executive committee unanimously.

"Can we allow Eastern propaganda to be encouraged on our athletic fields?" runs the question which the field manager submits in writing to the Unterrath Athletic Club.

"Our young athletes will not tolerate this state of affairs," maintains the honorary chairman at the bar in Dorotheenplatz. He knows Matern from before the war. "He made the same kind of trouble even then. Can't adapt himself. Poisons the atmosphere." In his opinion, which is seconded by nods and murmurs of "exactly," a true Unterrath athlete must not only give himself wholly and cheerfully to his elected sport, but must also be clean inside.

After soandso many dog years, for the soandsomanieth time in Matern's medium-length life, a court of honor takes up his case. Exactly like the Young Prussians on Heinrich Ehlers Field and the men of Langfuhr SA Sturm 84, the members of the Unterrath Athletic Club decide to expel Matern a second time. As in '39 the vote to exclude him from club and athletic field meets with no opposition. Only members Ankenrieb and Tolksdorf abstain, an attitude which meets with silent approval on all sides. In conclusion the honorary chairman remarks: "He can be glad that these proceedings will remain among ourselves. The last time the affair had further repercussions, police headquarters on Kavalleriestrasse, if that rings a bell." DON'T GO IN FOR SPORTS. YOU'LL BE MADE SPORT OF.

O Matern, how many defeats must you check off as victories? What environment spat you out after you had subjected it? Will they someday print maps of both Germanies and unroll them in school-rooms as a visual record of your battles, marked in the usual way—two crossed sabers? Will they say: Matern's victory at Witzenhausen became evident on the morning of the? The battle of Bielefeld saw the victor Matern in Cologne on the Rhine the following morning? When Matern triumphed in Düs-seldorf-Rath, the calendar read June 3, 1954? Or if your victories, marked with crosses and counted, do not find their way into history, will at least grandmothers surrounded by grandchildred remember half-truthfully: "Then, in the dog year '47 a poor dog, who had a black dog with him, came to see us and tried to make trouble for Grampa. But I took the fellow, not a bad sort really, quietly aside until he calmed down and began to purr like a kitten, all cuddly."

Inge Sawatzki, for example, has often revived the tired victor Matern and nursed him back to health, which is just what she does now that the wounds inflicted on the Unterrath athletic field are in need of being dressed. It was bound to happen. Inge can wait. Every warrior comes home now and then. Every woman welcomes with open arms. Every victory demands to be celebrated.

Even Jochen Sawatzki can see that. Accordingly he says to his wife Inge: "Go ahead if you can't help it." And they—the classical great lovers—do what they still can't help. The apartment is big enough after all. And now that he's kind of worn out, it's actually more fun than in the days when you only had to look at his knob for the machine to spring into action and finish the job much quicker than necessary. Always that craving for records: "I'll show you. I can do it any time, at high speed. I could show you seven times and climb the Feldberg when I'm through. That's the way I am. All the Materns have been like that. Simon Materna, for instance, always had a big chunk of meat up front, even on horseback when he was on his way to wreak vengeance between Dirschau, Danzig, and Elbing. That was a man. And as for his brother Gregor Materna, you can still read in the Danzig city archieves that 'after al manner of mysdeedes, murther, and the sheddyng of Christian blode, lorde Materna cam that autumn to Danczk for to wreak al manner of fiercenesse, and eke to hank Claus Bartusch by the neck, at which tyme he set vp his passyng styffe peter for a gallows, whereat wondyrment was of alle the robboures and marchants.' That's the kind he was. And in the old days, in the Army, for instance, you could have hung, well, maybe not a sack of pepper, but anyway a twenty-pound weight on my handle without preventing it from giving you the works quickly and very effectively."

Nevermore would he hammer nails into the wall with turgid tool. Now she takes him in hand—slowly and gently. "Mustn't panic right away, we have time. These are the best years of life, when potency levels off and we watch it like a savings account. After all there are other things in life. For instance, we could go to the theater sometime, you used to be an actor yourself. You don't feel like it? Never mind, we'll go to the movies, or we can go watch the Martinmas procession with Walli: lantern lantern, sun, moon, and stars. Or it's nice having coffee in Kaiserswerth and looking out over the Rhine. We could go to Dortmund for the six-day bicycle race, and this time we'll take Sawatzki with us. I've never been to the Moselle for the wine harvest. Ah, a beautiful beautiful year with you. It'll be something I can feed on for the rest of my life. You seem so much more settled than you used to be. You even leave the dog home once in a while. Of course there are always exceptions, like at the last Men's Garment Fair when we bumped into that tubby little Semrau man, and you went off your rocker and started arguing with him and Jochen behind our booth. But then you had a few beers together, and Jochen even closed a deal with Semrau: for several dozen duffel coats. Or in Cologne at the Mardi Gras parade: they've been marching by for over an hour, and then comes a float with a regular windmill on it, and a lot of nuns and knights in real armor are dancing around it. But headless the whole lot of them. They're carrying their heads under their arms. Or playing catch with them. I'm just on the point of asking you what they're suppose to symbolize when off you go, trying to break through the barrier and get at the nuns. Lucky they didn't let you through. Heaven knows what you would have done to them, and they to you, because they don't pull any punches on Mardi Gras. But then you calmed down, and at the station it was gay again. You went as some kind of medieval soldier; Sawatzki was a one-eyed admiral; and you made a regular robber's moll out of me. Too bad the picture turned out so fuzzy. Because if it were clear, you could see what a bay window you've put on, my sugarbun. That's because we take such good care of you. You've got nice and plump since you gave up athletics. It doesn't agree with you —clubs and meetings and all that stuff. You'll always be a lone wolf. The only reason you make out with Jochen is that he always does what you say. He's even against the atom bomb because you're against it and signed that petition. And I'm against it too, I wouldn't want to get bumped off now that we're so cozy together. Because I love you. Don't listen. I could eat you up, because I, do you hear? Everything about you. The way you look through walls and the way you clutch a glass. When you cut bacon against your thumb. When you talk like an actor, trying to grab hold of heaven knows what. Your voice, your shaving soap, or when you cut your, or the way you walk, you walk as if you had an appointment with God knows who. Because sometimes I can't make you out. But that doesn't matter. Just don't listen when I. But I would like to know how you spent the time with Jochen in the old days when. You don't have to start up with your teeth right away. Didn't I tell you not to listen? Say, there's a shooting match on the Rhine Meadows, hear? Should we go? Tomorrow? Without Jochen? I've got to be over there in the branch store until six. How about seven at the Rhine Bridge? On the Oberkassel side."

Matern is on his way to his date, without dog. Good old Pluto, he isn't allowed out in the street so often any more, for fear of his being run over. Matern walks quickly straight ahead, because he has an appointment at a definite time. He has bought cherries, a whole pound. Now he's spitting cherry pits in the direction of his appointment. People walking toward him have to dodge. The cherries and minutes grow fewer. When you cross the bridge on foot, you notice how wide the Rhine is: from the Planetarium on the Düsseldorf side to Oberkassel: a good pound of cherries wide. He spits in the head wind, which pushes the cherry pits in the direction of Cologne; but the Rhine carries them down to Duisburg or father still. Every cherry cries out for the next. Eating cherries puts you in a rage. Rage mounts from cherry to cherry. When Jesus chased the money-changers out of the Temple, He ate a pound of cherries before He. Othello also ate a whole pound before he. The Moor brothers, both of them, day in day out, even in winter. And if Matern had to play Jesus, Othello, or Franz Moor, he'd be obliged to eat a whole pound before each performance. How much hatred ripens with them or is preserved along with them in jars? They only seem to be so round; in reality cherries are pointed triangles. Especially sour cherries set the teeth on edge. As if he had any need of that. He thinks shorter than he spits. Ahead of him homeafteroffice-goers hold their hats tight and are afraid to look behind them. Those who look back have someone behind them. Only Inge Sawatzki, who also has an appointment, mirrors the ever more menacingly approaching Matern fearlessly and punctually in googoo eyes. How can she be expected to know that he has almost a pound of cherries under his belt? Freshwhite blows her flimsy dress. Tight above, wide below. Waist still twenty-one, though it takes a girdle. She can afford sleeveless expectation. Wind in Ingedress brushes jumpy knees, towardly knees: smiling toward, running toward, four-and-a-half Italian sandal steps: and then plunk between her towardly breasts; but nothing can get Inge Sawatzki down; under the impact she stands staunch and vertical: "Aren't I punctual? The spot looks good on my dress. It needed some red. Were they sweet or sour cherries?"

For the bag has vented all his rage. The cherry-pit spitter can drop it. "Should I buy you some more, there's a stand over there."

But Inge Sawatzki would like "to ride the high-flier, for ever and ever." So off across the Rhine Meadows. In amid the surge of others and instantly included in the count. But no description of the environment, for she doesn't want ice cream, she doesn't know how to shoot, the scenic railway appeals to her only when it's dark, sideshows are always a disappointment, all she wants is the high-flier, for ever and ever.

First he wins two roses and a tulip for her at the shooting gallery. Then she simply has to let herself be bumped around with him in a dodgem car. During which, hermetically sealed off against the outside world, he meditates on mass man, materialism, and transcendence. Then with three shots he wins her a little yellow bear for Walli, but it can't growl. Then he has to drink two consecutive beers standing up. Then he buys her burnt almonds whether she wants them or not. A try at a target—it'll only take a minute: two eights, a ten. At last she gets to ride the high-flier with him, but not for ever and ever. The high-flier is two-thirds empty, it's gradually going out of style. But Inge is wild about old-fashioned things. She collects music boxes, dancing bears, cutouts, magic lanterns, whistling tops, decalcomanias, she's just the type for the high-flier. Her dress and undies made specially to order for this circular journey. Hair loose, towardly knees anything but pressed together; for anyone who is as hot as Inge Sawatzki, obliged to carry a feverquiff around with her hour after hour, keeps wanting to hang it and herself out in the wind. But he doesn't enjoy subjection to the laws of gravitation. Round and round for two and a half minutes, regardless of whether or not you roll up and let the change of direction unwind you: round and round until the music stops. But Inge wants to hang herself in the wind: "One more time. One more time!" Not to be a spoilsport for once in his life. There's no cheaper way of making her dizzy. Take a look at the environment while it goes round and round. Still one and the same leaning St. Lambert's Tower means Düsseldorf over there. Still the same ugly mugs crowded in a circle, with or without ice cream, with objects bought or won by shooting or dicing, and waiting for Matern's return. Mass man believes in him and trembles at his approach. Slavish wisdom, slavish fears! all, without distinction, cooked according to the same recipe. Bankbooks in their hearts, jungle without claws, hygienic pipedreams, neither good nor evil, but *phenomenal,* all in one gravy. Scattered peas. Or if you prefer, raisins in a cake. Forgetful of Being, in search of an *ersatz* for transcendence. Taxpayers, all cut from the same cloth, excepting one. All identical; one stands out. Just an irregularity in the weave, but even so he stands out. From round to round, impossible to ignore. Got himself a sharpshooter's hat like all the other members of the rifle club, and is nonetheless here again, gone, back again, gone: a very special sharpshooter. O names! why, that's, of course, wait a minute! Gone—here again: that's all I needed. The jig is up, sharpshooter police major. The revels will soon be ended, Police Major Osterhues. Shall we ride the high-flier? Chase murder motives with leitmotives? What do you say, Heinrich, shall we?

Some of the sharpshooters want to, but this particular one doesn't. He wanted to before, but now that someone jumps off the starting high-flier and shouts his name plus his superannuated rank to the ends of the world, the meanwhile alderman and sharpshooter Heinrich Osterhues has lost all inclination and wants only to make himself scarce. "Police major";

those are words he doesn't like to hear. Even old friends aren't allowed to. That was once upon a time and has no business here.

Happened before and often filmed: nothing is easier than running away at a shooting match. For everywhere friendly fellow sharpshooters with their hats—half forester's hats, half sou'westers—stand in readiness and take him under cover. They even run a few steps to lead the wolf up a false trail. Fool him by scattering, which just about halves or quarters the wolf. Split into sixteenths—that's what Matern would have to do. Nab him, nab him! Leitmotive chases murder motive! Ah, if only he had Pluto with him, he'd know the way to Heinrich Osterhues. Ah, if only he had marked him, the police major of rib-smashing years, with cherry pit and cherry spot and not Ingedress. "Osterhues Osterhues!" Don't turn around—cherry pit's going around.

Only after an hour of Osterhues-screeching and Osterhues-searching —he must have seized a whole regiment of sharpshooters by the buttons of their uniforms and released them in disgust—does he find the trail again: he picks up a photograph, badly trampled, from the trampled grass. It doesn't show this one or that one or Osterhues the sharpshooter: no, it shows the onetime police major Osterhues, who in the year 1939 personally questioned Walter Matern, prisoner held for investigation, in the cellar of the Kavalleriestrasse police headquarters.

With this photograph—it must have slipped out of the fleeing sharpshooter's sharpshooter's jacket—Matern makes the rounds of the beer tents. No sign of him. Or he threw it away—evidence! Armed with this warrant, he races through sideshow booths, pokes around under the trailers. Night is falling over the Rhine Meadows—white Ingedress follows him pleading respectfully and wants to ride on the scenic railway, for ever and ever—when Osterhues-hungry, he enters a last beer tent. Whereas all the other tents, inflated like beer bellies, could scarcely hold the noise of the singing, under this tent silence prevails. "Psst!" warns the monitor at the entrance. "We're taking a picture." With catlike tread Matern treads on beer-sour sawdust. Neither folding chairs nor rows of tables. Osterhues-seeking eyes take in the scene: What a picture, what a photograph, the rifle club photographer is planning! Amidst hushed emptiness a platform raises one hundred thirty-two sharpshooters toward the tent roof. Arranged into tiers—kneeling, sitting, standing, and in the very back row towering-over. One hundred thirty-two sharpshooters wear their sharpshooter hats—half forester's hat, half sou'wester—slightly tilted to the right. Sharpshooter braid and rosettes are equitably distributed.

None silvers more strikingly, no chest is less bemedaled. Not one hundred thirty-one sharpshooters and one sharpshooter king, but one hundred thirty-two brother sharpshooters of equal rank smile slyly good-naturedly eagerly in the direction of Matern, who, armed with the police

930

major's photograph, is trying to distinguish and select. All resemblance is purely fortuitous. All resemblance is denied. All resemblance is admitted one hundred thirty-two times; for between raised platform and tent roof Sharpshooter Heinrich Osterhues smiles in tiers, kneels sits stands towers-over, wears his sharpshooter's hat tilted slightly to the right, and is photographed one hundred thirty-two times with one flash bulb. A family portrait. One hundred thirty-twolets. "That's all, gentlemen!" cries the photographer. One hundred thirty-two Heinrichs rise chatting lumbering beer-sodden, rise from the festival-photograph platform, all bent upon shaking hands immediately and one hundred thirty-twofold with an old friend from one-hundred-thirty-twofold police-major days: "How's it going? Back on the old stamping ground? Ribs mended O.K.? Those were rugged times all right. All hundred thirty-two of us will lay to that. It was hew to the line, boy, or else. But at least the guys sang when we took 'em in hand. They weren't pampered like nowadays . . ."

Whereupon Matern turns and runs, across beer-sour sawdust. "What's the hurry, man? A meeting like this wants to be celebrated!" The shooting match spews him out. O starry sky, with vanishing points! The tireless Inge and God in His heaven are waiting for him. In His hands and keeping, the Rhine Meadows are streaked with dawn by the time she has calmed him down—her teeth-chattering lover.

The Ninety-first, Halfway Sensible Materniad

What good is his cast-iron head if the walls to dash it against are made pervious on purpose? Is this an occupation: pushing revolving doors? Converting whores? Making holes in Swiss cheese? Who wants to tear open old wounds if the opening of wounds gives pleasure? Or dig a pit for the other guy so he can help you out of it afterward? Shadowboxing? Bending safety pins? Driving nails into solid-rubber enemies? Going through telephone directories or address books, name by name?—Call off the vengeance, Matern! Let Pluto rest by the fireside. Enough de-Nazification! Make your peace with this world; or combine your obligation to heed your heart, spleen, and kidneys with the security of a monthly income. Because you're not lazy. You've always worked full time: making the rounds, crossing-off, making the rounds. You've often strained yourself to the limit and beyond: women to take with you, women to drop. What else can you do, Matern? What have you learned at the mirror and against the wind? To speak loudly and distinctly on the stage. Well then, slip into roles, brush your teeth, knock three times, and get yourself hired: as a character actor, phenotype, Franz or Karl Moor depending on your mood—and announce to all the loges and to the orchestra as well: "But soon I will come among you and hold terrible muster!"

Too bad! Matern isn't prepared yet to make a halfway profitable business of revenge. In Sawatzki's easy chair he hatches out gaping nothings. He drags himself and his kidney stones from room to room. Friends support him. His mistress takes him to the movies. When he goes walking, with dog and on business, no one dares to turn around. What hammer blow will have to stun him before he learns to steer clear of people who hear him, the Grinder, behind them.

And then in 1955, when all the children born in '45, the year peace set in, turn ten years old, a cheap, mass-produced article floods the market. Secretly, though not illicitly, a well-oiled and hence soundless sales organization functions. No newspaper ads herald this hit of the season; in no shop window does it bait the eye; in no toyshops or department stores does this article sell like hotcakes; no mail-order house sends it out postage paid. Instead, peddlers peddle it on fairgrounds, on playgrounds, outside school buildings; wherever children condense; but also outside vocational schools, apprentice-homes and universities, a toy intended for the generation between seven and twenty-one is obtainable.

Not to make an additional mystery out of an already mysterious commodity, the object in question is a pair of glasses. No, not the kind of glasses through which you can study indecent goings-on in different colors and positions. No disreputable manufacturer is out to corrupt the West German postwar youth. No competent authorities or injunctions are called for or necessary. No pastor finds occasion to fling hair-raising parables from the pulpit. And yet the glasses that are offered for sale at strikingly low prices do not serve to correct the usual defects of vision. Glasses of a very different kind, which neither corrupt nor cure, approximately—we have only estimates to go by—one million four hundred thousand pairs of them, make their appearance on the market: price fifty pfennigs. Subsequently, after investigating commissions have had to concern themselves with this article in the provinces of Hesse and Lower Saxony, the official estimates are corroborated: a certain firm of Brauxel & Co., located in Grossgiessen near Hildesheim, has manufactured one million seven hundred forty thousand pairs of the wrongfully incriminated item and succeeded in selling exactly one million four hundred fifty-six thousand three hundred twelve of these mass-produced articles. Not a bad venture in view of the low production costs: crudely stamped plastic. Still, though the glasses are like windowpanes, without any special grind, they must have required long and painstaking research: Brauxel & Co. would seem to have employed the specialized skill of Jena-trained opticians, fugitives from the Democratic Republic. But Brauxel & Co.—a highly reputable firm I might add—is able to prove to both investigating commissions that no optician was working in the laboratory, but that a special mixture, patent applied for, had been brought to the melting point in the small glassworks connected with the enterprise: to the well-known mixture of quartz sand, sodium carbonate, sodium sulphate, and limestone is added a quantity, measured to the gram and therefore secret, of mica, such as may be gained from mica gneiss, mica slate, and mica granite. Thus no Devil's broth, nothing of a forbidden nature, is brewed; scientific data are confirmed by the affidavits of well-known chemists. The proceedings initiated by the provinces of Lower Saxony and Hesse are quashed. And yet there must be something special about the things—caused no doubt by the little mica mirrors. But only the younger generation from seven to twenty-one respond to the gimmick, for there is, in those glasses, a gimmick to which grownups and younger children are impervious.

What are the glasses called? Various names, not all of them developed by Brauxel & Co., are current. Originally the manufacturers present their article as a nameless toy, but once its appeal is obvious, they put out a name or two as slogans for vendors.

Matern, who has gone for a stroll hand in hand with the now eight-year-old Walli, hears of the "miracle glasses" for the first time at the Düsseldorf Christmas fair on Bolkerstrasse. Between the potato pancake booth and a stand selling Christmas stollen, an unobtrusive little man, who might just as well be selling Christmas cookies or cut-rate fountain pens or razor blades, is holding out a half-filled cardboard box.

But neither on the left where fat-saturated odors are meant to lure, nor on the right where powdered sugar is not being spared, are so many customers jostling as around the soon empty cardboard box. The vendor, doubtless a seasonal worker, doesn't shout but whispers: "Miracle glasses. Try them. Look through 'em." But for all its fairytale quality, the name is intended more for the grown-up pocket-book holders; for the nature of the miracle has got around among the younger generation: thirteen-year-old boys and sixteen-year-old girls mostly call the glasses "recognition glasses"; students in their last year of high school, newly licensed automobile mechanics, and students in their first year at the university speak of "knowledge glasses." Less current and probably not of juvenile origin are the terms: "father-recognition glasses" and "mother-recognition glasses" or "family unmaskers."

As the last names suggest, the glasses, which Brauxel & Co. has thrown on the market by the millions, enable the young to see through their families. The glasses uncover, recognize, worse, unmask father and mother, in fact, every adult who has reached the age of thirty. Only those who are not yet thirty or who are over twenty-one in the year '55 remain indifferent and can neither unmask nor be unmasked by their younger brothers and sisters. Is this crude arithmetical hocus-pocus supposed to solve the problem of the generations? Are the indifferent—nine complete

933

age groups—written off as incapable of essential knowledge? Has the firm of Brauxel & Co. ambitions; or is it not, quite simply, that modern market research has succeeded in spotting and satisfying the needs of the rising postwar generation?

On this controversial point as well, the counsel of the firm Brauxel & Co. has been able to produce affidavits whose acuteness and sociological insight dissipate the misgivings of two investigating commissions. "The coincidence between product and consumer," says one of these affidavits, "can be calculated only up to the moment of delivery, at which time the consumer begins to produce independently and to transform the acquired product into his means of production, in other words, into an inalienable possession."

Let skeptics hold their peace; for whatever motives may have been at work when it was decided to produce and distribute miracle glasses, the success of this passing fad is unquestionable and modified the social structure of West Germany considerably, regardless of whether the structural change, or consumer modification as Schelsky calls it, was intended or not.

The young people acquire knowledge. Even if over half of all the glasses sold are destroyed shortly after purchase, because the parents suspect that there's something fishy about these glasses, this leaves some seven hundred thousand eyeglass wearers, who are able at their leisure to form a complete picture of their parents. Favorable moments arise, for instance, after supper, on family excursions, or while Papa is running around in circles with the lawn mower. The presence of miracle glasses is registered throughout the Federal Republic; but alarming concentrations occur only in the provinces of North Rhine-Westphalia, Hesse, and Lower Saxony, whereas in the southwest and in Bavaria sales amount to no more than a steady but slow trickle. Only in the province of Schleswig-Holstein are there whole districts (Kiel and Lübeck are exceptions) which show no evidence of glasses, for there, in the districts of Eutin, Rendsburg, and Neumünster, the authorities have gone so far as to confiscate the glasses by the carton, straight from the wholesaler. An injunction was issued *post factum*. The firm of Brauxel & Co. was able to collect damages; but only in the cities and the vicinity of Itzehoe have the glasses found a clientele able and willing to form a picture, a picture of their parents.

But what exactly is seen through the miracle glasses? Inquiries have thrown little light on the question. Most of the youngsters who have formed, or are still engaged in rounding out, a picture of their parents, are reluctant to talk. At the most they admit that the miracle glasses have opened their eyes. Interviews on athletic fields or outside movie houses tend to go roughly as follows: "Would you kindly tell us, young man, how our glasses have affected you?"

"That's quite a question. Well, after wearing the glasses a few times, I knew my old man pretty well."

"It's the details we're interested in. Please speak freely and without reservation. We are from the firm of Brauxel & Co. In the interest of our customers we should be glad to perfect our glasses . . ."

"They don't need any perfecting. They're just fine. I looked through them a few times and now I know what's what. Nothing could be any clearer."

All those questioned answer evasively, but this much is certain: a young person sees his father differently with the naked eye and with an eye that takes aim through miracle glasses: the miracle glasses show youthful wearers varied images of their parents' past, often, though it takes a little patience, in chronological sequence. Episodes which are kept from the younger generation for one reason or another are made palpably clear. Here again questioning by the agents of Brauxel & Co., or by the school authorities, has not proved very fruitful. Nevertheless all indications are that, surprisingly enough, no staggering quantities of erotic secrets are aired—little beyond the customary escapades. The scenes that recur over and over again in the twin spheres of the father-recognition glasses are acts of violence performed tolerated instigated eleven twelve thirteen years ago: murders, often by the hundreds. Aiding and abetting. Smoking cigarettes and looking on while. Certified decorated applauded murderers. Murder motives become leitmotives. With murderers at one table, in the same boat, bed, and officers' club. Toasts, emergency directives. Record entries. Blowing on rubber stamps. Sometimes mere signatures and wastebaskets. Many roads lead to. Silence as well as words can. Every father has at least one to hide. Many lie buried curtained siloed, as if they had never happened until in the eleventh postwar year miracle glasses appear on the market.

No isolated cases. Here and there a young person consented to the statistical use of his "knowledge" but sons and daughters alike kept the concrete details secret, just as fathers and mothers had been discreet even in their dreams. Feelings of shame may have inhibited the youngsters. A boy who resembles his father physically may fear that people will infer other similarities. Furthermore, students are disinclined to jeopardize their educational careers, financed by their parents often at a great sacrifice, by calling their parents to account. Surely not the firm of Brauxel & Co., but someone who developed the miracle glasses, who obtained mica mirrors from gneiss and added them to the usual glass mixture, may have expected and even hoped that the eyeglass campaign would bring radical results. But a revolt of the children against their parents did not materialize. Family feeling, instinct of self-preservation, cold self-interest, and for that matter blind love of those who had been exposed prevented a revolution which might have netted our century a few headlines: "New edition of children's crusade!—Cologne Airfield seized by teen-ager organization!—Martial Law Decreed.—Bloody clashes in Bonn and Bad Godesberg.—Not until early morning did police detachments and Bundeswehr teams succeed in.—The Hessian Radio is still in the hands of. —To date, 47,000 young persons, including eight-year-old children, have been.—Suicide wave among youngsters cornered in the area of Lauenburg, Elbe.—France honors extradition treaty.—The fourteen- to sixteen-year-old ringleaders have already signed a confession.—Cleanup operations concluded. Tomorrow all stations will broadcast an address by.— The search for the Communist agents who instigated and led the uprising is being continued.—After an initial slump the stock market seems.— German securities again in demand in Zürich and London.—December 6 proclaimed a day of national mourning."

Nothing of the kind. Cases of illness are reported. The parental image is too much for a certain number of girls and boys: They leave home: emigration, Foreign Legion, the usual. Some return. In Hamburg four suicides are registered in rapid succession, in Hanover two, in Cassel six, causing Brauxel & Co. to suspend delivery of the so-called miracle glasses shortly before Easter.

The past flares up for a few months and then blacks out—forever, it is to be hoped. Only Matern, who is here being spoken of in Materniads, sees the daylight in spite of inner resistance; for when at the Düsseldorf Christmas fair he buys his daughter Walli a pair of these miracle glasses, the child puts them right on: Walli had just been laughing and nibbling Christmas cookies, now she sees Matern through the glasses, drops cookies and gold-beribboned package, starts to scream, and screaming runs away.

Matern with the dog after her. But both of them—for Walli sees the dog too accurately and terribly—become more and more terrifying in the eyes of the child, whom they overtake shortly before the Rating Gate. Passers-by feel sorry for the screaming little girl and demand that Matern identify himself as her father. Complications! Words begin to fall: "He was trying to rape the child, that's a sure thing. Just look at him. It's written over his face! Swine!" Then, at last, a policeman breaks up the crowd. Identities are established. Witnesses claim to have seen or not seen this and that. Walli is screaming and still has the glasses on. A patrol car deposits Matern, Pluto, and the horrified child at the Sawatzki residence. But even in the familiar apartment, surrounded by all her expensive toys, Walli doesn't feel at home, for she still has the glasses on: Walli sees not only Matern and the dog, but also Jochen and Inge Sawatzki with new eyes, accurately and terribly. Her screaming drives Pluto under the table, turns the grownups to stone, and fills the nursery. Intermittent words, grabled by screams yet charged with meaning. Walli stammers something about piles of snow and blood dripping in the snow, about teeth, about the poor nice fat man, whom Papa and Uncle Walter and other men, who all look awful, are hitting, hitting the whole time with their fists, most of all Uncle Walter. The nice fat man; he's not standing up any more, he's lying in the snow, because Uncle Walter . . . "Don't! It's not right. Hitting and being cruel to people flowers animals. It's forbidden. People who do that don't go to heaven. God sees it all. Stop stop . . ."

Only when Inge removes the glasses from the face of the delirious child does she calm down a little; but hours later, in her little bed and surrounded by all her dolls, she is still sobbing. Temperature is taken, she has a fever. A doctor is called. He speaks neither of incipient flu nor of the usual children's ailments, but thinks the crisis must have been brought on by a shock, something impossible to put your finger on, she needs rest, the adults should keep away from her. If she doesn't get better, she'll have to be taken to a hospital.

Which is just what happens. For two days the fever refuses to come down and indefatigably, without fear of repetitiousness, spawns the wintry scene: snow lies, blood drips, fists talk, fat man falls, tumbles time and again, into what? into the snow, because Uncle Walter and Papa too, into the snow, and so many teeth are spat out, one two five thirteen thirty-two!—No one can bear to count them any more. And so Walli with her two favorite dolls is taken to St. Mary's Hospital. The men, Sawatzki and Matern, don't sit beside the intolerably empty child's bed; they sit in the kitchen, drinking out of water glasses until they slide off their chairs. Jochen has retained his preference for the kitchen-livingroom environment: in the daytime he is a businessman, correctly clad in well-nigh wrinkleless material; in the evening he shuffles in bedroom slippers from icebox to stove and plucks at suspenders. In the daytime he speaks his brisk business German, to which vestiges of military jargon lend pithiness and time-saving succinctness: "Let's cut the goldbricking, let's wade in!" So, in his time, spoke Guderian, the military genius, and today Sawatzki takes a leaf from his book when he decides to flood the market with a certain single-breasted number; but toward evening, in kitchen and slippers, he eats crisp potato pancakes and speaks at great length and in broad dialect of the good old days and what it was like back home in the north. Matern too learns to appreciate the cozy warmth of the kitchen-livingroom. Tearfully two old buddies clap each other on the back. Emotion and unadulterated schnapps bring tears to their eyes. They push halfhearted feelings of guilt back and forth on the kitchen table, and quarrel only about dates. Matern says something or other happened in June '37. Sawatzki disagrees: "That was exactly in September. Who'da suspected the end was gonna be so rotten." But both are convinced that even then they were against it: "When you come right down to it, our sturm was kind of a hideout for the inner emikrashun. Don'tcha remember the way we slung the philosophy at the bar? Willy Eggers was there, the Dulleck brothers, naturally Fränzchen Wollschläger, Bublitz, Hoppe, and Otto Warnke. And you went on gassing about Being, until we wuz all nuts. Shoilem boil 'em! And now? Now what? Now a guy's own kid comes home saying: murderer murderer!"

After one of these laments, the kitchen-livingroom environment is as still as a mouse for a minute or two, except perhaps for the coffee water singing its peace-on-earthly song, until Sawatzki starts up again: "And all in all, what do you think, Walter, did we deserve that? Did we? No, we didn't. We don't."

When Walli was discharged from the hospital exactly four weeks later, the so-called miracle glasses had vanished from the apartment. Neither did Inge Sawatzki throw them in the garbage pail nor did Jochen and Walter demolish them in the kitchen-livingroom; maybe the dog chewed up, swallowed, digested them. But Walli asks no questions about her missing toy. Quietly the little girl sits at her desk and has to catch up, because she has missed a lot of school. Grown solemn and a little peaked, she can already multiply and add. All hope that the child has forgotten why she has grown so solemn and peaked, why she isn't plump and bumptious any more. Because that's what Walli was in the hospital for: good care to make Walli forget. Little by little this becomes the first principle of all concerned: Forget! Maxims are embroidered on handkerchiefs, pillow slips, and hat linings: Learn to forget. Forgetfulness is natural. The mind should be occupied by pleasant memories and not by nasty tormenting thoughts. It's hard to remember constructively. Ergo, people need something they can believe in: God, for instance; or if you can't manage that, there's beauty, progress, the good in man, etcetera. "We, here in the West, believe implicitly in freedom, always have."

In any event, activity! And what activity is more productive than forgetting? Matern buys a large eraser, stations himself on a kitchen chair, and begins to erase the names, crossed off and not crossed off, from his heart, spleen, and kidneys. As for Pluto, that four-legged hunk of past, feeble with age though still running around, he'd be glad to sell him, send him to a rest home for dogs, erase him; but who'd buy an elderly hound? Moreover, mother and child are opposed: not for any price would Inge Sawatzki. She's got used to the dog in the meantime. Walli cries and promises to get sick again if the dog. So, black and ineluctable, he stays. And the names, too, offer stubborn resistance to Matern's big eraser. For instance: while he effaces one and blows eraser crumbs from his spleen, he stumbles, in the course of his newspaper reading, across another, who writes articles about the theater. That's what comes of doing something else while erasing. Every article has an author. This one is a man of the theater, who has pondered his way to wisdom. He says and writes: "Just as man needs the theater, so, and in equal measure, the theater needs man." But a few lines later he deplores: "Today man finds himself in a state of increasing alienation." Yet this he knows for certain: "The history of mankind has its most exemplary parallel in the history of the theater." But if, as he anticipates: "The three-dimensional theater should once again flatten into a picture-frame stage," this man, who signs himself R. Z., can only second the great Lessing in crying out: "To what end have we toiled so bitterly to achieve dramatic form?" His article embodies at once a warning and an exhortation: "The theater does not stop when man ceases to be man; it is the other way around: Close the theaters and man will cease to be man!" In general Herr Rudolf Zander—Matern remembers him from his theatrical days—is hipped on the word "man." For example: "The man of coming decades." Or: "All this calls for a stormy reckoning with the problem of man." Or in a polemical vein: "Dehumanized theater? Never!" Be that as it may, R. Z., or Dr. Rolf Zander—onetime director of the Stadttheater in Schwerin—has forsaken the "theatrical mission"; of late he has been with the West German radio in an advisory function, an activity which does not deter him from writing articles for the Saturday supplements of several important newspapers: "It is not enough to show man the catastrophe; violent emotion remains an end in itself unless it culminates in exegesis, unless the purifying effect of catharsis tears the wreath from nihilism and lends meaning to chaos."

Salvation twinkles humanely between the lines. There's a man for Matern to turn to, all the more so as he knows him well from former days and carries the name of Rolf Zander around with him, incised somewhere: either in the heart or in the spleen or in kidney script; no eraser, not even the newly purchased one, can efface it.

Everybody has an address. R. Zander is no exception. He works in the beautiful new Radio Building in Cologne; and he resides—so whispers the phone book—in Cologne-Mariendorf.

With or without dog? To judge—or to ask advice in a situation of human-chaotic distress? With revenge in my baggage or with a little human question? Both. Matern cannot desist from. He is looking simultaneously for work and revenge. Carnage and entreaty slumber in the same fist. With identically black dog he calls on friend and enemy. Not that he makes a beeline to the door, saying: "Here I am, Zander, for better or for worse!"; several times he creeps—Don't turn around—through the old park, determined to strike, if not the former theater director, then at least the trees in his park.

One stormy evening in August—all this is perfectly true: it was August, it was hot, and a storm came up—he vaults the wall with dog and lands on the soft ground of Zander's park. He bears neither ax nor saw but a white powder. Oh, Matern has a hand with poison! He is experienced: exactly three hours later Harras was dead. No sprinkling of nux vomica; plain rat poison. This time it's plant poison. From tree to tree he scurries with dog shadow. A dance of nature worship. Minuet and gavotte determine the sequence of steps in the dusky, goblin-inhabited, ninefold green, nymphean lovers' maze of Zander's park. A figure bows low, a hand is held out: on dragon-thick roots he strews his powder without muttering spells. However, Matern grinds as usual:

> Don't turn around:
> the Grinder's around.

But how can the trees be expected to! They don't even feel like rustling, for not a breeze is stirring under the sultry sky. No magpie warns. No jay denounces. Moss-covered baroque putti are in no mood for giggling. Even Diana, with hunting dog at hastening heel, is disinclined to turn around and bend her unfailing bow; out of a dusky thinking-grotto Herr Zander in person addresses the winged powder strewer: "Gracious! Do my eyes deceive me? Matern, is it you? Goodness, and what amiable occupation are you engaged in? Putting chemical fertilizer on the roots of my giants? Aren't they big enough for you? But you've always been drawn to the colossal! Chemical fertilizer! How absurd and yet delightful. But you haven't taken the weather into account. Any minute a storm is going to pour down on us mortals and the park. The very first shower will wash away the traces of your horticultural enthusiasm. But let us not tarry! The first gusts of wind herald the storm. Undoubtedly the first drops have been released on high, they are coming, coming . . . May I invite you, as well as that magnificent specimen of a dog, to my modest home!"

A light tug at a reluctant arm, guidance in the direction of shelter. The last few steps, now over gravel paths, are rapid: only on the veranda is the conversation resumed: "Gracious, what a small world it is! How often I've wondered: what can Matern be doing? That child of nature, that—begging your pardon—ecstatic drinker?—And here you are, standing in my library, feeling my furniture, looking around, and your dog as well, both casting shadows in the lamplight, a warm human presence. Welcome!"

Herr Zander's housekeeper hastens to brew strong manly tea. Brandy is in readiness. Environment, undescribed, gains the upper hand again. While outside, as Herr Zander would put it, the storm hits the stage, a useful conversation about the theater runs its course in dry and comfortable armchairs. "My dear friend—you've done well to come right out with your grievances—but you're mistaken and you do me a grave injustice.

Admitted: it was I, I couldn't help myself, who canceled your contract with the Schwerin Stadttheater. However, the reason why all this was done to you—and had to be—was not, as you now suppose, political, but—how shall I put it?—purely and simply alcoholic. It just wouldn't do. Yes, yes, we all of us enjoyed a glass or two. But you went to extremes. Quite frankly: even today in our more or less democratic Federal Republic, any responsible director or stage manager would have to do the same: you came to rehearsals drunk, you came to performances drunk and without your lines. Yes, of course I remember your ringing speeches. No objection, not the slightest even then, to their content or expressiveness, but plenty, then and today as well, to the place and time of your resounding declamations. Nevertheless, my hat off to you: You pronounced, a hundred times, what the rest of us may have thought but didn't dare to state in public. I admired your magnificent courage, I still do; the freedom with which you spoke of certain very delicate matters would have been highly effective if not for your advanced alcoholic state. As it was, denunciations, mostly from stagehands, piled up on my desk. I stalled, smoothed things over, but in the end I had to take action, not least in order to protect you, yes, protect you; for if I hadn't, by a simple disciplinary measure, given you an opportunity to leave Schwerin, which had gradually got to be a very hot place for you, Lord, I don't like to think what would have happened to you. You know, Matern, when those people struck, it wasn't with kid gloves. The individual counted for nothing." Outside, the stage thunder doesn't miss a cue. Inside, Matern ponders what might have become of him but for the philanthropic Dr. Zander. Outside, wholesome rain washes away the plant-killing poison from the roots of age-old all-knowing trees. Inside, Pluto sighs out of dog dreams. Outside, Shakespearean rain functions like clockwork. Naturally a clock is ticking in the dryness too, no, three costly timepieces are ticking at once, variously pitched, into the silence between former theater director and former *jeune premier*. Peals of thunder do not traverse the footlights. Moistening of lips. Massaging of scalps. Inside, illuminated by outside lightning: Rolf Zander, an experienced host, gets back into the conversation: "Good Lord, Matern! Do you remember how you introduced yourself to us? Franz Moor, Act Five, Scene 1: Slavish wisdom, slavish fears! You were magnificent. No no, I mean it, shattering! An Iffland couldn't have wrung such horror from his entrails. A discovery, fresh from Danzig, which has given us full many an outstanding mime—think of Söhnker, or even, if you wish, of Dieter Borsche. Fresh and promising, you came to us. If I'm not mistaken, the excellent Gustav Nord, so lovable both as a man and as a colleague, who was to perish so wretchedly at the end of the war, was your teacher. Wait: You attracted my attention in a beastly play by Billinger. Didn't you play the son of Donata Opferkuch? Right, and

La Bargheer saved the show with her Donata. I could still die laughing when I think of Fritzchen Blumhoff playing the Prince of Arcadia, in '36-'37 I think it was, with his excruciating Saxon accent. Then there was Carl Kliever, the indestructible Dora Ottenburg. Heinz Brede, whom I remember in a very decent performance of *Nathan the Wise,* and of course your teacher: what a versatile Polonius! A fine Shakespearean actor and magnificent at Shaw too. Mighty courageous of your Stadttheater to put on *Saint Joan* as late as '38. I can only repeat: if it weren't for the provinces! What was it you people called the building? That's it. The Coffee Mill! I hear it was totally destroyed. Hasn't been rebuilt. But I'm told they're planning to on the same site and in the same neoclassical style. The Poles are amazing, always were. The heart of the Old City, too. I hear that Langgasse, Frauengasse, and Jopengasse have already been laid out. Why, I'm from the same neck of the woods: Memel. Am I thinking of? No, my friend, never marry the same. The spirit that presides over our West German theaters really doesn't. Theatrical mission? Theater as a medium of mass communication? The stage as a mere generic concept? And man as the measure of all things? Where everything becomes a purpose in itself and nothing culminates in exegesis? What of purification? Catharsis?—Gone, my dear Matern—or perhaps not, for my work on the radio satisfies me completely and leaves me time for short essays that have wanted to be written for years. And what about you? Enthusiasm gone? Act Five, Scene 1: Slavish wisdom, slavish fears!"

Matern sulks and drinks tea. Knotted in his entrails, twined round heart, spleen, and tortured kidneys, the rosary chatters: Opportunist! Potential Nazi! Phony! Opportunist! Potential Nazi! But over the teacup a sheepish voice: "Theater? Never again. Self-confidence gone? Possibly. There's also the leg injury. Hardly noticeable, yes I know, but on the stage? The rest is in good shape, organ of speech, energy, enthusiasm. Ah yes, everything but the opportunity."

Then, after three Empire clocks have been permitted to tick for a minute or two undisturbed, the redeeming words fall from Rolf Zander's mouth. The rather delicate little man paces the floor of the suitable room, speaking softly, sagely, sympathetically. Outside, in the park, trees drip a reminder of the short-lived August storm. As Dr. Zander talks, his hand caresses book spines on broad shelves, or he takes out a book, opens it, hesitates, imparts a quotation which fits easily into his monologue, puts the book away booklovingly. Outside, the dusk brings the trees closer together. Inside, Zander comes to rest among the fruits of a lifelong collector's passion—Balinese dance masks, demonic Chinese marionettes, colored morris house-keeper comes in with fresh tea and pastry; she too a rare piece like the Empire clocks, first editions, and musical instruments from Hindustan. Matern sprawls in the armchair. The standing lamp

942

communicates with his polished skull. Pluto makes rattling sounds in his sleep: a dog as old as the trees outside. Inside, Zander speaks of his work on the radio. He takes care of the early morning hours and bedtime: children's program and late night program. No contradiction for Zander, on the contrary. He speaks of tensions, of building bridges between. We must find our way back if we are to. At one time Matern too was allowed to sound off on a children's radio program. He was Little Red Riding Hood's Wolf; he devoured the seven kids. "Splendid!" Zander joins the threads: "We need voices, voices like yours, Matern. Voices that stand up in space. Voices that resemble the elements. Voices that carry, voices that bend the bow. Voices that give resonance to our past. For instance, we've been working up a new program, thinking of calling it 'Discussion with the Past,' or better still, 'DISCUSSION WITH OUR PAST.' A young colleague of mine, a countryman of yours, incidentally—talented, dangerously so, I'm almost inclined to think—is trying to develop new forms of radio entertainment. I can easily imagine that in our station you, my dear Matern, you in particular, might work your way into a vocation commensurate with your talents. Urgent search for truth. The eternal question of man. Whence come we—whither are we going? Silence has barred the way, but now speech will open the gate!—What do you say?"

Thereupon the age-old dog awakens hesitantly, and Matern says yes. Shake on it?—Shake on it. Day after tomorrow, 10 A.M. at the Radio Building?—Day after tomorrow at ten. But be punctual.—Punctual and sober. May I call you a cab?—Dr. Rolf Zander is entitled to charge the West German Radio. All expenses are deductible. All risks are tax-exempt. Every Matern finds his Zander.

He speaks rumbles roars. His voice enters every home. Matern, the popular radio speaker. The children dream of him and his voice, which awakens all their terrors. It will go rumbling on and little children grown into shriveling old folks will say: "In my childhood we had a radio uncle, whose voice gave me, took away from me, inspired me, forced me, so that sometimes even now, but that's how it is with any number of Maternoids, who in those days." But right now adults, upon whom other voices have set their stamp, make use of Matern's voice as an aid in child rearing; when the kids act up, their mother threatens: "Do you want me to turn the radio on again and let the wicked uncle speak?"

Over medium wave and short wave, a bogeyman can be brought into the room. His voice is in demand. And other stations want Matern to speak, rumble, and roar in their broadcasting rooms. His colleagues, it is true, remark in private that his pronunciation is bad, that he lacks training, but they have to admit that his voice has a certain something: "That atmospheric quality, that barbaric uncouthness, that voracious naïveté is worth its weight in gold—are sick of perfection nowadays."

Matern buys a date book, for every day, sometimes here sometimes there and at specified hours, his voice is recorded. He speaks rumbles roars mostly over the West German Radio, sometimes over the Hessian Radio, never over the Bavarian, occasionally on the North German, with alacrity and in Low German on the Bremen Station, very recently on the South German Radio in Stuttgart, and, when time permits, on the Southwestern Radio. He steers clear of trips to West Berlin. Consequently, RIAS and the Free Berlin Radio have had to drop their plans for live broadcasts that would rely on the very special character of Matern's voice, but within the exchange program they relay Matern's children's broadcasts from the West German Radio Station in Cologne, where his precious voice is at home.

He has set up housekeeping, he has an address: new building, two rooms, incinerator, kitchenette, built-in cupboards, bar, wide couch; for over the weekend inalienable Ingewife turns up, alone or with Walli. Sawatzki, the gentlemen's outfitter, sends his best. The dog is in the way. It's high time they had a little privacy. The mutt is a nuisance—like a grandmother who can't contain her water. Though still alert and well trained. How can there be any domestic well-being with this animal on the scene? Bleary-eyed, gone to fat in places, and even so, the skin sags on his neck. Still, no one says: "He ought to be done away with." On the contrary, Matern, Ingewife, and Wallichild are agreed: "Let him enjoy his pittance. Our Pluto won't be with us very long anyway. While there's enough for us, there'll always be enough for him." And Matern remembers at his shaving mirror: "He was always a friend in need. Stuck by me in hard times, when I was restless and unstable, when I was chasing a phantom that had many names and yet refused to be captured. The dragon. Evil. Leviathan. The Nothing. Errancy."

Yet occasionally, for all his fine-checked vests, Matern sighs over his omelet. At such times his hunter's eye excepts Ingewife and searches the wall for wallpaper script. But the Bauhaus pattern is unequivocal, and despite their ambivalent modernism the framed prints disclose no secrets. Or there's a pounding in the radiators, Matern pricks up an ear, Pluto stirs, the signals stop, and once again sighs blow copious bubbles. Not until early spring, when the first flies begin to stir, does he find an avocation that makes him forget to sigh for hours on end. Even the doughty little tailor started out with a flyswatter and went on to capture the unicorn. No one will ever know the names he gives to what he catches on the panes, what names he cracks between fingers, the names of his transmigrated enemies, from whom he plucks flyleg after flyleg and lastly the wings, without regret. The sighing persists, wakes up with Matern, goes to bed with him, sits with him at tables in the Radio Building canteen, while he is rehearsing his scoundrelly lines for the last time.

944

Because he'll be going on the air in a minute. Matern will have to speak rumble roar. He will have to abandon this half glass of beer. Around him the ladies of the forthcoming programs: the woman's touch. The farmer's voice. Music in the afternoon. The good word for Sunday. Band music. Fifteen minutes of meditation. Our sisters and brothers behind the Iron Curtain. Sports news and racetrack news. Poetry before midnight. Water-level report. Jazz. The Gürzenich Orchestra. The children's program. Colleagues and their colleagues: that one over there, or that one, or the one in the checked shirt without a tie. You know him. Or you might know him. Wasn't he the one who in '43 on the Mius front? Or the one in black and white with the milkshake? Didn't he once? Or wouldn't he have? The whole lot of them! Checked flies, black-and-white flies. Fat blue-bottles over skat chess crosswordpuzzles. Interchangeable. Keep cropping up. O Matern, slowly cicatrizing names are still itching you. There he sighs in serenely bored broadcasting room, and a colleague who hears Matern's heavily laden sigh rising from the center of the earth, pats him on the back: "Man, Matern. What have you got to sigh about? You have every reason to be pleased. You're working full time. Happened to turn on the agony box yesterday, and whom do I hear? This morning I look into the children's room. They've moved the box in there. The kids are sitting there with their tongues hanging out, and whose voice do I hear? You lucky bastard!"

Matern, the booming radio pedagogue, speaks rumbles roars as a permanent robber, wolf, rabble rouser, or Judas. Hoarse as a polar explorer in a snowstorm. Louder than wind velocity 12. As a coughing prisoner with rattling radio chains. As a grumbling miner just before the awful explosion. As the ragingly ambitious mountain climber on the inadequately organized Himalaya expedition. As the gold prospector, the refugee from the East zone, the martinet, the SS guard, the Foreign Legionary, the blasphemer, the slave overseer, and a reindeer in a Christmas play; this last role he has played once before, on the stage as a matter of fact, in his dramatic school days.

Harry Liebenau, his countryman, who directs the children's program under Dr. R. Zander's guidance, says to him: "I'm rather inclined to think that was my first meeting with you. Stadttheater. Children's show. The little Brunies girl, you remember, danced the part of the Snow Queen, and you did the talking reindeer. Made an enormous impression on me, a lasting impression. A fixed point in my development, so to speak. Decisive childhood experience. All sorts of things can be traced back to it."

That shithead with his file-card memory. Wherever he goes stands sits, always shuffling cards. Nothing he hasn't got the dope on: Proust and Henry Miller; Dylan Thomas and Karl Kraus; quotations from Adorno and sales figures; collector of details and tracker down of references; objective onlooker and layer-bare of cores; archive hound and connoisseur of environments; knows who thinks left and who has written right; writes asthmatic stuff about the difficulty of writing; flashbacker and time-juggler; caller-into-question and wise guy; but no writers' congress can dispense with his gift of formulation, his urge to recapitulate, his memory. And the way he looks at me: Interesting case! He thinks I'm grist for his mill. He pinpoints me, closely written, on file cards. Seems to think he knows all about me, because he saw me that time as a talking reindeer and maybe twice in uniform. He was much too young to. When Eddi and I. He couldn't have been more than. But his kind think they know. That capacity for patient listening, for playing the gumshoes with a knowing smile: "Never mind, Matern, I know. If I'd been born a couple of years sooner, I'd have fallen for it just like you. I'm certainly the last one to moralize. My generation, you know, has seen a thing or two. Besides, you adequately demonstrated that you could also. Someday we ought to go over the whole thing objectively and without the usual resentment. Maybe in the 'Discussion' series we've been planning. How does it appeal to you? These children's programs may be useful, but they can't satisfy us in the. Noises, to help people put their children to bed. When you come right down to it, they're nothing but ground-out hokum. The beep-beep between programs is more meaningful. Why not put some life on the air? What we need is facts. How about really spilling your guts? Unburdening your heart. Stuff that hits you in the kidneys!"

Only the spleen is missing. And what the asshole will wear! English custom-made shoes and ski sweater. Maybe a homo too. If I could only remember the guy. Goes on the whole time about his cousin and blinks at me: suggestively. Says his father was the carpenter with the dog— "Hm, you know!"—"And my cousin Tulla—her real name was Ursula —was crazy about you, back in the shore battery, remember, and later on in Kaiserhafen." He even claims that I was his gunnery instructor— "The Number 6 mans the fuze setter"—and that I introduced him to Heidegger's calendar mottoes—"Being withdraws, losing itself in the . . ." The guy has collecte more facts on the subject of Matern than Matern himself could dream up. Yet smooth and affable on the surface. Just thirty, going fat around the chin, and always ready for a joke. He'd have done fine as a Gestapo dick. He dropped in on me recently— ostensibly to go over a part with me—and what does he do? He grabs Pluto by the muzzle and feels his teeth or what's left of them. Like a vet. And with an air of mystery: "Strange, very strange. The stop too, and the line between withers and croup. Old as the animal is—my guess is twenty or more dog years—it's obvious from the structure of the fore-quarters and the excellent carriage of the ears. Tell me, Matern, where did you dig up that dog? No, better still, we'll discuss the question publicly. In my opinion this is a situation—I've told you about my pet idea—that ought to be developed dynamically and in public. But not in a dull naturalistic vein. The subject calls for formal ingenuity. If you want to hold an audience, you've got to stand your intellect on its head but still let it declaim. A kind of classical drama. Boiled down to one act, but keeping the good old structure: exposition peripeteia catastrophe. Here's how I visualize the set: a clearing in the woods, beeches if you like, birds twittering. You remember Jäschkental Forest, don't you? Well then: the clearing around the Gutenberg monument. We'll throw out old Gutenberg. But we'll keep the temple. And where the father of the printed book used to be, we'll put you. That's right, you, for a starter we drop you, the phenotype Matern, into the temple. So you're standing there under the roof, looking toward the Erbsberg, two hundred and fifty feet above sea level. On the other side of the Erbsberg there's Steffensweg, villa after villa, but we won't show that, only one set, the clearing. Facing the former Gutenberg monument, we'll put up a grandstand for the public, big enough for, well, in round numbers, thirty-two persons. All chicken and young people between the ages of ten and twenty-one. To the left we might have a small platform for the discussion leader. And Pluto—amazing animal, troubling resemblance—the dog can sit beside his master."

And that's exactly how this character—with hardly any musical trimmings—sets up his show. Zander is wildly enthusiastic, all he can talk about is this "exciting new form of broadcast." From the start he detects—"over and above the radio"—possibilities for the theater: "Neither picture-frame nor three-dimensional stage. Orchestra and stage merge for all time. After a centuries-long monologue, man finds a way back to dialogue; nay, more—this great Western debate warrants a new hope of exegesis and catharsis, interpretation and purification."

Rolf Zander points, in no end of articles, to the future; but the wisenheimer is thinking entirely of today. He isn't out to save the theater from subsidized stagnation, but to crucify Matern and dog. He is knitting a pitfall, but, questioned as to his intentions, he lays it on smoothly, confidentially: "Believe me, Matern, with your help we will work out a valid technique for getting at the truth. Not only for you, but for every one of our fellow men, this is a matter of vital necessity: we must break through between master and dog, design a window that will give us back our perspective; for even I—you can tell by my modest literary efforts—lack the vital grip, the quivering flesh of reality; the technique is there but not the substance: I've been unable to capture the this-is-how-it-was, the substantial reality that throws a shadow. Help me, Matern, or I'll lose myself in the subjunctive."

And this play is enacted under trees. The fellow has even succeeded in scaring up some beeches and a cast-iron temple, in which the phenotype Johannes Gutenberg waits for his relief. For six weeks, not counting rehearsals, Matern with dog is squeezed to the last drop in the presence of a changing audience. The final manuscript, with which this wisenheimer and his Dr. Rudolf Zander have tinkered a bit, but solely for artistic reasons, reads as follows. Matern—"You're an actor after all!"—is expected to memorize the main part, so as to be able to speak, rumble, roar it on the specified recording date.

An Open Forum

PRODUCER: West German Broadcasting Station, Cologne.
SCRIPT: R. Zander and H. Liebenau.
DATE OF BROADCAST: (approximate) May 8 1957.
PARTICIPANTS IN THE DISCUSSION:
    HARRY L.—Discussion leader.
    WALLI S.—Assistant with miracle glasses.
    WALTER MATERN.—The Topic under discussion.
    SUPPORTING ROLE: Pluto, the black shepherd.

Thirty-two children and young people of the postwar generation participate more or less actively in the open forum. None is under ten or over twenty-one.

TIME: Approximately one year ago, when the so-called miracle glasses, or knowledge glasses, were withdrawn from the market.

SCENE: An oval clearing in a beech forest. To the right rises a grandstand in four tiers, on which the children and young people, boys and girls, take their places without formality. A platform to the left bears a table, behind which sit the discussion leader and his assistant. To one side a blackboard. Between grandstand and platform, but somewhat farther to the rear, a small cast-iron temple with chain garlands and a mushroom roof. Three granite steps lead up to the temple.

Inside the temple a cast-iron statue—obviously of Johannes Gutenberg—is laid on its side by movingmen, wrapped in woolen blankets, and finally carried away. "Heave-ho," the workmen call to each other. A hubbub among the younger generation.

The discussion leader spurs on the workers with such cries as: "We've got to get started, gentlemen. The old man can't be any heavier than a Bechstein piano. You can have breakfast as soon as the temple is clear."

Over it all the twittering of birds.

As the movers exit, Matern enters the clearing with a black shepherd.

Walli S., the assistant, a little girl of ten, removes a pair of glasses from their case, but does not put them on.

948

Matern's entrance is greeted by enthusiastic stamping on the part of the younger generation. He does not know where to go.

The discussion leader points to the temple and the younger generation explains, speaking in chorus: "Matern will have to stay in the printer's house today. In Gutenberg's old place Matern will show his face! Matern just loves to answer questions. A topic will be discussed, where stood old Johann in his rust! With man and beast, we'll have a discussion feast! Matern has come. Welcome! Welcome!"

The verses of greeting are followed by applause and stamping. The assistant toys with her glasses. The discussion leader rises, makes a gesture that sweeps away all sound except for the twittering of the birds, and opens the discussion:

DISCUSSION LEADER: Fellow participants in this forum! Young friends! The word has become flesh again and has come to dwell among us. In other words: we have come here to discuss. Discussion is our generation's medium of expression par excellence. In former times discussions were carried on at the family board, in circles of friends, on playgrounds: they were secret, muffled, or aimlessly playful; but today we have succeeded in liberating the great, dynamic, never-ending discussion from the four walls that formerly confined it, and in putting it out into the open, under the sky, among the trees!

A BOY: The discussion leader. has forgotten the birds!

CHORUS OF BOYS AND GIRLS: A discussion feast
      with man and beast.

DISCUSSION LEADER: Yes indeed! They, too, the sparrows, blackbirds, and wood pigeons, answer us. Rookedykroo, rookedykroo! All speak! All demand to be informed. Every stone gives us information.

CHORUS: What's the stone's name today?
   Stones are people too, I say.

TWO BOYS: If it's Fritz, let him go,
   if it's Emil, let him blow.
   Let Hans and Ludwig run away,
   if it's Walter, let him stay.

DISCUSSION LEADER: That's it! Walter Matern has come among us in order that we may discuss him through and through. And when I say "him," I mean the reality that casts a shadow and leaves footprints.

A BOY: Has he come of his own free will?

DISCUSSION LEADER: Because we are alive, we discuss. We do not act, we . . .

CHORUS: . . . discuss!

DISCUSSION LEADER: We do not die . . .

CHORUS: We discuss death.

A BOY: I ask again: Has Matern come of his own free will?

DISCUSSION LEADER: We do not love . . .

CHORUS: We discuss love!

DISCUSSION LEADER: Consequently there is no topic we cannot discuss dynamically. God and liability insurance; the atomic bomb and Paul Klee; to us the past and the provisional constitution are not problems but topics of discussion. Only those who welcome discussion are fit . . .

CHORUS: . . . to be members of human society.

DISCUSSION LEADER: Only those who enjoy discussion become, through discussion, human beings. Therefore, to be a man is . . .

CHORUS: . . . to be willing to discuss!

A BOY: But is Matern?

CHORUS: Is Matern willing to discuss
his kidneys with us?

TWO GIRLS: We girls are curious to see
Matern's heart spout poetry.

TWO BOYS: And Matern's spleen we fondly hope
to study through a microscope.

CHORUS: Nibble nibble, crunch crunch,
from secret pockets let us munch.

TWO GIRLS: Another thing we wouldn't miss:
to see how thoughts and feelings kiss.

CHORUS: If Matern says: I'm willing!
it will be just thrilling.

DISCUSSION LEADER: And so we ask you, Matern, are you willing to be open, uncoded, and dynamically aired? Are you willing to think what you say; are you willing to speak out what you have buried? In other words: Are you willing to be the topic of this dynamic open forum? If so, answer loudly and plainly: I, Walter Matern, welcome discussion.

A BOY: He is not willing. I told you so: he's not willing.

A BOY: Or he hasn't understood yet.

A BOY: He doesn't want to understand.

CHORUS: If Matern won't lunderstand,
make him discuss by command.

DISCUSSION LEADER: I must request you to give your comments a choral form or to state them in writing. Mob emotions cannot be permitted to erupt in a public discussion. —I ask you for the second time: Walter Matern, do you feel the need of communicating yourself to us in order that the public . . .

(Whispering among the younger generation. Matern is silent.)

A BOY: Close the temple if he's not willing.

A BOY: I demand a compulsory discussion. The Matern case is of general interest and must be discussed.

DISCUSSION LEADER (to the assistant): Members number fourteen to twenty-two are obstructing discussion and therefore barred from discussion. (*Walli S. takes down the numbers on the margin of the blackboard.*) In line with the dynamism we are aiming at, the chair had decided to take account of certain comments that have not been cast in the proper form. If the topic of discussion persists in his hostility to discussion, a state of compulsory discussion will be declared. In other words: our assistant will make use of a special device, the so-called knowledge glasses, and so provide us with the facts, for every discussion must be based on facts.

CHORUS: If he keeps his secrets in,
　　　　glasses will see through his skin.

DISCUSSION LEADER: And so for the third time I ask Walter Matern: Are you willing, in this cast-iron temple, which only a short time ago housed Johannes Gutenberg, inventor of the printing press, to make yourself available as a topic of discussion, that is, to answer our questions? In a word: Do you welcome discussion?

MATERN: Hm . . . (*pause*) Damn it! . . . I . . . (*pause*) In the name of Satan and the Blessed Virgin . . . welcome discussion!
　　　　(*Walli S. writes on the blackboard: He welcomes discussion.*)

CHORUS: He says: I'm game,
　　　　he'll play our game.

MATERN: As in the Last Judgment,
　　　　where everyone speaks,
　　　　I have, I was,
　　　　I touched a hair,
　　　　I shot at the mirror, twice, struck home,
　　　　I wakened the mirror from purblind sleep.

TWO BOYS: He failed at butter with a spindle,
　　　　till water gushed, and cried: A swindle.

MATERN: I dashed the pigeon from the tower steep,
　　　　I buried the worm in the earth down deep.

TWO BOYS: Once when he'd stabbed an oven dead,
　　　　he saw an oven, he saw red.

TWO BOYS: He choked his towel, he was fit to be tied.
　　　　His towel was always a thorn in his side.

MATERN: I smothered the stone, I sweetened the salt.
　　　　I cut a goat's bleat out of her throat.

CHORUS: He wrote with chalk on the kitty's house:
　　　　Death in disgrace to Mister Mouse.

MATERN: And now I'm a topic of discussion;
　　　　being dragged to a foregone conclusion.
　　　　(*The younger generation clap and stamp. The discussion leader rises and motions for silence.*)

DISCUSSION LEADER: With great pleasure and interest we have just heard that Walter Matern is willing to unburden himself. But before question and answer, beginning as a rivulet but soon swelling into a broad-beamed torrent, carry him and us away, let us pray: (*The younger generation and the assistant rise with clasped hands.*) O great Creator of dynamic and everlasting world discussion, Thou who hast created question and answer, who givest and takest away the floor, sustain us this day as we proceed to discuss the discussion-welcoming topic of discussion, Walter Matern. O Lord of all discussions . . .

CHORUS: . . . give us this day the maturity indispensable to all discussion.

DISCUSSION LEADER: O wise and omniscient Creator of language, Thou who commandest the stars to discuss in the universe . . .

CHORUS: . . . loosen our tongues.

DISCUSSION LEADER: O Thou Creator of great sublime topics of discussion, Thyself the most sublime of all topics of discussion, loosen the tongue of the discussion-welcoming Walter Matern . . .

CHORUS: . . . loosen his tongue.

DISCUSSION LEADER: And let us in Thy name embark upon this discussion which honoreth Thee and Thee alone . . .

CHORUS: Amen. (*All sit down. Repressed murmurs. Matern wishes to speak. The discussion leader shakes his head.*)

DISCUSSION LEADER: The first question is the prerogative of the discussion club and not of the topic under discussion. But before we proceed to the usual exploratory questions, I wish to introduce Walli S., assistant to the chair, and to thank the firm of Brauxel & Co., which has supplied us, for purposes of the present discussion, with a pair of knowledge glasses, an article that has become extremely rare since it was taken off the market. (*Applause from the younger generation.*) But we intend to make use of this device only in case of necessity and on a motion supported by a majority of those present. Perhaps this will prove unnecessary since the topic under discussion has professed his readiness for discussion and since control by means of the Brauxel knowledge glasses is in order only if a state of compulsory discussion is declared. Nevertheless, by way of highlighting the efficient and every-ready presence of the glasses, the chair requests Walli S. to explain, for the benefit of our topic and of the new members of our discussion club, what these knowledge glasses are and how Walli S. first found occasion to put them to dynamic use.

WALLI S.: Approximately from the autumn of last year until shortly before Easter of the current year, the firm of Brauxel & Co. manufactured roughly one million four hundred forty thousand pairs of glasses, which were put on the market during this period under the name of miracle glasses and chalked up sensational sales. These miracles glasses, which are now known as knowledge glasses, cost fifty pfennigs a pair and enabled the purchaser, provided he was not under seven or over twenty-one years of age, to know all adults over thirty.

DISCUSSION LEADER: Walli, would you mind telling us more specifically what became known when you, for example, put the glasses on?

WALLI S.: Last year, on the third Sunday of Advent, my uncle Walter, who is the topic under discussion today, and to whom, because I know so much about him, I owe the honor of serving as assistant to the chair in spite of my tender years—my uncle Walter took me to the Düsseldorf Christmas fair. There were lots of colored electric signs and booths where you could buy everything under the sun: Christmas cookies and marchpane, antitank guns and Christmas buns, hand grenades, household articles, aerial bombs, cognac snifters, and suicide teams, leitmotives and murder motives, Christmas tree stands and close combat badges, dolls with washable hair, doll-houses, dolls' cradles, dolls' coffins, doll replacement parts, doll accessories, dolls' radar . . .

CHORUS: To the point! To the point!

WALLI S.: And the so-called miracle glasses were also on sale. My uncle Walter—there he is!—bought me a pair. I put the glasses on right away, because I always have to try things right away. I looked at him through the glasses and I saw him very plainly as he used to be: it was simply awful. Of course I began to scream and ran away. (*She lets out a short scream.*) But he—my uncle Walter—ran after me and caught me near Rating Gate. He had his dog with him. But since he didn't take the glasses off me, I kept seeing him and the dog too and their past. He looked like a terrible monster and I couldn't stop screaming. (*She screams again.*) After that my nerves were affected and I had to go to St. Mary's Hospital for four weeks. I had a nice time, though the food didn't amount to much. Because the nurses, one of them was called Sister Walburga like me, and another one was called Sister Dorothea, and the night nurse was called . . .

CHORUS: Please come to the point!

A BOY: No hospital stories!

A BOY: Such digressions are quite superfluous.

WALLI S.: Well, that is my experience with the miracle glasses, now known as knowledge glasses, which I shall put on today if the topic under discussion makes statements such as would inhibit discussion. Brauxel's knowledge glasses should be present at every public discussion. If speech should fail . . .

CHORUS: Brauxel's knowledge glasses never fail!

WALLI S.: Anyone who like my uncle is a topic under discussion . . .

CHORUS: . . . should never forget that Brauxel's knowledge glasses are always ready.

WALLI S.: Many thought the past was dead and buried . . .

CHORUS: . . . but Brauxel's knowledge glasses can make the past present.

WALLI S.: If, for instance, I were to put the glasses on now to look at my uncle Walter, I'd have to start screaming something awful like last year, on the third Sunday of Advent.—Want me to? (*Matern and dog grow restless. Matern pats the dog's neck. The discussion leader motions Walli S. to be seated.*)

DISCUSSION LEADER (*amiably*): Forgive us, Herr Matern, the members of our discussion club relapse occasionally into their usual childlike to adolescent state. Then what should be treated as work threatens to become a game; but for your peace of mind and our own, the chair will find means to prevent gruesome jokes from getting out of hand. —The discussion ban on members fourteen to twenty-two is lifted. We shall now open our discussion with exploratory questions which should be kept simple and as direct as possible! Questions, please! (*Several members raise their hands. The discussion leader calls on them successively.*)

A BOY: First series of exploratory questions, addressed to the topic under discussion: How many stations?

MATERN: Thirty-two.

A BOY: And counting backwards?

MATERN: Thirty-two.

A BOY: And how many have you forgotten?

MATERN: Thirty-two.

A BOY: Then you remember exactly. . .

MATERN: . . . thirty-two in all.

A BOY: What is your favorite dish?

MATERN: Thirty-stew.

A BOY: Your lucky number?

MATERN: Thirty-two times thirty-two.

A BOY: And your unlucky number?

MATERN: Ditto!

A BOY: Do you know your multiplication tables?

MATERN: Eight—sixteen—twenty-four—thirty-two.

A BOY: Thank you. The first series of exploratory questions is concluded.

DISCUSSION LEADER: Second series, please.

A BOY: Can you form simple sentences beginning with the indefinite pronoun "every"?

MATERN (*quickly*): Every tooth counts. Every witch burns better. Every knee hurts. Every station says bad things about the next. Every Vistula flows in retrospect wider than every Rhine. Every livingroom is always too rectangular. Every train pulls out. Every music begins. Every event casts its shadow. Every angel lisps. Every freedom dwells in mountains that are too high. Every miracle can be explained. Every athlete refurbishes his past. Every cloud has rained several times. Every word may be the last. Every candy is too sweet. Every hat fits. Every dog stands central. Every secret is ticklish . . .

DISCUSSION LEADER: That will do, thank you. And now, if you please, the third and last series of exploratory questions. Go ahead.

A BOY: Do you believe in God?

MATERN: I object; the question of God cannot be called an exploratory question.

DISCUSSION LEADER: The question of God is perfectly admissible as an exploratory question provided it is formulated without such modifiers as "triune" and "only true."

A BOY: Very well. Do you believe?

MATERN: In God?

A BOY: That's right. Do you believe in God?

MATERN: You mean . . . in God?

A BOY: Exactly: in God.

MATERN: In God up there?

A BOY: Not just up there. Everywhere, in general.

MATERN: You mean in something up there and elsewhere . . .

A BOY: We don't mean something, we mean God, neither more nor less. Out with it! Do you or don't you . . .?

CHORUS: Scissors or stone,
        yes or no!

MATERN: Every man, whether he likes it or not, every man, regardless of his upbringing and the color of his skin, regardless of the idea he lives by, every man who thinks, feels, eats, breathes, acts, in other words, lives . . .

DISCUSSION LEADER: Herr Matern, the question addressed by the members of the discussion group to the topic under discussion is: Do you believe in God?

MATERN: I believe in the Nothing. Because sometimes I have to ask myself in earnest: Why are these essents rather than nothing?

A BOY: That's a quotation from Heidegger. We're thoroughly familiar with it.

MATERN: So perhaps pure Being and pure Nothing are the same.

A BOY: Heidegger again!

MATERN: The Nothing never ceases to nihilate.

A BOY: Heidegger!

MATERN: The Nothing is the source of negation. The Nothing is more fundamental than the not and negation. The Nothing is acknowledged.

CHORUS: Heidegger hid, Heidegger hod!
        The question is: Do you believe in God?

955

MATERN: But sometimes I can't even believe in the Nothing; then again I think I could believe in God if I . . .

A BOY: Our question has been stated. There's no need to repeat it. Yes or no?

MATERN: Well . . . (*pause*) . . . In the name of the Father, the Son, and the Holy Ghost: No.

DISCUSSION LEADER: The third and last exploratory question may be considered answered. We sum up: The lucky and unlucky number of the topic under discussion is: thirty-two. The topic under discussion can form any number of sentences beginning with the indefinite pronoun "every." He does not believe in God. This constellation—thirty-two, every, God—justifies an additional question. Let's have it. (*Walli S. notes the answers to the exploratory questions on the blackboard.*)

MATERN: (*indignant*): Who sets up these rules? Who's running this discussion, who's pulling the strings? Who?

DISCUSSION LEADER: Our discussion, carried on by a discussion-loving group, has come to a point where it seems advisable to steer it in a direction that will lend it the necessary dynamic gradient, that will give promise of a catastrophe in the traditional classical sense. I therefore request a supplementary question, based on the conclusions drawn from our exploratory questions: Thirty-two, every, God.

A GIRL: Do you love animals?

MATERN: That's absurd! Can't you see I've got a dog?

A GIRL: That doesn't answer my supplementary question.

MATERN: The dog is well treated. Correctly and when the occasion arises firmly.

A GIRL: It seems hardly necessary to repeat, but I'll do it just the same: Do you love animals?

MATERN: Take a look, young lady. What do you see? An elderly, half-blind dog, hard to feed, because his scissors bite is, to say the least, incomplete, and yet . . .

A GIRL: Do you love animals?

MATERN: This dog . . .

DISCUSSION LEADER: Ruling from the chair. In view of the topic's obvious and deliberate evasiveness, appropriate subquestions will be permitted within the framework of the supplementary question. Questions, please!

A BOY: Did you ever kill an animal with your bare hands?

MATERN: Admitted: a canary with this hand, because the bird's owner —that was in Bielefeld—was an old-time Nazi and I as an anti-fascist . . .

A BOY: Did you ever shoot an animal?

MATERN: In the Army: rabbits and crows, but during the war everybody shot at animals, and those crows . . .

A BOY: Did you ever kill any animals with a knife?

MATERN: Like every boy who lays his hands on a pocketknife: rats and moles. A friend gave me the knife and with that knife we both of us . . .

A BOY: Did you ever poison an animal?

MATERN (*pause*): Yes.

A BOY: What kind of animal?

MATERN: A dog.

CHORUS: Was he white, blue, or purple?
Red, green, yellow, or purple?

MATERN: It was a black dog.

CHORUS: Was it a spitz, daschund, or pekinese?
A St. Bernard, boxer, or pekinese?

MATERN: It was a black-haired German shepherd answering to the name of Harras.

DISCUSSION LEADER: The supplementary question, supported by appropriate subquestions, has shown that Walter Matern, the topic under discussion, has killed a canary, several rabbits, a number of crows, moles, rats, and a dog; I therefore repeat the supplementary question based on thirty-two, every, and God: Do you love animals?

MATERN: Believe it or not: yes.

DISCUSSION LEADER (*motions to Walli, the assistant. She writes "loves animals" on the blackboard*): We note that on the one hand the topic under discussion has poisoned a black shepherd, and that on the other hand he takes excellent care of a black shepherd. Since he professes to love animals, dogs—as such and in this case a black shepherd—seem to become the fixed point of discussion in reference to the topic under discussion. For safety's sake may I request exploratory questions calculated to check the unquestionably dynamic result of our exposition, namely, a black-haired German shepherd, possibly the fixed point of this whole discussion. (*Walli S. writes "black-haired German shepherd" on the blackboard.*)

A BOY: For example: Are you afraid of death?

MATERN: I'm a bounceback man.

A BOY: Then perhaps you'd like to live a thousand years?

MATERN: A hundred thousand, because I'm a bounceback man.

A BOY: In case you should die notwithstanding, would you prefer to die in your room, in the open, in the kitchen, in the bathroom, or in the cellar?

MATERN: A bounceback man couldn't care less.

A BOY: What would you prefer: illness or traffic accident? Or do you favor battle, the duel as a form of existence, war as causality, revolution as potentiality, or a good honest free-for-all?

957

MATERN (*good-humoredly*): My good friend, for a bounceback man like me, all those are mere opportunities of showing what a bounceback man can do. You can discuss me to death with knives and firearms; you can hurl me from television towers; and even if you bury me fathoms deep and weigh me down with arguments as hard as granite—tomorrow I'll be standing on my lead soles again. Bounceback man, bounce!

CHORUS: Buried below and gladly we
          will take the bet: what's buried below
          comes out no more to the light, the sparkle,
          and stirs no more nor spoons;

MATERN: for the spoon too lay in the cellar
          melted down, but when outside
          Aurora with policeman's whistle
          blew back the darkness, Matern

CHORUS: stood on molded leaden soles
          with heart spleen kidneys, was hungry
          and spooned, ate, shat, and slept.

MATERN: The bolt struck low, I fell from the tower.
          The pigeons were troubled not at all.
          I was an epitaph, flat on the pavement,
          an inscription read by passers-by:

CHORUS: Here lies and lies and lies flat, lies he
          who fell from above and here he lies;
          no rain washes him, nor hail taps
          or types his letters, eyelashes,
          or open forums;

MATERN: but comes Aurora on two legs
          and blasts the pavement where I lie,
          first stands the pecker, then the man,
          and squirts and fathers and laughs himself sick.

CHORUS: Shot he was, through and through;
          a tunnel they had just been planning,
          and through him, through him, freshly shot,
          the railroad soon was running.

MATERN: The special trains, the kings,
          had to pass straight through me when
          they wished to visit other kings
          out past me, and the Pope
          spoke in nine languages through the hole.

CHORUS: He was funnel, tunnel, megaphone,
          and green grew the customhouses on either end;

MATERN: but when Aurora with the heavy
          far-famed hammer of resurrection
          plugged me up at both ends,

Matern, once freshly shot,
stood up and breathed spoke lived and hollered!

(*Pause. Walli S. writes "bounceback man" on the blackboard.*)

DISCUSSION LEADER: And so I take it that you're not afraid of death?

MATERN: Even bounceback men have their weak moments.

DISCUSSION LEADER: Then perhaps you wouldn't like to live for a thousand years or more?

MATERN: Good God! You have no idea what a bother lead soles can be.

DISCUSSION LEADER: Well, should the occasion arise and supposing you had your choice between death in bed and death out of doors?

MATERN: Definitely in the open air.

DISCUSSION LEADER: Heart disease, accident, or war injury?

MATERN: I'd like to be murdered.

DISCUSSION LEADER: With knives or firearms? Would you like to be hanged or electrocuted? Suffocate or drown?

MATERN: I'd like to be poisoned and collapse in the presence of a first-night audience in an open-air theater. Suddenly. (*He sketches the motion of collapsing.*)

CHORUS: Listen to that. Poison!
Matern swears by poison!

A BOY: What kind of poison?

A BOY: Old-fashioned toad's eyes?

A BOY: Snake venom?

A BOY: Arsenic or poisonous mushrooms: death cup, sickener, jack-o'-lantern, fly agaric, Satan's boletus?

MATERN: Plain ordinary rat poison.

DISCUSSION LEADER: The chair wishes to put a question: When you poisoned the black shepherd Harras, what poison did you select?

MATERN: Plain ordinary rat poison!

CHORUS: O strangest of men!
Rat poison again!

DISCUSSION LEADER (*to Walli S.*): Under "bounceback man" you'd better note: death urge, colon, poison. And branching off to the right: Harras' dogdeath, colon, rat poison. (*Walli S. writes in capitals.*) But for the present, rather than follow up this first confirmation of "black shepherd" as a fixed point, I suggest a second exploratory question that will place the fixed point in a more general perspective.

A BOY: Under what constellation were you born?

MATERN: I haven't the faintest idea. The date is April 19th.

WALLI S.: It is my duty as assistant to point out to the topic under discussion that false statements will result in immediate compulsory discussion: my uncle, that is, the topic under discussion, was born on April 20, 1917.

MATERN: That kid! That's what it says in my passport, but my mother

959

always insisted I was born on the nineteenth, at exactly ten minutes to twelve. The question is: Whom is the world going to believe, my mother or my passport?

A BOY: Nineteenth or twentieth of April, regardless, you were born in the sign of the Ram.

CHORUS: Passport date or mother's claim,
      in either case the Ram's the same.

A BOY: What famous men besides yourself were born when the sun was in the house of the Ram?

MATERN: How do I know? Professor Sauerbruch.

A BOY: Nonsense. Sauerbruch was Cancer.

MATERN: What about John Kennedy?

A BOY: A typical Gemini.

MATERN: His predecessor, then.

A BOY: I think it is generally known that General Eisenhower was born when the sun was in the sign of Libra?

DISCUSSION LEADER: Herr Walter Matern: Please concentrate. Who else was born in the sign of the Ram?

MATERN: You incompetents! You wisenheimers! This isn't a public discussion, it's degenerating into a witches' sabbath. In the same month and, as it says in my passport, on the twentieth of April, Adolf Hitler, the greatest criminal of all time, was whelped.

DISCUSSION LEADER: Exception! Cognizance is taken only of the name, not of the irrelevant apposition. We have come here not to sling mud but to discuss. The chair takes note of the fact that Walter Matern, the topic under discussion, was born in the same sign and on the same date as Adolf Hitler, builder of the Reichsautobahn, a topic recently discussed by our group. Very well then: in the sign of the Ram.

A BOY: Have you anything else in common with the Ram-born Adolf Hitler?

MATERN: All men have something in common with Hitler.

A BOY: We wish to make it clear that the topic under discussion is not "all men," and certainly not "mankind," but you and you alone.

WALLI S.: I know something. Something I can testify to without having to put on the knowledge glasses. Something he even does in his sleep and when shaving. He doesn't even have to suck a lemon to do it.

MATERN: Well, in school and later too, they called me "Grinder," because sometimes when I don't like the way things are going, I grind my teeth. Like this (*he grinds long and loud into the microphone*). And Hitler is also said to have ground his teeth now and then! (*Walli S. makes a note: "teeth grinding or the Grinder."*)

CHORUS: Don't turn around,
      the Grinder's around.

A BOY: Anything else in common with the builder of the Reichsautobahn?

CHORUS: Don't go to the woods,
in the woods are woods.
He who goes through the woods,
looking for trees,
seek him not in the woods.

A BOY: We wish to know whether the topic under discussion, Walter Matern, alias the Grinder, has other points in common with Adolf Hitler, topic of a previous discussion.

CHORUS: Have no fear,
fear smells of fear.
He who smells of fear
will be smelled
by heroes who smell like heroes.

A BOY: The topic under discussion is moistening his lips.

CHORUS: Don't drink of the sea,
it whets the appetite.
If you drink of the sea
you'll thirst eternally
for ocean.

A BOY: Dynamic compulsory discussion stands starkly menacing, without smoke trailer, on the horizon.

CHORUS: Don't build a home
or you'll be at home.
If you're at home,
you'll expect
late visitors and open up.

A BOY: Walli S., our assistant, has already begun to remove documents from the document case: postcards, blood spots, certificates, specimens of feces, affidavits, neckties, letters . . .

CHORUS: Don't write letters,
letters are filed away.
When you sign a letter,
you're signing
what you were yesterday.

A BOY: He who always stood central, whose phenotypes are the bounce-back man and the Grinder, whose posthumous papers we will examine in his lifetime, thinks he still stands central.

CHORUS: Don't stand in the light,
the light can't see you.

TWO BOYS: Don't have courage,
courage takes courage.

TWO GIRLS: Don't sing in the fire,
nobody sings in the fire.

961

TWO BOYS: Don't lapse into silence,
       or you'll break silence.
CHORUS: Don't turn around,
       the Grinder's around.
MATERN: To further your search for clarity, I'll talk again. What is it you wish to know, hear, nibble on?
A BOY: Facts. Characteristics in common with that other Ram-born topic. We know you grind your teeth.
CHORUS: Don't turn around.
MATERN: Always glad to oblige: this dog. Like me, Hitler was fond of black-haired German shepherds. And the black shepherd Harras, who belonged to a carpenter . . .
DISCUSSION LEADER: This definitely confirms the black-haired shepherd as our fixed point. Do any of our members, nevertheless and for safety's sake, wish to ask further questions? (*Walli S. notes and underlines the "fixed point."*)
A BOY: The fixed point, German shepherd, should at least be tested from the erotic standpoint.
A BOY: Member No. twenty-eight is surely referring to the sexual implications of the fixed point.
DISCUSSION LEADER: The supplementary exploratory question is approved. Go ahead.
A BOY: With what famous women have you, or would you like to have had, sexual intercourse?
MATERN: In the year 1806 with Queen Louise of Prussia, twice in quick succession. She was in flight from Napoleon at the time and spent the night with me in my father's windmill, which was guarded by a black shepherd by the name of Perkun.
A BOY: The queen in question is largely unknown to the members of this discussion club . . .
DISCUSSION LEADER: Nevertheless, Walli S., please make a note of the watchdog Perkun, but add the word "legendary" with a question mark.
MATERN: Furthermore, from late summer '38 to spring '39, I intercoursed fairly regularly with the Virgin Mary.
A BOY: Any good Catholic can re-enact fictious intercourse with the Virgin Mary; moreover, the same re-enaction is open to every so-called unbeliever.
MATERN: Just the same, it was she who persuaded me to poison the black shepherd Harras with rat poison, because this Harras . . .
DISCUSSION LEADER: Very well, at the request of the topic under discussion please note in parentheses "Marianic influence" before the key phrase "Harras' dogdeath by rat poison."
A BOY: We still need something more definite, something that isn't grounded in the irrational.

MATERN: All right, here's your candy. I slept with Eva Braun at a time when she was already his mistress.

A BOY: Please describe the coitus in every detail.

MATERN: A gentleman doesn't talk about his adventures in bed.

A BOY: The objection is unwarranted. After all, this is an open forum.

A GIRL: The topic's obscene secretiveness is an insult to the female members of this discussion club.

CHORUS: The discussion soon will be
            made compulsory.

DISCUSSION LEADER: Objection from the chair. The topic under discussion has adequately answered the question about coitus with celebrated women. After legendary intercourse with the here largely unknown Queen Louise of Prussia, after fictitious intercourse with the Virgin Mary, he has admitted to coitus with Fräulein Eva Braun. Consequently questions concerning the details of this coitus are superfluous; at most the topic under discussion might be asked whether the sexual act between the sexual subjects Matern and Braun was or was not performed in the presence of spectators.

A BOY: For instance: was the builder of the Reichsautobahn present?

MATERN: He and his black and favorite dog Prinz, as well as the Führer-photographer Hoffmann.

DISCUSSION LEADER: The exploratory question has been answered. The answer has confirmed the sexual implications of the "black-haired shepherd dog," already recognized as a fixed point of discussion. We can manage without the photographer, I should think. (Walli S. makes a note.) Before we proceed to discuss the ownership status of the dog here present, who not only functions as our topic's fixed point but is actually present at his feet, the topic under discussion is authorized to ask the members of our discussion club a question.

MATERN: What is all this? Why am I standing here in Johannes Gutenberg's place? How can you call this public third degree a public discussion? How can you say it's dynamic when I, talented and trained in dynamic striding, have to stand still between columns? For I, as actor and phenotype, as Karl Moor and Franz Moor: "Slavish wisdom, slavish fears!" hunger for pacings back and forth, for entrances sudden and unexpected, for phrases to hurl across footlights, exits that give promise of new and terrible entrances: "But soon I will come among you and hold terrible muster."—Instead of all this, statics and question games. By what right are these know-it-all snot-noses questioning me? Or, to put it more politely: What is the purpose of this discussion?

DISCUSSION LEADER: The last question is in order.

A BOY: Through discussion we inform ourselves.

A BOY: Public discussion plays a legitimate role in every democracy.

A BOY: Lest there be any misunderstanding, I wish to point out that public discussion, precisely because it is carried on in public, differs fundamentally from the Catholic institution of confession.

A BOY: Nor is there any justification for analogies between our efforts and the so-called public confessions of countries under Communist rule.

A BOY: Neither in the secular nor in the religious sense does democratic discussion culminate in absolution; it ends without commitment. Or it might be more accurate to say that true discussion doesn't end at all, for after every open forum we discuss our findings in small groups, and at the same time cast about for interesting topics to discuss in future open forums.

A BOY: When we have finished with topic Walter Matern, for example, we plan to discuss the denominational school, or we shall take up the question: Have savings encouraged by fiscal policy become of interest again?

A BOY: We recognize no taboos.

A BOY: Recently we discussed the philosopher Martin Heidegger, the man and his work. I feel justified in saying that this topic of discussion holds no further enigmas for us.

CHORUS: Stockingcap croaks
           metaphysical jokes.

A BOY: When you come right down to it, problems solve themselves. All you need is a little patience. Take the Jewish question. Such a thing could never happen in our generation. We'd have gone on discussing with the Jews until they emigrated of their own free will and conviction. We despise all violence. Even when we engage in compulsory discussion, the conclusion is in no way binding on the topic of compulsory discussion: when the discussion is over, he's perfectly free to hang himself or to drink beer if he prefers. We're living in a democracy after all.

A BOY: We live for discussion.

A BOY: In the beginning was discussion.

A BOY: We discuss in order not to have to soliloquize.

A BOY: For here and here alone are our social ties forged. Here no one is lonely.

A BOY: Neither class struggle ideology nor bourgeois political economy can replace the stratification mechanism of applied sociology, namely, free discussion.

A BOY: After all, the technical efficiency of our life apparatus depends on great social organizations such as the World League of Free and Discussion-welcoming Discussion Groups.

A BOY: To discuss is to master the problems of existence.

A BOY: Modern sociology has demonstrated that in a modern mass state free discussion alone offers the possibility of developing personalities mature enough for discussion.

CHORUS: We are one big happy public international independent dynamic discussion family.

TWO BOYS: If we didn't welcome discussion, there would be no democracy, no freedom, and consequently no life in a free democratic mass society.

A BOY: Let us sum up: (*All stand up.*) We have been asked by the topic under discussion why we discuss. Our answer is: We discuss in order to prove the existence of the topic under discussion; if we were silent, Walter Matern, the topic under discussion, would cease to exist!

CHORUS: Therefore we all agree:
without us Matern would not be! (*Walli S. writes on the blackboard.*)

DISCUSSION LEADER: The topic's question has been answered. And now we ask: Do you wish to ask a supplementary question?

MATERN: Don't mind me. I'm beginning to catch on, and I agree to play along—without reservation.

DISCUSSION LEADER: In that case let's get back to the fixed point, the black shepherd, who has proved himself three times, the last time in his erotic significance.

MATERN (*with pathos*): If you want me, friends, to spill
my guts, hold out the basin!
I'll vomit up without restraint
peas spooned up dog years ago.

DISCUSSION LEADER: We shall now proceed to clarify and discuss the ownership status of a black shepherd.

MATERN: Potatoes gobbled many dog years past
will demonstrate to you today
that even then potatoes grew.
Yesterday's murder motives
are today's leitmotives.

DISCUSSION LEADER: In other words, we shall check into a black shepherd who, present here in person, represents the fixed point of this discussion, which, as we have seen, is "black shepherd."

MATERN: For now the bars are down.
What tickled my palate then
makes me retch today.
What took the road to the high Caucasus
and down to pale Ladoga Lake,
shall now roll back: methodical, half-digested, gall-bitter,
and stink till it rises sour to your mouths.

DISCUSSION LEADER: And so I invite questions relating to the ownership status of the black shepherd here present.

MATERN: Murder: an old-fashioned word!

A BOY: What is the name of the black shepherd here present?

MATERN: Rear sight, front sight.
        The whites of their eyes.
        Holding enfolding squeezing.

A BOY: I repeat my question: The name of the dog here present?

MATERN: Corpses, who counts them any longer?
        The bones have all been processed.
        The blood flows on the stage.
        And hearts beat *moderato*.
        Death has been run out of town! (Pause)
        And the dog's name, as if you didn't know,
        is Pluto.

A BOY: To whom does Pluto belong?

MATERN: To the man who feeds him.

A BOY: Did you purchase Pluto?

MATERN: He attached himself to me.

A BOY: Did you make inquiries as to the dog's former owner?

MATERN: He attached himself to me shortly after the end of the war. There were lots of masterless dogs running around in those days.

A BOY: Has the topic under discussion any intimation as to whom Pluto may have belonged to, probably under another name?

MATERN: I'm willing to tell you what I've eaten, touched, done, experienced, but I refuse to let my intimations be discussed.

DISCUSSION LEADER: Since the topic under discussion, for reasons connoting hostility to discussion, wishes to remove his notions from the scope of our discussion, the members of our discussion club are authorized to question Pluto, the black shepherd, directly, since the dog, in fact and in his capacity as a fixed point, belongs to the topic under discussion. We shall submit three musical themes to the dog. Suggestions, please. (*Walli S. notes: "Musical interrogation of the dog Pluto."*)

A BOY: Why not begin the musical interrogation with *Eine Kleine Nachtmusik*? (*Walli S. puts on a record. Music plays briefly.*)

DISCUSSION LEADER: We observe that the dog Pluto does not react to Mozart. Second suggestion.

A BOY: How about Haydn? Or something of the sort, maybe *Deutschland, Deutschland über Alles*. (*Walli S. puts on the record. The dog wags his tail as soon as the music starts.*)

DISCUSSION LEADER: The dog reacts with pleasurable animation, so demonstrating that his former owner was a German national. This makes it clear that ownership cannot be imputed to members of the then occupying armies. Accordingly, we can dispense with Handel or with themes from the French opera *Carmen*. Neither *Nutcracker Suite* nor the Don Cossacks. Similarly there is no need to consider spirituals or ballads from American pioneering days. The third suggestion, please.

A BOY: Why beat about the bush? I suggest a direct approach: some typical Wagner, the Siegfried motif or the Helmsmen's Chorus . . .

A BOY: We might as well start right in with *Götterdämmerung*.

CHORUS: *Göt-ter-dämmerung!*

Göt-ter-dämmerung!

(Walli S. puts on the record. The music from Götterdämmerung *plays at length. The dog howls throughout.)*

DISCUSSION LEADER: Here we have conclusive proof that the dog Pluto must have belonged to an admirer of Wagner. On the strength of conclusions thus far arrived at in the course of our discussion—I call your attention to our notes—we shall make no mistake in presuming former Chancellor Adolf Hitler, whom we have recently discussed as the builder of the Reichsautobahn and whose predilection for Wagner is well known, to have been the rightful owner of the black shepherd here present, currently named Pluto. By way of avoiding unnecessary delay, we shall now proceed to a dynamic confrontation: black shepherd—Hitlerportrait, if you please.

MATERN: Preposterous. The dog is almost blind.

DISCUSSION LEADER: A dog's instinct never goes blind. My father, for example, an honorable carpenter, kept a shepherd as a watchdog; incidentally, he was black, his name was Harras, and he was poisoned with rat poison. Though he never studied cynology as a science, the chair, having grown up so to speak with this Harras, regards himself as a pretty fair judge of dogs, especially black shepherds. If you please, the confrontation! *(Walli S. stands up and unrolls a large color print of Hitler over the blackboard. Then she moves the blackboard forward until it faces the cast-iron temple. Long pause. The dog becomes restless, sniffs in the direction of the picture, suddenly breaks loose, stands whimpering in front of the picture, gets up on his hind legs, and begins to lick Hitler's colored face. At a sign from the discussion leader, Walli S. rolls up the picture. The dog continues to whimper and Walli S. has difficulty in leading him back to the temple. The blackboard is moved back to its former place. Clamor among the discussion club members.)*

A BOY: It's plain as day.

A BOY: Dynamic confrontation has again proved its value as a promoter of discussion.

CHORUS: Shrewdly confronted,

his instinct was unblunted.

He whimpered and licked the place

where he discovered a face.

DISCUSSION LEADER: Quite apart from its relevance to our discussion, the confrontation has obviously taken on the character of a historic event. We therefore request our members to rise and join me in a brief moment of meditation: O great Creator of everlasting world discussion, O Thou maker of sublime topics of discussion . . . *(Protracted silence. The members of the discussion club are filled with awe.)* Amen! *(The members sit down again.)* Meanwhile the archives of our discussion club have disclosed the following data:

WALLI S.: *(who has not joined in the prayer, is holding a sheaf of papers):* Among several shepherds in the kennels of former Chancellor Adolf Hitler, it was a black-haired shepherd by the name of Prinz who attracted the most attention. He was a present to the Chancellor from Adolf Forster, Gauleiter of Danzig. The first months of his life were spent in the police kennels at Danzig-Langfuhr. He was then transferred to the Führer's residence, the so-called Berghof, where, up to the outbreak of the war, he was free to romp and run untrammeled in God's great out-of-doors. Then, however, the vicissitudes of war led him from one Führer's Headquarters to another, and finally to the Führer's air-raid shelter in the Chancellery.

DISCUSSION LEADER: And there the following happened:

WALLI S.: On April 20, 1945 . . .

A BOY: On the day when the builder of the Reichsautobahn and our topic of discussion Walter Matern celebrate their birthdays . . .

WALLI S.: During the birthday celebration, attended by General Field Marshal Keitel, Lieutenant-Colonel von John . . .

A BOY: Naval Captain Lüdde-Neurath . . .

A BOY: Admirals Voss and Wagner . . .

A BOY: Generals Krebs and Burgdorf . . .

WALLI S.: Colonel von Below, Reichsleiter Bormann, Ambassador Hewel of the Foreign Office . . .

A BOY: Fräulein Braun!

WALLI S.: SS Hauptsturmführer Günsche and SS Obergruppenführer Fegelein . . .

A BOY: Dr. Morell . . .

WALLI S.: And Herr and Frau Dr. Goebbels with all their six children —while congratulations were still being tendered, the black-haired German shepherd Prinz ran away from his master.

A BOY: And then what? Was he halted, captured, shot?

A BOY: Did anyone see him running? Deserting?

A BOY: And to whom did he desert?

WALLI S.: After brief misgivings the dog decided to follow the movement of the hour and disengage in a westerly direction. Since at the time of his projected and executed flight violent finishfights were in progress all around the capital, it proved impossible to catch the dog Prinz despite the untiring efforts of the dogsearchtroops that were immediately set up. At 8:45 A.M. on May 8, 1945, the dog Prinz swam across the Elbe above Magdeburg and went looking for a new master on the west shore of the river.

CHORUS: Matern was the master he chose
        with his legs and eyes and nose.

WALLI S.: But since in his last will of April 29th, the then Führer and Chancellor bequeathed his black-haired shepherd Prinz to the German people . . .

DISCUSSION LEADER: . . . we are forced to conclude that Walter Matern, the topic under discussion, cannot be the rightful owner of the shepherd Prinz—presently known as Pluto. We can regard him at the very most as the administrator of the Führerlegacy, the aforesaid black shepherd Prinz.

MATERN: This is an outrage! I'm an antifascist.

DISCUSSION LEADER: Why shouldn't an antifascist be the administrator of the Führerlegacy? We shall be glad to hear the opinions of our members on the subject.

MATERN: I was with the Red Falcons. Later I was a card-carrying member of the C.P. . . .

A BOY: As administrator of the Führerlegacy, the topic under discussion can lay claim to qualities that predestine him to this historic task . . .

MATERN: I distributed leaflets as late as '36 . . .

A BOY: For instance, he was born in the sign of the Ram, like the dog's former owner.

MATERN: If I joined the SA later on, it was only for a year, a brief interlude.

A BOY: Like the dog's late owner, dogadministrator Matern can grind his teeth.

MATERN: And then the Nazis kicked me out. Court of honor.

A BOY: But must it not be taken as an argument to the contrary that the selfsame dogadministrator Matern once poisoned a black dog?

MATERN: Yes, and with rat poison, because that Nazi dog, who belonged to a carpenter, mated with a bitch in the police kennels who later . . .

A BOY: Yet the topic under discussion claims to love animals.

A BOY: Would it not be fruitful to discuss our fixed point, namely "black shepherd" and the ownership status of the black shepherd Prinz, now Pluto, in conjunction with the pedigree of the black shepherd Pluto and the dynamic past of the topic under discussion?

MATERN: As an antifascist, I protest forcefully against this association of unrelated and purely fortuitous factors.

DISCUSSION LEADER: Objection upheld. We amend our project as follows: The fixed point and the dog pedigree will be dynamically discussed in the light of our topic's antifascist past.

A BOY: But only the final outcome of our discussion can show whether the Führerlegacy Prinz—now Pluto—is in reliable hands with the present dogadministrator.

DISCUSSION LEADER: The member's motion is approved. Anticipating the probable existence of a second fixed point, the chair prefers for the present to invite questions without direct bearing on the fixed point or on the ownership status of the black shepherd. (*Walli S. notes: Fixed Point 2, colon.*)

A GIRL: Can the topic under discussion think of any important childhood experiences that left their mark on him?

MATERN: Actual happenings? Or are you more interested in atmosphere?

A GIRL: Every level of consciousness can provide us with discussion-promoting data.

MATERN (*with a sweeping gesture*): Here Nickelswalde—over there Schiewenhorst.

Perkunos, Pikollos, Potrimpos!
Twelve headless nuns and twelve headless knights.
Gregor Materna and Simon Materna.
The giant Miligedo and the robber Bobrowski.
Kujave wheat and Urtoba wheat.
Mennonites and breaches in the dikes . . .
And the Vistula flows,
and the mill mills,
and the narrow-gauge railway runs,
and the butter melts,
and the milk thickens,
a little sugar on top,
and the spoon stands upright,
and the ferry comes,
and the sun gone,
and the sun back again,
and the sea sand goes,
and the sea licks sand . . .
Barefoot barefoot run the children,
and find blueberries,
and look for amber,
and step on thistles,
and dig up mice,
and climb barefoot into hollow willows . . .
But he who looks for amber,
who steps on the thistle,
jumps into the willow,
and digs up the mouse,
will find a dead dried maiden in the dike:

that's Duke Swantopolk's daughter,
who was always shoveling about for mice in the sand,
who bit with two incisor teeth,
and never wore shoes or stockings . . .
Barefoot barefoot run the children,
and the willows shake themselves,
and the Vistula flows for evermore,
and the sun now gone, now back again,
and the ferry comes or goes
or lies fast and groans

while the milk thickens till the spoon stands, and slowly runs the narrow-gauge railway ringing fast on the bend. And the mill creaks when the wind at a rate of twenty-five feet a second. And the miller hears what the mealworm says. And teeth grind when Walter Matern from left to right. Same with his grandmother: all around the garden she chases poor Lorchen. Black and big with young, Senta crashes through a trellis of broad beans. For terrible she approaches, raising an angular arm: and in the hand on the arm the wooden cooking spoon casts its shadow on curly-headed Lorchen and grows bigger and bigger, fatter and fatter, more and more . . . also Eddi Amsel . . .

A BOY: Was this Eddi Amsel a friend of the topic under discussion?

MATERN: The only one I ever had.

A BOY: Did your friend die?

MATERN: I can't imagine Eddi Amsel being dead.

A BOY: Was the aforementioned Eddi Amsel an intimate friend?

MATERN: We were blood brothers! With one and the same pocketknife we scored each other's left . . .

A BOY: What became of the knife?

MATERN: No idea.

A BOY: The question is vital. We repeat: what happened to the pocket-knife?

MATERN: Actually I wanted to throw a *zellack* into the Vistula. In those parts we called stones *zellacken*.

A BOY: We are waiting for news of the pocketknife!

MATERN: Well, stone or *zellack*, I looked for one in both pockets, but didn't find anything but the . . .

A BOY: . . . pocketknife.

A BOY: The knife had . . .

MATERN: . . . three blades, a corkscrew, a saw, and a leather punch . . . Nevertheless, I threw it . . .

A BOY: . . . the knife!

MATERN: into the Vistula. What does a river like the Vistula carry away with it? Sunsets, friendships, pocketknives! What rises to memory, floating on its stomach, with the help of the Vistula? Sunsets, friend-ships, pocketknives! Not all friendships last. Rivers that set out for hell empty into the Vistula . . .

DISCUSSION LEADER: Therefore let us recapitulate: As children and with the help of a pocketknife, Walter Matern, the topic under discussion, and his friend Eddi Amsel swore blood brotherhood. Still a boy, Matern threw the same pocketknife into the Vistula. Why the pocketknife? Because no stone was available. But in a more general sense, why?

MATERN: Because the Vistula flowed straight ahead for evermore. Because the sunset behind the opposite dike, because after we had sworn blood brotherhood, my friend Eddi's blood flowed inside me, because— because . . .

A BOY: Was your friend a Negro, a Gypsy, or a Jew?

MATERN (*eagerly*): Only a half-Jew. His father was. His mother wasn't. He had reddish-blond hair from his mother and next to nothing from his father. A wonderful guy. You'd have liked him, boys. Always in a good humor, and what ideas he had! But he was kind of fat and I often had to protect him. All the same I loved him, admired him, even today I'd . . .

A BOY: If, for instance, you were annoyed with your friend, which must have happened now and then, what bad names did you call him?

MATERN: Well, at the worst, because he really was so monstrously fat, I'd call him a fat pig. Or to kid him, I'd call him fly shit, because he had millions of freckles all over. I'd also, but more as a joke and not when I was sore, call him milliner, because he was always building weird figures out of old rags, and the peasants used them for scarecrows and stood them up in their wheat.

A BOY: Can't you think of any other bad names?

A BOY: Something more specific.

MATERN: That was all.

A BOY: For instance, when you really wanted to wound him, to hurt his feelings?

MATERN: I never had any such intentions.

DISCUSSION LEADER: We are obliged to point out that we are discussing not intentions, but actions. So out with that big bad last dramatic dynamic word?

CHORUS: Let him cough up that little word,
      or under pressure he'll be heard.

WALLI S.: Perhaps I shall have to put on the knowledge glasses after all and peer into long past situations, in the course of which the topic under discussion, my uncle Walter, lost his temper.

MATERN (shakes his head): Then—at times when I couldn't control my-self, because he was starting up again, or because he wouldn't stop, or because Eddi—I called him sheeny.

DISCUSSION LEADER: The discussion will be suspended while the insulting word "sheeny" is being analyzed. (*Muttering among the members. Walli S. stands up.*) I request your attention for our assistant Walli S.

WALLI S.: "Sheeny" is a contemptuous term, meaning Jew, dating roughly from the middle of the nineteenth century. It is thought to derive from the Yiddish word *shane*, meaning "fine," "lovely," "very good," which is often overheard in conversation among Jews, though what reason they had for regarding anything as fine, lovely, or very good has not been established. Cf. the popular jingle which developed early in the twentieth century . . .

CHORUS: Jewish sheeny,
    his legs are skinny,
    Roman nose,
    shits in his close.

A BOY: But our topic's friend, whom he insulted by calling him a sheeny, was fat.

DISCUSSION LEADER: As we have seen in previous discussions, insulting epithets are not always used with the strictest logic. The Americans, for instance, call all Germans "krauts," although not all Germans love sauerkraut or eat it regularly. Consequently, the term "sheeny" can also be applied to a Jew or—as in the present case—a half-Jew with a tendency to corpulence.

A BOY: In any event we cannot fail to note our topic's penchant for anti-Semitic utterances.

MATERN: As a man and as a pronounced philo-Semite, I protest. Yes, I lost my temper now and then and said things I shouldn't have said, but I always defended Eddi when other people called him a sheeny; when, for instance, you, Herr Liebenau, aided and abetted by your snotnose cousin, grossly insulted my friend in the yard of your father's carpenter shop—for no reason at all, he was only sketching your watchdog Harras—I came to my friend's defense and rebuffed your childish but slanderous remarks.

A BOY: The topic under discussion apparently wishes to broaden the discussion by bringing up episodes from the private life of our discussion leader.

A BOY: He has called our discussion leader's cousin a snotnose.

A BOY: He has dragged in the carpenter shop where, as we know, our discussion leader enjoyed a carefree childhood amid lumber sheds and gluepots.

A BOY: He has likewise mentioned the carpenter's watchdog Harras, who is identical with the black shepherd Harras, later poisoned by the topic under discussion.

DISCUSSION LEADER: The chair can only interpret the unfair personal attacks to which it has just been subjected as a further indication of

973

our topic's uncontrolled reactions. We therefore ask a counterquestion: Was there any connection between the already-noted legendary dog Perkun, the likewise noted bitch Senta, who belonged to the father of the topic under discussion, namely, miller Matern, and the black shepherd Harras, who belonged to the discussion leader's father, namely carpenter Liebenau—was there, I ask, any connection between them apart from the fact that the miller's son Walter Matern on the one hand and on the other hand the carpenter's son Harry Liebenau and his cousin Tulla Pokriefke called the topic's friend a sheeny?

MATERN: O ye dog years, biting each other's tails! In the beginning there was a Lithuanian she-wolf. She was crossed with a male shepherd. The outcome of this unnatural act was a male whose name does not figure in any pedigree. And he, the nameless one, begat Perkun. And Perkun begat Senta . .

CHORUS: And Senta whelped Harras . . .

MATERN: And Harras sired Prinz, who is living on my charity today. O ye dog years hoarse from howling! What guarded a miller's mill, what watched over a carpenter shop, what in guise of favorite dog rubbed against the boots of your Reichsautobahn builder, attached itself to me, an antifascist. Have you fathomed the parable? Do your accounts of accursed dog years balance to the last decimal? Are you satisfied? Have you anything more to say? May Matern take his dog away and have a beer?

DISCUSSION LEADER: Our public and dynamic discussion is hurrying to a close. But though we take justified pride in our partial findings, it is too soon to speak of full satisfaction. There are still a few threads left to tie. Let us recollect. (*He points to the blackboard.*) The topic under discussion has killed many animals . . .

A BOY: He poisoned a dog!

DISCUSSION LEADER: And yet claimed . . .

A BOY: . . . to love animals . . .

DISCUSSION LEADER: . . . to be an animal lover. So far we know that on the one hand the topic under discussion, who likes to speak of himself as an antifascist and philo-Semite, protected his friend, the half-Jew Eddi Amsel, from the persecutions of ignorant children, and on the other hand insulted him by calling him a sheeny. We therefore ask:

CHORUS: Matern loves animals;
          does Matern also love the Jews?

MATERN (*with pathos*): By God and the Nothing! The Jews have been gravely wronged.

A BOY: Answer in so many words: Do you love the Jews as you love animals, or don't you?

MATERN: We have all of us gravely wronged the Jews.

A BOY: That is generally known. The statistics speak for themselves.

Reparation, a topic recently discussed by us, has been under way for years. But we are speaking of today. Do you love them today or haven't you come around to it?

MATERN: In an emergency I would defend every Jew with my life.

A BOY: What does the topic under discussion mean by an emergency?

MATERN: For instance, my friend Eddi Amsel was beaten up one cold day in January by nine SA men, and I was powerless to help him.

A BOY: What were the names of the nine assaulting SA men?

MATERN (*in an undertone*): As if names could stand for deeds! (*Aloud*) But never mind; Jochen Sawatzki. Paule Hoppe. Franz Wollschläger. Willy Eggers. Alfons Bublitz. Otto Warnke. Egon Dulleck and Bruno Dulleck.

CHORUS (*who have been counting on their fingers*):
> We've counted only eight.
> What was the name of the ninth?
> Nine foes, nine crows,
> nine symphonies,
> and nine holy kings
> adoring on their knees!

DISCUSSION LEADER: Though promised the names of nine thugs, our members have counted only eight names. May we, to obviate the need for dynamic compulsory discussion, assume that the topic under discussion was the ninth thug?

MATERN: No! No! You have no right . . .

WALLI S.: Aha, but we have the knowledge glasses! (*She puts on the glasses and moves halfway to the temple.*)
> Nine climbed the garden fence,
> my uncle was one.
> Nine trampled the January snow,
> my uncle in the snow was one.
> A black rag on every face,
> my uncle disguised was one.
> Nine fists battered a tenth face,
> my uncle's fist was one.
> And when nine fists were tired,
> my uncle wasn't done.
> And when all the teeth had been spat,
> my uncle stifled a cry.
> And sheeny sheeny sheeny was
> my uncle's litany.
> Nine men escaped over the fence,
> my uncle was one. (*Walli S. takes off the glasses, returns to the blackboard, and draws lines indicating nine little men.*)

DISCUSSION LEADER: We have only a few last questions:

A BOY: Which SA sturm?

MATERN (*crisply*): Langfuhr-North, Eighty-four, SA Brigade Six.

A BOY: Did your friend defend himself?

MATERN: At first he wanted to make us coffee, but we didn't want any.

A BOY: What then was the purpose of your visit?

MATERN: We wanted to teach him a little lesson.

A BOY: Why had you hidden your faces?

MATERN: Because it's the style: when you want to teach a lesson, you hide your face.

A BOY: What form did this lesson take?

MATERN: Hasn't that been made clear enough?—The sheeny got beaten up. Shoilem boil 'em! He got it square in the puss.

A BOY: Did your friend lose any teeth?

MATERN: All thirty-two of them!

CHORUS: To us the number isn't new.
        We keep on hearing thirty-two.

DISCUSSION LEADER: And so we find that the lucky and unlucky number obtained through our first series of exploratory questions is identical with the number of teeth that his friend Eddi Amsel had knocked out by nine disguised SA men. This makes it clear that in addition to "black shepherd," the personality of Walter Matern, the topic under discussion, has a second fixed point, which enables us to form a dynamic picture of him. This second fixed point is the number thirty-two. (*Walli S. writes on the blackboard with capital letters.*) The value of public discussion has again been fully confirmed.

A BOY: How, in conclusion, shall we characterize the topic under discussion?

DISCUSSION LEADER: How, if he were asked, would the topic under discussion characterize himself?

MATERN: Shoot the shit, crack wise, do what you like! I, Matern, was and am an out-and-out antifascist. I've proved it thirty-two times over, and . . .

DISCUSSION LEADER: Then we may characterize Walter Matern, the topic under discussion, as an antifascist who feeds Adolf Hitler's legacy, the black shepherd Pluto—formerly Prinz. Our discussion has brought results. Let us then give thanks and pray (*the boys and girls rise and clasp their hands*): O Thou great Guide and Creator of everlasting dynamic world discussion, Thou who hast given us a discussion-welcoming topic of discussion and shown us the way to a universally valid conclusion, let us offer up a hymn of thanksgiving, singing two and thirty times the praises of the black-haired German shepherd. As he was, and as he is:

CHORUS: Long-bodied, stiff-haired, with erect ears and a long tail.

TWO BOYS: A powerful muzzle with dry tight lips.

976

FIVE BOYS: Dark eyes slightly ovoid.

A BOY: Erect ears tilted slightly forward.

CHORUS: Neck firm, free from dewlap or throatiness.

TWO BOYS: Barrel length two inches in excess of shoulder height.

GIRLS: Seen from all angles, the legs are straight.

CHORUS: Toes well closed. His long, slightly sloping croup. Pads good and hard.

TWO BOYS: Shoulders hocks joints:

A GIRL: powerful, well muscled.

CHORUS: And every single hair: straight, smooth, harsh, and black.

FIVE BOYS: And black too the undercoat.

TWO GIRLS: No dark wolf markings on gray or yellow coat.

A BOY: No, all over him to the erect, slightly forward-tilting ears, on his deep curled chest, on the slightly fringed legs, his hair glistens black.

THREE BOYS: Umbrella-black, blackboard-black, priest-black, widow-black . . .

FIVE BOYS: SS-black, Falange-black, blackbird-black, Othello-black, Ruhr-black . . .

CHORUS: violet-black, tomato-black, lemon-black, flour-black, milk-black, snow-black . . .

DISCUSSION LEADER: Amen! (*The discussion club disbands.*)

The Hundred and First Fugitive Materniad

Matern reads this final broadcasting script of an open forum in the canteen of the Radio Building. But twenty-five minutes later—the members of the discussion group haven't yet reeled off their final prayer and the loudspeaker is summoning Matern to broadcasting room four—he leaves the brand-new Radio Building with Pluto. He doesn't want to speak. His tongue doesn't feel like it. He holds that Matern isn't a topic to be publicly discussed. From eagerly contributed discussion material, gumshoes and wisenheimers have built him a watertight house, in which he absolutely refuses to live, not even for the time of a single broadcast; but he still has a fat fee, earned with his popular children's-program voice, coming to him. The voucher, signature-blessed, may be presented at the cashier's office: bills fresh from the bank crackle shortly before he leaves the Cologne Radio Building.

In the beginning, when Matern was traveling to pass judgment, Cologne Central Station and Cologne Cathedral had been eloquent partners; now, with his final fee in his pocket and again in a mood for travel, he abandons the tension-charged triangle—Central Station, cathedral, Radio Building. Matern breaks away, withdraws, takes flight.

And finds reasons aplenty for flight: first, that revolting dynamic discussion; in the second place, he's had enough of the capitalistic, militaristic, revanchistic, and Nazi-logged West German rump state—he hears the call of the future-building, peaceloving, virtually classless, healthy, and East Elbian German Democratic Republic; and in the third place, Inge Sawatzki—the slut wants to divorce good old Jochen—has been getting flight-provokingly on his nerves.

Farewell to the Gothic pigeon-nourishing double prongs. Farewell to the still drafty railroad station. There's still time for a farewell glass of beer in Cologne's holy waiting room between the penitent and the hardened of heart. Just time for a last leak in Cologne's warm, tiled, sweet-and-pungent-smelling Catholic men's toilet. Oh no! No sentimentalities! The Devil and his philosophical equivalents take all the names which, scribbled in enamel bays, once made his heart thump, his spleen swell, his kidneys ache! A phenotype demands to be relieved. A bounce-back man wants to make a fresh bed for himself. A legacy administrator no longer feels responsible. Matern, who journeyed through the Western camp with black dog to judge, makes his way to the Eastern, peace-loving camp without dog: for he deposits Pluto, alias Prinz, with the station mission. Which mission? Two are in competition. But the Protestants are kinder to animals than the Catholics. Oh, Matern has meanwhile learned a thing or two about religions and ideologies. "Would you mind keeping this dog for me? Only for half an hour. I'm a war invalid. My certificate. I'm only passing through. I've got a business errand, and I can't take the. God will reward you. A cup of coffee? Gladly and gratefully when I get back. Be a good boy, Pluto. I won't be more than half an hour."

Parting of the ways. Heaves a sigh of relief in the hurried draft. Burns his ships in thought, word, and deed. Shakes off dust on the run: track four. The interzonal train via Düsseldorf, Duisburg, Essen, Dortmund, Hamm, Bielefeld, Hanover, Helmstedt, Magdeburg, to Berlin-Zoological Gardens and Berlin-East Station is about to pull out. All aboard!

O pipe-smoking certainty. While Pluto is probably lapping up his milk in the Protestant mission, Matern rides away dogless and second class. Nonstop to Düsseldorf. Adopts a candid foreign look; faustball players, sharpshooters, members of the Sawatzki family might come in and compel him by their mere presence to get out. But Matern is able to keep his seat and to go on carrying his well-known character actor's head unalienated on his shoulders. It's none too comfortable sharing a compartment with seven interzonal travelers. All peace lovers, as he soon finds out. None of whom wants to stay in the West, though it's ever so much cushier than.

Because they all have relatives over there. "There" is always where you aren't. "He was over there until last May, then he came over here. The people who stay over there have their reasons. And all the things you have to leave behind. Over here there's Italian tomato paste, over there you can get the Bulgarian stuff now and then." Conversations as far as Duisburg: palatal soft plaintive cautious. The one grandma from over there does all the complaining: "Over there at home they were out of brown thread for a while. So my son-in-law said: lay in a supply while you're over here, heaven only knows when you'll get another chance. At first I couldn't get used to it over here. Everything is so crowded. And the advertisements. But then when I saw the prices. They wanted to keep me over here: Grandma, why don't you stay? What's the use of going back over there, when over here with us. But I said no. I'm only a burden to you, I said, and over there at home maybe things will gradually get better. Young people are more adaptable. Last time I came over here, I said: My, how quickly you've settled into the life over here. And my second daughter's husband said: What do you think, Grandma. What kind of a life did we have over there? But neither of them thinks we'll ever be reunified. My second daughter's boss, who only came over four years ago, says when all's told, the Russians and the Amis are in cahoots. But everybody says something different. Not just over there at home, over here too. And every year come Christmas I think: Well, next Christmas. And every fall when I put up fruit from the garden, I say to my sister Lisbeth, maybe we'll all be peacefully unified by the time we have the plums for Christmas. Well, this time I brought two jars of preserves over. They were mighty pleased. Tastes like home, that's what they said. Though over here they've got plenty of everything. Every Sunday pineapple!"

This music in Matern's ears while outside a film unrolls: an industrial landscape working to capacity under the sign of the free-market economy. No commentary. Chimneys speak for themselves. Anyone who feels like it can count them. Not a one made of cardboard. All jutting skyward. Industry's Song of Songs. Sustained dynamic solemn; blast furnaces are no joke. Legal wages, subject to revocation. Capital and labor, eye to eye. Coalandchemicals ironandsteel RhineandRuhr.—Don't look out the window or, spooks is what you've got in store. The show begins in the coal basin and rises to a climax on the plains. In the smoking compartment plaintive palatal music: "My son-in-law over there says, and my second daughter over here wants to," while outside—Don't look out the window!—first from kitchen gardens, then from fields of spring-green grain, the uprising spreads. Mobilization—spook dynamics—scarecrow movements. They race along while the interzonal train runs on schedule. But they don't overtake it. No spooks jumping aboard a moving train in defiance of regulations. Just continuous running. While in the smoking compartment the grandma says: "I didn't want to come over without my sister, though she's always saying: Go on over, who knows when they'll close the border," outside—Don't look out the window—scarecrows tear themselves away from their fixed stations. Functionally dressed hatracks leave salad beds and knee-high wheat. Beanpoles buttoned up for winter start and take hurdles. What a moment before was blessing gooseberries with wide-sleeved arms, says amen and trots off. But it's not a flight, more like a relay race. It's not as if they were all hightailing it eastward to the Peaceloving Camp; no, their purpose is to pass something on over here, some news or a watchword; for scarecrows uproot themselves from their vegetable gardens, hand on the baton with the terrible message rolled in it, to other scarecrows who have hitherto been guarding rye, and as the vegetable scarecrows are catching their breath in rye, the rye scarecrows sprint beside the interzonal train until, in a good stand of barley, they encounter scarecrows ready to start, who take over the spook post, relieve breathless rye scarecrows, and with bold checks and beanpole joints keep pace with the on-schedule train, until once again herringbone-patterned rye scarecrows take over. One two six scarecrows—for teams are battling for victory—carry six handily rolled letters, an original and five copies—or is the treacherous import of one and the same message conveyed in six different versions?—to what address? But no Zatopek takes the baton from a Nurmi. No athletic uniforms suggest that Wersten (blue-and-white) is leading but that the Unterrath Athletic Club is coming up, passing the Derendorf boys, fighting neck and neck with Lohhausen 07. Distances are being devoured in civilian clothes of every conceivable style: under velours hats, nightcaps, and helmets of all sorts flutter coachmen's capes, Prussian Army coats, and carpets—chewed by whom?— long strides are taken by trouser legs ending in galoshes and buckled shoes, army boots, and friar's sandals. A duffel coat relays a Glasenapp Hussar. Loden passes on the baton to raglan. Rayon to muslin. Scarlet to synthetic fiber, poplin to herringbone, nankeen and piqué send brocade and chiffon on their way. Dutch bonnet and trenchcoat fall behind. A heavy ulster outdistances a wind-filled negligee and the Second Empire. Directoire and functional fashions are relayed by the twenties and by fusty furbelows. A genuine Gainsborough in collaboration with Prince Pückler-Muskau demonstrates the classical method of handing on the baton. Balzac catches up. Suffragettes hold their own. And then for quite some time a princess' skirt is in the lead. O bold and muted colors: shot silks, pastel shades, rainbow! O you prints: millefleurs and modest stripes. O you changing trends: the neoclassical note gives way to the functional, the military to the casual. The waist moves down again. The invention of the sewing machine contributes to the democratization of ladies' fashions. Crinolines have seen their day. But Makart opens the old chests, liberating velvet and plush, tassels and pompons: see how they run: Don't look out the window or, spooks is what you've got in store!, while in the smoking compartment!—O story without end!—the grandma from over here and over there is still at it when the Westphalian landscape passes on the baton with scarecrow-ease to the incoming Lower Saxon landscape, speeding it on its way from over here to over there: for scarecrows know no borders: parallel to Matern, the scarecrow message journeys to the Peace-loving Camp, shakes off the dust, leaves capitalistic rye behind it, is taken up by class-conscious scarecrows in socialized oats: from over here to over there without customs inspection or pass; for scarecrows don't, but Matern does have to show his papers, and so does the grandma, who was over there and is now coming back over here.

Matern sighs with relief: oh, how different the sausages smell in the Socialist Peaceloving Camp. Gone forever that capitalistic curry smell. Matern's heart bursts iron bands: Marienborn! How beautiful the people are here, and even the tenements, Vopos, windowboxes, and spittoons. And the well-fed redness of the flags, and the billowing streamers with their slogans. After all the bad years, with black dog at heel, at last socialism triumphs. No sooner is the interzonal train in motion than Matern wants to communicate the red jubilation of his heart. But as he starts to speak and to praise the Peaceloving Socialist Camp, quietly and suitcasedraggingly the smoking compartment empties. The smoke is getting too thick, there must be room in a compartment for nonsmokers. No offense and a pleasant trip.

All the fellow travelers on their way to Oschersleben, Halberstadt, and Magdeburg, and finally the grandma who is changing in Magdeburg for Dessau leave him. In his loneliness Matern is haunted by the rhythm of the rails: posts ghosts posts ghosts.

Message-bearing, they are on their way. Now clad like Spartacus or the toiling masses. Strike pickets hand on the baton. Sansculottes smell blood. Even in mixed forests Matern thinks he sees rebellious proletarians. Woods spit out scarecrows in windbreakers. Brooks are no obstacles. Hedges taken at a leap. Long-legged over knolls. Swallowed up, there again. Stockingless in wooden shoes, in Phrygian caps. Cross-country scarecrows. Field and stream scarecrows. Peasants' Revolt scarecrows: Bundschuh and Poor Konrad, vagabonds and iron miners, mendicant friars and Anabaptists, the monk Pfeiffer, Hipler and Geyer, the Fury of Allstedt, the peasants of Mansfeld and Eichsfeld, Balthasar and Bartel, Krumpf and Velten, on to Frankenhausen, where already the rainbow of rags and tatters, of leitmotives and murder motives . . . At this point Matern changes his view; but on the corridor side of the interzonal train he is horrified to find the same spooks behind sash windows, all moving in the same direction.

Out! At every station where the train doesn't stop, he wants to get out. Distrust germinates. Every train has a different destination. And will the Peaceloving Camp really take me to its bosom when this locomotive, hitched to first and second class, hitched to my dreams, says amen? Matern checks his ticket: all in order and paid for. What, seen through sash windows, is happening outside, is happening free of charge. Why should he have forebodings just because he sees a few plain ordinary scarecrows running? After all, it's the nationalized Magdeburg Bowl, famed for its sugarbeets, and not the capitalistic desert of Nevada that is being traversed by swift dynamic scarecrows. Besides, there have always been scarecrows. He wasn't the first and won't be the last to make dozens of them out of old rags and chicken-wire. But these here—a glance out of the window —might have been made by him. His style. His work. Eddi's deft fingers.

Thereupon Matern takes flight. Where can you run to on a speeding interzonal train, rendered transparent to left and right by sash windows, mostly stuck, if not to the john. He even manages to take a shit and so motivate his flight. Relax. Settle down. Put away all fear; for, generally speaking, the toilet windows of all trains, whether fast or slow, are made of frosted glass. Frosted glass windows negate spooks. O peaceful idyl. Almost holy and just as Catholic as the station toilet that Cologne held in readiness for him when he went to Cologne and was looking for a quiet place. Here too scribble-scrabble on damaged enamel. The usual: verses, confessions, suggestions for doing something this way or that way, names unknown to him; for neither heart, spleen, nor kidneys quiver as he tries to decipher individual words. But when the hand-sized and cross-hatched drawing catches his eye—the black-sketched dog Perkun Senta Harras Prinz Pluto jumping over a garden fence—his heart blackens, his purple spleen darkens, the urine curdles in his kidneys. Once again, this time from a skillfully sketched dog, Matern takes flight.

But where can you run to on a speeding interzonal train if you leave the one refuge which frosted glass windowpanes secure against the spook show? At first, quite logically, he wants to get out in Magdeburg, but then, like a hypnotized rabbit, remains faithful to the destination on his ticket, expecting salvation from the River Elbe. The Elbe forms a barrier. The Elbe is the natural frontier of the Peaceloving Camp. Bird-repellent spooks and anyone else who may be headed in that direction will halt at the Western shore of the Elbe and send their scarecrow screams or other spectral howlings heavenward, while the interzonal train hurries off across the not yet fully repaired Elbe bridge.

But as Matern and the meanwhile half-empty interzonal train—most of the travelers have got out in Magdeburg—leave behind that saving event, the Elbe bridge, multiplied evil burst forth from the rushes of the East-Elbian shore: not only are the usual news-pregnant scarecrows racing along as from Marathon to Athens; in addition, his coat still Elbe-wet, a dog glistening deep black knows only one direction: after the interzonal train! A race begins, neck and neck, dog versus express train roaring through the Peaceloving Camp. For a time the animal takes the lead— the train is running slightly late because the roadbed is soggy in the Peaceloving Camp and, timetable or not, can't afford to be in too much of a hurry—but then drops back, enabling Matern to feast his eyes on blackness.

Oh, if you had only left Pluto at the Catholic mission instead of its animal-loving competitor! If you had given him reliable poison, or if a club, properly handled, had destroyed the half-blind mutt's drive and his passion for the chase. But as it is, a black shepherd grows dog years younger between Genthin and Brandenburg. Rises in the ground swallow him up. Hollows spit him out. Fences split him into sixteenths. Fine steady driving gait. Soft landings. Powerful hind quarters. No one but he can jump like that. That line from the withers to the slightly sloping croup. Eight—twenty-four—thirty-two-legged. Pluto draws up and leads the field of scarecrows. Evening sun edges silhouettes. The Twelfth Army surges toward Beelitz. Götterdämmerung. Structure of the end. If I only had a camera: cut cut. Spook close-up. Final victory close-up. Dog close-up. But you're not allowed to take pictures of the Peaceloving Camp from moving trains. Unfilmed, the Wenck combat team, disguised as an army of scarecrows, and a dog by the name of Perkun Senta Harras Prinz Pluto remain on a level with the teeth-grinding Walter Matern behind a sash window: Beat it, dog. Scram, dog. Get thee behind me, *kyon!*

But only after Werder, near Potsdam, in among the vast expanse of lakes, do scarecrows and dog lose themselves in league with the land-engulfing darkness. Matern sticks to the plastic upholstery of his second-class seat and stares at the framed photograph across from him: in oblong the fissured landscape of the Elbsandstein Mountains advertises itself. Hikes through Saxon Switzerland. Something new for a change, especially as neither scarecrows nor Pluto are to be seen among the crags. Sturdy comfortable hiking shoes, if possible with double soles. Woolen stockings, undarned. Knapsack and map. Large deposits of granite, gneiss, and quartz. Brunies used to correspond with a geologist in Prina and exchange specimens of mica gneiss and mica granite. Quantities of Elbe sandstone besides. That's the place for you. It's quieter. There nothing will sneak up on you from behind. With or without dog, you've never been there. In general people should only go to places where they've never: to Flurstein, for instance, and then up the trail and along the Ziegenrück road to Polenz View, a rock platform without a railing, offering a marvelous view of the Polenz Valley: then follow Amsel Valley to Amsel Falls and the Hockstein. Stop for the night at the Amsel Valley Hunting Lodge.

I'm a stranger in these parts. Matern? Never heard of him. Why is Amsel Valley called Amsel Valley and Amsel Falls Amsel Falls? No connection with your friend by the same name. In addition we have here Amsel Gulch and Amsel Rock. We're not interested in your past. We have other, socialist worries. We're engaged in rebuilding the beautiful city of Dresden. The old Zwinger Palace with new Elbe sandstone. In people's quarries we're cutting house fronts for the Peaceloving Republic. Nobody grinds his teeth in these parts, and neither will you. So show your papers and turn in your pass. Steer clear of West Berlin, that bastion of capitalism. Go right on through to East Station, then come and see socialism being built in the Elbsandstein Mountains. Stay right in your seat when the train has to stop at the warmongers' and revanchists' station. Be patient until Friedrichstrasse Station bids you welcome. For God's sake don't get out at Zoological Gardens Station.

But shortly before the interzonal train stops at Zoological Gardens Station, Matern remembers that he still has a fat chunk of his radio fee in his pocket. He decides to stop for a minute, exchange his West marks for East marks at the profitable capitalistic rate, one to four, and take the "L" to the Peaceloving Camp. Besides, he has to buy a razor and blades, two pairs of socks, and a change of shirts; who knows whether these vital necessities are available over there at the moment?

With these modest desires he leaves the train. Along with him others, who doubtless have greater desires. relatives welcome relatives, taking no notice of Matern, whom, as he reflects with a note of bitterness, no relatives are expecting. Nevertheless, a reception has been provided for Matern. Reception jumps up on him with forepaws. Reception licks him with long tongue. Glad barking, whimpering jubilation. Don't you remember me? Don't you love me any more? Did you want me to stay in that station mission forever, until dog-death? Haven't I a right to be faithful as a dog?

Of course of course! It's all right, Pluto. Now you've got your master back again. Let's have a look at you. It's him and it isn't him. An obviously black stud dog answers to the name of Pluto, but the scissors bite is gapless to the touch. Gone are the ice-gray islands over the stop, the eyes are no longer bleary. Why, at the most that dog can't be a day over eight. Rejuvenated and new. Only the dog tag is still the same. Dog lost, dog found again; and—as usual in railroad stations—here comes the honest finder: "Pardon me, is this your dog?"

He removes the Borsalino from his smoothly combed hair: a slim, affected stringbean, as hoarse as a grater, which doesn't prevent him from sucking a coffin nail: "The animal ran up to me and insisted on dragging me to Zoological Gardens Station; he pulled me right through the entrance hall and up these stairs to where the big expresses come in."

Is he after a reward or does he wants to stike up an acquaintance? Still with hat in hand, he doesn't spare his vocal cords: "I don't wish to be obtrusive, but I am glad to have met you. Call me what you like. Here in Berlin most people call me Goldmouth. An allusion to my chronic hoarseness and the twenty-four-carat substitutes for teeth that I am obliged to wear in my mouth."

Thereupon Matern's internal cash drawer gets a checking over: coins of every kind jingle together. Inflamed with red only a moment before, his heart is now wrapped in gold leaf. Spleen and kidneys are heavy as ducats: "My, what a surprise! And in a railroad station of all places. I can't say what is more amazing, finding my Pluto again—I lost the dog in Cologne—or this momentous, I can't think of any other word, meeting."

"The pleasure is all mine!"—"But haven't we friends in common?" —"You think so?"—"Why yes, the Sawatzkis. Wouldn't they be flabbergasted if they."—"Why then I must be—or can I be mistaken?— talking to Herr Matern?"—"As he lives and breathes. What a coincidence! We really have to drink on it."—"Suits me."—"Where do you suggest?"—"Wherever you like."—"I'm pretty much of a stranger around here."—"Then let's start our little round at the Barfuss place."—"Anything you say. But first I'd like—my trip was unexpected—to buy a change of shirts and a razor. Heel, Pluto! My, is he happy!"

The Hundred and Second Fireproof Materniad

Here you see God's gigolo with his one and only prop! In between mincing pigeon steps, the guy is actually whirling an ebony cane with an ivory handle. In this station as in all others, familiar and welcomed: "Hi, Goldmouth. In town again? How's your love life?"

And smokes Navy Cut the whole time at high speed. While inside the station—the shops here are open until late—Matern buys his vital razor and the blades that go with it, the little fellow smokes without interruption and, when he runs out of matches, asks a policeman for a light: "Good evening, officer." And the officer salutes the idling smoker.

And everybody winks at Goldmouth and, so it seems to Matern, points to him and the rejuvenated dog: Among friends. Complicity. That's a hot one, Goldmouth. Some bird you've scared up.

Talk about birds! When Matern comes back with two pairs of woolen socks and a fresh shirt, five or six kids are surrounding his new friend. And what are they doing? Horsing around between the Heine Bookstore and the ticket windows of the "L," dancing around him while he offhandedly beats time with his cane, twittering like telegraph wires, cackling and chirping sound effects. They turn their jackets inside out; with the lining out they look like members of the scarecrow family that was

985

staging a relay race on both sides of the just-arrived interzonal train, as though intending, even before the train pulled in at Berlin-Zoological Gardens, to make known, deliver, and loudly proclaim the tidings, message, watchword: "He's coming! He's coming! He'll be here in a minute and needs to buy a razor and socks and a change of shirts."

But all the boys evaporate as soon as Matern steps up to Goldmouth with parcels and rejuvenated dog: "O.K. Let's go."

It's not far. The place is no longer in existence, but at the time when the trio is crossing Hardenbergstrasse is situated across the way from the Newsreel Theater, which today is projecting the news somewhere else. Not into the Bilka department store, but across Joachimstaler on the green light, and a few steps up Kantstrasse. After the Ski Hut sporting goods store, an electric sign over the usual Berlin pub makes it clear that ANNA HELENE BARFUSS—who by now must be rinsing glasses behind the heavenly bar—still reigns behind an earthly cash register as our trio is approaching. The place used to be a coachmen's hangout. Today traffic cops gather there after hours. Also teachers of art from Steinplatz and couples who are ahead of time for their movie. And now and then the kind who are often between jobs. They stand at the bar shifting their weight from leg to leg between glasses. For good measure one might mention a flighty old biddy who, always under the same hat, is enjoying a free lunch, in return for which she has to tell Anna Helene about the repertory at the Volksbühne from the latest Adamov to the last time Elsa Wagner brought the house down; for Anna Helene's cash register rings so steadily that she can never get out to the theater.

Here too Goldmouth is a familiar figure. His order: "A hot lemonade, please!" surprises no one but Matern. "For your throat, I suppose. That's a bad cold you've got. No, it must be smoker's cough. You sure smoke like a chimney."

Goldmouth listens attentively to the voice. He connects himself with the hot lemonade by means of a straw. But listening to Matern and sucking lemonade are only two activities; in addition, he smokes cigarettes, lights the fresh smoke-stick with the last third of the old one, and throws the burning butt behind him, whereupon la Barfuss, deep in retrospective theatricals at the free-lunch counter, motions the waiter with her eyebrows to stamp out the butt. The gentlemen pay for two beers, a hot lemonade, and three meatballs. Dutch, except that Matern pays for the dog.

But Goldmouth and Matern with newly found Pluto haven't far to go: up Joachimstaler, across Kurfürstendamm on the zebra stripes, and at the corner of Augsburger into the White Moor. There Matern consumes two beers and two schnapps; Goldmouth drains a hot lemonade to the sweet dregs; the dog is served a portion of fresh blood sausage—homemade! The waiter has to stamp out four butts in all behind the smoker's back. This time they don't cling to the bar but stand at a small table. Each becomes the other's opposite. And Matern counts as the waiter reduces to silence what Goldmouth flips smoking behind him. "You ought to quit smoking so much. It doesn't make sense when you're as hoarse as a grater."

But the several times admonished smoker expresses, as though in passing, the opinion that his constant smoking is not the cause of his chronic hoarseness, but that, thinking much further back, to a time when he was still a nonsmoker submitting to athletic discipline, something, a certain someone, had roughed up his vocal cords: "Hm, you surely remember. It happened early in January."

But strenuously as Matern swirls the remnant of beer in his glass, he can't seem to remember: "What am I supposed to? Are you trying to pull? But joking aside, you really ought to cut out the chain smoking. You won't have any voice left. Waiter, the check. Where do we go now?"

This time Goldmouth pays for everything, including the blood sausage for the newly found dog. Obviously their legs need no more stretching. A stone's throw up Augsburger. Scenes of welcome in the springtime air that has a hard time preserving its balminess against the curry vapors of nearby snack bars. Unaccompanied ladies are glad to see him, but not obtrusive: "Goldmouth here, Goldmouth there!" And the same song and dance at Paul's Taproom, where they sit on bar stools, because the circular sofa around the big table is fully occupied: trucking men with ladies and interminable stories which even Goldmouth's feted arrival can interrupt only briefly, and that because they feel obliged to say something about the dog. "Mine—sit, Hasso—is a good ten years old." Dog talk and curiosity: "That's a purebred. Where'd you get him?" As if the dog belonged not to Matern but to this smoker who, rising above all the questions, gives the order: "Hey, Hannchen. A beer for the gentleman. For me the usual. And a schnapps too for the gentleman, if it's all right."

It's all right. So long as he doesn't mix his drinks. Better be careful, keep a clear head and a steady hand in case of trouble. You never can tell.

Matern's refreshments are served. Goldmouth sucks the usual with a straw. The newly found dog, described as a purebred by one of the trucking men, receives a hard-boiled egg, which Hannchen in person peels for him behind the counter. A free and easy atmosphere: questions, answers, and somewhat ambiguous remarks are exchanged between tables. A three-lady table near the ventilator is curious to know whether Goldmouth is in town for business or pleasure. The round table—against a background adorned with photographs of wrestlers and boxers waiting, most of them at the vertical, for the next full nelson or left hook—

inquires, without so much as a lull in its internal conversation, how Goldmouth's business is doing. Trouble with the Internal Revenue Service is mentioned. Goldmouth complains of slow deliveries. The circular sofa counters: "What would you expect, with your export orders?" Hannchen wants to know how his love life is prospering. A question which was already asked by the bustling Zoological Gardens Station and which in both cases Goldmouth answers with a suggestive smoke line in the air.

But here again, in this pub, where everybody is in the know except for the hick Matern, the smoker insists on flipping his cigarette butts behind him every time Matern pushes up the ash tray: "Some manners you have, I must say. Oh well, these people are used to your routine. Why don't you try a filter for a change? Or try to fight it off with chewing gum? It's sheer nervousness. And that throat of yours. It's none of my business. But if I were you, I'd cut it out completely for two weeks. I'm really worried."

Goldmouth is pleased to hear Matern's concern expressed so prolixly. Though it keeps reminding him that his chronic hoarseness doesn't come from immoderate smoking, but can be dated with precision: "One January afternoon, years ago. You surely remember, my dear Matern. There was a lot of snow on the ground."

Matern counters that there's usually a lot of snow on the ground in January, that all this is a silly subterfuge to distract attention from his cigarette consumption, because the root of his throat trouble is coffin nails and not any perfectly normal winter cold he caught many years ago.

The next round is stood by the trucking men, whereupon Matern feels called upon to order seven slugs of gin—"because where it comes from is where I come from"—for the occupants of the round table. "From Nickelswalde, and Tiegenhof was our county seat." But despite rising spirits, Goldmouth, Matern, and newly found dog gather little moss at Paul's Taproom. Despite urgent pleas to hang around from the three-lady table—whose occupants change frequently—from the social stability of the trucking men's table, and from the universally popular Hannchen: "You're always dropping in for half a second; and you haven't told us a story in ages"—the gentlemen prefer to ask for the check, which doesn't mean that Goldmouth—he's already standing by the ventilator with Matern and dog—has no story up his sleeve.

"Tell us about the ballets you used to put on."

"Or when you were a so-called cultural-affairs officer in the occupation."

"The one about the worms is good too."

But this time Goldmouth's mood is running in a very different direction. Facing the round table, grazing the three-lady table, and taking in Hannchen, he hoarsely whispers words which the trucking men, nodding weightily weightily, load up.

"Just a very short story, because we're all so cozy here together. Once upon a time there were two little boys. One of them, out of friendship, gave the other a lovely pocketknife. With this gift the other boy did all sorts of things, and once, with that very same pocketknife, he scored his own arm and the arm of his friend whom friendship had made generous. And so the two little boys became blood brothers. But one day when the boy to whom the pocketknife had been given wanted to throw a stone in the river, but found no stone for throwingintheriver, he threw the pocketknife in the river. And it was gone forever."

The story makes Matern pensive. They're out in the street again: up Augsburger, across Nürnberger. The smoker is on the point of turning right to pay a visit to Rankestrasse and somebody he calls Prince Alexander, when he notices Matern's somber thoughtfulness and decides that he himself, Matern, and the newly found dog need a little exercise: up Fuggerstrasse, across Nollendorfplatz, and then to the left down Bülowstrasse.

"See here." That's Matern. "That story about the pocketknife sounds mighty familiar to me."

"That's perfectly natural, my friend," Goldmouth croaks. "It's a story out of a German schoolbook, so to speak. Everybody knows it. Even the men at the round table nodded in the right places, because they knew the story."

Matern suspects there's something behind all this and bores deep holes that are meant to get to the bottom of the enigma: "And what about the symbolism of it?"

"Nonsense! A common ordinary story. Just think, my good friend: two boys, a pocketknife, and a river. That's a story you can find in every German schoolbook. Edifying and easy to remember."

Even though the story oppresses him less since he has decided to call it symbolic, Matern can't help arguing some more: "You very much overestimate the quality of German schoolbooks. Still the same old rubbish as before. Nothing to enlighten the young people about the past and all that. Lies! Nothing but lies!"

Goldmouth smiles all around his cigarette: "My dear good friend, my story, too, though extremely edifying and easy to remember, is a lie. Jack look. The end of my fable goes: The boy threw the pocketknife in the river. And it was gone forever—But what have I here? Examine it closely. It's lost its sparkle after all these years. Well, what do you say?"

In the flat of his hand lies, as though conjured out of the air, a rusty pocketknife. The street lamp, under which Matern, the dog, and Goldmouth are standing, bends over the object: used to have three blades, a corkscrew, a saw, and a leather punch.

"And you think it's the same one as in your story?"

Gaily and always glad to do tricks with his ebony cane, Goldmouth replies in the affirmative: "That's the pocketknife out of my lying school-book story. You really oughtn't to make derogatory remarks about German schoolbooks. They're not so bad. If they mostly omit the point, as in the case of the knife that was found again, it's because the truth is too unbearable and might be harmful to a child's innocent mind. But German schoolbooks smell good, the stories are edifying and easy to remember."

Already the Hermitage is opening its arms to the trio, already Gold-mouth is about to give the recovered pocketknife back to the air, his spacious prop room, already the hasty imagination sees the trio standing at the bar or sitting in the Green Room, already the Hermitage is snapping its jaws at them with no intention of disgorging them before dawn—for none of the bars around the Church of the Apostles has a stomach better able to hold its guests—when a magnanimous mood carries the smoker away.

As they cross the street and, turning off to the right, succumb to the compulsion of Potsdamer Strasse, Goldmouth's gift-endowment-bequest is formulated: "Listen, my dear friend: the night—almost cloud-less and extravagantly supplied with moonlight—has put me in a generous mood: take it. Of course we're neither of us boys any more, and with rusty blades such as these it would be dangerous to score arms, to swear blood brotherhood, but take it just the same. It comes from the heart."

Late in the night—the month of May has populated all the drives and cemeteries, the Tiergarten and Kleist Park—Matern, who has already acquired a rejuvenated dog, receives a present of a heavy and, as he soon discovers, unopenable pocketknife. He thanks Goldmouth kindly but in return, as it were, can't refrain from expressing his sincere concern over Goldmouth's extreme hoarseness: "As a favor to me. I'm not a monster and I won't ask the impossible, but couldn't you skip every third cigarette? I've only known you a few hours, but even so. Maybe you think I should mind my own business. But I'm really worried."

What good can it do for the smoker to keep harping on the true source of his chronic hoarseness, that January frost which suddenly turned to a thaw; Matern continues to put the blame on cigarettes, which Gold-mouth persists in terming harmless and a vital necessity: "Not tonight, my dear friend. Your company stimulates me. But tomorrow, yes to-morrow, we shall live abstinently. And so, let us stop in here. I have to admit that a hot lemonade would do me and my throat good. Here, this wooden shed, temporary premises to be sure, will be glad to receive us and the dog. You shall have your beer and your *petits verres;* to me the usual will be served; and our good Pluto will be fed meatballs or weenies, hard-boiled eggs or a cutlet in aspic—ah, the world is so rich!"

What a set! In the background menaces the Sports Palace, a barn whose wheat was threshed years before; the foreground is occupied, with gaps in between, by wooden booths employed for various trades. One promises bargains. The second, amid undying curry aroma, provides shashlik and fried sausages. In the third, ladies can have ladders in their stockings picked up at any hour of the day. The fourth booth awakens hope of tombola winnings. And the seventh shed, hammered together from remnants of other sheds and bearing the name of Chez Jenny, will provide the trio with their next environment.

But before they go in, a question jells within Matern, a question that doesn't want to emerge in the seventh shanty, but to unfold in the balmy spring air: "Tell me this: This knife—it's mine now—where'd you get it? Because I can't really believe it's the same one as the little boy—the one in the story, I mean—is supposed to have thrown in the river."

Already the smoker has hooked the ivory crook of his cane into the door handle—he has opened the doors of all the joints in this way: Anna Helene Barfuss' place, Lauffersberger's White Moor, Paul's Taproom, and the Bülow Hermitage almost—already Jenny, the proprietress of the place that is not called Chez Jenny for nothing, is anticipating the arrival of new customers—she suspects who is coming and is starting to squeeze lemons—when Goldmouth's sandpapered vocal cords bring forth words of explanation: "Try to follow me, my good friend. We have been talking about a pocketknife. In the beginning every pocketknife is new. Then every pocketknife is used for what it is and ought to be, or it is alienated from its proper function and utilized as a paperweight, a counterweight, or—for lack of stone missiles—as a missile. Every pocketknife gets lost someday. It is stolen, forgotten, confiscated, or thrown away. Now, half of all the existing pocketknives in this world are found knives. These in turn may be be subdivided into common and preferred pocketknives. It is undoubtedly to the preferred class that we must assign the one I found in order to return it to you, its original owner. Or would you, here on the corner of Pallasstrasse and Potsdamer, here in the presence of the historical and actual Sports Palace, here, before this shed engulfs us, claim you never owned one, secondly that you never lost one, forgot one, or threw one away, and finally, that you haven't just recovered one?—And believe me, I had my troubles arranging this little reunion. My schoolbook story says: The pocketknife fell into a river and was gone forever. Forever is a lie. For there are fish that eat pocketknives and end, made manifest, on a kitchen table; what's more, there are dredges which bring everything to light, including pocketknives that have been thrown away; in addition there is chance, but that doesn't enter into the present case.—For years, just to give you an idea of the pains I've taken, for years and shunning no expense, I sent in petition after petition, I went so far as to bribe high officials of various flood-control commissions. Finally, and thanks to the complaisance of Polish officialdom, I obtained the desired permit: in the Vistula estuary—for as you and I know the knife was thrown into the Vistula—a dredge, put to work especially for me by a high-level bureau in Warsaw, brought the object to light approximately where it had taken leave of the light in March or April 1926: between the villages of Nickelswalde and Schiewenhorst, but nearer the Nickelswalde dike. No doubt was possible. And to think that I'd been having the Gulf of Bothnia and the southern coast of Sweden dredged for years, that the alluvial deposits off Hela Peninsula had been dug over any number of times at my expense and under my supervision. And so, to wind up our discussion of lost and found objects, there seems to be every reason to conclude that it's absurd to throw pocketknives into rivers. Every river gives back pocketknives without asking anything in return. And not only pocketknives! It was equally silly to sink the so-called Hoard of the Nibelungs in the Rhine. For if someone should come along who is seriously interested in the treasures hoarded by that restless race—as I, for instance, was in the fate of the pocketknife—the Hoard of the Nibelungs would come to light and, unlike the pocketknife whose rightful owner is still in the land of the living, find its way to a provincial museum.—But enough of this chatting in doorways. Don't thank me! Just bear with me and accept a little piece of advice: take better care of your newly found property. Don't throw it in the Spree as you once threw it in the Vistula; although the Spree surrenders pocketknives with less resistance than the Vistula, where you grew up—your accent still shows it."

And once more Matern stands at a bar, with dog at heel, anchored to a beer glass on the left and a double-decker schnapps on the right. While he ponders: How does he know all this, where did he . . . Goldmouth and the woman in charge of the otherwise empty bar play out a reunion scene, in which titles such as "Jennyofmyheart," "Jennymyconsolation," "dearest Jenny," show that the withered person behind the bar means more to Goldmouth than four plank walls can hold. While the faded spinster in the limp knitted jacket is squeezing the juice from lemon halves, Matern is told that this Jenny is among other things a silver Jenny and a Snow Queen to boot: "But we won't call her Angustri, though it's her real name, because that puts her in a melancholy frame of mind and reminds her of Bidandengero, in case you've heard of him."

Matern, who in his innermost soul is still arguing with the pocketknife, refuses to burden his memory with unpronounceable Gypsy names and to appraise a silver ring that has been worn thin. As far as he is concerned, this fulsomely praised Jenny—a single glance is enough—is some shopworn dancing girl; an acute observation that is confirmed by the décor of the shanty: while Paul's Taproom is graced with the photographs of flatnosed boxers and wrestlers, Jenny has decorated her joint with a *corps de ballet* of dance-worn ballet slippers: from the low ceiling they dangle pale-pink, once-silvery, and Swan Lake-white. Of course there are also pictures of various Giselles. With well-informed finger Goldmouth points to attitudes and arabesques: "That's la Deege at the lower left. Always lyrical, always lyrical. There's Svea Köller, la Skorik, Maria Fris in her first big part, as Dulcinea. And there, next to the ill-starred Leclerq, our Jenny Angustri with her partner Marcel, whose real name in those days, when Jenny was dancing the gardener's daughter, was just plain Fenchel."

A dancers' hangout. After the show you drop in for a moment Chez Jenny, and if you're in luck you'll meet little Bredow or Reinholm, the Vesco sisters, Kläuschen Geitel, or Rama the ballet photographer, who has retouched most of the photographs here displayed, for no neck must show strain and every instep wants to be the highest.

Ah, what ambition and ephemeral beauty these ballet slippers have danced away! And now the place, for all its tap beer, in spite of Mampe's Schnapps and Stobbe's Juniper, persists in smelling of chalk, sweat, and sour jersey. And that careworn goat face behind the bar, which, Goldmouth claims, is capable of making him the best and most soothing hot lemonade in the world. Even now, after the first greedy gulps, so the smoker assures us in his enthusiasm, relief is suffusing his throat, and his voice—as a boy, he inform me, he was able to sing steeple-high—is beginning to remember the most high-climbing of Mozart arias, and soon—only a few more glasses of Jennyhot Jennylemonade—he'll be able to awaken the angel within him and let him sing for joy.

Although Matern has ear enough to detect a few relatively smoothed-out notes in Goldmouth's voice, he can't help giving tongue once again to his concern: "It may be that the lemonade here is particularly good and, for my money, tasty as well. All the more reason why you should stick to soft drinks and give up that immoderate and, I might almost say, cynical smoking."

Back on the old subject: "Don't smoke too much or you'll smoke too much!" Whereupon the smoker with practiced fingernail tears open a fresh pack of Navy Cut, offers them neither to Matern nor to Jenny, helps himself, and dispense with a match, brightening his fresh weed with the remnant of his veteran smoke-stick: flip! over his shoulder flies the butt, landing on boards, where it is permitted to burn on, to burn out, or to find nourishment—who knows?

For this time no waiter creeps up behind Goldmouth, no heel worn to a slant grinds out the honored guest's afterglowing excrement; for that is what Goldmouth calls the cast-off butts he flips behind him: "They, my dear friend, are my existential bowel movements, so to speak. Which is not to disparage the term or, for that matter, the indispensable function

993

it connotes. Offal offal! Aren't we all? Or won't we be? Don't we live on it? Look, but without horror I beg of you, upon this glass of hot lemonade. I'm going—you won't mind, my dear Jenny?—to let you in on a secret. For what makes this glass, full of the usual, into something special is not selected lemons and choice water: a pinch of mica, got from mica gneiss and mica granite, is mixed—please observe the little silvery fishes!—into the lemonade; then—an old Gypsy recipe—three drops of precious and delicious essence, which my Jenny holds in readiness for me at all times, give this favorite drink of mine a magic, make it flow down my throat like balm. You've guessed. You've got the ugly yet grandiose word on the tip of your tongue and suspect the presence of a similar essence in your yellow beer, you're about to turn away, disgust in both corners of your mouth, and to cry out in horror: urine! urine! woman's urine!—but my Jenny and I are used to being suspected of operating an abominable witches' cauldron. No matter, you've already—right, Jenny?—been forgiven; already and once again harmony reigns between us under a sky of tired ballet slippers; already, and not for the last time, glasses are being filled; beer and clear grain spirits will suit my friend; meatballs will cheer the dog; and as for me, who smoke in order that the world may understand: Behold, he still lives, for he is still smoking!—for me, whose voice was sandpapered one January afternoon by a sudden thaw; for me, whose genius for retrieving no pocketknife can resist; for me, who have at my fingertips any number of schoolbook stories, such as the story of the burning christening goose or the one about the milk-drinking eels, the story of the twelve headless knights and the twelve headless nuns, not to mention the highly edifying tale about the scarecrows who were all created in man's image; for me, the surviving chain smoker, who tosses behind him what a moment before hung burning from his lips: excrement excrement! for me, Goldmouth, who as a child longed to wear two and thirty gold teeth in my mouth instead of my tiresome natural teeth; for me, then, the smoker with the gold teeth—a friend helped me to acquire them by redeeming me from my natural-grown dentition—for me, the redeemed one, let hot lemonade, to which biotite and muscovite have contributed a pinch of sparkling mica, let lemonade ennobled by Jenny's essence fill this glass, that we may drink—to what? To friendship, to the Vistula that flows for evermore, to all windmills, whether turning or standing still, to a black buckled patent-leather shoe that belonged to the little daughter of the village mayor, to the sparrows—sworraps!— over far-billowing wheatfields, to the grenadiers of Frederick II of Prussia, who was overly fond of pepper, to the button off a French grenadier's uniform, which, deep down under the Church of the Trinity, bore witness to history, to jumping frogs and quivering salamander tails, to the German game of schlagball, no, to Germany in general, to Germany's destiny sauces and Germany's cloud dumplings, to primordial pudding and noodle inwardness, likewise to Adebar the stork, who brings the babies, to the reaper who invented the hourglass, but also to Adler's Beer Hall and to the zeppelin high over Heinrich Ehlers Field, to master carpenters and concert pianists, to cough drops and the bone-glue imp, to oak paneling and Singer sewing machines, to the Municipal Coffee Mill and a hundred slim paperbacks, pregnant with roles, to Heidegger's Being and Heidegger's Time, similarly to Weininger's standard work, in other words, to song and the pure idea, to simplicity, modesty, and dignity, to awe of and emotion over, to honor and the profound Eros, to mercy love humor, to faith, to the oak tree and the Siegfried motif, to the trumpet and SA Sturm Eighty-four; let us then drink to that January day's snow man, who released me that smoking I might survive: I smoke, therefore I am! Let us drink to me and to you, Walter! Yet, it's me, so let us drink. You say something's burning; let us drink all the same. You say we ought to call the fire department; let us drink without the fire department! You say my excrement, which you call cigarette butts, has set fire to this haven of exhausted ballet slippers, which you call a shack; I beg of you, let us finally drink, because I'm thirsty: hot lemonade, delicious hot lemonade!"

The friends clink their glasses, while the fire on the floor spreads and begins to lick the plank walls. Beer glass and lemonade glass meet and tinkle obediently, while in the increasing heat the chorus of martyred ballet slippers under the ceiling begins a little dance: *échappé croisé, échappé effacé, assemblé assemblé, petits battements sur le cou-de-pied.* What an inspiring ballet master fire can be! But the truly applauseworthy miracle is wrought by the hot lemonade: Jenny's drops and the pinch of sparkling mica produce a miraculous effect: with a gentle voice, a trifle too high, rather too soft, so that whole words are drowned out by the ballet-directing work sounds of the fire, Goldmouth, who despite the flaming environment refuses to stop smoking, tells exciting schoolbook tales, with and without points. Not to be outdone, Matern tells stories of his own, which fill in certain gaps in Goldmouth's stories. And Jenny, too, knows stories. Around this quartet, busy entertaining each other—for Pluto listens— the fire tells a story which appeals to the hot-air ballet under the ceiling: the *corps de ballet* reacts with precise *pas de chat* and doesn't ever want to stop alternating feet: *pas de bourrée, pas de bourrée!* And while the photographs full of attitudes and arabesques turn brown at the lower edges; while at the bar the Goldmouth story, supported by Materniads, flows into a lemonade-hot Jenny story; while photographs curl, then shrivel, while stories find no end and the ballet unleashed above the fire executes daring glissades, outside the fire department begins to tell its hose-long story.

Presto! Goldmouth has to hurry through his scarecrow stories; Matern really ought to unwind his dog stories more quickly; Jenny would do well to hurry her mica-gneiss legends, in which forest hussars and Gypsies, tinkers and Tsiganes hunt hedgehogs, toward the final feast, the hedgehog banquet; for neither Goldmouth nor Jenny nor Matern, who takes a symbolic view of the dog, can narrate as fast as the blaze is devouring wood. Already attitudes and arabesques have left rigid photographed poses to join in the play of the fire. Already ingenious choreography mingles the *pas assemblés* of the slipper-dancers with the sweeping *pas jetés* of male flames. In a word, the whole shack, except for a small part of the story-obsessed bar, is going up in smoke. Quickly then the story about the scarecrows who turned the tables at the battle of Leuthen. And follow up with Matern's tale about how he poisoned a black dog with the help of the Virgin Mary. And Jenny—how the fire becomes the withered Giselle, what fine fresh bloom the heat lends her—in swift words set with tiny mica mirrors, a newly kindled beauty tells how a little seasoning transformed common hot lemonade into Goldmouth's elixir. With ever new cigarette, Goldmouth lashes on the company, now huddled on top of the bar with dozing dog. "More stories. More stories. Keep going! As long as we're telling stories, we're alive. As long as stories keep coming, with or without a point, dog stories, eel stories, scarecrow stories, rat stories, flood stories, recipe stories, stories full of lies and schoolbook stories, as long as stories have power to entertain us, no hell can take us in. Your turn, Walter. Tell stories as long as you love your life."

Gone the ballet, replaced by crackling applause. Nine-tailed flames wag their tails and mate. Shanty wood goes to meet its destiny. The fire department does its duty. The heat would be oppressive if not for Matern's frost-crunching January stories: "Only in the East are winters that cold. And when it snowed up there, it snowed in earnest, for days and days. The snow covered everything over, everything. That's why the snow men in the East were always bigger than the snow men in the West, even way back. And when it began to thaw, we had our hands full, believe me. It was in January, when the sea was frozen over from Hela to Weichsel-münde, that my ancestors, who still called themselves Materna, liked best to . . ."

Oh, Matern knows how to evoke the remote past when the lighting is right. The fire serves up its second course, spits out bone gnawed soft and red-hot nails, gobbles loudly, laps up rivers of beer, makes rows of bottles burst: Stobbe's Juniper, jugs of Steinhäger, Double Juniper, rot-gut schnapps and fine spirits, framboise and mild Bisquit, blended brandy and genuine arrack, Mampe's Half and Half, White Horse, sherry, black-berry brandy, chartreuse and gin, slender kümmel, curaçao so sweet, Hussar's Coffee . . . spirits! what a lovely, transcendence-caressing word.

Spirit kindles spirit while Matern, thinking back to the past, sets up a row of Materniads: "There were two of them, brothers. And the story begins with Gregor Materna in the year 1408. In that year he went from Danzig to London, where he was given short weight of salt, a mortal insult. Paid back in blood, by God! And he went back home and demanded justice, but didn't get it. And he raised hell outside the Artushof, where no one was allowed to bear arms, but he did, and used them. Whereupon they outlawed him, yes, outlawed him! But he didn't let the grass grow under his feet, he gathered henchmen: what was left of the dispersed band, once led by Hans Briger, the journeyman butcher, which had set fires such as this one and committed murders: Bobrowski joined him and Hildebrand Berwald, to mention only a few. To make a long story short: One thing happened near Subkau, something else was swung in Elbing; in January frost he raided the length and breadth of the Knights' country, cut the throat of the councillor Martin Rabenwald and filled him chock-full of lead. Then, because the cold refused to subside, he specialized in arson: Langgarten, along with the Church of St. Barbara and the howling Hospital of St. Barbara, went up in flames. He razed the beautiful, gaily painted Breitgasse. Finally Zantor, the voivod in Posen, caught him and hanged him. On September 14th, that's it, 1502. But if you think that was the end of it you're mistaken and doomed to burn. For now comes his brother, Simon Materna, avenges Gregor Materna, and regardless of the seasons sets fire to timber-frame houses and proud-gabled granaries. He maintains a storehouse for pitch, tar, and sulphur on Putzig Bay, and employs over three hundred maids, who all have to be maidens, winding tinder matches. He supplies the monastries of Oliva and Karthaus with funds, and zealous monks make him pitch torches. Thus equipped, he sets Petersiliengasse and Drehergasse flaming to high heaven. In this fire, laid especially for the purpose, he roasts twelve thousand pork sausages, a hundred and three sheep, and seventeen oxen to a fine crisp—not to mention the poultry, Island geese and Kashubian ducks—and feeds, yes by God, feeds the city's poor, the beggars from the suburbs, the cripples from Holy Ghost Hospital, and all those who come hobbling from Mattenbunden and the New City. And the houses of the patricians sizzle and sputter in rooster-red fire. Pepper sacks season the blaze, while food is roasted for the sick and hungry. Oh, Simon Materna—if they hadn't caught him and hanged him, he'd have set the world on fire to provide all the downtrodden with juicy roasts from the spit. And from him, the first class-conscious pyrotechnist, I am descended, yes, by God. And socialism will triumph, yes, by God."

This uproar, soon followed by endless gales of laughter—Goldmouth has launched a merry schoolbook story or two—lends the shanty fire, seen from outside, a touch of fiendish terror; for not only are the usual

997

onlookers, an easy prey for anything that smacks of ghosts, gripped with dread; but even the fire fighters of West Berlin, though good Protestants by birth and upbringing, have no thought but to cross themselves. The next wave of diabolical laughter sweeps away all four fire brigades. The helmeted men take barely time to roll up valuable hoses. Leaving the shanty fire to its own resources—strange to say, it shows no inclination to spread and consume the whole row of sheds—the fire fighters drive off with the well-known din. And not even a fire warden comes forward to hold vigil by the fire, for all ears are plugged with horror: in the heart of the furnace, diabolical guests are carousing; by turn they roar Communist slogans and burst into bestial laughter, after which the stage is taken over by a tenor, who sings higher than darting flames and fiery glow can sing: Latin, as sung in Catholic churches, desecrates Potsdamer Strasse from the Control Commission Building past Bülowstrasse.

The Sports Palace has never heard anything like it: a *Kyrie* that strikes sparks, a *Gloria in excelsis Deo* that teaches long-fingered flames to fold their hands. The arias are Goldmouth's offering. With mica-spiked, lemon-slim voice and childlike, forthright faith, he—the fire has finished the third course and is still nibbling hungrily at the dessert—believes: *in unum Deum*. The tenderly clinging *Sanctus* is followed by a *Hosanna* to which Goldmouth manages to lend an echolike polyphony. But when, in the velvety andante, the *Benedictus* breaks all altitude records, Matern, whose eyes have withstood all the smoke, can no longer hold back the tears: "Spare us the *Agnus Dei!*" But it's the jubilant round that pours Matern's emotion, which is threatening to spread to Jenny and Pluto, into a silk handkerchief: Goldmouth goes on singing *Dona nobis* until the grateful listeners have regained their composure and the flames, tongues, and sparks have all gone to sleep. The volutes of a pianissimo *amen* are spread like a blanket over the charred beams, molten glass, and the hot-air ballet that has sunk dead-tired to ashes.

Themselves tired, they crawl over the unharmed bar and leave the slumbering scene of the fire. Cautiously, step by little step, the dog in the lead, they reach the deserted Potsdamer Strasse, guarded only by street lamps. Jenny says how tired she is, and wants to go right off to bed. The drinks still have to be paid for. Goldmouth appoints himself host. Jenny wants to go home alone: "Nobody is interested in me." But the gentlemen insist on lending their protection. In Mansteinstrasse, across from Levdicke's, they say good night. At the house door Jenny, poor creature who is always being left behind, says: "You'd better go beddy-by too. You old night owls. Tomorrow's another day."

But for the two others, who are more likely to leave than to be left behind, the night is still young. And nature's immortal creation also stands fresh and attentive on four legs: "Heel, Pluto."

For there is still a leftover that wants to be tasted. On the one hand a leftover of cigarettes, lighted one from another, wish to go their way up Yorckstrasse past the Memorial Library, on the other hand an insubstantial leftover demands to be spoken of; it lodges between teeth and sets them on edge, all thirty-two of them.

But Goldmouth dotes on music such as this: "How happy it makes me, dear Walter, to hear you grind your teeth as in the blessed days of Amsel."

Matern, however, doesn't like to hear himself. In his innermost being—for the Grinder has an innermost being—he is staging wrestling bouts. Across Zossen Bridge, along Urban Harbor, the wrestlers grunt and groan. Lord knows who's trying to throw whom. Probably the whole Matern tribe is in there fighting: all conquering heroes on the lookout for worthy opponents. Is Goldmouth, for instance, fit for the ring? There he goes again with cynical talk, cynically smoking cigarettes that call everything into question. What in the fiery furnace was a jubilant credo without ambiguity, degenerates, not far from Admiral Bridge, into hoarse and cacophonous ifs and buts. Nothing in him is pure. Always standing values on their heads, so the pants slip down to the knees. his favorite theme: "The Prussians in general and the Germans in particular." Words of insidious praise for this people, among which he was doomed to suffer before and after the snow man. That won't do, Goldmouth! Even if it's May and the buds are popping: how can a man be in love with his murderers!

But even his love of Germany, when you listen carefully, is a twining of cynical laurel, taken from wax funeral wreaths. For instance, Goldmouth strews professions of faith across the Landwehr Canal: "I have found out, and you can take it from me, that the best and most long-lasting stamp pads are manufactured and utilized in the area bounded—as the song puts it—by the Adige and the Belt, the Meuse and the Memel."

With voice gone hoarse again, the smoker tosses sententious utterances into the claw-studded air along Maybach-Quay. His coffin nail participates in his remarks, shuttling from corner to corner of his mouth: "No, my dear Walter, you may still feel bitterness toward your great fatherland—but I love the Germans. Ah, how mysterious they are, how full of the forgetfulness which is pleasing to God! Not giving it a thought, they cook their pea soup on blue gas flames. And another thing: what other country in the world can boast such brown, velvety gravies?"

The scarcely flowing canal runs straight as a die. But then comes a fork: the left prong heads for the eastern port; up ahead lies the border of the Soviet sector; the right prong develops into the Neukölln Ship Canal. As the two of them with faithful dog stand on this memorable spot—across from them lies Treptow: everybody has heard of the war

999

memorial—Goldmouth indulges in words which, though worthy of the fork in the canal, carry noxious flotsam in their flow: "Of course you may say that every man is a potential scarecrow; for after all, and this should never be forgotten, the scarecrow was created in man's image. All nations are arsenals of scarecrows. But among them all it is the Germans, first and foremost, even more so than the Jews, who have it in them to give the world the archetypal scarecrow someday."

Not a word out of Matern. And the little birdies, who were already awake, pretend to be sleeping again. The usual grinding of teeth starts up. The aimless groping of a shoe on a flat pavement: no stone. What will I? Nowhere a *zellack*. My change of socks and shirts? I left my razor in the smoke-filled shanty. It looks like I'll have to. Or I'll clear out, beat it to the Soviet sector. That's where I was going in the first place, and I'm still hanging around here. So I'll just . . .

He thrusts his closed hand behind him, a wind-up: what a fine powerful thrower's stance! Goldmouth delights in the harmony of the movement. Pluto tenses. And Matern throws—well, what do you think?—the newly recovered pocketknife far away. What the Vistula, not without resistance, gave up, he gives to the Berlin Landwehr Canal, at the point where it forks. But no sooner has the pocketknife vanished with the usual splash, and seemingly for good, than Goldmouth is on the spot with well-meaning advice: "Don't worry, my dear Walter. For me it's the merest trifle. That section of the canal will be drained. There isn't much current at this point. You'll have your good old pocketknife back in two weeks at the most.—It made us into blood brothers, you know."

O impotence brooding eggs from which rage will hatch: naked and without fuzz. Matern releases a word. O human rage, always looking for words and finding one in the end. Matern flings a single word, which aims and strikes home. Human rage, which never has enough and heaps up repetitions intended as intensives. Several times in succession the word. The dog stands still. The canal forks. Goldmouth neglects to take a light from an almost burned-down cigarette. Leitmotive slips into murder motive. Matern takes aim and says: "SHEENY!"

At last the sparrows wake up. O lovely balmy May dawn under a bipartite sky. O night gone and day not yet come. O long in-between moment when the word "sheeny" is spoken, and doesn't feel like falling to the ground, but wants to hang in midair awhile!

It's Matern who sinks to the ground. He's overreached himself. It's really been too much for him: "First the interzonal trip with all the fuss and bother. Then the round from bar to bar. The change of air. The joy of finding his friend again. Most anybody would be floored. Every explanation applies only to the circumstances. Every word is too much. Do what you please with me."

And so Goldmouth's ebony cane summons a taxi. Tempelhof Airport. Departure gate. This gentleman, the dog, and I are in a hurry. We've got to catch the first plane for Hanover. We have to visit a plant that's situated below ground. The firm of Brauxel & Co. You've heard of it?"

The Hundred and Third and Bottommost Materniad

Anyone wishing to travel below ground will do well to take a start in the air: ergo, British-European Airways to Hanover-Langenfeld. The remaining miles on the flat surface are diminished by a company car: past cows and building sites, guided by detours and feeders, through a spring-green yet pallid countryside. A striking sight from the distance, the destination is stuck to the horizon: the conical waste pile, the brick-red buildings: lab, changehouse, boiler house, administration building, storehouse—and over all the roofs, towering above the waste pile and the dumping gear that goes with it: the stilt-legged headframe.

Who would want to build cathedrals in a day when the sky is held up by stagesets like this! This is Brauxel & Co., a firm which, though registered with the Hanover Potash Association and responsible to the Hanover Bureau of Mines, extracts not so much as a single ton of potash and yet lowers men in three shifts: powdermen, licensed muckers and drillers, all told one hundred and eighty-two miners.

And as long as pulleys in the headframe continue to drive cables over the whim, the man who alights first from the company car will no longer be called Goldmouth, but Herr Director or Herr Brauxel: so says the driver, so says the porter.

And the figure who gets out of the company car behind Brauxel is not yet Matern, but a black, full-grown shepherd, whom both Brauxel and the finally alighting Matern call Pluto.

But when they pass through the wrought-iron gate, which was installed in potash mining days, the porter takes his cap off to greet Herr Director Brauxel. Thereupon Matern, whom neither a night rich in wonders and not poor in startling conversations, nor a wonderfully serene flight along the Berlin-Hanover air corridor has deprived of his native capacity for amazement, cannot help asking a question: "How is it that the porter employed here looks so embarrassingly like my father, miller Anton Matern?"

To this Director Brauxel, who leads his guest straight to the changehouse, meanwhile whistling Pluto to heel as though the dog belonged to him, has the ultimate answer: "Porter Anton Matern does not look like miller Matern, he is the miller, he is your father."

Whereupon Matern, who likewise, but without results, whistles the dog to heel, draws the obscure but high-sounding conclusion: "In the end every father becomes a porter to every son."

The changehouse attendant submits to Matern a paper that has to be signed. Regulations prescribe that strangers to the mine, desirous of being lowered below ground with a view to visiting same, must confirm their intention with a signature. Matern signs and is led to a bathroom where, standing beside a dry tub, he is expected to remove his traveling clothes and put on light denims, woolen socks, high clodhoppers, a woolen scarf, and a new, yellow-varnished, and ill-fitting hard hat. He changes garment for garment and through the partition asks Director Brauxel in the adjoining bathroom: "What's become of Pluto?"

And Brauxel, who though director also has to exchange traveling clothes for a mine outfit, garment for garment, answers through the same partition: "Pluto's with me. Where else would he be?"

And thus attired, Brauxel and Matern, followed by Pluto, leave the changehouse. Each carries a carbide lamp in his left hand. The lamps as well as the denims and the twice-yellow hard hat efface the differences between director and visitor. But as they are passing the administration building, a hunchbacked little man, whom cuff protectors identify as the chief clerk, steps out of the door and obliges the gentlemen to pause. At the supposed chief clerk's request, Brauxel has to sign some papers that have accumulated during his absence. The chief clerk is glad to meet Herr Matern Junior. Then wishing them good luck, he lets them proceed to the headframe.

Followed by the dog, the two of them, Matern and Brauxel, cross a yard, where quantities of nailed-up crates are being hauled back and forth by forklift trucks; but there is no potash either in the crates or in warehouse bins.

And when they reach the foot of the headframe and Brauxel is about to step on the iron staircase leading to the shaft collar, Matern asks a question: "Is the dog going down too?" Brauxel isn't joking when he says: "Every dog comes from below and has to be lowered again in the end."

Matern has misgivings: "The dog has never been below ground." Whereupon Brauxel with authority: "The dog is company property and will have to get used to it."

This loss—a few hours ago he was still a dog owner—is too much for Matern: "He's my dog. Heel, Pluto!" But Brauxel whistles up ahead and the black shepherd takes the stairs to the shaft collar, which straddles the headframe at mid height. It's drafty on the platform. From obliquely below them, the drive wheel moves the pulleys above their heads: upper and lower cable tense in anticipation of the mine run.

But when strokes of a bell—four strokes meaning "go slow"—announce the arrival of the cage from the bottom, Matern wants to make a suggestion before it is too late: "Why not leave Pluto on the platform?

God knows what the rapid descent will do to him, and I hear it's hellishly hot down below."

Only when they are weighing down the cage—Pluto wedged in between Brauxel and Matern—is the director prepared to answer. The cage gate is closed. The trammer signals "ready" with three strokes, "go" with five strokes, and Brauxel says: "Every hell has its climate. The dog will have to get used to it."

And now the last daylight has been left upstairs. The descent from the platform (a hundred feet above the earth's surface) to the fill level on the pit bottom (twenty-eight hundred feet under the earth's surface) marks the beginning of the official tour of inspection, intended to give the stranger Walter Matern on-the-spot instruction.

He is advised to open his mouth and to breathe evenly. The pressure on his ears is explained by the speed of the lowering, the slight burnt smell by the friction between the falling cage and the guide rails of the shaft. The fingers of the updraft become more and more southerly; it finds it way through denim and up trouser legs. Matern claims to have noticed that Pluto is trembling; but Brauxel says everybody shivers who has to drop so far in barely one minute.

And before they reach the bottom, he enlightens Matern, for educational purposes, about the activities of potash-mining days and days within the memory of Brauxel & Co. The words "gangue rock" and "mine rock" drop fifty feet a second with them. At the same lowering speed there is talk of shutdowns and cable inspections: the cage cable consists of seven times thirty-two wire strands wound around a hempclad steel core. Loosening of the outer strands, overloaded steel cores, screw dislocations resulting in kinks, and cable jumping—these are the main causes of cable breaks, which, it should be added, are infrequent. Nor should rust erosion be forgotten, which digs its grooves even while the cable is running. For this reason grease, but it has to be non-acidic, must be applied to the cable, which has to be dry, and never must grease be applied to the whole length of the cable, but only in three-hundred-foot streches, for fear that fresh grease will get on the drive wheel, for this cable that's lowering us is the soul of the whole plant, its alpha and omega, it raises us to the light of day and carries us down below, so God help us if it.

And so Matern has no leisure to pay attention to the stomach flutter which is sometimes felt even in ordinary elevators. Pressure on the temples and watering of the eyes go unnoticed, because Brauxel is giving him a mental diagram of the shaft from the pulley covers to the return guides for cable and the so-called shaft sump.

With four warning strokes and the single stroke that calls the engine to halt, the trammer puts an end to the lesson which Brauxel has been able to funnel into the visitor in barely a minute; so vastly does a drop by cable enhance man's gift of assimilating and remembering.

The fill level has light, electric light, in readiness. And as they set foot on the pit bottom with Pluto in the lead, they return the *"Glück auf"* of Wernicke, the head foreman, who, in response to instructions from the surface, has come from the waste stall, where he had been checking the trap doors, to give Matern, the stranger, an account of the mine.

But Brauxel, who is as familiar with all scooped-out stalls, drifts, adits, and blind shafts as with the labyrinthine Old City where he went to school, admonishes the foreman: "Don't wander. Begin, as customary in our country, with a description of the situation after 1945; then come to the main point, how we stopped mining potash and began to turn out finished products bearing the trade mark of Brauxel & Co."

Thus admonished and accompanied by the three-tracked activity of the fill level, the foreman launches into his account of the mine: "Well then, in 1945, as our director has said, we in West Germany were left with only 39 per cent of Germany's over-all prewar potash production. The rest and, there's no denying it, the largest and most modern potash works were at the disposal of Soviet-occupied Central Germany. But even if things looked dark for us at first, West Germany had overtaken the East zone by the middle of '53, though by then our plant had given up potash and gone into the manufacture of finished products. But to get back to potash: Our operation was based on a large deposit extending from the Salzdetfurth Works in the eastern part of the Hildesheim Forest through Gross-Giessen, where our mine was located, to Hasede, Himmelsthür, Emmerke, and Sarstedt. As a rule, these salt veins are situated almost ten thousand feet below the surface, but here they are compressed into domes covered only by a layer of sandstone. Our mining rights covered roughly fourteen miles along the dome, some four miles of which had actually been tapped at the time when Brauxel & Co. gave up potash mining. Our company owns two shafts, two miles apart, going down to the twenty-eight-hundred-foot level. These two shafts, the one a mining, transportation, and fresh-air shaft, the other a vent shaft—are connected horizontally by four main galleries. On these galleries drifts lead to the stalls. Formerly the twenty-four-hundred-foot level was the pit bottom. There the rich Ronneberg deposit, containing for the most part 24 per cent of sylvinite and barely 14 per cent of carnallitite, was worked to a width of as much as sixty-five feet. In February 1952, when the drilling and blasting began on the Stassfurt reserve deposit, Wintershall AG took over the Burbach Potash Works, and our mine, allegedly because the Stassfurt deposit wasn't rich enough to be profitable, was first leased and then sold to Brauxel & Co. But most of the men stayed on because, in addition to our base pay and the tax-free miner's bonus of two marks fifty per shift, we were promised an extra indemnity for work unrelated to mining. But it wasn't until June 1953, after we had struck the plant for two weeks, that our bonus was paid regularly. It might also be worth mentioning that our own power plant, equipped with steam generators and substation, provides us with power and heat. Of the sixty-eight stalls, only a fraction of which had been worked out in mining days, thirty-six have had to be filled in with waste for reasons of safety. After a long-drawn-out inspection by the Bureau of Mines, Brauxel & Co. obtained permission to use the remaining thirty-two. Though at first it was hard for us experienced miners to give up our usual business of working muck holes, of operating scoops and shaking-conveyors, though the new working conditions struck us at first as unbefitting a miner, we finally got used to them. Thanks to Herr Brauxel's firmness, we were allowed to keep our membership in the miners' union."

Here Brauxel, the director, puts in: "That will do, Wernicke. And I hope no one will dare to set potash, coal, and iron ore above our finished products. What we raise from below can bear inspection from all sides."

But when Walter Matern, the stranger below, asks why it stinks so here at the fill level, where the smell comes from and what it's composed of, the director and foreman have to admit that the place still smells predominantly of potash-mining days: "The smell of brine oozing from the still damp waste blends with the earthy smell of sandstone and with lingering powder smoke, which is full of saltpeter because they used blasting gelatin to open up the roof. In addition, sulphur compounds deriving from algae and diatoms, mixed with the ozone generated by the sparks of electric cars and tramways, impregnate the air throughout the galleries and stalls. Further ingredients of the smell are: the salt dust that fills the air and settles everywhere, billows of acetylene from the lamps, traces of carbon dioxide, and stale grease. When the ventilation isn't too good, you can even guess what brand of beer was consumed here and is still being consumed in the era of Brauxel's finished products, namely, Herrenhäuser Pilsner, the bottled beer with the horse of Lower Saxony on the label."

And Matern, the stranger below, enlightened about the smell prevailing in all the well-ventilated galleries and in the poorly ventilated stalls, is of the opinion that in addition to the acrid smell there is also an oppressively warm draft blowing from the pit bottom to the fill level, although any amount of fresh spring air is available on the surface.

When they begin—and Pluto is not left behind—to move at first horizontally through the gallery on an electric trolley, and then vertically by cage to the waste stall—two thousand feet below the surface—they enter into a sultry August fug, the content of which is brine on top, sulphur compounds in the middle, and at the very bottom ancient blast smoke compounded with recent trolley ozone. The sweat dries faster than it breaks out.

"This is hell itself," says Matern.

But foreman Wernicke corrects him: "This is the place where our materials are made ready for the manufacturing process. This stall, which we call the first in accordance with the program of our visit, is where our new materials, requisitioned from above, are degraded, as we call it."

Dog in the lead, they enter the first stall through the narrow gangway. A room the size of a church nave opens up. Marked by neatly halved drill holes, layers of salt—overhanging cuts, face cuts, and underlying cuts—extend toward the far wall of the stall, which towers in such sacral remoteness as to suggest a chancel. But the room contains only two rows of enormous vats, sixteen on each side, extending at knee height from the narrow gangway to the far wall of the stall. In the narrow passage between the rows, Hinrich Schröter, formerly a powderman, services the vats with a long spoon-billed pole.

And the man in charge of the brine baths in stall No. 1 informs the stranger Matern: "We chiefly process cotton, synthetic wool, popeline, twill, calico, quick-shrinking flannel, jersey, taffeta, and tulle, but also raw silk and rayon. Not so long ago we handled a sizable lot of corduroy and twelve bolts of shot silk; occasionally there is a demand for small to medium lots of cashmere, cambric, and chiffon. Today, since the beginning of the night shift eight bolts of Irish linen, forty-eight inches in width before treatment, are in the first stage of degradation. We also have furs on hand, mostly pony, Persian lamb, and South African goat, and in the last three vats, on the upper left, a few brocades, an assortment of Brussels lace, and small quantities of piqué, crepe de Chine, and suede are in process of degradation. The remaining vats are degrading lining materials, denim, onion sacks, English sailcloth, and rope of every thickness. We work for the most part with cold caustic solutions, consisting of the usual waste brine with an admixture of magnesium choride. Only when intensive degradation of new materials is required to do we make use of a hot sylvinite solution to which magnesium bromide is added. Actually all our degradation baths, especially those containing bromide, call for above-average ventilation. But unfortunately, and Herr Wernicke, our foreman, will back me up, the ventilation on the two-thousand-foot level wasn't up to regulation even in the past, when they were still blasting open the stalls."

But Director Brauxel takes the reference to inadequate ventilation lightly. "Everything will be all right, boys, when the centrifugal ventilators come. They'll speed up the intake."

And they leave the first stall, over whose caustic solutions white vapors swirl, and find their way, foreman with raised lamp in the lead, to the second stall, where caustic-treated materials and new materials are subjected to dry degradation: a scoop driven by a sprocket wheel is moving a mountain of materials over loose muck, a leftover from potash-mining days.

But when with dog as chipper as ever they enter the third stall, no sprocket wheel is roaring, no magnesium chloride develops vapors; here, in lateral lockers, men's suits and overcoats and an assortment of uniforms are being devoured by moths. The articles here being degraded require attention only once a week. But Wernicke, the foreman, has the power of the keys and opens one of the lockers; moth silver sweeps up in a cloud. Quickly the door is closed.

In the fourth stall the visitors are introduced to an assortment of machines operated by former muckers and drillers, which on the one hand give caustic-scoop-moth-degraded materials an additional tearing, subject them to searing heat, and mark them with oil, ink, and wine spots, and on the other hand cut the now fully degraded materials to pattern, line them, and stitch them up. The director with dog, the overseer, and Matern the stranger are then received by the fifth stall, which rather resembles an engine room.

Scrap from the all-devouring surface, accumulated by auto grave-yards, engendered by wars and wrecking operations, scrap sorted out after boiler explosions, an anthology of scrap lies here in mounds, travels on conveyor belts, is disentangled with blow torches, takes rust-removing baths, hides a little while, and then returns galvanized to the conveyor belt: parts are assembled, ball joints play, gears come through the sand test unclogged, index wheels with chain hooks form a conveyor system that runs empty. Piston rods, clutches, bushings, governors, and suchlike gadgets obey electric motors. On man-high frames hang mechanical monsters. In busy skeletons elevators dawdle adagio from floor to floor. In stiffly vaulted thoraxes hammer mills have undertaken the never-ending task of crushing loud steel balls. Noise, noise!

And still more educational training in the sixth stall. Their ears are subjected to an experience which first makes Pluto restless, then sets him to howling under the steep late-Gothic roof.

And Matern, the stranger, says: "This is hell, indeed! We ought to have left the dog up top. The poor fellow is suffering."

But Brauxel, the director, is of the opinion that the dog's howling, flung vertically at the roof, blends admirably with the pretested electronic systems of the skeletons in process of manufacture: "Yet what has un-thinkingly been termed a hell gives bread and wages shift in shift out to thirty miners, trained by internationally known metal sculptors and sound experts. Our head foreman, the worthy Herr Wernicke, will bear me out when I say that muckers and drillers, who have been working in the mine for twenty years, are inclined to find hell anywhere on the surface, but no proof of hell below ground, not even when the ventilation is poor."

The mine-wise foreman nods several times and leads his director, the director's perseveringly howling dog, and the stranger out of the sixth stall, where the noise is unable to catch up with itself, through the muffling gangway, and out to the gallery, where the noise continues to recede.

They follow his buzzing carbide lamp to the mining shaft which at the beginning of the visit carried them from the pit bottom to the waste stall and the vent shaft.

Again descent is re-enacted, but only briefly, down to the level which the foreman traditionally calls the pit bottom but the director refers to as the "path of first-class disciplines."

In the seventh, eighth, and ninth stalls, the stranger below is exposed, in the interest of training, to the three cardinal emotions and their echo effects.

And once again Matern ventures to cry out: "This is hell, indeed!" although the weeping, every human variety of which is here represented, is tearless. Dry emotion turns the stall into a house of woe. Swathed in degraded mourning garments, frames, which only a little while before were scrap iron and then, resurrected as skeleton, were invested with noisy or soundless mechanisms and submitted to various mechanical and acoustical tests, now stand in weeping circles on the bare-scraped floor. Each circle has set itself a different tear-promoting yet desert-dry task. Here it begins. The next circle can't turn off the whimpering. This circle sobs deep within. Wailing, crescendo and decrescendo, dents and distends every circle. Muffled weeping, as into pillows. Blubbering as though the milk had been burned. Sniveling, handkerchief between teeth. Misery is contagious. Knotted into convulsions and threatened with hiccups. Plaintive to tearful: Bawling Suzy and Blubbering Lizzie. And above the shoulder-shaking, the breast-beating, the silent inward weeping, a voice on the verge of tears recites sob stories, snot-and-water stories, stories to often a stone: "And then the cruel bailiff said to the frozen little flower girl. But when the poor child held out her hands in supplication to the rich peasant. And when the famine was at its height, the king commanded that every third child in the land. The blind old woman was so lonely she thought she would have to. And when the brave young warrior lay thus miserably in his blood. Then grief spread like a shroud over the land. The ravens croaked. The wind moaned. The horses went lame. The deathwatch ticked in the beams. Woe! Woe! That will be your fate. There shall not be left one stone upon another, nor shall any eye remain dry. Woe!"

But those who in the seventh stall are subjected to the discipline of weeping, have no glands to open the floodgates. Here not even onion juice would help. These automats weep, but the coins refuse to jingle. And how indeed could this lacrimal discipline, encompassed as it is by salt above, below, and on all sides, be expected to release fountains with a crystalline residue, capable of seducing a goat?

And after so much futility, the director with dog and the foreman followed by the stranger leave the seventh chamber of the first emotion, to follow the busy gallery in silence until the foreman's lamp leads them through a gangway into the eighth stall, which seems almost too small to contain so much glee.

And once again Matern cannot hold back his cry: "What hellish laughter!" But actually—as Director Brauxel immediately points out—in the eighth stall only the gamut of the second emotion, human laughter, is assembled. We know the scale from tittering to splitting a gut. "It should be pointed out," says Wernicke, the foreman, "that the eighth stall is the only one in our entire plant which, because of the continuous explosions, has to be secured against cave-in with three rows of the finest mine props."

This is understandable. Frames, which sackcloth-clad were practicing grief and lamentation only a short time ago, are now guffawing bleating laughing in bright-colored, though also degraded, Scotch plaids and cowboy shirts. They double up, they lie down, they roll on the ground. Their built-in mechanisms permit belly-holding, thigh-slapping, and stamping. And while limbs make themselves independent, it bursts from a fist-size opening: the roar of people laughing themselves sick and sound, old men's laughter, tapped from beer barrels and wine cellars, staircase and lobby laughter, insolent, groundless, Satanic, sardonic laughter, nay more, insane and desperate laughter. It resounds in the cathedral with its forest of columns, mingles mates multiplies, a chorus struggling for breath: here laugh the company, the regiment, the army, the loons, homerically the gods, the people of the Rhineland, all Germany laughs at, with, in spite of, without end: German scarecrow laughter.

It is Walter Matern, the stranger below, who first speaks the characterizing word. And since neither the director nor the foreman corrected him when he spoke of hellish laughter, he calls the jokes that run back and forth between the laughing automats, which may as well be termed scarecrows, scarecrow jokes: "You heard this one? Two blackbirds and a starling meet in the Cologne Central Station . . . Or this one? A lark takes the interzonal train to Berlin for Corpus Christi, and when it gets to Marienborn . . . Or this one, it's really good: Three thousand two hundred and thirty-two sparrows decide to go to a whorehouse together, and when they come out, one of them has the clap. Which one? Wrong!

Once again now, listen carefully: Three thousand two hundred and thirty-two sparrows . . ."

Matern, the stranger below, pronounces this brand of humor too cynical for his taste. To his mind, humor should have a liberating, healing, often even a saving effect. He misses human warmth, or call it kindness, charity. Such qualities are promised him for the ninth stall. Whereupon all, including the never laughing Pluto, turn away from the scarecrow laughter and follow the gallery until a gangway branching off to the left announces the stall inhabited by the third cardinal emotion.

And Matern sighs, because the foretaste of dishes not yet served embitters his palate. At this Brauxel has to raise his curious lamp and ask what there is to sigh about. "I'm sorry for the dog, who hasn't a chance to romp about up above where the spring is green, who has to follow at heel down below and live through this meticulously organized inferno."

Brauxel, however, who is carrying not the usual plain walking stick but an ebony cane with an ivory crutch, which only a few hours before belonged to an immoderate smoker calling himself Goldmouth, never smokes below ground but says: "If this, our plant, absolutely has to be called an inferno by a stranger to the mine, it only goes to show that the company needs a hellhound of its own; just see how our light teaches the animal to cast a hellish shadow that devours the gallery: already the gangway is sucking him in. We must follow."

Here narrow-eyed hate, never oxidizing rage, cold and hot revenge keep school. In wind-inflated and consequently voluminous battle dress, which repeated caustic degradation has injected with the traces of seven boiler battles. Scarecrows which sackcloth-clad operated a tear pump that persistently said no, scarecrows which in bright checks and loud polka dots let their built-in humor-developer unwind, are standing in the empty stall, each scarecrow by himself. So this is the homework imposed on rage, hate, revenge: full-grown crowbars must be bent into question marks and suchlike gewgaws. Patched countless times, rage must burst and blow itself up again with its own lungs. Hate has to burn holes in its own knee with its narrow-set eyes. But cold and hot revenge must go round —Don't turn around, revenge is around—and grind whole spoonfuls of quartz pebbles between their teeth.

So that's what the meal sounds like that Matern, the stranger, had a foretaste of. School fare. Scarecrow fare. For not satisfied with bursting and with burning holes, not finding expression enough in the bending of crowbars, rage, the great valve burster, and hate, the blowtorch, spoon themselves full from feed troughs into which two employees of Brauxel & Co. hourly shovel a supply of the pebbles—food for grinding teeth— which are plentiful on the green surface of the earth.

Thereupon Matern, who from earliest childhood has ground his teeth whenever rage rode him, hate compelled him to stare at a fixed point, and revenge commanded him to make rounds, turns away from these scarecrows who have raised his particularity to the level of a universal discipline.

And to the foreman, who with upraised lamp is leading them from the ninth stall to the gallery, he says: "I should think that these immoderately expressive scarecrows would sell well. Man loves to see his mirror image in a blind rage."

But Wernicke, the foreman, counters: "It is true that formerly, in the early fifties, our odonto-acoustical models were in great demand both on the domestic and on the foreign market, but now that the decade has come of age, collections based on the third cardinal emotion find takers only in the young African states."

Whereupon Brauxel smiles subtly and pats Pluto on the neck: "Don't worry about the marketing problems of Brauxel & Co. Hate, rage, and roving revenge will be back in style one of these days. A cardinal emotion that promotes the grinding of teeth can't be a passing fad. To abolish revenge is to take revenge on revenge."

These words mount the electric trolley with them and demand to be mulled over during the long ride through two trap doors, past barred blind shafts and waste-filled stalls. Only at their destination, where the foreman promises a visit to the tenth to twenty-second stalls, is Brauxel's proposition about unabolishable revenge forgotten, though without loss to its succinctness.

For even in the tenth, eleventh, and twelfth stalls, where athletic, religious, and military exercises, in other words, relay races, skipping processions, and changes of the guard, are being performed, rage, hate, the revenge which, because it is always roving, cannot be rooted out, the futile tear pump, and the built-in humor-developer, in short, the cardinal emotions weeping, laughter, and the grinding of teeth provide the deep-seated foundation on which athletic scarecrows are able to break records at pole vaulting, penitent scarecrows at split-pea racing, and newly recruited scarecrows at close combat. How scarecrow outdoes scarecrow by a scarecrow head, how scarecrows keep bettering their time at elevating scarecrow crosses, how they overcome barbed-wire entanglements, not with old-fashioned wire cutters but by eating them up, barbs and all, then evacuate them barbless in scarecrow fashion, deserves to be recorded on charts, and recorded it is. Employees of Brauxel & Co. measure and enter: Scarecrow records and rosary lengths. Three stalls that were blasted in potash-mining days until they attained gymnasium length, church height, and the width of broad-shouldered antiaircraft dugouts, provide over four hundred team-spirited scarecrows, halleluia scarecrows, holdouttothelastgasp scarecrows per shift with room in which to develop their electronically guided energies. Remote-controlled for the present—the control room is where the windlass platform used to be—indoor sport festivals, pontifical offices, and autumn maneuvers, or the other way around, athletic events for recruits, divine services in the front lines, and the blessing of scrap-iron scarecrow weapons fill schedules in order that later on, when, as they say, an emergency arises, every record can be broken, every heretic unmasked, and every hero find his victory.

The director with his dog and the visitor with Wernicke, the mine-wise foreman, leave the caustic-degraded athletes, the moth-degraded monks' habits, and the scoop-degraded fatigue uniforms, which have to creep and crawl toward the enemy while the scarecrow enemy likewise creeps and crawls, for in the schedule it is written: Creeping and crawling. Creeping and crawling toward. Mutual creeping and crawling up to.

But when, as the visit continues, the thirteenth and fourteenth stalls are inspected, the scarecrow collections in training are no longer dressed in athletic costumes, altar-boy red, and camouflage fatigues; the goings-on in these two stalls are strictly civilian. For in a family stall and an administrative stall the democratic virtues of the scarecrow state, whose form of government is determined by the needs of its citizens, are in-culcated, developed, and put into daily practice. Harmoniously scarecrows sit at the table, at the television screen, and in moth-degraded camp tents. Scarecrow families—for the family is the germ cell of the state—are instructed concerning every article of the provisional constitution. Loudspeakers proclaim what polyphonic families repeat, the scarecrow preamble: "Conscious of its responsibility before God and men, inspired by the will to preserve our national and political scarecrow unity . . ." Then Article 1, dealing with the dignity of scarecrows, which is inviolable. Then the right, guaranteed in Article 2, of the scarecrow personality to develop freely.

Then one thing and another, and finally Article 8, which guarantees to all scarecrows the right to assemble peacefully and unarmed, without notice and permission. And nodding their heads, scarecrow families acquiesce in Article 27: "All German-blooded scarecrows are uniformly stamped with the trade mark of the firm of Brauxel & Co."; nor is there any opposition to Article 16, Paragraph 2: "Victims of persecution will enjoy the right of asylum below ground." And all this political science, from the "universal right to grouse" to "forced expatriation," is practiced in the fourteenth pit: scarecrow voters step into polling booths; discussion-welcoming scarecrows discuss the dangers of the welfare state; scarecrows whose journalistic talent condenses in a daily newspaper invoke the freedom of the press, Article 5; the parliament convenes; the Scarecrow Supreme Court rejects a last appeal; in questions of foreign policy, the opposition supports the government party; party discipline is exerted; the tax collector holds out his hand; freedom of coalition connects stalls that do not border on the same gallery; in accordance with Article 1 B, 3 a, scarecrow analysis with the help of the lie detector developed by Brauxel & Co. is declared unconstitutional; political life flourishes; nothing hampers communication; the self-government of scarecrows, guaranteed by Article 28 A 3, begins below ground and extends, on the flat and hilly surface, to the Canadian wheatfields, to the rice paddies of India, to the endless cornfields of the Ukraine, to every corner of the earth where the products of Brauxel & Co., namely, scarecrows of one variety or another, do their duty and put a stop to the depredations of birds.

But Walter Matern, the stranger below, says once again after the thirteenth and fourteenth stalls have shown themselves to be civilian and civic: "Heavens above, this is hell. It is hell itself!"

And so, in order to refute the stranger, Wernicke, the foreman, raising his lamp, leads Walter Matern and the director with compliant dog to the fifteenth, sixteenth, and seventeenth stalls, which house Eros unleashed, Eros inhibited, and phallic narcissism.

For here all uniformed discipline and civic dignity are defied, because hate, rage, and roving revenge, which only a short time before seemed to be checked by the administrative apparatus, bloom afresh, covered with degraded yet flesh-pink skin. Because all unleashed, inhibited, and narcissistic scarecrows nibble on the same cookie, the recipe for which makes dough of all lusts but satisfies no one regardless of how strenuously and in what positions the bare-assed mob fucks and squirts. Such results, to be sure, are registered only in the fifteenth stall, where the unleashed Eros permits none of the rutting scarecrows to ring the knell of an erection which has been at it for innumerable shifts. No stopper can withstand the flood. No intermission bell rings for this permanent orgasm. Unchecked flows the scarecrow snot, a sylvinite-containing product, as foreman Wernicke explains, which has been developed in the laboratories of Brauxel & Co and injected with gonococcuslike agents, so that the unleashed, steady-flowing scarecrows enjoy the benefit of irritation and itching similar to those observed in cases of common gonorrhea. But this pestilence is allowed to spread only in the fifteenth and not in the sixteenth and seventeenth stalls. For in these two there is no ejaculation and in the inhibited stall not even the indispensable erection. In the narcissistically phallic stall the solo scarecrows struggle in vain, despite the sultry music with prurient words which tries to help them, despite the sexy movie excerpts that occupy the screens which have been hung on the far walls of the repressed and narcissistic stalls. No sap may rise. Every snake lies dormant. All satisfaction has remained above ground; for Matern, the stranger below, says: "That's unnatural. Those are the torments of hell. Life, real life, has more to offer. I know. I've lived it!"

Suspecting at this point that the stranger is troubled by a lack of cultural life here below, Wernicke, the foreman, leads him and the director, who is smiling subtly to himself and holding Pluto loosely by the collar, to the eighteenth, nineteenth, and twentieth stalls, which are all situated on the next lower, the twenty-five-hundred-foot level, and provide room respectively for philosophical, sociological, and ideological knowledge, achievements, and antinomies.

No sooner has he arrived on this level than Matern turns away: the stranger doesn't want to go on; hell fatigues him; he would like to breathe in the daylight again; but sternly tapping his ebony cane, which only a few hours before belonged to a certain Goldmouth, Brauxel refers to something that Matern is supposed to have done up above: "Has the stranger forgotten under what circumstances he, in the early morning of this very day, threw a pocketknife into the Landwehr Canal, which flows through Berlin, a city situated on the sunlit surface?"

And so Matern, the stranger, is not allowed to turn away; he is obliged to pass through the gangway and face up to the philosophical insights that dwell loquaciously in the eighteenth stall.

But not Aristotle, not Descartes or Spinoza, from Kant to Hegel not a soul. From Hegel to Nietzsche: a vacuum! Nor any sign of a neo-Kantian or neo-Hegelian, no Rickert of the lion's mane, no Max Scheler, nor does the phenomenology of any goateed Husserl fill the stall with eloquence, permitting the stranger to forget what hellish torments the vulgarian Eros had to offer; no below-ground Socrates contemplates the world above ground; but He, the pre-Socratic, he multiplied a hundred-fold. He capped with a hundred caustic-degraded, once Alemannic stockingcaps, He in buckled shoes, in a linen smock: a hundred times He, coming and going. And thinks. And speaks. Has a thousand words for Being, for time, for essence, for world and ground, for the with and the now, for the Nothing, and for the scarecrow as existential frame. Accordingly: Scareness, being-scared, scare-structure, scare-view, primeval scare, scaring-away, counterscare, scare-vulnerable, scare-principle, scare-situation, unscared, final scare, scare-born time, scare-totality, foundation-scare, the law of scare. "For the essence of the scarecrow is the transcendental threefold dispersal of scarecrow suchness in the world project. Projecting itself into the Nothing, the scarecrow *physis,* or burgeoning, is at all times beyond the scarecrow such and the scarecrow at-hand . . ."

Transcendence drips from stockingcaps in the eighteenth stall. A hundred caustic-degraded philosophers are of one and the same opinion: "Scarecrow Being means: to be held-out-into Nothing." And the anxious question of Matern, the stranger below, who casts his voice into the stall: "But what of man, in whose image the scarecrow was created?" is answered by one and a hundred philosophers: "The scarecrow question calls ourselves—the askers—into question." At this Matern withdraws his voice. A hundred matching philosophers come and go on the salt floor, greeting each other essentially: "The scarecrow exists self-grounded."

With oldtime buckled shoes they have even trampled down paths. Now and then they fall silent, then Matern hears their mechanisms. The principle of sufficient scare is starting up again.

But before the hundred-times present, moth-scoop-and-caustic-degraded philosopher can run off his built-in sound tape again, Matern escapes to the gallery. He would gladly run for it, but can't, for he is still a stranger to the mine and would certainly go astray: "The scarecrow comes-to-be in errancy, where, erring in circles, it fosters error."

So thrown back upon Wernicke, the mine-wise foreman, and reminded of hell by Pluto's blackness, he is driven through stalls whose numbers make it clear that no stall is spared him.

Under the nineteenth roof sociological insights are gathered together. The forms of alienation, the theory of social stratification, the introspective method, the pragmatic nihilism that dispenses with values, pure behaviorism, factual statements, and analyses of concepts, the static and dynamic approach, not to mention sociological ambivalence and divers stratification structures, are embodied as mobiles. Degraded in a variety of ways, modern society listens to lectures on collective consciousness. Habit scarecrows develop into environment scarecrows. Secondary scarecrows correspond to the scarecrow norm. Determined scarecrows and undetermined scarecrows carry on a debate, the outcome of which neither Matern, the stranger below, nor Brauxel the mine-wise director, with dog and foreman, is inclined to wait for; for in the twentieth stall all ideological differences are argued out: a scarecrow controversy which Matern is able to follow, because a similar muddle prevails inside him. Here as in Matern's interior the question is: "Is there a hell? Or is hell already on earth? Do scarecrows go to heaven? Is the scarecrow descended from the angels, or were there scarecrows before the angels were conceived of? Are scarecrows themselves angels? Did the angels or the scarecrows invent the bird? Is there a God, or is God the first scarecrow? If man was created in God's image and the scarecrow in the image of man, is the scarecrow not the image and likeness of God?"—Oh, Matern would like to say yes to every question, he would like to hear a dozen more questions forthwith and to answer them all in the affirmative: "Are all scarecrows equal? Or are there elite scarecrows? Are scarecrows the property of the people? Or is every peasant entitled to claim scarecrow ownership? Of what race are scarecrows members? Is a Germanic scarecrow superior to a Slavic scarecrow? Is a German scarecrow allowed to buy from a Jewish one? Don't Jews lack the gift? Is a Semitic scarecrow even conceivable? Scarecrow sheeny, scarecrow sheeny!" And once again Matern escapes to the gallery; it asks no questions which he must answer blindly, all in the affirmative.

Soothingly, as though director and foreman wished to bandage the exhausted visitor's wounds, the twenty-first stall opens up to him: a feast for the eyes, to be contemplated in silence. Here the turning points in history are scarecrowified. Degraded yet dynamic, scarecrow history unfolds in its proper order, reciting dates, defenestrations, and peace treaties. After caustic bath and moth feast, old-time brooch and Wellington hat, Stuart collar and rakish sombrero, Dalmatic and two-cornered seafarer's hat embody fateful hours and years of destiny. They revolve and bow according to the fashion. Winged words—here Guelf, here Ghibelline! —Under my rule every man can save his soul according to his own lights . . . Give me four years' time . . . ! occupy the air and are replaced by others. And all the striking poses, still or in pantomime: The bloodbath at Verden. The victory on the Lechfeld. Canossa. Young Konradin rides and rides. Gothic madonnas make no attempt to economize on drapery. Sable predominates when the council of Electors is established. Who is stepping on the fathomslong train of that houppelande? Hussites and Turks influence customs. Knights and rust mate. Splendor-loving Burgundy contributes red, brocade, and silk tents lined with velvet. But when codpieces swell and braguettes can scarcely contain their exuberant contents, the monk nails his theses to the door. O Hapsburg lip casting its shadow on a century! Bundschuh goes round, scratching pictures from walls. But Maximilian tolerates slit doublets, jerkins, and low-crowned caps bigger than haloes. Above the Spanish black stand foam-born and thrice-starched ruffs. The rapier replaces the broadsword and ushers in the Thirty Years' War, which whimsically modifies the styles. Outlandish plumes, leather jerkins, and top boots move into winter quarters here and there. And no sooner have the Wars of Succession designed the full-bottomed periwig than the three-cornered hat, in the course of three Silesian wars, becomes more and more severe. But bag wig, *baigneuse,* and *trompeuse* are no safeguard against scissors-grinders and sansculottes: heads must fall. Represented in a striking mobile in the twenty-first stall. And yet, for all its discolored Bourbon white, the Directoire hatches the flowery Restoration. The Congress dances in split skirts and calf-pinching nankeen. The swallowtail survives the censorship and the riotous days of March. The men of the Paulskirche speak into their top hats. To the strains of the Yorck March, the Düppeln redoubts are scaled. The Ems Dispatch, teacher's pet of all history teachers. Bismarck resigns in a cape. In frock coats enter: Caprivi, Hohenlohe, and Bülow. The Kulturkampf, the Triple Alliance, and the Herero uprising yield three color-saturated images. And don't forget to mention the red dolman of the Zieten Hussars at Mars-la-Tour. And then in moth-degraded Balkan environment shots are fired. Victory bells are sounded. That little river is the Marne. Steel helmets replace spiked helmets. The gas mask has come to stay. In wartime crinoline and high boots, the Kaiser leaves for Holland, because of the dagger thrust from the rear. Whereupon cockadeless soldiers' councils.

Kapp makes his putsch. Spartacus rises up. Paper money crackles. The Stresemann suit votes for the Enabling Act. Torchlight parades. Books burn. Brown predominates. A November tableau: a kaftan stuffed with straw. Then fancy-dress balls. Then prison stripes. Then army boots, special communiqués, Winter Aid, earmuffs, snow hoods, camouflage uniforms, special communiqués . . . And in the end the radio symphony orchestra in its brown work clothes plays something from *Götterdämmerung*. That is always appropriate, a leit- and murder motive that flits like a spook through the entire history, imaged and resurrected in scarecrows, which fills the twenty-first stall.

Thereupon Matern, the stranger below, bares his head and with company-owned scarf dries the beads from his scalp. Even in his school-days, historical dates dropped from his book to the floor and vanished in cracks. Only his family history finds him in command of figures; but here scarecrows do not mime regional Materniads, here the war of investitures and Counterreformation are enacted; mechanically and by means of fist-size electric motors negotiations are carried on: the Peace of Westphalia; in scarecrow fashion assemble those who—when, where, with whom, against whom, without England—voice grievances, make proclamations, put under ban, in brief make history; appropriately costumed from turning point to turning point.

And when the corny round begins anew, flits across the Lechfeld to Canossa, and makes the young Hohenstaufen scarecrow ride again, the stranger is unable to behead his ever-ready comment: "A hell! This is indeed a hell!"

And he has similarly infernal words at his command when with dog they leave the twenty-second stall, which, made to look like the floor of a stock exchange, seems to be too small for the investing, market-con-quering, and prosperity-creating potential leaders. The mere sight of scarecrow-nimble trust formation, the acoustic charm of slight market fluctuations, the board of directors meeting raised to monumental stature wring from Matern the unminerly cry: "This is hell. Hell AG."

He is no more loquacious when discharged by the twenty-third stall, which, fifty feet in height, houses, between overhanging salt and under-lying salt, a highly acrobatic discipline that calls itself "internal emigra-tion." One might suppose that only scarecrows could knot themselves so inextricably, that only scarecrows would have the power to crawl into their own viscera, that scarecrows alone could give the subjunctive body within and clothing without. But since—according to the statutes—the scarecrow mirrors the image of man, there must be similar walking sub-junctives on the sunlit surface of the earth.

The stranger below has loaded his voice with scorn: "Your hell hasn't forgotten anybody. Not even the ichneumon."

And Brauxel, the director, replies with shadow-casting ebony cane:

"What can we do? The demand is great. The catalogues we distribute internationally are remarkable for their completeness. We have no remainders. The twenty-third stall is especially vital to our export program. People still emigrate internally. It's warm inside, you know your way around, there's nobody to bother you."

But though equally double-jointed, the goings-on are less sedentary in the twenty-fourth stall, the stall of the degraded opportunists. Here reaction speed is tested. At regular intervals, lamps hanging from the roof, not unlike the traffic lights of the upper world, flash sharp colors and political symbols: and naked scarecrows, whose inborn mechanism hangs unconcealed within their skeletons, have to change their rags at high speed under the prodding of the second hand and make parts in their caustic-degraded hair: for a time the hairdo was divided on the left side; now the part is worn on the right; shortly thereafter a part in the middle becomes the fashion; and every shading: half-left, half-right, and hairdo without any part at all can also, or might, be in demand.

This act amuses Matern—"What diabolical fun!"—all the more so as his yellow-varnished hard hat protects a skull, the forehead of which has been considerably heightened by the raging succession of opinions characteristic of conditions above ground, until with the help of the fair sex, as Matern has to admit, the whole meadow refuses to grow. The stranger is deeply relieved at the thought that no one will ever again be able to make him change his hairdo, to shift his part in accordance with a trend. "If you have rehearsed still other farces, I shall gladly look upon hell as a playhouse."

Matern is beginning to feel at home below ground. But Wernicke, the foreman, raises his buzzing carbide lamp. On the twenty-five-hundred-foot level, he has only one horror play left—in the twenty-fifth stall. This virtually plotless one-acter, which under the title *Atomic Particularities* has been on the program since potash-mining days, stifles Matern's high spirits at once, although the words of a classical poet provide the background for the silent action. What above ground is called absurd has the taste of reality below; separate members act independently. Jumping heads, for whose particularity even a neck was too much, are unable to scratch themselves. In short: each of the items that make the body a composite structure lives on independently. Arm and leg, hand and torso pose to an accompaniment of highsounding words which, ordinarily spoken in front of the footlights, are here recited behind the curtain: "O God, O God! This marriage is terrible, but eternal." "Welcome, my worthy friends. What important business brings you all to me?" "But soon I will come among you and hold terrible muster."

In Schiller, to be sure, there is the parenthetical instruction: "They exit trembling." But these obstinate scarecrow fragments are longplaying mimes, which never exit. An inexhaustible repertory of quotations permits of solitary genuflections. Solo hands speak for themselves. Heads heaped up like chunks of rock salt lament in chorus: "No greater sorrow than to recall happy days in a time of misery."

During a brief descent—with a double stroke of the bell, the trammer announces the pit bottom, where lies the fill level and hence also the hope that hell may be exhausted and ascent decided upon—Matern, wedged into the cage between director and foreman with dog, is informed that the mobile scarecrow fragments he has just seen have recently been in great demand, especially in the Argentine and in Canada, where the wide expanse of the wheatfields necessitates echeloned scarecrows.

And as the three of them with dog stand on the twenty-eight-hundred-foot level, the director gives Wernicke the cue for the lines introducing the final phase of the tour of inspection, and the foreman complies: "We have followed the stages of production on the three upper levels and have witnessed the various kinds of degradation as well as the assembly process. We have tried to make it clear that all the disciplines, from the athletic to the atomic-particular, are based upon the three central motives. We still have to show how the scarecrows are familiarized with the tasks they will have to perform on the surface. In the twenty-sixth, twenty-seventh, and twenty-eighth stalls we shall witness object lessons, tests from which no scarecrow produced by Brauxel & Co. has ever been exempted."

"That is cruelty to animals," says Matern even before the twenty-sixth stall is opened. "Leave the animals in peace," he shouts up at the roof when he is compelled to hear that sparrows, which Brauxel calls "our dear, unassuming citizens of the world," cannot stop chirping even below ground.

And the director says: "Here our export scarecrows are made acquainted with sparrows and with the varieties of wheat that they will soon have to guard against the depredations of birds. Each scarecrow to be tested—here a collection of Zealand rye scarecrows, whose sphere of action will be southwestern South Africa—is expected to protect a limited radius of attraction, rendered alluring by rye seed, from the incursion of test sparrows. In the course of this shift, as I see, still other collections are being tested: twelve assortments of Odessa scarecrows, which will have to prove their mettle over South Russian Girka wheat and Ukrainian Sandomir wheat. In addition our La Plata scarecrows, very much in demand, which have helped the Argentines to achieve record wheat harvests. Further, eight assortments of Kansas scarecrows will be familiarized with the protection of the Kubanka variety, a summer wheat which, I might add, is also grown in South Dakota. Smaller lots of wheat scarecrows will have to keep sparrows at a distance from Polish Sandomirka and from the bearded and frost-resistant Banat wheat. Here as in the twenty-seventh and twenty-eighth stalls, we shall test collections that are in demand for two-rowed Poltava barley, for Northern French brewer's barley, Scandinavian panicled oats, Moldavian corn, Italian cinquantino corn, and the North American and Soviet varieties of corn, grown in southern Russia and the Mississippi lowlands. While in this stall only sparrows are to be excluded from the radius of attraction, in the next stall birds of the pigeon family, especially rock pigeons, which also prey on rape seed, flax seed, and peas, are applied to the export scarecrows to be tested. Occasionally crows, daws, and meadowlarks are admitted as test material, while in the twenty-eighth stall thrushes and blackbirds test our orchard scarecrows and starlings our vineyard scarecrows.—But we can set the stranger's mind at rest: all of our test birds, from the sparrows to the rock pigeons, finches, larks, and starlings, have been brought down from the surface with the approval of the authorities. The S.P.C.A. of Hanover and Hildesheim inspects our testing stalls every three months. We are not unfriendly to birds. We co-operate with them. Our scarecrows have the utmost contempt for air rifles, lime twigs, and bird netting. Indeed, I am proud to say that Brauxel & Co. has repeatedly and publicly protested against the barbarous catching of song birds by the Italians. Our success on all continents, our Ohio and Maryland scarecrows, our Siberian Urtoba scarecrows, our scarecrows in Canadian Manitoba wheat, our rice scarecrows, which protect Javanese rice and the Italian ostiglione variety grown near Mantua, our corn scarecrows, which have helped Soviet corn harvests to approach the records set in America, all our scarecrows, whether they protect native rye, Moravian Hanna barley, the Milton oats of Minnesota, the celebrated Bordeaux wheat, the rice paddies of India, the Cuzco corn of southern Peru, or Chinese millet and Scottish buckwheat from the depredations of birds, all the products of Brauxel & Co. without exception are in harmony with nature; they themselves *are* nature: crows and scarecrows form a harmony; indeed, were it not for the scarecrow, there would be no crows; and both, crow and scarecrow—created by the same God —contribute to solving the mounting problem of feeding the world. The bird pecks the larvae of the corn fly, the black corn borer, and the malignant wild mustard seed, while over the ripening corn the scarecrow turns off all bird song, the cooing of pigeons and the chattering of sparrows, and banishes the starlings from vineyards, the blackbirds and thrushes from cherry trees."

And yet, eloquently as Director Brauxel lauds the harmony prevailing between birds and scarecrows, the words "cruelty to animals" keep falling from the lips of Matern, the stranger below. When he is now doomed to hear that Brauxel & Co., in line with its rationalization program, has begun to let sparrows, rock pigeons, and blackbirds nest, brood, and hatch in the mine, when it dawns on him that whole generations of birds have never seen the light of day and look upon rock salt ceilings as the sky, he speaks of the infernal torments of infernal birds, though all three stalls sound as merry as the merry month of May: the song of the finches and larks, the cooing of pigeons, the music of the daws, unorganized sparrow hubbub, in short, the sound effects of a sap-fomenting day in May fill the three stalls; and only very seldom, when the ventilation of the twenty-eight-hundred-foot level weakens, are employees of Brauxel & Co. obliged to gather up feathered folk, whose *joie de vivre* has been impaired by the atmospheric conditions.

The stranger affects indignation. He speaks of a "hellish outrage." If the foreman hadn't promised him that in the twenty-ninth stall he would witness the end of all scarecrow training, the graduation exercises, the great scarecrow mass meeting, he would run blindly for the fill level, there—if he ever made it—to scream for light and air, the light of day and the month of May.

But under the circumstances he consents to watch the shindig from the sidelines. In this scarecrow show the graduates of all the preceding stalls are represented. Halleluia scarecrows and close-combat scarecrows, and whatever scarecrow society has to offer: many-headed scarecrow families, the scarecrow cock at the head. Unleashed, inhibited, narcissistic scarecrow sex fiends. In degraded glad rags they have come to the scarecrow get-together, the scarecrow ball: the stockingcap scarecrow and the standardized secondary scarecrows, elite angelic scarecrows and the scarecrows of history: Burgundian nose and Hapsburg lip, Stuart collar and Suvorov boot, Spanish black and Prussian blue; in among them the touts of the free-market economy; internal refugees, almost indiscernible, because they have crawled back into their own wombs; who is speaking resolute language over there? Who is keeping up scarecrow morale and fostering scarecrow development? It's the universally popular opportunists, who wear red under brown and will slip into ecclesiastical black any minute. And with this gathering of the people for a republic is here represented by its average citizens—mingle the atomic and stage-struck particularities. A colorful gathering: scarecrow-colored. Beloved scarecrow German makes friends. Scarecrow music appeases hate, rage, and roving revenge, the cardinal emotions bred in stalls, which oil every scarecrow's mechanism and, serving as monitors, brandish the scarecrow whip: "God help you if. God help you if you!"

But the graduates are well mannered, though at all times ready for mischief. Pickaback scarecrows tease singing Salvation Army scarecrows. The scarecrow vulture can't stop thieving. The historical group, "Wallenstein's Death," has been joined by hospital-pale nurses. Who would have expected the pre-Socratic stockingcap scarecrow to be conversing with the stale theory of social stratification? Flirtations are in the making. Laughter, acquired in the seventh stall and unjustly called "infernal laughter," mingles with the weeping of the eighth stall and the teeth-grinding of the ninth; for where has there ever been a party at which jokes were not laughed at, the loss of a pocketbook wept over, and a sharp but soon settled quarrel ironed out amid a grinding of teeth?

But as now, accompanied by the mine director with dog and the stranger following the foreman, the graduates are led from the graduation celebrations into the nearby thirtieth stall, silence prevails for a moment.

A sense of shame commands Matern to avert his face, for the assembled guild of scarecrows, guided as he knows by remote control, "soulless automats," as he puts it, take the oath to the firm of Brauxel & Co. And the scarecrows have the audacity to babble: "So help me God." What begins with the customary "I solemnly swear . . ." ends, after scarecrows have taken the oath never to deny their origin, namely the pit below, never irresponsibly to desert the field assigned them, always to carry out their primary mission of firmly but fairly discouraging birds, ends with Him, whose eye also watches the pit below: "So help me God."

It remains to be mentioned only that in the thirty-first stall individual scarecrows and scarecrow collections are packed and bedded in crates for export; that in the thirty-second stall cases are labeled, bills of lading made out, and trucks dispatched.

"This," said Wernicke, the foreman, "brings us to the end of our long production process. We hope you have been able to form a rough idea. Certain features, such as all the laboratories situated on the surface, the automation, and our electrical workshops, are not included in the tour of inspection. Similarly our glassworks may be visited only by special permission. Perhaps you would like to ask Herr Brauxel."

But Walter Matern, the stranger below, has had enough. He craves to return to the light faster than the trolley can reach the shaft. Matern is supersaturated.

For that reason he has no heart to protest when Brauxel, the director, takes Pluto, the black shepherd, by the collar and chains him in the place where the tour of inspection began, where the view of the mine ends, where, as Brauxel has ordered, the mine-joyous inscription *"Glück auf"* has its place, but where, as Matern suggests, what ought to be written is: "Abandon hope all ye who enter here!"

Already the cage is opening for the ascent when the stranger drags up final words: "See here, that's my dog."

Whereupon Brauxel utters words of conclusion: "What object worthy of his guardianship has the bright surface of the earth to offer a dog such as this? This is his place. Here where the mining shaft says amen and the ventilators breathe forth spring air from above. He shall be guardian here, yet he will not bear the name of Cerberus. Orcus is up above."

O ascent two together—they have left the foreman below.

O ye fifty feet gained in every second.

O well-known feeling that every elevator imparts.

The roar in which they are silent stuffs cotton in every ear. And everyone smells the burnt smell. And every prayer beseeches the cable to remain united, in order that light, daylight, once again the sun-embroidered May . . .

But when they set foot on the platform of the shaft collar, it is raining outside and dusk is creeping over the land from the Harz Mountains.

And this man and that man—who now will call them Brauxel and Matern?—I and he, we stride with doused lamps to the changehouse, where the changehouse attendant takes our hard hats and carbide lamps. I and he are led to cabins where Matern's and Brauxel's clothes are in keeping. He and I strip off our mine outfits. For me and him bathtubs have been filled. I hear Eddi splashing next door. Now I too step into my bath. The water soaks me clean. Eddi whistles something indeterminate. I try to whistle something similar. But it's difficult. We're both naked. Each of us bathes by himself.

Notes

5   *Adalbert,* Bishop of Prague, 955-997, known as apostle of the Prussians, came down the Vistula, according to legend, and baptized more than a thousand pagans. He was killed by a pagan priest.—*Dukes Swantopolk* and *Mestwin II,* Dukes of Pomerelia, around whose castle Danzig was built. Mestwin II died in 1294 without a male heir.—*Duke Kynstute* (r. 1345-77) ruled Western Lithuania at a time when it was constantly raided by the Teutonic Knights (see below).

46   *Uniformed scarecrows:* the references are to the wars of Frederick the Great of Prussia. In the battle of Leuthen, 1747, the Prussians defeated the armies of the Austrian Empire.—The Poor Man of Toggenburg is the sobriquet of a Swiss mercenary who participated in the Seven Years' War, and later published his autobiography under this title.—*General Seydlitz,* one of Frederick's generals, pursued and defeated the head of the Austrian army, *Hildburghausen.*

57   *The Teutonic Knights,* a military and religious Order dedicated to the extension of the borders of Christendom. In 1208, Duke Conrad of Masovia invited the Order to settle along the Vistula in order to help protect his territories against the savage Prussians. In 1308, in alliance with the Poles, the Knights ousted the Prussians from Danzig, but forced their Polish allies out also. The Order established a Germanic military outpost on the Baltic which thrived at the expense of the Slavs. Eventually, the Order degenerated and its power waned. In 1410, the Knights were defeated by the combined Lithuanian and Polish forces in the battle of Tannenberg.—Hitler and his SS revived the mystique of the Order's mission as instrument of Germanic expansion in the East and the enslavement of the Slavs, and used the fortress castles of the Order as schools for the Nazi elite.—*Jagello,* Grand Duke of Lithuania, a pagan chieftain who brought about the union of Poland and Lithuania in 1386 and became Wladislaus II, Catholic King of Poland, founder of a dynasty which ruled Poland for two centuries, and devoted itself to keeping the Teutonic Order, the old enemy of their race, in check.—*Kasimir* III, *the Great* 1333-70, King of Poland.—*Stanislaus Lesczynski,* King of Poland 1704-09 and again 1733-34, besieged by the Russians in Danzig, his last refuge; vanquished and exiled.—*Kniprode, Letzkau, and von Plauen,* Grand Masters of the Teutonic

Knights.—*Albrecht Achilles,* 1414-86, Elector of Bradenburg, established his house as regnant over Pomerania.—*Zieten, Hans Joachim von,* 1699-1786, Prussian cavalry general under Frederick the Great.

63 ff   The Teutonic Order was joined by the flower of European chivalry in its crusade against the heathen. *Henry Derby,* Duke of Lancaster, later King Henry IV of England, made two journeys to Prussia, 1390-91 and 1392. Other foreign knights participating in raids against Lithuania were *Jacob Doutremer, Pege Peegott, Thomas Percy, Fitzwater.* At the time of Henry Derby's visits, *Konrad Wallenrod* was Grand Master of the Order (1391-93). *Engelhard Rabe,* Marshal of the Order (1387-92), led the Order's army into the trackless woods of Lithuania, starting his raids from one of the frontier castles, *Ragnit.* Traditionally, the *St. George's banner,* insigna of all Christian Knights, was carried by a German Knight, but Thomas Percy insisted on his own smaller banner. This led to bloody quarrels among German and English knights. Henry Derby also brought his own St. George's banner but was frustrated by Wallenrod, who conferred the privilege of carrying the banner on the German knight *Hattenstein. Simon Bache, Erik Cruse, Claus Schone, Richard Westrall, Spannerle, Tylman,* and *Robert Wendell* were artisans who supplied the Duke of Lancaster with various necessities on his Prussian campaigns.

102   *Sleeping lights:* candles made from the fat of stillborn children. Before breaking into a house, as many sleeping lights are lighted as there are sleepers in the house. If a light extinguishes, it is a sign that someone inside the house has woken up.

154   *Angela Raubal,* Hitler's widowed half-sister and housekeeper.—*Rudolf Hess,* Hitler's aide who helped him write *Mein Kampf,* and during the war undertook a sensational flight to Scotland.—*Ernst (Putzi) Hanfstaengl,* Harvard graduate, son of an American mother, befriended Hitler during his early Munich days and was later made chief of the Foreign Press Department of the Party.—*Hermann Rauschning,* President of the Danzig Senate 1933-35, helped National Socialism to victory in Danzig but was soon disillusioned. He went into exile and wrote *Conversations with Hilter* and *The Revolution of Nihilism.*—*Albert Forster,* National Socialist Gauleiter of Danzig. Proclaimed the annexation of Danzig to the German Reich on September 1, 1939, and appointed himself administrator of Danzig City and District.—*Wilhelm Brückner,* SA Commander and Hitler's personal adjutant.—*Gregor Strasser,* one of the earliest adherents of National Socialism and chief organizer of the nascent Party. He quarreled with Hitler and was liquidated in 1934.—*General Kurt von Schleicher,* last Chancellor of the Weimar Republic, who played a devious role in Hitler's rise to power. He was liquidated during the purge of June 30, 1934.—*Ernst Röhm,* one of Hitler's earliest supporters, who helped create and organize the SA, whose commander he was until his assassination at Hitler's orders on June 30, 1934.—*Count*

Joseph Arthur Gobineau, French man of letters, whose *Essay on the Inequality of Races* profoundly influenced Nazi racial theories.

169 *Franz and Karl Moor*, rebels against society in Schiller's early revolutionary drama *Die Räuber*.

177 *Arthur Greiser*, National Socialist, succeeded Hermann Rauschning as President of the Danzig Senate and signed a treaty with the Nationalist Socialists regularizing relations between Poland and Danzig.

185 *Houston Stewart Chamberlain*, 1855-1927, son-in-law of Richard Wagner, propagated Count Gobineau's racial theories. His main work, *Foundations of the Nineteenth Century*, exalts the Teutonic race and laid the groundwork for ideological anti-Semitism in Germany.

197 *SA man Brand*, propaganda figure of National Socialism, touted as hero and martyr of the Movement.—*Herbert Norkus*, Hitler youth, killed in 1932 in one of the bloody battles between Nazis and Communists.—*Horst Wessel*, SA leader of dubious morals, killed in a fight with Communists. Author and composer of the "Horst Wessel Lied," which became the second National Anthem in the Third Reich.

199 *Wilhelm Löbsack*, Nazi publicist and speaker, who edited the speeches and writings of the Danzig Gauleiter Albert Forster.

237 *Richard Billinger*, Austrian dramatist, dealt with the conflict between progress and mechanized city life on the one hand and the demonic world of the peasant on the other. In *The Giant* (1937), a peasant girl succumbs to the temptations of the city and finally drowns herself. Her seducer is the son of Donata Opferkuch.—*The phenomenology of a stockingcap*: the reference is to Martin Heidegger, who studied under Edmund Husserl, the founder of a new philosophical method which he called phenomenology. In 1927, Heidegger published his principal work, *Being and Time*. Soon after Hitler's rise to power, Heidegger came out in favor of the Nazi regime. His predilection for the stockingcap of the Alemannic peasant betokened his attachment to the simple life and the soil of his native Baden. He lives in Todtnau, in the Black Forest.—*Abstrusely secular lyric poetry* is a reference to the Expressionist poet Gottfried Benn (1886-1956) who also supported National Socialism from 1932 to 1934, but was later disillusioned and attacked by the regime. The fragments cited in the text are from his poem "Das späte Ich" (The late I). One of his early works is entitled "Morgue."

380 *The raving Beckmann* is a reference to the protagonist of the postwar play *Outside the Door* by Wolfgang Borchert, which describes the plight of the returning and unwanted soldier.

398 *Max Reimann*, Communist Party leader in postwar Germany.

402 *Quirinus Kuhlmann*, 1651-89, great lyric poet of the baroque, burnt in Moscow as a heretic.

410 ff   In Article 12 of the Postdam Pact, signed at the end of the war, the Allies outlawed "undue concentration of German economic power." A number of "decartelization laws" were issued, affecting all cartels, or trusts, and many other corporations and private businesses. Their purpose was to break the power of German heavy industry, which had helped establish Hilter's rule. It was argued the excessive concentrations of economic power impeded the functioning of democratic institutions and that German economic life should be guided by the spirit of free competition prevailing in the United States, France, and England. But the worm was in the economic system from the start—the expansion following the currency reform led to the formation of new trusts and monopolies. The old and new men of power: *Axel Springer,* who soon after the war founded the radio magazine *Hör Zu* (Tune In), published under British license, which today has the largest circulation of any German periodical (four million). He now directs the largest and most influential newspaper chain in Germany, which publishes the newspapers *Bild, Die Welt*, and the magazine *Kristall*. Springer also controls two publishing houses, Ullstein AG and Propyläen Verlag.—*Gerd Bucerius*, founder of Zeit-Verlag GmbH, which owns an interest in the Henry Nannen Verlag. These houses publish the weekly *Die Zeit* and *Stern*, one of the big illustrated magazines. From 1949 to 1962 Bucerius was a Christian Democratic member of the Bundestag.—*Rudolf Augstein*, after a short-lived experiment with the weekly *Die Woche,* in 1946 founded the news magazine *Der Spiegel* on the model of *Time* magazine.—*Otto-Ernst Flick,* son of the industrialist Friedrich Flick, who was sentenced to a prison term by the Nuremberg War Crimes court. Friedrich Flick KG was obliged by the decartelization law to withdraw from mining. Today it again holds an interest in Harpener Bergbau AG and is influential in numerous corporations, such as Daimler Benz AG. Otto-Ernst Flick is a board member and executive in these firms.—*Ernst Schneider,* chairman of the board and a large shareholder in Kohlensäure-Industrie AG, in which the C. G. Trinkhaus private bank also holds an interest—*The Michel group,* whose holdings in the Soviet zone were confiscated, built up a new soft-coal corporation on the basis of four mines it had retained in West Germany.—*Vicco von Bülow-Schwante,* landowner in Mecklenburg and retired ambassador, is chairman of the board of the Stumm family's mining company in the Saar.—*Bertold Beitz* was director of the Polish oil fields during the war. In 1953 he became chairman of the board of Friedrich Krupp von Bohlen und Halbach and directed the rebuilding of the Krupp Corporation, which was largely dissolved in 1945.—*Carl F. W. Borgward,* owner of the Borgward Automobile Corporation, which has meanwhile gone into bankruptcy.—*Heinrich Nordhoff,* chairman of the board of Volkswagen AG, Europe's largest producer of automobiles.—*Herbert Quand* directs in partnership with his brother Harald the concern inherited from their father, which has absorbed the Burbach Potash Works.—I-G *Successors*: In 1945 I-G Farben (the German Dye Trust) was the largest of German

corporations. On the strength of Law No. 35 of the Allied High Commission it was split up into the following concerns: Badische Anilin-u. Soda-Fabrik AG, Farbenfabriken Bayer AG, Farbwerke Höchst AG.—*Hjalmar Schacht*, economist, banker, former finance minister and president of the Reichsbank, in 1946 acquitted of war crimes charges by the Nuremberg court. Today he is part owner of the Schacht & Co. export-import bank, in Düsseldorf.—*Julius Münnemann* became, thanks to a new method of industrial financing, one of the most successful German financiers in the years after the war.—*Willy H. Schlieker* developed, in the same period, an important government enterprise in the Ruhr. After having built the world's most modern shipyard in Hamburg, his firm went into bankruptcy.—*Joseph Neckermann* in 1950 founded the Neckermann Versand KG, a mail-order house, which with ninety-one outlets is today the leading German enterprise of its kind.—*Max Grundig* developed after the war a small radio business into a large corporation which is now one of the world's foremost producers of radios, phonographs, and other electrical appliances.—*Hermann F. Reemtsma* vastly expanded the production of the Reemtsma cigarette factories after the war.—*Rudolf Brinckmann*, banker, part owner of the Brinckmann, Wirtz & Co. bank (formerly M. M. Warburg).—*Hermann J. Abs*, chairman of the Deutsche Bank AG, one of the three largest German banks. Member of the board of almost thirty leading corporations.—*Kurt Forberg*, banker, part owner of the C. G. Trinkhaus bank; member of the board in some twenty-five concerns.—*Robert Pferdmenges*, banker, part owner of Sal. Oppenheim Jr. & Cie. bank. Helped to found the Christian Democratic Party in the Rhineland. Long-time friend of Chancellor Konrad Adenauer.—*Rudolf August Oetker* expanded the flourishing baking powder factory inherited from his father and subsequently founded the largest German steamship company.—*Kurt Schumacher*, 1930-33 Social Democratic member of the Reichstag, spent the years 1933-45 in a concentration camp. He was the first postwar chairman of the German Socialist Party and up to the time of his death in 1952 the most prominent figure in the opposition.—*Erich Ollenhauer*, chairman of the German Socialist Party after Schumacher. During the war he was a member of the executive committee of the Socialist Party in exile.—*Dr. Eugen Gerstenmaier*, Protestant theologian and member of the German resistance movement during the war. Since 1949 a member of the Bundestag, of which he is now president.—*Dr. Otto Dibelius*, Protestant Bishop of Berlin since 1945. From 1954 to 1961 he was chairman of the World Council of Protestant Churches.—*Franz Joseph Würmeling* became Minister for Family Affairs in 1953. Known for his proposed legislation in favor of large families.—*Bruno Leuschner* became vice-chairman of the Council of Ministers of the German Democratic Republic in 1955, in 1960 a member of the state council, in charge of the co-ordination of economic plans. He died February 11, 1965.—*Otto Nuschke*, first chairman of the Communist Party in the German Democratic Republic, long vice-chairman of the Council of

Ministers.—*Kurt Mewis,* appointed in 1960 to the Council of State of the German Democratic Republic. In 1961 became a minister and first chairman of the State Planning Commission.—*Petersberg Agreement:* an agreement concluded in May 1952 between the three Western occupation powers and the German Federal Republic.—*Erich Kuby,* left-wing journalist.—*Hans Globke,* one of the jurists who formulated the notorious Nuremberg laws by which the Nazis deprived the Jews of the rights of citizenship. In postwar Germany, he became chief assistant to Chancellor Adenauer.

426 *Jan Wellem,* popular name of John William, elector palatine, 1679-1716 whose equestrian statue stands on Düsseldorf market place.— *Christian Dietrich Grabbe,* 1801-36 German dramatist, who visited Düsseldorf and left it after a quarrel. Among his historical tragedies is the unfinished drama *Hannibal.*

511f *Bundschuh and Poor Konrad, the monk Pfeiffer, Hipler and Geyer, the peasants of Mansfeld and Eichsfeld, etc.* are all references to the Peasants' War in South Germany in 1525. The Anabaptist Thomas Münzer (the Fury of Allstedt) was one of the leaders of the revolt. The insurgents were defeated at Frankenhausen and their leaders executed.